# Basic Standard Deduction Amounts

| Filing Status | Standard Deduction Amount | |
| --- | --- | --- |
| | 2004 | 2005 |
| Single | $4,850 | $5,000 |
| Married, filing jointly | 9,700 | 10,000 |
| Surviving spouse | 9,700 | 10,000 |
| Head of household | 7,150 | 7,300 |
| Married, filing separately | 4,850 | 5,000 |

# Amount of Each Additional Standard Deduction

*blind and/or over 65*

| Filing Status | 2004 | 2005 |
| --- | --- | --- |
| Single | $1,200 | $1,250 |
| Married, filing jointly | 950 | 1,000 |
| Surviving spouse | 950 | 1,000 |
| Head of household | 1,200 | 1,250 |
| Married, filing separately | 950 | 1,000 |

# Personal and Dependency Exemption

| 2004 | 2005 |
| --- | --- |
| $3,100 | $3,200 |

# Income Tax Rates—Corporations

| Taxable Income | Tax Rate |
| --- | --- |
| Not over $50,000 | 15% |
| Over $50,000 but not over $75,000 | 25% |
| Over $75,000 but not over $100,000 | 34% |
| Over $100,000 but not over $335,000 | 39%* (34% + 5% sur tax) |
| Over $335,000 but not over $10,000,000 | 34% |
| Over $10,000,000 but not over $15,000,000 | 35% |
| Over $15,000,000 but not over $18,333,333 | 38%** (35%+3% sur tax) |
| Over $18,333,333 | 35% |

*Five percent of this rate represents a phaseout of the benefits of the lower tax rates on the first $75,000 of taxable income.

**Three percent of this rate represents a phaseout of the benefits of the lower tax rate (34% rather than 35%) on the first $10 million of taxable income.

*If 38% or 39% use #'s in between! Ex: 39% use 15%, 25%, 34%, and 39%*

*use flat tax rate if any other number!*

West Federal Taxation

# Taxation of Business Entities

## 2006 EDITION

### General Editors

**James E. Smith**
*Ph.D., C.P.A.*
*College of*
*William and Mary*

**William A. Raabe**
*Ph.D., C.P.A.*
*The Ohio State University*

**David M. Maloney**
*Ph.D., C.P.A.*
*University of Virginia*

**Eugene Willis**
*Ph.D., C.P.A.*
*University of Illinois,*
*Urbana-Champaign*

THOMSON

SOUTH-WESTERN

Australia · Canada · Mexico · Singapore · Spain · United Kingdom · United States

**THOMSON**

**SOUTH-WESTERN**

*West Federal Taxation: Taxation of Business Entities, 2006 Edition*

James E. Smith, William A. Raabe, David M. Maloney, Eugene Willis

# Authors for West Federal Taxation Series

**James H. Boyd**
*Ph.D., CPA*
*Arizona State University*

**Steven C. Dilley**
*J.D., Ph.D., CPA*
*Michigan State University*

**Boyd C. Randall**
*J.D., Ph.D.*
*Brigham Young University*

**D. Larry Crumbley**
*Ph.D., CPA*
*Louisiana State University*

**William H. Hoffman, Jr.**
*J.D., Ph.D., CPA*
*University of Houston*

**Debra L. Sanders**
*Ph.D., CPA*
*Washington State University*

**Jon S. Davis**
*Ph.D., CPA*
*University of Wisconsin, Madison*

**Gary A. McGill**
*Ph.D., CPA*
*University of Florida*

**W. Eugene Seago**
*Virginia Polytechnic*
*Institute and State University*

**Mark B. Persellin**
*Ph.D., CPA, C.F.P.®*
*St. Mary's University*

**VP/Editorial Director**
Jack W. Calhoun

**Manager of Technology, Editorial**
Vicky True

**Internal and Cover Designer**
Ann Small/a small design studio

**Senior Acquisitions Editor**
Charles E. McCormick, Jr.

**Technology Project Editor**
Christine Wittmer

**Cover Images**
© William J. Hebert/Getty Images, Inc.

**Senior Developmental Editor**
Craig Avery

**Web Coordinator**
Scott Cook

**Production**
Litten Editing and Production, Inc.

**Marketing Manager**
Chris McNamee

**Manufacturing Coordinator**
Doug Wilke

**Composition**
TechBooks

**Senior Production Editor**
Tim Bailey

**Art Director**
Stacy Jenkins Shirley

**Printer**
Thomson-West
Eagan, MN

For more information about our products, contact us at:

Thomson Learning Academic Resource Center

1-800-423-0563

**Thomson Higher Education**
5191 Natorp Boulevard
Mason, OH 45040
USA

**Asia (including India)**
Thomson Learning
5 Shenton Way
#01-01 UIC Building
Singapore 068808

**Australia/New Zealand**
Thomson Learning Australia
102 Dodds Street
Southbank, Victoria 3006
Australia

**Canada**
Thomson Nelson
1120 Birchmount Road
Toronto, Ontario
M1K 5G4
Canada

**UK/Europe/Middle East/Africa**
Thomson Learning
High Holborn House
50/51 Bedford Row
London WC1R 4LR
United Kingdom

# To the Student

**YOUR SUCCESS** is our key goal at *West Federal Taxation.*

♦

*Taxation of Business Entities, 2006 Edition* comes from the most trusted and largest selling brand in college taxation—*West Federal Taxation* (*WFT*). Twenty-eight years after we started the *WFT* series, and **almost 1.4 million users** later, we are the market leader in college taxation texts and learning materials. That's because we are focused exclusively on providing the most useful, comprehensive, and up-to-date tax texts, online study aids, tax preparation tools, and print study guides to help you succeed in your tax education.

♦

You can be sure that the 2006 Edition contains everything you'll need to succeed in your tax course—up-to-date content developed by the most respected editors and authors in taxation, free tax preparation software from TurboTax® and TaxBrain®, free access to RIA Checkpoint® (the leading tax research database), and free online quizzing for every text chapter. *WFT* also provides you with free online updates for tax legislation that affect the text.

## YOUR TAX COURSE AND THIS TEXTBOOK

*WFT's Taxation of Business Entities, 2006 Edition* is the ideal basis for your tax course focusing on taxation of business entities and is perfect for both undergraduate and graduate accounting, business, and law students. It provides a thorough discussion of the structure of the Federal income tax, property transactions, business entities, special business topics, and taxation of individuals and contains material of critical interest to the serious tax practitioner. Because of its numerous straightforward examples and real-world problems, many users find it to be a valuable tool for self-study as well.

## FREE RESOURCES AND STUDY TOOLS

♦ **Free TurboTax® Business CD in every new copy. TurboTax® Business,** designed specifically for corporations, S corporations, partnerships of up to 100 partners, and LLCs as well as estates and trusts, covers corporation, partnership, and fiduciary income taxes and gives you practical, hands-on experience.

♦ **Free Online Access to TaxBrain® Tax Preparation Software—Filing Discount Included.** TaxBrain® online individual tax preparation software is used by more than 2,500 tax professionals every year. To access, log on to **http://www.taxbrain.com.** Take advantage of a 20 percent filing discount when filing your 2004 return with TaxBrain®—enter promotional code **SWL947.**

♦ **Exclusive Free Access to RIA's Checkpoint® Student Edition Online Tax Research Database.** Each *new* copy of the text contains an RIA Checkpoint® Student Edition access code, good for *six months* of free and unlimited access to content from the research database most widely used by tax professionals. As you use Checkpoint® to complete problems within the text, you are building research skills and familiarity with the database—valuable preparation for your professional future.

♦ **Free Tutorial for RIA's Checkpoint®.** This self-paced tutorial from RIA orients you to Checkpoint® features and walks you through the application of RIA research strategies—giving you a running start on your class assignments that use Checkpoint®.

♦ **Free Online Self-Quizzing, Updates, and Tax Links.** *WFT: Taxation of Business Entities, 2006 Edition* is supported by a text-specific Web site that offers student support and immediate access to current information. Students can take advantage of these key features:
   ✦ **Interactive Quizzing**—25 quiz items per chapter, with automatic grading and e-mailing of results to your instructor.
   ✦ **Tax newsletters** published twice a month written by the text authors.
   ✦ **NewsEdge** pulls from full text articles from over 1,200 online news sources on a continuous basis and includes the following features: topic organization, personalization with the "Select My Topics/View My Topics" feature, 30-day archive, links to full online articles, and robust search functionality. NewsEdge also offers access to "Company News by Ticker," which includes stock detail, charts, financials, management discussions, company profiles, competitor information, and company-specific news.

◆ **Tax Tips for the Recent Graduate** introduces the college graduate to some common tax considerations that could be beneficial in reducing the dreaded "tax-bite."

◆ **Tax Legislation Updates**—This resource, available to instructors and their students, provides up-to-the-minute tax information and major changes to the tax law. Tax Legislation Updates are posted as needed on the *WFT* Web site.

To start using these free study resources, go to **http://wft.swlearning.com** and select your *WFT* text.

**Download a Study Guide Chapter FREE before You Buy!**

**Get one chapter of the print Study Guide free online.** The Study Guide contains **questions and problems with solutions for self-study,** as well as **chapter highlights** that point you to the right place in the text for further study. Order it from your bookstore (ISBN 0-324-30508-7) or buy it online at **http://wft.swlearning.com.**

When you start using *Taxation of Business Entities, 2006 Edition,* its free online study aids, its time-saving Study Guide, and other supplements your instructor may assign, you'll experience how much a new textbook from *West Federal Taxation* can add to your success!

The *WFT* Taxation Team

# Contents in Brief

# Contents

**PART TWO**   STRUCTURE OF THE FEDERAL INCOME TAX

---

**PART FOUR**    **BUSINESS ENTITIES**

**PART FIVE** **SPECIAL BUSINESS TOPICS**

**PART SIX · TAXATION OF INDIVIDUALS**

# APPENDIXES

# The World of Taxation

**PART**

**1**

Part I provides an introduction to taxation in the United States. Various taxes imposed by Federal, state, and local governments are discussed. A unique tax planning framework is developed that is applied throughout the book in developing tax planning strategies for business entities and for individual taxpayers. This tax planning framework serves as a unifying theme throughout the book. The role of the IRS and the courts in the evolution of the Federal tax system is presented. The tax research process, including the relevance of the legislative, administrative, and judicial sources of the tax law, is discussed.

**CHAPTER 1**

Introduction to Taxation

**CHAPTER 2**

Working with the Tax Law

# Introduction to Taxation

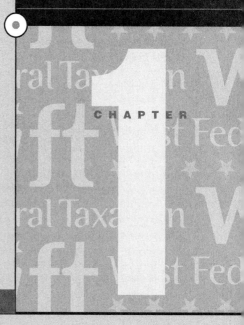

*After completing Chapter 1, you should be able to:*

## L O . 1
Understand the components of a tax.

## L O . 2
Identify the various taxes affecting business enterprises.

## L O . 3
Recall the basic tax formula for individuals and taxable business entities.

## L O . 4
Understand the relationship between business entities and their owners.

## L O . 5
Recognize tax planning opportunities and apply a general framework for tax planning.

## L O . 6
Recognize the economic, social, equity, and political considerations that underlie the tax law.

## L O . 7
Describe the role played by the IRS and the courts in the evolution of the Federal tax system.

http://wft.swlearning.com

## OUTLINE

> ## TAX TALK
>
> *How many people were taxed, who was taxed, and what was taxed tell more about a society than anything else.*
>
> —*Charles Adams*

Taxes have a pervasive impact on our lives. They affect every individual in the United States from birth to death, and even beyond death (through taxation of the individual's estate). Taxes likewise affect every business from formation of the business entity to its operations, distribution of profits to owners, and ultimate disposition or liquidation.

Despite the wide-ranging impact of taxes, most studies of the tax law overemphasize the provisions applying to individual taxpayers and ignore much of the tax law relevant to business. That approach fails to address the role of taxes in *business decisions*, and it fails to provide the broad knowledge base necessary to succeed in today's business environment. This text adopts a more balanced approach; it introduces the tax laws that apply to all business entities and surveys the tax rules specific to each type of entity. It also recognizes that both tax and nontax considerations are important in business planning and therefore presents the tax laws within the context of the business transactions to which they relate.

<table>
<tr><td>

**LO.1**

Understand the components of a tax.

</td><td>

# The Structure of Taxes

Most taxes have two components: a tax rate and a tax base (such as income, wages, value, or sales price). Tax liability is computed by multiplying these two components. Taxes vary by the structure of their rates and by the base subject to tax.

## TAX RATES

Tax rates can be either progressive, proportional, or regressive. A tax rate is *progressive* if it increases as the tax base increases. The Federal income tax and the Federal estate and **gift taxes** are progressive. For example, the Federal income tax rates for corporations range from 15 to 39 percent. These rates increase with increases in taxable income.

</td></tr>
</table>

**EXAMPLE 1**

Refer to the corporate Tax Rate Schedule inside the front cover of this text. If Abel Corporation has taxable income of $5,000, its income tax is $750 and its average tax rate is 15% ($750/$5,000, or the ratio of tax liability to the tax base). If, however, Abel's taxable income is $200,000, its income tax is $61,250 [$22,250 + 0.39($200,000 − $100,000)], and its average tax rate is 30.63% ($61,250/$200,000). The tax is progressive because the average tax rate increases with increases in the tax base (income). ■

A tax is *proportional* if the rate of tax is constant, regardless of the size of the tax base. State retail **sales taxes** are proportional, as is the Federal Medicare tax on salaries and wages. Proportional tax rates also underlie the various "flat tax" proposals recently in the news.[1]

**EXAMPLE 2**

Bob purchases an automobile for $6,000. If the sales tax on automobiles is 7% in Bob's state, he will pay a $420 tax. Alternatively, if Bob pays $20,000 for a car, his sales tax will be $1,400 (still 7% of the sales price). Because the average tax rate does not change with the tax base (sales price), the sales tax is proportional. ■

Finally, *regressive* tax rates decrease as the tax base increases. Federal **employment taxes,** such as FICA and FUTA, are regressive. When the tax base and the taxpayer's ability to pay generally are positively correlated (i.e., when they move in the same direction), many tax pundits view regressive tax rates as unfair. This is because the tax burden decreases as a *percentage* of the taxpayer's ability to pay.

**EXAMPLE 3**

In 2005, the combined Social Security and Medicare tax rate levied on the wages of employees is 7.65% up to a maximum of $90,000 and 1.45% on all wages over $90,000. Sarah earns a salary of $30,000. She will pay FICA taxes of $2,295, with an average tax rate of 7.65%. Alternatively, if Sarah earns $100,000, she will pay $7,030 [(0.0765 × $90,000) + 0.0145($100,000 − $90,000)], with an average tax rate of 7.03%. Once the FICA base exceeds the maximum amount subject to the Social Security part of FICA, the FICA tax is regressive since the average tax rate decreases as the tax base increases. ■

Under all three tax rate structures, the *amount* of taxes due increases as the tax base increases. The structure of tax rates only affects the *rate* of increase (i.e.,

---

[1]Flat tax proposals call for a new tax with one low, proportional rate (usually between 15% and 20%). Such a tax would have a very broad base, taxing almost all forms of income with few deductions.

To avoid taxing the poor, large personal exemptions would be provided (e.g., $30,000 for a family of four).

progressive taxes increase at an increasing rate, proportional taxes increase at a constant rate, and regressive taxes increase at a decreasing rate).

## TAX BASES

Most taxes are levied on one of four kinds of tax bases.

- Transactions (including sales or purchases of goods and services and transfers of wealth).
- Property or wealth (including ownership of specific kinds of property).
- Privileges and rights (including the ability to do business as a corporation, the right to work in a certain profession, and the ability to move goods between countries).
- Income, on a gross or net-of-expenses basis.

Because the Federal income tax usually has the most significant influence on business decisions, it is the principal focus of this text. Other taxes can play an important role, however, so it is important to have at least some familiarity with them. The next section introduces many of the taxes imposed on individuals and businesses in the United States.

**LO.2**

Identify the various taxes affecting business enterprises.

# Types of Taxes

After taxes on income, the various transaction taxes usually play the most important role in business (and personal) contexts. In many countries, transaction taxes are even more important than income taxes. There are three types of transaction taxes: sales and certain **excise taxes,** employment taxes, and taxes on the transfer of wealth.

## TAXES ON THE PRODUCTION AND SALE OF GOODS

Sales tax and some excise taxes are imposed on the production, sale, or consumption of commodities or the use of services. Excise taxes and general sales taxes differ by the breadth of their bases. An excise tax base is limited to a specific kind of good or service while a general sales tax is broad based (e.g., it might be levied on all retail sales). All levels of government impose excise taxes while state and local governments make heavy use of the general sales tax.

**Federal Excise Taxes.**   Together with customs duties, excise taxes served as the principal source of revenue for the United States during its first 150 years of existence. Since World War II, the role of excise taxes in the Federal government's fund-raising efforts has steadily declined, falling from about 30 to 40 percent of revenues just prior to the war to less than 4 percent now. During this time, the Federal government came to rely upon income and employment taxes as its principal sources of funds.

Despite the decreasing contribution of excise taxes to the Federal coffers, they continue to have a significant impact on specific industries. Currently, trucks, trailers, tires, liquor, tobacco, firearms, certain sporting equipment, air travel, and telephone service are all subject to Federal excise taxes. In the past, the sale and manufacture of a variety of other goods, including furs, jewelry, boats, luxury automobiles, and theater tickets, have been taxed. Excise taxes extend beyond sales transactions. They are also levied on privileges and rights, as discussed below.

The bases used for Federal excise taxes are as diverse as the goods that are taxed. Fuels are taxed by the gallon, vaccines by the dose, telephone service and air travel by the price paid for the service, water travel by the passenger, coal by the ton extracted or by the sales price, insurance by the premiums paid, and the gas guzzler tax by the mileage rating on the automobile produced. Some of these taxes are levied on producers, some on resellers, and some on consumers. In almost every circumstance, the tax rate structure is proportional.

With the exception of Federal excise taxes on alcohol, tobacco, and firearms, Federal excise taxes are due at least quarterly, when the Federal excise tax return (Form 720) is filed.

**State Excise Taxes.**  Many states levy excise taxes on the same items taxed by the Federal government. For example, most states have excise taxes on gasoline, liquor, and tobacco. However, the tax on specific goods can vary dramatically among states. Compare the state of New Jersey's $2.40 tax on each pack of cigarettes to Kentucky's $0.03 tax. These differences at the state level provide ample incentive for smuggling between states and for state-line enterprises specializing in taxed goods.[2]

Other goods and services subject to state and local excise taxes include admission to amusement facilities, hotel occupancy, rental of other facilities, and sales of playing cards, oleomargarine products, and prepared foods. Most states impose a tax on transfers of property that require recording of documents (such as real estate sales and sales of stock and securities).

**Local Excise Taxes.**  Over the last few years, two types of excise taxes imposed at the local level have become increasingly popular. These are the hotel occupancy tax and the rental car "surcharge." Since they tax the visitor who cannot vote, they are a political windfall and serve as a means of financing special projects that generate civic pride (e.g., convention centers, state-of-the-art sports arenas). That these levies can be significant is demonstrated by Houston's hotel tax of 17 percent and Boston's car rental tax of 28.7 percent.

**General Sales Tax.**  The broad-based general sales tax is a major source of revenue for most state and local governments. It is used in all but five states (Alaska, Delaware, Montana, New Hampshire, and Oregon). While specific rules vary from state to state, the sales tax typically employs a proportional tax rate and includes retail sales of tangible personal property (and occasionally personal services) in the base. Some states exempt medicine and food from the base, and sometimes tax rates vary with the good being sold (e.g., the sales tax rate for automobiles may differ from the rate on other goods). The sales tax is collected by the retailer and then paid to the state government.

Local general sales taxes, over and above those levied by the state, are common. It is not unusual to find taxpayers living in the same state who pay different general rates of sales taxes due to the location of their residence.

**EXAMPLE 4**

Pete and Sam both live in a state that has a general sales tax of 3%. Sam, however, resides in a city that imposes an additional general sales tax of 2%. Even though Pete and Sam live in the same state, one is subject to a rate of 3%, while the other pays a tax of 5%. ■

---

[2]Some excise taxes are referred to as "sin" taxes (because goods such as liquor and tobacco are subject to the tax). Although it is commonly believed that these taxes are imposed for the purpose of discouraging consumption, evidence frequently fails to show that sin taxes have a significant impact on consumption. Since demand for cigarettes and gasoline tends to be relatively inelastic (insensitive to price), the increase in price caused by excise taxes has little to do with rates of consumption.

## GLOBAL TAX ISSUES

### WHY IS GASOLINE EXPENSIVE? IT DEPENDS ON WHERE YOU LIVE

In recent years, increases in the cost of gasoline and fuel oil have sometimes aroused such a furor in the United States that supplies have been released from the national oil reserve. Whether such tactics reduce prices more than temporarily seems doubtful. But in the United States, unlike other countries, increases in the price of gasoline are largely attributable to the rising cost of crude oil. In 2004, the price of crude oil increased from approximately $30 to $50 per barrel. In January 2005, the average price per gallon in the United States was $1.85.

In other countries (and using selected European nations as examples), the real culprit is the amount of tax imposed. Consider the following situations.

| Country | Price per Gallon* |
|---|---|
| United Kingdom | $4.16 |
| France | 3.31 |
| Germany | 3.49 |
| Sweden | 3.41 |

*Converted to U.S. dollars

While other factors may contribute to the higher European prices, the primary factor is the amount of tax charged in those countries. For example, in the United Kingdom, approximately 75 percent of the cost of gasoline is attributable to taxes.

SOURCE: European prices and taxes as of June 2002, compiled by the Energy Information Administration.

For various reasons, some jurisdictions will suspend the application of a general sales tax. New York City does so to stimulate shopping. Illinois has permanently suspended the tax on construction materials used to build power-generating plants. Texas does so annually on clothing right before the beginning of the school year. Such suspensions are similar to the tax holidays granted for ad valorem tax purposes.

**Use Taxes.**   One obvious approach to avoiding state and local sales taxes is to purchase goods in a state that has little or no sales tax and then transport the goods back to one's home state. **Use taxes** exist to prevent this tax reduction ploy. The use tax is a value-based tax, usually imposed at the same rate as the sales tax, on the use, consumption, or storage of tangible property. Every state that imposes a general sales tax levied on the consumer also has a use tax.

**EXAMPLE 5**

Orange, Inc., is located in a jurisdiction that imposes a 5% general sales tax, but is located near a state that has no sales or use tax. Orange purchases an automobile for $10,000 from a dealer located in the neighboring tax-free state. Though Orange will pay no sales tax to the dealer upon purchase of the car, it will be assessed a use tax when it brings the automobile back to its home state and licenses it. ■

The use tax is difficult to enforce for many other purchases and is therefore often avoided. In some cases, for example, it may be worthwhile to make purchases through an out-of-state mail-order business. In spite of shipping costs, the avoidance of the local sales tax that otherwise might be incurred often makes the price of such products as computer components cheaper. Some states are taking steps to curtail this loss of revenue.

**Value Added Tax.** The **value added tax (VAT)** is a sales tax levied at each stage of production on value added by the producer. VAT is in widespread use in many countries around the world (most notably in the European Union and in Canada). The tax typically serves as a major source of revenue for governments that use it. Some proposals to reduce the Federal government's reliance on income tax have focused on VAT as an alternative tax system.

**EXAMPLE 6**

Farmer Brown sells wheat to a flour mill for $100. If the wheat cost $65 for Brown to produce and if the VAT rate is 10%, then Brown will owe a VAT of $3.50 [0.10($100 − $65)]. If the mill sells the flour for $200 to a baker and if it cost the mill $120 to make the flour (including the cost of Brown's wheat), then it will pay a VAT of $8 [0.10($200 − $120)]. If the baker sells the bread he makes from the flour for $400 and if it cost the baker $280 to make the bread, then he will pay a VAT of $12 [0.10($400 − $280)]. The consumer who buys the bread will not pay any VAT directly. It is likely, however, that some or all of the total VAT paid of $23.50 ($3.50 + $8 + $12) will be paid by the consumer in the form of higher prices for the bread.[3] ∎

## EMPLOYMENT TAXES

Both Federal and state governments tax the salaries and wages paid to employees. On the Federal side, employment taxes represent a major source of funds. For example, the **FICA tax** accounts for about one-third of revenues in the Federal budget, second only to the income tax in its contribution.

The Federal government imposes two kinds of employment tax. The Federal Insurance Contributions Act (FICA) imposes a tax on self-employed individuals, employees, and employers. The proceeds of the tax are used to finance Social Security and Medicare payments. The Federal Unemployment Tax Act (FUTA) imposes a tax on employers. The **FUTA tax** provides funds to state unemployment benefit programs. Most state employment taxes are similar to the FUTA tax, with proceeds used to finance state unemployment benefit payments.

**FICA Taxes.** The FICA tax has two components: old age, survivors, and disability insurance payments (commonly referred to as Social Security) and Medicare health insurance payments. The Social Security tax rate is 6.2 percent, and the Medicare tax rate is 1.45 percent. The maximum base for the Social Security tax is $90,000 for 2005 ($87,900 for 2004). There is no ceiling on the base amount for the Medicare tax. The employer must withhold the FICA tax from an employee's wages and must also pay a matching tax.

Payments are usually made through weekly or monthly deposits to a Federal depository. Employers must also file Form 941, Employer's Quarterly Federal Tax Return, by the end of the first month following each quarter of the calendar year (e.g., by July 31 for the quarter ending on June 30) and pay any remaining amount of employment taxes due for the previous quarter. Failure to pay can result in large and sometimes ruinous penalties.

**EXAMPLE 7**

Janet receives $95,000 in salary in 2005. She pays FICA taxes of $6,957.50 [(7.65% × $90,000) + 1.45%($95,000 − $90,000)]. Her employer is required to pay a matching FICA tax of $6,957.50.

---

[3] In the area of economics dealing with taxation (public finance), the issue of who ultimately pays a tax is known as *tax incidence*.

Janet's share of FICA taxes is withheld from her salary by her employer and deposited on a regular basis together with the employer's share of FICA. ■

Finally, FICA tax is not assessed on all wages paid. For example, wages paid to children under the age of 18 who are employed in a parent's trade or business are exempt from the tax.

**Self-Employment Tax.**   Self-employed individuals also pay FICA in the form of a self-employment (SE) tax (determined on Schedule SE, filed with Form 1040, U.S. Individual Income Tax Return). Self-employed individuals are required to pay both the employer and the employee portion of the FICA tax. Therefore, the 2005 SE tax rate is 15.3 percent ($2 \times 7.65\%$) on self-employment income up to $90,000 and 2.9 percent ($2 \times 1.45\%$) on all additional self-employment income. Self-employed individuals deduct half of the SE tax—the amount normally deductible by an employer as a business expense. The self-employment tax is discussed in more detail in Chapter 16.

**Unemployment Taxes.**   In 2005, FUTA applies at a rate of 6.2 percent on the first $7,000 of covered wages paid during the year to each employee. As with FICA, this represents a regressive rate structure. The Federal government allows a credit for unemployment tax paid (or allowed under a merit rating system)[4] to the state. The credit cannot exceed 5.4 percent of the covered wages. Thus, the amount required to be paid to the IRS could be as low as 0.8 percent (6.2% − 5.4%).

FUTA and state unemployment taxes differ from FICA in that the tax is imposed only on the employer. A few states, however, levy a special tax on employees to provide either disability benefits or supplemental unemployment compensation, or both.

Employers must file Form 940, Employer's Annual Federal Employment Tax Return, to determine the amount of Federal unemployment taxes due in a given year. The return is due on or before January 31 of the following year.[5] Most states also require unemployment tax returns to be filed with quarterly estimated payments.

## DEATH TAXES

A **death tax** is a tax on the transfer of property upon the death of the owner. If the death tax is imposed on the transferor at death, it is classified as an **estate tax.** If it taxes the recipient of the property, it is termed an **inheritance tax.** As is typical of other types of transaction taxes, the value of the property transferred provides the base for determining the amount of the death tax.

The Federal government imposes only an estate tax. State governments, however, levy inheritance taxes, estate taxes, or both.

**EXAMPLE 8**

At the time of her death, Wilma lived in a state that imposes an inheritance tax but not an estate tax. Mary, one of Wilma's heirs, lives in the same state. Wilma's estate is subject to the Federal estate tax, and Mary is subject to the state inheritance tax. ■

**The Federal Estate Tax.**   Never designed to generate a large amount of revenue, the estate tax was originally intended to prevent large concentrations of wealth from being kept within a family for many generations. Whether this objective has

---

[4]States follow a policy of reducing unemployment tax on employers with stable employment. Thus, an employer with no employee turnover might face state unemployment tax rates as low as 0.1% or, in some cases, zero. This *merit rating system* explicitly accounts for the savings generated by steady employment.

[5]Employers may be required to make more frequent payments of the tax (estimated payments) if their FUTA liability is sufficiently large.

been accomplished is debatable, because estate taxes can be substantially reduced (or deferred for decades) through careful planning.

Determination of the estate tax base begins with the gross estate, which includes property the decedent owned at the time of death. It also includes property interests, such as life insurance proceeds paid to the estate or to a beneficiary other than the estate if the deceased-insured had any ownership rights in the policy. Most property included in the gross estate is valued at fair market value as of the date of death.

Deductions from the gross estate in arriving at the taxable estate include funeral and administration expenses, certain taxes, debts of the decedent, transfers to charitable organizations, and, in some cases, an unlimited marital deduction. The marital deduction is available for amounts actually passing to a surviving spouse (a widow or widower).

Once the taxable estate has been determined and certain taxable gifts have been added to it, progressive estate tax rates ranging from 18 to 47 percent in 2005 are applied to determine a tentative tax liability. The tentative liability is reduced by a variety of credits to arrive at the amount due. Although many credits are available, probably the most significant is the *unified transfer tax credit*. This credit eliminates estate tax liability for most individuals. For 2005, the amount of the credit is $555,800. Based on the estate tax rates, the credit offsets a tax base of $1.5 million. The unified transfer tax credit is scheduled to increase until by 2009 it will be $3.5 million. By 2010, the Federal estate tax is scheduled to be eliminated.

**EXAMPLE 9**

Ildiko made no taxable gifts before her death in 2005. If Ildiko's taxable estate amounts to $1.5 million or less, no Federal estate tax is due because of the application of the unified transfer tax credit. Under the tax law, the tentative estate tax on a taxable estate of $1.5 million is $555,800, exactly equal to the maximum unified transfer tax credit allowed. ∎

**State Death Taxes.**  As noted earlier, states usually levy an inheritance tax, an estate tax, or both. The two forms of death taxes differ according to whether the tax is imposed on the heirs or on the estate.

Characteristically, an inheritance tax divides the heirs into classes based on their relationship to the decedent. The more closely related the heir, the lower the rates imposed and the greater the exemption allowed. Some states completely exempt amounts passing to a surviving spouse from taxation.

## GIFT TAXES

Like death taxes, the gift tax is an excise tax levied on the right to transfer property. In this case, however, the tax is imposed on transfers made during the owner's life rather than at death. A gift tax applies only to transfers that are not supported by full and adequate consideration (i.e., gifts).

**EXAMPLE 10**

Carl sells property worth $20,000 to his daughter for $1,000. Although property worth $20,000 has been transferred, only $19,000 represents a gift, since this is the portion not supported by full and adequate consideration. ∎

**The Federal Gift Tax.**  The Federal gift tax is intended to complement the estate tax. The gift tax base is the sum of all taxable gifts made *during one's lifetime*. Gifts are valued at the date of transfer. To compute the tax due in a year, the tax rate schedule is applied to the sum of all lifetime taxable gifts. The resulting tax is then reduced by gift taxes paid in prior years.

**EXAMPLE 11**

In 1995, Willie gave $700,000 of taxable gifts to his son. The gift tax paid in 1995 (before application of any credits) was $229,800. In 2005, Willie will give an additional $100,000 in taxable gifts to his son. The tax base in 2005 will be $800,000 of lifetime gifts, and the tax will be $267,800. However, the actual gift tax due in 2005 (before credits) will be $38,000 ($267,800 – $229,800 tax paid on prior-year gifts). ■

Under current law, the Federal gift tax and the Federal estate tax are *unified*.[6] The transfer of assets by a decedent at death is effectively treated as a final gift under the tax law. Thus, the unified transfer tax credit available under the estate tax is also available to reduce the tax liability generated by lifetime gifts. If the credit is exhausted during one's lifetime, it will not be available to reduce the estate tax liability, except to the extent of the excess of the credit amount for estate tax purposes over that for gift tax purposes. In addition, the same tax rate schedule applies to both lifetime gifts and the estate tax.

**EXAMPLE 12**

Before his death in 2005, Ben gives $1 million of taxable gifts. Because the unified transfer tax credit was used during his life to offset the tax due on these gifts, only a partial credit is left to reduce Ben's estate tax liability. ■

Annual taxable gifts are determined by reducing the fair market value of gifts given by an *annual exclusion* of $11,000 per donee. A married couple can elect *gift splitting*, which enables them to transfer twice the annual exclusion ($22,000) per donee per year.

**EXAMPLE 13**

On December 31, 2004, Vera (a widow) gives $11,000 to each of her four married children, their spouses, and her eight grandchildren. On January 3, 2005, she repeats the same procedure. Due to the annual exclusion, Vera has *not* made a taxable gift, although she transferred $176,000 [$11,000 × 16 (the number of donees)] in 2004 and $176,000 [$11,000 × 16 (the number of donees)] in 2005 for a total of $352,000 ($176,000 + $176,000). If Vera were married, she could have given twice as much ($704,000) by electing gift splitting with her husband. ■

As noted previously, the Tax Relief Reconciliation Act of 2001 proposes to phase out the Federal estate tax. The reason for the elimination of the estate tax does not apply to the gift tax. Unlike death, which is involuntary, the making of a gift is a voluntary parting of ownership. Thus, the ownership of a business can be transferred gradually without incurring drastic and immediate tax consequences. As a result, the Federal gift tax is to be retained with the unified transfer tax credit frozen at $345,800 (which covers a taxable gift of $1 million).

**State Gift Taxes.**    The states currently imposing a gift tax are Connecticut, Louisiana, North Carolina, and Tennessee. Most of the laws provide for lifetime exemptions and annual exclusions. Unlike the Federal version, the amount of state gift tax often depends on the relationship between the donor and the donee. As with state inheritance taxes, larger exemptions and lower rates apply when the donor and donee are closely related to each other.

## PROPERTY TAXES

A property tax can be a tax on the ownership of property or a tax on wealth, depending on the base used. Any measurable characteristic of the property being taxed can be used as a base (e.g., weight, size, number, or value). Most property taxes in the United States are taxes on wealth since they use value as a base. These value-based property taxes are known as **ad valorem taxes.** Property taxes are generally administered by state and local governments where they serve as a significant source of revenue.

---

[6]§§ 2010 and 2505.

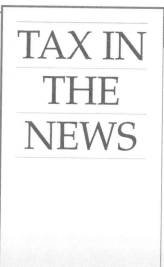

SOURCE: Adapted from "Cities Reconsidering Free Ride on Tax-Exempt College Property," *Houston Chronicle,* March 21, 2004, p. 2D.

## COLLEGE EXPANSION MAY CAUSE PROPERTY TAX EROSION

Municipalities are very sensitive to the acquisition of additional property by nonprofit organizations. An expansion by a nonprofit can be particularly detrimental to a city's tax base if the property acquired was formerly operated as an income-producing business. As a result of the acquisition, the city permanently loses valuable ad valorem tax revenue.

Recently, Duquesne University (a nonprofit tax-exempt organization) acquired an apartment building for $22 million and converted it to a dormitory facility. The city of Pittsburgh, for obvious reasons, is challenging the tax-exempt status of the new dorm. Hopefully, a compromise can be reached whereby Duquesne will continue to pay for certain city services in return for exemption from property taxes. Such an arrangement is not uncommon in university-dominated communities—Cambridge, Massachusetts, where Harvard is located is an example. Keep in mind that Pittsburgh is also home to the University of Pittsburgh and Carnegie Mellon University, both of which are nonprofit tax-exempt organizations.

**Taxes on Realty.**  Property taxes on **realty** are used exclusively by states and their local political subdivisions such as cities, counties, and school districts. They represent a major source of revenue for local governments, but their importance at the state level has waned over the past few years. Some states, for example, have imposed freezes on the upward revaluations of residential housing.

How realty is defined can have an important bearing on which assets are subject to tax. This is especially true in jurisdictions that do not impose ad valorem taxes on **personalty.** Although the definition is primarily a question of state property law, realty generally includes real estate and any capital improvements that are classified as fixtures. A fixture is something so permanently attached to the real estate that its removal will cause irreparable damage. A built-in bookcase might be a fixture, whereas a movable bookcase is not. Certain items such as electrical wiring and plumbing change from personalty to realty when installed in a building.

The following are some of the characteristics of ad valorem taxes on realty.

- Property owned by the Federal government is exempt from tax. Similar immunity usually is extended to property owned by state and local governments and by certain charitable organizations.
- Some states provide for lower valuations on property dedicated to agricultural use or other special uses (e.g., wildlife sanctuaries).
- Some states partially exempt the homestead, or personal residence, portion of property from taxation. Additionally, modern homestead laws normally protect some or all of a personal residence (including a farm or ranch) from the actions of creditors pursuing claims against the owner.
- Lower taxes may apply to a residence owned by a taxpayer age 65 or older.
- Some jurisdictions extend immunity from tax for a specified period of time (a tax holiday) to new or relocated businesses.

**Taxes on Personalty.**  Personalty includes all assets that are not realty. It may be helpful to distinguish between the classification of an asset (realty or personalty) and the use to which it is put. Both realty and personalty can be either business-use or personal-use property. Examples include a residence (personal-use realty), an

⊙ T A X   F A C T

## PROPERTY TAXES—IT MATTERS WHERE YOU LIVE!

A recent survey conducted by Runzheimer International (a Rochester, Wisconsin consulting firm) clearly shows that geography can cause a considerable difference in the amount of property taxes that one pays. Consider, for example, a four-bedroom, 2,200-square-foot residence appraised at $150,000. Located in Buffalo, New York, the house generates an ad valorem tax of $5,000 each year. The same house in Montgomery, Alabama, however, is taxed at $400. Based on the home's value, the effective tax rate is 3.3 percent in Buffalo but only 0.27 percent in Montgomery. Thus, real property taxes are approximately 12 times higher in Buffalo than in Montgomery.

Other high property tax areas include Rockford (Ill.), Pittsburgh (Pa.), and San Antonio (Tex.). Low-tax areas include Denver (Colo.), New Orleans (La.), and Salt Lake City (Utah).

office building (business-use realty), surgical instruments (business-use personalty), and casual clothing (personal-use personalty).

Personalty can also be classified as tangible property or intangible property. For property tax purposes, intangible personalty includes stocks, bonds, and various other securities (e.g., bank shares).

The following generalizations may be made concerning the property taxes on personalty.

* Particularly with personalty devoted to personal use (e.g., jewelry, household furnishings), taxpayer compliance ranges from poor to zero. Some jurisdictions do not even attempt to enforce the tax on these items. For automobiles devoted to personal use, many jurisdictions have converted from value as the tax base to a tax based on the weight of the vehicle. Some jurisdictions also consider the vehicle's age (e.g., automobiles six years or older are not subject to the ad valorem tax because they are presumed to have little value).
* For personalty devoted to business use (e.g., inventories, trucks, machinery, equipment), taxpayer compliance and enforcement procedures are notably better.
* Some jurisdictions impose an ad valorem property tax on intangibles.

### TAXES ON PRIVILEGES AND RIGHTS

Taxes on privileges and rights are usually considered excise taxes. A few of the most important of these taxes are reviewed here.

**Federal Customs Duties.**   Customs duties or tariffs can be characterized as a tax on the right to move goods across national borders. These taxes, together with selective excise taxes, provided most of the revenues needed by the Federal government during the nineteenth century. For example, tariffs and excise taxes alone paid off the national debt in 1835 and enabled the U.S. Treasury to pay a surplus of $28 million to the states. Today, however, customs duties account for only 1 percent of revenues in the Federal budget.

In recent years, tariffs have served the nation more as an instrument for carrying out protectionist policies than as a means of generating revenue. Thus, a particular U.S. industry might be saved from economic disaster, so the argument goes, by

> ◉ **T A X  F A C T**
>
> ## WHAT IS THE U.S. TAX BURDEN?
>
> One popular measure of the burden of taxes in the U.S. economy is the Tax Foundation's "Tax Freedom Day." This statistic is a determination of the day upon which an individual has completed the entire year's obligation to governmental units (i.e., if all earnings were paid as taxes to this point, annual taxes would be paid up, and one would now begin to "work for your own account").
>
> Being "free from taxes" may bring about a feeling of relief, but in reality tax burdens vary greatly from state to state. And as the U.S. economy has evolved and develops a more complex tax structure, adding emphasis on income and sales/use taxes, and reducing the relative reliance on tariffs and excise taxes, year-to-year comparisons become difficult. Nonetheless, as a rough measure of the presence of government in our lives, Tax Freedom Day carries some importance.
>
> | Year | Tax Freedom Day |
> |------|-----------------|
> | 1902 | 1/31 |
> | 1930 | 2/12 |
> | 1945 | 4/4 |
> | 1960 | 4/15 |
> | 1970 | 4/26 |
> | 1990 | 5/1 |
> | 1999 | 5/11 |
> | 2000 | 5/3 |
> | 2001 | 4/29 |
> | 2002 | 4/27 |
> | 2003 | 4/19 |
> | 2004 | 4/11 |

placing customs duties on the importation of foreign goods that can be sold at lower prices. Protectionists contend that the tariff therefore neutralizes the competitive edge held by the producer of the foreign goods.[7]

Protectionist policies seem more appropriate for less-developed countries whose industrial capacity has not yet matured. In a world where a developed country should have everything to gain by encouraging international free trade, such policies may be of dubious value since tariffs often lead to retaliatory action on the part of the nation or nations affected.

**Franchise Taxes and Occupational Taxes.** A **franchise tax** is a tax on the privilege of doing business in a state or local jurisdiction. Typically, the tax is imposed by states on corporations, but the tax base varies from state to state. While some states use a measure of corporate net income as part of the base, most states base the tax on the capitalization of the corporation (with or without certain long-term debt).

---

[7]The North American Free Trade Agreement (NAFTA) substantially reduced the tariffs on trade between Canada, Mexico, and the United States. General Agreement on Tariffs and Trade (GATT) legislation reduced tariffs on selected commodities among 124 countries.

■ **FIGURE 1–1**

Basic Formula for Federal
Income Tax

| | |
|---|---:|
| Income (broadly conceived) | $xxx,xxx |
| Less: Exclusions (income that is not subject to tax) | (xx,xxx) |
| Gross income (income that is subject to tax) | $xxx,xxx |
| Less: Deductions | (xx,xxx) |
| Taxable income | $xxx,xxx |
| Federal income tax on taxable income (see Tax Rate Schedules inside front cover of text) | $ xx,xxx |
| Less: Tax credits (including Federal income tax withheld and other prepayments of Federal income taxes) | (x,xxx) |
| Tax owed (or refund) | $ xxx |

Closely akin to the franchise tax are **occupational taxes** applicable to various trades or businesses, such as a liquor store license, a taxicab permit, or a fee to practice a profession such as law, medicine, or accounting. Most of these are not significant revenue producers and fall more into the category of licenses than taxes. The revenue derived is used to defray the cost incurred by the jurisdiction to regulate the business or profession for the public good.

**Severance Taxes.**   Severance taxes are based on the extraction of natural resources (e.g., oil, gas, iron ore, and coal). They are an important source of revenue for many states (e.g., Alaska).

## INCOME TAXES

Income taxes are levied by the Federal government, most states, and some local governments. In recent years, the trend in the United States has been to place greater reliance on this method of taxation while other countries are relying more heavily on transactions taxes such as the VAT.

Income taxes are generally imposed on individuals, corporations, and certain fiduciaries (estates and trusts). Most jurisdictions attempt to assure the collection of income taxes by requiring certain pay-as-you-go procedures, including withholding requirements for employees and estimated tax prepayments for all taxpayers.

**LO.3**

Recall the basic tax formula for individuals and taxable business entities.

**The Structure of the Federal Income Tax.**   Although some variations exist, the basic Federal income tax formula is similar for all taxable entities. This formula is shown in Figure 1–1.

The income tax is based on the assumption that all income is subject to tax and that no deductions are allowed unless specifically provided for in the law. Some types of income are specifically excluded on the basis of various economic, social, equity, and political considerations. Examples include gifts, inheritance, life insurance proceeds received by reason of death, and interest income from state and local bonds. All entities are allowed to deduct business expenses from gross income, but a number of limitations and exceptions are applied. A variety of credits against the tax are also allowed, again on the basis of economic, social, equity, or political goals of Congress.

Income tax rates for all entities are progressive. The corporate rates range from 15 percent on the lowest level of taxable income to 35 percent on the highest level. Individual rates range from 10 percent to 35 percent in 2005. Estates and trusts are also subject to taxation, with rates ranging from 15 percent to 35 percent in 2005.

Partnerships, qualifying small business corporations, and some limited liability companies are not taxable entities, but must file information returns. Owners of

■ **FIGURE 1–2**

Federal Income Tax Formula for Individuals

| | |
|---|---|
| Income (broadly conceived) | $xx,xxx |
| Less: Exclusions (income that is not subject to tax) | (x,xxx) |
| Gross income (income that is subject to tax) | $xx,xxx |
| Less: Certain business and investment deductions (usually referred to as deductions *for* adjusted gross income) | (x,xxx) |
| Adjusted gross income | $xx,xxx |
| Less: The greater of certain personal and employee deductions (usually referred to as *itemized deductions*) *or* | |
| The standard deduction (including any *additional* standard deduction) | (x,xxx) |
| Less: Personal and dependency exemptions | (x,xxx) |
| Taxable income | $xx,xxx |
| Federal income tax on taxable income (see Tax Rate Schedules inside front cover of text) | $ x,xxx |
| Less: Tax credits (including Federal income tax withheld and other prepayments of Federal income taxes) | (xxx) |
| Tax owed (or refund) | $ xxx |

these business entities then are taxed on the net taxable income of the enterprise, proportionate to their holdings.

In the case of individuals, deductions are separated into two categories—deductions *for* adjusted gross income (AGI) and deductions *from* AGI. Generally, deductions *for* AGI are related to business activities, while deductions *from* AGI are often personal in nature (e.g., medical expenses, mortgage interest and property taxes on a personal residence, charitable contributions, and personal casualty losses) or related to investment activities. Deductions *from* AGI take the form of *itemized deductions* and personal and dependency exemptions. Individuals may take a *standard deduction* (a specified amount based on filing status) rather than itemizing actual deductions. An overview of the individual income tax formula is provided in Figure 1–2.

**State Income Taxes.** Most states (except Alaska, Florida, Nevada, South Dakota, Texas, Washington, and Wyoming) impose a traditional income tax on individuals. Tennessee taxes only income from stocks and bonds, and New Hampshire taxes only dividend and interest income. Most states also impose either a corporate income tax or a franchise tax based in part on corporate income. The following additional points can be made about state income taxes.

- State income tax usually relies on Federal income tax laws to some degree—the states use Federal taxable income as a base, with a few adjustments (e.g., a few allow a deduction for Federal income taxes paid and sometimes an exclusion on interest income earned on Federal securities).
- For individuals, a few states impose a flat rate on Federal AGI.
- Several states piggyback directly on the Federal income tax system by using the Federal income tax liability as a base.
- Most states also require withholding of state income tax from salaries and wages and estimated payments by corporations and self-employed individuals.
- Most states have their own set of rates, exemptions, and credits.
- Many states also allow a credit for taxes paid to other states.

**BRIDGE DISCIPLINE**

**Bridge to Political Science and Sociology**

The tax law and its effects on citizens and businesses of the United States are included in many other academic disciplines. Tax burdens are part of American fiction, family studies, and minority issues, as well as economics, finance, and management courses.

In the Bridge feature found in most chapters of this text, we relate the concerns of other disciplines to a more specific review of tax law, as presented here. With the topical knowledge obtained in this text, the reader can better understand the issues raised by other disciplines, sometimes to support beliefs held by others, and sometimes to refute them.

For instance, the structure of the U.S. tax system raises many issues of equity and fairness. Politicians and journalists discuss these issues freely, often without the requisite tax knowledge to draw proper conclusions.

- Should the property tax on real estate be used to finance the local public education system? Why should elderly taxpayers with grown children, or parents who send their children to private schools, continue to pay for public schools through these taxes?
- How will the repeal of the Federal estate tax affect legacy gifts made to charitable organizations? Would the lack of a charitable contribution deduction impair the ability of charities to raise operating and capital funds?
- Does a regressive sales/use tax fall harder on individuals of color?

**Local Income Taxes.**   Cities imposing an income tax include Baltimore, Cincinnati, Cleveland, Detroit, Kansas City (Mo.), New York, Philadelphia, and St. Louis. City income taxes usually apply to anyone who earns income in a city. They are designed to collect contributions for government services from those who live in the suburbs but work in the city as well as from local residents.

**LO.4**

Understand the relationship between business entities and their owners.

# Income Taxation of Business Entities

## PROPRIETORSHIPS

The simplest form of business entity is a **proprietorship,** which is not a separate taxable entity. Instead, the proprietor reports the net profit of the business on his or her own individual tax return.

Individuals who own proprietorships often have specific tax goals with regard to their financial interactions with the business. Because a proprietorship is, by definition, owned by an individual, the individual has great flexibility in structuring the entity's transactions in a way that will minimize his or her income tax (or, in some cases, the income tax of the family unit).

**EXAMPLE 14**

Susan, a single individual, is the sole proprietor of Quality Fabrics, a retail store in which she works full-time. The business is her only source of income. Susan's taxable income in 2005 is $100,000, and her Federal income tax is $22,506.50 ($14,652.50 + 28% of the amount over $71,950). Thus, her *marginal tax rate* (the rate she pays on the highest *layer* of taxable income) is 28%. ■

**EXAMPLE 15**

Assume the same facts as in the previous example, except that Susan pays her nondependent 19-year-old son a $10,000 salary to work part-time at Quality Fabrics. This will reduce her 2005 taxable income by $10,000 and reduce her tax bill by $2,800 ($10,000 deduction × 28% marginal tax rate). Her son will have $1,800 in taxable income ($10,000 – $5,000 standard deduction – $3,200 personal exemption) and will be taxed at a 10% rate, which results in Federal income tax of $180. In summary, Susan (the individual taxpayer) is able to operate the business entity (Quality Fabrics) in a way that will save the family unit $2,620 in Federal income tax ($2,800 saved by Susan – $180 paid by her son). ■

Examples 14 and 15 reflect the fact that a proprietorship itself is not a taxpaying entity. The owner of the proprietorship must report the income and deductions of the business on a Schedule C (Profit or Loss from Business) and must report the net profit (or loss) of the proprietorship on his or her Form 1040 (U.S. Individual Income Tax Return). Specific issues related to the taxation of sole proprietorships are presented in detail in Chapter 16.

## CORPORATIONS

Some corporations pay tax on corporate taxable income while others pay no tax at the corporate level. Corporations that are separate taxable entities are referred to as **C corporations,** because they are governed by Subchapter C of the Internal Revenue Code. Corporations that meet certain requirements and pay no tax at the corporate level are referred to as **S corporations,** because they are governed by Subchapter S of the Code. S corporations are discussed in detail in Chapter 11. C corporations are addressed in Chapters 8 and 9.

A C corporation is required to file a tax return (Form 1120) and is subject to the Federal income tax. The shareholders then pay income tax on the dividends they receive when the corporation distributes its profits. Thus, the profits of the corporation can be seen as subject to double taxation, first at the corporate level and then at the shareholder level.

**EXAMPLE 16**

Joseph is single, has no dependents, and does not itemize deductions. He is the president and sole shareholder of Falcon Corporation. Falcon's taxable income for 2005 is $100,000, and its tax liability is $22,250. If Joseph has the corporation pay all of its after-tax income to him as a dividend, he will receive $77,750, have taxable income of $69,550 (after the $5,000 standard deduction and $3,200 personal exemption), and will pay Federal income tax of $10,432.50 ($69,550 × 15% rate applicable to qualified dividends). The combined Federal income tax paid by Joseph and the corporation is $32,682.50 ($22,250 corporate tax + $10,432.50 individual tax). ■

## PARTNERSHIPS

A partnership is not a separate taxable entity. The partnership is required to file a tax return (Form 1065) on which it summarizes the financial results of the business. Each partner then reports his or her share of the net income or loss and other special items that were reported on the partnership return.

**EXAMPLE 17**

Cameron and Connor form a partnership in which they are equal partners. The partnership reports a $100,000 net profit on its tax return, but is not subject to the Federal income tax. Cameron and Connor each report $50,000 net income from the partnership on their separate individual income tax returns. ■

## S CORPORATIONS

An S corporation is like a C corporation with regard to nontax factors. Shareholders have limited liability, shares are freely transferable, there is a centralized management (vested in the board of directors), and there is continuity of life (i.e., the corporation continues to exist after the withdrawal or death of a shareholder). With regard to tax factors, however, an S corporation is more like a partnership. The S corporation is not subject to the Federal *income tax*. Like a partnership, it does file a tax return (Form 1120S), but the shareholders report their share of net income or loss and other special items on their own tax returns.

**EXAMPLE 18**

Kay and Dawn form a corporation and elect to have it treated as an S corporation. Kay owns 60% of the stock of the corporation, and Dawn owns 40%. The S corporation reports a $100,000 net profit on its tax return, but is not subject to the income tax. Kay will report $60,000 net income from the S corporation on her individual income tax return, and Dawn will report $40,000 on her tax return. ∎

The S corporation, limited liability company, and partnership forms of organization, which are referred to as *flow-through* entities, avoid the double taxation problem associated with the C corporation.

## LIMITED LIABILITY COMPANIES AND LIMITED LIABILITY PARTNERSHIPS

Limited liability companies (LLCs) and limited liability partnerships (LLPs) have grown rapidly in popularity over the last few years. These organizations exist under state laws, and the specific rules vary somewhat from state to state. Both forms have limited liability and some (but not all) of the other nontax features of corporations. Additionally, both forms usually are treated as partnerships for tax purposes.

## DEALINGS BETWEEN INDIVIDUALS AND ENTITIES

Many of the provisions in the tax law deal with the relationships between owners and the business entities they own. The following are some of the major interactions between owners and business entities.

- Owners put assets into a business when they establish a business entity (e.g., a proprietorship, partnership, or corporation).
- Owners take assets out of the business during its existence in the form of salary, dividends, withdrawals, redemptions of stock, etc.
- Through their entities, owner-employees set up retirement plans for themselves, including IRAs, Keogh plans, and qualified pension plans.
- Owners dispose of all or part of a business entity.

Every major transaction that occurs between an owner and a business entity has important tax ramifications. The following are a few of the many tax issues that arise.

- How to avoid taxation at both the owner level and the entity level (i.e., the multiple taxation problem).
- How to get assets into the business with the least adverse tax consequences.
- How to get assets out of the business with the least adverse tax consequences.
- How to dispose of the business entity with the least adverse tax consequences.

When addressing these (and other) tax issues, a common set of tax planning tools can be applied. These tax planning fundamentals are introduced in the next section.

# Tax Planning Fundamentals

## OVERVIEW OF TAX PLANNING

Taxpayers generally attempt to minimize their tax liabilities, and it is perfectly acceptable to do so by using legal means. It is a long-standing principle that taxpayers have no obligation to pay more than their fair share of taxes. The now-classic words of Judge Learned Hand in *Commissioner v. Newman,* reflect the true values a taxpayer should have:

> Over and over again courts have said that there is nothing sinister in so arranging one's affairs as to keep taxes as low as possible. Everybody does so, rich or poor; and all do right, for nobody owes any public duty to pay more than the law demands; taxes are enforced exactions, not voluntary contributions. To demand more in the name of morals is mere cant.[8]

Minimizing taxes legally is referred to as **tax avoidance.** On the other hand, some taxpayers attempt to *evade* income taxes through illegal actions. There is a major distinction between tax avoidance and **tax evasion.** Though eliminating or reducing taxes is also a goal of tax evasion, the term *evasion* implies the use of subterfuge and fraud as a means to this end. Tax avoidance is legal, while tax evasion subjects the taxpayer to numerous civil and criminal penalties, including prison sentences.

Clients expect tax practitioners to provide advice to help them minimize their tax costs. This part of the tax practitioner's practice is referred to as *tax planning*. To structure a sound tax minimization plan, a practitioner must have a thorough knowledge of the tax law. Tax planning skill is based on knowledge of tax saving provisions in the tax law, as well as provisions that contain costly pitfalls for the unwary. Thorough study of the remainder of this text will provide a solid base of the knowledge required to recognize opportunities and avoid pitfalls. Tax planning requires the practitioner to have in mind both a framework for planning and an understanding of the tax planning implications of a client's situation.

## A GENERAL FRAMEWORK FOR INCOME TAX PLANNING

**TAX PLANNING FRAMEWORK**

The primary goal of tax planning is to design a transaction so as to minimize its tax costs, while meeting the other nontax objectives of the client. Generally, this means that the client attempts to maximize the present value of its after-tax income and assets. Selecting a specific form of transaction solely for the sake of tax minimization often leads to a poor business decision. Effective tax planning requires careful consideration of the nontax issues involved in addition to the tax consequences.

Careful analysis of the tax formula (refer to Figure 1–1) reveals a series of tax minimization strategies. Through creative tax planning that also takes into consideration a client's nontax concerns, each component of the tax formula can be managed in a way that will help to minimize the client's tax liability. The General Framework for Income Tax Planning in Figure 1–3 lists each element in the income tax formula, develops tax planning strategies designed to minimize taxes, and provides brief summaries of specific examples of tax planning. The framework is followed by a discussion of the tax planning strategies, along with detailed examples of how the strategies can be applied. In Chapters 3–16 of this book, these strategies and their tax formula components provide the framework for Planning Strategies features.

---

[8]47–1 USTC ¶9175, 35 AFTR 857, 159 F.2d 848 (CA-2, 1947).

**■ FIGURE 1–3**
General Framework for Income
Tax Planning

| Tax Formula | Tax Planning Strategy | Tax Planning Examples |
|---|---|---|
| Income and exclusions | ➤ **Avoid income recognition.** | Compensate employees with nontaxable fringe benefits (see Example 19). |
| | ➤ **Postpone recognition of income to achieve tax deferral.** | Postpone sale of assets (see Example 20). |
| – Deductions | ➤ **Maximize deductible amounts.** | Invest in stock of another corporation (see Example 21). |
| | ➤ **Accelerate recognition of deductions to achieve tax deferral.** | Elect to deduct charitable contribution in year of pledge rather than in year of payment (see Example 22). |
| = Taxable income | | |
| × Tax rate | ➤ **Shift net income from high-bracket years to low-bracket years.** | Postpone recognition of income to a low-bracket year (see Example 23). |
| | | Postpone recognition of deductions to a high-bracket year (see Example 24). |
| | ➤ **Shift net income from high-bracket taxpayers to low-bracket taxpayers.** | Pay children to work in the family business (see Example 25). |
| | ➤ **Shift net income from high-tax jurisdictions to low-tax jurisdictions.** | Establish subsidiary operations in countries with low tax rates (see Examples 26 and 27). |
| | ➤ **Control the character of income and deductions.** | Hold assets long enough to qualify for long-term capital gain rates before selling them (see Example 28). |
| | | Invest in small business stock to obtain ordinary loss treatment under § 1244 (see Example 29). |
| | ➤ **Avoid double taxation.** | Operate as a flow-through entity rather than a C corporation (see Example 30). |
| | | Maximize deductible expenses paid by a C corporation to a shareholder/employee (see Example 31). |
| = Federal income tax | | |
| – Tax credits | ➤ **Maximize tax credits.** | Hire employees who qualify the business for the work opportunity tax credit (see Example 33). |
| = Tax owed (or refund) | | |

FRAMEWORK FOCUS:
INCOME

## TAX MINIMIZATION STRATEGIES RELATED TO INCOME

TAX PLANNING STRATEGY   ➤AVOID INCOME RECOGNITION. Section 61(a) defines gross income as "all income from whatever source derived." However, the Code contains provisions that allow various types of income to be excluded from the tax base. Numerous exclusions are available for individuals, but very few are available for corporations. However, a corporation can provide excludible income for its owners at no tax cost to the corporation.

**EXAMPLE 19**

The average employee of Penguin Corporation is a 25% bracket taxpayer. In negotiations with the employees' union, Penguin proposes that it will increase the amount it spends on nontaxable fringe benefits by an average of $3,000 per employee in lieu of granting a $3,000 average salary increase. The average employee will be better off by $750 if the union accepts Penguin's offer, as shown below:

|  | Salary Increase | Fringe Benefit Increase |
| --- | --- | --- |
| Value of compensation received | $3,000 | $3,000 |
| Tax on employee's compensation | 750 | –0– |
| After-tax increase in compensation | $2,250 | $3,000 |

Although the average employee receives a $750 benefit, there is no tax cost to Penguin because both fringe benefits and salaries are deductible by the corporation. ■

TAX PLANNING STRATEGY

➤**POSTPONE RECOGNITION OF INCOME TO ACHIEVE TAX DEFERRAL.** The IRS requires that both income and expenses be reported in the proper year. If not for this requirement, taxpayers could freely shift income and expenses from year to year to take advantage of tax rate differentials or could defer tax liabilities indefinitely. Although various rules limit the shifting of income and deductions across time periods, some opportunities still exist.

**EXAMPLE 20**

In 1996, Turquoise Corporation acquired land for investment purposes at a cost of $500,000. In November 2005, Turquoise is negotiating to sell the land to Aqua Corporation for $800,000. Aqua insists that the transaction be completed in 2005, but Turquoise wants to delay the sale until 2006 in order to defer the tax on the gain. In an effort to compromise, Turquoise agrees to sell the land in November of 2005 and asks Aqua to pay for the land in two installments, $400,000 in December 2005 and $400,000 in January 2006. This will enable Turquoise to use the installment sale method, under which Turquoise will report $150,000 of the gain in 2005 and the remaining $150,000 in 2006. By electing the installment method, Turquoise will be able to defer the payment of tax on $150,000 of the gain for one year. Assuming that the marginal tax rate[9] (or marginal tax bracket) for Turquoise is 35%, this tax deferral strategy will provide $52,500 ($150,000 × 35%) to be invested or used in the business for a year. ■

FRAMEWORK FOCUS: DEDUCTIONS

## TAX MINIMIZATION STRATEGIES RELATED TO DEDUCTIONS

TAX PLANNING STRATEGY

➤**MAXIMIZE DEDUCTIBLE AMOUNTS.** A corporation that owns stock in another corporation is eligible for a *dividends received deduction (DRD)*. The DRD is equal to a specified percentage of the dividends received. The percentage is based on the amount of stock that the investor corporation owns in the investee corporation (70 percent deduction for ownership of less than 20 percent, 80 percent deduction for ownership of 20 percent or more but less than 80 percent, and 100 percent deduction for ownership of 80 percent or more).

**EXAMPLE 21**

Falcon Corporation invests in bonds of Sparrow Corporation and receives interest of $20,000 in 2005. Red Hawk Corporation acquires 15% of the stock of Pheasant Corporation and receives a $20,000 dividend in 2005. Falcon's taxable income is increased by $20,000 of

---

[9]A taxpayer's *marginal tax rate* (or *marginal tax bracket*) is the rate that would be paid on an additional dollar of taxable income.

interest received. Red Hawk's income is increased by $20,000 in dividend income, but it is allowed a $14,000 dividends received deduction, thus increasing taxable income by only $6,000. ■

Example 21 clearly demonstrates the *tax* advantage of dividend income versus interest income. However, it is also important to consider *nontax* factors. Is the investment in bonds safer than the investment in stock? Does the potential growth in the value of stock outweigh the possible risk of investing in stock versus bonds?

**TAX PLANNING STRATEGY**   ▶**ACCELERATE RECOGNITION OF DEDUCTIONS TO ACHIEVE TAX DEFERRAL.** Both corporate and noncorporate taxpayers may deduct charitable contributions if the recipient is a qualified charitable organization. Generally, a deduction is allowed only for the year in which the payment is made. However, an important exception is available for *accrual basis corporations*. They may claim the deduction in the year *preceding* payment if two requirements are met. First, the contribution must be authorized by the board of directors by the end of that year. Second, the contribution must be paid on or before the fifteenth day of the third month of the next year.

**EXAMPLE 22**   Blue, Inc., a calendar year, accrual basis corporation, wants to make a $10,000 donation to the Atlanta Symphony Association (a qualified charitable organization), but does not have adequate funds to make the contribution in 2005. On December 28, 2005, Blue's board of directors *authorizes* a $10,000 contribution to the Association. The donation is made on March 14, 2006. Because Blue is an accrual basis corporation, it may claim the $10,000 donation as a deduction for calendar year 2005, even though payment is not made until 2006. ■

In the preceding example, Blue Corporation was able to take advantage of a tax provision and reduce taxable income for 2005 by $10,000. Assuming that Blue is in the 35 percent marginal bracket, the corporation has been able to defer payment of $3,500 in Federal income tax. The $3,500 can be invested or used in the business for a year.

**FRAMEWORK FOCUS: TAX RATES**

## TAX MINIMIZATION STRATEGIES RELATED TO TAX RATES

**TAX PLANNING STRATEGY**   ▶**SHIFT NET INCOME FROM HIGH-BRACKET YEARS TO LOW-BRACKET YEARS.** One objective of shifting income is to defer the payment of income tax (refer to Example 20). A second time-shifting strategy is to shift *net* income from high-tax to low-tax years. This can be accomplished by shifting income from high-bracket years to low-bracket years or by shifting deductions from low-bracket years to high-bracket years.

**EXAMPLE 23**   Egret Corporation, a calendar year taxpayer, is in the 34% bracket in 2005, but expects to be in the 25% bracket in 2006. The corporation, which is negotiating a $10,000 service contract with a client, decides to wait until 2006 to sign the contract and perform the services. The client is indifferent as to when the contract is completed. Thus, Egret saves $900 in income tax by deferring the service contract income to 2006, when it will be taxed at the 25% rate instead of the current 34% rate. In this case, the income-shifting strategy is used to accomplish two tax planning objectives. First, shifting the income defers the payment of income tax from 2005 to 2006. Second, the shifting strategy results in the income being taxed at a rate of 25% rather than 34%. ■

**EXAMPLE 24**   Macaw Corporation has been sued for $125,000 damages by a customer, and the parties decided to settle out of court for $100,000. Macaw expects to be in the 25% bracket in 2005 and the 35% bracket in 2006. Macaw will save $10,000 in income tax if it finalizes the agreement in January 2006 rather than December 2005 [$100,000 × (35% − 25%)]. ■

TAX PLANNING STRATEGY ▶**SHIFT NET INCOME FROM HIGH-BRACKET TAXPAYERS TO LOW-BRACKET TAX-PAYERS.** Individual income tax rates range from 10 to 35 percent. Although several provisions in the tax law prevent shifting income from high-bracket taxpayers to low-bracket taxpayers, many opportunities to do so remain. Business entities can be effective vehicles for shifting income to low-bracket taxpayers.

**EXAMPLE 25**

Bill Gregory is the president and sole shareholder of Grayhawk, Inc., an S corporation. He projects that Grayhawk will earn $400,000 in 2005. Bill will be taxed on this income at a 35% marginal rate. Bill and his wife have four teenage children, all of whom are dependents. Bill decides to employ the children as part-time workers throughout 2005 and pay them $11,000 each. This will reduce Bill's income from Grayhawk by $44,000 and reduce his Federal income tax by $15,400 ($44,000 × 35%). Each child will have taxable income of $6,000 ($11,000 − $5,000 standard deduction) and will pay $600 of Federal income tax ($6,000 × 10% rate). As a result of this income-shifting strategy, the family unit will save $13,000 ($15,400 tax saved by Bill − $2,400 tax paid by children). ∎

TAX PLANNING STRATEGY ▶**SHIFT NET INCOME FROM HIGH-TAX JURISDICTIONS TO LOW-TAX JURISDIC-TIONS.** The state or country where income is earned (or where a deduction is incurred) can have a large impact on an entity's overall tax liability. Hence, shifting income from high-tax jurisdictions to low-tax jurisdictions or shifting deductions from low-tax jurisdictions to high-tax jurisdictions is an important tax planning strategy.

**EXAMPLE 26**

Gold International owns a sales subsidiary in Texas and a manufacturing subsidiary in Ireland (which imposes a 10% tax rate on certain types of business income). The Irish subsidiary makes drill presses and sells them for $4 million to the Texas subsidiary, which then modifies them and offers them for sale to businesses in the United States for $8.4 million. The cost of manufacturing and modifying each drill press is $3 million. Of the $5.4 million of profit earned, $1 million is attributable to the Irish corporation (which is subject to a 10% tax rate), and $4.4 million is attributable to the U.S. corporation (which is subject to a 34% tax rate). Gold's total tax liability is $1,596,000 [($1,000,000 × 10%) + ($4,400,000 × 34%)]. ∎

**EXAMPLE 27**

Assume the same facts as in the previous example, except $5 million of the profit is attributable to the Irish corporation and $400,000 is attributable to the U.S. corporation. In this case, Gold's total tax liability is $636,000 [($5,000,000 × 10%) + ($400,000 × 34%)]. Thus, by altering the amount of work done in each of the two subsidiaries and the amount of income generated by each, Gold's tax liability is decreased by $960,000 ($1,596,000 − $636,000). ∎

TAX PLANNING STRATEGY ▶**CONTROL THE CHARACTER OF INCOME AND DEDUCTIONS.** For various policy reasons, Congress has chosen to treat certain categories of income and losses more favorably than others. For instance, the provisions that tax long-term capital gains at a maximum rate of 15 percent, compared to a 35 percent rate on ordinary income, were enacted to encourage individuals to make long-term investments of capital in the economy.

**EXAMPLE 28**

Lisa is the proprietor of Designer Enterprises. Because a proprietorship is a flow-through entity, Lisa must report all of Designer's transactions on her individual income tax return. On October 9, 2005, Lisa invested $25,000 of Designer's excess cash in Lavender Corporation stock. On October 1, 2006, the stock was worth $35,000.

Lisa, who is a 35% bracket taxpayer, has decided to sell the stock and use the cash to increase Designer's inventory. She must hold the stock until October 10, 2006, for the gain to qualify as long term (held more than a year). If she sells the stock before October 10, 2006, the gain will be short term, and she will pay 35% tax on the gain. If she sells the stock after October 9, 2006, the gain will be long term, and she will pay 15% tax on the gain. ∎

To encourage investment in small businesses, Congress enacted the § 1244 provisions, which provide favorable treatment of losses incurred on the sale of qualifying small business stock. Generally, losses on the sale of stock are treated as capital losses. Individuals with capital losses in excess of capital gains are permitted to deduct only $3,000 of such losses against ordinary income in a tax year. To make small business stock more attractive as an investment, § 1244 allows up to $50,000 ($100,000 if married filing jointly) of losses on such stock to be treated as ordinary losses, thus exempting the § 1244 losses from being offset against capital gains and then from the $3,000 limit that would otherwise apply to any excess capital losses.

**EXAMPLE 29**

Roberto invested $80,000 in Mauve Corporation stock and sold the stock in 2005 for $40,000. He has no other capital asset transactions and does not expect to have any in future years. If the Mauve stock qualifies as § 1244 stock, Roberto may deduct the entire $40,000 loss in 2005 as an ordinary loss. If the stock does not qualify as § 1244 stock, Roberto may deduct only $3,000 as a capital loss in 2005 and must carry the remaining loss of $37,000 forward. In future years, the loss will continue to be subject to the $3,000 per year limitation. ∎

**TAX PLANNING STRATEGY**

➤**AVOID DOUBLE TAXATION.** The owners of a corporation can choose between two entity forms. A C corporation, also referred to as a regular corporation, is a taxable entity that pays tax on corporate profits. Shareholders also pay tax on dividends received from a C corporation, resulting in what is commonly referred to as *double taxation* (refer to Example 16). Note, however, as discussed in Chapter 3, the dividends may be eligible for a beneficial tax rate.

Shareholders can avoid double taxation by electing to have a corporate entity become an S corporation. Unlike a C corporation, an S corporation is not a taxable entity. Instead, the profits and losses of the S corporation flow through to the shareholders and are reported on their tax returns (see Chapter 11).

**EXAMPLE 30**

Chickadee, Inc., a C corporation with net income of $100,000 in 2005, pays Carl, its sole shareholder, a $77,750 dividend. Chickadee must pay corporate income tax of $22,250 on the net income of $100,000, and Carl must pay tax on the $77,750 dividend. Sparrow, Inc., an S corporation, earns $100,000 in 2005. Sparrow is not a taxable entity, so it pays no income tax on the $100,000 net income. Sam, who is the sole shareholder of Sparrow, must include $100,000 in computing his taxable income. ∎

There are other entity choices that can be used to avoid double taxation, including partnerships and limited liability companies. Partnerships and limited liability companies, like S corporations, are flow-through entities rather than taxable entities (see Chapter 10).

Choosing to operate as a flow-through entity is not the only way to avoid double taxation. Double taxation can be avoided or minimized by having the corporation make payments, such as salaries, rent, and interest to the shareholders.

**EXAMPLE 31**

Walt is the president and sole shareholder of Meadowlark, Inc., a C corporation. Meadowlark's taxable income before any payment to Walt is $600,000. Walt, a skilled manager, is primarily responsible for the profitability of the corporation. If Meadowlark pays Walt a dividend of $400,000, the corporation must pay Federal income tax on $600,000, and Walt must include the $400,000 dividend in gross income. However, if Meadowlark pays Walt a salary of $400,000, the salary is deductible, and the corporation has only $200,000 of taxable income. Walt must include the $400,000 salary in gross income. In either case, Walt must include $400,000 in gross income (the dividends, however, may be eligible for a beneficial tax rate). Meadowlark, on the other hand, will have $400,000 less taxable income if the payment to Walt is a salary payment rather than a dividend payment. ∎

<table>
<tr><td>

FRAMEWORK FOCUS:
CREDITS

TAX PLANNING STRATEGY

</td></tr>
</table>

## TAX MINIMIZATION STRATEGIES RELATED TO CREDITS

➤**MAXIMIZE TAX CREDITS.** For many years, Congress has used the tax credit provisions of the Internal Revenue Code liberally in implementing tax policy. It is important to understand the difference between a credit and a deduction, both of which reduce a taxpayer's tax liability. A deduction reduces taxable income, which results in a reduction of the tax paid. The tax benefit of the deduction depends on the amount of the qualifying expenditure and the taxpayer's tax rate. A tax credit reduces the tax liability dollar for dollar and is not affected by the taxpayer's tax rate.

**EXAMPLE 32**

Oriole Corporation, which is in the 25% marginal bracket, has a $6,000 deduction for expenditures made to repair a machine. The deduction will reduce taxable income by $6,000 and will result in a tax liability reduction of $1,500 ($6,000 deduction × 25% marginal rate). Oriole also incurred expenditures of $6,000 to rehabilitate a building, which qualifies the corporation for a tax credit of $600 ($6,000 rehabilitation expenditures × 10% rate for the credit). The rehabilitation expenditures credit results in a $600 reduction of Oriole's tax liability. In addition, Oriole's depreciable basis for the building will increase by $5,400 ($6,000 expenditures – $600 credit). ■

One example of the use of credits to influence taxpayer behavior is the work opportunity tax credit, which was enacted to encourage employers to hire employees from several targeted and economically disadvantaged groups, including high-risk youths, summer youth employees, and military veterans. The employee is certified to be a member of a qualifying targeted group. The work opportunity tax credit is 40 percent of the first $6,000 of wages paid during the first 12 months of employment.[10]

**EXAMPLE 33**

Robin Corporation hired a high-risk youth for four months at a cost of $6,000. Robin will qualify for the work opportunity tax credit and will be allowed a credit of $2,400 ($6,000 wages × 40% credit rate) and a wage deduction of $3,600 ($6,000 wages – $2,400 credit). Robin is a 34% bracket taxpayer. The $3,600 deduction will reduce Robin's income tax by $1,224 ($3,600 × 34%). The total tax saving will be $3,624 ($1,224 + $2,400 credit).

If the employee does not qualify Robin for the work opportunity tax credit, Robin will be allowed a deduction of $6,000, which will result in a tax saving of $2,040 ($6,000 × 34%). Thus, hiring an employee who qualifies Robin for the work opportunity tax credit will save an additional $1,584 in tax ($3,624 – $2,040). ■

## THINKING OUTSIDE THE FRAMEWORK

Although the General Framework for Income Tax Planning in Figure 1–3 is broad and covers most tax planning strategies, some strategies fall outside the framework. In addition, other planning ideas can supplement the strategies in the framework. Some of these ideas are discussed below.

**Determining the Tax Burden.** To engage in effective tax planning, one must be able to identify the relevant tax rate that will be applied to a transaction. There are three kinds of tax rates. A taxpayer's *marginal* tax rate (or tax bracket) is the rate that would be paid on an additional dollar of taxable income. Referring to the corporate income tax rate schedule inside the front cover of this text, a corporation's marginal tax rate on its first dollar of income is 15 percent. Similarly, the marginal tax rate faced by a corporation with $100,001 of income is 39 percent. The *average*

---

[10]The work opportunity tax credit was extended through December 31, 2005, by the Working Families Tax Relief Act of 2004.

tax rate is the ratio of taxes paid to the tax base. Thus, a corporation with $100,000 of taxable income is subject to an average tax rate of 22.25 percent ($22,250 in tax divided by $100,000 in taxable income). A third kind of tax rate, the *effective* tax rate, can be seen as either (1) the ratio of taxes paid to financial net income before tax or (2) the sum of currently payable and deferred tax expense divided by net income before tax. Of these approaches to determining a taxpayer's tax rate, the marginal tax rate is most appropriate for tax planning purposes.

**EXAMPLE 34**

Azure Corporation has taxable income of $80,000. Azure also has $10,000 of tax-free interest income from municipal bonds. Using the corporate tax rate schedule inside the front cover of this text, one can determine that the company's tax liability is $15,450. If Azure were to earn an additional dollar in taxable income, it would pay $0.34 in tax. Thus, the company's marginal tax rate is 34%. Azure's average tax rate is the ratio of taxes paid to taxable income or 19.3% ($15,450/$80,000). Finally, the company has an effective rate of tax of 17.2% ($15,450/$90,000), the ratio of taxes paid to financial net income before tax (here, the sum of taxable income and tax-free income). ■

The actual tax paid may not always be apparent. For example, the amount of taxes paid should include both current taxes and the present value of future taxes generated by a transaction.

**EXAMPLE 35**

Magenta Corporation is a publishing company that specializes in electronic media. It is a new corporation that was formed on January 1, 2003. During that year, it generated a net operating loss (NOL) of $300,000. The NOL can be carried forward to offset future years' taxable income and thereby reduce Magenta's future tax liabilities. Magenta expects to earn $100,000 of income each year over the next four years. The NOL should completely offset the company's taxable income for the first three of these years.

At the beginning of 2004, Magenta must decide whether to invest in a project that will earn an additional $40,000 of taxable income during 2004 or a project that will generate $36,000 of tax-free income. The company's president reasons that, since the company has an NOL carryforward, the applicable tax rate is 0%, so the taxable project should be chosen.

The president's reasoning is incorrect, because an additional $40,000 of income now will result in $40,000 of taxable income in 2006 (since there will be $40,000 less NOL available in that year).

| | 2004 | 2005 | 2006 | 2007 |
|---|---|---|---|---|
| *Alternative 1 (tax-free investment)* | | | | |
| Pre-NOL taxable income | $ 100,000 | $ 100,000 | $ 100,000 | $100,000 |
| NOL carryforward (from 2003) | (300,000) | (200,000) | (100,000) | –0– |
| Taxable income | $　–0– | $　–0– | $　–0– | $100,000 |
| *Alternative 2 (taxable investment)* | | | | |
| Pre-NOL taxable income | $ 140,000 | $ 100,000 | $ 100,000 | $100,000 |
| NOL carryforward (from 2003) | (300,000) | (160,000) | (60,000) | –0– |
| Taxable income | $　–0– | $　–0– | $ 40,000 | $100,000 |

The tax on the $40,000 project equals the discounted value of the tax due in 2006. Assuming a 10% discount rate and a 15% corporate tax rate, the present value of taxes paid in three years is $4,508, and the discounted tax rate is 11.27%. Thus, the after-tax proceeds on the taxable project will be $35,492, or $508 *less* than the $36,000 earnings on the tax-free project. ■

Finally, the amount of tax paid includes both *explicit* taxes (paid directly to the government) and **implicit taxes** (paid through higher prices or lower returns on tax-favored investments).

Sunflower, Inc., a C corporation with a 15% marginal tax rate, has accumulated excess cash of $100,000 that it wants to invest in bonds. Sunflower has the option of investing in taxable corporate bonds that yield 9% or tax-free municipal bonds that yield 6%. Assume that the bonds are identical, except for their tax status.

Sunflower's tax rate on the corporate bonds is explicit at 15%. The tax rate on the municipal bonds is implicit, evidenced by the lower return on the bonds. Since the bonds are identical, if the municipal bonds were taxable, they would yield a 9% pre-tax rate. Their after-tax rate is 6% because they are tax-free. Hence, the implicit tax rate on the municipal bonds equals 33%, or the tax rate that would generate a 6% after-tax return on a 9% bond [9% − (0.33 × 9%)].

Since Sunflower is in the 15%, tax bracket, it should invest in the taxable bonds because it would face a higher marginal tax rate (a 33% implicit rate) if it invested in the municipal bonds. Stated another way, Sunflower's after-tax return on the taxable bonds is greater than the 6% return available on the tax-free bonds. ■

## LO.6

Recognize the economic, social, equity, and political considerations that underlie the tax law.

# Understanding the Federal Tax Law

The Federal tax law is a mosaic of statutory laws, administrative pronouncements, and court decisions. Anyone who has attempted to work with these provisions would have to admit to their complexity. For the person who has to trudge through a mass of rules to find the solution to a tax problem, it may be of some consolation to know that the law's complexity can generally be explained. Whether sound or not, there are reasons for the formulation of every rule. Knowing these reasons, therefore, is an important step toward understanding the Federal tax law.

## REVENUE NEEDS

The foundation of the income tax system is the raising of revenue to cover the cost of government operations. Ideally, annual outlays should not exceed anticipated revenues, thereby leading to a balanced budget with no resulting deficit. Many states have achieved this objective by passing laws or constitutional amendments precluding deficit spending.

The U.S. Constitution allows deficit spending, and politicians often find it hard to resist the temptation to spend more than the tax system collects currently. Congress uses several approaches to reduce a tax bill's net revenue loss. When tax reductions are involved, the full impact of the legislation can be phased in over a period of years. Or, as an alternative, the tax reduction can be limited to a period of years. When the period expires, Congress can then renew or not renew the provision in light of budget considerations.

## ECONOMIC CONSIDERATIONS

Using the tax system in an effort to accomplish economic objectives has become increasingly popular in recent years. Generally, proponents of this approach use tax legislation to promote measures designed to help control the economy or encourage certain economic activities and businesses.

**Encouragement of Certain Activities.**   Without passing judgment on the wisdom of any such choices, it is quite clear that the tax law does encourage certain types of economic activity or segments of the economy. For example, the favorable treatment (immediate deduction) allowed research and development expenditures can be explained by the desire to foster technological progress.

---

**⊙ T A X   F A C T**

## WHO PAYS THE FEDERAL INCOME TAX?

**A** Tax Foundation study of 2002 IRS data shows that nearly 54 percent of all Federal individual income taxes is paid by the top 5 percent of earners. Actually, the top 1 percent of U.S. earners pay about a third of all such taxes collected. These amounts are up from similar amounts in 1988, when the top 1 percent paid over a quarter of the Federal individual income taxes, and the top 5 percent paid over 45 percent.

Skews of this sort in the tax-payment data are consistent with the trend since 1980 to shift tax liabilities disproportionately to the top income and wealth groups. Such results likely were purposefully a part of the elder Bush and Clinton tax increases. But they also speak to the effort to relieve low-income taxpayers of all income tax liabilities, as collecting these relatively small amounts likely costs the government more than the revenues it generates.

Selected data from Tax Foundation studies follow.

**Federal Individual Income Taxes**

| 2002 | Returns (000s) | Tax Paid (Millions) | Income Split Point | Share of Total AGI | Share of Tax | Average Tax Rate |
|---|---|---|---|---|---|---|
| All taxpayers | 128,324 | $796,862 | | 100.0% | 100.0% | 13.03% |
| Top 1% AGI | 1,283 | 268,608 | $285,424 | 16.1 | 33.7 | 27.3 |
| Top 5% | 6,416 | 428,680 | 126,525 | 30.6 | 53.8 | 23.0 |
| Top 10% | 12,832 | 523,812 | 92,663 | 41.8 | 65.7 | 20.5 |
| Top 25% | 32,080 | 668,558 | 56,401 | 64.4 | 83.9 | 17.0 |
| Top 50% | 64,162 | 768,963 | 28,654 | 85.8 | 96.5 | 14.7 |
| Bottom 50% | 64,162 | 27,899 | | 14.2 | 3.5 | 3.2 |

| 1988 | Returns (000s) | Tax Paid (Millions) | Income Split Point | Share of Total AGI | Share of Tax | Average Tax Rate |
|---|---|---|---|---|---|---|
| All taxpayers | 108,872 | $412,761 | | 100.0% | 100.0% | 13.2% |
| Top 1% AGI | 1,089 | 113,841 | $157,136 | 15.2 | 27.6 | 24.0 |
| Top 5% | 5,444 | 188,303 | 72,735 | 28.5 | 45.6 | 21.1 |
| Top 10% | 10,887 | 236,411 | 55,437 | 39.5 | 57.3 | 19.2 |
| Top 25% | 27,218 | 321,297 | 35,398 | 62.4 | 77.8 | 16.5 |
| Top 50% | 54,436 | 389,145 | 18,367 | 85.1 | 94.3 | 14.6 |
| Bottom 50% | 54,436 | 23,616 | | 14.9 | 5.7 | 5.1 |

Similarly, Congress has used depreciation deductions as a means of encouraging investment in business capital. Theoretically, shorter asset lives and accelerated methods should encourage additional investment in depreciable property acquired for business use. Conversely, longer asset lives and the required use of the straight-line method of depreciation dampen the tax incentive for capital outlays.

Is preserving the environment a desirable objective? Ecological considerations explain why the tax law permits favorable treatment for costs incurred in the installation of pollution control facilities.

Is it wise to stimulate U.S. exports of goods and services? Considering the pressing and continuing problem of a deficit in the U.S. balance of payments, the answer should be clear. Along this line, Congress has created an exclusion designed to encourage domestic exports of goods by reducing the effective tax rate. Also in an international setting, Congress has deemed it advisable to establish incentives for U.S. citizens who accept employment overseas.

Is saving desirable for the economy? Saving leads to capital formation and thereby makes funds available to finance home construction and industrial expansion. The tax law encourages saving by according preferential treatment to private retirement plans. Not only are contributions to Keogh (H.R. 10) plans and certain Individual Retirement Accounts (IRAs) deductible, but income on the contributions is not taxed until withdrawn.

**Encouragement of Certain Industries.**   No one can question the proposition that a sound agricultural base is necessary for a well-balanced national economy. Undoubtedly, this explains why farmers are accorded special treatment under the Federal income tax system. Among the benefits available to farmers are the election to expense rather than capitalize certain soil and water conservation expenditures and fertilizers and the election to defer the recognition of gain on the receipt of crop insurance proceeds.

**Encouragement of Small Business.**   At least in the United States, a consensus exists that what is good for small business is good for the economy as a whole. Whether valid or not, this assumption has led to a definite bias in the tax law favoring small business. Several income tax provisions can be explained by the desire to benefit small business, including the low marginal tax rates applied to the first dollars of the entity's income.

## SOCIAL CONSIDERATIONS

Some provisions of the Federal tax law, particularly those dealing with the income tax of individuals, can be explained by a desire to encourage certain social results.

- Certain benefits provided to employees through accident and health plans financed by employers are nontaxable to employees. Encouraging such plans is considered socially desirable since they provide medical benefits in the event of an employee's illness or injury.
- A contribution made by an employer to a qualified pension or profit sharing plan for an employee may receive special treatment. The contribution and any income it generates are not taxed to the employee until the funds are distributed. Such an arrangement also benefits the employer by allowing a tax deduction when the contribution is made to the qualified plan. Various types of retirement plans are encouraged to supplement the subsistence income level the employee would otherwise have under the Social Security system.
- A deduction is allowed for contributions to qualified charitable organizations. The deduction attempts to shift some of the financial and administrative burden of socially desirable programs from the public (government) to the private (citizens) sector.
- Various tax credits, deductions, and exclusions that are designed to encourage taxpayers to obtain or extend the level of education are allowed.
- A tax credit is allowed for amounts spent to furnish care for certain minor or disabled dependents to enable the taxpayer to seek or maintain gainful employment. Who could deny the social desirability of encouraging taxpayers to provide care for their children while they work?
- A tax deduction is denied for certain expenditures deemed to be contrary to public policy. This disallowance extends to such items as fines, penalties, illegal kickbacks, bribes to government officials, and gambling losses in excess of gains. Social considerations dictate that the tax law should not encourage these activities by permitting a deduction.

**Bridge to Economics**

Economists refer to taxes as a "dead weight loss," in that a tax levy of any sort withdraws money from the overall economy after it has been earned as part of the Gross Domestic Product. A more modern view of the taxing process would counter that most tax collections are recirculated through the economy as wage payments to government workers, benefit payments to retirees, and interest payments to investors.

But how much tax is too much? History is littered with tax rebellions, including the Boston Tea Party and a property tax revolt started in California in the mid-1970s. According to 2000 data from the Tax Foundation, taxes continue to rank as the highest single outlay for the U.S. family, exceeding the combined totals spent for housing and health care. A full analysis of the data is available at **http://www.taxfoundation.org** under the most current version of the report titled "The Price of Civilized Society."

| Category | | Amount |
|---|---|---|
| Taxes | | |
| Federal | $7,237 | |
| State and local | 3,210 | $10,447 |
| Housing, household | | 5,913 |
| Health care, medical | | 4,133 |
| Food | | 2,713 |
| Transportation | | 2,552 |
| Recreation | | 1,994 |
| Clothing | | 1,436 |

## EQUITY CONSIDERATIONS

The concept of equity is relative. Reasonable persons can, and often do, disagree about what is fair or unfair. In the tax area, moreover, equity is most often tied to a particular taxpayer's personal situation. To illustrate, compare the tax positions of those who rent their personal residences with those who own their homes. Renters may not take a Federal income tax deduction for the rent they pay. For homeowners, however, a large portion of the house payments they make may qualify for the Federal mortgage interest and property tax deductions. Although renters may have difficulty understanding this difference in tax treatment, the encouragement of home ownership can be justified on both economic and social grounds.

In many other parts of the law, however, equity concerns are evident. The concept of equity appears in tax provisions that alleviate the effect of multiple taxation and postpone the recognition of gain when the taxpayer lacks the ability or **wherewithal to pay** the tax. Provisions that mitigate the effect of the application of the annual accounting period concept and help taxpayers cope with the eroding results of inflation also reflect equity considerations.

**Alleviating the Effect of Multiple Taxation.**　The income earned by a taxpayer may be subject to taxes imposed by different taxing authorities. If, for example, the taxpayer is a resident of New York City, income might be subject to Federal, state of New York, and city of New York income taxes. To compensate for this apparent inequity, the Federal tax law allows a taxpayer to claim a deduction for state and local income taxes.

The deduction does not, however, neutralize the effect of multiple taxation, since the benefit derived depends on the taxpayer's Federal income tax rate. Only a tax credit, rather than a deduction, would completely eliminate the effects of multiple taxation on the same income. Equity considerations can also explain the Federal tax treatment of certain income from foreign sources.

**The Wherewithal to Pay Concept.**    The wherewithal to pay concept recognizes the inequity of taxing a transaction when the taxpayer lacks the means to pay the tax. The wherewithal to pay concept underlies a provision in the tax law dealing with the treatment of gain resulting from an involuntary conversion. An involuntary conversion occurs when property is destroyed by casualty or taken by a public authority through condemnation. If gain results from the conversion, it need not be recognized if the taxpayer replaces the property within a specified time period. The replacement property must be similar or related in service or use to that involuntarily converted.

**EXAMPLE 37**

Ron, a rancher, has some pasture land that is condemned by the state for use as a game preserve. The condemned pasture land cost Ron $120,000, but the state pays him $150,000 (its fair market value). Shortly thereafter, Ron buys more pasture land for $150,000.

Ron has realized gain of $30,000 [$150,000 (condemnation award) – $120,000 (cost of land)]. It would be inequitable to require Ron to pay a tax on this gain for two reasons. First, without disposing of the property acquired (the new land), Ron would be hard-pressed to pay the tax. Second, his economic position has not changed. ▪

**EXAMPLE 38**

Assume the same facts as in Example 37, except that Ron reinvests only $140,000 of the award in new pasture land. Now, Ron has a taxable gain of $10,000. Instead of ending up with only replacement property, Ron now has $10,000 in cash. ▪

**Mitigating the Effect of the Annual Accounting Period Concept.**    For purposes of effective administration of the tax law, all taxpayers must report to and settle with the Federal government at periodic intervals. Otherwise, taxpayers would remain uncertain as to their tax liabilities, and the government would have difficulty judging revenues and budgeting expenditures. The period selected for final settlement of most tax liabilities is one year.

The application of this annual accounting period concept can lead to dissimilar tax treatment for taxpayers who are, from a long-range standpoint, in the same economic position.

**EXAMPLE 39**

José and Alicia, both sole proprietors, experienced the following results during the indicated three tax years.

| | Profit (or Loss) | |
|---|---|---|
| Year | José | Alicia |
| 2003 | $50,000 | $ 150,000 |
| 2004 | 60,000 | 60,000 |
| 2005 | 60,000 | (40,000) |

Although José and Alicia have the same profit of $170,000 over the period from 2003 through 2005, the annual accounting period concept places Alicia at a disadvantage for tax purposes. However, the net operating loss deduction generated in 2005 offers Alicia some relief by allowing her to carry back some or all of her 2005 loss to the earlier profitable years (in this case, 2003). Thus, with an NOL carryback, Alicia can obtain an immediate refund for some of the taxes she paid on the $150,000 profit reported for 2003. ■

The installment method of recognizing gain on the sale of property allows a taxpayer to spread tax consequences over the payout period. The harsh effect of taxing all the gain in the year of sale is thereby avoided. The installment method can also be explained by the wherewithal to pay concept, since recognition of gain is tied to the collection of the installment notes received from the sale of the property.

**Coping with Inflation.**   Because of the progressive nature of the income tax, a wage adjustment to compensate for inflation can push the recipient into a higher income tax bracket without increasing real income. Known as *bracket creep*, this phenomenon's overall impact is an erosion of purchasing power. Congress recognized this problem and began to adjust various income tax components, such as marginal tax brackets, standard deduction amounts, and personal and dependency exemptions. Indexation usually is based upon the rise in the consumer price index over the prior year.

## POLITICAL CONSIDERATIONS

A large segment of the Federal tax law is made up of statutory provisions. Since these statutes are enacted by Congress, is it any surprise that political considerations influence tax law? For purposes of discussion, the effect of political considerations on the tax law is divided into the following topics: special interest legislation, political expediency, and state and local government influences.

**Special Interest Legislation.**   There is no doubt that certain provisions of the tax law can largely be explained by the political influence some groups have had on Congress. For example, is there any other realistic reason that prepaid subscription and dues income is not taxed until earned, while prepaid rents are taxed to the landlord in the year received?

Special interest legislation is not necessarily to be condemned if it can be justified on economic, social, or some other utilitarian grounds. At any rate, it is an inevitable product of our political system.

**Political Expediency.**   Various tax reform proposals rise and fall in favor with the shifting moods of the American public. That Congress is sensitive to popular feeling is an accepted fact. Therefore, certain provisions of the tax law can be explained by the political climate at the time they were enacted.

Measures that deter more affluent taxpayers from obtaining so-called preferential tax treatment have always had popular appeal and, consequently, the support of Congress. Provisions such as the limitation on the deductibility of interest on investment indebtedness can be explained on this basis.

**State and Local Government Influences.**   State law has had an influence in shaping our present Federal tax law. One example of this effect is the evolution of Federal tax law in response to states with community property systems. The states with community property systems are Louisiana, Texas, New Mexico, Arizona, California, Washington, Idaho, Nevada, and Wisconsin. Spouses in Alaska can elect community property treatment. The rest of the states are common law jurisdictions. The difference between common law and community property systems centers around the property rights possessed by married persons. In a common law system, each spouse owns whatever he or she earns. Under a community property system, one-half of the earnings of each spouse is considered owned by the other spouse.

**EXAMPLE 40**

Al and Fran are husband and wife, and their only income is the $60,000 annual salary Al receives. If they live in New Jersey (a common law state), the $60,000 salary belongs to Al. If, however, they live in Arizona (a community property state), the $60,000 is divided equally, in terms of ownership, between Al and Fran. ■

At one time, the tax position of the residents of community property states was so advantageous that many common law states actually adopted community property systems. Needless to say, the political pressure placed on Congress to correct the disparity in tax treatment was considerable. To a large extent, this was accomplished in 1948 when the law extended many of the community property tax advantages to residents of common law jurisdictions.

The major advantage extended was the provision allowing married taxpayers to file joint returns and compute the tax liability as if the income had been earned one-half by each spouse. This result is automatic in a community property state, since half of the income earned by one spouse belongs to the other spouse. The income-splitting benefits of a joint return are now incorporated as part of the tax rates applicable to married taxpayers.

**LO.7**

Describe the role played by the IRS and the courts in the evolution of the Federal tax system.

## INFLUENCE OF THE INTERNAL REVENUE SERVICE

The influence of the IRS on tax law is apparent in many areas beyond its role in issuing the administrative pronouncements that make up a considerable portion of our tax law. The IRS has been instrumental in securing the passage of much legislation designed to curtail the most flagrant tax avoidance practices (to close tax loopholes). In addition, the IRS has sought and obtained legislation to make its own job easier (to attain administrative feasibility).

**Closing Perceived Tax Loopholes.** Certain tax provisions are intended to prevent a loophole from being used to avoid the tax consequences intended by Congress. Working within the letter of existing law, ingenious taxpayers and their advisers devise techniques that accomplish indirectly what cannot be accomplished directly. As a consequence, legislation is enacted to close the loopholes that taxpayers have located and exploited. Some tax law can be explained in this fashion and is discussed in the chapters to follow.

**Administrative Feasibility.** Some tax law is justified on the grounds that it simplifies the task of the IRS in collecting the revenue and administering the law. With regard to collecting the revenue, the IRS long ago realized the importance of placing taxpayers on a pay-as-you-go basis. Elaborate withholding procedures apply to wages, and accrual basis taxpayers often must pay taxes on prepaid income in the year received and not when earned. The approach may be contrary to generally accepted accounting principles, but it is consistent with the wherewithal to pay concept.

Of considerable aid to the IRS in collecting revenue are the numerous provisions that impose interest and penalties on taxpayers for noncompliance with the tax law. Provisions such as the penalties for failure to pay a tax or to file a return that is due, the negligence penalty for intentional disregard of rules and regulations, and various penalties for civil and criminal fraud serve as deterrents to taxpayer noncompliance.

One of the keys to an effective administration of our tax system is the audit process conducted by the IRS. To carry out this function, the IRS is aided by provisions that reduce the chance of taxpayer error or manipulation and therefore reduce the audit effort that is necessary. An increase in the amount of the standard

---

### ⊙ T A X   F A C T

## THE COSTS OF COMPLEXITY

**A** tax system that is designed to accomplish so many, sometimes contradictory, goals is bound to be a complex animal. According to the University of Michigan's Office of Tax Policy Research, the current system may actually be so complex as to be self-defeating. By one measure, the costs of complying with the individual income tax portions of the Internal Revenue Code—taxpayers' time, record-keeping systems and software, and costs for tax advisers and preparers—equal 12 cents for every dollar collected by the Treasury for the tax year. Office director Joel Slemrod says that "The U.S. personal income tax system is probably the most complicated in the world," even after years of tax reform measures have worked to decrease marginal rates and reduce the number of available deductions and credits.

---

deduction, for example, reduces the number of individual taxpayers who will choose the alternative of itemizing their personal deductions. With fewer deductions to check, the audit function is simplified.

## INFLUENCE OF THE COURTS

In addition to interpreting statutory provisions and the administrative pronouncements issued by the IRS, the Federal courts have influenced tax law in two other respects.[11] First, the courts have formulated certain judicial concepts that serve as guides in the application of various tax provisions. Second, certain key decisions have led to changes in the Internal Revenue Code.

**Judicial Concepts Relating to Tax.**   Particularly in dealings between related parties, the courts test transactions by looking to whether the taxpayers acted in an arm's length manner. The question to be asked is: Would unrelated parties have handled the transaction in the same way?

**EXAMPLE 41**

Rex, the sole shareholder of Silver Corporation, leases property to the corporation for a yearly rent of $6,000. To test whether the corporation should be allowed a rent deduction for this amount, the IRS and the courts will apply the arm's length concept. Would Silver Corporation have paid $6,000 a year in rent if it had leased the same property from an unrelated party (rather than from Rex)? Suppose it is determined that an unrelated third party would have paid an annual rent for the property of only $5,000. Under these circumstances, Silver Corporation will be allowed a deduction of only $5,000. The other $1,000 it paid for the use of the property represents a nondeductible dividend. Accordingly, Rex will be treated as having received rent income of $5,000 and dividend income of $1,000. ■

**Judicial Influence on Statutory Provisions.**   Some court decisions have been of such consequence that Congress has incorporated them into statutory tax law. For example, many years ago the courts found that stock dividends distributed to

---

[11]A great deal of case law is devoted to ascertaining congressional intent. The courts, in effect, ask: What did Congress have in mind when it enacted a particular tax provision?

the shareholders of a corporation were not taxable as income. This result was largely accepted by Congress, and a provision in the tax statutes now addresses the issue.

On occasion, however, Congress has reacted negatively to judicial interpretations of the tax law.

**EXAMPLE 42**

Nora leases unimproved real estate to Wade for 40 years. At a cost of $200,000, Wade erects a building on the land. The building is worth $100,000 when the lease terminates and Nora takes possession of the property. Does Nora have any income either when the improvements are made or when the lease terminates? In a landmark decision, a court held that Nora must recognize income of $100,000 upon the termination of the lease. ■

Congress felt that the result reached in Example 42 was inequitable in that it was not consistent with the wherewithal to pay concept. Consequently, the tax law was amended to provide that a landlord does not recognize any income either when the improvements are made (unless made in lieu of rent) or when the lease terminates.

## SUMMARY

In addition to its necessary revenue-raising objective, the Federal tax law has developed in response to several other factors.

- *Economic considerations.* The emphasis here is on tax provisions that help regulate the economy and encourage certain activities and types of businesses.
- *Social considerations.* Some tax provisions are designed to encourage (or discourage) socially desirable (or undesirable) practices.
- *Equity considerations.* Of principal concern in this area are tax provisions that alleviate the effect of multiple taxation, recognize the wherewithal to pay concept, mitigate the effect of the annual accounting period concept, and recognize the eroding effect of inflation.
- *Political considerations.* Of significance in this regard are tax provisions that represent special interest legislation, reflect political expediency, and reflect the effect of state and local law.
- *Influence of the IRS.* Many tax provisions are intended to aid the IRS in the collection of revenue and the administration of the tax law.
- *Influence of the courts.* Court decisions have established a body of judicial concepts relating to tax law and have, on occasion, led Congress to enact statutory provisions to either clarify or negate their effect.

# Suggested Further Readings

Barry H. Frank and Jeffrey Cooper, "Courts Approve of Treating Doctors as Independent Contractors," *Practical Tax Strategies,* July 2003, pp. 36–42.

Chaim V. Kofinas, "State & Local Taxation—Sales Tax Treatment of Internet Commerce," *The CPA Journal,* January 2004, pp. 36–40.

Michael Lafferty, editor, "Tough Love from the New Guard," *The Accountant,* September 2004, pp. 6–7.

## KEY TERMS

| | | |
|---|---|---|
| Ad valorem tax, 1–10 | FUTA tax, 1–7 | S corporation, 1–17 |
| C corporation, 1–17 | Gift tax, 1–3 | Sales tax, 1–3 |
| Death tax, 1–8 | Implicit tax, 1–26 | Tax avoidance, 1–19 |
| Employment tax, 1–3 | Inheritance tax, 1–8 | Tax evasion, 1–19 |
| Estate tax, 1–8 | Occupational tax, 1–14 | Use tax, 1–6 |
| Excise tax, 1–4 | Personalty, 1–11 | Value added tax (VAT), 1–7 |
| FICA tax, 1–7 | Proprietorship, 1–16 | Wherewithal to pay, 1–30 |
| Franchise tax, 1–13 | Realty, 1–11 | |

## PROBLEM MATERIALS

### Problems

**Issue ID**

1. Aqua Corporation believes that it will have a better distribution location for its product if it relocates the corporation to another state. What considerations (both tax and nontax) should Aqua Corporation weigh before making a decision on whether to make the move?

2. Give several examples of taxes that are *proportional*. That are *progressive*.

3. Is the Medicare component of FICA a proportional or a progressive tax? Explain.

4. Compare FICA and FUTA in connection with each of the following.
   a. Incidence of taxation.
   b. Justification for taxation.
   c. Rates and base involved.

5. Jim, a resident of Washington (which imposes a general sales tax), goes to Oregon (which does not impose a general sales tax) to purchase his automobile. Will Jim successfully avoid the Washington sales tax? Explain.

6. In 2003, Horace makes a taxable gift of $250,000 upon which he pays a Federal gift tax of $70,800. In 2005, Horace makes another taxable gift of $250,000. Will the 2005 taxable gift result in the same gift tax as the 2003 gift? Why or why not?

7. How much property can Herman, a widower, give to his four married children, their spouses, and eight grandchildren over a period of 10 years without making a taxable gift?

**Issue ID**

8. Once its new facilities are finished, the Church of the Good Samaritan moves from downtown Madison City to the suburbs. Instead of disposing of the old location, the church leases it to a former mayor of Madison City who converts the church building and its parking lot into a high-end restaurant. Comment on any tax ramifications of this arrangement.

**Ethics**

9. The Toth family lives in a residence that they have owned for several years. They purchased the residence from St. Matthew's Catholic Church, which had used the house as a rectory for its priest. To the Toths' surprise, since they purchased the residence, they have not received any ad valorem property tax bills from either the city or the county. Is there a plausible explanation for this? Explain. What, if anything, should the Toths do about the property tax matter?

**Issue ID**

10. Until recently, Hunter College has relied on privately owned dormitories to provide housing for its out-of-state students. After a successful fund-raising campaign, the board of regents is considering purchasing and operating most of the privately owned dormitories. The city where Hunter College is located opposes the project. Why?

**Issue ID**

11. Shaquille O'Neal, a perennial All-Star in the National Basketball Association, was traded by the Los Angeles Lakers to the Miami Heat. Discuss Shaq's state income tax situation both before and after the trade.

**Issue ID**

12. Before she entered a nursing home, Doris signed a deed transferring title to her personal residence to her only son, Walt. Walt has never filed the deed with the county clerk's office and continues to pay the property taxes in his mother's name. Walt and his family are the only occupants of the property. Is there an explanation for Walt's actions?

13. The commissioners for Colby County are actively negotiating with Eagle Industries regarding the location of a new manufacturing facility in the county. As Eagle has several sites from which to pick, a "generous tax holiday" may be needed to influence its choice. The local school district is opposed to any "generous tax holiday."
    a. What might a proposal for a "generous tax holiday" entail?
    b. Why should the school district be opposed?

**Issue ID**

14. The Mayo family is selected for ABC's *Extreme Makeover: Home Edition*. The program gives the Mayos' California home the royal treatment, increasing the living area from 1,200 square feet to about 4,300—more than doubling the value of the property. Do you envision any tax problems?

**Issue ID**

15. During a social event, Muriel and Earl are discussing the home computer each recently purchased. Although the computers are identical makes and models, Muriel is surprised to learn that she paid a sales tax, while Earl did not. Comment as to why this could happen.

**Issue ID**

16. Jared wants to give his wife a $30,000 diamond necklace for her birthday. To avoid the state and local general sales tax of 8.5%, he asks his aunt (who lives in New Hampshire) to make the purchase. Has Jared saved $2,550 (8.5% × $30,000)?

17. Jill is a single individual. In 2005, she has total income of $220,000, credits of $19,000, exclusions of $30,000, deductions *for* AGI of $38,000, itemized deductions of $20,000 (assume no AGI limitations are applicable), a standard deduction of $5,000, a personal exemption equal to $3,200, and estimated tax payments of $16,500.
    a. What is her tax due?
    b. If Jill were a corporation instead of an individual, and if all of her deductions were business related, what would be the tax due?

**Decision Making**

**Communications**

18. Cory and Cynthia have decided to go into business together. They will operate a sandwich delivery business. They expect to have a loss in the first and second years of the business and subsequently expect to make a substantial profit. Both are also concerned about potential liability if a customer ever gets sick. They have called your office and asked for advice about whether they should run their business as a partnership or as a corporation. Write a letter to Cynthia Clay, at 1206 Seventh Avenue, Fort Worth, TX 76101, describing the alternative forms of business that they can select. In your letter, explain what form or forms of business you recommend and why.

**Decision Making**

19. Ashley runs a small business in Boulder, Colorado, that makes snow skis. She expects the business to grow substantially over the next three years. Because she is concerned about product liability and is planning to take the company public in the year 2005, she is currently considering incorporating the business. Financial data are as follows.

|  | 2004 | 2005 | 2006 |
|---|---|---|---|
| Sales revenue | $150,000 | $320,000 | $600,000 |
| Tax-free interest income | 5,000 | 8,000 | 15,000 |
| Deductible cash expenses | 30,000 | 58,000 | 95,000 |
| Tax depreciation | 25,000 | 20,000 | 40,000 |

Ashley expects her marginal tax rate to be 35% over the next three years before any profits from the business are considered. Her cost of capital is 10%.

a. Compute the present value of the future cash flows for 2004 to 2006, assuming Ashley incorporates the business and pays all after-tax income as dividends (that qualify for the 15% rate).

b. Compute the present value of the future cash flows for 2004 to 2006, assuming Ashley continues to operate the business as a sole proprietorship.

c. Should Ashley incorporate the business this year? Why or why not?

20. Sienna, Inc., faces a marginal tax rate of 25%, an average tax rate of 17.5%, and an effective marginal tax rate of 16.8%. Sienna is considering investing in Kiowa County bonds, which currently pay a 5% return (equivalent taxable bonds are paying an 8% return).

a. What is the implicit tax rate on the Kiowa County bonds?

b. Are the Kiowa County bonds a good investment for Sienna? Why or why not?

21. Chartreuse, Inc., has a net operating loss carryforward of $100,000. If Chartreuse continues its business with no changes, it will have $50,000 of taxable income (before the NOL) in both 2005 and 2006. If Chartreuse decides to invest in a new product line instead, it expects to have taxable income of $70,000 in 2005 and $50,000 in 2006. What marginal tax rate does the new product line face in 2005?

22. Mauve Supplies, Inc., reports total income of $120,000. The corporation's taxable income is $105,000. What are Mauve's marginal, average, and effective tax rates?

23. What is the justification for the annual exclusion from the Federal gift tax?

24. Discuss the possible justification for the following provisions of the tax law:

a. The preferential treatment allowed U.S. citizens who work overseas.

b. An election that enables certain corporations to avoid the corporate income tax and pass losses through to their shareholders.

c. The tax treatment of premiums for group term life insurance paid by an employer for employees.

d. The carryback and carryover provisions relating to net operating losses.

25. What purpose is served by allowing individuals to deduct home mortgage interest and property taxes?

26. Some tax rules can be justified on multiple grounds (e.g., economic, social, etc.). In this connection, comment on the possible justification for the rules governing the following:

a. Pension plans.

b. Education.

c. Home ownership.

d. Installment sales.

e. Unearned income.

27. The state has condemned grazing land belonging to Justin, a rancher, for use as a roadside park and campground. Justin paid $20,000 for the land 30 years ago. He is delighted with the condemnation award of $140,000, as he thinks the land is not worth more than $80,000. Shortly thereafter, Justin purchases additional grazing land. What are Justin's tax consequences if the replacement land costs:

a. $15,000?

b. $150,000?

c. $130,000?

28. In what manner does the tax law mitigate the effect of the annual accounting period concept for installment sales?

29. How does the tax law cope with the impact of inflation?

**EXTENDER**    30. Go to **http://www.taxfoundation.org** and determine Tax Freedom Day for your state for 1950, 1960, 1970, 1980, 1990, 2000, and 2004.

**EXTENDER**    31. Contrast a value added tax (VAT) with a national sales tax in terms of anticipated taxpayer compliance.

1. Consider the Tax Foundation data in the Bridge feature on page 1–30.
   a. Convert the data to a pie chart.
   b. Redraw the pie chart, showing your own preferences for the spending patterns of a U.S. family.
   c. If you were a politician, how would you move the country's economy from the chart in (a) to the one in (b)?

# Working with the Tax Law

*After completing Chapter 2, you should be able to:*

## L O . 1
Understand the statutory, administrative, and judicial sources of the tax law and the purpose of each source.

## L O . 2
Locate and work with the tax law and understand the tax research process.

## L O . 3
Communicate the results of the tax research process in a client letter and a tax file memorandum.

## L O . 4
Have an awareness of computer-assisted tax research.

http://wft.swlearning.com

## OUTLINE

---

## TAX TALK

*The less people know about how sausages and laws are made, the better they'll sleep at night.*

—Otto von Bismarck

---

**LO.1**

Understand the statutory, administrative, and judicial sources of the tax law and the purpose of each source.

# Tax Sources

Understanding taxation requires a mastery of the sources of the *rules of tax law*. These sources include not only legislative provisions in the form of the Internal Revenue Code, but also congressional Committee Reports, Treasury Department Regulations, other Treasury Department pronouncements, and court decisions. Thus, the *primary sources* of tax information include pronouncements from all three branches of government: legislative, executive, and judicial.

In addition to being able to locate and interpret the sources of the tax law, a tax professional must understand the relative weight of authority within these sources. The tax law is of little significance, however, until it is applied to a set of facts and circumstances. This chapter, therefore, both introduces the statutory, administrative, and judicial sources of the tax law *and* explains how the law is applied to individual and business transactions. It also explains how to apply research techniques effectively.

Tax research is necessary because the application of the law to a specific situation is often not clear. As complicated as the Internal Revenue Code is, it cannot clearly address every conceivable situation. Accordingly, the tax professional must search other sources (such as administrative rulings and judicial decisions) to determine the most likely tax treatment of a transaction.

Often, this search process will yield widely differing results for similar fact patterns. One of the goals of tax research is to discover which facts and which legal rules are most relevant in determining the ultimate tax consequences. Working with such knowledge, a tax professional can then advise the client about the tax consequences of several possible courses of action. Tax research, in other words, is of critical importance not only in properly characterizing completed events but also in planning proposed transactions.

## STATUTORY SOURCES OF THE TAX LAW

**Origin of the Internal Revenue Code.**   Before 1939, the statutory provisions relating to taxation were contained in the individual revenue acts enacted by

## MEASURING TAX SYSTEM COMPLEXITY

A recent report by the Joint Economic Committee (JEC) of Congress provides several measures of the complexity of the U.S. tax system. Some of these issues also were addressed in testimony to Congress by the Tax Foundation. Here are some of the JEC's observations that justify a conclusion that the U.S. tax system has become too complex.

| | | |
|---|---|---|
| **Internal Revenue Code in 2000** | 2,840 pages | 2.8 million words |
| **Tax Regulations in 2000** | 8,920 pages | 10.7 million words |
| **CCH Federal Tax Reporter** | 6,900 pages in 2000 | 400 pages in 1913 |
| **Cost of complying with the Federal tax system, all taxpayers and forms** | 6.1 billion hours | $183 billion in value of such time, at $30 per hour |
| **Individuals using paid tax preparers** | 53% in 1997 40% in 1990 | 19% in 1960 |
| **Telephone calls to IRS tax "help lines"** | 110 million | 73% received "correct" responses |
| **IRS budget** | $8.2 billion in 2000 | $12 million in 1900 |
| **IRS employees** | 100,000 workers in 2000 | 10,000 workers in 1900 |

Congress. The inconvenience and confusion that resulted from dealing with many separate acts led Congress to codify all of the Federal tax laws. Known as the Internal Revenue Code of 1939, this codification arranged all Federal tax provisions in a logical sequence and placed them in a separate part of the Federal statutes. A further rearrangement took place in 1954 and resulted in the Internal Revenue Code of 1954, which continued in effect until it was replaced by the Internal Revenue Code of 1986.[1]

Now, statutory amendments to the tax law are integrated into the existing Code. Thus, subsequent tax legislation, such as the Working Families Tax Relief Act of 2004 and the American Jobs Creation Act of 2004, has become part of the Internal Revenue Code of 1986.

**The Legislative Process.**   Federal tax legislation generally originates in the House of Representatives, where it is first considered by the House Ways and Means Committee. Tax bills can originate in the Senate if they are attached as riders to other legislative proposals. If acceptable to the committee, the proposed bill is referred to the entire House of Representatives for approval or disapproval. Approved bills are sent to the Senate, where they initially are considered by the Senate Finance Committee.

---

[1]Aside from changes due to a large tax act, the organization of the Internal Revenue Code of 1986 is not substantively different from the organization of the 1954 Code. In contrast, the numbering scheme of sections in the 1939 Code differs from that used in the 1954 Code.

## THOSE DISAPPEARING DEPENDENTS

Tax law changes can have unforeseen or peculiar impacts. In 1986, 77 million dependents were claimed on U.S. individual income tax returns, but a year later, in 1987, more than 7 million of those dependents had disappeared. More than 11,000 taxpayers who claimed seven or more dependents in 1986 claimed none in 1987. Had some disaster or plague occurred?

No, according to former IRS Commissioner Donald C. Alexander. A 1987 tax law change required taxpayers to provide a dependent's Social Security number on their tax returns. Apparently, those 7 million disappearing dependents were fakes who never existed.

Two years later 2.6 million babysitters disappeared. Kidnapped maybe? No, a change in the tax law required taxpayers to provide the babysitter's name, address, and Social Security number on the income tax return. Alexander says that tax laws must be enforced to be effective.

The next step is referral from the Senate Finance Committee to the entire Senate. Assuming no disagreement between the House and Senate, passage by the Senate means referral to the President for approval or veto. If the bill is approved or if the President's veto is overridden, the bill becomes law and part of the Internal Revenue Code. Recently, the passage of JGTRRA of 2003 required the vote of the Vice President to break a 50–50 tie in the Senate.

When the Senate version of the bill differs from that passed by the House, the Conference Committee, which includes members of both the House Ways and Means Committee and the Senate Finance Committee, is called upon to resolve the differences. House and Senate versions of major tax bills frequently differ. One reason bills are often changed in the Senate is that each senator has considerable latitude to make amendments when the Senate as a whole is voting on a bill referred to it by the Senate Finance Committee. In contrast, the entire House of Representatives either accepts or rejects what is proposed by the House Ways and Means Committee, and changes from the floor are rare.

The deliberations of the Conference Committee usually produce a compromise between the two versions, which is then voted on by both the House and the Senate. If both bodies accept the revised bill, it is referred to the President for approval or veto. The typical legislative process dealing with tax bills is summarized in Figure 2–1.

The role of the Conference Committee indicates the importance of compromise in the legislative process. As an example of the practical effect of the compromise process, consider what happened to a provision allowing the amortization of certain intangible assets in the Revenue Reconciliation Act of 1993 (see Figure 2–2).

Referrals from the House Ways and Means Committee, the Senate Finance Committee, and the Conference Committee are usually accompanied by *Committee Reports*. These Committee Reports often explain the provisions of the proposed legislation and are therefore a valuable source for ascertaining the *intent of Congress*. What Congress had in mind when it considered and enacted tax legislation is the key to interpreting legislation. Since Regulations interpreting new legislation normally are not issued immediately after a statute is enacted, taxpayers and the courts look to Committee Reports to determine congressional intent.

■ **FIGURE 2–1**
Legislative Process for Tax Bills

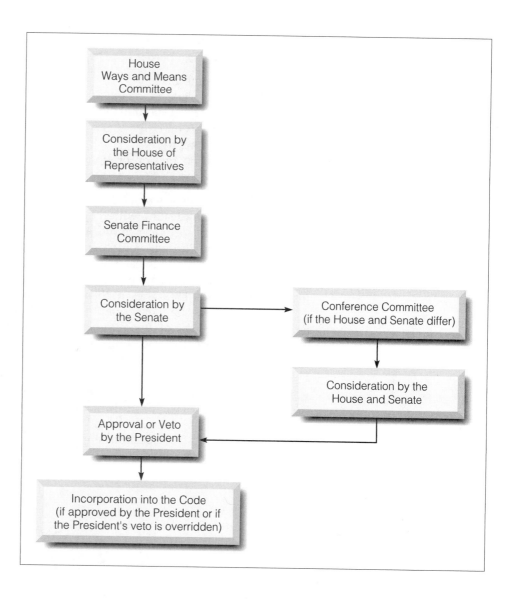

■ **FIGURE 2–2**

Example of Compromise in the
Conference Committee

**Arrangement of the Code.**   The Internal Revenue Code is found in Title 26 of the U.S. Code. Here is a partial table of contents.

> Subtitle A. Income Taxes
>> Chapter 1. Normal Taxes and Surtaxes
>>> Subchapter A. Determination of Tax Liability
>>>> Part I. Tax on Individuals
>>>>> Sections 1–5
>>>> Part II. Tax on Corporations
>>>>> Sections 11–12

In referring to a provision of the Code, the key is usually the Section number. In citing Section 2(a) (dealing with the status of a surviving spouse), for example, it is unnecessary to include Subtitle A, Chapter 1, Subchapter A, Part I. Merely mentioning Section 2(a) will suffice, since the Section numbers run consecutively and do not begin again with each new Subtitle, Chapter, Subchapter, or Part. Not all Code Section numbers are used, however. Part I ends with Section 5 and Part II starts with Section 11 (at present there are no Sections 6, 7, 8, 9, and 10).[2]

Tax practitioners commonly refer to certain areas of income tax law by Subchapter designation. Some of the more common Subchapter designations include Subchapter C ("Corporate Distributions and Adjustments"), Subchapter K ("Partners and Partnerships"), and Subchapter S ("Tax Treatment of S Corporations and Their Shareholders"). Particularly in the last situation, it is much more convenient to describe the effect of the applicable Code provisions (Sections 1361–1379) as "Subchapter S" than as the "Tax Treatment of S Corporations and Their Shareholders."

**Citing the Code.**   Code Sections are often broken down into subparts.[3] Section 2(a)(1)(A) serves as an example.

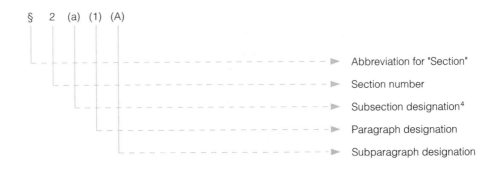

§   2   (a)   (1)   (A)

- ▶ Abbreviation for "Section"
- ▶ Section number
- ▶ Subsection designation[4]
- ▶ Paragraph designation
- ▶ Subparagraph designation

---

[2] When the Code was drafted, Section numbers were intentionally omitted so that later changes could be incorporated into the Code without disrupting its organization. When Congress does not leave enough space, subsequent Code Sections are given A, B, C, etc., designations. A good example is the treatment of Sections 280A through 280H.

[3] Some Code Sections do not have subparts. See, for example, Sections 211 and 241.

[4] Some Code Sections omit the subsection designation and use, instead, the paragraph designation as the first subpart. See, for example, Sections 212(1) and 1222(1).

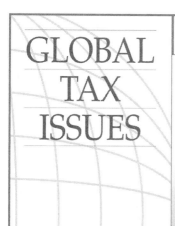

## TAX TREATIES

The United States has entered into treaties with most of the major countries of the world, to eliminate possible double taxation. For example, nonresident alien students wishing to claim exemption from taxation are required to provide an information statement as set forth in several Revenue Procedures. The withholding agent must also certify the form.

Chinese students are required to prepare a four-part statement. Part 3 of the student's statement is as follows.

> I will receive compensation for personal services performed in the United States. This compensation qualifies for exemption from withholding of Federal income tax under the tax treaty between the United States and the People's Republic of China in an amount not in excess of $5,000 for any taxable year.

Broken down by content, a citation for Code Section 2(a)(1)(A) appears as follows.

§ 2 — Definitions and special rules (relating to the income tax imposed on individuals).

(a) — Definition of a surviving spouse.

(1) — For purposes of § 1 (the determination of the applicable rate schedule), a surviving spouse must meet certain conditions.

(A) — One of the conditions necessary to qualify as a surviving spouse is that the taxpayer's spouse must have died during either of his or her two taxable years immediately preceding the present taxable year.

Throughout the text, references to the Code Sections are in the form given above. The symbols "§" and "§§" are used in place of "Section" and "Sections." The following table summarizes the format used in the text.

| Complete Reference | Text Reference |
|---|---|
| Section 2(a)(1)(A) of the Internal Revenue Code of 1986 | § 2(a)(1)(A) |
| Sections 1 and 2 of the Internal Revenue Code of 1986 | §§ 1 and 2 |
| Section 2 of the Internal Revenue Code of 1954 | § 2 of the Internal Revenue Code of 1954 |
| Section 12(d) of the Internal Revenue Code of 1939[5] | § 12(d) of the Internal Revenue Code of 1939 |

**Effect of Treaties.**   The United States signs certain tax treaties (sometimes called tax conventions) with foreign countries to render mutual assistance in tax enforcement and to avoid double taxation. These treaties affect transactions involving U.S. persons and entities operating or investing in a foreign country, as well as persons and entities of a foreign country operating or investing in the United States. Although these bilateral agreements are not codified in any one source, they are published in various Internal Revenue Service publications as well as in privately published tax services.

---

[5]Section 12(d) of the Internal Revenue Code of 1939 is the predecessor to § 2 of the Internal Revenue Codes of 1954 and 1986.

■ **EXHIBIT 2–1**
Administrative Sources

| Source | Location | Authority† |
|---|---|---|
| Regulations | *Federal Register*<br>*Internal Revenue Bulletin*<br>*Cumulative Bulletin* | Force and effect of law. May be cited as precedent. |
| Temporary Regulations | *Federal Register*<br>*Internal Revenue Bulletin*<br>*Cumulative Bulletin* | May be cited as a precedent. |
| Proposed Regulations | *Federal Register*<br>*Internal Revenue Bulletin*<br>*Cumulative Bulletin* | Preview of final Regulations. Not precedent. |
| Revenue Rulings<br>Revenue Procedures<br>Treasury Decisions<br>Actions on Decisions | *Internal Revenue Bulletin***<br>*Cumulative Bulletin* | Do not have the force and effect of law. Not precedent. |
| General Counsel Memoranda<br>Technical Advice Memoranda | Tax Analysts' *Tax Notes*; RIA's *Internal Memoranda of the IRS*; CCH's *IRS Position Reporter* | May not be cited as precedent. |
| Letter Rulings | Research Institute of America and Commerce Clearing House loose-leaf services** | Applicable only to taxpayer addressed. Not precedent. |

*Final, Temporary, and Proposed Regulations are published in soft-cover form and on CD-ROM by several publishers (including *RIA OnPoint*).

**Revenue Rulings, Revenue Procedures, and letter rulings are also published on CD-ROM by several publishers (including *RIA OnPoint*).

†Each of these sources may be substantial authority for purposes of the accuracy-related penalty in § 6662. Notice 90–20, 1990–1 C.B. 328.

Neither a tax law nor a tax treaty automatically takes precedence. When there is a direct conflict, the most recent item will take precedence. With certain exceptions, a taxpayer must disclose on the tax return any position where a treaty overrides a tax law.[6] There is a $1,000 per *failure to disclose* penalty for individuals and a $10,000 per failure to disclose penalty for corporations.[7]

## ADMINISTRATIVE SOURCES OF THE TAX LAW

The administrative sources of the Federal tax law can be grouped as follows: Treasury Department Regulations, Revenue Rulings and Revenue Procedures, and various other administrative pronouncements (see Exhibit 2–1). All are issued by either the U.S. Treasury Department or the IRS.

**Treasury Department Regulations.** Regulations are issued by the U.S. Treasury Department under authority granted by Congress.[8] Usually interpretive by nature, they provide taxpayers with considerable guidance on the meaning and application of the Code and often include examples. Regulations carry considerable authority as the official interpretation of tax statutes. They are an important factor to consider in complying with the tax law.

Treasury Regulations are arranged in the same sequence as the Code. A number is added at the beginning, however, to indicate the type of tax or other matter to which they relate. For example, the prefix 1 designates the Regulations under the

[6]§ 7852(d).
[7]§ 6712.

[8]§ 7805.

income tax law. Thus, the Regulations under Code § 2 would be cited as Reg. § 1.2, with subparts added for further identification. The numbering pattern of these subparts often has no correlation with the Code subsections. The prefix 20 designates estate tax Regulations, 25 addresses gift tax Regulations, 31 relates to employment taxes, and 301 refers to procedure and administration. This list is not all-inclusive. Reg. § 1.351–1(a)(2) is an example of a citation.

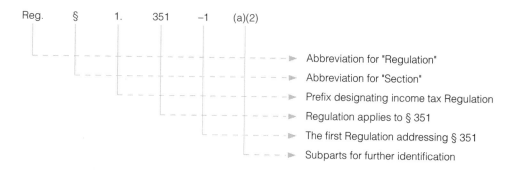

Reg. § 1. 351 –1 (a)(2)

- Abbreviation for "Regulation"
- Abbreviation for "Section"
- Prefix designating income tax Regulation
- Regulation applies to § 351
- The first Regulation addressing § 351
- Subparts for further identification

New Regulations and changes in existing Regulations are usually issued in proposed form before they are finalized. The interval between the proposal of a Regulation and its finalization permits taxpayers and other interested parties to comment on the propriety of the proposal. These comments are usually provided in writing, but oral comments can be offered at hearings held by the IRS on the Regulations in question pursuant to a public notice. This practice of notice-and-comment is a major distinction between Regulations and other forms of Treasury guidance such as Revenue Rulings, Revenue Procedures, and the like.

**Proposed Regulations** under Code § 2, for example, are cited as Prop.Reg. § 1.2. The Tax Court indicates that Proposed Regulations carry little weight—no more than a position advanced in a written brief prepared by a litigating party before the Tax Court.[9]

Sometimes the Treasury Department issues **Temporary Regulations** relating to matters where immediate guidance is important. These Regulations are issued without the comment period required for Proposed Regulations. Temporary Regulations have the same authoritative value as final Regulations and may be cited as precedents. Since 1989, Temporary Regulations also are issued as Proposed Regulations and automatically expire within three years after the date of their issuance.[10]

Proposed, Temporary, and **Final Regulations** are published in the *Federal Register*, the *Internal Revenue Bulletin*, and major tax services.

Regulations may also be classified as *legislative, interpretive,* or *procedural.* This classification scheme is discussed later in the chapter.

**Revenue Rulings and Revenue Procedures.** **Revenue Rulings** are official pronouncements of the National Office of the IRS.[11] Like Regulations, they are designed to provide interpretation of the tax law. However, they do not carry the same legal force and effect as Regulations and usually deal with more restricted problems. In addition, Regulations are approved by the Secretary of the Treasury, whereas Revenue Rulings generally are not.

Both Revenue Rulings and Revenue Procedures serve an important function in providing *guidance* to IRS personnel and taxpayers in handling routine tax matters. Revenue Rulings and Revenue Procedures generally apply retroactively

---

[9] *F. W. Woolworth Co.,* 54 T.C. 1233 (1970); *Harris M. Miller,* 70 T.C. 448 (1978); and *James O. Tomerlin Trust,* 87 T.C. 876 (1986).

[10] § 7805(e).

[11] § 7805(a).

and may be revoked or modified by subsequent rulings or procedures, Regulations, legislation, or court decisions.

Revenue Rulings typically provide one or more examples of how the IRS would apply a law to specific fact situations. Revenue Rulings may arise from technical advice memoranda of the IRS, court decisions, suggestions from tax practitioner groups, and various tax publications. A Revenue Ruling may also arise from a specific taxpayer's request for a letter ruling. If the IRS believes that a taxpayer's request for a letter ruling deserves official publication due to its widespread impact, the letter ruling will be converted into a Revenue Ruling and issued for the information and guidance of taxpayers, tax practitioners, and IRS personnel. Names, identifying descriptions, and money amounts are changed to conceal the identity of the requesting taxpayer.

**Revenue Procedures** are issued in the same manner as Revenue Rulings, but deal with the internal management practices and procedures of the IRS. Familiarity with these procedures increases taxpayer compliance and helps make the administration of the tax laws more efficient. The failure of a taxpayer to follow a Revenue Procedure can result in unnecessary delay or, in a discretionary situation, can cause the IRS to decline to act on behalf of the taxpayer.

Some recent Revenue Procedures dealt with the following matters.

- Deduction limits on luxury automobile depreciation.
- Revised procedures for the issuance of letter rulings.
- Automatic consent procedure for a change in accounting method.

Revenue Rulings and Revenue Procedures are published weekly by the U.S. Government in the *Internal Revenue Bulletin* (I.R.B.). Semiannually, the *Bulletins* for a six-month period are gathered together and published in a bound volume called the *Cumulative Bulletin* (C.B.).[12]

The proper form for citing Rulings and Procedures depends on whether the item has been published in the *Cumulative Bulletin* or is available only in I.R.B. form. Consider, for example, the following sequence.

| Temporary Citation | { | Rev.Rul. 2004–18, I.R.B. No. 8, 509. *Explanation:* Revenue Ruling Number 18, appearing on page 509 of the 8th weekly issue of the *Internal Revenue Bulletin* for 2004. |
|---|---|---|
| Permanent Citation | { | Rev.Rul. 2004–18, 2004–1 C.B. 509. *Explanation:* Revenue Ruling Number 18, appearing on page 509 of Volume 1 of the *Cumulative Bulletin* for 2004. |

Until the first volume of the 2004 *Cumulative Bulletin* is published, the I.R.B. citation is used. After the publication of the *Cumulative Bulletin*, the C.B. citation is preferred. Note that the page reference of 509 is the same for both the I.R.B. (temporary) and C.B. (permanent) versions of the citation. The IRS numbers the pages of the I.R.B.'s consecutively for each six-month period so as to facilitate their conversion to C.B. form. Revenue Procedures are cited in the same manner, except that "Rev.Proc." is substituted for "Rev.Rul."

**Letter Rulings.**   **Letter rulings** are issued for a fee upon a taxpayer's request and describe how the IRS will treat a *proposed* transaction for tax purposes. Letter rulings can be useful to taxpayers who wish to be certain of how a transaction will be taxed before proceeding with it. Letter rulings allow taxpayers to avoid

---

[12]Usually, only two volumes of the *Cumulative Bulletin* are published each year. However, when Congress has enacted major tax legislation, additional volumes may be published containing the congressional Committee Reports supporting the Revenue Act.

unexpected tax costs. The procedure for requesting a ruling can be quite cumbersome, although it sometimes is the most effective way to carry out tax planning. The IRS limits the issuance of individual rulings to restricted, pre-announced areas of taxation and generally will not rule on situations that are fact-intensive. Thus, a ruling may not be obtained on many of the problems that are particularly troublesome to taxpayers.[13]

Although letter rulings once were private and not available to the public, the law now requires the IRS to make such rulings available for public inspection after identifying details are deleted.[14] Published digests of private letter rulings can be found in RIA's *Private Letter Rulings*, BNA *Daily Tax Reports*, and Tax Analysts' *Tax Notes*. *IRS Letter Rulings Reports* (published by Commerce Clearing House) contain both digests and full texts of all letter rulings. *Letter Ruling Review* (published by Tax Analysts), a monthly publication, selects and discusses the most important of the approximately 40 letter rulings issued each week. In addition, computerized databases of letter rulings are also available through several private publishers.

Letter rulings are issued multidigit file numbers, which indicate the year and week of issuance as well as the number of the ruling during that week. Consider, for example, Ltr.Rul. 200414039, which ruled that grants awarded under a tax-exempt theology school's scholarship program do not represent compensation for services.

| **2004** | **14** | **039** |
| --- | --- | --- |
| Year 2004 | 14th week of issuance | 39th ruling issued during the 14th week |

**Other Administrative Pronouncements.** *Treasury Decisions* (TDs) are issued by the Treasury Department to promulgate new Regulations, amend or otherwise change existing Regulations, or announce the position of the Government on selected court decisions. Like Revenue Rulings and Revenue Procedures, TDs are published initially in the *Internal Revenue Bulletin* and subsequently transferred to the *Cumulative Bulletin*.

The IRS publishes other administrative communications in the *Internal Revenue Bulletin*, such as Announcements, Notices, LRs (Proposed Regulations), Termination of Exempt Organization Status, Practitioner Disciplinary Actions, and Prohibited Transaction Exemptions.

Like letter rulings, **determination letters** are issued at the request of taxpayers and provide guidance on the application of the tax law. They differ from letter rulings in that the issuing source is an IRS Director rather than the National Office of the IRS. Further, determination letters usually involve *completed* (as opposed to proposed) transactions. Determination letters are not regularly published and are made known only to the party making the request.

**EXAMPLE 1**

The shareholders of Red Corporation and Green Corporation want assurance that the consolidation of their corporations into Blue Corporation will be a nontaxable reorganization. The proper approach is to ask the National Office of the IRS to issue a letter ruling concerning the income tax effect of the proposed transaction. ■

**EXAMPLE 2**

Chris operates a barber shop in which he employs eight barbers. To comply with the rules governing income tax and payroll tax withholdings, Chris wants to know whether the

---

[13]The first *Internal Revenue Bulletin* issued each year contains a list of areas in which the IRS will not issue advance rulings. This list may be modified throughout the year. See, for example, Rev.Proc.

2004–3, I.R.B. No. 1, 114. From time to time, subsequent Revenue Procedures will modify or amplify Rev.Proc. 2004–3.
[14]§ 6110.

### CHANGING THE FACE OF RUSSIA

Peter the Great, the ruler of Russia from 1682 to 1725, imposed a tax on beards (except for clergy) because he felt that beards were "unnecessary, uncivilized, and ridiculous." If an individual did not pay the tax, a tax official would scrape off the beard. Without warning Peter himself would take a straight razor to the faces of bearded men appearing before him. When Peter attended a ceremony or banquet, anyone arriving with a beard would depart without it.

SOURCE: Adapted from Erik Jensen, "Taxation of Beards," *Tax Notes* (January 5, 2004): 153–157.

barbers working for him are employees or independent contractors. The proper procedure is to request a determination letter on their status from the appropriate IRS Director. ▪

The National Office of the IRS releases **Technical Advice Memoranda (TAMs)** weekly. TAMs resemble letter rulings in that they give the IRS's determination of an issue. Letter rulings, however, are responses to requests by taxpayers, whereas TAMs are issued by the National Office of the IRS in response to questions raised by IRS field personnel during audits. TAMs deal with completed rather than proposed transactions and are often requested for questions relating to exempt organizations and employee plans.

The law requires that several internal memoranda that constitute the working law of the IRS be released. TAMs and General Counsel Memoranda (GCMs) are not officially published, and the IRS indicates that they may not be cited as precedents by taxpayers.[15] However, these working documents do explain the IRS's position on various issues.

## JUDICIAL SOURCES OF THE TAX LAW

**The Judicial Process in General.**   After a taxpayer has exhausted some or all of the remedies available within the IRS (no satisfactory settlement has been reached at the agent level or at the Appeals Division level), the dispute can be taken to the Federal courts. The dispute is first considered by a **court of original jurisdiction** (known as a trial court), with any appeal (either by the taxpayer or the IRS) taken to the appropriate appellate court. In most situations, the taxpayer has a choice of four trial courts: a **District Court,** the **Court of Federal Claims,** the **Tax Court,** or the **Small Cases Division** of the Tax Court. The court system for Federal tax litigation is illustrated in Figure 2–3.

The broken line between the Tax Court and the Small Cases Division indicates that there is no appeal from the Small Cases Division. Decisions from the Small Cases Division have no precedential value. Some of these cases can now be found on the U.S. Tax Court Internet Web site. They may not be relied upon by other taxpayers or even by the taxpayer in question in subsequent years. The jurisdiction of the Small Cases Division is limited to cases involving amounts of $50,000 or less.

---

[15]These are unofficially published by the sources listed in Exhibit 2–1. Internal memoranda may constitute substantial authority for purposes of the § 6662 accuracy-related penalty. Notice 90–20, 1990–1 C.B. 328.

■ **FIGURE 2–3**
Federal Judicial System

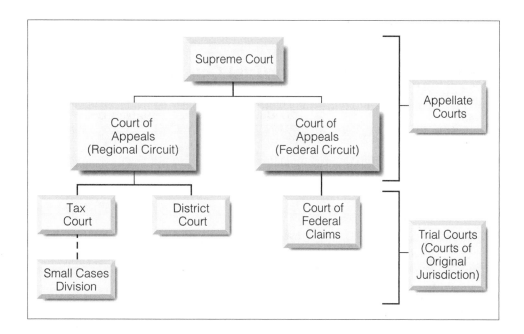

**Trial Courts.** The differences among the various trial courts (courts of original jurisdiction) can be summarized as follows.

- *Number of courts.* There is only one Court of Federal Claims and only one Tax Court, but there are many District Courts. The taxpayer does not select the District Court that will hear the dispute but must sue in the one that has jurisdiction where the taxpayer resides.
- *Number of judges.* A case tried in a District Court is heard before only 1 judge. The Court of Federal Claims has 16 judges, and the Tax Court has 19 regular judges. The entire Tax Court, however, reviews a case (the case is sent to court conference) only when important or novel tax issues are involved. Most cases are heard and decided by 1 of the 19 judges.
- *Location.* The Court of Federal Claims meets most often in Washington, D.C., while a District Court meets at a prescribed seat for the particular district. Each state has at least one District Court, and many of the populous states have more than one. Choosing the District Court usually minimizes the inconvenience and expense of traveling for the taxpayer and his or her counsel. The Tax Court is based in Washington, D.C., but various judges travel to different parts of the country and hear cases at predetermined locations and dates. This procedure eases the distance problem for the taxpayer, but it can mean a delay before the case comes to trial.
- *Jurisdiction of the Court of Federal Claims.* The Court of Federal Claims has jurisdiction over any claim against the United States that is based upon the Constitution, any Act of Congress, or any Regulation of an executive department. Thus, the Court of Federal Claims hears nontax litigation as well as tax cases.
- *Jurisdiction of the Tax Court and District Courts.* The Tax Court hears only tax cases and is the most popular forum. The District Courts hear a wide variety of nontax cases, including drug crimes and other Federal violations, as well as tax cases. For this reason, some people suggest that the Tax Court has more expertise in tax matters.
- *Jury trial.* The only court in which a taxpayer can obtain a jury trial is a District Court. Juries can decide only questions of fact and not questions of law. Therefore, taxpayers who choose the District Court route often do not

## CONCEPT SUMMARY 2–1

### Federal Judicial System: Trial Courts

| Issue | Tax Court | District Court | Court of Federal Claims |
|---|---|---|---|
| Number of judges per court | 19* | 1 per case | 16 |
| Payment of deficiency before trial | No | Yes | Yes |
| Jury trial available | No | Yes | No |
| Types of disputes | Tax cases only | Mostly criminal and civil issues | Claims against the United States |
| Jurisdiction | Nationwide | Location of taxpayer | Nationwide |
| IRS acquiescence policy | Yes | Yes | Yes |
| Appeal route | U.S. Court of Appeals | U.S. Court of Appeals | Court of Appeals for the Federal Circuit |

*There are also 14 special trial judges and 9 senior judges.

request a jury trial. If a jury trial is not elected, the judge will decide all issues. Note that a District Court decision is controlling only in the district in which the court has jurisdiction.

- *Payment of deficiency.* Before the Court of Federal Claims or a District Court can have jurisdiction, the taxpayer must pay the tax deficiency assessed by the IRS and then sue for a refund. If the taxpayer wins (assuming no successful appeal by the Government), the tax paid plus appropriate interest will be recovered. Jurisdiction in the Tax Court, however, is usually obtained without first paying the assessed tax deficiency.

 DIGGING DEEPER ①  *Find more information on this topic at our Web site:* ***http://wft-entities.swlearning.com.***

- *Appeals.* Appeals from a District Court or a Tax Court decision go to the Court of Appeals for the circuit in which the taxpayer resides. Appeals from the Court of Federal Claims go to the Court of Appeals for the Federal Circuit. Few Tax Court cases are appealed, and when appeals are made, most are filed by the taxpayers rather than the IRS.
- *Bankruptcy.* When a taxpayer files a bankruptcy petition, the IRS, like other creditors, is prevented from taking action against the taxpayer. Sometimes a bankruptcy court may settle a tax claim.

For a summary of the Federal trial courts, see Concept Summary 2–1.

**Appellate Courts.**   The losing party can appeal a trial court decision to a **Circuit Court of Appeals.** The 11 geographic circuits, the circuit for the District of Columbia, and the Federal Circuit[16] are shown in Figure 2–4.

If the Government loses at the trial court level (District Court, Tax Court, or Court of Federal Claims), it need not (and frequently does not) appeal. The fact that an appeal is not made, however, does not indicate that the IRS agrees with the result and will not litigate similar issues in the future. The IRS may decide not

---

[16]The Court of Appeals for the Federal Circuit was created to hear decisions appealed from the Claims Court (now the Court of Federal Claims).

**■ FIGURE 2–4**
The Circuit Courts of Appeals

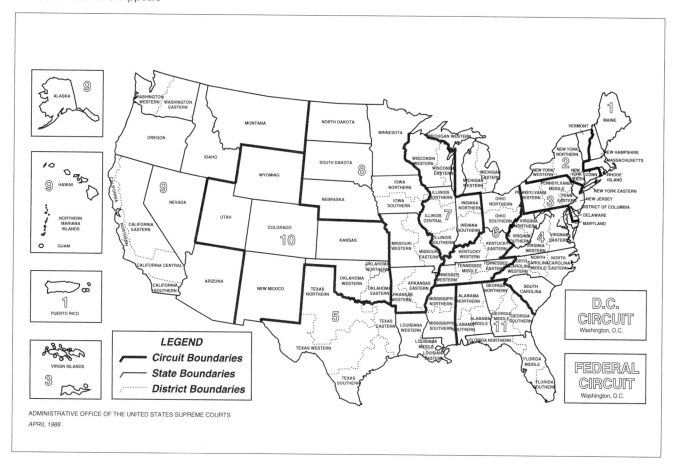

ADMINISTRATIVE OFFICE OF THE UNITED STATES SUPREME COURTS
*APRIL 1988*

to appeal for a number of reasons. First, its current litigation load may be heavy. As a consequence, the IRS may decide that available personnel should be assigned to other, more important cases. Second, the IRS may not appeal for strategic reasons. For example, the taxpayer may be in a sympathetic position, or the facts may be particularly strong in his or her favor. In that event, the IRS may wait for a weaker case to test the legal issues involved. Third, if the appeal is from a District Court or the Tax Court, the Court of Appeals of jurisdiction could have some bearing on whether the IRS decides to pursue an appeal. Based on past experience and precedent, the IRS may conclude that the chance for success on a particular issue might be more promising in another Court of Appeals. If so, the IRS will wait for a similar case to arise in a different jurisdiction.

The Federal Circuit at the appellate level provides a taxpayer with an alternative forum to the Court of Appeals of his or her home circuit. When a particular circuit has issued an adverse decision, the taxpayer may prefer the Court of Federal Claims route since any appeal will be to the Court of Appeals for the Federal Circuit.

District Courts, the Tax Court, and the Court of Federal Claims must abide by the **precedents** set by the Court of Appeals of their jurisdiction. A particular Court of Appeals need not follow the decisions of another Court of Appeals. All courts, however, must follow decisions of the **Supreme Court.**

This pattern of appellate precedents raises an issue for the Tax Court. Because the Tax Court is a national court, it decides cases from all parts of the country. Appeals from its decisions, however, go to all of the Courts of Appeals except the Court of Appeals for the Federal Circuit. Accordingly, identical Tax Court cases might be appealed to different circuits with different results. As a result of the *Golsen*[17] case, the Tax Court will not follow its own precedents in a subsequent case if the Court of Appeals with jurisdiction over the taxpayer in question has previously reversed the Tax Court on the specific issue at hand.

**EXAMPLE 3**

Emily lives in Texas and sues in the Tax Court on Issue A. The Fifth Circuit Court of Appeals is the appellate court with jurisdiction. The Fifth Circuit has already decided, in a case involving similar facts but a different taxpayer, that Issue A should be resolved against the Government. Although the Tax Court feels that the Fifth Circuit is wrong, under its *Golsen* policy it will render judgment for Emily. Shortly thereafter, in a comparable case, Rashad, a resident of New York, sues in the Tax Court on Issue A. Assume that the Second Circuit Court of Appeals, the appellate court with jurisdiction in New York, has never expressed itself on Issue A. Presuming the Tax Court has not reconsidered its position on Issue A, it will decide against Rashad. Thus, it is entirely possible for two taxpayers suing in the same court to end up with opposite results merely because they live in different parts of the country. ■

Appeal to the Supreme Court is not automatic. It must be applied for via a **Writ of Certiorari.** If the Court agrees to hear the case, it will grant the Writ (*Cert. granted*). Most often, it will decline to hear the case (*Cert. denied*). In fact, the Supreme Court rarely hears tax cases. The Court usually grants certiorari to resolve a conflict among the Courts of Appeals (e.g., two or more appellate courts have opposing positions on a particular issue) or where the tax issue is extremely important. The granting of a *Writ of Certiorari* indicates that at least four members of the Supreme Court believe that the issue is of sufficient importance to be heard by the full Court.

The *role* of appellate courts is limited to a review of the record of trial compiled by the trial courts. Thus, the appellate process usually involves a determination of whether the trial court applied the proper law in arriving at its decision, rather than a consideration of the trial court's factual findings.

An appeal can have any of a number of possible outcomes. The appellate court may approve (affirm) or disapprove (reverse) the lower court's finding, or it may send the case back for further consideration (remand). When many issues are involved, a mixed result is not unusual. Thus, the lower court may be affirmed (*aff'd.*) on Issue A and reversed (*rev'd.*) on Issue B, while Issue C is remanded (*rem'd.*) for additional fact finding.

When more than one judge is involved in the decision-making process, disagreements are not uncommon. In addition to the majority view, one or more judges may concur (agree with the result reached but not with some or all of the reasoning) or dissent (disagree with the result). In any one case, the majority view controls. But concurring and dissenting views can influence other courts or, at some subsequent date when the composition of the court has changed, even the same court.

Knowledge of several terms is important in understanding court decisions. The plaintiff is the party requesting action in a court, and the defendant is the party against whom the suit is brought. Sometimes a court uses the terms *petitioner* and *respondent*. In general, "petitioner" is a synonym for "plaintiff," and "respondent" is a synonym for "defendant." At the trial court level, a taxpayer is normally the plaintiff (or petitioner), and the government is the defendant (or respondent). If the taxpayer wins and the Government appeals as the new petitioner (or appellant), the taxpayer now is the respondent.

**Judicial Citations—General.** Having briefly described the judicial process, it is appropriate to consider the more practical problem of the relationship of case

---

[17]*Jack E. Golsen*, 54 T.C. 742 (1970).

law to tax research. As previously noted, court decisions are an important source of tax law. The ability to locate a case and to cite it is therefore a must in working with the tax law. Judicial citations usually follow a standard pattern: case name, volume number, reporter series, page or paragraph number, court (where necessary), and the year of decision.

**Judicial Citations—The Tax Court.** The Tax Court issues two types of decisions: Regular and Memorandum. The Chief Judge decides whether the opinion is issued as a Regular or Memorandum decision. The distinction between the two involves both substance and form. In terms of substance, *Memorandum* decisions deal with situations necessitating only the application of already established principles of law. *Regular* decisions involve novel issues not previously resolved by the court. In actual practice, however, this distinction is not always so clear. Be that as it may, both Regular and Memorandum decisions represent the position of the Tax Court and, as such, can be relied on.

Regular and Memorandum decisions issued by the Tax Court also differ in form. Memorandum decisions are not officially published while Regular decisions are published by the U.S. Government in a series called *Tax Court of the United States Reports* (T.C.). Each volume of these *Reports* covers a six-month period (January 1 through June 30 and July 1 through December 31) and is given a succeeding volume number. But there is usually a time lag between the date a decision is rendered and the date it appears in official form. A temporary citation may be necessary to help the researcher locate a recent Regular decision. Consider, for example, the temporary and permanent citations for *Estate of Leona Engelman*, a decision filed on July 24, 2003.

| Temporary Citation | { | *Estate of Leona Engelman*, 121 T.C. ____, No. 4 (2003). *Explanation:* Page number left blank because not yet known. |
|---|---|---|
| Permanent Citation | { | *Estate of Leona Engelman*, 121 T.C. 54 (2003). *Explanation:* Page number now available. |

Both citations tell us that the case will ultimately appear in Volume 121 of the *Tax Court of the United States Reports*. Until this volume becomes available to the general public, however, the page number must be left blank. Instead, the temporary citation identifies the case as being the 4th Regular decision issued by the Tax Court since Volume 120 ended. With this information, the decision can easily be located in either of the special Tax Court services published by Commerce Clearing House and Research Institute of America (formerly by Prentice-Hall). Once Volume 121 is released, the permanent citation can be substituted and the number of the case dropped. Starting in 1999, both Regular decisions and Memorandum decisions are published on the U.S. Tax Court Web site (**http://www.usataxcourt.gov**).

Before 1943, the Tax Court was called the Board of Tax Appeals, and its decisions were published as the *United States Board of Tax Appeals Reports* (B.T.A.). These 47 volumes cover the period from 1924 to 1942. For example, the citation *Karl Pauli*, 11 B.T.A. 784 (1928) refers to the 11th volume of the *Board of Tax Appeals Reports*, page 784, issued in 1928.

If the IRS loses a decision, it may indicate whether it agrees or disagrees with the results reached by the court by publishing an **acquiescence** ("A" or "*Acq.*") or **nonacquiescence** ("NA" or "*Nonacq.*"), respectively. The acquiescence program is used where guidance is helpful, regardless of the court that issued the opinion. The acquiescence or nonacquiescence is published in the *Internal Revenue Bulletin* and the *Cumulative Bulletin* as an *Action on Decision*. The IRS can retroactively revoke an acquiescence.

Although Memorandum decisions were not published by the U.S. Government until recently (now published on the U.S. Tax Court Web site), they were and continue to be published by Commerce Clearing House (CCH) and Research Institute of America. Consider, for example, the three different ways that *Jack D. Carr* can be cited.

*Jack D. Carr*, T.C.Memo. 1985–19.
> The 19th Memorandum decision issued by the Tax Court in 1985.

*Jack D. Carr*, 49 TCM 507.
> Page 507 of Vol. 49 of the CCH *Tax Court Memorandum Decisions*.

*Jack D. Carr*, RIA T.C.Mem.Dec. ¶85,019.
> Paragraph 85,019 of the RIA *T.C. Memorandum Decisions*.

The third citation contains the same information as the first. Thus, ¶85,019 indicates the following information about the case: year 1985, 19th T.C. Memo. decision. Although the RIA citation does not include a specific volume number, the paragraph citation (85,019) indicates that the decision can be found in the 1985 volume of the RIA Memorandum Decision service.

Starting in 2001, U.S. Tax Court Summary Opinions are published on the U.S. Tax Court Web site, with the warning that they may not be treated as precedent for any other case. For example, *Edward Charles Jones*, filed on May 27, 2003, is cited as follows.

*Edward Charles Jones*, T.C. Summary Opinion, 2003–61.

### Judicial Citations—The District Courts, Court of Federal Claims, and Courts of Appeals.

District Court, Court of Federal Claims, and Court of Appeals decisions dealing with Federal tax matters are reported in both the CCH *U.S. Tax Cases* (USTC) and the RIA *American Federal Tax Reports* (AFTR) series.

District Court decisions, dealing with *both* tax and nontax issues, are also published by West Publishing Company in its *Federal Supplement Series* (F.Supp.). Volume 999, published in 1998, is the last volume of the Federal Supplement Series. It is followed by the *Federal Supplement Second Series* (F.Supp.2d). A District Court case can be cited in three different forms.

*Simons-Eastern Co. v. U.S.*, 73–1 USTC ¶9279 (D.Ct.Ga., 1972).

> *Explanation:* Reported in the first volume of the *U.S. Tax Cases* (USTC) published by Commerce Clearing House for calendar year 1973 (73–1) and located at paragraph 9279 (¶9279).

*Simons-Eastern Co. v. U.S.*, 31 AFTR2d 73–640 (D.Ct.Ga., 1972).

> *Explanation:* Reported in the 31st volume of the second series of the *American Federal Tax Reports* (AFTR2d) published by RIA, beginning on page 640. The "73" preceding the page number indicates the year the case was published but is a designation used only in recent decisions.

*Simons-Eastern Co. v. U.S.*, 354 F.Supp. 1003 (D.Ct.Ga., 1972).

> *Explanation:* Reported in the 354th volume of the *Federal Supplement Series* (F.Supp.) published by West Publishing Company, beginning on page 1003.

In all of the preceding citations, the name of the case is the same (Simons-Eastern Co. being the taxpayer), as are the references to the District Court of Georgia (D.Ct.Ga.) and the year the decision was rendered (1972).

Decisions of the Court of Federal Claims and the Courts of Appeals are published in the USTCs, AFTRs, and the *Federal Second Series* (F.2d). Volume 999, published in 1993, is the last volume of the *Federal Second Series*. It is followed by the *Federal Third Series* (F.3d). Beginning with October 1982, decisions of the Court of Federal Claims are published in the *Claims Court Reporter* (abbreviated as Cl.Ct.). Beginning with Volume 27 on October 30, 1992, the name of the reporter changed to the *Federal Claims Reporter* (abbreviated as Fed.Cl.).

*Finkbohner, Jr. v. U.S.,* (CA–11, 1986).

86–1 USTC ¶9393 (CCH citation)
57 AFTR2d 86–1400 (RIA citation)
788 F.2d 723 (West citation)

*Apollo Computer, Inc. v. U.S.,* (Fed.Cl., 1994).

95–1 USTC ¶50,015 (CCH citation)
74 AFTR2d 94–7172 (RIA citation)
32 Fed.Cl. 334 (West citation)

*Finkbohner, Jr.* is a decision rendered by the Eleventh Circuit Court of Appeals in 1986 (CA–11, 1986), while *Apollo Computer, Inc.* was issued by the Court of Federal Claims in 1994 (Fed.Cl., 1994).

**Judicial Citations—The Supreme Court.** Like all other Federal tax decisions (except those rendered by the Tax Court), Supreme Court decisions dealing with Federal tax matters are published by Commerce Clearing House in the USTCs and by RIA in the AFTRs. The U.S. Government Printing Office publishes all Supreme Court decisions in the *United States Supreme Court Reports* (U.S.), as do West Publishing Company in its *Supreme Court Reporter* (S.Ct.) and the Lawyer's Co-operative Publishing Company in its *United States Reports, Lawyer's Edition* (L.Ed.).

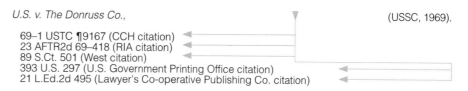

*U.S. v. The Donruss Co.,* (USSC, 1969).

69–1 USTC ¶9167 (CCH citation)
23 AFTR2d 69–418 (RIA citation)
89 S.Ct. 501 (West citation)
393 U.S. 297 (U.S. Government Printing Office citation)
21 L.Ed.2d 495 (Lawyer's Co-operative Publishing Co. citation)

The parenthetical reference (USSC, 1969) identifies the decision as having been rendered by the U.S. Supreme Court in 1969. In this text, the citations of Supreme Court decisions are limited to the CCH (USTC), RIA (AFTR), and West (S.Ct.) versions.

**LO.2**

Locate and work with the tax law and understand the tax research process.

# Working with the Tax Law—Tax Research

Tax research is undertaken to determine the best available solution to a situation that has tax consequences. In the case of a completed transaction, the objective of the research is to determine the tax result of what has already taken place. For example, is the expenditure incurred by the taxpayer deductible or not deductible for tax purposes? When dealing with proposed transactions, tax research is concerned with the determination of possible alternative tax consequences to facilitate effective tax planning.

Tax research involves the following procedures.

* Identifying and refining the problem.
* Locating the appropriate tax law sources.
* Assessing the tax law sources.
* Arriving at the solution or at alternative solutions while giving due consideration to nontax factors.
* Effectively communicating the solution to the taxpayer or the taxpayer's representative.
* Following up on the solution (where appropriate) in light of new developments.

This process is depicted schematically in Figure 2–5. The broken lines indicate steps of particular interest when tax research is directed toward proposed, rather than completed, transactions.

### Bridge to Business Law

U.S. income tax laws change daily by the action of Congress, tax administrators, and the courts. This process matches the three-branch structure of the rest of the government, with the legislative, executive, and judicial branches each having a say in making tax law. But this distinction among the functions of government is perhaps less clear when it involves the tax law.

- Presidential vetoes of tax legislation are rare.
- The Tax Court is a creation of the Congress in the Internal Revenue Code, not of the U.S. Constitution.
- The cost of tax litigation and the time that it takes for a case to work its way through the judicial system render the courts unavailable to most taxpayers.

Under the U.S. Constitution, legislation involving government revenues must start in the House of Representatives. This provision likely was included so that the public would have greater control over those who want greater access to their pocketbooks. Several recent pieces of tax legislation, though, have been initiated as bills in the Senate. And during the years of the deepest Federal deficits, all bills introduced in both houses of Congress were required to be "revenue neutral" (i.e., they had to include provisions by which the legislation's new programs would be paid for). In both houses, this resulted in amendments to the Internal Revenue Code being attached to legislation involving clean air and water standards, child care programs, and product import and export limitations.

In a few cases, the courts considered a taxpayer challenge to the way this tax legislation was crafted. But so far the courts have failed to overturn any tax provisions solely because they were initiated in the Senate. The courts' rationale for this seemingly unconstitutional position is that (1) the House and its committees heard a full discussion of the proposal, and (2) too much time has passed since adoption of the legislation to easily un-wind it and undertake a refund procedure.

## IDENTIFYING THE PROBLEM

Problem identification starts with a compilation of the relevant facts involved. In this regard, *all* of the facts that may have a bearing on the problem must be gathered, as any omission could modify the solution reached. To illustrate, consider what appears to be a very simple problem.

**EXAMPLE 4**

In reviewing their tax and financial situation, Fred and Megan, a married couple, notice that Fred's investment in Airways stock has declined from its purchase price of $8,000 to a current market value of $5,500. Megan wants to sell this stock now and claim the $2,500 loss ($5,500 value − $8,000 cost) as a deduction this year. Fred, however, believes that Airways Co. will yet prosper and does not want to part with its stock. Their daughter suggests that they sell the Airways Co. stock to Maple, Inc., a corporation owned equally by Fred and Megan. That way, they can claim the deduction this year while still holding the stock through their corporation. Will this suggestion work? ■

## REFINING THE PROBLEM

Fred and Megan in Example 4 face three choices: (1) sell the Airways stock through their regular investment broker and get a deduction in the current year (Megan's plan); (2) continue to hold the Airways stock (Fred's plan); and (3) sell the Airways

■ **FIGURE 2–5**
Tax Research Process

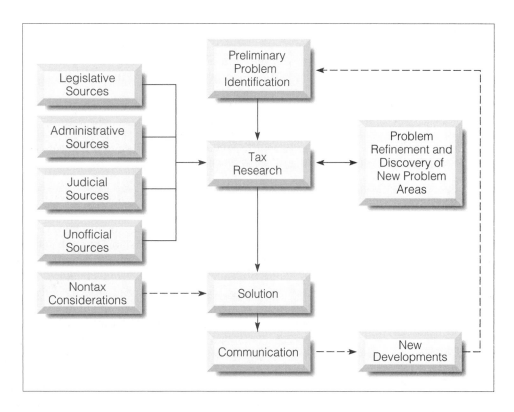

■ **FIGURE 2–5**
Tax Research Process

stock to a corporation owned 50–50 by Fred and Megan (their daughter's suggestion). The tax consequences of plans (1) and (2) are clear, but the question that Fred and Megan want to resolve is whether plan (3) will work as anticipated. Refining the problem further, can shareholders deduct a loss from the sale of an asset to a corporation that they control? Section 267(a)(1) indicates that losses from the sale of property between persons specified in § 267(b) are not deductible. This subsection lists 12 different relationships, including, in § 267(b)(2): "an individual and a corporation more than 50 percent in value of the outstanding stock of which is owned, directly or indirectly, by or for such individual." Thus, if Fred and Megan each own 50 percent of Maple, neither owns *more than* 50 percent, as § 267(b) requires. Accordingly, the loss disallowance rule would not apply to Fred, and their daughter's suggestion would appear to be sound.

The language of the statute, however, indicates that any stock owned *directly or indirectly* by an individual is counted toward the 50 percent test. Might Megan's stock be considered owned "indirectly" by Fred? Further research is necessary. Section 267(c) contains rules for determining "constructive ownership of stock," or when stock owned by one person will be attributed to someone else. One of the rules in this subsection declares that an individual is considered to own any stock that is owned by that person's *family*, and family is defined in § 267(c)(4) as including a person's spouse, among others. Therefore, Megan's stock will be attributed to Fred, so that Fred is treated as owning all of the stock of Maple, Inc. As a result, § 267(a) would indeed apply, and no loss would be deductible if Fred sells his Airways stock to Maple. In short, the daughter's suggestion will not work.

## LOCATING THE APPROPRIATE TAX LAW SOURCES

Once the problem is clearly defined, what is the next step? While it is a matter of individual judgment, most tax research begins with the index volume of a paper-based tax service or a keyword search of an online or CD-ROM tax service. If the problem is not complex, the researcher may bypass the tax service and turn directly to the Internal Revenue Code and the Treasury Regulations. For the beginner, the latter procedure saves time and will solve many of the more basic problems. If the researcher does not have a personal copy of the Code or Regulations, use of the appropriate volume(s) of a tax service, an online service, or a CD-ROM is necessary.[18] The major tax services and their publishers are:

*Standard Federal Tax Reporter*, Commerce Clearing House.

*United States Tax Reporter*, Research Institute of America.

*Federal Tax Coordinator 2d*, Research Institute of America.

*Tax Management Portfolios*, Bureau of National Affairs.

*Mertens Law of Federal Income Taxation*, Callaghan and Co.

**Working with Tax Services.**   In this text, it is not feasible to explain the use of any particular tax service—this ability can be obtained with experience. However, several important observations about the use of tax services cannot be overemphasized. First, always check for current developments. The main text of any paper-based service is revised too infrequently to permit reliance on that portion as the *latest* word on any subject. Where current developments can be found depends on which service is being used. Commerce Clearing House's *Standard Federal Tax Reporter* contains a special volume devoted to current matters. Both RIA's *United States Tax Reporter* and *Federal Tax Coordinator 2d* integrate the new developments into the body of the service throughout the year. Second, there is no substitute for the original source. Do not base a conclusion solely on a tax service's commentary. If the Code Section, Regulation, or case is vital to the research, read it.

**Tax Periodicals.**   Various tax periodicals are another source of information. The easiest way to locate a journal article on a particular tax problem is through CCH's *Federal Tax Articles*. This six-volume service includes a subject index, a Code Section number index, and an author's index. In addition, RIA's tax service has a topical "Index to Tax Articles" section that is organized using the RIA paragraph index system. *The Accounting & Tax Index* also is available in three quarterly issues plus a cumulative year-end volume covering all four quarters.

The following are some of the more useful tax periodicals.

*The Journal of Taxation*
Warren, Gorham and Lamont
395 Hudson Street
4th Floor
New York, NY 10014

*Tax Law Review*
Warren, Gorham and Lamont
395 Hudson Street
4th Floor
New York, NY 10014

*Oil, Gas, and Energy Quarterly*
Matthew Bender & Co.
1275 Broadway
Albany, NY 12204

*Practical Tax Strategies*
Warren, Gorham and Lamont
395 Hudson Street
4th Floor
New York, NY 10014

*The International Tax Journal*
Aspen Publishing, Inc.
1185 Avenue of the Americas
New York, NY 10036

*The Tax Executive*
1200 G Street NW
Suite 300
Washington, D.C. 20005

---

[18]Several of the major tax services publish paperback editions of the Code and Treasury Regulations that can be purchased at modest prices. These editions are usually revised twice each year. For an annotated and abridged version of the Code and Regulations that is published annually, see James E. Smith, *West's Internal Revenue Code of 1986 and Treasury Regulations: Annotated and Selected* (West/South-Western College Publishing, 2006). The complete Code and Regulations are also available in *RIA Checkpoint*.

*TAXES—The Tax Magazine*
Commerce Clearing House, Inc.
2700 Lake Cook Road
Riverwood, IL 60015

*National Tax Journal*
725 15th Street NW
Suite 600
Washington, D.C. 20005

*The Tax Adviser*
AICPA
Harborside Financial Center
201 Plaza III
Jersey City, NJ 07311-3881

*Estate Planning*
Warren, Gorham and Lamont
395 Hudson Street
4th Floor
New York, NY 10014

*Journal of Corporate Taxation*
Warren, Gorham and Lamont
395 Hudson Street
4th Floor
New York, NY 10014

*Journal of Taxation for Individuals*
Warren, Gorham and Lamont
395 Hudson Street
4th Floor
New York, NY 10014

*Journal of the American Taxation Association*
American Accounting Association
5717 Bessie Drive
Sarasota, FL 34233

*Tax Notes*
6830 Fairfax Drive
Arlington, VA 22213

## ASSESSING TAX LAW SOURCES

Once a source has been located, the next step is to assess it in light of the problem at hand. Proper assessment involves careful interpretation of the tax law and consideration of its relevance and significance.

**Interpreting the Internal Revenue Code.**  The language of the Code is often difficult to comprehend fully. Contrary to many people's suspicions, the Code is not written deliberately to confuse. Nevertheless, it often has that effect. The Code is intended to apply to more than 275 million citizens, most of whom are willing to exploit any linguistic imprecision to their benefit—to find a "loophole," in popular parlance. Moreover, many of the Code's provisions are limitations or restrictions involving two or more variables. Expressing such concepts algebraically would be more direct; using words to accomplish this task instead is often quite cumbersome. Among the worst such attempts was former § 341(e) relating to so-called collapsible corporations, which included one sentence with more than 450 words.

Nevertheless, the Code is the governing law, the only source of tax law (other than treaties) that has received the actual approval of Congress and the President. Accordingly, it is usually the first source to be consulted, and often it is the only source needed.

**Assessing the Significance of a Treasury Regulation.**  Treasury Regulations are the official interpretation of the Code and are entitled to great deference. Occasionally, however, a court will invalidate a Regulation or a portion thereof on the grounds that the Regulation is contrary to the intent of Congress. Usually, courts do not question the validity of Regulations because of the belief that "the first administrative interpretation of a provision as it appears in a new act often expresses the general understanding of the times or the actual understanding of those who played an important part when the statute was drafted."[19]

---

[19]*Augustus v. Comm.*, 41–1 USTC ¶9255, 26 AFTR 612, 118 F.2d 38 (CA–6, 1941).

**INTERNAL REVENUE CODE: INTERPRETATION PITFALLS**

One author has noted 10 common pitfalls in interpreting the Code:

1. Determine the limitations and exceptions to a provision. Do not permit the language of the Code Section to carry greater or lesser weight than was intended.
2. Just because a Section fails to mention an item does not necessarily mean that the item is excluded.
3. Read definitional clauses carefully.
4. Do not overlook small words such as *and* and *or*. There is a world of difference between these two words.
5. Read the Code Section completely; do not jump to conclusions.
6. Watch out for cross-referenced and related provisions, since many Sections of the Code are interrelated.
7. At times Congress is not careful when reconciling new Code provisions with existing Sections. Conflicts among Sections, therefore, do arise.
8. Be alert for hidden definitions; terms in a particular Code Section may be defined in the same Section or in a separate Section.
9. Some answers may not be found in the Code; therefore, a researcher may have to consult the Regulations and/or judicial decisions.
10. Take careful note of measuring words such as *less than 50 percent, more than 50 percent*, and *at least 80 percent*.

SOURCE: Adapted by permission from Henry G. Wong, "Ten Common Pitfalls in Reading the Internal Revenue Code," *Journal of Business Strategy* (July–August 1972): 30–33. Reprinted with permission by Faulkner & Gray, Inc., 11 Penn Plaza, New York, NY 10001.

Keep in mind the following observations when assessing the significance of a Regulation.

- IRS agents *must* give the Code and the Regulations issued thereunder equal weight when dealing with taxpayers and their representatives.
- Proposed Regulations provide a preview of future final Regulations, but they are not binding on the IRS or taxpayers.
- In a challenge, the burden of proof is on the taxpayer to show that a Regulation varies from the language of the statute and has no support in the Committee Reports.
- Final Regulations can be classified as procedural, interpretive, or legislative. **Procedural Regulations** neither establish tax laws nor attempt to explain tax laws. Procedural Regulations often include procedural instructions, indicating information that taxpayers should provide the IRS, as well as information about the internal management and conduct of the IRS itself.
- **Interpretive Regulations** rephrase and elaborate what Congress stated in the Committee Reports that were issued when the tax legislation was enacted. Such Regulations are *hard and solid* and almost impossible to overturn unless they do not clearly reflect the intent of Congress.
- In some Code Sections, Congress has given the *Secretary or his delegate* the specific authority to prescribe Regulations to carry out the details of administration or to otherwise create rules not included in the Code. Under such circumstances, Congress is effectively delegating its legislative powers to the Treasury Department. Regulations issued pursuant to this type of authority

possess the force and effect of law and are often called **Legislative Regulations** [e.g., see § 385(a)].

**Assessing the Significance of Other Administrative Sources of the Tax Law.**   Revenue Rulings issued by the IRS carry much less weight than Treasury Department Regulations. Revenue Rulings are important, however, in that they reflect the position of the IRS on tax matters. In any dispute with the IRS on the interpretation of tax law, taxpayers should expect agents to follow the results reached in applicable Revenue Rulings. It is not unusual, however, for courts to overturn Revenue Rulings as incorrect applications of the law to the facts presented.

*Actions on Decisions* further tell the taxpayer the IRS's reaction to certain court decisions. Recall that the IRS follows a practice of either acquiescing (agreeing) or nonacquiescing (not agreeing) with selected judicial decisions. A nonacquiescence does not mean that a particular court decision is of no value, but it does indicate that the IRS may choose to litigate the issue involved.

**Assessing the Significance of Judicial Sources of the Tax Law.**   The judicial process as it relates to the formulation of tax law has been described. How much reliance can be placed on a particular decision depends upon the following factors.

- *The level of the court*. A decision rendered by a trial court (e.g., a District Court) carries less weight than one issued by an appellate court (e.g., the Fifth Circuit Court of Appeals). Unless Congress changes the Code, decisions by the U.S. Supreme Court represent the last word on any tax issue.
- *The legal residence of the taxpayer*. If, for example, a taxpayer lives in Texas, a decision of the Fifth Circuit Court of Appeals means more than one rendered by the Second Circuit Court of Appeals. This is the case because any appeal from a District Court or the Tax Court would be to the Fifth Circuit Court of Appeals and not to the Second Circuit Court of Appeals.
- *The type of decision*. A Tax Court Regular decision carries more weight than a Memorandum decision because the Tax Court does not consider Memorandum decisions to have precedential value.[20]
- *The weight of the decision*. A decision that is supported by cases from other courts carries more weight than a decision that is not supported by other cases.
- *Subsequent events*. Was the decision affirmed or overruled on appeal?

In connection with the last two factors, a citator is helpful to tax research.[21] A citator provides the history of a case and lists subsequent published opinions that refer to the case being assessed. Reviewing these references enables the tax researcher to determine whether the decision in question has been reversed, affirmed, followed by other courts, or distinguished in some way. If one plans to rely on a judicial decision to any significant degree, "running" the case through a citator is imperative.

**Understanding Judicial Opinions**   Reading judicial opinions can be more productive if certain conventions of usage are understood. Some courts, including the Tax Court, apply the terms *petitioner* and *respondent* to the plaintiff and defendant, respectively, particularly when the case does not involve an appellate proceeding. Appellate courts often use the terms *appellant* and *appellee* instead.

---

[20]*Severino R. Nico, Jr.*, 67 T.C. 647 (1977).

[21]The major citators are published by Commerce Clearing House, RIA, and Shepard's Citations, Inc. These citators are available in published and electronic formats. WESTLAW has a citator that is available only in electronic format.

It is also important to distinguish between a court's final determination, or *holding*, and passing comments made in the course of its opinion. These latter remarks, examples, and analogies, often collectively termed *dicta*, are not part of the court's conclusion and do not have precedential value. Nevertheless, they often facilitate one's understanding of the court's reasoning and can enable a tax adviser to better predict how the court might resolve some future tax case.

*Find more information on this topic at our Web site: http://wft-entities.swlearning.com.*

**Assessing the Significance of Other Sources.** *Primary sources* of tax law include the Constitution, legislative history materials (e.g., Committee Reports), statutes, treaties, Treasury Regulations, IRS pronouncements, and judicial decisions. In general, the IRS regards only primary sources as substantial authority. However, reference to *secondary materials* such as legal periodicals, treatises, legal opinions, General Counsel Memoranda, and written determinations may be useful. In general, secondary sources are not authority.

Although the statement that the IRS regards only primary sources as substantial authority is generally true, there is one exception. Substantial authority *for purposes of* the accuracy-related penalty in § 6662 includes a number of secondary materials (e.g., letter rulings and General Counsel Memoranda).[22] "Authority" does not include conclusions reached in treatises, legal periodicals, and opinions rendered by tax professionals.

A letter ruling or determination letter can be relied upon *only* by the taxpayer to whom it is issued, except as noted above with respect to the accuracy-related penalty.

*Find more information on this topic at our Web site: http://wft-entities.swlearning.com.*

## ARRIVING AT THE SOLUTION OR AT ALTERNATIVE SOLUTIONS

Example 4 raises the question of whether taxpayers would be denied a loss deduction from the sale of stock to a corporation that they own. The solution depends, in part, on the relationship of the corporation's shareholders to each other. Since Fred and Megan are married to each other, § 267(c)(2) attributes Megan's stock to Fred in applying the "more than 50 percent" test of § 267(b)(2). Accordingly, Fred and Maple, Inc., are considered related parties under § 267(a), and a sale between them does not provide a deductible loss. If Fred and Megan were not related to each other, the constructive stock ownership rules would not apply, and a loss could be deducted on a sale by Fred to Maple.

If Maple, Inc., were a *partnership* instead of a corporation, § 267 would not apply, per Regulation § 1.267(b)–1(b)(1). That Regulation, however, references a different Code Section, namely § 707, which produces the same result: no deduction of the loss from a sale between a "more than 50 percent" partner and the partnership. This additional research prevents Fred and Megan from erroneously selling their Airways stock to a partnership in hopes of obtaining a loss deduction from the sale. Accordingly, Fred must sell the Airways stock to an unrelated party in order to deduct the loss.

Since Fred still wants to own Airways stock, he might consider purchasing new Airways Co. stock to replace the stock he sells. Additional research reveals that for the loss on the sale to be deductible, the "wash sale" rule of § 1091 requires

---

[22]Reg. § 1.6661–3(b)(2).

that 30 days elapse between the purchase of the new stock and the sale of the old stock. This section applies to purchases and sales of *substantially identical stock or securities*. As a result, to deduct the loss on the Airways stock, Fred must either wait at least 30 days after selling this stock to buy new Airways stock or acquire stock in a different company at any time. This new company can even be in the same general business as is Airways.[23]

## LO.3

*Communicate the results of the tax research process in a client letter and a tax file memorandum.*

## COMMUNICATING TAX RESEARCH

Once the problem has been researched adequately, a memorandum, letter, or speech setting forth the result may need to be prepared. The form the communication takes could depend on a number of considerations. For example, does an employer or instructor recommend a particular procedure or format for tax research memos? Is the memo to be given directly to the client or will it first go to the preparer's employer? If the communication is a speech, who is the audience? How long should one speak?[24] Whatever form it takes, a good research communication should contain the following elements.

* A clear statement of the issue.
* In more complex situations, a short review of the fact pattern that raises the issue.
* A review of the pertinent tax law sources (e.g., Code, Regulations, Revenue Rulings, judicial authority).
* Any assumptions made in arriving at the solution.
* The solution recommended and the logic or reasoning supporting it.
* The references consulted in the research process.

Illustrations of the memo for the tax file and the client letter associated with Example 4 appear in Figures 2–6 and 2–7.

### FOLLOW-UP PROCEDURES

Because tax research may involve a proposed (as opposed to a completed) transaction, a change in the tax law (either legislative, administrative, or judicial) could alter the original conclusion. Additional research may be necessary to test the solution in light of current developments (refer to the broken lines at the right in Figure 2–5).

## LO.4

*Have an awareness of computer-assisted tax research.*

## COMPUTER-ASSISTED TAX RESEARCH

Computer-based tax research tools hold a prominent position in tax practice. Electronic tax resources allow the tax library to better reflect the tax law's dynamic and daily changes. Nevertheless, using a computer to locate tax law sources cannot substitute for developing and maintaining a thorough knowledge of the tax law or for careful analysis when addressing tax research issues.

Accessing tax documents electronically offers several important advantages over a paper-based approach.

---

[23]Rev.Rul. 59–44, 1959–1 C.B. 205.
[24]See W. A. Raabe and G. E. Whittenburg, "Talking Tax: How to Make a Tax Presentation," *The Tax Adviser*, March 1997, pp. 179–182.

■ **FIGURE 2–6**
Tax File Memorandum

August 16, 2005

**TAX FILE MEMORANDUM**

FROM:      John J. Jones

SUBJECT: Fred and Megan Taxpayer
              Engagement: Issues

Today I talked to Fred Taxpayer with respect to his August 14, 2005 letter requesting tax assistance. He wishes to know if he can sell his stock in Airways Co. to Maple, Inc., and deduct the $2,500 loss on his Airways stock.

FACTS: Maple, Inc., is owned 50% by Fred and 50% by Megan. Fred wants to continue holding Airways stock in anticipation of a rebound in its value, and that is why he has asked about a proposed sale of this stock to Maple.

ISSUE: Can shareholders deduct a loss on the sale of an asset to a corporation all of whose stock they own?

ANALYSIS: Section 267(a) provides that no loss will be deductible on a sale or exchange between certain related parties. One of these relationships involves a corporation and a shareholder who owns "more than 50 percent" of that corporation's stock [see § 267(b)(2)]. Although Fred owns only 50% of Maple, Inc., his wife, Megan, owns the other 50%. The constructive ownership rule of § 267(c)(2) attributes stock held by family members, and a spouse is part of a taxpayer's family for this purpose, according to § 267(c)(4). Consequently, Megan's stock will be attributed to Fred, who is then treated as owning 100% of Maple, Inc. The related-party disallowance rule would then apply to the loss from Fred's selling his Airways stock to Maple. Accordingly, Fred must sell this stock to an unrelated party to make his loss deductible.

Since Fred really wants to retain an investment in Airways, he can purchase replacement stock either before or after he sells his original Airways stock. Section 1091(a), however, requires that at least 30 days elapse between the purchase and the sale, or the sale and the purchase, as the case may be. Moreover, for this purpose, an option to buy the stock is treated as equivalent to the stock itself. As a result, Fred must wait at least 30 days between transactions and cannot utilize stock options in the interim to minimize his stock market exposure.

A final alternative might be to replace the Airways stock with securities of a comparable company in the same industry. Although no two companies are exactly alike, there may be another company whose management philosophy, marketing strategy, and financial data are sufficiently similar to Airways to provide an equivalent return on investment. Under this alternative, Fred could acquire the new company's shares immediately without waiting the 30 days mandated by § 1091(a). Despite the two companies' investment similarity, they would not be treated as "substantially identical" for this purpose [see Rev.Rul. 59–44, 1959–1 C.B. 205].

CONCLUSION: Fred should *not* sell his Airways stock to Maple. Instead, he should sell this stock via his regular broker and either acquire new Airways stock at least 30 days before or after the date of sale, or acquire stock of a similar company whenever he chooses.

- Materials generally are available to the practitioner faster through an electronic system.
- Some tax documents, such as slip opinions of trial-level court cases and interviews with policymakers, are available *only* through electronic means.
- Commercial subscriptions to electronic tax services sometimes provide, at little or no cost, additional tax law sources to which the researcher would not have access through stand-alone purchases of traditional material. For example, the full text of private letter rulings is costly to acquire in a paper-based format, but electronic publishers may bundle the rulings with other materials for a reasonable cost.

Strict cost comparisons of paper and electronic tax research materials are difficult to make, especially when the practitioner uses computers that are already in place and employed elsewhere in the practice. Over time, however, the convenience,

■ **FIGURE 2–7**
Client Letter

---

Smith, Raabe, Maloney, and Willis, CPAs
5191 Natorp Boulevard
Mason, OH 45040

August 30, 2005

Mr. and Ms. Fred Taxpayer
111 Boulevard
Williamsburg, Virginia 23185

Dear Mr. and Ms. Taxpayer:

This letter is in response to your request for us to review your family's financial and tax situation. Our conclusions are based upon the facts as outlined in your August 14th letter. Any change in the facts may affect our conclusions.

Mr. Taxpayer owns stock in Airways Co. that has declined in value, but he would like to retain this stock in anticipation of a rebound in its worth. You have proposed a sale of this stock at its current market value to Maple, Inc., a corporation owned 50–50 by Mr. and Mrs. Taxpayer. Such a sale, however, would not permit the loss to be deducted.

A better approach would be to sell the Airways stock before year-end and repurchase this stock through your regular stockbroker. Please understand that the loss will not be deductible unless at least 30 days elapse between the sale and the repurchase of the stock. You can either sell the old stock first and then buy the new stock, or buy the new stock first and then sell the old stock. However, it is essential that at least 30 days elapse between the sale and purchase transactions. Using options during this 30-day period is ineffective and will prevent the loss from being deducted in the current taxable year.

If the 30-day requirement is unacceptable, you might consider replacing the Airways stock with securities of some other company, perhaps even a company in the same general business as is Airways. Your regular stockbroker should be able to suggest appropriate possibilities. In that situation, your loss on the Airways stock can be deducted without regard to when you buy the new stock.

Should you need more information or need to clarify our conclusions, do not hesitate to contact me.

Sincerely yours,

John J. Jones, CPA

Partner

---

cost, and reliability of electronic research tools clearly make them the dominant means of finding and analyzing tax law.

**Using Electronic Tax Services.**    Usually, tax professionals use one of the following strategies when performing computer-based tax research.

- *Search* various databases using keywords that are likely to be found in the underlying documents, as written by Congress, the judiciary, or administrative sources.
- *Link* to tax documents for which all or part of the proper citation is known.
- *Browse* the tax databases, examining various tables of contents and indexes in a traditional manner or using cross-references in the documents to jump from one tax law source to another.

Virtually all of the major commercial tax publishers and most of the primary sources of the law itself, such as the Supreme Court and some of the Courts of Appeals, provide tax material in a variety of electronic formats, including CD-ROM services and online services. Exhibit 2–2 summarizes the most popular of the electronic tax services on the market today.

⊙ **T A X   F A C T**

## AN ELECTRONIC IRS

The IRS is pushing for greater numbers of taxpayers to file their tax returns electronically. For tax year 2003 over one-half of all individuals filed their Forms 1040 using an electronic format. From the taxpayer's standpoint, electronic filing offers several advantages.

- Electronic filing better matches taxpayers' increasingly computer-oriented lifestyles. As many taxpayers use software to manage their bank and brokerage accounts, the transfer of tax data among programs becomes more effective.
- Refunds are processed and paid more quickly. Forty percent of returns receiving significant refunds and 60 percent of those using the earned income tax credit were e-filed. Nearly all of the e-filers chose to receive refunds by direct deposit.

The IRS benefits from electronic filing too.

- IRS computers capture all of the data submitted by an e-filing taxpayer, but only 40 percent from those filing returns on paper.
- The error rate for data entry into IRS computers is less than 2 percent for e-filed returns, but it is about 20 percent for paper-based returns.

Increases in the use of e-filing are obvious, and such increases may be traceable to taxpayer familiarity with computer usage, approximated by taxpayer age.

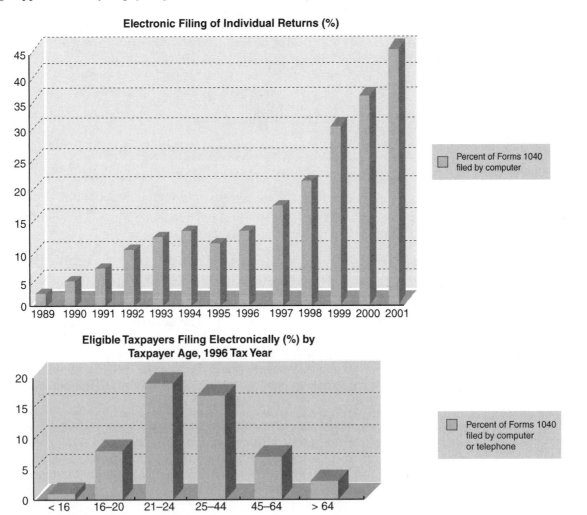

**Electronic Filing of Individual Returns (%)**

Percent of Forms 1040 filed by computer

**Eligible Taxpayers Filing Electronically (%) by Taxpayer Age, 1996 Tax Year**

Percent of Forms 1040 filed by computer or telephone

■ **EXHIBIT 2–2**
Electronic Tax Services

| Electronic Service | Description |
|---|---|
| CCH | Includes the CCH tax service, primary sources including treatises, and other subscription materials. Ten to 20 discs and online. |
| RIA | Includes primary sources, the *Federal Tax Coordinator,* and the *United States Tax Reporter.* The citator has elaborate document-linking features. Major tax treatises and other subscription materials are provided. One to 10 discs and online. |
| WESTLAW | Code, Regulations, *Cumulative Bulletins,* cases, citator, and editorial material are included. Twelve discs and online. |
| Kleinrock's | A single disc with statutory, administrative, and judicial tax law. Another disc provides tax forms and instructions for Federal and state jurisdictions. |

**CD-ROM Services.**   The CD-ROM has been a medium for tax data for about a decade. CCH, RIA, WESTLAW, and others offer vast tax libraries to the practitioner, often in conjunction with a subscription to traditional paper-based resources and accompanied by newsletters, training seminars, and ongoing technical support.

At its best, a CD-ROM tax library provides the archival data that make up a permanent, core library of tax documents. For about $300 a year, a CD-ROM is updated quarterly, providing more comprehensive tax resources than the researcher is ever likely to need. The CD-ROM is comparable in scope to a paper-based library of a decade ago costing perhaps $20,000 to establish and $5,000 per year in perpetuity to maintain. If the library is contained on a small number of discs, it also can offer portability through use on notebook computers.

**Online Services.**   Online research systems allow practitioners to obtain virtually instantaneous use of tax law sources by accessing databases via a modem connection

■ **EXHIBIT 2–3**
Online Tax Services

| Online Service | Description |
|---|---|
| LEXIS/NEXIS | Includes Federal and state statutory, administrative, and judicial material. Extensive libraries of newspapers, magazines, patent records, and medical and economic databases, both U.S. and foreign-based. |
| RIA | Includes the RIA tax services, major tax treatises, Federal and state statutes, administrative documents, and court opinions. Extensive citator access, editorial material, and practitioner aids. |
| CCH | Includes the CCH tax service, primary sources including treatises, and other subscription materials. Tax and economic news sources, extensive editorial material, and practitioner support tools. |
| WESTLAW | Federal and state statutes, administrative documents, and court opinions. Extensive citator access, editorial material, and gateways to third-party publications. Extensive government document databases. |

Online quizzing @ http://wft.swlearning.com

**■ EXHIBIT 2–4**
Tax-Related Web Sites

| Web Site | WWW Address at Press Date | Description |
| --- | --- | --- |
| Internal Revenue Service | http://www.irs.gov/ | News releases, downloadable forms and instructions, tables, and e-mail |
| Court opinions | http://www.law.emory.edu/caselaw | Allows the researcher to link to the site of the jurisdiction (other than the Tax Court) that is the subject of the query. |
| Tax Analysts | http://www.taxanalysts.com | Policy-oriented readings on tax laws and proposals to change it, moderated bulletins on various tax subjects. |
| *Tax Sites Directory* | http://www.taxsites.com | References and links to tax sites on the Internet, including state and Federal tax sites, academic and professional pages, tax forms, and software. |
| Tax laws online | http://cfr.law.cornell.edu/cfr/ http://www4.law.cornell.edu/uscode/ http://uscode.house.gov/ search/criteria.php | Treasury Regulations. Internal Revenue Code. |
| *Motley Fool Tax Page* | http://www.fool.com/taxes | References and links to tax sites on the Internet. |
| Commercial tax publishers | For example, http://www.taxlibrary.com and http://cch.com | Information about products and services available by subscription and newsletter excerpts. |
| Large accounting firms and professional organizations | For example, the AICPA's page is at http://www.aicpa.org, Ernst & Young is at http://www.ey.com/ home.asp, and KPMG is at http://www.kpmg.com | Tax planning newsletters, descriptions of services offered and career opportunities, and exchange of data with clients and subscribers. |
| Thomson South-Western | http://wft.swlearning.com | Informational updates, newsletters, support materials for students and adopters, and continuing education. |
| Tax Court decisions | http://www.ustaxcourt.gov/ | Recent Tax Court decisions. |

Caution: Addresses change frequently.

or via the Internet. Online services generally employ price-per-search cost structures, which can be as much as $200 per hour, significantly higher than the cost of CD materials. Thus, unless a practitioner can pass along related costs to clients or others, online searching generally is limited to the most important issues and to the researchers with the most experience and training in search techniques.

Perhaps the best combination of electronic tax resources is to conduct day-to-day work on a CD system, so that the budget for the related work is known in advance, and augment the CD search with online access where it is judged to be critical. Exhibit 2–3 provides details about the most commonly used commercial online tax services.

**The Internet.** The Internet provides a wealth of tax information in several popular forms, sometimes at no direct cost to the researcher. Using web browser software and an Internet connection, the tax professional can access information provided around the world that can aid the research process.

- *The World Wide Web (WWW)* provides access to a number of sites maintained by accounting and consulting firms, publishers, tax academics and libraries, and governmental bodies. The best sites offer links to other sites and direct contact to the site providers. Exhibit 2–4 lists some of the Web sites that may be most useful to tax researchers and their Internet addresses as of press date.
- *Newsgroups* provide a means by which information related to the tax law can be exchanged among taxpayers, tax professionals, and others who subscribe to the group's services. Newsgroup members can read the exchanges among other members and offer replies and suggestions to inquiries as desired. Discussions address the interpretation and application of existing law, analysis of proposals and new pronouncements, and reviews of tax software.

While tax information on the Internet is plentiful, freely accessed information should never be relied upon without referring to other, more reliable sources. Always remember that anyone can set up a Web site and quality control is often lacking.

In many situations, solutions to research problems benefit from, or require, the use of various electronic tax research tools. A competent tax professional must become familiar and proficient with these tools and be able to use them to meet the expectations of clients and the necessities of work in the modern world.[25]

# Suggested Further Readings

Sheldon I. Banoff and Richard M. Lipton, editors Shop Talk, "Will Withdrawal of a Letter Ruling Request Lead to § 6662 Penalties?" *Journal of Taxation*, November 2003, pp. 316–317.

Richard Lipton and Elena S. Mossina, "Proposed Regulations on Withholding for Partnerships with Foreign Partners Would Ease Burdens," *Journal of Taxation*, December 2003, pp. 334–341.

Ted Needleman, "What's New in Tax Research," *Practical Accountant,* June 2004, pp. 35–38.

Robert W. Scott, editor, "Navigating the Research Stream," *Practical Accountant—2004 Year in Review,* pp. 6–11.

Michael G. Stevens, "What Are You Overlooking in Your Tax Tools?" *Practical Accountant*, June 2003, pp. 38–41.

## KEY TERMS

| | | |
|---|---|---|
| Acquiescence, 2–17 | Legislative Regulations, 2–25 | Small Cases Division, 2–12 |
| Circuit Court of Appeals, 2–14 | Letter rulings, 2–10 | Supreme Court, 2–15 |
| Court of Federal Claims, 2–12 | Nonacquiescence, 2–17 | Tax Court, 2–12 |
| Court of original jurisdiction, 2–12 | Precedents, 2–15 | Technical Advice Memoranda (TAMs), 2–12 |
| Determination letters, 2–11 | Procedural Regulations, 2–24 | |
| District Court, 2–12 | Proposed Regulations, 2–9 | Temporary Regulations, 2–9 |
| Final Regulations, 2–9 | Revenue Procedures, 2–10 | Writ of Certiorari, 2–16 |
| Interpretive Regulations, 2–24 | Revenue Rulings, 2–9 | |

---

[25]For a more detailed discussion of the use of electronic tax research in the modern tax practice, see W. A. Raabe, G. E. Whittenburg, and D. L. Sanders, *West's Federal Tax Research*, 7th ed. (Thomson/Southwestern, 2006).

## PROBLEM MATERIALS

### Problems

1. What is a primary source of tax information?

*Communications*

2. Barbara Brown operates a small international firm named Mallard, Inc. A new treaty between the United States and Ukraine conflicts with a Section of the Internal Revenue Code. Barbara asks you for advice. If she follows the treaty position, does she need to disclose this on her tax return? If she is required to disclose, are there any penalties for failure to disclose? Prepare a letter in which you respond to Barbara. Mallard's address is 100 International Drive, Tampa, FL 33620.

3. What is the function of the Joint Conference Committee of the House Ways and Means Committee and the Senate Finance Committee?

4. Distinguish between the following.
   a. Treasury Regulations and Revenue Rulings.
   b. Revenue Rulings and Revenue Procedures.
   c. Revenue Rulings and letter rulings.
   d. Letter rulings and determination letters.

5. Rank the following items from the highest authority to the lowest in the Federal tax law system.
   a. Interpretive Regulation.
   b. Legislative Regulation.
   c. Letter ruling.
   d. Revenue Ruling.
   e. Internal Revenue Code.
   f. Proposed Regulation.

6. Explain how Regulations are arranged. How would the following Regulations be cited?
   a. Finalized Regulations under § 442.
   b. Proposed Regulations under § 318.
   c. Temporary Regulations under § 446.

7. Interpret each of the following citations.
   a. Prop.Reg. § 1.280A–3(c)(4).
   b. Rev.Rul. 67–74, 1967–1 C.B. 194.
   c. Ltr.Rul. 200409001.

8. Which of the following would be considered advantages of the Small Cases Division of the Tax Court?
   a. Appeal to the Tax Court is possible.
   b. A hearing of a deficiency of $65,000 is considered on a timely basis.
   c. Taxpayer can handle the litigation without using a lawyer or certified public accountant.
   d. Taxpayer can use Small Cases Division decisions for precedential value.
   e. The actual hearing is conducted informally.
   f. Travel time will probably be reduced.

9. List an advantage and a disadvantage of using the U.S. District Court as the trial court for Federal tax litigation.

*Communications*

10. Carl Jensen is considering litigating a tax deficiency of approximately $274,000 in the court system. He asks you to provide him with a short description of his alternatives indicating the advantages and disadvantages of each. Prepare your response to Carl in the form of a letter. His address is 200 Mesa Drive, Tucson, AZ 85714.

11. A taxpayer lives in Michigan. In a controversy with the IRS, the taxpayer loses at the trial court level. Describe the appeal procedure for each of the following trial courts.
    a. Small Cases Division of the Tax Court.
    b. Tax Court.

    c. District Court.

    d. Court of Federal Claims.

12. Suppose the U.S. Government loses a tax case in the U.S. Tax Court and does not appeal the result. What does the failure to appeal signify?

13. For the Tax Court, District Court, and the Court of Federal Claims, indicate the following.
    a. Number of regular judges per court.
    b. Availability of a jury trial.
    c. Whether the deficiency must be paid before the trial.

14. In which of the following states could a taxpayer appeal the decision of a U.S. District Court to the Ninth Circuit Court of Appeals?
    a. Alaska.
    b. Arkansas.
    c. Florida.
    d. New York.
    e. South Carolina.

15. What is the Supreme Court's policy on hearing tax cases?

16. In assessing the validity of a prior court decision, discuss the significance of the following on the taxpayer's issue.
    a. The decision was rendered by the U.S. District Court of Wyoming. Taxpayer lives in Wyoming.
    b. The decision was rendered by the Court of Federal Claims. Taxpayer lives in Wyoming.
    c. The decision was rendered by the Second Circuit Court of Appeals. Taxpayer lives in California.
    d. The decision was rendered by the Supreme Court.
    e. The decision was rendered by the Tax Court. The IRS has acquiesced in the result.
    f. Same as (e), except that the IRS has nonacquiesced in the result.

17. What is the difference between a Regular decision, a Memorandum decision, and a Summary Opinion of the Tax Court?

18. Interpret each of the following citations.
    a. 54 T.C. 1514 (1970).
    b. 408 F.2d 117 (CA–2, 1969).
    c. 69–1 USTC ¶9319 (CA–2, 1969).
    d. 23 AFTR2d 69–1090 (CA–2, 1969).
    e. 293 F.Supp. 1129 (D.Ct.Miss., 1967).
    f. 67–1 USTC ¶9253 (D.Ct.Miss., 1967).
    g. 19 AFTR2d 647 (D.Ct.Miss., 1967).
    h. 56 S.Ct. 289 (USSC, 1935).
    i. 36–1 USTC ¶9020 (USSC, 1935).
    j. 16 AFTR 1274 (USSC, 1935).
    k. 422 F.2d 1336 (Ct.Cls., 1970).

19. Explain the following abbreviations.
    a. CA–2          i. USTC
    b. Fed.Cl.       j. AFTR
    c. *aff'd.*         k. F.3d
    d. *rev'd.*         l. F.Supp.
    e. *rem'd.*       m. USSC
    f. *Cert. denied*   n. S.Ct.
    g. *acq.*          o. D.Ct.
    h. B.T.A.

20. Give the Commerce Clearing House citation for each of the following courts.
    a. Small Cases Division of the Tax Court.
    b. District Court.
    c. Supreme Court.

    d.  Court of Federal Claims.
    e.  Tax Court Memorandum decision.

21. Where can you locate a published decision of the U.S. Court of Federal Claims?

22. Which of the following items can probably be found in the *Cumulative Bulletin*?
    a.  Action on Decision.
    b.  Small Cases Division of the Tax Court decision.
    c.  Letter ruling.
    d.  Revenue Procedure.
    e.  Final Regulation.
    f.  Court of Appeals decision.
    g.  Senate Finance Committee Report.
    h.  Acquiescences to Tax Court decisions.
    i.  U.S. Circuit Court of Appeals decision.

23. Answer the following questions based upon this citation: *United Draperies, Inc. v. Comm.*, 340 F.2d 936 (CA–7, 1964), *aff'g* 41 T.C. 457 (1963), *cert. denied* 382 U.S. 813 (1965).
    a.  In which court did this decision first appear?
    b.  Did the appellate court uphold the trial court?
    c.  Who was the plaintiff?
    d.  Did the Supreme Court uphold the appellate court decision?

**Issue ID**  24. Ashley is preparing a research paper discussing the differences between alimony and child care support for her tax class. Explain to Ashley how she can research these differences.

25. James has just been audited by the IRS and, as a result, has been assessed a substantial deficiency (which he has not yet paid) in additional income taxes. In preparing his defense, James advances the following possibilities.
    a.  Although a resident of Texas, James plans to sue in a District Court in Oregon that appears to be more favorably inclined toward taxpayers.
    b.  If (a) is not possible, James plans to take his case to a Texas state court where an uncle is the presiding judge.
    c.  Since James has found a B.T.A. decision that seems to help his case, he plans to rely on it under alternative (a) or (b).
    d.  If he loses at the trial court level, James plans to appeal to either the Court of Federal Claims or the Eleventh Circuit Court of Appeals because he has relatives in both Washington, D.C., and Atlanta. Staying with these relatives could save James lodging expense while his appeal is being heard by the court selected.
    e.  Even if he does not win at the trial court or appeals court level, James feels certain of success on an appeal to the Supreme Court.

    Evaluate James's notions concerning the judicial process as it applies to Federal income tax controversies.

26. Using the legend provided, classify each of the following statements (more than one answer per statement may be appropriate).

    **Legend**

    D = Applies to the District Court
    T = Applies to the Tax Court
    C = Applies to the Court of Federal Claims
    A = Applies to the Circuit Court of Appeals
    U = Applies to the Supreme Court
    N = Applies to none of the above

    a.  Decides only Federal tax matters.
    b.  Decisions are reported in the F.3d Series.
    c.  Decisions are reported in the USTCs.

d. Decisions are reported in the AFTRs.
e. Appeal is by *Writ of Certiorari*.
f. Court meets most often in Washington, D.C.
g. Offers the choice of a jury trial.
h. Is a trial court.
i. Is an appellate court.
j. Allows appeal to the Court of Appeals for the Federal Circuit, and bypasses the tax-payer's particular Circuit Court of Appeals.
k. Has a Small Cases Division.
l. Is the only trial court where the taxpayer does not have to first pay the tax assessed by the IRS.

27. Using the legend provided, classify each of the following citations as to the type of court.

**Legend**

D = Applies to the District Court
T = Applies to the Tax Court
C = Applies to the Court of Federal Claims
A = Applies to the Circuit Court of Appeals
U = Applies to the Supreme Court
N = Applies to none of the above

a. *Peter M. Schaeffer*, T.C.Memo. 1997–263.
b. Rev.Rul. 83–78, 1983–1 C.B. 245.
c. *Tufts v. Comm.*, 52 AFTR2d 83–5759 (CA–5, 1983).
d. *Farm Service Cooperative*, 70 T.C. 145 (1978).
e. *Korn Industries v. U.S.*, 532 F.2d 1352 (Ct.Cl., 1976).
f. *Zeeman v. Comm.*, 275 F.Supp. 235 (D.Ct. N.Y., 1967).
g. *Clark v. Comm.*, 489 U.S. 726 (1989).
h. Rev.Proc. 2001–43, 2001–2 C.B. 191.
i. 3 B.T.A. 1042 (1926).

28. Using the legend provided, classify each of the following tax sources.

**Legend**

P = Primary tax source
S = Secondary tax source
B = Both
N = Neither

a. Sixteenth Amendment to the Constitution.
b. Tax Treaty between the United States and France.
c. Revenue Procedure.
d. General Counsel Memoranda (1989).
e. Tax Court memorandum decision.
f. *Tax Notes* article.
g. Temporary Regulations (issued 2004).
h. Tax Court Memorandum decision.
i. Small Cases Division of the Tax Court decision.
j. Senate Finance Committee Report.

**Ethics**

29. An accountant friend of yours tells you that he "almost never" does any tax research, because he feels that "research usually reveals that some tax planning idea has already been thought up and shot down." Besides, he points out, most tax returns are never audited by the IRS. Can a tax adviser who is dedicated to reducing his client's tax liability justify the effort to engage in tax research? Do professional ethics *demand* such efforts? Which approach would a client probably prefer?

Ethics

30. Another friend of yours, who is a philosophy major, has overheard the conversation described in the previous problem and declares that all tax research is "immoral." She says that tax research enables people with substantial assets to shift the burden of financing public expenditures to those who "get up every morning, go to work, play by the rules, and pay their bills." How do you respond?

31. In general, most tax research can now be conducted and conclusions reached with the use of materials available on the Internet. Assess the validity of this statement.

**EXTENDER** 32. Under what circumstances can court decisions lead to changes in the Code?

**EXTENDER** 33. Locate the following Code provisions and give a brief description of each.
    a. § 61(a)(13).
    b. § 643(a)(2).
    c. § 2503(g)(2)(A).

 **BRIDGE DISCIPLINE**

1. Comment on these statements.
    a. The tax law is created and administered in the same way as other Federal provisions.
    b. Most taxpayers find it too expensive and time-consuming to sue the government in a tax dispute.

## Research Problems

**THOMSON**

**RIA**

*Note: Solutions to Research Problems can be prepared by using the **RIA Checkpoint® Student Edition** online research product, which is available to accompany this text. It is also possible to prepare solutions to the Research Problems by using tax research materials found in a standard tax library.*

**Research Problem 1.**   In *Bank One Corp.*, 120 T.C. 174 (2003), what was the position of the court with respect to the mark-to-market rule?

**Research Problem 2.**   Locate the following Code citations and give a brief topical description of each.
    a. § 708(a).
    b. § 1371(a)(1).
    c. § 2503(a).

**Research Problem 3.**   Locate the following Regulations and give a brief topical description of each.
    a. Reg. § 1.170A–4A(b)(2)(ii)(C).
    b. Reg. § 1.672(b)–1.
    c. Reg. § 20.2031–7(f).

**Research Problem 4.**   Locate the following items and give a brief summary of the results.
    a. *Charles Y. Choi*, T.C.Memo. 2002–183.
    b. Ltr.Rul. 200231003.
    c. Action on Decision 2000–004, May 10, 2000.

**Research Problem 5.**   Complete the following citations.
    a. *Figgie International, Inc.*, T.C.Memo. 1985– _____ .
    b. *S. Morton*, 38 B.T.A. _____ (1938).
    c. *Northern Coal & Dock Co.*, 12 T.C. _____ (1949).
    d. *Winn-Dixie Stores, Inc.*, 254 F.3d _____ (CA–11, 2001).
    e. Rev.Rul. 59–_____ , 1959–2 C.B. 87.
    f. *Upjohn Co. v. U.S.*, 449 U.S. _____ (1981).
    g. *In re Sealed Case*, 737 F.2d 94 (_____ , 1984).

**Research Problem 6.**   Find *Kathryn Bernal*, 120 T.C. 102 (2003) and answer the following questions.
   a.   What was the docket number?
   b.   When was the dispute filed?
   c.   Who is the respondent?
   d.   Who was the attorney for the taxpayers?
   e.   Who was the judge who wrote the opinion?
   f.   What was the disposition of the dispute?

**Research Problem 7.**   Determine how the term *person* is defined in the *Internal Revenue Code*. Specify the Code Section in which the term is defined.

**Research Problem 8.**   Go to page 44,274 of the August 25, 1995 issue of the *Federal Register*. What action was taken by the IRS, and what was the subject matter?

**Internet Activity**

*Use the tax resources of the Internet to address the following questions. Do not restrict your search to the World Wide Web, but include a review of newsgroups and general reference materials, practitioner sites and resources, primary sources of the tax law, chat rooms and discussion groups, and other opportunities.*

**Research Problem 9.**   Go to each of the following Internet locations.
   a.   Several primary sources of the tax law, including the U.S. Supreme Court, a Circuit Court of Appeals, the Internal Revenue Service, and final Regulations.
   b.   Sources of proposed Federal tax legislation.
   c.   A collection of tax rules for your state.

**Research Problem 10.**   Go to the U.S. Tax Court Internet site.
   a.   What different types of cases can be found on the site?
   b.   What is a Summary Opinion? Find one.
   c.   What is a Memorandum Opinion? Find one.
   d.   Find the "Rules of Practice and Procedure."
   e.   Is the site user friendly? E-mail suggested improvements to the webmaster.

# Structure of the Federal Income Tax

Part II introduces the components of the basic tax model. The gross income component, including the effect of exclusions, the accounting period, and the accounting method, are presented. This presentation is followed by an analysis of business deductions, including deductions that are allowed, deductions that are disallowed, and the effect of the accounting period and the accounting method on the timing of deductions. Included in the presentation are the deduction for charitable contributions, research and experimental expenditures, interest and taxes, cost recovery, amortization, and depletion. Part II concludes with a discussion of losses. Included are coverage on bad debts, casualty and theft losses, net operating losses, the tax shelter issue, the at-risk limitations, and the passive activity loss limitations.

**CHAPTER 3**

Gross Income

**CHAPTER 4**

Business Deductions

**CHAPTER 5**

Losses and Loss Limitations

http://wft.swlearning.com

# Gross Income

CHAPTER 3

## LEARNING OBJECTIVES

*After completing Chapter 3, you should be able to:*

**LO.1**

Explain the concepts of gross income and realization and distinguish between the economic, accounting, and tax concepts of gross income.

**LO.2**

Understand when the cash, accrual, and hybrid methods of accounting are used and how they are applied.

**LO.3**

Identify who should pay the tax on an item of income.

**LO.4**

Understand that statutory authority is required to exclude an item from gross income.

**LO.5**

Apply the Internal Revenue Code provisions on loans made at below-market interest rates.

**LO.6**

Determine the extent to which receipts can be excluded under the tax benefit rule.

**LO.7**

Understand the Internal Revenue Code provision that excludes interest on state and local government obligations from gross income.

**LO.8**

Use the Internal Revenue Code's exclusion of leasehold improvements from gross income.

**LO.9**

Determine the extent to which life insurance proceeds are excluded from gross income.

**LO.10**

Describe the circumstances under which income must be reported from the discharge of indebtedness.

**LO.11**

Describe the tax consequences of property transactions.

http://wft.swlearning.com

## OUTLINE

---

### TAX TALK

*The first nine pages of the Internal Revenue Code define income. The remaining 1,100 pages spin the web of exceptions and preferences.*

—*Warren G. Magnuson*

---

**M**ary purchases a number of computer components from a supplier for $500. She hires an employee to assemble them into a computer that has a market value of $1,100. Keith, one of Mary's long-time customers, has been especially effective in sending new business to Mary's operation, so Mary sells the computer to Keith for $950. Direct labor costs for the computer totaled $150, and an allocable share of Mary's overhead for the current sale was determined to be $40.

Keith called in his order on December 15, 2005. Because he was going to be out of town, Keith told Mary to bring the computer to his office on January 6, 2006. The computer was fully assembled on December 22, 2005, but Mary delivered the machine on January 6, 2006.

Mary does business in a storefront in the local strip mall, using the name Home-Made Computers. Home-Made is a partnership, owned equally by Mary and her sister Sherry.

Some variation of this simple scenario is carried out millions of times every day in today's global economy. Several broad tax questions, such as the following, arise as a result of these transactions.

- What: What is income?
- When: In which tax period is the income recognized?
- Who: Who is taxed on the income?

# The Tax Formula

The basic income tax formula was introduced in Chapter 1 and summarized in Figure 1–1. This chapter, together with Chapters 4 through 7, examines the elements of this formula in detail. However, before embarking on a detailed study of the income tax, a brief introduction of each component of the tax formula is provided below as an overview.

## COMPONENTS OF THE TAX FORMULA

**Income (Broadly Conceived).** This includes all of the taxpayer's income, both taxable and nontaxable. Although it is essentially equivalent to gross receipts, it does not include a return of capital or borrowed funds.

**Exclusions.** For various reasons, Congress has chosen to exclude certain types of income from the income tax base. The principal income exclusions that apply to all entities (e.g., life insurance proceeds received by reason of death of the insured and state and local bond interest) are discussed later in this chapter, while exclusions that are unique to individuals are addressed in Chapters 15 and 16.

**Gross Income.** Section 61 of the Internal Revenue Code provides the following definition of **gross income.**

> Except as otherwise provided in this subtitle, gross income means all income from whatever source derived.

This language is derived from the Sixteenth Amendment to the Constitution. The "except as otherwise provided" phrase refers to exclusions.

Supreme Court decisions have made it clear that *all* sources of income are subject to tax unless Congress specifically excludes the type of income received.

> The starting point in all cases dealing with the question of the scope of what is included in "gross income" begins with the basic premise that the purpose of Congress was to use the full measure of its taxing power.[1]

While it is clear that income is to be broadly construed, the statutory law fails to provide a satisfactory definition of the term and lists only a small set of items that are specifically included in income, including:

- Compensation for services.
- Business income.
- Gains from sales and other disposition of property.
- Interest.
- Dividends.
- Rents and royalties.
- Certain income arising from discharge of indebtedness.
- Income from partnerships.

**Deductions.** Generally, all ordinary and necessary trade or business expenses are deductible by taxpaying entities. Such expenses include the cost of goods sold, salaries, wages, operating expenses (such as rent and utilities), research and

---

[1]*James v. U.S.,* 61–1 USTC ¶9449, 7 AFTR2d 1361, 81 S.Ct. 1052 (USSC, 1961).

development expenditures, interest, taxes, depreciation, amortization, and depletion.

As noted in Chapter 1, individuals can use two categories of deductions—deductions *for* AGI and deductions *from* AGI. In addition, individuals are unique among taxpaying entities in that they are permitted to deduct a variety of personal expenses (i.e., expenses unrelated to business or investment), they are allowed a standard deduction if this amount exceeds the deductible personal expenses, and they are allowed a deduction for personal and dependency exemptions.

**Determining the Tax.**   Taxable income is determined by subtracting deductions (after any applicable limitations) from gross income. The tax rates (located inside the front cover of this text) are then applied to determine the tax. Finally, tax prepayments (such as Federal income tax withholding on salaries and estimated tax payments) and a wide variety of credits are subtracted from the tax to determine the amount due to the Federal government or the refund due to the taxpayer.

**L0.1**

Explain the concepts of gross income and realization and distinguish between the economic, accounting, and tax concepts of gross income.

# Gross Income—What Is It?

## ECONOMIC AND ACCOUNTING CONCEPTS OF INCOME

As noted above, Congress failed to provide in the Code a clear definition of income. Instead, it was left to the judicial and administrative branches of government to thrash out the meaning of income. As the income tax law developed, two competing models of income were considered by these agencies: economic income and accounting income.

The term **income** is used in the Code but is defined very broadly. Early in the history of our tax laws, the courts were required to interpret "the commonly understood meaning of the term which must have been in the minds of the people when they adopted the Sixteenth Amendment."[2]

Economists measure income (**economic income**) by determining the change (increase or decrease) in the fair market value of the entity's net assets from the beginning to the end of the year. This focus on change in *net worth* as a measure of income (or loss) requires no disposition of assets. For *individual* taxpayers, one adds the value of the year's personal consumption of goods and services (e.g., food, the rental value of owner-occupied housing, etc.).[3]

**EXAMPLE 1**

Helen's economic income is calculated by comparing her net worth at the end of the year (December 31) with her net worth at the beginning of the year (January 1) and adding her personal consumption.

| | | |
|---|---:|---:|
| Fair market value of Helen's assets on December 31 | $220,000 | |
| Less liabilities on December 31 | (40,000) | |
| Net worth on December 31 | | $ 180,000 |
| Fair market value of Helen's assets on January 1 | $200,000 | |
| Less liabilities on January 1 | (80,000) | |
| Net worth on January 1 | | (120,000) |
| Increase in net worth | | $  60,000 |

---

[2] *Merchants Loan and Trust Co. v. Smietanka*, 1 USTC ¶42, 3 AFTR 3102, 41 S.Ct. 386 (USSC, 1921).

[3] See Henry C. Simons, *Personal Income Taxation* (Chicago: University of Chicago Press, 1933), Chapters 2–3.

BRIDGE DISCIPLINE

### Bridge to Financial Accounting

Accountants use a definition of income that relies on the realization principle.[4] **Accounting income** is not recognized until it is realized. For realization to occur:

- An exchange of goods or services must take place between the entity and some independent, external party, and
- The goods or services received by the entity must be capable of being objectively valued.[5]

Thus, an increase in the fair market value of an asset before its sale or other disposition is not sufficient to trigger the recognition of accounting income. Similarly, the imputed savings that arise when an entity creates assets for its own use (e.g., feed grown by a farmer for his or her livestock) do not constitute accounting income because no exchange has occurred.

Business taxpayers often reconcile their annual income computations for financial accounting and tax law purposes. Taxpayers required to prepare audited financial statements must explain in the footnotes to the statements (1) the most important accounting principles used in computing book income, and (2) the most important tax elections and other consequences of the tax law on earnings per share.

| | | |
|---|---|---|
| Consumption | | |
| Food, clothing, and other personal expenditures | $25,000 | |
| Imputed rental value of the home Helen owns and occupies | 12,000 | |
| Total consumption | | 37,000 |
| Economic income | | $97,000 |

The tax law relies to some extent on net worth as a measure of income.[6] Potentially, anything that increases net worth is income, and anything that decreases net worth is deductible (if permitted by statute). Thus, *windfall income* such as buried treasure found in one's backyard is taxable under the theory that net worth has been increased.[7] Likewise, a lender does *not* recognize gross income on receipt of loan principal repayments. The lender's investment simply changes from a loan receivable to cash, so net worth does not change.

Because the strict application of a tax based on economic income would require taxpayers to determine the value of their assets annually, compliance would be burdensome. Controversies between taxpayers and the IRS would inevitably arise under an economic approach to income determination because of the subjective nature of valuation in many circumstances. In addition, using market values to determine income for tax purposes could result in liquidity problems. That is, a taxpayer's assets could increase in value but not be easily converted into the cash

---

[4]See the American Accounting Association Committee Report on the "Realization Concept," *The Accounting Review* (April 1965): 312–322.
[5]Valuation is carried out in the local currency of the reporting entity.
[6]*Comm. v. Glenshaw Glass Co.*, 55–1 USTC ¶9308, 47 AFTR 162, 348 U.S. 426 (USSC, 1955).

[7]*Cesarini v. U.S.*, 69–1 USTC ¶9270, 23 AFTR2d 69–997, 296 F.Supp. 3 (D.Ct. Oh., 1969), *aff'd* 70–2 USTC ¶9509, 26 AFTR2d 70–5107, 428 F.2d 812 (CA–6, 1970); Rev.Rul. 61, 1953–1 C.B. 17.

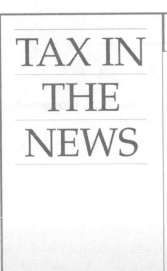

## YOUR SILENT GAMBLING PARTNER: IF YOU WIN!

Gambling has become big business in the United States. But many folks fail to understand that when you win, Uncle Sam wins too, or at least he's supposed to win. Gambling payoffs, no matter how large or small, are taxable and should be reported on your Federal income tax return. This includes the fair market value of noncash prizes such as cars, trips, and dinner coupons. The provision applies to winnings from all sources, from casinos to office pools.

No one knows for sure how much in gambling winnings goes unreported. For winnings of $600 or more ($1,200 from bingo or slot machines, $1,500 from keno), however, the payer is required to notify the IRS and issue the player an IRS Form W–2G.

But what happens to all those bets you placed that didn't pay off? A person's gambling losses can be used only to offset his or her gambling gains. So, if you have a net gain, the IRS wins, and if you have a net loss, you lose.

SOURCE: Adapted from Armond Budish, "Bet On Paying Taxes When You Gamble and Win," *Cleveland Plain Dealer,* August 10, 2004, p. C5.

needed to pay the resulting tax (e.g., increases in the value of commercial real estate).[8] Thus, the IRS, Congress, and the courts have rejected broad application of the economic income concept as impractical.

## COMPARISON OF THE ACCOUNTING AND TAX CONCEPTS OF INCOME

Although income tax rules frequently parallel financial accounting measurement concepts, differences do exist. Of major significance, for example, is the fact that unearned (prepaid) income received by an accrual basis taxpayer often is taxed in the year of receipt. For financial accounting purposes, such prepayments are not treated as income until earned. Because of this and other differences, many corporations report financial accounting income that is substantially different from the amounts reported for tax purposes.

The Supreme Court provided an explanation for some of the variations between accounting and taxable income in a decision involving inventory and bad debt adjustments.

> The primary goal of financial accounting is to provide useful information to management, shareholders, creditors, and others properly interested; the major responsibility of the accountant is to protect these parties from being misled. The primary goal of the income tax system, in contrast, is the equitable collection of revenue. . . . Consistently with its goals and responsibilities, financial accounting has as its foundation the principle of conservatism, with its corollary that "possible errors in measurement [should] be in the direction of understatement rather than overstatement of net income and net assets." In view of the Treasury's markedly different goals and responsibilities, understatement of income is not destined to be its guiding light. . . .
>
> Financial accounting, in short, is hospitable to estimates, probabilities, and reasonable certainties; the tax law, with its mandate to preserve the revenue, can give no quarter to uncertainty.[9]

---

[8]In Chapter 1, this was identified as a justification of the wherewithal to pay concept.

[9]*Thor Power Tool Co. v. Comm.,* 79–1 USTC ¶9139, 43 AFTR2d 79–362, 99 S.Ct. 773 (USSC, 1979).

## FORM OF RECEIPT

Gross income is not limited to cash received. "It includes income realized in any form, whether in money, property, or services. Income may be realized [and recognized], therefore, in the form of services, meals, accommodations, stock or other property, as well as in cash."[10]

**EXAMPLE 2**

Ostrich Corporation allows Cameron, an employee, to use a company car for his vacation. Cameron realizes income equal to the rental value of the car for the time and mileage. ∎

**EXAMPLE 3**

Plover, Inc., owes $10,000 on a mortgage. The creditor accepts $8,000 in full satisfaction of the debt. Plover realizes income of $2,000 from retiring the debt.[11] ∎

**EXAMPLE 4**

Donna is a CPA specializing in individual tax return preparation. Her neighbor, Jill, is a dentist. Each year, Donna prepares Jill's tax return in exchange for two dental checkups. Jill and Donna both have gross income equal to the fair market value of the services they provide. ∎

# Year of Inclusion

## TAXABLE YEAR

The annual accounting period or **taxable year** is a basic component of our tax system. Generally, an entity must use the *calendar year* to report its income. However, a *fiscal year* (a period of 12 months ending on the last day of any month other than December) can be elected if the taxpayer maintains adequate books and records. This fiscal year option generally is not available to partnerships, S corporations, and personal service corporations.

Determining the tax year in which the income is recognized is important for determining the tax consequences of the income.

- With a progressive tax rate system, a taxpayer's marginal tax rate can change from year to year.
- Congress may change the tax rates.
- The relevant rates may change because of a change in the entity's status (e.g., a proprietorship may incorporate).
- Several provisions in the Code depend on the taxpayer's income for the year (e.g., the charitable contribution deduction).

**LO.2**

Understand when the cash, accrual, and hybrid methods of accounting are used and how they are applied.

## ACCOUNTING METHODS

The year in which an item of income is subject to tax often depends upon the **accounting method** the taxpayer employs. The three primary methods of accounting are (1) the cash receipts and disbursements method, (2) the accrual method, and (3) the hybrid method. Most individuals use the cash receipts and disbursements method of accounting, whereas most corporations use the accrual method. Because the Regulations require the accrual method for determining purchases and sales when inventory is an income-producing factor,[12] some businesses employ a hybrid method that is a combination of the cash and accrual methods.

---

[10]Reg. § 1.61–1(a).

[11]Reg. § 1.61–12. See *U.S. v. Kirby Lumber Co.,* 2 USTC ¶814, 10 AFTR 458, 52 S.Ct. 4 (USSC, 1931). Exceptions to this general rule exist.

[12]Reg. § 1.446–1(c)(2)(i).

In addition to these overall accounting methods, a taxpayer may choose to spread the gain from an installment sale of property over the collection period by using the *installment method* of income recognition. Contractors may either spread profits from contracts over the period in which the work is done (the *percentage of completion method*) or defer all profit until the year in which the project is completed (the *completed contract method*) in limited circumstances.[13]

The IRS has the power to prescribe the accounting method to be used by the taxpayer. The IRS holds broad powers to determine if the accounting method used *clearly reflects income*.

> If no method of accounting has been regularly used by the taxpayer, or *if the method used does not clearly reflect income, the computation of taxable income shall be made under such method as, in the opinion of the Secretary . . . does clearly reflect income.*[14]

**Cash Receipts Method.**　Under the **cash receipts method,** property or services received are included in the taxpayer's gross income in the year of actual or constructive receipt by the taxpayer or agent, regardless of whether the income was earned in that year.[15] The income received need not be reduced to cash in the same year. All that is necessary for income recognition is that property or services received have a fair market value—a cash equivalent.[16] Thus, a cash basis taxpayer that receives a note in payment for services has income in the year of receipt equal to the fair market value of the note. However, a creditor's mere promise to pay (e.g., an account receivable), with no supporting note, is not usually considered to have a fair market value.[17] Thus, the cash basis taxpayer defers income recognition until the account receivable is collected.

**EXAMPLE 5**

Finch & Thrush, a CPA firm, uses the cash receipts method of accounting. In 2005, the firm performs an audit for Orange Corporation and bills the client for $5,000, which is collected in 2006. In 2005, the firm also performs an audit for Blue Corporation. Because of Blue's precarious financial position, Finch & Thrush requires Blue to issue an $8,000 secured negotiable note in payment of the fee. The note has a fair market value of $6,000. The firm collects $8,000 on the note in 2006. Finch & Thrush has the following gross income for the two years.

|  | 2005 | 2006 |
|---|---|---|
| Fair market value of note received from Blue | $6,000 | |
| Cash received | | |
| From Orange on account receivable | | $ 5,000 |
| From Blue on note receivable | | 8,000 |
| Less: Recovery of capital | –0– | (6,000) |
| Total gross income | $6,000 | $ 7,000 |

Generally, a check received is considered a cash equivalent. Thus, a cash basis taxpayer must recognize the income when the check is received. This is true even if the taxpayer receives the check after banking hours.[18]

---

[13]§§ 453 and 460.

[14]§ 446(b).

[15]*Julia A. Strauss,* 2 B.T.A. 598 (1925). The doctrine of *constructive receipt* holds that if income is unqualifiedly available although not physically in the taxpayer's possession, it is subject to the income tax. An example is accrued interest on a savings account. Under the doctrine of constructive receipt, the interest is taxed to a depositor in

the year available, rather than the year actually withdrawn. The fact that the depositor uses the cash basis of accounting for tax purposes is irrelevant. Reg. § 1.451–2.

[16]Reg. §§ 1.446–1(a)(3) and (c)(1)(i).

[17]*Bedell v. Comm.,* 1 USTC ¶359, 7 AFTR 8469, 30 F.2d 622 (CA–2, 1929).

[18]*Charles F. Kahler,* 18 T.C. 31 (1952).

Certain taxpayers are not permitted to use the cash method of accounting regardless of whether inventories are material. Specifically, the accrual basis must be used to report the income earned by (1) corporations (other than S corporations), (2) partnerships with a corporate partner, and (3) tax shelters.[19] A number of other businesses still can use the cash method. Included are:

- A farming business.
- A qualified personal service corporation (e.g., a corporation performing services in health, law, engineering, architecture, accounting, actuarial science, performing arts, or consulting).
- Any entity that is not a tax shelter whose average annual gross receipts for the most recent three-year period are $5 million or less.[20]

## Cash Receipts Method

**FRAMEWORK FOCUS: INCOME**

STRATEGY ➤ POSTPONE RECOGNITION OF INCOME TO ACHIEVE TAX DEFERRAL.

**FRAMEWORK FOCUS: TAX RATE**

STRATEGY ➤ SHIFT NET INCOME FROM HIGH-BRACKET YEARS TO LOW-BRACKET YEARS.

The timing of income from services can often be controlled through the cash method of accounting. Although taxpayers are somewhat constrained by the constructive receipt doctrine, seldom will customers and clients offer to pay before they are asked. The usual lag between billings and collections (e.g., December's billings collected in January) will result in a deferral of some income until the last year of operations. For example, before rendering services, a corporate officer approaching retirement may contract with the corporation to defer a portion of his or her compensation to the lower tax bracket retirement years.

**Accrual Method.**    Under the **accrual method,** an item generally is included in gross income for the year in which it is earned, regardless of when the income is collected. The income is earned when (1) all the events have occurred that fix the right to receive the income and (2) the amount to be received can be determined with reasonable accuracy.[21]

Generally, the taxpayer's rights to the income accrue when title to property passes to the buyer or the services are performed for the customer or client.[22] If the rights to the income have accrued but are subject to a potential refund claim (e.g., under a product warranty), the income is reported in the year of sale, and a deduction is allowed in subsequent years when actual claims accrue.[23]

Where the taxpayer's rights to the income are being contested (e.g., when a contractor fails to meet specifications), gross income is recognized only when payment has been received.[24] If the payment is received before the dispute is settled,

---

[19]§ 448(a).

[20]§ 448(b). Rev.Proc. 2002–28, I.R.B. No. 18, 815.

[21]Reg. § 1.451–1(a).

[22]*Lucas v. North Texas Lumber Co.,* 2 USTC ¶484, 8 AFTR 10276, 50 S.Ct. 184 (USSC, 1930).

[23]*Brown v. Helvering,* 4 USTC ¶1222, 13 AFTR 851, 54 S.Ct. 356 (USSC, 1933).

[24]*Burnet v. Sanford and Brooks,* 2 USTC ¶636, 9 AFTR 603, 51 S.Ct. 150 (USSC, 1931).

however, the court-made **claim of right doctrine** requires the taxpayer to recognize the income in the year of receipt.[25]

**EXAMPLE 6**

Tangerine Construction, Inc., completes construction of a building in 2005 and presents a bill to the customer. The customer refuses to pay the bill and claims that Tangerine has not met specifications. A settlement with the customer is not reached until 2006. No income accrues to Tangerine until 2006. Alternatively, if the customer pays for the work and then files suit for damages, Tangerine cannot defer the income, and it is taxable in 2005. ■

**EXAMPLE 7**

Assume the same facts as in Example 5, except that Finch & Thrush uses the accrual basis of accounting. The firm must recognize $13,000 ($8,000 + $5,000) income in 2005, the year its rights to the income accrue. ■

**Hybrid Method.**   The Regulations require that the accrual method be used for determining sales and cost of goods sold. To simplify record keeping, some taxpayers account for inventory using the accrual method and use the cash method for all other income and expense items. This approach, called the **hybrid method,** is used primarily by small businesses when inventory is an income-producing factor.

## SPECIAL RULES FOR CASH BASIS TAXPAYERS

**Constructive Receipt.**   Income that has not actually been received by the taxpayer is taxed as though it had been received—the income is constructively received—under the following conditions.

* The amount is made readily available to the taxpayer.
* The taxpayer's actual receipt is not subject to substantial limitations or restrictions.[26]

The rationale for the **constructive receipt** doctrine is that if the income is available, the taxpayer should not be allowed to postpone income recognition. For instance, a taxpayer is not permitted to defer income for December services by refusing to accept payment until January.

**EXAMPLE 8**

Rob, a physician, conducts his medical practice as a sole proprietorship. Rob is also a member of a barter club. In 2005, Rob provided medical care for other club members and earned 3,000 points. Each point entitles him to $1 in goods and services sold by other members of the club; the points can be used at any time. In 2006, Rob exchanged his points for a new high definition TV. Rob recognizes $3,000 of gross income in 2005 when the 3,000 points were credited to his account.[27] ■

**EXAMPLE 9**

On December 31, an employer issued a bonus check to an employee but asked her to hold it for a few days until the company could make deposits to cover the check. The income was not constructively received on December 31 since the issuer did not have sufficient funds in its account to pay the debt.[28] ■

**EXAMPLE 10**

Mauve, Inc., an S corporation, owned interest coupons that matured on December 31. The coupons can be converted to cash at any bank at maturity. Thus, the income was constructively received on December 31, even though Mauve failed to cash in the coupons until the following year.[29] ■

---

[25]*North American Oil Consolidated Co. v. Burnet*, 3 USTC ¶943, 11 AFTR 16, 52 S.Ct. 613 (USSC, 1932).
[26]Reg. § 1.451–2(a).

[27]Rev.Rul. 80–52, 1980–1 C.B. 100.
[28]*L. M. Fischer*, 14 T.C. 792 (1950).
[29]Reg. § 1.451–2(b).

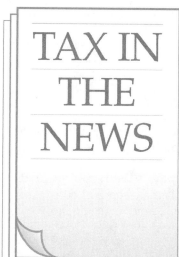

**CONGRESS RESCUES LOTTERY WINNERS FROM CONSTRUCTIVE RECEIPT PROBLEMS**

Under the general rules of constructive receipt, a lottery winner who elected to receive the winnings in installments could face horrendous tax problems. If the winner had the right to receive the entire amount, but elected to be paid in installments, tax was due on all the amounts to be received in the future as well as the amount received currently. Frequently, the winner made the election without being aware of the tax consequences. To protect poorly advised, or unadvised, lottery winners, Congress changed § 451(h) so that the constructive receipt doctrine will not apply to "qualified prizes," a term crafted specifically to address the lottery and prize winner's situation. Thus, lottery winnings can be received in installments and included in gross income as the installments are actually received.

**EXAMPLE 11**

Flamingo Company mails dividend checks on December 31, 2005. The checks will not be received by the shareholders until January. The shareholders do not realize gross income until 2006.[30] ■

The constructive receipt doctrine does not reach income that the taxpayer is not yet entitled to receive even though the taxpayer could have contracted to receive the income at an earlier date.

**EXAMPLE 12**

Murphy offers to pay Peach Corporation (a cash basis taxpayer) $100,000 for land in December 2005. Peach Corporation refuses but offers to sell the land to Murphy on January 1, 2006, when the corporation will be in a lower tax bracket. If Murphy accepts Peach's offer, the gain is taxed to Peach in 2006 when the sale is completed.[31] ■

**Original Issue Discount.** Lenders frequently make loans that require a payment at maturity of more than the amount of the original loan. The difference between the amount due at maturity and the amount of the original loan is actually interest but is referred to as **original issue discount.** Under the general rules of tax accounting, a cash basis lender would not report the original issue discount as interest income until the year the amount is collected, although an accrual basis borrower would deduct the interest as it is earned. However, the Code puts the lender and borrower on parity by requiring that the original issue discount be reported when it is earned, regardless of the taxpayer's accounting method.[32] The *interest earned* is calculated by the effective interest rate method.

**EXAMPLE 13**

On January 1, 2005, Blue and White, a cash basis partnership, pays $82,645 for a 24-month certificate of deposit. The certificate is priced to yield 10% (the effective interest rate) with interest compounded annually. No interest is paid until maturity, when Blue and White

---

[30]Reg. § 1.451–2(b).

[31]*Cowden v. Comm.*, 61–1 USTC ¶9382, 7 AFTR2d 1160, 289 F.2d 20 (CA–5, 1961).

[32]§§ 1272(a)(3) and 1273(a).

receives $100,000. Thus, the partnership's gross income from the certificate is $17,355 ($100,000 – $82,645). Blue and White calculates income earned each year as follows.

| | |
|---|---|
| 2005: (0.10 × $82,645) = | $ 8,264 |
| 2006: [0.10($82,645 + $8,264)] = | 9,091 |
| | $17,355 |

The original issue discount rules do not apply to U.S. savings bonds or to obligations with a maturity date of one year or less from the date of issue.[33]

**Amounts Received under an Obligation to Repay.**   The receipt of funds with an obligation to repay that amount in the future is the essence of borrowing. The taxpayer's assets and liabilities increase by the same amount, so no income is realized when the borrowed funds are received.

**EXAMPLE 14**

A landlord receives a damage deposit from a tenant. The landlord does not recognize income until the deposit is forfeited because the landlord has an obligation to repay the deposit if no damage occurs.[34] However, if the deposit is in fact a prepayment of rent, it is taxed in the year of receipt. ■

## SPECIAL RULES FOR ACCRUAL BASIS TAXPAYERS

**Prepaid Income.**   For financial reporting purposes, advance payments received from customers are reflected as prepaid income and as a liability of the seller. For tax purposes, however, the prepaid income often is taxed in the year of receipt.

**EXAMPLE 15**

In December 2005, a company pays its January 2006 rent of $1,000. The accrual basis landlord must include the $1,000 in 2005 gross income for tax purposes, although the unearned rent income is reported as a liability on the landlord's balance sheet for December 31, 2005. ■

**Deferral of Advance Payments for Goods.**   Generally, an accrual basis taxpayer can elect to defer recognition of income from advance payments for goods if the method of accounting for the sale is the same for tax and financial reporting purposes.[35]

**EXAMPLE 16**

Brown Company ships goods only after payment for the goods has been received. In December 2005, Brown receives $10,000 for goods that are not shipped until January 2006. Brown can elect to report the income in 2006 for tax purposes, assuming the company reports the income in 2006 for financial reporting purposes. ■

**Deferral of Advance Payments for Services.**   Revenue Procedure 2004–34[36] permits an accrual basis taxpayer to defer recognition of income for *advance payments for services* to be performed after the end of the tax year of receipt. The portion of the advance payment that relates to services performed in the tax year of receipt is included in gross income in the tax year of receipt. The portion of the advance payment that relates to services to be performed after the tax year of receipt is included in gross income in the tax year following the tax year of receipt of the advance payment.

---

[33]§ 1272(a)(2).
[34]*John Mantell*, 17 T.C. 1143 (1952).
[35]Reg. § 1.451–5(b). See Reg. § 1.451–5(c) for exceptions to this deferral opportunity.

[36]2004 I.R.B. 13, 991.

**EXAMPLE 17**

Yellow Corporation, an accrual basis calendar year taxpayer, sells its services under 12-month, 24-month, and 36-month contracts. The corporation provides services to each customer every month. On May 1, 2005, Yellow Corporation sold the following customer contracts:

| Length of Contract | Total Proceeds |
|---|---|
| 12 months | $3,000 |
| 24 months | 4,800 |
| 36 months | 7,200 |

Yellow may defer until 2006 all of the income that will be earned after 2005.

| Length of Contract | Income Recorded in 2005 | Income Recorded in 2006 |
|---|---|---|
| 12 months | $2,000 ($3,000 × 8/12) | $1,000 ($3,000 × 4/12) |
| 24 months | 1,600 ($4,800 × 8/24) | 3,200 ($4,800 × 16/24) |
| 36 months | 1,600 ($7,200 × 8/36) | 5,600 ($7,200 × 28/36) |

Revenue Procedure 2004–34 does not apply to prepaid rent or prepaid interest. Advance payments for these items are always taxed in the year of receipt.

**PLANNING STRATEGIES**

## Prepaid Income

**FRAMEWORK FOCUS: INCOME**

**STRATEGY ▶ POSTPONE RECOGNITION OF INCOME TO ACHIEVE TAX DEFERRAL.**

The accrual basis taxpayer who receives advance payments from customers should structure the transactions using the rules discussed above to avoid having to pay tax on income before the time the income is actually earned. In addition, both cash and accrual basis taxpayers can sometimes defer income by stipulating that the payments are deposits rather than prepaid income. For example, a landlord might consider requiring an equivalent damage deposit rather than prepayment of the last month's rent.

**LO.3**

Identify who should pay the tax on an item of income.

# Income Sources

## PERSONAL SERVICES

It is a well-established principle of taxation that income from personal services must be included in the gross income of the person who performs the services. This principle was first established in a Supreme Court decision, *Lucas v. Earl*.[37] Mr. Earl entered into a binding agreement with his wife under which Mrs. Earl was to receive one-half of Mr. Earl's salary. Justice Holmes used the celebrated **fruit and tree metaphor** to explain that the fruit (income) must be attributed to the tree from which it came (Mr. Earl's services). A mere **assignment of income** does not shift the liability for the tax.

---

[37]2 USTC ¶496, 8 AFTR 10287, 50 S.Ct. 241 (USSC, 1930).

**Services of an Employee.**   Services performed by an employee for the employer's customers are considered performed by the employer. Thus, the employer is taxed on the income from the services provided to the customer, and the employee is taxed on any compensation received from the employer.[38]

EXAMPLE 18

Dr. Carey incorporates her medical practice and enters into a contract to work for the corporation for a salary. All patients contract to receive their services from the corporation, and those services are provided through the corporation's employee, Dr. Carey. The corporation must include the patients' fees in its gross income. Dr. Carey must include her salary in her gross income. The corporation is allowed a deduction for a reasonable salary paid to Dr. Carey. ■

## INCOME FROM PROPERTY

Income earned from property (interest, dividends, rent) must be included in the gross income of the owner of the property. If a shareholder clips interest coupons from bonds shortly before the interest payment date and transfers the coupons to his or her solely owned corporation, the interest still is taxed to the shareholder. Similarly, a parent who assigns rents from income-producing property to a child is taxed on the rent, since the parent retains ownership of the property.[39]

Often income-producing property is transferred after income from the property has accrued but before the income is recognized under the transferor's method of accounting. The IRS and the courts have developed rules to allocate the income between the transferor and the transferee. These allocation rules are addressed below. Other allocation rules address income in community property states.

DIGGING DEEPER (1)   *Find more information on this topic at our Web site: **http://wft-entities.swlearning.com**.*

**Interest.**   According to the IRS, interest accrues daily. Therefore, the interest for the period that includes the date of the transfer is allocated between the transferor and the transferee based on the number of days during the period that each owned the property.

EXAMPLE 19

Floyd, a cash basis taxpayer, gives his son, Seth, bonds with a face amount of $10,000 and an 8% stated annual interest rate, payable December 31. The gift is made on January 31, 2005. Floyd recognizes $68 in interest income ($8\% \times \$10,000 \times {}^{31}\!/_{365}$). Seth recognizes $732 in interest income ($800 − $68). ■

When the transferor recognizes gross income from the property depends upon the method of accounting and the manner in which the property was transferred. In the case of a gift of income-producing property, the donor's share of the accrued income is recognized at the time it would have been recognized had the donor continued to own the property.[40] If the transfer is a sale, however, the transferor recognizes the accrued income at the time of the sale because the accrued interest is included in the sales proceeds.

[38]*Sargent v. Comm.*, 91–1 USTC ¶50,168, 67 AFTR2d 91–718, 929 F.2d 1252 (CA–8, 1991).

[39]*Galt v. Comm.*, 54–2 USTC ¶9457, 46 AFTR 633, 216 F.2d 41 (CA–7, 1954); *Helvering v. Horst*, 40–2 USTC ¶9787, 24 AFTR 1058, 61 S.Ct. 144 (USSC, 1940).

[40]Rev.Rul. 72–312, 1972–1 C.B. 22.

**TAX FACT**

## HOW MUCH AND WHAT TYPE OF INCOME?

Of the 127 million individual income tax returns filed for the 1999 tax year, 85 percent included wage or salary income, and over half included some amount of taxable interest income. But except for these two categories, no other type of income was found in even a quarter of the returns filed. Sales of business assets were found on 1 percent of the returns, and about 5 percent of the returns included flow-through income or loss from partnerships and S corporations. Capital gains showed up on about a quarter of the returns, but only when distributions from mutual fund investments were included.

**EXAMPLE 20**

Assume the same facts as in the preceding example, except that the interest payable on December 31 is not actually or constructively received by the bondholders until January 3, 2006. As a cash basis taxpayer, Floyd generally does not recognize interest income until it is received. If Floyd had continued to own the bonds, he would have included the interest in his gross income in 2006, the year he would have received it. Therefore, Floyd includes the $68 accrued income in his gross income as of January 3, 2006.

Further assume that Floyd sells identical bonds on the date of the gift. The bonds sell for $9,900, including accrued interest. On January 31, 2005, Floyd recognizes the accrued interest of $68 on the bonds sold. Thus, the selling price of the bonds is $9,832 ($9,900 − $68). ■

**Dividends.**  A corporation is taxed on its earnings, and the shareholders are taxed on the dividends paid to them from the corporation's after-tax earnings. The dividend can take the form of an actual dividend or a constructive dividend (e.g., shareholder use of corporate assets).

Partial relief from the double taxation of dividends has been provided in the Jobs and Growth Tax Relief Reconciliation Act of 2003. Generally, dividends received in taxable years beginning after 2002 are taxed at the same marginal rate that is applicable to a net capital gain.[41] Individuals subject to the 25, 28, 33, or 35 percent marginal tax rate pay a 15 percent tax on qualified dividends received. Individuals otherwise subject to the 10 or 15 percent marginal tax rate pay only a 5 percent tax on qualified dividends received. Thus, qualified dividends receive favorable treatment as compared to interest income.

Note that qualified dividends are not treated as capital gains in the gains and losses netting process; thus, they are *not* reduced by capital losses. Qualified dividend income is merely taxed at the rates that would apply to the taxpayer if he or she had an excess of net long-term capital gain over net short-term capital loss.

Because the beneficial tax rate is intended to mitigate double taxation, only certain dividends are eligible for the beneficial treatment. Excluded are certain dividends from foreign corporations, dividends from tax-exempt entities, and dividends that do not satisfy the holding period requirement.

A dividend from a foreign corporation is eligible for qualified dividend status only if one of the following requirements is met: (1) the foreign corporation's stock

---

[41]§ 1(h)(11).

is traded on an established U.S. securities market, or (2) the foreign corporation is eligible for the benefits of a comprehensive income tax treaty between its country of incorporation and the United States.

To satisfy the holding period requirement, the stock on which the dividend is paid must have been held for more than 60 days during the 120-day period beginning 60 days before the ex-dividend date.[42] The purpose of this requirement is to prevent the taxpayer from buying the stock shortly before the dividend is paid, receiving the dividend, and then selling the stock at a loss (a capital loss) after the stock goes ex-dividend. A stock's price often declines after the stock goes ex-dividend.

**EXAMPLE 21**

In June 2005, Green Corporation pays a dividend of $1.50 on each share of its common stock. Madison and Daniel, two unrelated shareholders, each own 1,000 shares of the stock. Consequently, each receives $1,500 (1,000 shares × $1.50). Assume Daniel satisfies the 60/120-day holding period rule, but Madison does not. The $1,500 Daniel receives is subject to preferential 15%/5% treatment. The $1,500 Madison receives, however, is not. Because Madison did not comply with the holding period rule, her dividend is not a *qualified dividend* and is taxed at ordinary income rates. ■

**EXAMPLE 22**

Assume that both Madison and Daniel in Example 21 are in the 35% tax bracket. Consequently, Madison pays a tax of $525 (35% × $1,500) on her dividend, while Daniel pays a tax of $225 (15% × $1,500) on his. The $300 saving that Daniel enjoys underscores the advantages of a qualified dividend. ■

Unlike interest, dividends do not accrue on a daily basis because the declaration of a dividend is at the discretion of the corporation's board of directors. Generally, dividends are taxed to the person who is entitled to receive them—the shareholder of record as of the corporation's record date.[43] Thus, if a taxpayer sells stock after a dividend has been declared but before the record date, the dividend generally will be taxed to the purchaser.

If a donor makes a gift of stock to someone (e.g., a family member) after the declaration date but before the record date, the Tax Court has held that the donor does not shift the dividend income to the donee. The *fruit* has sufficiently ripened as of the declaration date to tax the dividend income to the donor of the stock.[44] In a similar set of facts, the Fifth Circuit Court of Appeals concluded that the dividend income should be included in the gross income of the donee (the owner at the record date). In this case, the taxpayer gave stock to a qualified charity (a charitable contribution) after the declaration date and before the record date.[45]

*Find more information on this topic at our Web site:* ***http://wft-entities.swlearning.com***.

**EXAMPLE 23**

On June 20, the board of directors of Black Corporation declares a $10 per share dividend. The dividend is payable on June 30, to shareholders of record on June 25. As of June 20, Kathleen owns 200 shares of Black Corporation's stock. On June 21, Kathleen sells 100 of the shares to Jon for their fair market value and gives 100 of the shares to Andrew (her son). Both Jon and Andrew are shareholders of record as of June 25. Jon (the purchaser) is taxed on $1,000 since he is entitled to receive the dividend. However, Kathleen (the donor) is taxed on the $1,000 received by Andrew (the donee) because the gift was made after the declaration date of the dividend. ■

---

[42]The ex-dividend date is the date following the record date on which the corporation finalizes the list of shareholders who will receive the dividends.

[43]Reg. § 1.61–9(c). The record date is the cutoff for determining the shareholders who are entitled to receive the dividend.

[44]*M. G. Anton*, 34 T.C. 842 (1960).

[45]*Caruth Corporation v. U.S.*, 89–1 USTC ¶9172, 63 AFTR2d 89–716, 865 F.2d 644 (CA–5, 1989).

○ T A X   F A C T

## BUSINESS INCOME AND LOSS

**S**ole proprietors reporting net business income on Form 1040 constitute about 10 percent of all returns filed. Flow-through income from partnerships and S corporations is found on only half as many returns, but the income reported is essentially the same in nominal dollars. Flow-through income has increased dramatically and consistently since the 1987 tax year, when changes in marginal tax rates shifted to favor individual rather than C corporation taxpayers. It will be interesting to see what effect, if any, the beneficial tax rates for qualified dividends will have on the choice of the form of business entity.

## INCOME RECEIVED BY AN AGENT

Income received by the taxpayer's agent is considered to be received by the taxpayer. A cash basis principal must recognize the income at the time it is received by the agent.[46]

**EXAMPLE 24**

Longhorn, Inc., a cash basis corporation, delivers cattle to the auction barn in late December. The auctioneer, acting as the corporation's agent, sells the cattle and collects the proceeds in December. The auctioneer does not pay Longhorn until the following January. The corporation must include the sales proceeds in its gross income in the year the auctioneer received the funds. ■

PLANNING STRATEGIES

## Techniques for Reducing Gross Income

FRAMEWORK FOCUS: INCOME

STRATEGY ➤ AVOID INCOME RECOGNITION.

FRAMEWORK FOCUS: TAX RATE

STRATEGY ➤ SHIFT NET INCOME FROM HIGH-BRACKET YEARS TO LOW-BRACKET YEARS.

FRAMEWORK FOCUS: INCOME

STRATEGY ➤ POSTPONE RECOGNITION OF INCOME TO ACHIEVE TAX DEFERRAL.

## NONTAXABLE ECONOMIC BENEFITS

Home ownership is the prime example of economic income from capital that is not subject to tax. If the taxpayer uses his or her capital to purchase investments, but pays rent on a personal residence, the taxpayer would pay the rent from after-tax income. However, if the taxpayer purchases a personal residence instead of the investments, he or she would give up gross income from the forgone investments in exchange for the rent savings. The savings in rent enjoyed as a result of owning the home are not subject to tax. Thus, the homeowner will have substituted nontaxable for taxable income.

## TAX DEFERRAL

**General**  Since deferred taxes are tantamount to interest-free loans from the government, the deferral of taxes is a worthy goal of the tax planner. However, the tax planner must also consider the tax rates for the years the income is shifted from and to. For example, a one-year deferral of income from a year in which a corporate taxpayer's tax rate was 25 percent to a year in which the tax rate will be 35 percent would not be advisable if the taxpayer expects to earn less than a 10 percent after-tax return on the deferred tax dollars.

---

[46]Rev.Rul. 79–379, 1979–2 C.B. 204.

The taxpayer can often defer the recognition of income from appreciated property by postponing the event triggering realization (the final closing on a sale or an exchange of property). If the taxpayer needs cash, obtaining a loan by using the appreciated property as collateral may be the least costly alternative. When the taxpayer anticipates reinvesting the proceeds, a sale may be inadvisable.

---

**EXAMPLE 25**

Ira owns 100 shares of Pigeon Company common stock with a cost of $20,000 and a fair market value of $50,000. Although the stock's value has increased substantially in the past three years, Ira thinks the growth days are over. If he sells the Pigeon stock, Ira will invest the proceeds from the sale in other common stock. If Ira's marginal tax rate on the sale is 15%, he will have only $45,500 [$50,000 – .15($50,000 – $20,000)] to reinvest. The alternative investment must substantially outperform Pigeon in the future in order for the sale to be beneficial. ■

**Selection of Investments** Because no tax is due until a gain has been recognized, the law favors investments that yield appreciation rather than annual income.

---

**EXAMPLE 26**

Vera can buy a corporate bond or an acre of land for $10,000. The bond pays $1,000 of interest (10%) each year, and Vera expects the land to increase in value 10% each year for the next 10 years. She is in the 40% (combined Federal and state) tax bracket for ordinary income and 26% for qualifying capital gains. If the bond would mature or the land would be sold in 10 years and Vera would reinvest the interest at a 10% before-tax return, she would accumulate the following amount at the end of 10 years.

|  |  | Bond | Land |
|---|---|---|---|
| Original investment |  | $10,000 | $10,000 |
| Annual income | $1,000 |  |  |
| Less tax | (400) |  |  |
|  | $ 600 |  |  |
| Compound amount reinvested for 10 years at 6% after-tax | ×13.18 | 7,908 |  |
| Future value |  | $17,908 |  |
| Compound amount, 10 years at 10% |  |  | × 2.59 |
|  |  |  | $25,900 |
| Less tax on sale: 26%($25,900 – $10,000) |  |  | (4,134) |
| Future value |  |  | $21,766 |

Therefore, the value of the deferral that results from investing in the land rather than in the bond is $3,858 ($21,766 – $17,908). ■

---

**LO.4**

Understand that statutory authority is required to exclude an item from gross income.

# Specific Items of Gross Income

The all-inclusive principles of gross income determination as applied by the IRS and the courts have, on occasion, been expanded or modified by Congress through legislation. This legislation generally provides more specific rules for determining gross income from certain sources. Most of these special rules appear in §§ 71–90 of the Code.

In addition to provisions describing how specific sources of gross income are to be taxed, several specific rules *exclude* items from gross income. Authority for excluding specific items is provided in §§ 101–150 and in various other provisions in the Code.

Many statutory exclusions are unique to *individual taxpayers* (e.g., gifts and inheritances,[47] scholarships,[48] and a variety of fringe benefits paid to *employees*). These exclusions are discussed in Chapters 15 and 16. Other exclusions are broader and apply to all entities. These exclusions include interest on state and local bonds (§ 103), life insurance proceeds received by reason of death of the insured (§ 101), the fair market value of leasehold improvements received by the lessor when a lease is terminated (§ 109),[49] and income from discharge of indebtedness (§ 108). Some of the broadly applied statutory rules describing inclusions and exclusions are discussed below.

---

[47]§ 102.
[48]§ 117.

[49]If the tenant made the improvements in lieu of rent, the value of the improvements is not eligible for exclusion.

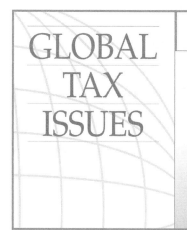

## FROM "ALL SOURCES" IS A BROAD DEFINITION

When § 61 refers to "income from whatever source derived," the taxing authorities are reaching far beyond the borders of the United States. Although one interpretation of "source" in this context is type of income (wages, interest, etc.), a broader interpretation revolves around the place where the income is generated. In this context, citizens and residents of the United States are subject to taxation on income earned from sources both inside and outside the country. This "worldwide income" tax base can cause potential double taxation problems when other countries also tax income earned within their borders. Beneficially, mechanisms such as the foreign tax credit can alleviate some or all of these tax burdens.

**LO.5**

Apply the Internal Revenue Code provisions on loans made at below-market interest rates.

## IMPUTED INTEREST ON BELOW-MARKET LOANS

As discussed earlier in the chapter, generally no income is recognized unless it is realized. Realization occurs when the taxpayer performs services or sells goods and thus becomes entitled to a payment from the other party. It follows that no income is realized if the goods or services are provided at no charge. Under this interpretation of the realization requirement, before 1984, interest-free loans were used to shift income between taxpayers.

**EXAMPLE 27**

Brown Corporation is in the 35% tax bracket and has $200,000 in a money market account earning 10% interest. Jack is the sole shareholder of Brown. He is in the 15% tax bracket and has no investment income. In view of the difference in tax rates, Jack believes that it would be better for him to receive and pay tax on the earnings from Brown's $200,000 investment. Jack does not wish to receive the $200,000 from Brown as a dividend because that would trigger a tax.

Before 1984, Jack could achieve his goals as follows. He could receive the money market account from Brown Corporation in exchange for a $200,000 non-interest-bearing note, payable on Brown's demand. As a result, Jack would receive the $20,000 earnings on the money market account, and the combined taxes of Brown Corporation and Jack would be decreased by $4,000.

| | |
|---|---|
| Decrease in Brown's tax—(0.10 × $200,000) × 0.35 | ($7,000) |
| Increase in Jack's tax—(0.10 × $200,000) × 0.15 | 3,000 |
| Overall decrease in tax liability | $4,000 |

Under 1984 amendments to the Code, Brown Corporation in the preceding example is deemed to have received an interest payment from Jack even though no interest was actually paid.[50] This payment of imputed interest is taxable to Brown. Jack may be able to deduct the imaginary interest payment on his return as investment interest if he itemizes deductions. To complete the fictitious series of transactions, Brown is deemed to return the interest to Jack in the form of a taxable dividend.

Imputed interest is calculated using rates the Federal government pays on new borrowings and is compounded semiannually. The Federal rates are adjusted monthly and are published by the IRS.[51] There are three Federal rates: short-term (not over three years and including demand loans), mid-term (over three years but not over nine years), and long-term (over nine years).

---

[50]§ 7872(a)(1).

[51]§§ 7872(b)(2) and (f)(2).

## CONCEPT SUMMARY 3-1

### Effect of Certain Below-Market Loans on the Lender and Borrower

| Type of Loan | | Lender | Borrower |
|---|---|---|---|
| Gift | Step 1 | Interest income | Interest expense |
| | Step 2 | Gift made* | Gift received |
| Compensation related | Step 1 | Interest income | Interest expense |
| | Step 2 | Compensation expense | Compensation income |
| Corporation to shareholder | Step 1 | Interest income | Interest expense |
| | Step 2 | Dividend paid | Dividend income |

*The gift may be subject to the gift tax (refer to Chapter 1).

**EXAMPLE 28**

Assume the Federal rate applicable to the loan in the preceding example is 7% through June 30 and 8% from July 1 through December 31. Brown Corporation made the loan on January 1, and the loan is still outstanding on December 31. Brown must recognize interest income of $15,280, and Jack has interest expense of $15,280. Brown is deemed to have paid a $15,280 dividend to Jack.

| Interest Calculations | |
|---|---|
| January 1 to June 30—(0.07 × $200,000) (½ year) | $ 7,000 |
| July 1 to December 31—[0.08($200,000 + $7,000)] (½ year) | 8,280 |
| | $15,280 |

If interest is charged on the loan but is less than the Federal rate, the imputed interest is the difference between the amount that would have been charged at the Federal rate and the amount actually charged.

**EXAMPLE 29**

Assume the same facts as in Example 28, except that Brown Corporation charged 6% interest, compounded annually.

| | |
|---|---|
| Interest at the Federal rate | $ 15,280 |
| Less interest charged (0.06 × $200,000) | (12,000) |
| Imputed interest | $ 3,280 |

The imputed interest rules apply to the following types of below-market loans.[52]

1. Gift loans (made out of love, affection, or generosity).
2. Compensation-related loans (employer loans to employees).
3. Corporation-shareholder loans (a corporation's loans to its shareholders, as in Example 27).
4. Tax avoidance loans and other loans that significantly affect the borrower's or lender's Federal tax liability (discussed in the following paragraphs).

The effects of the first three types of loans on the borrower and lender are summarized in Concept Summary 3-1.

---

[52]§ 7872(c).

## CONCEPT SUMMARY 3–2

### Exceptions to the Imputed Interest Rules for Below-Market Loans

| Exception | Eligible Loans | Ineligible Loans and Limitations |
|---|---|---|
| *De minimis*—aggregate loans of $10,000 or less | Gift loans | Proceeds used to purchase income-producing assets. |
| | Employer-employee | Principal purpose is tax avoidance. |
| | Corporation-shareholder | Principal purpose is tax avoidance. |
| Aggregate loans of $100,000 or less | Gift loans between individuals | Principal purpose is tax avoidance. For all other loans, interest is imputed to the extent of the borrower's net investment income, if it exceeds $1,000. |

**Exceptions and Limitations.** No interest is imputed on total outstanding *compensation-related loans* or *corporation-shareholder loans* of $10,000 or less unless the purpose of the loan is tax avoidance.[53] This vague tax avoidance standard exposes practically all compensation-related and corporation-shareholder loans to possible imputed interest problems. Nevertheless, the $10,000 exception should apply when an employee's borrowing was necessitated by personal needs (e.g., to meet unexpected expenses) rather than tax considerations.

Similarly, no interest is imputed on outstanding *gift loans* of $10,000 or less between individuals, unless the loan proceeds are used to purchase income-producing property.[54] This exemption eliminates from these complex provisions immaterial amounts that do not result in sizable shifts of income.

On loans of $100,000 or less between individuals, the imputed interest cannot exceed the borrower's net investment income for the year (gross income from all investments less the related expenses).[55] Through the gift loan provision, the imputed interest rules are designed to prevent high-income individuals from shifting income to relatives in a lower marginal bracket. This shifting of investment income is considered to occur only to the extent that the borrower has net investment income. Thus, the income imputed to the lender is limited to the borrower's net investment income. As a further limitation or exemption, if the borrower's net investment income for the year does not exceed $1,000, no interest is imputed on loans of $100,000 or less. However, these limitations for loans of $100,000 or less do not apply if a principal purpose of a loan is tax avoidance. In such a case, interest is imputed, and the imputed interest is not limited to the borrower's net investment income.[56]

These exceptions to the imputed interest rules are summarized in Concept Summary 3–2.

**LO.6**

Determine the extent to which receipts can be excluded under the tax benefit rule.

### TAX BENEFIT RULE

Generally, if a taxpayer obtains a deduction for an item in one year and in a later year recovers all or a portion of the prior deduction, the recovery is included in gross income in the year received.[57]

---

[53]§ 7872(c)(3).
[54]§ 7872(c)(2).
[55]§ 7872(d). The $100,000 provision applies only to gift loans.

[56]*Deficit Reduction Tax Bill of 1984: Explanation of the Senate Finance Committee* (April 2, 1984), p. 484.
[57]§ 111(a).

## LOANS TO EXECUTIVES PROHIBITED

Interest-free loans have become a popular form of compensation for executives. Several examples of multimillion dollar loans have come to light as a result of recent bankruptcies by large corporations. The board of directors often justifies the loans as necessary to enable the executive to be able to purchase a residence or to buy stock in the company.

Loans by publicly held corporations to their executives are now generally prohibited by Federal law. The Sarbanes-Oxley Act of 2002 (Public Law No. 107–294) places a general prohibition on loans by corporations to their executives. However, an exception permits corporate loans to finance the acquisition of a personal residence for an executive.

---

**EXAMPLE 30**

A business deducted as a loss a $1,000 receivable from a customer when it appeared the amount would never be collected. The following year, the customer paid $800 on the receivable. The business must report the $800 as gross income in the year it is received. ■

However, the § 111 **tax benefit rule** limits income recognition when a deduction does not yield a tax benefit in the year it is taken. If the taxpayer in Example 30 has no tax liability in the year of the deduction, the $800 receipt will be excluded from gross income in the year of the recovery.

**EXAMPLE 31**

Before deducting a $1,000 loss from an uncollectible business receivable, Tulip Company had taxable income of $200. The business bad debt deduction yields only a $200 tax benefit (assuming no loss carryback is made). That is, taxable income is reduced by only $200 (to zero) as a result of the bad debt deduction. Therefore, if the customer makes a payment on the previously deducted receivable in the following year, only the first $200 is a taxable recovery of a prior deduction. Any additional amount collected is nontaxable because only $200 of the loss yielded a reduction in taxable income (i.e., a tax benefit). ■

---

**LO.7**

Understand the Internal Revenue Code provision that excludes interest on state and local government obligations from gross income.

## INTEREST ON CERTAIN STATE AND LOCAL GOVERNMENT OBLIGATIONS

At the time the Sixteenth Amendment was ratified by the states, there was some question as to whether the Federal government possessed the constitutional authority to tax interest on state and local government obligations. Taxing such interest was thought to violate the doctrine of intergovernmental immunity because the tax would impair the ability of state and local governments to finance their operations.[58] Thus, interest on state and local government obligations was specifically exempted from Federal income taxation.[59] However, the Supreme Court has concluded that there is no constitutional prohibition against levying a nondiscriminatory Federal income tax on state and local government obligations.[60] Nevertheless, the statutory exclusion still exists.

The current exempt status applies solely to state and local government bonds. Thus, income received from the accrual of interest on a condemnation award or

---

[58]*Pollock v. Farmer's Loan & Trust Co.,* 3 AFTR 2602, 15 S.Ct. 912 (USSC, 1895).

[59]§ 103(a).

[60]*South Carolina v. Baker III,* 88–1 USTC ¶9284, 61 AFTR2d 88–995, 108 S.Ct. 1355 (USSC, 1988).

an overpayment of state tax is fully taxable.[61] Nor does the exemption apply to gains on the sale of tax-exempt securities.

*Find more information on this topic at our Web site: **http://wft-entities.swlearning.com**.*

**EXAMPLE 32**

Macaw Corporation purchases State of Virginia bonds for $10,000 on July 1, 2004. The bonds pay $400 interest each June 30 and December 31. On March 31, 2005, Macaw sells the bonds for $10,500 plus $200 of accrued interest. Macaw must recognize a $500 taxable gain ($10,500 − $10,000), but the $200 accrued interest is exempt from taxation. ■

Obviously, the interest exclusion reduces the cost of borrowing for state and local governments. A taxpayer with a 35 percent marginal tax rate requires only a 5.2 percent yield on a tax-exempt bond to obtain the same after-tax income as a taxable bond paying 8 percent interest [5.2% ÷ (1 − 0.35) = 8%].

State and local governments have developed sophisticated financial schemes to attract new industry. For example, local municipalities have issued bonds to finance construction of plants to be leased to private enterprise. By arranging the financing with low-interest municipal obligations, the plants could be leased at lower cost than other facilities the private business could obtain. However, Congress has placed limitations on the use of tax-exempt securities to finance private business.[62]

## State and Municipal Bonds

**FRAMEWORK FOCUS: INCOME AND EXCLUSIONS**

**STRATEGY ▶ AVOID INCOME RECOGNITION.**

Tax-exempt state and local bonds are almost irresistible investments for taxpayers with high marginal tax rates. To realize the maximum benefit from the exemption, the investor can purchase zero coupon bonds, which pay interest only at maturity. The advantage of the zero coupon feature is that the investor can earn tax-exempt interest on the accumulated principal and interest. If the investor purchases a tax-exempt bond that pays the interest each year, the interest received may be such a small amount that an additional tax-exempt investment cannot be made. In addition, reinvesting the interest may entail transaction costs (broker's fees). The zero coupon feature avoids these problems. However, certain state and municipal bond interest may increase the base of the alternative minimum tax, as discussed in Chapter 13.

## LO.8

Use the Internal Revenue Code's exclusion of leasehold improvements from gross income.

## IMPROVEMENTS ON LEASED PROPERTY

When a real property lease expires, the landlord regains control of both the real property and any improvements to the property (e.g., buildings and landscaping) made by the tenant during the term of the lease. In 1940, the Supreme Court held that the fair market value of improvements made by a tenant to the landlord's property should be included in the landlord's gross income upon termination of the lease.[63] Congress effectively reversed this decision by enacting § 109, which

---

[61]*Kieselbach v. Comm.,* 43–1 USTC ¶9220, 30 AFTR 370, 63 S.Ct. 303 (USSC, 1943); *U.S. Trust Co. of New York v. Anderson,* 3 USTC ¶1125, 12 AFTR 836, 65 F.2d 575 (CA–2, 1933).

[62]See § 103(b). The alternative minimum tax may apply to some of this interest income.

[63]*Helvering v. Bruun,* 40–1 USTC ¶9337, 24 AFTR 652, 60 S.Ct. 631 (USSC, 1940).

defers tax on the value of the improvements until the property is sold. More specifically, any improvements made to the leased property are excluded from the landlord's gross income unless the improvement is made to the property in lieu of rent.

**EXAMPLE 33**

Mahogany Corporation leases office space to Zink and Silver, Attorneys-at-Law. When the law firm took possession of the office space, it added wall partitions, an in-wall computer network, and a variety of other improvements to the space. The improvements were not made in lieu of rent payments to Mahogany. When the lease expires and Mahogany regains possession of the space, the value of the improvements will be excluded from Mahogany's gross income. ■

**LO.9**

Determine the extent to which life insurance proceeds are excluded from gross income.

## LIFE INSURANCE PROCEEDS

**General Rule.**  **Life insurance proceeds** paid to the beneficiary because of the death of the insured are exempt from income tax.[64] Congress chose to exempt life insurance proceeds from gross income for the following reasons.

- For family members, life insurance proceeds serve much the same purpose as a nontaxable inheritance.
- In a business context (as well as in a family situation), life insurance proceeds replace an economic loss suffered by the beneficiary.

Thus, Congress concluded that, in general, making life insurance proceeds exempt from income tax was a good policy.

**EXAMPLE 34**

Sparrow Corporation purchased an insurance policy on the life of its CEO and named itself as the beneficiary. Sparrow paid $24,000 in premiums. When the company's CEO died, Sparrow collected the insurance proceeds of $60,000. The $60,000 is excluded from Sparrow's gross income. ■

**Exceptions to Exclusion Treatment.**  The income tax exclusion applies only when the insurance proceeds are received because of the death of the insured. If the owner cancels the policy and receives the cash surrender value, he or she must recognize gain to the extent of the excess of the amount received over the cost of the policy.[65]

Another exception to exclusion treatment applies if the policy is transferred after the insurance company issues it. If the policy is transferred for valuable consideration, the insurance proceeds are includible in the gross income of the transferee to the extent the proceeds received exceed the amount paid for the policy by the transferee plus any subsequent premiums paid.

**EXAMPLE 35**

Platinum Corporation pays premiums of $5,000 for an insurance policy with a face amount of $12,000 on the life of Beth, an officer of the corporation. Subsequently, Platinum sells the policy to Beth's husband for $5,500. On Beth's death, her husband receives the proceeds of $12,000. Beth's husband can exclude from gross income $5,500 plus any premiums he paid subsequent to the transfer. ■

The Code, however, provides four exceptions to the rule illustrated in the preceding example.[66] These exceptions permit exclusion treatment for transfers to

---

[64]*Estate of D. R. Daly*, 3 B.T.A. 1042 (1926).

[65]*Landfield Finance Co. v. U.S.*, 69–2 USTC ¶9680, 24 AFTR2d 69–5744, 418 F.2d 172 (CA–7, 1969).

[66]§ 101(a)(2).

the following. The first three exceptions facilitate the use of insurance contracts to fund **buy-sell agreements.**

1. A partner of the insured.
2. A partnership in which the insured is a partner.
3. A corporation in which the insured is an officer or shareholder.
4. A transferee whose basis in the policy is determined by reference to the transferor's basis, such as a gift or a transfer due to a divorce.

**EXAMPLE 36**

Rick and Sam are equal partners who have a buy-sell agreement that allows either partner to purchase the interest of a deceased partner for $500,000. Neither partner has sufficient cash to actually buy the other partner's interest, but each has a life insurance policy on his own life in the amount of $500,000. Rick and Sam could exchange their policies (usually at little or no taxable gain), and upon the death of either partner, the surviving partner could collect tax-free insurance proceeds. The proceeds could then be used to purchase the decedent's interest in the partnership. ■

*Investment earnings* arising from the reinvestment of life insurance proceeds are generally subject to income tax. For example, the beneficiary may elect to collect the insurance proceeds in installments that include taxable interest income. The interest portion of each installment is included in gross income.

## PLANNING STRATEGIES

## Life Insurance

**FRAMEWORK FOCUS: INCOME AND EXCLUSIONS**

**STRATEGY ➤ AVOID INCOME RECOGNITION.**

Life insurance is a tax-favored investment. The annual increase in the cash surrender value of the policy is not taxable because it is subject to substantial restrictions (no income has been actually or constructively received). By borrowing on the policy's cash surrender value, the owner can receive the policy's increase in value in cash without recognizing income.

---

**LO.10**

Describe the circumstances under which income must be reported from the discharge of indebtedness.

## INCOME FROM DISCHARGE OF INDEBTEDNESS

Income is generated when appreciated property is used to pay a debt or when the creditor cancels debt. If appreciated property is used to pay a debt, the transaction is treated as a sale of the appreciated property followed by payment of the debt.[67] Foreclosure by a creditor is also treated as a sale or exchange of the property.[68]

**EXAMPLE 37**

Juan owed the State Bank $100,000 on an unsecured note. Juan satisfied the note by transferring to the bank common stock with a basis of $60,000 and a fair market value of $100,000. Juan recognizes a $40,000 gain on the transfer. Juan also owed the bank $50,000 on a note secured by land. When Juan's basis in the land was $20,000 and the land's fair market value was $50,000, the bank foreclosed on the loan and took title to the land. Juan recognizes a $30,000 gain on the foreclosure. ■

A creditor may cancel debt to assure the vitality of the debtor. In such cases, the debtor's net worth is increased by the amount of debt forgiven.

---

[67]Reg. § 1.1001–2(a).

[68]*Estate of Delman v. Comm.*, 73 T.C. 15 (1979).

**EXAMPLE 38**

Brown Corporation is unable to meet the mortgage payments on its factory building. Both the corporation and the mortgage holder are aware of the depressed market for industrial property in the area. Foreclosure would only result in the creditor's obtaining unsellable property. To improve Brown's financial position and thus improve its chances of obtaining the additional credit necessary for survival from other lenders, the creditor agrees to forgive all amounts past due and to reduce the principal amount of the mortgage. Brown's net worth is increased by the amount of past due debt that was forgiven *plus* the reduction in the mortgage balance. ■

Generally, the debtor recognizes gross income equal to the amount of debt canceled.[69] The following two examples illustrate additional circumstances where gross income results from cancellation of indebtedness.

**EXAMPLE 39**

A corporation issues bonds with a face value of $500,000. Subsequently, the corporation repurchases the bonds in the market for $150,000. It has effectively canceled its $500,000 debt with a $150,000 payment, so it recognizes $350,000 in gross income.[70] ■

**EXAMPLE 40**

In 2000, Turquoise Corporation borrowed $60,000 from National Bank to purchase a warehouse. Turquoise agreed to make monthly principal and interest payments for 15 years. The interest rate on the note was 7%. When the balance on the note had been reduced through monthly payments to $48,000, the bank offered to accept $45,000 in full settlement of the note. The bank made the offer because interest rates had increased to 11%. Turquoise accepted the bank's offer. As a result, Turquoise recognizes $3,000 ($48,000 − $45,000) of gross income.[71] ■

Though discharge of indebtedness generally increases the taxpayer's gross income, in the following cases, the reduction in debt is excluded from gross income.[72]

1. Creditors' gifts.
2. Discharges under Federal bankruptcy law.
3. Discharges that occur when the debtor is insolvent.
4. Discharge of the farm debt of a solvent taxpayer.
5. Discharge of **qualified real property business indebtedness.**
6. A seller's cancellation of a buyer's indebtedness.
7. A shareholder's cancellation of a corporation's indebtedness.
8. Forgiveness of certain loans to students.

**Creditors' Gifts.** If the creditor reduces the debt as an act of *love, affection or generosity*, the debtor has simply received a nontaxable gift (situation 1). Such motivations generally arise only on loans between friends or family members. Rarely will a gift be found to have occurred in a business context. A businessperson may settle a debt for less than the amount due, but as a matter of business expediency (e.g., high collection costs or disputes as to contract terms) rather than generosity.[73]

**Insolvency and Bankruptcy.** Cancellation of indebtedness income is excluded when the debtor is insolvent (i.e., the debtor's liabilities exceed the fair market value of the assets) or when the cancellation of debt results from a bankruptcy proceeding (situations 2 and 3). The insolvency exclusion is limited to the amount of insolvency. The tax law permits this exclusion to avoid imposing undue hardship on the debtor (wherewithal to pay) and the debtor's limited resources.

---

[69]§ 61(a)(12).
[70]See *U.S. v. Kirby Lumber Co.*, 2 USTC ¶814, 10 AFTR 458, 52 S.Ct. 4 (USSC, 1931).
[71]Rev.Rul. 82–202, 1982–1 C.B. 35.

[72]§§ 108 and 1017.
[73]*Comm. v. Jacobson*, 49–1 USTC ¶9133, 37 AFTR 516, 69 S.Ct. 358 (USSC, 1949).

The law imposes a cost for the insolvency and bankruptcy exclusion. More specifically, the debtor must decrease certain tax benefits (capital loss carryforwards, net operating loss carryforwards, some tax credits, and suspended passive losses)[74] by the amount of income excluded. In addition, if the amount of excluded income exceeds these tax benefits, the debtor must then reduce the basis in assets.[75] Thus, excluded cancellation of indebtedness income either accelerates recognition of future income (by reducing tax benefit carryforwards) or is deferred until the debtor's assets are sold (or depreciated).

**EXAMPLE 41**

Before any debt cancellation, Maroon Corporation has assets with a fair market value of $500,000 and liabilities of $600,000. A creditor agrees to cancel $125,000 of liabilities. Maroon excludes $100,000 of the debt cancellation income (the amount of insolvency) and is taxed on $25,000. Maroon also reduces any tax benefits and the basis of its assets by $100,000 (the excluded income). ■

**Qualified Real Property Indebtedness.**  Taxpayers (other than C corporations) can elect to exclude income from cancellation of indebtedness if the canceled debt is secured by real property used in a trade or business (situation 5). In addition, the debt must have been used to acquire or improve real property in a trade or business to qualify for the exclusion.[76] The amount of the exclusion is limited to the *lesser of* (1) the excess of the debt over the fair market value of the real property or (2) the adjusted basis of all depreciable real property held. In addition, the basis of all depreciable real property held by the debtor must be reduced by the amount excluded.

**EXAMPLE 42**

Blue, Inc., owns a warehouse worth $5 million, with a $3 million basis. The warehouse is subject to a $7 million mortgage that was incurred in connection with the acquisition of the warehouse. In lieu of foreclosure, the lender decides that it will reduce the mortgage to $4.5 million. Blue may elect to exclude $2 million from gross income ($7 million – $5 million). If Blue makes the election, it must reduce the aggregate basis of its depreciable realty by $2 million. ■

**EXAMPLE 43**

Assume the same facts as in the preceding example, except that the basis of the warehouse is $1 million. If the warehouse is the only piece of depreciable realty that Blue owns, only $1 million of the debt cancellation income may be excluded. ■

**Seller Cancellation.**  When a seller of property cancels debt previously incurred by a buyer in a purchase transaction, the cancellation generally is not treated as income to the buyer (situation 6). Instead, the reduction in debt is considered to be a reduction in the purchase price of the asset. Consequently, the basis of the asset is reduced in the hands of the buyer.[77]

**EXAMPLE 44**

Snipe, Inc., purchases a truck from Sparrow Autos for $10,000 in cash and a $25,000 note payable. Two days after the purchase, Sparrow announces a sale on the same model truck, with a sales price of $28,000. Snipe contacts Sparrow and asks to be given the sales price on the truck. Sparrow complies by canceling $7,000 of the note payable. The $7,000 is excluded from Snipe's gross income, and the basis of the truck to Snipe is $28,000. ■

**Shareholder Cancellation.**  If a shareholder cancels the corporation's indebtedness to him or her (situation 7) and receives nothing in return, the cancellation usually is considered a contribution of capital to the corporation by the shareholder.

---

[74]See Chapter 5 for a discussion of net operating loss carryforwards and suspended passive losses. Chapter 7 discusses capital loss carryforwards. Chapter 13 discusses tax credits.

[75]§ 108(b).
[76]§ 108(a)(1)(D).
[77]§ 108(e)(5).

Thus, the corporation recognizes no income. Instead, its paid-in capital is increased, and its liabilities are decreased by the same amount.[78]

*Find more information on this topic at our Web site:* ***http://wft-entities.swlearning.com.***

**Student Loans.** Many states make loans to students on the condition that the loan will be forgiven if the student practices a profession in the state upon completing his or her studies. The amount of the loan that is forgiven (situation 8) is excluded from gross income.[79]

## GAINS AND LOSSES FROM PROPERTY TRANSACTIONS

LO.11

Describe the tax consequences of property transactions.

**In General.** When property is sold or otherwise disposed of, gain or loss may result. Such gain or loss has an effect on the gross income of the party making the sale or other disposition when the gain or loss is *realized* and *recognized* for tax purposes. The concept of realized gain or loss is expressed as follows.

$$\begin{matrix} \text{Amount realized} \\ \text{from the sale} \end{matrix} - \begin{matrix} \text{Adjusted basis of} \\ \text{the property} \end{matrix} = \begin{matrix} \text{Realized gain} \\ \text{(or loss)} \end{matrix}$$

The amount realized is the selling price of the property less any costs of disposition (e.g., brokerage commissions) incurred by the seller. The adjusted basis of the property is determined as follows.

Cost (or other original basis) at date of acquisition[80]
Add:      Capital additions
Subtract:   Depreciation (if appropriate) and other capital recoveries (see Chapter 4)
Equals:     Adjusted basis at date of sale or other disposition

Without realized gain or loss, generally, there can be no recognized (taxable) gain or loss. All realized gains are recognized unless some specific part of the tax law provides otherwise. Realized losses may or may not be recognized (deductible) for tax purposes, depending on the circumstances involved. For example, losses realized from the disposition of personal-use property (property held by individuals and not used for business or investment purposes) are not recognized.

**EXAMPLE 45**

During the current year, Ted sells his sailboat (adjusted basis of $4,000) for $5,500. Ted also sells one of his personal automobiles (adjusted basis of $8,000) for $5,000. Ted's realized gain of $1,500 from the sale of the sailboat is recognized. The $3,000 realized loss on the sale of the automobile, however, is not recognized. Thus, the gain is taxable, but the loss is not deductible. ■

Once it has been determined that the disposition of property results in a recognized gain or loss, the next step is to classify the gain or loss as capital or ordinary. Although ordinary gain is fully taxable and ordinary loss is fully deductible, the same is not true for capital gains and capital losses.

**Capital Gains and Losses.** Gains and losses from the disposition of capital assets receive special tax treatment. Capital assets are defined in the Code as any property held by the taxpayer *other than* property listed in § 1221. The list in § 1221

---

[78]§ 108(e)(6).
[79]§ 108(f).
[80]Cost usually means purchase price plus expenses related to the acquisition of the property and incurred by the purchaser (e.g.,

brokerage commissions). For the basis of property acquired by gift or inheritance and other basis rules, see Chapter 6.

includes, among other things, inventory, accounts receivable, and depreciable property or real estate used in a business. The sale or exchange of assets in these categories usually results in ordinary income or loss treatment (see Chapter 7). The sale of any other asset generally creates a capital gain or loss.

**EXAMPLE 46**

Cardinal, Inc., owns a pizza parlor. During the current year, Cardinal sells an automobile. The automobile, which had been used as a pizza delivery car for three years, was sold at a loss of $1,000. Because this automobile was a depreciable asset used in its business, Cardinal has an ordinary loss of $1,000, rather than a capital loss. Cardinal also sold securities held for investment during the current year. The securities were sold for a gain of $800. The securities are capital assets. Therefore, Cardinal has a capital gain of $800. ■

Individuals and corporations are taxed differently on capital gains and losses. An individual's *net capital gain* is subject to the following *maximum* tax rates in 2005.[81]

|                                                      | **Maximum Rate**[82] |
| ---------------------------------------------------- | :------------------: |
| Short-term gains (assets held for one year or less)  | 35%                  |
| Long-term gains (assets held for more than one year) | 15%                  |

A corporation's net capital gain does not receive any beneficial tax treatment.

The net capital losses of individuals can be used to offset up to $3,000 of ordinary income each year. Any remaining capital loss is carried forward indefinitely until it is exhausted. Corporations may deduct capital losses only to the extent of capital gains. Capital losses of corporations in excess of capital gains may not be deducted against ordinary income. A corporation's unused capital losses can be carried back three years and then carried forward five years to offset capital gains in those years.[83]

**EXAMPLE 47**

Jones has a short-term capital loss of $5,000 during 2005 and no capital gains. If Jones is an individual, she can deduct $3,000 of this amount as an ordinary loss. The remaining $2,000 loss is carried over to 2006 and will continue to be carried forward until it is fully deducted.

If Jones is a corporation, none of the capital loss is deductible in 2005. All of the $5,000 loss is carried back and offset against capital gains in 2002, 2003, and 2004 (generating an immediate tax refund). Any unused capital loss is carried forward and offset against capital gains in 2006 to 2010. ■

 DIGGING DEEPER 5

*Find more information on this topic at our Web site:* **http://wft-entities.swlearning.com.**

# Suggested Further Readings

Louis Lavelle, "Everybody Should Be a Little Nervous," *Business Week,* December 22, 2003, p. 42.

Howard Wolosky, editor, "Tax Briefing—Telecommunications Fees Taxable Income," *Practical Accountant,* October 2004, p. 17.

Robert W. Wood and Dominic L. Daher, "Contingent Attorney's Fees in Class Action Cases—From Bad to Worse for Taxpayer-Plaintiffs," *Journal of Taxation,* October 2003, pp. 228–233.

Alan S. Zipp, "Stock Redemption in Divorce—Someone Will Have to Recognize Gain under the Final Regs.," *Journal of Taxation,* September 2003, pp. 172–178.

---

[81]§ 1(h). Net capital gain is defined in § 1222(11) as the excess of the net long-term capital gain over the net short-term capital loss.

[82]Certain assets, such as collectibles (e.g., art, antiques, stamps, etc.) and some real estate, receive special treatment. Collectibles gain is taxed at a maximum rate of 28%, and certain real estate gain is taxed at a maximum rate of 25%.

[83]§§ 1211 and 1212.

## KEY TERMS

## PROBLEM MATERIALS

### Problems

**Issue ID**

1. Cecil buys wrecked cars and stores them on his property. Recently, he purchased a 1990 Ford Taurus for $250. If he can sell all of the usable parts, his total proceeds from the Taurus will be over $2,000. As of the end of the year, he has sold only the radio for $50, and he does not know how many, if any, of the remaining parts will ever be sold. What are Cecil's income recognition issues?

2. In each of the following, determine the taxpayer's "income" for the current year as computed by an economist and as computed for tax purposes. Explain any differences.
   a. In the previous year, the taxpayer purchased stock for $5,000. At the beginning of the current year, the market value of the stock was $7,000. During the current year, the taxpayer sold the stock for $8,000.
   b. The individual made improvements to his personal residence. The cost of the materials was $10,000, and he provided the labor. The improvements increased the value of the house by $18,000.
   c. The controlling shareholder in a corporation sold property to the corporation for $15,000. The value of the property was $10,000, and the shareholder's cost was $15,000.
   d. The taxpayer found a suitcase containing $25,000 in cash, and she could not determine the true owner.

**Ethics**

3. The roof of your corporation's office building recently suffered some damage as the result of a storm. You, the president of the corporation, are negotiating with a carpenter who has quoted two prices for the repair work: $600 if you pay in cash ("folding money") and $700 if you pay by check. The carpenter observes that the IRS can more readily discover his receipt of a check. Thus, he hints that he will report the receipt of the check (but not the cash). The carpenter has a full-time job and will do the work after hours and on the weekend. He comments that he should be allowed to keep all he earns after regular working hours. Evaluate what you should do.

4. Jared, a self-employed insect exterminator, uses the cash method of accounting to report his income. In December 2005, Jared received a check for $400 from a client. Jared deposited the check near the end of December. In early January 2006, the bank notified him that the check did not clear because of insufficient funds in the customer's account. The bank sent the check through a second time, and it cleared in January 2006. Jared computes his income using his deposit records. Therefore, he included the $400 in his 2005 gross income.
   a. In what year should Jared report the $400 of income?
   b. Why does it matter to Jared whether he reports the income in 2005 or 2006, as long as he actually reports it?

**Decision Making**

**Communications**

5. Kevin, a cash basis taxpayer, received the following from his employer during 2005.

   • Salary of $80,000.

   • 2004 bonus of $12,000 received in 2005.

The 2004 bonus was not paid until 2005 because Kevin's employer suffered a computer crash and could not complete the bonus calculations in a timely manner. In addition, Kevin earned a 2005 bonus of $15,000 that was to be paid by the end of December 2005. However, in December, Kevin told his employer to delay the payment of the bonus until January 2006, when Kevin plans to retire.

a. Determine the effect of the above on Kevin's gross income in 2005.

b. Assume that Kevin is your client and he tells you that he now does not plan to retire until 2007. He is reasonably certain that he will be in a lower marginal tax bracket in that year. Write a memorandum explaining what you plan to advise Kevin regarding his 2006 bonus.

6. Evaluate the following alternative proposals for taxing the income from property.

a. All assets would be valued at the end of the year, any increase in value that occurred during the year would be included in gross income, and any decrease in value would be deductible from gross income.

b. No gain or loss would be recognized until the taxpayer sold or exchanged the property.

c. Increases or decreases in the value of property traded on a national exchange (e.g., the New York Stock Exchange) would be reflected in gross income for the years in which the changes in value occur. For all other assets, no gain or loss would be recognized until the owner disposes of the property.

**Decision Making**

**Communications**

7. Which of the following investments of $10,000 each will yield the greatest after-tax value, assuming the taxpayer is in the 35% tax bracket for ordinary income and 15% for qualifying capital gains in all years? The investments will be liquidated at the end of five years.

a. Land that will increase in value by 6% each year.

b. A taxable bond yielding 6% before tax. The interest can be reinvested at 6% before tax.

c. Common stock paying a 5% dividend each year that can be reinvested in common stock paying a 5% dividend each year. The value of the stock will not change.

Prepare a brief speech for your tax class in which you explain why the future value of the land will exceed the future value of the taxable bond. Also explain why the after-tax return on the stock will exceed the after-tax return earned on the bond.

Compound amount of $1 and compound value of annuity payments at the end of five years are given as:

| Interest Rate | $1 Compounded for Five Years | $1 Annuity Compounded for Five Years |
|:---:|:---:|:---:|
| 6% | $1.34 | $5.64 |
| 3.90% | 1.20 | 5.39 |
| 4.25% | 1.23 | 5.44 |

8. Determine the taxpayer's gross income for tax purposes in each of the following situations:

a. Olga, a cash basis taxpayer, sold a corporate bond with accrued interest of $200 for $10,500. Olga's cost of the bond was $10,000.

b. Olga needed $10,000 to make a down payment on her house. She instructed her broker to sell some stock to raise the $10,000. Olga's cost for the stock is $3,000. Based on her broker's advice, instead of selling the stock, she borrowed the $10,000 using the stock as collateral for the debt.

c. Olga owns a vacant lot that has been zoned for residential housing. She spends $900 in attorney fees to get the property rezoned as commercial. The property's value increases by $10,000 as a result of the rezoning.

**Decision Making**

9. Al is an attorney who conducts his practice as a sole proprietor. During 2005, he received cash of $150,000 for legal services. Of the amount collected, $25,000 was for services provided in 2004. At the end of 2005, Al had accounts receivable of $45,000, all for services rendered in 2005. During the year, Al billed a client $20,000, but the client died and Al has no hope of collecting the balance due. At the end of the year, Al received

$5,000 as a deposit on property a client was in the process of selling. Compute Al's gross income for 2005:

a.  Using the cash basis of accounting.

b.  Using the accrual basis of accounting.

c.  Advise Al on which method of accounting he should use.

10.  Autumn Company began operating a grocery store during the year. Autumn's only books and records are based on cash receipts and disbursements, but the company president has asked you to compute the company's gross profit from the business for tax purposes.

| | |
|---|---|
| Sale of merchandise | $480,000 |
| Purchases of merchandise | 220,000 |

You determine that as of the end of the year Autumn has accounts payable for merchandise of $20,000 and accounts receivable from customers totaling $12,000. The cost of merchandise on hand at the end of the year was $9,000. Compute Autumn's accrual method gross profit for the year.

**Communications**

11.  Color Paint Shop, Inc. (459 Ellis Avenue, Harrisburg, PA 17111), is an accrual basis taxpayer that paints automobiles. During 2005, the company painted Samuel's car and was to receive a $1,000 payment from his insurance company. Samuel was not satisfied with the work, however, and the insurance company refused to pay. In December 2005, Color and Samuel agreed that Color would receive $800 for the work, subject to final approval by the insurance company. In the past, Color had come to terms with customers only to have the insurance company negotiate an even smaller amount. In May 2006, the insurance company reviewed the claim and paid the $800 to Color. An IRS agent thinks that Color should report $1,000 of income in 2005 and deduct a $200 loss in 2006. Prepare a memo to Susan Apple, a tax partner for whom you are working, with the recommended treatment for the disputed income.

12.  Dance, Inc., is a dance studio that sells dance lessons for cash, on open account, and for notes receivable. The company also collects interest on bonds held as an investment. The company's cash receipts for the year totaled $219,000.

| | |
|---|---|
| Cash sales | $ 70,000 |
| Collections on accounts receivable | 120,000 |
| Collections on notes receivable | 20,000 |
| Interest on bonds | 9,000 |
| | $219,000 |

The balances in accounts receivable, notes receivable, and accrued interest on bonds at the beginning and end of the year were as follows.

| | 1–1 | 12–31 |
|---|---|---|
| Accounts receivable | $24,000 | $24,000 |
| Notes receivable | 9,000 | 13,000 |
| Accrued interest on bonds | 2,500 | 4,000 |
| | $35,500 | $41,000 |

The fair market value of the notes is equal to 60% of their face amount. There were no bad debts for the year, and all notes were for services performed during the year. Compute the corporation's gross income:

a.  Using the cash basis of accounting.

b.  Using the accrual basis of accounting.

c.  Using a hybrid method—accrual basis for lessons and cash basis for interest income.

13. Determine the effect of the following on a cash basis taxpayer's gross income for 2005.
    a. Received his paycheck for $3,000 from his employer on December 31, 2005. He deposited the paycheck on January 2, 2006.
    b. Received a bonus of $5,000 from his employer on January 10, 2006. The bonus was for the outstanding performance of his division during 2005.
    c. Received a dividend check from IBM on November 28, 2005. He mailed the check back to IBM in December requesting that additional IBM stock be issued to him under IBM's dividend reinvestment plan.

14. Swan Appliance Company, an accrual basis taxpayer, sells home appliances and service contracts. Determine the effects of each of the following transactions on the company's 2005 gross income assuming that the company uses any available options to defer its taxes.
    a. In December 2004, the company received a $1,200 advance payment from a customer for an appliance that Swan special ordered from the manufacturer. The appliance did not arrive from the manufacturer until January 2005, and Swan immediately delivered it to the customer. The sale was reported in 2005 for financial accounting purposes.
    b. In June 2005, the company sold a 12-month service contract for $240. The company also sold a 24-month service contract for $480 in December 2005.
    c. On December 31, 2005, the company sold an appliance for $1,200. The company received $500 cash and a note from the customer for $700 and $260 interest, to be paid at the rate of $40 a month for 24 months. Because of the customer's poor credit record, the fair market value of the note was only $600. The cost of the appliance was $750.

**Ethics**

15. Dr. Randolph, a cash basis taxpayer, knows that he will be in a lower marginal tax bracket in 2006 than in 2005. To take advantage of the expected decrease in his tax rate, Dr. Randolph instructs his office manager to delay filing the medical insurance claims for services performed in November and December until January 2006. This will assure that the receipts will not be included in his 2005 gross income. Is Dr. Randolph abusing the cash method of accounting rules?

**Decision Making**

16. The Bonhaus Apartments is a new development and is in the process of structuring its lease agreements. The company would like to set the damage deposits high enough that tenants will keep the apartments in good condition. The company is actually more concerned about damage than about tenants not paying their rent.
    a. Discuss the tax effects of the following alternatives.

    • $400 damage deposit and $400 rent for the final month of the lease.

    • $800 rent for the final two months of the lease and no damage deposit.

    • $800 damage deposit with no rent prepayment.

    b. Which option do you recommend?

17. In 2005, Alva received dividends on her stocks as follows:

| | |
|---|---|
| Amur Corporation (a French corporation whose stock is traded on an established U.S. securities market) | $55,000 |
| Blaze, Inc., a Delaware corporation | 25,000 |
| Grape, Inc., a Virginia corporation | 12,000 |

    a. Alva purchased the Grape stock four years ago, and she purchased the Amur stock two years ago. She purchased the Blaze stock 15 days before it went ex-dividend and sold it 20 days later at a $22,000 loss. Alva had no other capital gains and losses for the year. She is in the 35% marginal tax bracket. Compute Alva's tax on her dividend income for 2005.
    b. Alva's daughter, who is not Alva's dependent, had taxable income of $10,000, which included $1,000 of dividends on Grape, Inc. stock. The daughter had purchased the stock two years ago. Compute the daughter's tax liability on the dividends.

18. Bethany Investment Partners is a cash basis taxpayer. It purchased a 20-year zero-coupon bond (no annual interest is paid) for $4,291 on January 1, 2005. The maturity value of the bond in 20 years is $20,000, which is the principal plus 8% interest compounded annually.
    a. What is Bethany's interest income from the bond for 2005?
    b. What is its basis for the bond on December 31, 2005?
    c. Will the interest income from the bond be greater in 2014 than it was in 2005? Explain.

**Issue ID**

19. Brad is the president of the Zinc Corporation. He and other members of his family control the corporation. Brad has a temporary need for $50,000, and the corporation has excess cash. He could borrow the money from a bank at 9%, and Zinc is earning 6% on its temporary investments. Zinc has made loans to other employees on several occasions. Therefore, Brad is considering borrowing $50,000 from the corporation. He will repay the loan principal in two years plus interest at 5%. Identify the relevant tax issues for Brad and Zinc Corporation.

20. On June 30, 2005, Ridge borrowed $62,000 from his employer. On July 1, 2005, Ridge used the money as follows.

| | |
|---|---:|
| Interest-free loan to Ridge's controlled corporation (operated by Ridge on a part-time basis) | $31,000 |
| Interest-free loan to Tab (Ridge's son) | 11,000 |
| National Bank of Grundy 6% CD ($14,840 due at maturity, June 30, 2006) | 14,000 |
| National Bank of Grundy 6.25% CD ($6,773 due at maturity, June 30, 2007) | 6,000 |
| | $62,000 |

Ridge's employer did not charge him interest. The applicable Federal rate was 7% throughout the relevant period. Tab had investment income of $800 for the year, and he used the loan proceeds to pay medical school tuition. There were no other outstanding loans between Ridge and Tab. What are the effects of the preceding transactions on Ridge's 2005 taxable income?

21. Indicate whether the imputed interest rules apply in the following situations.
    a. Mitch is a cash basis attorney who charges his clients based on the number of hours it takes to do the job. The bill is due upon completion of the work. However, for clients who make an initial payment when the work begins, Mitch grants a discount on the final bill. The discount is equal to 10% interest on the deposit.
    b. Local Telephone Company requires that customers make a security deposit. The deposit is refunded after the customer has established a good record for paying the telephone bill. The company pays 6% interest on the deposits.
    c. Lynn asked Kelly for a $125,000 loan to purchase a new home. Kelly made the loan and did not charge interest. Kelly never intended to collect the loan, and at the end of the year Kelly told Lynn that the debt was forgiven.

22. Vito is the sole shareholder of Vito, Inc. The corporation also employs him. On June 30, 2005, Vito borrowed $8,000 from Vito, Inc., and on July 1, 2006, he borrowed an additional $3,000. Both loans were due on demand. No interest was charged on the loans, and the Federal rate was 10% for all relevant dates. Vito used the money to purchase stock, and he had no investment income. Determine the tax consequences to Vito and Vito, Inc., if:
    a. The loans are considered employer-employee loans.
    b. The loans are considered corporation-shareholder loans.

23. White and Swan Modeling is a partnership. How does the tax benefit rule apply to White and Swan in the following transactions?
    a. In 2005, White and Swan paid Vera $5,000 for locating a potential client. The deal fell through, and in 2006, Vera refunded the $5,000 to the partnership.
    b. In 2005, White and Swan paid an attorney $300 for services in connection with a title search. Because the attorney was negligent, the partnership incurred some additional costs in acquiring the land. In 2006, the attorney refunded his $300 fee to White and Swan.

24. Rita is a CPA. Her clients frequently ask her for advice about investing. The current rate quoted on tax-exempt state and local government bond funds is 4.4%, and the rate on taxable U.S. government obligations is 6.6%. Both types of accounts are considered "risk-free." What is the minimum marginal tax bracket in which clients can benefit from investing in the tax-exempt funds in 2005?

**Ethics**

25. The exclusion of state and local bond interest from Federal income tax is often criticized as creating a tax haven for the wealthy. Critics, however, often fail to take into account the effect of market forces. In recent months, the long-term tax-exempt interest rate has been 4.45% while the long-term taxable rate for bonds of comparable risk was approximately 6.4%. On the other hand, state and local governments do enjoy a savings in interest costs because of the tax-favored status of their bonds. To date, Congress has concluded that the benefits gained by the states and municipalities and their residents outweigh any damages to our progressive income tax system. Do you agree with the proponents of the exclusion? Why or why not?

**Decision Making**

26. Tedra, a C corporation, is in the 35% marginal tax bracket, is very risk adverse, and is considering purchasing U.S. government bonds due in 10 years that yield 5.6% before tax. Triple A rated State of Virginia bonds due in 10 years yield 4%. Which is the better alternative, assuming the bonds are of equal risk?

27. Determine the taxable life insurance proceeds in the following cases.
    a. When Monty died, his wife collected $50,000 on a group term insurance policy purchased by Monty's employer. Monty had never included the premiums in gross income.
    b. The Cardinal Software Company purchased an insurance policy on the life of a key employee. The company paid $50,000 in premiums and collected $500,000 of insurance proceeds.
    c. When Barbara died, she and her husband owed $15,000 on a loan. Under the terms of the loan, Barbara was required to purchase life insurance to pay the creditor the amount due at the date of Barbara's death. The creditor collected from the life insurance company the amount due at the time of Barbara's death. Is the creditor required to recognize income from the collection of the life insurance proceeds?

**Decision Making**

28. The Egret Company, which has a 40% (combined Federal and state) marginal tax rate, estimated that if its current president should die, the company would incur $200,000 in costs to find a suitable replacement. In addition, profits on various projects the president is responsible for would likely decrease by $300,000. The president has recommended that Egret purchase a $500,000 life insurance policy. How much insurance should the company carry on the life of its president to compensate for the after-tax loss that would result from the president's death, assuming the $200,000 costs of finding a president are deductible and the lost profits would have been taxable?

29. Fay and Edward are partners in an accounting firm. The partners have entered into an arm's length agreement requiring Fay to purchase Edward's partnership interest from Edward's estate if he dies before Fay. The price is set at 150% of the book value of Edward's partnership interest at the time of his death. Fay purchased an insurance policy on Edward's life to fund this agreement. After Fay had paid $40,000 in premiums, Edward was killed in an automobile accident, and Fay collected $1.5 million of life insurance proceeds. Fay used the life insurance proceeds to purchase Edward's partnership interest.
    a. What amount should Fay include in her gross income from receiving the life insurance proceeds?
    b. The insurance company paid Fay $15,000 interest on the life insurance proceeds during the period Edward's estate was in administration. During this period, Fay had left the insurance proceeds with the insurance company. Is this interest taxable?
    c. When Fay purchased Edward's partnership interest for $1.5 million, as determined by specifications in the agreement, the fair market value of Edward's interest was $2 million. How much should Fay include in her gross income from this bargain purchase?

**Issue ID**

30. Hawk Industries, Inc., has experienced financial difficulties as a result of its struggling business. The corporation has been behind on its mortgage payments for the last six

months. The mortgage holder has offered to accept $80,000 in full payment of the $100,000 owed on the mortgage and payable over the next 10 years. The interest rate of the mortgage is 7%, and the market rate is now 8%. What tax issues are raised by the creditor's offer?

**EXTENDER** 31. During 2005, Wanda had the following transactions involving capital assets:

| | |
|---|---:|
| Short-term gain on the sale of a stock investment | $6,000 |
| Long-term gain on the sale of a sailing boat owned for 4 years (used for pleasure) | 3,000 |
| Long-term loss on the sale of a power boat owned for 2 years (used for pleasure) | 1,000 |
| Long-term gain on the sale of real estate held for 3 years as an investment | 7,000 |

a. If Wanda is in the 28% tax bracket, how much income tax do these transactions generate?
b. What if Wanda is in the 15% tax bracket?
c. What if Wanda is a C corporation in the 35% tax bracket? Assume that the power boat is used in the corporation's business.

**EXTENDER** 32. During 2005, Cole had the following gains and losses from the sale of capital assets.

| | |
|---|---:|
| Loss on Pigeon Corporation stock (held 9 months) | ($4,000) |
| Gain on painting (held for 2 years as an investment) | 5,000 |
| Gain on unimproved land (held for 3 years as an investment) | 3,000 |

a. If Cole is in the 35% tax bracket, how much income tax do these transactions generate?
b. What if Cole is in the 15% tax bracket?
c. What if Cole is a C corporation in the 35% tax bracket?

**EXTENDER** 33. Selma opened a farm implements store in 2005. The only accounting records she maintains are her cash receipts and disbursements for the business. Cash receipts for 2005 total $500,000, and cash disbursements total $350,000. The cash receipts include the $50,000 Selma originally invested in the business and a $5,000 customer deposit on a new tractor that was to be delivered by the factory in January 2006. You determine that there were no accounts receivable at the beginning of the year. At the end of the year, receivables total $15,000. The inventory at the end of the year is $75,000, and the accounts payables are $40,000. Determine the gross income for the store for 2005 for tax purposes.

**BRIDGE DISCIPLINE**

1. Using an online research service, find the audited financial statements of a major U.S. corporation.
   a. Summarize its most important financial accounting policies.
   b. Describe two elements of the Federal income tax law that significantly affected the corporation's earnings per share for the operating year.

**Decision Making**
**Communications**

2. Your client is a new partnership, Aspen Associates, which is an engineering consulting firm. Generally, Aspen bills clients for services at the end of each month. Client billings are about $50,000 each month. On average, it takes 45 days to collect the receivables. Aspen's expenses are primarily for salary and rent. Salaries are paid on the last day of each month, and rent is paid on the first day of each month. The partnership has a line of credit with a bank, which requires monthly financial statements. These must be prepared using the accrual method. Aspen's managing partner, Amanda Sims, has

suggested that the firm should also use the accrual method for tax purposes and thus reduce accounting fees by $500. Write a letter to your client explaining why you believe it would be worthwhile for Aspen to file its tax return on the cash basis even though its financial statements are prepared on the accrual basis. Aspen's address is 100 James Tower, Denver, CO 80208.

## Research Problems

*Note: Solutions to Research Problems can be prepared by using the **RIA Checkpoint® Student Edition** online research product, which is available to accompany this text. It is also possible to prepare solutions to the Research Problems by using tax research materials found in a standard tax library.*

**Communications**

**Research Problem 1.** Tranquility Funeral Home, Inc., your client, is an accrual basis taxpayer that sells pre-need funeral contracts. Under these contracts, the customer pays in advance for goods and services to be provided at the contract beneficiary's death. These payments are refundable at the contract purchaser's request, pursuant to state law, at any time until the goods and services are furnished. Tranquility, consistent with its financial accounting reporting, includes the payments in income for the year the funeral service is provided. The IRS agent insists that the payments are prepaid income subject to tax in the year of receipt. Your client believes the amounts involved are customer deposits. Write a letter to Tranquility that contains your advice about how the issue should be resolved. The client's address is 400 Rock Street, Memphis, TN 38152.

**Research Problem 2.** Sales personnel employed by Ivory Sales, Inc., accumulate substantial frequent-flyer miles traveling for the company. Since Ivory Sales reimburses its employees for travel expenses incurred, the company, rather than the employee, is entitled to the frequent-flyer miles. The company is considering a change in policy that would permit the employees to retain the miles for their personal use. Ivory Sales would like to know the income tax implications to the employees of the proposed change in policy.

**Communications**

**Research Problem 3.** Your client, the Cheyenne Golf and Tennis Club, requires its newly admitted members to purchase stock in the corporation and to make a deposit of $10,000. The deposit is to be repaid in 30 years, and no interest is charged. Is the deposit subject to the imputed interest rules for below-market loans? Outline the points you intend to make when you call the client back next week.

*Partial list of research aids:*
TAM 9735002.

**Communications**

**Research Problem 4.** Debra is a cash basis taxpayer. In December 2004, she purchased a used piano for $400. In 2005, she discovered $4,500 hidden inside the piano. Debra was unable to determine who placed the funds in the piano. She included the $4,500 in her 2005 gross income. When her 2005 return was examined, she explained the source of the $4,500 of other income she reported. Upon hearing the story, the IRS agent contended that Debra should have included the $4,500 on her 2004 return. Since she bought the piano in 2004, that is when her wealth actually increased. Debra was in the 35% marginal tax bracket in 2004, but was only in the 10% marginal tax bracket in 2005.

Debra has asked your advice about the correct year for reporting the $4,500. Summarize your analysis in a memo to the tax research file.

*Partial list of research aids:*
*Cesarini v. U.S.*, 70–2 USTC ¶9509, 26 AFTR2d 70–5107, 428 F.2d 812 (CA–6, 1970).

**Internet Activity**

*Use the tax resources of the Internet to address the following questions. Do not restrict your search to the World Wide Web, but include a review of newsgroups and general reference materials, practitioner sites and resources, primary sources of the tax law, chat rooms and discussion groups, and other opportunities.*

**Research Problem 5.** Determine the applicable Federal rate as of today for purposes of below-market loans.

**Research Problem 6.**   Go to the Web page for a securities broker or mutual fund. Use a "calculator" provided there to indicate the following.

| Taxable Interest Rate | Your Marginal Tax Rate | Breakeven Exempt Interest Rate |
|---|---|---|
| 6% | 35% | ? |
| 6% | 15% | ? |
| 8% | 28% | ? |
| 8% | 33% | ? |

**Research Problem 7.**   Find an article about the tax and nontax advantages of a buy-sell agreement and summarize it.

# Business Deductions

CHAPTER 4

## LEARNING OBJECTIVES

*After completing Chapter 4, you should be able to:*

### L O . 1
Understand the meaning and application of the ordinary, necessary, and reasonableness requirements for the deduction of business expenses.

### L O . 2
Describe the cash and accrual methods of accounting for business deductions.

### L O . 3
Apply a variety of Internal Revenue Code deduction disallowance provisions.

### L O . 4
Understand the limitations applicable to the charitable contribution deduction for corporations.

### L O . 5
Recognize and apply the alternative tax treatments for research and experimental expenditures.

### L O . 6
Determine the amount of cost recovery under MACRS, and apply the § 179 expensing election and the deduction limitations on listed property and automobiles when making the MACRS calculation.

### L O . 7
Identify intangible assets that are eligible for amortization and calculate the amount of the deduction.

### L O . 8
Determine the amount of depletion expense and recognize the alternative tax treatments for intangible drilling and development costs.

## OUTLINE

---

**TAX TALK**

*Last year I had difficulty with my income tax. I tried to take my analyst off as a business deduction. The Government said it was entertainment. We compromised finally and made it a religious contribution.*

—*Woody Allen*

---

**LO.1**

Understand the meaning and application of the ordinary, necessary, and reasonableness requirements for the deduction of business expenses.

# Overview of Business Deductions

## ORDINARY AND NECESSARY REQUIREMENT

*Definition page C-12*

Section 162(a) permits a deduction for all **ordinary and necessary** expenses paid or incurred in carrying on a trade or business. To understand the scope of this provision, it is necessary to understand the meanings of the terms ordinary and necessary.

Neither ordinary nor necessary is defined in the Code or Regulations. However, the courts have had to deal with these terms on numerous occasions and have held that an expense is necessary if a prudent business person would incur the same expense and the expense is expected to be appropriate and helpful in the taxpayer's business.[1] Many expenses that are necessary are not ordinary.

**EXAMPLE 1**

Welch felt that it would be helpful for the development of his new business if he repaid the debts owed by a bankrupt corporation that he had worked for. Consequently, over a period of years, he took a portion of his income and repaid these debts, even though he was under no legal obligation to do so. Welch claimed these repayments as ordinary and necessary business expenses. The Supreme Court indicated that the payments were *necessary* for the development of Welch's business because they contributed toward Welch's reputation and built goodwill. However, the Court also indicated that the expenses were *not ordinary*, since the act of repaying the debts of a bankrupt company was unusual and not a normal method of doing business. Instead, the repayments were more appropriately classified as capital expenditures for goodwill.[2] ■

An expense is ordinary if it is normal, usual, or customary in the type of business conducted by the taxpayer and is not capital in nature.[3] However, an expense need not be recurring to be deductible as ordinary.

**EXAMPLE 2**

Zebra Corporation engaged in a mail-order business. The post office judged that Zebra's advertisements were false and misleading. Under a fraud order, the post office stamped "fraudulent" on all letters addressed to Zebra's business and returned them to the senders. Zebra spent $30,000 on legal fees in an unsuccessful attempt to force the post office to stop. The legal fees (though not recurring) were ordinary business expenses because they were normal, usual, or customary in the circumstances.[4] ■

## REASONABLENESS REQUIREMENT

Although § 162 is intended to allow taxpayers to deduct a broad range of trade or business expenses, certain expenses are mentioned specifically:

- *Reasonable* salaries paid for services.
- Expenses for the use of business property. *Definition Page C-15*

The Code applies the **reasonableness requirement** solely to salaries and other compensation for services.[5] However, the courts have held that for *any* business expense to be ordinary and necessary, it must also be reasonable in amount.[6]

What constitutes reasonableness is a question of fact.[7] If an expense is unreasonable, the excess amount is not allowed as a deduction. The question of reasonableness usually arises with respect to closely held corporations with no separation of ownership and management.

Transactions between shareholders and a closely held corporation may result in the disallowance of deductions for excessive salaries, rent, and other expenses paid by the corporation to the shareholders. The courts will view an unusually large salary in light of all relevant circumstances and may find that the salary is reasonable

---

[1]*Welch v. Helvering,* 3 USTC ¶1164, 12 AFTR 1456, 54 S.Ct. 8 (USSC, 1933).

[2]*Welch v. Helvering,* 3 USTC ¶1164, 12 AFTR 1456, 54 S.Ct. 8 (USSC, 1933). For a contrasting decision, see *Dunn and McCarthy, Inc. v. Comm.,* 43–2 USTC ¶9688, 31 AFTR 1043, 139 F.2d 242 (CA–2, 1943), involving an *existing* business, where repayments to employees of a bankrupt corporation were held to be both ordinary and necessary.

[3]*Deputy v. DuPont,* 40–1 USTC ¶9161, 23 AFTR 808, 60 S.Ct. 363 (USSC, 1940).

[4]*Comm. v. Heininger,* 44–1 USTC ¶9109, 31 AFTR 783, 64 S.Ct. 249 (USSC, 1943).

[5]§ 162(a)(1).

[6]*Comm. v. Lincoln Electric Co.,* 49–2 USTC ¶9388, 38 AFTR 411, 176 F.2d 815 (CA–6, 1949).

[7]*Kennedy, Jr. v. Comm.,* 82–1 USTC ¶9186, 49 AFTR2d 82–628, 671 F.2d 167 (CA–6, 1982), *rev'g* 72 T.C. 793 (1979).

despite its size. If excessive payments for salaries, rent, and other expenses are closely related to the percentage of stock owned by the recipients, the payments are generally treated as dividends.[8] Since dividends are not deductible by the corporation, the disallowance results in an increase in corporate taxable income. Deductions for reasonable salaries will not be disallowed solely because the corporation has paid insubstantial portions of its earnings as dividends to its shareholders.

**EXAMPLE 3**

Sparrow Corporation, a closely held corporation, is owned equally by Lupe, Carlos, and Ramon. The company has been highly profitable for several years and has not paid dividends. Lupe, Carlos, and Ramon are key officers of the company, and each receives a salary of $200,000. Salaries for similar positions in comparable companies average only $100,000. Amounts paid the owners in excess of $100,000 may be deemed unreasonable, and, if so, a total of $300,000 in salary deductions by Sparrow is disallowed. The disallowed amounts are treated as dividends rather than salary income to Lupe, Carlos, and Ramon because the payments are proportional to stock ownership. Salaries are deductible by the corporation, but dividends are not. ■

## PLANNING STRATEGIES    Unreasonable Compensation

**FRAMEWORK FOCUS: TAX RATE**

STRATEGY ➤ AVOID DOUBLE TAXATION.

In substantiating the reasonableness of a shareholder-employee's compensation, an internal comparison test is sometimes useful. If it can be shown that nonshareholder-employees and shareholder-employees in comparable positions receive comparable compensation, it is indicative that compensation is not unreasonable.

Another possibility is to demonstrate that the shareholder-employee has been underpaid in prior years. For example, the shareholder-employee may have agreed to take a less-than-adequate salary during the unprofitable

formative years of the business. He or she would expect the "postponed" compensation to be paid in later, more profitable years. The agreement should be documented, if possible, in the corporate minutes.

Keep in mind that in testing for reasonableness, the total pay package must be considered. Compensation includes all fringe benefits or perquisites, such as contributions by the corporation to a qualified pension plan, regardless of when the funds are available to the employee.

**Common Business Deductions.**   The language of § 162 is broad enough to permit the deduction of many different types of ordinary and necessary business expenses. Some of the more common deductions are listed in Exhibit 4–1.

**LO.2**

Describe the cash and accrual methods of accounting for business deductions.

# Timing of Expense Recognition

A taxpayer's accounting method is a major factor in determining taxable income. The method used determines *when* an item is includible in income and *when* an item is deductible on the tax return. Usually, the taxpayer's regular method of

---

[8]Reg. § 1.162–8.

■ **EXHIBIT 4–1**
Partial List of Business
Deductions

| | |
|---|---|
| Advertising | Pension and profit sharing plans |
| Bad debts | Rent or lease payments |
| Commissions and fees | Repairs and maintenance |
| Depletion | Salaries and wages |
| Depreciation | Supplies |
| Employee benefit programs | Taxes and licenses |
| Insurance | Travel and transportation |
| Interest | Utilities |

record keeping is used for income tax purposes.[9] The taxing authorities require that the method used clearly reflect income and that items be handled consistently.[10] The most common methods of accounting are the cash method and the accrual method.

Throughout the portions of the Code dealing with deductions, the phrase "paid or incurred" is used. A cash basis taxpayer is allowed a deduction only in the year an expense is *paid*. An accrual basis taxpayer is allowed a deduction in the year in which the liability for the expense is *incurred* (becomes certain).

## CASH METHOD REQUIREMENTS

The expenses of cash basis taxpayers are deductible only when they are actually paid with cash or other property. Promising to pay or issuing a note does not satisfy the actually paid requirement.[11] However, the payment can be made with borrowed funds. Thus, taxpayers are allowed to claim the deduction at the time they charge expenses on credit cards. They are deemed to have simultaneously borrowed money from the credit card issuer and constructively paid the expenses.[12]

Although the cash basis taxpayer must have actually or constructively paid the expense, payment does not assure a current deduction. The Regulations require capitalization of any expenditure that creates an asset having a useful life that extends substantially beyond the end of the tax year.[13] Thus, cash basis and accrual basis taxpayers cannot take a current deduction for capital expenditures except through amortization, depletion, or depreciation over the tax life of the asset.

**E X A M P L E  4**

Redbird, Inc., a cash basis taxpayer, rents property from Bluejay, Inc. On July 1, 2005, Redbird pays $24,000 rent for the 24 months ending June 30, 2007. The prepaid rent extends 18 months after the close of the tax year—substantially beyond the year of payment. Therefore, Redbird must capitalize the prepaid rent and amortize the expense on a monthly basis. Redbird's deduction for 2005 is $6,000. ■

DIGGING DEEPER ①

*Find more information on this topic at our Web site:* ***http://wft-entities.swlearning.com.***

---

[9]§ 446(a).
[10]§§ 446(b) and (e); Reg. § 1.446–1(a)(2).
[11]*Page v. Rhode Island Trust Co., Exr.,* 37–1 USTC ¶9138, 19 AFTR 105, 88 F.2d 192 (CA–1, 1937).

[12]Rev.Rul. 78–39, 1978–1 C.B. 73. See also Rev.Rul. 80–335, 1980–2 C.B. 170, which applies to pay-by-phone arrangements.
[13]Reg. § 1.461–1(a).

## Time Value of Tax Deductions

**FRAMEWORK FOCUS: DEDUCTIONS**

STRATEGY ➤ ACCELERATE RECOGNITION OF DEDUCTIONS TO ACHIEVE TAX DEFERRAL.

Cash basis taxpayers often have the ability to make early payments for their expenses at the end of the tax year. This may permit the payments to be deducted in the year of payment instead of in the following tax year. In view of the time value of money, a tax deduction this year may be worth more than the same deduction next year. Before employing this strategy, the taxpayer must consider next year's expected income and tax rates and whether a cash-flow problem may develop from early payments. Thus, a variety of considerations must be taken into account when planning the timing of tax deductions.

### ACCRUAL METHOD REQUIREMENTS

The period in which an accrual basis taxpayer can deduct an expense is determined by applying the *all events test* and the *economic performance test*. A deduction cannot be claimed until (1) all the events have occurred to create the taxpayer's liability and (2) the amount of the liability can be determined with reasonable accuracy. Once these requirements are satisfied, the deduction is permitted only if economic performance has occurred. The economic performance test is met only when the service, property, or use of property giving rise to the liability is actually performed for, provided to, or used by the taxpayer.[14]

**EXAMPLE 5**

On December 22, 2005, Robin, Inc., an entertainment business, sponsored a jazz festival in a rented auditorium at City College. Robin is responsible for cleaning up the auditorium after the festival and for reinstalling seats that were removed so more people could attend the festival. Since the college is closed over the Christmas holidays, the company hired by Robin to perform the work did not begin these activities until January 2, 2006. The cost to Robin is $1,200. Robin cannot deduct the $1,200 until 2006, when the services are performed. ■

As illustrated in Examples 6 and 7, an exception to the economic performance requirement allows some *recurring* items to be deducted if certain conditions are met.[15]

*Find more information on this topic at our Web site: **http://wft-entities.swlearning.com.***

**EXAMPLE 6**

Towhee Company, an accrual basis, calendar year taxpayer, entered into a monthly maintenance contract during the year. Towhee makes a monthly accrual at the end of every month for this service and pays the fee sometime between the first and fifteenth of the following month when services are performed. The December 2005 accrual is deductible in 2005 even though the service is performed on January 12, 2006. ■

**EXAMPLE 7**

Tanager, Inc., an accrual basis, calendar year taxpayer, shipped merchandise sold on December 30, 2005, via Greyhound Van Lines on January 2, 2006, and paid the freight charges at

---

[14]§ 461(h).                    [15]§ 461(h)(3)(A).

that time. Since Tanager reported the sale of the merchandise in 2005, the shipping charge should also be deductible in 2005. This procedure results in a better matching of income and expenses. ■

Reserves for estimated expenses (frequently employed for financial accounting purposes) generally are not allowed for tax purposes because the economic performance test cannot be satisfied.

**EXAMPLE 8**

Oriole Airlines is required by Federal law to test its engines after 3,000 flying hours. Aircraft cannot return to flight until the tests have been conducted. An unrelated aircraft maintenance company does all of the company's tests for $1,500 per engine. For financial reporting purposes, the company accrues an expense based upon $.50 per hour of flight and credits an allowance account. The actual amounts paid for maintenance are offset against the allowance account. For tax purposes, the economic performance test is not satisfied until the work has been done. Therefore, the reserve method cannot be used for tax purposes. ■

**LO.3**

Apply a variety of Internal Revenue Code deduction disallowance provisions.

# Disallowance Possibilities

While most ordinary and necessary business expenses are deductible, the tax law contains provisions that disallow a deduction for certain expenditures. The most frequently encountered disallowance provisions are discussed below.

## PUBLIC POLICY LIMITATIONS

**Justification for Denying Deductions.** The courts developed the principle that a payment that is in violation of public policy is not a necessary expense and is not deductible.[16] Although a bribe or fine may be appropriate, helpful, and even contribute to the profitability of an activity, allowing a deduction for such expenses would frustrate clearly defined public policy. A deduction would effectively represent an indirect governmental subsidy for taxpayer wrongdoing.

Under legislation enacted based on this principle, deductions are disallowed for specific types of expenditures that are considered contrary to public policy:

- Bribes and kickbacks illegal under either Federal or state law, including those associated with Medicare or Medicaid.
- Two-thirds of the treble damage payments made to claimants resulting from violation of antitrust law.[17]
- Fines and penalties paid to a government for violation of law.

**EXAMPLE 9**

Brown Corporation, a moving company, consistently loads its trucks with weights in excess of the limits allowed by state law. The additional revenue more than offsets the fines levied. The fines are for a violation of public policy and are not deductible. ■

DIGGING DEEPER 3

*Find more information on this topic at our Web site: **http://wft-entities.swlearning.com**.*

**Legal Expenses Incurred in Defense of Civil or Criminal Penalties.** To deduct legal expenses as trade or business expenses, the taxpayer must be able to show that the origin and character of the claim are directly related to a trade or business. Personal legal expenses are not deductible. Thus, legal fees incurred in

---

[16]*Tank Truck Rentals, Inc. v. Comm.*, 58–1 USTC ¶9366, 1 AFTR2d 1154, 78 S.Ct. 507 (USSC, 1958).

[17]§§ 162(c), (f), and (g).

connection with a criminal defense are deductible only if the crime is associated with the taxpayer's trade or business.[18]

**EXAMPLE 10**

Debra, a majority shareholder and chief financial officer of Blue Corporation, incurs legal expenses in connection with her defense in a criminal indictment for evasion of Blue's income taxes. Debra may deduct her legal expenses because she is deemed to be in the trade or business of being an executive. The legal action impairs her ability to conduct this business activity.[19] ■

**Expenses Related to an Illegal Business.** The usual expenses of operating an illegal business (e.g., a numbers racket) are deductible.[20] However, § 162 disallows a deduction for fines, bribes to public officials, illegal kickbacks, and other illegal payments.

**EXAMPLE 11**

Grizzly, Inc., owns and operates a saloon. In addition, Grizzly operates an illegal gambling establishment out of the saloon's back room. In connection with the illegal gambling activity, Grizzly has the following expenses during the year:

| | |
|---|---:|
| Rent | $ 60,000 |
| Payoffs to police | 40,000 |
| Depreciation on equipment | 100,000 |
| Wages | 140,000 |
| Interest | 30,000 |
| Criminal fines | 50,000 |
| Illegal kickbacks | 10,000 |
| Total | $430,000 |

All of the usual expenses (rent, depreciation, wages, and interest) are deductible; payoffs, fines, and kickbacks are not deductible. Of the $430,000 spent, $330,000 is deductible and $100,000 is not. ■

An exception applies to expenses incurred in illegal trafficking in drugs.[21] Drug dealers are not allowed a deduction for ordinary and necessary business expenses incurred in their business. In arriving at gross income from the business, however, dealers may reduce total sales by the cost of goods sold.[22]

## POLITICAL CONTRIBUTIONS AND LOBBYING ACTIVITIES

**Political Contributions.** Generally, no business deduction is permitted for direct or indirect payments for political purposes.[23] Historically, the government has been reluctant to extend favorable tax treatment to political expenditures by businesses. Allowing deductions might encourage abuses and enable businesses to have undue influence upon the political process.

---

[18]*Comm. v. Tellier*, 66–1 USTC ¶9319, 17 AFTR2d 633, 86 S.Ct. 1118 (USSC, 1966).
[19]Rev.Rul. 68–662, 1968–2 C.B. 69.
[20]*Comm. v. Sullivan*, 58–1 USTC ¶9368, 1 AFTR2d 1158, 78 S.Ct. 512 (USSC, 1958).

[21]§ 280E.
[22]Reg. § 1.61–3(a). Gross income is defined as sales minus cost of goods sold. Thus, while § 280E prohibits any deductions for drug dealers, it does not modify the normal definition of gross income.
[23]§ 276.

**Lobbying Expenditures.**    The Code places severe restrictions on the deductibility of expenses incurred in connection with lobbying activities.[24] These provisions deny deductions for expenditures incurred in connection with:

- influencing state or Federal legislation;
- participating or intervening in any political campaign on behalf of, or in opposition to, any candidate for public office;
- attempting to influence voters with respect to elections, legislative matters, or referendums; and
- attempting to influence the actions of certain high-ranking public officials (including the President, Vice President, and cabinet-level officials).

There are three exceptions to the disallowance provisions. First, an exception is provided for influencing *local* legislation (e.g., city and county governments). Second, the disallowance provision does not apply to activities devoted solely to *monitoring* legislation. Third, a *de minimis* exception allows the deduction of up to $2,000 of annual *in-house expenditures*, if the expenditures are not otherwise disallowed under the provisions discussed above. In-house lobbying expenditures do not include expenses paid to professional lobbyists or any portion of dues used by associations for lobbying. If in-house expenditures exceed $2,000, none of the in-house expenditures can be deducted.

**EXAMPLE 12**

Egret Company pays a $10,000 annual membership fee to the Free Trade Group, a trade association for plumbing wholesalers. The trade association estimates that 70% of its dues are allocated to lobbying activities. Thus, Egret's deduction is limited to $3,000 ($10,000 × 30%), the amount that is not associated with lobbying activities.  ■

## EXCESSIVE EXECUTIVE COMPENSATION

The Code contains a *millionaires' provision* that applies to compensation paid by *publicly held* corporations.[25] The provision does not limit the amount of compensation that can be *paid* to an employee. Instead, it limits the amount the employer can *deduct* for the compensation of a covered executive to $1 million annually. Covered employees include the chief executive officer and the four other most highly compensated officers. Employee compensation for this purpose *excludes* the following:

- Commissions based on individual performance.
- Certain performance-based compensation based on company performance according to a formula approved by a board of directors compensation committee (comprised solely of two or more outside directors) and by shareholder vote. The performance attainment must be certified by this compensation committee.
- Payments to tax-qualified retirement plans.
- Payments that are excludible from the employee's gross income (e.g., certain fringe benefits).

## DISALLOWANCE OF DEDUCTIONS FOR CAPITAL EXPENDITURES

The Code specifically disallows a deduction for "any amount paid out for new buildings or for permanent improvements or betterments made to increase the value of any property or estate."[26] The Regulations further define capital expenditures to

---

[24]§ 162(e).
[25]§ 162(m).

[26]§ 263(a)(1).

## EXECUTIVE PAY ABUSE

The IRS has increased its scrutiny of executive pay practices. Its examination of 24 big companies found that several were evading the millionaires' limit on executive pay. Most of the abuses involve the exception for performance-based compensation. By paying bonuses based on performance, a corporation can exceed the general $1 million deduction cap. Some companies achieve this by changing the bonus plan formula or target throughout the year or, even worse, by paying the bonus even though the performance goals are not reached.

According to Catherine Livingston Fernandez, a speaker at a compensation conference, "some pretty large adjustments have been proposed" to correct such abuses. The Senate Finance Committee, in its report on the Enron investigation, proposed repealing the $1 million cap because it was not modifying corporate behavior as intended. Robert McIntyre, the director of Citizens for Tax Justice, believes that if the goal is to limit executive compensation deductions to $1 million, then nobody should be paid more than $1 million, and no exceptions should be allowed.

SOURCES: Adapted from Joan S. Lublin, "IRS Is Cracking Down on Abuse of Executive Bonus Tax Breaks," *Wall Street Journal*, June 18, 2004, p. B5; Jessee Drucker, "As CEOs Miss Bonus Goals, Goalposts Move," *Wall Street Journal*, July 7, 2004, p. C1.

include expenditures that add to the value or prolong the life of property or adapt the property to a new or different use.[27] Incidental repairs and maintenance of the property are not capital expenditures and can be deducted as ordinary and necessary business expenses. Repairing a roof is a deductible expense, but replacing a roof is a capital expenditure subject to depreciation deductions over its useful life. The tune-up of a delivery truck is an expense; a complete overhaul probably is a capital expenditure.

**Capitalization versus Expense.** When an expenditure is capitalized rather than expensed, the deduction is at best deferred and at worst lost forever. Although an immediate tax benefit for a large cash expenditure is lost, the cost may be deductible in increments over a longer period of time.

If the expenditure is for a tangible asset that has an ascertainable life, it is capitalized and may be deducted as depreciation over the life of the asset or as a cost recovery allowance over a specified statutory period under MACRS.[28] Land is not subject to depreciation (or cost recovery) since it does not have an ascertainable life.

**EXAMPLE 13**

Buffalo Corporation purchases a prime piece of land and an old but usable apartment building located in an apartment-zoned area. Buffalo pays $500,000 for the property and immediately has the building demolished at a cost of $100,000. The $500,000 purchase price and the $100,000 demolition costs must be capitalized, and the tax basis of the land is $600,000. Since land is a nondepreciable asset, no deduction is allowed. More favorable tax treatment might result if Buffalo rents the apartments in the old building for a period of time to attempt to establish that there is no intent to demolish the building. If Buffalo's attempt is successful, it might be possible to allocate a substantial portion of the original

---

[27]Reg. § 1.263(a)–1(b).

[28]Depreciation and cost recovery allowances are discussed later in this chapter.

purchase price of the property to the building (a depreciable asset). When the building is later demolished, any remaining adjusted basis can be deducted as an ordinary (§ 1231) loss. ■

## INVESTIGATION OF A BUSINESS

Investigation expenses are paid or incurred to determine the feasibility of entering a new business or expanding an existing business. They include such costs as travel, engineering and architectural surveys, marketing reports, and various legal and accounting services. How such expenses are treated for tax purposes depends on a number of variables, including the following:

* The current business, if any, of the taxpayer.
* The nature of the business being investigated.
* Whether or not the acquisition actually takes place.

If the taxpayer is in a business the same as or similar to that being investigated, all investigation expenses are deductible in the year paid or incurred. The tax result is the same whether or not the taxpayer acquires the business being investigated.[29]

**EXAMPLE 14**

Terry, an accrual basis sole proprietor, owns and operates three motels in Georgia. In the current year, Terry incurs expenses of $8,500 in investigating the possibility of acquiring several additional motels located in South Carolina. The $8,500 is deductible in the current year whether or not Terry acquires the motels in South Carolina. ■

When the taxpayer is not in a business that is the same as or similar to the one being investigated, the tax result depends on whether the new business is acquired. If the business is not acquired, all investigation expenses generally are nondeductible.[30]

**EXAMPLE 15**

Lynn, president and sole shareholder of Marmot Corporation, incurs expenses when traveling from Rochester, New York, to California to investigate the feasibility of acquiring several auto care centers. Marmot is in the residential siding business. If no acquisition takes place, Marmot may not deduct any of the expenses. ■

If the taxpayer is not in a business that is the same as or similar to the one being investigated and actually acquires the new business, the expenses must be capitalized. At the election of the taxpayer, the first $5,000 of the expenses can be immediately deducted. Any excess expenses can be amortized over a period of not less than 180 months (15 years). In arriving at the $5,000 immediate deduction allowed, a dollar-for-dollar reduction must be made for those expenses in excess of $50,000.[31]

**EXAMPLE 16**

Tina, a sole proprietor, owns and operates 10 restaurants located in various cities throughout the Southeast. She travels to Atlanta to discuss the acquisition of an auto dealership. In addition, she incurs legal and accounting costs associated with the potential acquisition. After incurring total investigation costs of $52,000, she acquires the auto dealership on October 1, 2005.

Tina may immediately deduct $3,000 [$5,000 − ($52,000 − $50,000)] and amortize the balance of $49,000 ($52,000 − $3,000) over a period of 180 months. For calendar year 2005, therefore, Tina can deduct $3,817 [$3,000 + ($49,000 × 3/180)]. ■

 *Find more information on this topic at our Web site: http://wft-entities.swlearning.com.*

[29]*York v. Comm.,* 58–2 USTC ¶9952, 2 AFTR2d 6178, 261 F.2d 421 (CA–4, 1958).
[30]Rev.Rul. 57–418, 1957–2 C.B. 143; *Morton Frank,* 20 T.C. 511 (1953); and *Dwight A. Ward,* 20 T.C. 332 (1953).
[31]§ 195(b). Prior to October 22, 2004 (the effective date of the American Jobs Creation Act), no immediate deduction was available, but the amortization period was 60 months.

## TRANSACTIONS BETWEEN RELATED PARTIES

The Code places restrictions on the recognition of gains and losses from **related-party transactions.** Without these restrictions, relationships created by birth, marriage, and business would provide endless possibilities for engaging in financial transactions that produce tax savings with no real economic substance or change. For example, to create an artificial loss, a corporation could sell investment property to its sole shareholder at a loss and deduct the loss on the corporate return. The shareholder could then hold the asset indefinitely. Although title to the property has changed, there has been no real economic loss if the shareholder and corporation are considered as an economic unit. A complex set of laws has been designed to eliminate such possibilities.

**Losses.**   The Code provides for the disallowance of any losses from sales or exchanges of property directly or indirectly between related parties.[32] In addition to specified family relationships (e.g., brothers and sisters), certain business relationships are subject to this disallowance rule. For instance, a corporation and a shareholder are considered related parties if the shareholder owns more than 50 percent of the corporation.

When the property is subsequently sold to an unrelated party, any gain recognized is reduced by the loss previously disallowed. Any disallowed loss not used by the related-party buyer to offset his or her recognized gain on a subsequent sale or exchange to an unrelated party is permanently lost.

**EXAMPLE 17**

Anna, sole shareholder of Leopard Corporation, sells common stock with a basis of $1,000 to the corporation for $800. Leopard sells the stock several years later for $1,100. Anna's $200 loss is disallowed upon the sale to Leopard, and only $100 of gain ($1,100 selling price – $800 basis – $200 disallowed loss) is taxable to Leopard upon the subsequent sale. ■

**EXAMPLE 18**

George sells common stock with a basis of $1,050 to his wholly owned corporation for $800. George's $250 loss is disallowed under the related-party rules. The corporation sells the stock eight months later to an unrelated party for $900. The corporation's gain of $100 ($900 selling price – $800 basis) is not recognized because of the offset from George's previously disallowed loss of $250. Note that the offset may result in only a partial tax benefit upon the subsequent sale (as in this case). If George had not sold the property to the corporation, he could have recognized a $150 loss upon the sale to the unrelated party ($900 selling price – $1,050 basis). ■

**Unpaid Expenses and Interest.**   The law prevents related taxpayers from engaging in tax avoidance schemes where one related taxpayer uses the accrual method of accounting and the other uses the cash basis. The accrual basis allows the deduction of expenses when incurred, while the cash method requires that income be reported when received. In the absence of restrictions, an accrual basis, closely held corporation, for example, could borrow funds from a cash basis individual shareholder. At the end of the year, the corporation would accrue and deduct the interest expense, but the cash basis lender would not recognize interest income since no interest had been paid. Section 267 specifically defers the accrual of an interest deduction until the lender is required to include the interest in income; that is, when it is actually received by the cash basis taxpayer. This matching provision also applies to other expenses, such as salaries and bonuses.

---

[32]§ 267(a)(1).

The deduction deferral provision does not apply if both of the related taxpayers use the accrual method or both use the cash method. Likewise, it does not apply if the related party reporting income uses the accrual method and the related party taking the deduction uses the cash method.

**Relationships and Constructive Ownership.**   Section 267 operates to disallow losses and defer deductions only between *related parties*. Losses or deductions generated by similar transactions with an unrelated party are allowed. Related parties include the following:

- Brothers and sisters (whether whole, half, or adopted), spouse, ancestors (parents, grandparents), and lineal descendants (children, grandchildren) of the taxpayer.
- A corporation owned more than 50 percent (directly or indirectly) by the taxpayer.
- Two corporations that are members of a controlled group.
- A series of other complex relationships between trusts, corporations, and individual taxpayers.

*Constructive ownership* provisions are applied to determine whether the taxpayers are related. Under these provisions, stock owned by certain relatives or related entities is deemed to be owned by the taxpayer for purposes of applying the loss and expense deduction disallowance provisions. A taxpayer is deemed to own not only his or her stock but also the stock owned by his or her lineal descendants, ancestors, brothers and sisters or half-brothers and half-sisters, and spouse. The taxpayer is also deemed to own his or her proportionate share of stock owned by any partnership, corporation, estate, or trust of which he or she is a member. An individual is deemed to own any stock owned, directly or indirectly, by his or her partner. However, constructive ownership by an individual of the other partner's shares does not extend to the individual's spouse or other relatives (no double attribution).

| | |
|---|---|
| *EXAMPLE 19* | The stock of Sparrow Corporation is owned 20% by Ted, 30% by Ted's father, 30% by Ted's mother, and 20% by Ted's sister. On July 1 of the current year, Ted loaned $10,000 to Sparrow Corporation at 8% annual interest, principal and interest payable on demand. For tax purposes, Sparrow uses the accrual basis, and Ted uses the cash basis. Both report on a calendar year basis. Since Ted is deemed to own the 80% owned by his parents and sister, he actually and constructively owns 100% of Sparrow. If the corporation accrues the interest within the taxable year, no deduction can be taken until payment is made to Ted. ■ |

## LACK OF ADEQUATE SUBSTANTIATION

The tax law is built on a voluntary system. Taxpayers file their tax returns, report income and take deductions to which they are entitled, and pay their taxes through withholding or estimated tax payments during the year. The taxpayer has the burden of proof for substantiating expenses deducted on the returns and must retain adequate records. Upon audit, the IRS will disallow any undocumented or unsubstantiated deductions. These requirements have resulted in numerous conflicts between taxpayers and the IRS.

Some events throughout the year should be documented as they occur. For example, it is generally advisable to receive a pledge payment statement from a charity, in addition to a canceled check (if available), for proper documentation of a charitable contribution.[33] In addition, for a charitable contribution of $250 or more, a donor must obtain a *receipt* from the donee. Other types of deductible expenditures (such as travel and entertainment expenses, and depreciation on property used for both business and personal purposes) may require receipts or some other type of support.

## EXPENSES AND INTEREST RELATED TO TAX-EXEMPT INCOME

Certain income, such as interest on municipal bonds, is tax-exempt.[34] The law also allows the taxpayer to deduct expenses incurred for the production of income.[35] Deduction disallowance provisions, however, make it impossible to make money at the expense of the government by excluding interest income and deducting interest expense.[36]

**EXAMPLE 20**

Oriole, Inc., a corporation in the 35% bracket, purchased $100,000 of 6% municipal bonds. At the same time, Oriole used the bonds as collateral on a bank loan of $100,000 at 8% interest. A positive cash flow would result from the tax benefit as follows:

| | |
|---|---:|
| Cash paid out on loan | ($8,000) |
| Cash received from bonds | 6,000 |
| Tax savings from deducting interest expense ($8,000 × 35%) | 2,800 |
| Net positive cash flow | $  800 |

To eliminate the possibility illustrated in the preceding example, the Code specifically disallows a deduction for the expenses of producing tax-exempt income. Interest on any indebtedness incurred or continued to purchase or carry tax-exempt obligations also is disallowed.

**Judicial Interpretations.**   It is often difficult to show a direct relationship between borrowings and investment in tax-exempt securities. Suppose, for example, that a taxpayer borrows money, adds it to existing funds, buys inventory and stocks, then later sells the inventory and buys municipal bonds. A series of transactions such as these can completely obscure any connection between the loan and the tax-exempt investment. One solution would be to disallow interest on any debt to the extent that the taxpayer holds any tax-exempt securities. The law was not intended to go to such extremes. As a result, judicial interpretations have tried to be reasonable in disallowing interest deductions.[37]

 *Find more information on this topic at our Web site:* ***http://wft-entities.swlearning.com.***

**EXAMPLE 21**

In January of the current year, Crane Corporation borrowed $100,000 at 8% interest. Crane used the loan proceeds to purchase 5,000 shares of stock in White Corporation. In July, Crane sold the stock for $120,000 and reinvested the proceeds in City of Denver bonds, the income from which is tax-exempt. Assuming the $100,000 loan remained outstanding throughout the entire year, Crane cannot deduct the interest attributable to the period when it held the bonds. ■

---

[33]Rev.Proc. 92–71, 1992–2 C.B. 437, addresses circumstances where checks are not returned by a financial institution or where electronic transfers are made.

[34]§ 103.

[35]§ 212.

[36]§ 265.

[37]See, for example, *The Wisconsin Cheeseman, Inc. v. U.S.,* 68–1 USTC ¶9145, 21 AFTR2d 383, 388 F.2d 420 (CA–7, 1968).

LO.4

Understand the limitations applicable to the charitable contribution deduction for corporations.

# Charitable Contributions

Corporations and individuals are allowed to deduct contributions made to qualified domestic charitable organizations.[38] Qualified organizations include:[39]

- A state or possession of the United States or any subdivisions thereof.
- A corporation, trust, or community chest, fund, or foundation that is situated in the United States and is organized and operated exclusively for religious, charitable, scientific, literary, or educational purposes or for the prevention of cruelty to children or animals.

DIGGING DEEPER 6

*Find more information on this topic at our Web site: **http://wft-entities.swlearning.com**.*

← Definition page C-4

Generally, a deduction for a **charitable contribution** will be allowed only for the year in which the payment is made. However, an important exception is made for *accrual basis* corporations. They may claim the deduction in the year preceding payment if two requirements are met. First, the contribution must be *authorized* by the board of directors by the end of that year. Second, it must be *paid* on or before the fifteenth day of the third month of the following year.

**EXAMPLE 22**

On December 28, 2005, Blue Company, a calendar year, accrual basis partnership, authorizes a $5,000 donation to the Atlanta Symphony Association (a qualified charitable organization). The donation is made on March 14, 2006. Because Blue Company is a partnership, the contribution can be deducted only in 2006.[40] However, if Blue Company is a corporation and the December 28, 2005 authorization was made by its board of directors, Blue may claim the $5,000 donation as a deduction for calendar year 2005. ■

## PROPERTY CONTRIBUTIONS

Definitions:
* Capital Gain Property
  – page C-4
* Ordinary Income Property
  – Page C-12

The amount that can be deducted for a noncash charitable contribution depends on the type of property contributed. Property must be identified as long-term **capital gain property** or ordinary income property. Long-term capital gain property is property that, if sold, would result in long-term capital gain for the taxpayer. Such property generally must be a capital asset and must be held for the long-term holding period (more than one year). **Ordinary income property** is property that, if sold, would result in ordinary income for the taxpayer. Examples of ordinary income property include inventory and capital assets held short term (one year or less). Refer to Chapter 3 for a brief introduction to the distinction between capital and ordinary assets.

The deduction for a charitable contribution of long-term capital property is generally measured by its *fair market value.*

**EXAMPLE 23**

In 2005, Mallard Corporation donates a parcel of land (a capital asset) to Oakland Community College. Mallard acquired the land in 1988 for $60,000, and the fair market value on the date of the contribution is $100,000. The corporation's charitable contribution deduction (subject to a percentage limitation discussed later) is measured by the asset's fair market

---

[38]§ 170.
[39]§ 170(c).
[40]Each calendar year partner will report an allocable portion of the charitable contribution deduction as of December 31, 2006 (the end of the partnership's tax year). See Chapter 10.

value of $100,000, even though the $40,000 of appreciation on the land has never been included in Mallard's income. ■

In two situations, a charitable contribution of long-term capital gain property is measured by the basis of the property, rather than fair market value. If a corporation contributes tangible personal property and the charitable organization puts the property to an *unrelated use,* the appreciation on the property is not deductible. Unrelated use is defined as use that is not related to the purpose or function that qualifies the organization for exempt status.

**EXAMPLE 24**

White Corporation donates a painting worth $200,000 to Western States Art Museum (a qualified charity), which exhibits the painting. White had acquired the painting in 1980 for $90,000. Because the museum put the painting to a related use, White is allowed to deduct $200,000, the fair market value of the painting. ■

**EXAMPLE 25**

Assume the same facts as in the previous example, except that White Corporation donates the painting to the American Cancer Society, which sells the painting and deposits the $200,000 proceeds in the organization's general fund. White's deduction is limited to the $90,000 basis because it contributed tangible personal property that was put to an unrelated use by the charitable organization. ■

The deduction for charitable contributions of long-term capital gain property to certain private nonoperating foundations (defined in §§ 4942 and 509) is also limited to the basis of the property.

As a general rule, the deduction for a contribution of ordinary income property is limited to the basis of the property. On certain contributions, however, corporations enjoy two special exceptions that allow a deduction for basis plus 50 percent of the appreciation on the property. The first exception concerns inventory if the property is used in a manner related to the exempt purpose of the donee. The charity must use the property solely for the care of the ill, the needy, or infants.

**EXAMPLE 26**

Lark Corporation, a grocery chain, donates canned goods to the Salvation Army to be used to feed the needy. Lark's basis in the canned goods is $2,000, and the fair market value (the sales price to customers) is $3,000. Lark's deduction is $2,500 [$2,000 basis + 50%($3,000 − $2,000)]. ■

The second exception involves gifts of scientific property to colleges and certain scientific research organizations for use in research, provided certain conditions are met.[41]

## LIMITATIONS IMPOSED ON CHARITABLE CONTRIBUTION DEDUCTIONS

Both corporations and individuals are subject to percentage limits on the charitable contribution deduction.[42] The complex limitations for individual taxpayers are covered in Chapter 15.

For any one year, a corporate taxpayer's contribution deduction is limited to 10 percent of taxable income. For this purpose, taxable income is computed without regard to the charitable contribution deduction, any net operating loss carryback or capital loss carryback, and the dividends received deduction. Any contributions in excess of the 10 percent limitation may be carried forward to the five succeeding

---

[41]These conditions are set forth in § 170(e)(4). For the inventory exception, see § 170(e)(3).

[42]The percentage limitations applicable to individuals and corporations are set forth in § 170(b).

---

> ◉ **T A X  F A C T**
>
> ## WHAT TEN PERCENT CEILING?
>
> Just how generous is corporate America? Based on recent data, of the $635 billion of corporate income subject to tax, contributions and gifts totaled nearly $11.4 billion. In other words, approximately 1.8 percent of a corporation's income subject to tax, on average, goes to charity.
>
> **Source:** Corporation Income Tax Returns, 2001; Table 2—Selected Balance Sheet, Income Statement, and Tax Items by Asset Size; September 2004.

---

tax years. Any carryforward must be added to subsequent contributions and will be subject to the 10 percent limitation. In applying this limitation, the current year's contributions must be deducted first, with excess deductions from previous years deducted in order of time.[43]

**EXAMPLE 27**

During 2005, Orange Corporation (a calendar year taxpayer) had the following income and expenses.

| | |
|---|---|
| Income from operations | $140,000 |
| Expenses from operations | 110,000 |
| Dividends received | 10,000 |
| Charitable contributions made in May 2005 | 5,000 |

For purposes of the 10% limitation only, Orange Corporation's taxable income is $40,000 ($140,000 − $110,000 + $10,000). Consequently, the allowable charitable contribution deduction for 2005 is $4,000 (10% × $40,000). The $1,000 unused portion of the contribution can be carried forward to 2006, 2007, 2008, 2009, and 2010 (in that order) until exhausted. ■

**EXAMPLE 28**

Assume the same facts as in the previous example. In 2006, Orange Corporation has taxable income (for purposes of the 10% limitation) of $50,000 and makes a charitable contribution of $4,500. The maximum deduction allowed for 2006 is $5,000 (10% × $50,000). The entire 2006 contribution of $4,500 and $500 of the 2005 charitable contribution carryforward are currently deductible. The remaining $500 of the 2005 carryforward may be carried over to 2007 (and later years, if necessary). ■

---

**LO.5**

Recognize and apply the alternative tax treatments for research and experimental expenditures.

# Research and Experimental Expenditures

*Definition Page C-15*

Section 174 covers the treatment of **research and experimental expenditures.** The Regulations define research and experimental expenditures as follows:

> all such costs incident to the development of an experimental or pilot model, a plant process, a product, a formula, an invention, or similar property, and the improvement of already existing property of the type mentioned. The term does not include expenditures such as those for the ordinary testing or inspection of materials or products for quality control or those for efficiency surveys, management studies, consumer surveys, advertising, or promotions.[44]

---

[43]The carryover rules relating to all taxpayers are in § 170(d).

[44]Reg. § 1.174–2(a)(1).

The law permits three alternatives for the handling of research and experimental expenditures:

- Expense in the year paid or incurred.
- Defer and amortize.
- Capitalize.

If the costs are capitalized, a deduction is not available until the research project is abandoned or is deemed worthless. Since many products resulting from research projects do not have a definite and limited useful life, a taxpayer should ordinarily elect to write off the expenditures immediately or to defer and amortize them. It is generally preferable to elect an immediate write-off of the research expenditures because of the time value of the tax deduction.

The law also provides for a research activities credit. The credit amounts to 20 percent of certain research and experimental expenditures.[45]

## EXPENSE METHOD

A taxpayer can elect to expense all of the research and experimental expenditures incurred in the current year and all subsequent years. The consent of the IRS is not required if the method is adopted for the first taxable year in which such expenditures were paid or incurred. Once the election is made, the taxpayer must continue to expense all qualifying expenditures unless a request for a change is made to, and approved by, the IRS. In certain instances, a taxpayer may incur research and experimental expenditures before actually engaging in any trade or business activity. In such instances, the Supreme Court has applied a liberal standard of deductibility and permitted a deduction in the year of incurrence.[46]

## DEFERRAL AND AMORTIZATION METHOD

Alternatively, research and experimental expenditures may be deferred and amortized if the taxpayer makes an election.[47] Under the election, research and experimental expenditures are amortized ratably over a period of not less than 60 months. A deduction is allowed beginning with the month in which the taxpayer first realizes benefits from the research and experimental expenditures. The election is binding, and a change requires permission from the IRS.

**EXAMPLE 29**

Gold Corporation decides to develop a new line of adhesives. The project begins in 2005. Gold incurs the following expenses in 2005 and 2006 in connection with the project:

|  | 2005 | 2006 |
|---|---|---|
| Salaries | $25,000 | $18,000 |
| Materials | 8,000 | 2,000 |
| Depreciation and machinery | 6,500 | 5,700 |

The benefits from the project will be realized starting in March 2007. If Gold Corporation elects a 60-month deferral and amortization period, there is no deduction prior to March 2007, the month benefits from the project begin to be realized. The deduction for 2007 is $10,867, computed as follows.

---

[45]§ 41. See Chapter 13 for a more detailed discussion of the research activities credit.

[46]*Snow v. Comm.*, 74–1 USTC ¶9432, 33 AFTR2d 74–1251, 94 S.Ct. 1876 (USSC, 1974).

[47]§ 174(b)(2).

| | |
|---|---|
| Salaries ($25,000 + $18,000) | $43,000 |
| Materials ($8,000 + $2,000) | 10,000 |
| Depreciation ($6,500 + $5,700) | 12,200 |
| Total | $65,200 |
| $65,200 × (10 months/60 months) | $10,867 |

The option to treat research and experimental expenditures as a deferred expense is usually employed when a company does not have sufficient income to offset the research and experimental expenses. Rather than create net operating loss carryovers that might not be utilized because of the 20-year limitation on such carryovers, the deferral and amortization method may be used. The deferral of research and experimental expenditures should also be considered if the taxpayer expects higher tax rates in the future.

# Other Expense Rules

In addition to the provisions related to charitable contributions and research and experimental expenditures, a variety of other expenses are subject to special rules and limitations. Some of these rules are noted briefly in the paragraphs that follow.

## INTEREST EXPENSE

Generally, corporations are not limited in the amount of interest expense they may deduct. However, the deductibility of expenses (including interest) from certain activities may be limited.[48] In contrast, individuals generally may not deduct interest expense on loans used for personal purposes, unless the loan is secured by a home. Furthermore, individuals may only deduct interest expense associated with investments to the extent of net investment income and interest on qualified education loans.[49]

Because the deductibility of interest expense associated with certain activities is limited, the IRS provides rules for allocating interest expense among activities. Under these rules, interest is allocated in the same manner as the debt with respect to which the interest is paid, and debt is allocated by tracing disbursements of the debt proceeds to specific expenditures. The interest tracing rules are complex and depend on whether loan proceeds are commingled with other cash and the length of time the loan proceeds are held before they are spent.

## TAXES

As with interest expense, tax payments in a business or investment context are generally deductible. However, most Federal taxes are not deductible. Individuals may also deduct tax payments, subject to limitations (discussed in Chapter 15). One unique problem associated with determining the deductibility of taxes relates to real estate taxes paid during a year when the real estate is sold.

Real estate taxes for the entire year are apportioned between the buyer and seller based on the number of days the property was held by each during the real property tax year. This apportionment is required whether the tax is paid by the buyer or the seller or is prorated according to the purchase agreement. It is the apportionment that determines who is entitled to deduct the real estate taxes in

---

[48]See, for example, the discussion of the passive activity limits in Chapter 5.

[49]See Chapter 15 for a more detailed discussion of the deductibility of interest by individuals.

the year of sale. The required apportionment prevents the shifting of the deduction for real estate taxes from buyer to seller, or vice versa.

In making the apportionment, the assessment date and the lien date are disregarded. The date of sale counts as a day the property is owned by the buyer. In leap years, the taxes are prorated over 366 days.

**EXAMPLE 30**

A county's real property tax year runs from April 1 to March 31. Nuthatch Corporation, the owner on April 1, 2005, of real property located in the county, sells the real property to Crane, Inc., on June 30, 2005. Crane owns the real property from June 30, 2005, through March 31, 2006. The tax for the real property tax year April 1, 2005, through March 31, 2006, is $3,650. The portion of the real property tax treated as imposed upon Nuthatch, the seller, is $900 [(90/365) × $3,650, April 1 through June 29, 2005], and $2,750 [(275/365) × $3,650, June 30, 2005, through March 31, 2006] of the tax is treated as imposed upon Crane, the purchaser. ■

If the actual real estate taxes are not prorated between the buyer and seller as part of the purchase agreement, adjustments are required. The adjustments are necessary to determine the amount realized by the seller and the adjusted basis of the property to the buyer. If the buyer pays the entire amount of the tax, it effectively has paid the seller's portion of the real estate tax and has therefore paid more for the property than the actual purchase price. Thus, the amount of real estate tax that is apportioned to the seller (for Federal income tax purposes) and paid by the buyer is added to the buyer's adjusted basis. The seller must increase the amount realized on the sale by the same amount.

**EXAMPLE 31**

Seth sells real estate on October 3, 2006, for $100,000. The buyer, Winslow Company, pays the real estate taxes of $3,650 for the 2006 calendar year, which is the real estate property tax year. Of the real estate taxes, $2,750 (for 275 days) is apportioned to and is deductible by the seller, Seth, and $900 (for 90 days) of the taxes is deductible by Winslow. The buyer has paid Seth's real estate taxes of $2,750 and has therefore paid $102,750 for the property. Winslow's basis is increased to $102,750, and the amount realized by Seth from the sale is increased to $102,750. ■

The opposite result occurs if the seller (rather than the buyer) pays the real estate taxes. In this case, the seller reduces the amount realized from the sale by the amount that has been apportioned to the buyer. The buyer is required to reduce his or her adjusted basis by a corresponding amount.

**EXAMPLE 32**

Silver Corporation sells real estate to Butch for $50,000 on October 3, 2006. While Silver held the property, it paid the real estate taxes of $1,095 for the calendar year, which is the real estate property tax year. Although Silver paid the entire $1,095 of real estate taxes, $270 of that amount is apportioned to Butch, based on the number of days he owned the property, and is therefore deductible by him. The effect is that the buyer, Butch, has paid only $49,730 ($50,000 − $270) for the property. The amount realized by Silver, the seller, is reduced by $270, and Butch reduces his basis in the property to $49,730. ■

## MANUFACTURERS' DEDUCTION

The American Jobs Creation Act of 2004 was enacted to replace certain tax provisions that our world trading partners regarded as allowing unfair advantage to U.S. exports. Among other changes, the Act creates a new deduction based on the income from manufacturing activities (designated as *production activities*). The new **manufacturers' deduction** is contained in § 199 and is effective for taxable years beginning after December 31, 2004.

*Definition Page C-10* ←

**Operational Rules.** At present, the manufacturers' deduction is based on the following formula:

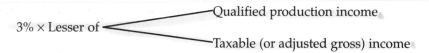

$$3\% \times \text{Lesser of} \begin{cases} \text{Qualified production income} \\ \text{Taxable (or adjusted gross) income} \end{cases}$$

The deduction, however, cannot exceed 50 percent of an employer's W–2 wages.

A phase-in provision increases the 3 percent rate that is applicable for 2005–2006 to 6 percent for 2007 through 2009 and to 9 percent for 2010 and thereafter. Ultimately, therefore, the deduction will be determined under a 9 percent rate.

*Eligible Taxpayers.* The deduction is available to a variety of taxpayers including individuals, partnerships, S corporations, C corporations, cooperatives, estates, and trusts. For a pass-through entity (e.g., partnerships, S corporations), the deduction flows through to the individual owners. In the case of a sole proprietor, a deduction *for* AGI results and probably will be reflected as a Schedule C item.

**EXAMPLE 33**

Amanda, a calendar year taxpayer, owns and operates a shop that manufactures costume jewelry. For 2005, she has AGI of $360,000 and qualified production income of $380,000. Amanda's manufacturers' deduction is $10,800 [3% × $360,000 (the lesser of $380,000 or $360,000)]. Thus, Amanda's AGI becomes $349,200 ($360,000 – $10,800). (It has been assumed that the W–2 wage limitation is not a problem.) ■

~Definition page (14

*Eligible Income.* **Qualified production income** is the total of qualified production receipts reduced by:

- Cost of goods sold that are attributable to such receipts.
- Other deductions, expenses, or losses that are directly allocable to such receipts.
- A share of other deductions, expenses, and losses that are not directly allocable to such receipts or another class of income.

The term also includes receipts for certain services rendered in connection with construction projects in the United States.

Qualified production receipts do not include proceeds from the sale of food and beverages prepared at a retail establishment.

**Observations and Operational Problems.** Although it is called the "manufacturers' deduction," note the broad definition of production receipts. Not only is traditional manufacturing included, but so are other activities such as agriculture, extraction, and construction. Also note that the manufacturers' deduction, unlike the export subsidies it replaced, is not conditioned on the foreign sale of the goods produced. In this regard, domestic and foreign activities will be treated alike.

Because many of the concepts introduced by the manufacturers' deduction are unique, current tax law offers little assistance in resolving the problems that are bound to arise. Some of these are noted in the observations that follow.

- How much activity must take place before manufacturing occurs? For example, is the mere packaging of another's product enough? The law recognizes that production *in part* will suffice, but only if such production is *significant*.
- As to construction projects, qualifying activities are limited to structural improvements—cosmetic changes will not be enough. So, can repainting a house (cosmetic) be accompanied by some sheet rock replacement to make it structural?

- When a taxpayer has integrated businesses with some that qualify as manufacturing and others that do not, manipulation is to be expected. Income will be shifted *to* and expenses will be shifted *from* the businesses that qualify. What safeguards will be imposed to preclude this type of manipulation?

The IRS can be expected to provide answers to these questions and to issue guidelines that will aid taxpayers in utilizing the manufacturers' deduction correctly.

**LO.6**

Determine the amount of cost recovery under MACRS, and apply the § 179 expensing election and the deduction limitations on listed property and automobiles when making the MACRS calculation.

# Cost Recovery Allowances

## OVERVIEW

Taxpayers may write off the cost of certain assets that are used in a trade or business or held for the production of income. A write-off may take the form of a *cost recovery allowance* (depreciation under prior law), depletion, or amortization. Tangible assets, other than natural resources, are written off through cost recovery allowances. Natural resources, such as oil, gas, coal, and timber, are *depleted*. Intangible assets, such as copyrights and patents, are *amortized*. Generally, no write-off is allowed for an asset that does not have a determinable useful life.

The tax rules for writing off the cost of business assets differ from the accounting rules. Several methods are available for determining depreciation for accounting purposes, including the straight-line, declining-balance, and sum-of-the-years' digits methods. Historically, *depreciation* for tax purposes was computed using variations of these accounting methods. Congress completely overhauled the **depreciation rules** in 1981 tax legislation by creating the **accelerated cost recovery system (ACRS)**. Substantial modifications were made to ACRS in 1986 tax legislation, which resulted in the **modified accelerated cost recovery system (MACRS)** replacing ACRS.

The statutory changes that have taken place since 1980 have widened the gap that exists between the accounting and tax versions of depreciation. The tax rules that existed prior to 1981 were much more compatible with generally accepted accounting principles. This chapter focuses on the MACRS rules because they cover more recent property acquisitions (i.e., after 1986) and their use is more widespread.

## CONCEPTS RELATING TO DEPRECIATION

**Nature of Property.**    Property includes both realty (real property) and personalty (personal property). *Realty* generally includes land and buildings permanently affixed to the land. *Personalty* is defined as any asset that is not realty. Personalty includes furniture, machinery, equipment, and many other types of assets. Do not confuse personalty (or personal property) with personal-use property. Personal-use property is any property (realty or personalty) that is held for personal use rather than for use in a trade or business or an income-producing activity. Cost recovery is not allowed for personal-use assets.

In summary, both realty and personalty can be either business-use/income-producing property or personal-use property. Examples include a residence (realty that is personal use), an office building (realty that is business use), a dump truck (personalty that is business use), and regular wearing apparel (personalty that is personal use). It is imperative that this distinction between the classification of an asset (realty or personalty) and the use to which the asset is put (business or personal) be understood.

*[Handwritten margin notes: "Definitions: Depreciation Rules Page C-6, Accelerated Cost Recovery System (ACRS) Page C-1, Modified Accelerated Cost Recovery System (MACRS) Page C-11"]*

**TAX FACT**

## COST RECOVERY BY ANY OTHER NAME

Not surprisingly, the most prevalent write-off of assets used in a trade or business or in the production of income comes in the form of the cost recovery or depreciation allowances. Of the approximately $770 billion of corporate deductions in a recent year, the relative use of the three broad types of write-offs is shown below.

| | Percentage |
|---|---|
| Amortization | 14.34 |
| Cost recovery or depreciation | 84.39 |
| Depletion | 1.27 |
| | 100.00 |

**Source:** Corporation Income Tax Returns, 2001; Table 2—Selected Balance Sheet, Income Statement, and Tax Items by Asset Size; September 2004.

Assets used in a trade or business or for the production of income are eligible for cost recovery if they are subject to wear and tear, decay or decline from natural causes, or obsolescence. Assets that do not decline in value on a predictable basis or that do not have a determinable useful life (e.g., land, stock, antiques) are not eligible for cost recovery.

**Placed in Service Requirement.** The key date for the commencement of depreciation is the date an asset is placed in service. This date, and not the purchase date of an asset, is the relevant date. This distinction is particularly important for an asset that is purchased near the end of the tax year, but not placed in service until after the beginning of the following tax year.

**Cost Recovery Allowed or Allowable.** The basis of cost recovery property must be reduced by the cost recovery *allowed* and by not less than the *allowable* amount. The allowed cost recovery is the cost recovery actually taken, whereas the allowable cost recovery is the amount that could have been taken under the applicable cost recovery method. If the taxpayer does not claim any cost recovery on property during a particular year, the basis of the property must still be reduced by the amount of cost recovery that should have been deducted (the *allowable* cost recovery).

**EXAMPLE 34**

On March 15, Heron Corporation paid $10,000 for a copier to be used in its business. The copier is five-year property. Heron elected to use the straight-line method of cost recovery, but did not take any cost recovery allowance in year 3 or 4. Therefore, the allowed cost recovery (cost recovery actually deducted) and the allowable cost recovery are as follows:[50]

---

[50]The cost recovery allowances are based on the half-year convention, which allows a half-year's cost recovery in the first and last years of the recovery period.

**Bridge to Finance**

For many business entities, success in producing goods for sale is dependent on the efficient use of fixed assets, such as machinery and equipment. An important question for such businesses to resolve is how they should gain access to the required complement of fixed assets: that is, whether the assets should be purchased or leased. To answer this question, the taxpayer must determine which alternative is more cost-effective. Critical to this assessment is quantifying the after-tax cost (including the associated tax benefits) of each option.

Purchasing productive assets for business use often necessitates an immediate cash outflow. However, the tax savings resulting from the available depreciation expense deductions mitigate the impact of that outflow, by reducing the taxpayer's taxable income and the income tax paid for the year. Consequently, the tax savings from the depreciation calculation associated with the purchase of an asset reduce the after-tax cost of employing the asset. The analysis can be refined further by evaluating the tax savings from the depreciation deductions in present value terms by quantifying the tax savings from the depreciation expense over the life of the asset. The asset's purchase also can be financed with debt.

Taxpayers who lease rather than buy an asset benefit by not giving up the use of funds that otherwise would have gone to purchase the asset. Lessees also forgo the opportunity to claim depreciation deductions; however, they reduce the cost of the leasing option by claiming the lease expense as a deduction against their tax base.

| | Cost Recovery Allowed | Cost Recovery Allowable |
|---|---|---|
| Year 1 | $1,000 | $ 1,000 |
| Year 2 | 2,000 | 2,000 |
| Year 3 | –0– | 2,000 |
| Year 4 | –0– | 2,000 |
| Year 5 | 2,000 | 2,000 |
| Year 6 | 1,000 | 1,000 |
| Totals | $6,000 | $10,000 |

The adjusted basis of the copier at the end of year 6 is $0 ($10,000 cost – $10,000 *allowable* cost recovery). If Heron sells the copier for $800 in year 7, it will recognize an $800 gain ($800 amount realized – $0 adjusted basis). ■

**Cost Recovery Basis for Personal-Use Assets Converted to Business or Income-Producing Use.** If personal-use assets are converted to business or income-producing use, the basis for cost recovery and for loss is the lower of the adjusted basis or the fair market value at the time the property was converted. As a result of this basis rule, losses that occurred while the property was personal-use property will not be recognized for tax purposes through the cost recovery of the property.

**EXAMPLE 35**

Hans acquires a personal residence for $120,000. Four years later, when the fair market value is only $100,000, he establishes a consulting company and uses the residence solely for office space. The basis for cost recovery is $100,000, since the fair market value is less than

■ **EXHIBIT 4–2**

Cost Recovery Periods: MACRS Personalty

| Class | Examples |
|-------|----------|
| 3-year | Tractor units for use over-the-road<br>Any horse that is not a racehorse and is more than 12 years old at the time it is placed in service<br>Special tools used in the manufacturing of motor vehicles, such as dies, fixtures, molds, and patterns |
| 5-year | Automobiles and taxis<br>Light and heavy general-purpose trucks<br>Typewriters, calculators, and copiers<br>Computers and peripheral equipment |
| 7-year | Office furniture, fixtures, and equipment<br>Agricultural machinery and equipment |
| 10-year | Vessels, barges, tugs, and similar water transportation equipment<br>Assets used for petroleum refining or for the manufacture of grain and grain mill products, sugar and sugar products, or vegetable oils and vegetable oil products<br>Single-purpose agricultural or horticultural structures |
| 15-year | Land improvements<br>Assets used for industrial steam and electric generation and/or distribution systems<br>Assets used in the manufacture of cement |
| 20-year | Farm buildings except single-purpose agricultural and horticultural structures<br>Water utilities |

the adjusted basis. The $20,000 decline in value is deemed to be personal (since it occurred while Hans held the property for personal use). Therefore, depreciation deductions will be based on $100,000 rather than $120,000. ■

## MODIFIED ACCELERATED COST RECOVERY SYSTEM (MACRS)

MACRS provides separate cost recovery tables for realty (real property) and personalty (personal property). Write-offs are not available for land because it does not have a determinable useful life. Cost recovery allowances for real property, other than land, are based on recovery lives specified in the law. The IRS provides tables that specify cost recovery allowances for personalty and for realty.

## COST RECOVERY FOR PERSONAL PROPERTY

MACRS provides that the cost recovery basis of eligible personalty (and certain realty) is recovered over 3, 5, 7, 10, 15, or 20 years.[51] Examples of property in the different cost recovery categories are shown in Exhibit 4–2.[52]

Accelerated depreciation is allowed for these six MACRS classes of property. The appropriate computational methods and conventions are built into the tables, so, in general, it is not necessary to perform any calculations. To determine the amount of the cost recovery allowance, simply identify the asset by class and go

---

[51]Property is classified by recovery period under MACRS based on asset depreciation range (ADR) midpoint lives provided by the IRS. Rev.Proc. 87–56, 1987–2 C.B. 674 is the source for the ADR midpoint lives.

[52]§ 168(e).

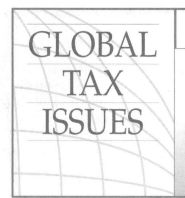

**CHANGING THE LIFE OF A TRUCK**

The Australian Tax Office changed the life of a truck, for depreciation computations, from five years to seven and one-half years with the effective date being January 1, 2005. Because of this change, truck operators could reduce their tax liability by buying a new truck before the end of 2004. Under the diminishing value of depreciation method, the write-off was 30 percent for 2004. Starting in 2005, the write-off is only 20 percent.

SOURCE: Adapted from MATP, "Truckload of Tax Savings," *The Daily Telegraph* (Sydney, Australia), September 25, 2004, p. G42.

*Definition*
*Half-Year Convention*
*Page C-8*

to the appropriate table.[53] The MACRS percentages for personalty are shown in Table 4–1 (MACRS tables begin at the end of the chapter prior to the Problem Materials).

Taxpayers may *elect* the straight-line method to compute cost recovery allowances for each of these classes of property. Certain property is not eligible for accelerated cost recovery and must be depreciated under an alternative depreciation system (ADS). Both the straight-line election and ADS are discussed later in the chapter.

MACRS views property as placed in service in the middle of the first year and allows a half-year of cost recovery in the year of acquisition and in the final year of cost recovery (the **half-year convention**).[54] Thus, for example, the statutory recovery period for three-year property begins in the middle of the year the asset is placed in service and ends three years later. In practical terms, this means the actual write-off periods cover 4, 6, 8, 11, 16, and 21 tax years. MACRS also allows for a half-year of cost recovery in the year of disposition or retirement.

**EXAMPLE 36**

Robin Corporation acquires a five-year class asset on April 10, 2005, for $30,000. Robin's cost recovery deduction for 2005 is $6,000, computed as follows:

MACRS calculation based on Table 4–1
    ($30,000 × .20)                                    $6,000

**EXAMPLE 37**

Assume the same facts as in Example 36 and that Robin disposes of the asset on March 5, 2007. Robin's cost recovery deduction for 2007 is $2,880 [$30,000 × ½ × .192 (Table 4–1)]. ■

*Definition*
*Additional First-Year*
*Depreciation*
*Page C-2*

**Additional First-Year Depreciation.**   The Job Creation and Worker Assistance Act of 2002 provided for **additional first-year depreciation** on qualified property acquired after September 10, 2001, and before September 11, 2004, and placed in service before January 1, 2005. The provision allows for an additional 30 percent cost recovery in the year the asset is placed in service. The term *qualified property* includes most types of *new* property other than buildings. The term *new* means original or first use of the property. Property that is used but new to the taxpayer does not qualify. The Jobs and Growth Tax Relief Reconciliation Act of 2003 increased the additional first-year depreciation allowance percentage from 30 percent to 50 percent. The higher percentage applies to property acquired after May 5, 2003, and placed in service before January 1, 2005. Fifty percent additional first-year

---

[53]§ 168(b).                              [54]§ 168(d)(4)(A).

property must meet the same requirements as the 30 percent additional first-year property except for the May 5, 2003 acquisition date.[55]

The additional first-year depreciation applies to the year in which the qualifying property was placed in service and is claimed in addition to the otherwise available depreciation deduction. After calculating the additional first-year depreciation, the standard cost recovery allowance under MACRS is calculated by multiplying the cost recovery basis (original cost recovery basis less additional first-year depreciation) by the percentage that reflects the applicable cost recovery method and the applicable cost recovery convention.

**EXAMPLE 38**

Morgan acquires a five-year class asset on March 20, 2004, for $50,000. Morgan's cost recovery deduction for 2004 is $30,000, computed as follows:

| | |
|---|---:|
| 50% additional first-year depreciation | |
| ($50,000 × .50) | $25,000 |
| MACRS cost recovery | |
| [($50,000 − $25,000) × .20 (Table 4–1)] | 5,000 |
| Total cost recovery | $30,000 |

**EXAMPLE 39**

Assume the same facts as in Example 38, except that the asset was acquired on April 24, 2005. Because additional first-year depreciation is not allowed on property placed in service after December 31, 2004, Morgan's cost recovery deduction for 2005 is $10,000 [$50,000 × .20 (Table 4–1)]. ■

**EXAMPLE 40**

Assume the same facts as in Example 39 and that Morgan disposes of the asset on October 17, 2007. Morgan's cost recovery deduction for 2007 is $4,800 [$50,000 × ½ × .192 (Table 4–1)]. ■

**Mid-Quarter Convention.** If more than 40 percent of the value of property other than eligible real estate[56] is placed in service during the last quarter of the year, a **mid-quarter convention** applies.[57] Under the convention, property acquisitions are grouped by the quarter they were acquired for cost recovery purposes. Acquisitions during the first quarter are allowed 10.5 months of cost recovery; the second quarter, 7.5 months; the third quarter, 4.5 months; and the fourth quarter, 1.5 months. The percentages are shown in Table 4–2.

*[handwritten: * Definition Mid-Quarter Convention - page C11]*

**EXAMPLE 41**

Silver Corporation acquires the following five-year class property in 2005.

| Acquisition Dates | Cost |
|---|---:|
| February 15 | $ 200,000 |
| July 10 | 400,000 |
| December 5 | 600,000 |
| Total | $1,200,000 |

If Silver Corporation uses the statutory percentage method, the cost recovery allowances for the first two years are computed as indicated below. Because more than 40% ($600,000/

---

[55]§ 168(k).
[56]See Cost Recovery for Real Estate later in this chapter for a discussion of eligible real estate.

[57]§ 168(d)(3).

## CAPITAL INVESTMENT WRITE-OFFS REDUCE CORPORATE TAXES

A study by the Citizens for Tax Justice and its affiliate, the Institute on Taxation and Economic Policy, found that over the last three years the largest and most profitable U.S. companies paid less in corporate income taxes. This decline in tax liability occurred as corporate profits increased. The study attributed the decline in tax payments in part to the changes in the tax laws allowing additional first-year depreciation and increased expensing under § 179.

SOURCE: Adapted from Lynnley Browning, "Study Finds Accelerating Decline in Corporate Taxes," *New York Times*, September 23, 2004, p. C3.

$1,200,000 = 50%) of the acquisitions are in the last quarter, the mid-quarter convention applies.

**2005**

| | Mid-Quarter Convention Depreciation | | Total Depreciation |
|---|---|---|---|
| February 15 | $200,000 × .35 (Table 4–2) | = | $ 70,000 |
| July 10 | $400,000 × .15 | = | 60,000 |
| December 5 | $600,000 × .05 | = | 30,000 |
| Total | | | $160,000 |

**2006**

| | Mid-Quarter Convention Depreciation | | Total Depreciation |
|---|---|---|---|
| February 15 | $200,000 × .26 (Table 4–2) | = | $ 52,000 |
| July 10 | $400,000 × .34 | = | 136,000 |
| December 5 | $600,000 × .38 | = | 228,000 |
| Total | | | $416,000 |

When property to which the mid-quarter convention applies is disposed of, the property is treated as though it were disposed of at the midpoint of the quarter. Hence, in the quarter of disposition, cost recovery is allowed for one-half of the quarter.

**EXAMPLE 42**

Assume the same facts as in Example 41, except that Silver Corporation sells the $400,000 asset on November 30, 2006. The cost recovery allowance for 2006 is computed as follows.

| | | | |
|---|---|---|---|
| February 15 | $200,000 × .26 (Table 4–2) | = | $ 52,000 |
| July 10 | $400,000 × .34 × (3.5/4) | = | 119,000 |
| December 5 | $600,000 × .38 | = | 228,000 |
| Total | | | $399,000 |

## COST RECOVERY FOR REAL ESTATE

Under MACRS, the cost recovery period for residential rental real estate is 27.5 years, and the straight-line method is used for computing the cost recovery allowance. **Residential rental real estate** includes property where 80 percent or

Definition page C-16

## CONCEPT SUMMARY 4–1

### MACRS Computational Rules: Statutory Percentage and Straight-Line Methods

|  | Personal Property | Real Property |
|---|---|---|
| Convention | Half-year or mid-quarter | Mid-month |
| Cost recovery deduction in the year of disposition | Half-year for year of disposition or half-quarter for quarter of disposition | Half-month for month of disposition |

*Dehnihon*
*Mid-Month Convention*
*Page C-11*

more of the gross rental revenues are from nontransient dwelling units (e.g., an apartment building). Hotels, motels, and similar establishments are not residential rental property. Nonresidential real estate has a recovery period of 39 years (31.5 years for such property placed in service before May 13, 1993) and is also depreciated using the straight-line method.[58]

Some items of real property are not treated as real estate for purposes of MACRS. For example, single-purpose agricultural structures are in the 10-year MACRS class. Land improvements are in the 15-year MACRS class.

All eligible real estate placed in service after June 22, 1984 (under both ACRS and MACRS) is depreciated using the **mid-month convention.** Regardless of when during the month the property is placed in service, it is deemed to have been placed in service at the middle of the month. This allows for one-half month's cost recovery for the month the property is placed in service. If the property is disposed of before the end of the recovery period, one-half month's cost recovery is permitted for the month of disposition regardless of the specific date of disposition.

Cost recovery is computed by multiplying the applicable rate (taken from a table) by the cost recovery basis. The MACRS real property rates are provided in Table 4–3.

**EXAMPLE 43**

Badger Rentals, Inc., acquired a building on April 1, 1993, for $800,000. If the building is classified as residential rental real estate, the cost recovery allowance for 2005 is $29,088 (.03636 × $800,000). If the building is classified as nonresidential real estate, the 2005 cost recovery allowance is $25,400 (.03175 × $800,000). (See the first two sections of Table 4–3 for the percentages.) ■

**EXAMPLE 44**

Assume the same facts as in Example 43, except that Badger acquired the nonresidential building on November 19, 2005. The 2005 cost recovery allowance is $2,568 [$800,000 × .00321 (Table 4–3)]. (See the last section of Table 4–3 for the percentage.) ■

An overview of MACRS rules is provided in Concept Summary 4–1.

### STRAIGHT-LINE ELECTION

Although MACRS requires straight-line depreciation for all eligible real estate as previously discussed, the taxpayer may *elect* to use the straight-line method for personal property.[59] The property is depreciated using the class life (recovery period) of the asset with a half-year convention or a mid-quarter convention, whichever is applicable. The election is available on a class-by-class and year-by-year basis. The percentages for the straight-line election with a half-year convention appear in Table 4–4.

---

[58]§§ 168(b), (c), and (e).          [59]§ 168(b)(5).

**EXAMPLE 45**

Terry acquires a 10-year class asset on August 4, 2005, for $100,000. He elects the straight-line method of cost recovery. Terry's cost recovery deduction for 2005 is $5,000 ($100,000 × .05). His cost recovery deduction for 2006 is $10,000 ($100,000 × .10). (See Table 4–4 for the percentages.) ■

*[handwritten margin note: Definition — § 179 Expensing Election — Page C-16]*

## ELECTION TO EXPENSE ASSETS UNDER § 179

Section 179 (Election to Expense Certain Depreciable Business Assets) permits a taxpayer to elect to deduct up to $105,000 in 2005[60] of the acquisition cost of *tangible personal property* used in a trade or business. Amounts that are expensed under § 179 may not be capitalized and depreciated. The **§ 179 expensing election** is an annual election and applies to the acquisition cost of property placed in service that year. The immediate expense election is not available for real property or for property used for the production of income.[61] In addition, any elected § 179 expense is taken *before* the 50 or 30 percent additional first-year depreciation is computed. The base for calculating the standard MACRS deduction is net of the § 179 expense and the 50 or 30 percent additional first-year depreciation.

**EXAMPLE 46**

Kodiak Corporation acquires machinery (five-year class asset) on February 1, 2004, at a cost of $152,000 and elects to expense $102,000 under § 179. Kodiak also takes the 50% additional first-year depreciation and the statutory percentage cost recovery (see Table 4–1 for the percentage) for 2004. As a result, the total deduction for the year is calculated as follows.

| | |
|---|---|
| § 179 expense | $102,000 |
| 50% additional first-year depreciation [($152,000 − $102,000) × .50] | 25,000 |
| Standard MACRS calculation [($152,000 − $102,000 − $25,000) × .20] | 5,000 |
| Total | $132,000 |

■

**EXAMPLE 47**

Assume the same facts as in Example 46, except that the machinery is acquired on February 15, 2005, and Kodiak elects to expense $105,000 under § 179. Kodiak also takes the statutory percentage cost recovery for 2005. As a result, the total deduction for the year is calculated as follows.

| | |
|---|---|
| § 179 expense | $105,000 |
| Standard MACRS calculation [($152,000 − $105,000) × .20] | 9,400 |
| Total | $114,400 |

■

**Annual Limitations.**   Two additional limitations apply to the amount deductible under § 179. First, the ceiling amount on the deduction is reduced dollar-for-dollar when property (other than ineligible real estate) placed in service during the taxable year exceeds $420,000 ($410,000 in 2004). Second, the amount expensed under § 179 cannot exceed the aggregate amount of taxable income derived from the conduct of any trade or business by the taxpayer. Taxable income of a trade or business is computed without regard to the amount expensed under § 179. Any § 179 deduction in excess of taxable income is carried forward to future taxable years and added to other amounts eligible for expensing. The § 179 amount eligible for expensing in a carry-forward year is limited to the *lesser* of (1) the appropriate statutory dollar amount ($105,000 in 2005) reduced by the cost of § 179 property placed in service in excess

---

[60]The expense amount was $100,000 for assets placed in service in 2003 and $102,000 for assets placed in service in 2004.

[61]§§ 179(b) and (d).

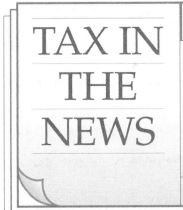

## CHANGING BUSINESS DEDUCTIONS

The Oregon legislature is considering a bill to increase revenues so as to balance the state budget for the next three years. The new law, if enacted, would require companies using sport utility vehicles to add back, in computing Oregon taxable income, the § 179 expense deduction and the bonus depreciation deduction allowed under Federal tax law. The changes affecting business taxes would provide $146 million of the $800 million additional revenue required to balance the state budget.

SOURCE: Adapted from Boaz Herzog, "Businesses Split on Merits of Measure 30," *The Oregonian*, January 19, 2004, p. E01.

of $420,000 in the carryforward year or (2) the business income limitation in the carryforward year.

**EXAMPLE 48**

Jill owns a computer service and operates it as a sole proprietorship. In 2005, she will net $11,000 before considering any § 179 deduction. If Jill spends $491,000 on new equipment, her § 179 expense deduction is computed as follows.

| | |
|---|---:|
| § 179 deduction before adjustment | $105,000 |
| Less: Dollar limitation reduction ($491,000 − $420,000) | (71,000) |
| Remaining § 179 deduction | $ 34,000 |
| Business income limitation | $ 11,000 |
| § 179 deduction allowed | $ 11,000 |
| § 179 deduction carryforward ($34,000 − $11,000) | $ 23,000 |

**Effect on Basis.** The basis of the property for cost recovery purposes is reduced by the § 179 amount after it is adjusted for property placed in service in excess of $420,000. This adjusted amount does not reflect any business income limitation.

**EXAMPLE 49**

Assume the same facts as in Example 48 and that the new equipment is five-year class property. After considering the § 179 deduction, Jill's cost recovery deduction for 2005 is calculated as follows. (See Table 4–1 for the percentage.)

| | |
|---|---:|
| Standard MACRS calculation [($491,000 − $34,000) × .20] | $91,400 |

### BUSINESS AND PERSONAL USE OF AUTOMOBILES AND OTHER LISTED PROPERTY

Limits exist on MACRS deductions for automobiles and other **listed property** used for both personal and business purposes.[62] These limits would apply, for example, to an automobile used by a sole proprietor partly for business purposes and partly for personal use.

If the listed property is *predominantly* used for business, the taxpayer is allowed to use the *statutory percentage method* to recover the cost. In cases where the property is *not predominantly* used for business, the cost is recovered using the *straight-line*

---

[62]§ 280F.

*method.* The statutory percentage method results in a faster recovery of cost than the straight-line method. Listed property includes the following:

- Any passenger automobile.
- Any other property used as a means of transportation.
- Any property of a type generally used for purposes of entertainment, recreation, or amusement.
- Any computer or peripheral equipment, with the exception of equipment used exclusively at a regular business establishment, including a qualifying home office.
- Any cellular telephone or other similar telecommunications equipment.
- Any other property specified in the Regulations.

### Automobiles and Other Listed Property Used Predominantly in Business.

For listed property to be considered as predominantly used in business, its *business usage* must exceed 50 percent.[63] The use of listed property for production of income does not qualify as business use for purposes of the more-than-50 percent test. However, both production-of-income and business-use percentages are used to compute the cost recovery deduction.

EXAMPLE 50

On September 1, 2005, Emma places in service listed five-year recovery property. The property cost $10,000. If Emma uses the property 40% for business and 25% for the production of income, the property is not considered as predominantly used for business. The cost is recovered using straight-line cost recovery. Emma's cost recovery allowance for the year is $650 ($10,000 × .10 × .65). If, however, Emma uses the property 60% for business and 25% for the production of income, the property is considered as used predominantly for business. Therefore, she may use the statutory percentage method. Emma's cost recovery allowance for the year is $1,700 ($10,000 × .20 × .85). ■

The method for determining the percentage of business usage for listed property is specified in the Regulations. The Regulations provide that for automobiles a mileage-based percentage is to be used. Other listed property is to use the most appropriate unit of time (e.g., hours) the property is actually used (rather than available for use).[64]

### Limits on Cost Recovery for Automobiles.

The law places special limitations on the cost recovery deduction for *passenger automobiles*.[65] These statutory dollar limits were imposed on passenger automobiles because of the belief that the tax system was being used to underwrite automobiles whose cost and luxury far exceeded what was needed for their business use.

The following limits apply to the cost recovery deductions for passenger automobiles for 2004.[66]

| Year of Use | Recovery Limitation* |
|---|---|
| 1 | $2,960 |
| 2 | 4,800 |
| 3 | 2,850 |
| Succeeding years until all cost is recovered | 1,675 |

*The indexed amounts for 2005 were not available at the time of this writing.

---

[63]§ 280F(b)(3).
[64]Reg. § 1.280F–6T(e).
[65]§ 280F(d)(5).

[66]§ 280F(a)(1). Because the 2005 indexed amounts were not available at the time of this writing, the 2004 amounts are used in the Examples and Problem Materials.

There are also separate cost recovery limitations for trucks and vans and for electric automobiles. Because these limitations are applied in the same manner as those imposed on passenger automobiles, these additional limitations are not discussed further in this chapter.

The limits are imposed before any percentage reduction for personal use. In addition, the limitation in the first year includes any amount the taxpayer elects to expense under § 179.[67] If the passenger automobile is used partly for personal use, the personal-use percentage is ignored for the purpose of determining the unrecovered cost available for deduction in later years.

**EXAMPLE 51**

On July 1, 2005, Dan places in service a new automobile that cost $40,000. He does not elect § 179 expensing. The car is always used 80% for business and 20% for personal purposes. Dan chooses the MACRS 200% declining-balance method of cost recovery (see the 5-year column in Table 4–1). The depreciation computation for 2005–2010 is summarized below:

| Year | MACRS Amount | Recovery Limitation | Depreciation Allowed |
|------|--------------|---------------------|----------------------|
| 2005 | $6,400 ($40,000 × 20% × 80%) | $2,368 ($2,960 × 80%) | $2,368 |
| 2006 | $10,240 ($40,000 × 32% × 80%) | $3,840 ($4,800 × 80%) | $3,840 |
| 2007 | $6,144 ($40,000 × 19.2% × 80%) | $2,280 ($2,850 × 80%) | $2,280 |
| 2008 | $3,686 ($40,000 × 11.52% × 80%) | $1,340 ($1,675 × 80%) | $1,340 |
| 2009 | $3,686 ($40,000 × 11.52% × 80%) | $1,340 ($1,675 × 80%) | $1,340 |
| 2010 | $1,843 ($40,000 × 5.76% × 80%) | $1,340 ($1,675 × 80%) | $1,340 |

The cost recovery allowed is the lesser of the MACRS amount or the recovery limitation. If Dan continues to use the car after 2010, his cost recovery is limited to the lesser of the recoverable basis or the recovery limitation (i.e., $1,675 × business use percentage). For this purpose, the recoverable basis is computed as if the full recovery limitation was allowed even if it was not. Thus, the recoverable basis as of January 1, 2011, is $24,365 ($40,000 − $2,960 − $4,800 − $2,850 − $1,675 − $1,675 − $1,675). ■

The cost recovery limitations are maximum amounts. If the regular calculation produces a lesser amount of cost recovery, the lesser amount is used.

**EXAMPLE 52**

On April 2, 2005, Gail places in service a pre-owned automobile that cost $10,000. The car is always used 70% for business and 30% for personal use. Therefore, the cost recovery allowance for 2005 is $1,400 ($10,000 × .20 × .70), which is less than $2,072 ($2,960 × .70). ■

The cost recovery limitations apply *only* to passenger automobiles and not to other listed property.

**Special Limitation.** The American Jobs Creation Act of 2004 (AJCA) placed a limit on the § 179 deduction for certain vehicles not subject to the statutory dollar

---

[67]§ 280F(d)(1).

limits on cost recovery deductions that are imposed on passenger automobiles. This new limit is $25,000. The limit applies to sport utility vehicles with an unloaded GVW rating of more than 6,000 pounds and not more than 14,000 pounds.[68]

**EXAMPLE 53**

During 2005, Jay acquires and places in service a sport utility vehicle that cost $70,000 and has a GVW of 8,000 pounds. Jay uses the vehicle 100% of the time for business purposes. The total deduction for 2005 with respect to the SUV is $34,000, computed as follows:

| | |
|---|---:|
| § 179 expense | $25,000 |
| Standard MACRS calculation | |
| [($70,000 − $25,000) × .20 (Table 4–1)] | 9,000 |
| Total | $34,000 |

**Automobiles and Other Listed Property Not Used Predominantly in Business.** The cost of listed property that does not pass the more-than-50 percent business usage test in the year the property is placed in service must be recovered using the straight-line method.[69] The straight-line method to be used is that required under the alternative depreciation system (introduced later in the chapter). This system requires a straight-line recovery period of five years for automobiles. However, even though the straight-line method is used, the cost recovery allowance for passenger automobiles cannot exceed the dollar limitations noted above.

If the listed property fails the more-than-50 percent business usage test, the straight-line method must be used for the remainder of the property's life. This applies even if at some later date the business usage of the property increases to more than 50 percent. Even though the straight-line method must continue to be used, however, the amount of cost recovery will reflect the increase in business usage.

**Change from Predominantly Business Use.** If the business-use percentage of listed property falls to 50 percent or lower after the year the property is placed in service, the property is subject to *cost recovery recapture*. The amount required to be recaptured and included in the taxpayer's return as ordinary income is the excess cost recovery. *Excess cost recovery* is the excess of the cost recovery deduction taken in prior years using the statutory percentage method over the amount that would have been allowed if the straight-line method had been used since the property was placed in service.[70]

After the business usage of the listed property drops below the more-than-50 percent level, the straight-line method must be used for the remaining life of the property.

**Leased Automobiles.** A taxpayer who leases a passenger automobile for business purposes must report an *inclusion amount* in gross income. The inclusion amount is computed from an IRS table for each taxable year for which the taxpayer leases the automobile. The purpose of this provision is to prevent taxpayers from circumventing the cost recovery dollar limitations by leasing, instead of purchasing, an automobile.

---

[68]§ 179(b)(6). The effective date for this provision is for vehicles placed in service after October 22, 2004, the date of enactment for the AJCA.

[69]§ 280F(b)(1).
[70]§ 280F(b)(2).

The dollar amount of the inclusion is based on the fair market value of the automobile and is prorated for the number of days the auto is used during the taxable year. The prorated dollar amount is then multiplied by the business and income-producing usage percentage to determine the amount to be included in gross income.[71] The taxpayer deducts the lease payments, multiplied by the business and income-producing usage percentage. The net effect is that the annual deduction for the lease payment is reduced by the inclusion amount.

**EXAMPLE 54**

On April 1, 2005, Jim leases and places in service a passenger automobile worth $40,000. The lease is to be for a period of five years. During the taxable years 2005 and 2006, Jim uses the automobile 70% for business and 30% for personal use. Assuming the dollar amounts from the IRS table for 2005 and 2006 are $83 and $184, Jim must include $44 in gross income for 2005 and $129 for 2006, computed as follows.

| | |
|---|---|
| 2005 | $83 \times (275/365) \times .70 = $44 |
| 2006 | $184 \times (365/365) \times .70 = $129 |

In addition, Jim can deduct 70% of the lease payments each year because this is the business-use percentage. ■

**Substantiation Requirements.** Listed property is subject to the substantiation requirements of § 274. This means that the taxpayer must prove the business usage as to the amount of expense or use, the time and place of use, the business purpose for the use, and the business relationship to the taxpayer of persons using the property. Substantiation requires adequate records or sufficient evidence corroborating the taxpayer's statement. However, these substantiation requirements do not apply to vehicles that, by reason of their nature, are not likely to be used more than a *de minimis* amount for personal purposes.[72]

## ALTERNATIVE DEPRECIATION SYSTEM (ADS)

The **alternative depreciation system (ADS)** must be used in lieu of MACRS for the following:[73]

* To calculate the portion of depreciation treated as an alternative minimum tax (AMT) adjustment for purposes of the corporate and individual AMT (see Chapter 13).[74]
* To compute depreciation allowances for property for which any of the following is true:
  * Used predominantly outside the United States.
  * Leased or otherwise used by a tax-exempt entity.
  * Financed with the proceeds of tax-exempt bonds.
  * Imported from foreign countries that maintain discriminatory trade practices or otherwise engage in discriminatory acts.
* To compute depreciation allowances for earnings and profits purposes (see Chapter 9).

---

[71]Reg. § 1.280F–7(a).
[72]§§ 274(d) and (i).
[73]§ 168(g).
[74]This AMT adjustment applies for real and personal property placed in service before 1999. However, it will continue to apply for personal property placed in service after 1998, if the taxpayer uses the 200% declining-balance method for regular income tax purposes. See Chapter 13.

Tables 4–5, 4–6, and 4–7 provide cost recovery rates under the ADS method. Additional details of the ADS method are beyond the scope of this chapter.

L O . 7

Identify intangible assets that are eligible for amortization and calculate the amount of the deduction.

*Definition
Amortization
— page C-2

# Amortization

Taxpayers can claim an **amortization** deduction on certain intangible assets. The amount of the deduction is determined by amortizing the adjusted basis of such intangibles ratably over a 15-year period beginning in the month in which the intangible is acquired.[75]

An amortizable § 197 intangible is any § 197 intangible acquired after August 10, 1993, and held in connection with the conduct of a trade or business or for the production of income. Section 197 intangibles include goodwill and going-concern value, franchises, trademarks, and trade names. Covenants not to compete, copyrights, and patents are also included if they are acquired in connection with the acquisition of a business. Generally, self-created intangibles are not § 197 intangibles. The 15-year amortization period applies regardless of the actual useful life of an amortizable § 197 intangible. No other depreciation or amortization deduction is permitted with respect to any amortizable § 197 intangible except those permitted under the 15-year amortization rules.

**EXAMPLE 55**

On June 1, 2005, Sally purchased and began operating the Falcon Café. Of the purchase price, $90,000 is correctly allocated to goodwill. The amortization deduction for 2005 is $3,500 [($90,000/15) × (7/12)]. ∎

**PLANNING STRATEGIES**

## Structuring the Sale of a Business

**FRAMEWORK FOCUS: TAX RATE**

**STRATEGY ➤ CONTROL THE CHARACTER OF INCOME AND DEDUCTIONS.**

On the sale of a sole proprietorship where the sales price exceeds the fair market value of the tangible assets and stated intangible assets, a planning opportunity may exist for both the seller and the buyer.

The seller's preference is for the excess amount to be allocated to *goodwill* because goodwill is a capital asset whose sale may result in favorably taxed long-term capital gain. Amounts received for a *covenant not to compete,* however, produce ordinary income, which is not subject to favorable long-term capital gain rates.

Because a covenant and goodwill both are amortized over a statutory 15-year period, the tax results of a covenant

not to compete versus goodwill are the same for the *buyer.* However, the buyer should recognize that an allocation to goodwill rather than a covenant may provide a tax benefit to the seller. Therefore, the buyer, in negotiating the purchase price, should factor in the tax benefit to the seller of having the excess amount labeled goodwill rather than a covenant not to compete. Of course, if the noncompetition aspects of a covenant are important to the buyer, a portion of the excess amount can be assigned to a covenant.

---

[75]§ 197(a).

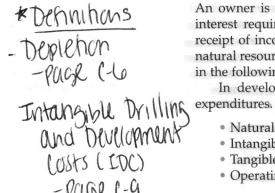

\* Definitions

- Depletion
  - Page C-6

Intangible Drilling
and Development
Costs (IDC)
  - Page C-9

**LO.8**

Determine the amount of depletion expense and recognize the alternative tax treatments for intangible drilling and development costs.

# Depletion

Natural resources (e.g., oil, gas, coal, gravel, timber) are subject to **depletion,** which is simply a form of depreciation applicable to natural resources. Land generally cannot be depleted.

The owner of an interest in the natural resource is entitled to deduct depletion. An owner is one who has an economic interest in the property.[76] An economic interest requires the acquisition of an interest in the resource in place and the receipt of income from the extraction or severance of that resource. Although all natural resources are subject to depletion, oil and gas wells are used as an example in the following paragraphs to illustrate the related costs and issues.

In developing an oil or gas well, the producer must make four types of expenditures.

- Natural resource costs.
- Intangible drilling and development costs.
- Tangible asset costs.
- Operating costs.

Natural resources are physically limited, and the costs to acquire them (e.g., oil under the ground) are, therefore, recovered through depletion. Costs incurred in making the property ready for drilling such as the cost of labor in clearing the property, erecting derricks, and drilling the hole are **intangible drilling and development costs (IDC).** These costs generally have no salvage value and are a lost cost if the well is not productive (dry). Costs for tangible assets such as tools, pipes, and engines are capital in nature. These costs must be capitalized and recovered through depreciation (cost recovery). Costs incurred after the well is producing are operating costs. These costs would include expenditures for such items as labor, fuel, and supplies. Operating costs are deductible when incurred (on the accrual basis) or when paid (on the cash basis).

The expenditures for depreciable assets and operating costs pose no unusual problems for producers of natural resources. The tax treatment of depletable costs and intangible drilling and development costs is quite a different matter.

## INTANGIBLE DRILLING AND DEVELOPMENT COSTS (IDC)

Intangible drilling and development costs can be handled in one of two ways at the option of the taxpayer. They can be either charged off as an expense in the year in which they are incurred or capitalized and written off through depletion. The taxpayer makes the election in the first year such expenditures are incurred either by taking a deduction on the return or by adding them to the depletable basis. No formal statement of intent is required. Once made, the election is binding on both the taxpayer and the IRS for all such expenditures in the future. If the taxpayer fails to make the election to expense IDC on the original timely filed return the first year such expenditures are incurred, an automatic election to capitalize them has been made and is irrevocable.

As a general rule, it is more advantageous to expense IDC. The obvious benefit of an immediate write-off (as opposed to a deferred write-off through depletion) is not the only advantage. Since a taxpayer can use percentage depletion, which is calculated without reference to basis, the IDC may be completely lost as a deduction if they are capitalized.

---

[76]Reg. § 1.611–1(b).

*Definitions*

Cost Depletion
- Page C-5

Percentage Depletion
- Page C-13

## DEPLETION METHODS

There are two methods of calculating depletion: cost and percentage. **Cost depletion** can be used on any wasting asset (and is the only method allowed for timber). **Percentage depletion** is subject to a number of limitations, particularly for oil and gas deposits. Depletion should be calculated both ways, and generally the method that results in the larger deduction is used. The choice between cost and percentage depletion is an annual election.

**Cost Depletion.** Cost depletion is determined by using the adjusted basis of the asset.[77] The basis is divided by the estimated recoverable units of the asset (e.g., barrels, tons) to arrive at the depletion per unit. The depletion per unit then is multiplied by the number of units sold (not the units produced) during the year to arrive at the cost depletion allowed. Cost depletion, therefore, resembles the units-of-production method of calculating depreciation.

**EXAMPLE 56**

On January 1, 2005, Pablo purchases the rights to a mineral interest for $1 million. At that time, the remaining recoverable units in the mineral interest are estimated to be 200,000. The depletion per unit is $5 [$1,000,000 (adjusted basis)/200,000 (estimated recoverable units)]. If during the year 60,000 units are mined and 25,000 are sold, the cost depletion is $125,000 [$5 (depletion per unit) × 25,000 (units sold)]. ■

If the taxpayer later discovers that the original estimate was incorrect, the depletion per unit for future calculations must be redetermined based on the revised estimate.[78]

**EXAMPLE 57**

Assume the same facts as in Example 56. In 2006, Pablo realizes that an incorrect estimate was made. The remaining recoverable units now are determined to be 400,000. Based on this new information, the revised depletion per unit is $2.1875 [$875,000 (adjusted basis)/400,000 (estimated recoverable units)]. The adjusted basis is the original cost ($1,000,000) reduced by the depletion claimed in 2005 ($125,000). If 30,000 units are sold in 2006, the depletion for the year is $65,625 [$2.1875 (depletion per unit) × 30,000 (units sold)]. ■

**Percentage Depletion.** Percentage depletion (also referred to as statutory depletion) is a specified percentage provided for in the Code. The percentage varies according to the type of mineral interest involved. A sample of these percentages is shown in Exhibit 4–3. The rate is applied to the gross income from the property, but in no event may percentage depletion exceed 50 percent of the taxable income from the property before the allowance for depletion.[79]

**EXAMPLE 58**

Assuming gross income of $100,000, a depletion rate of 22%, and other expenses relating to the property of $60,000, the depletion allowance is determined as follows:

| | |
|---|---:|
| Gross income | $100,000 |
| Less: Other expenses | (60,000) |
| Taxable income before depletion | $ 40,000 |
| Depreciation allowance [the lesser of $22,000 (22% × $100,000) or $20,000 (50% × $40,000)] | (20,000) |
| Taxable income after depletion | $ 20,000 |

---

[77]§ 612.

[78]§ 611(a).

[79]§ 613(a). Special rules apply for certain oil and gas wells under § 613A (e.g., the 50% ceiling is replaced with a 100% ceiling, and the percentage depletion may not exceed 65% of the taxpayer's taxable income from all sources before the allowance for depletion).

■ **EXHIBIT 4–3**
Sample of Percentage Depletion
Rates

| **22% Depletion** | |
| --- | --- |
| Cobalt | Sulfur |
| Lead | Tin |
| **15% Depletion** | |
| Copper | Oil and gas |
| Gold | Silver |
| **10% Depletion** | |
| Coal | Perlite |
| **5% Depletion** | |
| Gravel | Sand |

The adjusted basis of the property is reduced by $20,000, the depletion allowed. If the other expenses had been only $55,000, the full $22,000 could have been deducted, and the adjusted basis would have been reduced by $22,000. ■

Note that percentage depletion is based on a percentage of the gross income from the property and makes no reference to cost. Thus, when percentage depletion is used, it is possible to deduct more than the original cost of the property. If percentage depletion is used, however, the adjusted basis of the property (for computing cost depletion) must be reduced by the amount of percentage depletion taken until the adjusted basis reaches zero.

**PLANNING STRATEGIES**

## Switching Depletion Methods

**FRAMEWORK FOCUS: DEDUCTIONS**

**STRATEGY ➤ MAXIMIZE DEDUCTIBLE AMOUNTS.**

Since the election to use the cost or percentage depletion method is an annual election, a taxpayer can use cost depletion (if higher) until the basis is exhausted and then switch to percentage depletion in the following years.

| | |
| --- | --- |
| Remaining depletable basis | $ 11,000 |
| Gross income (10,000 units) | 100,000 |
| Expenses (other than depletion) | 30,000 |
| Percentage depletion rate | 22% |

Since cost depletion is limited to the basis of $11,000 and the percentage depletion is $22,000, Warbler would choose the latter. The company's basis is then reduced to zero. In future years, however, Warbler can continue to take percentage depletion since percentage depletion is taken without reference to the remaining basis. ■

**EXAMPLE 59**

Assume the following facts for Warbler Company.

# Cost Recovery Tables

## Summary of Cost Recovery Tables

Table 4–1     MACRS statutory percentage table for personalty.

Applicable depreciation methods: 200 or 150 percent declining-balance switching to straight-line.

Applicable recovery periods: 3, 5, 7, 10, 15, 20 years.

Applicable convention: half-year.

Table 4–2     MACRS statutory percentage table for personalty.

Applicable depreciation method: 200 percent declining-balance switching to straight-line.

Applicable recovery periods: 3, 5, 7 years.

Applicable convention: mid-quarter.

Table 4–3     MACRS straight-line table for realty.

Applicable depreciation method: straight-line.

Applicable recovery periods: 27.5, 31.5, 39 years.

Applicable convention: mid-month.

Table 4–4     MACRS optional straight-line table for personalty.

Applicable depreciation method: straight-line.

Applicable recovery periods: 3, 5, 7, 10, 15, 20 years.

Applicable convention: half-year.

Table 4–5     Alternative minimum tax declining-balance table for personalty.

Applicable depreciation method: 150 percent declining-balance switching to straight-line.

Applicable recovery periods: 3, 5, 7, 9.5, 10, 12 years.

Applicable convention: half-year.

Table 4–6     ADS straight-line table for personalty.

Applicable depreciation method: straight-line.

Applicable recovery periods: 5, 9.5, 12 years.

Applicable convention: half-year.

Table 4–7     ADS straight-line table for realty.

Applicable depreciation method: straight-line.

Applicable recovery period: 40 years.

Applicable convention: mid-month.

■ **TABLE 4–1**
MACRS Accelerated
Depreciation for Personal
Property Assuming Half-Year
Convention

### For Property Placed in Service after December 31, 1986

| Recovery Year | 3-Year (200% DB) | 5-Year (200% DB) | 7-Year (200% DB) | 10-Year (200% DB) | 15-Year (150% DB) | 20-Year (150% DB) |
|---|---|---|---|---|---|---|
| 1 | 33.33 | 20.00 | 14.29 | 10.00 | 5.00 | 3.750 |
| 2 | 44.45 | 32.00 | 24.49 | 18.00 | 9.50 | 7.219 |
| 3 | 14.81* | 19.20 | 17.49 | 14.40 | 8.55 | 6.677 |
| 4 | 7.41 | 11.52* | 12.49 | 11.52 | 7.70 | 6.177 |
| 5 | | 11.52 | 8.93* | 9.22 | 6.93 | 5.713 |
| 6 | | 5.76 | 8.92 | 7.37 | 6.23 | 5.285 |
| 7 | | | 8.93 | 6.55* | 5.90* | 4.888 |
| 8 | | | 4.46 | 6.55 | 5.90 | 4.522 |
| 9 | | | | 6.56 | 5.91 | 4.462* |
| 10 | | | | 6.55 | 5.90 | 4.461 |
| 11 | | | | 3.28 | 5.91 | 4.462 |
| 12 | | | | | 5.90 | 4.461 |
| 13 | | | | | 5.91 | 4.462 |
| 14 | | | | | 5.90 | 4.461 |
| 15 | | | | | 5.91 | 4.462 |
| 16 | | | | | 2.95 | 4.461 |
| 17 | | | | | | 4.462 |
| 18 | | | | | | 4.461 |
| 19 | | | | | | 4.462 |
| 20 | | | | | | 4.461 |
| 21 | | | | | | 2.231 |

*Switchover to straight-line depreciation.

■ **TABLE 4–2**
MACRS Accelerated
Depreciation for Personal
Property Assuming Mid-Quarter
Convention

### For Property Placed in Service after December 31, 1986 (Partial Table*)

| | 3-Year | | | |
|---|---|---|---|---|
| Recovery Year | First Quarter | Second Quarter | Third Quarter | Fourth Quarter |
|---|---|---|---|---|
| 1 | 58.33 | 41.67 | 25.00 | 8.33 |
| 2 | 27.78 | 38.89 | 50.00 | 61.11 |

| | 5-Year | | | |
|---|---|---|---|---|
| Recovery Year | First Quarter | Second Quarter | Third Quarter | Fourth Quarter |
|---|---|---|---|---|
| 1 | 35.00 | 25.00 | 15.00 | 5.00 |
| 2 | 26.00 | 30.00 | 34.00 | 38.00 |

| | 7-Year | | | |
|---|---|---|---|---|
| Recovery Year | First Quarter | Second Quarter | Third Quarter | Fourth Quarter |
|---|---|---|---|---|
| 1 | 25.00 | 17.85 | 10.71 | 3.57 |
| 2 | 21.43 | 23.47 | 25.51 | 27.55 |

*The figures in this table are taken from the official tables that appear in Rev.Proc. 87–57, 1987–2 C.B. 687. Because of their length, the complete tables are not presented.

■ **TABLE 4–3**
MACRS Straight-Line Depreciation for Real Property
Assuming Mid-Month Convention*

**For Property Placed in Service after December 31, 1986: 27.5-Year Residential Real Property**

| Recovery Year(s) | The Applicable Percentage Is (Use the Column for the Month in the First Year the Property Is Placed in Service): | | | | | | | | | | | |
| | 1 | 2 | 3 | 4 | 5 | 6 | 7 | 8 | 9 | 10 | 11 | 12 |
|---|---|---|---|---|---|---|---|---|---|---|---|---|
| 1 | 3.485 | 3.182 | 2.879 | 2.576 | 2.273 | 1.970 | 1.667 | 1.364 | 1.061 | 0.758 | 0.455 | 0.152 |
| 2–18 | 3.636 | 3.636 | 3.636 | 3.636 | 3.636 | 3.636 | 3.636 | 3.636 | 3.636 | 3.636 | 3.636 | 3.636 |
| 19–27 | 3.637 | 3.637 | 3.637 | 3.637 | 3.637 | 3.637 | 3.637 | 3.637 | 3.637 | 3.637 | 3.637 | 3.637 |
| 28 | 1.970 | 2.273 | 2.576 | 2.879 | 3.182 | 3.485 | 3.636 | 3.636 | 3.636 | 3.636 | 3.636 | 3.636 |
| 29 | 0.000 | 0.000 | 0.000 | 0.000 | 0.000 | 0.000 | 0.152 | 0.455 | 0.758 | 1.061 | 1.364 | 1.667 |

**For Property Placed in Service after December 31, 1986, and before May 13, 1993: 31.5-Year Nonresidential Real Property**

| Recovery Year(s) | The Applicable Percentage Is (Use the Column for the Month in the First Year the Property Is Placed in Service): | | | | | | | | | | | |
| | 1 | 2 | 3 | 4 | 5 | 6 | 7 | 8 | 9 | 10 | 11 | 12 |
|---|---|---|---|---|---|---|---|---|---|---|---|---|
| 1 | 3.042 | 2.778 | 2.513 | 2.249 | 1.984 | 1.720 | 1.455 | 1.190 | 0.926 | 0.661 | 0.397 | 0.132 |
| 2–19 | 3.175 | 3.175 | 3.175 | 3.175 | 3.175 | 3.175 | 3.175 | 3.175 | 3.175 | 3.175 | 3.175 | 3.175 |
| 20–31 | 3.174 | 3.174 | 3.174 | 3.174 | 3.174 | 3.174 | 3.174 | 3.174 | 3.174 | 3.174 | 3.174 | 3.174 |
| 32 | 1.720 | 1.984 | 2.249 | 2.513 | 2.778 | 3.042 | 3.175 | 3.175 | 3.175 | 3.175 | 3.175 | 3.175 |
| 33 | 0.000 | 0.000 | 0.000 | 0.000 | 0.000 | 0.000 | 0.132 | 0.397 | 0.661 | 0.926 | 1.190 | 1.455 |

**For Property Placed in Service after May 12, 1993: 39-Year Nonresidential Real Property**

| Recovery Year(s) | The Applicable Percentage Is (Use the Column for the Month in the First Year the Property Is Placed in Service): | | | | | | | | | | | |
| | 1 | 2 | 3 | 4 | 5 | 6 | 7 | 8 | 9 | 10 | 11 | 12 |
|---|---|---|---|---|---|---|---|---|---|---|---|---|
| 1 | 2.461 | 2.247 | 2.033 | 1.819 | 1.605 | 1.391 | 1.177 | 0.963 | 0.749 | 0.535 | 0.321 | 0.107 |
| 2–39 | 2.564 | 2.564 | 2.564 | 2.564 | 2.564 | 2.564 | 2.564 | 2.564 | 2.564 | 2.564 | 2.564 | 2.564 |
| 40 | 0.107 | 0.321 | 0.535 | 0.749 | 0.963 | 1.177 | 1.391 | 1.605 | 1.819 | 2.033 | 2.247 | 2.461 |

*The official tables contain a separate row for each year. For ease of presentation, certain years are grouped in these tables. In some instances, this will produce a difference of .001 for the last digit when compared with the official tables.

■ **TABLE 4–4**
MACRS Straight-Line Depreciation for Personal Property Assuming Half-Year Convention*

**For Property Placed in Service after December 31, 1986**

| MACRS Class | Percent First Recovery Year | Other Recovery Years | | Last Recovery Year | |
| | | Years | % | Year | % |
|---|---|---|---|---|---|
| 3-year | 16.67 | 2–3 | 33.33 | 4 | 16.67 |
| 5-year | 10.00 | 2–5 | 20.00 | 6 | 10.00 |
| 7-year | 7.14 | 2–7 | 14.29 | 8 | 7.14 |
| 10-year | 5.00 | 2–10 | 10.00 | 11 | 5.00 |
| 15-year | 3.33 | 2–15 | 6.67 | 16 | 3.33 |
| 20-year | 2.50 | 2–20 | 5.00 | 21 | 2.50 |

*The official table contains a separate row for each year. For ease of presentation, certain years are grouped in this table. In some instances, this will produce a difference of .01 for the last digit when compared with the official table.

■ **TABLE 4–5**

Alternative Minimum Tax: 150% Declining-Balance Assuming Half-Year Convention

### For Property Placed in Service after December 31, 1986 (Partial Table*)

| Recovery Year | 3-Year 150% | 5-Year 150% | 7-Year 150% | 9.5-Year 150% | 10-Year 150% | 12-Year 150% |
|---|---|---|---|---|---|---|
| 1 | 25.00 | 15.00 | 10.71 | 7.89 | 7.50 | 6.25 |
| 2 | 37.50 | 25.50 | 19.13 | 14.54 | 13.88 | 11.72 |
| 3 | 25.00** | 17.85 | 15.03 | 12.25 | 11.79 | 10.25 |
| 4 | 12.50 | 16.66** | 12.25** | 10.31 | 10.02 | 8.97 |
| 5 | | 16.66 | 12.25 | 9.17** | 8.74** | 7.85 |
| 6 | | 8.33 | 12.25 | 9.17 | 8.74 | 7.33** |
| 7 | | | 12.25 | 9.17 | 8.74 | 7.33 |
| 8 | | | 6.13 | 9.17 | 8.74 | 7.33 |
| 9 | | | | 9.17 | 8.74 | 7.33 |
| 10 | | | | 9.16 | 8.74 | 7.33 |
| 11 | | | | | 4.37 | 7.32 |
| 12 | | | | | | 7.33 |
| 13 | | | | | | 3.66 |

*The figures in this table are taken from the official table that appears in Rev.Proc. 87–57, 1987–2 C.B. 687. Because of its length, the complete table is not presented.

**Switchover to straight-line depreciation.

■ **TABLE 4–6**

ADS Straight-Line for Personal Property Assuming Half-Year Convention

### For Property Placed in Service after December 31, 1986 (Partial Table*)

| Recovery Year | 5-Year Class | 9.5-Year Class | 12-Year Class |
|---|---|---|---|
| 1 | 10.00 | 5.26 | 4.17 |
| 2 | 20.00 | 10.53 | 8.33 |
| 3 | 20.00 | 10.53 | 8.33 |
| 4 | 20.00 | 10.53 | 8.33 |
| 5 | 20.00 | 10.52 | 8.33 |
| 6 | 10.00 | 10.53 | 8.33 |
| 7 | | 10.52 | 8.34 |
| 8 | | 10.53 | 8.33 |
| 9 | | 10.52 | 8.34 |
| 10 | | 10.53 | 8.33 |
| 11 | | | 8.34 |
| 12 | | | 8.33 |
| 13 | | | 4.17 |

*The figures in this table are taken from the official table that appears in Rev.Proc. 87–57, 1987–2 C.B. 687. Because of its length, the complete table is not presented. The tables for the mid-quarter convention also appear in Rev.Proc. 87–57.

■ **TABLE 4–7**
ADS Straight-Line for Real
Property Assuming Mid-Month
Convention

**For Property Placed in Service after December 31, 1986**

| Recovery Year(s) | Month Placed in Service | | | | | | | | | | | |
|---|---|---|---|---|---|---|---|---|---|---|---|---|
| | 1 | 2 | 3 | 4 | 5 | 6 | 7 | 8 | 9 | 10 | 11 | 12 |
| 1 | 2.396 | 2.188 | 1.979 | 1.771 | 1.563 | 1.354 | 1.146 | 0.938 | 0.729 | 0.521 | 0.313 | 0.104 |
| 2–40 | 2.500 | 2.500 | 2.500 | 2.500 | 2.500 | 2.500 | 2.500 | 2.500 | 2.500 | 2.500 | 2.500 | 2.500 |
| 41 | 0.104 | 0.312 | 0.521 | 0.729 | 0.937 | 1.146 | 1.354 | 1.562 | 1.771 | 1.979 | 2.187 | 2.396 |

# Suggested Further Readings

Dennis J. Gaffney, Richard O. Davis, Richard P. Weber, and Maureen H. Smith-Gaffney, "Advance Payments: Rev.Proc. 2004–34 Expands Rev.Proc. 71–21 and Provides Needed Clarity," *Journal of Taxation,* August 2004, pp. 84–94.

Timothy R. Koski, "Business—Not Investor—Status Helps Develop R&D Deductions," *Practical Tax Strategies,* January 2004, pp. 33–38.

Edward J. Schnee and Lisa H. McKinney "Independent Contractor Compensation Deferral Can Delay Deduction," *Practical Tax Strategies,* June 2004, pp. 324–337.

W. Eugene Seago, "IRS Takes a Unique Approach in New Rules for Change in Accounting Method for Depreciation," *Journal of Taxation,* June 2004, pp. 350–356.

## KEY TERMS

Accelerated cost recovery system (ACRS), 4–22

Additional first-year depreciation, 4–26

Alternative depreciation system (ADS), 4–35

Amortization, 4–36

Capital gain property, 4–15

Charitable contribution, 4–15

Cost depletion, 4–38

Depletion, 4–37

Depreciation rules, 4–22

Half-year convention, 4–26

Intangible drilling and development costs (IDC), 4–37

Listed property, 4–31

Manufacturers' deduction, 4–20

Mid-month convention, 4–29

Mid-quarter convention, 4–27

Modified accelerated cost recovery system (MACRS), 4–22

Ordinary and necessary, 4–2

Ordinary income property, 4–15

Percentage depletion, 4–38

Qualified production income, 4–21

Reasonableness requirement, 4–3

Related-party transactions, 4–12

Research and experimental expenditures, 4–17

Residential rental real estate, 4–28

Section 179 expensing election, 4–30

## PROBLEM MATERIALS

### Problems

West Federal Taxation

**Issue ID**

1. Ted is an agent for Waxwing Corporation, an airline manufacturer, and is negotiating a sale with a representative of the U.S. government and with a representative of a developing country. Waxwing has sufficient capacity to handle only one of the orders. Both orders will have the same contract price. Ted believes that if Waxwing will authorize a $500,000 payment to the representative of the foreign country, he can guarantee the sale. He is not sure that he can obtain the same result with the U.S. government. Identify the relevant tax issues for Waxwing.

2. Linda operates a drug-running operation. Which of the following expenses she incurs can reduce taxable income?
   a. Bribes paid to border guards.
   b. Salaries to employees.
   c. Price paid for drugs purchased for resale.
   d. Kickbacks to police.
   e. Rent on an office.
   f. Depreciation on office furniture and equipment.
   g. Tenant's casualty insurance.

**Ethics**

3. Cardinal Corporation is a trucking firm that operates in the Mid-Atlantic states. One of Cardinal's major customers frequently ships goods between Charlotte and Baltimore. Occasionally, the customer sends last-minute shipments that are outbound for Europe on a freighter sailing from Baltimore. To satisfy the delivery schedule in these cases, Cardinal's drivers must substantially exceed the speed limit. Cardinal pays for any related speeding tickets. During the past year, two drivers had their licenses suspended for 30 days each for driving at such excessive speeds. Cardinal continues to pay each driver's salary during the suspension periods.

   Cardinal believes that it is necessary to conduct its business in this manner if it is to be profitable, maintain the support of the drivers, and maintain the goodwill of customers. Evaluate Cardinal's business practices.

4. Quail Corporation anticipates that being positively perceived by the individual who is elected mayor will be beneficial for business. Therefore, Quail contributes to the campaigns of both the Democratic and the Republican candidates. The Republican candidate is elected mayor. Can Quail deduct any of the political contributions it made?

5. Melissa, the owner of a sole proprietorship, does not provide health insurance for her 20 employees. She plans to spend $1,500 lobbying in opposition to legislation that would require her to provide health insurance for her employees. Discuss the tax advantages and disadvantages of paying the $1,500 to a professional lobbyist rather than spending the $1,500 on in-house lobbying expenditures.

**Issue ID**

6. Ella owns 60% of the stock of Peach, Inc. The stock has declined in value since Ella purchased it five years ago. She is going to sell 5% of the stock to a relative to pay her 12-year-old daughter's private school tuition. Ella is also going to make a gift of 10% of her stock to another relative. Identify the relevant tax issues for Ella.

7. Jake owns City of Charleston bonds with an adjusted basis of $100,000. During the year, he receives interest payments of $4,000. Jake partially financed the purchase of the bonds by borrowing $70,000 at 6% interest. Jake's interest payments on the loan this year are $4,100, and his principal payments are $1,000.
   a. Should Jake report any interest income this year?
   b. Can Jake deduct any interest expense this year?

8. Drew and his wife Cassie own all of the stock of Thrush, Inc. Cassie is the president and Drew is the vice president. Cassie and Drew are paid salaries of $400,000 and $300,000, respectively, each year. They consider the salaries to be reasonable based on a comparison with salaries paid for comparable positions in comparable companies. They project Thrush's taxable income for next year, before their salaries, to be $800,000.

They decide to place their four teenage children on the payroll and to pay them total salaries of $100,000. The children will each work about five hours per week for Thrush.

a. What are Drew and Cassie trying to achieve by hiring the children?
b. Calculate the tax consequences of hiring the children on Thrush, Inc., and on Drew and Cassie's family.

9. Polly made the following political contributions:

| | |
|---|---|
| To national Republican Party | $1,000 |
| To national Democratic Party | 1,000 |
| To local candidate for mayor | 700 |
| To candidate for state Senate | 200 |
| To candidate for school board | 250 |

How much can Polly deduct?

10. Jenny, the owner of a very successful restaurant chain, is exploring the possibility of expanding the chain into a city in the neighboring state. She incurs $25,000 of expenses associated with this investigation. Based on the regulatory environment for restaurants in the city, she decides not to do so. During the year, she also investigates opening a hotel that will be part of a national hotel chain. Her expenses for this are $51,000. The hotel begins operations on November 1. Determine the amount that Jenny can deduct in the current year for investigating these two businesses.

**Decision Making**

**Communications**

11. Janet Saxon sold stock (basis of $82,000) to her brother, Fred, for $70,000, the fair market value.

a. What are the tax consequences to Janet?
b. What are the tax consequences to Fred if he later sells the stock for $90,000? For $50,000? For $75,000?
c. Write a letter to Janet in which you inform her of the tax consequences if she sells the stock to Fred for $70,000 and explain how a sales transaction could be structured that would produce better tax consequences for her. Janet's address is 32 Country Lane, Lawrence, KS 66045.

12. Coyote, Inc. (a calendar year C corporation) had the following income and expenses in 2006.

| | |
|---|---|
| Income from operations | $200,000 |
| Expenses from operations | 80,000 |
| Dividends received (less than 20% ownership) | 16,000 |
| Charitable contribution | 16,000 |

a. How much is Coyote, Inc.'s charitable contribution deduction for 2006?
b. What happens to the portion of the contribution not deductible in 2006?

**Decision Making**

**Communications**

13. Dan Simms is the president and sole shareholder of Simms Corporation, 1121 Madison Street, Seattle, WA 98121. Dan plans for the corporation to make a charitable contribution to the University of Washington, a qualified public charity. He will have the corporation donate Jaybird Corporation stock, held for five years, with a basis of $8,000 and a fair market value of $20,000. Dan projects a $200,000 net profit for Simms Corporation in 2005 and a $100,000 net profit in 2006. Dan calls you on December 3, 2005, and asks whether he should make the contribution in 2005 or 2006. Write a letter advising Dan about the timing of the contribution.

14. Blue Corporation, a manufacturing company, decided to develop a new line of merchandise. The project began in 2005. Blue had the following expenses in connection with the project.

|                                                   | **2005**  | **2006**  |
| ------------------------------------------------- | --------- | --------- |
| Salaries                                          | $300,000  | $400,000  |
| Materials                                         | 80,000    | 70,000    |
| Insurance                                         | 10,000    | 15,000    |
| Utilities                                         | 7,000     | 8,000     |
| Cost of inspection of materials for quality control | 4,000   | 4,000     |
| Promotion expenses                                | 10,000    | 7,000     |
| Advertising                                       | –0–       | 30,000    |
| Equipment depreciation                            | 10,000    | 12,000    |
| Cost of market survey                             | 8,000     | –0–       |

The new product will be introduced for sale beginning in July 2007. Determine the amount of the deduction for research and experimental expenditures for 2005, 2006, and 2007 if:
a.  Blue Corporation elects to expense the research and experimental expenditures.
b.  Blue Corporation elects to amortize the research and experimental expenditures over 60 months.

15. On November 4, 2003, Blue Company acquired an asset (27.5-year residential real property) for $100,000 for use in its business. In 2003 and 2004, respectively, Blue took $321 and $2,564 of cost recovery. These amounts were incorrect because Blue applied the wrong percentages (i.e., those for 39-year rather than 27.5-year property). Blue should have taken $455 and $3,636 of cost recovery in 2003 and 2004. On January 1, 2005, the asset was sold for $98,000. Calculate the gain or loss on the sale of the asset in 2005.

16. Juan, a sole proprietor, acquires a new five-year class asset on March 14, 2005, for $200,000. This is the only asset acquired by Juan during the year. He does not elect immediate expensing under § 179. On July 15, 2006, Juan sells the asset.
    a.  Determine Juan's cost recovery for 2005.
    b.  Determine Juan's cost recovery for 2006.

17. On November 5, 2005, Chris, a sole proprietor, acquires land with a warehouse on it for $3 million. The land was valued at $1 million. On January 10, 2016, Chris sells the land and warehouse for $4.5 million. Calculate Chris's cost recovery for 2005. For 2016.

18. Janice acquired an apartment building on June 4, 2005, for $1.4 million. The value of the land is $200,000. Janice sold the apartment building on November 29, 2011.
    a.  Determine Janice's cost recovery for 2005.
    b.  Determine Janice's cost recovery for 2011.

**EXTENDER**

19. On July 10, 1996, Wade purchased and placed in service a warehouse. The warehouse cost $850,000. On May 7, 2005, Wade sold the warehouse.
    a.  Determine Wade's cost recovery for 1996.
    b.  Determine Wade's cost recovery for 2005.

**Decision Making**

20. Lori, who is single, purchased a new copier (five-year class property) for $30,000 and new furniture (seven-year class property) for $112,000 on May 20, 2005. Lori expects the taxable income derived from her business (without regard to the amount expensed under § 179) to be about $200,000. Lori wants to elect immediate § 179 expensing, but she doesn't know which asset she should expense under § 179.
    a.  Determine Lori's total deduction if the § 179 expense is first taken with respect to the copier.
    b.  Determine Lori's total deduction if the § 179 expense is first taken with respect to the furniture.
    c.  What is your advice to Lori?

21. Jack owns a small business that he operates as a sole proprietor. In 2005, Jack will net $80,000 of business income before consideration of any § 179 deduction. Jack spends $428,000 on new equipment in 2005. If Jack also has $4,000 of § 179 deduction carryforwards from 2004, determine his § 179 expense deduction for 2005 and the amount of any carryforward.

22. Olga is the proprietor of a small business. In 2005, the business income, before consideration of any cost recovery or § 179 deduction, is $180,000. Olga spends $132,000 for new furniture and elects to take the § 179 deduction on the furniture. Olga's cost recovery deduction for 2005, except for the cost recovery deduction with respect to the furniture, is $86,000. Determine Olga's total cost recovery for 2005 with respect to the furniture and the amount of any § 179 carryforward.

**Decision Making**

23. On March 10, 2005, Yoon purchased three-year class property for $20,000. On December 15, 2005, he purchased five-year class property for $127,000. Yoon has net business income of $140,000 before consideration of any § 179 deduction.
    a. Calculate Yoon's cost recovery for 2005, assuming he does not make the § 179 election or use straight-line cost recovery.
    b. Calculate Yoon's cost recovery for 2005, assuming he does elect to use § 179 and does not elect to use straight-line cost recovery.
    c. Assuming Yoon's marginal tax rate is 33%, determine his tax benefit from electing § 179.

**Communications**

24. John Johnson is considering acquiring an automobile at the beginning of 2005 that he will use 100% of the time as a taxi. The purchase price of the automobile is $35,000. John has heard of cost recovery limits on automobiles and wants to know the maximum amount of the $35,000 he can deduct in the first year. Write a letter to John in which you present your calculations. Also, prepare a memo for the tax files. John's address is 100 Morningside, Clinton, MS 39058.

25. On October 15, 2005, Jon purchased and placed in service a new car. The purchase price was $30,000. This was the only business-use asset Jon acquired in 2005. He used the car 80% of the time for business and 20% for personal use. Jon used the statutory percentage method of cost recovery. Calculate the total deduction Jon may take for 2005 with respect to the car.

26. On June 5, 2005, Leo purchased and placed in service a new car that cost $18,000. The business-use percentage for the car is always 100%. Compute Leo's cost recovery deduction in 2005 and 2006.

**EXTENDER**

27. On May 28, 2005, Mary purchased and placed in service a new $20,000 car. The car was used 60% for business, 20% for production of income, and 20% for personal use. In 2006, the usage changed to 40% for business, 30% for production of income, and 30% for personal use. Mary did not elect immediate expensing under § 179. Compute the cost recovery and any cost recovery recapture in 2006.

28. At the beginning of the current year, Abdel purchased a new computer (five-year class property) for $8,000. During the year, Abdel used the computer 80% of the time for his personal investments and 20% of the time for personal use. Calculate the maximum total deduction Abdel can take with respect to the computer for the current tax year.

29. Midway through 2005, Abdel leases and places in service a passenger automobile. The lease will run for five years, and the payments are $700 per month. During 2005, Abdel uses the car 65% for business use and 35% for personal use. Assuming the inclusion dollar amount from the IRS table is $80, determine the tax consequences to Abdel from the lease for the year 2005.

**Decision Making**

**Communications**

30. Mike Saxon is negotiating the purchase of a business. The final purchase price has been agreed upon, but the allocation of the purchase price to the assets is still being discussed. Appraisals on a warehouse range from $1,200,000 to $1,500,000. If a value of $1,200,000 is used for the warehouse, the remainder of the purchase price, $800,000, will be allocated to goodwill. If $1,500,000 is allocated to the warehouse, goodwill will be $500,000. Mike wants to know what effect each alternative will have on cost recovery and amortization

during the first year. Under the agreement, Mike will take over the business on January 1 of next year. Write a letter to Mike in which you present your calculations and recommendation. Also, prepare a memo for the tax files. Mike's address is 200 Rolling Hills Drive, Shavertown, PA 18708.

**Ethics**

31. Sam Jones owns a granite stone quarry. When he acquired the land, Sam allocated $800,000 of the purchase price to the quarry's recoverable mineral reserves, which were estimated at 10 million tons of granite stone. Based on these estimates, the cost depletion was $.08 per ton. In April of the current year, Sam received a letter from the State Department of Highways notifying him that part of his property was being condemned so the state could build a new road. At that time, the recoverable mineral reserves had an adjusted basis of $600,000 and 7.5 million tons of granite rock. Sam estimates that the land being condemned contains about 2 million tons of granite. Therefore, for the current year, Sam has computed his cost depletion at $.11 [$600,000/(7,500,000 − 2,000,000)] per ton. Evaluate the appropriateness of what Sam is doing.

32. Wes acquired a mineral interest during the year for $10 million. A geological survey estimated that 250,000 tons of the mineral remained in the deposit. During the year, 80,000 tons were mined, and 45,000 tons were sold for $12 million. Other expenses amounted to $5 million. Assuming the mineral depletion rate is 22%, calculate Wes's lowest taxable income.

**BRIDGE DISCIPLINE**

**Decision Making**

1. Sparrow Corporation is considering the acquisition of an asset for use in its business over the next five years. However, Sparrow must decide whether it would be better served by leasing the asset or buying it. An appropriate asset could be purchased for $15,000, and it would qualify as a three-year asset under the MACRS classification. Assume that the election to expense assets under § 179 is not available and that the asset is not expected to have a salvage value at the end of its use by Sparrow. Alternatively, Sparrow could lease the asset for a $3,625 annual cost over the five-year period. If Sparrow is in the 34% tax bracket, would you recommend that Sparrow buy or lease the asset? In your calculations, assume that 10% is an appropriate discount factor.

**Decision Making**

2. Lark Corporation is considering the acquisition of an asset for use in its business over the next five years. However, Lark must decide whether it would be better served by leasing the asset or buying it. An appropriate asset could be purchased for $15,000, and it would qualify as a three-year asset under the MACRS classification. Assume that the election to expense assets under § 179 is made and that the asset is not expected to have a salvage value at the end of its use by Lark. Alternatively, Lark could lease the asset for a $3,625 annual cost over the five-year period. If Lark is in the 34% tax bracket, would you recommend that Lark buy or lease the asset? In your calculations, assume that 10% is an appropriate discount factor.

3. Wayside Fruit Company is a sole proprietorship owned by Neil Stephenson. The company's records reflect the following.

| | |
|---|---|
| Sales revenue | $185,000 |
| Operating expenses | 125,000 |
| Depreciation expense for book | 13,000 |
| Cost recovery allowance for tax | 17,500 |
| Loss on the sale of delivery truck to Neil's brother | 5,000 |
| Amount paid to fruit inspector to overlook below-standard fruit shipped to various vendors | 3,000 |

Compute the net income before tax for book purposes and the amount of taxable income for Wayside Fruit Company.

## Research Problems

*Note: Solutions to Research Problems can be prepared by using the RIA Checkpoint® Student Edition online research product, which is available to accompany this text. It is also possible to prepare solutions to the Research Problems by using tax research materials found in a standard tax library.*

**Research Problem 1.** Green Motor Transportation Corporation is a nationwide long-haul freight concern that owns and operates approximately 15,000 trucks. For tax purposes, Green uses a calendar year and the accrual method of accounting.

Every year, Green is required to pay for a large number of fees, licenses, insurance, and permits (designated as FLIP expenses) in order to legally operate its fleet of vehicles in the large number of states in which it does business. Although the FLIP expenses are accrued for financial accounting purposes, they are expensed for tax purposes. None of the FLIP expenses covers a period of more than one year in duration. This practice has been followed consistently by Green for many years and, until recently, has never been questioned by the IRS.

Upon audit of Green's tax return, the IRS disallowed approximately 55% of the FLIP expenses that had been claimed as a deduction. Although the disallowed expenses were paid in 2002, the IRS held that they were applicable to year 2003. Because Green used the accrual method both for accounting and for tax purposes, the IRS found that a prorating of these expenses was necessary. Green disputed the proration based on the notion that the expenses did not provide a "substantial" benefit to future years. Under an informal policy followed by the IRS, prepaid expenses of less than a year can be expensed in the year paid if certain conditions are met. Green contended that these conditions were met as the FLIP expenses were routine in nature, did not distort income, and were not designed to be manipulative.

The IRS disputed the existence of any such "one-year rule" being available to preclude deducting prepaid expenses. But regardless of whether the rule existed, it would, in any event, not apply to *accrual basis* taxpayers.

Who is right? Can Green Motor Transportation Corporation deduct all of the FLIP expenses paid in 2002, or must 55% of this amount be deferred to 2003?

**Research Problem 2.** Bud purchased farmland from Enos. Bud paid Enos $400,000 for the land. Bud also paid Enos $100,000 for the peanut base acres and payment yield assigned to the land. Bud would like to know whether he can take cost recovery or amortization on the $100,000 payment.

**Research Problem 3.** Keith has just finished building a new golf course. He would like to know whether he can take a cost recovery deduction with respect to the golf course greens.

**Research Problem 4.** Juan owns a business that acquires exotic automobiles that are high-tech, state-of-the-art vehicles with unique design features or equipment. The exotic automobiles are not licensed nor are they set up to be used on the road. Rather, the cars are used exclusively for car shows or related promotional photography. Juan would like to know whether he can take a cost recovery deduction with respect to the exotic automobiles on his Federal income tax return.

*Partial list of research aids:*
*Bruce Selig,* 70 TCM 1125, T.C.Memo. 1995–519.

**Research Problem 5.** Osprey Corporation operates a pipeline system to transport unprocessed "raw" or "wet" natural gas from the gas wellheads to its natural gas processing plant. The pipeline system consists of a central line leading into the processing plant. The central line is fed by lateral adjoining pipelines that link specific wellheads. At all times, Osprey has owned and operated the pipeline system while the "raw" natural gas remains the property of its producer. The producers compensate Osprey for the use of the pipeline on a contractual "fee-for-service" basis.

Determine whether Osprey should depreciate the pipeline over a 7-year period or a 15-year period. Explain.

**Internet Activity**

*Use the tax resources of the Internet to address the following questions. Do not restrict your search to the World Wide Web, but include a review of newsgroups and general reference materials, practitioner sites and resources, primary sources of the tax law, chat rooms and discussion groups, and other opportunities.*

**Research Problem 6.** The $1 million maximum compensation deduction does not seem to have deterred large corporations from remunerating their executives at very high levels. What techniques are being used to work around the millionaires' provision? Are executives taking pay cuts, or are their salaries being deferred or changed in nature due to § 162(m)?

**Research Problem 7.** Changes to depreciation systems often are discussed by policy makers and observers of the tax system. Outline the terms and policy objectives of one of the changes currently proposed by the Treasury, a member of Congress, or a tax policy think tank.

# Losses and Loss Limitations

**CHAPTER 5**

http://wft.swlearning.com

**TAX TALK**

*The income tax has made more liars out of the American people than golf has. Even when you make a tax form out on the level, you don't know when it's through if you are a crook or a martyr.*

—Will Rogers

**C**hapter 4 introduced rules governing the deductibility of trade and business expenses. This chapter extends the notion of deductibility to losses occurring in the course of business operations. In particular, special rules concerning the tax treatment of bad debts, casualty losses, and operating losses are reviewed. In addition, tax shelters and the rules that limit their usefulness as tax avoidance devices are discussed.

**LO.1**

Determine the amount, classification, and timing of the bad debt deduction.

# Bad Debts

If a taxpayer lends money or purchases a debt instrument and the debt is not repaid, a **bad debt** deduction is allowed. Similarly, if an accrual basis taxpayer sells goods or provides services on credit and the account receivable subsequently becomes worthless, a bad debt deduction is permitted.[1] No deduction is allowed, however, for a bad debt arising from the sale of a product or service when the taxpayer is on the cash basis because no income is reported until the cash has been collected. Permitting a bad debt deduction for a cash basis taxpayer would amount to a double deduction because the expenses of the product or service rendered are

---

[1]Reg. § 1.166–1(e).

---

**⊙ T A X   F A C T**

## JUST HOW GOOD IS YOUR CREDIT?

To be successful, a business must generate sales among customers who are willing and able to pay their obligations. Nonetheless, if a sale is made and it is determined that the related account receivable is uncollectible, the business is allowed to claim a bad debt deduction. Recently, corporations claimed bad debt deductions of approximately $142.2 billion against business receipts of over $17.5 trillion.

**Source:** Corporation Income Tax Returns, 2001; Table 2—Selected Balance Sheet, Income Statement, and Tax Items, by Asset Size; Summer 2004.

---

deducted when payments are made to suppliers and to employees or at the time of the sale.

**EXAMPLE 1**

Ella, a sole proprietor engaged in the practice of accounting, performed services for Pat for which she charged $8,000. Pat never paid the bill, and his whereabouts are unknown.

If Ella is an accrual basis taxpayer, she includes the $8,000 in income when the services are performed. When she determines that Pat's account will not be collected, she deducts the $8,000 as a bad debt.

If Ella is a cash basis taxpayer, she does not include the $8,000 in income until payment is received. When she determines that Pat's account will not be collected, she cannot deduct the $8,000 as a bad debt expense because it was never recognized as income. ▪

## SPECIFIC CHARGE-OFF METHOD

Most taxpayers are required to use the **specific charge-off method** when accounting for bad debts. Some financial institutions are permitted to use an alternative **reserve method** for computing bad debt deductions.

A taxpayer using the specific charge-off method may claim a deduction when a specific *business* debt becomes either partially or wholly worthless or when a specific *nonbusiness* debt becomes wholly worthless.[2] For a business debt, the taxpayer must satisfy the IRS that the debt is partially worthless and must demonstrate the amount of worthlessness. If a business debt previously deducted as partially worthless becomes totally worthless in a future year, only the remainder not previously deducted can be deducted in the future year.

In the case of total worthlessness, a deduction is allowed for the entire amount in the year that the debt becomes worthless. The amount of the deduction depends on the taxpayer's basis in the bad debt. If the debt arose from the sale of services or products and the face amount was previously included in income, that amount is deductible. If the taxpayer purchased the debt, the deduction equals the amount the taxpayer paid for the debt instrument.

Determining when a bad debt becomes worthless can be a difficult task. Legal proceedings need not be initiated against the debtor when the surrounding facts indicate that such action will not result in collection.

---

[2]§ 166(a) and Reg. § 1.166.

### A DEDUCTION FOR BAD DEBTS

When computing Federal taxable income, a business is allowed a deduction for bad debts. The city of Los Angeles, however, does not allow a deduction for bad debts when determining the city's business tax. Los Angeles city councilman Greig Smith feels this treatment of bad debts does not promote a business-friendly environment in the city. In his opinion, not allowing a deduction is "just plain bad policy."

SOURCE: Adapted from "Business Taxes," *City News Service*, May 4, 2004.

**EXAMPLE 2**

In 2003, Partridge Company lent $1,000 to Kay, who agreed to repay the loan in two years. In 2005, Kay disappeared after the note became delinquent. If a reasonable investigation by Partridge indicates that Kay cannot be found or that a suit against Kay would not result in collection, Partridge can deduct the $1,000 in 2005. ■

Bankruptcy is generally an indication of at least partial worthlessness of a debt. Bankruptcy may create worthlessness before the settlement date. If this is the case, the deduction may be taken in the year of worthlessness.

**EXAMPLE 3**

In Example 2, assume that Kay filed for personal bankruptcy in 2004 and that the debt is a business debt. At that time, Partridge learned that unsecured creditors (including Partridge) were ultimately expected to receive 20 cents on the dollar. In 2005, settlement is made and Partridge receives only $150. Partridge should deduct $800 ($1,000 loan − $200 expected settlement) in 2004 and $50 in 2005 ($200 balance − $150 proceeds). ■

If a receivable is written off as uncollectible and is subsequently collected during the same tax year, the write-off entry is reversed. If a receivable has been written off as uncollectible, collection in a later tax year may result in income being recognized. Income will result if the deduction yielded a tax benefit in the year it was taken (the tax benefit rule).

## BUSINESS VERSUS NONBUSINESS BAD DEBTS

The nature of a debt depends upon whether the lender is engaged in the business of lending money or whether there is a proximate relationship between the creation of the debt and the *lender's* trade or business. Where either of these conditions is true, a bad debt is classified as a **business bad debt.** If these conditions are not met, a bad debt is classified as a **nonbusiness bad debt.** The use to which the borrowed funds are put is of no consequence when making this classification decision.

**EXAMPLE 4**

Jamil lent his friend, Esther, $1,500. Esther used the money to start a business, which subsequently failed. Even though the proceeds of the loan were used in a business, the loan is a nonbusiness bad debt, because the business was Esther's, and not Jamil's. ■

**EXAMPLE 5**

Horace operates a sole proprietorship that sells premium stereo equipment. Horace uses the accrual basis to account for sales of the stereo equipment. During the year, he sold a $4,000 stereo system to Herbie on credit. Later that year, the account receivable becomes worthless. The loan is a business bad debt, because the debt was related to Horace's business. ■

## CONCEPT SUMMARY 5–1

# The Tax Treatment of Bad Debts Using the Specific Charge-Off Method

| | Business Bad Debts | Nonbusiness Bad Debts |
|---|---|---|
| Timing of deduction | A deduction is allowed when the debt becomes either partially or wholly worthless. | A deduction is allowed *only* when the debt becomes wholly worthless. |
| Character of deduction | The bad debt may be deducted as an ordinary loss. | The bad debt is classified as a short-term capital loss, subject to the $3,000 capital loss limitation for individuals. |
| Recovery of amounts previously deducted | If the account recovered was written off during the current tax year, the write-off entry is reversed. If the account was written off in a previous tax year, income is created subject to the tax benefit rule. | If the account recovered was written off during the current tax year, the write-off entry is reversed. If the account was written off in a previous tax year, income is created subject to the tax benefit rule. |

Generally, nonbusiness bad debts are incurred only by individuals. It is assumed that any loans made by a corporation are related to its trade or business. Therefore, any bad debts resulting from loans made by a corporation are automatically business bad debts.

The distinction between a business bad debt and a nonbusiness bad debt is important. A business bad debt is deductible as an ordinary loss in the year incurred, whereas a nonbusiness bad debt is always treated as a short-term capital loss. Thus, regardless of the age of a nonbusiness bad debt, the deduction may be of limited benefit due to the $3,000 capital loss limitation for individuals (refer to the discussion in Chapter 3).

### LOANS BETWEEN RELATED PARTIES

Loans between related parties raise the issue of whether the transaction was a *bona fide* loan or some other transfer, such as a gift, a disguised dividend payment, or a contribution to capital. The Regulations state that a bona fide debt arises from a debtor-creditor relationship based on a valid and enforceable obligation to pay a fixed or determinable sum of money. Thus, individual circumstances must be examined to determine whether advances between related parties are loans. Some considerations are these:

* Was a note properly executed?
* Was there a reasonable rate of interest?
* Was collateral provided?
* What collection efforts were made?
* What was the intent of the parties?

*EXAMPLE 6*

Ted, who is the sole shareholder of Penguin Corporation, lends the corporation $10,000 so that it can continue business operations. The note specifies a 2% interest rate and is payable on demand. Penguin has shown losses in each year of its five-year existence. The corporation also has liabilities greatly in excess of its assets. It is likely that Ted's transfer to the corporation would be treated as a contribution to capital rather than a liability. Consequently, no bad debt deduction would be allowed upon default by Penguin. ∎

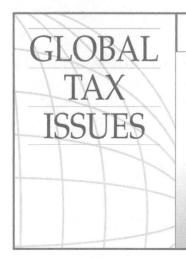

## MACAU—THE NEW LAS VEGAS?

Recently, the Las Vegas Sands opened the first U.S.-operated casino in the People's Republic of China in Macau, the former Portuguese colony handed over to the People's Republic by Portugal in 1999. Because gambling is illegal in most of East Asia, including the rest of China, Macau's casino industry is expected to grow rapidly. Some believe that Macau, once best known for its seedy gambling dens, will become the Las Vegas of the East. An issue facing the gambling industry, however, is the fact that casinos cannot write off bad debts against profits. The authorities are reluctant to allow this deduction because Macau gets two-thirds of its tax revenue from gambling profits.

SOURCE: Adapted from Keith Bradsher, "Macau Famously Seedy, Now Bets on Vegas Plush," *The International Herald Tribune*, May 26, 2004, News, p. 1.

---

**LO.2**

Understand the tax treatment of worthless securities including § 1244 stock.

## Worthless Securities

A loss is allowed for securities that become *completely* worthless during the year (**worthless securities**).[3] Such securities are shares of stock, bonds, notes, or other evidence of indebtedness issued by a corporation or government. The losses generated are treated as capital losses (refer to Chapter 3) deemed to have occurred on the *last day* of the tax year. By treating losses as having occurred on the last day of the tax year, a loss that would otherwise have been classified as short term (if the date of worthlessness were used) may be classified as long term.

**EXAMPLE 7**

Falcon Company, a calendar year taxpayer, owns stock in Owl Corporation (a publicly held company). The stock was acquired as an investment on May 31, 2004, at a cost of $5,000. On April 1, 2005, the stock became worthless. Because the stock is deemed to have become worthless as of December 31, 2005, Falcon has a capital loss from an asset held for 19 months (a long-term capital loss). ■

### SMALL BUSINESS STOCK

The general rule is that shareholders receive capital loss treatment for losses from the sale or exchange of corporate stock. As noted in Chapter 3, the deductibility of capital losses is limited. However, it is possible to avoid capital loss limitations if the loss is sustained on **small business stock (§ 1244 stock)**. Such a loss could arise from a sale of the stock or from the stock becoming worthless. Only *individuals*[4] who acquired the stock *from* the issuing corporation are eligible to receive ordinary loss treatment under § 1244. The ordinary loss treatment is limited to $50,000 ($100,000 for married individuals filing jointly) per year. Losses on § 1244 stock in excess of the statutory limits are treated as capital losses.

The issuing corporation must meet certain requirements for the loss on § 1244 stock to be treated as an *ordinary*—rather than a capital—loss. The principal requirement is that the total capitalization of the corporation is limited to a maximum of

---

[3]§ 165(g).
[4]The term *individuals* for this purpose includes a partnership but not a trust or an estate.

$1 million. This capital limit includes all money and other property received by the corporation for stock and all capital contributions made to the corporation. The $1 million test is made at the time the stock is issued. There are no requirements regarding the kind of stock issued. Section 1244 stock can be either common or preferred.

Section 1244 applies only to losses. If § 1244 stock is sold at a gain, the provision does not apply and the gain is capital gain (which, for individuals, may be subject to preferential tax treatment, as discussed in Chapter 3).

**EXAMPLE 8**

On July 1, 2003, Iris, a single individual, purchased 100 shares of Eagle Corporation common stock for $100,000. The Eagle stock qualifies as § 1244 stock. On June 20, 2005, Iris sells all of the Eagle stock for $20,000, which results in a loss of $80,000. Because the Eagle stock is § 1244 stock, Iris has $50,000 of ordinary loss and $30,000 of long-term capital loss. ■

## PLANNING STRATEGIES

## Maximizing the Benefits of § 1244

**FRAMEWORK FOCUS: TAX RATE**

STRATEGY ➤ CONTROL THE CHARACTER OF INCOME AND DEDUCTIONS.

Because § 1244 limits the amount of loss classified as ordinary loss on a yearly basis, a taxpayer might maximize the benefits of § 1244 by selling the stock in more than one taxable year.

**EXAMPLE 9**

Mitch, a single individual, purchased small business stock in 2003 for $150,000 (150 shares at $1,000 per share). On December 20, 2005, the stock is worth $60,000 (150 shares at $400 per share). Mitch wants to sell the stock at this time. He earns a salary of $80,000 a year, has no other capital transactions, and does not expect any in the future. If Mitch sells all of the small business stock in 2005,

his recognized loss will be $90,000 ($60,000 selling price − $150,000 cost). The loss will be characterized as a $50,000 ordinary loss and a $40,000 long-term capital loss. In computing taxable income for 2005, Mitch could deduct the $50,000 ordinary loss but could deduct only $3,000 of the capital loss (assuming he has no capital gains). The remainder of the capital loss could be carried over and used in future years subject to the capital loss limitations.

Alternatively, if Mitch sells 82 shares in 2005, he will recognize an ordinary loss of $49,200 [82 × ($400 − $1,000)]. If Mitch then sells the remainder of the shares in 2006, he will recognize an ordinary loss of $40,800 [68 × ($400 − $1,000)], successfully avoiding the capital loss limitation. Mitch could deduct the $49,200 ordinary loss in computing 2005 taxable income and the $40,800 ordinary loss in computing 2006 taxable income. ■

---

**LO.3**

Identify a casualty and determine the amount, classification, and timing of casualty and theft losses.

# Casualty and Theft Losses

Losses on business property are deductible, whether attributable to casualty, theft, or some other cause (e.g., rust, termite damage). While all *business* property losses are generally deductible, the amount and timing of casualty and theft losses are determined using special rules. Furthermore, for individual taxpayers, who may deduct casualty losses on personal-use (nonbusiness) property as well as on business and investment property (held in partnerships and S corporations or in an individual capacity), a set of special limitations applies. Casualty gains are also afforded special consideration in the tax law.

## DEFINITION OF CASUALTY

The term *casualty* generally includes *fire, storm, shipwreck,* and *theft.* In addition, losses from *other casualties* are deductible. Such losses generally include any loss resulting from an event that is (1) identifiable; (2) damaging to property; and (3) sudden, unexpected, and unusual in nature. The term also includes accidental loss of property provided the loss qualifies under the same rules as any other casualty.

A *sudden event* is one that is swift and precipitous and not gradual or progressive. An *unexpected event* is one that is ordinarily unanticipated and occurs without the intent of the taxpayer who suffers the loss. An *unusual event* is one that is extraordinary and nonrecurring and does not commonly occur during the activity in which the taxpayer was engaged when the destruction occurred.[5] Examples include hurricanes, tornadoes, floods, storms, shipwrecks, fires, sonic booms, vandalism, and mine cave-ins. A taxpayer also can take a deduction for a casualty loss from an automobile accident if the accident is not attributable to the taxpayer's willful act or willful negligence. Weather that causes damage (drought, for example) must be unusual and severe for the particular region to qualify as a casualty. Furthermore, damage must be to the *taxpayer's* property to be deductible.

**Events That Are Not Casualties.**   Not all acts of God are treated as **casualty losses** for income tax purposes. Because a casualty must be sudden, unexpected, and unusual, progressive deterioration (such as erosion due to wind or rain) is not a casualty because it does not meet the suddenness test.

An example of an event that generally does not qualify as a casualty is insect damage. When termites caused damage over a period of several years, some courts have disallowed a casualty loss deduction.[6] On the other hand, some courts have held that termite damage over periods of up to 15 months after infestation constituted a sudden event and was, therefore, deductible as a casualty loss.[7] Despite the existence of some judicial support for the deductibility of termite damage as a casualty loss, the current position of the IRS is that termite damage is not deductible.[8]

Other examples of events that are not casualties are losses resulting from a decline in value rather than an actual loss of the property. For example, a taxpayer was allowed a loss for the actual flood damage to his property but not for the decline in market value due to the property's being flood-prone.[9] Similarly, a decline in value of an office building due to fire damage to nearby buildings is not deductible as a casualty.

## DEFINITION OF THEFT

Theft includes, but is not necessarily limited to, larceny, embezzlement, and robbery.[10] Theft does not include misplaced items.[11]

**Theft losses** are treated like other casualty losses, but the *timing* of recognition of the loss differs. A theft loss is deducted in the *year of discovery,* not the year of the theft (unless, of course, the discovery occurs in the same year as the theft). If, in the year of the discovery, a claim exists (e.g., against an insurance company)

---

[5]Rev.Rul. 72–592, 1972–2 C.B. 101.

[6]*Fay v. Helvering,* 41–2 USTC ¶9494, 27 AFTR 432, 120 F.2d 253 (CA–2, 1941); *U.S. v. Rogers,* 41–1 USTC ¶9442, 27 AFTR 423, 120 F.2d 244 (CA–9, 1941).

[7]*Rosenberg v. Comm.,* 52–2 USTC ¶9377, 42 AFTR 303, 198 F.2d 46 (CA–8, 1952); *Shopmaker v. U.S.,* 54–1 USTC ¶9195, 45 AFTR 758, 119 F.Supp. 705 (D.Ct. Mo., 1953).

[8]Rev.Rul. 63–232, 1963–2 C.B. 97.

[9]*S. L. Solomon,* 39 TCM 1282, T.C.Memo. 1980–87.

[10]Reg. § 1.165–8(d).

[11]*Mary Francis Allen,* 16 T.C. 163 (1951).

and there is a reasonable expectation of recovering the adjusted basis of the asset from the insurance company, no deduction is permitted.[12] If, in the year of settlement, the recovery is less than the asset's adjusted basis, a deduction may be available. If the recovery is greater than the asset's adjusted basis, *casualty gain* may be recognized.

**EXAMPLE 10**

Sakura, Inc., owned a computer that was stolen from its offices in December 2003. The theft was discovered on June 3, 2004, and the corporation filed a claim with its insurance company that was settled on January 30, 2005. Assuming there is a reasonable expectation of full recovery, no deduction is allowed in 2004. A deduction may be available in 2005 if the actual insurance proceeds are less than the adjusted basis of the asset. (Loss measurement rules are discussed later in this chapter.) ■

## Documentation of Related-Taxpayer Loans, Casualty Losses, and Theft Losses

**PLANNING STRATEGIES**

**FRAMEWORK FOCUS: DEDUCTIONS**

**STRATEGY ➤ MAXIMIZE DEDUCTIBLE AMOUNTS.**

Since the validity of loans between related taxpayers might be questioned, adequate documentation is needed to substantiate a bad debt deduction if the loan subsequently becomes worthless. Documentation should include proper execution of the note (legal form) and the establishment of a bona fide purpose for the loan. In addition, it is desirable to stipulate a reasonable rate of interest and a fixed maturity date.

Because a theft loss deduction is not permitted for misplaced items, a police report and evidence of the value of the property (e.g., appraisals, pictures of the property, purchase receipts) are necessary to document a theft.

Similar documentation of the value of property should be provided to support a casualty loss deduction because the amount of loss is measured, in part, by the decline in fair market value of the property.

## WHEN TO DEDUCT CASUALTY LOSSES

**General Rule.** Generally, a casualty loss is deducted in the year the loss occurs. However, no casualty loss is permitted if a reimbursement claim with a reasonable *prospect of full recovery* exists.[13] If the taxpayer has a partial claim, only part of the loss can be claimed in the year of the casualty, and the remainder is deducted in the year the claim is settled.

**EXAMPLE 11**

Fuchsia Corporation's new warehouse was completely destroyed by fire in 2005. Its cost and fair market value were $250,000. Fuchsia's only claim against the insurance company was on a $70,000 policy that was not settled by year-end. The following year, 2006, Fuchsia settled with the insurance company for $60,000. Fuchsia is entitled to a $180,000 deduction in 2005 and a $10,000 deduction in 2006. ■

If a taxpayer receives reimbursement for a casualty loss sustained and deducted in a previous year, an amended return is not filed for that year. Instead, the taxpayer must include the reimbursement in gross income on the return for the year in which

---

[12]Reg. §§ 1.165–1(d)(2) and 1.165–8(a)(2).                    [13]Reg. § 1.165–1(d)(2)(i).

it is received to the extent that the previous deduction resulted in a tax benefit (refer to Chapter 3).

**EXAMPLE 12**

Golden Hawk, Inc., had a deductible casualty loss of $15,000 on its 2004 tax return. Golden Hawk's taxable income for 2004 was $60,000 after deducting the $15,000 loss. In June 2005, the corporation is reimbursed $13,000 for the prior year's casualty loss. Golden Hawk includes the entire $13,000 in gross income for 2005 because the deduction in 2004 produced a tax benefit. ■

**Disaster Area Losses.**    An exception to the general rule for the time of deduction is allowed for **disaster area losses,** which are casualties or disaster-related business losses sustained in an area designated as a disaster area by the President of the United States.[14] In such cases, the taxpayer may *elect* to treat the loss as having occurred in the taxable year immediately *preceding* the taxable year in which the disaster actually occurred. The rationale for this exception is to provide immediate relief to disaster victims in the form of accelerated tax benefits.

If the due date, plus extensions, for the prior year's return has not passed, a taxpayer makes the election to claim the disaster area loss on the prior year's tax return. If a disaster area is designated after the prior year's return has been filed, it is necessary to file either an amended return or a refund claim. In any case, the taxpayer must show clearly that such an election is being made.

## MEASURING THE AMOUNT OF LOSS

**Amount of Loss.**    The rules for determining the amount of a loss depend in part on whether business, investment, or personal-use (nonbusiness) property was involved. Another factor that must be considered is whether the property was partially or completely destroyed.

If business property or investment property (e.g., rental property) is *completely destroyed*, the loss is equal to the adjusted basis[15] (typically cost less depreciation) of the property at the time of destruction.

**EXAMPLE 13**

Monty's Movers owned a truck, which was used only for business purposes. The truck was destroyed by fire. Monty, the proprietor, had unintentionally allowed his insurance coverage to expire. The fair market value of the truck was $39,000 at the time of the fire, and its adjusted basis was $40,000. Monty is allowed a loss deduction of $40,000 (the adjusted basis of the truck). ■

A different measurement rule applies for *partial destruction* of business and investment property and for *partial* or *complete destruction* of personal-use property held by individuals. In these situations, the loss is the *lesser* of:

• the adjusted basis of the property, or
• the difference between the fair market value of the property before the event and the fair market value immediately after the event.

**EXAMPLE 14**

Wynd and Rain, a law firm, owned an airplane that was used only for business purposes. The airplane was damaged in a crash. At the date of the crash, the fair market value of the plane was $52,000, and its adjusted basis was $32,000. After the crash, the plane was appraised

---

[14]§ 165(h).

[15]See Chapter 6 for a detailed discussion of basis rules.

at \$24,000. The law firm's loss deduction is \$28,000 (the lesser of the adjusted basis or the decrease in fair market value). ■

Any insurance recovery reduces the loss for business, investment, and personal-use losses. In fact, a taxpayer may realize a gain if the insurance proceeds exceed the adjusted basis of the property. Chapter 7 discusses the treatment of net gains and losses on business property and income-producing property.

A special rule on insurance recovery applies to *personal-use property*. In particular, individuals are not permitted to deduct a casualty loss for damage to insured personal-use property unless an insurance claim is filed. This rule applies, whether the insurance provides partial or full reimbursement for the loss.[16]

Generally, an appraisal before and after the casualty is needed to measure the amount of loss. However, the *cost of repairs* to the damaged property generally is acceptable as a method of establishing the loss in value.[17]

*Find information on this topic at our Web site: **http://wft-entities.swlearning.com**.*

**Multiple Losses.** When multiple casualty losses occur during the year, the amount of each loss is computed separately. The rules for computing loss deductions where multiple losses have occurred are illustrated in Example 15.

**EXAMPLE 15**

During the year, Swan Enterprises had the following business casualty losses:

| | | Fair Market Value of the Asset | | |
|---|---|---|---|---|
| Asset | Adjusted Basis | Before the Casualty | After the Casualty | Insurance Recovery |
| A | \$900 | \$600 | \$–0– | \$400 |
| B | 300 | 800 | 250 | 150 |

The following losses are allowed:

- Asset A: \$500. The complete destruction of a business asset results in a deduction of the adjusted basis of the property (reduced by any insurance recovery) regardless of the asset's fair market value.
- Asset B: \$150. The partial destruction of a business asset results in a deduction equal to the lesser of the adjusted basis (\$300) or the decline in value (\$550), reduced by any insurance recovery (\$150). ■

## CASUALTY AND THEFT LOSSES OF INDIVIDUALS

Recall from Chapter 3 that the individual income tax formula distinguishes between deductions *for* AGI and deductions *from* AGI. Casualty and theft losses incurred by an individual in connection with a business or with rental and royalty activities are deductible *for* AGI and are limited only by the rules previously discussed.[18] Losses from most other investment activities and personal-use losses are generally deducted *from* AGI. Investment casualty and theft losses (e.g., the theft of a security) are classified as other miscellaneous itemized deductions (not subject to a 2 percent-of-AGI floor as explained in Chapter 15). Casualty and theft losses of personal-use property are subject to special limitations discussed on the following page.

---

[16]§ 165(h)(4)(E).
[17]Reg. § 1.165–7(a)(2)(ii).

[18]§ 62(a)(1).

## CONCEPT SUMMARY 5–2

### Casualty Gains and Losses

| | Business-Use or Income-Producing Property | Personal-Use Property |
|---|---|---|
| Event creating the loss | Any event. | Casualty or theft. |
| Amount | The lesser of the decline in fair market value or the adjusted basis, but always the adjusted basis if the property is totally destroyed. | The lesser of the decline in fair market value or the adjusted basis. |
| Insurance | Insurance proceeds received reduce the amount of the loss. | Insurance proceeds received (or for which there is an unfiled claim) reduce the amount of the loss. |
| $100 floor | Not applicable. | Applicable per event. |
| Gains and losses | Gains and losses are netted (see detailed discussion in Chapter 7). | Personal casualty and theft gains and losses are netted. |
| Gains exceeding losses | | The gains and losses are treated as gains and losses from the sale of capital assets. |
| Losses exceeding gains | | The gains—and the losses to the extent of gains—are treated as ordinary items in computing AGI. The losses in excess of gains, to the extent that they exceed 10% of AGI, are itemized deductions (*from* AGI). |

**Personal-Use Property.** In addition to the valuation rules discussed above, casualty and theft loss deductions from personal-use property must be reduced by a $100 *per event* floor and a 10 percent-of-AGI *aggregate* floor.[19] The $100 floor applies separately to each casualty or theft and applies to the entire loss from each casualty (e.g., if a storm damages both a taxpayer's residence and automobile, only $100 is subtracted from the total amount of the loss) or theft. All personal-use losses incurred during the year are then added together, and the total is reduced by 10 percent of the taxpayer's AGI. The resulting amount is the taxpayer's itemized deduction for personal-use casualty and theft losses.

**EXAMPLE 16**

Rocky, who had AGI of $30,000, was involved in a motorcycle accident. His motorcycle, which was used only for personal use and had a fair market value of $12,000 and an adjusted basis of $9,000, was completely destroyed. He received $5,000 from his insurance company. Rocky's casualty loss deduction is $900 [$9,000 basis − $5,000 insurance − $100 floor − $3,000 (.10 × $30,000 AGI)]. The $900 casualty loss is an itemized deduction (*from* AGI). ■

Where there are both casualty and theft gains and losses from personal-use property, special netting rules apply. Generally, if casualty and theft gains exceed losses during the year, the gains and losses are treated as capital gains and losses. Alternatively, if losses exceed gains, the casualty and theft gains (and losses to the

---

[19]§§ 165(c)(3) and (h).

extent of gains) are treated as ordinary gains and losses. Any excess losses are deductible as personal-use casualty and theft losses.

*Find more information on this topic at our Web site:* ***http://wft-entities.swlearning.com.***

**LO.4**

Recognize the impact of the net operating loss carryback and carryover provisions.

# Net Operating Losses

## INTRODUCTION

The requirement that every taxpayer file an annual income tax return (whether on a calendar year or a fiscal year) can lead to inequities for taxpayers who experience uneven income over a series of years. These inequities result from the application of progressive tax rates to taxable income determined on an annual basis.

**EXAMPLE 17**

Orange, Inc., realizes the following taxable income or loss over a five-year period: Year 1, $50,000; Year 2, ($30,000); Year 3, $100,000; Year 4, ($200,000); and Year 5, $380,000. Blue Corporation has taxable income of $60,000 every year. Note that both corporations have total taxable income of $300,000 over the five-year period. Assume there is no provision for carryback or carryover of net operating losses. Orange and Blue would have the following five-year tax liabilities:

| Year | Orange's Tax | Blue's Tax |
| --- | --- | --- |
| 1 | $ 7,500 | $10,000 |
| 2 | –0– | 10,000 |
| 3 | 22,250 | 10,000 |
| 4 | –0– | 10,000 |
| 5 | 129,200 | 10,000 |
| | $158,950 | $50,000 |

The computation of tax is made without regard to any NOL benefit. Rates applicable to 2005 are used to compute the tax.

Even though Orange and Blue realized the same total taxable income ($300,000) over the five-year period, Orange would have to pay taxes of $158,950, while Blue would pay taxes of only $50,000. ■

To provide partial relief from this inequitable tax treatment, a deduction is allowed for **net operating losses (NOLs)**.[20] This provision permits an NOL for any one year to offset taxable income in other years. The NOL provision provides relief only for losses from the operation of a trade or business or from casualty and theft.

Only C corporations and individuals are permitted an NOL deduction, since losses of partnerships and S corporations pass through to their owners. For C corporations, the NOL equals any negative taxable income for the year, with an adjustment for the dividends received deduction (see Chapter 8). In addition, deductions for prior-year NOLs are not allowed when determining a current-year NOL.

---

[20]§ 172.

⊙ **T A X   F A C T**

## THE UTILITY OF THE NOL DEDUCTION

**R**ecently, corporations claimed net operating loss deductions of approximately $60.5 billion against business receipts of over $17.5 trillion.

**Source:** Corporation Income Tax Returns, 2001; Table 2—Selected Balance Sheet, Income Statement, and Tax Items, by Asset Size; Summer 2004.

NOLs of individuals are computed by adding back to negative taxable income the excess of nonbusiness deductions (e.g., the standard deduction, charitable contributions, alimony payments) over nonbusiness income, personal and dependency exemptions, and any net capital loss deducted in calculating taxable income. Business deductions that are allowed for determining the NOL include moving expenses, losses on rental property, loss on the sale of small business stock, one-half of the self-employment tax (refer to Chapter 1), and losses from a sole proprietorship, partnership, or S corporation.

### CARRYBACK AND CARRYOVER PERIODS

**General Rules.** A current-year NOL is usually carried back and deducted against income over the two preceding tax years.[21] It is carried back first to the second year before the loss year and then to the year immediately preceding the loss year (until it fully offsets income). If the loss is not completely used against income in the carryback period, it is carried forward for 20 years following the loss year. NOLs that are not used within the 20-year carryforward period are lost. Thus, an NOL sustained in 2005 is used first in 2003 and then 2004. Then, the loss is carried forward and offsets income in 2006 through 2025.

When an NOL is carried back, the taxpayer requests an immediate refund of prior years' taxes by filing an amended return for the previous two years. When an NOL is carried forward, the current return shows an NOL deduction for the prior year's loss. Thus, a struggling business with an NOL can receive rapid cash-flow assistance.

**NOLs from Multiple Tax Years.** When there are NOLs in two or more years, the earliest year's loss is used first. Later years' losses can then be used until they are offset against income or lost. Thus, one year's return could show NOL carryovers from two or more years. Each loss is computed and applied separately.

**Election to Forgo Carryback.** A taxpayer can *irrevocably elect* not to carry back an NOL. The election is made on a corporate tax return (Form 1120) by checking the appropriate box. Individuals can make the election by attaching a statement to their tax return. If the election is made, the loss can *only* be carried forward for

---

[21]A three-year carryback period is available for any portion of an individual's NOL resulting from a casualty or theft loss. The three-year carryback rule also applies to NOLs that are attributable to presidentially declared disaster areas that are incurred by a small business or a taxpayer engaged in farming. For purposes of this provision, a small business is one whose average annual gross receipts for a three-year period are $5 million or less.

### INCREASED NET OPERATING LOSS CAP

The Pennsylvania General Assembly is considering a measure that would increase the cap on the net operating loss carryover provision. The change would increase the amount from $2 million to $5 million.

SOURCE: Adapted from "Manufacturing Initiatives May Pass Before Summer Recess," *Pennsylvania Law Weekly*, May 10, 2004, News, p. 13.

20 years. This election may be desirable in circumstances where marginal tax rates in future years are expected to exceed rates in prior years.

**LO.5**

Discuss tax shelters and the reasons for at-risk and passive loss limitations.

## The Tax Shelter Problem

Before Congress enacted legislation to reduce or eliminate their effectiveness, **tax shelters** were popular investments for tax avoidance purposes because they could generate losses and other benefits that could be used to offset income from other sources. Because of the tax avoidance potential of many tax shelters, they were attractive to wealthy taxpayers with high marginal tax rates. Many tax shelters merely provided an opportunity for "investors" to buy deductions and credits in ventures that were not expected to generate a profit, even in the long run.

Although it may seem odd that a taxpayer would intentionally invest in an activity that was designed to produce losses, there is a logical explanation. The typical tax shelter operated as a partnership and relied heavily on nonrecourse financing.[22] Accelerated depreciation and interest expense deductions generated large losses in the early years of the activity. At the very least, the tax shelter deductions deferred the recognition of any net income from the venture until the activity was sold. In the best of situations, the investor could realize additional tax savings by offsetting other income (e.g., salary, interest, and dividends) with losses flowing from the tax shelter. Ultimately, the sale of the investment would result in *tax-favored* capital gain. The following examples illustrate what was possible *before* Congress enacted legislation to curb tax shelter abuses.

**EXAMPLE 18**

Bob, who earned a salary of $400,000 as a business executive and dividend income of $15,000, invested $20,000 for a 10% interest in a cattle-breeding tax shelter. He did not participate in the operation of the business. Through the use of $800,000 of nonrecourse financing and available cash of $200,000, the partnership acquired a herd of an exotic breed of cattle costing $1 million. Depreciation, interest, and other deductions related to the activity resulted in a loss of $400,000, of which Bob's share was $40,000. Bob was allowed to deduct the $40,000 loss, even though he had invested and stood to lose only $20,000 if the investment turned sour. The net effect of the $40,000 deduction from the partnership was that a portion of Bob's salary and dividend income was "sheltered," and as a result, he was required to calculate his tax liability on only $375,000 of income [$415,000 (salary and dividends) − $40,000 (deduction)] rather than $415,000. If this deduction were available under current

---

[22]Nonrecourse debt is an obligation for which the borrower is not personally liable. An example of nonrecourse debt is a liability on real estate acquired by a partnership without the partnership or any of the partners assuming any liability for the mortgage. The acquired property generally is pledged as collateral for the loan.

## WITH TAX SHELTERS IN THE SPOTLIGHT, TAXPAYERS SHOULD BE CAUTIOUS!

Over the years, the at-risk and passive loss rules have gone a long way to curb abusive tax shelters. To the IRS's chagrin, however, some tax shelters are not restricted by these rules and continue to be a problem, as many reports in the media have shown. In response, the IRS has directed its attention toward those abusive tax shelters marketed by well-known and respected members of the financial community.

The publicity surrounding the IRS's efforts has driven a wedge between shelter marketers and their clients. As a consequence, many clients have sought damages from the accounting and law firms that developed the questionable shelters. Those corporations and executives whose shelters are under scrutiny by the IRS are at risk of losing enormous amounts of money.

But just because some taxpayers have been a bit "too creative" in using the tax law for financial advantage does not mean that all tax shelters are illegal or somehow immoral. Many "tax minimization strategies," such as pursuing well-timed property transactions that postpone taxes or sheltering assets in a § 401(k) account, are well within the bounds of appropriate tax planning. Nonetheless, in the current environment, taxpayers need to be prudent. As a safety precaution, be wary of schemes that take place only on paper and reflect no true economic gain or loss. Particularly problematic are schemes that involve so-called offshore trusts or partnerships. Remember that when something seems too good to be true, it often is!

law and if Bob was in a combined Federal and state income tax bracket of 40%, a tax savings of $16,000 ($40,000 × 40%) would be generated in the first year alone! ∎

A review of Example 18 shows that the taxpayer took a two-for-one write-off ($40,000 deduction, $20,000 investment). In the heyday of tax shelters, promoters often promised even larger write-offs for the investor.

The first major provision aimed at tax shelters is the **at-risk limitation**. Its objective is to limit a taxpayer's deductions to the amount that the taxpayer could actually lose from the investment (the amount "at risk") if it turns out to be a financial disaster.

**EXAMPLE 19**

Returning to the facts of the preceding example, under the current at-risk rules Bob would be allowed to deduct $20,000 (i.e., the amount that he could lose if the business failed). This deduction would reduce his other income, and as a result, Bob would report $395,000 of income ($415,000 – $20,000). The remaining nondeductible $20,000 loss and any future losses flowing from the partnership would be suspended under the at-risk rules and would be deductible in the future only as Bob's at-risk amount increased. ∎

The second major attack on tax shelters came with the passage of the **passive loss** rules. These rules are intended to halt an investor's ability to benefit from the mismatching of an entity's expenses and income that often occurs in the early years of the business. Congress observed that despite the at-risk limitations, investors could still deduct losses flowing from an entity and thereby defer their tax liability on other income. These passive loss rules have, to a great degree, made the term *tax shelter* obsolete by suspending the deductibility of losses.

**Bridge to Finance**

An overarching requirement to maximizing wealth is to reduce the present value cost of taxation. One way to reduce the cost of taxation in present value terms is to defer the payment of a tax into the future for as long as possible. This can be accomplished by reducing the taxpayer's tax base (i.e., taxable income) either by deferring the recognition of income or by accelerating the timing of deductions. As a result, to the extent that the tax cost associated with an investment alternative is reduced, the after-tax benefit from that investment and the investor's wealth position are enhanced.

For example, a common attribute of many tax-advantaged investments is the availability of tax losses that investors may claim on their own income tax returns. Many times, these tax losses are the result of investment-level deductions, such as interest and depreciation expenses, that are bunched in the early years of the life of the investment rather than being due to economic woes of the investment itself.

Through the at-risk limitations and the passive loss rules, the tax law works to scale back the ability of taxpayers to claim tax losses flowing from certain investments. These limitations have a direct impact on *when* investors can claim loss deductions flowing from affected investments. The typical result of these provisions is that the loss deductions are deferred. As a result, when evaluating competing investment alternatives, taxpayers must address the impact of these tax limitations in projecting the after-tax benefits that can be expected to follow.

The passive loss rules require the taxpayer to segregate all income and losses into three categories: active, passive, and portfolio. In general, the passive loss limits *disallow* the deduction of passive losses *against active or portfolio income*, even when the taxpayer is at risk to the extent of the loss. In general, passive losses can only offset passive income.

**EXAMPLE 20**

Returning to the facts of Example 18, the passive activity loss rules further restrict Bob's ability to claim the $20,000 tax deduction shown in Example 19. Because Bob is a passive investor and does not materially participate in any meaningful way in the activities of the cattle-breeding operation, the $20,000 loss allowed under the at-risk rules is disallowed under the passive loss rules. The passive loss is disallowed because Bob does not generate any passive income that could absorb his passive loss. His salary (active income) and dividends (portfolio income) cannot be sheltered by any of the passive loss. Consequently, Bob's current-year taxable income is $415,000, and he receives no current benefit for his share of the partnership loss. However, all is not lost because Bob's share of the entity's loss is *suspended*. That is, it is carried forward and can be deducted in the future when he has passive income or sells his interest in the activity. ■

The following two sections explore the nature of the at-risk limits and passive activity loss rules and their impact on investors. Congress intentionally structured these rules so that investors evaluating potential investments must consider mainly the *economics* of the venture instead of the *tax benefits* or tax avoidance possibilities that an investment may generate.

LO.6

Describe how the at-risk limitation and the passive loss rules limit deductions for losses and identify taxpayers subject to these restrictions.

# At-Risk Limitations

The at-risk provisions limit the deductibility of losses from business and income-producing activities. These provisions, which apply to individuals and closely held corporations, are designed to prevent taxpayers from deducting losses in excess of their actual economic investment in an activity. In the case of an S corporation or a partnership, the at-risk limits apply at the owner level. Under the at-risk rules, a taxpayer's deductible loss from an activity for any taxable year is limited to the amount the taxpayer has at risk at the end of the taxable year (i.e., the amount the taxpayer could actually lose in the activity).

While the amount at risk generally vacillates over time, the initial amount considered at risk consists of the following:[23]

- The amount of cash and the adjusted basis of property contributed to the activity by the taxpayer.
- Amounts borrowed for use in the activity for which the taxpayer is personally liable.
- The adjusted basis of property pledged as security that is not used in the activity.

This amount generally is increased each year by the taxpayer's share of income and is decreased by the taxpayer's share of losses and withdrawals from the activity. In addition, because *general partners* are jointly and severally liable for recourse debts of the partnership, their at-risk amounts are increased when the partnership increases its debt and are decreased when the partnership reduces its debt. However, a taxpayer generally is not considered at risk with respect to borrowed amounts if either of the following is true:

- The taxpayer is not personally liable for repayment of the debt (e.g., nonrecourse debt).
- The lender has an interest (other than as a creditor) in the activity.

An important exception provides that, in the case of an activity involving the holding of real property, a taxpayer is considered at risk for his or her share of any *qualified nonrecourse financing* that is secured by real property used in the activity.[24]

Subject to the passive activity rules discussed later in the chapter, a taxpayer may deduct a loss as long as the at-risk amount is positive. However, once the at-risk amount is exhausted, any remaining loss cannot be deducted until a later year. Any losses disallowed for any given taxable year by the at-risk rules may be deducted in the first succeeding year in which the rules do not prevent the deduction—that is, when there is, and to the extent of, a positive at-risk amount.

EXAMPLE 21

In 2005, Sue invests $40,000 in an oil partnership. The partnership, through the use of nonrecourse loans, spends $60,000 on deductible intangible drilling costs applicable to Sue's interest. Assume Sue's interest in the partnership is subject to the at-risk limits but is not subject to the passive loss limits. Since Sue has only $40,000 of capital at risk, she cannot deduct more than $40,000 against her other income and must reduce her at-risk amount to zero ($40,000 at-risk amount − $40,000 loss deducted). The nondeductible loss of $20,000 ($60,000 loss generated − $40,000 loss allowed) can be carried over to 2006.

---

[23]§ 465(b)(1).

[24]Section 465(b)(6) defines qualified nonrecourse financing.

| CONCEPT SUMMARY 5–3 |
|---|

## Calculation of At-Risk Amount

Increases to a taxpayer's at-risk amount:

* Cash and the adjusted basis of property contributed to the activity.
* Amounts borrowed for use in the activity for which the taxpayer is personally liable.
* The adjusted basis of property pledged as security that is not used in the activity.
* Taxpayer's share of amounts borrowed for use in the activity that are qualified nonrecourse financing.
* Taxpayer's share of the activity's income.

Decreases to a taxpayer's at-risk amount:

* Withdrawals from the activity.
* Taxpayer's share of the activity's loss.
* Taxpayer's share of any reductions of debt for which recourse against the taxpayer exists or reductions of qualified nonrecourse debt.

In 2006, Sue has taxable income of $15,000 from the oil partnership and invests an additional $10,000 in the venture. Her at-risk amount is now $25,000 ($0 beginning balance + $15,000 taxable income + $10,000 additional investment). This enables Sue to deduct the $20,000 carryover loss and requires her to reduce her at-risk amount to $5,000 ($25,000 at-risk amount – $20,000 carryover loss allowed). ■

An additional complicating factor is that previously allowed losses must be recaptured as income to the extent the at-risk amount is reduced below zero.[25] This rule applies in situations such as when the amount at risk is reduced below zero by distributions to the taxpayer or when the status of indebtedness changes from recourse to nonrecourse.

# Passive Loss Limits

### CLASSIFICATION AND IMPACT OF PASSIVE INCOME AND LOSS

**Classification.**   The passive loss rules require income and loss to be classified into one of three categories: *active, passive,* or *portfolio*. **Active income** includes the following:

* Wages, salary, commissions, bonuses, and other payments for services rendered by the taxpayer.
* Profit from a trade or business in which the taxpayer is a material participant.

**Portfolio income** includes the following:

* Interest, dividends, annuities, and royalties not derived in the ordinary course of a trade or business.
* Gain or loss from the disposition of property that produces portfolio income or is held for investment purposes.

---

[25]§ 465(e).

Section 469 provides that income or loss from the following activities is treated as *passive:*

- Any trade or business or income-producing activity in which the taxpayer does not materially participate.
- Subject to certain exceptions, all rental activities, whether the taxpayer materially participates or not.

Although the Code defines rental activities as passive activities, several exceptions allow losses from certain real estate rental activities to offset nonpassive (active or portfolio) income. The exceptions are discussed under Special Rules for Real Estate later in the chapter.

**General Impact.**   Losses or expenses generated by passive activities can only be deducted to the extent of income from passive activities. Any excess may not be used to offset income from active or portfolio income. Instead, any unused passive losses are suspended and carried forward to future years to offset passive income generated in those years. Otherwise, suspended losses may be used only when a taxpayer disposes of his or her entire interest in an activity. In that event, all current and suspended losses related to the activity may offset active and portfolio income.

**EXAMPLE 22**

Kim, a physician, earns $150,000 from her full-time practice. She also receives $10,000 in dividends and interest from various portfolio investments, and her share of a passive loss from a tax shelter not limited by the at-risk rules is $60,000. Because the loss is a passive loss, it is not deductible against her other income. The loss is suspended and is carried over to the future. If Kim has passive income from this investment or from other passive investments in the future, she can offset the suspended loss against that passive income. If she does not have passive income to offset this suspended loss in the future, she will be allowed to offset the loss against other types of income when she eventually disposes of the passive activity. ■

**Impact of Suspended Losses.**   The actual economic gain or loss from a passive investment (including any suspended losses) can be determined when a taxpayer disposes of his or her entire interest in the investment. As a result, under the passive loss rules, upon a fully taxable disposition, any overall loss realized from the activity by the taxpayer is recognized and can be offset against passive, active, and portfolio income.

A fully taxable disposition generally involves a sale of the property to a third party at arm's length and thus, presumably, for a price equal to the property's fair market value. Gain recognized upon a transfer of an interest in a passive activity generally is treated as passive and is first offset by the suspended losses from that activity.

**EXAMPLE 23**

Rex sells an apartment building, a passive activity, with an adjusted basis of $100,000 for $180,000. In addition, he has suspended passive losses of $60,000 associated with the building. His total gain, $80,000, and his taxable gain, $20,000, are calculated as follows:

| | |
|---|---|
| Net sales price | $ 180,000 |
| Less: Adjusted basis | (100,000) |
| Total gain | $  80,000 |
| Less: Suspended losses | (60,000) |
| Taxable gain (passive) | $  20,000 |

■

---

**◯ T A X   F A C T**

## THE DECLINING INTEREST IN LIMITED PARTNERSHIPS

**B**ased on the most recently available data compiled by the IRS, the number of taxpayers investing in limited partnerships appears to have peaked at about the time the passive activity loss rules were enacted by Congress. Since that time, the number of limited partnership interests has declined. It may well be no accident that with the constraints placed on a taxpayer's ability to claim losses by the passive activity provisions, fewer taxpayers are interested in investment opportunities that promote tax losses.

| Year | Number of Partners in Limited Partnerships |
|------|-------------------------------------------|
| 1985 | 13,244,824 |
| 1990 | 11,986,542 |
| 1995 | 10,223,901 |
| 1998 | 9,325,111 |
| 2000 | 6,468,292 |
| 2002 | 6,918,515 |

**Sources:** Partnership Returns: Selected Balance Sheet and Income Statement Items for Specified Income Years, 1985–2001, Table 11, *SOI Bulletin*, Summer 2003; Partnership Returns: Selected Balance Sheet and Income Statement Items for Specified Income Years, 1990–2002, Table 11, *SOI Bulletin*, Summer 2004.

---

If current and suspended losses of the passive activity exceed the gain realized from the sale or if the sale results in a realized loss, the amount of

- any loss from the activity for the tax year (including losses suspended in the activity disposed of)

in excess of

- net income or gain for the tax year from all passive activities (without regard to the activity disposed of)

is treated as a loss that is not from a passive activity. In computing the loss from the activity for the year of disposition, any gain or loss recognized is included in the calculation.

**EXAMPLE 24**

Dean sells an apartment building with an adjusted basis of $100,000 for $150,000. In addition, he has current and suspended passive losses of $60,000 associated with the building and has no other passive activities. His total gain of $50,000 and his deductible loss of $10,000 are calculated as follows:

| | |
|---|---|
| Net sales price | $ 150,000 |
| Less: Adjusted basis | (100,000) |
| Total gain | $ 50,000 |
| Less: Suspended losses | (60,000) |
| Deductible loss (not passive) | ($ 10,000) |

The $10,000 loss can be deducted against Dean's active and portfolio income. ■

**Carryovers of Suspended Losses.**   In the above examples, it was assumed that the taxpayer had an interest in only one passive activity, and as a result, the suspended loss was related exclusively to the activity that was disposed of. When a taxpayer owns more than one passive activity, however, any suspended losses must be allocated among the activities. The allocation to an activity is made by multiplying the disallowed passive activity loss from all activities by the following fraction:

$$\frac{\text{Loss from activity}}{\text{Sum of losses for taxable year from all activities having losses}}$$

**EXAMPLE 25**

Diego has investments in three passive activities with the following income and losses for 2004:

| | |
|---|---:|
| Activity A | ($ 30,000) |
| Activity B | (20,000) |
| Activity C | 25,000 |
| Net passive loss | ($ 25,000) |
| Net passive loss allocated to: | |
|     Activity A [$25,000 × ($30,000/$50,000)] | ($ 15,000) |
|     Activity B [$25,000 × ($20,000/$50,000)] | (10,000) |
| Total suspended losses | ($ 25,000) |

Suspended losses are carried over indefinitely and are offset in the future against any passive income from the activities to which they relate.[26]

**EXAMPLE 26**

Assume the same facts as in the preceding example and that Activity A produces $10,000 of income in 2005. Of the suspended loss of $15,000 from 2004 for Activity A, $10,000 is offset against the income from this activity. If Diego sells Activity A in early 2006, then the remaining $5,000 suspended loss is used in determining his final gain or loss. ■

**Passive Credits.**   Credits arising from passive activities are limited in much the same way as passive losses. Passive credits can be utilized only against regular tax attributable to passive income,[27] which is calculated by comparing the tax on all income (including passive income) with the tax on income excluding passive income.

**EXAMPLE 27**

Sam owes $50,000 of tax, disregarding net passive income, and $80,000 of tax, considering both net passive and other taxable income (disregarding the credits in both cases). The amount of tax attributable to the passive income is $30,000.

| | |
|---|---:|
| Tax due (before credits) including net passive income | $ 80,000 |
| Less: Tax due (before credits) without including net passive income | (50,000) |
| Tax attributable to passive income | $ 30,000 |

Sam in the preceding example can claim a maximum of $30,000 of passive activity credits; the excess credits are carried over. These passive activity credits (such as the low-income housing credit and rehabilitation credit) can be used only

---

[26]§ 469(b).

[27]§ 469(d)(2).

against the *regular* tax attributable to passive income. If a taxpayer has a net loss from passive activities during a given year, no credits can be used.

**Carryovers of Passive Credits.** Tax credits attributable to passive activities can be carried forward indefinitely, much like suspended passive losses. Unlike passive losses, however, passive credits are lost forever when the activity is disposed of in a taxable transaction where loss is recognized. Credits are allowed on dispositions only when there is sufficient tax on passive income to absorb them.

**EXAMPLE 28**

Alicia sells a passive activity for a gain of $10,000. The activity had suspended losses of $40,000 and suspended credits of $15,000. The $10,000 gain is offset by $10,000 of the suspended losses, and the remaining $30,000 of suspended losses is deductible against Alicia's active and portfolio income. The suspended credits are lost forever because the sale of the activity did not generate any tax after considering the effect of the suspended losses. This is true even if Alicia has positive taxable income or is subject to the alternative minimum tax (discussed in Chapter 13). ■

**EXAMPLE 29**

If Alicia in the preceding example had realized a $100,000 gain on the sale of the passive activity, the suspended credits could have been used to the extent of regular tax attributable to the net passive income.

| | |
|---|---|
| Gain on sale | $100,000 |
| Less: Suspended losses | (40,000) |
| Net gain | $ 60,000 |

If the tax attributable to the net gain of $60,000 is $15,000 or more, the entire $15,000 of suspended credits can be used. If the tax attributable to the gain is less than $15,000, the excess of the suspended credits over the tax attributable to the gain is lost forever. ■

When a taxpayer has an adequate regular tax liability from passive activities to trigger the use of suspended credits, the credits lose their character as passive credits. They are reclassified as regular tax credits and made subject to the same limits as other credits (see Chapter 13).

**Passive Activity Changes to Active.** If a formerly passive activity becomes active, suspended losses are allowed to the extent of income from the now active business.[28] If any of the suspended loss remains, it continues to be treated as a loss from a passive activity. The excess suspended loss can be deducted against passive income or carried over to the next tax year and deducted to the extent of income from the now active business in the succeeding year(s).

## TAXPAYERS SUBJECT TO THE PASSIVE LOSS RULES

The passive loss rules apply to individuals, estates, trusts, personal service corporations, and closely held C corporations.[29] Passive income or loss from investments in partnerships or S corporations (see Chapters 10 and 11) flows through to the owners, and the passive loss rules are applied at the owner level. Consequently, it is necessary to understand how the passive activity rules apply to both entities *and* their owners (including individual taxpayers).

---

[28]§ 469(f).

[29]§ 469(a).

**Personal Service Corporations.**   Application of the passive loss limitations to **personal service corporations** is intended to prevent taxpayers from sheltering personal service income by creating personal service corporations and acquiring passive activities at the corporate level.

**EXAMPLE 30**

Five tax accountants, who earn a total of $1 million a year in their individual practices, form a personal service corporation. Shortly after its formation, the corporation invests in a passive activity that produces a $200,000 loss during the year. Because the passive loss rules apply to personal service corporations, the corporation may not deduct the $200,000 loss against the $1 million of active income. ■

Determination of whether a corporation is a *personal service corporation* is based on rather broad definitions. A personal service corporation is a corporation that meets both of the following conditions:

* The principal activity is the performance of personal services.
* Such services are substantially performed by owner-employees.

Generally, personal service corporations include those in the fields of health, law, engineering, architecture, accounting, actuarial science, performing arts, and consulting.[30]

*Find more information on this topic at our Web site: **http://wft-entities.swlearning.com**.*

**Closely Held C Corporations.**   Application of the passive loss rules to closely held (non-personal service) C corporations is also intended to prevent individuals from incorporating to avoid the passive loss limitations. A corporation is classified as a **closely held C corporation** if at any time during the taxable year, more than 50 percent of the value of its outstanding stock is owned, directly or indirectly, by or for five or fewer individuals. Closely held C corporations (other than personal service corporations) may use passive losses to offset *active* income, but *not portfolio* income.

**EXAMPLE 31**

Silver Corporation, a closely held (non-personal service) C corporation, has a $500,000 passive loss from a rental activity, $400,000 of active income, and $100,000 of portfolio income. The corporation may offset $400,000 of the $500,000 passive loss against the $400,000 of active business income, but may not offset the remainder against the $100,000 of portfolio income. Thus, $100,000 of the passive loss is suspended ($500,000 passive loss − $400,000 offset against active income). ■

Application of the passive loss limitations to closely held C corporations prevents shareholders from transferring their portfolio investments to such corporations in order to offset passive losses against portfolio income.

**LO.7**

Discuss and be able to apply the definitions of activity, material participation, and rental activity under the passive loss rules.

### ACTIVITY DEFINED

Identifying what constitutes an activity is a necessary first step in applying the passive loss limitation. The current rules used to delineate an activity state that, in general, a taxpayer can treat one or more trade or business activities or rental activities as a single activity if those activities form an *appropriate economic unit* for measuring gain or loss. The Regulations provide guidelines for identifying

---

[30]§ 448(d)(2)(A).

appropriate economic units.[31] These guidelines are designed to prevent taxpayers from arbitrarily combining different businesses in an attempt to circumvent the passive loss limitation. For example, combining a profitable active business and a passive business generating losses into one activity would allow the taxpayer to offset passive losses against active income.

*Find more information on this topic at our Web site: **http://wft-entities.swlearning.com**.*

To determine which ventures form an appropriate economic unit, all of the relevant facts and circumstances must be considered. However, special rules restrict the grouping of rental and nonrental activities.[32] The example below, adapted from the Regulations, illustrates the application of the activity grouping rules.[33]

**EXAMPLE 32**

George owns a men's clothing store and a video game parlor in Chicago. He also owns a men's clothing store and a video game parlor in Milwaukee. Reasonable methods of applying the facts and circumstances test may result in any of the following groupings:

- All four businesses may be grouped into a single activity.
- The clothing stores may be grouped into an activity, and the video game parlors may be grouped into an activity.
- The Chicago businesses may be grouped into an activity, and the Milwaukee businesses may be grouped into an activity.
- Each of the four businesses may be treated as a separate activity. ■

Once a set of activities has been grouped by the taxpayer using the above rules, the grouping cannot be changed unless a material change in the facts and circumstances occurs or the original grouping was clearly inappropriate. In addition, the Regulations also grant the IRS the right to regroup activities when one of the primary purposes of the taxpayer's grouping is to avoid the passive loss limitation and the grouping fails to reflect an appropriate economic unit.[34]

## MATERIAL PARTICIPATION

If a taxpayer materially participates in a nonrental trade or business activity, any loss from that activity is treated as an active loss that can offset active or portfolio income. If a taxpayer does not materially participate, however, the loss is treated as a passive loss, which can only offset passive income. Therefore, controlling whether a particular activity is treated as active or passive is an important part of the tax strategy of a taxpayer who owns an interest in one or more businesses. Consider the following examples.

**EXAMPLE 33**

Cameron, a corporate executive, earns a salary of $600,000 per year. In addition, he owns a separate business in which he participates. The business produces a loss of $100,000 during the year. If Cameron materially participates in the business, the $100,000 loss is an active loss that may offset his active income from his corporate employer. If he does not materially participate, the loss is passive and is suspended. Cameron may use the suspended loss in the future only when he has passive income or disposes of the activity. ■

**EXAMPLE 34**

Connor, an attorney, earns $350,000 a year in his law practice. He owns interests in two activities, A and B, in which he participates. Activity A, in which he does not *materially*

---

[31]Reg. § 1.469–4.
[32]Reg. § 1.469–4(d).

[33]Reg. § 1.469–4(c)(3).
[34]Reg. § 1.469–4(f).

participate, produces a loss of $50,000. Connor has not yet met the material participation standard for Activity B, which produces income of $80,000. However, he can meet the material participation standard if he spends an additional 50 hours in Activity B during the year. Should Connor attempt to meet the material participation standard for Activity B? If he continues working in Activity B and becomes a material participant, the $80,000 of income from the activity is active, and the $50,000 passive loss from Activity A must be suspended. A more favorable tax strategy is for Connor to *not meet* the material participation standard for Activity B, thus making the income from that activity passive. This enables him to offset the $50,000 passive loss from Activity A against the passive income from Activity B. ■

It is possible to devise numerous scenarios in which the taxpayer could control the tax outcome by increasing or decreasing participation in different activities. Examples 33 and 34 demonstrate two of the possibilities. The conclusion reached in most analyses of this type is that taxpayers will benefit by having profitable activities classified as passive so that any passive losses can be used to offset that passive income. If the activity produces a loss, however, the taxpayer will benefit if it is classified as active so that the loss is not subject to the passive loss limitations.

Temporary Regulations[35] provide seven tests that are intended to help taxpayers determine when **material participation** is achieved.

**Tests Based on Current Participation.**   The first four tests are quantitative tests that require measurement, in hours, of the individual's participation in the activity during the year.

1. *Does the individual participate in the activity for more than 500 hours during the year?*

The purpose of the 500-hour requirement is to restrict deductions from the types of trade or business activities that Congress intended to treat as passive activities. The 500-hour standard for material participation was adopted for the following reasons:[36]

- Few investors in traditional tax shelters devote more than 500 hours a year to such an investment.
- The IRS believes that income from an activity in which the taxpayer participates for more than 500 hours a year should not be treated as passive.

2. *Does the individual's participation in the activity for the taxable year constitute substantially all of the participation in the activity of all individuals (including nonowner employees) for the year?*

**EXAMPLE 35**

Ned, a physician, operates a separate business in which he participates for 80 hours during the year. He is the only participant and has no employees in the separate business. Ned meets the material participation standard of Test 2. If he had employees, it could be difficult to apply Test 2, because the Temporary Regulations do not define the term "substantially all." ■

3. *Does the individual participate in the activity for more than 100 hours during the year, and is the individual's participation in the activity for the year not less than the participation of any other individual (including nonowner employees) for the year?*

---

[35]Temp.Reg. § 1.469–5T(a).

[36]T.D. 8175, 1988–1 C.B. 191.

<table>
<tr><td>

**EXAMPLE 36**

</td><td>

Adam, a college professor, owns a separate business in which he participates 110 hours during the year. He has an employee who works 90 hours during the year. Adam meets the material participation standard under Test 3, but probably does not meet it under Test 2 because his participation is only 55% of the total participation. It is unlikely that 55% would meet the substantially all requirement of Test 2. ■

</td></tr>
</table>

Tests 2 and 3 are included because the IRS recognizes that the operation of some activities does not require more than 500 hours of participation during the year.

4. *Is the activity a significant participation activity for the taxable year, and does the individual's aggregate participation in all significant participation activities during the year exceed 500 hours?*

A **significant participation activity** is a trade or business in which the individual's participation exceeds 100 hours during the year. This test treats taxpayers as material participants if their aggregate participation in several significant participation activities exceeds 500 hours. Test 4 thus accords the same treatment to an individual who devotes an aggregate of more than 500 hours to several significant participation activities as to an individual who devotes more than 500 hours to a single activity.

<table>
<tr><td>

**EXAMPLE 37**

</td><td>

Mike owns five different businesses. He participates in each activity during the year as follows:

| Activity | Hours of Participation |
|----------|------------------------|
| A | 110 |
| B | 140 |
| C | 120 |
| D | 150 |
| E | 100 |

Activities A, B, C, and D are significant participation activities, and Mike's aggregate participation in those activities is 520 hours. Therefore, Activities A, B, C, and D are *not* treated as passive activities. Activity E is not a significant participation activity (not more than 100 hours), so it is not included in applying the 500-hour test. Activity E is treated as a passive activity, unless Mike meets one of the other material participation tests for that activity. ■

</td></tr>
</table>

<table>
<tr><td>

**EXAMPLE 38**

</td><td>

Assume the same facts as in the preceding example, except that Activity A does not exist. All of the activities are now treated as passive. Activity E is not counted in applying the more-than-500-hour test, so Mike's aggregate participation in significant participation activities is 410 hours (140 in Activity B + 120 in Activity C + 150 in Activity D). He could meet the significant participation test for Activity E by participating for one more hour in the activity. This would cause Activities B, C, D, and E to be treated as nonpassive activities. However, before deciding whether to participate for at least one more hour in Activity E, Mike should assess how the participation would affect his overall tax liability. ■

</td></tr>
</table>

**Tests Based on Prior Participation.** Tests 5 and 6 are based on material participation in prior years. Under these tests, a taxpayer no longer participating in an activity can continue to be *classified* as a material participant. The IRS takes the position that material participation in a trade or business for a long period of time is likely to indicate that the activity represents the individual's principal livelihood, rather than a passive investment. Consequently, withdrawal from the activity or reduction of participation to the point where it is not material does not change the classification of the activity from active to passive.

5. *Did the individual materially participate in the activity for any five taxable years (whether consecutive or not) during the 10 taxable years that immediately precede the taxable year?*

**EXAMPLE 39**

Dawn, who owns a 50% interest in a restaurant, was a material participant in the operations of the restaurant from 1999 through 2003. She retired at the end of 2003 and is no longer involved in the restaurant except as an investor. Dawn will be treated as a material participant in the restaurant in 2004. Even if she does not become involved in the restaurant as a material participant again, she will continue to be treated as a material participant in 2005, 2006, 2007, and 2008. In 2009 and later years, Dawn's share of income or loss from the restaurant will be classified as passive unless she materially participates in those years. ▨

6. *Is the activity a personal service activity, and did the individual materially participate in the activity for any three preceding taxable years (whether consecutive or not)?*

As indicated above, the material participation standards for personal service activities differ from other businesses. An individual who was a material participant in a personal service activity for *any three years* prior to the taxable year continues to be treated as a material participant after withdrawal from the activity.

**EXAMPLE 40**

Evan, a CPA, retires from the EFG Partnership after working full-time in the partnership for 30 years. As a retired partner, he will continue to receive a share of the profits of the firm for the next 10 years, even though he will not participate in the firm's operations. Evan also owns an interest in a passive activity that produces a loss for the year. Because he continues to be treated as a material participant in the EFG Partnership, his income from the partnership is active income. Therefore, he is not allowed to offset the loss from his passive investment against the income from the EFG Partnership. ▨

**Test Based on Facts and Circumstances.**   Test 7 assesses the facts and circumstances to determine whether the taxpayer has materially participated.

7. *Based on all the facts and circumstances, did the individual participate in the activity on a regular, continuous, and substantial basis during the year?*

*Find more information on this topic at our Web site: **http://wft-entities.swlearning.com**.*

Unfortunately, the Temporary Regulations do not define what constitutes regular, continuous, and substantial participation.[37]

**Participation Defined.**   Participation generally includes any work done by an individual in an activity that he or she owns. Participation does not include work if it is of a type not customarily done by owners *and* if one of its principal purposes is to avoid the disallowance of passive losses or credits. Also, work done in an individual's capacity as an investor (e.g., reviewing financial reports in a non-managerial capacity) is not counted in applying the material participation tests. However, participation by an owner's spouse counts as participation by the owner.[38]

---

[37]Temp.Reg. § 1.469–5T(b)(2).

[38]Temp.Reg. § 1.469–5T(f)(3).

**EXAMPLE 41**

Tom, who is a partner in a CPA firm, owns a computer store that has operated at a loss during the year. In order to offset this loss against the income from his CPA practice, Tom would like to avoid having the computer business classified as a passive activity. Through December 15, he has worked 400 hours in the business in management and selling activities. During the last two weeks of December, he works 80 hours in management and selling activities and 30 hours doing janitorial chores. Also during the last two weeks in December, Tom's wife participates 40 hours as a salesperson. She has worked as a salesperson in the computer store in prior years, but has not done so during the current year. If any of Tom's work is of a type not customarily done by owners and if one of its principal purposes is to avoid the disallowance of passive losses or credits, it is not counted in applying the material participation tests. It is likely that Tom's 480 hours of participation in management and selling activities will count as participation, but the 30 hours spent doing janitorial chores will not. However, the 40 hours of participation by his wife will count, and as a result, Tom will qualify as a material participant under the more-than-500-hour rule (480 + 40 = 520). ■

**Limited Partners.** A *limited* partner is one whose liability to third-party creditors of the partnership is limited to the amount the partner has invested in the partnership. Such a partnership must have at least one *general* partner, who is fully liable in an individual capacity for the debts of the partnership to third parties. Generally, a *limited partner* is not considered a material participant unless he or she qualifies under Test 1, 5, or 6 in the above list. However, a *general partner* may qualify as a material participant by meeting any of the seven tests. If a general partner also owns a limited interest in the same limited partnership, all interests are treated as a general interest.[39]

**Corporations.** Personal service corporations and closely held C corporations cannot directly participate in an activity. However, a corporation is deemed to materially participate if its owners materially participate in an activity of the corporation. Together, the participating owners must own directly or indirectly more than 50 percent of the value of the outstanding stock of the corporation.[40] Alternatively, a closely held C corporation may be deemed to materially participate in an activity if, during the entire year, it has at least one full-time employee actively managing the business and at least three full-time nonowner employees working for the business. In addition, the corporation's trade or business expenses must exceed the gross income from that business by 15 percent for the year.[41]

## RENTAL ACTIVITIES

The Code specifies that, subject to certain exceptions, all rental activities are to be treated as passive activities.[42] A **rental activity** is defined as any activity where payments are received principally for the use of tangible (real or personal) property.[43] Importantly, an activity that is classified as a rental activity is subject to the passive activity loss rules, even if the taxpayer involved is a material participant.

**EXAMPLE 42**

Sarah owns an apartment building and spends an average of 60 hours a week in its operation. Assuming that the apartment building operation is classified as a rental activity, it is automatically subject to the passive activity rules, even though Sarah spends more than 500 hours a year in its operation. ■

---

[39]Temp.Reg. § 1.469–5T(e)(3)(ii).
[40]Temp.Reg. § 1.469–1T(g)(3)(i)(A).
[41]Temp.Reg. § 1.469–1T(g)(3)(i)(B).

[42]§ 469(c)(2).
[43]§ 469(j)(8).

## CONCEPT SUMMARY 5–4

### Passive Activity Loss Rules: General Concepts

| | |
|---|---|
| What is the fundamental passive activity rule? | Passive activity losses may be deducted only against passive activity income and gains. Losses not allowed are suspended and used in future years. |
| Who is subject to the passive activity rules? | Individuals.<br>Estates.<br>Trusts.<br>Personal service corporations.<br>Closely held C corporations. |
| What is a passive activity? | Trade or business or income-producing activity in which the taxpayer does not materially participate during the year, or rental activities, subject to certain exceptions, regardless of the taxpayer's level of participation. |
| What is an activity? | One or more trades or businesses or rental activities that comprise an appropriate economic unit. |
| How is an appropriate economic unit determined? | Based on a reasonable application of the relevant facts and circumstances. |
| What is material participation? | In general, the taxpayer participates on a regular, continuous, and substantial basis. More specifically, when the taxpayer meets the conditions of one of the seven tests provided in the Regulations. |
| What is a rental activity? | In general, an activity where payments are received for the use of tangible property. More specifically, a rental activity that does *not* meet one of the six exceptions provided in the Regulations. Special rules apply to rental real estate. |

Temporary Regulations, however, provide exceptions for certain situations where activities involving rentals of real and personal property are *not* to be treated as rental activities.[44] Activities covered by any of the exceptions provided by the Temporary Regulations are not *automatically* treated as passive activities because they would not be classified as rental activities. Instead, the activities are subject to the material participation tests.

*Find more information on this topic at our Web site:* ***http://wft-entities.swlearning.com.***

**EXAMPLE   43**

Dan owns a DVD rental business. Because the average period of customer use is seven days or less, Dan's business is not treated as a rental activity. ■

The fact that Dan's DVD business in the previous example is not treated as a rental activity does not necessarily mean that it is classified as a nonpassive activity. Instead, the DVD business is treated as a trade or business activity subject to the material participation standards. If Dan is a material participant, the business is treated as active. If he is not a material participant, it is treated as a passive activity.

---

[44]Temp.Reg. § 1.469–1T(e)(3)(ii).

## LO.8

Recognize the relationship between the at-risk and passive activity limitations.

## INTERACTION OF AT-RISK AND PASSIVE ACTIVITY LIMITS

The determination of whether a loss is suspended under the passive loss rules is made *after* application of the at-risk rules, as well as other provisions relating to the measurement of taxable income. A loss that is not allowed for the year because the taxpayer is not at risk with respect to it is suspended under the at-risk provision and not under the passive loss rules. Further, a taxpayer's basis is reduced by deductions (e.g., depreciation) even if the deductions are not currently usable because of the passive loss rules.

**EXAMPLE 44**

Jack's adjusted basis in a passive activity is $10,000 at the beginning of 2004. His loss from the activity in 2004 is $4,000. Since Jack has no passive activity income, the $4,000 cannot be deducted. At year-end, Jack has an adjusted basis and an at-risk amount of $6,000 in the activity and a suspended passive loss of $4,000. ■

**EXAMPLE 45**

Jack in the preceding example has a loss of $9,000 in the activity in 2005. Since the $9,000 exceeds his at-risk amount ($6,000) by $3,000, that $3,000 loss is disallowed by the at-risk rules. If Jack has no passive activity income, the remaining $6,000 is suspended under the passive activity rules. At year-end, he has:

- A $3,000 loss suspended under the at-risk rules.
- $10,000 of suspended passive losses.
- An adjusted basis and at-risk amount in the activity of zero. ■

**EXAMPLE 46**

Jack in Example 45 realizes $1,000 of passive income from the activity in 2006. Because the $1,000 increases his at-risk amount, $1,000 of the $3,000 unused loss is reclassified as a passive loss. If he has no other passive income, the $1,000 income is offset by $1,000 of suspended passive losses. At the end of 2006, Jack has:

- No taxable passive income.
- $2,000 ($3,000 − $1,000) of unused losses under the at-risk rules.
- $10,000 of (reclassified) suspended passive losses ($10,000 + $1,000 of reclassified unused at-risk losses − $1,000 of passive losses offset against passive income).
- An adjusted basis and an at-risk amount in the activity of zero. ■

**EXAMPLE 47**

In 2007, Jack has no gain or loss from the activity in Example 46. He contributes $5,000 more to the passive activity. Because the $5,000 contribution increases his at-risk amount, the $2,000 of losses suspended under the at-risk rules is reclassified as passive. Jack gets no passive loss deduction in 2007. At year-end, he has:

- No suspended losses under the at-risk rules.
- $12,000 of suspended passive losses ($10,000 + $2,000 of reclassified suspended at-risk losses).
- An adjusted basis and an at-risk amount of $3,000 ($5,000 additional investment − $2,000 of reclassified losses). ■

## LO.9

Discuss the special treatment available to real estate activities.

## SPECIAL RULES FOR REAL ESTATE

The passive loss rules contain two exceptions related to real estate activities. These exceptions allow all or part of real estate rental losses to offset active or portfolio income, even though the activity otherwise is defined as a passive activity.

## NEWLY DEVELOPED TAX SHELTER STRATEGIES NOW PROTECTED BY PATENTS

A patent is generally thought of as an intangible asset that protects the intellectual property underlying a new drug, manufacturing process, or consumer item. In such cases, the U.S. Patent and Trademark Office grants a patent that legally protects the holder's exclusive right to the invention. Now, tax and financial planners are patenting their newest tax shelters and strategies to prevent competitors from using them. Some of the patented strategies involve making mixed gifts of art to charities and family or transferring appreciated assets to heirs with minimal tax consequences.

The applicant for a patent should be aware of the potential costs associated with acquiring such legal protection, however. Even if the Patent and Trademark Office grants a so-called business method patent, there is no assurance that the IRS will approve of the technique. In addition, obtaining a patent can be an expensive and involved process that can take years. Nonetheless, last year over 6,000 patent applications involving business methods were submitted for approval.

SOURCE: Adapted from Rachel Emma Silverman, "The Patented Tax Shelter," *Wall Street Journal*, June 24, 2004, pp. D1 and D2.

**Real Estate Professionals.**   The first exception allows certain real estate professionals to avoid passive loss treatment for losses from real estate rental activities.[45] To qualify for nonpassive treatment, a taxpayer must satisfy both of the following requirements:

- More than half of the personal services that the taxpayer performs in trades or businesses are performed in real property trades or businesses in which the taxpayer materially participates.
- The taxpayer performs more than 750 hours of services in these real property trades or businesses as a material participant.

Taxpayers who do not satisfy the above requirements must continue to treat losses from real estate rental activities as passive losses.

**EXAMPLE 48**

During the current year, Della performs personal service activities as follows: 900 hours as a personal financial planner, 550 hours in a real estate development business, and 600 hours in a real estate rental activity. Any loss Della incurs in the real estate rental activity will not be subject to the passive loss rules, since more than 50% of her personal services are devoted to real property trades or businesses and her material participation in those real estate activities exceeds 750 hours. Thus, any loss from the real estate rental activity can offset active and portfolio income. ■

As discussed earlier, a spouse's work is taken into consideration in satisfying the material participation requirement. However, the hours worked by a spouse are not taken into account when ascertaining whether a taxpayer has worked for more than 750 hours in real property trades or businesses during a year. Services performed by an employee are not treated as being related to a real estate trade or business unless the employee performing the services owns more than a

---

[45]§ 469(c)(7).

5 percent interest in the employer. Additionally, a closely held C corporation may also qualify for the passive loss relief if more than 50 percent of its gross receipts for the year are derived from real property trades or businesses in which it materially participates.[46]

**Rental Real Estate Deduction.** The second exception is more significant in that it is not restricted to real estate professionals. This exception allows individuals to deduct up to $25,000 of losses from real estate rental activities against active and portfolio income.[47] The potential annual $25,000 deduction is reduced by 50 percent of the taxpayer's adjusted gross income (AGI) in excess of $100,000. Thus, the entire deduction is phased out at $150,000. If married individuals file separately, the $25,000 deduction is reduced to zero unless they lived apart for the entire year. If they lived apart for the entire year, the loss amount is $12,500 each, and the phaseout begins at $50,000.

To qualify for the $25,000 exception, a taxpayer must:[48]

* *Actively participate* in the real estate rental activity.
* Own 10 percent or more (in value) of all interests in the activity during the entire taxable year (or shorter period during which the taxpayer held an interest in the activity).

The difference between *active participation* and *material participation* is that the former can be satisfied without regular, continuous, and substantial involvement in operations as long as the taxpayer participates in making management decisions in a significant and bona fide sense. In this context, relevant management decisions include such decisions as approving new tenants, deciding on rental terms, and approving capital or repair expenditures.

The $25,000 allowance is available after all active participation rental losses and gains are netted and applied to other passive income. If a taxpayer has a real estate rental loss in excess of the amount that can be deducted under the real estate rental exception, that excess is treated as a passive loss.

**EXAMPLE 49**

Brad, who has $90,000 of AGI before considering rental activities, has $85,000 of losses from a real estate rental activity in which he actively participates. He also actively participates in another real estate rental activity from which he has $25,000 of income. He has other passive income of $36,000. Of the net rental loss of $60,000, $36,000 is absorbed by the $36,000 of passive income, leaving $24,000 that can be deducted against active or portfolio income because of the availability of the $25,000 allowance. ■

The $25,000 offset allowance is an aggregate of both deductions and credits in deduction equivalents. The deduction equivalent of a passive activity credit is the amount of deductions that reduces the tax liability for the taxable year by an amount equal to the credit.[49] A taxpayer with $5,000 of credits and a marginal tax rate of 25 percent would have a deduction equivalent of $20,000 ($5,000/25%).

If total deductions and deduction equivalents exceed $25,000, the taxpayer must allocate the benefit on a pro rata basis. First, the allowance must be allocated among the losses (including real estate rental activity losses suspended in prior years) and then to credits.

**EXAMPLE 50**

Kevin is an active participant in a real estate rental activity that produces $8,000 of income, $26,000 of deductions, and $1,500 of credits. Kevin, whose marginal tax rate is 25%, may deduct the net passive loss of $18,000 ($8,000 − $26,000). After deducting the loss, he has an available deduction equivalent of $7,000 ($25,000 − $18,000 passive loss). Therefore, the

---

[46]§ 469(c)(7)(B) and Reg. § 1.469–9.
[47]§ 469(i).

[48]§ 469(i)(6).
[49]§ 469(j)(5).

maximum amount of credits that he may claim is $1,750 ($7,000 × 25%). Since the actual credits are less than this amount, Kevin may claim the entire $1,500 credit. ■

**EXAMPLE 51**

Kelly, whose marginal tax rate is 25%, actively participates in three separate real estate rental activities. The relevant tax results for each activity are as follows:

- Activity A: $20,000 of losses.
- Activity B: $10,000 of losses.
- Activity C: $4,200 of credits.

Kelly's deduction equivalent from the credits is $16,800 ($4,200/25%). Therefore, the total passive deductions and deduction equivalents are $46,800 ($20,000 + $10,000 + $16,800), which exceeds the maximum allowable amount of $25,000. Consequently, Kelly must allocate pro rata first from among losses and then from among credits. Deductions from losses are limited as follows:

- Activity A: $25,000 × [$20,000/($20,000 + $10,000)] = $16,667.
- Activity B: $25,000 × [$10,000/($20,000 + $10,000)] = $8,333.

Since the amount of passive deductions exceeds the $25,000 maximum, the deduction balance of $5,000 and passive credits of $4,200 must be carried forward. Kelly's suspended losses and credits by activity are as follows:

|                    | Total     | Activity A | Activity B | Activity C |
|--------------------|-----------|------------|------------|------------|
| Allocated losses   | $ 30,000  | $ 20,000   | $ 10,000   | $  –0–     |
| Allocated credits  | 4,200     | –0–        | –0–        | 4,200      |
| Utilized losses    | (25,000)  | (16,667)   | (8,333)    | –0–        |
| Suspended losses   | 5,000     | 3,333      | 1,667      | –0–        |
| Suspended credits  | 4,200     | –0–        | –0–        | 4,200      |

## DISPOSITION OF PASSIVE ACTIVITIES

Recall from an earlier discussion that if a taxpayer disposes of an entire interest in a passive activity, any suspended losses (and in certain cases, suspended credits) may be utilized when calculating the final economic gain or loss on the investment. In addition, if a loss ultimately results, that loss can offset other types of income. However, the consequences may differ if the activity is disposed of in a transaction that is not fully taxable. The following discusses the treatment of suspended passive losses in two such dispositions.

**Disposition of a Passive Activity at Death.**   A transfer of a taxpayer's interest in an activity by reason of the taxpayer's death results in suspended losses being allowed (to the decedent) to the extent they exceed the amount, if any, of the step-up in basis allowed.[50] Suspended losses are lost to the extent of the amount of the basis increase. The losses allowed generally are reported on the final return of the deceased taxpayer.

**EXAMPLE 52**

A taxpayer dies with passive activity property having an adjusted basis of $40,000, suspended losses of $10,000, and a fair market value at the date of the decedent's death of $75,000. The increase (i.e., step-up) in basis (see Chapter 6) is $35,000 (fair market value at date of death

---

[50]§ 469(g)(2).

in excess of adjusted basis). None of the $10,000 suspended loss is deductible by either the decedent or the beneficiary. The suspended losses ($10,000) are lost because they do not exceed the step-up in basis ($35,000). ■

**EXAMPLE 53**

A taxpayer dies with passive activity property having an adjusted basis of $40,000, suspended losses of $10,000, and a fair market value at the date of the decedent's death of $47,000. Since the step-up in basis is only $7,000 ($47,000 − $40,000), the suspended losses allowed are limited to $3,000 ($10,000 suspended loss at time of death − $7,000 increase in basis). The $3,000 loss available to the decedent is reported on the decedent's final income tax return. ■

**Disposition of a Passive Activity by Gift.** In a disposition of a taxpayer's interest in a passive activity by gift, the suspended losses are added to the basis of the property.[51]

**EXAMPLE 54**

A taxpayer makes a gift of passive activity property having an adjusted basis of $40,000, suspended losses of $10,000, and a fair market value at the date of the gift of $100,000. The taxpayer cannot deduct the suspended losses in the year of the disposition. However, the suspended losses of $10,000 transfer with the property and are added to the adjusted basis of the property in the hands of the donee. ■

**PLANNING STRATEGIES**

## Utilizing Passive Losses

**FRAMEWORK FOCUS: TAX RATE**

STRATEGY ➤ CONTROL THE CHARACTER OF INCOME AND DEDUCTIONS.

Perhaps the biggest challenge individuals face with the passive loss rules is to recognize the potential impact of the rules and then to structure their affairs to minimize this impact. Taxpayers who have passive activity losses (PALs) should adopt a strategy of generating passive activity income that can be sheltered by existing passive losses. One approach is to buy an interest in a passive activity that is generating income (referred to as a passive income generator, or PIG). Then the PAL can offset income from the PIG. From a tax perspective, it would be foolish to buy a loss-generating passive activity (PAL) unless one has passive income to shelter or the activity is rental real estate that can qualify for the $25,000 exception or the exception available to real estate professionals.

If a taxpayer does invest in an activity that produces losses subject to the passive loss rules, the following strategies may help to minimize the loss of current deductions:

- If money is borrowed to finance the purchase of a passive activity, the associated interest expense is generally treated as part of any passive loss. Consequently, by increasing the amount of cash used to purchase the passive investment, the investor will need less debt and will incur less interest expense. By incurring less interest expense, a possible suspended passive loss deduction is reduced.

- If the investor does not have sufficient cash readily available for the larger down payment, it can be obtained by borrowing against the equity in his or her personal residence. The interest expense on such debt will be deductible under the qualified residence interest provisions (see Chapter 15) and will not be subject to the passive loss limitations. Thus, the taxpayer avoids the passive loss limitation and secures a currently deductible interest expense.

---

[51]§ 469(j)(6).

Often unusable passive losses accumulate and provide no current tax benefit because the taxpayer has no passive income. When the taxpayer disposes of the entire interest in a passive activity, however, any suspended losses from that activity are used to reduce the taxable gain. If any taxable gain still remains, it can be offset by losses from other passive activities. As a result, the taxpayer should carefully select the year in which a passive activity is disposed of. It is to the taxpayer's advantage to wait until sufficient passive losses have accumulated to offset any gain recognized on the asset's disposition.

### EXAMPLE 55

Bill, a calendar year taxpayer, owns interests in two passive activities: Activity A, which he plans to sell in December of this year at a gain of $100,000; and Activity B, which he plans to keep indefinitely. Current and suspended losses associated with Activity B total $60,000, and Bill expects losses from the activity to be $40,000 next year. If Bill sells Activity A this year, the $100,000 gain can be offset by the current and suspended losses of $60,000 from Activity B, producing a net taxable gain of $40,000. However, if Bill delays the sale of Activity A until January of next year, the $100,000 gain will be fully offset by the $100,000 of losses generated by Activity B ($60,000 current and prior losses + $40,000 next year's loss). Consequently, by postponing the sale by one month, he could avoid recognizing $40,000 of gain that would otherwise result. ▪

Taxpayers with passive losses should consider the level of their involvement in all other trades or businesses in which they have an interest. If they show that they do not materially participate in a profitable activity, the activity becomes a passive activity. Current and suspended passive losses then could shelter any income generated by the profitable business. Family partnerships in which certain members do not materially participate would qualify. The silent partner in any general partnership engaged in a trade or business would also qualify.

### EXAMPLE 56

Gail has an investment in a limited partnership that produces annual passive losses of approximately $25,000. She also owns a newly acquired interest in a convenience store where she works. Her share of the store's income is $35,000. If she works enough to be classified as a material participant, her $35,000 share of income is treated as active income. This results in $35,000 being subject to tax every year, while her $25,000 loss is suspended. However, if Gail reduces her involvement at the store so that she is not a material participant, the $35,000 of income receives passive treatment. Consequently, the $35,000 of income can be offset by the $25,000 passive loss, resulting in only $10,000 being subject to tax. Thus, by reducing her involvement, Gail ensures that the income from the profitable trade or business receives passive treatment and can then be used to absorb passive losses from other passive activities. ▪

The passive loss rules can have a dramatic effect on a taxpayer's ability to claim passive losses currently. As a result, it is important to keep accurate records of all sources of income and losses, particularly any suspended passive losses and credits and the activities to which they relate, so that their potential tax benefit will not be lost.

## Suggested Further Readings

Claudia L. Kelley and John M. Norman, "Repayments of Business Debt after Business Ceases," *The Tax Adviser*, September 2004, pp. 566–570.

Alvin D. Lurie, "How Tax Shelters Evolved: The Road from *Crane* Has Been Paved with Bad Contentions," *Journal of Taxation*, May 2004, pp. 274–286.

Susan Megaard, "Recent Corporate Scandals Focus Attention on Tax Treatment of Stock Losses," *Journal of Taxation*, August 2004, pp. 101–109.

"Service Intends to Disallow Theft Loss Deductions for Declining Stock Prices," *The Tax Adviser*, June 2004, p. 394.

## KEY TERMS

| | | |
|---|---|---|
| Active income, 5–19 | Casualty loss, 5–8 | Net operating loss (NOL), 5–13 |
| At-risk limitation, 5–16 | Closely held C corporation, 5–24 | Nonbusiness bad debt, 5–4 |
| Bad debt, 5–2 | Disaster area losses, 5–10 | Passive loss, 5–16 |
| Business bad debt, 5–4 | Material participation, 5–26 | Personal service corporation, 5–24 |

## PROBLEM MATERIALS

### Problems

**Communications**

1. Several years ago, Loon Finance Company, which is in the lending business, loaned Sara $30,000 to purchase an automobile to be used for personal purposes. In August of the current year, Sara filed for bankruptcy, and Loon was notified that it could not expect to receive more than $4,000. As of the end of the current year, Loon has received $1,000. Loon has contacted you about the possibility of taking a bad debt deduction for the current year.

    Write a letter to Loon Finance Company that contains your advice as to whether it can claim a bad debt deduction for the current year. Also, prepare a memo for the tax files. Loon's address is 100 Tyler Lane, Erie, PA 16563.

2. Sue loaned her sister Janice $10,000 three years ago. Janice has never made any payments to Sue, and Sue has never tried to collect from Janice. This year, Janice filed for bankruptcy and told Sue that she would not be able to repay any of the $10,000 loan. Determine Sue's tax treatment for the loan for the current year.

**Issue ID**

3. John was the sole shareholder of Blonde, Inc. The corporation had 26 salaried employees, which included John. Several years ago, Blonde began experiencing financial difficulties. As a result, John made several loans to the corporation in an attempt to continue business operations and pay employee salaries. The corporation eventually filed for bankruptcy under Chapter 7 of the bankruptcy code. Upon the final discharge of the corporation's debts, John's loans remained unpaid and were worthless. Identify the relevant tax issues for John with respect to his loans to Blonde, Inc.

4. Mable and Jack file a joint return. For the current year, they had the following items:

| | |
|---|---|
| Salaries | $180,000 |
| Loss on sale of § 1244 stock acquired two years ago | 95,000 |
| Gain on sale of § 1244 stock acquired six months ago | 12,000 |
| Nonbusiness bad debt | 16,000 |

    Determine the impact of the above items on Mable and Jack's income for the current year.

**Decision Making**

5. Mary, a single taxpayer, purchased 10,000 shares of § 1244 stock several years ago at a cost of $20 per share. In November of the current year, Mary receives an offer to sell the stock for $12 per share. She has the option of either selling all of the stock now or selling half of the stock now and half of the stock in January of next year. Mary's salary is $80,000 for the current year, and it will be $90,000 next year. Mary has long-term capital gains of $8,000 for the current year and will have $10,000 next year. If Mary's goal is to minimize her AGI for the two years, determine whether she should sell all of her stock this year or half of her stock this year and half next year.

**EXTENDER**

**Communications**

6. Paul Sanders, a married taxpayer who files a joint return with his wife, acquired stock in a corporation that qualified as a small business corporation under § 1244. The stock cost $30,000 and was acquired three years ago. A few months after he acquired the stock he gave it to his brother, Mike Sanders. The stock was worth $30,000 on the date

of the gift. Mike, who is married and files a joint return with his wife, sells the stock for $10,000 in the current tax year. You represent Mike who asks you whether he can take a loss deduction on the sale of the stock. If so, how will the loss be treated for tax purposes? Prepare a letter to your client and a memo to the files. Mike's address is 2600 Riverview Drive, Plank, MO 63701.

**Ethics**

7.  In the case of a casualty loss, if property used in a trade or business is damaged, the amount of the loss is the lesser of the decline in fair market value or the adjusted basis of the property.

    Many years ago, Joe purchased a parcel of land for $300,000. The land was to be used in Joe's business. On the land was an existing road that was in poor condition. Joe made improvements to the road that cost $40,000. He computed his basis for the road to be $50,000—$40,000 from the improvements and $10,000 allocated from the original purchase price of the land. Joe has taken depreciation on the road, and consequently, at the beginning of the current year, the road has an adjusted basis of $20,000. During the current year, severe rainstorms washed out the road, and Joe paid $80,000 to have it repaired. Joe is considering claiming a loss deduction of $80,000 for the damage to the road. Evaluate Joe's plan.

**Decision Making**

8.  Grackle Farming, Inc., owns a 500-acre farm in Minnesota. A tornado hit the area and destroyed a farm building and some farm equipment and damaged a barn. Fortunately for Grackle, the tornado occurred after the company had harvested its corn crop. Applicable information is as follows:

| Asset | Basis | FMV Before | FMV After | Insurance Recovery |
|-------|-------|-----------|-----------|--------------------|
| Building | $90,000 | $ 70,000 | $   –0– | $70,000 |
| Equipment | 40,000 | 50,000 | –0– | 25,000 |
| Barn | 90,000 | 120,000 | 70,000 | 25,000 |

Because of the extensive damage caused by the tornado, the President of the United States designated the area as a disaster area.

    Grackle had $95,000 of taxable income last year. The company's taxable income for the current year, excluding the loss from the tornado, is $250,000. Determine the amount of the corporation's loss and the year in which it should take the loss.

**Issue ID**

9.  Marydale Farms, Inc., owned 1,000 acres of unimproved farmland. During the spring of the current year, shortly after the company had tilled the ground, a storm blew away four inches of topsoil from 60% of the acreage. Identify the relevant tax issues for Marydale Farms.

**Decision Making**

**Communications**

10.  On November 1 of the current year, Sam dropped off to sleep while driving home from a business trip. Luckily, he was only slightly injured in the resulting accident, but the company car that he was driving was completely destroyed.

    Sam is an employee of Snipe Industries. The corporation purchased the car new two years ago for $40,000. The automobile had a fair market value of $30,000 before the accident and $12,000 after the accident. The car was covered by an insurance policy that had a $3,000 deductible clause. The corporation is afraid that the policy will be canceled if it makes a claim for the damages. Therefore, Snipe is considering not filing a claim. The company believes that the casualty loss deduction will help mitigate the loss of the insurance reimbursement. The corporation's taxable income for the current year is $25,000.

    Write a letter to Snipe Industries that contains your advice regarding the filing of an insurance claim for reimbursement for the damage to the company's car. Snipe Industries' address is 450 Colonel's Way, Warrensburg, MO 64093.

**EXTENDER**

11.  Mary, a single taxpayer with two dependent children, has the following items of income and expense during 2005:

| Gross receipts from business | $144,000 |
|---|---|
| Business expenses | 180,000 |
| Alimony received | 22,000 |
| Interest income | 25,000 |
| Itemized deductions (no casualty or theft) | 28,000 |

a. Determine Mary's taxable income for 2005.
b. Determine Mary's NOL for 2005.

12. In 2004, Fred invested $50,000 in a general partnership. Fred's interest is not considered to be a passive activity. His share of the partnership losses was $35,000 in 2004 and $25,000 in 2005. How much can Fred deduct in 2004 and 2005?

**Communications**

13. In the current year, Bill Parker (54 Oak Drive, St. Paul, MN 55162) is considering making an investment of $60,000 in Best Choice Partnership. The prospectus provided by Bill's broker indicates that the partnership investment is not a passive activity and that Bill's share of the entity's loss in the current year will likely be $40,000, while his share of the partnership loss next year will probably be $25,000. Write a letter to Bill in which you indicate how the losses would be treated for tax purposes in the current and next years.

**Issue ID**

14. In the current year, George and Susie Melvin, both successful CPAs, made a cash investment in a limited partnership interest in a California orange grove. In addition to the cash generated from the investors, the venture borrowed a substantial sum to purchase assets necessary for its operation. The Melvins' investment adviser told them that their share of the tax loss in the first year alone would be in excess of their initial cash investment. This result would be followed by several more years of losses. They feel confident that their interest in the orange grove is a sound investment. Identify the tax issues facing the Melvins.

15. In 2000, Russell acquired an interest in a partnership in which he is not a material participant. The partnership was profitable through 2003, and Russell's basis in his partnership interest at the beginning of 2004 was $40,000. In 2004, Russell's share of the partnership loss was $35,000, and in 2005, his share of the partnership income is $15,000. How much can Russell deduct for 2004 and 2005?

16. Ray acquired an activity several years ago, and in 2005, it generated a loss of $50,000. Ray has AGI of $140,000 before considering the loss from the activity. If the activity is a bakery and Ray is not a material participant, what is his AGI?

17. Rachel sells rental property with an adjusted basis of $75,000 for $125,000, its fair market value. Associated with this investment are suspended losses that have not been deducted in prior years. The anticipated tax loss from the property in the current year is expected to be $4,000. What is the current taxable gain or deductible loss on the sale of the rental property if the suspended losses from prior years total:
a. $35,000?
b. $60,000?

18. Saundra has investments in four passive activity partnerships purchased several years ago. Last year, the income and losses were as follows:

| Activity | Income (Loss) |
|---|---|
| A | $ 10,000 |
| B | (5,000) |
| C | (25,000) |
| D | (20,000) |

In the current year, she sold her interest in Activity D for a $19,000 gain. Activity D, which had been profitable until last year, had a current loss of $1,000. How will the sale of Activity D affect Saundra's taxable income in the current year?

19. Brown Corporation, a personal service corporation, earns active income of $200,000 in the current year. The corporation receives $60,000 in dividends during the year. In addition, Brown incurs a loss of $45,000 from an investment in a passive activity acquired three years ago. What is Brown's income for the current year after considering the passive investment?

20. White, Inc., earns $400,000 from operations in the current year. White also receives $36,000 in interest on various investments. During the year, White pays $150,000 to acquire a 20% interest in a passive activity that produces a $200,000 loss. How will these facts affect White's taxable income, assuming the corporation is:
    a. A personal service corporation?
    b. A closely held (non-personal service) C corporation?

**Decision Making**
**Communications**

21. Greg Horne (431 Maple Avenue, Cincinnati, OH 45229), a syndicated radio talk show host, earns an annual salary of $400,000. He works approximately 30 hours per week in this job, which leaves him time to participate in several businesses newly acquired in 2005. He owns a movie theater and a drugstore in Cincinnati, a movie theater and a drugstore in Indianapolis, and a drugstore in Louisville. A preliminary analysis on December 1, 2005, shows the following projected income and losses and time spent for these various businesses:

|  | **Income (Loss)** |
| --- | --- |
| Cincinnati movie theater (95 hours participation) | $ 56,000 |
| Cincinnati drugstore (140 hours participation) | (89,000) |
| Indianapolis movie theater (90 hours participation) | 34,000 |
| Indianapolis drugstore (170 hours participation) | (41,000) |
| Louisville drugstore (180 hours participation) | (15,000) |

Greg has full-time employees in each of the five businesses. Write a letter to Greg suggesting a grouping method and other strategies that will provide the greatest tax advantage. As Greg is not knowledgeable about tax law, provide a nontechnical explanation.

**Decision Making**

22. Suzanne owns interests in a bagel shop, a lawn and garden store, and a convenience store. Several full-time employees work at each of the enterprises. As of the end of November of the current year, Suzanne has worked 150 hours in the bagel shop, 250 hours at the lawn and garden store, and 70 hours at the convenience store. In reviewing her financial records, you learn that she has no passive investments that are generating income and that she expects these three ventures collectively to produce a loss. What recommendation would you offer Suzanne as she plans her activities for the remainder of the year?

**Issue ID**

23. Rene retired from public accounting after a long and successful career of 45 years. As part of her retirement package, she continues to share in the profits and losses of the firm, albeit at a lower rate than when she was working full-time. Because Rene wants to stay busy during her retirement years, she has invested and works in a local hardware business, operated as a partnership. Unfortunately, the business has recently gone through a slump and has not been generating profits. Identify relevant tax issues for Rene.

**EXTENDER**

**Decision Making**

24. Last year, Juan, a real estate developer, purchased 25 acres of farmland on the outskirts of town for $100,000. He expects that the land's value will appreciate rapidly as the town expands in that direction. Since the property was recently reappraised at $115,000, some of the appreciation has already taken place. To enhance his return from the investment, Juan decides he will begin renting the land to a local farmer. He has determined that a

fair rent would be at least $1,500 but no more than $3,500 per year. Juan also has an interest in a passive activity that generates a $2,800 loss annually. How do the passive loss rules affect Juan's decision on how much rent to charge for the farmland?

**Decision Making**

25. The end of the year is approaching, and Maxine has begun to focus on ways of minimizing her income tax liability. Several years ago, she purchased an investment in Teal Limited Partnership, which is subject to both the at-risk and the passive activity loss rules. (Last year, Maxine sold a different investment that was subject to these rules but produced passive income.) She believes that her investment in Teal has good long-term economic prospects. However, it has been generating tax losses for several years in a row. In fact, when she was discussing last year's income tax return with her tax accountant, he said that unless "things change" with respect to her investments, she would not be able to deduct losses this year.
    a. What was the accountant referring to in his comment?
    b. You learn that Maxine's current at-risk basis in her investment is $1,000 and her share of the current loss is expected to be $13,000. Based on these facts, how will her loss be treated?
    c. After reviewing her situation, Maxine's financial adviser suggests that she invest at least an additional $12,000 in Teal in order to ensure a full loss deduction in the current year. How do you react to his suggestion?
    d. What would you suggest Maxine consider as she attempts to maximize her current-year deductible loss?

26. A number of years ago, Lee acquired a 20% interest in the BlueSky Partnership for $60,000. The partnership was profitable through 2004, and Lee's amount at risk in the partnership interest was $120,000 at the beginning of 2005. BlueSky incurred a loss of $400,000 in 2005 and reported income of $200,000 in 2006. Assuming Lee is not a material participant, how much of his loss from BlueSky Partnership is deductible in 2005 and 2006?

27. Last year, Fran invested $40,000 for an interest in a partnership in which she is a material participant. Her share of the partnership's loss for the year was $50,000. In the current year, Fran's share of the partnership's income is $30,000. What is the effect on her taxable income for the current year?

**Issue ID**

28. During the current year, Alan is determined to make better use of the tax losses that tend to flow from the various businesses that he owns. He is particularly sensitive to the limitations that the passive loss rules place on the deductibility of losses because of the disaster that occurred last year. His accountant informed him that he would not be able to claim any of the losses on his income tax return because of his lack of material participation. He has even suggested to his wife that she may have to put in some time at the businesses if his goals are to be accomplished. Identify the tax issues that Alan faces.

29. Jonathan, a physician, earns $200,000 from his practice. He also receives $18,000 in dividends and interest on various portfolio investments. During the year, he pays $45,000 to acquire a 20% interest in a partnership that produces a $300,000 loss.
    a. Compute Jonathan's AGI, assuming he does not participate in the operations of the partnership.
    b. Compute Jonathan's AGI, assuming he is a material participant in the operations of the partnership.

30. Five years ago, Gerald invested $150,000 in a passive activity, his sole investment venture. On January 1, 2004, his amount at risk in the activity was $30,000. His shares of the income and losses were as follows:

| Year | Income (Loss) |
| --- | --- |
| 2004 | ($40,000) |
| 2005 | (30,000) |
| 2006 | 50,000 |

How much can Gerald deduct in 2004 and 2005? What is his taxable income from the activity in 2006? Consider the at-risk rules as well as the passive loss rules.

31. During the year, Roger performs personal services in three separate activities: 800 hours as a CPA in his tax practice, 400 hours in a real estate development business (i.e., not a material participant), and 600 hours in an apartment leasing operation. He expects that losses will be realized from the two real estate ventures while his tax practice will show a profit. Roger files a joint return with his wife who has salary income of $200,000. What is the character of the income and losses generated by these activities?

**Ethics**

**Communications**

32. You have just met with Scott Myers (603 Pittsfield Dr., Champaign, IL 61821), a successful full-time real estate developer and investor. During your meeting you discussed his tax situation, because you are starting to prepare his 2005 Federal income tax return. During your meeting, Scott mentioned that he and his wife, Susan, went to great lengths to maximize their participation in an apartment complex that they own and manage. In particular, Scott included the following activities in the 540 hours of participation for the current year:

  * Time spent thinking about the rentals.

  * Time spent by Susan on weekdays visiting the apartment complex to oversee operations of the buildings (i.e., in a management role).

  * Time spent by both Scott and Susan on weekends visiting the apartment complex to assess operations. Scott and Susan always visited the complex together on weekends and both counted their hours (i.e., one hour at the complex was two hours of participation).

  * Time spent on weekends driving around the community looking for other potential rental properties to purchase. Again, both Scott's hours and Susan's hours were counted, even when they drove together.

  After reviewing Scott's records, you note that the apartment complex generated a significant loss this year. Prepare a letter to Scott describing your position on the deductibility of the loss.

**Decision Making**

33. Ruth and Mike are married with no dependents and live in Vermont (not a community property state). Since Ruth has large medical expenses, they seek your advice about filing separately to save taxes. Their income and expenses for 2005 are as follows:

| | |
|---|---:|
| Ruth's salary | $ 30,000 |
| Mike's salary | 50,000 |
| Interest income (joint) | 1,800 |
| Rental loss from actively managed rental property | (20,000) |
| Ruth's unreimbursed medical expenses | 6,500 |
| All other itemized deductions:* | |
|    Ruth | 2,000 |
|    Mike | 8,000 |

*None subject to limitations.

  Determine whether Ruth and Mike should file jointly or separately for 2005.

34. During the current year, Gene performs services as follows: 1,800 hours as a CPA in his tax practice and 50 hours in an apartment leasing operation in which he has a 15% interest. Because of his oversight duties, Gene is considered to be an active participant in the leasing operation. He expects that his share of the loss realized from the apartment leasing operation will be $30,000 while his tax practice will show a profit of approximately $80,000. Gene is single and has no other income besides that stated above. Discuss the character of income and losses generated by these activities.

35. Ida, who has AGI of $80,000 before considering rental activities, is active in three separate real estate rental activities. Ida has a marginal tax rate of 28%. She has $12,000 of losses from Activity A, $18,000 of losses from Activity B, and income of $10,000 from Activity C. She also has $2,100 of tax credits from Activity A. Calculate her deductions and credits allowed and the suspended losses and credits.

36. Ella has $105,000 of losses from a real estate rental activity in which she actively participates. She has other rent income of $25,000 and other passive income of $32,000. How much rental loss can Ella deduct against active and portfolio income (ignoring the at-risk rules)? Does she have any suspended losses to carry over?

**Ethics**

37. Lucien dies in the current year owning a limited partnership interest in a partnership that owns and operates an apartment complex. Associated with Lucien's interest is a $10,000 suspended passive activity loss that he had not been able to claim. Ron, the executor of Lucien's estate, learns from the partnership's general partner that she is not aware of any recent qualified appraisals or sales that would help determine the fair market value of the limited partnership interest. Ron feels that the cost of hiring a qualified appraiser to determine the value of the interest is not necessary because Lucien's estate is not large enough to be subject to the Federal estate tax. Lucien's records reflect a basis of $65,000 for the partnership interest immediately before his death.

    The partnership's bookkeeper has a "gut feeling" that the partnership interest is worth anywhere between $65,000 and $80,000. This is good news to Ron. Based on her "guesstimate," Ron sets the value of the interest at $65,000.

    What is Ron trying to accomplish in setting this valuation? What ethical issues arise?

**BRIDGE DISCIPLINE**

1. Marketplace, Inc., has recognized over time that a certain percentage of its customer accounts receivable will not be collected. To ensure the appropriate matching of revenues and expenditures in its financial reports, Marketplace uses the reserve method for bad debts. Records show the following pertaining to its treatment of bad debts.

    | | |
    |---|---|
    | Beginning allowance for bad debts | $120,000 |
    | Ending allowance for bad debts | 123,000 |
    | Bad debts written off during the year | 33,000 |

    a. What was the bad debt expense for financial accounting purposes during the year?
    b. What was the bad debt expense for income tax purposes during the year?
    c. Assuming the before-tax net income for financial accounting purposes was $545,000, what is the taxable income for the year if the treatment of bad debts is the only book/tax difference?

**Decision Making**

2. Amanda wishes to invest $40,000 in a relatively safe venture and has discovered two alternatives that would produce the following ordinary income and loss over the next three years:

    | Year | Alternative 1 Income (Loss) | Alternative 2 Income (Loss) |
    |---|---|---|
    | 1 | ($ 24,000) | ($48,000) |
    | 2 | (24,000) | 32,000 |
    | 3 | 72,000 | 40,000 |

    She is interested in the after-tax effects of these alternatives over a three-year horizon. Assume that:

    • Amanda's investment portfolio produces sufficient passive income to offset any potential passive loss that may arise from these alternatives.

    • Amanda's marginal tax rate is 25%, and her cost of capital is 8% (the present value factors are 0.92593, 0.85734, and 0.79383).

    • Each investment alternative possesses equal growth potential and comparable financial risk.

* In the loss years for each alternative, there is no cash flow from or to the investment (i.e., the loss is due to depreciation), while in those years when the income is positive, cash flows to Amanda equal the amount of the income.

Based on these facts, compute the present value of these two investment alternatives and determine which option Amanda should choose.

**Decision Making**

3. Emily has $100,000 that she wishes to invest and is considering the following two options:

* Option A: Investment in Redbird Mutual Fund, which is expected to produce interest income of $8,000 per year.
* Option B: Investment in Cardinal Limited Partnership (buys, sells, and operates wine vineyards). Emily's share of the partnership's ordinary income and loss over the next three years would be:

| Year | Income (Loss) |
|------|---------------|
| 1    | ($ 8,000)     |
| 2    | (2,000)       |
| 3    | 34,000        |

Emily is interested in the after-tax effects of these alternatives over a three-year horizon. Assume that Emily's investment portfolio produces ample passive income to offset any passive losses that may be generated. Her cost of capital is 8% (the present value factors are 0.92593, 0.85734, and 0.79383), and she is in the 28% tax bracket. The two investment alternatives possess equal growth potential and comparable financial risk. Based on these facts, compute the present value of these two investment alternatives and determine which option Emily should choose.

## Research Problems

*Note: Solutions to Research Problems can be prepared by using the **RIA Checkpoint**® **Student Edition** online research product, which is available to accompany this text. It is also possible to prepare solutions to the Research Problems by using tax research materials found in a standard tax library.*

**Communications**

**Research Problem 1.**   Jeb Simmons operated an illegal gambling business out of his home. While executing a search warrant, the local sheriff seized gambling paraphernalia and $200,000 in cash. Subsequently, Jeb voluntarily consented to forfeit to the state the cash that had been seized in connection with the execution of the search warrant. Write a letter to Jeb advising him as to whether he can claim a loss under § 165 for the seized cash. Also, prepare a memo for the tax files. Jeb's address is 100 Honey Lane, Macon, GA 62108.

**Research Problem 2.**   George and Judy Cash own a 30-foot yacht that is moored at Oregon Inlet on the Outer Banks of North Carolina. The yacht is offered for rent to tourists during March through November every year. George and Judy live too far away to be involved in the yacht's routine operation and maintenance. They are, however, able to perform certain periodic tasks, such as cleaning and winterizing it. Routine daily management, operating, and chartering responsibilities have been contracted to "Captain Mac." George and Judy are able to document spending 120 hours on the yacht chartering activities during the year. Determine how any losses resulting from the activity are treated under the passive activity loss rules.

**Communications**

**Research Problem 3.**   Lane Mitchell (77 Lakeview Drive, Salt Lake City, UT 84109) is a married individual who files a separate return for the taxable year. He is employed full-time as an accountant and also owns an interest in a minor league baseball team. He does no work in connection with the activity and anticipates that the activity will produce a loss. He pays his wife to work as an office receptionist in connection with the activity. Her work requires an average of 20 hours a week. Write a letter to Lane and explain whether he will be allowed to deduct his share of the loss from the minor league baseball team activity.

**Internet Activity**

*Use the tax resources of the Internet to address the following questions. Do not restrict your search to the World Wide Web, but include a review of newsgroups and general reference materials, practitioner sites and resources, primary sources of the tax law, chat rooms and discussion groups, and other opportunities.*

**Research Problem 4.**  Scan several publications that are read by owners of small businesses. Some of the articles in these publications address tax-related issues such as how to structure a new business. Do these articles do an adequate job of conveying the benefits of issuing § 1244 small business stock? Prepare a short memo explaining the use of § 1244 stock and post it to a newsgroup that is frequented by inventors, engineers, and others involved in start-up corporations.

**Research Problem 5.**  Scan the materials offered in several newsgroups frequented by tax advisers and consultants. In what context are "tax shelters" still discussed by these professionals? Do these advisers and consultants adequately take into account the rules of §§ 465 and 469?

# Property Transactions

Part III presents the tax treatment of sales, exchanges, and other dispositions of property. Included are the determination of the realized gain or loss, recognized gain or loss, and the classification of the recognized gain or loss as capital or ordinary. The topic of basis is evaluated both in terms of its effect on the calculation of the gain or loss and in terms of the determination of the basis of any contemporaneous or related subsequent acquisitions of property.

http://wft.swlearning.com

# Property Transactions: Basis, Gain and Loss, and Nontaxable Exchanges

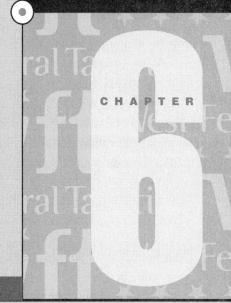

CHAPTER

6

*After completing Chapter 6, you should be able to:*

### L O . 1
Understand the computation of realized gain or loss on property dispositions.

### L O . 2
Distinguish between realized and recognized gain or loss.

### L O . 3
Explain how basis is determined for various methods of asset acquisition.

### L O . 4
Describe various loss disallowance provisions.

### L O . 5
Apply the nonrecognition provisions and basis determination rules for like-kind exchanges.

### L O . 6
Explain the nonrecognition provisions available on the involuntary conversion of property.

### L O . 7
Identify other nonrecognition provisions contained in the Code.

## OUTLINE

---

## TAX TALK

*To base all of your decisions on tax consequences is not necessarily to maintain the proper balance and perspective on what you are doing.*

*—Barber Conable*

---

This chapter and the following chapter are concerned with the income tax consequences of property transactions, including the sale or other disposition of property. The following questions are considered with respect to the sale or other disposition of property:

- Is there a realized gain or loss?
- If so, is that gain or loss recognized for tax purposes?
- If that gain or loss is recognized, is it ordinary or capital?
- What is the basis of any replacement property that is acquired?

This chapter discusses the determination of realized and recognized gain or loss and the basis of property. The following chapter covers the classification of recognized gain or loss as ordinary or capital.

For the most part, the rules discussed in Chapters 6 and 7 apply to all types of taxpayers. Individuals, partnerships, closely held corporations, limited liability companies, and publicly held corporations all own assets for use in business activities or as investments in entities that themselves conduct business activities. Individuals, however, are unique among taxpayers because they also own assets that are used in daily life and have no significant business or investment component. Because of that possibility, some property transaction concepts apply somewhat differently to individual taxpayers depending upon how a person uses the specific asset in question. Nevertheless, the material that follows pertains to taxpayers generally except where otherwise noted.

**L O . 1**

Understand the computation of realized gain or loss on property dispositions.

# Determination of Gain or Loss

## REALIZED GAIN OR LOSS

For tax purposes, gain or loss is the difference between the *amount realized* from the sale or other disposition of property and the property's *adjusted basis* on the date of disposition. If the amount realized exceeds the property's adjusted basis, the result is a **realized gain.** Conversely, if the property's adjusted basis exceeds the amount realized, the result is a **realized loss.**[1]

**EXAMPLE 1**

Lavender, Inc., sells Swan Corporation stock with an adjusted basis of $3,000 for $5,000. Lavender's realized gain is $2,000. If Lavender had sold the stock for $2,000, it would have had a realized loss of $1,000. ■

**Sale or Other Disposition.** The term *sale or other disposition* is defined broadly to include virtually any disposition of property. Thus, trade-ins, casualties, condemnations, thefts, and bond retirements are all treated as dispositions of property. The most common disposition of property is a sale or exchange. Usually, the key factor in determining whether a disposition has taken place is whether an identifiable event has occurred[2] as opposed to a mere fluctuation in the value of the property.[3]

**EXAMPLE 2**

Heron & Associates owns Tan Corporation stock that cost $3,000. The stock has appreciated in value by $2,000 since Heron purchased it. Heron has no realized gain since mere fluctuation in value is not a disposition or identifiable event for tax purposes. Nor would Heron have a realized loss had the stock declined in value. ■

**Amount Realized.** The **amount realized** from a sale or other disposition of property is the sum of any money received plus the fair market value of other property received. The amount realized also includes any real property taxes treated as imposed on the seller that are actually paid by the buyer.[4] The reason for including these taxes in the amount realized is that by paying the taxes, the purchaser is, in effect, paying an additional amount to the seller of the property.

The amount realized also includes any liability on the property disposed of, such as a mortgage debt, if the buyer assumes the mortgage or the property is sold subject to the mortgage.[5] The amount of the liability is included in the amount realized, even if the debt is nonrecourse and even if the amount of the debt is greater than the fair market value of the mortgaged property.[6]

---

[1]§ 1001(a) and Reg. § 1.1001–1(a).
[2]Reg. § 1.1001–1(c)(1).
[3]*Lynch v. Turrish,* 1 USTC ¶18, 3 AFTR 2986, 38 S.Ct. 537 (USSC, 1918).
[4]§ 1001(b) and Reg. § 1.1001–1(b).
[5]*Crane v. Comm.,* 47–1 USTC ¶9217, 35 AFTR 776, 67 S.Ct. 1047 (USSC, 1947). Although a legal distinction exists between the direct

assumption of a mortgage and taking property subject to a mortgage, the tax consequences in calculating the amount realized are the same.
[6]*Comm. v. Tufts,* 83–1 USTC ¶9328, 51 AFTR2d 83–1132, 103 S.Ct. 1826 (USSC, 1983).

## REEVALUATING YOUR INVESTMENT STRATEGY

One of the many ways stocks are distinguished for investment purposes is by growth potential versus income yield. A growth stock is expected to appreciate over time and to pay few, if any, dividends. In contrast, an income stock pays regular dividends but is not expected to appreciate significantly.

Historically, growth and income stocks have also been taxed differently. The long-term capital gain on growth stocks was eligible for beneficial alternative tax treatment, whereas the dividend income on income stocks was taxed as ordinary income.

The Jobs and Growth Tax Relief Reconciliation Act of 2003 changed this historical difference. Long-term capital gains continue to be eligible for the beneficial alternative tax treatment but with rates reduced from 20%/10% to 15%/5%. Under the Act, moreover, qualified dividends are now eligible for a beneficial 15%/5% tax rate.

These changes may well cause some taxpayers to rethink their investment strategy regarding the choice between growth and income stocks.

**EXAMPLE 3**

Bunting & Co. sells property to Orange, Inc., for $50,000 cash. There is a $20,000 mortgage on the property. Bunting's amount realized from the sale is $70,000 if Orange assumes the mortgage or takes the property subject to the mortgage. ■

The **fair market value** of property received in a sale or other disposition has been defined by the courts as the price at which the property will change hands between a willing seller and a willing buyer when neither is compelled to sell or buy.[7] Fair market value is determined by considering the relevant factors in each case.[8] An expert appraiser is often required to evaluate these factors in arriving at fair market value. When the fair market value of the property received cannot be determined, the value of the property given up by the taxpayer may be used.[9]

In calculating the amount realized, selling expenses such as advertising, commissions, and legal fees relating to the disposition are deducted. The amount realized is the net amount that the taxpayer received directly or indirectly, in the form of cash or anything else of value, from the disposition of the property.

**Adjusted Basis.** The **adjusted basis** of property disposed of is the property's original basis adjusted to the date of disposition.[10] Original basis is the cost or other basis of the property on the date the property is acquired by the taxpayer. Considerations involving original basis are discussed later in this chapter. *Capital additions* increase and *recoveries of capital* decrease the original basis so that on the date of disposition the adjusted basis reflects the unrecovered cost or other basis of the property.[11] Adjusted basis is determined as follows:

Cost (or other adjusted basis) on date of acquisition
+ Capital additions
− Capital recoveries
= Adjusted basis on date of disposition

[7]*Comm. v. Marshman,* 60–2 USTC ¶9484, 5 AFTR2d 1528, 279 F.2d 27 (CA–6, 1960).

[8]*O'Malley v. Ames,* 52–1 USTC ¶9361, 42 AFTR 19, 197 F.2d 256 (CA–8, 1952).

[9]*U.S. v. Davis,* 62–2 USTC ¶9509, 9 AFTR2d 1625, 82 S.Ct. 1190 (USSC, 1962).

[10]§ 1011(a) and Reg. § 1.1011–1.

[11]§ 1016(a) and Reg. § 1.1016–1.

**Capital Additions.**    Capital additions include the cost of capital improvements and betterments made to the property by the taxpayer. These expenditures are distinguishable from expenditures for the ordinary repair and maintenance of the property, which are neither capitalized nor added to the original basis (refer to Chapter 4). The latter expenditures are deductible in the current taxable year if they are related to business or income-producing property. Amounts representing real property taxes treated as imposed on the seller but paid or assumed by the buyer are part of the cost of the property.[12] Any liability on property that is assumed by the buyer is also included in the buyer's original basis of the property. The same rule applies if property is acquired subject to a liability. In a similar fashion, amortization of the discount on bonds increases the adjusted basis of the bonds.[13]

**EXAMPLE 4**

Bluebird Corporation purchased some manufacturing equipment for $25,000. Whether Bluebird uses $25,000 from the business's cash account to pay for this equipment or uses $5,000 from that account and borrows the remaining $20,000, the basis of this equipment will be the same—namely, $25,000. Moreover, it does not matter whether Bluebird borrowed the $20,000 from the equipment's manufacturer, from a local bank, or from any other lender. ■

**Capital Recoveries.**    Capital recoveries decrease the adjusted basis of property. The following are examples of capital recoveries:

1. *Depreciation and cost recovery allowances.* The original basis of depreciable property is reduced by the annual depreciation charges (or cost recovery allowances) while the property is held by the taxpayer. The amount of depreciation that is subtracted from the original basis is the greater of the *allowed* or *allowable* depreciation calculated on an annual basis.[14] In most circumstances, the allowed and allowable depreciation amounts are the same (refer to Chapter 4).
2. *Casualties and thefts.* A casualty or theft may result in the reduction of the adjusted basis of property.[15] The adjusted basis is reduced by the amount of the deductible loss. In addition, the adjusted basis is reduced by the amount of insurance proceeds received. However, the receipt of insurance proceeds may result in a recognized gain rather than a deductible loss. The gain increases the adjusted basis of the property.[16]

**EXAMPLE 5**

An insured truck owned by the Falcon Corporation is destroyed in an accident. The adjusted basis is $8,000, and the fair market value is $6,500. Falcon received insurance proceeds of $6,500. The amount of the casualty loss is $1,500 ($6,500 insurance proceeds − $8,000 adjusted basis). The adjusted basis becomes $0 ($8,000 pre-accident adjusted basis, reduced by the $1,500 casualty loss and the $6,500 of insurance proceeds received). ■

**EXAMPLE 6**

Osprey, Inc., owned an insured truck that was destroyed in an accident. The adjusted basis and fair market value of the truck were $6,500 and $8,000, respectively. Osprey received insurance proceeds of $8,000. The amount of the casualty *gain* is $1,500 ($8,000 insurance proceeds − $6,500 adjusted basis). The adjusted basis is increased by the $1,500 casualty gain and is reduced by the $8,000 of insurance proceeds received ($6,500 basis before casualty + $1,500 casualty gain − $8,000 insurance proceeds = $0 basis). ■

---

[12]Reg. §§ 1.1001–1(b)(2) and 1.1012–1(b). Refer to Chapter 4 for a discussion of this subject.

[13]See Chapter 3 for a discussion of bond discount and the related amortization.

[14]§ 1016(a)(2) and Reg. § 1.1016–3(a)(1)(i).

[15]Refer to Chapter 5 for the discussion of casualties and thefts.

[16]Reg. § 1.1016–6(a).

### Bridge to Financial Accounting

Certain property transactions discussed later in this chapter are treated differently for tax purposes than for financial accounting purposes. For example, the category of transactions generally referred to as "nontaxable exchanges," such as like-kind exchanges and involuntary conversions, gives taxpayers the opportunity to defer the recognition of income on the disposition of property in qualifying transactions. The gains or losses deferred under tax law, however, are not deferred for financial reporting purposes. Instead, the actual gain or loss realized is reflected in the entity's financial reports.

Identifying and calculating the book-tax differences that arise from *taxable* dispositions of certain other property may not be so easy. For example, as discussed in Chapter 4, cost recovery (i.e., depreciation) rules provided by the tax law specify various ways in which an asset's cost may be recovered over time. These methods often differ from the methods used to depreciate an asset for book purposes. Consequently, the annual book-tax differences in these depreciation expense calculations are noted in the financial reports. But, in addition, these cumulative differences, as reflected in the accumulated depreciation account, will also produce a book-tax difference on the asset's disposition. That is, because an asset's accumulated depreciation may differ for book and tax purposes, its adjusted basis will also differ. Consequently, when the asset is sold, the amount of gain or loss for book purposes will differ from that recognized for tax purposes.

3. *Certain corporate distributions.* A corporate distribution to a shareholder that is not taxable is treated as a return of capital, and it reduces the basis of the shareholder's stock in the corporation.[17] Once the basis of the stock is reduced to zero, the amount of any subsequent distributions is a capital gain if the stock is a capital asset. See Chapter 9.
4. *Amortizable bond premium.* The basis in a bond purchased at a premium is reduced by the amortizable portion of the bond premium.[18] Investors in taxable bonds may *elect* to amortize the bond premium.[19] The amount of the amortized premium on taxable bonds is permitted as an interest deduction. Therefore, the election enables the taxpayer to take an annual interest deduction to offset ordinary income in exchange for a larger capital gain or smaller capital loss on the disposition of the bond (due to the basis reduction).

*Find more information on this topic at our Web site: **http://wft-entities.swlearning.com**.*

In contrast to the treatment of taxable bonds, the premium on tax-exempt bonds *must* be amortized, and no interest deduction is permitted. Furthermore, the basis of tax-exempt bonds is reduced even though the amortization is not allowed as a deduction. No amortization deduction is permitted on tax-exempt bonds because the interest income is exempt from tax, and the amortization of the bond premium merely represents an adjustment of the effective amount of such income.

---

[17]§ 1016(a)(4) and Reg. § 1.1016–5(a).

[18]§ 1016(a)(5) and Reg. § 1.1016–5(b). The accounting treatment of bond premium amortization is the same as for tax purposes. The amortization results in a decrease in the bond investment account.

[19]§ 171(c).

## CONCEPT SUMMARY 6–1

### Recognized Gain or Loss

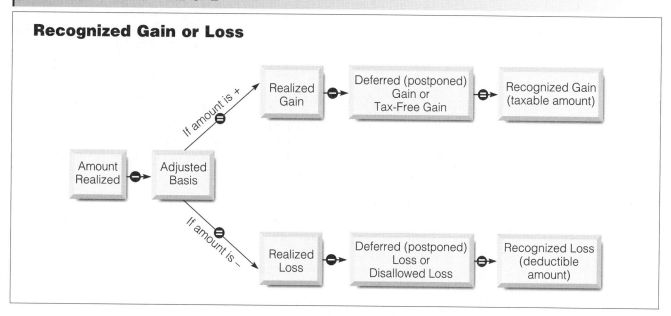

---

**EXAMPLE 7**

Navy, Inc., purchases Eagle Corporation taxable bonds with a face value of $100,000 for $110,000, thus paying a premium of $10,000. The annual interest rate is 7%, and the bonds mature 10 years from the date of purchase. The annual interest income is $7,000 (7% × $100,000). If Navy elects to amortize the bond premium, the $10,000 premium is deducted over the 10-year period. Navy's basis for the bonds is reduced each year by the amount of the amortization deduction. If the bonds were tax-exempt, amortization of the bond premium and the basis adjustment would be mandatory, and no deduction would be allowed for the amortization. ■

5. *Easements.* An easement is the legal right to use another's land for a special purpose. Historically, easements were commonly used to obtain rights-of-way for utility lines and roads. In recent years, grants of conservation easements have become a popular means of obtaining charitable contribution deductions and reducing the value of real estate for transfer tax (i.e., estate and gift) purposes. Likewise, scenic easements are used to reduce the value of land as assessed for ad valorem property tax purposes.

If the taxpayer does not retain any right to the use of the land, all of the basis is assigned to the easement. However, if the use of the land is only partially restricted, an allocation of some of the basis to the easement is appropriate.

**L0.2**

Distinguish between realized and recognized gain or loss.

### RECOGNIZED GAIN OR LOSS

**Recognized gain** is the amount of the realized gain that is included in the taxpayer's gross income.[20] A **recognized loss**, on the other hand, is the amount of a realized loss that is deductible for tax purposes.[21] As a general rule, the entire amount of a realized gain or loss is recognized when it is realized.[22]

Concept Summary 6–1 summarizes the realized gain or loss and recognized gain or loss concepts.

---

[20]§ 61(a)(3) and Reg. § 1.61–6(a).
[21]§ 165(a) and Reg. § 1.165–1(a).

[22]§ 1001(c) and Reg. § 1.1002–1(a).

## NONRECOGNITION OF GAIN OR LOSS

In certain cases, a realized gain or loss is not recognized upon the sale or other disposition of property. One such case involves nontaxable exchanges, which are covered later in this chapter. In addition, realized losses from the sale or exchange of property between certain related parties are not recognized.[23]

**Dispositions of Personal-Use Assets.**   For individual taxpayers, special rules apply to *personal-use* assets, that is, assets such as a residence or automobile that are not used in any business or investment activity. A loss from the sale, exchange, or condemnation of such assets is not recognized for tax purposes. An exception exists for casualty or theft losses from personal-use assets (refer to Chapter 5). In contrast, any gain realized from the disposition of personal-use assets is generally taxable.

**EXAMPLE 8**

Freda sells an automobile, which she has held exclusively for personal use, for $6,000. The adjusted basis of the automobile is $5,000. Freda has a realized and recognized gain of $1,000. If she sold this automobile for $4,500, she would have a realized loss of $500, but the loss would not be recognized for tax purposes. ▪

## RECOVERY OF CAPITAL DOCTRINE

**Doctrine Defined.**   The **recovery of capital doctrine** pervades all the tax rules relating to property transactions. The doctrine derives its roots from the very essence of the income tax—a tax on income or profit. Because the focus of the tax is on profit, a taxpayer is entitled to recover the cost or other original basis of property acquired without being taxed on that amount.

The cost or other original basis of depreciable property is recovered through annual depreciation deductions. The basis is reduced as the cost is recovered over the period the property is held. Therefore, when property is sold or otherwise disposed of, it is the adjusted basis (unrecovered cost or other basis) that is compared with the amount realized from the disposition to determine realized gain or loss.

**EXAMPLE 9**

Cardinal Corporation purchased a machine for $20,000 four years ago and has deducted depreciation totaling $13,000 during those years. Since Cardinal has recovered $13,000 through depreciation, the adjusted basis of this machine is $7,000 ($20,000 − $13,000). If Cardinal sells this machine, it subtracts the $7,000 adjusted basis from the amount realized when determining whether it realized a gain or loss upon the disposition. ▪

*Find more information on this topic at our Web site: http://wft-entities.swlearning.com.*

**LO.3**

Explain how basis is determined for various methods of asset acquisition.

# Basis Considerations

## DETERMINATION OF COST BASIS

As noted earlier, the basis of property is generally the property's cost. Cost is the amount paid for the property in cash or other property.[24] This general rule follows logically from the recovery of capital doctrine; that is, the cost or other basis of property is to be recovered tax-free by the taxpayer.

---

[23]§ 267(a)(1).

[24]§ 1012 and Reg. § 1.1012–1(a).

A *bargain purchase* of property is an exception to the general rule for determining basis. A bargain purchase may result when an employer transfers property to an employee at less than the property's fair market value (as compensation for services) or when a corporation transfers property to a shareholder at less than the property's fair market value (a dividend). These transfers create taxable income for the purchaser equal to the difference between fair market value and purchase price. The basis of property acquired in a bargain purchase is the property's fair market value.[25] If the basis of the property were not increased by the bargain amount, the taxpayer would be taxed on this amount again at disposition.

**EXAMPLE 10**

Wade buys land from his employer for $10,000. The fair market value of the land is $15,000. Wade must include the $5,000 difference between the cost and the fair market value of the land in his gross income. The bargain element represents additional compensation to Wade. His basis for the land is $15,000, the land's fair market value. ∎

**Identification Problems.** Sometimes, it can be difficult to determine the cost of an asset being sold. This problem is frequently encountered in sales of corporate stock, because a taxpayer may purchase separate lots of a company's stock on different dates and at different prices. When the stock is sold, if the taxpayer cannot identify the specific shares being sold, the stock sold is determined on a first-in, first-out (FIFO) basis. Thus, the holding period and cost of the stock sold are determined by referring to the purchase date and cost of the first lot of stock acquired.[26] But if the stock being sold can be adequately identified, then the basis and holding period of the specific stock sold are used in determining the nature and amount of gain or loss.[27] Thus, to avoid FIFO treatment when the sold securities are held by a broker, it is often necessary to provide specific instructions and receive written confirmation of the securities being sold.

**EXAMPLE 11**

Pelican, Inc., purchases 100 shares of Olive Corporation stock on July 1, 2003, for $5,000 ($50 a share) and another 100 shares of Olive stock on July 1, 2004, for $6,000 ($60 a share). Pelican sells 50 shares of the stock on January 2, 2005. The cost of the stock sold, assuming Pelican cannot adequately identify the shares, is $50 a share (from shares purchased on July 1, 2003), or $2,500. This is the cost Pelican will compare with the amount realized in determining the gain or loss from the sale. ∎

**Allocation Problems.** When a taxpayer acquires *several assets in a lump-sum purchase*, the total cost must be allocated among the individual assets.[28] Allocation is necessary for several reasons:

- Some of the assets acquired may be depreciable (e.g., buildings), while others may not be (e.g., land).
- Only a portion of the assets acquired may be sold.
- Some of the assets may be capital or depreciable assets that receive special tax treatment upon subsequent sale or other disposition.

The lump-sum cost is allocated on the basis of the fair market values of the individual assets acquired.

**EXAMPLE 12**

Magenta Corporation purchases a building and land for $800,000. Because of the depressed nature of the industry in which the seller was operating, Magenta was able to negotiate a very favorable purchase price. Appraisals of the individual assets indicate that the fair

---

[25]Reg. §§ 1.61–2(d)(2)(i) and 1.301–1(j).
[26]*Kluger Associates, Inc.,* 69 T.C. 925 (1978).

[27]Reg. § 1.1012–1(c)(1).
[28]Reg. § 1.61–6(a).

market value of the building is $600,000 and that of the land is $400,000. Magenta's basis for the building is $480,000 [($600,000/$1,000,000) × $800,000], and its basis for the land is $320,000 [($400,000/$1,000,000) × $800,000]. ■

If a business is purchased and **goodwill** (or any other § 197 intangible asset) is involved, a special *residual allocation* rule applies. Initially, the purchase price of the business is allocated to four classes of assets in the following order:

- Class 1—cash, demand deposits, etc.
- Class 2—marketable securities, certificates of deposit, and foreign currency.
- Class 3—all other assets, except for § 197 intangible assets.
- Class 4—goodwill and other § 197 intangible assets.

Within each class of assets, the purchase price is allocated among the assets on the basis of their respective fair market values, and the amount allocated to any specific asset cannot exceed its fair market value. Therefore, any amount paid in excess of fair market value for tangible assets (classes 1 through 3) is allocated to goodwill and other intangible assets of the acquired business (class 4). This allocation of purchase price is applicable to both the buyer and the seller.[29]

| | |
|---|---|
| **EXAMPLE 13** | Roadrunner, Inc., sells its business to Coyote Corporation. The two companies agree that the values of the specific assets are as follows: |

| | |
|---|---|
| Cash | $ 10,000 |
| Marketable securities | 5,000 |
| Inventory | 35,000 |
| Building | 500,000 |
| Land | 200,000 |

After negotiations, Roadrunner and Coyote agree on a sales price of $1 million. Applying the residual method, the purchase price is allocated first to cash, then to marketable securities up to their fair market value. Next, the purchase price is allocated to inventory, building, and land, all on the basis of their fair market values. The residual purchase price is allocated to goodwill, resulting in the following basis of assets to Coyote Corporation:

| | |
|---|---|
| Cash | $ 10,000 |
| Marketable securities | 5,000 |
| Inventory | 35,000 |
| Building | 500,000 |
| Land | 200,000 |
| Goodwill | 250,000 |

In the case of *nontaxable stock dividends*, the allocation depends on whether the dividend is a common stock dividend on common stock or a preferred stock dividend on common stock. If the dividend is common on common, the cost of the original common shares is allocated to the total shares owned after the dividend.[30]

| | |
|---|---|
| **EXAMPLE 14** | Yellow, Inc., owns 100 shares of Sparrow Corporation common stock for which it paid $1,100. Yellow receives a 10% common stock dividend, giving it a new total of 110 shares. Before the stock dividend, Yellow's basis was $11 per share ($1,100 ÷ 100 shares). The basis of each share after the stock dividend is $10 ($1,100 ÷ 110 shares). ■ |

---

[29]§ 1060 and Temp.Reg. § 1.338(b)–1T.
[30]§§ 305(a) and 307(a). The holding period of the new shares includes the holding period of the old shares. § 1223(5) and Reg.

§ 1.1223–1(e). See Chapter 7 for a discussion of the importance of the holding period.

If the nontaxable stock dividend is preferred stock on common, the cost of the original common shares is allocated between the common and preferred shares on the basis of their relative fair market values on the date of distribution.[31]

**EXAMPLE 15**

Brown Company owns 100 shares of Cardinal Corporation common stock for which it paid $1,000. Brown receives a nontaxable stock dividend of 50 shares of preferred stock on the Cardinal common stock. The fair market values on the date of distribution of the preferred stock dividend are $30 a share for common stock and $40 a share for preferred stock.

| | |
|---|---|
| Fair market value of common ($30 × 100 shares) | $3,000 |
| Fair market value of preferred ($40 × 50 shares) | 2,000 |
| | $5,000 |
| Basis of common: ⅗ × $1,000 | $ 600 |
| Basis of preferred: ⅖ × $1,000 | $ 400 |

The basis per share for the common stock is $6 ($600/100 shares). The basis per share for the preferred stock is $8 ($400/50 shares). ■

## GIFT BASIS

Although business entities can neither make nor receive gratuitous transfers, ownership interests in such entities are frequently the subject of lifetime and testamentary gifts. Partnership interests, stock in closely or publicly held corporations, and other assets are regularly passed from one generation of owners to another for a variety of family and business reasons. Special basis rules apply to such transfers.

When a taxpayer receives property as a gift, there is no cost to the donee (recipient). Thus, under the cost basis provision, the donee's basis would be zero. With a zero basis, if the donee sold the property, the entire amount realized would be treated as taxable gain. Instead, the Code[32] assigns a basis to the property received that depends upon the following:

- The date of the gift.
- The basis of the property to the donor.
- The fair market value of the property.
- The amount of the gift tax paid, if any.

**Gift Basis Rules if No Gift Tax Is Paid.** If a property's fair market value on the date of gift exceeds the donor's basis in the property, the donor's basis carries over to the new owner.[33] This basis is called a *carryover basis* and is used in determining the donee's gain or loss.

**EXAMPLE 16**

Melissa purchased stock two years ago for $10,000. She gave the stock to her son, Joe, this year, when the fair market value was $15,000. No gift tax was paid on the transfer. Joe subsequently sells the property for $15,000. Joe's basis is $10,000, and he has a realized gain of $5,000. ■

If the property's fair market value on the date of gift is *lower* than the donor's basis in the property, the donee's basis cannot be determined until the donee

---

[31]Reg. § 1.307–1(a).
[32]§ 1015(a).
[33]§ 1015(a) and Reg. § 1.1015–1(a)(1). See Reg. § 1.1015–1(a)(3) for cases in which the facts necessary to determine the donor's adjusted

basis are unknown. See Example 22 for the effect of depreciation deductions by the donee.

disposes of the property. For the purpose of determining *gain*, the donor's basis will carry over, as in the preceding example. But for determining *loss*, the property's basis will be its fair market value when the gift was made.

**EXAMPLE 17**

Burt purchased stock three years ago for $10,000. He gave the stock to his son, Cliff, this year, when the fair market value was $7,000. No gift tax was paid on the transfer. Cliff later sells the stock for $6,000. For determining loss, Cliff's basis is $7,000, and the realized loss from the sale is $1,000 ($6,000 amount realized – $7,000 basis). ■

Note that this loss basis rule prevents the donee from receiving a tax benefit from a decline in value that occurred while the donor held the property. Therefore, in the preceding example, Cliff has a loss of only $1,000 rather than a loss of $4,000. The $3,000 difference represents the decline in value that occurred while Burt held the property. Ironically, however, a donee might be subject to income tax on the appreciation that occurred while the donor held the property, as illustrated in Example 16.

In any case, the operation of this dual basis rule produces a curious anomaly: if the sales proceeds fall *between* the donor's adjusted basis and the property's fair market value at the date of gift, no gain or loss is recognized.

**EXAMPLE 18**

Assume the same facts as in the preceding example, except that Cliff sells the stock for $8,000. To calculate gain, he would use a basis of $10,000, the donor's adjusted basis. But when a $10,000 basis is compared to $8,000 of sales proceeds, a *loss* is produced. Yet in determining loss, Cliff must use the property's fair market value at the date of gift—namely, $7,000. When a $7,000 basis is compared to sales proceeds of $8,000, a *gain* is produced. Accordingly, no gain or loss is recognized on this transaction. ■

**PLANNING STRATEGIES**    ## Gift Planning

**FRAMEWORK FOCUS: TAX RATE; DEDUCTIONS**

STRATEGY ➤ SHIFT NET INCOME FROM HIGH-BRACKET TAXPAYERS TO LOW-BRACKET TAXPAYERS.
➤ MAXIMIZE DEDUCTIBLE AMOUNTS.

Gifts of *appreciated property* can produce tax savings if the donee is in a lower tax bracket than the donor. The carryover basis rule effectively shifts the tax on the property's appreciation to the new owner, even if all of the appreciation arose while the property was owned by the donor.

On the other hand, donors should generally avoid making gifts of property that is worth less than the donor's adjusted basis (loss property). The operation of the basis rule for losses may result in either (1) a realized loss that is not deductible by either the donor or the donee or (2) reduced tax benefits when the loss is recognized by a donee facing lower marginal tax rates. Unless the property is expected to rebound in value before it is sold, a donor would be better advised to sell the property that has declined in value, deduct the resulting loss, and then transfer the proceeds to the prospective donee.

**Adjustment for Gift Tax.**  If gift taxes are paid by the donor, the donee's basis may exceed the donor's basis. This occurs only if the fair market value of the property at the date of the gift exceeds the donor's adjusted basis (i.e., the property has appreciated in value). The portion of the gift tax paid that is related to the appreciation is added to the donor's basis in calculating the donee's basis for the property. In this circumstance, the following formula is used for calculating the donee's basis:[34]

*The taxable gift is the fair market value of the gift less the per donee annual exclusion.

**EXAMPLE 19**

Bonnie made a gift of stock (adjusted basis of $15,000) to Peggy earlier this year. The stock had a fair market value of $50,000, and the transfer resulted in a gift tax of $4,000. The unrealized appreciation of the stock is $35,000 ($50,000 fair market value − $15,000 adjusted basis), while the taxable gift is $39,000 ($50,000 fair market value of gift − $11,000 per donee annual exclusion). Peggy's basis in the stock is $18,600, determined as follows:

| | |
|---|---|
| Donor's adjusted basis | $15,000 |
| Gift tax attributable to appreciation— | |
| $35,000/$39,000 = 90% (rounded) × $4,000 | 3,600 |
| Donee's gain basis | $18,600 |

**EXAMPLE 20**

Don made a gift of stock to Matt earlier this year, when the fair market value of the stock was $50,000. Don paid gift tax of $4,000. Don had purchased the stock in 1986 for $65,000. Because there is no unrealized appreciation at the date of the gift, none of the gift tax paid is added to Don's basis in calculating Matt's basis. Thus, Matt's gain basis is $65,000. ∎

For *gifts made before 1977*, the full amount of the gift tax paid is added to the donor's basis. However, the ceiling on this total is the fair market value of the property at the date of the gift. Thus, in Example 19, if the gift had been made before 1977, the basis of the property would be $19,000 ($15,000 + $4,000). In Example 20, the donee's basis would still be $65,000 ($65,000 + $0) for gain and $50,000 for loss.

**Holding Period.**   The **holding period** for property acquired by gift begins on the date the donor acquired the property,[35] unless the special circumstance requiring use of the property's fair market value at the date of gift applies. If so, the holding period starts on the date of the gift.[36] The significance of the holding period for capital assets is discussed in Chapter 7.

The following example summarizes the basis and holding period rules for gift property.

**EXAMPLE 21**

Jill acquired 100 shares of Wren Corporation stock on December 30, 1996, for $40,000. On January 3 of this year, when the stock has a fair market value of $38,000, Jill gives it to Dennis and pays gift tax of $4,000. The basis is not increased by a portion of the gift tax paid because the property has not appreciated in value at the time of the gift. Therefore, Dennis's basis for determining gain is $40,000. Dennis's basis for determining loss is $38,000 (fair market value), because the fair market value on the date of the gift is less than the donor's adjusted basis.

---

[34]§ 1015(d)(6) and Reg. § 1.1015–5(c)(2).
[35]§ 1223(2) and Reg. § 1.1223–1(b).

[36]Rev.Rul. 59–86, 1959–1 C.B. 209.

- If Dennis sells the stock for $45,000, he has a recognized gain of $5,000. The holding period for determining whether the capital gain is short term or long term begins on December 30, 1996, the date Jill acquired the property.
- If Dennis sells the stock for $36,000, he has a recognized loss of $2,000. The holding period for determining whether the capital loss is short term or long term begins on January 3 of this year, the date of the gift.
- If Dennis sells the property for $39,000, no gain or loss is recognized because the amount realized is between the property's fair market value when given ($38,000) and the donor's adjusted basis of $40,000. ■

**Basis for Depreciation.** The basis for depreciation on depreciable gift property is the donee's basis for determining gain.[37] This rule is applicable even if the donee later sells the property at a loss and uses the property's fair market value at the date of gift in calculating the amount of the realized loss.

EXAMPLE 22

Vito gave a machine to Tina earlier this year. At that time, the adjusted basis was $32,000 (cost of $40,000 – accumulated depreciation of $8,000), and the fair market value was $26,000. No gift tax was due. Tina's basis for determining gain is $32,000, and her loss basis is $26,000. During this year, Tina deducts depreciation (cost recovery) of $6,400 ($32,000 × 20%). (Refer to Chapter 4 for the cost recovery tables.) At the end of this year, Tina's basis determinations are calculated as follows:

|  | Gain Basis | Loss Basis |
| --- | --- | --- |
| Donor's basis or fair market value | $32,000 | $26,000 |
| Depreciation | (6,400) | (6,400) |
|  | $25,600 | $19,600 |

■

## PROPERTY ACQUIRED FROM A DECEDENT

**General Rules.** The basis of property acquired from a decedent is generally the property's fair market value at the date of death (referred to as the *primary valuation amount*).[38] The property's basis is the fair market value six months after the date of death if the executor or administrator of the estate *elects* the alternate valuation date for estate tax purposes. This amount is referred to as the *alternate valuation amount*.

*Find more information on this topic at our Web site: **http://wft-entities.swlearning.com**.*

EXAMPLE 23

Linda and various other family members inherited stock in a closely held corporation from Linda's father, who died earlier this year. At the date of death, her father's adjusted basis for the stock Linda inherited was $35,000. The stock's fair market value at the date of death was $50,000. The alternate valuation date was not elected. Linda's basis for income tax purposes is $50,000. This is commonly referred to as a *stepped-up basis*. ■

EXAMPLE 24

Assume the same facts as in the preceding example, except that the stock's fair market value at the date of death was $20,000. Linda's basis for income tax purposes is $20,000. This is commonly referred to as a *stepped-down basis*. ■

No estate tax return must be filed for estates below a threshold amount (refer to Chapter 1). In such cases, the alternate valuation date and amount are not available. Even if an estate tax return is filed and the executor elects the alternate

---

[37]§ 1011 and Reg. §§ 1.1011–1 and 1.167(g)–1.       [38]§ 1014(a).

## TAX IN THE NEWS

### EFFECT OF 2001 TAX LEGISLATION ON THE BASIS OF INHERITED PROPERTY: BAD NEWS/GOOD NEWS!

The *bad news* is that the Tax Relief Reconciliation Act of 2001 repeals the current step-up or step-down (i.e., fair market value) rules for the beneficiary's basis in inherited property and replaces them with a modified carryover basis. By itself, this change significantly increases the complexity of the tax law. A potential decedent will need to maintain detailed records on the cost of his or her assets and have such data readily available for the executor. Otherwise, the executor will be unable to determine the cost of many assets included in the estate.

So what is the *good news*? First, the effective date for this new carryover basis provision is deferred to deaths occurring after December 31, 2009. Second, the carryover basis approach for inherited property has been tried before. The results were so unsuccessful that the legislation was repealed retroactively by Congress. Hopefully, if the new carryover basis ever becomes effective, history will repeat itself, and another retroactive repeal by Congress will occur.

valuation date, the six-months-after-death date is available only for property that the executor has not distributed before this date. For any property distributed or otherwise disposed of by the executor during the six-month period preceding the alternate valuation date, the adjusted basis to the beneficiary will equal the fair market value on the date of distribution or other disposition.[39]

The alternate valuation date can be elected *only if*, as a result of the election, *both* the value of the gross estate and the estate tax liability are lower than they would have been if the primary valuation date had been used. This provision prevents the alternate valuation election from being used to increase the basis of the property to the beneficiary for income tax purposes without simultaneously increasing the estate tax liability (because of estate tax deductions or credits).[40]

**EXAMPLE 25**

Nancy inherited investment real estate from her father, who died earlier this year. Her father's adjusted basis for the property at the date of death was $350,000. The property's fair market value was $1,750,000 at the date of death and $1,760,000 six months after death. The alternate valuation date cannot be elected because the value of the gross estate has increased during the six-month period. Nancy's basis for income tax purposes is $1,750,000. ■

**EXAMPLE 26**

Assume the same facts as in Example 25, except that the property's fair market value six months after death was $1,745,000. If the executor elects the alternate valuation date, Nancy's basis for income tax purposes is $1,745,000. ■

**EXAMPLE 27**

Assume the same facts as in Example 26, except that the property is distributed four months after the date of the decedent's death. At the distribution date, the property's fair market value is $1,747,500. Since the executor elected the alternate valuation date, Nancy's basis for income tax purposes is $1,747,500. ■

*Find more information on this topic at our Web site: **http://wft-entities.swlearning.com.***

---

[39]§ 2032(a)(1) and Rev.Rul. 56–60, 1956–1 C.B. 443.          [40]§ 2032(c).

## Property from a Decedent

STRATEGY ➤ AVOID INCOME RECOGNITION.
　　　　 ➤ MAXIMIZE DEDUCTIBLE AMOUNTS.

If a taxpayer *retains appreciated property* until death, the property's basis will be "stepped up" to its fair market value at that time. Thus, no income tax will be paid on the property's appreciation by either the former owner (the decedent) or the new owner (the heir).

On the other hand, *depreciated property should be sold* prior to death. Otherwise, the property's basis in the heir's hands will be its declined fair market value, and neither the decedent nor the heir will be able to deduct the loss that occurred while the property was owned by the decedent.

**Deathbed Gifts.**   The Code contains a provision designed to eliminate a tax avoidance technique occasionally described as *deathbed gifts*. With this technique, a donor makes a gift of appreciated property to a dying person with the understanding that the donor (or the donor's spouse) will inherit the property on the donee's death. If a person (or that person's spouse) receives from a decedent property that this person gave to the decedent during the year before the decedent's death, the property does *not* get a stepped-up basis. Instead, the basis of that property is the donor's adjusted basis.[41]

**EXAMPLE 28**

Ned gives stock to his uncle, Vern, this year. Ned's basis for the stock is $1,000, and the fair market value is $9,000. No gift tax is due. Eight months later, Ned inherits the stock from Vern. At the date of Vern's death, the fair market value of the stock is $12,000. Ned's adjusted basis for the stock is $1,000. ∎

**Holding Period of Property Acquired from a Decedent.**   The holding period of property acquired from a decedent is *deemed to be long term* (held for the required long-term holding period). This provision applies regardless of whether the property is disposed of at a gain or at a loss.[42]

**LO.4**

Describe various loss disallowance provisions.

## DISALLOWED LOSSES

**Related Taxpayers.**   Section 267 provides that realized losses from sales or exchanges of property between certain related parties are not recognized. This loss disallowance provision applies to several types of related-party transactions. The most common involve (1) members of a family and (2) an individual and a corporation in which the individual owns, directly or indirectly, more than 50 percent in value of the corporation's outstanding stock. Section 707 provides a similar loss disallowance provision where the related parties are a partner and a partnership in which the partner owns, directly or indirectly, more than 50 percent of the capital interests or profits interests in the partnership. Neither provision, however, prevents the recognition of *gains* between related parties. The rules governing the relationships covered by § 267 were discussed in Chapter 4.

If income-producing or business property is transferred to a related party and a loss is disallowed, the basis of the property to the recipient is the property's cost

---

[41]§ 1014(e).

[42]§ 1223(11).

to the transferee. However, if a subsequent sale or other disposition of the property by the original transferee results in a realized gain, the amount of gain is reduced by the loss that was previously disallowed. This *right of offset* is not applicable if the original sale involved the sale of a personal-use asset (e.g., a personal residence). Furthermore, the right of offset is available only to the original transferee (the related-party buyer). See Example 17 and Example 18 in Chapter 4.

*Find more information on this topic at our Web site: **http://wft-entities.swlearning.com.***

**Wash Sales.** Section 1091 stipulates that in certain cases, a realized loss on the sale or exchange of stock or securities is not recognized. Specifically, if a taxpayer sells or exchanges stock or securities and within 30 days before *or* after the date of the sale or exchange acquires *substantially identical* stock or securities, any loss realized from the sale or exchange is not recognized because the transaction is a **wash sale.**[43] The term *acquire* means acquire by purchase or in a taxable exchange and includes an option to purchase substantially identical securities. *Substantially identical* means the same in all important particulars. Corporate bonds and preferred stock are normally not considered substantially identical to a corporation's common stock. However, if the bonds and preferred stock are convertible into common stock, they may be considered substantially identical under certain circumstances.[44] Attempts to avoid the application of the wash sale rules by having a related taxpayer repurchase the securities have been unsuccessful.[45] The wash sale provisions do *not* apply to gains.

Recognition of the loss is disallowed because the taxpayer is considered to be in substantially the same economic position after the sale and repurchase as before. This disallowance rule does not apply to taxpayers engaged in the business of buying and selling securities.[46] Investors, however, are not allowed to create losses through wash sales to offset income for tax purposes.

A realized loss that is not recognized is added to the *basis* of the substantially identical stock or securities whose acquisition resulted in the nonrecognition of loss.[47] In other words, the basis of the replacement stock or securities is increased by the amount of the unrecognized loss. If the loss were not added to the basis of the newly acquired stock or securities, the taxpayer would never recover the entire basis of the old stock or securities. As a result, the wash sale rule operates to *defer* the recognition of the taxpayer's loss.

**EXAMPLE 29**

Oriole Manufacturing Company sold 50 shares of Green Corporation stock (adjusted basis of $10,000) for $8,000. Ten days later, Oriole purchased 50 shares of the same stock for $7,000. Oriole's realized loss of $2,000 ($8,000 amount realized − $10,000 adjusted basis) is not recognized because it resulted from a wash sale. Oriole's basis in the newly acquired stock is $9,000 ($7,000 purchase price + $2,000 unrecognized loss from the wash sale). ■

The basis of the new stock or securities includes the unrecovered portion of the basis of the formerly held stock or securities. Therefore, the *holding period* of the new stock or securities begins on the date of acquisition of the old stock or securities.[48]

A taxpayer may acquire fewer shares than the number sold in a wash sale. In this case, the loss from the sale is prorated between recognized and unrecognized loss on the basis of the ratio of the number of shares acquired to the number of shares sold.[49]

---

[43]§ 1091(a) and Reg. §§ 1.1091–1(a) and (f).
[44]Rev.Rul. 56–406, 1956–2 C.B. 523.
[45]*McWilliams v. Comm.*, 47–1 USTC ¶9289, 35 AFTR 1184, 67 S.Ct. 1477 (USSC, 1947).

[46]Reg. § 1.1091–1(a).
[47]§ 1091(d) and Reg. § 1.1091–2(a).
[48]§ 1223(4) and Reg. § 1.1223–1(d).
[49]§ 1091(b) and Reg. § 1.1091–1(c).

# Avoiding Wash Sales

**FRAMEWORK FOCUS: DEDUCTIONS**

STRATEGY ➤ MAXIMIZE DEDUCTIBLE AMOUNTS.

The wash sale restriction can be avoided by replacing the sold security with a *similar* but not "substantially identical" security. For example, if IBM common stock is sold to claim an unrealized loss, the taxpayer could immediately acquire Intel common stock without triggering the wash sale rule.

*Nontax considerations* must also come into play, however, because IBM and Intel are two different companies with different investment prospects. Though both securities will be affected by many of the same factors, they will also be subject to different factors that may be even more significant than the ones they share.

## CONVERSION OF PROPERTY FROM PERSONAL USE TO BUSINESS OR INCOME-PRODUCING USE

As discussed previously, losses from the sale of personal-use assets are not recognized for tax purposes, but losses from the sale of business and income-producing assets are deductible. Can a taxpayer convert a personal-use asset that has declined in value to business or income-producing use and then sell the asset to recognize a business or income-producing loss? The tax law prevents this practice by specifying that the *basis for determining loss* on personal-use assets converted to business or income-producing use is the *lower* of the property's adjusted basis or its fair market value on the date of conversion.[50] The *gain basis* for converted property is the property's adjusted basis on the date of conversion, regardless of whether the property's use is business, income-producing, or personal in nature.

**EXAMPLE 30**

Diane's personal residence has an adjusted basis of $175,000 and a fair market value of $160,000. When she converts the personal residence to residential rental property on January 1, her basis for determining loss is $160,000 (lower of $175,000 adjusted basis and fair market value of $160,000). The $15,000 decline in value is a personal loss and can never be recognized for tax purposes. Diane's basis for determining gain is $175,000. ■

The basis for determining loss is also the *basis for depreciating* the converted property.[51] This is an exception to the general rule that the basis for depreciation is the basis for determining gain (e.g., property received by gift). This exception prevents the taxpayer from recovering a personal loss indirectly through depreciation of the higher original basis. Once property is converted, both its basis for loss and its basis for gain are adjusted for depreciation deductions from the date of conversion to the date of disposition.

**EXAMPLE 31**

Assume the same facts as in Example 30. The MACRS cost recovery deduction for the current year is $5,576 ($160,000 × 3.485%). Thus, at the end of the current year, Diane's adjusted basis for gain for the rental property is $169,424 ($175,000 − $5,576), and her adjusted basis for loss is $154,424 ($160,000 − $5,576). ■

DIGGING DEEPER 6   DIGGING DEEPER 7

*Find more information on these topics at our Web site: **http://wft-entities.swlearning.com**.*

---

[50]Reg. § 1.165–9(b)(2).

[51]Reg. § 1.167(g)–1.

## CONCEPT SUMMARY 6–2

# Adjustments to Basis

| Item | Effect | Refer to Chapter | Explanation |
|------|--------|------------------|-------------|
| Amortization of bond discount. | Increase | 6 | Amortization is mandatory for certain taxable bonds and elective for tax-exempt bonds. |
| Amortization of bond premium. | Decrease | 6 | Amortization is mandatory for tax-exempt bonds and elective for taxable bonds. |
| Amortization of covenant not to compete. | Decrease | 4 | Covenant must be for a definite and limited time period. The amortization period is a statutory period of 15 years. |
| Amortization of intangibles. | Decrease | 4 | Intangibles are amortized over a 15-year period. |
| Bad debts. | Decrease | 5 | Most taxpayers must use the specific charge-off method. |
| Capital additions. | Increase | 6 | Certain items, at the taxpayer's election, can be capitalized or deducted. |
| Casualty. | Decrease | 6 | For a casualty loss, the amount of the adjustment is the sum of the deductible loss and the insurance proceeds received. For a casualty gain, the amount of the adjustment is the insurance proceeds received reduced by the recognized gain. |
| Condemnation. | Decrease | 6 | See casualty explanation. |
| Cost recovery. | Decrease | 4 | § 168 is applicable to tangible assets placed in service after 1980 whose useful life is expressed in terms of years. |
| Depletion. | Decrease | 4 | Use the greater of cost or percentage depletion. Percentage depletion can be deducted even when the basis is zero. |
| Depreciation. | Decrease | 4 | § 167 is applicable to tangible assets placed in service before 1981 and to tangible assets not depreciated in terms of years. |
| Easement. | Decrease | 6 | If the taxpayer does not retain any use of the land, all of the basis is allocable to the easement transaction. However, if only part of the land is affected by the easement, only part of the basis is allocable to the easement transaction. |
| Improvements by lessee to lessor's property. | Increase | 3 | Adjustment occurs only if the lessor is required to include the fair market value of the improvements in gross income under § 109. |
| Imputed interest. | Decrease | | Amount deducted is not part of the cost of the asset. |
| Inventory: lower of cost or market. | Decrease | | Not available if the LIFO method is used. |
| Limited expensing under § 179. | Decrease | 4 | Occurs only if the taxpayer elects § 179 treatment. |
| Medical capital expenditure deducted as a medical expense. | Decrease | 15 | Adjustment is the amount of the deduction (the effect on basis is to increase it by the amount of the capital expenditure net of the deduction). |

## SUMMARY OF BASIS ADJUSTMENTS

Some of the more common items that either increase or decrease the basis of an asset appear in Concept Summary 6–2.

In discussing the topic of basis, a number of specific techniques for determining basis have been presented. Although the various techniques are responsive to

| Item | Effect | Refer to Chapter | Explanation |
|------|--------|------------------|-------------|
| Real estate taxes: apportionment between the buyer and seller. | Increase or decrease | 4 | To the extent the buyer pays the seller's pro rata share, the buyer's basis is increased. To the extent the seller pays the buyer's pro rata share, the buyer's basis is decreased. |
| Rebate from manufacturer. | Decrease | | Since the rebate is treated as an adjustment to the purchase price, it is not included in the buyer's gross income. |
| Stock dividend. | Decrease | 6 | Adjustment occurs only if the stock dividend is nontaxable. While the basis per share decreases, the total stock basis does not change. |
| Stock rights. | Decrease | 9 | Adjustment to stock basis occurs only for nontaxable stock rights and only if the fair market value of the rights is at least 15% of the fair market value of the stock or, if less than 15%, the taxpayer elects to allocate the basis between the stock and the rights. |
| Theft. | Decrease | 5 | See casualty explanation. |

and mandated by transactions occurring in the marketplace, they possess enough common characteristics to be categorized as follows:

- The basis of the asset may be determined by its cost.
- The basis of the asset may be determined by the basis of another asset.
- The basis of the asset may be determined by its fair market value.
- The basis of the asset may be determined by the basis of the asset in the hands of another taxpayer.

# General Concept of a Nontaxable Exchange

A taxpayer who is going to replace a productive asset (e.g., machinery) used in a trade or business may structure the transaction as a sale of the old asset and the purchase of a new asset. When this approach is used, any realized gain or loss on the sale of the old asset is recognized. The basis of the new asset is its cost. Alternatively, the taxpayer may be able to trade the old asset for the new asset. This exchange of assets may produce beneficial tax consequences as a nontaxable exchange.

The tax law recognizes that nontaxable exchanges result in a change in the *form* but not the *substance* of a taxpayer's relative economic position. The replacement property received in the exchange is viewed as essentially a continuation of the old investment.[52] Additional justification for nontaxable treatment is that this type of transaction does not provide the taxpayer with the wherewithal to pay the tax on any realized gain.

The nonrecognition provisions for nontaxable exchanges do not apply to realized losses from the sale or exchange of personal-use assets. Such losses are never recognized (i.e., they are disallowed) because they are personal in nature.

In contrast, in a **nontaxable exchange**, recognition of gains or losses is *postponed* (i.e., deferred) until the new property received in the nontaxable exchange is

---

[52]Reg. § 1.1002–1(c).

subsequently disposed of in a taxable transaction. This is accomplished by assigning a carryover basis to the replacement property.

*E X A M P L E   3 2*

Starling Management Company exchanges property with an adjusted basis of $10,000 and a fair market value of $12,000 for property with a fair market value of $12,000. The transaction qualifies for nontaxable exchange treatment. Starling has a realized gain of $2,000 ($12,000 amount realized – $10,000 adjusted basis). Its recognized gain is $0. Starling's basis in the replacement property is a carryover basis of $10,000. Assume the replacement property is nondepreciable and Starling subsequently sells it for $12,000. The realized and recognized gain will be the $2,000 gain that was postponed (deferred) in the nontaxable transaction. If the replacement property is depreciable, the carryover basis of $10,000 is used in calculating depreciation. ∎

In some nontaxable exchanges, only some of the property involved in the transaction qualifies for nonrecognition treatment. If the taxpayer receives cash or other nonqualifying property, part or all of the realized gain from the exchange is recognized. In these situations, gain is recognized because the taxpayer has changed or improved its relative economic position and has the wherewithal to pay income tax to the extent of cash or other property received.

It is important to distinguish between a nontaxable disposition (or nonrecognition transaction, as the term is used in the statute) and a tax-free transaction. As previously mentioned, the term *nontaxable* refers to postponement of recognition via some version of carryover basis. In a *tax-free* transaction, the nonrecognition is permanent (e.g., see the discussion later in this chapter of the exclusion of gain from the sale of a principal residence).

Either way, nontaxable and tax-free transactions must be understood as exceptions to the Code's general rule that gains and losses are recognized when they are realized. These exceptions have their own sets of requirements, limitations, and restrictions, all of which must be satisfied for a transaction to be characterized as nontaxable or tax-free. Otherwise, the general rule of recognition applies to the gain or loss at hand.

LO.5

Apply the nonrecognition provisions and basis determination rules for like-kind exchanges.

# Like-Kind Exchanges—§ 1031

Section 1031 provides for nontaxable exchange treatment if the following requirements are satisfied:[53]

- The form of the transaction is an exchange.
- Both the property transferred and the property received are held either for productive use in a trade or business or for investment.
- The property is like-kind property.

Qualifying **like-kind exchanges** include exchanges of business for business, business for investment, investment for business, or investment for investment property. Property held for personal use does not qualify under the like-kind exchange provisions. Thus, the purpose for which the property is held by the taxpayer in question is critical. For example, if Janet uses a small truck in her trade or business, it may qualify for like-kind treatment, but if she uses this truck as her personal-use vehicle, it is ineligible for nonrecognition treatment under § 1031.

---

[53]§ 1031(a) and Reg. § 1.1031(a)–1(a).

Some assets are excluded from like-kind treatment by statute. These excluded assets include a taxpayer's inventory or "stock in trade," as well as most forms of investment other than real estate. Thus, stocks, bonds, partnership interests (whether general or limited), and other securities, even though held for investment, do not qualify for like-kind exchange treatment.

The nonrecognition provision for like-kind exchanges is *mandatory* rather than elective. A taxpayer who wants to recognize a realized gain or loss will have to structure the transaction in a form that does not satisfy the statutory requirements for a like-kind exchange.

## Like-Kind Exchanges

**FRAMEWORK FOCUS: DEDUCTIONS**

STRATEGY ➤ MAXIMIZE DEDUCTIBLE AMOUNTS.

Because nonrecognition of gain or loss is mandatory in like-kind exchanges, a taxpayer must affirmatively *avoid such exchanges* if nonrecognition treatment is not desired. If an asset is worth less than its adjusted basis, a *loss would result* from its disposition. Accordingly, the taxpayer should sell this property outright to ensure the deductibility of the loss, assuming it would otherwise be deductible.

Even if *disposition would result in a gain*, a taxpayer might want to recognize this gain in the current taxable year. If so, a like-kind exchange should be avoided. Circumstances suggesting this strategy include:

- Unused capital loss carryovers, especially if the taxpayer is a corporation for which such carryovers are limited in duration (see Chapters 3 and 7).
- Unused net operating loss carryovers (see Chapter 5).
- Unused general business credit carryovers (see Chapter 13).
- Suspended or current passive activity losses (see Chapter 5).
- Expectations of higher tax rates in future years.

## LIKE-KIND PROPERTY

The term *like-kind* is explained in the Regulations as follows: "The words 'like-kind' refer to the nature or character of the property and not to its grade or quality. One kind or class of property may not . . . be exchanged for property of a different kind or class."[54] The Regulations go on to explain that although real estate can be exchanged only for other real estate, the definition of real estate is quite broad. *Real estate* (or realty) includes principally rental buildings, office and store buildings, manufacturing plants, warehouses, and land. It is immaterial whether real estate is improved or unimproved. Thus, unimproved land can be exchanged for an apartment house. On the other hand, real property located in the United States exchanged for foreign real property (and vice versa) does not qualify as like-kind property. A similar provision applies to exchanges of foreign and domestic personalty.

In any case, real estate cannot be exchanged in a like-kind transaction for personalty. *Personalty* includes tangible assets other than real estate, such as

---

[54]Reg. § 1.1031(a)–1(b).

machinery, equipment, trucks, automobiles, furniture, and fixtures. Thus, an exchange of a machine (personalty) for a small office building (realty) is not a like-kind exchange. Finally, the Code mandates that livestock of different sexes are not like-kind property.

Pheasant, Inc., made the following exchanges during the taxable year:

  a.  Inventory for a machine used in business.
  b.  Land held for investment for a building used in business.
  c.  Stock held for investment for equipment used in business.
  d.  A business truck for a business truck.
  e.  Livestock for livestock of a different sex.
  f.  Land held for investment in New York for land held for investment in London.

Exchanges (b), investment real property for business real property, and (d), business personalty for business personalty, qualify as exchanges of like-kind property. Exchanges (a), inventory; (c), stock; (e), livestock of different sexes; and (f), U.S. and foreign real estate do not qualify.  ■

*Find more information on this topic at our Web site:* ***http://wft-entities.swlearning.com***.

The Regulations dealing with § 1031 like-kind exchanges provide greater specificity when determining whether depreciable tangible personalty is of a like kind. Such property held for productive use in a business is of like kind only if the exchanged property is within the same *general business asset class* (as specified by the IRS in Rev.Proc. 87–56 or as subsequently modified) or the same *product class* (as specified by the Department of Commerce). Property included in a general business asset class is evaluated exclusively under the Revenue Procedure, rather than under the product class system.

The following are examples of general business asset classes:

  • Office furniture, fixtures, and equipment.
  • Information systems (computers and peripheral equipment).
  • Airplanes.
  • Automobiles and taxis.
  • Buses.
  • Light general-purpose trucks.
  • Heavy general-purpose trucks.

These Regulations narrow the range of depreciable tangible personalty subject to § 1031 like-kind exchange treatment. For example, the exchange of office equipment for a computer does not qualify as an exchange of like-kind property. Even though both assets are depreciable tangible personalty, they are not like-kind property because they are in different general business asset classes. Accordingly, any realized *gain or loss* on the office equipment would be recognized currently.

*Find more information on this topic at our Web site:* ***http://wft-entities.swlearning.com***.

Finally, a special provision applies if the taxpayers involved in the exchange are *related parties* under § 267(b). To qualify for like-kind exchange treatment, the taxpayer and the related party must not dispose of the like-kind property received in the exchange for two years after the date of the exchange. If such a disposition does occur, the postponed gain is recognized as of the date of that disposition. Dispositions due to death, involuntary conversions, and certain non-tax avoidance transactions are excepted from this rule.

## EXCHANGE REQUIREMENT

The transaction must generally involve a direct exchange of property to qualify as a like-kind exchange. The sale of old property and the purchase of new property, even though like kind, is not an exchange. However, the Code does provide a limited procedure for real estate to be exchanged for qualifying property that is acquired subsequent to the exchange.[55]

Of course, the taxpayer may want to avoid nontaxable exchange treatment. Recognition of gain gives the taxpayer a higher basis for depreciation. To the extent that such gains would, if recognized, either receive favorable capital gain treatment or be passive activity income that could be offset by passive activity losses, it might be preferable to avoid the nonrecognition provisions through an indirect exchange transaction. For example, a taxpayer may sell property to one company, recognize the gain, and subsequently purchase similar property from another company. The taxpayer may also want to avoid nontaxable exchange treatment so that a realized loss can be recognized.

*Find more information on this topic at our Web site: **http://wft-entities.swlearning.com**.*

## BOOT

If the taxpayer in a like-kind exchange gives or receives some property that is not like-kind property, recognition may occur. Property that is not like-kind property, including cash, is often referred to as **boot.** Although the term *boot* does not appear in the Code, tax practitioners commonly use it rather than saying "property that does not qualify as like-kind property."

The *receipt* of boot will trigger recognition of gain if there is realized gain. The amount of the recognized gain is the *lesser* of the boot received or the realized gain (realized gain serves as the ceiling on recognition).

**EXAMPLE 34**

Blue, Inc., and White Corporation exchange machinery, and the exchange qualifies as like kind under § 1031. Since Blue's machinery (adjusted basis of $20,000) is worth $24,000 and White's machine has a fair market value of $19,000, White also gives Blue cash of $5,000. Blue's recognized gain is $4,000, the lesser of the realized gain of $4,000 ($24,000 amount realized – $20,000 adjusted basis) or the fair market value of the boot received of $5,000. ■

**EXAMPLE 35**

Assume the same facts as in the preceding example, except that White's machine is worth $21,000 (not $19,000). Under these circumstances, White gives Blue cash of $3,000 to make up the difference. Blue's recognized gain is $3,000, the lesser of the realized gain of $4,000 ($24,000 amount realized – $20,000 adjusted basis) or the fair market value of the boot received of $3,000. ■

The receipt of boot does not result in recognition if there is realized loss.

**EXAMPLE 36**

Assume the same facts as in Example 34, except that the adjusted basis of Blue's machine is $30,000. Blue's realized loss is $6,000 ($24,000 amount realized – $30,000 adjusted basis). The receipt of the boot of $5,000 does not trigger recognition of Blue's loss. ■

The *giving* of boot does not trigger recognition if the boot consists solely of cash.

**EXAMPLE 37**

Flicker, Inc., and Gadwall Corporation exchange equipment in a like-kind exchange. Flicker receives equipment with a fair market value of $25,000 and transfers equipment worth

[55]§ 1031(a)(3).

$21,000 (adjusted basis of $15,000) and cash of $4,000. Flicker's realized gain is $6,000 ($25,000 amount realized − $15,000 adjusted basis − $4,000 cash), none of which is recognized. ■

If, however, the boot given is appreciated or depreciated property, gain or loss is recognized to the extent of the difference between the adjusted basis and the fair market value of the boot. For this purpose, *appreciated or depreciated property* is property with an adjusted basis that differs from fair market value.

**EXAMPLE 38**

Assume the same facts as in the preceding example, except that Flicker transfers equipment worth $10,000 (adjusted basis of $12,000) and boot worth $15,000 (adjusted basis of $9,000). Flicker's realized gain appears to be $4,000 ($25,000 amount realized − $21,000 adjusted basis). Since realization previously has served as a ceiling on recognition, it appears that the recognized gain is $4,000 (lower of realized gain of $4,000 or amount of appreciation on boot of $6,000). However, the recognized gain actually is $6,000 (full amount of the appreciation on the boot). In effect, Flicker must calculate the like-kind and boot parts of the transaction separately. That is, the realized loss of $2,000 on the like-kind property *is not* recognized ($10,000 fair market value − $12,000 adjusted basis), but the $6,000 realized gain on the boot *is* recognized ($15,000 fair market value − $9,000 adjusted basis). ■

## BASIS AND HOLDING PERIOD OF PROPERTY RECEIVED

If an exchange does not qualify as nontaxable under § 1031, gain or loss is recognized, and the basis of property received in the exchange is the property's fair market value. If the exchange qualifies for nonrecognition, the basis of property received must be adjusted to reflect any postponed (deferred) gain or loss. The *basis of like-kind property* received in the exchange is the property's fair market value less postponed gain or plus postponed loss. The *basis* of any *boot* received is the boot's fair market value.

**EXAMPLE 39**

Vireo Property Management Company exchanges a building (used in its business) with an adjusted basis of $30,000 and a fair market value of $38,000 for land with a fair market value of $38,000. The land is to be held as an investment. The exchange qualifies as like kind (an exchange of business real property for investment real property). Thus, the basis of the land is $30,000 (the land's fair market value of $38,000 less the $8,000 postponed gain on the building). If the land is later sold for its fair market value of $38,000, the $8,000 postponed gain is recognized. ■

**EXAMPLE 40**

Assume the same facts as in the preceding example, except that the building has an adjusted basis of $48,000 and a fair market value of only $38,000. The basis in the newly acquired land is $48,000 (fair market value of $38,000 plus the $10,000 postponed loss on the building). If the land is later sold for its fair market value of $38,000, the $10,000 postponed loss is recognized. ■

The Code provides an alternative approach for determining the basis of like-kind property received:

> Adjusted basis of like-kind property surrendered
> + Adjusted basis of boot given
> + Gain recognized
> − Fair market value of boot received
> − Loss recognized
> = *Basis of like-kind property received*

This approach accords with the recovery of capital doctrine. That is, the unrecovered cost or other basis is increased by additional cost (boot given) or decreased by cost recovered (boot received). Any gain recognized is included in the basis of the new property. The taxpayer has been taxed on this amount and is now entitled to recover it tax-free. Any loss recognized is deducted from the basis of the new property since the taxpayer has already received a tax benefit on that amount.

The holding period of the property surrendered in the exchange carries over and *tacks on* to the holding period of the like-kind property received.[56] This rule derives from the basic concept that the new property is a continuation of the old investment. The boot received has a new holding period (from the date of exchange) rather than a carryover holding period.

Depreciation recapture potential carries over to the property received in a like-kind exchange.[57] See Chapter 7 for a discussion of this topic.

*Find more information on this topic at our Web site: **http://wft-entities.swlearning.com**.*

If the taxpayer either assumes a liability or takes property subject to a liability, the amount of the liability is treated as boot given. For the taxpayer whose liability is assumed or whose property is taken subject to the liability, the amount of the liability is treated as boot received. The following example illustrates the effect of such a liability. In addition, the example illustrates the tax consequences for both parties involved in the like-kind exchange.

**EXAMPLE 41**

Jaeger & Company and Lark Enterprises, Inc., exchange real estate investments. Jaeger gives up property with an adjusted basis of $250,000 (fair market value of $400,000) that is subject to a mortgage of $75,000 (assumed by Lark). In return for this property, Jaeger receives property with a fair market value of $300,000 (adjusted basis of $200,000) and cash of $25,000.[58]

|  | Jaeger | Lark |
|---|---|---|
| Amount realized: |  |  |
| Like-kind property received | $ 300,000 | $ 400,000 |
| Boot received: |  |  |
| Cash | 25,000 |  |
| Mortgage assumed | 75,000 |  |
|  | $ 400,000 | $ 400,000 |
| Adjusted basis: |  |  |
| Like-kind property given | (250,000) | (200,000) |
| Boot given: |  |  |
| Cash |  | (25,000) |
| Mortgage assumed |  | (75,000) |
| Realized gain | $ 150,000 | $ 100,000 |
| Recognized gain | 100,000* | –0–** |
| Deferred gain | $ 50,000 | $ 100,000 |

*Lesser of boot received ($25,000 cash + $75,000 mortgage assumed = $100,000) or gain realized ($150,000).
**No boot received.

---

[56]§ 1223(1) and Reg. § 1.1223–1(a). For like-kind exchanges after March 1, 1954, the tacked-on holding period applies only if the like-kind property surrendered was either a capital asset or § 1231 property. See Chapter 7 for the discussion of capital assets and § 1231 property.

[57]Reg. §§ 1.1245–2(a)(4) and 1.1250–2(d)(1).
[58]Example (2) of Reg. § 1.1031(d)–2 illustrates a special situation in which both the buyer and the seller transfer liabilities that are assumed by the other party or both parties acquire property that is subject to a liability.

**Bridge to Economics**

One can assert that the "tax variable" is neutralized in nontaxable exchanges when taxable gains or losses do not arise. Neutralizing potential tax consequences can have a positive result given that tax costs tend to dampen economic activity. For example, in a like-kind exchange, a taxpayer can exchange one asset for another asset of like kind without having to recognize a gain or pay a tax. The justification for the tax deferral is that the taxpayer is viewed as having an equivalent economic investment after the transaction as before the transaction. But the tax-neutral result changes when the taxpayer receives property that is not "like kind" because the taxpayer's economic standing has changed.

If, for example, the taxpayer receives investment land *and* cash in exchange for investment land, her ownership in the land given up has, at least in part, been converted to cash, and to that degree, her investment has substantively changed. That is, the taxpayer's economic investment has changed from an ownership exclusively in land to ownership in land *and* cash. Alternatively, if the taxpayer gives up her investment land for corporate stock in a high-tech venture, the nature of her investment also would substantially change as a result of the transaction. These differences in the taxpayer's economic position after the transaction lead to the transactions being taxed.

|  | **Jaeger** | **Lark** |
|---|---|---|
| Basis of property transferred: | | |
| Like-kind property | $ 250,000 | $200,000 |
| Cash | | 25,000 |
| Mortgage assumed | | 75,000 |
| | $ 250,000 | $300,000 |
| Plus: Gain recognized | 100,000 | |
| Less: Boot received | (100,000) | |
| Basis of new property | $ 250,000 | $300,000 |

LO.6

Explain the nonrecognition provisions available on the involuntary conversion of property.

# Involuntary Conversions—§ 1033

Section 1033 provides that a taxpayer who suffers an involuntary conversion of property may postpone recognition of *gain* realized from the conversion, if that taxpayer *reinvests* the amount realized from the conversion in replacement property. Thus, if the amount reinvested in replacement property is *less than* the amount realized, realized gain *is recognized*, but only to the extent of the amount not reinvested. Any realized gain not recognized reduces the taxpayer's basis in the replacement property.[59] Thus, recognition of the gain is deferred until the replacement property is disposed of.

**EXAMPLE 42**

Sandpiper, Inc., receives insurance proceeds of $29,000 when some of its manufacturing equipment (adjusted basis of $25,000) is destroyed by fire. Sandpiper purchases new

---

[59]§ 1033(b)(2).

equipment costing $30,000, so none of its $4,000 realized gain ($29,000 amount realized – $25,000 adjusted basis) is recognized. Sandpiper's basis in the new equipment is $26,000 ($30,000 cost – $4,000 deferred gain). ■

**EXAMPLE 43**

If Sandpiper, Inc., in the preceding example purchases new equipment that costs $28,000, it would recognize gain of $1,000, the difference between the $29,000 of insurance proceeds realized on the conversion and the $28,000 cost of the new equipment. The remaining $3,000 of realized gain would not be recognized; instead, it would reduce the company's basis in the new equipment to $25,000 ($28,000 cost – $3,000 deferred gain). ■

By its terms, § 1033 is *elective*. A taxpayer need not postpone recognition of gain, even if replacement property is acquired. In essence, a taxpayer has three options:

* Reinvest the proceeds and elect § 1033's nonrecognition of gain.
* Reinvest the proceeds and not elect § 1033, thereby triggering recognition of realized gain under the customary rules applicable to property transactions.
* Not reinvest the proceeds and recognize the realized gain accordingly.

If a *loss* occurs on an involuntary conversion, § 1033 does not apply, and the general rules for loss recognition are effective. See Chapter 5 for the discussion of the deduction of losses.

**PLANNING STRATEGIES**

## Recognizing Involuntary Conversion Gains

**FRAMEWORK FOCUS: TAX RATE; DEDUCTIONS**

**STRATEGY** ➤ **SHIFT NET INCOME FROM HIGH-BRACKET YEARS TO LOW-BRACKET YEARS.**
         ➤ **MAXIMIZE DEDUCTIBLE AMOUNTS.**

Sometimes, a taxpayer may prefer to *recognize a gain from an involuntary conversion* and will choose not to elect § 1033, even though replacement property is acquired. Circumstances suggesting this strategy would include:

* The taxpayer realized the gain in a low-bracket tax year, quite possibly because of the events that caused the involuntary conversion, such as a flood and its aftermath that seriously disrupted the business.
* The taxpayer has an expiring net operating loss carryover that can offset most, if not all, of the gain from the involuntary conversion.
* The replacement property is depreciable, and the taxpayer would prefer an unreduced basis for this

asset to maximize depreciation deductions in future years.

*Nontax considerations* might also come into play, perhaps suggesting that the property not be replaced at all. Even before the event that produced the involuntary conversion, the taxpayer might have been wanting to downsize the business or terminate it outright. In any case, the taxpayer might prefer to recognize the gain, pay the tax involved, and thereby free up the remaining proceeds for other uses—business, investment, or even personal—especially if the gain is small compared to the amount of proceeds received.

## INVOLUNTARY CONVERSION DEFINED

An **involuntary conversion** results from the destruction (complete or partial), theft, seizure, requisition or condemnation, or sale or exchange under threat or imminence of requisition or condemnation of the taxpayer's property.[60] This description

---

[60]§ 1033(a) and Reg. §§ 1.1033(a)–1(a) and –2(a).

# TAX IN THE NEWS

## A COURT LIMITS THE GOVERNMENT'S TAKING OF PROPERTY

Under eminent domain, governmental units have the right to take private property for public use. As fair compensation must be paid, disagreement often arises over the fair market value of condemned property.

In recent years, there has also been controversy over what constitutes "public use." Courts have expanded the definition of public use beyond the traditional public projects (such as roads, bridges, schools, hospitals, and slum clearance) to allow the taking of unblighted property for commercial development purposes. The objective in taking such property is to create jobs and increase tax revenues by means of new office parks, big box stores, racetracks, and other businesses. For example, one Mississippi case dealt with the right of a governmental agency to condemn farmland for use by Nissan as a site for a truck factory.

Recently, though, the Michigan Supreme Court in a unanimous decision refused to allow the taking of 1,300 acres near the Detroit airport for a business complex. The effect of this decision was to reverse the position the court had taken in the 1981 landmark *Poletown* case (so called for the ethnic neighborhood involved). The *Poletown* decision had permitted the city of Detroit to condemn 1,000 homes and 600 businesses to enable General Motors to acquire the land necessary for a plant. The public use was determined to be the economic benefits that resulted. In effect, the Michigan Supreme Court has now overturned the precedential value of *Poletown*.

Other courts, however, are continuing to follow the rationale set forth in *Poletown*. The time seems right for the U.S. Supreme Court to address and resolve this issue.

SOURCES: Adapted from Dean Starkman, "Michigan Upholds Property Rights in Broad Ruling," *Wall Street Journal*, August 2, 2004, p. A6; Editorial, "Poletown's Revenge," *Wall Street Journal*, August 3, 2004, p. A10.

---

includes fires (other than arson),[61] tornadoes, hurricanes, earthquakes, floods, and other natural disasters. In these circumstances, *gain* can result from insurance proceeds received in an amount that exceeds the taxpayer's historical cost of the property, especially if depreciation deductions have lowered the property's adjusted basis.

For requisitions and condemnations, the amount realized includes the compensation paid by the public authority acquiring the taxpayer's property. To prove the existence of a threat or imminence of condemnation, the taxpayer must obtain confirmation that there has been a decision to acquire the property for public use. In addition, the taxpayer must have reasonable grounds to believe the property will be taken.[62] The property does not have to be sold to the authority threatening to condemn it to qualify for § 1033 postponement. If the taxpayer satisfies the confirmation and reasonable grounds requirements, he or she can sell the property to another party.[63] Likewise, the sale of property to a condemning authority by a taxpayer who acquired the property from its former owner with the knowledge

---

[61]Rev.Rul. 82–74, 1982–1 C.B. 110.

[62]Rev.Rul. 63–221, 1963–2 C.B. 332, and *Joseph P. Balistrieri*, 38 TCM 526, T.C.Memo. 1979–115.

[63]Rev.Rul. 81–180, 1981–2 C.B. 161.

that the property was under threat of condemnation also qualifies as an involuntary conversion under § 1033.[64]

*Find more information on this topic at our Web site:* ***http://wft-entities.swlearning.com***.

## REPLACEMENT PROPERTY

The requirements for replacement property under the involuntary conversion rules generally are more restrictive than those for like-kind property under § 1031. The basic requirement is that the replacement property be similar or related in service or use to the involuntarily converted property.[65]

Different interpretations of the phrase *similar or related in service or use* apply depending on whether the involuntarily converted property is held by an *owner-user* or by an *owner-investor* (e.g., lessor). For an owner-user, the *functional use test* applies, and for an owner-investor, the *taxpayer use test* applies.

**Functional Use Test.**   Under this test, a taxpayer's use of the replacement property and of the involuntarily converted property must be the same. Replacing a manufacturing plant with a wholesale grocery warehouse does not meet this test. Instead, the plant must be replaced with another facility of similar functional use.

**Taxpayer Use Test.**   The taxpayer use test for owner-investors provides the taxpayer with more flexibility in terms of what qualifies as replacement property than does the functional use test for owner-users. Essentially, the properties must be used by the taxpayer (the owner-investor) in similar endeavors. For example, rental property held by an owner-investor qualifies if replaced by other rental property, regardless of the type of rental property involved. The test is met when an investor replaces a manufacturing plant with a wholesale grocery warehouse if both properties are held for the production of rental income.[66] The replacement of a rental residence with a personal residence does not meet the test.[67]

**Special Real Property Test.**   In addition to the functional and taxpayer use tests, the Code provides a special rule for business or investment real property *that is condemned*. This rule applies the broad like-kind classification for real estate to such circumstances. Accordingly, improved real property can be replaced with unimproved real property.

The rules concerning the nature of replacement property are illustrated in Concept Summary 6–3.

## TIME LIMITATION ON REPLACEMENT

The taxpayer normally has a two-year period after the close of the taxable year in which gain is realized from an involuntary conversion to replace the property (*the latest date*).[68] This rule affords as much as three years from the date of realization of gain to replace the property if the realization of gain took place on the first day of the taxable year.[69] If the involuntary conversion involved the condemnation of real property used in a trade or business or held for investment, the Code substitutes a three-year period for the normal two-year period. In this case, a taxpayer might

---

[64]Rev.Rul. 81–181, 1981–2 C.B. 162.

[65]§ 1033(a) and Reg. § 1.1033(a)–1.

[66]*Loco Realty Co. v. Comm.*, 62–2 USTC ¶9657, 10 AFTR2d 5359, 306 F.2d 207 (CA–8, 1962).

[67]Rev.Rul. 70–466, 1970–2 C.B. 165.

[68]§§ 1033(a)(2)(B) and (g)(4) and Reg. § 1.1033(a)–2(c)(3).

[69]A taxpayer can apply for an extension of this time period anytime before its expiration [Reg. § 1.1033(a)–2(c)(3)]. Also, the period for filing the application for extension can be extended if a taxpayer shows reasonable cause.

---

| **CONCEPT SUMMARY 6–3** |
| --- |

## Replacement Property Tests

| Type of Property and User | Like-Kind Test | Taxpayer Use Test | Functional Use Test |
| --- | --- | --- | --- |
| Land used by a manufacturing company is condemned by a local government authority. | X | | |
| Apartment and land held by an investor are sold due to the threat or imminence of condemnation. | X | | |
| An investor's rented shopping mall is destroyed by fire; the mall may be replaced by other rental properties (e.g., an apartment building). | | X | |
| A manufacturing plant is destroyed by fire; replacement property must consist of another manufacturing plant that is functionally the same as the property converted. | | | X |
| Personal residence of taxpayer is condemned by a local government authority; replacement property must consist of another personal residence. | | | X |

have as much as four years from the date of realization of gain to replace the property.

**EXAMPLE 44**

Magpie, Inc.'s warehouse is destroyed by fire on December 16, 2004. The adjusted basis is $325,000. Magpie receives $400,000 from the insurance company on January 10, 2005. The company is a calendar year taxpayer. The latest date for replacement is December 31, 2007 (the end of the taxable year in which realized gain occurred plus two years). The critical date is not the date the involuntary conversion occurred, but rather the date of gain realization (when the insurance proceeds are received). ■

**EXAMPLE 45**

Assume the same facts as in the preceding example, except that Magpie's warehouse is condemned. The latest date for replacement is December 31, 2008 (the end of the taxable year in which realized gain occurred plus three years). ■

The *earliest date* for replacement typically is the date the involuntary conversion occurs. However, if the property is condemned, it is possible to replace the condemned property before this date. In this case, the earliest date is the date of the threat or imminence of requisition or condemnation of the property. The purpose of this provision is to enable the taxpayer to make an orderly replacement of the condemned property.

**LO.7**

Identify other nonrecognition provisions contained in the Code.

# Other Nonrecognition Provisions

Several additional nonrecognition provisions are treated briefly in the remainder of this chapter.

### TRANSFER OF ASSETS TO BUSINESS ENTITY—§§ 351 AND 721

Taxpayers can transfer assets to corporations in exchange for stock without recognizing gain or loss on the transfer according to § 351. See Chapter 8 for the applicable restrictions and corresponding basis adjustments for the stock acquired. A similar provision (§ 721) allows the nontaxable transfer of assets to a partnership in exchange for an interest in that partnership. See Chapter 10 for a description of § 721.

## EXCHANGE OF STOCK FOR PROPERTY—§ 1032

Under § 1032, a corporation does not recognize gain or loss on the receipt of money or other property in exchange for its stock (including treasury stock). In other words, a corporation does not recognize gain or loss when it deals in its own stock. This provision accords with the accounting treatment of such transactions.

## CERTAIN EXCHANGES OF INSURANCE POLICIES—§ 1035

Under § 1035, no gain or loss is recognized from the exchange of certain insurance contracts or policies. The rules relating to exchanges not solely in kind (i.e., with boot) and the basis of the property acquired are the same as under § 1031. Exchanges qualifying for nonrecognition include the following:

- The exchange of life insurance contracts.
- The exchange of a life insurance contract for an endowment or annuity contract.
- The exchange of an endowment contract for another endowment contract that provides for regular payments beginning at a date not later than the date payments would have begun under the contract exchanged.
- The exchange of an endowment contract for an annuity contract.
- The exchange of annuity contracts.

## EXCHANGE OF STOCK FOR STOCK OF THE SAME CORPORATION—§ 1036

Section 1036 provides that a shareholder does not recognize gain or loss on the exchange of common stock solely for common stock in the same corporation or from the exchange of preferred stock for preferred stock in the same corporation. Exchanges between individual shareholders as well as between a shareholder and the corporation are included under this nonrecognition provision. The rules relating to exchanges not solely in kind and the basis of the property acquired are the same as under § 1031. For example, a nonrecognition exchange occurs when common stock with different rights, such as voting for nonvoting, is exchanged. A shareholder usually recognizes gain or loss from the exchange of common for preferred or preferred for common even though the stock exchanged is in the same corporation.

## ROLLOVERS INTO SPECIALIZED SMALL BUSINESS INVESTMENT COMPANIES—§ 1044

Section 1044 provides a postponement opportunity associated with the sale of publicly traded securities. If the amount realized is reinvested in the common stock or partnership interest of a specialized small business investment company (SSBIC), the realized gain is not recognized. Gain will be recognized, however, to the extent of any amount not reinvested. To qualify, the taxpayer must reinvest the proceeds within 60 days of the date of sale. In calculating the basis of the SSBIC stock, the amount of the purchase price is reduced by the amount of the postponed gain.

Statutory ceilings are imposed on the amount of realized gain that can be postponed for any taxable year as follows:

- For an individual taxpayer, the lesser of:
  - $50,000 ($25,000 for married filing separately).
  - $500,000 ($250,000 for married filing separately) reduced by the amount of such nonrecognized gain in all preceding taxable years.
- For a corporate taxpayer, the lesser of:
  - $250,000.
  - $1 million reduced by the amount of such nonrecognized gain in all preceding taxable years.

Investors ineligible for this postponement treatment include partnerships, S corporations, estates, and trusts.

*Find more information on this topic at our Web site: **http://wft-entities.swlearning.com**.*

### SALE OF A PRINCIPAL RESIDENCE—§ 121

Section 121 allows individual taxpayers to exclude gain from the sale of a *principal residence*. This provision applies to the first $250,000 of realized gain, or $500,000 on a joint return. For this purpose, the residence must have been owned and used by the taxpayer as the primary residence for at least two of the five years preceding the date of sale. In addition, the exclusion is not available for sales occurring within two years of its last use. This exclusion can be prorated, however, if a taxpayer failed to meet one or more of these time period requirements due to a change in his or her place of employment or health. Moreover, a surviving spouse counts the ownership and usage periods of the decedent spouse in meeting the two-year test. This provision applies only to gains; losses on residences, like those of other personal-use assets, are not recognized for tax purposes.

*Find more information on these topics at our Web site: **http://wft-entities.swlearning.com**.*

### TRANSFERS OF PROPERTY BETWEEN SPOUSES OR INCIDENT TO DIVORCE—§ 1041

Section 1041 provides for nontaxable exchange treatment on property transfers *between spouses during marriage*. The basis to the recipient spouse is a carryover basis.

Section 1041 also provides that transfers of property *between spouses or former spouses incident to divorce* are nontaxable transactions. Therefore, the basis to the recipient is a carryover basis. To be treated as incident to the divorce, the transfer must be related to the cessation of marriage or must occur within one year after the date on which the marriage ceases.

## Suggested Further Readings

Steven Dilley, "Tax Planning for the Sale of a Principal Residence (Part I)," *The Tax Adviser,* January 2004, pp. 30–34.

Steven Dilley, "Tax Planning for the Sale of a Principal Residence (Part II)," *The Tax Adviser,* February 2004, pp. 90–94.

Carolyn Hartwell, Russell H. Hereth, and John C. Talbott, "Unraveling a Stock's Basis Is Not Necessarily Basic," *Practical Tax Strategies,* June 2003, pp. 356–360.

"IRS Approves 1031 Exchange of Water Rights for Farmland," *Journal of Taxation,* June 2004, pp. 370–371.

## KEY TERMS

| | | |
|---|---|---|
| Adjusted basis, 6–4 | Holding period, 6–13 | Realized loss, 6–3 |
| Amount realized, 6–3 | Involuntary conversion, 6–28 | Recognized gain, 6–7 |
| Boot, 6–24 | Like-kind exchange, 6–21 | Recognized loss, 6–7 |
| Fair market value, 6–4 | Nontaxable exchange, 6–20 | Recovery of capital doctrine, 6–8 |
| Goodwill, 6–10 | Realized gain, 6–3 | Wash sale, 6–17 |

## PROBLEM MATERIALS

### Problems

1. If a taxpayer sells property for cash, the amount realized consists of the net proceeds from the sale. For each of the following, indicate the effect on the amount realized:
   a. The property is sold on credit.
   b. A mortgage on the property is assumed by the buyer.
   c. The buyer acquires the property subject to a mortgage of the seller.
   d. The seller pays real property taxes that are treated as imposed on the purchaser.
   e. Stock that has a basis to the purchaser of $6,000 and a fair market value of $10,000 is received by the seller as part of the consideration.

2. Black, Inc., owns a building (adjusted basis of $375,000 on January 1) that it rents to Lapwing & Longspur, which operates a restaurant in the building. The municipal health department closed the restaurant for two months this year because of health code violations. Under MACRS, the cost recovery deduction for this year would be $24,000. However, Black deducted cost recovery only for the 10 months the restaurant was open since it waived the rent income during the two-month period the restaurant was closed.
   a. What is the amount of the cost recovery deduction that Black should report on this year's income tax return?
   b. Calculate the adjusted basis of the building at the end of this year.

3. Nina owns a personal-use boat that has a fair market value of $12,500 and an adjusted basis of $17,000. Nina's AGI is $60,000. Calculate the realized and recognized loss if:
   a. Nina sells the boat for $12,500.
   b. Nina exchanges the boat for another boat worth $12,500.
   c. The boat is stolen and Nina receives insurance proceeds of $12,500.

4. Hubert's personal residence is condemned as part of an urban renewal project. His adjusted basis for the residence is $325,000. He receives condemnation proceeds of $300,000 and invests the proceeds in stock.
   a. Calculate Hubert's realized and recognized gain or loss.
   b. If the condemnation proceeds are $355,000, what are Hubert's realized and recognized gain or loss?
   c. What are Hubert's realized and recognized gain or loss in (a) if the house was rental property?

**Issue ID**   5. A warehouse owned by Marmot & Squirrel (a partnership) and used in its business (i.e., to store inventory) is being condemned by the city to provide a right of way for a highway. The warehouse has appreciated by $100,000 based on an estimate of fair market value. In the negotiations, the city is offering $40,000 less than what Marmot & Squirrel believes the property is worth. Alan, a real estate broker, has offered to purchase the property for $25,000 more than the city's offer. The partnership plans to invest the proceeds it will receive in an office building that it will lease to various tenants. Identify the relevant tax issues for Marmot & Squirrel.

6. Finch, Inc., purchases 100 shares of Bluebird Corporation stock on June 3, 2005, for $150,000. On August 25, 2005, Finch purchases an additional 50 shares of Bluebird stock for $60,000. According to market quotations, Bluebird stock is selling for $1,100 per share on December 31, 2005. Finch sells 60 shares of Bluebird stock on March 1, 2006, for $51,000.
   a. What is the adjusted basis of Finch's Bluebird stock on December 31, 2005?
   b. What is Finch's recognized gain or loss from the sale of Bluebird stock on March 1, 2006, assuming the shares sold are from the shares purchased on June 3, 2005?
   c. What is Finch's recognized gain or loss from the sale of Bluebird stock on March 1, 2006, assuming Finch cannot adequately identify the shares sold?

**Communications**

7. Rod Mitchell purchases Agnes's sole proprietorship for $975,000 on August 15, 2005. The assets of the business are as follows:

| Asset | Agnes's Adjusted Basis | FMV |
|---|---|---|
| Accounts receivable | $ 70,000 | $ 70,000 |
| Inventory | 90,000 | 100,000 |
| Equipment | 150,000 | 160,000 |
| Furniture and fixtures | 95,000 | 130,000 |
| Building | 190,000 | 250,000 |
| Land | 25,000 | 75,000 |

Rod and Agnes agree that $50,000 of the purchase price is for Agnes's five-year covenant not to compete.
   a. Calculate Agnes's realized and recognized gain.
   b. Determine Rod's basis for each of the assets.
   c. Write a letter to Rod informing him of the tax consequences of the purchase. His address is 300 Riverview Drive, Delaware, OH 43015.

8. Juanita has decided to dispose of the following assets that she received as gifts:
   a. In 1990, she received land worth $62,000. The donor's adjusted basis was $75,000. Juanita sells the land for $58,000 this year.
   b. In 1996, she received stock worth $50,000. The donor's adjusted basis was $65,000. Juanita sells the stock this year for $59,000.

What is the recognized gain or loss from each of the preceding transactions? Assume in each transaction that no gift tax was paid.

**Ethics**

9. Holly owns stock with an adjusted basis of $2,500 and fair market value of $9,500. Holly expects the stock to continue to appreciate. Alice, Holly's best friend, has recently been operated on for cancer. Alice's physicians have told her that her life expectancy is between six months and one and a half years. One day at lunch, the two friends were discussing their tax situations (both feel they pay too much), when Alice mentioned that she had read a newspaper article about a tax planning opportunity that might be suitable for Holly. Holly would make a gift of the appreciated stock to Alice. In her will, Alice would bequeath the stock back to Holly. Since Alice is confident that she will live longer than a year, the basis of the stock to Holly would be the fair market value on the date of Alice's death. Alice would "feel good" because she had helped Holly "beat the tax system." You are Holly's tax adviser. How will you respond to Alice's proposal? Would your response change if the stock were a painting that Alice could enjoy for her remaining days?

10. Beth receives a car from Sam as a gift. Sam paid $18,000 for the car. He had used it for business purposes and had deducted $8,000 for depreciation up to the time he gave the car to Beth. The fair market value of the car is $6,000.
   a. Assuming Beth uses the car for business purposes, what is her basis for depreciation?
   b. If the estimated useful life is two years (from the date of the gift), what is her depreciation deduction for each year? Use the straight-line method.

    c. If Beth sells the car for $900 one year after receiving it, what is her gain or loss?

    d. If Beth sells the car for $6,000 one year after receiving it, what is her gain or loss?

11. In 2005, Rhett receives a gift of property with a fair market value of $100,000 (adjusted basis to the donor of $32,000). Assume the donor paid gift tax of $20,000 on the transfer.

    a. What is Rhett's basis for gain and loss and for depreciation?

    b. If the gift occurred in 1975, what is Rhett's basis for gain and loss and for depreciation?

**Issue ID**

12. Simon, who is retired, owns Teal, Inc. stock that has declined in value since he purchased it. He has decided either to give the stock to his nephew, Fred, who is a high school teacher, or to sell the stock and give the proceeds to Fred. Because nearly all of his wealth is invested in tax-exempt bonds, Simon faces a 15% marginal tax rate. Fred will use the cash or the proceeds from his sale of the stock to make the down payment on the purchase of a house. Based on a recent conversation, Simon is aware that Fred is in the 25% marginal tax bracket. Identify the tax issues relevant to Simon in deciding whether to give the stock or the sale proceeds to Fred.

13. On September 18, 2005, Gerald received land and a building from his Uncle Frank as a gift. Uncle Frank's adjusted basis and the fair market value at the date of the gift were as follows:

| Asset | Adjusted Basis | FMV |
| --- | --- | --- |
| Land | $100,000 | $211,000 |
| Building | 80,000 | 100,000 |

Uncle Frank paid gift tax of $45,000.

    a. Determine Gerald's adjusted basis for the land and building.

    b. Assume instead that the fair market value of the land was $87,000 and that of the building was $65,000. Determine Gerald's adjusted basis for the land and building.

14. Catherine died in March 2005 leaving real estate (adjusted basis of $500,000) to her niece, Amanda. The fair market value of the real estate at the date of Catherine's death is $1,825,000. The executor of the estate does not distribute the real estate to Amanda until November 2005, when its fair market value is $1,813,000. The fair market value of the real estate six months after Catherine's death is $1,815,000.

    a. What are the possibilities as to Amanda's adjusted basis in the real estate?

    b. What purpose does the alternate valuation date serve?

    c. Assume instead that the fair market value six months after Catherine's death is $1,860,000. What is Amanda's basis in the real estate?

15. Dan bought a hotel for $2,720,000 in January 2002. In January 2005, he died and left the hotel to Ed. Dan had deducted $20,930 of cost recovery on the hotel before his death. The fair market value in January 2005 was $2,780,000. The fair market value six months later was $2,850,000.

    a. What is the basis of the property to Ed?

    b. What is the basis of the property to Ed if the fair market value six months later was $2,500,000 and the objective of the executor was to minimize the estate tax liability?

16. Sheila sells land to Elane, her sister, for the fair market value of $40,000. Six months later when the land is worth $42,000, Elane gives it to Jacob, her son. No gift taxes are paid. Shortly thereafter, Jacob sells the land for $43,000.

    a. Assuming Sheila's adjusted basis for the land is $25,000, what are Sheila's and Jacob's recognized gain or loss on their respective sales?

    b. Assuming Sheila's adjusted basis for the land is $50,000, what are Sheila's and Jacob's recognized gain or loss on their respective sales?

**Decision Making**

17. Justin owns 1,000 shares of Oriole Corporation common stock (adjusted basis of $9,800). On April 27, 2005, he sells 300 of these shares for $2,800. On May 5, 2005, Justin purchases 200 shares of Oriole Corporation common stock for $2,500.

    a. What is Justin's recognized gain or loss resulting from these transactions?
    b. What is Justin's basis for the stock acquired on May 5?
    c. Could Justin have obtained different tax consequences in (a) and (b) if he had sold the 300 shares on December 27, 2005, and purchased the 200 shares on January 5, 2006?

18. Jeffrey leaves a public accounting firm to enter private practice. He had bought a home two years earlier for $56,000 (ignore land). When starting his business, he converts one-fourth of the home into an office. The fair market value of the home on the date of the conversion (January 1, 2000) is $75,000, while the adjusted basis remains at $56,000. Jeffery lives and works in the home for six years and sells it at the end of the sixth year. He deducted $2,124 of cost recovery (using the statutory percentage method). How much gain or loss is recognized if Jeffrey sells the home for:
    a. $44,000?
    b. $70,000?

19. Surendra's personal residence originally cost $180,000 (ignore land). After living in the house for five years, he converts it to rental property. At the date of conversion, the fair market value of the house is $150,000. As to the rental property, calculate Surendra's basis for:
    a. Loss.
    b. Depreciation.
    c. Gain.

20. Heron Industries, Inc., owns undeveloped land with an adjusted basis of $212,000. Heron exchanges this land for other undeveloped land worth $290,000.
    a. What are Heron's realized and recognized gain or loss?
    b. What is Heron's basis in the undeveloped land it receives?

**Decision Making**

**Communications**

21. Tex Watson owns undeveloped land (basis of $350,000) held as an investment. On October 7, 2005, he exchanges the land with his 27-year-old daughter, Porchia, for other undeveloped land also to be held as an investment. The appraised value of Porchia's land is $500,000.
    a. On February 15, 2006, Tex sells the land to Baxter, a real estate broker, for $600,000. Calculate Tex's realized and recognized gain or loss from the exchange with Porchia and on the subsequent sale of the land to Baxter.
    b. Calculate Tex's realized and recognized gain or loss on the exchange with Porchia if Tex does not sell the land. Instead, on February 15, 2006, Porchia sells the land received from Tex. Calculate Tex's basis for the land on October 7, 2005, and on February 15, 2006.
    c. Write a letter to Tex advising him on how he could avoid any recognition of gain associated with the October 7, 2005 exchange. His address is The Corral, El Paso, TX 79968.

22. Starling Corporation owns a computer with an adjusted basis of $3,000. Starling exchanges the computer and cash of $5,000 for a laser printer worth $14,000.
    a. Calculate Starling's recognized gain or loss on the exchange.
    b. Calculate its basis for the printer.

23. Redfern Investments, Inc., owns land and a building with an adjusted basis of $125,000 and a fair market value of $275,000. Redfern exchanges the land and building for land with a fair market value of $175,000 that it will use as a parking lot. In addition, Redfern receives stock worth $100,000.
    a. What is the company's realized gain or loss?
    b. Its recognized gain or loss?
    c. The basis of the land and the stock received?
    d. How would the answers in (a), (b), and (c) change if the stock is worth $175,000 (not $100,000) and the land Redfern Investments receives has a fair market value of $100,000 (not $175,000)?

**Issue ID**

24. Tulip, Inc., would like to dispose of some land that it acquired four years ago because the land will not continue to appreciate. Its value has increased by $50,000 over the four-year period. The company also intends to sell stock that has declined in value by $50,000 during the six months since its purchase. Tulip has four offers to acquire the stock and land:

Buyer number 1:   Exchange land.

Buyer number 2:   Purchase land for cash.

Buyer number 3:   Exchange stock.

Buyer number 4:   Purchase stock for cash.

Identify the tax issues relevant to Tulip in disposing of this land and stock.

25. What is the basis of the new property in each of the following exchanges?
    a. Apartment building held for investment (adjusted basis, $145,000) for office building to be held for investment (fair market value, $225,000).
    b. Land and building used as a barber shop (adjusted basis, $190,000) for land and building used as a grocery store (fair market value, $350,000).
    c. Office building (adjusted basis, $45,000) for bulldozer (fair market value, $42,000), both held for business use.
    d. IBM common stock (adjusted basis, $20,000) for ExxonMobil common stock (fair market value, $28,000).
    e. Rental house (adjusted basis, $90,000) for mountain cabin to be held for personal use (fair market value, $225,000).

**Decision Making**

**Communications**

26. Hyacinth Realty Company owns land in Iowa that was originally purchased for $130,000. Hyacinth has received an all-cash offer in the amount of $400,000 from a well-known shopping center developer. An international real estate broker has now offered some land located outside Florence, Italy, that is worth $400,000 in exchange for the Iowa property. Please write the company a letter analyzing these options from a tax stand-point. Hyacinth's address is 2501 Longview Lane, Des Moines, IA 50311.

**Decision Making**

27. Redbud Company owns Machine A (adjusted basis of $12,000 and fair market value of $15,000), which it uses in its business. Redbud sells Machine A for $15,000 to Oak, Inc. (a dealer). Redbud then purchases Machine B for $15,000 from Cutting Edge Company (also a dealer). Machine B would normally qualify as like-kind property.
    a. What are Redbud's realized and recognized gain on the sale of Machine A?
    b. What is Redbud's basis for Machine B?
    c. What factors would motivate Redbud to sell Machine A and purchase Machine B rather than exchange one machine for the other?
    d. Assume that the adjusted basis of Machine A is $15,000 and the fair market value of both machines is $12,000. Respond to (a) through (c).

28. Cardinal Properties, Inc., exchanges real estate held for investment plus stock for real estate to be held for investment. The stock transferred has an adjusted basis of $30,000 and a fair market value of $20,000. The real estate transferred has an adjusted basis of $30,000 and a fair market value of $90,000. The real estate acquired has a fair market value of $110,000.
    a. What is Cardinal's realized gain or loss?
    b. Its recognized gain or loss?
    c. The basis of the newly acquired real estate?

**Decision Making**

29. Avocet Management Company exchanges a warehouse and the related land with Indigo, Inc., for an office building and the related land. Avocet's adjusted basis for the warehouse and land is $420,000. The fair market value of Indigo's office building and land is $410,000. Avocet's property has a $90,000 mortgage that Indigo assumes.
    a. Calculate Avocet's realized and recognized gain or loss.
    b. Calculate Avocet's adjusted basis for the office building and land received.
    c. As an alternative, Indigo has proposed that rather than assuming the mortgage, it will transfer cash of $90,000 to Avocet, which would use the cash to pay off the mortgage. Advise Avocet on whether this alternative would be beneficial to it from a tax perspective.

30. Determine the realized, recognized, and postponed gain or loss and the new basis for each of the following like-kind exchanges:

| | Adjusted Basis of Old Asset | Boot Given | Fair Market Value of New Asset | Boot Received |
|---|---|---|---|---|
| a. | $ 7,000 | $ –0– | $12,000 | $4,000 |
| b. | 14,000 | 2,000 | 15,000 | –0– |
| c. | 3,000 | 7,000 | 8,000 | 500 |
| d. | 22,000 | –0– | 32,000 | –0– |
| e. | 10,000 | –0– | 11,000 | 1,000 |
| f. | 10,000 | –0– | 8,000 | –0– |

31. Turquoise Realty Company owns an apartment house that has an adjusted basis of $950,000 but is subject to a mortgage of $240,000. Turquoise transfers the apartment house to Dove, Inc., and receives from Dove $150,000 in cash and an office building with a fair market value of $975,000 at the time of the exchange. Dove assumes the $240,000 mortgage on the apartment house.
    a. What is Turquoise's realized gain or loss?
    b. What is its recognized gain or loss?
    c. What is the basis of the newly acquired office building?

32. For each of the following involuntary conversions, indicate whether the property acquired qualifies as replacement property, the recognized gain, and the basis for the property acquired:
    a. A warehouse is destroyed by a tornado. The space in the warehouse was rented to various tenants. The adjusted basis was $470,000. The owner of the warehouse uses all of the insurance proceeds of $700,000 to build a shopping mall in a neighboring community where no property has been damaged by tornadoes. The shopping mall is rented to various tenants.
    b. A warehouse is destroyed by fire. The adjusted basis is $300,000. Because of economic conditions in the area, the owner decides not to rebuild the warehouse. Instead, it uses all of the insurance proceeds of $400,000 to build a warehouse in another state.
    c. Swallow Fashions, Inc., owns a building that is destroyed by a hurricane. The adjusted basis is $250,000. Because of an economic downturn in the area caused by the closing of a military base, Swallow decides to rent space for its retail outlet rather than to replace the building. It uses all of the insurance proceeds of $300,000 to buy a four-unit apartment building in another city. A realtor in that city will handle the rental of the apartments.
    d. Susan and Rick's personal residence is destroyed by a tornado. The adjusted basis was $170,000. Since they would like to travel, they decide not to acquire a replacement residence. Instead, they invest all of the insurance proceeds of $200,000 in a duplex, which they rent to tenants.

**Ethics**

33. The City of Richmond is going to condemn some buildings to build a park. Steve's principal residence is among those to be condemned. His adjusted basis for the house and land is $120,000. The appraised value of the house and land is $104,000. Steve is unaware of the future condemnation proceedings, but would like his family to move to a better neighborhood. Therefore, when Ross, a realtor, mentions that he may have a corporate client who would like to purchase the property for $130,000, Steve is ecstatic and indicates a willingness to sell.

    Ross is having some "second thoughts" about his conversation with Steve. The potential corporate purchaser is a company owned by Ross and his wife. Ross is aware of the future condemnation proceedings. He considers himself a skilled negotiator and thinks he can negotiate a $260,000 price for the house. Ross is considering telling Steve that the corporate client has changed its mind. Ross would then indicate that he has learned the city will be condemning several buildings in order to create a park, but has not yet established the prices it will pay for the condemned property. He would also tell Steve that because he believes he can get more from the city than Steve would obtain, he is willing to gamble and purchase the property now from Steve for $130,000.

Ross will point out several benefits available to Steve. These include (1) not having to deal with the city, (2) receiving an amount that exceeds both the appraised value and the original purchase cost of the home, and (3) receiving the money now. While admitting that he could reap a substantial profit, Ross would emphasize that he would also be taking on substantial risks. In addition, Ross would explain that when he sells the property to the city, he will defer the taxes by reinvesting the sales proceeds (due to involuntary conversion).

Should Ross make a new proposal to Steve based on his "second thoughts"? How do you think Steve will respond?

34. Lark Corporation's office building is destroyed by a hurricane in September. The adjusted basis is $210,000. Lark receives insurance proceeds of $390,000 in October.
   a. Calculate Lark's realized gain or loss, recognized gain or loss, and basis for the replacement property if it acquires an office building for $390,000 in October.
   b. Calculate Lark's realized gain or loss, recognized gain or loss, and basis for the replacement property if it acquires a warehouse for $350,000 in October.
   c. Calculate Lark's realized gain or loss and recognized gain or loss if it does not acquire replacement property.

**Decision Making**

35. Magenta, Inc.'s warehouse, which has an adjusted basis of $300,000 and a fair market value of $420,000, is condemned by an agency of the Federal government to make way for a highway interchange. The initial condemnation offer is $400,000. After substantial negotiations, the agency agrees to transfer to Magenta a surplus warehouse that it believes is worth $420,000.
   a. What are the recognized gain or loss and the basis of the replacement warehouse if Magenta's objective is to recognize as much gain as possible?
   b. Advise Magenta regarding what it needs to do by what date in order to achieve its objective.

36. What are the *maximum* postponed gain or loss and the basis for the replacement property for the following involuntary conversions?

|     | Property | Type of Conversion | Amount Realized | Adjusted Basis | Amount Reinvested |
|-----|----------|--------------------|-----------------|----------------|-------------------|
| a. | Drugstore (business) | Condemned | $160,000 | $120,000 | $100,000 |
| b. | Apartments (investment) | Casualty | 100,000 | 120,000 | 200,000 |
| c. | Grocery store (business) | Casualty | 400,000 | 300,000 | 350,000 |
| d. | Residence (personal) | Casualty | 16,000 | 18,000 | 17,000 |
| e. | Vacant lot (investment) | Condemned | 240,000 | 160,000 | 240,000 |
| f. | Residence (personal) | Casualty | 20,000 | 18,000 | 19,000 |
| g. | Residence (personal) | Condemned | 18,000 | 20,000 | 26,000 |
| h. | Apartments (investment) | Condemned | 150,000 | 100,000 | 200,000 |

**EXTENDER**

37. Milton, who is single, listed his personal residence with a realtor on March 3, 2005, at a price of $250,000. He rejected several offers in the $200,000 range during the summer. Finally, on August 16, 2005, he and the purchaser signed a contract to sell for $245,000. The sale (i.e., closing) took place on September 7, 2005. The closing statement showed the following disbursements:

| | |
|---|---|
| Realtor's commission | $ 14,000 |
| Appraisal fee | 500 |
| Exterminator's certificate | 300 |
| Recording fees | 400 |
| Mortgage to First Bank | 180,000 |
| Cash to seller | 49,800 |

Milton's adjusted basis for the house is $150,000. He owned and occupied the house for eight years. On October 1, 2005, Milton purchases another residence for $210,000.

a. Calculate Milton's recognized gain on the sale.
b. What is Milton's adjusted basis for the new residence?
c. Assume instead that the selling price is $735,000. What is Milton's recognized gain? His adjusted basis for the new residence?

**EXTENDER**

**Decision Making**

38. Roby and Sid have been married for 12 years. Roby sells Peach, Inc. stock that she has owned for four years to Sid for its fair market value of $120,000. Her adjusted basis is $150,000.
a. Calculate Roby's recognized gain or recognized loss.
b. Calculate Sid's adjusted basis for the stock.
c. How would the tax consequences in (a) and (b) differ if Roby had made a gift of the stock to Sid? Which form of the transaction would you recommend?

**BRIDGE DISCIPLINE**

1. In April of the current year, Blue Corporation purchased an asset to be used in its manufacturing operations for $100,000. Blue's management expects the asset to ratably provide valuable services in the production process for eight years and have a salvage value of $12,000. The asset is a five-year asset for tax purposes. Blue has adopted the half-year convention for book purposes in the year of acquisition and disposition; Blue uses MACRS for tax purposes.
a. Compute the depreciation expense in the year of acquisition for book and tax purposes.
b. Identify the book-tax difference related to the depreciation expense in the year of acquisition.

2. Refer to the facts in the preceding problem. Assume Blue Corporation disposes of the manufacturing asset at the beginning of year seven for $40,000. Compute the amount of gain or loss recognized for book and tax purposes. What is the book-tax difference in the year of disposition?

3. Identify whether the taxpayer's economic position has changed in the following exchanges such that they are subject to current taxation. That is, identify whether the following qualify as like-kind exchanges under § 1031.
a. Improved for unimproved real estate.
b. Vending machine (used in business) for inventory.
c. Rental house for personal residence.
d. Business equipment for securities.
e. Warehouse for office building (both used for business).
f. Truck for computer (both used in business).
g. Rental house for land (both held for investment).
h. Ten shares of stock in Blue Corporation for 10 shares of stock in Red Corporation.
i. Office furniture for office equipment (both used in business).
j. Unimproved land in Jackson, Mississippi, for unimproved land in Toledo, Spain.

## Research Problems

**THOMSON**

**RIA**

*Note: Solutions to Research Problems can be prepared by using the **RIA Checkpoint® Student Edition** online research product, which is available to accompany this text. It is also possible to prepare solutions to the Research Problems by using tax research materials found in a standard tax library.*

**Research Problem 1.** Abner gives stock worth $400,000 to Hattie. Abner's adjusted basis in the stock is $95,000, and the gift taxes generated as a result of the transfer are $122,400. As a condition for receiving the stock, Hattie agrees to pay the gift tax. The stock is transferred to Hattie on February 5, 2005.
a. What are the income tax consequences to Abner?
b. What are the income tax consequences to Abner if the gift was made on February 5, 1981?

**Research Problem 2.**   Asa operated his business in a building on Mason Drive. Due to changing residential housing patterns in the city, he decided to move the business to a new location on Leigh Lane. His adjusted basis for the Mason Drive property is $120,000, and the fair market value is $500,000. He purchased the Leigh Lane property for $500,000 on September 1, 2005. Asa quitclaimed title to the Leigh Lane property to Ivory Enterprises on September 1, 2005, in exchange for a nonrecourse and non-interest-bearing single payment note for $500,000 (to be paid at the second closing). Ivory was to have a building constructed on the Leigh Lane property in accordance with specifications provided by Asa. The construction of the building was financed by a $700,000 note that was guaranteed by Asa and was nonrecourse to Ivory.

Another agreement provided that Asa would convey the Mason Drive property to Ivory on completion of the building in exchange for the Leigh Lane property and the new building. At that time, Asa would assume the $700,000 note.

On December 1, the Leigh Lane property was conveyed to Asa, the Mason Drive property was conveyed to Ivory, and Ivory paid the $500,000 note to Asa (the second closing). Asa assumed the $700,000 note associated with the construction and reported his recognized gain as follows:

|  | **Exchange of Mason Drive** | **Sale of Leigh Lane** |
|---|---|---|
| Amount realized | $ 500,000 | $ 1,210,000 |
| Basis | (120,000) | (1,200,000) |
| Realized gain | $ 380,000 | $ 10,000 |
| Recognized gain | $ –0–* | $ 10,000 |

* § 1031 like-kind exchange.

An IRS agent treated the transactions as the sale of the Mason Drive property and a § 1031 exchange of the Leigh Lane property, producing a recognized gain of $380,000 rather than $10,000.

Evaluate the position of the IRS and of Asa.

**Research Problem 3.**   Brown Construction, Inc., is in the road construction business. Brown exchanges a grader used in its business and $45,000 in cash for a scraper to be used in its business. The adjusted basis of the grader is $50,000, and the fair market value of the scraper is $102,000. What are the tax consequences to Brown of the exchange?

**Internet Activity**

*Use the tax resources of the Internet to address the following questions. Do not restrict your search to the World Wide Web, but include a review of newsgroups and general reference materials, practitioner sites and resources, primary sources of the tax law, chat rooms and discussion groups, and other opportunities.*

**Research Problem 4.**   A number of public policy think tanks, taxpayer unions, and other private interest groups have proposed changes to the tax rules that apply to like-kind exchanges of realty. Summarize several of these proposals, including your assessment of the motivations underlying the suggested changes.

**Research Problem 5.**   When taxpayers sell some of their mutual fund shares, they may compute their basis in the shares sold by utilizing the specific identification method. Go to the site of an investment adviser or mutual fund to find instructions on how to apply the specific identification method. What other options are described in the information you find? Illustrate each of the alternatives.

# Property Transactions: Capital Gains and Losses, Section 1231, and Recapture Provisions

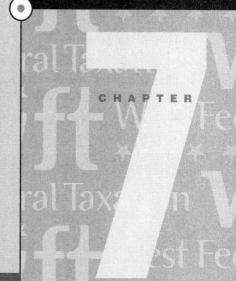

CHAPTER **7**

http://wft.swlearning.com

## OUTLINE

## TAX TALK

*Governments likely to confiscate wealth are unlikely to find much wealth to confiscate in the long run.*

—*Thomas Sowell*

# General Considerations

## RATIONALE FOR SEPARATE REPORTING OF CAPITAL GAINS AND LOSSES

Since the earliest days of the Federal income tax, **capital assets** have received special treatment upon their disposition. Gains from these assets have historically received *preferential treatment* in the form of either partial exclusion of gain, lower

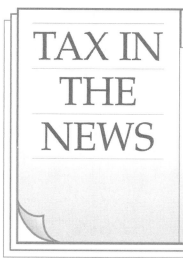

## SWITCHING FUNDS CREATES A LOSS

Many individual taxpayers own shares in mutual funds, which invest in a wide variety of stocks and bonds. These mutual fund shares are a capital asset to the individual investor. Many mutual funds that invest in stocks have suffered severe losses since 2000; consequently, the lower value of their shares may lead investors to sell out of the fund.

A taxpayer can usually switch between mutual funds in the same "family" of funds without any charge. For instance, a taxpayer may switch out of a stock fund and into a bond fund that is, hopefully, a "safer" investment. The switch is a sale of the shares in the stock fund and a purchase of the shares in the bond fund. The sale of the stock fund shares is taxable and, in this example, results in a capital loss. The loss may be long term or short term depending upon how long the taxpayer held the shares of the stock fund.

rates, or a maximum tax rate. Losses from capital assets, however, have historically received less desirable treatment than losses from other assets. Further, because a taxpayer has complete control over the timing of dispositions, the Code imposes limitations on when capital losses can be deducted to prevent taxpayers from manipulating their tax liability excessively.

During World War II, capital asset treatment was extended to other assets. These assets are now called "§ 1231 assets" after the Code Section that prescribes their special treatment. Several years after World War II ended, Congress believed that this special treatment was no longer entirely warranted. Instead of repealing § 1231, however, Congress left that section in place but eroded many—but not all—of its benefits through *recapture provisions* in § 1245 and § 1250. Together, these Code Sections constitute one of the most complicated areas of tax law affecting both individual taxpayers and business entities.

As already intimated, one concern is that taxpayers can time the realization of gains and losses by choosing when or even whether to sell the asset in question. If Lark Enterprises, Inc., owns stock with a basis of $20 per share and a current value of $80 per share, it does not pay tax on the $60 gain until it chooses to dispose of this stock in a taxable transaction. And for the most part, Lark has complete control over that decision. When it does dispose of the stock, however, its $60 gain is taxable in full, even though this gain may have accrued over many years. To mitigate the impact of this *bunching* of income in a single year and to offset the effect of inflation over the period of Lark's ownership of the stock, preferential treatment is prescribed for this **capital gain.**

The nature of this preferential treatment is discussed later in this chapter, but the essential point for now is that preferential treatment is confined to the excess of net long-term capital gains over net short-term **capital losses.** This cumbersome description requires taxpayers to separate their capital asset transactions from their transactions involving noncapital assets. It further requires taxpayers to separate their long-term (i.e., more than one year) transactions from their short-term (i.e., one year or less) transactions. Moreover, certain types of capital assets (principally real estate and "collectibles") receive specific treatment apart from the rates generally applicable to capital assets.

## GENERAL SCHEME OF TAXATION

Recognized gains and losses must be properly classified. Proper classification depends upon three characteristics.

- The tax status of the property, including the specific type of asset.
- The manner of the property's disposition.
- The holding period of the property.

The three possible tax statuses are capital asset, § 1231 asset, and ordinary asset. Property disposition may be by sale, exchange, casualty, theft, or condemnation. The two relevant holding periods are one year or less (short term) and more than one year (long term).

**LO.1**

Distinguish capital assets from ordinary assets.

# Capital Assets

## DEFINITION OF A CAPITAL ASSET

*Investments* comprise the most typical category of capital assets and include corporate stocks and bonds, mutual funds, partnership interests, government securities, and vacant land. These assets can be held by any type of taxpayer—individuals, partnerships, limited liability companies, and corporations, whether closely held or publicly held. In addition, individuals own certain capital assets that are part of their daily life, such as residences, automobiles, furniture, and artwork. The classification of these *personal-use* assets as capital assets is relevant only when their disposition produces a recognized gain. Losses from the disposition of personal-use assets are not recognized for tax purposes, as explained in the preceding chapter.

Capital assets are not directly defined in the Code. Instead, § 1221(a) defines what is *not* a capital asset. A capital asset is property held by the taxpayer that is *not* any of the following.

- Inventory or property held primarily for sale to customers in the ordinary course of a business. The Supreme Court, in *Malat v. Riddell*,[1] defined *primarily* as meaning *of first importance* or *principally*.
- Accounts and notes receivable acquired from the sale of inventory or acquired for services rendered in the ordinary course of business.
- Depreciable property or real estate used in a business.
- Certain copyrights; literary, musical, or artistic compositions; or letters, memoranda, or similar property held by (1) a taxpayer whose efforts created the property; (2) in the case of a letter, memorandum, or similar property, a taxpayer for whom it was produced; or (3) a taxpayer who received the property as a lifetime gift from someone described in (1) or (2).
- U.S. government publications that are (1) received by a taxpayer from the U.S. government other than by purchase at the price at which they are offered for sale to the public or (2) held by a taxpayer who received the publication as a lifetime gift from someone described in (1).
- Supplies of a type regularly used or consumed in the ordinary course of a business.

**Inventory.**   What constitutes inventory is determined by reference to the taxpayer's business.

---

[1]66–1 USTC ¶9317, 17 AFTR2d 604, 86 S.Ct. 1030 (USSC, 1966).

**EXAMPLE 1**

Green Company buys and sells used cars. Its cars are inventory. Its gains from the sale of the cars are ordinary income. ■

**EXAMPLE 2**

Soong sells her personal-use automobile at a $500 gain. The automobile is a personal-use asset and, therefore, a capital asset. The gain is a capital gain. ■

No asset is inherently capital or ordinary. If Soong in Example 2 sells her capital asset automobile to Green Company in Example 1, that very same automobile loses its capital asset status, because it is inventory to Green Company. Similar transformations can occur if, for example, an art dealer sells a painting (inventory; *not* a capital asset) to a private collector (now a capital asset). Whether an asset is capital or ordinary, therefore, depends entirely on the relationship of *that asset* to the taxpayer who sold it. This classification dilemma is but one feature of capital asset treatment that makes this area so confused and perennially complicated.

**Accounts and Notes Receivable.** Collection of an accrual basis account receivable usually does not result in a gain or loss because the amount collected equals the receivable's basis. The *sale* of an account or note receivable may generate a gain or loss, however, because it will probably be sold for more or less than its basis. That gain or loss will be ordinary because the receivable is not a capital asset. A cash basis account receivable has no basis, so sale of such a receivable generates a gain, and that gain is ordinary income. Collection of a cash basis receivable also generates ordinary income.

**EXAMPLE 3**

Oriole Company, an accrual basis taxpayer, has accounts receivable of $100,000. Revenue of $100,000 was recorded and a $100,000 basis was established when the receivable was created. Because Oriole needs working capital, it sells the receivables for $83,000 to a financial institution. Accordingly, it has a $17,000 ordinary loss. If Oriole is a cash basis taxpayer, it has $83,000 of ordinary income because it would not have recorded any revenue earlier and the receivable would have no tax basis. ■

**Business Fixed Assets.** Depreciable personal property and real estate (both depreciable and nondepreciable) used by a business are not capital assets. Thus, *business fixed assets* are not capital assets. Business fixed assets can sometimes be treated as capital assets pursuant to § 1231, however, as discussed later in this chapter.

**Copyrights and Creative Works.** Generally, the person whose efforts led to the copyright or creative work has an ordinary asset, not a capital asset. This rule makes the creator comparable to a taxpayer whose customary activity (salary, business profits) is taxed as ordinary income. *Creative works* include the works of authors, composers, and artists. Also, the person for whom a letter, memorandum, or other similar property was created has an ordinary asset. Finally, a person receiving a copyright, creative work, letter, memorandum, or similar property by lifetime gift from the creator or the person for whom the work was created also has an ordinary asset.

**EXAMPLE 4**

Wanda is a part-time music composer. A music publisher purchases one of her songs for $5,000. Wanda has a $5,000 ordinary gain from the sale of an ordinary asset. ■

**EXAMPLE 5**

Ed received a letter from the President of the United States in 1994. In the current year, Ed sells the letter to a collector for $300. Ed has a $300 ordinary gain from the sale of an ordinary asset (because the letter was created for Ed). ■

### AN ARTIST'S DILEMMA

Artist Peter Max was the creator of valuable paintings that had a zero tax basis. If he sold the paintings, the entire proceeds from the sale would be ordinary income. Instead, Max *exchanged* the paintings for valuable real estate in the United States and in several other countries. The IRS contended that the exchange of the paintings was taxable and charged Max with failing to report more than $1 million of ordinary income.

**EXAMPLE 6**

Isabella gives a song she composed to her son. Her son sells the song to a music publisher for $5,000. Her son has a $5,000 ordinary gain from the sale of an ordinary asset. If he inherits the song from Isabella, his basis for the song is its fair market value at Isabella's death. The song is a capital asset because the son's basis is not related to Isabella's basis for the song (i.e., the song was not a *lifetime* gift). ■

**U.S. Government Publications.**   U.S. government publications received from the U.S. government (or its agencies) for a reduced price are not capital assets. This prevents a taxpayer from later donating the publications to charity and claiming a charitable contribution equal to the fair market value of the publications. A charitable contribution of a capital asset generally yields a deduction equal to the asset's fair market value. If such property is received by gift from the original purchaser, the property is not a capital asset to the donee. (For a more comprehensive explanation of charitable contributions of property, refer to Chapter 4.)

### STATUTORY EXPANSIONS

Because of the uncertainty often associated with capital asset status, Congress has occasionally enacted Code Sections to clarify the definition in particular circumstances. These statutory expansions of the capital asset definition are discussed in this section.

*Find more information on this topic at our Web site: **http://wft-entities.swlearning.com.***

**Dealers in Securities.**   As a general rule, securities (stocks, bonds, and other financial instruments) held by a dealer are considered to be inventory and are, therefore, not subject to capital gain or loss treatment. A *dealer in securities* is a merchant (e.g., a brokerage firm) that regularly engages in the purchase and resale of securities to customers. However, under the following circumstances, a dealer will have capital gain or capital loss. If a dealer clearly identifies certain securities as held for investment purposes by the close of business on the acquisition date, gain from the securities' sale will be capital gain. The gain will be ordinary if the dealer ceases to hold the securities for investment prior to the sale. Losses are capital losses if at any time the securities have been clearly identified by the dealer as held for investment.[2]

*Find more information on this topic at our Web site: **http://wft-entities.swlearning.com.***

---

[2]§§ 1236(a) and (b) and Reg. § 1.1236–1(a).

**Real Property Subdivided for Sale.** Substantial real property development activities may result in the owner being considered a dealer for tax purposes. If so, income from the sale of real estate property lots will be treated as the sale of inventory and therefore will be taxed as ordinary income. However, § 1237 allows real estate investors to claim capital gain treatment if they engage *only* in *limited* development activities. To be eligible for § 1237 treatment, the following requirements must be met.

- The taxpayer is not a corporation.
- The taxpayer is not a real estate dealer.
- No substantial improvements have been made to the lots sold. *Substantial* generally means more than a 10 percent increase in the value of a lot. Shopping centers and other commercial or residential buildings are considered substantial, while filling, draining, leveling, and clearing operations are not.
- The taxpayer has held the lots sold for at least 5 years, except for inherited property. The substantial improvements test is less stringent if the property is held at least 10 years.

If the preceding requirements are met, all gain is capital gain until the taxable year in which the *sixth* lot is sold. Sales of contiguous lots to a single buyer in the same transaction count as the sale of one lot. Beginning with the taxable year in which the *sixth* lot is sold, 5 percent of the revenue from lot sales is potential ordinary income. That potential ordinary income is offset by any selling expenses from the lot sales. Practically, sales commissions often are at least 5 percent of the sales price, so usually none of the gain is treated as ordinary income.

Section 1237 does not apply to losses. A loss from the sale of subdivided real property is ordinary loss unless the property qualifies as a capital asset under § 1221. The following example illustrates the application of § 1237.

**EXAMPLE 7**

Ahmed owns a large tract of land and subdivides it for sale. Assume Ahmed meets all the requirements of § 1237 and during the tax year sells the first 10 lots to 10 different buyers for $10,000 each. Ahmed's basis in each lot sold is $3,000, and he incurs total selling expenses of $4,000 on the sales. Ahmed's gain is computed as follows.

| | | |
|---|---:|---:|
| Selling price (10 × $10,000) | $100,000 | |
| Less: Selling expenses (10 × $400) | (4,000) | |
| Amount realized | | $ 96,000 |
| Basis (10 × $3,000) | | (30,000) |
| Realized and recognized gain | | $ 66,000 |
| Classification of recognized gain: | | |
| Ordinary income | | |
| Five percent of selling price (5% × $100,000) | $ 5,000 | |
| Less: Selling expenses | (4,000) | |
| Ordinary gain | | 1,000 |
| Capital gain | | $ 65,000 |

**LO.2**

Understand the relevance of a sale or exchange to classification as a capital gain or loss.

# Sale or Exchange

Recognition of capital gain or loss usually requires a **sale or exchange** of a capital asset. The Code uses the term *sale or exchange*, but does not define it. Generally, a property sale involves the receipt of money by the seller and/or the assumption by the purchaser of the seller's liabilities. An exchange involves the transfer of property for other property. Thus, an involuntary conversion (casualty, theft, or condemnation) is not a sale or exchange. In several situations, the determination of whether or when a sale or exchange has taken place has been clarified by the enactment of Code Sections that specifically provide for sale or exchange treatment. These situations are discussed below.

Recognized gains or losses from the cancellation, lapse, expiration, or any other termination of a right or obligation with respect to personal property (other than stock) that is or would be a capital asset in the hands of the taxpayer are capital gains or losses.[3] See the discussion under Options later in the chapter for more details.

## WORTHLESS SECURITIES AND § 1244 STOCK

Occasionally, securities such as stock and bonds may become worthless due to the insolvency of their issuer. If the security is a capital asset, the loss is deemed to have occurred as the result of a sale or exchange on the *last day* of the tax year.[4] This last-day rule may have the effect of converting a short-term capital loss into a long-term capital loss. See Capital Losses later in this chapter.

Section 1244 allows an *ordinary* deduction on disposition of stock at a loss. The stock must be that of a small business company, and the ordinary deduction is limited to $50,000 ($100,000 for married individuals filing jointly) per year.

## RETIREMENT OF CORPORATE OBLIGATIONS

A debt obligation (e.g., a bond or note payable) may have a tax basis different from its redemption value because it may have been acquired at a premium or discount. Consequently, the collection of the redemption value may result in a loss or a gain. Generally, the collection of a debt obligation is *treated* as a sale or exchange.[5] Therefore, any loss or gain is capital because a sale or exchange has taken place.

DIGGING DEEPER ③  *Find more information on this topic at our Web site:* **http://wft-entities.swlearning.com.**

**EXAMPLE 8**   Osprey, Inc., purchases $1,000 of General Motors Corporation bonds for $1,020 in the open market. If the bonds are held to maturity, the $20 difference between Osprey's collection of the $1,000 redemption value and its cost of $1,020 is treated as capital loss. ■

## OPTIONS

Frequently, a potential buyer of property wants to defer a final purchase decision, but wants to control the sale and/or the sale price in the meantime. **Options** are used to achieve such control. The potential purchaser (grantee) pays the property owner (grantor) for an option on the property. The grantee then becomes the option holder. An option usually sets the price at which a grantee can buy the property and expires after a specified period of time.

**Sale of an Option.**   In addition to exercising an option or letting it expire, a grantee can often arrange for its sale or exchange. Such a sale or exchange generally results in capital gain or loss if the option property is (or would be) a capital asset to the grantee.[6]

---

[3]§ 1234A.
[4]§ 165(g)(1).

[5]§ 1271.
[6]§ 1234(a) and Reg. § 1.1234–1(a)(1).

Robin & Associates wants to buy some vacant land for investment purposes, but cannot afford the full purchase price. Instead, the firm convinces the landowner (grantor) to sell it the right to purchase the land for $100,000 anytime in the next two years. Robin & Associates (grantee) pays $3,000 for this option to buy the land. The option is a capital asset to Robin because if the firm actually purchased the land (the option property), the land would be a capital asset. Three months after purchasing the option, Robin sells it for $7,000. The firm has a $4,000 ($7,000 – $3,000) capital gain on this sale. ■

**Failure to Exercise Options.** If an option holder (grantee) fails to exercise the option, the lapse of the option is considered a sale or exchange on the option expiration date. Thus, the resulting loss is a capital loss if the property subject to the option is (or would be) a capital asset in the hands of the grantee.

The grantor of an option on *stocks, securities, commodities, or commodity futures* receives short-term capital gain treatment upon the expiration of the option.[7] For example, an individual investor who owns stock (a capital asset) may sell a call option, entitling the buyer of the option to acquire the stock at a specified price higher than the stock's value at the date the option is granted. The writer of the call (the grantor) receives a premium for writing the option. If the price of the stock does not increase during the option period, the option will expire unexercised. Upon the expiration of the option, the grantor must recognize a short-term capital gain equal to the premium received. These provisions do not apply to options held for sale to customers (the inventory of a securities dealer).

Options on property *other than* stocks, securities, commodities, or commodity futures result in ordinary income to the grantor when the option expires. For instance, the landowner in the preceding example would have ordinary income of $3,000 if Robin (the grantee) had allowed the option to expire.

**Exercise of Options by Grantee.** If an option is exercised, the amount paid for the option is added to the optioned property's selling price. This increases the gain (or reduces the loss) to the grantor resulting from the sale of the property. The grantor's gain or loss is capital or ordinary depending on the tax status of the property. The grantee adds the cost of the option to the basis of the property purchased.

Several years ago, Indigo, Inc., purchased 100 shares of Eagle Company stock for $5,000. On April 1 of this year, Indigo writes a call option on the stock, giving the grantee the right to buy the stock for $6,000 during the following six-month period. Indigo (the grantor) receives a call premium of $500 for writing the call.

- If the call is exercised by the grantee on August 1, Indigo has $1,500 ($6,000 + $500 – $5,000) of long-term capital gain from the sale of the stock. The grantee has a $6,500 ($500 option premium + $6,000 purchase price) basis for the stock.
- Assume that the option expired unexercised. Indigo has a $500 short-term capital gain equal to the call premium received for writing the option. This gain is not recognized until the option expires. The grantee has a loss from expiration of the option. The nature of that loss will depend upon whether the option was a capital asset or an ordinary asset in the hands of the grantee. ■

## PATENTS

Transfer of a **patent** is treated as the sale or exchange of a long-term capital asset when *all substantial rights* to the patent (or an undivided interest that includes all

---

[7]§ 1234(b)(1).

## Concept Summary 7-1

### Options

|  | Effect on | |
| Event | Grantor | Grantee |
|---|---|---|
| Option is granted. | Receives value and has a contract obligation (a liability). | Pays value and has a contract right (an asset). |
| Option expires. | Has a short-term capital gain if the option property is stocks, securities, commodities, or commodity futures. Otherwise, gain is ordinary income. | Has a loss (capital loss if option property would have been a capital asset for the grantee). Otherwise, loss is ordinary. |
| Option is exercised. | Amount received for option increases proceeds from sale of the option property. | Amount paid for option becomes part of the basis of the option property purchased. |
| Option is sold or exchanged by grantee. | Result depends upon whether option later expires or is exercised (see above). | Could have gain or loss (capital gain or loss if option property would have been a capital asset for the grantee). |

such rights) are transferred by a *holder*.[8] The transferor/holder may receive payment in virtually any form. Lump-sum or periodic payments are most common. The amount of the payments may also be contingent on the transferee/purchaser's productivity, use, or disposition of the patent. If the transfer meets these requirements, any gain or loss is *automatically a long-term* capital gain or loss. Whether the asset was a capital asset for the transferor, whether a sale or exchange occurred, and how long the transferor held the patent are all irrelevant.

**EXAMPLE 11**

Mei-Yen, a druggist, invents a pill-counting machine, which she patents. In consideration of a lump-sum payment of $200,000 plus $10 per machine sold, Mei-Yen assigns the patent to Drug Products, Inc. Assuming Mei-Yen has transferred all substantial rights, she automatically has a long-term capital gain from both the lump-sum payment and the $10 per machine royalty to the extent these proceeds exceed her basis for the patent. ■

This special long-term capital gain or loss treatment for patents is intended to encourage technological development and scientific progress. In contrast, books, songs, and artists' works may be copyrighted, but copyrights and the assets they represent are not capital assets. Thus, the disposition of these assets by their creators usually results in ordinary gain or loss.

**Substantial Rights.**　To receive favorable capital gain treatment, all *substantial rights* to the patent (or an undivided interest in it) must be transferred. All substantial rights to a patent means all rights that are valuable at the time the patent rights (or an undivided interest in the patent) are transferred. All substantial rights have not been transferred when the transfer is limited geographically within the issuing country or when the transfer is for a period less than the remaining legal life of the patent. The circumstances of the entire transaction, rather than merely the language used in the transfer instrument, are to be considered in deciding whether all substantial rights have been transferred.[9]

---

[8]§ 1235.

[9]Reg. § 1.1235–2(b)(1).

**EXAMPLE 12**

Assume Mei-Yen, the druggist in the preceding example, only licensed Drug Products, Inc., to manufacture and sell the invention in Michigan. She retained the right to license the machine elsewhere in the United States. Mei-Yen has retained a substantial right and is not eligible for automatic long-term capital gain treatment. ■

**Holder Defined.**   The *holder* of a patent must be an *individual* and is usually the invention's creator. A holder may also be an individual who purchases the patent rights from the creator before the patented invention has been reduced to practice. However, the creator's employer and certain parties related to the creator do not qualify as holders. Thus, in the common situation where an employer has all rights to an employee's inventions, the employer is not eligible for long-term capital gain treatment. More than likely, the employer will have an ordinary asset because the patent was developed as part of its business.

## FRANCHISES, TRADEMARKS, AND TRADE NAMES

A mode of operation, a widely recognized brand name (trade name), and a widely known business symbol (trademark) are all valuable assets. These assets may be licensed (commonly known as *franchising*) by their owner for use by other businesses. Many fast-food restaurants (such as McDonald's and Taco Bell) are franchises. The franchisee usually pays the owner (franchisor) an initial fee plus a contingent fee. The contingent fee is often based upon the franchisee's sales volume.

For Federal income tax purposes, a **franchise** is an agreement that gives the franchisee the right to distribute, sell, or provide goods, services, or facilities within a specified area.[10] A franchise transfer includes the grant of a franchise, a transfer by one franchisee to another person, or the renewal of a franchise.

Section 1253 provides that a transfer of a franchise, trademark, or trade name is *not* a sale or exchange of a capital asset when the transferor retains any significant power, right, or continuing interest in the property transferred.

*Find more information on this topic at our Web site:* **http://wft-entities.swlearning.com**.

**Significant Power, Right, or Continuing Interest.**   *Significant powers, rights, or continuing interests* include control over assignment of the franchise, trademark, or trade name, as well as the quality of the transferee's products or services. The following rights also are included.

- Right to require the transferee to sell or advertise *only* the transferor's products or services.
- Right to require the transferee to purchase substantially all supplies and equipment from the transferor.
- Right to receive substantial contingent payments.
- Right to terminate the franchise, trademark, or trade name at will.

In the unusual case where no significant power, right, or continuing interest is retained by the transferor, a sale or exchange may occur, and capital gain or loss treatment may be available. For capital gain or loss treatment to be available, the asset transferred must still qualify as a capital asset.

**EXAMPLE 13**

Orange, Inc., a franchisee, sells the franchise to a third party. Payments to Orange are not contingent, and all significant powers, rights, and continuing interests are transferred. The gain (payments – adjusted basis) on the sale is a capital gain to Orange. ■

---

[10]§ 1253(b)(1).

| CONCEPT SUMMARY 7–2 |
| --- |

## Franchises

| | Effect on | |
| --- | --- | --- |
| **Event** | **Franchisor** | **Franchisee** |
| **Franchisor Retains Significant Powers and Rights** | | |
| Noncontingent payment | Ordinary income. | Capitalized and amortized over 15 years as an ordinary deduction; if franchise is sold, amortization is subject to recapture under § 1245. |
| Contingent payment | Ordinary income. | Ordinary deduction. |
| **Franchisor Does *Not* Retain Significant Powers and Rights** | | |
| Noncontingent payment | Ordinary income if franchise rights are an ordinary asset; capital gain if franchise rights are a capital asset (unlikely). | Capitalized and amortized over 15 years as an ordinary deduction; if the franchise is sold, amortization is subject to recapture under § 1245. |
| Contingent payment | Ordinary income. | Ordinary deduction. |

**Noncontingent Payments.**　When the transferor retains a significant power, right, or continuing interest, the transferee's noncontingent payments to the transferor are ordinary income to the transferor. The franchisee capitalizes the payments and amortizes them over 15 years. The amortization is subject to recapture under § 1245, discussed later in this chapter.

**EXAMPLE 14**

Grey Company signs a 10-year franchise agreement with DOH Donuts. Grey (the franchisee) makes payments of $3,000 per year for the first 8 years of the franchise agreement—a total of $24,000. Grey cannot deduct $3,000 per year as the payments are made. Instead, Grey must amortize the $24,000 total over 15 years. Thus, Grey may deduct $1,600 per year for each of the 15 years of the amortization period. The same result would occur if Grey had made a $24,000 lump-sum payment at the beginning of the franchise period. Assuming DOH Donuts (the franchisor) retains significant powers, rights, or a continuing interest, it will have ordinary income when it receives the payments from Grey. ■

**Contingent Payments.**　Whether or not the transferor retains a significant power, right, or continuing interest, contingent franchise payments are ordinary income for the franchisor and an ordinary deduction for the franchisee.

**EXAMPLE 15**

TAK, a spicy chicken franchisor, transfers an eight-year franchise to Egret Corporation. TAK retains a significant power, right, or continuing interest. Egret, the franchisee, agrees to pay TAK 15% of sales. This contingent payment is ordinary income to TAK and a business deduction for Egret as the payments are made. ■

### LEASE CANCELLATION PAYMENTS

The tax treatment of payments received for canceling a lease depends on whether the recipient of the payments is the **lessor** or the **lessee** and whether the lease is a capital asset or not.

## TAX IN THE NEWS

### CANCELLATION OF A LEASE AGREEMENT

Opaque Company (a sole proprietorship) has a lease agreement with Orange Company, a real estate management firm, for Opaque's store in a strip shopping mall. A national corporation has offered to purchase the shopping mall, but only if all the current tenants have waived their remaining lease rights. The new owner wants to renegotiate all of the existing leases in a manner that would increase the profitability of the mall.

Orange has offered Opaque $440,000 to cancel its lease and move out within three months. The lease is not a capital asset, because Opaque uses the property in its business. Opaque recognizes ordinary income of $440,000 if it accepts Orange's offer.

**Lessee Treatment.**   Lease cancellation payments received by a lessee (the tenant) are treated as an exchange.[11] Thus, these payments are capital gains if the lease is a capital asset. Generally, a lessee's lease is a capital asset if the property (either personalty or realty) is used for the lessee's personal use (e.g., his or her residence). A lease held one year or less is an ordinary income asset if the property is used in the lessee's trade or business.[12]

**EXAMPLE 16**

Merganser, Inc., owns an apartment building that it is going to convert into an office building. Vicki is one of the apartment tenants and receives $1,000 from Merganser to cancel the lease. Vicki has a capital gain of $1,000 (which is long term or short term depending upon how long she has held the lease). Merganser has an ordinary deduction of $1,000. ■

**Lessor Treatment.**   Payments received by a lessor (the landlord) for a lease cancellation are always ordinary income because they are considered to be in lieu of rental payments.[13]

**EXAMPLE 17**

Finch & Company owns an apartment building near a university campus. Hui-Fen is one of the tenants. Hui-Fen is graduating early and offers Finch $800 to cancel the apartment lease. Finch accepts the offer. Finch has ordinary income of $800. Hui-Fen has a nondeductible payment since the apartment was personal-use property. ■

**LO.3**

Determine the applicable holding period for a capital asset.

## Holding Period

Property must be held more than one year to qualify for long-term capital gain or loss treatment.[14] Property not held for the required long-term period results in short-term capital gain or loss. To compute the **holding period,** start counting on the day after the property was acquired and include the day of disposition.

**EXAMPLE 18**

Mallard & Co. purchases a capital asset on January 15, 2005, and sells it on January 16, 2006. Mallard's holding period is more than one year. If Mallard had sold the asset on January

---

[11]§ 1241 and Reg. § 1.1241–1(a).
[12]Reg. § 1.1221–1(b), PLR 200045019. If the lease was held for more than one year before cancellation, it is a § 1231 asset.

[13]*Hort v. Comm.*, 41–1 USTC ¶9354, 25 AFTR 1207, 61 S.Ct. 757 (USSC, 1941).
[14]§ 1222.

15, 2006, the holding period would have been exactly one year, and the gain or loss would have been short term. ■

To be held for more than one year, a capital asset acquired on the last day of any month must not be disposed of until on or after the first day of the thirteenth succeeding month.[15]

**EXAMPLE 19**

Purple, Inc., purchases a capital asset on March 31, 2005. If Purple sells the asset on March 31, 2006, the holding period is one year, and Purple will have a short-term capital gain or loss. If Purple sells the asset on April 1, 2006, the holding period is more than one year, and it will have a long-term capital gain or loss. ■

## SPECIAL HOLDING PERIOD RULES

There are several special holding period rules.[16] The application of these rules depends on the type of asset and how it was acquired.

**Nontaxable Exchanges.** The holding period of property received in a like-kind exchange (and certain other qualified nontaxable exchanges) includes the holding period of the former asset if the property that was exchanged was either a capital asset or a § 1231 asset.

**EXAMPLE 20**

Red Manufacturing Corporation exchanges some vacant real estate it owns (a capital asset) for land closer to its factory. The transaction is a like-kind exchange, so the holding period of the new land includes the holding period of the old land. ■

**EXAMPLE 21**

A lightning strike destroyed Vireo Company's generator (a § 1231 asset) in March. Vireo uses the entire insurance proceeds it received to acquire a comparable generator. The holding period of the new generator includes the holding period of the old generator. ■

**Nontaxable Transactions Involving Carryover of Another Taxpayer's Basis.** If a transaction is nontaxable and the former owner's basis carries over to the present owner, the former owner's holding period is included in (tacked on to) the present owner's holding period.

**EXAMPLE 22**

Kareem acquired 100 shares of Robin Corporation stock for $1,000 on December 31, 2001. He transferred the shares by gift to Megan on December 31, 2005, when the stock was worth $2,000. Kareem's basis of $1,000 becomes the basis for determining gain or loss on a subsequent sale by Megan. Megan's holding period begins with the date the stock was acquired by Kareem. ■

**EXAMPLE 23**

Assume the same facts as in the preceding example, except that the fair market value of the shares was only $800 on the date of the gift. If Megan sells the stock for a loss, its value at the date of the gift is her basis. Accordingly, the tacked-on holding period rule does not apply, and Megan's holding period begins with the date of the gift. So, if she sells the shares for $500 on April 1, 2006, Megan has a $300 recognized capital loss, and the holding period is from December 31, 2005, to April 1, 2006. The loss is short term. ■

---

[15]Rev.Rul. 66–7, 1966–1 C.B. 188.  [16]§ 1223.

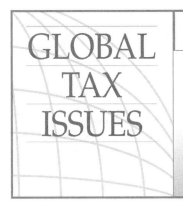

## TRADING ADRS ON U.S. STOCK EXCHANGES

Many non-U.S. companies now have subsidiaries that were formerly U.S. companies. For instance, Chrysler Corporation is now a subsidiary of DaimlerChrysler (formed when the German company Daimler-Benz acquired Chrysler). Shares in such non-U.S. companies generally cannot be traded directly on U.S. stock exchanges. Instead, the offshore companies issue instruments called American Depository Receipts (ADRs) that can be traded on U.S. stock exchanges. Purchases and sales of ADRs are treated for tax purposes as though the ADRs were shares in the corporation that issued them.

**Disallowed Loss Transactions.** Under several Code provisions, realized losses are disallowed. When a loss is disallowed, there is no carryover of holding period. Losses can be disallowed under § 267 (sale or exchange between related taxpayers) and § 262 (sale or exchange of personal-use assets) as well as other Code Sections. Taxpayers who acquire property in a disallowed loss transaction begin a new holding period and have a basis equal to the purchase price.

**EXAMPLE 24**

Janet sells her personal automobile at a loss. She may not deduct the loss because it arises from the sale of personal-use property. Janet purchases a replacement automobile for more than the selling price of her former automobile. Janet has a basis equal to the cost of the replacement automobile, and her holding period begins when she acquires the replacement automobile. ∎

**Inherited Property.** The holding period for inherited property is treated as long term no matter how long the property is actually held by the heir. The holding period of the decedent or the decedent's estate is not relevant to the heir's holding period.

**EXAMPLE 25**

Shonda inherits Blue Company stock from her father. She receives the stock on April 1, 2005, and sells it on November 1, 2005. Even though Shonda did not hold the stock more than one year, she receives long-term capital gain or loss treatment on the sale. ∎

## SHORT SALES

A **short sale** occurs when a taxpayer sells borrowed property and repays the lender with substantially identical property either held on the date of the sale or purchased after the sale. Short sales typically involve corporate stock. The seller's objective is to make a profit in anticipation of a decline in the stock's price. If the price declines, the seller in a short sale recognizes a profit equal to the difference between the sales price of the borrowed stock and the price paid for its replacement.

Section 1233 provides that a short sale gain or loss is a capital gain or loss to the extent that the short sale property constitutes a capital asset of the taxpayer. This gain or loss is not recognized until the short sale is closed. Generally, the holding period of the short sale property is determined by how long the property used to close the short sale was held.

**EXAMPLE 26**

On January 4, Green & Associates sold short 100 shares of Osprey Corporation for $1,500. Green closed the transaction on July 28 of the same year by purchasing 100 shares of Osprey for $1,000 and delivering them to the broker from whom the securities were borrowed. Because this stock was held less than one year (actually less than a day), Green's gain ($1,500 sale price – $1,000 cost) is short term. ■

**EXAMPLE 27**

Assume the same facts as in the preceding example, except that the January 4 short sale was not closed until January 28 of the *following* year. The result is the same, because the stock was acquired and used to close the transaction on the same day; that is, it was not held more than a year. ■

If a taxpayer owns securities that are "substantially identical" to those sold short, § 1259 subjects the short sale to potential *constructive sale treatment*, and the taxpayer recognizes gain (but not loss) as of that date. If the taxpayer has not closed the short sale by delivering the short sale securities to the broker from whom the securities were borrowed before January 31 of the year following the short sale, the short sale is deemed to have closed on the short sale date. The holding period in such circumstances is determined by how long the securities in question were held.

**EXAMPLE 28**

Assume the same facts as in Example 26, except that Green & Associates owned 100 shares of Osprey Corporation when it sold short 100 shares on January 4. Green does not close the short sale before January 31 of the following year. Green must recognize any gain on its 100 shares of Osprey as of January 4 of the current year. If Green owned those shares more than one year as of that date, the gain is long term. ■

*Find more information on this topic at our Web site: **http://wft-entities.swlearning.com**.*

**LO.4**

Describe the tax treatment of capital gains and losses for noncorporate taxpayers.

# Tax Treatment of Capital Gains and Losses of Noncorporate Taxpayers

This section discusses how capital gains and losses are taxed to noncorporate taxpayers, that is, individuals, noncorporate partners, trusts, and estates. The rules applicable to corporations are considered in the following section of this chapter.

## CAPITAL GAINS

Gains from the sale or exchange of capital assets are taxed at various rates, depending upon the holding period, the taxpayer's regular tax rate, and the type of asset involved.

**Short-Term Gains.**   Gains on capital assets held one year or less are taxed as *ordinary income*. Accordingly, the applicable tax rates vary from 10 percent to 35 percent. Although short-term capital gains receive no preferential tax treatment compared to ordinary income, they do have one advantage: they can absorb capital losses without limit. As discussed later in this section, *capital losses* are deducted first against capital gains (without limit) and then against ordinary income, but

## ⊙ TAX FACT

### INDIVIDUAL RETURNS REPORTING CAPITAL GAINS

The number of individual income tax returns including net capital gain in AGI is as follows. About 130 million individual returns are filed annually, so about 7.5 percent of all returns report capital gain income. During the stock market boom of the late 1990s, though, this number was much higher.

| Year | Number of Returns (in Millions) |
|------|-------------------------------|
| 1975 | 5.8 |
| 1980 | 7.0 |
| 1985 | 10.0 |
| 1990 | 9.2 |
| 1995 | 14.8 |
| 2000 | 22.7 |
| 2002 | 10.0 |

only up to $3,000 per year.[17] Thus, someone with a large capital loss will find short-term capital gains attractive, even though such gains do not qualify for lower tax rates.

**PLANNING STRATEGIES**          **Timing Capital Gains**

**FRAMEWORK FOCUS: INCOME AND EXCLUSIONS**

STRATEGY ➤ POSTPONE RECOGNITION OF INCOME TO ACHIEVE TAX DEFERRAL.

**FRAMEWORK FOCUS: DEDUCTIONS**

STRATEGY ➤ MAXIMIZE DEDUCTIBLE AMOUNTS.

Taxpayers have considerable control over the timing of their capital gains through the mechanism of realization. Accordingly, a taxpayer might want to defer recognizing a large capital gain in a year with *substantial itemized deductions,* such as large personal casualty losses or the purchase of a new residence with large up-front interest expenses. In so doing, the taxpayer minimizes the loss of such deductions due to AGI limitations and deduction phaseouts applicable to some high-income individuals.

*Nontax considerations,* of course, often dictate when assets are sold. If a particular stock is peaking in popularity, selling it might be a wise investment strategy, even if the taxpayer's current tax situation is not optimal. Similarly, if a taxpayer needs cash to start a business, purchase a home, or pay for a child's education or medical costs, the capital asset might need to be sold at a time when investment *and* tax considerations counsel otherwise. In these circumstances, however, a taxpayer might choose to *borrow* the money required and use the capital asset as collateral for the loan, rather than sell the asset. A loan does not trigger tax consequences, and the taxpayer can continue to hold the asset until a more opportune time—albeit at the cost of paying interest, which may be nondeductible.

---

[17]§ 1211(b).

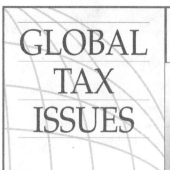

### CAPITAL GAIN TREATMENT IN THE UNITED STATES AND OTHER COUNTRIES

Few other countries apply an alternative tax rate or other incentive to long-term capital gains. Instead, those gains are taxed in the same manner as other income. Consequently, even though the U.S. system of identifying and taxing capital assets is complex, it may be preferable because of the lower tax rates, and because the lower rates are available to taxpayers in all tax brackets.

**Long-Term Gains.**  Gains on capital assets held more than one year are classified as *long-term* gains and are eligible for a special 15 percent tax rate, or 5 percent rate for taxpayers in the 10 or 15 percent tax bracket. The benefit of these long-term capital gain tax rates, therefore, is as follows.

| Ordinary Income | Capital Gain | Differential (Percentage Points) |
|---|---|---|
| 10% | 5% | 5 |
| 15 | 5 | 10 |
| 25 | 15 | 10 |
| 28 | 15 | 13 |
| 33 | 15 | 18 |
| 35 | 15 | 20 |

In point of fact, relatively few capital gains are realized by persons in the 10 or 15 percent tax bracket. Thus, the tax rate that generally applies to long-term capital gains is 15 percent.

There are two major exceptions, however, to this general treatment. The first exception is so-called *28% property,* which consists of the following items.

- **Collectibles** (works of art, rugs, antiques, gems, coins, stamps, and alcoholic beverages) held more than one year.[18]
- The taxable half of the gain on sales of *qualified small business stock* (see the end of this section).

These assets are labeled *28% property,* because the gains that they produce are taxed at 28 percent. But this 28 percent rate is a *maximum* rate, so a taxpayer in a lower tax bracket would pay at that rate. As a result, the benefit of the applicable tax rates for gains on 28% property is as follows.

| Ordinary Income | Applicable Rate | Differential (Percentage Points) |
|---|---|---|
| 10% | 10% | None |
| 15 | 15 | None |
| 25 | 25 | None |
| 28 | 28 | None |
| 33 | 28 | 5 |
| 35 | 28 | 7 |

---

[18]§ 408(m) and Reg. § 1.408–10(b).

Gains on 28% property receive preferential tax treatment only when realized by taxpayers in the top two tax brackets.

## Gifts of Appreciated Securities

**FRAMEWORK FOCUS: TAX RATE**

STRATEGY ➤ SHIFT NET INCOME FROM HIGH-BRACKET TAXPAYERS TO LOW-BRACKET TAXPAYERS.

Persons with appreciated securities that have been held over one year may reduce the tax due on their sale by giving the securities to someone (often a child) who is in the *lowest tax bracket*. The donor's holding period carries over, along with his or her basis, and the donee's lower tax rate applies when the securities are sold. As a result, the gain could be taxed at the donee's 5 percent, rather than the donor's 15 percent. The donee should be over age 13 by year-end, however, or a *kiddie tax* will nullify most of the tax advantage being sought. The kiddie tax subjects the gain to the parents' tax rate. See Chapter 15.

Such gifts usually bear no gift tax due to the annual $11,000 exclusion. But the property received after payment of the tax belongs to the donee. It is not available to the donor, nor may it be used to pay a parent's essential support obligations. Moreover, these assets may affect a child's eligibility for need-based financial aid when applying to college.

The second major exception involves depreciable real estate that has been held more than one year. Some—but not all—of the gain attributable to depreciation deductions on apartments, office buildings, shopping centers, and warehouses is taxable at 25 percent rather than 5 or 15 percent. The amount that is taxed in this manner depends upon how much depreciation is "recaptured" as ordinary income under § 1250, as explained later in this chapter. Accordingly, these gains are called *unrecaptured § 1250 gain* [§ 1(h)(7)]. In any case, the 25 percent rate is a *maximum* rate, so the benefit of the applicable tax rates for gains from the sale of depreciable real estate is as follows.

| Ordinary Income | Applicable Rate | Differential (Percentage Points) |
|---|---|---|
| 10% | 10% | None |
| 15 | 15 | None |
| 25 | 25 | None |
| 28 | 25 | 3 |
| 33 | 25 | 8 |
| 35 | 25 | 10 |

### CAPITAL LOSSES

As explained above, capital gains can be classified into four general categories.

- Short term—taxed as ordinary income.
- 28% property—taxed at no more than 28 percent.
- Unrecaptured § 1250 gain—taxed at no more than 25 percent.
- Regular long term—taxed at 5 percent or 15 percent.

A taxpayer can also have losses from capital assets in *three* of these four categories. The *unrecaptured § 1250 gain* category contains only gain. When both gains and

## CONCEPT SUMMARY 7–3

### Capital Gains of Noncorporate Taxpayers

| Type of Asset | Applicable Rate |
| --- | --- |
| Held not more than one year. | 10%–35%, same as ordinary income. |
| Collectibles held more than one year. | 10/15/25% for lowest bracket taxpayers, 28% for all others. |
| Taxable portion (50%) of gain on qualified small business stock held more than five years. | 10/15/25% for lowest bracket taxpayers, 28% for all others. |
| Unrecaptured § 1250 gain on depreciable real estate held more than one year. | 10/15% for lowest bracket taxpayers, 25% for all others. |
| Other capital assets held more than one year. | 5% for lowest bracket taxpayers, 15% for all others. |

losses occur in the year, they must be netted against each other in the order specified below.

> *Step 1.* Group all gains and losses into short-term, 28% property, unrecaptured § 1250, and regular long-term categories.
>
> *Step 2.* Net the gains and losses within each category to obtain net short-term, 28% property, unrecaptured § 1250, and regular long-term gain or loss.
>
> *Step 3.* Offset the net 28% property and unrecaptured § 1250 amounts if they are of opposite sign. Add them if they have the same sign. Then, offset the resulting amount against the regular net long-term amount if they are of opposite sign, or add the amounts if they have the same sign.
>
> *Step 4.* Offset the result of step 3 with the net short-term gain or loss from step 2 if they are of opposite sign.

These netting rules offset net short-term capital loss against the *highest taxed gain first*. Consequently, if there is a net short-term capital loss, it first offsets any net 28% property gain, any remaining loss offsets unrecaptured § 1250 gain, and then any remaining loss offsets regular long-term gain.

If the result of step 4 is *only* a short-term capital gain, the taxpayer is not eligible for a reduced tax rate. If the result of step 4 is a loss, a **net capital loss** exists, and the taxpayer may be eligible for a *capital loss deduction* (discussed later in this chapter). If there was no offsetting in step 4 because the short-term and step 3 results were both gains *or* if the result of the offsetting is either a 28% property, an unrecaptured § 1250 property, and/or a regular long-term gain, a **net capital gain** exists, and the taxpayer may be eligible for a reduced tax rate. The net capital gain may consist of regular *long-term gain, unrecaptured § 1250 gain,* and/or *28% property gain*. Each of these gains may be taxed at a different rate.

**EXAMPLE 29**

Joe is in the 35% Federal income tax bracket. He is taxed as follows.

| | |
| --- | --- |
| Ordinary income | 35% |
| Unrecaptured § 1250 gain | 25% |
| 28% gain | 28% |
| Short-term capital gain | 35% |
| Other long-term capital gain | 15% |

<table>
<tr><td>**EXAMPLE 30**</td><td>This example shows how a net long-term capital loss is applied.</td></tr>
</table>

| Step | Short Term | 28% Gain | Unrecaptured § 1250 Gain | Regular Long Term | Comment |
|---|---|---|---|---|---|
| 1 | $ 3,000 | $ 1,000 | | $ 3,000 | |
| | | | | (8,000) | |
| 2 | $ 3,000 | $ 1,000 | | ($ 5,000) | |
| 3 | | (1,000) | → | 1,000 | Netted because of opposite sign. |
| | | $ –0– | | ($ 4,000) | |
| 4 | (3,000) | → | → | 3,000 | The net short-term gain is netted against the net regular long-term loss, and the remaining loss is eligible for the capital loss deduction. |
| | $ –0– | | | ($ 1,000) | |

| **EXAMPLE 31** | This example shows how net short-term and regular long-term capital losses are applied. |
|---|---|

| Step | Short Term | 28% Gain | Unrecaptured § 1250 Gain | Regular Long Term | Comment |
|---|---|---|---|---|---|
| 1 | $ 3,000 | $15,000 | $4,000 | $ 3,000 | |
| | (5,000) | (7,000) | | (8,000) | |
| 2 | ($ 2,000) | $ 8,000 | $4,000 | ($ 5,000) | |
| 3 | | (5,000) | ← | 5,000 | Net regular long-term loss is netted against 28% gain first. |
| | | $ 3,000 | | $ –0– | |
| 4 | $ 2,000 → | (2,000) | | | Short-term loss is netted against 28% gain first. |
| | $ –0– | $ 1,000 | $4,000 | | |
| | | Net 28% gain | Net 25% gain | | |

If a net loss remains after applying these rules for offsetting losses, a noncorporate taxpayer may deduct up to $3,000 of that loss against ordinary income.[19] Losses in excess of $3,000 are carried over to future years where they are applied first against capital gains and then deducted up to $3,000 per year. Capital loss carryovers expire, however, when the taxpayer dies.

| **EXAMPLE 32** | James incurred a $10,000 loss on his only capital asset transaction in 2005. If he has no other capital asset transactions from that point on, his $10,000 loss is deducted as follows. |
|---|---|

| Year | Deduction |
|---|---|
| 2005 | $3,000 |
| 2006 | 3,000 |
| 2007 | 3,000 |
| 2008 | 1,000 |

---

[19]§ 1211(b)(1). Married persons filing separate returns are limited to a $1,500 deduction per tax year.

## TAX FACT

### DETRIMENTAL TAX TREATMENT FOR CAPITAL LOSSES

A corporate taxpayer cannot deduct a net capital loss against ordinary income. It can carry the loss back three years and forward five years in search of capital gains. An individual taxpayer can deduct a maximum of $3,000 of net capital loss against ordinary income in the current tax year. Any excess can be carried forward indefinitely in search of capital gains. After capital gains are exhausted in each carryforward year, a maximum of $3,000 of the remaining net capital loss can be deducted against ordinary income.

The number of individual income tax returns with a net capital loss in AGI is as follows. These numbers are much higher lately, due to drops in stock market prices.

| Year | Number of Returns (in Millions) |
|------|--------------------------------|
| 1975 | 2.5 |
| 1980 | 2.0 |
| 1985 | 2.7 |
| 1990 | 5.0 |
| 1995 | 5.1 |
| 2000 | 6.9 |
| 2002 | 13.3 |

**EXAMPLE 33**

Assume the same facts as in the preceding example, except that James realizes a capital gain of $4,500 in 2007. At that time, his remaining capital loss carryover is $4,000 ($10,000 – $6,000 deducted previously). Since his capital gain in 2007 (i.e., $4,500) exceeds this loss carryforward, James can deduct the entire $4,000 against that year's capital gain. ■

**EXAMPLE 34**

Assume the same facts as in Example 32, except that James died in late 2006. His remaining capital loss carryforward of $4,000 ($10,000 – $6,000 deducted in 2005 and 2006) expires unused. ■

When a taxpayer's capital loss exceeds $3,000 and derives from more than one category, it is used in the following order: first, short term; then, 28% property; then, unrecaptured § 1250 property; and finally, regular long term. Unused losses are carried forward as follows: short-term losses carry forward as short-term losses, and long-term losses carry forward as long-term losses.

**EXAMPLE 35**

Nancy incurs a long-term capital loss of $8,500 this year, of which $3,000 is deducted against her ordinary income. The remaining $5,500 ($8,500 loss – $3,000 deducted) carries forward as a long-term capital loss. ■

DIGGING DEEPER 6   *Find more information on this topic at our Web site: **http://wft-entities.swlearning.com**.*

## Matching Gains with Losses

**FRAMEWORK FOCUS: INCOME AND EXCLUSIONS**

STRATEGY ➤ AVOID INCOME RECOGNITION.

A taxpayer who has already realized a large capital gain may want to *match this gain* with an *offsetting capital loss.* Doing so will shelter the capital gain from taxation and will also free up an asset that has declined in value. Without the capital gain, after all, the taxpayer might hesitate to sell a loss asset, because the resulting capital loss may be deductible only in $3,000 annual increments.

Similarly, a taxpayer with a large realized capital loss might use the occasion to sell some appreciated assets. Doing so would enable the taxpayer to use the capital loss immediately and at the same time realize the benefit of the asset appreciation at little or no tax cost.

On the other hand, matching capital losses and long-term capital gains means that the taxpayer utilizes the capital loss against income that would otherwise qualify for a preferential tax rate of 5 or 15 percent. If the taxpayer's ordinary income is taxed at a higher rate, he or she might prefer to deduct the loss against that higher taxed income, even on a schedule of $3,000 per year. The *time value of money* must be considered; a current-year deduction at 5 or 15 percent might be worth more than a series of annual deductions at higher rates spread over several years.

*Nontax considerations,* such as investment prospects for the assets in question, are also important. Future investment prospects are often unknowable or at least highly speculative, while tax effects can be determined with relative certainty—which explains some of the late December selling activity in publicly traded securities and mutual funds.

## SMALL BUSINESS STOCK

A special 50 percent *exclusion* is available to noncorporate taxpayers who derive capital gains from the sale or exchange of **qualified small business stock.**[20] Half of the gain is excluded from the taxpayer's gross income, and the other half is subjected to a maximum tax rate of 28 percent, as noted earlier.

*EXAMPLE 36*

Yolanda realized a $100,000 gain on the sale of qualified small business stock. Yolanda has a 35% marginal tax rate without considering this gain. So $50,000 of this gain is excluded from her gross income, and the other $50,000 is taxed at a maximum tax rate of 28%. Thus, Yolanda owes tax of $14,000 ($50,000 × 28%), an effective tax rate of 14% on the entire $100,000 capital gain. ■

This treatment is more favorable than the capital gain tax treatment explained previously. Accordingly, Congress imposed additional restrictions to ensure that the gains receiving this treatment were derived in the circumstances that Congress intended to promote. These restrictions include the following.

- The stock must have been newly issued *after* August 10, 1993.
- The taxpayer must have held the stock *more than five years*.
- The issuing corporation must use at least 80 percent of its assets, determined by their value, in the *active conduct* of a trade or business.
- When the stock was issued, the issuing corporation's assets must not have exceeded $50 million, at adjusted basis, including the proceeds of the stock issuance.

[20]§ 1202(a).

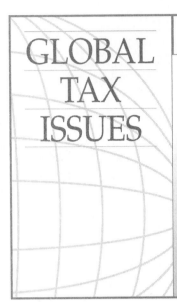

## GLOBAL TAX ISSUES

### CAPITAL GAIN TREATMENT AND NON-U.S. STOCK

U.S. shareholders of certain non-U.S. corporations may find that they are denied capital gain treatment upon sale or other disposal of their stock. If the entity that issued the stock is considered a controlled foreign corporation (CFC) because certain U.S. shareholders as a group own more than 50 percent by vote or value, any gain recognized upon disposition of the stock is recharacterized as dividend income to the extent of the entity's earnings and profits yet to be taxed in the United States.

U.S. persons investing in non-U.S. corporations ultimately receive income taxable in the United States through dividends or capital gains upon disposition of the stock. If an offshore corporation pays no dividends, the U.S. shareholder's entire return from the stock investment is in the form of a gain on disposition of the stock, with the accumulated earnings of the non-U.S. corporation reflected in that gain. This provision protects the ability of the United States to tax these accumulated earnings as ordinary dividend income when they ultimately are realized by U.S. persons.

- The corporation does not engage in banking, financing, insurance, investing, leasing, farming, mineral extraction, hotel or motel operation, restaurant operation, or any business whose principal asset is the *reputation or skill* of its employees (such as accounting, architecture, health, law, engineering, or financial services).

Even if each of these requirements is met, the amount of gain eligible for the exclusion is limited to the *greater* of 10 times the taxpayer's basis in the stock or $10 million per taxpayer per company,[21] computed on an aggregate basis.

**EXAMPLE 37**

Vanita purchased $100,000 of qualified small business stock when it was first issued in October 1996. This year, she sells the stock for $4 million. Her gain is $3.9 million ($4,000,000 − $100,000). Although this amount exceeds 10 times her basis ($100,000 × 10 = $1,000,000), it is *less* than $10 million, so the entire $3.9 million gain is eligible for the 50% exclusion. ■

Transactions that fail to satisfy *any one* of the applicable requirements are taxed as capital gains (and losses) realized by noncorporate taxpayers generally.

Gains are also eligible for *nonrecognition* treatment if the sale proceeds are invested in other qualified small business stock within 60 days.[22] To the extent that the sale proceeds are not so invested, gain is recognized, but the 50 percent exclusion still applies. To be eligible for this treatment, the stock sold must have been held more than six months.

**EXAMPLE 38**

Assume the same facts as in the preceding example, except that Vanita sold her stock in January 2006 and used $3.5 million of the sale proceeds to purchase other qualified small business stock one month later. Vanita's gain is recognized to the extent that the sale proceeds were not reinvested—namely, $500,000 ($4,000,000 sale proceeds − $3,500,000 reinvested). The 50% exclusion will apply, however, to this amount. ■

DIGGING DEEPER (7)     *Find more information on this topic at our Web site: **http://wft-entities.swlearning.com**.*

---

[21]For married persons filing separately, the limitation is $5 million.          [22]§ 1045(a).

## LO.5

Describe the tax treatment of capital gains and losses for corporate taxpayers.

# Tax Treatment of Capital Gains and Losses of Corporate Taxpayers

The treatment of a corporation's net capital gain or loss differs dramatically from the rules for noncorporate taxpayers discussed in the preceding section. Briefly, the differences are as follows.

- Capital gains are taxed at the ordinary income tax rates.[23]
- Capital losses offset only capital gains. No deduction of capital losses is permitted against ordinary taxable income.
- There is a three-year carryback and a five-year carryforward period for net capital losses.[24] Capital loss carrybacks and carryforwards are always treated as short term, regardless of their original nature.

**EXAMPLE 39**

Sparrow Corporation has a $15,000 long-term capital loss for the current year and $57,000 of ordinary taxable income. Sparrow may not offset the $15,000 long-term capital loss against its ordinary income by taking a capital loss deduction. The $15,000 long-term capital loss becomes a $15,000 short-term capital loss for carryback and carryforward purposes. This amount may offset capital gains in the three-year carryback period or, if not absorbed there, offset capital gains in the five-year carryforward period. Any amount remaining after this carryforward period expires is permanently lost. ■

## LO.6

Distinguish § 1231 assets from ordinary and capital assets, and calculate § 1231 gain or loss.

# Section 1231 Assets

Businesses own many assets that are used in the business rather than held for resale. In financial accounting, such assets are known as "fixed assets." For example, a foundry's 30,000-pound stamping machine is a fixed asset. It is also a depreciable asset. The building housing the foundry is another fixed asset. The remainder of this chapter largely deals with how to *classify* the gains and losses from the disposition of fixed assets. Chapter 4 discussed how to depreciate such assets. Chapter 6 discussed how to determine the adjusted basis and the amount of gain or loss from their disposition.

### RELATIONSHIP TO CAPITAL ASSETS

At first glance, the *classification of fixed assets* ought to be straightforward. Section 1221(a)(2) specifically excludes from the capital asset definition any property that is depreciable or that is real estate "used in a trade or business." Accordingly, the foundry's stamping machine and the building housing the foundry described above are not capital assets. Therefore, one would expect gains to be taxed as ordinary income and losses to be deductible as ordinary losses. Since World War II, however, certain business assets have received more favorable treatment.

Section 1231 provides that business assets held for more than one year can receive the best of both worlds: capital gain treatment on gains and ordinary loss treatment on losses. More specifically, this provision requires that gains and losses

---

[23]§ 1201. The alternative tax rate of 35% produces no beneficial results.    [24]§ 1212(a)(1).

## TAX FACT

### CAPITAL GAINS FOR THE WEALTHY?

Economists and other observers of society often accuse the Code of favoring those with higher levels of income and wealth, despite a fairly substantial progressivity in the Federal income tax rate structure. The claim is that the wealthy are the sole possessors of capital assets, and that capital gains are subject to highly favorable tax treatment. Current tax return data may confirm those assertions.

**Net Capital Gain Income as a Percentage of AGI, 2002 Returns**

from **§ 1231 property** be compiled at the end of the taxable year; the *net result* is then classified as capital gain if a net gain is produced, or as ordinary loss if a net loss is produced. As a result, a particular disposition's character as capital or ordinary is not determined until the taxable year has concluded and all of the taxpayer's **§ 1231 gains and losses** are tabulated.

**EXAMPLE 40**

Brown & Co. sells business land and building at a $5,000 gain and equipment at a $3,000 loss. Both properties were held for more than one year. Brown's net gain is $2,000, and that net gain may be treated as a long-term capital gain under § 1231. ∎

**EXAMPLE 41**

Chickadee, Inc., sells equipment at a $10,000 loss and business land at a $2,000 gain. Both properties were held for more than one year. Chickadee's net loss is $8,000, and that net loss is an ordinary loss. ∎

*Find more information on this topic at our Web site: **http://wft-entities.swlearning.com**.*

After World War II, Congress decided that § 1231's highly favorable treatment was no longer entirely appropriate. Rather than repeal § 1231, however, Congress chose to take back some—but not all—of its benefits through the *recapture provisions* of §§ 1245 and 1250, which are discussed later in this chapter.

## PROPERTY INCLUDED

Section 1231 property includes the following.

- Depreciable or real property used in business (principally machinery and equipment, buildings, and land).
- Property held for the production of income if it has been involuntarily converted.
- Timber, coal, or domestic iron ore to which § 631 applies.
- Livestock held for draft, breeding, dairy, or sporting purposes.
- Unharvested crops on land used in business.
- Certain *purchased* intangible assets (such as patents and goodwill) that are eligible for amortization.

*Find more information on these topics at our Web site: **http://wft-entities.swlearning.com**.*

## PROPERTY EXCLUDED

Section 1231 property generally does *not* include the following.

- Property not held more than one year. Livestock must be held at least 12 months (24 months in some cases). Unharvested crops do not have to be held more than one year, but the land must be so held.
- Property not put to a personal use, where casualty losses exceed casualty gains for the taxable year. If a taxpayer has a net casualty loss, the casualty gains and losses are treated as ordinary gains and losses.
- Inventory and property held primarily for sale to customers.
- Copyrights; literary, musical, or artistic compositions, etc.; and certain U.S. government publications.
- Accounts receivable and notes receivable arising in the ordinary course of the trade or business.

## CASUALTY OR THEFT AND NONPERSONAL-USE CAPITAL ASSETS

When § 1231 assets are disposed of by casualty or theft, a special netting rule is applied. For simplicity, the term *casualty* is used to mean both casualty and theft dispositions. First, the casualty gains and losses from § 1231 assets *and* the casualty gains and losses from **long-term nonpersonal-use capital assets** are determined. For business entities, virtually any capital asset is a nonpersonal-use capital asset, because partnerships, limited liability companies, and corporations are incapable of using assets *personally*. This classification, therefore, is most significant to individual taxpayers who might use certain capital assets as part of their daily life.

Once the casualty gains and losses from § 1231 assets and nonpersonal-use capital assets are determined, they are netted together. If the result is a *net gain*, the net gain is treated as § 1231 gain, but if the result is a *net loss*, the net loss is deducted outside § 1231. Thus, whether these casualties get § 1231 treatment depends on the results of the casualty netting process.

Casualties and thefts are *involuntary conversions*, it should be recalled, and gains from such conversions need not be recognized if the proceeds are timely reinvested in similar property. Thus, the netting process described above would not consider any casualty and theft gains that are being deferred because insurance proceeds were reinvested according to the requirements of § 1033 (see Chapter 6). Section 1231, in other words, has no effect on whether a *realized* gain or loss is recognized. Instead, § 1231 merely dictates how a *recognized* gain will be classified.

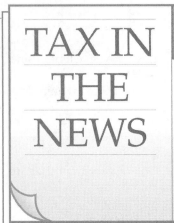

## SALE OF "CAMPUS" LAND YIELDS POTENTIAL LONG-TERM CAPITAL GAIN

Recently, a large suburban Chicago insurance corporation announced that it was planning to sell 500 acres of land surrounding its headquarters "campus." The land contains lakes, a golf course, tennis courts, and a farm. All of these facilities were available for use by the corporation's employees. Now, however, the corporation has significantly downsized its workforce and moved many of its operations to other cities. Consequently, it is going to sell the 500 acres to a developer who will build luxury homes there. Since the land has been used in the corporation's business and has been held more than a year, it is a § 1231 asset. The gain from disposition of the land is a § 1231 gain.

This special netting process for casualties and thefts does not apply to *condemnation* gains and losses. As a result, if a § 1231 asset is disposed of by condemnation, any resulting gain or loss will get § 1231 treatment.

### GENERAL PROCEDURE FOR § 1231 COMPUTATION

The tax treatment of § 1231 gains and losses depends on the results of a rather complex *netting* procedure. The steps in this netting procedure are as follows.

**Step 1: Casualty Netting.** Net all recognized long-term gains and losses from casualties of § 1231 assets and nonpersonal-use capital assets. This casualty netting is beneficial because if there is a net gain, the gain may receive long-term capital gain treatment. If there is a net loss, it receives ordinary loss treatment.

    a. If the casualty gains exceed the casualty losses, add the net gain to the other § 1231 gains for the taxable year.

    b. If the casualty losses exceed the casualty gains, exclude all casualty losses and gains from further § 1231 computation. The casualty gains are ordinary income and the casualty losses are deductible. For individual taxpayers, the casualty losses must be classified further. Section 1231 asset casualty losses are deductible *for* AGI, while other casualty losses are deductible *from* AGI.

**Step 2: § 1231 Netting.** After adding any net casualty gain from Step 1a to the other § 1231 gains and losses (including *recognized* § 1231 asset condemnation gains and losses), net all § 1231 gains and losses.

    a. If the gains exceed the losses, the net gain is offset by the "lookback" nonrecaptured § 1231 losses (see step 3 below) from the prior five tax years. To the extent of this offset, the net § 1231 gain is classified as ordinary income. Any remaining gain is long-term capital gain.

    b. If the losses exceed the gains, the net loss is deducted against ordinary income. For individual taxpayers only, the gains are ordinary income, the § 1231 asset losses are deductible *for* AGI, and the other casualty losses are deductible *from* AGI.

| EXAMPLE 42 | Falcon Management, Inc., recognized the following gains and losses this year. |

| **Capital Gains and Losses** | |
| --- | --- |
| Long-term capital gain | $ 3,000 |
| Long-term capital loss | (400) |
| Short-term capital gain | 1,000 |
| Short-term capital loss | (200) |

| **Casualties** | |
| --- | --- |
| Gain from insurance recovery on fire loss to building, owned five years | $ 1,200 |
| Loss from theft of computer (uninsured), owned two years | (1,000) |

| **§ 1231 Gains and Losses from Depreciable Business Assets Held Long Term** | |
| --- | --- |
| Asset A | $ 300 |
| Asset B | 1,100 |
| Asset C | (500) |

| **Gains and Losses from Sale of Depreciable Business Assets Held Short Term** | |
| --- | --- |
| Asset D | $ 200 |
| Asset E | (300) |

Falcon had no net § 1231 losses in prior tax years.

Disregarding the recapture of depreciation (discussed later in this chapter), Falcon's gains and losses receive the following tax treatment.

* The casualty netting of the § 1231 and nonpersonal-use capital assets contains two items—the $1,200 gain from the business building and the $1,000 loss from the computer. Consequently, there is a $200 net gain and that gain is treated as a § 1231 gain (added to the § 1231 gains).
* The gains from § 1231 transactions (Assets A, B, and C and the § 1231 asset casualty gain) exceed the losses by $1,100 ($1,600 – $500). This excess is a long-term capital gain and is added to Falcon's other long-term capital gains.
* Falcon's net long-term capital gain is $3,700 ($3,000 + $1,100 from § 1231 transactions – $400 long-term capital loss). Its net short-term capital gain is $800 ($1,000 – $200). The result is capital gain income of $4,500, which will be taxed at ordinary rates. If Falcon were an individual rather than a corporation, the $3,700 net long-term capital gain portion would be eligible for preferential capital gain treatment, and the $800 net short-term capital gain would be taxed as ordinary income.
* Falcon treats the gain and loss from Assets D and E as ordinary gain and loss, because § 1231 does not apply unless the assets have been held more than one year.[25]

| **Results of the Gains and Losses on Falcon's Tax Computation** | |
| --- | --- |
| Net long-term capital gain | $3,700 |
| Net short-term capital gain | 800 |
| Ordinary gain from sale of Asset D | 200 |
| Ordinary loss from sale of Asset E | (300) |
| Gross income | $4,400 |

---

[25]§ 1231(b)(1).

**EXAMPLE 43**

Assume the same facts as in the preceding example, except that the loss from Asset C was $1,700 instead of $500.

- The treatment of the casualty gains and losses is the same.
- The losses from § 1231 transactions now exceed the gains by $100 ($1,700 – $1,600). As a result, the net loss is deducted in full as an ordinary loss.
- Capital gain income is $3,400 ($2,600 long term + $800 short term).

| **Results of the Gains and Losses on Falcon's Tax Computation** | |
| --- | ---: |
| Net long-term capital gain | $2,600 |
| Net short-term capital gain | 800 |
| Net ordinary loss on Assets A, B, and C and § 1231 casualty gain | (100) |
| Ordinary gain from sale of Asset D | 200 |
| Ordinary loss from sale of Asset E | (300) |
| Gross income | $3,200 |

**Step 3: § 1231 Lookback Provision.**   The net § 1231 gain from step 2a is offset by the nonrecaptured net § 1231 losses for the five preceding taxable years.[26] For 2005, the lookback years are 2000, 2001, 2002, 2003, and 2004. To the extent of the nonrecaptured net § 1231 loss, the current-year net § 1231 gain is ordinary income. The *nonrecaptured* net § 1231 losses are those that have not already been used to offset net § 1231 gains. Only the net § 1231 gain exceeding this net § 1231 loss carryforward is given long-term capital gain treatment. The **§ 1231 lookback** provision reduces the taxpayer's ability to gain a tax advantage by "timing" sales artificially.

**EXAMPLE 44**

Komodo Manufacturing Corporation sold various used machines and some business real estate during 2005 for a net § 1231 gain of $25,000. During 2004, Komodo had no § 1231 transactions, but in 2003, it had a net § 1231 loss of $17,000. This loss causes $17,000 of the 2005 gain to be classified as ordinary income. The remaining 2005 gain of $8,000 ($25,000 of § 1231 gain – $17,000 nonrecaptured loss) is § 1231 gain. ∎

**EXAMPLE 45**

Assume the same facts as in the preceding example, except that Komodo had a net § 1231 loss of $37,000 in 2003 and a net § 1231 gain of $10,000 in 2004.

- The 2003 net § 1231 loss of $37,000 would cause the net § 1231 gain of $10,000 in 2004 to be classified as ordinary income, and $27,000 ($37,000 loss – $10,000 recaptured) would carry over to 2005.
- The remaining nonrecaptured § 1231 loss of $27,000 from 2003 completely offsets the § 1231 gain of $25,000 from 2005, making that entire gain ordinary income.
- The remaining nonrecaptured § 1231 loss from 2003 is $2,000 ($27,000 carried to 2005 – $25,000 recaptured). This recapture potential carries over to 2006. ∎

**LO.7**

Determine when recapture provisions apply and derive their effects.

# Section 1245 Recapture

As the preceding section explained, when Congress determined that § 1231 was unduly generous, it chose to *recapture* some of § 1231's benefits rather than repeal that section altogether. This recapture phenomenon applies exclusively to the gain

---

[26]§ 1231(c).

**CONCEPT SUMMARY 7–4**

## Section 1231 Netting Procedure

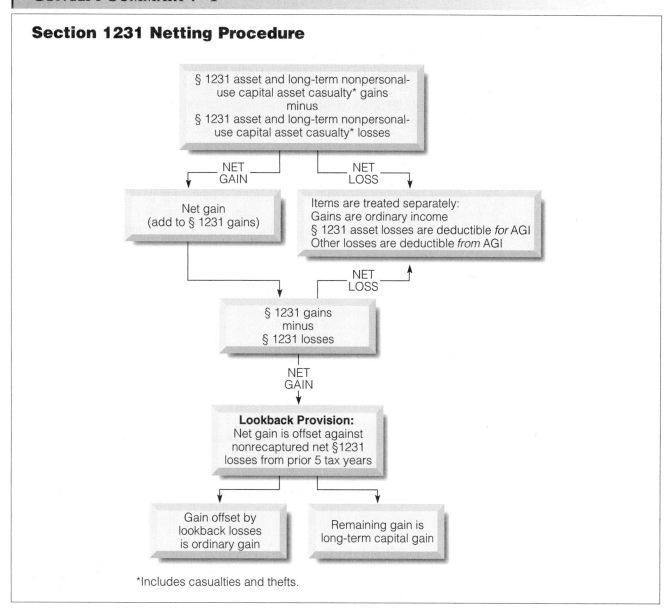

*Includes casualties and thefts.

side of § 1231; the ordinary loss feature applicable to § 1231 property is not affected by the Code's recapture provisions. In essence, recapture takes part—often all—of the gain from the sale or exchange of a § 1231 asset and classifies it as *ordinary income* before the netting process of § 1231 begins. Accordingly, recaptured gain is computed *first*, without considering the other § 1231 transactions that occurred during the taxable year. This section discusses the § 1245 recapture rules, and the next section discusses the § 1250 recapture rules.

Section 1245 requires taxpayers to treat all gain as ordinary gain unless the property is sold for more than its original cost. This result is accomplished by requiring that all gain be treated as ordinary gain to the extent of the depreciation taken on the property disposed of. Section 1231 gain results only if the property is disposed of for more than its original cost. The excess of the sales price over the original cost is § 1231 gain. Section 1245 applies primarily to personalty such as machinery, trucks, and office furniture.

**Bridge to Financial Accounting**

The essence of much of the tax code is to create definitions that discriminate among certain types of income or expenditure, so that special tax treatment can be afforded to one of the definitional groups. For instance, municipal bond interest might be favored over corporate bond interest income, long-term capital gains over short-term capital gains or ordinary income, and processing fees to bribes. In each case, the former generally allows a reduction of taxable income or the tax liability and helps the taxpayer to meet its goal of maximizing the available after-tax income that it generates.

Maximizing net income also is a goal of financial accounting, at least from the viewpoint of current and potential shareholders. In the long run, stock prices may advance solely because of the positive earnings that the corporation generates relative to the rest of the capital markets. The greater the net earnings, the greater the increase in stock price and private wealth.

But financial accounting makes far fewer distinctions when classifying the reporting entity's revenues and expenses. Most of the tax code's definitions and distinctions are politically or economically motivated means by which to reduce the effective tax rate of the taxpayer, perhaps without affecting its nominal rate.

The preferential treatment of long-term capital gains is one of the most long-lived of these tax fictions. The "best of both worlds" § 1231 treatment is over 60 years old itself. Whereas the gain or loss generated by the sale of a business or investment asset is merely included in the body of the income statement of the reporting entity, § 1221 and § 1231 can reduce the taxpayer's effective tax rate, and § 1245 and § 1250 can increase it.

Differences in classification of income and deductions created solely by the tax code constitute most of the items to be reconciled in the Schedule M–1 or M–3 of the C corporation, S corporation, partnership, and limited liability entity. Many of these items must be reported as permanent or timing differences in the Deferred Tax Liability account regulated by APB 23 and SFAS 109.

---

**EXAMPLE 46**

Avocet, Inc., purchased a $100,000 machine and deducted $70,000 depreciation before selling it for $80,000. Avocet's gain is $50,000 [$80,000 amount realized – $30,000 adjusted basis ($100,000 cost – $70,000 depreciation taken)]. Section 1245 treats as ordinary income (not as § 1231 gain) any gain to the extent of depreciation taken. In this example, the entire $50,000 gain would be ordinary income. ■

**EXAMPLE 47**

If Avocet, Inc., in the preceding example sold the machine for $120,000, it would have a gain of $90,000 ($120,000 amount realized – $30,000 adjusted basis). The § 1245 gain would be $70,000 (equal to the depreciation taken), and the remaining gain of $20,000 (equal to the excess of the sales price over the original cost) would be § 1231 gain. ■

**EXAMPLE 48**

Assume the same facts as in Example 46, except that the asset is sold for $25,000 instead of $80,000. Avocet's loss is $5,000 ($25,000 amount realized – $30,000 adjusted basis). Since there is a loss, there is no depreciation recapture. All of the loss is § 1231 loss. ■

**Section 1245 recapture** applies to the portion of *recognized* gain from the sale or other disposition of § 1245 property that represents depreciation, including § 167 depreciation, § 168 cost recovery, 30 and 50 percent additional first-year depreciation, § 179 immediate expensing, and § 197 amortization. Section 1245 merely *classifies* gain as ordinary income; it does not cause gain to be recognized. Thus, in Example 46, Avocet, Inc., recaptures as ordinary income only the $50,000 of actual

**TAX IN THE NEWS**

### MORE DEPRECIATION AND MORE DEPRECIATION RECAPTURE

The combination of the 30 and 50 percent special depreciation allowances and the $102,000 (in 2004) § 179 immediate expense election dramatically increases the amount of depreciation that may be taken in the first year for new property (see Chapter 4). However, the increased depreciation means that the adjusted basis of the property is reduced more quickly. Consequently, if the property is sold early in its useful life, there will very likely be a gain on its disposition, and the § 1245 depreciation recapture will be greater because the depreciation taken is greater.

gain, not the entire $70,000 of depreciation taken. In other words, § 1245 recaptures the *lower* of the depreciation taken or the gain recognized.

The method of depreciation (e.g., accelerated or straight-line) does not matter. All depreciation taken is potentially subject to recapture. Thus, § 1245 recapture is often referred to as *full recapture*. Any remaining gain after subtracting the amount recaptured as ordinary income will usually be § 1231 gain. The remaining gain is casualty gain, however, if the asset is disposed of in a casualty event. For example, if the machine in Example 47 had been disposed of by casualty and the $120,000 received had been an insurance recovery, Avocet would still have a gain of $90,000, and $70,000 of that gain would still be recaptured by § 1245 as ordinary gain. The other $20,000 of gain, however, would be casualty gain.

If § 1245 property is disposed of in a transaction other than a sale, exchange, or involuntary conversion, the maximum amount recaptured is the excess of the property's fair market value over its adjusted basis. See the discussion under Exceptions to §§ 1245 and 1250 later in this chapter.

## SECTION 1245 PROPERTY

Generally, **§ 1245 property** includes all depreciable personal property (e.g., machinery and equipment), including livestock. Buildings and their structural components usually are not § 1245 property. The following property is *also* subject to § 1245 treatment.

* Amortizable personal property such as goodwill, patents, copyrights, and leaseholds of § 1245 property.
* Professional baseball and football player contracts.
* Expensing of costs to remove architectural and transportation barriers that restrict the handicapped and/or elderly.
* Section 179 immediate expensing of depreciable tangible personal property.
* Certain depreciable tangible real property (other than buildings and their structural components) employed as an integral part of certain activities such as manufacturing and production. For example, a natural gas storage tank where the gas is used in the manufacturing process is § 1245 property.
* Pollution control facilities, railroad grading and tunnel bores, on-the-job training facilities, and child care facilities on which amortization is taken.
* Single-purpose agricultural and horticultural structures and petroleum storage facilities (e.g., a greenhouse or silo).

## OBSERVATIONS ON § 1245

* In most instances, the total depreciation taken will exceed the recognized gain. Therefore, the disposition of § 1245 property usually results in ordinary income rather than § 1231 gain. Refer to Example 46.

- Recapture applies to the total amount of depreciation allowed or allowable regardless of the depreciation method used (i.e., full recapture).
- Recapture applies regardless of the holding period of the property. Of course, the entire recognized gain would be ordinary income if the property was not held more than one year, because then § 1231 would not apply.
- Section 1245 does not apply to losses, which receive § 1231 treatment.
- Gains from the disposition of § 1245 assets may also be treated as passive activity gains (refer to Chapter 5).

**EXAMPLE 49**

Upon sale of some business equipment held for five years, Pink Corporation recognized a $7,500 loss. All of the $20,000 § 1245 depreciation recapture potential for the asset disappears as a result of the disposition. The transaction receives § 1231 loss treatment, and none of Pink's cost recovery deductions are recaptured into ordinary income for this asset. ■

**PLANNING STRATEGIES**

## Depreciation Recapture and § 179

**FRAMEWORK FOCUS: DEDUCTIONS**

**STRATEGY ▶ ACCELERATE RECOGNITION OF DEDUCTIONS TO ACHIEVE TAX DEFERRAL.**

Section 1245 recapture applies to all types of depreciation, including § 179 *immediate expensing*. Expensing under § 179, however, is elective and entirely within the discretion of the taxpayer. Choosing this option accelerates depreciation on the affected property but increases the potential recapture as well. Therefore, if a taxpayer anticipates that an asset will generate a gain when it is sold and that such sale will occur in the early years of the asset's life, the taxpayer might decide to forgo electing the additional depreciation under § 179.

On the other hand, electing § 179 remains attractive if little or no gain is anticipated upon an asset's disposition. After all, § 1245 recapture applies only to the extent that gain is actually realized. Moreover, even if a substantial gain is anticipated upon an asset's disposition, the *time value of money* might suggest that § 179 be elected if the disposition is expected to be many years away. In any case, the taxpayer can usually control when an asset is sold or exchanged and can thereby extend the time before the taxes saved by electing § 179 must be returned as § 1245 recapture.

## Section 1250 Recapture

Some depreciable property that is not subject to § 1245 recapture faces a separate recapture computation mechanism in § 1250. For the most part, § 1250 applies to *depreciable real property* (principally buildings and their structural components), such as apartments, office buildings, factories, stores, and warehouses. Intangible real property, such as leaseholds of **§ 1250 property,** also is included.

**Section 1250 recapture** is much less onerous than § 1245 recapture, but it is also much more complex. Section 1250 recaptures only a property's **additional depreciation,** which is the excess of the depreciation actually deducted over the amount that would have been allowed under the straight-line method of depreciation. For this reason, § 1250 recapture is often referred to as *partial recapture*, in contrast to § 1245's full recapture.

Since § 1250 recaptures only the excess over straight-line depreciation, the concept does not apply to properties that were depreciated using the straight-line method (unless they were held for one year or less). Real property placed in service *after 1986* can only be depreciated using the straight-line method, so there is *no § 1250 recapture* upon the disposition of such properties that are held for longer than one year.

---

## CONCEPT SUMMARY 7–5

### Comparison of § 1245 and § 1250 Depreciation Recapture

|  | § 1245 | § 1250 |
|---|---|---|
| Property affected | All depreciable personal property, including items such as § 179 expense and § 197 amortization of intangibles such as goodwill, patents, and copyrights. | Nonresidential real property acquired after 1969 and before 1981, on which accelerated depreciation was taken. Residential rental real property acquired after 1975 and before 1987, on which accelerated depreciation was taken. |
| Depreciation recaptured | Potentially all depreciation taken. If the selling price is greater than or equal to the original cost, all depreciation is recaptured. If the selling price is between the adjusted basis and the original cost, only some depreciation is recaptured. | Additional depreciation (the excess of accelerated depreciation over straight-line depreciation). All depreciation taken if property disposed of in first year. |
| Limit on recapture | Lower of depreciation taken or gain recognized. | Lower of additional depreciation or gain recognized. |
| Treatment of gain exceeding recapture gain | Usually § 1231 gain. | Usually § 1231 gain. |
| Treatment of loss | No depreciation recapture; loss is usually § 1231 loss. | No depreciation recapture; loss is usually § 1231 loss. |

But real estate is particularly long-lived, and many dispositions of such assets involve properties placed in service *before 1987*, when accelerated depreciation was often available for real estate. Finally, § 1250 does not affect the § 1231 treatment of realized losses.

When straight-line depreciation is used, there is no § 1250 recapture potential unless the property is disposed of in the first year of use. For real property placed in service after 1986, only straight-line depreciation is allowed. Therefore, the application of § 1250 is limited to first-year dispositions.

**EXAMPLE 50**

Sanjay Enterprises, Ltd., acquires a residential rental building on January 1, 2004, for $300,000. It receives an offer of $450,000 for the building and sells it on December 23, 2005.

- Sanjay takes $20,909 [($300,000 × .03485) + ($300,000 × .03636 × $^{11.5}/_{12}$) = $20,909] of total depreciation for 2004 and 2005. The adjusted basis of the property is $279,091 ($300,000 − $20,909).
- Sanjay's recognized gain is $170,909 ($450,000 − $279,091).
- All of the gain is § 1231 gain. ∎

Concept Summary 7–5 compares and contrasts the § 1245 and § 1250 depreciation recapture rules.

### UNRECAPTURED § 1250 GAIN (REAL ESTATE 25% GAIN)

As noted previously, *noncorporate taxpayers* pay tax at a maximum rate of 25 percent on their **unrecaptured § 1250 gain.** This gain represents that part of the gain on § 1250 property that is attributable to depreciation that was not recaptured by § 1250.

The procedure for computing this amount involves three distinct steps.

*Step 1.* Determine the part of the recognized gain that is attributable to *depreciation deductions* claimed in prior years.

*Step 2.* Apply § 1250 to determine the portion of the gain calculated in step 1 that is recaptured as ordinary income.

*Step 3.* Subtract the gain recaptured under § 1250 (step 2) from the gain derived in step 1. This amount is the *unrecaptured § 1250 gain.*

**EXAMPLE 51**

Linda placed two apartment buildings in service at a cost of $100,000 each. On each building, she claimed accelerated depreciation deductions of $78,000, and straight-line depreciation would have been $64,000. Thus, her adjusted basis for each building is $22,000 ($100,000 cost − $78,000 depreciation deducted), and her potential § 1250 recapture on each building is $14,000 ($78,000 accelerated depreciation − $64,000 straight-line). She now sells these buildings for $96,000 and $110,000, respectively, and computes her gain as follows.

|                                          | Building A | Building B |
|------------------------------------------|-----------:|-----------:|
| Amount realized                          | $ 96,000   | $110,000   |
| Adjusted basis                           | (22,000)   | (22,000)   |
| Recognized gain                          | $ 74,000   | $ 88,000   |
| Depreciation recaptured per § 1250       | (14,000)   | (14,000)   |
| Remaining gain                           | $ 60,000   | $ 74,000   |
| Unrecaptured § 1250 gain                 | (60,000)   | (64,000)   |
| § 1231 gain                              | None       | $ 10,000   |

For property placed in service after 1986, § 1250 generally does not apply, because such property may use only straight-line depreciation under MACRS. As a result, *all* of the gain attributable to depreciation on such assets is unrecaptured § 1250 gain.

**PLANNING STRATEGIES**

## Selling Depreciable Real Estate

**FRAMEWORK FOCUS: DEDUCTIONS**

> STRATEGY ➤ MAXIMIZE DEDUCTIBLE AMOUNTS.

**FRAMEWORK FOCUS: TAX RATE**

> STRATEGY ➤ CONTROL THE CHARACTER OF INCOME AND DEDUCTIONS.

A building depreciated on an accelerated method eventually generates annual allowances that are smaller than the amount that the straight-line method would have produced. Beyond that "cross-over" point, the *cumulative* amount of "additional depreciation" is reduced every year the asset is operated. Doing so effectively converts gain that would otherwise be subject to § 1250 recapture into "unrecaptured § 1250 gain," enabling the taxpayer to save the difference between the applicable tax rate on ordinary income and 25 percent.

Continuing to operate the building, however, brings forth an array of important *nontax considerations*. Each year a building is used subjects it to additional maintenance expenses to keep it in operating condition. Moreover, a building's appeal to current and prospective tenants tends to decline over time as newer structures appear offering more modern amenities, such as wireless high-speed Internet access, and other conveniences. Finally, local real estate developments might produce lower resale prices that offset much, if not all, of the tax advantage obtained by holding the property for the additional time.

## ADDITIONAL RECAPTURE FOR CORPORATIONS

Although depreciation recapture is generally the same for all taxpayers, corporations that sell depreciable real estate face an additional amount of depreciation recapture. Section 291(a)(1) requires recapture of 20 percent of the excess of the amount that would be recaptured under § 1245 over the amount actually recaptured under § 1250.

**EXAMPLE 52**

Franklin Corporation purchased an apartment building for $300,000. Accelerated depreciation was taken in the amount of $260,000 before the building was sold for $250,000. Straight-line depreciation would have been $245,000. The corporation's depreciation recapture and § 1231 gain are computed as follows.

| | |
|---|---:|
| Sales price | $250,000 |
| Less: Adjusted basis [$300,000 (cost of building) – $260,000 (MACRS depreciation)] | (40,000) |
| Recognized gain | $210,000 |
| Ordinary income if property were § 1245 property | $210,000 |
| Less: Gain recaptured under § 1250 ($260,000 – $245,000) | (15,000) |
| Excess § 1245 gain | $195,000 |
| Percentage that is ordinary gain | × 20% |
| Additional § 291 gain recaptured | $ 39,000 |
| Ordinary income from depreciation recapture ($15,000 + $39,000) | $ 54,000 |
| Section 1231 gain ($210,000 – $54,000) | 156,000 |
| Total recognized gain | $210,000 |

**EXAMPLE 53**

If the building in the preceding example were commercial property and straight-line depreciation was used, no § 1250 recapture results. A corporate taxpayer still must recapture as ordinary income 20% of the depreciation that would be ordinary income if the property were § 1245 property.

| | |
|---|---:|
| Sales price | $250,000 |
| Less: Adjusted basis [$300,000 (cost of building) – $245,000 (straight-line depreciation)] | (55,000) |
| Recognized gain | $195,000 |
| Ordinary income if property were § 1245 property | $195,000 |
| Less: Ordinary income under § 1250 | (–0–) |
| Excess ordinary income under § 1245 | $195,000 |
| Apply § 291 percentage | × 20% |
| Ordinary income under § 291 | $ 39,000 |

Thus, $39,000 of the $195,000 gain would be ordinary income, and $156,000 would be § 1231 gain. ▪

# Exceptions to §§ 1245 and 1250

Recapture under §§ 1245 and 1250 does not apply to the following transactions.

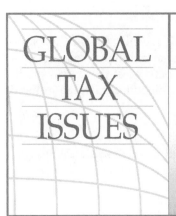

## EXCHANGE FOR FOREIGN PROPERTY YIELDS RECOGNIZED RECAPTURE GAIN

Tangible personal property used in a trade or business may be the subject of a like-kind exchange, and the postponed gain is most likely postponed § 1245 gain. However, tangible personal property used predominantly within the United States cannot be exchanged for tangible personal property used predominantly outside the United States. Thus, such an exchange would cause recognized gain, and, as long as the fair market value of the property given up does not exceed its original cost, all of the gain is § 1245 depreciation recapture gain.

## GIFTS

Depreciation recapture potential carries over to the donee.[27]

**EXAMPLE 54**

Wade gives his daughter, Helen, § 1245 property with an adjusted basis of $1,000. The amount of recapture potential is $700. Helen uses the property in her business and claims further depreciation of $100 before selling it for $1,900. Helen's recognized gain is $1,000 [$1,900 amount realized – $900 adjusted basis ($1,000 carryover basis – $100 depreciation taken by Helen)], of which $800 is recaptured as ordinary income ($100 depreciation taken by Helen + $700 recapture potential carried over from Wade). The remaining gain of $200 is § 1231 gain. Even if Helen had used the property for personal purposes, the $700 recapture potential would have carried over. ■

## DEATH

Although not an attractive tax planning approach, death eliminates all recapture potential.[28] Depreciation recapture potential does not carry over from a decedent to an estate or an heir.

**EXAMPLE 55**

Assume the same facts as in the preceding example, except that Helen receives the property as a result of Wade's death. The $700 recapture potential from Wade is extinguished at his death. Helen has a basis in the property equal to its fair market value (assume $1,700) at Wade's death. She will have a $300 gain when the property is sold because the selling price ($1,900) exceeds the property's adjusted basis of $1,600 ($1,700 basis to Helen – $100 depreciation) by $300. Because of § 1245, Helen has ordinary income of $100. The remaining gain of $200 is § 1231 gain. ■

## CHARITABLE TRANSFERS

Depreciation recapture potential reduces the amount of any charitable contribution deduction.[29]

---

[27]§§ 1245(b)(1) and 1250(d)(1) and Reg. §§ 1.1245–4(a)(1) and 1.1250–3(a)(1).
[28]§§ 1245(b)(2) and 1250(d)(2).

[29]§ 170(e)(1)(A) and Reg. § 1.170A–4(b)(1). In certain circumstances, § 1231 gain also reduces the amount of the charitable contribution. See § 170(e)(1)(B).

*EXAMPLE 56*

Bullfinch Corporation donates to a museum § 1245 property with a fair market value of $10,000 and an adjusted basis of $7,000. Depreciation recapture potential is $2,000 (the amount of recapture that would occur if the property were sold). The company's charitable contribution deduction (subject to the limitations discussed in Chapter 4) is $8,000 ($10,000 fair market value – $2,000 recapture potential). ◼

## CERTAIN NONTAXABLE TRANSACTIONS

In certain transactions, the transferor's adjusted basis for the property carries over to the transferee. Then, depreciation recapture potential also carries over to the transferee.[30] Included in this category are transfers of property pursuant to the following.

- Nontaxable incorporations under § 351.
- Certain liquidations of subsidiary companies under § 332.
- Nontaxable contributions to a partnership under § 721.
- Nontaxable corporate reorganizations.

Gain may be recognized in these transactions if boot is received. If gain is recognized, it is treated as ordinary income to the extent of the recapture potential or the recognized gain, whichever is lower.[31]

## LIKE-KIND EXCHANGES AND INVOLUNTARY CONVERSIONS

As explained in Chapter 6, realized gain is recognized to the extent of boot received in a like-kind exchange. Realized gain is also recognized to the extent the proceeds from an involuntary conversion are not reinvested in similar property. Such recognized gain is subject to recapture as ordinary income under §§ 1245 and 1250. Any remaining recapture potential carries over to the property received in the exchange.

*EXAMPLE 57*

Crane Corporation exchanges § 1245 property with an adjusted basis of $300 for § 1245 property with a fair market value of $6,000 plus $1,000 cash (boot). The exchange qualifies as a like-kind exchange under § 1031. Crane's realized gain is $6,700 ($7,000 amount realized – $300 adjusted basis of property).

Since Crane received boot of $1,000, it recognizes gain to this extent. Assuming the recapture potential is $7,500, Crane recognizes § 1245 gain of $1,000. The remaining recapture potential of $6,500 carries over to the like-kind property received. ◼

 *Find more information on this topic at our Web site: **http://wft-entities.swlearning.com.***

# Reporting Procedures

Noncapital gains and losses are reported on Form 4797, Sales of Business Property. Before filling out Form 4797, however, Form 4684, Casualties and Thefts, Part B, must be completed to determine whether any casualties will enter into the § 1231 computation procedure. Recall that gains from § 1231 asset casualties may be recaptured by § 1245 or § 1250. These gains do not appear on Form 4684. The § 1231 gains

---

[30]§§ 1245(b)(3) and 1250(d)(3). Reg. §§ 1.1245–2(a)(4) and (c)(2), 1.1245–4(c), 1.1250–2(d)(1) and (3).

[31]§§ 1245(b)(3) and 1250(d)(3), and Reg. §§ 1.1245–4(c) and 1.1250–3(c).

and nonpersonal-use long-term capital gains are netted against § 1231 and nonpersonal-use long-term capital losses on Form 4684 to determine if there is a net gain to transfer to Form 4797, Part I.

*Find more information on this topic at our Web site: **http://wft-entities.swlearning.com**.*

## Timing of Recapture

### FRAMEWORK FOCUS: TAX RATE

STRATEGY ➤ SHIFT NET INCOME FROM HIGH-BRACKET YEARS TO LOW-BRACKET YEARS.
➤ SHIFT NET INCOME FROM HIGH-BRACKET TAXPAYERS TO LOW-BRACKET TAXPAYERS.

Since recapture is usually not triggered until the property is sold or disposed of, it may be possible to plan for recapture in low-bracket or loss years. If a taxpayer has net operating loss carryovers that are about to expire, the recognition of ordinary income from recapture may be advisable to absorb the loss carryovers.

### EXAMPLE 58

Angel Corporation has a $15,000 net operating loss carryover that will expire this year. It owns a machine that it plans to sell in the early part of next year. The expected gain of $17,000 from the sale of the machine will be recaptured as ordinary income under § 1245. Angel sells the machine before the end of this year and offsets $15,000 of the ordinary income against the net operating loss carryover. ■

### POSTPONING AND SHIFTING RECAPTURE

It is also possible to postpone recapture or to shift the burden of recapture to others. For example, recapture is avoided upon the disposition of a § 1231 asset if the taxpayer replaces the property by entering into a like-kind exchange. In this instance, recapture potential is merely carried over to the newly acquired property (refer to Example 57).

Recapture can be shifted to others through the gratuitous transfer of § 1245 or § 1250 property to family members. A subsequent sale of such property by the donee will trigger recapture to the donee rather than the donor (refer to Example 54). This technique is advisable when the donee is in a lower income tax bracket than the donor.

## Summary

The lower tax rates afforded long-term capital gains present numerous definitional and computational challenges. Most of these rules are found in court decisions and regulations rather than in the Code. The tax professional needs to use good software to analyze all of the possibilities that are available.

## Suggested Further Readings

Charles F. Carroll, "Tax Loss Selling: Look Before You Leap," *Estate Planning*, February 2002, pp. 89–92.

Michael Schlesinger, "Consider Consulting and Noncompete Agreements When Selling a Business," *Practical Tax Strategies*, May 2002, pp. 260–270.

Louis S. Weller and Dean A. Halfacre, "Depreciating Replacement Property in Nonrecognition Exchanges," *Journal of Taxation*, May 2004, pp. 262–273.

## KEY TERMS

Additional depreciation, 7–34

Capital asset, 7–2

Capital gain, 7–3

Capital loss, 7–3

Collectibles, 7–18

Franchise, 7–11

Holding period, 7–13

Lessee, 7–12

Lessor, 7–12

Long-term nonpersonal-use capital assets, 7–27

Net capital gain, 7–20

Net capital loss, 7–20

Options, 7–8

Patent, 7–9

Qualified small business stock, 7–23

Sale or exchange, 7–7

Section 1231 gains and losses, 7–26

Section 1231 lookback, 7–30

Section 1231 property, 7–26

Section 1245 property, 7–33

Section 1245 recapture, 7–32

Section 1250 property, 7–34

Section 1250 recapture, 7–34

Short sale, 7–15

Unrecaptured § 1250 gain, 7–35

## PROBLEM MATERIALS

### Problems

1. Mariah had three property transactions during the year. She sold a vacation home used only for personal purposes at a $35,000 loss. The home had been held for five years and had never been rented. Mariah also sold an antique clock for $13,500 that she had inherited from her grandmother. The clock was valued in Mariah's grandmother's estate at $12,000. Mariah owned the clock for only four months. She sold these assets to finance her full-time occupation as a songwriter. Near the end of the year, Mariah sold one of the songs she had written two years earlier. She received cash of $50,000 and a royalty interest in revenues derived from the merchandising of the song. Mariah had no tax basis for the song. What is Mariah's gross income?

2. All of the following assets are held by Chuck, not in his trade or business. Which are capital assets?
   a. Ten shares of Green Motors common stock.
   b. A note Chuck received when he loaned $3,000 to a friend.
   c. Chuck's personal-use automobile.
   d. A letter written by Abraham Lincoln that Chuck purchased at an auction. Chuck is a collector of Lincoln memorabilia.

**Communications**

3. Hyacinth, Inc., is a dealer in securities. The firm has spotted a fast-rising company and would like to buy and hold its stock for investment. The stock is currently selling for $15 per share, and Hyacinth thinks it will climb to $63 a share within two years. How can Hyacinth ensure that any gain it realizes will be taxed as long-term capital gain? Draft a letter responding to Hyacinth's inquiry. The firm's address is 200 Morningside Drive, Hattisburg, MS 39406.

4. Eagle Partners has owned a large tract of land for 15 years and subdivides it for sale. Assume Eagle meets all the requirements of § 1237. During the first year of sales, Eagle sells 20 lots for $60,000 each. Its selling expenses are 7% of the sale price of each lot. Eagle has a basis of $51,000 in each lot. Compute the total gain from the sale of these lots and indicate the nature of the gain.

**Decision Making**

5. Swan Songs, Inc., is in the business of buying song copyrights from struggling songwriters, holding those copyrights, and then reselling the songs to major record companies and singers. Swan has a four-month option to purchase a song copyright. The firm paid $2,000 for this option. A famous singer has heard the song and is willing to buy the option for $10,000. Swan thinks the song may be worth $35,000 in six months. If Swan

exercises the option, it will have to pay $20,000 for the song. Assuming Swan is in the 34% tax bracket, which of these alternatives will give it a better after-tax cash flow?

**Issue ID**

6. Daffodil Enterprises Company purchased a one-year option on 20 acres of farmland for $245,000. Daffodil's plans for the property did not work out, so it let the option expire unexercised. What tax issues does the company face in determining how to treat the $245,000?

7. An investment partnership is looking for vacant land to buy. For $20,000, it is granted an 11-month option to buy 20 acres of vacant land for $400,000. The owner (who is holding the land for investment) paid $62,000 for the land several years ago.
   a. Does the landowner have gross income when $20,000 is received for granting the option?
   b. Does the partnership have an asset when the option is granted?
   c. If the option lapses, does the landowner have a recognized gain? If so, what type of gain? Does the partnership have a recognized loss? If so, what type of loss?
   d. If the option is exercised and an additional $400,000 is paid for the land, how much recognized gain does the seller have? What type of gain? What is the partnership's tax basis for the property?

8. Freys, Inc., sells a 12-year franchise to Red Company. The franchise contains many restrictions on how Red may operate its store. For instance, Red cannot use less than Grade 10 Idaho potatoes, must fry the potatoes at a constant 410 degrees, dress store personnel in Freys-approved uniforms, and have a Freys sign that meets detailed specifications on size, color, and construction. When the franchise contract is signed, Red makes a noncontingent $40,000 payment to Freys. During the same year, Red pays Freys $25,000—14% of Red's sales. How does Freys treat each of these payments? How does Red treat each of the payments?

**Issue ID**

9. Meredith, the owner of a sole proprietorship, is selling the assets of her business. The buyer is willing to pay $2,600 for various supplies (copy paper, folders, toner cartridges, etc.). Meredith deducted the $3,000 cost of these supplies as they were acquired. What issues does Meredith face from the sale of these supplies?

10. Tricia sells an automobile used in her business to her daughter, Felicia. Tricia has a realized loss of $9,000 on the sale even though the sale was for the full fair market value of the automobile. Tricia is unable to deduct this loss because of the loss disallowance rules for sales between related taxpayers. When does Felicia's holding period begin?

11. Magenta is an accrual basis corporation that is having cash-flow problems. It sells its account receivable to a financing company for 85% of the receivable's $236,000 face value. What is the nature of the loss from the disposition of the receivable?

**Communications**

12. Latisha Case has the following transactions this year.

| | |
|---|---|
| Long-term capital gain | $ 32,000 |
| Long-term capital loss | (25,000) |
| Short-term capital gain | 29,000 |
| Short-term capital loss | (33,000) |

What is her net capital gain or loss? Draft a letter to Latisha describing how the net capital gain or loss will be treated on her tax return. Assume Latisha's income from other sources puts her in the 35% bracket. Her address is 300 Ireland Avenue, Shepherdstown, WV 25443.

**Decision Making**

13. Sally has taxable income of $160,000 as of November 30 of this year. She wants to sell a Rodin sculpture that has appreciated $90,000 since she purchased it six years ago, but she does not want to pay more than $15,000 of additional tax on the transaction. Sally also owns various stocks, some of which are currently worth less than their basis. How can she achieve her desired result?

14. Platinum, Inc., has determined its taxable income as $215,000 before considering the results of its capital gain or loss transactions. Platinum has a short-term capital loss of

$24,000, a long-term capital loss of $38,000, and a short-term capital gain of $39,000. What is Platinum's taxable income, and what (if any) are the amount and nature of its capital loss carryover?

**Ethics**

15. The taxpayer is an antiques collector and is going to sell an antique purchased many years ago for a large gain. The facts and circumstances indicate that the taxpayer might be classified as a dealer rather than an investor in antiques. The taxpayer will save $40,000 in taxes if the gain is treated as long-term capital gain rather than as ordinary income. The taxpayer is considering the following options as ways to assure the $40,000 tax savings.

   * Give the antique to his daughter, who is an investment banker, to sell.
   * Merely assume that he has held the antique as an investment.
   * Exchange the antique in a like-kind exchange for another antique he wants.

   One of the tax preparers the taxpayer has contacted has said he would be willing to prepare the return under the second option. Would you? Why? Evaluate the other options.

**Issue ID**

16. Bridgette is known as the "doll lady." She started collecting dolls as a child, always received one or more dolls as gifts on her birthday, never sold any dolls, and eventually owned 600 dolls. She is retiring and moving to a small apartment and has decided to sell her collection. She lists the dolls on an Internet auction site and, to her great surprise, receives an offer from another doll collector of $45,000 for the entire collection. Bridgette sells the entire collection, except for five dolls that she purchased during the last year. She had owned all the dolls sold for more than a year. What tax factors should Bridgette consider in deciding how to report the sale?

**Communications**

17. A painting that Tulip & Co. held for investment was destroyed in a flood. The painting was insured, and Tulip had a $30,000 gain from this casualty. It also had a $27,000 loss from an uninsured antique vase that was destroyed by the flood. The vase was also held for investment. Tulip had no other property transactions during the year and has no nonrecaptured § 1231 losses from prior years. Compute Tulip's net gain or loss and identify how it would be treated. Write a letter to Tulip explaining the nature of the gain or loss. Tulip's address is 2000 Meridian Road, Hannibal Point, MO 34901.

18. During the year, Eric had the four property transactions summarized below. Eric is a collector of antique automobiles and occasionally sells one to get funds to buy another. What are the amount and nature of the gain or loss from each of these transactions?

| Property | Date Acquired | Date Sold | Adjusted Basis | Sale Price |
|---|---|---|---|---|
| Antique truck | 06/18/97 | 05/23/05 | $47,000 | $35,000 |
| Blue Growth Fund (100 shares) | 12/23/99 | 11/22/05 | 12,000 | 23,000 |
| Orange bonds | 02/12/00 | 04/11/05 | 34,000 | 42,000* |
| Green stock (100 shares) | 02/14/05 | 11/23/05 | 13,000 | 11,000 |

*The sale price included $750 of accrued interest income.

**Decision Making**

19. Mateen, an inventor, obtained a patent on a chemical process to clean old aluminum siding so that it can be easily repainted. Mateen has a zero tax basis in the patent. Mateen does not have the capital to begin manufacturing and selling this product, so he has done nothing with the patent since obtaining it two years ago.

   Now a group of individuals has approached him and offered two alternatives. Under one alternative, they will pay Mateen $400,000 (payable evenly over the next 10 years) for the exclusive right to manufacture and sell the product. Under the other, they will form a business and contribute capital to it to begin manufacturing and selling the product; Mateen will receive 20% of the company's shares of stock in exchange for all of his patent rights. Discuss which alternative is better for Mateen.

**Decision Making**

20. Sylvia owns two items of business equipment. They were both purchased in 2001 for $100,000, both have a seven-year recovery period, and both have an adjusted basis of $37,490. Sylvia is considering selling these assets in 2005. One of them is worth $40,000, and the other is worth $23,000. Since both items were used in her business, Sylvia simply assumes that the loss on one will be offset against the gain from the other and the net gain or loss will increase or reduce her business income. Is she correct?

**Ethics**

21. Harold, a CPA, has a new client who recently moved to town. Harold prepares the client's current-year tax return, which shows a net § 1231 gain. Harold calls the client to request copies of the returns for the preceding five years to determine if there are any § 1231 lookback losses. The client says that the returns are "still buried in the moving mess somewhere" and cannot be found. The client also says that he does not remember any § 1231 net losses on the prior-year returns. What should Harold do? Justify your answer.

22. Geranium, Inc., has the following net § 1231 results for each of the years shown. What is the nature of the net gain in 2004 and 2005?

| Tax Year | Net § 1231 Loss | Net § 1231 Gain |
|----------|-----------------|-----------------|
| 2000 | $16,000 | |
| 2001 | 43,000 | |
| 2002 | 32,000 | |
| 2003 | | $41,000 |
| 2004 | | 30,000 |
| 2005 | | 39,000 |

**Decision Making**

23. Delphinium Company owns two parcels of land (§ 1231 assets). One parcel can be sold at a loss of $30,000, and the other parcel can be sold at a gain of $40,000. The company has no nonrecaptured § 1231 losses from prior years. The parcels could be sold at any time because potential purchasers are abundant. The company has a $25,000 short-term capital loss carryover from a prior tax year and no capital assets that could be sold to generate long-term capital gains. What should Delphinium do based upon these facts?

24. Green Industries (a sole proprietorship) sold three § 1231 assets on October 10, 2005. Data on these property dispositions are as follows.

| Asset | Cost | Acquired | Depreciation | Sold for |
|-------|------|----------|--------------|----------|
| Rack | $100,000 | 10/10/01 | $60,000 | $75,000 |
| Forklift | 35,000 | 10/16/02 | 23,000 | 5,000 |
| Bin | 87,000 | 3/12/04 | 34,000 | 60,000 |

a. Determine the amount and the character of the recognized gain or loss from the disposition of each asset in 2005.
b. Assuming Green has no nonrecaptured net § 1231 losses from prior years, how much of the recognized gains are treated as long-term capital gains?

**Communications**

25. On December 1, 2003, Gray Manufacturing Company (a corporation) purchased another company's assets, including a patent. The patent was used in Gray's manufacturing operations; $40,500 was allocated to the patent, and it was amortized at the rate of $225 per month. On June 30, 2005, Gray sold the patent for $70,000. Twenty months of amortization had been taken on the patent. What are the amount and nature of the gain Gray recognizes on the disposition of the patent? Write a letter to Gray discussing the treatment of the gain. Gray's address is 6734 Grover Street, Back Bay Harbor, ME 23890. The letter should be addressed to Siddim Sadatha, Controller.

26. Dave is the sole proprietor of a trampoline shop. During 2005, the following transactions occurred.

- Unimproved land adjacent to the store was condemned by the city on February 1. The condemnation proceeds were $25,000. The land, acquired in 1983, had an allocable basis of $40,000. Dave has additional parking across the street and plans to use the condemnation proceeds to build his inventory.

- A truck used to deliver trampolines was sold on January 2 for $3,500. The truck was purchased on January 2, 2001, for $6,000. On the date of sale, the adjusted basis was $2,509.

- Dave sold an antique rowing machine at an auction. Net proceeds were $3,900. The rowing machine was purchased as used equipment 17 years ago for $5,200 and is fully depreciated.

- Dave sold an apartment building for $200,000 on September 1. The rental property was purchased on September 1, 2002, for $150,000 and was being depreciated over a 27.5-year life using the straight-line method. At the date of sale, the adjusted basis was $124,783.

- Dave's personal yacht was stolen on September 5. The yacht had been purchased in August at a cost of $25,000. The fair market value immediately preceding the theft was $20,000. Dave was insured for 50% of the original cost, and he received $12,500 on December 1.

- Dave sold a Buick on May 1 for $9,600. The vehicle had been used exclusively for personal purposes. It was purchased on September 1, 2001, for $20,800.

- Dave's trampoline stretching machine (owned two years) was stolen on May 5, but the business's insurance company will not pay any of the machine's value because Dave failed to pay the insurance premium. The machine had a fair market value of $8,000 and an adjusted basis of $6,000 at the time of theft.

- Dave had AGI of $402,000 from sources other than those described above.

- Dave has no nonrecaptured § 1231 lookback losses.

  a. For each transaction, what are the amount and nature of recognized gain or loss?
  b. What is Dave's 2005 AGI?

27. Vermilion Corporation sold a machine used in its business for $453,000 on the installment basis. It received a $53,000 down payment in 2005 and will receive payments of $100,000 (plus fair market value interest) for each of the next four years. The machine was originally purchased for $1 million in 1993 and had a zero adjusted basis at the time of its sale. How much gain must be recognized, when must it be recognized, and what is the nature of the gain from this sale?

28. Nicholas owns business equipment with a $155,000 adjusted basis; he paid $200,000 for the equipment, and it is currently worth $173,000. Nicholas dies suddenly, and his son Alvin inherits the property. What is Alvin's basis for the property, and what happens to the § 1245 depreciation recapture potential?

**EXTENDER** 29. Two years ago, Hsui Company (an unincorporated entity) developed a process for preserving fresh fruit that gives the fruit a much longer shelf life. The process is not patented or copyrighted, and only Hsui knows how it works. A conglomerate has approached Hsui with an offer to purchase the formula for the process. Specifically, the offer allows Hsui to choose between the following. Which option should Hsui accept?

  - $850,000 cash for the formula and a 10-year covenant not to compete, paying Hsui $45,000 per year for 10 years.

  - $850,000 cash for a 10-year covenant not to compete, and an annual $45,000 royalty for the formula, payable for 10 years.

**EXTENDER** 30. In March 2003, the Sue-Jen Partnership contracted for $100,000 to cut timber on a 100-acre tract of undeveloped South Dakota land. On January 1, 2004, the timber was worth $110,000. The value in November 2004 when the timber was cut was $115,000. On January 30, 2005, the wood was sold for $78,000.

a. If Sue-Jen elects to treat the timber cutting as a sale, what is its recognized gain or loss for 2003, 2004, and 2005?

b. In each case, what is the character of this gain or loss?

c. How does the result change if the wood is sold in December 2004? Why?

d. If the timber was worth only $48,000 on January 1, 2004, was cut in November when worth $21,000, and was sold in December for $49,000, how would the answers in (a) and (b) change?

**EXTENDER**   31. Thrasher Corporation sells short 100 shares of ARC stock at $20 per share on January 15, 2005. It buys 200 shares of ARC stock on April 1, 2005, at $25 per share. On May 2, 2005, Thrasher closes the short sale by delivering 100 of the shares purchased on April 1.

a. What are the amount and nature of Thrasher's loss upon closing the short sale?

b. When does the holding period for the remaining 100 shares begin?

c. If Thrasher sells (at $27 per share) the remaining 100 shares on January 20, 2006, what will be the nature of its gain or loss?

**BRIDGE DISCIPLINE**

1. Using an online research service, find the audited financial statements of a major U.S. corporation.

a. List some of the items that the corporation reports as having different treatment for tax and financial accounting purposes. These items often are mentioned in the footnotes to the statements.

b. List two or more such items that seem to increase the taxpayer's after-tax income and two or more that seem to decrease it.

## Research Problems

**THOMSON**
**RIA**

*Note: Solutions to Research Problems can be prepared by using the **RIA Checkpoint® Student Edition** online research product, which is available to accompany this text. It is also possible to prepare solutions to the Research Problems by using tax research materials found in a standard tax library.*

**Research Problem 1.**   Siva Nathaniel owns various plots of land in Fulton County, Georgia. He acquired the land at various times during the last 20 years. About every fourth year, Siva subdivides one of the properties he owns into lots. He then has water, sewer, natural gas, and electricity hookups put in on each lot and paves the new streets. Siva has always treated his sales of such lots as sales of capital assets. His previous tax returns were prepared by an accountant whose practice you recently purchased. Has the proper tax treatment been used on the prior tax returns?

*Partial list of research aids:*
*§§ 1221 and 1237.*
*Jesse W. and Betty J. English, 65 TCM 2160, T.C.Memo. 1993–111.*

**Research Problem 2.**   Ali owns 100 shares of Brown Corporation stock. He purchased the stock at five different times and at five different prices per share as indicated.

| Share Block | Number of Shares | Per Share Price | Purchase Date |
|---|---|---|---|
| A | 10 | $60 | 10/10/94 |
| B | 20 | 20 | 8/11/95 |
| C | 15 | 15 | 10/24/95 |
| D | 35 | 30 | 4/23/97 |
| E | 20 | 25 | 7/28/97 |

On April 28, 2005, Ali will sell 40 shares of Brown stock for $40 per share. All of Ali's shares are held by his stockbroker. The broker's records track when the shares were purchased. May Ali designate the shares he sells, and, if so, which shares should he sell? Assume Ali wants to maximize his gain because he has a capital loss carryforward.

**Research Problem 3.**  Sidney owns a professional football franchise. He has received an offer of $80 million for the franchise, all the football equipment, the rights to concession receipts, the rights to a stadium lease, and the rights to all the player contracts he owns. Most of the players have been with the team for quite a long time and have contracts that were signed several years ago. The contracts have been substantially depreciated. Sidney is concerned about potential § 1245 recapture when the contracts are sold. He has heard about "previously unrecaptured depreciation with respect to initial contracts" and would like to know more about it. Find a definition for that phrase and apply it to Sidney's situation.

**Communications**

**Research Problem 4.**  Clean Corporation runs a chain of dry cleaners. Borax is used heavily in Clean's dry cleaning process and has been in short supply several times in the past. Several years ago, Clean Corporation bought a controlling interest in Dig Corporation—a borax mining concern—to assure Clean of a continuous supply of borax if another shortage developed. Clean has just sold the stock at a loss because Dig is in difficult financial straits and because Clean has obtained an alternative source of borax. What is the nature of Clean's loss on the disposition of the Dig Corporation stock? Write a letter to the controller, Salvio Guitterez, that contains your advice and prepare a memo for the tax files. The mailing address of Clean Corporation is 4455 Whitman Way, San Mateo, CA 44589.

**Research Problem 5.**  Walter is both a real estate developer and the owner and manager of residential rental real estate. Walter is retiring and is going to sell both the land he is holding for future development and the rental properties he owns. Straight-line depreciation was used to depreciate the rental real estate. The rental properties will be sold at a substantial loss, and the development property will be sold at a substantial gain. What is the nature of these gains and losses?

*Partial list of research aids:*
§§ 1221 and 1231.
*Zane R. Tollis,* 65 TCM 1951, T.C.Memo. 1993–63.

**Communications**

**Research Problem 6.**  In 2005, a taxpayer made leasehold improvements that were eligible for a 15-year MACRS life. Straight-line depreciation will be taken on the improvements. Will these leasehold improvements be subject to either § 1245 or § 1250 depreciation recapture if they are eventually disposed of at a gain? Summarize your findings in an e-mail to your instructor.

**Internet Activity**

*Use the tax resources of the Internet to address the following question. Do not restrict your search to the World Wide Web, but include a review of newsgroups and general reference materials, practitioner sites and resources, primary sources of the tax law, chat rooms and discussion groups, and other opportunities.*

**Communications**

**Research Problem 7.**  Summarize tax planning strategies related to each of the following topics that are presented on the Internet by tax advisers looking for clients. Send your findings in an e-mail to your instructor.
a. A strategy for maximizing gains that are eligible for the 5%/15% alternative tax rate rather than the 25% rate.
b. A strategy for maximizing gains that are eligible for the 5%/15% alternative tax rate rather than the 28% rate.

**Communications**

**Research Problem 8.**  Find a Web site that discusses the income tax in England. Determine whether England has an alternative tax on net long-term capital gains similar to that in the United States. Summarize your findings in an e-mail to your instructor.

**Research Problem 9.**  Investors are flooded with performance data and rankings of mutual funds. The "tax efficiency" of these funds is much more difficult to determine, even though this information often has an enormous impact on taxable accounts (i.e., non-retirement-oriented accounts). Examine various Web sites to determine recent distribution history of mutual funds and compare their pre-tax and after-tax performance data to assess the impact of this information on investment planning.

**Research Problem 10.**   Go to the the IRS Web site and download a Form 4797 and its instructions. Use the form to complete Problem 24.

**Research Problem 11.**   How does your state tax the sale of a plot of investment land, owned by a resident of your state, but located in Arizona?

# Business Entities

PART

4

The materials in Parts I through III have dealt with tax concepts that generally are taxpayer neutral with respect to the different types of business entities. Some of these tax concepts are equally applicable to individual taxpayers. Part IV focuses on the different types of business entities and includes a life cycle coverage of formation, operations, and termination. The specific business entities covered are the C corporation, the S corporation, the partnership, and the LLC.

**CHAPTER 8**

Corporations: Organization, Capital Structure, and Operating Rules

**CHAPTER 9**

Corporations: Earnings & Profits and Dividend Distributions

**CHAPTER 10**

Partnerships and Limited Liability Entities

**CHAPTER 11**

S Corporations

http://wft.swlearning.com

# Corporations: Organization, Capital Structure, and Operating Rules

**CHAPTER 8**

## OUTLINE

---

## TAX TALK

*Taxes owing to the Government . . . are the price that business has to pay for protection and security.*

—Benjamin N. Cardozo

---

**B**usiness operations may be conducted in a number of different forms. As with many business decisions, consideration must be given to the tax consequences of choosing a particular business entity. This chapter deals with the unique tax consequences of operating an entity as a regular corporation, including:

- Classification of the entity as a corporation.
- The tax consequences to the shareholders and the corporation upon the formation of the corporation.
- The capital structure of the corporation.
- Determination of the corporate income tax liability.
- Corporate tax filing requirements.

---

# An Introduction to Corporate Tax

Corporations are governed by Subchapter C or Subchapter S of the Internal Revenue Code. Those governed by Subchapter C are referred to as **C corporations** or **regular corporations**. Corporations governed by Subchapter S are referred to as **S corporations.**

S corporations, which generally do not pay Federal income tax, are similar to partnerships in that net profit or loss flows through to the shareholders to be reported on their separate returns. Also like partnerships, S corporations do not aggregate all income and expense items in computing net profit or loss. Certain

## GLOBAL TAX ISSUES

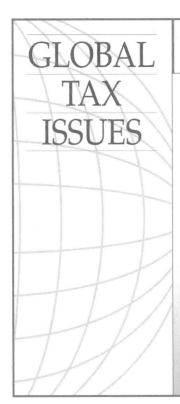

### CHOICE OF ORGANIZATIONAL FORM WHEN OPERATING OVERSEAS

When the management of a corporation decides to expand its business by establishing a presence in a foreign market, the new business venture may take one of several organizational forms. As each form comes with its respective advantages and disadvantages, making the best choice can be difficult.

One common approach is to conduct the foreign activity as a *branch* operation of the U.S. corporation. The foreign branch is not a separate legal entity, but a division of the U.S. corporation established overseas. As a result, any gains and losses produced by the foreign unit are included in the corporation's overall financial results.

Another possibility is to organize the foreign operations as a *subsidiary* of the U.S. parent corporation. If this route is chosen, the subsidiary may be either a *domestic* subsidiary (i.e., organized in the United States) or a *foreign* subsidiary (organized under the laws of a foreign country).

One fundamental tax difference between these two approaches is that the gains and losses of a domestic subsidiary may be consolidated with the operations of the U.S. parent, while the operations of a foreign subsidiary may not. Thus, the use of a domestic subsidiary to conduct foreign operations will yield generally the same final result as the use of a branch. With both approaches, the financial statements of the U.S. parent reflect the results of its worldwide operations.

items flow through to the shareholders and retain their separate character when reported on the shareholders' returns. See Chapter 11 for detailed coverage of S corporations.

### DOUBLE TAXATION OF CORPORATE INCOME

Unlike proprietorships, partnerships, and S corporations, C corporations are tax-paying entities. This results in what is known as a *double tax* effect. A C corporation reports its income and expenses on Form 1120 (or Form 1120–A, the corporate short form). The corporation computes tax on the taxable income reported on the corporate tax return using the rate schedule applicable to corporations (refer to the rate schedule inside the front cover of this text). When a corporation distributes its income, the corporation's shareholders report dividend income on their own tax returns. Thus, income that has already been taxed at the corporate level is also taxed at the shareholder level. The effects of double taxation are illustrated in Examples 1 and 2.

**EXAMPLE 1**

*⋆ Differences between C-Corp &*

Lavender Corporation earned net profit of $100,000 in 2005. It paid corporate tax of $22,250 (refer to the corporate rate schedule on the inside front cover of this text). This left $77,750, all of which was distributed as a dividend to Mike, the corporation's sole shareholder. Mike had taxable income of $69,550 ($77,750 – $5,000 standard deduction – $3,200 personal exemption). He paid tax at the 15% rate applicable to dividends. His tax was $10,433 ($69,550 × 15%). The combined tax on the corporation's net profit was $32,683 ($22,250 paid by the corporation + $10,433 paid by the shareholder). ■

**EXAMPLE 2**

*Sole Proprietorship*

Assume the same facts as in Example 1, except that the business is organized as a sole proprietorship. Mike reports the $100,000 net profit from the business on his tax return. He has taxable income of $91,800 ($100,000 – $5,000 standard deduction – $3,200 personal exemption) and pays tax of $20,211. Therefore, operating the business as a sole proprietorship resulted in tax *savings* of $12,472 in 2005 ($32,683 tax from Example 1 – $20,211). ■

## CORPORATIONS' REPORTING RESPONSIBILITIES

Like individuals, corporations are required to report their taxable income and other financial information to the IRS on an annual basis. The forms used depend on the type and size of the corporation. Based on projections, the IRS expects to receive over 6 million corporate income tax returns during the 2005 filing season.

| Type of Corporation | Form | Percentage |
|---------------------|------|-----------|
| C Corporation | 1120 | 36.4% |
| C Corporation | 1120–A | 3.6 |
| S Corporation | 1120S | 60.0 |
|  |  | 100.0% |

Interestingly, only about 1.1 percent of C and S corporations are expected to submit their returns electronically.

**Source:** Projections of Returns That Will Be Filed in Calendar Years 2004–2010, *SOI Bulletin*, Winter 2003–2004.

Examples 1 and 2 deal with a specific set of facts. The conclusions reached in this situation cannot be extended to all decisions about a form of business organization. Each specific set of facts and circumstances requires a thorough analysis of the tax factors. In many cases, the tax burden will be greater if the business is operated as a corporation (as in Example 1), but sometimes operating as a corporation can result in tax savings, as illustrated in Examples 3 and 4.

**EXAMPLE 3**

In 2005, Tan Corporation filed Form 1120 reporting net profit of $100,000. The corporation paid tax of $22,250 and distributed the remaining $77,750 as a dividend to Carla, the sole shareholder of the corporation. Carla had income from other sources and was in the top individual tax bracket of 35% in 2005. As a result, she paid tax of $11,663 ($77,750 × 15% rate on dividends) on the distribution. The combined tax on the corporation's net profit was $33,913 ($22,250 paid by the corporation + $11,663 paid by the shareholder). ■

**EXAMPLE 4**

Assume the same facts as in Example 3, except that the business is a sole proprietorship. Carla reports the $100,000 net profit from the business on her tax return and pays tax of $35,000 ($100,000 net profit × 35% marginal rate). Therefore, operating the business as a sole proprietorship resulted in a tax *cost* of $1,087 in 2005 ($35,000 – $33,913 tax from Example 3). ■

Shareholders in closely held corporations frequently attempt to avoid double taxation by paying out all the profit of the corporation as salary to themselves.

**EXAMPLE 5**

Orange Corporation has net income of $180,000 during the year ($300,000 revenue – $120,000 operating expenses). Emilio is the sole shareholder of Orange Corporation. In an effort to avoid tax at the corporate level, Emilio has Orange pay him a salary of $180,000, which results in zero taxable income for the corporation. ■

**TAX IN THE NEWS**

## IMPACT OF THE DIVIDEND TAX CUT

The Bush administration's 2003 reduction of the tax rate on dividends to 15 percent led to much speculation as to how the cut would affect corporate dividend policy. Here is some information gleaned from the financial press on the impact to date.

- On December 2, 2004, Microsoft paid a special dividend of $32 billion to its shareholders, representing the largest dividend payout on record.
- At least 10 major corporations, including Reebok, Viacom, and Costco, paid dividends for the first time.
- Many corporations, including more than 250 of the Standard and Poor's 500, have increased the rate of dividend payouts.
- Prices of dividend-paying stocks have increased considerably relative to prices of stocks that do not pay dividends.

Although the linkage between the dividend tax cut and increased dividend payouts appears strong, additional research is needed to determine the strength of the cause-and-effect relationship.

Will the strategy described in Example 5 effectively avoid double taxation? The answer depends on whether the compensation paid to the shareholder is *reasonable*. Section 162 provides that compensation is deductible only to the extent that it is reasonable in amount. The IRS is aware that many taxpayers use this strategy to bail out corporate profits and, in an audit, looks closely at compensation expense.

If the IRS believes that compensation is too high based on the amount and quality of services performed by the shareholder, the compensation deduction of the corporation is reduced to a reasonable amount. Compensation that is determined to be unreasonable is usually treated as a constructive dividend to the shareholder and is not deductible by the corporation.

**EXAMPLE 6**

Assume the same facts as in Example 5, and that the IRS determines that $80,000 of the amount paid to Emilio is unreasonable compensation. As a result, $80,000 of the corporation's compensation deduction is disallowed and treated as a constructive dividend to Emilio. Orange has taxable income of $80,000. Emilio would report salary of $100,000 and a taxable dividend of $80,000. The net effect is that $80,000 would be subject to double taxation. ■

**Taxation of Dividends.** The Jobs and Growth Tax Relief Reconciliation Act (JGTRRA) of 2003 reduced the impact of double taxation. Before 2003, dividends received by individuals were subject to the same rates as ordinary income. JGTRRA changed the top individual rate from 38.6 percent to 35 percent and the rate on dividend income to 15 percent (5 percent for low-income taxpayers).

The new tax-favored treatment of dividends will have a marked impact on many closely held corporations. Prior to JGTRRA, the motivation was to avoid paying dividends, as they were nondeductible to the corporation and fully taxed to the shareholders (as illustrated in Examples 1 and 3 above). To counter this problem of double taxation, corporate profits were bailed out in a manner that provided tax benefits to the corporation (refer to Example 5). Hence, liberal use was made of compensation, loan, and lease arrangements, as salaries, interest, and rent are deductible items. Now, a new variable has been interjected. Who should benefit? Shareholders will prefer dividends because salaries, interest, and rent are fully

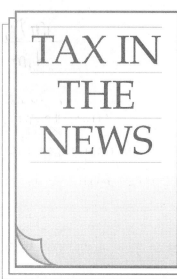

### CORPORATE TAX BREAKS

Although rates in the corporate tax schedule range from 15 percent to 39 percent, a recent Government Accountability Office study found that fewer than 40 percent of U.S. corporations paid *any* Federal income taxes from 1996 to 2000. The Commerce Department provides additional evidence of the low tax burden borne by U.S. corporations. Throughout the 1990s, the average rate paid by U.S. corporations was approximately 30 percent. Since 2001, the rate has been approximately 20 percent. A Duke University study found that the rate in 2002 was 12 percent, compared to 15 percent in 1999 and 18 percent in 1995. All of these studies show that the actual rate of Federal income tax paid by corporations is low and that it has declined steadily from the early 1990s through 2002.

SOURCE: "Corporate Tax Burden Shows Sharp Decline," *Wall Street Journal*, April 13, 2004, pp. C1–C3.

taxed, while dividends are taxed at the new 15 percent rate (5 percent for low-income taxpayers). Corporations, however, will continue to favor distributions that are deductible (e.g., salaries, interest, and rent). The ideal will be a good mix of the two approaches. Besides being attractive to shareholders, the payment of dividends helps the corporation ease the problems of unreasonable compensation, thin capitalization, and meeting the arm's length test as to rents. Chapter 9 presents a detailed discussion of the taxation of dividends.

## COMPARISON OF CORPORATIONS AND OTHER FORMS OF DOING BUSINESS

Chapter 14 presents a detailed comparison of sole proprietorships, partnerships, S corporations, and C corporations as forms of doing business. However, it is appropriate at this point to consider some of the tax and nontax factors that favor corporations over other business entities.

Consideration of tax factors requires an examination of the corporate rate structure. The income tax rate schedule applicable to corporations is reproduced on the inside front cover of the text. As this schedule shows, corporate rates on taxable income up to $75,000 are lower than individual rates for persons in the 28 percent and higher brackets. Therefore, corporate tax will be lower than individual tax. Furthermore, only the corporate marginal rates of 38 and 39 percent are higher than the 35 percent top bracket for individuals. When dividends are paid, however, the double taxation problem occurs.

Another tax consideration involves the nature of dividend income. All income and expense items of a proprietorship retain their character when reported on the proprietor's tax return. In the case of a partnership, several separately reported items (e.g., charitable contributions and long-term capital gains) retain their character when passed through to the partners. However, the tax attributes of income and expense items of a corporation do not pass through the corporate entity to the shareholders.

Losses of a C corporation are treated differently than losses of a proprietorship, partnership, or S corporation. A loss incurred by a proprietorship may be deductible by the owner, because all income and expense items are reported by the proprietor. Partnership and S corporation losses are passed through the entity and may be deductible by the partners or shareholders. C corporation losses, however, have no effect on the taxable income of the shareholders.

**Bridge to Finance**

Investment brokers and promoters often try to entice individuals to invest their disposable income in ventures designed to produce handsome returns. In most situations, the type of business entity in which the funds are invested takes the form of a "flow-through" entity, such as a limited partnership. Such investment ventures rarely operate as regular corporations.

A limited partnership is the favored investment vehicle for several reasons. One of the most significant reasons is that the investors who become limited partners are protected from exposure to unlimited liability. In addition, any operating losses of the entity (which may be expected in the venture's early years) flow through to the partners and, as a result, may provide an immediate tax benefit on the partners' returns. Another major advantage of the partnership form, in contrast to the corporate form, is that the business earnings are subject to only one level of tax—at the partner or investor level. If the investments were housed in a corporation, a tax would be levied first on the corporate earnings and then at the investor level when the corporation makes distributions to the shareholders.

**EXAMPLE 7**

Franco plans to start a business this year. He expects the business will incur operating losses for the first three years and then become highly profitable. Franco decides to operate as an S corporation during the loss period because the losses will flow through and be deductible on his personal return. When the business becomes profitable, he intends to switch to C corporation status. ■

## NONTAX CONSIDERATIONS

Nontax considerations will sometimes override tax considerations and lead to the conclusion that a business should be operated as a corporation. The following are some of the more important nontax considerations:

- Sole proprietors and *general* partners in partnerships face the danger of *unlimited liability*. That is, creditors of the business may file claims not only against the assets of the business but also against the *personal* assets of proprietors or general partners. Shareholders are protected from claims against their personal assets by state corporate law.
- The corporate form of business organization can provide a vehicle for raising large amounts of capital through widespread stock ownership. Most major businesses in the United States are operated as corporations.
- Shares of stock in a corporation are freely transferable, whereas a partner's sale of his or her partnership interest is subject to approval by the other partners.
- Shareholders may come and go, but a corporation can continue to exist. Death or withdrawal of a partner, on the other hand, may terminate the existing partnership and cause financial difficulties that result in dissolution of the entity. Thus, *continuity of life* is a distinct advantage of the corporate form of doing business.
- Corporations have *centralized management*. All management responsibility is assigned to a board of directors, which appoints officers to carry out the corporation's business. Partnerships, by contrast, may have decentralized management, in which every owner has a right to participate in the organization's business decisions; **limited partnerships**, though, may have centralized management. Centralized management is essential for the smooth operation of a widely held business.

*Definition
Limited Partnerships
Page C-10*

*[handwritten margin note:]* *Definition Limited Liability Company –Page C-10*

## LIMITED LIABILITY COMPANIES

The **limited liability company (LLC)** has proliferated greatly in recent years, particularly since 1988 when the IRS first ruled that it would treat qualifying LLCs as partnerships for tax purposes. All 50 states and the District of Columbia have passed laws that allow LLCs, and thousands of companies have chosen LLC status. As with a corporation, operating as an LLC allows its owners to avoid unlimited liability, which is a primary *nontax* consideration in choosing this form of business organization. The tax advantage of LLCs is that qualifying businesses may be treated as partnerships for tax purposes, thereby avoiding the problem of double taxation associated with regular corporations.

Some states allow an LLC to have centralized management, but not continuity of life or free transferability of interests. Other states allow LLCs to adopt any or all of the corporate characteristics of centralized management, continuity of life, and free transferability of interests. The comparison of business entities in Chapter 14 includes a discussion of LLCs.

## ENTITY CLASSIFICATION

*[handwritten margin note:]* *Definition Check-The-Box Regulation –Page C-4*

In late 1996, the IRS issued its so-called **check-the-box Regulations.**[1] Effective beginning in 1997, the Regulations enable taxpayers to choose the tax status of a business entity without regard to its corporate (or noncorporate) characteristics. These rules have simplified tax administration considerably and eliminated the type of litigation that arose under prior law.

Under these rules, entities with more than one owner can elect to be classified as either a partnership or a corporation. An entity with only one owner can elect to be classified as a sole proprietorship or as a corporation. In the event of default (i.e., no election is made), multi-owner entities are classified as partnerships and single-person businesses as sole proprietorships.

The election is not available to entities that are actually incorporated under state law or to entities that are required to be corporations under Federal law (e.g., certain publicly traded partnerships). Otherwise, LLCs are not treated as being incorporated under state law. Consequently, they can elect either corporation or partnership status.

DIGGING DEEPER 1    *Find more information on this topic at our Web site:* ***http://wft-entities.swlearning.com.***

---

**PLANNING STRATEGIES**

## Consolidated Groups May Utilize Check-the-Box Regulations

**FRAMEWORK FOCUS: THINKING OUTSIDE THE FRAMEWORK**

The check-the-box Regulations allow a single-owner eligible entity to be treated as a corporation or a division. Since LLCs are eligible entities, a C corporation that owns 100 percent of an LLC can treat the LLC as a division. At the same time, the parent corporation can enjoy the benefit of limited liability in the LLC operations. By electing division treatment, the income of the LLC flows directly to the parent corporation for tax purposes. Consequently, the parent corporation is able to avoid detailed and complex consolidated return Regulations and filing requirements.

---

[1]Reg. §§ 301.7701–1 through –4, and –7.

## LO.1

Identify the tax consequences of incorporating and transferring assets to controlled corporations.

*Gain/Loss = Fair Market Value − Tax Basis of Property Transferred*

# Organization of and Transfers to Controlled Corporations

## IN GENERAL

Property transactions normally produce tax consequences if a gain or loss is realized. As a result, unless special provisions in the Code apply, a transfer of property to a corporation in exchange for stock is a taxable transaction. The amount of gain or loss is measured by the difference between the fair market value of the stock received and the tax basis of the property transferred.

The Code, however, does permit nonrecognition of gain or loss in limited circumstances. For example, when a taxpayer exchanges some of his or her property for other property of a like kind, § 1031 provides that gain (or loss) on the exchange is deferred because there has not been a substantive change in the taxpayer's investment. The deferral of gain or loss is accomplished by calculating a substituted basis for the like-kind property received. With this substituted basis, the potential gain or loss on the property given up is recognized when the property received in the exchange is sold.

In a similar fashion, § 351 provides for the nonrecognition of gain or loss upon the transfer of property to a corporation in exchange for stock. The nonrecognition of gain or loss under § 351 reflects the principle that gain should not be recognized when a taxpayer's investment has not substantively changed. When a business is incorporated, the owner's economic status remains the same; only the *form* of the investment has changed. The investment in the business assets carries over to an investment in corporate stock. When only stock in the corporation is received, the shareholder is hardly in a position to pay a tax on any realized gain. As noted later, however, when the taxpayer receives property other than stock (i.e., *boot*) from the corporation, realized gain may be recognized.

The same principles govern the nonrecognition of gain or loss under § 1031 and § 351. The concept of nonrecognition of gain or loss, present in both provisions, causes gain or loss to be deferred until a substantive change in the taxpayer's investment occurs (such as a sale to or a taxable exchange with third parties). This approach is justified under the wherewithal to pay concept discussed in Chapter 1. A further justification for the nonrecognition of gain or loss provisions under § 351 is that tax rules should not impede the exercise of sound business judgment (e.g., choice of business entity).

**EXAMPLE 8**

Ron is considering incorporating his donut shop. He is concerned about his personal liability for the shop's obligations. Ron realizes that if he incorporates the shop, he will be liable only for the debts of the business that he has personally guaranteed. If Ron incorporates, the following assets will be transferred to the corporation:

|  | Tax Basis | Fair Market Value |
|---|---|---|
| Cash | $10,000 | $ 10,000 |
| Furniture and fixtures | 20,000 | 60,000 |
| Land and building | 40,000 | 100,000 |
|  | $70,000 | $170,000 |

In exchange, Ron will receive stock in the newly formed corporation worth $170,000. Without the nonrecognition provisions of § 351, Ron would recognize a taxable gain of $100,000 ($170,000 − $70,000) on the transfer. Under § 351, however, Ron does not recognize any gain because his economic status has not changed. Ron's investment in the assets of his unincorporated donut shop ($70,000) carries over to his investment in the incorporated donut shop, which is now represented by his ownership of stock in the incorporated donut shop. Thus, § 351 provides for tax neutrality on the initial incorporation of Ron's donut shop. ■

*wherewithal to Pay – Page C-19*

When a taxpayer participates in a like-kind exchange, gain is deferred to the extent that the taxpayer receives like-kind property. The taxpayer must recognize any realized gain when receiving "boot" (i.e., property of an unlike kind). For example, if a taxpayer exchanges a truck used in a business for another truck to be used in the business and also receives cash, the taxpayer has the wherewithal to pay an income tax on the cash involved. Further, the taxpayer's economic status has changed to the extent of the cash (not like-kind property) received. Thus, any "realized" gain on the exchange is recognized to the extent of the cash received. In like manner, if a taxpayer transfers property to a corporation and receives money or property other than stock, § 351(b) provides that gain is recognized to the extent of the lesser of the gain realized or the boot received (the amount of money and the fair market value of other property received). Gain is characterized according to the type of asset transferred.[2] Loss on a § 351 transaction is never recognized. The nonrecognition of gain or loss is accompanied by a substituted basis in the shareholder's stock.[3]

**EXAMPLE 9**

Abby and Bill form White Corporation. Abby transfers property with an adjusted basis of $30,000 and a fair market value of $60,000 for 50% of White's stock. Bill transfers property with an adjusted basis of $70,000 and a fair market value of $60,000 for the remaining 50% of the stock. The transfers qualify under § 351. Abby has a deferred gain of $30,000, and Bill has a deferred loss of $10,000. Both have a substituted basis in the stock of White Corporation. Abby has a basis of $30,000 in her stock, and Bill has a basis of $70,000 in his stock. Assume instead that Abby receives stock and cash of $10,000. Abby would recognize a gain of $10,000. ■

Section 351 is mandatory if a transaction satisfies the provision's requirements. There are three requirements for nonrecognition of gain or loss: (1) *property* is transferred (2) in exchange for *stock* and (3) the transferors must be in *control* of the transferee corporation immediately after the transfer. These three requirements are discussed below.

## TRANSFER OF PROPERTY

*Definition Property – page C-14*

Questions have arisen concerning what constitutes **property** for purposes of § 351. The Code specifically excludes services rendered from the definition of property. With this exception, the definition of property is comprehensive. For example, along with plant and equipment, unrealized receivables for a cash basis taxpayer and installment obligations are considered property.[4] The transfer of an installment obligation in a transaction qualifying under § 351 is not a disposition of the installment obligation. Thus, gain is not recognized to the transferor. Secret processes and formulas, as well as secret information in the general nature of a patentable invention, also qualify as property under § 351.[5]

Services are not considered to be property under § 351 for a critical reason. A taxpayer must report as income the fair market value of any consideration received

---

[2]Rev.Rul. 68–55, 1968–1 C.B. 140.
[3]§ 358(a). See the discussion preceding Example 28.
[4]*Hempt Brothers, Inc. v. U.S.*, 74–1 USTC ¶9188, 33 AFTR2d 74–570, 490 F.2d 1172 (CA–3, 1974), and Reg. § 1.453–9(c)(2).

[5]Rev.Rul. 64–56, 1964–1 C.B. 133; Rev.Rul. 71–564, 1971–2 C.B. 179.

as compensation for services rendered.[6] Thus, if a taxpayer receives stock in a corporation as consideration for rendering services to the corporation, the taxpayer has taxable income. In this case, the amount of income recognized by the taxpayer is equal to the fair market value of the stock received. The taxpayer's basis in the stock received is its fair market value.

**EXAMPLE 10**

Ann and Bob form Brown Corporation and transfer the following consideration:

| | Consideration Transferred | | |
| --- | --- | --- | --- |
| | Basis to Transferor | Fair Market Value | Number of Shares Issued |
| From Ann: | | | |
| Personal services rendered to Brown Corporation | $ –0– | $20,000 | 200 |
| From Bob: | | | |
| Installment obligation | 5,000 | 40,000 | |
| Inventory | 10,000 | 30,000 | 800 |
| Secret process | –0– | 10,000 | |

The value of each share in Brown Corporation is $100.[7] Ann has taxable income of $20,000 on the transfer because services do not qualify as "property." She has a basis of $20,000 in her 200 shares of stock in Brown. Bob recognizes no gain on the transfer because all of the consideration he transferred to Brown qualifies as "property" and he has "control" of Brown after the transfer. (See the discussion concerning control below.) Bob has a substituted basis of $15,000 in the Brown stock. ∎

If property is transferred to a corporation in exchange for any property other than stock, the property received constitutes boot. The boot is taxable to the transferor-shareholder to the extent of any realized gain.[8]

## STOCK

Generally, the term "stock" needs no clarification. It includes both common stock and most preferred stock. However, the Regulations state that the term "stock" does not include stock rights and stock warrants.[9] In addition, it does not include "nonqualified preferred stock," which possesses many of the attributes of debt.[10]

Thus, any corporate debt or **securities** (i.e., long-term debt, such as bonds) are treated as boot because they are not an equity interest or stock. Thus, the receipt of debt in exchange for the transfer of appreciated property to a controlled corporation causes recognition of gain.

*Definition
Securities
– Page C-17

## CONTROL OF THE CORPORATION

For a transaction to qualify as nontaxable under § 351, the transferor(s) of the property must be in **control** of the corporation immediately after the exchange. Control means that the person or persons transferring *property* must have at least

*Definition
control
– Page C-5

---

[6]§§ 61 and 83.

[7]The value of closely held stock normally is presumed to be equal to the value of the property transferred.

[8]§ 351(b).

[9]Reg. § 1.351–1(a)(1)(ii).

[10]§ 351(g). Examples of nonqualified preferred stock include preferred stock that is redeemable within 20 years of issuance and whose dividend rate is based on factors other than corporate performance. Therefore, gain is recognized up to the fair market value of the nonqualified preferred stock received. Loss may be recognized when the transferor receives *only* nonqualified preferred stock (or nonqualified preferred stock and other boot) in exchange for property. See also Reg. § 1.351–1(a)(1)(ii).

an 80 percent stock ownership in the transferee corporation. The transferor-shareholders must own stock possessing at least 80 percent of the total combined voting power of all classes of stock entitled to vote *and* at least 80 percent of the total *number* of shares of all other classes of stock.[11]

### Control Immediately after the Transfer.

Immediately after the exchange, the property transferors must control the corporation. Control can apply to a single person or to several taxpayers if they are all parties to an integrated transaction. The Regulations provide that when more than one person is involved, the exchange does not necessarily require simultaneous exchanges by two or more persons. The Regulations do, however, require that the rights of the parties (i.e., those transferring property to the corporation) be previously set out and determined. Also, the agreement to transfer property should be executed "with an expedition consistent with orderly procedure."[12]

If two or more persons transfer property to a corporation for stock, the transfers should occur close together in time and should be made in accordance with an agreement among the parties.

**EXAMPLE 11**

Jack exchanges property with a basis of $60,000 and a fair market value of $100,000 for 70% of the stock of Gray Corporation. The other 30% is owned by Jane, who acquired it several years ago. The fair market value of Jack's stock is $100,000. Jack recognizes a taxable gain of $40,000 on the transfer because he does not have control immediately after the exchange and his transaction cannot be integrated with Jane's for purposes of the control requirement. ■

**EXAMPLE 12**

Lana, Leo, and Lori incorporate their respective businesses by forming Green Corporation. Lana exchanges her property for 300 shares in Green on January 6, 2005. Leo exchanges his property for 400 shares in Green on January 12, 2005, and Lori exchanges her property for 300 shares in Green on March 5, 2005. The three exchanges are part of a prearranged plan, so the control requirement is met. The nonrecognition provisions of § 351 apply to all of the exchanges. ■

Stock need not be issued to the property transferors in the same proportion as the relative value of the property transferred by each. However, when stock received is not proportionate to the value of the property transferred, the actual effect of the transaction must be properly characterized. For example, in such situations one transferor may actually be making a gift of valuable consideration to another transferor.

**EXAMPLE 13**

Ron and Shelia, father and daughter, form Oak Corporation. Ron transfers property worth $50,000 in exchange for 100 shares of stock, while Shelia transfers property worth $50,000 for 400 shares of stock. The transfers qualify under § 351 because Ron and Shelia have control of the Oak stock immediately after the transfers of property. However, the implicit gift by Ron to Shelia must be recognized and appropriately characterized. As such, the value of the gift might be subject to the gift tax. ■

Once control has been achieved, it is not necessarily lost if stock received by shareholders in a § 351 exchange is sold or given to persons who are not parties to the exchange shortly after the transaction. However, failure to meet the control requirement might result if a *plan* for the ultimate disposition of the stock existed *before* the exchange.[13]

---

[11]§ 368(c). Nonqualified preferred stock is treated as stock, and not boot, for purposes of this control test.
[12]Reg. § 1.351–1(a)(1).

[13]*Wilgard Realty Co. v. Comm.*, 42–1 USTC ¶9452, 29 AFTR 325, 127 F.2d 514 (CA–2, 1942).

**EXAMPLE 14**

Mark and Carl form Black Corporation. They transfer appreciated property to the corporation with each receiving 50 shares of the stock. Shortly after the formation, Mark gives 25 shares to his son. Because Mark was not committed to make the gift, he is considered to own his original shares of Black Corporation stock and, along with Carl, to control Black Corporation "immediately after the exchange." The requirements of § 351 are met, and neither Mark nor Carl is taxed on the exchange. Alternatively, had Mark immediately given 25 shares to a business associate pursuant to a plan to satisfy an outstanding obligation, the formation of Black would be taxable to Mark and Carl because of their lack of control. ∎

## PLANNING STRATEGIES — Utilizing § 351

**FRAMEWORK FOCUS: INCOME AND EXCLUSIONS**

**STRATEGY ➤ AVOID INCOME RECOGNITION.**

When using § 351(a), ensure that all parties transferring property (including cash) receive control of the corporation. Simultaneous transfers are not necessary, but a long period of time between transfers makes the transaction vulnerable to taxation if the transfers are not properly documented as part of a single plan. To do this, the parties should document and preserve evidence of their intentions. Also, it is helpful to have some reasonable explanation for any delay in the transfers.

To meet the requirements of § 351, mere momentary control on the part of the transferor may not suffice if loss of control is compelled by a prearranged agreement.[14]

**EXAMPLE 15**

For many years, Todd operated a business as a sole proprietor employing Linda as manager. To dissuade Linda from quitting and going out on her own, Todd promised her a 30% interest in the business. To fulfill this promise, Todd transferred the business to newly formed Green Corporation in return for all its stock. Immediately thereafter, Todd transfers 30% of the stock to Linda. As a consequence, he no longer meets the 80% control requirement. Section 351 probably does not apply to Todd's transfer to Green Corporation. It appears that Todd was under an obligation to relinquish control. If this is not the case and the loss of control was voluntary on Todd's part, momentary control would suffice.[15] ∎

Be sure that later transfers of property to an existing corporation satisfy the 80 percent control requirement if recognition of gain is to be avoided. Also with respect to later transfers, a transferor's interest cannot be counted if the value of stock received is relatively small compared with the value of stock already owned. Further, the primary purpose of the transfer may not be to qualify other transferors for § 351 treatment.[16]

**Transfers for Property and Services.** Section 351 treatment is lost if stock is transferred to persons who did not contribute property, causing those who did to lack control immediately after the exchange.

**EXAMPLE 16**

Kate transfers property with a value of $60,000 and a basis of $5,000 for 600 shares of stock in newly formed Wren Corporation. Brian receives 400 shares in Wren for services rendered to the corporation. Each share of stock is worth $100. Both Kate and Brian have taxable gain on the transaction. Brian is not part of the control group because he does not transfer property for stock. He has taxable income of $40,000 (400 shares × $100). Kate has a taxable gain of $55,000 [$60,000 (fair market value of the stock in Wren Corporation) − $5,000 (basis in the transferred property)]. Kate is taxed on the exchange because she receives only 60% of the stock in Wren Corporation. ∎

[14]Rev.Rul. 54–96, 1954–1 C.B. 111.
[15]Compare *Fahs v. Florida Machine and Foundry Co.*, 48–2 USTC ¶9329, 36 AFTR 1161, 168 F.2d 957 (CA–5, 1948), with *John C. O'Connor*, 16 TCM 213, T.C.Memo. 1957–50, *aff'd* in 58–2 USTC ¶9913, 2 AFTR2d 6011, 260 F.2d 358 (CA–6, 1958).
[16]Reg. § 1.351–1(a)(1)(ii).

A person who performs services for the corporation in exchange for stock and also transfers some property is treated as a member of the transferring group. That person is taxed on the value of the stock issued for services but not on the stock issued for property. In such a case, all the stock received by the person transferring both property and services is counted in determining whether the transferors acquired control of the corporation.[17]

**EXAMPLE 17**

Assume the same facts as in Example 16, except that Brian transfers property worth $30,000 (basis of $3,000) in addition to services rendered to the corporation (valued at $10,000). Now Brian becomes a part of the control group. Kate and Brian together receive 100% of the stock in Wren Corporation. Consequently, § 351 is applicable to the exchanges. Kate has no recognized gain. Brian does not recognize gain on the transfer of the property, but he has taxable income to the extent of the value of the shares issued for services rendered. Thus, Brian recognizes income of $10,000.  ■

**Transfers for Services and Nominal Property.**    To be a member of the group and aid in qualifying all transferors under the 80 percent control test, the person contributing services must transfer property having more than a "relatively small value" compared to the value of services performed. Section 351 will not apply when a small amount of property is transferred and the primary purpose of the transfer is to qualify the transaction under § 351 for concurrent transferors.[18]

**EXAMPLE 18**

Kim and Eric transfer property to Redbird Corporation, each in exchange for one-third of the stock. Howie receives the other one-third of the stock for services rendered. The transaction will not qualify under § 351 because Howie is not a member of the group transferring property and Kim and Eric together received only 66⅔% of the stock. Thus, the post-transfer control requirement is not met.

Assume instead that Howie also transfers property. Then he is a member of the group, and the transaction qualifies under § 351. Howie is taxed on the value of the stock issued for services, but the remainder of the transaction is tax-free. However, if the property transferred by Howie is of a relatively small value in comparison to the stock he receives for his services, and the primary purpose for transferring the property is to cause the transaction to be tax-free for Kim and Eric, the exchange does not qualify under § 351. Gain or loss is recognized by all parties.  ■

The IRS generally requires that before a transferor who receives stock for both property and services can be included in the control group, the value of the property transferred must be at least 10 percent of the value of the services provided.[19] If the value of the property transferred is less than this amount, the IRS will not issue an advance ruling that the exchange meets the requirements of § 351.

**EXAMPLE 19**

Sara and Rick form White Corporation. Sara transfers land (worth $100,000, basis of $20,000) for 50% of the stock in White. Rick transfers equipment (worth $5,000, adjusted basis of $1,000) and provides services worth $95,000 for 50% of the stock. Rick's stock in White Corporation is unlikely to be counted in determining control for purposes of § 351; thus, the control requirement is not met. None of Rick's stock is counted in determining control because the property he transfers has a nominal value in comparison to the value of the services he renders. Sara recognizes $80,000 of gain on the transfer of the land. She has a basis of $100,000 in her White stock. Rick must recognize income of $95,000 on the transfer

---

[17]Reg. § 1.351–1(a)(2), Ex. 3.
[18]Reg. § 1.351–1(a)(1)(ii).

[19]Rev.Proc. 77–37, 1977–2 C.B. 568.

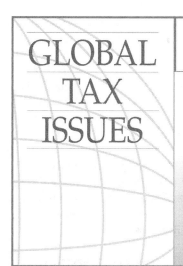

## GLOBAL TAX ISSUES

### DOES § 351 COVER THE INCORPORATION OF A FOREIGN BUSINESS?

When a taxpayer wishes to incorporate a business overseas by moving assets across U.S. borders, the deferral mechanism of § 351 applies in certain situations, but not in others. In general, § 351 is available to defer gain recognition when starting up a new corporation outside the United States unless so-called tainted assets are involved. Under § 367, tainted assets, which include assets such as inventory and accounts receivable, are treated as having been sold by the taxpayer prior to the corporate formation; therefore, their transfer results in the current recognition of gain. The presence of tainted assets triggers gain because Congress does not want taxpayers to be able to shift the gain outside of U.S. jurisdiction. The gain recognized is ordinary or capital, depending on the nature of the asset involved.

for services rendered and a gain of $4,000 for the property transferred. Rick also has a $100,000 basis in his White stock. ■

**Transfers to Existing Corporations.**   Once a corporation is in operation, § 351 also applies to any later transfers of property for stock by either new or existing shareholders.

**EXAMPLE 20**

Sam and Beth formed Blue Corporation three years ago. Both Sam and Beth transferred appreciated property to Blue in exchange for 500 shares each in the corporation. The original transfers qualified under § 351, and neither Sam nor Beth was taxed on the exchange. In the current year, Sam transfers property (worth $100,000, adjusted basis of $5,000) for 500 additional Blue shares. Sam has a taxable gain of $95,000 on the transfer. The exchange does not qualify under § 351 because Sam does not have 80% control of Blue Corporation immediately after the transfer; he owns 1,000 shares of the 1,500 shares outstanding, or a 66⅔% interest. ■

If current shareholders transfer property with a small value relative to the value of stock already owned, a special rule applies (similar to the nominal property rule noted previously). In particular, if the purpose of the transfer is to qualify a transaction under § 351, the ownership of the current shareholders is not counted when determining control. Thus, in the preceding example, if Beth had contributed $200 for one share of stock at the time of Sam's contribution, Beth's ownership would not count toward the 80 percent control requirement and Sam would still have a taxable exchange.

**LO.2**

Understand the special rules that apply when a corporation assumes a shareholder's liability.

### ASSUMPTION OF LIABILITIES—§ 357

Without a provision to the contrary, the transfer of mortgaged property to a controlled corporation could require recognition of gain by the transferor if the corporation took over the mortgage. This would be consistent with the rule in like-kind exchanges under § 1031. Liabilities assumed by the other party are considered the equivalent of cash and treated as boot received. Section 357(a) provides, however, that when the acquiring corporation **assumes a liability** in a § 351 transaction, the transfer does *not* result in boot to the transferor-shareholder. Nevertheless, liabilities assumed by the transferee corporation are treated as boot in determining the

*Definition
Assumes a
liability
—page C-3

basis of the stock received. As a result, the basis of the stock received is reduced by the amount of the liabilities assumed by the corporation.

**EXAMPLE 21**

Vera transfers property with an adjusted basis of $60,000, fair market value of $100,000, to Gray Corporation for 100% of the stock in Gray. The property is subject to a liability of $25,000 that Gray Corporation assumes. The exchange is tax-free under §§ 351 and 357. However, the basis to Vera of the Gray stock is $35,000 [$60,000 (basis of property transferred) – $25,000 (amount of the liability assumed by Gray)]. ∎

The general rule of § 357(a) has two exceptions: (1) § 357(b) provides that if the principal purpose of the assumption of the liabilities is to avoid tax *or* if there is no bona fide business purpose behind the exchange, the liabilities are treated as boot; and (2) § 357(c) provides that if the sum of the liabilities exceeds the adjusted basis of the properties transferred, the excess is taxable gain.

**Exception (1): Tax Avoidance or No Bona Fide Business Purpose.** Unless liabilities are incurred shortly before incorporation, § 357(b) generally poses few problems. A tax avoidance purpose for transferring liabilities to a controlled corporation normally is not a concern in view of the basis adjustment as noted above. Since the liabilities transferred reduce the basis of the stock received, any realized gain merely is deferred and not completely eliminated. Any postponed gain is recognized when and if the stock is disposed of in a taxable sale or exchange.

Satisfying the bona fide business purpose is not difficult if the liabilities were incurred in connection with the transferor's normal course of conducting a trade or business. But the bona fide business purpose requirement can cause difficulty if the liability is taken out shortly before the property is transferred and the proceeds are utilized for personal purposes.[20] This type of situation is analogous to a cash distribution by the corporation, which is taxed as boot.

**EXAMPLE 22**

Dan transfers real estate (basis of $40,000 and fair market value of $90,000) to a controlled corporation in return for stock in the corporation. Shortly before the transfer, Dan mortgages the real estate and uses the $20,000 of proceeds to meet personal obligations. Thus, along with the real estate, the mortgage is transferred to the corporation. In this case, the assumption of the mortgage lacks a bona fide business purpose. Consequently, the release of the liability is treated as boot received, and Dan has a taxable gain on the transfer of $20,000, computed as follows:[21]

| | |
|---|---:|
| Stock | $ 70,000 |
| Release of liability—treated as boot | 20,000 |
| Total amount realized | $ 90,000 |
| Less: Basis of real estate | (40,000) |
| Realized gain | $ 50,000 |
| Recognized gain | $ 20,000 |

∎

The effect of the application of § 357(b) is to taint *all* liabilities transferred, even if some are supported by a bona fide business purpose.

---

[20]See, for example, *Campbell, Jr. v. Wheeler*, 65–1 USTC ¶9294, 15 AFTR2d 578, 342 F.2d 837 (CA–5, 1965).

[21]§ 351(b).

**EXAMPLE 23**

Tim, an accrual basis taxpayer, incorporates his sole proprietorship. Among the liabilities transferred to the new corporation are trade accounts payable of $100,000 and a credit card bill of $5,000. Tim had used the credit card to purchase a wedding anniversary gift for his wife. Under these circumstances, the *entire* $105,000 of liabilities is boot and triggers the recognition of gain to the extent gain is realized. ■

**Exception (2): Liabilities in Excess of Basis.** Section 357(c) states that, if the amount of the liabilities assumed *exceeds* the total of the adjusted bases of the properties transferred, the excess is taxable gain. Without this provision, if liabilities exceed basis in property exchanged, a taxpayer would have a negative basis in the stock received in the controlled corporation.[22] Section 357(c) precludes the negative basis possibility by treating the excess over basis as gain to the transferor.

**EXAMPLE 24**

Andre transfers land and equipment with adjusted bases of $35,000 and $5,000, respectively, to a newly formed corporation in exchange for 100% of the stock. The corporation assumes $50,000 of liabilities on the transferred land. Without § 357(c), Andre's basis in the stock of the new corporation would be a negative $10,000 [$40,000 (bases of properties transferred) + $0 (gain recognized) – $0 (boot received) – $50,000 (liabilities assumed)]. Section 357(c), however, causes Andre to recognize a gain of $10,000 ($50,000 liabilities assumed – $40,000 bases of assets transferred). As a result, the stock has a zero basis in Andre's hands, determined as follows:

| | |
|---|---|
| Bases in the properties transferred ($35,000 + $5,000) | $ 40,000 |
| Plus: Gain recognized | 10,000 |
| Less: Boot received | (–0–) |
| Less: Liabilities assumed | (50,000) |
| Basis in the stock received | $  –0– |

Thus, Andre recognizes $10,000 of gain, and a negative stock basis is avoided. ■

The definition of liabilities under § 357(c) excludes obligations that would have been deductible to the transferor had those obligations been paid before the transfer. Thus, accounts payable of a cash basis taxpayer that give rise to a deduction are not considered to be liabilities for purposes of § 357(c). In addition, they are not considered in the computation of stock basis.

**EXAMPLE 25**

Tina, a cash basis taxpayer, incorporates her sole proprietorship. In return for all of the stock of the new corporation, she transfers the following items:

| | Adjusted Basis | Fair Market Value |
|---|---|---|
| Cash | $10,000 | $10,000 |
| Unrealized accounts receivable (amounts due to Tina but not yet received by her) | –0– | 40,000 |
| Trade accounts payable | –0– | 30,000 |
| Note payable | 5,000 | 5,000 |

---

[22]*Jack L. Easson,* 33 T.C. 963 (1960), *rev'd* in 61–2 USTC ¶9654, 8 AFTR2d 5448, 294 F.2d 653 (CA–9, 1961).

Unrealized accounts receivable and trade accounts payable have a zero basis. Under the cash method of accounting, no income is recognized until the receivables are collected, and no deduction materializes until the payables are satisfied. The note payable has a basis because it was issued for consideration received.

In this situation, the trade accounts payable are disregarded for gain recognition purposes and in determining Tina's stock basis. Thus, because the balance of the note payable does not exceed the basis of the assets transferred, Tina does not have a problem of liabilities in excess of basis (i.e., the note payable of $5,000 does not exceed the aggregate basis in the cash and accounts receivable of $10,000). ■

If §§ 357(b) and (c) both apply to the same transfer, § 357(b) dominates.[23] This could be significant because § 357(b) does not create gain on the transfer, as does § 357(c), but merely converts the liability to boot. Thus, the realized gain limitation continues to apply to § 357(b) transactions.

**EXAMPLE 26**

Chris owns land with a basis of $100,000 and a fair market value of $1 million. The land is subject to a mortgage of $300,000. One month prior to transferring the land to Robin Corporation, Chris borrows an additional $200,000 for personal purposes and gives the lender a second mortgage on the land. Therefore, upon the incorporation, Robin Corporation issues stock worth $500,000 to Chris and assumes the mortgages on the land.

Both § 357(c) and § 357(b) apply to the transfer. The mortgages on the property ($500,000) exceed the basis of the property ($100,000). Thus, Chris has a gain of $400,000 under § 357(c). Chris borrowed $200,000 just prior to the transfer and used the loan proceeds for personal purposes. Under § 357(b), Chris has boot of $500,000 in the amount of the liabilities. Note that *all* of the liabilities are treated as boot, not just the "tainted" $200,000 liability. He has realized gain of $900,000 [$1,000,000 (stock of $500,000 and assumption of liabilities of $500,000) – $100,000 (basis in the land)]. Gain is recognized to the extent of the boot of $500,000. Section 357(b) dominates over § 357(c). ■

## PLANNING STRATEGIES

# Avoiding § 351

**FRAMEWORK FOCUS: TAX RATE**

**STRATEGY** ▶ **SHIFT NET INCOME FROM HIGH-BRACKET YEARS TO LOW-BRACKET YEARS.**
▶ **CONTROL THE CHARACTER OF INCOME AND DEDUCTIONS.**

Section 351(a) provides for the nonrecognition of gain on transfers to controlled corporations. As such, it is often regarded as a relief provision favoring taxpayers. In some situations, however, avoiding § 351(a) may produce a more advantageous tax result. The transferors might prefer to recognize gain on the transfer of property if the tax cost is low. For example, they may be in low tax brackets, or the gain may be a capital gain from which substantial capital losses can be offset. Also, recognition of gain will lead to a stepped-up basis in the transferred property in the corporation.

Another reason a particular transferor might wish to avoid § 351 concerns possible loss recognition. Recall that § 351 refers to the nonrecognition of both gains and losses. Section 351(b)(2) specifically states: "No loss to such recipient shall be recognized." A transferor who wishes to recognize loss has several alternatives:

——————————
[23]§ 357(c)(2)(A).

- Sell the property to the corporation for its stock. The IRS could attempt to collapse the "sale," however, by taking the approach that the transfer really falls under § 351(a).[24]
- Sell the property to the corporation for other property or boot. Because the transferor receives no stock, § 351 is inapplicable.
- Transfer the property to the corporation in return for securities or nonqualified preferred stock. Recall that § 351 does not apply to a transferor who receives securities or nonqualified preferred stock. In both this and the previous alternatives, watch for the possible disallowance of the loss under the related-party rules.

Suppose loss property is to be transferred to the corporation and no loss is recognized by the transferor due to § 351(a). This could present an interesting problem in terms of assessing the economic realities involved.

---

**EXAMPLE 27**

Iris and Ivan form Wren Corporation with the following investments: property by Iris (basis of $40,000 and fair market value of $50,000) and property by Ivan (basis of $60,000 and fair market value of $50,000). Each receives 50% of the Wren stock. Has Ivan acted wisely in settling for only 50% of the stock? At first, it would appear so, since Iris and Ivan each invested property of the same value ($50,000). But what about tax considerations? Due to the carryover basis rules, the corporation now has a basis of $40,000 in Iris's property and $60,000 in Ivan's property. In essence, Iris has shifted a possible $10,000 gain to the corporation while Ivan has transferred a $10,000 potential loss. With this in mind, an equitable allocation of the Wren stock would call for Ivan to receive a greater percentage interest than Iris. ■

---

## LO.3

Recognize the basis issues relevant to the shareholder and the corporation.

## BASIS DETERMINATION AND OTHER ISSUES

Recall that § 351(a) postpones gain or loss recognition until the taxpayer's investment changes substantively. By virtue of the basis rules described below, the postponed gain or loss is recognized when the stock is disposed of in a taxable transaction.

**Basis of Stock to Shareholder.**  For a taxpayer transferring property to a corporation in a § 351 transaction, the basis of *stock* received in the transaction is the same as the basis the taxpayer had in the property transferred, increased by any gain recognized on the exchange and decreased by boot received. For basis purposes, boot received includes any liabilities transferred by the shareholder to the corporation. Also note that if the shareholder receives any *other property* (i.e., boot) along with the stock, it takes a basis equal to its fair market value.[25]

**Basis of Property to Corporation.**  The basis of property received by the corporation is the basis of the exchanged property in the hands of the transferor increased by the amount of any gain recognized by the transferor-shareholder.[26]

The basis rules are summarized in Figures 8–1 and 8–2 and illustrated in Examples 28 and 29.

**EXAMPLE 28**

Maria and Ned form Brown Corporation. Maria transfers land (basis of $30,000 and fair market value of $70,000); Ned invests cash ($60,000). They each receive 50 shares in Brown Corporation, worth $1,200 per share, but Maria also receives $10,000 cash from Brown. The transfers of property, the realized and recognized gain on the transfers, and the basis of the stock in Brown Corporation to Maria and Ned are as follows:

---

[24]*U.S. v. Hertwig,* 68–2 USTC ¶9495, 22 AFTR2d 5249, 398 F.2d 452 (CA–5, 1968).

[25]§ 358(a).
[26]§ 362(a).

| | |
|---|---|
| Adjusted basis of property transferred | $xx,xxx |
| Plus: Gain recognized | x,xxx |
| Minus: Boot received (including any liabilities transferred) | (x,xxx) |
| Equals: Basis of stock received | $xx,xxx |

| | |
|---|---|
| Adjusted basis of property transferred | $xx,xxx |
| Plus: Gain recognized by transferor-shareholder | xxx |
| Equals: Basis of property to corporation | $xx,xxx |

| | A | B | C | D | E | F |
|---|---|---|---|---|---|---|
| | Basis of Property Transferred | FMV of Stock Received | Boot Received | Realized Gain (B + C − A) | Recognized Gain (Lesser of C or D) | Basis of Stock in Brown (A − C + E) |
| **From Maria:** | | | | | | |
| Land | $30,000 | $60,000 | $10,000 | $40,000 | $10,000 | $30,000 |
| **From Ned:** | | | | | | |
| Cash | 60,000 | 60,000 | –0– | –0– | –0– | 60,000 |

Brown Corporation has a basis of $40,000 in the land: Maria's basis of $30,000 plus her recognized gain of $10,000. ■

**EXAMPLE 29**

Assume the same facts as in Example 28 except that Maria's basis in the land is $68,000 (instead of $30,000). Because recognized gain cannot exceed realized gain, the transfer generates only $2,000 of gain to Maria. The realized and recognized gain and the basis of the stock in Brown Corporation to Maria are as follows:

| | A | B | C | D | E | F |
|---|---|---|---|---|---|---|
| | Basis of Property Transferred | FMV of Stock Received | Boot Received | Realized Gain (B + C − A) | Recognized Gain (Lesser of C or D) | Basis of Stock in Brown (A − C + E) |
| Land | $68,000 | $60,000 | $10,000 | $2,000 | $2,000 | $60,000 |

Brown's basis in the land is $70,000 ($68,000 basis to Maria + $2,000 gain recognized by Maria). ■

## Stock Issued for Services Rendered.

A corporation's transfer of stock for property is not a taxable exchange.[27] A transfer of shares for services is also not a

---

[27]§ 1032.

taxable transaction to a corporation.[28] Can a corporation deduct the fair market value of the stock it issues in consideration of services as a business expense? Yes, unless the services are such that the payment is characterized as a capital expenditure.[29]

**EXAMPLE 30**

Carol and Carl form White Corporation. Carol transfers cash of $500,000 for 100 shares of White Corporation stock. Carl transfers property worth $400,000 (basis of $90,000) and agrees to serve as manager of the corporation for one year; in return, Carl receives 100 shares of stock in White. The value of Carl's services to White Corporation is $100,000. Carol's and Carl's transfers qualify under § 351. Neither Carol nor Carl is taxed on the transfer of their property. However, Carl has income of $100,000, the value of the services he will render to White Corporation. White has a basis of $90,000 in the property it acquired from Carl, and it may claim a compensation expense deduction under § 162 for $100,000. Carl's stock basis is $190,000 ($90,000 + $100,000). ■

**EXAMPLE 31**

Assume, in the preceding example, that Carl receives the 100 shares of White Corporation stock as consideration for the appreciated property and for providing legal services in organizing the corporation. The value of Carl's legal services is $100,000. Carl has no gain on the transfer of the property but has income of $100,000 for the value of the services rendered. White Corporation has a basis of $90,000 in the property it acquired from Carl and must capitalize the $100,000 as an organizational expense. Carl's stock basis is $190,000 ($90,000 + $100,000). ■

**Holding Period for Shareholder and Transferee Corporation.** The shareholder's holding period for stock received for a capital asset or for § 1231 property includes the holding period of the property transferred to the corporation. The holding period of the property is *tacked on* to the holding period of the stock. The holding period for stock received for any other property (e.g., inventory) begins on the day after the exchange. The transferee corporation's holding period for property acquired in a § 351 transfer is the holding period of the transferor-shareholder regardless of the character of the property to the transferor.[30]

### RECAPTURE CONSIDERATIONS

In a pure § 351(a) nontaxable transfer (no boot involved) to a controlled corporation, the recapture of accelerated cost recovery rules do not apply.[31] Instead, any recapture potential of the property carries over to the corporation as it steps into the shoes of the transferor-shareholder for purposes of basis determination. However, to the extent that gain is recognized, the recapture rules are applied.

**EXAMPLE 32**

Paul transfers equipment (adjusted basis of $30,000, original cost of $120,000, and fair market value of $100,000) to a controlled corporation in return for additional stock. If Paul had sold the equipment, it would have yielded a gain of $70,000, all of which would be recaptured as ordinary income under § 1245. If the transfer comes within § 351(a), Paul has no recognized gain and no accelerated cost recovery to recapture. If the corporation later disposes of the equipment in a taxable transaction, it must take into account the § 1245 recapture potential originating with Paul.

---

[28]Reg. § 1.1032–1(a).
[29]Rev.Rul. 62–217, 1962–2 C.B. 59, modified by Rev.Rul. 74–503, 1974–2 C.B. 117.

[30]§§ 1223(1) and (2).
[31]§§ 1245(b)(3) and 1250(d)(3).

If Paul had received boot of $60,000 on the transfer, all of the recognized gain would be recaptured as ordinary income. The remaining $10,000 of recapture potential would carry over to the corporation. ■

## Other Considerations When Incorporating a Business

### FRAMEWORK FOCUS: TAX RATE

STRATEGY ➤ CONTROL THE CHARACTER OF INCOME AND DEDUCTIONS.
        ➤ SHIFT NET INCOME FROM HIGH-BRACKET TAXPAYERS TO LOW-BRACKET TAXPAYERS.

### FRAMEWORK FOCUS: DEDUCTIONS

STRATEGY ➤ MAXIMIZE DEDUCTIBLE AMOUNTS.

### FRAMEWORK FOCUS: INCOME AND EXCLUSIONS

STRATEGY ➤ AVOID INCOME RECOGNITION.

When a business is incorporated, the organizers must determine which assets and liabilities should be transferred to the corporation. A transfer of assets that produce passive income (rents, royalties, dividends, and interest) can cause the corporation to be a personal holding company in a tax year when operating income is low. Thus, the corporation could be subject to the personal holding company penalty tax (see the discussion in Chapter 9).

A transfer of the accounts payable of a cash basis taxpayer may prevent the taxpayer from taking a tax deduction when the accounts are paid. These payables should generally be retained.

Leasing property to the corporation may be a more attractive alternative than transferring ownership. Leasing provides the taxpayer with the opportunity of withdrawing money from the corporation in a deductible form without the payment being characterized as a nondeductible dividend. If the property is donated to a family member in a lower tax bracket, the lease income can be shifted as well. If the depreciation and other deductions available in connection with the property are larger than the lease income, a high tax rate taxpayer could retain the property until the income exceeds the deductions.

Another way to shift income to other taxpayers is by the use of corporate debt. Shareholder debt in a corporation can be given to family members with low marginal tax rates. This technique also shifts income without a loss of control of the corporation.

---

**LO.4**

Understand the tax aspects of the capital structure of a corporation.

# Capital Structure of a Corporation

## CAPITAL CONTRIBUTIONS

When a corporation receives money or property in exchange for capital stock (including treasury stock), neither gain nor loss is recognized by the recipient corporation.[32] The corporation's gross income also does not include shareholders' contributions of money or property to the capital of the corporation. Additional funds received from shareholders through voluntary pro-rata payments are not income to the corporation. This is the case even though there is no increase in the number of outstanding shares of stock of the corporation. The payments represent

---

[32]§ 1032.

an additional price paid for the shares held by the shareholders (increasing their basis) and are treated as additions to the operating capital of the corporation.[33]

Contributions by nonshareholders, such as land contributed to a corporation by a civic group or a governmental group to induce the corporation to locate in a particular community, are also excluded from the gross income of a corporation.[34] However, property that is transferred to a corporation by a nonshareholder in exchange for goods or services rendered is taxable income to the corporation.[35]

**EXAMPLE 33**

A cable company charges its customers an initial fee to hook up to a new cable system installed in the area. These payments are used to finance the total cost of constructing the cable facilities. The customers will make monthly payments for the cable service. The initial payments are used for capital expenditures, but they represent payments for services to be rendered by the cable company. As such, they are taxable income and not contributions to capital by nonshareholders. ∎

*Definition capital contribution — pages C-3- C-4*

The basis of property received by a corporation from a shareholder as a **capital contribution** is equal to the basis of the property in the hands of the shareholder. The basis of property transferred to a corporation by a nonshareholder as a contribution to capital is zero.

If a corporation receives *money* as a contribution to capital from a nonshareholder, a special rule applies. The basis of any property acquired with the money during a 12-month period beginning on the day the contribution was received is reduced by the amount of the contribution. The excess of money received over the cost of new property is used to reduce the basis of other property held by the corporation and is applied in the following order:

* Depreciable property.
* Property subject to amortization.
* Property subject to depletion.
* All other remaining properties.

The basis of property within each category is reduced in proportion to the relative bases of the properties.[36]

**EXAMPLE 34**

A city donates land to Brown Corporation as an inducement for Brown to locate in the city. The receipt of the land produces no taxable income to Brown, and the land's basis to the corporation is zero. If, in addition, the city gives the corporation $10,000 in cash, the money is not taxable income to the corporation. However, if the corporation purchases property with the $10,000 within the next 12 months, the basis of the property is reduced by $10,000. Any excess cash not used is handled according to the ordering rules noted above. ∎

**LO.5**

Recognize the tax differences between debt and equity investments.

## DEBT IN THE CAPITAL STRUCTURE

**Advantages of Debt.** Significant tax differences exist between debt and equity in the capital structure, and shareholders must be aware of these differences. The advantages of issuing long-term debt are numerous. Interest on debt is deductible by the corporation, while dividend payments are not. Further, the shareholders are

---

[33]§ 118 and Reg. § 1.118–1.

[34]See *Edwards v. Cuba Railroad Co.*, 1 USTC ¶139, 5 AFTR 5398, 45 S.Ct. 614 (USSC, 1925).

[35]Reg. § 1.118–1. See also *Teleservice Co. of Wyoming Valley*, 27 T.C. 722 (1957), *aff'd* in 58–1 USTC ¶9383, 1 AFTR2d 1249, 254 F.2d 105 (CA–3, 1958), *cert. den.* 78 S.Ct. 1360 (USSC, 1958).

[36]§ 362(c); Reg. §§ 1.362–2(b) and 1.118–1.

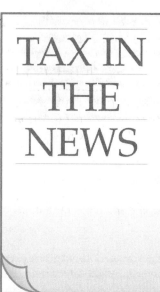

## CONFLICT ARISES BETWEEN CORPORATIONS AND THEIR SHAREHOLDERS

Throughout the history of income taxation in the United States, applicable law has favored financing regular corporations with debt rather than equity. This corporate preference for debt exists because interest is deductible by the corporation, while dividends are not. Thus, if a corporation raises capital by issuing debt, the deductibility of the interest reduces the after-tax cost of obtaining financing. From the shareholders' perspective, the difference between debt and equity was not important because both interest and dividend income were taxed at ordinary income tax rates.

Now, with most dividend income being taxed at lower rates than interest income, investors will have a bias toward dividends. In contrast, corporations will still prefer debt financing because interest payments remain deductible while dividend payments are not. The chart in Example 35 illustrates this divergence between corporate and shareholder preferences. It will be interesting to see how the market will respond.

not taxed on debt repayments unless the repayments exceed basis. An investment in stock usually cannot be withdrawn tax-free as long as a corporation has earnings and profits. Withdrawals will be deemed to be taxable dividends to the extent of earnings and profits of the distributing corporation. (The concept of earnings and profits is discussed in Chapter 9.) Beginning in 2003, the advantages of debt over equity from the investor's perspective have lessened. Dividend income on equity holdings now is taxed to individual investors at the low capital gains rates, while interest income on debt continues to be taxed at the higher ordinary income rates.

**EXAMPLE 35**

Wade transfers cash of $100,000 to a newly formed corporation for 100% of the stock. In the first year of operations, the corporation has net income of $40,000. If the corporation distributes $9,500 to Wade, the distribution is a taxable dividend with no corresponding deduction to the corporation. Assume, instead, that Wade transfers to the corporation cash of $50,000 for stock. In addition, he lends the corporation $50,000. The note is payable in equal annual installments of $5,000 and bears interest at the rate of 9%. At the end of the year, the corporation pays Wade interest of $4,500 ($50,000 × 9%), and a note repayment of $5,000. The interest payment is taxable to Wade and deductible to the corporation. The $5,000 principal repayment on the loan is neither taxed to Wade nor deductible by the corporation. The after-tax impact to Wade and the corporation under each alternative is illustrated below.

|  | If the Distribution Is | |
| --- | --- | --- |
|  | **$9,500 Dividend** | **$5,000 Note Repayment and $4,500 Interest** |
| *After-tax benefit to Wade** | | |
| [$9,500 × (1 − 15%)] | $8,075 | |
| {$5,000 + [$4,500 × (1 − 35%)]} | | $7,925 |
| *After-tax cost to corporation*** | | |
| No deduction to corporation | 9,500 | |
| {$5,000 + [$4,500 × (1 − 35%)]} | | 7,925 |

\*Assumes Wade's dividend income is taxed at the 15% capital gains rate and his interest income is taxed at the 35% ordinary income rate.
\*\*Assumes the corporation is in the 35% marginal tax bracket.

**Reclassification of Debt as Equity (Thin Capitalization Problem).** In situations where the corporation is said to be thinly capitalized, the IRS contends that debt is really an equity interest and denies the corporation the tax advantages of debt financing. If a debt instrument has too many features of stock, it may be treated as a form of stock by the IRS. As a result, the principal and interest payments are considered dividends. Under § 385, the IRS has the authority to characterize corporate debt wholly as equity or as part debt and part equity. In the current environment, however, the IRS may be less inclined to raise the thin capitalization issue because the conversion of interest income to dividend income would produce a tax benefit to individual investors.

For the most part, the principles used to classify debt as equity developed in connection with closely held corporations where the holders of the debt are often shareholders. The rules have often proved inadequate for dealing with large, publicly traded corporations.

Section 385 lists several factors that *may* be used to determine whether a debtor-creditor relationship or a shareholder-corporation relationship exists. The thrust of § 385 is to authorize the Treasury to prescribe Regulations that provide more definite guidelines for determining when debt should be reclassified as equity. To date, the Treasury Department has not drafted final Regulations. Consequently, taxpayers must rely on judicial decisions to determine whether a true debtor-creditor relationship exists.

The courts have identified the following factors to be considered when classifying a security as debt or equity:

- Whether the debt instrument is in proper form. An open account advance is more easily characterized as a contribution to capital than a loan evidenced by a properly written note executed by the shareholder.[37]
- Whether the debt instrument bears a reasonable rate of interest and has a definite maturity date. When a shareholder advance does not provide for interest, the return expected is that inherent in an equity interest (e.g., a share of the profits or an increase in the value of the shares).[38] Likewise, a lender unrelated to the corporation will usually be unwilling to commit funds to the corporation for an indefinite period of time (i.e., no definite due date).
- Whether the debt is paid on a timely basis. A lender's failure to insist upon timely repayment (or satisfactory renegotiation) indicates that the return sought does not depend upon interest income and the repayment of principal.
- Whether payment is contingent upon earnings. A lender ordinarily will not advance funds that are likely to be repaid only if the venture is successful.
- Whether the debt is subordinated to other liabilities. Subordination tends to eliminate a significant characteristic of the creditor-debtor relationship. Creditors should have the right to share with other general creditors in the event of the corporation's dissolution or liquidation. Subordination also destroys another basic attribute of creditor status—the power to demand payment at a fixed maturity date.[39]
- Whether holdings of debt and stock are proportionate (e.g., each shareholder owns the same percentages of debt and stock). When debt and equity obligations are held in the same proportion, shareholders are, apart from tax

[37]*Estate of Mixon, Jr. v. U.S.,* 72–2 USTC ¶9537, 30 AFTR2d 72–5094, 464 F.2d 394 (CA–5, 1972).
[38]*Slappey Drive Industrial Park v. U.S.,* 77–2 USTC ¶9696, 40 AFTR2d 77–5940, 561 F.2d 572 (CA–5, 1977).
[39]*Fin Hay Realty Co. v. U.S.,* 68–2 USTC ¶9438, 22 AFTR2d 5004, 398 F.2d 694 (CA–3, 1968).

considerations, indifferent as to whether corporate distributions are in the form of interest or dividends.

- Whether funds loaned to the corporation are used to finance initial operations or capital asset acquisitions. Funds used to finance initial operations or to acquire capital assets the corporation needs to operate are generally obtained through equity investments.
- Whether the corporation has a high ratio of shareholder debt to shareholder equity. **Thin capitalization** occurs when shareholder debt is high relative to shareholder equity. This indicates the corporation lacks reserves to pay interest and principal on debt when corporate income is insufficient to meet current needs.[40] In determining a corporation's debt-equity ratio, courts look at the relation of the debt both to the book value of the corporation's assets and to their actual fair market value.[41]

Section 385 also authorizes the Treasury to issue Regulations classifying an instrument either as *wholly* debt or equity or as *part* debt and *part* equity. This flexible approach is important because some instruments cannot readily be classified either wholly as stock or wholly as debt. It may also provide an avenue for the IRS to address problems in publicly traded corporations.

*\*Definition*
*Thin Capitalization*
*– page C-18*

# Corporate Operations

The rules related to gross income, deductions, and losses discussed in previous chapters of this text generally apply to corporations. In a few instances, it was noted that corporations face unique limitations such as the 10 percent of taxable income limitation for charitable contributions and the limitation allowing corporate capital losses to be deductible only against capital gains. Corporations also are permitted some deductions not generally available to other entities. These special deductions and other special rules regarding the determination of corporate income tax liability are discussed in the following pages.

**LO.6**

Understand the tax rules unique to corporations.

*\*Definition*
*Dividends received*
*Deduction*
*– page C-6*

## DEDUCTIONS AVAILABLE ONLY TO CORPORATIONS

**Dividends Received Deduction.** The purpose of the **dividends received deduction** is to mitigate multiple levels of taxation. Without the deduction, dividends paid between corporations could be subject to several levels of tax. For example, if Corporation A pays Corporation B a dividend, and B passes the dividend on to its shareholders, the dividend is taxed at three levels: Corporation A, Corporation B, and Corporation B's shareholders. The dividends received deduction alleviates this inequity by limiting or eliminating the amount of dividend income taxable to corporations.

As the following table illustrates, the amount of the dividends received deduction depends on the percentage of ownership the recipient corporate shareholder holds in a domestic corporation making the dividend distribution.[42]

---

[40]A court held that a debt-equity ratio of approximately 14.6:1 was not excessive. See *Tomlinson v. 1661 Corp.*, 67–1 USTC ¶9438, 19 AFTR2d 1413, 377 F.2d 291 (CA–5, 1967). A 26:1 ratio was found acceptable in *Delta Plastics, Inc.*, 85 TCM 940, T.C.Memo. 2003–54.

[41]In *Bauer v. Comm.*, 84–2 USTC ¶9996, 55 AFTR2d 85–433, 748 F.2d 1365 (CA–9, 1984), a debt-equity ratio of 92:1 resulted when book

value was used. But the ratio ranged from 2:1 to 8:1 when equity included both paid-in capital and accumulated earnings.

[42]§ 243(a).

| Percentage of Ownership by Corporate Shareholder | Deduction Percentage |
|---|---|
| Less than 20% | 70% |
| 20% or more (but less than 80%) | 80% |
| 80% or more* | 100% |

*The payor corporation must be a member of an affiliated group with the recipient corporation.

The dividends received deduction is limited to a percentage of the taxable income of the shareholder-corporation. For this purpose, taxable income is computed without regard to the net operating loss (NOL), the dividends received deduction, and any capital loss carryback to the current tax year. The percentage of taxable income limitation corresponds to the deduction percentage. Thus, if a corporate shareholder owns less than 20 percent of the stock in the distributing corporation, the dividends received deduction is limited to 70 percent of taxable income. However, the taxable income limitation does not apply if the corporation has an NOL for the current taxable year.[43]

The following steps summarize the computation of the deduction:

1. Multiply the dividends received by the deduction percentage.
2. Multiply the taxable income by the deduction percentage.
3. The deduction is limited to the lesser of Step 1 or Step 2, unless subtracting the amount derived in Step 1 from taxable income *generates* an NOL. If so, the amount derived in Step 1 should be used. This is referred to as the *NOL rule*.

**EXAMPLE 36**

Red, White, and Blue Corporations, three unrelated calendar year corporations, have the following transactions for the year:

|  | Red Corporation | White Corporation | Blue Corporation |
|---|---|---|---|
| Gross income from operations | $ 400,000 | $ 320,000 | $ 260,000 |
| Expenses from operations | (340,000) | (340,000) | (340,000) |
| Dividends received from domestic corporations (less than 20% ownership) | 200,000 | 200,000 | 200,000 |
| Taxable income before the dividends received deduction | $ 260,000 | $ 180,000 | $ 120,000 |

In determining the dividends received deduction, use the three-step procedure described above:

|  | Red | White | Blue |
|---|---|---|---|
| Step 1 (70% × $200,000) | $140,000 | $140,000 | $140,000 |
| Step 2 |  |  |  |
| 70% × $260,000 (taxable income) | $182,000 |  |  |
| 70% × $180,000 (taxable income) |  | $126,000 |  |
| 70% × $120,000 (taxable income) |  |  | $ 84,000 |
| Step 3 |  |  |  |
| Lesser of Step 1 or Step 2 | $140,000 | $126,000 |  |
| Step 1 amount generates an NOL |  |  | $140,000 |

---

[43]§ 246(b)(2).

White Corporation is subject to the 70% of taxable income limitation. It does not qualify for NOL rule treatment since subtracting $140,000 (Step 1) from $180,000 (100% of taxable income before the dividends received deduction) does not yield a negative figure. Blue Corporation qualifies under the NOL rule because subtracting $140,000 (Step 1) from $120,000 (100% of taxable income before the dividends received deduction) yields a negative figure. In summary, each corporation has a dividends received deduction for the year as follows: $140,000 for Red Corporation, $126,000 for White Corporation, and $140,000 for Blue Corporation. ■

**Deduction of Organizational Expenditures.** Expenses incurred in connection with the organization of a corporation normally are chargeable to a capital account. That they benefit the corporation during its existence seems clear. But over what period should organizational expenses be amortized? The lack of a determinable and limited estimated useful life makes such a determination difficult. Section 248 was enacted to solve this problem.

Under § 248, a corporation may elect to amortize **organizational expenditures** over a period of 180 months or more. The period begins with the month in which the corporation begins business.[44] Organizational expenditures *subject to the election* include:

- Legal services incident to organization (e.g., drafting the corporate charter, bylaws, minutes of organizational meetings, terms of original stock certificates).
- Necessary accounting services.
- Expenses of temporary directors and of organizational meetings of directors or shareholders.
- Fees paid to the state of incorporation.

Expenditures that *do not qualify* include those connected with issuing or selling shares of stock or other securities (e.g., commissions, professional fees, and printing costs) or with the transfer of assets to a corporation. Such expenditures reduce the amount of capital raised and are not deductible.

A special exception allows the corporation to immediately expense the first $5,000 of organizational costs. The exception, however, is phased out on a dollar-for-dollar basis when these expenses exceed $50,000. A corporation, for example, with $52,000 of organizational expenditures could elect to expense $3,000 [$5,000 − ($52,000 − $50,000)] of this amount and amortize the $49,000 balance ($52,000 − $3,000) over 180 months.[45]

To qualify for the election, the expenditure must be *incurred* before the end of the tax year in which the corporation begins business. In this regard, the corporation's method of accounting is of no consequence. Thus, an expense incurred by a cash basis corporation in its first tax year qualifies even though not paid until a subsequent year.

The election is made in a statement attached to the corporation's tax return for its first tax year. The return and statement must be filed no later than the due date of the return (including any extensions).

If the election is not made on a timely basis, organizational expenditures cannot be deducted until the corporation ceases to do business and liquidates. These expenditures will be deductible if the corporate charter limits the life of the corporation.

---

[44]The month in which a corporation begins business may not be immediately apparent. See Reg. § 1.248–1(a)(3). For a similar problem in the Subchapter S area, see Chapter 11.

[45]Organizational expenditures incurred before October 23, 2004, could not be immediately expensed but could be amortized over a period of 60 months or more. The change to § 248 was made by the American Jobs Creation Act of 2004.

EXAMPLE 37

Black Corporation, an accrual basis, calendar year taxpayer, was formed and began operations on May 1, 2005. The following expenses were incurred during its first year of operations (May 1–December 31, 2005):

| | |
|---|---|
| Expenses of temporary directors and of organizational meetings | $15,000 |
| Fee paid to the state of incorporation | 2,000 |
| Accounting services incident to organization | 18,000 |
| Legal services for drafting the corporate charter and bylaws | 32,000 |
| Expenses incident to the printing and sale of stock certificates | 48,000 |

Because of the dollar cap (i.e., dollar-for-dollar reduction for amounts in excess of $50,000), no immediate expensing under the $5,000 rule is available. Assume, however, that Black Corporation elects to amortize the qualifying organizational expenses over a period of 180 months. The monthly amortization is $372 [($15,000 + $2,000 + $18,000 + $32,000) ÷ 180 months], and $2,976 ($372 × 8 months) is deductible for tax year 2005. Note that the $48,000 of expenses incident to the printing and sale of stock certificates does not qualify for the election. These expenses cannot be deducted. Instead, they reduce the amount of the capital realized from the sale of stock. ∎

Organizational expenditures are distinguished from start-up expenditures covered by § 195. Start-up expenditures include various investigation expenses involved in entering a new business, whether incurred by a corporate or a noncorporate taxpayer. Start-up expenses also include operating expenses, such as rent and payroll, that are incurred by a corporation before it actually begins to produce any gross income. At the election of the taxpayer, such expenditures (e.g., travel, market surveys, financial audits, legal fees) can be treated in the same manner as organizational expenditures. Thus, up to $5,000 can be immediately expensed (subject to the dollar cap and excess-of-$50,000 phaseout) and any remaining amounts amortized over a period of 180 months or longer.

PLANNING STRATEGIES

## Organizational Expenditures

FRAMEWORK FOCUS: DEDUCTIONS

STRATEGY ▶ MAXIMIZE DEDUCTIBLE AMOUNTS.

To qualify for the 180-month amortization procedure of § 248, only organizational expenditures incurred in the first taxable year of the corporation can be considered. This rule could prove to be an unfortunate trap for corporations formed late in the year.

EXAMPLE 38

Thrush Corporation is formed in December 2005. Qualified organizational expenditures are incurred as follows: $62,000 in December

2005 and $30,000 in January 2006. If Thrush uses the calendar year for tax purposes, only $62,000 of the organizational expenditures qualify for amortization. ∎

A solution to the problem posed by Example 38 may be for Thrush Corporation to adopt a fiscal year that ends on or beyond January 31. All organizational expenditures will then have been incurred before the close of the first tax year.

LO.7

Compute the corporate income tax.

## DETERMINING THE CORPORATE INCOME TAX LIABILITY

**Corporate Income Tax Rates.** Corporate income tax rates have fluctuated widely over past years. Refer to the inside front cover of the text for a schedule of current corporate income tax rates.

**EXAMPLE 39**

Gold Corporation, a calendar year taxpayer, has taxable income of $90,000 for 2005. Its income tax liability is $18,850, determined as follows:

| | |
|---|---|
| Tax on $75,000 | $13,750 |
| Tax on $15,000 × 34% | 5,100 |
| Tax liability | $18,850 |

For a corporation that has taxable income in excess of $100,000 for any tax year, the amount of the tax is increased by the lesser of (1) 5 percent of the excess or (2) $11,750. In effect, the additional tax means a 39 percent rate for every dollar of taxable income from $100,000 to $335,000.

**EXAMPLE 40**

Silver Corporation, a calendar year taxpayer, has taxable income of $335,000 for 2005. Its income tax liability is $113,900, determined as follows:

| | |
|---|---|
| Tax on $100,000 | $ 22,250 |
| Tax on $235,000 × 39% | 91,650 |
| Tax liability | $113,900 |

Note that the tax liability of $113,900 is 34% of $335,000. Thus, due to the 39% rate (34% normal rate + 5% additional tax on taxable income between $100,000 and $335,000), the benefit of the lower rates on the first $75,000 of taxable income completely phases out at $335,000. The normal rate drops back to 34% on taxable income between $335,000 and $10 million.

Section 11(b) provides that qualified **personal service corporations (PSCs)** are taxed at a flat 35 percent rate on all taxable income. Thus, PSCs do not enjoy the tax savings of being in the 15 percent to 34 percent brackets applicable to other corporations. For this purpose, a PSC is a corporation that is substantially employee owned. Also, it must engage in one of the following activities: health, law, engineering, architecture, accounting, actuarial science, performing arts, or consulting.

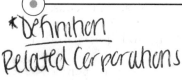

*Definition
Personal Service
Corporations (PSCs)
– Page C-13

**LO.8**

Explain the tax rules unique to multiple corporations.

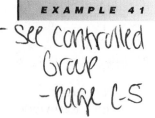

*Definition
Related Corporations

## TAX LIABILITY OF RELATED CORPORATIONS

**Related corporations** are subject to special rules for computing the income tax, the AMT exemption, and the § 179 election to expense certain depreciable assets.[46] If these restrictions did not exist, the shareholders of a corporation could gain significant tax advantages by splitting a single corporation into *multiple* corporations. The next two examples illustrate the potential *income tax* advantage of multiple corporations.

**EXAMPLE 41**

- See controlled
Group
– page C-5

Gray Corporation annually yields taxable income of $300,000. The corporate tax on $300,000 is $100,250, computed as follows:

| | |
|---|---|
| Tax on $100,000 | $ 22,250 |
| Tax on $200,000 × 39% | 78,000 |
| Tax liability | $100,250 |

---

[46]§ 1561(a). Small corporations are not subject to the AMT. See Chapter 13 for details.

**EXAMPLE 42**

Assume that Gray Corporation in the previous example is divided equally into four corporations. Each corporation would have taxable income of $75,000, and the tax for each (absent the special provisions for related corporations) would be computed as follows:

| | |
|---|---|
| Tax on $50,000 | $ 7,500 |
| Tax on $25,000 × 25% | 6,250 |
| Tax liability | $13,750 |

The total liability for the four corporations would be $55,000 ($13,750 × 4). Consequently, the savings would be $45,250 ($100,250 − $55,000). ■

To preclude the advantages that could be gained by using multiple corporations, the tax law requires special treatment for *controlled groups* of corporations. A comparison of Examples 41 and 42 reveals that the income tax savings that could be achieved by using multiple corporations result from having more of the total income taxed at lower rates. To close this potential loophole, the law limits a controlled group's taxable income in the tax brackets below 35 percent to the amount the corporations in the group would have if they were one corporation. Thus, in Example 42, under the controlled corporation rules, only $12,500 (one-fourth of the first $50,000 of taxable income) for each of the four related corporations would be taxed at the 15 percent rate. The 25 percent rate would apply to the next $6,250 (one-fourth of the next $25,000) of taxable income of each corporation. This equal allocation of the $50,000 and $25,000 amounts is required unless all members of the controlled group consent to an apportionment plan providing for an unequal allocation.

Similar limitations apply to the § 179 expense election (see Chapter 4) and to the $40,000 exemption amount for purposes of computing the AMT (see Chapter 13).

## CONTROLLED GROUPS

A **controlled group** of corporations includes parent-subsidiary groups, brother-sister groups, combined groups, and certain insurance companies. Groups of the first two types are discussed in the following sections.

**Parent-Subsidiary Controlled Group.** A **parent-subsidiary controlled group** consists of one or more *chains* of corporations connected through stock ownership with a common parent corporation. The ownership connection can be established through either a *voting power test* or a *value test*. The voting power test requires ownership of stock possessing at least 80 percent of the total voting power of all classes of stock entitled to vote. The value test requires ownership of at least 80 percent of the total value of all shares of all classes of stock of each of the corporations, except the parent corporation, by one or more of the other corporations.[47]

**EXAMPLE 43**

Aqua Corporation owns 80% of White Corporation. Aqua and White Corporations are members of a parent-subsidiary controlled group. Aqua is the parent corporation and White is the subsidiary. ■

The parent-subsidiary relationship described in Example 43 is easy to recognize because Aqua Corporation is the direct owner of White Corporation. Real-world

[47]§ 1563(a)(1).

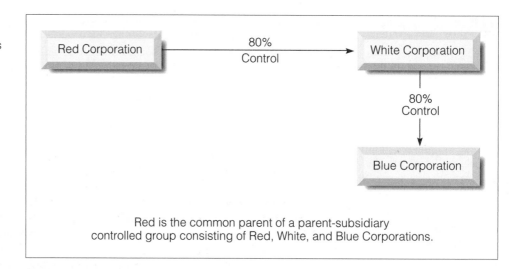

■ **FIGURE 8–3**
Controlled Groups—
Parent-Subsidiary Corporations

Red is the common parent of a parent-subsidiary
controlled group consisting of Red, White, and Blue Corporations.

business organizations are often much more complex, sometimes including numerous corporations with chains of ownership connecting them. In these complex corporate structures, determining whether the controlled group classification is appropriate becomes more difficult. The ownership requirements can be met through direct ownership (refer to Example 43) or through indirect ownership, as illustrated in the following example.

**EXAMPLE 44**

Red Corporation owns 80% of the voting stock of White Corporation, and White Corporation owns 80% of the voting stock of Blue Corporation. Red, White, and Blue Corporations constitute a controlled group in which Red is the common parent and White and Blue are subsidiaries. This parent-subsidiary relationship is diagrammed in Figure 8–3. The same result would occur if Red Corporation, rather than White Corporation, owned the Blue Corporation stock. ■

**Brother-Sister Corporations.**   A **brother-sister controlled group** *may* exist if two or more corporations are owned by five or fewer *persons* (individuals, estates, or trusts).[48] The ownership test is met if the shareholder group possesses stock representing more than 50 percent of the total combined voting power of all classes of stock entitled to vote *or* more than 50 percent of the total value of shares of all classes of stock of each corporation.

In applying the more than 50 percent ownership tests, the stock held by each person is considered only to the extent that the stock ownership is *identical* for each corporation. That is, if a shareholder owns 30 percent of Silver Corporation and 20 percent of Gold Corporation, that shareholder has identical ownership of 20 percent of each corporation.

**EXAMPLE 45**

The outstanding stock of Hawk, Eagle, Crane, and Dove Corporations, each of which has only one class of stock outstanding, is owned by the following unrelated individuals:

[48]§ 1563(a)(2). AJCA of 2004 changed the definition of brother-sister controlled groups only with respect to computing the corporate income tax, accumulated earnings credit, and AMT exemption. For other purposes, an 80% total ownership test and the 50% identical ownership test apply.

| Shareholders | Corporations | | | | Identical Ownership |
|---|---|---|---|---|---|
| | Hawk | Eagle | Crane | Dove | |
| Allen | 10% | 20% | 30% | 25% | 20% |
| Barton | 20% | 20% | 15% | 20% | 15% |
| Carter | 10% | 15% | 10% | 10% | 10% |
| Dixon | 10% | 10% | 15% | 10% | 10% |
| Total | 50% | 65% | 70% | 65% | 55% |

In determining whether a brother-sister controlled group exists, a corporation is considered only if the shareholder group of five or fewer persons owns more than 50% of the stock of the corporation. Therefore, Hawk Corporation is not considered as a potential member of the brother-sister group because the shareholder group does not own *more than* 50% of that corporation. It is then necessary to apply the identical ownership test to the shareholders' ownership in the remaining corporations. Under the identical ownership test, five or fewer persons (Allen, Barton, Carter, and Dixon) own 55% of all classes of stock in Eagle, Crane, and Dove Corporations. Consequently, Eagle, Crane, and Dove are regarded as members of a brother-sister controlled group. ■

**Application of § 482.**   Congress has recognized that a parent corporation has the power to shift income among its subsidiaries. Likewise, shareholders who control brother-sister groups can shift income and deductions among the related corporations.

When the true taxable income of a subsidiary or other related corporation has been understated or overstated, the IRS can reallocate the income and deductions of the related corporations under § 482. Section 482 permits the IRS to allocate gross income, deductions, and credits between any two or more organizations, trades, or businesses that are owned or controlled by the same interests. This is appropriate when the allocation is necessary to prevent avoidance of taxes or to reflect income correctly. Controlled groups of corporations, especially multinational corporations, are particularly vulnerable to § 482.

**L0.9**

Describe the reporting process for corporations.

# Procedural Matters

## FILING REQUIREMENTS FOR CORPORATIONS

A corporation must file a Federal income tax return whether or not it has taxable income.[49] A corporation that was not in existence throughout an entire annual accounting period is required to file a return for the fraction of the year during which it was in existence. In addition, a corporation must file a return even though it has ceased to do business if it has valuable claims for which it will bring suit. A corporation is relieved of filing income tax returns only when it ceases to do business and retains no assets.

DIGGING DEEPER 2   *Find more information on this topic at our Web site:* ***http://wft-entities.swlearning.com.***

The return must be filed on or before the fifteenth day of the third month following the close of a corporation's tax year. A regular corporation, other than a PSC, can use either a calendar or a fiscal year to report its taxable income. The tax year of the shareholders has no effect on the corporation's tax year.

---

[49]§ 6012(a)(2).

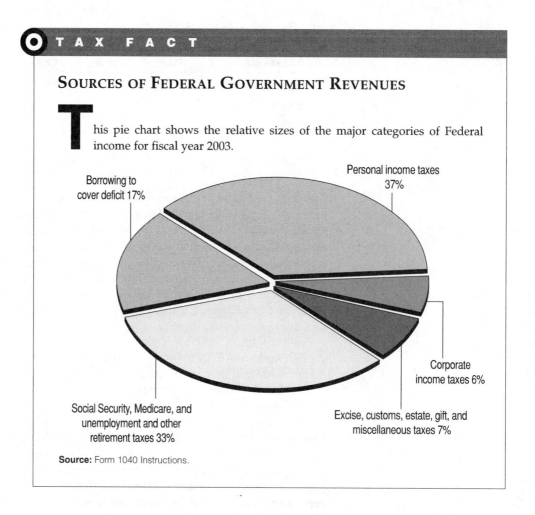

**T**AX **F**ACT

## SOURCES OF FEDERAL GOVERNMENT REVENUES

**T**his pie chart shows the relative sizes of the major categories of Federal income for fiscal year 2003.

Personal income taxes 37%

Borrowing to cover deficit 17%

Corporate income taxes 6%

Social Security, Medicare, and unemployment and other retirement taxes 33%

Excise, customs, estate, gift, and miscellaneous taxes 7%

**Source:** Form 1040 Instructions.

## ESTIMATED TAX PAYMENTS

A corporation must make payments of estimated tax unless its tax liability can reasonably be expected to be less than $500. The required annual payment (which includes any estimated AMT liability) is the lesser of (1) 100 percent of the corporation's final tax or (2) 100 percent of the tax for the preceding year (if that was a 12-month tax year and the return filed showed a tax liability).[50] Estimated payments can be made in four installments due on or before the fifteenth day of the fourth month, the sixth month, the ninth month, and the twelfth month of the corporate taxable year. The full amount of the unpaid tax is due on the due date of the return without regard to extensions. A corporation failing to pay its required estimated tax payments will be subjected to a nondeductible penalty on the amount by which the installments are less than the tax due.

## RECONCILIATION OF TAXABLE INCOME AND FINANCIAL NET INCOME

**Conventional Reconciliations.**   **Schedule M–1** on the last page of Form 1120 is used to reconcile net income as computed for financial accounting purposes with taxable income reported on the corporation's income tax return. The starting point on Schedule M–1 is net income per books (financial accounting net income). Additions and subtractions are entered for items that affect net income per books

*Definition

Schedule M-1
-page C-16

---

[50]§§ 6655(d) and (e).

and taxable income differently. The following items are entered as additions (see lines 2 through 5 of Schedule M–1 below):

- Federal income tax expense (deducted in computing net income per books but not deductible in computing taxable income).
- The excess of capital losses over capital gains (deducted for financial accounting purposes but not deductible by corporations for income tax purposes).
- Income that is reported in the current year for tax purposes that is not reported in computing net income per books (e.g., prepaid income).
- Various expenses that are deducted in computing net income per books but are not deducted in computing taxable income (e.g., charitable contributions in excess of the 10 percent ceiling applicable to corporations).

The following subtractions are entered on lines 7 and 8 of Schedule M–1:

- Income reported for financial accounting purposes but not included in taxable income (e.g., tax-exempt interest).
- Expenses deducted on the tax return but not deducted in computing net income per books (e.g., a charitable contributions carryover deducted in a prior year for financial accounting purposes but deductible in the current year for tax purposes).

The result is taxable income (before the NOL deduction and the dividends received deduction).

**EXAMPLE 46**

During the current year, Tern Corporation had the following transactions:

| | |
|---|---|
| Net income per books (after tax) | $92,400 |
| Taxable income | 50,000 |
| Federal income tax expense per books | 7,500 |
| Interest income from tax-exempt bonds | 5,000 |
| Interest paid on loan, the proceeds of which were used to purchase the tax-exempt bonds | 500 |
| Life insurance proceeds received as a result of the death of a key employee | 50,000 |
| Premiums paid on key employee life insurance policy | 2,600 |
| Excess of capital losses over capital gains | 2,000 |

For book and tax purposes, Tern Corporation determines depreciation under the straight-line method. Tern's Schedule M–1 for the current year is as follows:

| Schedule M-1 | Reconciliation of Income (Loss) per Books With Income per Return | | | | |
|---|---|---|---|---|---|
| 1 | Net income (loss) per books | 92,400 | 7 | Income recorded on books this year not included on this return (itemize): | |
| 2 | Federal income tax per books | 7,500 | | | |
| 3 | Excess of capital losses over capital gains | 2,000 | | Tax-exempt interest $ *5,000* | |
| 4 | Income subject to tax not recorded on books this year (itemize): | | | *Life insurance proceeds on key* *employee $50,000* | 55,000 |
| 5 | Expenses recorded on books this year not deducted on this return (itemize): | | 8 | Deductions on this return not charged against book income this year (itemize): | |
| a | Depreciation . . $ | | a | Depreciation . . $ | |
| b | Charitable contributions $ | | b | Charitable contributions $ | |
| c | Travel and entertainment $ | | | | |
| | *Prem.–life ins. $2,600; Int.–exempt bonds $500* | 3,100 | 9 | Add lines 7 and 8 | 55,000 |
| 6 | Add lines 1 through 5 | 105,000 | 10 | Income (page 1, line 28)—line 6 less line 9 | 50,000 |

Schedule M–2 reconciles unappropriated retained earnings at the beginning of the year with unappropriated retained earnings at year-end. Beginning balance plus net income per books, as entered on line 1 of Schedule M–1, less dividend distributions during the year equals ending retained earnings. Other sources of increases or decreases in retained earnings are also listed on Schedule M–2.

> ### BRIDGE DISCIPLINE
>
> ### Bridge to Financial Accounting
>
> Measures of corporate income for financial reporting and income tax purposes differ because the objectives of these measures differ. Income measures for financial reporting purposes are intended to help various stakeholders have a clear view of the corporation's financial position and operational results. Income measures for Federal income tax purposes, on the other hand, must comply with the relevant provisions of the Internal Revenue Code. The tax law is intended not only to raise revenues to fund government operations, but to reflect the objectives of government fiscal policy as well.
>
> As a consequence of these differing objectives, revenue and expense measurements used to determine taxable income may differ from those used in financial reporting. In most cases, differences between book and tax measurements are temporary in nature. Two such temporary differences relate to the different methods of calculating depreciation expense and the limits placed on the deductibility of net capital losses for tax purposes. Permanent differences between book and tax income, such as the dividends received deduction, also may exist.
>
> Accounting standards for reporting income tax expenses and liabilities require that the tax impact of *temporary* differences be recognized currently in the financial statements. Because many temporary differences allow a firm to postpone its tax payments to later years, the financial statements must show the amount of the expense that is paid currently and that portion that is to be paid in a later period. The portion of the taxes to be paid in a later period is shown as a liability for such future income taxes. The liability for future income taxes is referred to as a deferred income tax liability.

**EXAMPLE 47**

Assume the same facts as in the preceding example. Tern Corporation's beginning balance in unappropriated retained earnings is $125,000. During the year, Tern distributed a cash dividend of $30,000 to its shareholders. Based on these further assumptions, Tern's Schedule M–2 for the current year is as follows:

| Schedule M-2 | Analysis of Unappropriated Retained Earnings per Books (Line 25, Schedule L) | | | | | | |
|---|---|---|---|---|---|---|---|
| 1 | Balance at beginning of year . . . | *125,000* | 5 | Distributions: | a Cash . . . | | *30,000* |
| 2 | Net income (loss) per books . . . | *92,400* | | | b Stock . . . | | |
| 3 | Other increases (itemize): _____ | | | | c Property . . | | |
| | ------------------------------- | | 6 | Other decreases (itemize): _____ | | | |
| | ------------------------------- | | 7 | Add lines 5 and 6 . . . . . | | *30,000* |
| 4 | Add lines 1, 2, and 3 . . . . . | *217,400* | 8 | Balance at end of year (line 4 less line 7) | | | *187,400* |

*Find more information on these topics at our Web site: **http://wft-entities.swlearning.com**.*

### Expanded Reconciliation of Book and Tax Differences—Schedule M–3.

Corporate taxpayers with total assets of $10 million or more are now required to report much greater detail relative to differences between income (loss) reported for financial purposes and income (loss) reported for tax purposes. This expanded reconciliation of book and tax income (loss) is reported on new **Schedule M–3,** which must be filed for years ending on or after December 31, 2004. One objective of Schedule M–3 is to create greater transparency between corporate financial statements and tax returns. Another objective is to identify corporations that engage in aggressive tax practices by requiring that transactions that create book/tax differences be disclosed on corporate tax returns. Comparison of Schedule M–3 (available at **http://www.irs.gov**) with Schedule M–1 (demonstrated in Example 46) reveals the significantly greater disclosure requirements that now apply to corporations with total assets of $10 million or more.

*Find more information on these topics at our Web site: **http://wft-entities.swlearning.com**.*

*[handwritten margin note: ]* *Definition Schedule M-3 — page L-16*

## SUMMARY

The evolution of the check-the-box Regulations has provided taxpayers with a simplified method for determining an entity's tax classification. Nevertheless, taxpayers should not discount the importance of choosing the appropriate form of entity. As demonstrated in this chapter and Chapter 9, a variety of tax provisions applicable to corporations do not extend to other entities. Of particular importance are the different deductions available to corporations and the corporate income tax rate structure. Corporations must also be aware of their levels of debt to avoid equity reclassification. Such reclassification causes deductible interest paid on debt to become nondeductible dividend payments. Equally important are the timing and completeness requirements of the corporate filing provisions. Failure to comply with the appropriate filing provisions may result in heavy penalties and interest.

# Suggested Further Readings

Brian E. Keller, "Sec. 351 Transfers Involving Boot and Encumbered Assets," *The Tax Adviser,* September 2004, pp. 536–539.

Phillip J. Korb, John N. Sigler, and Thomas E. Vermeer, "Dividend Tax Rate Cuts Benefits Closely Held Corporations," *The CPA Journal,* October 2004, pp. 40–41.

Robert Willens, "IRS Alters the Landscape with Respect to the 351 'Control Immediately After' Requirement," *Journal of Taxation*, June 2003, pp. 325–332.

## KEY TERMS

Assumption of liabilities, 8–15

Brother-sister controlled group, 8–32

C corporation, 8–2

Capital contribution, 8–23

Check-the-box Regulations, 8–8

Control, 8–11

Controlled group, 8–31

Dividends received deduction, 8–26

Limited liability company (LLC), 8–8

Limited partnership, 8–7

Organizational expenditures, 8–28

Parent–subsidiary controlled group, 8–31

Personal service corporation (PSC), 8–30

Property, 8–10

Regular corporation, 8–2

Related corporations, 8–30

S corporation, 8–2

Schedule M–1, 8–34

Schedule M–3, 8–36

Securities, 8–11

Thin capitalization, 8–26

## PROBLEM MATERIALS

### Problems

1. Harry is the sole shareholder of Purple Corporation, which is an S corporation. Purple earned net operating income of $60,000 during the year and had a long-term capital loss of $8,000. Harry withdrew $30,000 of the profit from the corporation. How much income must Harry report on his individual tax return for 2005?

2. On June 17, 2005, Susan and Valerie started an investment firm called B & W Investments. During 2005, both Susan and Valerie lived and conducted their business in Illinois. B & W Investments is an unincorporated entity under Illinois state law. Neither Susan nor Valerie filed an election regarding the Federal tax classification of B & W Investments.

Susan's husband, Bill, told Valerie and Susan that they must file a Form 1120 for the 2005 taxable year and will be taxed twice on B & W's earnings. Is Bill correct in his assessment?

3. Emu Company, which was formed in 2005, had operating income of $100,000 and operating expenses of $80,000 in 2005. In addition, Emu had a long-term capital loss of $5,000. How does Andrew, the owner of Emu Company, report this information on his individual tax return under the following assumptions?
   a. Emu Company is a proprietorship, and Andrew does not withdraw any funds from Emu during the year.
   b. Emu Company is a corporation and pays no dividends during the year.

4. Lewis and Burton are equal partners in Wolverine Enterprises, a calendar year partnership. During the year, Wolverine Enterprises had $500,000 of gross income and $350,000 of operating expenses. In addition, the partnership sold land that had been held for investment purposes for a long-term capital gain of $60,000. During the year, Lewis withdrew $40,000 from the partnership, and Burton withdrew $45,000. Discuss the impact of this information on the taxable income of Wolverine, Lewis, and Burton.

5. Pink Company had $100,000 of net profit from operations in 2005 and paid Sandra Pink, its sole shareholder, a dividend of $77,750 ($100,000 net profit − $22,250 corporate tax). Sandra has a large amount of income from other sources and is in the 35% marginal tax bracket. Would Sandra's tax situation be better or worse if Pink Company were a proprietorship and Sandra withdrew $77,750 from the business during the year?

**Issue ID**

6. Emily incorporates her sole proprietorship, but does not transfer a building used by the business to the corporation. Instead, the building is leased to the corporation for an annual rent. What tax reasons might Emily have for not transferring the building to the corporation when the business was incorporated?

7. John, Brad, Kate, and Marta form Martin Corporation with the following consideration:

|  | Consideration Transferred | | |
|---|---|---|---|
|  | Basis to Transferor | Fair Market Value | Number of Shares Issued |
| From John— | | | |
|   Personal services rendered to Martin Corporation | $ –0– | $ 30,000 | 30 |
| From Brad— | | | |
|   Equipment | 345,000 | 300,000 | 270* |
| From Kate— | | | |
|   Cash | 60,000 | 60,000 | |
|   Unrealized accounts receivable | –0– | 90,000 | 150 |
| From Marta— | | | |
|   Land and building | 210,000 | 450,000 | |
|   Mortgage on land and building | 300,000 | 300,000 | 150 |

*Brad receives $30,000 in cash in addition to the 270 shares.

Martin Corporation assumes the mortgage transferred by Marta. The value of each share of Martin Corporation stock is $1,000. As to these transactions, provide the following information:
   a. John's recognized gain or loss.
   b. John's basis in the Martin Corporation stock.
   c. Brad's recognized gain or loss.
   d. Brad's basis in the Martin Corporation stock.
   e. Martin Corporation's basis in the equipment.
   f. Kate's recognized gain or loss.

g. Kate's basis in the Martin Corporation stock.
h. Martin Corporation's basis in the unrealized accounts receivable.
i. Marta's recognized gain or loss.
j. Marta's basis in the Martin Corporation stock.
k. Martin Corporation's basis in the land and building.

8. Mark and Gail form Maple Corporation with the following consideration:

| | Consideration Transferred | | |
| | Basis to Transferor | Fair Market Value | Number of Shares Issued |
| --- | --- | --- | --- |
| From Mark— | | | |
| Cash | $ 50,000 | $ 50,000 | |
| Installment obligation | 140,000 | 250,000 | 30 |
| From Gail— | | | |
| Cash | 150,000 | 150,000 | |
| Equipment | 125,000 | 250,000 | |
| Patent | 10,000 | 300,000 | 70 |

The installment obligation has a face amount of $250,000 and was acquired last year from the sale of land held for investment purposes (adjusted basis of $140,000). As to these transactions, provide the following information:
a. Mark's recognized gain or loss.
b. Mark's basis in the Maple Corporation stock.
c. Maple Corporation's basis in the installment obligation.
d. Gail's recognized gain or loss.
e. Gail's basis in the Maple Corporation stock.
f. Maple Corporation's basis in the equipment and the patent.
g. How would your answers to the preceding questions change if Mark received common stock and Gail received preferred stock?
h. How would your answers change if Gail was a partnership?

**Decision Making**

9. Jane, Jon, and Clyde incorporate their respective businesses and form Starling Corporation. On March 1 of the current year, Jane exchanges her property (basis of $100,000 and value of $400,000) for 200 shares in Starling Corporation. On April 15, Jon exchanges his property (basis of $140,000 and value of $600,000) for 300 shares in Starling. On May 10, Clyde transfers his property (basis of $1,180,000 and value of $1 million) for 500 shares in Starling.
a. If the three exchanges are part of a prearranged plan, what gain will each of the parties recognize on the exchanges?
b. Assume Jane and Jon exchanged their property for stock four years ago while Clyde transfers his property for 500 shares in the current year. Clyde's transfer is not part of a prearranged plan with Jane and Jon to incorporate their businesses. What gain or loss will Clyde recognize on the transfer?
c. What arrangement—part (a) or part (b)—would the parties prefer?

**Communications**

10. Andrew Boninti (1635 Maple Street, Syracuse, NY 13201) exchanges property, basis of $30,000 and fair market value of $600,000, for 60% of the stock of Gray Corporation. The other 40% is owned by Kendall Smith, who acquired her stock several years ago. You represent Andrew, who asks whether he must report gain on the transfer. Prepare a letter to Andrew and a memorandum for the tax files documenting your response.

**Issue ID**

11. Barbara exchanges property, basis of $20,000 and fair market value of $500,000, for 65% of the stock of Pelican Corporation. Alice, Barbara's daughter, who acquired her stock last year, owns the other 35% of Pelican. What are the tax issues?

12. Dan and Vera form Crane Corporation. Dan transfers land (worth $200,000, basis of $60,000) for 50% of the stock in Crane. Vera transfers machinery (worth $150,000, adjusted basis of $30,000) and provides services worth $50,000 for 50% of the stock.

    a. Will the transfers qualify under § 351?

    b. What are the tax consequences to Dan and Vera?

    c. What is Crane Corporation's basis in the land and the machinery?

13. Juan organized Red Corporation 10 years ago. He contributed property worth $1 million (basis of $200,000) for 2,000 shares of stock in Red (representing 100% ownership). Juan later gave each of his children, Julie and Rachel, 500 shares of the stock. In the current year, Juan transfers property worth $400,000 (basis of $150,000) to Red for 500 more of its shares. What gain, if any, will Juan recognize on the transfer?

14. Ann and Bob form Robin Corporation. Ann transfers property worth $420,000 (basis of $150,000) for 70 shares in Robin Corporation. Bob receives 30 shares for property worth $165,000 (basis of $30,000) and for legal services in organizing the corporation; the services are worth $15,000.

    a. What gain, if any, will the parties recognize on the transfer?

    b. What basis do Ann and Bob have in the stock in Robin Corporation?

    c. What is Robin Corporation's basis in the property and services it received from Ann and Bob?

15. Assume in Problem 14 that the property Bob transfers to Robin Corporation is worth $15,000 (basis of $3,000) and his services in organizing the corporation are worth $165,000. What are the tax consequences to Ann, Bob, and Robin Corporation?

**Decision Making**

16. Rhonda Johnson owns 50% of the stock of Peach Corporation. She and the other 50% shareholder, Rachel Powell, have decided that additional contributions of capital are needed if Peach is to remain successful in its competitive industry. The two shareholders have agreed that Rhonda will contribute assets having a value of $200,000 (adjusted basis of $15,000) in exchange for additional shares of stock. After the transaction, Rhonda will hold 75% of Peach Corporation and Rachel's interest will fall to 25%.

    a. What gain is realized on the transaction? How much of the gain will be recognized?

    b. Rhonda is not satisfied with the transaction as proposed. How would the consequences change if Rachel agrees to transfer $1,000 of cash in exchange for additional stock? In this case, Rhonda will own slightly less than 75% of Peach and Rachel's interest will be slightly more than 25%.

    c. If Rhonda still is not satisfied with the result, what should be done to avoid any gain recognition?

17. Paul transfers property with an adjusted basis of $50,000, fair market value of $400,000, to Swift Corporation for 90% of the stock. The property is subject to a liability of $60,000, which Swift assumes. What is the basis of the Swift stock to Paul? What is the basis of the property to Swift Corporation?

**Issue ID**

18. Three years ago, Chris exchanged an apartment building worth $1,500,000 (basis of $300,000), which was subject to a mortgage of $200,000, for land worth $1,150,000, subject to a mortgage of $150,000, and cash of $300,000. In the current year, Chris transfers the land that he received in the exchange to newly formed Amber Corporation for all of the stock in Amber. Amber Corporation assumes the original mortgage on the land, currently in the amount of $100,000, and another mortgage in the amount of $20,000 that Chris later placed on the land to secure his purchase of some equipment that he uses in this business. What are the tax issues?

19. Allie forms Blue Corporation by transferring land with a basis of $125,000 (fair market value of $775,000). The land is subject to a mortgage of $375,000. One month prior to incorporating Blue, Allie borrows $100,000 for personal purposes and gives the lender a second mortgage on the land. Blue Corporation issues stock worth $300,000 to Allie and assumes the mortgages on the land.

    a. What are the tax consequences to Allie and to Blue Corporation?

    b. How would the tax consequences to Allie differ if she had not borrowed the $100,000?

20. Fay, a sole proprietor, is engaged in a cash basis, service business. In the current year, she incorporates the business to form Robin Corporation. She transfers assets with a basis of $400,000 (fair market value of $1.2 million), a bank loan of $360,000 (which Robin assumes), and $80,000 in trade payables in return for all of Robin's stock. What are the tax consequences of the incorporation of the business?

Issue ID

21. Nancy and her daughter, Margaret, have been working together in a cattery called "The Perfect Cat." Nancy formed the business in 1990 as a sole proprietorship. Because of the high quality and exotic lineage of the cats that Nancy breeds, the business has been very successful. It currently has assets with a fair market value of $250,000 and a basis of $180,000. On the advice of her tax accountant, Nancy decides to incorporate "The Perfect Cat." Because of Margaret's loyalty, Nancy would like her to have shares in the corporation. What are the relevant tax issues?

Ethics

22. Jean incorporates her sole proprietorship. Inadvertently, she transfers to the new corporation a credit card charge for a family dinner she hosted. After the corporation pays the bill, she realizes her mistake and issues a note payable to the corporation for the charge. Has Jean avoided § 357(c)? Has she acted properly?

23. Sara and Jane form Wren Corporation. Sara transfers property, basis of $25,000 and fair market value of $200,000, for 50 shares in Wren Corporation. Jane transfers property, basis of $10,000 and fair market value of $185,000, and agrees to serve as manager of Wren for one year; in return Jane receives 50 shares in Wren. The value of Jane's services to Wren is $15,000.
    a. What gain will Sara and Jane recognize on the exchange?
    b. What basis will Wren Corporation have in the property transferred by Sara and Jane? How should Wren treat the value of the services Jane renders?

24. Assume in Problem 23, that Jane receives the 50 shares of Wren Corporation stock in consideration for the appreciated property and for providing legal services in organizing the corporation. The value of Jane's services is $15,000.
    a. What gain does Jane recognize?
    b. What is Wren Corporation's basis in the property transferred by Jane? How should Wren treat the value of the services Jane renders?

25. On January 10, 2005, Carol transferred machinery worth $100,000 (adjusted basis of $20,000) to a controlled corporation, Lark. The transfer qualified under § 351. Carol had deducted $85,000 of depreciation on the machinery while it was used in her proprietorship. On November 15, 2005, Lark Corporation sells the machinery for $95,000. What are the tax consequences to Carol and to Lark Corporation on the sale of the machinery?

26. Blue Corporation desires to set up a manufacturing facility in a southern state. After considerable negotiations with a small town in Arkansas, Blue accepts the following offer: land (fair market value of $3 million) and cash of $1 million.
    a. How much gain, if any, must Blue Corporation recognize?
    b. What basis will Blue Corporation have in the land?
    c. Within one year of the contribution, Blue constructs a building for $800,000 and purchases inventory for $300,000. What basis will Blue Corporation have in each of these assets?

EXTENDER

Communications

27. Emily Patrick (36 Paradise Road, Northampton, MA 01060) formed Teal Corporation a number of years ago with an investment of $200,000 of cash, for which she received $20,000 in stock and $180,000 in bonds bearing interest of 8% and maturing in nine years. Several years later, Emily lent the corporation an additional $50,000 on open account. In the current year, Teal Corporation becomes insolvent and is declared bankrupt. During the corporation's existence, Emily was paid an annual salary of $60,000. Write a letter to Emily in which you explain how she should treat her losses for tax purposes.

28. In each of the following independent situations, determine the dividends received deduction. Assume that none of the corporate shareholders owns 20% or more of the stock in the corporations paying the dividends.

| | Red Corporation | White Corporation | Blue Corporation |
| --- | --- | --- | --- |
| Income from operations | $ 700,000 | $ 800,000 | $ 700,000 |
| Expenses from operations | (600,000) | (900,000) | (740,000) |
| Qualifying dividends | 100,000 | 200,000 | 200,000 |

29. Owl Corporation was formed on December 1, 2005. Qualifying organizational expenses were incurred and paid as follows:

| | |
|---|---:|
| Incurred and paid in December 2005 | $12,000 |
| Incurred in December 2005 but paid in January 2006 | 6,000 |
| Incurred and paid in February 2006 | 3,600 |

Assuming that Owl Corporation makes a timely election under § 248 to expense and amortize its organizational expenditures, what amount may be deducted in the corporation's first tax year under each of the following assumptions?

a. Owl Corporation adopts a calendar year and the cash basis of accounting for tax purposes.

b. Same as (a), except that Owl Corporation chooses a fiscal year of December 1–November 30.

c. Owl Corporation adopts a calendar year and the accrual basis of accounting for tax purposes.

d. Same as (c), except that Owl Corporation chooses a fiscal year of December 1–November 30.

30. Hummingbird Corporation, an accrual basis taxpayer, was formed and began operations on July 1, 2005. The following expenses were incurred during the first tax year (July 1 to December 31, 2005) of operations:

| | |
|---|---:|
| Expenses of temporary directors and of organizational meetings | $12,000 |
| Fee paid to the state of incorporation | 3,000 |
| Accounting services incident to organization | 15,000 |
| Legal services for drafting the corporate charter and bylaws | 21,000 |
| Expenses incident to the printing and sale of stock certificates | 18,000 |
| | $69,000 |

Assume Hummingbird Corporation makes an appropriate and timely election under § 248 and the related Regulations. What is the maximum organizational expense Hummingbird may write off for tax year 2005?

31. In each of the following *independent* situations, determine the corporation's income tax liability. Assume that all corporations use a calendar year for tax purposes and that the tax year involved is 2005.

| | Taxable Income |
|---|---:|
| Violet Corporation | $ 38,000 |
| Indigo Corporation | 180,000 |
| Orange Corporation | 335,000 |
| Blue Corporation | 4,620,000 |
| Green Corporation | 18,500,000 |

32. The outstanding stock in Red, Blue, and Green Corporations, each of which has only one class of stock, is owned by the following unrelated individuals:

| | Corporations | | |
|---|---|---|---|
| Shareholders | Red | Blue | Green |
| Marrin | 20% | 10% | 30% |
| Murray | 10% | 50% | 20% |
| Moses | 50% | 30% | 35% |

a. Determine whether Red, Blue, and Green Corporations constitute a brother-sister controlled group.

b. Assume that Murray does not own stock in any of the corporations. Would a brother-sister controlled group exist?

33. Adams, Burke, and Chan, who are unrelated individuals, have voting stock in Pink, Purple, and Red Corporations as follows:

| | Corporations | | |
|---|---|---|---|
| **Shareholder** | **Pink** | **Purple** | **Red** |
| Adams | 20% | 20% | 10% |
| Burke | 15% | 25% | 35% |
| Chan | 30% | 25% | 20% |

Are Pink, Purple, and Red Corporations treated as a brother-sister controlled group?

34. The outstanding stock in Amber, Sand, Tan, Beige, and Purple Corporations, which have only one class of stock outstanding, is owned by the following unrelated individuals:

| | Corporations | | | | |
|---|---|---|---|---|---|
| **Individuals** | **Amber** | **Sand** | **Tan** | **Beige** | **Purple** |
| Anna | 25% | 20% | 15% | 15% | 25% |
| Bill | 15% | 20% | 10% | 10% | 10% |
| Carol | 10% | 20% | 15% | 10% | 18% |
| Don | 10% | 20% | 20% | 5% | 17% |
| Eve | 10% | 20% | 15% | 5% | 20% |

Determine if Amber, Sand, Tan, Beige, and Purple Corporations constitute a brother-sister controlled group.

**EXTENDER** 35. Indicate in each of the following *independent* situations whether the corporation may file Form 1120–A:

| | Jay Corporation | Shrike Corporation | Martin Corporation |
|---|---|---|---|
| Sales of merchandise | $600,000 | $400,000 | $300,000 |
| Total assets | 200,000 | 360,000 | 400,000 |
| Total income (gross profit plus other income, including gains) | 480,000 | 490,000 | 380,000 |
| Member of controlled group | no | yes | no |
| Ownership in foreign corporation | no | no | no |

36. The following information for 2005 relates to Oak Corporation, a calendar year, accrual basis taxpayer. You are to determine the amount of Oak's taxable income for the year using this information. You may use Schedule M–1, which is available on the IRS Web site.

| | |
|---|---|
| Net income per books (after tax) | $209,710 |
| Federal income tax expense per books | 30,050 |
| Interest income from tax-exempt bonds | 12,000 |
| Interest paid on loan incurred to purchase tax-exempt bonds | 1,200 |
| Life insurance proceeds received as a result of the death of the president of the corporation | 120,000 |
| Premiums paid on policy on the life of the president of the corporation | 6,240 |
| Excess of capital losses over capital gains | 4,800 |

37. For 2006, Cedar Corporation, an accrual basis, calendar year taxpayer, had net income per books of $172,750 and the following special transactions:

| | |
|---|---:|
| Life insurance proceeds received as a result of the death of the corporation's president | $100,000 |
| Premiums paid on the life insurance policy on the president | 10,000 |
| Prepaid rent received and properly taxed in 2005 but credited as rent income in 2006 | 15,000 |
| Rent income received in 2006 ($10,000 is prepaid and relates to 2007) | 25,000 |
| Interest income on tax-exempt bonds | 5,000 |
| Interest on loan to carry tax-exempt bonds | 3,000 |
| MACRS depreciation in excess of straight-line (straight-line was used for book purposes) | 4,000 |
| Capital loss in excess of capital gains | 6,000 |
| Federal income tax liability and accrued tax provision for 2006 | 22,250 |

Using Schedule M–1 of Form 1120 (the most recent version available), determine Cedar Corporation's taxable income for 2006.

38. For years ending after December 31, 2004, corporate taxpayers with total assets of $10 million or more are required to report much greater detail relative to differences between book and tax income (loss). What were the government's objectives in creating this new reporting requirement?

**Issue ID**

39. In January, Don and Steve each invested $100,000 of cash to form a corporation to conduct business as a retail golf equipment store. On January 5, they paid Bill, an attorney, to draft the corporate charter, file the necessary forms with the state, and write the bylaws. They leased a store building and began to acquire inventory, furniture, display equipment, and office equipment in February. They hired a sales staff and clerical personnel in March and conducted training sessions during the month. They had a successful opening on April 1, and sales increased steadily throughout the summer. The weather turned cold in October, and all local golf courses closed by October 15, which resulted in a drastic decline in sales. Don and Steve expect business to be very good during the Christmas season and then to taper off significantly from January 1 through February 28. The corporation accrued bonuses to Don and Steve on December 31, payable on April 15 of the following year. The corporation made timely estimated tax payments throughout the year. The corporation hired a bookkeeper in February, but he does not know much about taxation. Don and Steve have hired you as a tax consultant and have asked you to identify the tax issues that they should consider.

## Comprehensive Tax Return Problem

**Tax Return Problem**

40. On September 9, 1992, Jennifer Jones and Jeff Shurts formed SnowPro Corporation to sell ski equipment. Pertinent information regarding SnowPro is summarized as follows:

- The business address is 2120 Adobe Drive, Las Cruces, NM 88011.

- The employer identification number is 75–3392543; the principal business activity code is 451110.

- Jennifer and Jeff each own one-half of the outstanding common stock; no other class of stock is authorized. Jennifer is president of the company, and Jeff is secretary-treasurer. Both are full-time employees of the corporation, and each receives a salary of $189,500. Jennifer's Social Security number is 399–50–2953; Jeff's Social Security number is 400–30–4495.

- The corporation uses the accrual method of accounting and reports on a calendar year basis. Inventories are determined using the lower of cost or market method. For book and tax purposes, the straight-line method of depreciation is used.

- During 2004, the corporation distributed a cash dividend of $72,000.

Selected portions of SnowPro's profit and loss statement for 2004 reflect the following debits and credits:

| Account | Debit | Credit |
|---|---|---|
| Gross sales | | $2,556,000 |
| Sales returns and allowances | $ 72,000 | |
| Cost of goods sold | 925,000 | |
| Dividends received from stock investments in less-than-20%-owned U.S corporations | | 108,000 |
| Interest income | | |
| State bonds | $12,600 | |
| Certificates of deposit | 23,000 | 35,600 |
| Premiums on term life insurance policies on the lives of Jennifer and Jeff; SnowPro Corporation is the designated beneficiary | 14,000 | |
| Salaries—officers | 379,000 | |
| Salaries—clerical  and sales | 370,000 | |
| Taxes (state, local, and payroll) | 92,000 | |
| Repairs | 72,500 | |
| Interest expense | | |
| Loan to purchase state bonds | $ 7,200 | |
| Other business loans | 16,800 | 24,000 |
| Advertising | 83,400 | |
| Rental expense | 177,700 | |
| Depreciation | 36,000 | |

A comparative balance sheet for SnowPro Corporation reveals the following information:

| Assets | January 1, 2004 | December 31, 2004 |
|---|---|---|
| Cash | $  369,000 | $  251,194 |
| Trade notes and accounts receivable | 790,560 | 956,140 |
| Inventories | 540,000 | 640,800 |
| Federal bonds | 127,000 | 154,000 |
| State bonds | 143,000 | 186,000 |
| Prepaid Federal tax | — | 1,620 |
| Buildings and other depreciable assets | 216,000 | 216,000 |
| Accumulated depreciation | (79,920) | (115,920) |
| Land | 18,500 | 18,500 |
| Other assets | 2,740 | 1,300 |
| Total assets | $2,126,880 | $2,309,634 |

| Liabilities and Equity | | |
|---|---|---|
| Accounts payable | $  208,000 | $  214,004 |
| Other current liabilities | 134,270 | 69,600 |
| Mortgages | 214,000 | 205,000 |
| Capital stock | 425,000 | 425,000 |
| Retained earnings | 1,145,610 | 1,396,030 |
| Total liabilities and equity | $2,126,880 | $2,309,634 |

Net income per books (before any income tax accrual) is $454,000. During 2004, SnowPro Corporation made estimated tax payments of $133,200 to the IRS. Prepare a Form 1120 for SnowPro Corporation for tax year 2004.

**BRIDGE DISCIPLINE**

1. Charles is planning to invest $10,000 in a venture whose management is undecided as to whether it should be structured as a regular corporation or as a partnership. Charles will hold a 10% interest in the entity. Determine the treatment to Charles if the entity is a corporation and if it is a partnership. In the analysis, assume Charles is in the 35% marginal tax bracket, and the entity, if operating as a corporation, is in the 34% marginal tax bracket. Also, assume that the passive activity rules do not apply to Charles.
   a. If the entity incurs an $80,000 operating loss in year 1, what is Charles's cash outflow if the entity is a corporation? A partnership?
   b. In year 2, the entity earns operating income of $200,000 and makes no distribution to any of the owners. What is the tax burden on Charles if the investment is a corporation? A partnership?
   c. In year 3, the entity earns operating income of $200,000 and distributes all of that year's after-tax proceeds to the owners. What amount of cash is available to Charles if the entity operates as a corporation (assume any distribution is a qualified dividend)? A partnership?

2. On your review of the books and records of Ridge Corporation, you note the following information pertaining to its tax provision.

| | |
|---|---|
| Net income per books | $525,400 |
| Book income tax expense | 234,600 |
| Dividends received deduction | 70,000 |
| Capital gains | 50,000 |
| Capital losses | (60,000) |
| MACRS depreciation | 80,000 |
| Book depreciation | 65,000 |

   a. Calculate Ridge's taxable income and Federal income tax liability for the year.
   b. Calculate Ridge's deferred income tax liability.

## Research Problems

**THOMSON**

**RIA**

**Decision Making**

**Communications**

*Note: Solutions to Research Problems can be prepared by using the **RIA Checkpoint® Student Edition** online research product, which is available to accompany this text. It is also possible to prepare solutions to the Research Problems by using tax research materials found in a standard tax library.*

**Research Problem 1.**   Lynn Jones, Shawn, Walt, and Donna are trying to decide whether they should organize a corporation and transfer their shares of stock in several corporations to this new corporation. All their shares are listed on the New York Stock Exchange and are readily marketable. Lynn would transfer shares in Brown Corporation; Shawn would transfer stock in Rust Corporation; Walt would transfer stock in White Corporation; and Donna would transfer stock in several corporations. The stock would be held by the newly formed corporation for investment purposes. Lynn asks you, her tax adviser, if she would have gain on the transfer of her substantially appreciated shares in Brown Corporation if she transfers the shares to a newly formed corporation. She also asks whether there will be tax consequences if she, Shawn, Walt, and Donna form a partnership, rather than a corporation, to which they would transfer their readily marketable stock. Your input will be critical as they make their decision. Prepare a letter to the client, Lynn Jones, and a memo for the firm's files. Lynn's address is 1540 Maxwell Avenue, Highland, KY 41099.

**Communications**

**Research Problem 2.**   Joe and Tom Moore are brothers and equal shareholders in Black Corporation, a calendar year taxpayer. In 2002, they incurred certain travel and entertainment expenditures, as employees, on behalf of Black Corporation. Because Black was in a precarious financial condition, Joe and Tom decided not to seek reimbursement for these expenditures. Instead, each brother deducted what he spent on his own individual return (Form 1040). Upon audit of the returns filed by Joe and Tom for 2002, the IRS disallowed these expenditures. Write a letter to Joe at 568 Inwood Avenue, Waynesburg, PA 15370, and indicate whether he should challenge the IRS action. Explain your conclusion using nontechnical language.

**Decision Making**

**Research Problem 3.**   Skeeter has owned and operated an accrual basis golf driving range for a number of years. The sole proprietorship has been successful and has grown to the point where it now also offers golf lessons and sponsors tournaments and other activities. Skeeter has been advised that incorporating his proprietorship would give him an opportunity to restructure the business debt and to acquire additional working capital at more favorable rates.

Based on this advice, Skeeter transfers the business assets (fair market value $1 million, adjusted basis $200,000) along with the associated debt ($325,000) to the newly formed corporation. As far as he is concerned, nothing has really changed in his relationship with the creditor bank: he still feels personally obligated to pay off the debt. In fact, before the debt is assigned to the newly formed corporation, the bank insists that Skeeter remain secondarily responsible for its payment. Even though the proprietorship's liabilities transferred exceed the basis of the assets transferred, Skeeter regards the transaction as tax-free because:

- nothing has changed with his business other than its form of operation,

- a business justification exists for changing its form to that of a corporation, and

- he has enjoyed no personal gain from the transaction.

Determine if Skeeter's belief is justified. If you believe that the transaction as currently planned would be taxable, identify strategies that could be employed to eliminate or minimize any recognition of gain.

*Partial list of research aids:*
§ 357(c).

**Internet Activity**

*Use the tax resources of the Internet to address the following questions. Do not restrict your search to the World Wide Web, but include a review of newsgroups and general reference materials, practitioner sites and resources, primary sources of the tax law, chat rooms and discussion groups, and other opportunities.*

**Research Problem 4.**   Find the IRS Web site and print a copy of Schedule M–3. Compare it with the Schedule M–1 used in Example 46 and discuss the differences.

**Research Problem 5.**   Fundamental differences exist in the attributes underlying common stock and preferred stock. For example, preferred stock generally pays dividends at a higher rate than common stock. This makes preferred stock an attractive investment choice given the current preferential income tax rate applicable to dividend income. However, some preferred stock is treated as long-term debt that generates interest rather than as stock that produces dividends. Investigate the current IRS position regarding the factors used to distinguish preferred stock that is treated as stock from preferred stock that is treated as debt. In addition, identify planning guidelines offered by various investment houses that may be relevant when making preferred stock investments. Is this category of preferred stock similar to "nonqualified preferred stock" as defined by § 351(g)?

# Corporations: Earnings & Profits and Dividend Distributions

*After completing Chapter 9, you should be able to:*

### LO.1
Understand the role that earnings and profits play in determining the tax treatment of distributions.

### LO.2
Compute a corporation's earnings and profits.

### LO.3
Apply the rules for allocating earnings and profits to distributions.

### LO.4
Understand the tax impact of property dividends on the recipient shareholder and the corporation making the distribution.

### LO.5
Understand the nature and treatment of constructive dividends.

### LO.6
Distinguish between taxable and nontaxable stock dividends.

### LO.7
Discuss the tax treatment of stock redemptions.

http://wft.swlearning.com

## OUTLINE

**TAX TALK**

*The relative stability of profits after taxes is evidence that the corporation profits tax is, in effect, almost entirely shifted; the government simply uses the corporation as a tax collector.*

—*K. E. Boulding*

Generally, a corporation cannot deduct distributions made to its shareholders. In contrast, shareholders may be required to treat distributions as fully subject to tax, a nontaxable recovery of capital, or capital gain.

Since distributions provide no deduction to the paying corporation and often require income recognition by the shareholders, a double tax seemingly results (i.e., at both the corporate and the shareholder levels). Because of the possibility of a double tax when dealing with corporations, the tax treatment of distributions often raises issues such as the following.

- The availability of earnings to be distributed.
- The basis of the stock in the hands of the shareholder.
- The character of the property being distributed.
- Whether the shareholder gives up ownership in return for the distribution.
- Whether the distribution is liquidating or nonliquidating.

**LO.1**

Understand the role that earnings and profits play in determining the tax treatment of distributions.

\* Dehmhen
Dividend
- page C-6

## Corporate Distributions—In General

To the extent that a distribution is made from corporate earnings and profits (E & P), the shareholder is deemed to receive a **dividend**, usually taxed in a preferential manner.[1] Generally, corporate distributions are presumed to be paid out of E & P (defined later in this chapter) and are treated as dividends, *unless* the parties to the transaction can show otherwise.

The portion of a corporate distribution that is not taxed as a dividend (because of insufficient E & P) is nontaxable to the extent of the shareholder's basis in the stock. The stock basis is reduced accordingly. The excess of the distribution over the shareholder's basis is treated as a gain from the sale or exchange of the stock.[2]

---

[1]§§ 301(c)(1) and 316(a). Corporate shareholders claim a dividends received deduction. Others typically pay a tax on dividends at a 15% rate.

[2]§ 301(c).

### COMPANIES PAY RECORD DIVIDENDS IN 2004

In response to the 2003 tax cut on dividend income, companies in the Standard & Poor's 500 stock index were expected to pay out a record $183 billion in dividends in 2004. This continues a trend that started in late 2003, when corporations paid out a then-record $161 billion. A new paper published by the National Bureau of Economic Research suggests that the increase in dividend payments in the last two years extends beyond the companies in the S&P 500.

According to equity market analysts, the growth in dividend payments is being fueled both by larger dividends from companies with an established dividend-paying history (e.g., Wal-Mart, Coca-Cola, and Harley-Davidson) and by first-time dividends from growth companies that haven't paid dividends in the past (such as Staples, Cendant Corporation, and Costco Wholesale Corporation). In 2004, 374 of the S&P 500 were expected to pay dividends, up from 351 in 2002 and 370 in 2003. This is the highest rate since 1999.

The biggest dividend payers in the S&P 500 are usually Citigroup (which pays out $8.27 billion annually), General Electric (about $8.17 billion annually), and ExxonMobil (around $7 billion each year). The standout in 2004, however, was Microsoft, which paid a record one-time $32 billion dividend in December and doubled its usual quarterly dividend to boot. Some have speculated that Microsoft's large dividend reflected concerns that John Kerry might be elected president. (He was expected to eliminate the preferential tax rate on dividends.)

**EXAMPLE 1**

At the beginning of the year, Amber Corporation (a calendar year taxpayer) has accumulated E & P of $30,000. The corporation has no current E & P. During the year, the corporation distributes $40,000 to its *equal* shareholders, Bob and Bonnie. Only $30,000 of the $40,000 distribution is a taxable dividend. Suppose Bob's basis in his stock is $8,000, while Bonnie's basis is $4,000. Under these conditions, Bob recognizes a taxable dividend of $15,000 and reduces the basis of his stock from $8,000 to $3,000. The $20,000 Bonnie receives from Amber Corporation is accounted for as follows.

- Taxable dividend of $15,000.
- Reduction in stock basis from $4,000 to zero.
- Taxable gain of $1,000. ■

**LO.2**

Compute a corporation's earnings and profits.

*Definition Earnings and Profits –page C–7*

## Earnings and Profits (E & P)

The notion of **earnings and profits** is similar in many respects to the accounting concept of retained earnings. Both are measures of the firm's accumulated capital. However, these two concepts differ in a fundamental way. The computation of retained earnings is based on financial accounting rules, while E & P is determined using rules specified in the tax law.

E & P fixes the upper limit on the amount of dividend income that shareholders must recognize as a result of a distribution by the corporation. In this sense, E & P represents the corporation's economic ability to pay a dividend without impairing its capital. Thus, the effect of a specific transaction on the E & P account often can be determined by considering whether the transaction increases or decreases the corporation's capacity to pay a dividend.

## COMPUTATION OF E & P

The Code does not explicitly define the term *earnings and profits*. Instead, a series of adjustments to taxable income are identified to provide a measure of the corporation's economic income.[3] In general, E & P determinations are applied in the same manner for cash and accrual basis taxpayers.

Accumulated E & P is fixed as of the beginning of the tax year, which is the sum of the undistributed earnings of the entity since February 28, 1913. **Current E & P** is that portion of E & P attributable to the current tax year's operations. It is computed by using the corporation's Federal taxable income and then applying a series of adjustments to more closely approximate the cash flow of the entity.[4]

**Additions to Taxable Income.**   It is necessary to add certain previously excluded income items back to taxable income to determine current E & P. Included among these positive adjustments are interest income on municipal bonds, excluded life insurance proceeds (in excess of cash surrender value), Federal income tax refunds from taxes paid in prior years, the deduction for domestic manufacturing income, and the dividends received deduction.

**EXAMPLE 2**

A corporation collects $100,000 on a key employee life insurance policy (the corporation is the owner and beneficiary of the policy). At the time the policy matured on the death of the insured employee, it possessed a cash surrender value of $30,000. None of the $100,000 is included in the corporation's taxable income, but $70,000 is added to taxable income when computing current E & P. ■

**Subtractions from Taxable Income.**   Some of the corporation's nondeductible expenditures are subtracted from taxable income to arrive at E & P. These negative adjustments include related-party losses, expenses incurred to produce tax-exempt income, Federal income taxes paid, nondeductible key employee life insurance premiums (net of increases in cash surrender value), and nondeductible fines and penalties.

**EXAMPLE 3**

A corporation sells property (basis of $10,000) to its sole shareholder for $8,000. Because of § 267 (disallowance of losses on sales between related parties), the $2,000 loss cannot be deducted in arriving at the corporation's taxable income. But since the overall economic effect of the transaction is a decrease in the corporation's assets by $2,000, the loss reduces the current E & P for the year of the sale. ■

**EXAMPLE 4**

A corporation pays a $10,000 premium on a key employee life insurance policy covering the life of its president. As a result of the payment, the cash surrender value of the policy is increased by $7,000. Although none of the $10,000 premium is deductible for tax purposes, current E & P is reduced by $3,000. ■

---

[3] Reg. § 1.312–6(a).
[4] Section 312 describes most of the adjustments to taxable income necessary to determine E & P. Regulations relating to E & P begin at Reg. § 1.312–6.

**Timing Adjustments.** Some E & P adjustments shift the effect of a transaction from the year of its inclusion in or deduction from taxable income to the year in which it has an economic effect on the corporation. Charitable contribution carryovers, net operating loss carryovers, and capital loss carryovers all give rise to this kind of adjustment.

**EXAMPLE 5**

During 2005, Raven Corporation makes charitable contributions, $12,000 of which cannot be deducted in arriving at the taxable income for the year because of the 10% taxable income limitation. Consequently, the $12,000 is carried forward to 2006 and fully deducted in that year. The excess charitable contribution reduces the corporation's current E & P for 2005 by $12,000 and increases its current E & P for 2006, when the deduction is allowed, by a like amount. The increase in E & P in 2006 is necessary because the charitable contribution carryover reduces the taxable income for that year (the starting point for computing E & P) and already has been taken into account in determining the E & P for 2005. ■

Gains and losses from property transactions generally affect the determination of E & P only to the extent that they are recognized for tax purposes. Thus, gains and losses deferred under the like-kind exchange provision and deferred involuntary conversion gains do not affect E & P until recognized. Accordingly, no adjustment is required for these items.

**Accounting Method Adjustments.** In addition to the above adjustments, accounting methods used for determining E & P are generally more conservative than those allowed under the income tax rules. For example, the installment method is not permitted for E & P purposes even though, in some cases, it is allowed when computing taxable income. Thus, an adjustment is required for the deferred gain attributable to sales of property made during the year under the installment method. Specifically, all principal payments are treated as having been received in the year of sale.[5]

**EXAMPLE 6**

In 2005, Cardinal Corporation, a calendar year taxpayer, sells unimproved real estate (basis of $20,000) for $100,000. Under the terms of the sale, beginning in 2006, Cardinal will receive two annual payments of $50,000 each with interest of 9%. Cardinal Corporation does not elect out of the installment method. Since Cardinal's taxable income for 2005 will not reflect any of the gain from the sale, the corporation must make an $80,000 positive adjustment for 2005 (the deferred gain from the sale) in computing E & P. Similarly, $40,000 negative adjustments will be required in 2006 and 2007 when the deferred gain is recognized under the installment method. ■

The alternative depreciation system (ADS) must be used for purposes of computing E & P.[6] This method requires straight-line depreciation over a recovery period equal to the Asset Depreciation Range (ADR) midpoint life.[7] If MACRS cost recovery is used for income tax purposes, a positive or negative adjustment equal to the difference between MACRS and ADS must be made each year. Finally, none of the 30 or 50 percent additional first-year depreciation is allowed under the ADS.[8]

Likewise, when assets are disposed of, an additional adjustment to taxable income is required to allow for the difference in gain or loss resulting from the difference in income tax basis and E & P basis.[9] The adjustments arising from depreciation are illustrated in the following example.

---

[5]§ 312(n)(5).
[6]§ 312(k)(3)(A).
[7]See § 168(g)(2). The ADR midpoint life for most assets is set out in Rev.Proc. 87–56, 1987–2 C.B. 674. The recovery period is 5 years for

automobiles and light-duty trucks and 40 years for real property. For assets with no class life, the recovery period is 12 years.
[8]§ 168(k)(2)(C).
[9]§ 312(f)(1).

**EXAMPLE 7**

On January 2, 2005, White Corporation purchased equipment with an ADR midpoint life of 10 years for $30,000. The equipment was then depreciated over its 7-year MACRS class life. The asset was sold on July 2, 2007, for $27,000. For purposes of determining taxable income and E & P, cost recovery claimed on the equipment is summarized below.

| Year | Cost Recovery Computation | MACRS | ADS | Adjustment Amount |
|------|---------------------------|-------|-----|-------------------|
| 2005 | $30,000 × 14.29% | $ 4,287 | | |
| | $30,000 ÷ 10-year ADR recovery period × ½ (half-year for first year of service) | | $1,500 | $2,787 |
| 2006 | $30,000 × 24.49% | 7,347 | | |
| | $30,000 ÷ 10-year ADR recovery period | | 3,000 | 4,347 |
| 2007 | $30,000 × 17.49% × ½ (half-year for year of disposal) | 2,624 | | |
| | $30,000 ÷ 10-year ADR recovery period × ½ (half-year for year of disposal) | | 1,500 | 1,124 |
| | Total cost recovery | $14,258 | $6,000 | $8,258 |

Each year White Corporation increases its taxable income by the adjustment amount indicated above to determine E & P. In addition, when computing E & P for 2007, White reduces taxable income by $8,258 to account for the excess gain recognized for income tax purposes.

| | Income Tax | E & P |
|---|-----------|-------|
| Amount realized | $ 27,000 | $ 27,000 |
| Adjusted basis for income tax ($30,000 cost − $14,258 MACRS) | (15,742) | |
| Adjusted basis for E & P ($30,000 cost − $6,000 ADS) | | (24,000) |
| Gain on sale | $ 11,258 | $ 3,000 |
| Adjustment amount ($3,000 − $11,258) | ($ 8,258) | |

In addition to more conservative depreciation methods, the E & P rules impose limitations on the deductibility of § 179 expense.[10] In particular, this expense is deducted over a period of five years for E & P purposes. Thus, in any year that § 179 is elected, 80 percent of the resulting expense is added back to taxable income to determine current E & P. In each of the following four years, a negative adjustment equal to 20 percent of the § 179 expense is made.

A variety of other accounting method adjustments is also required to determine current E & P. For example, cost depletion is required for E & P purposes, so an adjustment must be made to taxable income in cases where percentage depletion is used. Similarly, the percentage of completion method is required for E & P purposes when accounting for long-term contracts, so an adjustment is required when the completed contract method is employed. Intangible drilling costs and mine exploration and development costs may be deducted currently for income tax purposes, but must be capitalized for E & P. Once capitalized, these expenditures can be amortized under the E & P rules over 60 months for intangible drilling costs and over 120 months for mine exploration and development costs.[11]

---

[10]§ 312(k)(3)(B).

[11]§ 312(n)(2).

**CONCEPT SUMMARY 9–1**

## Computing E & P

| Transaction | Adjustment to Taxable Income to Determine Current E & P | |
|---|---|---|
| | **Addition** | **Subtraction** |
| Tax-exempt income | X | |
| Dividends received deduction | X | |
| Collection of proceeds from insurance policy on life of corporate officer (in excess of cash surrender value) | X | |
| Deferred gain on installment sale (all gain is added to E & P in year of sale) | X | |
| Future recognition of installment sale gross profit | | X |
| Excess capital loss and excess charitable contribution (over 10% limitation) in year incurred | | X |
| Deduction of charitable contribution, NOL, or capital loss carryovers in succeeding taxable years (increase E & P because deduction reduces taxable income while E & P was reduced in a prior year) | X | |
| Federal income taxes paid | | X |
| Federal income tax refund | X | |
| Loss on sale between related parties | | X |
| Nondeductible fines, penalties, meals, and entertainment | | X |
| Payment of premiums on insurance policy on life of corporate officer (in excess of increase in cash surrender value of policy) | | X |
| Realized gain (not recognized) on an involuntary conversion | No effect | |
| Realized gain or loss (not recognized) on a like-kind exchange | No effect | |
| Percentage depletion (only cost depletion can reduce E & P) | X | |
| Accelerated depreciation (E & P is reduced only by straight-line, units-of-production, or machine hours depreciation) | X | X |
| Deduction for domestic manufacturing income | X | |
| § 179 expense in year elected (80%) | X | |
| § 179 expense in four years following election (20% each year) | | X |
| Intangible drilling costs deducted currently (reduce E & P in future years by amortizing costs over 60 months) | X | |
| Mine exploration and development costs (reduce E & P in future years by amortizing costs over 120 months) | X | |

### SUMMARY OF E & P ADJUSTMENTS

E & P serves as a measure of the earnings of the corporation that are available for distribution as taxable dividends to the shareholders. Current E & P is determined by making a series of adjustments to the corporation's taxable income. These adjustments are reviewed in Concept Summary 9–1.

**LO.3**

Apply the rules for allocating earnings and profits to distributions.

### ALLOCATING E & P TO DISTRIBUTIONS

When a positive balance exists in both the current and the accumulated E & P accounts, corporate distributions are deemed to be made first from current E & P and then from accumulated E & P. When distributions exceed the amount of current E & P, it becomes necessary to allocate current and accumulated E & P to each

---

**CONCEPT SUMMARY 9–2**

## Allocating E & P to Distributions

1. Current E & P is allocated first to distributions on a pro rata basis; then, accumulated E & P is applied (to the extent necessary) in chronological order beginning with the earliest distribution. See Example 8.

2. Unless and until the parties can show otherwise, it is presumed that current E & P covers all distributions. See Example 9.

3. When a deficit exists in accumulated E & P and a positive balance exists in current E & P, distributions are regarded as dividends to the extent of current E & P. See Example 10.

4. When a deficit exists in current E & P and a positive balance exists in accumulated E & P, the two accounts are netted at the date of distribution. If the resulting balance is zero or a deficit, the distribution is treated as a return of capital, first reducing the basis of the stock to zero, then generating taxable gain. If a positive balance results, the distribution is a dividend to the extent of the balance. Any loss in current E & P is allocated ratably during the year unless the parties can show otherwise. See Example 11.

---

distribution made during the year. Current E & P is allocated on a pro rata basis to each distribution. Accumulated E & P is applied in chronological order, beginning with the earliest distribution. This allocation is important if any shareholder sells stock during the year.

**EXAMPLE 8**

As of January 1 of the current year, Black Corporation has accumulated E & P of $10,000. Current E & P for the year amounts to $30,000. Megan and Matt are sole *equal* shareholders of Black from January 1 to July 31. On August 1, Megan sells all of her stock to Helen. Black makes two distributions to shareholders during the year: $40,000 to Megan and Matt ($20,000 to each) on July 1, and $40,000 to Matt and Helen ($20,000 to each) on December 1. Current and accumulated E & P are allocated to the two distributions as follows.

| | Source of Distribution | | |
| --- | --- | --- | --- |
| | **Current E & P** | **Accumulated E & P** | **Return of Capital** |
| July 1 distribution ($40,000) | $15,000 | $10,000 | $15,000 |
| December 1 distribution ($40,000) | 15,000 | –0– | 25,000 |

Thus, since 50% of the total distributions are made on July 1 and December 1, respectively, one-half of current E & P is allocated to each of the two distributions. Accumulated E & P is applied in chronological order, so the entire amount is attributed to the July 1 distribution. The tax consequences to the shareholders are presented below.

| | Shareholder | | |
| --- | --- | --- | --- |
| | **Megan** | **Matt** | **Helen** |
| July distribution ($40,000) | | | |
|   Dividend income— | | | |
|     From current E & P ($15,000) | $ 7,500 | $ 7,500 | $ –0– |
|     From accumulated E & P ($10,000) | 5,000 | 5,000 | –0– |
|   Return of capital ($15,000) | 7,500 | 7,500 | –0– |

| | Shareholder | | |
| --- | --- | --- | --- |
| | **Megan** | **Matt** | **Helen** |
| December distribution ($40,000) | | | |
| Dividend income— | | | |
| From current E & P ($15,000) | $ –0– | $ 7,500 | $ 7,500 |
| From accumulated E & P ($0) | –0– | –0– | –0– |
| Return of capital ($25,000) | –0– | 12,500 | 12,500 |
| Total dividend income | $12,500 | $20,000 | $ 7,500 |
| Nontaxable return of capital (assuming sufficient basis in the stock investment) | $ 7,500 | $20,000 | $12,500 |

Because the balance in the accumulated E & P account is exhausted when it is applied to the July 1 distribution, Megan has more dividend income than Helen, even though both receive equal distributions during the year. In addition, each shareholder's basis is reduced by the nontaxable return of capital; any excess over basis results in taxable gain. ■

When the tax years of the corporation and its shareholders are not the same, it may be impossible to determine the amount of current E & P on a timely basis. For example, if shareholders use a calendar year and the corporation uses a fiscal year, then current E & P may not be ascertainable until after the shareholders' tax returns have been filed. To address this timing problem, the allocation rules presume that current E & P is sufficient to cover every distribution made during the year unless or until the parties can show otherwise.

**EXAMPLE 9**

Green Corporation uses the fiscal year of July 1 through June 30 for tax purposes. Carol, Green's only shareholder, uses a calendar year. As of July 1, 2006, Green Corporation has a zero balance in its accumulated E & P account. For fiscal year 2006–2007, the corporation incurs a $5,000 deficit in current E & P. On August 1, 2006, Green distributed $10,000 to Carol. The distribution is dividend income to Carol and is reported when she files her income tax return for the 2006 calendar year, on or before April 15, 2007.

Because Carol cannot prove until June 30, 2007, that the corporation has a deficit for the 2006–2007 fiscal year, she must assume the $10,000 distribution is fully covered by current E & P. When Carol learns of the deficit, she can file an amended return for 2006 showing the $10,000 as a return of capital. Alternatively, Carol can file for an extension for her return, while she awaits Green Corporation's fiscal year-end. ■

Additional difficulties arise when either the current or the accumulated E & P account has a deficit balance. In particular, when current E & P is positive and accumulated E & P has a deficit balance, accumulated E & P is *not* netted against current E & P. Instead, the distribution is deemed to be a taxable dividend to the extent of the positive current E & P balance.

**EXAMPLE 10**

At the beginning of the current year, Brown Corporation has a deficit of $30,000 in accumulated E & P. For the year, it has current E & P of $10,000 and distributes $5,000 to its shareholders. The $5,000 distribution is treated as a taxable dividend since it is deemed to have been made from current E & P. This is the case even though Brown Corporation still has a deficit in accumulated E & P at the end of the year. ■

In contrast to the above rule, when a deficit exists in current E & P and a positive balance exists in accumulated E & P, the accounts are netted at the date of distribution. If the resulting balance is zero or negative, the distribution is a

### Bridge to Finance

Investors often have tried to read the dividend policies of a corporation as indicators of the strength of the entity: Constant dividend payments indicated a stable financial structure for the corporation, while dividend increases were a predictor of good times and triggered stock price increases. Reductions in historic dividend payment patterns foreshadowed financial difficulties and often caused a quick and sizable drop in share price.

Nobel Prize winners Merton Miller, University of Chicago, and Franco Modigliani, MIT, disagreed. They viewed dividends as a remnant of various financing sources available to the corporation: If it was cheaper to finance future growth by retaining profits and decreasing or eliminating dividend payments, so be it. The entity must reduce its cost of capital wherever possible, and, under this interpretation, a dividend decrease might indicate the internal financial strength of the corporation. Conversely, the payment of a dividend reduces the capital available to the entity, thereby forcing the entity to finance its operations and growth from some third-party source and risking future weakness if the cost of that capital increases.

Miller and Modigliani held that stock price and dividend policy were unrelated, and that changes in dividend patterns should not affect the capitalized value of the business. Their original studies are more than 40 years old, but the market seems to have adopted them. Even with lower tax rates on dividends, few shareholders complain that the typical growth stock never pays dividends.

---

return of capital. If a positive balance results, the distribution is a dividend to the extent of the balance. Any current E & P deficit is allocated ratably during the year unless the parties can show otherwise.

**EXAMPLE 11**

At the beginning of the current year, Gray Corporation (a calendar year taxpayer) has accumulated E & P of $10,000. During the year, the corporation incurs a $15,000 deficit in current E & P that accrues ratably. On July 1, Gray Corporation distributes $6,000 in cash to Hal, its sole shareholder. To determine how much of the $6,000 cash distribution represents dividend income to Hal, the balances of both accumulated and current E & P as of July 1 are determined and netted. This is necessary because of the deficit in current E & P.

|  | Source of Distribution | |
|---|---|---|
|  | Current E & P | Accumulated E & P |
| January 1 |  | $10,000 |
| July 1 (½ of $15,000 deficit in current E & P) | ($7,500) | 2,500 |
| July 1 distribution—$6,000 |  |  |
| Dividend income: $2,500 |  |  |
| Return of capital: $3,500 |  |  |

The balance in E & P on July 1 is $2,500. Thus, of the $6,000 distribution, $2,500 is taxed as a dividend, and $3,500 represents a return of capital. ■

## Corporate Distributions

In connection with the discussion of corporate distributions, the following points need reinforcement.

- Because E & P is the measure of dividend income, its periodic determination is essential to corporate planning. Thus, an E & P account should be established and maintained, particularly if the possibility exists that a corporate distribution might be a return of capital.
- Accumulated E & P is the sum of all past years' current E & P. There is no statute of limitations on the computation of E & P. The IRS can, for example, redetermine a corporation's current E & P for a tax year long since passed. Such a change affects accumulated E & P and has a direct impact on the taxability of current distributions to shareholders.
- Distributions can be planned to avoid or minimize dividend exposure.

### EXAMPLE 12

Flicker Corporation has accumulated E & P of $100,000 as of January 1 of the current year. During the year, it expects to have earnings from operations of $80,000 and to sell an asset for a loss of $100,000. Thus, it anticipates a current E & P deficit of $20,000. Flicker also expects to make a cash distribution of $60,000. The best approach is to recognize the loss as soon as possible and immediately thereafter make the cash distribution to the shareholders. Suppose these two steps take place on January 1. Because the current E & P has a deficit, the accumulated E & P account must be brought up to date (refer to Example 11). Thus, at the time of the distribution, the combined E & P balance is zero [$100,000 (beginning balance in accumulated E & P) – $100,000 (existing deficit in current E & P)], and the $60,000 distribution to the shareholders constitutes a return of capital. Current deficits are allocated pro rata throughout the year unless the parties can prove otherwise. Here they can. ■

### EXAMPLE 13

After several unprofitable years, Darter Corporation has a deficit in accumulated E & P of $100,000 as of January 1, 2004. Starting in 2004, Darter expects to generate annual E & P of $50,000 for the next four years and would like to distribute this amount to its shareholders. The corporation's cash position (for dividend purposes) will correspond to the current E & P generated. Compare the following possibilities.

1. On December 31 of 2004, 2005, 2006, and 2007, Darter Corporation distributes a cash dividend of $50,000.
2. On December 31 of 2005 and 2007, Darter Corporation distributes a cash dividend of $100,000.

The two alternatives are illustrated as follows.

| Year | Accumulated E & P (First of Year) | Current E & P | Distribution | Amount of Dividend |
|------|------|------|------|------|
| | | *Alternative 1* | | |
| 2004 | ($100,000) | $50,000 | $50,000 | $50,000 |
| 2005 | (100,000) | 50,000 | 50,000 | 50,000 |
| 2006 | (100,000) | 50,000 | 50,000 | 50,000 |
| 2007 | (100,000) | 50,000 | 50,000 | 50,000 |
| | | *Alternative 2* | | |
| 2004 | ($100,000) | $50,000 | $ –0– | $ –0– |
| 2005 | (50,000) | 50,000 | 100,000 | 50,000 |
| 2006 | (50,000) | 50,000 | –0– | –0– |
| 2007 | –0– | 50,000 | 100,000 | 50,000 |

Alternative 1 produces $200,000 of dividend income because each $50,000 distribution is fully covered by current E & P. Alternative 2, however, produces only $100,000 of dividend income to the shareholders. The remaining $100,000 is a return of capital. Why? At the time Darter Corporation made its first distribution of $100,000 on December 31, 2005, it had a deficit of $50,000 in accumulated E & P (the original deficit of $100,000 is reduced by the $50,000 of current E & P from 2004). Consequently, the $100,000 distribution yields a $50,000 dividend (the current E & P for 2005), and $50,000 is treated as a return of capital. As of January 1, 2006, Darter's accumulated E & P now has a deficit balance of $50,000, since a distribution cannot increase a deficit in E & P. Adding the remaining $50,000 of current E & P from 2006, the balance as of January 1, 2007, is zero. Thus, the second distribution of $100,000 made on December 31, 2007, also yields $50,000 of dividends (the current E & P for 2007) and a $50,000 return of capital. ■

**Bridge to Investments**

Most investors look to the stocks of utilities, real estate investment trusts, and tobacco companies as the source of steady dividend payments. This is a prudent decision on the investor's part, as the typical S&P 500 stock offers a dividend yield of just over 1 percent. But an investor could put together a fairly diversified portfolio using only stocks that regularly produce dividend yields of at least 2 percent. Using recent data, these companies include the following.

- Bank of America
- Dow Chemical
- Hong Kong Telecommunications
- Emerson Electric
- Telefonos de Mexico
- Weyerhauser

- General Electric
- ChevronTexaco
- Citigroup
- BellSouth
- Honeywell
- Kimberly–Clark
- Sara Lee

Dividends can be important to the investor because:

- They can be used in a tax-sheltered account, like a § 401(k) plan, such that the tax inefficiency of the dividends is not recognized immediately by the investor.
- Even today, about 40 percent of the total return from an investment can be traced to holding stocks that make regular distributions.
- Generally, a dividend-paying company is a profitable company, and corporate profits often are hard to come by.
- Earning and reinvesting dividends is an easy way to put into place an investment policy of dollar-cost averaging, a technique that forces the investor to buy more shares when prices are low and fewer shares when prices are high. Dollar-cost averaging often implements a contrarian investment strategy.

---

**LO.4**

Understand the tax impact of property dividends on the recipient shareholder and the corporation making the distribution.

*Definition
Property Dividend
–page C-14*

# Property Dividends

The previous discussion assumed that all distributions by a corporation to its shareholders are in the form of cash. Although most corporate distributions are paid in cash, a corporation may distribute a **property dividend** for various reasons. The shareholders may want a particular property that is held by the corporation. Or a corporation that is strapped for cash may want to distribute a dividend to its shareholders.

Property distributions have the same tax impact as distributions of cash except for effects attributable to any difference between the basis and the fair market value of the distributed property. In most situations, distributed property is appreciated, so its sale would result in a gain to the corporation. Distributions of property with a basis that differs from fair market value raise several tax questions.

- For the shareholder:
  - What is the amount of the distribution?
  - What is the basis of the property in the shareholder's hands?
- For the corporation:
  - Is a gain or loss recognized as a result of the distribution?
  - What is the effect of the distribution on E & P?

## PROPERTY DIVIDENDS—EFFECT ON THE SHAREHOLDER

When a corporation distributes property rather than cash to a shareholder, the amount distributed is measured by the fair market value of the property on the date of distribution.[12] As with a cash distribution, the portion of a property distribution covered by existing E & P is a dividend, and any excess is treated as a return of capital. If the fair market value of the property distributed exceeds the corporation's E & P and the shareholder's basis in the stock investment, a capital gain usually results.

The amount distributed is reduced by any liabilities to which the distributed property is subject immediately before and immediately after the distribution and by any liabilities of the corporation assumed by the shareholder. The basis in the distributed property to the shareholder is the fair market value of the property on the date of the distribution.

**EXAMPLE 14**

Robin Corporation has E & P of $60,000. It distributes land with a fair market value of $50,000 (adjusted basis of $30,000) to its sole shareholder, Charles. The land is subject to a liability of $10,000, which Charles assumes. Charles has a taxable dividend of $40,000 [$50,000 (fair market value) – $10,000 (liability)]. The basis of the land to Charles is $50,000. ■

**EXAMPLE 15**

Red Corporation owns 10% of Tan Corporation. Tan has ample E & P to cover any distributions made during the year. One distribution made to Red consists of a vacant lot with a basis of $50,000 and a fair market value of $30,000. Red recognizes a taxable dividend of $30,000, and its basis in the lot becomes $30,000. ■

Distributing property that has depreciated in value as a property dividend may reflect poor planning. Note what happens in Example 15. Basis of $20,000 disappears due to the loss (basis $50,000, fair market value $30,000). As an alternative, if Tan Corporation sells the lot, it could use the loss to reduce its taxes. Then Tan could distribute the $30,000 of proceeds to its shareholders.

## PROPERTY DIVIDENDS—EFFECT ON THE CORPORATION

As noted earlier, the distribution of a property dividend raises two questions related to the corporation's tax position: Is a gain or loss recognized? What is the effect on E & P?

**Recognition of Gain or Loss.** All distributions of appreciated property generate gain to the distributing corporation.[13] In effect, a corporation that distributes appreciated property is treated as if it had sold the property to the shareholder for its fair market value. However, the distributing corporation does *not* recognize loss on distributions of property.

**EXAMPLE 16**

A corporation distributes land (basis of $10,000 and fair market value of $30,000) to a shareholder. The corporation recognizes a gain of $20,000. ■

**EXAMPLE 17**

Assume the property in Example 16 has a basis of $30,000 and a fair market value of $10,000. The corporation does not recognize a loss on the distribution. ■

If the distributed property is subject to a liability in excess of basis or the shareholder assumes such a liability, a special rule applies. The fair market value

[12]§ 301.
[13]§ 311.

### Bridge to Public Finance

The double tax on corporate income has always been controversial. Reformers have argued that taxing corporate profits twice creates several distortions in the economy, including:

- An incentive to invest in noncorporate rather than corporate businesses.
- An incentive for corporations to finance operations with debt rather than new equity because interest payments are deductible.
- An incentive for corporations to retain earnings and to structure distributions of profits to avoid the double tax.

Taken together, these distortions raise the cost of capital for corporate investments and increase the vulnerability of corporations in economic downturns due to excessive debt financing. Reformers argue that eliminating the double tax would remove these distortions, stimulate the economy (with estimated gains of up to $25 billion annually), and increase capital stock in the corporate sector by as much as $500 billion. They also argue that elimination of the double tax would make the United States more competitive internationally, because the majority of our trading partners assess only one tax on corporate income.

In contrast, supporters of the double tax argue that in view of the economic power held by publicly traded corporations, the tax is appropriate, especially since the income tax is based on notions of ability to pay and fairness. They also argue that many of the distortions can already be avoided through the use of deductible payments by closely held C corporations and through partnerships, limited liability companies, and S corporations.

---

of the property for purposes of determining gain on the distribution is treated as not being less than the amount of the liability.[14]

**EXAMPLE 18**

Assume the land in Example 16 is subject to a liability of $35,000. The corporation recognizes gain of $25,000 on the distribution ($35,000 − $10,000). ■

**Effect of Corporate Distributions on E & P.**   Corporate distributions reduce E & P by the amount of money distributed or by the greater of the fair market value or the adjusted basis of property distributed, less the amount of any liability on the property.[15] E & P is increased by gain recognized on appreciated property distributed as a property dividend.

**EXAMPLE 19**

Crimson Corporation distributes property (basis of $10,000 and fair market value of $20,000) to Brenda, its shareholder. Crimson Corporation recognizes a gain of $10,000, which is added to its E & P. E & P is then reduced by $20,000, the fair market value of the property. Brenda has dividend income of $20,000 (presuming sufficient E & P). ■

**EXAMPLE 20**

Assume the same facts as in Example 19, except that the property's adjusted basis in the hands of Crimson Corporation is $25,000. Because loss is not recognized and the property's adjusted basis is greater than its fair market value, E & P is reduced by $25,000. Brenda reports dividend income of $20,000 (the fair market value of the property received). ■

---

[14]§ 311(b)(2).                    [15]§§ 312(a), (b), and (c).

**EXAMPLE 21**

Assume the same facts as in Example 20, except that the property is subject to a liability of $6,000. E & P is now reduced by $19,000 [$25,000 (adjusted basis) − $6,000 (liability)]. Brenda has a dividend of $14,000 [$20,000 (amount of the distribution) − $6,000 (liability)], and her basis in the property is $20,000. ■

Under no circumstances can a distribution, whether cash or property, either generate a deficit in E & P or add to a deficit in E & P. Deficits can arise only through recognized corporate losses.

**EXAMPLE 22**

Teal Corporation has accumulated E & P of $10,000 at the beginning of the current tax year. During the year, it has current E & P of $15,000. At the end of the year, it distributes cash of $30,000 to its sole shareholder, Walter. Teal's E & P at the end of the year is zero. The accumulated E & P of $10,000 is increased by current E & P of $15,000 and reduced $25,000 by the dividend distribution. The remaining $5,000 of the distribution to Walter does not reduce E & P because a distribution cannot generate a deficit in E & P. ■

**LO.5**

Understand the nature and treatment of constructive dividends.

*Dennihan
Constructive
Dividend
– page G-5*

# Constructive Dividends

Any measurable economic benefit conveyed by a corporation to its shareholders can be treated as a dividend for Federal income tax purposes even though it is not formally declared or designated as a dividend. A distribution need not be issued pro rata to all shareholders.[16] Nor must the distribution satisfy the legal requirements of a dividend as set forth by applicable state law. This benefit, often described as a **constructive dividend,** is distinguishable from actual corporate distributions of cash and property in form only.

Constructive dividend situations usually arise in closely held corporations. Here, the dealings between the parties are less structured, and frequently, formalities are not preserved. The constructive dividend serves as a substitute for actual distributions. Usually, it is intended to accomplish some tax objective not available through the use of direct dividends. The shareholders may be attempting to distribute corporate profits in a form deductible to the corporation, like compensation.[17] Alternatively, the shareholders may be seeking benefits for themselves while avoiding the recognition of income. Some constructive dividends are, in reality, disguised dividends. But not all constructive dividends are deliberate attempts to avoid actual and formal dividends; many are inadvertent. Thus, an awareness of the various constructive dividend situations is essential to protect the parties from unanticipated, undesirable tax consequences.

## TYPES OF CONSTRUCTIVE DIVIDENDS

The most frequently encountered types of constructive dividends are summarized on the following pages.

---

[16]See *Lengsfield v. Comm.,* 57–1 USTC ¶9437, 50 AFTR 1683, 241 F.2d 508 (CA–5, 1957).

[17]Recall that dividend distributions do not provide the distributing corporation with an income tax deduction, although they do reduce E & P.

**Shareholder Use of Corporate-Owned Property.**  A constructive dividend can occur when a shareholder uses the corporation's property for personal purposes at no cost. Personal use of corporate-owned automobiles, airplanes, yachts, fishing camps, hunting lodges, and other entertainment facilities is commonplace in some closely held corporations. The shareholder has dividend income to the extent of the fair rental value of the property for the period of its personal use.

**Bargain Sale of Corporate Property to a Shareholder.**  Shareholders often purchase property from a corporation at a cost below the fair market value of the property. These bargain sales produce dividend income to the extent that the property's fair market value on the date of sale differs from the amount the shareholder paid for the property.[18] These situations might be avoided by appraising the property on or about the date of the sale. The appraised value should become the price to be paid by the shareholder.

**Bargain Rental of Corporate Property.**  A bargain rental of corporate property by a shareholder also produces dividend income. Here the measure of the constructive dividend is the excess of the property's fair rental value over the rent actually paid. Again, appraisal data should be used to avoid any questionable situations.

**Payments for the Benefit of a Shareholder.**  If a corporation pays an obligation of a shareholder, the payment is treated as a constructive dividend. The obligation involved need not be legally binding on the shareholder; it may, in fact, be a moral obligation.[19] Forgiveness of shareholder indebtedness by the corporation creates an identical problem.[20] Excessive rentals paid by a corporation for the use of shareholder property also are treated as constructive dividends.

**Unreasonable Compensation.**  A salary payment to a shareholder-employee that is deemed to be **unreasonable compensation** is frequently treated as a constructive dividend. As a consequence, it is not deductible by the corporation. In determining the reasonableness of salary payments, the following factors are considered.

* The employee's qualifications.
* A comparison of salaries with dividend distributions.
* The prevailing rates of compensation for comparable positions in comparable business concerns.
* The nature and scope of the employee's work.
* The size and complexity of the business.
* A comparison of salaries paid with both gross and net income.
* The taxpayer's salary policy toward all employees.
* For small corporations with a limited number of officers, the amount of compensation paid to the employee in question in previous years.
* For large corporations, whether a reasonable shareholder would have agreed to the level of compensation paid.[21]

**Loans to Shareholders.**  Advances to shareholders that are not bona fide loans are constructive dividends. Whether an advance qualifies as a bona fide loan is a question of fact to be determined in light of the particular circumstances. Factors

---

[18]Reg. § 1.301–1(j).

[19]*Montgomery Engineering Co. v. U.S.*, 64–2 USTC ¶9618, 13 AFTR2d 1747, 230 F.Supp. 838 (D.Ct. N.J., 1964), *aff'd* in 65–1 USTC ¶9368, 15 AFTR2d 746, 344 F.2d 996 (CA–3, 1965).

[20]Reg. § 1.301–1(m).

[21]*Mayson Manufacturing Co. v. Comm.*, 49–2 USTC ¶9467, 38 AFTR 1028, 178 F.2d 115 (CA–6, 1949) and *Alpha Medical v. Comm.*, 99–1 USTC ¶50,461, 83 AFTR2d 99–697, 172 F.3d 942 (CA–6, 1999).

## TAX IN THE NEWS

### THE $6,000 SHOWER CURTAIN: COMPENSATION OR CONSTRUCTIVE DIVIDEND?

Recently, there have been several well-publicized accounts of compensation abuse (to some) and illegal looting of corporate coffers (to others) by corporate executives. At the forefront of these scandals are the payments to L. Dennis Kozlowski by Tyco International (a large multinational conglomerate).

Kozlowski, during a four-year stint as CEO of Tyco, received about $400 million from the company in salary and stock-related compensation. In addition, Kozlowski received fringe benefits valued at $135 million. The benefits purportedly included:

- A new 15,000-square-foot home in Boca Raton, Florida, complete with pool, tennis court, and fountain. Tyco initially loaned the money interest-free to Kozlowski and then later forgave the entire loan. It paid him an extra $13 million to help him handle the income taxes on the income that resulted from forgiveness of the debt.
- More than $11 million in corporate funds used to decorate an $18 million Fifth Avenue apartment that Kozlowski stayed in when visiting New York. The funds were used to purchase antiques, art, a $17,000 umbrella stand, and a $6,000 gold-and-burgundy floral-patterned shower curtain.
- Half the cost of a $2.1 million birthday party for Kozlowski's wife, on the island of Sardinia. The weeklong party included a performance by singer Jimmy Buffett.
- Flowers costing $96,943 for Kozlowski's homes.

Kozlowski and other officers of Tyco are facing criminal indictments alleging that the compensation represents theft of the corporation's assets. Tyco is suing Kozlowski, seeking repayment of $244 million in back pay and benefits.

How should the compensation payments be treated? Kozlowski owned stock in his employer. Should Tyco treat the payments as compensation, a constructive dividend, or a theft loss? Avoidance of the double tax does not seem to have been a motive for the payments (recall that compensation in excess of $1 million is not deductible unless it is contingent on performance), and the corporation is publicly traded. Consequently, it would be difficult for the IRS to argue for constructive dividend treatment. The payments to Kozlowski were apparently not authorized, so they may be treated as a theft of Tyco's assets.

considered in determining whether the advance is a bona fide loan include the following.[22]

- Whether the advance is on open account or is evidenced by a written instrument.
- Whether the shareholder furnished collateral or other security for the advance.
- How long the advance has been outstanding.
- Whether any repayments have been made.
- The shareholder's ability to repay the advance.
- The shareholder's use of the funds (e.g., payment of routine bills versus nonrecurring, extraordinary expenses).
- The regularity of the advances.
- The dividend-paying history of the corporation.

---

[22]*Fin Hay Realty Co. v. U.S.*, 68–2 USTC ¶9438, 22 AFTR2d 5004, 398 F.2d 694 (CA–3, 1968).

# TAX IN THE NEWS

## HARD WORK PAYS OFF!

By 1985, William Rogers, a pharmacist with 25 years of experience in health care, had successfully developed and sold two businesses—a pharmacy chain and a medical supply company. In 1986, after turning down a $1 million offer to manage the home health care division of a large corporation, Rogers founded Alpha Medical, Inc., with a $1,000 contribution. Over the next four years, Rogers built Alpha Medical into a business with 60 employees, a taxable income of almost $7 million, and a 1990 return on equity of almost 100 percent. The business provided both financial management and medical consulting services to hospitals and home health care companies. Rogers was the company's sole shareholder and president. He regularly worked 12 hours a day and was on call 24 hours a day. Rogers made all major decisions for Alpha Medical, acquired all of the company's clients, and personally negotiated all of the company's contracts. In addition, he personally developed many of the company's products and collaborated with programmers to develop proprietary software used by the company.

In 1986, Rogers received only $67,000 in compensation. The amount increased to $431,000 in 1988 and $928,000 in 1989. In 1990, Rogers was paid over $4.4 million, 64 percent of the company's taxable income, while the company paid only a $1,500 dividend.

During an audit of Alpha Medical, the IRS argued that only $400,000 of Rogers' compensation in 1990 was reasonable and that the remaining $4 million was not deductible. As a result, the IRS assessed a $1.3 million tax deficiency and an accuracy-related penalty.

The Tax Court split the difference between the IRS and the taxpayer, holding that $2.3 million of Rogers' pay was reasonable. On appeal, however, the Sixth Circuit Court of Appeals ruled that all $4.4 million of the compensation paid to Rogers was reasonable. In its decision, the Court of Appeals said that "in light of Rogers' record of accomplishment, risks he assumed, and amazing growth, reasonable shareholders would have gladly agreed to Rogers' level of compensation." The Court of Appeals also explicitly noted that Rogers had been undercompensated in prior years and that he had incurred a substantial opportunity cost when he refused the $1 million job offer so that he could start Alpha Medical.

SOURCE: *Alpha Medical, Inc. v. Comm.*, 99–1 USTC ¶50,461, 83 AFTR2d 99–697, 172 F.3d 942 (CA–6, 1999).

Even when a corporation makes a bona fide loan to a shareholder, a constructive dividend may be triggered, equal to the amount of any imputed (forgone) interest on the loan.[23] Imputed interest equals the amount of interest (using the rate the Federal government pays on new borrowings, compounded semiannually) that exceeds the interest charged on the loan. When the imputed interest provision applies, the shareholder is deemed to have made an interest payment to the corporation equal to the amount of imputed interest, and the corporation is deemed to have repaid the imputed interest to the shareholder through a constructive dividend. As a result, the corporation receives interest income and makes a nondeductible dividend payment, and the shareholder has taxable dividend income that may be offset with an interest deduction.

---

[23]See § 7872. A more detailed discussion of imputed interest is found in Chapter 3.

---

### ⊙ TAX FACT

## EXECUTIVE COMPENSATION: AMOUNT AND COMPOSITION

Median executive compensation exceeds $2 million in the following five industries: insurance, communications, telecommunications, energy, and financial services. While stock options accounted for less than 20 percent of a CEO's direct pay in 1980, long-term compensation—mostly from exercised stock options—now makes up 80 percent of the average CEO's pay package.

---

**EXAMPLE 23**

Mallard Corporation lends its principal shareholder, Henry, $100,000 on January 2 of the current year. The loan is interest-free and payable on demand. On December 31, the imputed interest rules are applied. Assuming the Federal rate is 6%, compounded semiannually, the amount of imputed interest is $6,090. This amount is deemed paid by Henry to Mallard in the form of interest. Mallard is then deemed to return the amount to Henry as a constructive dividend. Thus, Henry has dividend income of $6,090, which may be offset with a deduction for the interest deemed paid to Mallard. Mallard has interest income of $6,090 for the interest received, with no offsetting deduction for the dividend payment. ■

**Loans to a Corporation by Shareholders.** Shareholder loans to a corporation may be reclassified as equity if the debt has too many features of stock. Any interest and principal payments made by the corporation to the shareholder are then treated as constructive dividends. This topic was covered more thoroughly in the discussion of "thin capitalization" in Chapter 8.

### TAX TREATMENT OF CONSTRUCTIVE DIVIDENDS

For tax purposes, constructive distributions are treated the same as actual distributions.[24] Thus, a corporate shareholder is entitled to the dividends received deduction (refer to Chapter 8). The constructive distribution is taxable as a dividend only to the extent of the corporation's current and accumulated E & P. The burden of proving that the distribution constitutes a return of capital because of inadequate E & P rests with the taxpayer.[25]

---

## Constructive Dividends

### FRAMEWORK FOCUS: INCOME AND EXCLUSIONS

STRATEGY ➤ AVOID INCOME RECOGNITION.

---

Tax planning can be particularly effective in avoiding constructive dividend situations. Shareholders should try to structure their dealings with the corporation on an arm's length basis. For example, reasonable rent should be paid for the use of corporate property, and a fair price should be paid for its purchase. The parties should make every effort to support the amount involved with appraisal data or market information obtained from reliable sources at or near the time of the transaction. Dealings between shareholders and a closely held corporation should be as formal as possible. In

---

[24]*Simon v. Comm.*, 57–2 USTC ¶9989, 52 AFTR 698, 248 F.2d 869 (CA–8, 1957).

[25]*DiZenzo v. Comm.*, 65–2 USTC ¶9518, 16 AFTR2d 5107, 348 F.2d 122 (CA–2, 1965).

the case of loans to shareholders, for example, the parties should provide for an adequate rate of interest and written evidence of the debt. Shareholders also should establish and follow a realistic repayment schedule.

If shareholders wish to distribute corporate profits in a form deductible to the corporation, a balanced mix of the possible alternatives lessens the risk of constructive dividend treatment. Rent for the use of shareholder property, interest on amounts borrowed from shareholders, or salaries for services rendered by shareholders are all feasible substitutes for dividend distributions. But overdoing any one approach may attract the attention of the IRS. Too much interest, for example, may mean the corporation is thinly capitalized, and some of the debt may be reclassified as equity.

Much can be done to protect against the disallowance of unreasonable compensation. Example 24 is an illustration, all too common in a family corporation, of what *not* to do.

### EXAMPLE 24

Bob Cole wholly owns Eagle Corporation. Corporate employees and annual salaries include Mrs. Cole ($30,000), Cole, Jr. ($20,000), Bob Cole ($160,000), and Ed ($80,000). The operation of Eagle Corporation is shared about equally between Bob Cole and Ed, who is an unrelated party. Mrs. Cole performed significant services for Eagle during its formative years but now merely attends the annual meeting of the board of directors. Cole, Jr., Bob Cole's son, is a full-time student and occasionally signs papers for the corporation in his capacity as treasurer. Eagle Corporation has not distributed a dividend for 10 years, although it has accumulated substantial E & P. Mrs. Cole, Cole, Jr., and Bob Cole run the risk of a finding of unreasonable compensation, based on the following factors.

- Mrs. Cole's salary is vulnerable unless proof is available that some or all of her $30,000 annual salary is payment for services rendered to the corporation in prior years and that she was underpaid for those years.[26]

- Cole, Jr.'s salary is also vulnerable; he does not appear to earn the $20,000 paid to him by the corporation. Although neither Cole, Jr., nor Mrs. Cole is a shareholder, each one's relationship to Bob Cole is enough of a tie-in to raise the unreasonable compensation issue.

- Bob Cole's salary appears susceptible to challenge. Why is he receiving $80,000 more than Ed when it appears that they share equally in the operation of the corporation?

- The fact that Eagle Corporation has not distributed dividends over the past 10 years, even though it is capable of doing so, increases the likelihood of a constructive dividend. ■

What could have been done to improve the tax position of the parties in Example 24? Mrs. Cole and Cole, Jr., are not entitled to a salary as neither seems to be performing any services for the corporation. Paying them a salary simply aggravates the problem. The IRS is more apt to consider *all* the salaries to members of the family as being excessive under the circumstances. Bob Cole should probably reduce his compensation to correspond to that paid Ed. He can then attempt to distribute corporate earnings to himself in some other form.

Paying some dividends to Bob Cole would also help alleviate the problems raised in Example 24. The IRS has been successful in denying a deduction for salary paid to a shareholder-employee, even when the payment was reasonable, in a situation where the corporation had not distributed any dividends.[27] Most courts, however, have not denied deductions for compensation solely because a dividend was not paid. A better approach is to compare an employee's compensation with the level of compensation prevalent in the particular industry.

The corporation can substitute *indirect* compensation for Bob Cole by paying expenses that benefit him personally but are nevertheless deductible to the corporation. For example, premiums paid by the corporation for sickness, accident, and hospitalization insurance for Bob Cole are deductible to the corporation and generally nontaxable to him.[28] Any payments under the policy are not taxable to Bob Cole unless they exceed his medical expenses.[29] The corporation can also pay for travel and entertainment expenses incurred by Cole on behalf of the corporation. If these expenditures are primarily for the benefit of the corporation, Bob Cole will not recognize any taxable income and the corporation will receive a deduction.[30] The tax treatment of these benefits is discussed in more detail in Chapter 16.

When testing for reasonableness, the IRS looks at the total compensation package, including indirect compensation payments to a shareholder-employee. Thus, indirect payments must not be overlooked.

---

[26]See, for example, *R. J. Nicoll Co.*, 59 T.C. 37 (1972).

[27]*McCandless Tile Service v. U.S.*, 70–1 USTC ¶9284, 25 AFTR2d 70–870, 422 F.2d 1336 (Ct.Cls., 1970). The court in *McCandless* concluded that a return on equity of 15% of net profits was reasonable.

[28]Reg. § 1.162–10.

[29]The medical reimbursement plan must meet certain nondiscrimination requirements of § 105(h)(2).

[30]Reg. § 1.62–2(c)(4).

**EXAMPLE 25**

Cora, the president and sole shareholder of Willet Corporation, is paid an annual salary of $100,000 by the corporation. Cora would like to draw funds from the corporation but is concerned that additional salary payments might cause the IRS to contend her salary is unreasonable. Cora does not want Willet to pay any dividends. She also wishes to donate $50,000 to her alma mater to establish scholarships for needy students. Willet Corporation could make the contribution on Cora's behalf. The payment clearly benefits Cora, but the amount of the contribution will not be taxed to her.[31] Willet can take a charitable contribution deduction for the payment. ■

**EXAMPLE 26**

Assume in Example 25 that Cora has made an individual pledge to the university to provide $50,000 for scholarships for needy students. Willet Corporation satisfies Cora's pledge by paying the $50,000 to the university. The $50,000 will be taxed to Cora.[32] In this context, the $50,000 payment to the university may be treated as *indirect* compensation to Cora. In determining whether Cora's salary is unreasonable, both the *direct* payment of $100,000 and the *indirect* $50,000 payment will be considered. Cora's total compensation package is $150,000. Cora may be eligible for a charitable contribution deduction, up to 50% of her adjusted gross income. However, the phaseout of itemized deductions for high-income individuals may limit the deduction (see Chapter 15). ■

---

**LO.6**

Distinguish between taxable and nontaxable stock dividends.

DIGGING DEEPER 1

*Definition*

*Stock Dividends*

*—page C-17*

# Stock Dividends

As a general rule, **stock dividends** are excluded from income if they are pro rata distributions of stock or stock rights, paid on common stock.[33] However, there are five exceptions to this general rule. These exceptions to nontaxability of stock dividends deal with various disproportionate distribution situations.

*Find more information on this topic at our Web site: http://wft-entities.swlearning.com.*

If a stock dividend is not taxable, the corporation's E & P is not reduced.[34] If a stock dividend is taxable, the distributing corporation treats the distribution in the same manner as any other taxable property dividend.

If a stock dividend is taxable, the shareholder's basis of the newly received shares is fair market value, and the holding period starts on the date of receipt. If a stock dividend is not taxable, the basis of the stock on which the dividend is distributed is reallocated.[35] If the dividend shares are identical to these formerly held shares, basis in the old stock is reallocated by dividing the taxpayer's cost in the old stock by the total number of shares. If the dividend stock is not identical to the underlying shares (e.g., a stock dividend of preferred on common), basis is determined by allocating the basis of the formerly held shares between the old and new stock according to the fair market value of each. The holding period includes the holding period of the previously held stock.[36]

**EXAMPLE 27**

Gail bought 1,000 shares of common stock two years ago for $10,000. In the current tax year, Gail receives 10 shares of common stock as a nontaxable stock dividend. Gail's basis of $10,000 is divided by 1,010. Consequently, each share of stock has a basis of $9.90 instead of the pre-dividend $10 basis. ■

---

[31]*Henry J. Knott*, 67 T.C. 681 (1977).

[32]*Schalk Chemical Co. v. Comm.*, 62–1 USTC ¶9496, 9 AFTR2d 1579, 304 F.2d 48 (CA–9, 1962).

[33]Companies often issue stock dividends or authorize stock splits to keep the stock price in an affordable range. Stock splits do not change the total value of an investment. For example, 100 shares

at $100 will become 200 shares at $50 after the split. However, some studies show that a stock split often leads to an upward price trend over the year following the split.

[34]§ 312(d)(1).

[35]§ 307(a).

[36]§ 1223(5).

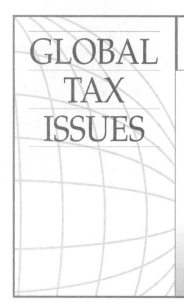

## DEEMED DIVIDENDS FROM CONTROLLED FOREIGN CORPORATIONS

It is not uncommon for U.S. multinational companies to conduct business overseas through the use of foreign corporations. Most often, these foreign corporations are controlled by the U.S. parent. Called controlled foreign corporations (CFCs), such entities would be ideal for income avoidance if incorporated in a low-tax jurisdiction (i.e., a tax haven country). Further, U.S. income tax on their profits would be deferred if no dividends are distributed to the U.S. parent.

Well aware of the latter possibility, the tax law compels a U.S. shareholder to recognize as income the profits of a CFC that are not distributed. In contrast to constructive dividends, the "deemed dividend" distribution increases the basis the U.S. company has in the foreign corporation's stock. Furthermore, when the deemed dividend is ultimately distributed to the parent (i.e., repatriated), no income results. Thus, the CFC rules prevent deferral but are not intended to lead to double taxation.

**EXAMPLE 28**

Assume instead that Gail received a nontaxable preferred stock dividend of 100 shares. The preferred stock has a fair market value of $1,000, and the common stock, on which the preferred is distributed, has a fair market value of $19,000. After the receipt of the stock dividend, the basis of the common stock is $9,500, and the basis of the preferred is $500, computed as follows.

| | |
|---|---|
| Fair market value of common | $19,000 |
| Fair market value of preferred | 1,000 |
| | $20,000 |
| Basis of common: $19/20 \times \$10,000$ | $ 9,500 |
| Basis of preferred: $1/20 \times \$10,000$ | $   500 |

*Find more information on this topic at our Web site: **http://wft-entities.swlearning.com**.*

**LO.7**

Discuss the tax treatment of stock redemptions.

# Stock Redemptions

Many investors are tempted to use a "no dividends" strategy in working with a healthy corporation whose accumulated profits and market value continue to rise over time.

**EXAMPLE 29**

Sally invests $100,000 in the new Cream Corporation. Cream is successful in generating operating profits, and it reinvests its accumulated profits in the business rather than paying dividends. Fifteen years later, Sally's shares are worth $300,000, and her share of Cream's E & P exceeds $1 million. Sally sells the shares for a $200,000 long-term capital gain, taxed at a rate of only 15%. By selling her stock to a third party, Sally can reduce the sales proceeds by her stock basis, resulting in a significant tax savings to her, at no detriment to Cream. ■

A similar strategy would seem to work where several shareholders can act in concert. Using a **stock redemption** to carry out this strategy, the corporation buys back shares from its shareholders in a market transaction.

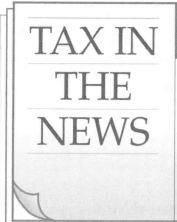

### CORPORATE CASH RESERVES AFFECT THE FREQUENCY OF STOCK REDEMPTIONS

The economic and financial market slumps of 2001 and 2002, along with the uneven economic recovery that followed, prompted many corporate executives to build up corporate cash reserves to record levels. However, finding productive uses for this cash in the current economic environment can be challenging. One consequence of the higher cash reserves has been an increase in stock buybacks (i.e., redemptions) over the last two years. Many corporations have also increased their dividend payouts in response to the reduction in tax rates applicable to dividends. Debt reduction also appears to have been a favorite use for the excess cash reserves.

**EXAMPLE 30**

Mike and Cheryl are husband and wife, and each owns 100 shares in Mauve Corporation, the total of all of Mauve's outstanding stock. Mauve's operations have produced a sizable aggregated operating profit over the years, such that its E & P exceeds $5 million. Mike and Cheryl both have realized appreciation of $600,000 on their original investment of $100,000 each, and they would like to enjoy some of the cash that Mauve has accumulated during their holding period. At Mike's request, instead of paying a dividend, Mauve buys back one-half of Mike's shares for $350,000. This seems to produce a $300,000 long-term capital gain [$350,000 (sales proceeds) − $50,000 (basis in 50 shares of Mauve stock)], rather than a $350,000 dividend for Mike. ■

Stock redemptions, however, generally result in dividend income for the shareholder whose stock is redeemed, rather than a sale or exchange, unless the shareholder surrenders significant control in the entity as a result of the redemption. Section 302 allows sale or exchange treatment where either:

- All of the shareholder's stock is redeemed.[37]
- After the redemption, the investor is a minority shareholder and owns less than 80 percent of the interest owned in the corporation before the redemption.[38]

*Find more information on this topic at our Web site: **http://wft-entities.swlearning.com.***

When the transaction is treated as a dividend, the investor's basis in the redeemed shares *does not disappear* but attaches to any remaining shares that he or she owns.

Other provisions also allow sale or exchange treatment for a stock redemption.[39] In measuring the investor's stock holdings before and after the redemption, shares owned by related taxpayers also are counted.[40]

*Find more information on this topic at our Web site: **http://wft-entities.swlearning.com.***

Stock redemptions occur for numerous reasons, including the following.

- To acquire the holdings of a retiring or deceased shareholder.
- To carry out a property settlement related to a divorce.
- To increase the per-share price of the stock as it trades in a market.

---

[37]§ 302(b)(3).
[38]§ 302(b)(2).

[39]For example, see §§ 302(b)(1), 302(b)(4), and 303.
[40]§ 318 is used for this purpose.

The tax consequences for the redeeming corporation are summarized as follows.

- If noncash property is used to acquire the redeemed shares, the corporation recognizes any realized gain (but not loss) on the distributed assets.[41]
- E & P of the redeeming corporation *disappears* to the extent of the number of shares redeemed as a percentage of the shares outstanding before the buyback.[42]

Thus, a dividend likely results in Example 30. The strategy illustrated in Example 29, though, can be effective in avoiding dividend income and converting it instead into a long-term capital gain.

# Restrictions on Corporate Accumulations

Two provisions of the Code are designed to prevent corporations and their shareholders from avoiding the double tax on dividend distributions. Both provisions impose a penalty tax on undistributed income retained by the corporation. The rules underlying these provisions are complex and beyond the scope of this text. However, a brief description is provided as an introduction.

The *accumulated earnings tax* (in §§ 531–537) imposes a 15 percent tax on the current year's corporate earnings that have been accumulated without a reasonable business need. The burden of proving what constitutes a reasonable need is borne by the taxpayer. In determining accumulated income, most businesses are allowed a $250,000 minimum credit. Thus, most corporations can accumulate $250,000 in earnings over a series of years without fear of an accumulated earnings tax. Beyond the minimum credit, earnings can be accumulated for:

- Working capital needs (to purchase inventory),
- Retirement of debt incurred in connection with the business,
- Investment or loans to suppliers or customers (if necessary to maintain the corporation's business), or
- Realistic business contingencies, including lawsuits or self-insurance.

The *personal holding company (PHC) tax* (described in §§ 541–547) was enacted to discourage the sheltering of certain kinds of passive income in corporations owned by individuals with high marginal tax rates. Historically, the tax was aimed at "incorporated pocketbooks" that were frequently found in the entertainment and construction industries. For example, a taxpayer could shelter income from securities in a corporation, which would pay no dividends, and allow the corporation's stock to increase in value. Like the accumulated earnings tax, the PHC tax employs a 15 percent rate and is designed to force a corporation to distribute earnings to shareholders. However, in any single year, the IRS cannot impose both the PHC tax and the accumulated earnings tax. Generally, a company is considered a PHC and may be subject to the tax if:

- More than 50 percent of the value of the outstanding stock was owned by five or fewer individuals at any time during the last half of the year, and
- A substantial portion (60 percent or more) of the corporation's income is comprised of passive types of income, including dividends, interest, rents, royalties, or certain personal service income.

---

[41]§ 311.                              [42]§ 312(n)(7).

# Suggested Further Readings

Richard W. Bailine, "When Is a Dividend Not a Dividend?" *Journal of Corporate Taxation*, March/April 2004.

"Exclusive Discounts Treated as Constructive Distributions," *Business Entities*, July/August 2002, p. 51.

Andrew R. Lee, "Dividend Planning Strategies for Shareholders and Corporations," *Practical Tax Strategies*, October 2003, pp. 204–211.

## KEY TERMS

| | | |
|---|---|---|
| Accumulated earnings and profits, 9–4 | Dividend, 9–2 | Stock dividends, 9–21 |
| Constructive dividend, 9–15 | Earnings and profits, 9–3 | Stock redemption, 9–22 |
| Current earnings and profits, 9–4 | Property dividend, 9–12 | Unreasonable compensation, 9–16 |

## PROBLEM MATERIALS

### Problems

1. At the start of the current year, Swan Corporation (a calendar year taxpayer) has accumulated E & P of $200,000. Its current E & P is $60,000. During the year, Swan distributes $280,000 ($140,000 each) to its equal shareholders, George and Albert. George has a basis of $48,000 in his stock, and Albert has a basis of $8,000 in his stock. How is the distribution treated for tax purposes?

2. During the year, Vireo Corporation received dividend income of $300,000 from a corporation in which it holds a 10% interest. Vireo also received interest income of $50,000 from municipal bonds. The municipality used the proceeds from the sale of the bonds to construct a needed facility to house county documents and to provide office space for several county officials. Vireo borrowed funds to purchase the municipal bonds and paid $25,000 in interest on the loan this year. Vireo's taxable income exclusive of the items noted above was $225,000.
   a. What is Vireo Corporation's taxable income after considering the dividend income, the interest from the municipal bonds, and the interest paid on the indebtedness to purchase the municipals?
   b. What is Vireo Corporation's E & P as of December 31 if its E & P account balance was $80,000 as of January 1?

**Ethics**

3. In 1998, Beige Corporation made a cash distribution to its shareholders, one of whom was Steve Jordan. At that time, the parties involved believed that the distribution was a return of capital because Beige had no E & P. Accordingly, none of the shareholders reported dividend income. In Steve's case, he reduced the $200,000 original basis of his stock investment by $40,000, his share of the distribution. In 2006, it is discovered that E & P had been incorrectly computed. The 1998 distribution was fully covered by E & P and *should not have been treated as a return of capital.*

   In 2007, Steve sells his stock in Beige Corporation for $350,000. He plans to report a gain of $150,000 [$350,000 (selling price) − $200,000 (original basis)] on the sale. Although Steve realizes that he should have recognized dividend income of $40,000 for 1998, the statute of limitations has made this a closed year.

   Comment on Steve's situation.

4. On November 15, 2006, Red Corporation sold a parcel of land. The land had a basis of $350,000, and Red received a $900,000 note as consideration in the sale. The note is to

be paid in five installments, the first of which is due on December 15, 2007. Because Red did not elect out of the installment method, none of the $550,000 gain is included in taxable income for 2006.

Red Corporation had a deficit in accumulated E & P of $280,000 on January 1, 2006. For 2006, before considering the effect of the land sale, Red had a deficit in current E & P of $120,000.

Buck, the sole shareholder in Red, has a basis of $100,000 in his stock. If Red distributes $300,000 to Buck on December 31, 2006, how much gross income must Buck report from the distribution?

5.  In determining Greene Corporation's current E & P for 2006, how should taxable income be adjusted by the following transactions?
    a.  Sale of inventory on installment in 2006, with the first payment due in 2007.
    b.  A net operating loss carryover from 2005, fully used in 2006.
    c.  Excess capital losses incurred in 2006 that are carried forward to 2007.
    d.  Gain deferred in a qualifying like-kind exchange that occurred in 2006.
    e.  A Federal income tax refund received in 2006.
    f.  Section 179 expenses elected and deducted in 2004.

6.  Gadwall Corporation is a calendar year taxpayer. At the beginning of the current year, Gadwall has accumulated E & P of $350,000. The corporation incurs a current E & P deficit of $400,000 that accrues ratably throughout the year. On September 30, Gadwall distributes $200,000 to its sole individual shareholder, Richard. If Richard has a basis in his stock of $15,000, how is the distribution taxed to him?

7.  Complete the following schedule. For each case, assume the shareholder has ample basis in the stock investment.

|    | Accumulated E & P Beginning of Year | Current E & P | Cash Distributions (All on Last Day of Year) | Dividend Income | Return of Capital |
|----|----|----|----|----|----|
| a. | $ 100,000 | ($ 30,000) | $150,000 | $ | $ |
| b. | (200,000) | 40,000 | 90,000 | | |
| c. | 90,000 | 140,000 | 220,000 | | |
| d. | 140,000 | (60,000) | 120,000 | | |
| e. | Same as (d), except the distribution of $120,000 is made on June 30 and the corporation uses the calendar year for tax purposes. | | | | |

8.  Complete the following schedule. For each case, assume that there is one shareholder whose basis in the corporate stock is $20,000. Any current losses accrue ratably throughout the year.

|    | Accumulated E & P Beginning of Year | Current E & P | Cash Distributions (All on Last Day of Year) | Dividend Income | Capital Gain |
|----|----|----|----|----|----|
| a. | ($ 100,000) | $ 120,000 | $150,000 | $ | $ |
| b. | 70,000 | 30,000 | 110,000 | | |
| c. | (100,000) | 80,000 | 70,000 | | |
| d. | 210,000 | (160,000) | 90,000 | | |
| e. | Same as (d), except the distribution of $90,000 is made on June 30 and the corporation uses the calendar year for tax purposes. | | | | |

9.  Carrie Lynn, the sole shareholder of Junco Corporation, had a basis of $50,000 in Junco stock that she sold to Rajib on July 30 for $200,000. Junco had accumulated E & P of $95,000 on January 1 and current E & P of $80,000. During the year, Junco made the following distributions: $150,000 of cash to Carrie Lynn on July 1, and $150,000 of cash to Rajib on December 30. How will the distributions be taxed to Carrie Lynn and Rajib? What gain will Carrie Lynn recognize on the sale of her stock to Rajib?

10. In each of the following *independent* situations, indicate the effect on taxable income and E & P, stating the amount of any increase (or decrease) as a result of the transaction. Assume E & P has already been increased by the taxable amount.

|   | Transaction | Taxable Income Increase (Decrease) | E & P Increase (Decrease) |
|---|---|---|---|
| a. | Recognition of $20,000 gain from payment received on installment note from sale in prior year. | | |
| b. | Payment of $27,000 in Federal income taxes. | | |
| c. | $8,000 in premiums paid for life insurance on corporate officer's life. As a result of premium payment, cash surrender value of policy increased $500. | | |
| d. | Capital loss, $43,000. No capital gains were recognized in the current year. | | |
| e. | Disallowed portion (50%) of meals and entertainment expenses, $8,500. | | |
| f. | Realized gain on involuntary conversion of $175,000 ($25,000 of gain is recognized). | | |

11. In each of the following *independent* situations, indicate the effect on taxable income and E & P, stating the amount of any increase (or decrease) as a result of the transaction. Assume E & P has already been increased by the taxable income.

|   | Transaction | Taxable Income Increase (Decrease) | E & P Increase (Decrease) |
|---|---|---|---|
| a. | Sale of unimproved real estate to the sole shareholder of the corporation at a realized loss of $40,000. | | |
| b. | Intangible drilling costs incurred on May 1 of the current year; $30,000 is deductible from current-year taxable income. | | |
| c. | Sale of unimproved real estate to unrelated third party; basis is $200,000, fair market value is $400,000 (no election out of installment method; payments in year of sale total $100,000). | | |

|  | Transaction | Taxable Income Increase (Decrease) | E & P Increase (Decrease) |
|---|---|---|---|
| d. | Dividends of $10,000 received from 10%-owned corporation, together with dividends received deduction (assume taxable income limit does not apply). | | |
| e. | Realized gain of $150,000 from qualifying like-kind exchange ($30,000 of gain is recognized). | | |
| f. | Section 179 expense deduction of $12,000 in current year. | | |
| g. | Impact of current-year § 179 expense deduction in succeeding year. | | |
| h. | MACRS depreciation of $80,000. ADS depreciation would have been $50,000. | | |
| i. | A $60,000 refund of Federal income taxes paid in previous year. | | |

12. Taylor, an individual, owns all of the outstanding stock in Violet Corporation. Taylor purchased his stock in Violet 11 years ago, and his basis is $15,000. At the beginning of this year, the corporation has $35,000 of accumulated E & P and no current E & P (before considering the effect of distributions). What are the tax consequences to Taylor (amount of dividend income and basis in property received) and Violet Corporation (gain or loss and effect on E & P) in each of the following situations?
   a. Violet distributes land to Taylor. The land was held as an investment and has a fair market value of $25,000 and an adjusted basis of $18,000.
   b. Violet Corporation has no current or accumulated E & P prior to the distribution. How would your answer to (a) change?
   c. The land distributed in (a) is subject to a $22,000 mortgage (which Taylor assumes). How would your answer change?
   d. The land has a fair market value of $25,000 and an adjusted basis of $28,000 on the date of distribution. How would your answer to (a) change?
   e. Instead of distributing land, Violet decides to distribute furniture used in its business. The furniture has a $6,000 fair market value and $500 adjusted basis for income tax purposes and a $2,500 adjusted basis for E & P purposes. The original fair market value of the furniture when it was purchased four years ago was $8,000.

13. At the beginning of the current year, Northern Fulmar Corporation (a calendar year taxpayer) has accumulated E & P of $46,000. During the year, Northern Fulmar incurs a $34,000 loss from operations that accrues ratably. On July 1, Northern Fulmar distributes $38,000 in cash to Adriana, its sole shareholder. How will the $38,000 be taxed to Adriana?

14. Pearl Corporation, with E & P of $600,000, distributes land worth $175,000, adjusted basis of $220,000, to Azure, a corporate shareholder. The land is subject to a liability of $50,000, which Azure assumes.
   a. What is the amount of dividend income to Azure?
   b. What is Azure's basis in the land it received?
   c. How does the distribution affect Pearl Corporation's E & P account?

**Decision Making**  15. Crimson Corporation owns three automobiles that it uses in its business. It no longer needs two of these cars and is considering the possibility of distributing them to its two shareholders as a property dividend. All three automobiles have a fair market value of $15,000. Automobile A has a basis of $8,000; automobile B has a basis of $15,000; and automobile C has a basis of $20,000. The corporation has asked you for advice. What actions do you recommend?

16. Petrel Corporation has accumulated E & P of $63,000 at the beginning of the year. Its current-year taxable income is $300,000. On December 31, Petrel distributed business property (worth $120,000, adjusted basis of $270,000) to Juan, its sole shareholder. Juan assumes a $78,000 liability on the property. Included in the determination of Petrel's current taxable income is $14,000 of income recognized from an installment sale in a previous year. In addition, the corporation incurred a Federal income tax liability of $108,050, paid life insurance premiums of $3,000, and received term life insurance proceeds of $54,300 on the death of an officer.
    a. What is the amount of taxable income to Juan?
    b. What is the E & P of Petrel Corporation after the property distribution?
    c. What is Juan's tax basis in the property received?
    d. How would your answers to (a) and (b) change if Petrel had sold the property at its fair market value, used $78,000 of the proceeds to pay off the liability, and then distributed the remaining cash and any tax savings to Juan?

**Issue ID**

17. Copper Corporation has two equal shareholders, Cybil and Sally. Cybil acquired her Copper stock three years ago by transferring property worth $600,000, basis of $200,000, for 60 shares of the stock. Sally acquired 60 shares in Copper Corporation two years ago by transferring property worth $620,000, basis of $70,000. Copper Corporation's accumulated E & P as of January 1 of the current year is $300,000. On March 1 of the current year, the corporation distributed to Cybil property worth $100,000, basis to Copper of $30,000. It distributed cash of $200,000 to Sally. On July 1 of the current year, Sally sold her stock to Dana for $800,000. On December 1 of the current year, Copper distributed cash of $80,000 each to Dana and to Cybil. What are the tax issues?

18. Redwing Corporation is a closely held company with accumulated E & P of $500,000 and current E & P of $55,000. Mike and Royce are brothers, and each owns a 50% share in Redwing. On a day-to-day basis, Mike and Royce share management responsibilities equally. What are the tax consequences of the following *independent* transactions involving Redwing, Mike, and Royce? How does each transaction affect Redwing's E & P?
    a. Redwing sells a parking lot (adjusted basis $33,000, fair market value $18,000) to Mike for $5,000.
    b. Redwing lends Royce $200,000 on July 1 of this year. The loan, evidenced by a note, is due on demand. No interest is charged on the loan. The current applicable Federal interest rate is 9%.
    c. Redwing owns a yacht in Miami, Florida. It rents the yacht to vacationers throughout the year. During the current year, Mike and Royce each use the yacht for one month and pay no rent to Redwing. The rental value of the yacht is $7,500 per week. Mike has indicated that the average maintenance cost per week for the rental is $500.
    d. Mike leases equipment to Redwing for $20,000 per year. If the corporation were to lease the same equipment from another company, the rent would be $13,000.

19. Whether compensation paid to a corporate employee is reasonable is a question of fact to be determined from the surrounding circumstances. How would the resolution of this problem be affected by each of the following factors?
    a. The employee is not a shareholder but is related to the sole owner of the corporate employer.
    b. The shareholder-employee never completed high school.
    c. The shareholder-employee is a full-time college student.
    d. The shareholder-employee was underpaid for her services during the formative period of the corporate employer.
    e. The corporate employer pays only a nominal dividend each year.
    f. Year-end bonuses are paid to all shareholder-employees, but not to nonshareholder-employees.

**Decision Making**

20. Condor Corporation would like to transfer excess cash to its sole shareholder, Jen, who is also an employee. Jen is in the 35% tax bracket, and Condor is in the 34% tax bracket. Because Jen's contribution to the business is substantial, Condor believes that a $50,000

bonus in the current year would be viewed as reasonable compensation and would be deductible by the corporation. However, Condor is leaning toward paying Jen a $50,000 dividend, because the tax rate on dividends is lower than that on compensation. Is Condor correct in the belief that a dividend is the better choice? Why or why not?

21. Verdigris Corporation owns 25% of the stock of Rust Corporation. Rust Corporation, with E & P of $150,000 on December 20, distributes land with a fair market value of $60,000 and a basis of $90,000 to Verdigris. The land is subject to a liability of $50,000, which Verdigris assumes.
    a.  How is Verdigris Corporation taxed on the distribution?
    b.  What is Rust Corporation's E & P after the distribution?

22. At the beginning of its taxable year, Bunting Corporation had E & P of $175,000. Bunting Corporation sold an asset at a loss of $175,000 on June 30. Bunting incurred a deficit in current E & P of $195,000, which includes the $175,000 loss on the sale of the asset, for the calendar year. Assume Bunting made a distribution of $40,000 to its sole individual shareholder on July 1. How will the shareholder be taxed on the $40,000?

23. Teal Corporation is a calendar year taxpayer. At the beginning of the current year, Teal had a deficit in accumulated E & P of $130,000. Its net profit for the period January 1 through September 30 was $160,000, but its E & P for the entire taxable year was only $20,000. Teal made a distribution of $50,000 to its sole individual shareholder on December 31. How will the shareholder be taxed on this distribution?

24. Stan purchased 6,000 shares of Robin Corporation common stock five years ago for $30,000. In the current year, Stan receives a nontaxable preferred stock dividend of 300 shares. The preferred stock has a fair market value of $10,000. Stan's common stock in Robin has a fair market value of $50,000. What is Stan's basis in the preferred stock and common stock after the dividend is received?

**EXTENDER**

**Communications**

25. Your client, Cormorant Corporation, declares a dividend permitting its common stockholders to elect to receive 8 shares of cumulative preferred stock or 2 additional shares of common stock for every 10 shares of common stock currently held. Cormorant currently has only common stock outstanding, with a fair market value of $50 per share. Two shareholders elect to receive preferred stock, and all the remaining shareholders elect to receive common stock. Cormorant asks you whether the shareholders must recognize any taxable income on the receipt of the stock. Prepare a letter to Cormorant and a memo to the file. Cormorant's address is 6730 Pima Drive, Madison, WI 53708.

**Communications**

26. Sarah Beckert bought 3,000 shares of Grebe Corporation stock two years ago for $10,000. Last year, Sarah received a nontaxable stock dividend of 1,000 shares in Grebe. In the current tax year, Sarah sold all of the stock received as a dividend for $8,000. Prepare a letter to Sarah and a memo to the file describing the tax consequences of the stock sale. Sarah's address is 1822 N. Sarnoff Road, Tucson, AZ 85710.

**EXTENDER**

27. Stork Corporation declares a nontaxable dividend payable in rights to subscribe to common stock. One right and $50 entitle the holder to subscribe to one share of stock. One right is issued for every two shares of stock owned. At the date of distribution of the rights, the market value of the stock was $100 per share, and the market value of the rights was $45 per right. Cindy, a shareholder, owns 200 shares of stock that she purchased two years ago for $6,000. Cindy received 100 rights, of which she exercises 70 to purchase 70 additional shares. She sells the remaining 30 rights for $1,650. What are the tax consequences of these transactions to Cindy?

**EXTENDER**

**Decision Making**

28. Becca is a shareholder in Blue Corporation. This year, she receives a $4,000 qualified dividend from Blue. Becca is in the 35% tax bracket, has investment interest expense of $8,000, and net investment income of $4,500 (not including the qualified dividend). Assume that Becca expects to have more than enough net investment income next year to permit the deduction of any investment interest expense that is carried forward. Should Becca subject the qualified dividend to a 15% tax rate or treat it as net investment income?

**Decision Making**

29. Ivana, the president and a shareholder of Robin Corporation, has earned a salary bonus of $15,000 for the current year. Because of the recent reduction in tax rates on qualified

dividends, Robin is considering substituting a dividend for the bonus. Pertinent tax rates are 28% for Ivana and 34% for Robin Corporation.

a. How much better off would Ivana be if she were paid a dividend rather than salary?

b. How much better off would Robin Corporation be if it paid Ivana salary rather than a dividend?

c. If Robin Corporation pays Ivana a salary bonus of $20,000 instead of a $15,000 dividend, how would your answers to (a) and (b) change?

d. What should Robin do?

30. Shonda owns 110 shares of the 200 outstanding shares of Hawk Corporation. Shonda paid $1,000 per share for the stock five years ago. The remaining Hawk stock is owned by several unrelated individuals. In the current year, Hawk redeems 20 of Shonda's shares for $60,000 ($3,000 per share). Hawk's E & P at the time of the redemption was $200,000.

a. How does Shonda report the $60,000?

b. What is Shonda's basis in her remaining shares?

c. What is Hawk's E & P after the redemption?

31. Teal Corporation's 100 shares of outstanding common stock are held equally by Ann and Bonnie. The shareholders are not related to each other. Each paid $1,000 per share for the Teal stock 10 years ago. Teal shows $20,000 of current E & P and $100,000 of accumulated E & P. Teal distributes $80,000 of cash to Ann in exchange for 25 of her shares.

a. What are the tax consequences of the exchange for Ann?

b. What is Teal's E & P balance after the exchange?

**EXTENDER**

32. Blue Jay Corporation was organized eight years ago to construct family dwellings. Six years ago, it began selling furniture. Because of a glut in the real estate market, Blue Jay discontinues its construction business in the current year. Blue Jay sells all the assets used in the construction business for $4 million and distributes the proceeds to its two equal shareholders, Walt (an individual) and Redbird Corporation, in the redemption of half of their stock. Walt has a basis of $110,000 in his redeemed stock, and Redbird has a basis of $200,000 in its redeemed stock. Blue Jay's E & P was $7 million on the date of the distribution. What are the tax consequences of the redemption to Walt, Redbird, and Blue Jay?

**EXTENDER**

**Communications**

33. Stork Corporation has 1,000 shares of common stock outstanding. The shares are owned as follows.

- Leo Jones, 700 shares

- Lori Johnson, 100 shares

- Lana Pierce, 200 shares

Lori is Lana's mother. Leo is not related to the two other shareholders. Stork redeems 100 of Lana's shares for $45,000. Lana paid $100 per share for her stock two years ago. On the date of the redemption, Stork's E & P was $400,000.

Prepare a memo to the tax research file and a letter to Lana (1000 Main Street, Oldtown, MN 55166) outlining the tax effects of the redemption to her.

**EXTENDER**

34. Thrush Corporation has 2,000 shares of common stock outstanding. The shares are owned as follows: Jacque Jones, 800 shares; Monique Jones (Jacque's daughter), 800 shares; and Enrique Jones (Jacque's brother), 400 shares. In the current year, Thrush redeems all of Jacque's shares. Determine whether the redemption can qualify for sale or exchange treatment under the complete termination redemption rules in the following independent circumstances.

a. Jacque remains as a director of Thrush Corporation.

b. Jacque resigns as director of Thrush Corporation; Monique becomes a director of Thrush to replace Jacque.

c. Two years after the redemption, Jacque acquires 25 shares in Thrush Corporation as a gift from Enrique.

**EXTENDER**

35. Cardinal Corporation has 200 shares of common stock outstanding. Hubert owns 80 of the shares, Hubert's mother owns 50 shares, Hubert's brother owns 20 shares, and Redbird Corporation owns 20 shares. Hubert owns 80% of the stock in Redbird.

a. Applying the § 318 stock attribution rules, how many shares does Hubert own in Cardinal?
b. Assume Hubert owns only 25% of Redbird. How many shares does Hubert own directly and indirectly in Cardinal?
c. Assume the same facts as in (a) above, but in addition, Hubert owns 40% of Yellow Partnership. The partnership owns 30 shares in Cardinal. How many shares does Hubert own directly and indirectly in Cardinal?

 BRIDGE DISCIPLINE

1. Using an online research service, find the audited financial statements of five major U.S. corporations, each in a different operating industry (e.g., manufacturing, energy, financial services, health care).
   a. Compute the total return on each corporation's stock for the past two years.
   b. Compute the dividend yield of the stock for the past two years.

## Research Problems

**THOMSON**
*
™
**RIA**

*Note: Solutions to Research Problems can be prepared by using the **RIA Checkpoint**® **Student Edition** online research product, which is available to accompany this text. It is also possible to prepare solutions to the Research Problems by using tax research materials found in a standard tax library.*

**Communications**

**Research Problem 1.**   Spifficar, Inc., owns and operates several car washes in Tucson, Arizona. A married couple, Joe and Simone Simpson, are the sole shareholders of Spifficar, and they have been your clients for the last decade. Over the course of several years, Joe and Simone made weekly deposits of their receipts from the car washes to corporate and personal bank accounts. In a recent phone conversation with Joe, he told you some very disturbing news. It turns out that the Simpsons regularly took a portion of the weekly collections home rather than depositing them at the bank. These amounts were hidden in shoe boxes under the Simpsons' bed and were not reported as taxable income by them. The total hidden under their bed amounts to approximately $250,000. Joe says that the IRS notified them that criminal tax evasion charges under § 7201 are being brought against them. The IRS believes that the Simpsons' actions provide prima facie evidence that they intended to defraud the government.

As Joe and Simone's accountant, you recognize that Spifficar has a deficit in its current and accumulated E & P accounts and that a deficit has existed over the period at issue with the IRS. In addition, your records indicate that the Simpsons' basis in the Spifficar stock is $300,000 (before taking into consideration the money hidden under their bed). You believe that these facts may have some bearing on the evasion charges being made against them. Investigate the tax law related to this situation and prepare a letter to the Simpsons' attorney reporting the results of your research. Their attorney is Monty Davis, 1212 S. Camino Seco, Tucson, AZ 85710.

**Communications**

**Research Problem 2.**   Patrick Zimbrick and his son, Dan, own all of the outstanding stock of Osprey Corporation. Both Dan and Patrick are officers in the corporation and, together with their uncle, John, comprise the entire board of directors. Osprey uses the cash method of accounting and a calendar year-end. In late 2004, the board of directors adopted the following legally enforceable resolution (agreed to in writing by each of the officers).

Salary payments made to an officer of the corporation that are disallowed in whole or in part as a deductible expense for Federal income tax purposes shall be reimbursed by such officer to the corporation to the full extent of any disallowance. It is the duty of the board of directors to enforce repayment of each such amount.

In 2006, Osprey paid Patrick $560,000 in compensation. Dan received $400,000. On audit, the IRS found the compensation of both officers to be excessive. It disallowed deductions for $200,000 of the payment to Patrick and $150,000 of the payment to Dan. The IRS recharacterized the disallowed payments as constructive dividends. Complying with the resolution by the board of directors, both Patrick and Dan repaid the disallowed compensation to Osprey Corporation. Dan and Patrick have asked you to determine how their repayments should be treated for tax purposes. Prepare a memo to your files describing the results of your research.

**Communications**

**Research Problem 3.** Aqua Corporation wholly owns Egret Corporation. Aqua formed Egret four years ago with the transfer of several assets to the corporation, together with a substantial amount of cash. Aqua's basis in Egret stock is $5.5 million. Since it was formed, Egret has been a very profitable software company and currently has accumulated E & P of $4 million. The company's principal assets are software patents currently worth $5 million and cash and marketable securities of approximately $4.5 million (a total fair market value of $9.5 million).

Aqua and Egret are members of an affiliated group and have made the election under § 243(b) so that Aqua is entitled to a 100% dividends received deduction. From a strategic perspective, Aqua is no longer interested in the software industry and so is considering a sale of Egret. In anticipation of a sale in the next year or two, the management of Aqua has contacted you for advice. If Egret is sold outright, then Aqua Corporation will have a capital gain of $4 million ($9.5 million fair market value less a basis of $5.5 million). As an alternative, it has been suggested that taxes on a future sale would be minimized if Egret pays Aqua a dividend (using existing cash and securities) equal to its E & P. With the 100% dividends received deduction, this payment would be a tax-free transfer from Egret to Aqua. Subsequent to the dividend payment, Egret could be sold for its remaining value of $5.5 million ($5 million in software patents plus $500,000 in cash), generating no additional loss or gain to Aqua.

a. Prepare a letter to the president of Aqua Corporation describing the results of your research on the proposed plan. The president's name and address is Bill Gateson, 601 Pittsfield Dr., Champaign, IL 61821.
b. Prepare a memo for your firm's client files.

*Partial list of research aids:*

*Waterman Steamship Corp. v. Comm.*, 70–2 USTC ¶9514, 26 AFTR2d 70–5185, 430 F.2d 1185 (CA–5, 1970).

**Research Problem 4.** In the summer of this year, Tangerine Corporation announced that it would pay a special one-time dividend of about $32 billion ($3 per share) on December 2 (with an ex-dividend date of November 15). It also announced that it would double its regular quarterly per-share dividend from $0.04 to $0.08, for the dividends payable on September 14 (with an ex-dividend date of August 23) and December 2 (with an ex-dividend date of November 15). Motivated by these announcements, Samantha (a high-income taxpayer) purchased 50,000 shares of Tangerine stock on August 20 at $27 per share and sold the stock in late December (after receiving the dividends) for $26 per share. The highest trading price reached by Tangerine stock during the year was $29.98 per share on the day before the special dividend ex-dividend date. Before considering the Tangerine sale, Samantha has $50,000 of short-term capital gains and $50,000 of 15% long-term capital gains. Assume that the dividend paid by Tangerine qualifies for the 15% dividend tax rate. What are the tax consequences of the dividends and stock sale to Samantha?

**Internet Activity**

*Use the tax resources of the Internet to address the following questions. Do not restrict your search to the World Wide Web, but include a review of newsgroups and general reference materials, practitioner sites and resources, primary sources of the tax law, chat rooms and discussion groups, and other opportunities.*

**Research Problem 5.** Just how common are dividend distributions? Are dividends concentrated in the companies traded on the New York Stock Exchange, or do closely held corporations pay dividends with the same frequency and at the same rates? Financial institutions and observers are acutely interested in these issues. Search for comments on such questions at various commercial Web sites as well as one or two academic journals or newsgroups.

**Communications**

**Research Problem 6.** Investigate Web sites of for-profit investment managers and summarize the information you find in a two-page discussion, entitled "The Market in Stock Splits: How You Can Profit." Submit the summary to your professor.

**Communications**

**Research Problem 7.** Write an e-mail query to two tax consultants who practice in your state. Ask each for an example or two of a constructive dividend that a client recently has paid. Give your instructor copies of your query and the responses you receive.

**Research Problem 8.** Many believe that the reduced tax rate on dividends will be made permanent during President Bush's second term in office. Use the Web to search for evidence about the effects of the dividend tax cut to date. Have dividend-paying stocks experienced any increased demand relative to growth stocks? Have any other economic effects (or lack thereof) been observed by the media or by academics? On the basis of your research, would you label the dividend tax cut a success?

# Partnerships and Limited Liability Entities

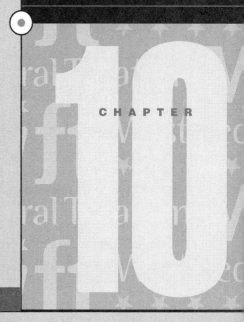

CHAPTER

10

http://wft.swlearning.com

## OUTLINE

---

### TAX TALK

*Today is the first day of the rest of your taxable year.*

*—Jeffrey L. Yablon*

---

# Overview of Partnership Taxation

**M**uch of the new business in today's world of commerce is conducted in what the Internal Revenue Code would classify as *partnerships*. As evidence of their popularity, more than 2 million partnership tax returns are filed with the IRS annually.

Whether termed a *joint venture, working agreement, shared operating arrangement,* or some other designation, a partnership is formed when individuals or separate business entities get together for the specific purpose of earning profits by jointly operating a trade or business. For example, a partnership likely exists when a U.S. business enters into a joint venture with a foreign distributor to gain access to an overseas consumer market. Or a number of businesses located in a blighted downtown area might work together to boost sales and customer traffic by forming a group that unifies and improves the appearance of the storefronts in the area, conducts joint advertising, and coordinates sales and coupon activities.

Partnerships allow a great degree of flexibility in the conduct of business: for example, a group can limit its goals to a specific list of agreed-to projects or to a given time period, or businesses can work together without altering any of their underlying capital structures. In many service professions, such as law, medicine, and accounting, state laws prohibit the owners from using a corporation to limit their liability to clients or patients, so the partnership form prevails.

The tax law addressing the transactions of partners and partnerships is found in Subchapter K of the Code. These provisions comprise only a few short pages

---

**◉ T A X   F A C T**

---

## PARTNERSHIP POWER

**P**artnerships represent a sizable number of tax entities, and they generate a significant part of the net income of the economy, especially in the investment sectors.

| Partnership Activities, Tax Year 2002 | |
| --- | --- |
| Number of partnerships | 2,250,000 |
| Number of partners | 14,350,000 |
| Reported partnership net income—total | $272 billion |
| Reported partnership business income | $126 billion |
| Reported partnership portfolio income | $106 billion |
| Reported partnership rental real estate income | $40 billion |

---

in the Code, however. Most of the details of partnership tax law have evolved through extensive Regulations and a healthy number of court cases.

## FORMS OF DOING BUSINESS—FEDERAL TAX CONSEQUENCES

This chapter and the next chapter analyze business forms that offer certain advantages over C corporations. These entities are partnerships and S corporations, which are called *flow-through* or *pass-through* entities because the owners of the trade or business elect to avoid treating the enterprise as a separate taxable entity. Instead, the owners are taxed on a proportionate share of the firm's taxable income at the end of each of its taxable years, regardless of the amount of cash or property distributions the owners receive during the year. The entity serves as an information provider to the IRS and its owners with respect to the proportionate income shares, and the tax falls directly upon the owners of those shares.

A partnership may be especially advantageous in many cases. A partnership's income is subject to only a single level of taxation, whereas C corporation income is subject to *double taxation*. Corporate income is taxed at the entity level at rates up to 35 percent. Any after-tax income that is distributed to corporate owners is taxed again as a dividend at the owner level. Though partnership income may be subject to high individual rates, the resulting tax will likely be lower than a combined corporate-level tax and a second tax on dividends.

In addition, administrative and filing requirements are relatively simple for a partnership, and the entity offers certain planning opportunities not available to other entities. Both C and S corporations are subject to rigorous allocation and distribution requirements (generally, each allocation or distribution is proportionate to the ownership interest of the shareholder). A partnership, though, may adjust its allocations of income and cash flow among the partners each year according to their needs, as long as certain standards are met. Any previously unrealized income (such as appreciation of corporate assets) of a C corporation is taxed at the entity level when the corporation liquidates, but a partnership generally may liquidate tax-free. Finally, many states impose reporting and licensing requirements on corporate entities, including S corporations. These include franchise or capital stock tax returns that may require annual assessments and costly professional preparation

**BRIDGE DISCIPLINE**

### Bridge to Finance

As movies have become more expensive to produce, many production studios have turned to limited partnerships as a lucrative source of investment capital. For example, DreamWorks and the Walt Disney Company have sold limited partnership or LLC interests in entities formed to produce specific movies.

The sponsoring studio usually injects capital for a small (1–5 percent) general partnership interest, and the limited partners contribute the remaining capital—millions of dollars in most cases. The partnership agreement spells out the number and types of films the partnership intends to produce and provides a formula for allocating cash flows to the partners. The agreement includes various benefits for the general partner (studio), such as a preferred allocation of cash flows (the first $1 million per year, for example), distribution fees for marketing the movies, and/or reimbursement of specified amounts of corporate overhead. Any cash remaining after these expenses is allocated under a fixed formula between the general and limited partners (for example, the limited partners may receive 90 percent of remaining cash flows).

These film-financing partnerships are not necessarily private operations. A layperson with a well-connected tax or investment adviser can become a partner in the next Julia Roberts project, perhaps financed by Silver Screen Partners XXII. Partnership shares sell for multiples of $100,000 or more, and in return the investor can become part-owner in an entity that is certain to throw off operating losses for many years to come.

Especially interested in movie financing of this type can be non-U.S. investors. The use of partnerships and limited liability entities is a common way to attract cross-border investment, as many developed countries treat such joint ventures favorably under their tax laws, allowing deferral of income recognition and lower tax withholding on the income of these entities. U.S. investors are attracted to joint venture financing of film projects in several countries, including Canada, that offer generous tax credits for projects that are filmed and processed chiefly within their borders. The partnership tax regime can offer an immediate flow-through of these tax benefits.

Think about traditional bank financing of manufacturing or distribution activities in comparison, and you will see why the movie studio finds partnerships so appealing: How many banks would allow the general partner to receive reimbursements and allocations before debt principal and interest are paid?

This capital-raising technique has proved so advantageous to the studios that some related industries, such as movie lighting contractors and special effects companies, have also used limited partnerships to raise capital. The next time you go to a movie, watch the credits at the end and think about the large number of people who invested cash in the movie hoping for a blockbuster!

---

assistance. Partnerships, on the other hand, often have no reporting requirements beyond Federal and state informational tax returns.

Although partnerships may avoid many of the income tax and reporting burdens faced by other entities, they are subject to all other taxes in the same manner as any other business. Thus, the partnership files returns and pays the outstanding amount of pertinent sales taxes, property taxes, and payroll taxes.

In summary, partnerships offer advantages to both large and small businesses. For smaller business operations, a partnership enables several owners to combine their resources at low cost. It also offers simple filing requirements, the taxation of income only once, and the ability to discontinue operations relatively inexpensively. For larger business operations, a partnership offers a unique ability to raise capital with low filing and reporting costs (compared to corporate bond issuances, for example).

## WHAT IS A PARTNERSHIP?

A partnership is an association of two or more persons formed to carry on a trade or business, with each contributing money, property, labor, or skill, and with all expecting to share in profits and losses. A "person" can be an individual, a corporation, or another partnership. For Federal income tax purposes, a partnership includes a syndicate, group, pool, joint venture, or other unincorporated organization, through which any business, financial operation, or venture is carried on. The entity must not be otherwise classified as a corporation, trust, or estate.[1]

An eligible entity can "check the box" on the partnership tax return indicating that the entity wants to be taxed as a partnership.[2] A partnership must have at least two owners, so a sole proprietor or one-shareholder corporation cannot "check the box" and be taxed as a partnership.[3]

Businesses operating in several forms are taxed as partnerships. Provisions controlling these legal forms of doing business typically are dictated by the laws of the states in which the businesses operate.

- In a **general partnership,** the partners share profits and losses in some specified manner, as dictated by the partnership agreement. Creditors can reach the assets of the business and the personal assets of the general partners to satisfy any outstanding debts. A general partner can be bankrupted by a judgment against the entity, even though the partner did not cause the violation triggering the damages.
- In a **limited partnership,** profits and losses are shared as the partners agree, but ownership interests are either general (creditors can reach the personal assets of the partner) or limited (a partner's exposure to entity liabilities is limited to the partner's own capital contributions). Usually, the general partners conduct most of the partnership business, and they have a greater say in making decisions that affect the entity operations.
- The **limited liability partnership (LLP)** is used chiefly in the service professions, such as accounting and consulting. The primary difference between an LLP and a general partnership is that an LLP partner is not personally liable for acts of negligence, fraud, or malpractice committed by other partners.
- The **limited liability company (LLC)** is discussed in more detail later in this chapter. This entity is taxed as a partnership, but its capital structure resembles that of a corporation, with shares for sale and an owner's liability limited almost strictly to the extent of capital contributions. Some states allow LLCs to be owned solely by one person.

**LO.1**

Discuss governing principles and theories of partnership taxation.

## PARTNERSHIP TAXATION AND REPORTING

A partnership is not a taxable entity.[4] Rather, the taxable income or loss of the partnership flows through to the partners at the end of the entity's tax year.[5] Partners report their allocable share of the partnership's income or loss for the year

---

[1]§ 7701(a)(2).
[2]Reg. §§ 301.7701–1 to 301.7701–3, as discussed in Chapter 8 of this text.

[3]§ 761(a).
[4]§ 701.
[5]§ 702.

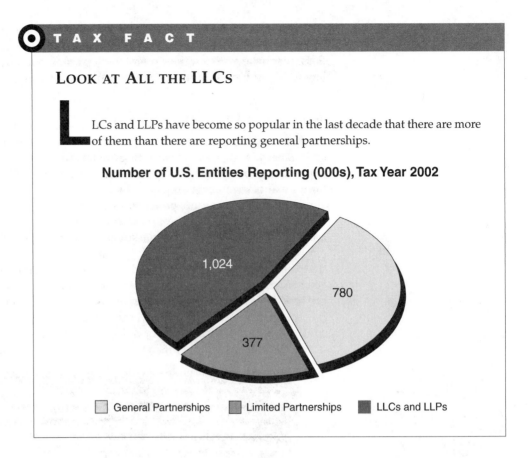

**TAX FACT**

## LOOK AT ALL THE LLCS

LCs and LLPs have become so popular in the last decade that there are more of them than there are reporting general partnerships.

**Number of U.S. Entities Reporting (000s), Tax Year 2002**

1,024

780

377

☐ General Partnerships    ☐ Limited Partnerships    ■ LLCs and LLPs

on their tax returns. As a result, the partnership itself pays no Federal income tax on its income; instead, the partners' individual tax liabilities are affected by the activities of the entity.

**EXAMPLE 1**

Adam is a 40% partner in the ABC Partnership. Both Adam's and the partnership's tax years end on December 31. This year, the partnership generates $200,000 of ordinary taxable income. However, because the partnership needs capital for expansion and debt reduction, Adam makes no cash withdrawals during the year. He meets his living expenses by reducing his investment portfolio. Adam is taxed on his $80,000 allocable share of the partnership's income ($200,000 × 40%), even though he received no distributions from the entity during the year. This allocated income is included in Adam's gross income. ■

**EXAMPLE 2**

Assume the same facts as in Example 1, except that the partnership realizes a taxable loss of $100,000. Adam's $40,000 proportionate share of the loss flows through to him from the partnership, and he can deduct the loss. (Note: Loss limitation rules discussed later in the chapter may result in some or all of this loss being deducted by Adam in a later year.) ■

Many items of partnership income, expense, gain, or loss retain their tax identity as they flow through to the partners. These **separately stated items** include those items that may affect any two partners' tax liability computations differently.[6] For example, the § 179 expense of a partnership is separately stated because one partner

*Definition
Separately Stated
Items
—page

[6]§ 703(a)(1). Certain large partnerships can elect to limit the number of separately stated items.

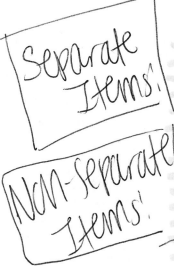

might be able to deduct his or her share of the expense completely, while another's deduction might be limited. Separately stated items include recognized gains and losses from property transactions, dividend income, preferences and adjustments for the alternative minimum tax (see Chapter 13), foreign tax payments, and expenditures that individual partners would treat as itemized deductions (e.g., charitable contributions).

Items that are not separately stated, because all partners will treat them the same on their individual tax returns, are aggregated and form the *ordinary income* of the partnership. Thus, profits from product sales, advertising expenses, and depreciation recapture amounts are combined to form the entity's ordinary income. This amount is then allocated among the partners and flows through to their tax returns. The ordinary income that flows through to a general partner, as well as any salary-like guaranteed payments (discussed in a later section) received, usually is subject to self-employment tax, as well as Federal income tax.[7]

**EXAMPLE 3**

Beth is a 25% partner in the BR Partnership. The cash basis entity collected sales income of $60,000 and incurred $15,000 in business expenses. In addition, it sold a corporate bond for a $9,000 long-term capital gain. Finally, the partnership made a $1,000 contribution to the local Performing Arts Fund drive. The fund is a qualifying charity. BR and all of its partners use a calendar tax year.

Beth is allocated ordinary taxable income of $11,250 [($60,000 − $15,000) × 25%] from the partnership. She also is allocated a flow-through of a $2,250 long-term capital gain and a $250 charitable contribution deduction. The ordinary income increases Beth's gross income, and the capital gain and charitable contribution are combined with her other similar activities for the year as though she had incurred them herself. These items could be treated differently on the tax returns of the various partners (e.g., because a partner may be subject to a percentage limitation on charitable contribution deductions), so they are not included in the computation of ordinary partnership income. Instead, the items flow through to the partners separately. ■

*Find more information on this topic at our Web site: **http://wft-entities.swlearning.com**.*

Even though it is not a taxpaying entity, the partnership files an information tax return, Form 1065. Look at Form 1065 in Appendix B, and refer to it during the following discussion. The ordinary income and expense items generated by the partnership's trade or business activities are netted to produce a single income or loss amount. The partnership reports this ordinary income or loss from its trade or business activities on Form 1065, page 1. Schedule K (page 3 of Form 1065) accumulates all items that must be separately reported to the partners, including net trade or business income or loss (from page 1). The amounts on Schedule K are allocated to all the partners. Each partner receives a Schedule K–1, which shows that partner's share of partnership items.

**EXAMPLE 4**

The BR Partnership in Example 3 reports its $60,000 of sales income on Form 1065, page 1, line 1. The $15,000 of business expenses are reported in the appropriate amounts on page 1, line 2 or lines 9–20. Partnership ordinary income of $45,000 is shown on page 1, line 22, and on Schedule K, line 1. The $9,000 capital gain and the $1,000 charitable contribution are reported only on Schedule K, on lines 9a and 13, respectively.

Beth receives a Schedule K–1 from the partnership that shows her shares of partnership ordinary income of $11,250, long-term capital gain of $2,250, and charitable contributions of $250 on lines 1, 9a, and 13, respectively.

---

[7]§ 1402(a).

She combines these amounts with similar items from other sources on her personal tax return. For example, if she has a $5,000 long-term capital loss from a stock transaction during the year, her overall net capital loss is $2,750. She then evaluates this net amount to determine the amount she may deduct on her Form 1040. ■

Thus, one must look at both page 1 and Schedule K to get complete information regarding a partnership's operations for the year.

Certain items reported on Schedule K are netted and entered on line 1 of the Analysis of Net Income (Loss) on page 4. This total agrees with the total amount on line 9 of Schedule M–1, Reconciliation of Income (Loss) per Books with Income (Loss) per Return. Schedule L generally shows an accounting-basis balance sheet, and Schedule M–2 reconciles beginning and ending partners' capital accounts.

## PARTNER'S OWNERSHIP INTEREST IN A PARTNERSHIP

Each partner typically owns both a **capital interest** and a **profits (loss) interest** in the partnership. A capital interest is measured by a partner's **capital sharing ratio,** which is the partner's percentage ownership of the capital of the partnership. A partner's capital interest can be determined in several ways. The most widely accepted method measures the capital interest as the percentage of net asset value (asset value remaining after payment of all partnership liabilities) a partner would receive on immediate liquidation of the partnership.

A profits (loss) interest is simply the partner's percentage allocation of current partnership operating results. **Profit and loss sharing ratios** usually are specified in the partnership agreement. They are used to determine each partner's allocation of partnership ordinary taxable income and separately stated items.[8] The partnership can change its profit and loss allocations at any time by amending the partnership agreement.

The partnership agreement may, in some cases, provide for a **special allocation** of certain items to specified partners, or it may allocate items in a different proportion from the general profit and loss sharing ratios. These items are separately reported to the partner receiving the allocation. For a special allocation to be recognized for tax purposes, it must produce nontax economic consequences to the partners receiving the allocation.[9]

> *Handwritten margin note:*
> *Definitions
> Capital Interest
>   – page C-4
> Profit (loss) Interest
>   – page C-14
> Capital Sharing ratio
>   – page C-4
> Profit and loss sharing
>   ratios
>   – pages C-13-14
> Special Allocation
>   – page C-17*

**EXAMPLE 5**

When the George-Helen Partnership was formed, George contributed cash and Helen contributed some City of Iuka bonds that she had held for investment purposes. The partnership agreement allocates all of the tax-exempt interest income from the bonds to Helen as an inducement for her to remain a partner. This is an acceptable special allocation for income tax purposes; it reflects the differing economic circumstances that underlie the partners' contributions to the capital of the entity. Since Helen would have received the tax-exempt income if she had not joined the partnership, she can retain the tax-favored treatment via the special allocation. ■

**EXAMPLE 6**

Assume the same facts as in Example 5. Three years after it was formed, the George-Helen Partnership purchased some City of Butte bonds. The municipal bond interest income of $15,000 flows through to the partners as a separately stated item, so it retains its tax-exempt status. The partnership agreement allocates all of this income to George because he is subject to a higher marginal income tax rate than is Helen. The partnership then allocates $15,000 more of the partnership's ordinary income to Helen than to George. These allocations are

---

[8] § 704(a).      [9] § 704(b).

**Bridge to Financial Accounting**

The equivalent in financial accounting to the partner's basis in his or her partnership interest is the **capital account.** A partner's ending balance in the capital account rarely is the same as his or her basis in the partnership interest. Just as the tax and accounting bases of a specific asset may differ, a partner's capital account and basis in the partnership interest usually are not equal.

Whereas contributions and most distributions from the partnership do not create financial accounting income, the capital account is "written up" or down to aggregate fair market value when the entity is formed. For most partnerships with simple financial transactions, *changes* to the capital account parallel closely the annual changes to the partner's basis in the partnership. Basis in one's partnership interest cannot be a negative number, but the capital account can become negative.

Oddly, the Schedules K–1 for the partners require an accounting for their capital accounts, but there is no required reconciliation for the partner's tax basis on the Schedule K–1. As a result, the tax adviser may find that a new partnership client has poor records with respect to the basis amounts of the partners, and a reconstruction must take place so that future computations will be correct. Sometimes, lacking adequate information with which to make this computation, the capital account is used because it is "close enough" and forms a good surrogate for the partner's basis in the partnership.

not effective for income tax purposes because they have no purpose other than a reduction of the partners' combined income tax liability. ■

*Definition: basis in the Partnership Interest —page C-3*

A partner has a **basis in the partnership interest,** just as he or she would have a tax basis in any asset owned. When income flows through to a partner from the partnership, the partner's basis in the partnership interest increases accordingly. When a loss flows through to a partner, basis is reduced.[10] A partner's basis is important when determining the treatment of distributions from the partnership to the partner, establishing the deductibility of partnership losses, and calculating gain or loss on the disposition of the partnership interest.

**EXAMPLE 7**

Paul contributes $20,000 of cash to acquire a 30% capital and profits interest in the Red Robin Partnership. In its first year of operations, the partnership earns ordinary income of $40,000 and makes no distributions to Paul. Paul's initial basis is the $20,000 he paid for the interest. He reports ordinary income of $12,000 (30% × $40,000 partnership income) on his individual return and increases his basis by the same amount, to $32,000. ■

The Code provides for increases and decreases in a partner's basis so that the income or loss from partnership operations is taxed only once. In Example 7, if Paul sold his interest at the end of the first year for $32,000, he would have no gain or loss. If the Code did not provide for an adjustment of a partner's basis, Paul's basis would still be $20,000, and he would be taxed on the gain of $12,000 in addition to being taxed on his $12,000 share of income.

---

[10]§§ 705, 722, and 723.

*Find more information on this topic at our Web site: http://wft-entities.swlearning.com.*

**L O . 2**

Describe the tax effects of
forming a partnership with
cash and property
contributions.

*Handwritten note:* Gain/Loss= FMV- Adjusted Basis of Property Transferred

# Formation of a Partnership: Tax Effects

## GAIN OR LOSS ON CONTRIBUTIONS TO THE PARTNERSHIP

When a taxpayer transfers property to an entity in exchange for valuable consideration, a taxable exchange usually results. Typically, both the taxpayer and the entity realize and recognize gain or loss on the exchange.[11] The gain or loss recognized by the transferor is the difference between the fair market value of the consideration received and the adjusted basis of the property transferred.[12]

In most situations, however, neither the partner nor the partnership recognizes the gain or loss that is realized when a partner contributes property to a partnership in exchange for a partnership interest. Instead, recognition of any realized gain or loss is deferred.[13]

There are two reasons for this nonrecognition treatment. First, forming a partnership allows investors to combine their assets toward greater economic goals than could be achieved separately. Only the form of ownership, rather than the amount owned by each investor, has changed. Requiring that gain be recognized on such transfers would make the formation of some partnerships economically unfeasible. Second, because the partnership interest received is typically not a liquid asset, the partner may not be able to generate the cash to pay the tax. Thus, deferral of the gain recognizes the economic realities of the business world and follows the wherewithal to pay principle.

**E X A M P L E   8**

Alicia transfers two assets to the Wren Partnership on the day the entity is created, in exchange for a 60% profits and loss interest worth $60,000. She contributes cash of $40,000 and retail display equipment (basis to her as a sole proprietor, $8,000; fair market value, $20,000). Since an exchange has occurred between two parties, Alicia *realizes* a $12,000 gain on this transaction. The gain realized is the fair market value of the partnership interest of $60,000 less the basis of the assets that Alicia surrendered to the partnership [$40,000 (cash) + $8,000 (equipment)].

Under § 721, Alicia *does not recognize* the $12,000 realized gain in the year of contribution. Alicia might not have had sufficient cash if she had been required to pay tax on the $12,000 gain. All that she received from the partnership was an illiquid partnership interest; she received no cash with which to pay any resulting tax liability. ■

**E X A M P L E   9**

Assume the same facts as in Example 8, except that the equipment Alicia contributes to the partnership has an adjusted basis of $25,000. She has a $5,000 *realized* loss [$60,000 − ($40,000 + $25,000)], but she cannot deduct the loss. Realized losses, as well as realized gains, are deferred by § 721.

Unless it was essential that the partnership receive Alicia's display equipment rather than similar equipment purchased from an outside supplier, Alicia should have considered selling the equipment to a third party. This would have allowed her to deduct a $5,000 loss in the year of the sale. Alicia then could have contributed $60,000 of cash (including the proceeds from the sale) for her interest in the partnership, and the partnership would have funds to purchase similar equipment. ■

---

[11]§ 1001(c).
[12]§ 1001(a).

[13]§ 721.

**EXAMPLE  10**

Five years after the Wren Partnership (Examples 8 and 9) was created, Alicia contributes another piece of equipment to the entity. This property has a basis of $35,000 and a fair market value of $50,000. Alicia will defer the recognition of the $15,000 realized gain. Section 721 is effective *whenever* a partner makes a contribution to the capital of the partnership, not just when the partnership is formed.  ■

## EXCEPTIONS TO NONRECOGNITION

The nonrecognition provisions of § 721 do *not* apply where:

- the transaction is essentially a taxable exchange of properties;
- the transaction is a disguised sale of properties; or
- the partnership interest is received in exchange for services rendered to the partnership by the partner.[14]

**Exchange.**   If a transaction is essentially a taxable exchange of properties, tax on the gain is not deferred under the nonrecognition provisions of § 721.[15]

**EXAMPLE  11**

Sara owns land, and Bob owns stock. Sara would like to have Bob's stock, and Bob wants Sara's land. If Sara and Bob both contribute their property to newly formed SB Partnership in exchange for interests in the partnership, the tax on the transaction appears to be deferred under § 721. The tax on a subsequent distribution by the partnership of the land to Bob and the stock to Sara also appears to be deferred under § 731. According to a literal interpretation of the statutes, no taxable exchange has occurred. Sara and Bob will find, however, that this type of tax subterfuge is not permitted. The IRS will disregard the passage of the properties through the partnership and will hold, instead, that Sara and Bob exchanged the land and stock directly. Thus, the transactions will be treated as any other taxable exchange.  ■

**Disguised Sale.**   A similar result (i.e., recognition) occurs in a **disguised sale** of properties. A disguised sale is deemed to occur when a partner contributes property to a partnership and soon thereafter receives a distribution from the partnership. This distribution could be viewed as a payment by the partnership for purchase of the property.[16]

*Definition
Disguised Sale
→ Page C-6*

**EXAMPLE  12**

Kim transfers property to the KLM Partnership. The property has an adjusted basis of $10,000 and a fair market value of $30,000. Two weeks later, the partnership makes a distribution of $30,000 of cash to Kim. Under the rules of § 731, the distribution would not be taxable to Kim if the basis for her partnership interest prior to the distribution was greater than the $30,000 of cash distributed. However, the transaction appears to be a disguised purchase-sale transaction, rather than a contribution and distribution. Therefore, Kim must recognize gain of $20,000 on transfer of the property, and the partnership is deemed to have purchased the property for $30,000.  ■

A disguised sale is presumed to exist when a contribution by one partner is followed within two years by a specified distribution to him or her from the partnership.

**Services.**   Another exception to the nonrecognition provision of § 721 occurs when a partner receives an interest in the partnership as compensation for services rendered to the partnership. This is not a tax-deferred transaction because services

---

[14]§ 721(b). A few other exceptions to § 721 treatment also exist.
[15]Reg. § 1.731–1(c)(3).

[16]§ 707(a)(2)(B).

are not treated as "property" that can be transferred to a partnership on a tax-free basis. Instead, the partner performing the services recognizes ordinary compensation income equal to the fair market value of the partnership interest received.[17]

The partnership may deduct the amount included in the *service partner's* income if the services are of a deductible nature. If the services are not deductible by the partnership, they are capitalized. For example, architectural plans created by a partner are capitalized to the structure built with those plans. Alternatively, day-to-day management services performed by a partner for the partnership usually are deductible by the partnership.

**EXAMPLE 13**

Bill, Carol, and Dave form the BCD Partnership, with each receiving a one-third interest in the entity. Dave receives his one-third interest as compensation for the accounting and tax planning services he will render after the formation of the partnership. The value of a one-third interest in the partnership (for each of the parties) is $20,000. The partnership deducts $20,000 for Dave's services in computing ordinary income. Dave recognizes $20,000 of compensation income, and he has a $20,000 basis in his partnership interest. The same result would occur if the partnership had paid Dave $20,000 for his services and he immediately contributed that amount to the entity for a one-third ownership interest. ■

## TAX ISSUES RELATED TO CONTRIBUTED PROPERTY

When a partner makes a tax-deferred contribution of an asset to the capital of a partnership, the entity assigns a *carryover basis* to the property.[18] The partnership's basis in the asset is equal to the basis the partner held in the property prior to its transfer to the partnership. The partner's basis in the new partnership interest equals the prior basis in the contributed asset. The tax term for this basis concept is *substituted basis*. Thus, two assets are created out of one when a partnership is formed, namely, the property in the hands of the new entity and the new asset (the partnership interest) in the hands of the partner. Both assets are assigned a basis that is derived from the partner's basis in the contributed property.

The holding period of a partner's interest includes that of the contributed property when the property was a § 1231 asset or capital asset in the partner's hands. Otherwise, the holding period starts on the day the interest is acquired. The holding period of an interest acquired by a cash contribution starts at acquisition.

To understand the logic of these rules, consider what Congress was attempting to accomplish in this deferral transaction. For both parties, realized gain is deferred, under the wherewithal to pay concept, until the asset or ownership interest is subsequently disposed of in a taxable transaction. The deferral is accomplished through the use of a substituted basis by the partner and a carryover basis by the partnership. This treatment is similar to the treatment of assets transferred to a controlled corporation and the treatment of like-kind exchanges.[19]

**EXAMPLE 14**

On June 1, José transfers property to the JKL Partnership in exchange for a one-third interest in the partnership. The property has an adjusted basis to José of $10,000 and a fair market value of $30,000. José has a $20,000 realized gain on the exchange ($30,000 − $10,000), but he does not recognize any of the gain. José's basis for his partnership interest is the amount necessary to recognize the $20,000 deferred gain if his partnership interest is subsequently sold for its $30,000 fair market value. This amount, $10,000, is the substituted basis. The basis of the property contributed to the partnership is the amount necessary to allow for

*Carryover Basis* *Substituted Basis*

---

[17]§ 83(a).
[18]§ 723.

[19]§§ 351 and 1031.

the recognition of the $20,000 deferred gain if the property is subsequently sold for its $30,000 fair market value. This amount, also $10,000, is the carryover basis. ■

The holding period for the contributed asset also carries over to the partnership. Thus, the partnership's holding period for the asset includes the period during which the partner owned the asset individually.

**Depreciation Method and Period.**   If depreciable property is contributed to the partnership, the partnership usually is required to use the same cost recovery method and life used by the partner. The partnership merely "steps into the shoes" of the partner and continues the same cost recovery calculations. Thus, the partnership may not expense any part of the basis of depreciable property it receives from the transferor partner under § 179.

**Intangible Assets.**   If a partner contributes an existing "§ 197" intangible asset to the partnership, the partnership generally will "step into the shoes" of the partner in determining future amortization deductions. Section 197 intangible assets include goodwill, going-concern value, information systems, customer- or supplier-related intangible assets, patents, licenses obtained from a governmental unit, franchises, trademarks, covenants not to compete, and other items.

**Receivables, Inventory, and Losses.**   To prevent ordinary income from being converted into capital gain, gain or loss is treated as ordinary when the partnership disposes of either of the following.[20]

- Contributed receivables that were unrealized in the contributing partner's hands at the contribution date. Such receivables include the right to receive payment for goods or services.
- Contributed property that was inventory in the contributor's hands on the contribution date, if the partnership disposes of the property within *five years of the contribution*. For this purpose, inventory includes all tangible property except capital and real or depreciable business assets.

| **EXAMPLE 15** | Tyrone operates a cash basis retail electronics and television store as a sole proprietor. Ramon is an enterprising individual who likes to invest in small businesses. On January 2 of the current year, Tyrone and Ramon form the TR Partnership. Their partnership contributions are listed below. |

|  | **Adjusted Basis** | **Fair Market Value** |
| --- | --- | --- |
| From Tyrone: |  |  |
| Receivables | $  –0– | $ 2,000 |
| Inventory | 2,500 | 5,000 |
| Land used as parking lot* | 1,200 | 5,000 |
| From Ramon: |  |  |
| Cash | 12,000 | 12,000 |

*The parking lot had been held for nine months at the contribution date.

---

[20]§ 724. For this purpose, § 724(d)(2) waives the holding period requirement in defining § 1231 property.

Within 30 days of formation, TR collects the receivables and sells the inventory for $5,000. It uses the land for the next 10 months as a parking lot, then sells it for $3,500. TR realized the following income in the current year from these transactions.

- Ordinary income of $2,000 from collecting the receivables.
- Ordinary income of $2,500 from the sale of inventory.
- § 1231 gain of $2,300 from the sale of land.

Since the land takes a carryover holding period, it is treated as having been held 19 months at the sale date. ∎

A similar rule is designed to prevent a capital loss from being converted into an ordinary loss. Under the rule, if contributed property is disposed of at a loss and the property had a "built-in" capital loss on the contribution date, the loss is treated as a capital loss if the partnership disposes of the property *within five years of the contribution*. The capital loss is limited to the "built-in" loss on the date of contribution.[21]

**EXAMPLE 16**

Assume the same facts as Example 15, except for the following.

- Tyrone held the land as an investment. It had a fair market value of $800 at the contribution date.
- TR used the land as a parking lot for 10 months and sold it for $650.

TR realizes the following income and loss from these transactions.

- Ordinary income of $2,000 from collecting the receivables.
- Ordinary income of $2,500 from the sale of inventory.
- Capital loss of $400 from the sale of land ($800 – $1,200).
- § 1231 loss of $150 from the sale of land ($650 – $800).

Since the land was sold within five years of the contribution date, the $400 built-in loss is a capital loss. The postcontribution loss of $150 is a § 1231 loss since TR used the property in its business. ∎

## INSIDE AND OUTSIDE BASES

In this chapter, reference is made to the partnership's inside basis and the partners' outside basis. **Inside basis** refers to the adjusted basis of each partnership asset, as determined from the partnership's tax accounts. **Outside basis** represents each partner's basis in the partnership interest. Each partner "owns" a share of the partnership's inside basis for all its assets, and all partners should maintain a record of their respective outside bases.

In many cases—especially on formation of the partnership—the total of all the partners' outside bases equals the partnership's inside bases for all its assets. Differences between inside and outside basis arise when a partner's interest is sold to another person for more or less than the selling partner's share of the inside basis of partnership assets. The buying partner's outside basis equals the price paid for the interest, but the buyer's share of the partnership's inside basis is the same amount as the seller's share of the inside basis.

Concept Summary 10–1 reviews the rules that apply to partnership asset contributions and basis adjustments.

---

[21]§ 724(c).

## CONCEPT SUMMARY 10–1

## Partnership Formation and Basis Computation

1. Generally, partners or partnerships do not recognize gain or loss when property is contributed for capital interests.

2. Partners contributing property for partnership interests take the contributed property's adjusted basis for their *outside basis* in their partnership interest. The partners are said to take a substituted basis in their partnership interest.

3. The partnership will continue to use the contributing partner's basis for the *inside basis* in property it receives. The contributed property is said to take a carryover basis.

4. The partnership's holding period for contributed property may include the contributing partner's holding period.

5. Gain is recognized by a contributing partner when services are contributed or when the capital contribution is a disguised sale or exchange.

6. Special rules may apply when the partnership disposes of contributed receivables, inventory, or loss assets.

**LO.3**

Examine the tax treatment of expenditures of a newly formed partnership and identify elections available to the partnership.

## TAX ACCOUNTING ELECTIONS

A newly formed partnership must make numerous tax accounting elections. These elections are formal decisions on how a particular transaction or tax attribute should be handled. Most of these elections must be made by the partnership rather than by the partners individually.[22] The *partnership* makes the elections involving the following items.

- Inventory method.
- Cost or percentage depletion method, excluding oil and gas wells.
- Accounting method (cash, accrual, or hybrid).
- Cost recovery methods and assumptions.
- Tax year.
- Amortization of organization costs and amortization period.
- Amortization of start-up expenditures and amortization period.
- First-year cost recovery deductions for certain tangible personal property.
- Nonrecognition treatment for gains from involuntary conversions.

Each partner is bound by the decisions made by the partnership relative to the elections. If the partnership fails to make an election, a partner cannot compensate for the error by making the election individually.

Though most elections are made by the partnership, each *partner* individually makes a specific election on the following relatively narrow tax issues.

- Whether to take a deduction or a credit for taxes paid to foreign countries.
- Whether to claim the cost or percentage depletion method for oil and gas wells.
- Whether to reduce the basis of depreciable property first when excluding income from discharge of indebtedness.

### INITIAL COSTS OF A PARTNERSHIP

In its initial stages, a partnership incurs expenses relating to some or all of the following: forming the partnership (organization costs), admitting partners to the partnership, marketing and selling partnership units to prospective partners

---

[22]§ 703(b).

*[handwritten margin note: Definition Syndication Costs —page C-18]*

(**syndication costs**), acquiring assets, starting business operations (start-up costs), negotiating contracts, and other items. Many of these expenditures are not currently deductible. However, the Code permits a deduction for or a ratable (straight-line) amortization of "organization" and "start-up" costs; acquisition costs incurred to acquire depreciable assets are included in the initial basis of the acquired assets; and costs related to some intangible assets may be amortized. "Syndication costs" may be neither amortized nor deducted.[23]

**Organization Costs.**   Organization costs are incurred incident to the creation of the partnership and are capital in nature. Such costs include accounting and legal fees associated with the partnership formation.[24] Costs incurred for the following purposes are *not* organization costs.

- Acquiring assets for the partnership.
- Transferring assets to the partnership.
- Admitting partners, other than at formation.
- Removing partners, other than at formation.
- Negotiating operating contracts.

For organization costs incurred after October 22, 2004, a partnership may elect to deduct up to $5,000 of the costs in the year in which it begins business. This amount is reduced, however, by the organization costs that exceed $50,000. Any organization costs that cannot be deducted under this provision are amortizable over 180 months beginning with the month in which the partnership begins business. For organization costs incurred before that date, the taxpayer could elect to amortize the amount over 60 months, commencing with the month the taxpayer began business.

The election to deduct or amortize these amounts must be made by the due date (including extensions) of the partnership return for the year in which it begins business. Failure to make a proper election results in no deduction or amortization of the organization costs until the partnership is liquidated.

**EXAMPLE 17**

The Bluejay Partnership, which was formed on March 1, 2006, incurs $52,000 in organization costs. On its first tax return for the period March–December 2006, Bluejay can deduct $5,722 for these items. This deduction is the sum of:

- $5,000 reduced by the $2,000 ($52,000 − $50,000) amount by which the organization costs exceed $50,000.
- $2,722 ($49,000 × 10/180) amortization of the remaining $49,000 ($52,000 − $3,000) of organization costs for 10 months.

If Bluejay had failed to make a proper election to deduct or amortize the organization costs, none of these costs would be deductible until the partnership liquidated. ■

**Start-up Costs.**   Operating costs that are incurred after the entity is formed but before it begins business are known as start-up costs. Like organization costs, start-up costs are capitalized and may be immediately expensed and/or amortized.[25] Such costs include marketing surveys prior to conducting business, pre-operating advertising expenses, costs of establishing an accounting system, and salaries paid to executives and employees before the start of business.

A partnership may elect to deduct up to $5,000 of start-up costs in the year in which it begins business. This amount is reduced, however, by the start-up costs that exceed $50,000. Costs that are not deductible under this provision are amortizable

---

[23]§ 709(a).
[24]§ 709(b)(2).

[25]§ 195.

over 180 months beginning with the month in which the partnership begins business. Failure to make a proper election results in no deduction or amortization of the start-up costs until the partnership is liquidated. For start-up costs incurred before October 23, 2004, the taxpayer could elect to amortize them over 60 months, commencing with the month the taxpayer began business.

*Find more information on this topic at our Web site: http://wft-entities.swlearning.com.*

**LO.4**

Calculate partnership taxable income and describe how partnership items affect a partner's income tax return.

# Operations of the Partnership

A key consideration in the taxation of partnerships is that a variety of entities can be partners and each may be affected differently by the partnership's operations. In particular, any combination of individuals, corporations, trusts, estates, or other partnerships may be partners. Furthermore, at the end of each year, every partner receives a share of the partnership's income, deductions, credits, and alternative minimum tax (AMT) preferences and adjustments.[26] These flow-through items ultimately may be reported and taxed on a wide variety of income tax returns [e.g., Forms 1040 (Individuals), 1041 (Fiduciaries), 1120 (C corporations), and 1120S (S corporations)], each facing different limitations and rules. Thus, the ultimate tax treatment of partnership operations is directly affected by how the partnership reports its operating results.

## REPORTING OPERATING RESULTS

Form 1065 is due on the fifteenth day of the fourth month following the close of the partnership's tax year; for a calendar year partnership, this is April 15.

**Classifying Income and Deductions.** The measurement and reporting of partnership income require a two-step approach. Some items are not reported separately. These are netted at the partnership level and flow through to the partners as an aggregate number. Other items must be segregated and reported separately on the partnership return and each partner's Schedule K–1. Items passed through separately include the following.[27]

- Net short-term and net long-term capital gains or losses.
- Section 1231 gains and losses.
- Charitable contributions.
- Portfolio income items (qualified and ordinary dividends, interest, and royalties).
- Expenses related to portfolio income.
- Immediately expensed tangible personal property (§ 179).
- Deduction for domestic manufacturing income.[28]
- Items allocated differently from the general profit and loss ratio.
- Recovery of items previously deducted (tax benefit items).
- AMT preference and adjustment items.
- Self-employment income.
- Passive activity items (e.g., rental real estate income or loss).
- Intangible drilling and development costs.
- Taxes paid to foreign countries and U.S. possessions.

*Separate Items!* (handwritten)

---

[26]§ 702(a).
[27]§ 702(b).

[28]§ 199.

A partnership is not allowed the following deductions.

- Net operating loss.
- Dividends received deduction.

In addition, items that are allowed only to individuals, such as standard deductions or personal exemptions, are not allowed to the partnership.

**EXAMPLE 18**

Tiwanda is a one-third partner in the TUV Partnership. The partnership experienced a $20,000 net loss from operations last year, its first year of business. The partnership's transactions for this year are summarized below.

| | |
|---|---:|
| Fees received | $100,000 |
| Salaries paid | 30,000 |
| Cost recovery deductions | 10,000 |
| Supplies, repairs | 3,000 |
| Payroll taxes paid | 9,000 |
| Contribution to art museum | 6,000 |
| Short-term capital gain | 12,000 |
| Passive income (rental operations) | 7,500 |
| Qualified dividends received | 1,500 |
| Tax-exempt income (bond interest) | 2,100 |
| AMT adjustment (private activity bond interest) | 3,600 |
| Payment of partner Vern's alimony obligations | 4,000 |

The two-step computational process that is used to determine partnership income is applied in the following manner.

| **Nonseparately Stated Items (Ordinary Income)** | |
|---|---:|
| Fees received | $100,000 |
| Salaries paid | (30,000) |
| Cost recovery deductions | (10,000) |
| Supplies, repairs | (3,000) |
| Payroll taxes paid | (9,000) |
| Ordinary income | $ 48,000 |

| **Separately Stated Items** | |
|---|---:|
| Contribution to art museum | $ 6,000 |
| Short-term capital gain | 12,000 |
| Passive income (rental operations) | 7,500 |
| Qualified dividends received | 1,500 |
| Tax-exempt income (bond interest) | 2,100 |
| AMT adjustment (private activity bond interest) | 3,600 |

Each of the separately stated items passes through proportionately to each partner and is included on the appropriate schedule or netted with similar items that the partner generated for the year. Thus, in determining her tax liability, Tiwanda includes a $2,000 charitable contribution, a $4,000 short-term capital gain, $2,500 of passive rent income, $500 of qualified dividend income, and a $1,200 positive adjustment in computing alternative minimum taxable income. Tiwanda treats these items as if she had generated them herself. She must disclose her $700 share of tax-exempt interest on the first page of her Form 1040. In addition, Tiwanda reports $16,000 as her share of the partnership's ordinary income, the net amount of the nonseparately stated items.

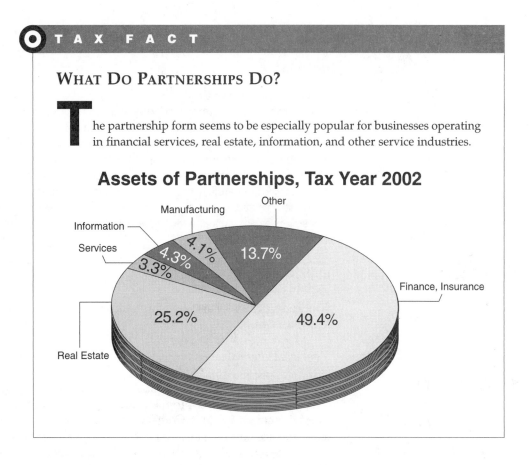

TAX FACT

## WHAT DO PARTNERSHIPS DO?

The partnership form seems to be especially popular for businesses operating in financial services, real estate, information, and other service industries.

**Assets of Partnerships, Tax Year 2002**

The partnership is not allowed a deduction for last year's $20,000 net operating loss—this item was passed through to the partners in the previous year. Moreover, the partnership is not allowed a deduction for personal expenditures (payment of Vern's alimony). ■

**Withdrawals.**   Capital withdrawals by partners during the year do not affect the partnership's income classification and reporting process.[29] These items usually are treated as distributions made on the last day of the partnership's tax year. In Example 18, the payment of Vern's alimony by the partnership is probably treated as a distribution from the partnership to Vern.

 DIGGING DEEPER 4   *Find more information on this topic at our Web site: http://wft-entities.swlearning.com.*

### PARTNERSHIP ALLOCATIONS

Two key special allocation rules also can affect a partner's Schedule K–1 results.[30]

**Economic Effect.**   The partnership agreement can provide that any partner may share capital, profits, and losses in different ratios.[31] For example, a partner could have a 25 percent capital sharing ratio, yet be allocated 30 percent of the profits and 20 percent of the losses of the partnership, or, as in Examples 5 and 6, a partner could be allocated a specific amount or items of income, deduction, gain, or loss. Such special allocations are permissible if they meet the **economic effect test.**[32]

---

[29]§ 731(a).
[30]The Code requires certain other allocations not discussed here.

[31]§ 704(a).
[32]Reg. § 1.704–1(b).

**Bridge to Business Law**

Although a written partnership agreement is not required, many rules governing the tax consequences to partners and their partnerships refer to such an agreement. Remember that a partner's distributive share of income, gain, loss, deduction, or credit is determined in accordance with the partnership agreement. Consequently, if taxpayers operating a business in partnership form want a measure of certainty as to the tax consequences of their activities, a carefully drafted partnership agreement is crucial. An agreement that sets forth the obligations, rights, and powers of the partners should prove invaluable in settling controversies among them and provide some degree of certainty as to the tax consequences of the partners' actions.

The rules prevent partners from shifting income and loss items merely to reduce current taxes.

*Find more information on this topic at our Web site: **http://wft-entities.swlearning.com**.*

**Precontribution Gain or Loss.**   Certain income, gain, loss, and deductions relative to contributed property may not be allocated under the economic effect rules.[33] Instead, **precontribution gain or loss** is allocated among the partners to take into account the variation between the basis of the property and its fair market value on the date of contribution.[34] For nondepreciable property, this means that *built-in* gain or loss on the date of contribution is allocated to the contributing partner when the property is eventually disposed of by the partnership in a taxable transaction.

**EXAMPLE 19**

Seth and Tim form the equal profit and loss sharing ST Partnership. Seth contributes cash of $10,000, and Tim contributes land purchased two years ago and held for investment. The land has an adjusted basis of $6,000 and fair market value of $10,000 at the contribution date. For accounting purposes, the partnership records the land at its fair market value of $10,000. For tax purposes, the partnership takes a carryover basis of $6,000 in the land. After using the land as a parking lot for five months, ST sells it for $10,600. No other transactions have taken place.

The accounting and tax gain from the land sale are computed as follows.

|  | Accounting | Tax |
|---|---|---|
| Amount realized | $ 10,600 | $10,600 |
| Less: Adjusted basis | (10,000) | (6,000) |
| Gain realized | $    600 | $  4,600 |
| Built-in gain to Tim | (–0–) | (4,000) |
| Remaining gain (split equally) | $    600 | $    600 |

Seth recognizes $300 of the gain ($600 remaining gain ÷ 2), and Tim recognizes $4,300 [$4,000 built-in gain + ($600 remaining gain ÷ 2)]. ■

---

[33]§ 704(b).                    [34]§ 704(c)(1)(A).

CONCEPT SUMMARY 10–2

## Tax Reporting of Partnership Activities

| Event | Partnership Level | Partner Level |
|---|---|---|
| 1. Compute partnership ordinary income. | Form 1065, line 22, page 1. Schedule K, Form 1065, line 1, page 3. | Schedule K–1 (Form 1065), line 1. Each partner's share is passed through for separate reporting. Each partner's basis is increased. |
| 2. Compute partnership ordinary loss. | Form 1065, line 22, page 1. Schedule K, Form 1065, line 1, page 3. | Schedule K–1 (Form 1065), line 1. Each partner's share is passed through for separate reporting. Each partner's basis is decreased. The amount of a partner's loss deduction may be limited. Losses that may not be deducted are carried forward for use in future years. |
| 3. Separately reported items like portfolio income, capital gain and loss, and § 179 deductions. | Schedule K, Form 1065, various lines, page 3. | Schedule K–1 (Form 1065), various lines. Each partner's share of each item is passed through for separate reporting. |
| 4. Net earnings from self-employment. | Schedule K, Form 1065, line 14, page 3. | Schedule K–1 (Form 1065), line 14. |

**LO.5**

Determine a partner's basis in the partnership interest.

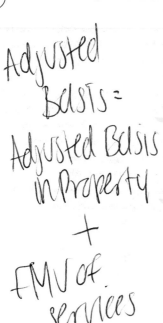

Adjusted Basis =
Adjusted Basis in Property
+
FMV of services

## BASIS OF A PARTNERSHIP INTEREST

A partner's adjusted basis in a newly formed partnership usually equals (1) the adjusted basis in any property contributed to the partnership plus (2) the fair market value of any services the partner performed for the partnership (i.e., the amount of ordinary income reported by the partner for services rendered to the partnership).

A partnership interest also can be acquired after the partnership has been formed. The method of acquisition controls how the partner's initial basis is computed. If the partnership interest is purchased from another partner, the purchasing partner's basis is the amount paid (cost basis) for the partnership interest. The basis of a partnership interest acquired by gift is the donor's basis for the interest plus, in certain cases, some or all of the transfer (gift) tax paid by the donor. The basis of a partnership interest acquired through inheritance generally is the fair market value of the interest on the date the partner dies.

After the partnership begins its activities, or after a new partner is admitted to the partnership, the partner's basis is adjusted for numerous items. The following operating results *increase* a partner's adjusted basis.

- The partner's proportionate share of partnership income (including capital gains and tax-exempt income).
- The partner's proportionate share of any increase in partnership liabilities.

The following operating results *decrease* the partner's adjusted basis in the partnership. A partner's adjusted basis for the partnership interest cannot be reduced below zero.

- The partner's proportionate share of partnership deductions and losses (including capital losses).

- The partner's proportionate share of nondeductible expenses.
- The partner's proportionate share of any reduction in partnership liabilities.[35]

Increasing the adjusted basis for the partner's share of partnership taxable income is logical since the partner has already been taxed on the income. By increasing the partner's basis, the Code ensures that the partner is not taxed again on the income when he or she sells the interest or receives a distribution from the partnership.

It is also logical that tax-exempt income should increase the partner's basis. If the income is exempt in the current period, it should not contribute to the recognition of gain when the partner either sells the interest or receives a distribution from the partnership.

Decreasing the adjusted basis for the partner's share of deductible losses, deductions, and noncapitalizable, nondeductible expenditures is logical for the same reasons.

| **EXAMPLE 20** | Yuri is a one-third partner in the XYZ Partnership. His proportionate share of the partnership income during the current year consists of $20,000 of ordinary taxable income and $10,000 of tax-exempt income. None of the income is distributed to Yuri. The adjusted basis of Yuri's partnership interest before adjusting for his share of income is $35,000, and the fair market value of the interest before considering the income items is $50,000. |

The unrealized gain inherent in Yuri's investment in the partnership is $15,000 ($50,000 – $35,000). Yuri's proportionate share of the income items should increase the fair market value of the interest to $80,000 ($50,000 + $20,000 + $10,000). By increasing the adjusted basis of Yuri's partnership interest to $65,000 ($35,000 + $20,000 + $10,000), the Code ensures that the unrealized gain inherent in Yuri's partnership investment remains at $15,000. This makes sense because the $20,000 of ordinary taxable income is taxed to Yuri this year and should not be taxed again when Yuri either sells his interest or receives a distribution. Similarly, the tax-exempt income is exempt this year and should not increase Yuri's gain when he either sells his interest or receives a distribution from the partnership. ■

**Partnership Liabilities.**    A partner's adjusted basis is affected by the partner's share of partnership debt.[36] Partnership debt includes most debt that is considered a liability under financial accounting rules except for accounts payable of a cash basis partnership and certain contingent liabilities.

Two major types of partnership debt exist.[37] **Recourse debt** is partnership debt for which the partnership or at least one of the partners is personally liable. This liability can exist, for example, through the operation of state law or through personal guarantees that a partner makes to the creditor. Personal liability of a party related to a partner (under attribution rules) is treated as the personal liability of the partner. **Nonrecourse debt** is debt for which no partner (or party related to a partner) is personally liable. Lenders of nonrecourse debt generally require that collateral be pledged against the loan. Upon default, the lender can claim only the collateral, not the partners' personal assets.

| **EXAMPLE 21** | The Bay Partnership financed its asset acquisitions with debt. If the partnership defaults on the debt, the lender can place a lien on the partners' salaries and personal assets. This constitutes recourse debt. ■ |

| **EXAMPLE 22** | The Tray Partnership financed its asset acquisitions with debt. If the partnership defaults on the debt, the lender can repossess the equipment purchased with the loan proceeds. This constitutes nonrecourse debt. ■ |

---

[35]§§ 705 and 752.
[36]§ 752.

[37]Reg. § 1.752–1(a).

When Ray bought into the Sleigh Partnership, the entity was in the midst of settling litigation as to its liability to those who had purchased its products and were making warranty claims against the entity. Ray's basis in his partnership interest does not include his share of these contingent liabilities. ■

A partner's share of entity-level debt usually increases as a result of increases in outstanding partnership debt.

Jim and Becky contribute property to form the JB Partnership. Jim contributes cash of $30,000. Becky contributes land with an adjusted basis and fair market value of $45,000, subject to a liability of $15,000. The partnership borrows $50,000 to finance construction of a building on the contributed land. At the end of the first year, the accrual basis partnership owes $3,500 in trade accounts payable to various vendors. No other operating activities occurred. If Jim and Becky share equally in liabilities, the partners' bases in their partnership interests are determined as follows.

| Jim's Basis | | Becky's Basis | |
|---|---|---|---|
| Contributed cash | $30,000 | Basis in contributed land | $ 45,000 |
| Share of debt on land (assumed by partnership) | 7,500 | Less: Debt assumed by partnership | (15,000) |
| Share of construction loan | 25,000 | Share of debt on land (assumed by partnership) | 7,500 |
| Share of trade accounts payable | 1,750 | Share of construction loan | 25,000 |
| | | Share of trade accounts payable | 1,750 |
| Basis, end of Year 1 | $64,250 | Basis, end of Year 1 | $ 64,250 |

In this case, it is reasonable that the parties have an equal basis after contributing their respective properties, because each is a 50% owner and they contributed property with identical net bases and identical *net* fair market values. ■

A decrease in a partner's share of partnership debt decreases the partner's basis. A partner's share of partnership debt decreases as a result of (1) decreases in total partnership debt and (2) assumption of a partner's debt by the entity. This limits the partner's ability to deduct current-year flow-through losses.

*Find more information on this topic at our Web site: **http://wft-entities.swlearning.com**.*

## PARTNER'S BASIS, GAIN, AND LOSS

The partner's basis is also affected by (1) postacquisition contributions of cash or property to the partnership and (2) postacquisition distributions of cash or property from the partnership.

Ed is a one-third partner in the ERM Partnership. On January 1, 2005, Ed's basis in his partnership interest was $50,000. During 2005, the calendar year, accrual basis partnership generated ordinary taxable income of $210,000. It also received $60,000 of tax-exempt interest income from City of Buffalo bonds. It paid $3,000 in nondeductible bribes to local law enforcement officials, so that the police would not notify the Federal government about the products that the entity had imported without paying the proper tariffs. On July 1, 2005, Ed contributed $20,000 cash and a computer (zero basis to him) to the partnership. Ed's monthly draw from the partnership is $3,000; this is not a guaranteed payment. The only liabilities that the partnership has incurred are trade accounts payable. On January 1, 2005, the trade accounts payable totaled $45,000; this account balance was $21,000 on December 31, 2005. Ed shares in one-third of the partnership liabilities for basis purposes.

Ed's basis in the partnership on December 31, 2005, is $115,000, computed as follows.

| | |
|---|---:|
| Beginning balance | $ 50,000 |
| Share of ordinary partnership income | 70,000 |
| Share of tax-exempt income | 20,000 |
| Share of nondeductible expenditures | (1,000) |
| Ed's basis in noncash capital contribution (computer) | –0– |
| Additional cash contributions | 20,000 |
| Capital withdrawal ($3,000 per month) | (36,000) |
| Share of net decrease in partnership liabilities<br>[⅓ × ($45,000 – $21,000)] | (8,000) |
| | $115,000 |

**EXAMPLE 26**

Assume the same facts as in Example 25. If Ed withdraws cash of $115,000 from the partnership on January 1, 2006, the withdrawal is tax-free to him and reduces his basis to zero. The distribution is tax-free because Ed has recognized his share of the partnership's net income throughout his association with the entity via the annual flow-through of his share of the partnership's income and expense items to his personal tax return. Note that the $20,000 cash withdrawal of his share of the municipal bond interest retains its nontaxable character in this distribution. Ed receives the $20,000 tax-free because his basis was increased in 2005 when the partnership received the interest income. ■

**Distributions.** When a distribution involves something other than cash, the recipient partner (1) reduces the basis in the partnership interest and (2) assigns a basis to the asset received, both by the amount of the inside basis of the distributed asset. When cash and another asset are distributed at the same time, the partner first accounts for the cash received. Loss is never recognized when a partnership makes a distribution other than in its own liquidation. A partner recognizes gain only when receiving cash in an amount in excess of the partner's basis.

*Loss is never recognized when a partnership makes a distribution other than it's own liquidation.*

**EXAMPLE 27**

Pert Corporation has a $100,000 basis in the PQR Partnership. Pert receives a distribution from PQR in the form of a plot of land (basis to PQR of $40,000, fair market value of $50,000). Pert recognizes no income from the distribution. Pert's basis in the land is $40,000 (i.e., a carryover basis), and its basis in PQR now is $60,000 ($100,000 – $40,000). ■

**EXAMPLE 28**

Pert Corporation has a $100,000 basis in the PQR Partnership. Pert receives a distribution from PQR in the form of a plot of land (basis to PQR of $40,000, fair market value of $50,000), and $75,000 of cash. Pert recognizes no income from the distribution because the cash received ($75,000) does not exceed Pert's partnership basis ($100,000). Pert's basis in the land is $25,000, the basis in PQR remaining after accounting for the cash ($100,000 partnership basis – $75,000 cash = $25,000 basis assigned to land). Pert's basis in the partnership now is zero ($25,000 basis after accounting for the cash – $25,000 assigned to the land). ■

**EXAMPLE 29**

Pert Corporation has a $100,000 basis in the PQR Partnership. Pert receives a distribution from PQR in the form of a plot of land (basis to PQR of $40,000, fair market value of $50,000), and $125,000 of cash. Pert recognizes $25,000 of income from the distribution ($125,000 cash received – $100,000 basis in PQR). Pert's basis in the land is $0, as there is no basis in PQR remaining after accounting for the cash. Pert's basis in the partnership also is zero. ■

■ **FIGURE 10–1**

Partner's Basis in Partnership Interest

**Basis is generally adjusted in the following order.**

Initial basis. Amount paid for partnership interest, or gift or inherited basis (including share of partnership debt).

+ Partner's subsequent asset contributions.
+ Since interest acquired, partner's share of the partnership's

- Debt increase.
- Income items.
- Tax-exempt income items.
- Excess of depletion deductions over adjusted basis of property subject to depletion.

– Partner's distributions and withdrawals.
– Since interest acquired, partner's share of the partnership's

- Debt decrease.
- Nondeductible items not chargeable to a capital account.
- Special depletion deduction for oil and gas wells.
- Loss items.

**The basis of a partner's interest can never be negative.**

Entity-level liabilities, and thus a partner's interest basis, change from day to day, but the partner's interest basis generally needs to be computed only once or twice a year.

**Capital Changes.** When a partnership interest is sold, exchanged, or retired, the partner must compute the adjusted basis as of the date the transaction occurs. The partner recognizes gain or loss on the disposition of the partnership interest, and this usually is a capital gain or loss. Income "bunching" may occur if the partner recognizes the pass-through of operating income in the same tax year during which the sale of the interest occurs. To the extent that the partner is allocated a share of ordinary income items that have yet to be recognized by the partnership (i.e., "hot assets"), some of the capital gain is converted to ordinary income.[38]

**EXAMPLE 30**

When its basis in the TUV Partnership is $100,000, taking into account all earnings to date and the sale-date liabilities of the partnership, Kurt Corporation sells its interest in the entity to Gloria for $120,000. Kurt recognizes a $20,000 capital gain [$120,000 (amount realized) − $100,000 (basis in partnership interest)]. ■

**EXAMPLE 31**

When its basis in the TUV Partnership is $100,000, taking into account all earnings to date and the sale-date liabilities of the partnership, Kurt Corporation sells its interest in the entity to Gloria for $120,000. At the time of the sale, Kurt's share of the TUV hot assets is $8,000. Kurt recognizes $8,000 of ordinary income and $12,000 of capital gain (i.e., total gain of $20,000 is comprised of $8,000 of ordinary income and $12,000 of capital gain). ■

**EXAMPLE 32**

When its basis in the TUV Partnership is $100,000, taking into account all earnings to date and the sale-date liabilities of the partnership, Kurt Corporation sells its interest in the entity to Gloria for $120,000. At the time of the sale, Kurt's share of the TUV hot assets is $28,000. Kurt recognizes $28,000 of ordinary income and $8,000 of capital loss (i.e., total gain of $20,000 is comprised of $28,000 of ordinary income and $8,000 of capital loss). ■

Figure 10–1 summarizes the rules for computing a partner's basis in a partnership interest.

---

[38]Partnership items that hold unrecognized ordinary income are known as *hot assets*. Hot assets include the unrealized receivables of a cash basis partnership, and a broadly defined concept of appreciated inventory. §§ 751(a) and (d).

**LO.6**

Describe the limitations on deducting partnership losses.

## LOSS LIMITATIONS

Partnership losses flow through to the partners for use on their tax returns. However, the amount and nature of the losses that may be used in a partner's tax computations may be limited. When limitations apply, all or a portion of the losses are suspended and carried forward until the rules allow them to be used. Only then can the losses decrease the partner's tax liability.

Three different limitations may apply to partnership losses that are passed through to a partner. The first allows the deduction of *losses* only to the extent the partner has adjusted basis for the partnership interest. Losses that are deductible under this basis limitation may then be subject to the *at-risk* limitations. Losses are deductible under this provision only to the extent the partner is at risk for the partnership interest. Any losses that survive this second limitation may be subject to a third limitation, the *passive* loss rules. Only losses that make it through all of these applicable limitations are eligible to be deducted on the partner's tax return.

**EXAMPLE 33**

Meg is a partner in a partnership that does not invest in real estate. On January 1, Meg's adjusted basis for her partnership interest is $50,000, and her at-risk amount is $35,000. Her share of losses from the partnership for the year is $60,000, all of which is passive. She has one other passive income-producing investment that produced $25,000 of passive income during the year. Meg can deduct $25,000 of partnership losses on her Form 1040.

| Applicable Provision | Deductible Loss | Suspended Loss |
|---|---|---|
| Basis limitation | $50,000 | $10,000 |
| At-risk limitation | 35,000 | 15,000 |
| Passive loss limitation | 25,000 | 10,000 |

Meg can deduct only $50,000 under the basis limitation. Of this $50,000, only $35,000 is deductible under the at-risk limitation. Under the passive loss limitation, passive losses can only be deducted against passive income. Thus, Meg can deduct only $25,000 on her return. The remaining $35,000 of losses is suspended. ■

**Basis Limitation.**   A partner may only deduct losses flowing through from the partnership to the extent of the partner's adjusted basis in the partnership.[39] A partner's adjusted basis in the partnership is determined at the end of the partnership's taxable year. It is adjusted for distributions and any partnership gains during the year, but it is determined *before considering any losses for the year.*

Losses that cannot be deducted because of this rule are suspended and carried forward (never back) for use against future increases in the partner's adjusted basis. Such increases might result from additional capital contributions, from sharing in additional partnership debts, or from future partnership income.

**EXAMPLE 34**

Carol and Dan do business as the CD Partnership, sharing profits and losses equally. All parties use the calendar year. At the start of the current year, the basis of Carol's partnership interest is $25,000. The partnership sustains an operating loss of $80,000 in the current year. Only $25,000 of Carol's $40,000 allocable share of the partnership loss can be deducted under the basis limitation. As a result, the basis of Carol's partnership interest is zero as of January 1 of the following year, and Carol must carry forward the remaining $15,000 of partnership losses. ■

---

[39]§ 704(d).

**EXAMPLE 35**

Assume the same facts as in Example 34, and that the partnership earns a profit of $70,000 for the next calendar year. Carol reports net partnership income of $20,000 ($35,000 distributive share of income – $15,000 carryforward loss). The basis of Carol's partnership interest becomes $20,000. ■

## Make Your Own Tax Shelter

**FRAMEWORK FOCUS: DEDUCTIONS**

STRATEGY ➤ MAXIMIZE DEDUCTIBLE AMOUNTS.

In Example 34, Carol's entire $40,000 share of the current-year partnership loss could have been deducted under the basis limitation in the current year if she had contributed an additional $15,000 or more in capital by December 31. Alternatively, if the partnership had incurred additional debt by the end of the current year, Carol's basis might have been increased to permit some or all of the loss to be deducted in that year. Thus, if partnership losses are projected for a given year, careful tax planning can ensure their deductibility under the basis limitation.

Notice that, in Figure 10–1, contributions to capital, partnership income items, and distributions from the partnership are taken into account before loss items. This *losses last* rule can produce some unusual results in taxation of partnership distributions and deductibility of losses.

**EXAMPLE 36**

The Ellen-Glenn Partnership is owned equally by partners Ellen and Glenn. At the beginning of the year, Ellen's basis in her partnership interest is exactly $0. Her share of partnership income is $10,000 for the year, and she receives a $10,000 distribution from the partnership.

Under the basis adjustment ordering rules of Figure 10–1, Ellen's basis is first increased by the $10,000 of partnership income; then it is decreased by her $10,000 distribution. She reports her $10,000 share of partnership taxable income on her personal tax return. Her basis at the end of the year is exactly $0 ($0 + $10,000 income – $10,000 distribution). ■

**EXAMPLE 37**

Assume the same facts as in Example 36, except that Ellen's share of partnership operating results is a $10,000 loss instead of $10,000 income. She again receives a $10,000 distribution.

A distribution of cash in excess of basis in the partnership interest results in a gain to the distributee partner to the extent of the excess. Ellen's distribution is considered before the deductibility of the loss is evaluated under the basis limitation.

Therefore, Ellen recognizes gain on the $10,000 distribution because she has no basis in her partnership interest. The gain effectively ensures that she still has a $0 basis after the distribution. The loss cannot be deducted under the basis limitation rule because Ellen has no basis in her partnership interest. ■

Given this $20,000 difference in partnership earnings in the two examples ($10,000 income versus $10,000 loss), does income taxed to Ellen differ in the same way? Actually, she reports $10,000 of income (gain) in each case: ordinary income in Example 36, and (probably) a capital gain from the distribution in Example 37. In Example 37, she also has a $10,000 suspended loss carryforward. These results are due solely to the basis adjustment ordering rules.

**At-Risk Limitation.** Under the at-risk rules, the partnership losses from business and income-producing activities that individual partners and closely held C corporation partners can deduct are limited to amounts that are economically

**TAX FACT**

## WHOSE MONEY ARE WE LOSING?

Net operating losses are more likely to be found in the limited partnership and LLC/LLP than in the general partnership.

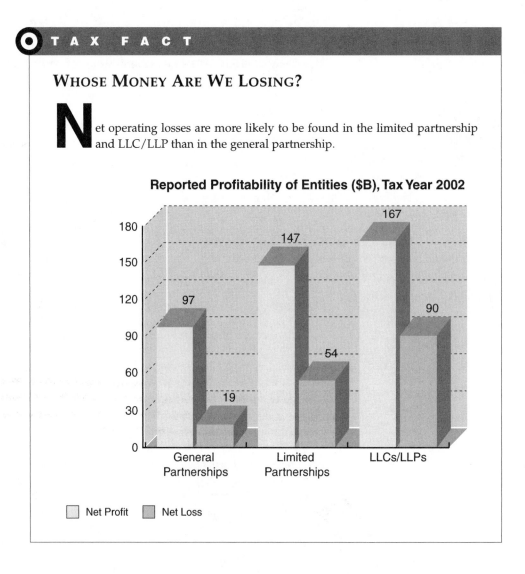

**Reported Profitability of Entities ($B), Tax Year 2002**

General Partnerships: Net Profit 97, Net Loss 19
Limited Partnerships: Net Profit 147, Net Loss 54
LLCs/LLPs: Net Profit 167, Net Loss 90

☐ Net Profit   ■ Net Loss

invested in the partnership. Invested amounts include the cash and the adjusted basis of property contributed by the partner and the partner's share of partnership earnings that has not been withdrawn.[40] A closely held C corporation exists when five or fewer individuals own more than 50 percent of the entity's stock under appropriate attribution and ownership rules.

When some or all of the partners are personally liable for partnership recourse debt, that debt is included in the adjusted basis of those partners. Usually, those partners also include the debt in their amount at risk.

No partner, however, carries any financial risk on nonrecourse debt. Therefore, as a general rule, partners cannot include nonrecourse debt in their amount at risk even though that debt is included in the adjusted basis of their partnership interest. This rule has an exception, however, that applies in many cases. Real estate nonrecourse financing provided by a bank, retirement plan, or similar party or by a Federal, state, or local government generally is deemed to be at risk.[41] Such debt is termed **qualified nonrecourse debt.** In summary, although the general rule provides that nonrecourse debt is not at risk, the overriding exception may provide that it is deemed to be at risk.

---

[40]§ 465(a).

[41]§ 465(b)(6).

**EXAMPLE 38**

Kelly invests $5,000 in the Kelly Green Limited Partnership as a 5% general partner. Shortly thereafter, the partnership acquires the master recording of a well-known vocalist for $250,000 ($50,000 from the partnership and $200,000 secured from a local bank via a *recourse* mortgage). Kelly's share of the recourse debt is $10,000, and her basis in her partnership interest is $15,000 ($5,000 cash investment + $10,000 debt share). Since the debt is recourse, Kelly's at-risk amount also is $15,000. Kelly's share of partnership losses in the first year of operations is $11,000. Kelly is entitled to deduct the full $11,000 of partnership losses under both the basis and the at-risk limitations because this amount is less than both her outside basis and at-risk amount. ■

**EXAMPLE 39**

Assume the same facts as in Example 38, except the bank loan is nonrecourse (the partners have no direct liability under the terms of the loan in the case of a default). Kelly's basis in her partnership interest still is $15,000, but she can deduct only $5,000 of the flow-through loss. The amount she has at risk in the partnership does not include the nonrecourse debt. (The debt does not relate to real estate so it is not qualified nonrecourse debt.) ■

**Passive Activity Rules.** A partnership loss share may also be disallowed under the passive activity rules. Recall from Chapter 5 that an activity is considered passive if the taxpayer (in this case, a partner) does not materially participate or if the activity is considered a rental activity. Losses from passive partnership activities are aggregated by each partner with his or her other passive income and losses. Any net loss is suspended and carried forward to future years. Thus, the passive activity limitation applies at the partner level and is computed after the basis and at-risk limitations.

**PLANNING STRATEGIES**

## Formation and Operation of a Partnership

**FRAMEWORK FOCUS: INCOME AND EXCLUSIONS**

**STRATEGY ▶ POSTPONE RECOGNITION OF INCOME TO ACHIEVE TAX DEFERRAL.**

In transferring assets to a partnership, potential partners should be cautious to ensure that they are not required to recognize any gain upon the creation of the entity. The nonrecognition provisions of § 721 are relatively straightforward and resemble the provisions under § 351. However, any partner can make a tax-deferred contribution of assets to the entity either at the inception of the partnership or later. This possibility is not available to less-than-controlling shareholders in a corporation.

The partners should anticipate the tax benefits and pitfalls that are presented in Subchapter K and should take appropriate actions to resolve any resulting problems. Typically, all that is needed is an appropriate provision in the partnership agreement (e.g., with respect to differing allocation percentages for gains and losses). Recall, however, that a special allocation of income, expense, or credit items in the partnership agreement must satisfy certain requirements before it is acceptable to the IRS.

**L0.7**

Review the treatment of transactions between a partner and the partnership.

## Transactions between Partner and Partnership

Many types of transactions occur between a partnership and its partners. A partner may contribute property to the partnership, perform services for the partnership, or receive distributions from the partnership. A partner may borrow money from or lend money to the partnership. Property may be bought and sold between a partner and the partnership. Several of these transactions were discussed earlier in the chapter. The remaining types of partner-partnership transactions are the focus of this section.

## GUARANTEED PAYMENTS

If a partnership makes a payment to a partner in his or her capacity as a partner, the payment may be a draw against the partner's share of partnership income; a return of some or all of the partner's original capital contribution; or a guaranteed payment, among other treatments. A **guaranteed payment** is a payment for services performed by the partner or for the use of the partner's capital. The payment may not be determined by reference to partnership income. Guaranteed payments are usually expressed as a fixed-dollar amount or as a percentage of capital that the partner has invested in the partnership. Whether the partnership deducts or capitalizes the guaranteed payment depends on the nature of the payment.

**EXAMPLE 40**

David, Donald, and Dale formed the accrual basis DDD Partnership. The partnership and each of the partners are calendar year taxpayers. According to the partnership agreement, David is to manage the partnership and receive a $21,000 distribution from the entity every year, payable in 12 monthly installments. Donald is to receive an amount that is equal to 18% of his capital account, as it is computed by the firm's accountant at the beginning of the year, payable in 12 monthly installments. Dale is the partnership's advertising specialist. He withdraws about 3% of the partnership's net income every month for his personal use. David and Donald receive guaranteed payments from the partnership, but Dale does not. ∎

Guaranteed payments resemble the salary or interest payments of other businesses and receive somewhat similar income tax treatment.[42] In contrast to the provision that usually applies to withdrawals of assets by partners from their partnerships, guaranteed payments are deductible (or capitalized) by the entity. Deductible guaranteed payments, like any other deductible expenses of a partnership, can create an ordinary loss for the entity. Partners receiving a guaranteed payment report ordinary income, treated as paid on the last day of the entity's tax year.

**EXAMPLE 41**

Continue with the situation introduced in Example 40. For calendar year 2005, David receives the $21,000 as provided by the partnership agreement, Donald's guaranteed payment for 2005 is $17,000, and Dale withdraws $20,000 under his personal expenditures clause. Before considering these amounts, the partnership's ordinary income for 2005 is $650,000.

The partnership can deduct its payments to David and Donald, so the final amount of its 2005 ordinary income is $612,000 ($650,000 − $21,000 − $17,000). Thus, each of the equal partners is allocated $204,000 of ordinary partnership income for their 2005 individual income tax returns ($612,000 ÷ 3). In addition, David reports the $21,000 guaranteed payment as income, and Donald includes the $17,000 guaranteed payment in his 2005 income. Dale's partnership draw is deemed to have come from his allocated $204,000 (or from the accumulated partnership income that was taxed to him in prior years) and is not taxed separately to him. ∎

**EXAMPLE 42**

Assume the same facts as in Example 41, except that the partnership's tax year ends on March 31, 2006. The total amount of the guaranteed payments is taxable to the partners on that date. Thus, even though David received 9 of his 12 payments for fiscal 2006 in the 2005 calendar year, all of his guaranteed payments are taxable to him in 2006. Similarly, all of Donald's guaranteed payments are taxable to him in 2006, rather than when they are received. The deduction for, and the gross income from, guaranteed payments is allowed on the same

---

[42]§ 707(c).

## CONCEPT SUMMARY 10–3

### Partner-Partnership Transactions

1. Partners can transact business with their partnerships in a nonpartner capacity. These transactions include the sale and exchange of property, rentals, loans of funds, etc.

2. A payment to a partner may be classified as a guaranteed payment if it is for services or use of the partner's capital and is not based on partnership income. A guaranteed payment usually is deductible by the partnership and is included in the partner's income on the last day of the partnership's tax year.

3. A payment to a partner may be treated as being to an outside (though related) party. Such a payment is deductible or capitalizable by the partnership at the time it must be included in income under the partner's method of accounting.

4. Guaranteed payments and payments to a partner that are treated as being to an outside party are deductible if the payment constitutes an ordinary and necessary (rather than capitalizable) business expense.

5. Losses are disallowed between a partner or related party and a partnership when the partner or related party owns more than a 50% interest in the partnership's capital or profits.

6. Income from a related-party sale is treated as ordinary income if the property is not a capital asset to both the transferor and the transferee.

7. Partners are not employees of their partnership, so the entity cannot deduct payments for partner fringe benefits, nor need it withhold or pay any payroll tax for payments to partners.

date that all of the other income and expense items relative to the partnership are allocated to the partners (i.e., on the last day of the entity's tax year). ■

### OTHER TRANSACTIONS BETWEEN A PARTNER AND A PARTNERSHIP

Certain transactions between a partner and the partnership are treated as if the partner were an outsider, dealing with the partnership at arm's length.[43] Loan transactions, rental payments, and sales of property between the partner and the partnership are generally treated in this manner.

**EXAMPLE 43**

Emilio, a one-third partner in the ABC Partnership, owns a tract of land that the partnership wishes to purchase. The land has a fair market value of $30,000 and an adjusted basis to Emilio of $17,000. If Emilio sells the land to the partnership, he recognizes a $13,000 gain on the sale, and the partnership takes a $30,000 cost basis in the land. If the land has a fair market value of $10,000 on the sale date, Emilio recognizes a $7,000 loss. ■

 DIGGING DEEPER (7)

*Find more information on this topic at our Web site: **http://wft-entities.swlearning.com**.*

**Sales of Property.** No loss is recognized on a sale of property between a person and a partnership when the person owns, directly or indirectly, more than 50 percent of partnership capital or profits.[44] The disallowed loss may not vanish entirely, however. If the person eventually sells the property at a gain, the disallowed loss reduces the gain that would otherwise be recognized.[45]

**EXAMPLE 44**

Barry sells land (adjusted basis, $30,000; fair market value, $45,000) to a partnership in which he controls a 60% capital interest. The partnership pays him only $20,000 for the land. Barry cannot deduct his $10,000 realized loss. The sale apparently was not at arm's length, but the taxpayer's intentions are irrelevant. Barry and the partnership are related parties, and the loss is disallowed.

---

[43]§ 707(a).
[44]§ 707(b).

[45]This is similar to treatment under § 267.

When the partnership sells the land to an outsider at a later date, it receives a sales price of $44,000. The partnership can offset the recognition of its $24,000 realized gain on the subsequent sale ($44,000 sales proceeds − $20,000 adjusted basis) by the amount of the $10,000 prior disallowed loss ($20,000 − $30,000). Thus, the partnership recognizes a $14,000 gain on its sale of the land. ■

Using a similar rationale, any gain that is realized on a sale or exchange between a partner and a partnership in which the partner controls a capital or profits interest of more than 50 percent is recognized as ordinary income, unless the asset is a capital asset to both the seller and the purchaser.[46]

**EXAMPLE 45**

Kristin purchases some land (adjusted basis, $30,000; fair market value, $45,000) for $45,000 from a partnership in which she controls a 90% profits interest. The land was a capital asset to the partnership. If Kristin holds the land as a capital asset, the partnership recognizes a $15,000 capital gain. However, if Kristin is a land developer and the property is not a capital asset to her, the partnership must recognize $15,000 of ordinary income from the sale, even though the property was a capital asset to the partnership. ■

## PARTNERS AS EMPLOYEES

A partner usually does not qualify as an employee for tax purposes. For example, a partner receiving guaranteed payments is not regarded as an employee of the partnership for purposes of payroll taxes (e.g., FICA or FUTA). Moreover, since a partner is not an employee, the partnership cannot deduct its payments for the partner's fringe benefits. Nonetheless, a general partner's distributive share of ordinary partnership income and guaranteed payments for services are generally subject to the Federal self-employment tax.[47]

**PLANNING STRATEGIES**     ## Transactions between Partners and Partnerships

**FRAMEWORK FOCUS: DEDUCTIONS**

STRATEGY ➤ MAXIMIZE DEDUCTIBLE AMOUNTS.

Partners should be careful when engaging in transactions with the partnership to ensure that no negative tax results occur. A partner who owns a majority of the partnership generally should not sell property at a loss to the partnership because the loss is disallowed. Similarly, a majority partner should not sell a capital asset to the partnership at a gain, if the asset is to be used by the partnership as other than a capital asset. The gain on this transaction is taxed as ordinary income to the selling partner rather than as capital gain.

As an alternative to selling property to a partnership, the partner may lease it to the partnership. The partner recognizes rent income, and the partnership has a rent expense.

A partner who needs more cash immediately can sell the property to an outside third party; then the third party can lease the property to the partnership for a fair rental.

The timing of the deduction for payments by accrual basis partnerships to cash basis partners varies depending on whether the payment is a guaranteed payment or is treated as a payment to an outsider. If the payment is a guaranteed payment, the deduction occurs when the partnership properly accrues the payment. If the payment is treated as a payment to an outsider, the actual date the payment is made controls the timing of the deduction.

---

[46]§ 707(b)(2).

[47]§ 1402(a).

## LO.8

Describe the application of partnership tax law provisions to limited liability companies (LLCs) and limited liability partnerships (LLPs).

# Limited Liability Entities

## LIMITED LIABILITY COMPANIES

The *limited liability company (LLC)* combines partnership taxation with limited personal liability for all owners of the entity. All states and the District of Columbia have passed legislation permitting the establishment of LLCs.

**Taxation of LLCs.**  A properly structured LLC may be taxed as a partnership under the "check-the-box" rules. Because LLC members are not personally liable for the debts of the entity, the LLC is effectively treated as a limited partnership with no general partners. This may result in unusual application of partnership taxation rules. The IRS has not specifically ruled on most aspects of LLC taxation, so several of the following comments are based on speculation about how a partnership with no general partners would be taxed.

- Formation of a new LLC is treated in the same manner as formation of a partnership. Generally, no gain or loss is recognized by the LLC member or the LLC, the member takes a substituted basis in the LLC interest, and the LLC takes a carryover basis in the assets it receives.
- An LLC's income and losses are allocated proportionately. Special allocations are permitted, as long as they demonstrate economic effect.
- Contributed property with built-in gains can be subject to tax on certain distributions within five years of the contribution.
- A loss must meet the basis, at-risk, and passive loss limitations to be currently deductible. Because debt of an LLC is considered nonrecourse to each of the members, it may not be included in the at-risk limitation unless it is "qualified nonrecourse financing." The IRS has not issued rulings as to whether a member is treated as a material or active participant of an LLC for passive loss purposes. Presumably, passive or active status will be based on the time the member spends in LLC activities.
- The initial accounting period and accounting method elections are available to an LLC.
- An LLC member's share of partnership income is *not* subject to self-employment taxes.
- Property takes a carryover or substituted basis when distributed from an LLC.

**Advantages of an LLC.**  An LLC offers certain advantages over a limited partnership.

- Generally, none of the members of an LLC is personally liable for the entity's debts. General partners in a limited partnership have personal liability for partnership recourse debts.
- Limited partners cannot participate in the management of a partnership. All owners of an LLC have the legal right to participate in the entity's management.

An LLC also offers certain advantages over an S corporation (see Chapter 11), including the following.

- An LLC can have an unlimited number of owners, while an S corporation is limited to 100 shareholders.

## CONCEPT SUMMARY 10–4

### Advantages and Disadvantages of the Partnership Form

The partnership form may be attractive when one or more of the following factors is present:

* The entity is generating net taxable losses and/or valuable tax credits, which will be of use to the owners.
* The owners want to avoid complex corporate administrative and filing requirements.
* Other means of reducing the effects of the double taxation of corporate business income (e.g., compensation to owners, interest, and rental payments) have been exhausted.
* The entity does not generate material amounts of tax preference and adjustment items, which increase the alternative minimum tax liabilities of its owners.
* The entity is generating net passive income, which its owners can use to claim immediate deductions for net passive losses that they have generated from other sources.
* Given the asset holdings and distribution practices of the entity, the possibility of liability under the accumulated earnings and personal holding company taxes is significant.
* The owners wish to make special allocations of certain income or deduction items that are not possible under the C or S corporation forms.
* The owners have adequate bases in their ownership interests to facilitate the deduction of flow-through losses and the assignment of an adequate basis to assets distributed in-kind to the owners.

The partnership form may be less attractive when one or more of the following factors is present:

* The tax paid by the owners on the entity's income is greater than that payable by the entity as a C corporation, and the income is not expected to be distributed soon. (If distributed by a C corporation, double taxation would likely occur.)
* The entity is generating net taxable income without distributing any cash to the owners. The owners may not have sufficient cash with which to pay the tax on the entity's earnings.
* The type of income that the entity is generating (e.g., business and portfolio income) is not as attractive to its owners as net passive income would be because the owners could use net passive income to offset the net passive losses that they have generated on their own.
* The entity is in a high-exposure business, and the owners desire protection from personal liability. An LLC or LLP structure may be available, however, to limit personal liability.
* The owners want to avoid Federal self-employment tax.

---

* Any taxpayers, including corporations, nonresident aliens, other partnerships, and trusts, can be owners of an LLC. S corporation shares can be held only by specified parties.
* The transfer of property to an LLC in exchange for an ownership interest in the entity is governed by partnership tax provisions rather than corporate tax provisions. Thus, the transfers need not satisfy the 80 percent control requirement needed for tax-free treatment under the corporate tax statutes.
* The S corporation taxes on built-in gains and passive income do not apply to LLCs.
* An owner's basis in an LLC includes the owner's share of almost all LLC liabilities under § 752. Only certain entity liabilities are included in the S corporation shareholder's basis.
* An LLC may make special allocations, whereas S corporations must allocate income, loss, etc., only on a per share/per day basis.

**Disadvantages of an LLC.**   The disadvantages of an LLC stem primarily from the entity's relative newness. There is no established body of case law interpreting the various state statutes, so the application of specific provisions is uncertain. An additional uncertainty for LLCs that operate in more than one jurisdiction is which state's law will prevail and how it will be applied.

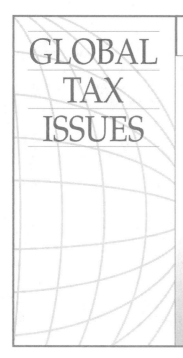

## PARTNERSHIPS AROUND THE WORLD—AND BEYOND

Technology continues to act as a catalyst—and incentive—for the creation of joint ventures. From Web kiosks at gas stations to global satellite networks, high-tech companies are forging alliances to bring technology to consumers.

Microsoft has teamed up with BP to provide news, weather, and other content for customers to watch while they fill up at the gas station. TimeWarner and Radiant Systems, Inc., formed their own venture to offer programming at other gas stations, pizza parlors, and numerous other retail outlets. These ventures appear to be spurred by a desire to capture larger shares of the ever-expanding global market.

Meanwhile, various domestic telephone companies are continuing to align themselves with partners in foreign telecommunications markets: each wants to have the widest possible service coverage area so it can offer efficient communications and computer networking to business clients with a global presence.

Primestar is a partnership formed by several media and cable companies to offer digital satellite television services on numerous channels to customers for a monthly rental fee. And several partnerships have been formed to establish satellite-based Web communications around the world.

Among other factors, statutes differ from state to state as to the type of business an LLC can conduct—primarily the extent to which a service-providing firm can operate as an LLC. A service entity may find it cannot operate as an LLC in several jurisdictions where it conducts business. Despite these uncertainties and limitations, LLCs are being formed at increasing rates, and the ranks of multistate LLCs are rising quickly.

### LIMITED LIABILITY PARTNERSHIPS

The difference between a general partnership and a limited liability partnership (LLP) is small, but very significant. Recall that general partners are jointly and severally liable for all partnership debts. Partners in a registered LLP are jointly and severally liable for contractual liability (i.e., they are treated as general partners for commercial debt). They are also personally liable for their own malpractice or other torts. They are not, however, personally liable for the malpractice and torts of their partners. As a result, the exposure of their personal assets to lawsuits filed against other partners and the partnership is considerably reduced.

An LLP must have formal documents of organization and register with the state. LLPs are taxed as partnerships under Federal tax rules.

## Summary

Partnerships are popular among business owners because formation of the entity is relatively simple and tax-free. The Code places very few restrictions on who can be a partner. Partnerships are especially attractive when operating losses are anticipated, or when marginal rates that would apply to partnership income are less than those that would be paid by a C corporation. Partnerships do not offer the limited liability of a corporate entity, but the use of limited partnerships, LLCs, and LLPs can offer some protection to the owners.

Partnerships are tax-reporting, not taxpaying, entities. Distributive shares of ordinary income and separately stated items are taxed to the partners on the last day of the tax year. Special allocations and guaranteed payments are allowed and offer partners the ability to tailor the cash-flow and taxable amounts that are distributed by the entity to its owners. Deductions for flow-through losses may be limited by the passive activity, related-party, and at-risk rules, as well as by the partner's interest basis. The flexibility of the partnership rules makes this form continually attractive to new businesses, especially in a global setting.

# Suggested Further Readings

"Are LLC Members GPs or LPs for Federal or State Tax Purposes?" *Journal of Taxation*, January 2003, p. 62.

C. Curry, S. Harrington, and K. Milani, "Tax Choice When Receiving Partnership Interest for Services," *Practical Tax Strategies*, February 2004, pp. 112–118.

Peter C. Mahoney and Elizabeth Williams, "Opportunities, Pitfalls, and Developments in the Disguised Sale Rules," *Real Estate Taxation*, WG&L Online, 2005.

Charles I. Middleton, "Use of a Partnership in International Dealings Can Be Beneficial for Both Inbound and Outbound Transactions," *Journal of Partnership Taxation*, Winter 1999, pp. 306–334.

## KEY TERMS

| | | |
|---|---|---|
| Basis in partnership interest, 10–9 | Inside basis, 10–14 | Profit and loss sharing ratios, 10–8 |
| Capital account, 10–9 | Limited liability company (LLC), 10–5 | Profits (loss) interest, 10–8 |
| Capital interest, 10–8 | | Qualified nonrecourse debt, 10–28 |
| Capital sharing ratio, 10–8 | Limited liability partnership (LLP), 10–5 | Recourse debt, 10–22 |
| Disguised sale, 10–11 | Limited partnership, 10–5 | Separately stated item, 10–6 |
| Economic effect test, 10–19 | Nonrecourse debt, 10–22 | Special allocation, 10–8 |
| General partnership, 10–5 | Outside basis, 10–14 | Syndication costs, 10–16 |
| Guaranteed payment, 10–30 | Precontribution gain or loss, 10–20 | |

## PROBLEM MATERIALS

### Problems

**Issue ID**

1. Justin and Tiffany will contribute property to form the equal TJ Partnership. Justin will contribute cash of $20,000 plus land with a fair market value of $80,000 and an adjusted basis of $65,000. Tiffany currently operates a sole proprietorship with assets valued at $100,000 and an adjusted basis of $125,000. Tiffany will contribute these assets in-kind to the partnership. Describe the tax consequences of the formation to Tiffany, Justin, and the partnership.

2. Larry and Ken form an equal partnership with a cash contribution of $50,000 from Larry and a property contribution (adjusted basis of $30,000 and a fair market value of $50,000) from Ken.
   a. How much gain, if any, must Larry recognize on the transfer? Must Ken recognize any gain?
   b. What is Larry's basis in his partnership interest?
   c. What is Ken's basis in his partnership interest?
   d. What basis does the partnership take in the property transferred by Ken?

**Decision Making**

3. Tom and Katie form an equal partnership with an $80,000 cash contribution from Tom and a contribution of property (basis of $100,000, fair market value of $80,000) from Katie.
   a. Compute Katie's realized and recognized gain or loss from the contribution.
   b. Compute Tom's basis in his partnership interest.
   c. Compute Katie's basis in her partnership interest.
   d. What basis does the partnership take in Katie's contributed asset?
   e. Are there more tax-effective ways to structure the transaction?

4. Three years after the S&P Partnership is formed, Sylvia, a 25% partner, contributes an additional $50,000 of cash and land she has held for investment. Sylvia's basis in the land is $60,000, and its fair market value is $100,000. Her basis in the partnership interest was $50,000 before this contribution. The partnership uses the land as a parking lot for four years and then sells it for $120,000.
   a. How much gain or loss does Sylvia recognize on the contribution?
   b. What is Sylvia's basis in her partnership interest immediately following this contribution?
   c. How much gain or loss does S&P recognize on this contribution?
   d. What is S&P's basis in the property it receives from Sylvia?
   e. How much gain or loss does the partnership recognize on the later sale of the land, and what is the character of the gain or loss? How much is allocated to Sylvia?

**Issue ID**

5. Block, Inc., a calendar year general contractor, and Strauss, Inc., a development corporation with a July 31 year-end, formed the equal SB Partnership on January 1 of the current year. Both partners are C corporations. The partnership was formed to construct and lease shopping centers in Wilmington, Delaware. Block contributed equipment (basis of $650,000, fair market value of $650,000), building permits, and architectural designs created by Block's employees (basis $0, fair market value $100,000). Strauss contributed land (basis $50,000, fair market value $250,000) and cash of $500,000. The cash was used as follows.

| | |
|---|---:|
| Legal fees for drafting partnership agreement | $ 10,000 |
| Materials and labor costs for construction in progress on shopping center | 400,000 |
| Office expense (utilities, rent, overhead, etc.) | 90,000 |

What issues must the partnership address in preparing its initial tax return?

**Decision Making**

6. Craig and Beth are equal members of the CB Partnership, formed on June 1 of the current year. Craig contributed land that he inherited from his father three years ago. Craig's father purchased the land in 1946 for $6,000. The land was worth $50,000 when the father died. The fair market value of the land was $75,000 at the date it was contributed to the partnership.
   Beth has significant experience developing real estate. After the partnership is formed, she will prepare a plan for developing the property and secure zoning approvals for the partnership. She would normally bill a third party $25,000 for these efforts. Beth will also contribute $50,000 of cash in exchange for her 50% interest in the partnership. The value of her 50% interest is $75,000.
   a. How much gain or income will Craig recognize on his contribution of the land to the partnership? What is the character of any gain or income recognized?
   b. What basis will Craig take in his partnership interest?
   c. How much gain or income will Beth recognize on the formation of the partnership? What is the character of any gain or income recognized?
   d. What basis will Beth take in her partnership interest?
   e. Construct an opening balance sheet for the partnership reflecting the partnership's basis in the assets and the fair market value of these assets.
   f. Outline any planning opportunities that may minimize current taxation to any of the parties.

7. Continue with the facts presented in Problem 6. At the end of the first year, the partnership distributes the $50,000 of cash to Craig. No distribution is made to Beth.

a. Under general tax rules, how would the payment to Craig be treated?

b. How much income or gain would Craig recognize as a result of the payment?

c. Under general tax rules, what basis would the partnership take in the land Craig contributed?

8. The SJ Partnership was formed to acquire land and subdivide it as residential housing lots. On July 1, 2005, Sarah contributed land valued at $200,000 to the partnership in exchange for a 50% interest. She had purchased the land in 2000 for $160,000 and held it for investment purposes (capital asset). The partnership holds the land as inventory.

On the same date, Joe contributed land valued at $200,000 that he had purchased in 1999 for $240,000. He also became a 50% owner in SJ. Joe is a real estate developer, but he held this land personally for investment purposes. The partnership holds this land as inventory.

In 2006, the partnership sells the land contributed by Sarah for $220,000.

In 2007, the partnership sells half of the subdivided real estate contributed by Joe for $88,000. The other half is finally sold in 2012 for $108,000.

a. What is each partner's initial basis in his or her partnership interest?

b. What is the amount of gain or loss recognized on the sale of the land contributed by Sarah? What is the character of this gain or loss?

c. What is the amount of gain or loss recognized each year on the sale of the land contributed by Joe? What is the character of this gain or loss?

9. The partnership agreement for the SJ Partnership in Problem 8 provides that all gains and losses are allocated equally between the partners unless otherwise required under the tax law.

a. How will the gains or losses determined in (b) and (c) in Problem 8 be allocated to each of the partners?

b. Calculate each partner's basis in his or her partnership interest at December 31, 2012. Assume the partnership has no transactions through the end of the year 2012 other than the transactions described in Problem 8. Why are these balances the same or different?

10. On July 1 of the current year, the R&R Partnership was formed to operate a bed and breakfast inn. The partnership paid $3,000 in legal fees for drafting the partnership agreement, and $5,000 for accounting fees related to organizing the entity. It also paid $10,000 in syndication costs to locate and secure investments from limited partners. In addition, before opening the inn for business, the entity paid $15,500 for advertising and $36,000 in costs related to an open house just before the grand opening of the property. The partnership opened the inn for business on October 1.

a. How are these expenses classified?

b. How much may the partnership deduct in its initial year of operations?

c. How are costs treated that are not deducted currently?

d. What elections must the partnership make in its initial tax return?

11. Lisa and Lori are equal members of the Redbird Partnership. They are real estate investors who formed the partnership several years ago with equal cash contributions. Redbird then purchased a piece of land.

On January 1 of the current year, to acquire a one-third interest in the entity, Lana contributed some land she had held for investment to the partnership. Lana purchased the land three years ago for $30,000; its fair market value at the contribution date was $40,000. No special allocation agreements were in effect before or after Lana was admitted to the partnership. The Redbird Partnership holds all land for investment.

Immediately before Lana's property contribution, the balance sheet of the Redbird Partnership was as follows.

|      | Basis | FMV |              | Basis | FMV |
|------|-------|-----|--------------|-------|-----|
| Land | $5,000 | $80,000 | Lisa, capital | $2,500 | $40,000 |
|      |        |         | Lori, capital | 2,500 | 40,000 |
|      | $5,000 | $80,000 |              | $5,000 | $80,000 |

a. At the contribution date, what is Lana's basis in her interest in the Redbird Partnership?
b. When does the partnership's holding period begin for the contributed land?
c. On June 30 of the current year, the partnership sold the land contributed by Lana for $40,000. How much is the recognized gain or loss, and how is it allocated among the partners?
d. Prepare a balance sheet reflecting basis and fair market value for the partnership immediately after the land sale.

12. Assume the same facts as in Problem 11, with the following exceptions.

   • Lana purchased the land three years ago for $50,000. Its fair market value was $40,000 when it was contributed to the partnership.

   • Redbird sold the land contributed by Lana for $34,000.

   a. How much is the recognized gain or loss, and how is it allocated among the partners?
   b. Prepare a balance sheet reflecting basis and fair market value for the partnership immediately after the land sale. Complete schedules that support the amount in each partner's capital account.

13. Earl and Zelda are equal partners in the accrual basis EZ Partnership. At the beginning of the current year, Earl's capital account has a balance of $10,000, and the partnership has recourse debts of $30,000 payable to unrelated parties. All partnership recourse debt is shared equally between the partners. The following information about EZ's operations for the current year is obtained from the partnership's records.

| | |
|---|---|
| Taxable income | $10,000 |
| § 1231 gain | 6,000 |
| Long-term capital gain | 2,000 |
| Short-term capital loss | 600 |
| Charitable contribution to Red Cross | 200 |
| Cash distribution to Earl | 14,000 |
| Payment of Earl's medical expenses | 6,000 |

   Assume that year-end partnership debt payable to unrelated parties is $40,000.
   a. If all transactions are reflected in his beginning capital and basis in the same manner, what is Earl's basis in the partnership interest at the beginning of the year?
   b. What is Earl's basis in the partnership interest at the end of the current year?

14. Martin and Morgan formed the equal M&M Partnership on January 1. Martin contributed $25,000 cash, and land with a fair market value of $10,000 and an adjusted basis of $2,000. Morgan contributed equipment with a fair market value of $35,000 and an adjusted basis of $20,000. Morgan previously had used the equipment in his sole proprietorship. As to the partnership formation:
   a. How much gain or loss will Martin, Morgan, and the partnership realize?
   b. How much gain or loss will Martin, Morgan, and the partnership recognize?
   c. What bases will Martin and Morgan take in their partnership interests?
   d. What bases will M&M take in the assets it receives?
   e. Are there any differences between inside and outside basis?
   f. How will the partnership depreciate any assets it receives from the partners?

**Decision Making**

**Communications**

15. Your client, the Williams Institute of Technology (WIT), is a 60% partner in the Research Industries Partnership (RIP). WIT is located at 76 Bradford Lane, St. Paul, MN 55164. The controller, Jeanine West, has sent you the following note and a copy of WIT's 2005 Schedule K–1 from the partnership.

   **Excerpt from client's note**
   "RIP" expects its 2006 operations to include the following.

| | |
|---|---|
| Net loss from operations | $200,000 |
| Capital gain from sale of land | 100,000 |

The land was contributed by DASH, the other partner, when its value was $260,000. The partnership sold the land for $300,000. The partnership used this cash to repay all the partnership debt and pay for research and development expenditures, which a tax partner in your firm has said RIP can deduct this year.

We want to be sure we can deduct our full share of this loss, but we do not believe we will have enough basis. We are a material participant in this partnership's activities.

---

### Items Reported on the 2005 Schedule K–1

| | |
|---|---|
| WIT's share of partnership recourse liabilities | $90,000 |
| WIT's ending capital account balance | 30,000 |

---

Draft a letter to the controller that describes the following.

- WIT's allocation of partnership items.

- WIT's basis in the partnership interest following the allocation.

- Any limitations on loss deductions.

- Any recommendations you have that would allow WIT to claim the full amount of losses in 2006.

WIT's 2005 Schedule K–1 accurately reflects the information needed to compute its basis in the partnership interest. The research expenditures are fully deductible this year, as the partner said.

Your client has experience researching issues in the Internal Revenue Code, so you may use some citations. However, be sure that the letter is written in layperson's terms and that legal citations are minimized.

16. Lee, Brad, and Rick form the LBR Partnership on January 1 of the current year. In return for a 25% interest, Lee transfers property (basis of $15,000, fair market value of $17,500) subject to a nonrecourse liability of $10,000. The liability is assumed by the partnership. Brad transfers property (basis of $16,000, fair market value of $7,500) for a 25% interest, and Rick transfers cash of $15,000 for the remaining 50% interest.
    a. How much gain must Lee recognize on the transfer?
    b. What is Lee's basis in his interest in the partnership?
    c. How much loss may Brad recognize on the transfer?
    d. What is Brad's basis in his interest in the partnership?
    e. What is Rick's basis in his interest in the partnership?
    f. What basis does the LBR Partnership take in the property transferred by Lee?
    g. What is the partnership's basis in the property transferred by Brad?

17. Assume the same facts as in Problem 16, except that the property contributed by Lee has a fair market value of $27,500 and is subject to a nonrecourse mortgage of $20,000.
    a. What is Lee's basis in his partnership interest?
    b. How much gain must Lee recognize on the transfer?
    c. What is Brad's basis in his partnership interest?
    d. What is Rick's basis in his partnership interest?
    e. What basis does the LBR Partnership take in the property transferred by Lee?

**Issue ID**

18. Sam has operated a microbrewery (sole proprietorship) in southern Oregon for the past 15 years. The business has been highly profitable lately, and demand for the product will soon exceed the amount Sam can produce with his present facilities. Marcie, a long-time fan of the brewery, has offered to invest $1,500,000 for equipment to expand production. The assets and goodwill of the brewery are currently worth $1,000,000 (tax basis is only $200,000). Sam will continue to manage the business. He is not willing to own less than 50% of whatever arrangement they arrive at. What issues should Sam and Marcie address and document before finalizing their venture?

**Issue ID**

**Decision Making**

19. The BCD Partnership plans to distribute cash of $20,000 to partner Brad at the end of the tax year. The partnership reported a loss for the year, and Brad's share of the loss is $10,000. Brad has a basis of $15,000 in the partnership interest, including his share

of partnership liabilities. The partnership expects to report substantial income in future years.

a. What rules are used to calculate Brad's ending basis in his partnership interest?
b. How much income or loss will Brad report for the tax year?
c. Will any of the $10,000 be suspended?
d. Could any planning opportunities be used to minimize the tax ramifications of the distribution?

20. The Warbler Partnership was formed on July 1 of the current year and admitted Ross and Rachel as equal partners on that date. The partners contributed $100,000 of cash each to establish an apparel shop in the local mall. The partners spent July and August buying inventory, equipment, supplies, and advertising for their "Grand Opening" on September 1. The partnership will use the accrual method of accounting. The partnership incurred the following costs during its first year of operations.

- Purchased all assets of Jenny B. Apparel of New York, which was going out of business, including:

| | |
|---|---|
| Trade name and logo | $ 30,000 |
| Inventory | 95,000 |
| Shop fixtures, racks, shelves, etc. | 25,000 |

- Other costs:

| | |
|---|---|
| Additional inventory | $ 40,000 |
| Legal fees to form partnership | 3,000 |
| Advertising for "Grand Opening" | 10,000 |
| Advertising after opening | 6,000 |
| Consulting fees for establishing accounting system | 3,000 |
| Rent, at $3,000 per month | 18,000 |
| Utilities, at $400 per month | 2,400 |
| Salaries to sales clerks | 15,000 |
| Payments to Ross and Rachel for services ($3,500 per month each for four months) | 28,000 |
| Tax return preparation expense | 3,000 |

- Revenues during the year included the following.

| | |
|---|---|
| Sales revenues | $200,000 |
| Interest income on bank balances | 1,500 |

- Inventory remaining at the end of the year was valued at $35,000 on a FIFO basis.

a. Determine how each of the above costs and revenues is treated by the partnership, and identify the period over which the costs can be deducted, if any.
b. Calculate the deduction for start-up and organization costs.
c. Identify any elections the partnership should make on its initial tax return.

21. Four Lakes Partnership is owned by four sisters. Anne holds a 70% interest; each of the others owns 10%. Anne sells investment property to the partnership for its fair market value of $100,000. Her tax basis was $150,000.
a. How much loss, if any, may Anne recognize?
b. If the partnership later sells the property for $160,000, how much gain must it recognize?
c. If Anne's basis in the investment property was $20,000 instead of $150,000, how much, if any, gain would she recognize on the sale, and how would it be characterized?

22. Comment on the validity of each of the following statements.
a. Since a partnership is not a taxable entity, it is not required to file any type of tax return.

b. Each partner can choose a different method of accounting and depreciation computation in determining the gross income from the entity.

c. Generally, a transfer of appreciated property to a partnership results in recognized gain to the contributing partner at the time of the transfer.

d. A partner can carry forward, for an unlimited period of time, the partner's share of any partnership operating losses that exceed the partner's basis in the entity, provided the partner retains an ownership interest in the partnership.

e. When a partner renders services to the entity in exchange for an unrestricted interest, that partner does not recognize any gross income.

f. Losses on sales between a partner and the partnership always are nondeductible.

g. A partnership may choose a year that results in the least aggregate deferral of tax to the partners, unless the IRS requires the use of a natural business year.

h. A partner's basis in a partnership interest includes that partner's share of partnership recourse and nonrecourse liabilities.

i. Built-in loss related to nondepreciable property contributed to a partnership must be allocated to the contributing partner to the extent the loss is eventually recognized by the partnership.

j. Property that was held as inventory by a contributing partner, but is a capital asset in the hands of the partnership, results in a capital gain if the partnership immediately sells the property.

23. Sonya is a 20% owner of Philadelphia Cheese Treats, Inc., a C corporation that was formed on February 1, 2005. She receives a $5,000 monthly salary from the corporation, and Cheese Treats generates $200,000 of taxable income (after the salary payment) for its tax year ending January 31, 2006.

a. How do these activities affect Sonya's 2005 adjusted gross income?

b. Assume, instead, that Cheese Treats is a partnership with a January 31 year-end and consider Sonya's salary to be a guaranteed payment. How do these activities affect Sonya's 2005 and 2006 adjusted gross income?

24. As of January 1 of last year, the outside basis and at-risk limitation of Rashad's 25% interest in the RST Partnership were $24,000. Rashad and the partnership use the calendar year for tax purposes. The partnership incurred an operating loss of $100,000 for last year and a profit of $8,000 for the current year. Rashad is a material participant in the partnership.

a. How much loss, if any, may Rashad recognize for last year?

b. How much net reportable income must Rashad recognize for the current year?

c. What is Rashad's basis in the partnership interest as of January 1 of the current year?

d. What is Rashad's basis in the partnership interest as of January 1 of the next year?

e. What year-end tax planning would you suggest to ensure that Rashad can deduct his share of the partnership losses?

**EXTENDER**

25. Melinda, Gabe, and Pat each contributed $10,000 cash to start up the MGP General Partnership on January 1 this year. Each partner shares equally in partnership income, losses, deductions, gains, and credits. At the end of the year, the partnership balance sheet reads as follows.

|  | Basis | FMV |  | Basis | FMV |
|---|---|---|---|---|---|
| Assets | $60,000 | $75,000 | Recourse debt | $30,000 | $30,000 |
|  |  |  | Melinda, capital | 14,000 | 19,000 |
|  |  |  | Gabe, capital | 14,000 | 19,000 |
|  |  |  | Pat, capital | 2,000 | 7,000 |
|  |  |  |  | $60,000 | $75,000 |

How will the basis computations of the partners' interests be affected by the partnership debt?

**EXTENDER**
**Communications**

26. The Cardinal Partnership leases apartments to individuals. Chris is a 15% partner in Cardinal, and her share of this year's operating losses totals $70,000. Before accounting for this loss, Chris reported the following amounts.

| Share of partnership recourse liabilities | $10,000 |
| Share of partnership nonrecourse liabilities | 6,000 |
| Capital account in Cardinal | 40,000 |

Chris also is a partner in the Bluebird Partnership, which earns income from equipment rentals of more than 30 days. Chris's share of Bluebird's income this year is $23,000.

Chris performs substantial services for Bluebird and spends several hundred hours a year working for Cardinal. Chris's AGI before accounting for the partnership investments totals $100,000.

Your manager has asked you to determine how much of the Cardinal loss that Chris can deduct this year. Draft a memo to the tax research file describing the various loss limitations that apply to Chris.

## Comprehensive Tax Return Problem

**Tax Return Problem**

27. Craig Howard (623–98–0123), Josh Edwards (410–63–4297), and Dana Prosky (896–49–1235) are equal partners in TDP—the "Tile Doctors Partnership"—a general partnership engaged in residential tile installation in Baton Rouge, Louisiana. TDP's Federal ID number is 42–1234598. The partnership uses the accrual method of accounting and the calendar year for reporting purposes. It began business operations on October 15, 2002. Its current address is 5917 La Rue, Baton Rouge, LA 70825. The 2004 income statement for the partnership reflected net income of $161,520. The following information was taken from the partnership's financial statements for the current year.

| Receipts | |
| --- | --- |
| Sales revenues | $740,925 |
| Qualified dividend income | 2,700 |
| Long-term capital gain | 1,275 |
| Long-term capital loss | (300) |
| Total revenues | $744,600 |

| Cash payments related to cost of goods sold | |
| --- | --- |
| Materials purchases | $162,250 |
| Direct job costs | 26,450 |
| Additional § 263A costs | 2,950 |
| Contract labor | 278,300 |
| Total cash payments—work-in-progress | $469,950 |

| Other cash disbursements (net of additional § 263A costs) | |
| --- | --- |
| Rent | $ 8,400 |
| Utilities | 6,580 |
| Office employee salaries | 25,400 |
| Contribution to Red Cross | 1,500 |
| Meals and entertainment, subject to 50% disallowance | 1,200 |
| Guaranteed payment, Dana Prosky, managing partner | 30,000 |
| Office expense | 2,820 |
| Accounting fees | 3,500 |
| Payroll taxes | 2,680 |
| Business interest on operating line of credit | 9,500 |
| Repairs | 1,420 |
| Payment of beginning accounts payable | 8,200 |
| Tile cutting equipment | 9,000 |
| Total other cash disbursements | $110,200 |

| Noncash expenses | |
|---|---|
| Amortization | $  600 |
| Accrual of ending accounts payable | –0– |
| Depreciation on equipment owned previously (reported on Schedule A) | 16,620 |

The beginning and ending balance sheets for the partnership were as follows for 2004.

| | **Beginning** | **Ending** |
|---|---|---|
| Cash | $  28,730 | $  38,180 |
| Inventory (jobs in progress) | 36,850 | 42,940 |
| Long-term investments | 46,000 | 42,000 |
| Equipment | 95,000 | 104,000 |
| Accumulated depreciation | (26,660) | (52,280) |
| Organization fees | 3,000 | 3,000 |
| Accumulated amortization | (750) | (1,350) |
| Total assets | $182,170 | $176,490 |
| Accounts payable | $  8,200 | $   –0– |
| Recourse operating line of credit (note payable in less than one year) | 75,000 | 60,000 |
| Capital, Howard | 32,990 | 38,830 |
| Capital, Edwards | 32,990 | 38,830 |
| Capital, Prosky | 32,990 | 38,830 |
| Total liabilities and capital | $182,170 | $176,490 |

The partnership uses the lower of cost or market method for valuing inventory. TDP is subject to § 263A; for simplicity, assume § 263A costs are reflected in the same manner for book and tax purposes. TDP did not change its inventory accounting method during the year. There were no writedowns of inventory items, and TDP does not use the LIFO method.

The partnership claimed $16,620 of depreciation expense for both tax and financial accounting purposes; all $16,620 should be reported on Schedule A. None of the depreciation creates a tax preference. The partnership will claim a § 179 deduction for the tile cutting equipment purchased during the year.

None of the long-term capital gain or loss is taxable at a 28% rate. All line-of-credit borrowings were used exclusively for business operations; consequently, none of the interest expense is considered investment interest expense.

No guaranteed payments were paid to partners other than Dana Prosky. Instead, each partner (including Prosky) withdrew $4,000 per month as a distribution (draw) of operating profits. There were no distributions of noncash property.

All debts are recourse debt. The partners share equally in all partnership liabilities, since all initial contributions and all ongoing allocations and distributions are pro rata. All partners are considered "active" for purposes of the passive loss rules.

None of the partners sold any portion of their interests in the partnership during 2004. The partnership's operations are entirely restricted to southern Louisiana. All partners are U.S. citizens. The partnership had no foreign operations, no foreign bank accounts, and no ownership of any foreign trusts or other partnerships. The partnership is not publicly traded and is not a statutory tax shelter. No Forms 8865 are required to be attached to the return.

The IRS's business code for "tile contractors" is 238340. The partnership is not subject to the consolidated audit procedures and does not have a tax matters partner. The partnership files its tax return in Ogden, Utah. Partner Dana Prosky lives at 1423 N. Louisiana Boulevard, Baton Rouge, LA 70823. The capital account reconciliation on Schedules K–1 is prepared according to GAAP, which, in this case, corresponds to the tax basis.

a. Prepare pages 1–4 of Form 1065 for TDP. Do not prepare Form 4562. Leave any items blank where insufficient information has been provided. Prepare supporting schedules as necessary if adequate information is provided. (You will not be able to prepare a schedule for additional § 263A costs.) *Hint:* Prepare Schedule A first to determine cost of goods sold.

b. Prepare Schedule K–1 for partner Dana Prosky.

BRIDGE DISCIPLINE

1. Jim Dunn, Amy Lauersen, and Tony Packard have agreed to form a partnership. In return for a 30% capital interest, Dunn transferred machinery (basis $268,000, fair market value $400,000) subject to a liability of $100,000. The liability was assumed by the partnership. Lauersen transferred land (basis $450,000, fair market value $300,000) for a 30% capital interest. Packard transferred cash of $400,000 for the remaining 40% interest. Compute the initial values of Dunn's basis and capital account.

## Research Problems

THOMSON
＊
RIA

*Note: Solutions to Research Problems can be prepared by using the **RIA Checkpoint® Student Edition** online research product, which is available to accompany this text. It is also possible to prepare solutions to the Research Problems by using tax research materials found in a standard tax library.*

**Decision Making**

**Communications**

**Research Problem 1.**   Your clients, Mark Henderson and John Burton, each contributed $10,000 of cash to form the Realty Management Partnership, a limited partnership. Mark is the general partner, and John is the limited partner. The partnership used the $20,000 of cash to make a down payment on a building. The rest of the building's $200,000 purchase price was financed with an interest-only nonrecourse loan of $180,000, which was obtained from an independent third-party bank. The partnership allocates all partnership items equally between the partners except for the MACRS deductions and building maintenance, which are allocated 70% to John and 30% to Mark. The partnership definitely wishes to satisfy the "economic effect" requirements of Reg. § 1.704–1 and Reg. § 1.704–2 and will reallocate MACRS, if necessary, to satisfy the requirements of the Regulations.

Under the partnership agreement, liquidation distributions will be paid in proportion to the partners' positive capital account balances. Capital accounts are maintained as required in the Regulations. Mark has an unlimited obligation to restore his capital account while John is subject to a qualified income offset provision.

All partnership items, except for MACRS, net to zero throughout the first three years of the partnership operations. Each year's MACRS deduction is $10,000 (to simplify the calculations).

Draft a letter to the partnership evaluating the allocation of MACRS in each of the three years under Reg. § 1.704–1 and Reg. § 1.704–2. The partnership's address is 53 East Marsh Ave., Smyrna, GA 30082. Do not address the "substantial" test.

**Decision Making**

**Communications**

**Research Problem 2.**   Harrison has considerable experience as a leasing agent for residential rental properties. He is disappointed, though, that his salary with his present employer does not reflect the effort he puts forth.

Alameda Properties has offered Harrison a position handling leasing activities for a new limited partnership that is being formed to construct and manage three apartment complexes in southern California. Alameda is willing to hire Harrison for two years to lease the properties, but is unable to pay the $60,000 salary Harrison requires without impairing its ability to pay necessary cash distributions to the limited partners.

Alameda is willing to pay a $30,000 salary for two years, increasing to a market salary thereafter. Alameda is also willing to allow Harrison to purchase a 10% interest in the partnership, but Harrison cannot afford the required $20,000 capital contribution.

The partnership expects to distribute cash flows from operations of approximately $150,000 per year, for an estimated seven-year holding period (taxable income will be much lower because depreciation and interest deductions will be greater than mortgage payments).

Harrison and Alameda Properties have approached you for assistance in structuring a mutually satisfactory arrangement. You are aware that a partner can be awarded an interest in the future profits of a partnership and have learned from a colleague that in 1993 the IRS issued a Revenue Procedure that outlines the types of profits interests that will not be subject to current taxation. Present a structure to Harrison and Alameda Properties that meets their respective goals, and outline the advantages and disadvantages to each party.

**Research Problem 3.** Cameron, an individual, and Totco, Inc., a domestic C corporation, form CT, a California LLC. The new LLC will produce a product that Cameron has recently developed and patented. Cameron and Totco, Inc., each take a 50% capital and profits interest in the LLC. Cameron is a calendar year taxpayer, while Totco uses a fiscal year ending June 30. The LLC does not have a "natural business year" and elects to be taxed as a partnership.
a. Determine the taxable year of the LLC under existing Code and Regulations.
b. Two years after formation of the LLC, Cameron sells half of his interest (25%) to Totco, Inc. Can the LLC retain the taxable year determined in (a)?

**Research Problem 4.** Fred and Grady have formed the FG Partnership as a retail establishment to sell antique household furnishings. Fred is the general partner, and Grady is the limited partner. Both partners contribute $15,000 to form the partnership. The partnership uses the $30,000 contributed by the partners and a recourse loan of $100,000 (obtained from an unrelated third-party lender) to acquire $130,000 of initial inventory.

The partners believe they will have extensive losses in the first year due to advertising and initial cash-flow requirements. Fred and Grady have agreed to share losses equally. To make sure the losses can be allocated to both partners, they have included a provision in the partnership agreement requiring each partner to restore any deficit balance in his partnership capital account upon liquidation of the partnership.

Fred was also willing to include a provision that requires him to make up any deficit balance within 90 days of liquidation of the partnership. As a limited partner, Grady argued that he should not be subject to such a time requirement. The partners compromised and included a provision that requires Grady to restore a deficit balance in his capital account within two years of liquidation of the partnership. No interest will be owed on the deferred restoration payment.

Determine whether FG can allocate the $100,000 recourse debt equally to the two partners, to ensure they will be able to deduct their respective shares of partnership losses.

**Internet Activity**

*Use the tax resources of the Internet to address the following questions. Do not restrict your search to the World Wide Web, but include a review of newsgroups and general reference materials, practitioner sites and resources, primary sources of the tax law, chat rooms and discussion groups, and other opportunities.*

**Communications**

**Research Problem 5.** Find a solicitation for funds posted by investors in an Internet start-up company. Summarize the partner's rights to profits and any tax implications discussed in the prospectus, in a PowerPoint presentation to your class.

**Research Problem 6.** Find a discussion group that concentrates on the taxation of partners and partnerships. Post to the group a message defining the terms "inside and outside basis" and illustrating why the distinction between them is important. Respond to any replies you receive. Print your message and one or two of the replies.

**Communications**

**Research Problem 7.** Determine the statutory tax treatment in your state of a one-member LLC. Write an e-mail message to your professor, comparing this rule with Federal tax law.

**Communications**

**Research Problem 8.** Graph the increases in the numbers of LLCs and LLPs filing Federal tax returns, for five-year periods beginning with 1970. Explain any trends in the data that you identify. Send your report as an e-mail to your instructor.

# S Corporations

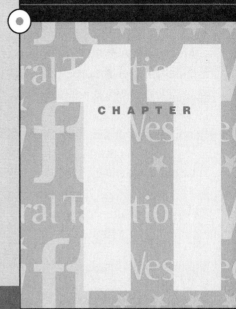

CHAPTER

11

http://wft.swlearning.com

## LEARNING OBJECTIVES

*After completing Chapter 11, you should be able to:*

**LO.1**

Explain the tax effects associated with S corporation status.

**LO.2**

Identify corporations that qualify for the S election.

**LO.3**

Understand how to make and terminate an S election.

**LO.4**

Compute nonseparately stated income and allocate income, deductions, and credits to shareholders.

**LO.5**

Understand how distributions to S corporation shareholders are taxed.

**LO.6**

Calculate a shareholder's basis in S corporation stock.

**LO.7**

Explain the tax effects of losses on S shareholders.

**LO.8**

Compute the entity-level taxes on S corporations.

## OUTLINE

---

### TAX TALK

*In levying taxes and in shearing sheep it is well to stop when you get down to the skin.*

—*Austin O'Malley*

---

**LO.1**

Explain the tax effects associated with S corporation status.

An individual establishing a business has a number of choices as to the form of business entity under which to operate. Chapters 8 and 9 outline many of the rules, advantages, and disadvantages of operating as a regular C corporation. Chapter 10 discusses the partnership entity, as well as the limited liability company (LLC) and limited liability partnership (LLP) forms.

Another alternative, the **S corporation,** provides many of the benefits of partnership taxation and at the same time gives the owners limited liability protection from creditors. The S corporation rules, which are contained in **Subchapter S** of the Internal Revenue Code (§§ 1361–1379), were enacted to minimize the role of tax considerations in the entity choice that businesspeople face. Thus, S status combines the legal environment of C corporations with taxation similar to that applying to partnerships. S corporation status is obtained through an election by a *qualifying* corporation with the consent of its shareholders.

S corporations are treated as corporations under state law. They are recognized as separate legal entities and generally provide shareholders with the same liability protection afforded by C corporations. Some states (such as Michigan) treat S corporations as C corporations for tax purposes, resulting in a state corporate income or franchise tax liability. For Federal income tax purposes, however, taxation of S corporations resembles that of partnerships. As with partnerships, the income, deductions, and tax credits of an S corporation flow through to shareholders annually, regardless of whether distributions are made. Thus, income generally is taxed at the shareholder level and not at the corporate level. Distributions made to S shareholders by the corporation are tax-free to the extent that the distributed earnings were previously taxed.

Although the tax treatment of S corporations and partnerships is similar, it is not identical. For example, liabilities affect an owner's basis differently, and S corporations may incur a tax liability at the corporate level. In addition, a variety of C corporation provisions apply to S corporations. For example, the liquidation of C and S corporations is taxed in the same way. As a rule, where the S corporation provisions are silent, C corporation rules apply.

*[handwritten margin note: ★Definitions / S Corporation / –page C-16 / Subchapter S / –page C17]*

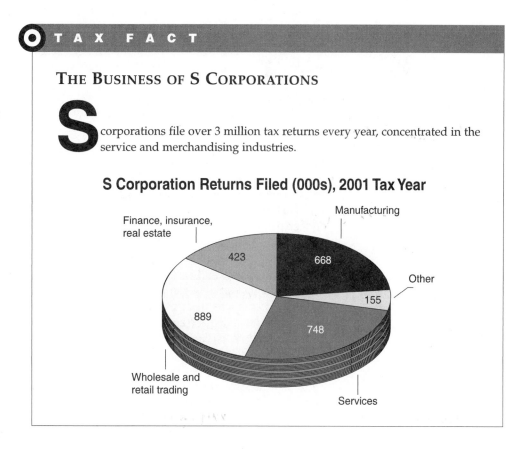

**TAX FACT**

## THE BUSINESS OF S CORPORATIONS

S corporations file over 3 million tax returns every year, concentrated in the service and merchandising industries.

**S Corporation Returns Filed (000s), 2001 Tax Year**

Manufacturing

Finance, insurance, real estate — 423

668

Other — 155

889

748

Wholesale and retail trading

Services

---

# An Overview of S Corporations

Since the inception of S corporations in 1958, their popularity has waxed and waned with changes in the tax law. Before the Tax Reform Act of 1986, their ranks grew slowly. In contrast, in the two years following the 1986 law change, the number of S corporations increased by 52 percent. Now, over 3 million of the country's 5.5 million corporations have elected S status. The IRS projects that S corporations and limited liability companies (LLCs) will be the most-chosen forms of business entity for the next decade.

**EXAMPLE 1**

An S corporation earns $300,000, and all after-tax income is distributed currently. The marginal individual tax rate applicable to its shareholders is 35% for ordinary income and 15% for dividend income. The marginal corporate tax rate is 34%. The entity's available after-tax earnings, compared with those of a similar C corporation, are computed below.

|  | **C Corporation** | **S Corporation** |
|---|---|---|
| Earnings | $ 300,000 | $ 300,000 |
| Less: Corporate income tax | (102,000) | (–0–) |
| Amount available for distribution | $ 198,000 | $ 300,000 |
| Less: Income tax at owner level | (29,700)* | (105,000)** |
| Available after-tax earnings | $ 168,300 | $ 195,000 |

*$198,000 × 15% dividend income tax rate.
**$300,000 × 35% ordinary income tax rate.

**Bridge to Business Law**

An S corporation is a corporation for all purposes other than its Federal and state income tax law treatment. The entity registers as a corporation with the secretary of state of the state of its incorporation. It issues shares and may hold some treasury stock. Dealings in its own stock are not taxable to the S corporation.

The corporation itself is attractive as a form of business ownership because it offers limited liability to all shareholders from the claims of customers, employees, and others. This is not the case for any type of partnership, where there always is at least one general partner bearing the ultimate personal liability for the operations of the entity. Forming an entity as an S corporation facilitates the raising of capital for the business, as an infinite number of shares can be divided in any way imaginable, so as to pass income and deductions, gains, losses, and credits through to the owners, assuming that the fairly generous "type of shareholder" requirements continue to be met.

An S corporation must comply with all licensing and registration requirements of its home state under the rules applicable to corporate entities. Some states levy privilege taxes on the right to do business in the corporate form, and the S corporation typically is not exempted from this tax.

Because an S corporation is a separate legal entity from its owners, shareholders can be treated as employees and receive qualified retirement and fringe benefits under the Code, as well as unemployment and worker's compensation protection through the corporation. Some limitations apply to the deductibility of fringe benefits, though.

The tax fiction of the S corporation is attractive to investors, as over one-half of all U.S. corporations have an S election in effect.

---

The S corporation generates an extra $26,700 of after-tax earnings ($195,000 − $168,300), when compared with a similar C corporation. The C corporation might be able to reduce this disadvantage, however, by paying out its earnings as compensation, rents, or interest to its owners. In addition, tax at the owner level can also be deferred or avoided by not distributing after-tax earnings. ▪

**EXAMPLE 2**

A new corporation elects S status and incurs a net operating loss (NOL) of $300,000. The shareholders may use their proportionate shares of the NOL to offset other taxable income in the current year, providing an immediate tax savings. In contrast, a newly formed C corporation is required to carry the NOL forward for up to 20 years and receives no tax benefit in the current year. Hence, an S corporation can accelerate the use of NOL deductions and thereby provide a greater present value for the tax savings generated by the loss. ▪

Limited liability companies can provide tax results similar to those of an S corporation, while avoiding some of the key restrictions that are imposed on S corporations and their shareholders. However, recent changes to a number of S corporation election and operating rules provide greater flexibility in using S corporations as a viable alternative to LLCs.

## When to Elect S Corporation Status

### PLANNING STRATEGIES

**FRAMEWORK FOCUS: DEDUCTIONS; TAX RATE**

STRATEGY ➤ MAXIMIZE DEDUCTIBLE AMOUNTS.
➤ SHIFT NET INCOME FROM HIGH-BRACKET TAXPAYERS TO LOW-BRACKET TAXPAYERS.
➤ SHIFT NET INCOME FROM HIGH-TAX JURISDICTIONS TO LOW-TAX JURISDICTIONS.

The planner begins by determining whether an S election is appropriate for the entity. The following factors should be considered.

- If shareholders are subject to high marginal rates relative to C corporation rates, it may be desirable to avoid S corporation status. Although a C corporation may be subject to double taxation, this result can be mitigated by paying compensation to employee-shareholders. Likewise, profits of the corporation may be taken out by the shareholders through other compensation arrangements, as interest, or as rent income. Corporate profits can be transferred to shareholders as capital gain income through capital structure changes, such as stock redemptions, liquidations, or sales of stock to others. Alternatively, profits may be paid out as dividends at a 15 percent tax rate. Any distribution of profits or sale of stock can be deferred to a later year, thereby reducing the present value of shareholder taxes. Finally, potential shareholder-level tax on corporate profits can be eliminated by a step-up in the basis of the stock upon the shareholder's death.

- S corporation status allows shareholders to realize tax benefits from corporate losses immediately—an important consideration in new business enterprises where operating losses are common. Thus, if corporate NOLs are anticipated and there is unlikely to be corporate income over the near term to offset with the NOLs, S corporation status is advisable. However, the deductibility of the losses to shareholders must also be

considered. The at-risk and passive loss limitations (refer to Chapter 5) apply to losses generated by an S corporation. In addition, as discussed later in this chapter, shareholders may not deduct losses in excess of the tax basis in their S corporation stock. Together with the time value of money considerations of deferring any loss deduction, these limits may significantly reduce the benefits of an S corporation election in a loss setting.

- If the entity electing S status is currently a C corporation, NOL carryovers from prior years (refer to Chapter 5) generally cannot be used in an S corporation year. Even worse, S corporation years use up the 20-year carryover period.

- Distributions of earnings from C corporations are usually taxed using the preferential 15 percent tax rate. In contrast, because S corporations are flow-through entities, all deduction and income items retain any special tax characteristics when they are reported on shareholders' returns. Whether this consideration favors S status depends upon the character of income and deductions of the S corporation.

- The S corporation rules impose significant requirements for qualifying as an S corporation. When electing S status, one should consider whether any of these requirements are likely to be violated at some point in the future.

- State and local tax laws also should be considered when making the S corporation election. Although an S corporation usually escapes Federal income tax, it may not be immune from all state and local income taxes.

---

### LO.2

Identify corporations that qualify for the S election.

## Qualifying for S Corporation Status

### DEFINITION OF A SMALL BUSINESS CORPORATION

To achieve S corporation status, a corporation must *first* qualify as a **small business corporation**. A small business corporation:

- Is a domestic corporation (incorporated and organized in the United States).
- Is eligible to elect S corporation status.
- Issues only one class of stock.
- Is limited to a maximum of 100 shareholders.

*Definition
Small Business
Corporation
- page 1-17*

- Has only individuals, estates, and certain trusts and exempt organizations as shareholders.
- Has no nonresident alien shareholders.

Unlike other small business provisions in the tax law (e.g., § 1244), no maximum or minimum dollar sales or capitalization restrictions apply to S corporations.

**Ineligible Corporations.**  S status is not permitted for foreign corporations, certain banks, or insurance companies. S corporations are permitted to have wholly owned C and S corporation subsidiaries.[1]

**One Class of Stock.**  A small business corporation may have only one class of stock issued and outstanding.[2] This restriction permits differences in voting rights, but not differences in distribution or liquidation rights.[3] Thus, two classes of common stock that are identical except that one class is voting and the other is nonvoting would be treated as a single class of stock for small business corporation purposes. In contrast, voting common stock and voting preferred stock (with a preference on dividends) would be treated as two classes of stock. Authorized and unissued stock or treasury stock of another class does not disqualify the corporation. Likewise, unexercised stock options, phantom stock, stock appreciation rights, warrants, and convertible debentures usually do not constitute a second class of stock.[4]

DIGGING DEEPER 1

*Find more information on this topic at our Web site: **http://wft-entities.swlearning.com**.*

**\*Safe Harbor Provisions!**

Although the one-class-of-stock requirement seems straightforward, it is possible for debt to be reclassified as stock, resulting in an unexpected loss of S corporation status.[5] To mitigate concern over possible reclassification of debt as a second class of stock, the law provides a set of *safe harbor* provisions. Neither straight debt[6] nor short-term advances[7] constitute a second class of stock.

DIGGING DEEPER 2

*Find more information on this topic at our Web site: **http://wft-entities.swlearning.com**.*

**Number of Shareholders.**  A small business corporation is limited to 100 shareholders. If shares of stock are owned jointly by two individuals, they will generally be treated as separate shareholders. However, family members (ancestors, descendants, spouses, and former spouses) of the investor can elect to be counted as one shareholder for purposes of determining the number of shareholders.[8]

**EXAMPLE 3**

Fred and Wilma (husband and wife) jointly own 10 shares in Oriole, Inc., an S corporation, with the remaining 90 shares outstanding owned by 99 other shareholders. Fred and Wilma are divorced. Both before and after the divorce, the 100-shareholder limit is met, and Oriole can qualify as a small business corporation.  ■

**Type of Shareholder Limitation.**  Small business corporation shareholders may be individuals, estates, or certain trusts and exempt organizations.[9] This limitation prevents partnerships, corporations, LLCs, LLPs, and IRAs from owning S corporation stock. Without this rule, partnerships and corporate shareholders could easily circumvent the 100-shareholder limitation.

---

[1]Other eligibility rules exist. § 1361(b).
[2]§ 1361(b)(1)(D).
[3]§ 1361(c)(4).
[4]Reg. § 1.1361–1(l)(2).
[5]Refer to the discussion of debt-versus-equity classification in Chapter 8.

[6]§ 1361(c)(5)(A).
[7]Reg. § 1.1361–1(l)(4).
[8]§ 1361(c)(1). Narrower rules applied for tax years prior to 2005.
[9]§ 1361(b)(1)(B).

*EXAMPLE 4*

Paul and 200 other individuals wish to form an S corporation. Paul reasons that if the group forms a partnership, the partnership can then form an S corporation and act as a single shareholder, thereby avoiding the 100-shareholder rule. Paul's plan will not work, because partnerships cannot own stock in an S corporation. ■

## Beating the 100-Shareholder Limit

**FRAMEWORK FOCUS: TAX RATE**

STRATEGY ➤ AVOID DOUBLE TAXATION.

Although partnerships and corporations cannot own small business corporation stock, S corporations themselves can be partners in a partnership or shareholders in a corporation. In this way, the 100-shareholder requirement can be bypassed in a limited sense. For example, if two S corporations, each with 80 shareholders, form a partnership, then the shareholders of both corporations can enjoy the limited liability conferred by S corporation status and a single level of tax on the resulting profits.

**Nonresident Aliens.** Nonresident aliens cannot own stock in a small business corporation.[10] Thus, individuals who are not U.S. citizens *must live in the United States* to own S corporation stock. Shareholders with nonresident alien spouses in community property states[11] cannot own S corporation stock because the nonresident alien spouse is treated as owning half of the stock.[12] Similarly, if a resident alien shareholder moves outside the United States, the S election is terminated.

### LO.3

Understand how to make and terminate an S election.

## MAKING THE ELECTION

To become an S corporation, the entity must file a valid election with the IRS. The election is made on Form 2553. For the election to be valid, it must be filed on a timely basis and all shareholders must consent. For S corporation status to apply in the current tax year, the election must be filed either in the previous year or on or before the fifteenth day of the third month of the current year.[13]

*EXAMPLE 5*

In 2006, a calendar year C corporation decides to become an S corporation beginning January 1, 2007. The S corporation election can be made at any time in 2006 or by March 15, 2007. An election after March 15, 2007, will not be effective until the 2008 tax year. ■

Even if the 2½-month deadline is met, a current election is not valid unless the corporation qualifies as a small business corporation for the *entire* tax year. Otherwise, the election will be effective for the following tax year. Late current-year

---

[10]§ 1362(b)(1)(C).

[11]Assets acquired by a married couple are generally considered community property in these states: Alaska (by election), Arizona, California, Idaho, Louisiana, Nevada, New Mexico, Texas, Washington, and Wisconsin.

[12]See *Ward v. U.S.*, 81–2 USTC ¶9674, 48 AFTR2d 81–5942, 661 F.2d 226 (Ct.Cls., 1981), where the court found that the stock was owned

as community property. Since the taxpayer-shareholder (a U.S. citizen) was married to a citizen and resident of Mexico, the nonresident alien prohibition was violated. If the taxpayer-shareholder had held the stock as separate property, the S election would have been valid.

[13]§ 1362(b).

elections, after the 2½-month deadline, may be considered timely if there is reasonable cause for the late filing.

A corporation that does not yet exist cannot make an S corporation election.[14] Thus, for new corporations, a premature election may not be effective. A new corporation's 2½-month election period begins at the earliest occurrence of any of the following events.

- When the corporation has shareholders.
- When it acquires assets.
- When it begins doing business.[15]

## SHAREHOLDER CONSENT

A qualifying election requires the consent of all of the corporation's shareholders.[16] Consent must be in writing, and it must generally be filed by the election deadline. However, although no statutory authority exists for obtaining an extension of time for filing an S election (Form 2553), a shareholder may receive an extension of time to file a consent. Both husband and wife must consent if they own their stock jointly (as joint tenants, tenants in common, tenants by the entirety, or community property).[17]

**EXAMPLE 6**

Vern and Yvonne decide to convert their C corporation into a calendar year S corporation for 2006. At the end of February 2006 (before the election is filed), Yvonne travels to Ukraine and forgets to sign a consent to the election. Yvonne will not return to the United States until June and cannot be reached by fax or e-mail. Vern files the S election on Form 2553 and also requests an extension of time to file Yvonne's consent to the election. Vern indicates that there is a reasonable cause for the extension: a shareholder is out of the country. Since the government's interest is not jeopardized, the IRS probably will grant Yvonne an extension of time to file the consent. Vern must file the election on Form 2553 on or before March 15, 2006, for the election to be effective for the 2006 calendar year. ■

**PLANNING STRATEGIES**     ## Making a Proper Election

**FRAMEWORK FOCUS: TAX RATE**

**STRATEGY ➤ AVOID DOUBLE TAXATION.**

- Because S corporation status is *elected*, strict compliance with the requirements is demanded by both the IRS and the courts. Any failure to meet a condition in the law may lead to loss of the S election and raise the specter of double tax.
- Make sure all shareholders consent. If any doubt exists concerning the shareholder status of an individual, it would be wise to request that he or she sign a consent

anyway.[18] Missing consents are fatal to the election; the same cannot be said for too many consents.
- Be sure that the election is timely and properly filed. Either deliver the election to an IRS office in person, or send it by certified or registered mail or via a major overnight delivery service. The date used to determine timeliness is the postmark date, not the date the IRS receives the election.

---

[14]See, for example, *T.H. Campbell & Bros., Inc.*, 34 TCM 695, T.C.Memo. 1975–149; Ltr.Rul. 8807070.

[15]Reg. § 1.1372–2(b)(1). Also see, for example, *Nick A. Artukovich*, 61 T.C. 100 (1973).

[16]§ 1362(a)(2).

[17]Rev.Rul. 60–183, 1960–1 C.B. 625; *William Pestcoe*, 40 T.C. 195 (1963); Reg. § 1.1362–6(b)(3)(iii). This rule likely applies to all family members electing to be treated as one shareholder.

[18]See *William B. Wilson*, 34 TCM 463, T.C.Memo. 1975–92.

## LOSS OF THE ELECTION

An S election remains in force until it is revoked or lost. Election or consent forms are not required for future years. However, an S election can terminate if any of the following occurs.[19]

- Shareholders owning a majority of shares (voting and nonvoting) voluntarily revoke the election.
- A new shareholder owning more than one-half of the stock affirmatively refuses to consent to the election.
- The corporation no longer qualifies as a small business corporation.
- The corporation does not meet the passive investment income limitation.

**Voluntary Revocation.** A **voluntary revocation** of the S election requires the consent of shareholders owning a majority of shares on the day that the revocation is to be made.[20] A revocation filed up to and including the fifteenth day of the third month of the tax year is effective for the entire tax year, unless a later date is specified. Similarly, unless an effective date is specified, revocation made after the first 2½ months of the current tax year is effective for the following tax year.

*[handwritten: *Definition Voluntary Revocation —page C-19]*

**EXAMPLE 7**

The shareholders of Petunia Corporation, a calendar year S corporation, voluntarily revoke the S election on January 5, 2005. They do not specify a future effective date in the revocation. Assuming the revocation is properly executed and timely filed, Petunia will be a C corporation for the entire 2005 tax year. If the revocation is not made until June 2005, Petunia remains an S corporation in 2005 and becomes a C corporation at the beginning of 2006. ■

A corporation can revoke its S status *prospectively* by specifying a future date when the revocation is to be effective. A revocation that designates a future effective date splits the corporation's tax year into a short S corporation year and a short C corporation year. The day on which the revocation occurs is treated as the first day of the C corporation year. The corporation allocates income or loss for the entire year on a pro rata basis, based on the number of days in each short year.

**EXAMPLE 8**

Assume the same facts as in the preceding example, except that Petunia designates July 1, 2005, as the revocation date. Accordingly, June 30, 2005, is the last day of the S corporation's tax year. The C corporation's tax year runs from July 1, 2005, to December 31, 2005. Income or loss for the 12-month period is allocated between the two short years (i.e., 184/365 to the C corporation year). ■

Rather than using pro rata allocation, the corporation can elect to compute the actual income or loss attributable to the two short years. This election requires the consent of everyone who was a shareholder at any time during the S corporation's short year and everyone who owns stock on the first day of the C corporation's year.[21]

**Loss of Small Business Corporation Status.** If an S corporation fails to qualify as a small business corporation at any time after the election has become effective, its status as an S corporation ends. The termination occurs on the day that the corporation ceases to be a small business corporation.[22] Thus, if the corporation ever has more than 100 shareholders, a second class of stock, or a nonqualifying shareholder, or otherwise fails to meet the definition of a small business corporation, the S election is terminated immediately.

---

[19]§ 1362(d).
[20]§ 1362(d)(1)(B).

[21]§ 1362(e)(3).
[22]§ 1362(d)(2)(B).

**EXAMPLE 9**

Peony Corporation has been a calendar year S corporation for three years. On August 13, 2006, one of its 100 shareholders sells *some* of her stock to an outsider. Peony now has 101 shareholders, and it ceases to be a small business corporation. Peony is an S corporation through August 12, 2006, and a C corporation from August 13 to December 31, 2006. ■

*Definition
Passive Investment
Income
—page C-13*

**Passive Investment Income Limitation.**    The Code provides a **passive invest- ment income (PII)** limitation for S corporations that were previously C corporations or for S corporations that have merged with C corporations. If an S corporation has C corporation E & P and passive income in excess of 25 percent of its gross receipts for three consecutive taxable years, the S election is terminated as of the beginning of the fourth year.[23]

**EXAMPLE 10**

For 2003, 2004, and 2005, Chrysanthemum Corporation, a calendar year S corporation, derived passive income in excess of 25% of its gross receipts. If Chrysanthemum holds accumulated E & P from years in which it was a C corporation, its S election is terminated as of January 1, 2006. ■

PII includes dividends, interest, rents, gains and losses from sales of securities, and royalties net of investment deductions. Rents are not considered PII if the corporation renders significant personal services to the occupant.

**EXAMPLE 11**

Violet Corporation owns and operates an apartment building. The corporation provides utilities for the building, maintains the lobby, and furnishes trash collection for tenants. These activities are not considered significant personal services, so any rent income earned by the corporation will be considered PII.

Alternatively, if Violet also furnishes maid services to its tenants (personal services beyond what normally would be expected from a landlord in an apartment building), the rent income would no longer be PII. ■

**Reelection after Termination.**    After an S election has been terminated, the corporation must wait five years before reelecting S corporation status. The five-year waiting period is waived if:

- there is a more-than-50-percent change in ownership of the corporation after the first year for which the termination is applicable, or
- the event causing the termination was not reasonably within the control of the S corporation or its majority shareholders.

**PLANNING STRATEGIES**    **Preserving the S Election**

**FRAMEWORK FOCUS: TAX RATE**

STRATEGY ➤ **AVOID DOUBLE TAXATION.**

Unexpected loss of S corporation status can be costly to a corporation and its shareholders. Given the complexity of the rules facing these entities, constant vigilance is necessary to preserve the S election.

- As a starting point, the corporation's management and shareholders should be made aware of the various transactions that can lead to the loss of an election.

---

[23]§ 1362(d)(3)(A)(ii).

- Prevent violations of the small business corporation limitations. Since most such violations result from transfers of stock, the corporation and its shareholders should consider adopting a set of stock transfer restrictions. A carefully designed set of restrictions could prevent sale of stock to nonqualifying entities or violation of the 100-shareholder rule. Similarly, stock could be repurchased by the corporation under a buy-sell agreement upon the death of a shareholder, thereby preventing nonqualifying trusts from becoming shareholders.[24]

---

**LO.4**

Compute nonseparately stated income and allocate income, deductions, and credits to shareholders.

# Operational Rules

S corporations are treated much like partnerships for tax purposes. With a few exceptions, S corporations generally make tax accounting and other elections at the corporate level.[25] Each year, the S corporation determines nonseparately stated income or loss and separately stated income, deductions, and credits. These items are taxed only once, as they pass through to shareholders. All items are allocated to each shareholder based on average ownership of stock throughout the year.[26] The flow-through of each item of income, deduction, and credit from the corporation to the shareholder is illustrated in Figure 11–1.

■ **FIGURE 11–1**
Flow-Through of Items of Income and Loss to S Corporation Shareholders

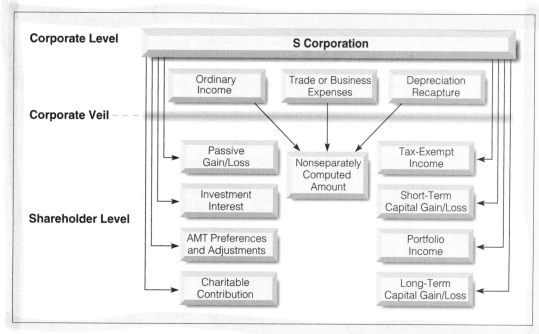

---

[24]Most such agreements do not create a second class of stock. Rev.Rul. 85–161, 1985–2 C.B. 191; *Portage Plastics Co. v. U.S.*, 72–2 USTC ¶9567, 30 AFTR2d 72–5229, 470 F.2d 308 (CA–7, 1973).

[25]Certain elections are made at the shareholder level (e.g., the choice between a foreign tax deduction or credit).
[26]§§ 1366(a), (b), and (c).

## COMPUTATION OF TAXABLE INCOME

Subchapter S taxable income or loss is determined in a manner similar to the tax rules that apply to partnerships, except that S corporations recognize gains (but not losses) on distributions of appreciated property to shareholders.[27] Other special provisions affecting only the computation of C corporation income, such as the dividends received deduction, do not extend to S corporations.[28] Finally, as with partnerships, certain deductions of individuals are not permitted, including alimony payments, personal moving expenses, certain dependent care expenses, the personal exemption, and the standard deduction.

In general, S corporation items are divided into (1) nonseparately stated income or loss and (2) separately stated income, losses, deductions, and credits that could uniquely affect the tax liability of any shareholder. In essence, nonseparate items are aggregated into an undifferentiated amount that constitutes Subchapter S taxable income or loss.

**EXAMPLE 12**

The following is the income statement for Larkspur, Inc., an S corporation.

| | | |
|---|---:|---:|
| Sales | | $ 40,000 |
| Less: Cost of goods sold | | (23,000) |
| Gross profit on sales | | $ 17,000 |
| Less: Interest expense | $1,200 | |
|     Charitable contributions | 400 | |
|     Advertising expenses | 1,500 | |
|     Other operating expenses | 2,000 | (5,100) |
| | | $ 11,900 |
| Add: Tax-exempt interest | $  300 | |
|     Dividend income | 200 | |
|     Long-term capital gain | 500 | 1,000 |
| Less: Short-term capital loss | | (150) |
| Net income per books | | $ 12,750 |

Subchapter S taxable income for Larkspur is calculated as follows, using net income for book purposes as the starting point.

| | | |
|---|---:|---:|
| Net income per books | | $12,750 |
| *Separately stated items* | | |
| Deduct: Tax-exempt interest | $300 | |
|     Dividend income | 200 | |
|     Long-term capital gain | 500 | (1,000) |
| | | $11,750 |
| Add: Charitable contributions | $400 | |
|     Short-term capital loss | 150 | 550 |
| Subchapter S taxable income | | $12,300 |

The $12,300 of Subchapter S taxable income, as well as each of the five separately stated items, are divided among the shareholders based upon their stock ownership. ■

---

[27]§ 1363(d).

[28]§ 703(a)(2).

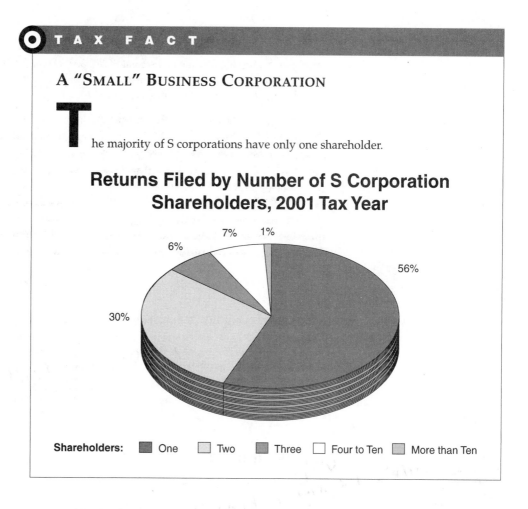

**⊙ T A X F A C T**

## A "SMALL" BUSINESS CORPORATION

The majority of S corporations have only one shareholder.

**Returns Filed by Number of S Corporation Shareholders, 2001 Tax Year**

7%  1%
6%
56%
30%

Shareholders: ■ One  ▢ Two  ■ Three  ▢ Four to Ten  ▨ More than Ten

## ALLOCATION OF INCOME AND LOSS

Each shareholder is allocated a pro rata portion of nonseparately stated income or loss and all separately stated items. The pro rata allocation method assigns an equal amount of each of the S items to each day of the year. If a shareholder's stock holding changes during the year, this allocation assigns the shareholder a pro rata share of each item for each day the stock is owned. On the date of transfer, the transferor (not the transferee) is considered to own the stock.[29]

| S corporation item | **⊗** | Percentage of shares owned | **⊗** | Percentage of year shares were owned | **=** | Amount of item to be reported |

The per-day allocation must be used, unless the shareholder disposes of his or her entire interest in the entity.[30] In case of a complete termination, a short year may result, as discussed below. If a shareholder dies during the year, his or her share of the pro rata items up to the date of death is reported on the final individual income tax return.

---

[29]Reg. § 1.1377–1(a)(2)(ii).

[30]§§ 1366(a)(1) and 1377(a)(1).

**EXAMPLE 13**

Pat, a shareholder, owned 10% of Larkspur's stock (from Example 12) for 100 days and 12% for the remaining 265 days. Using the required per-day allocation method, Pat's share of the Subchapter S taxable income is the total of $12,300 × [10% × (100/365)] plus $12,300 × [12% × (265/365)], or $1,409. All of Pat's Schedule K–1 totals flow through to the corresponding lines on his individual income tax return (Form 1040). ■

**The Short-Year Election.**   If a shareholder's interest is completely terminated during the tax year by disposition or death, all shareholders owning stock during the year and the corporation may elect to treat the S taxable year as two taxable years. The first year ends on the date of the termination. Under this election, an interim closing of the books is undertaken, and the shareholders report their shares of the S corporation items as they occurred during the short tax year.[31]

The short-year election provides an opportunity to shift income, losses, and credits among shareholders. The election is desirable in circumstances where more loss can be allocated to taxpayers with higher marginal rates.

(DIGGING DEEPER 3)   *Find more information on this topic at our Web site:* ***http://wft-entities.swlearning.com.***

**EXAMPLE 14**

Alicia, the owner of all of the shares of an S corporation, transfers her stock to Cindy halfway through the tax year. There is a $100,000 NOL for the entire tax year, but $30,000 of the loss occurs during the first half of the year. Without a short-year election, $50,000 of the loss is allocated to Alicia and $50,000 is allocated to Cindy. If the corporation makes the short-year election, Cindy is allocated $70,000 of the loss. The sales price of the stock probably would be increased to recognize the tax benefits being transferred from Alicia to Cindy. ■

## PLANNING STRATEGIES        Salary Structure

**FRAMEWORK FOCUS: TAX RATE**

STRATEGY ➤ SHIFT NET INCOME FROM HIGH-BRACKET TAXPAYERS TO LOW-BRACKET TAXPAYERS.
➤ AVOID DOUBLE TAXATION.

The amount of salary paid to a shareholder-employee of an S corporation can have varying tax consequences and should be considered carefully. Larger amounts might be advantageous if the maximum contribution allowed under the retirement plan has not been reached. Smaller amounts may be beneficial if the parties are trying to shift taxable income to lower-bracket shareholders, reduce payroll taxes, curtail a reduction of Social Security benefits, or restrict losses that do not pass through because of the basis limitation.

A strategy of decreasing compensation and correspondingly increasing distributions to shareholder-employees often results in substantial savings in employment taxes. However, a shareholder of an S corporation cannot always perform substantial services and arrange to receive distributions rather than compensation so that the corporation may avoid paying employment taxes. The shareholder may be deemed an employee, and any distributions will be recharacterized as wages subject to FICA and FUTA taxes.[32] For planning purposes, some level of compensation should be paid to all shareholder-employees to avoid any recharacterization of distributions as deductible salaries—especially in personal service corporations.

Use of S corporations as an income-shifting device within a family (e.g., through a gift of stock from a high-marginal-rate taxpayer to a low-marginal-rate taxpayer) may be ineffective. The IRS can ignore such transfers unless the stock is purchased at fair market value.[33] Effectively, the IRS can require that reasonable compensation be paid to family members who render services or provide capital to the S corporation.

[31]§ 1377(a)(2).
[32]Rev.Rul. 74–44, 1974–1 C.B. 287; *Spicer Accounting, Inc. v. U.S.*, 91–1 USTC ¶50,103, 66 AFTR2d 90–5806, 918 F.2d 90 (CA–9, 1990);

*Radtke v. U.S.*, 90–1 USTC ¶50,113, 65 AFTR2d 90–1155, 895 F.2d 1196 (CA–7, 1990).
[33]§ 1366(e) and Reg. § 1.1373–1(a).

## AN ABUSIVE TAX SHELTER?

During the 2004 presidential campaign, some tax practitioners pointed out that Democratic vice presidential candidate John Edwards had approximately $20 million of legal fees inside his S corporation in 1995. By paying himself a salary of only $360,000, he avoided paying almost $600,000 for the Medicare portion of FICA taxes (imposed at a rate of 2.9 percent).

There was considerable discussion of Edwards's tax situation in the media, and Vice President Dick Cheney mentioned the issue in the vice presidential debate. Reactions tended to follow the party affiliation of the commentator. In general, the $360,000 was probably less than reasonable compensation for Edwards (less than 2 percent of his legal fees), and the IRS could deem any distributions (i.e., recharacterize them) as wages subject to the FICA and FUTA taxes.

Even one of Edwards's defenders said that if these funds were distributed to the senator, he "was making use of an alleged 'tax shelter' and the IRS would be quite justified in treating the distributions as salary." Another commentator said that it was somewhat hypocritical for Edwards to express concern about the solvency of Medicare and Social Security when he had engaged in what seemed to be an attempt to evade the Medicare tax.

---

**LO.5**

Understand how distributions to S corporation shareholders are taxed.

## TAX TREATMENT OF DISTRIBUTIONS TO SHAREHOLDERS

S corporations do not generate earnings and profits (E & P) while the S election is in effect. Indeed, all profits are taxed in the year earned, as though they were distributed on a pro rata basis to the shareholders. Thus, distributions from S corporations do not constitute dividends in the traditional sense—there is no corporate E & P to distribute.

It is possible, however, for S corporations to have an accumulated E & P (AEP) account. This can occur when:

- the S corporation was previously a C corporation, or
- a C corporation with its own AEP merged into the S corporation.

Distributions from S corporations are measured as the cash received plus the fair market value of any other distributed property. The tax treatment of distributions differs, depending upon whether the S corporation has AEP.

**S Corporation with No AEP.**   If the S corporation has no AEP, the distribution is a tax-free recovery of capital to the extent that it does not exceed the adjusted basis of the shareholder's stock. When the amount of the distribution exceeds the adjusted basis of the stock, the excess is treated as a gain from the sale or exchange of property (capital gain in most cases).

**EXAMPLE 15**

Hyacinth, Inc., a calendar year S corporation, has no AEP. During the year, Juan, an individual shareholder of the corporation, receives a cash distribution of $12,200 from Hyacinth. Juan's basis in his stock is $9,700. Juan recognizes a capital gain of $2,500, the excess of the distribution over the stock basis ($12,200 − $9,700). The remaining $9,700 is tax-free, but it reduces Juan's basis in his stock to zero. ∎

**S Corporation with AEP.**   For S corporations with AEP, a more complex set of rules applies. These rules blend the entity and conduit approaches to taxation, treating distributions of pre-election (C corporation) and postelection (S corporation)

## CONCEPT SUMMARY 11–1

### Distributions from an S Corporation

| Where Earnings and Profits Exist | Where No Earnings and Profits Exist |
|---|---|
| 1. Distributions are tax-free to the extent of the AAA.* | |
| 2. Any PTI from pre-1983 tax years can be distributed tax-free. | |
| 3. The remaining distribution constitutes dividend income from AEP.† | |
| 4. Distributions are tax-free to the extent of the other adjustments account (OAA). | |
| 5. Any residual amount is applied as a tax-free reduction in basis of stock. | 1. Distributions are nontaxable to the extent of adjusted basis in stock. |
| 6. Excess is treated as gain from a sale or exchange of stock (capital gain in most cases). | 2. Excess is treated as gain from a sale or exchange of stock (capital gain in most cases). |

\* A shareholder's stock basis serves as a limit on the amount that may be received tax-free.
†The AAA bypass election is available to pay out AEP before reducing the AAA [§ 1368(e)(3)].

*[handwritten: \*Definition Accumulated Adjustments Account – page C-1]*

earnings differently. Distributions of C corporation AEP are taxed as dividends (5/15 percent rate), while distributions of previously taxed S corporation earnings are tax-free to the extent of the shareholder's adjusted basis in the stock.

The treatment of distributions is determined by their order. Specifically, distributions are deemed to be first from previously taxed, undistributed earnings of the S corporation. Such distributions are tax-free and are determined by reference to a special account, the **accumulated adjustments account (AAA)**.[34] Next, AEP is distributed as taxable dividends. Remaining amounts of the distribution are received tax-free to the extent of the shareholder's remaining stock basis,[35] with any excess being treated as capital gain.

**EXAMPLE 16**

Salvia, a calendar year S corporation, distributes $1,300 of cash to its only shareholder, Otis, on December 31. Otis's basis in his stock is $1,400, AAA is $500, and the corporation has AEP of $750 before the distribution.

The first $500 of the distribution is a tax-free recovery of basis from the AAA. The next $750 is a taxable dividend distribution from AEP. Finally, the remaining $50 of cash is a tax-free recovery of basis. Immediately after the distribution, Salvia has no AAA or AEP. Otis's stock basis now is $850.

| | Corporate AAA | Corporate AEP | Otis's Stock Basis |
|---|---|---|---|
| Beginning balance | $ 500 | $ 750 | $1,400 |
| Distribution from AAA | (500) | | (500) |
| Distribution from AEP | | (750) | |
| Distribution of capital | | | (50) |
| Ending balance | $ –0– | $ –0– | $ 850 |

---

[34]For S corporations in existence prior to 1983, an account similar to the AAA was used. This account, called *previously taxed income* (PTI), can be distributed in cash tax-free to shareholders after AAA has been distributed. See §§ 1368(c)(1) and (e)(1).

[35]§ 1368(c).

■ **EXHIBIT 11–1**
Adjustments to the Corporate
AAA

*Increase by:*
1. Positive separately stated items other than tax-exempt income.
2. Nonseparately computed income.

*Decrease by:*
3. Distribution(s) from AAA and OAA (but not below zero).
4. Adjustments other than distributions (e.g., losses, deductions).

**EXAMPLE 17**

*AAA Bypass Election*

Assume the same facts as in the preceding example. The next year, Salvia has no earnings and distributes $1,000 to Otis. Of the distribution, $850 is a tax-free recovery of the stock basis, and then $150 is taxed to Otis as a capital gain. ■

With the consent of all of its shareholders, an S corporation can elect to have a distribution treated as if it were made from AEP rather than from the AAA. This mechanism is known as an AAA *bypass election*. This election may be desirable when making distributions to move the entity to the no-AEP system of accounting for distributions, at a tax cost of 15 percent of the AEP.

**EXAMPLE 18**

Rotor is a valid S corporation. It has $50 of AEP. An AAA bypass election for Rotor's next shareholder distribution would eliminate the need to track the AAA and would greatly simplify the accounting for future distributions. The cost for this simplification is the tax on $50 of dividend income. ■

**The Accumulated Adjustments Account.**   The AAA is the cumulative total of undistributed nonseparately and separately stated income and deduction items for S corporation years beginning after 1982. As noted above, it provides a mechanism to ensure that earnings of an S corporation are taxed only once. Changes to the AAA are reported annually in Schedule M–2 on page 4 of the Form 1120S.

AAA is computed at the end of each tax year rather than at the time of a distribution. First, add to the year's beginning balance any current nonseparately computed income and positive separately stated items (except tax-exempt income). Next, account for distributions *prior* to subtracting the negative items.

AAA is applied to the distributions made during the year on a pro rata basis (in a fashion similar to the application of current E & P, discussed in Chapter 9). The determination of AAA is summarized in Exhibit 11–1.

Although adjustments to AAA and stock basis adjustments are similar, there are some important differences between the two amounts. In particular,

* The AAA is not affected by tax-exempt income and related expenses.
* Unlike stock basis, the AAA can have a negative balance. All losses decrease the AAA balance, even those in excess of the shareholder's basis. However, distributions may not make the AAA negative or increase a negative balance in the account.
* Every shareholder has a proportionate interest in the AAA, regardless of the amount of his or her stock basis.[36] In fact, AAA is a corporate account, so there is no connection between the amount and any specific shareholder.[37] Thus, the benefits of AAA can be shifted from one shareholder to another. For example, when an S corporation shareholder sells stock to another party, any AAA balance on the purchase date can be distributed tax-free to the purchaser.

---

[36]§ 1368(c).                                    [37]§ 1368(e)(1)(A).

**Schedule M–2.** Schedule M–2 (reproduced below) also contains a column labeled *Other adjustments account (OAA)*. This account includes items that affect basis but not the AAA, such as tax-exempt income and any related nondeductible expenses. Distributions are made from the OAA after AEP and the AAA are reduced to zero. Distributions from this account are tax-free.

**EXAMPLE 19**

Poinsettia, an S corporation, records the following items.

| | |
|---|---|
| AAA, beginning of the year | $ 8,500 |
| Ordinary income | 25,000 |
| Tax-exempt interest | 4,000 |
| Key employee life insurance proceeds received | 5,000 |
| Payroll penalty expense | 2,000 |
| Charitable contributions | 3,000 |
| Unreasonable compensation | 5,000 |
| Premiums on key employee life insurance | 2,100 |
| Distributions to shareholders | 16,000 |

Poinsettia's Schedule M–2 appears as follows.

| **Schedule M-2** Analysis of Accumulated Adjustments Account, Other Adjustments Account, and Shareholders' Undistributed Taxable Income Previously Taxed | | |
|---|---|---|
| | **(a)** Accumulated adjustments account | **(b)** Other adjustments account |
| 1 Balance at beginning of tax year . . . | 8,500 | |
| 2 Ordinary income from page 1, line 21 . . | 25,000 | |
| 3 Other additions . . . . . . . . . | | 9,000** |
| 4 Loss from page 1, line 21 . . . . . . | ( ) | |
| 5 Other reductions . . . . . . . . | ( 10,000* ) | ( 2,100 ) |
| 6 Combine lines 1 through 5 . . . . . | 23,500 | 6,900 |
| 7 Distributions other than dividend distributions . | 16,000 | |
| 8 Balance at end of tax year. Subtract line 7 from line 6 | 7,500 | 6,900 |

\* *$2,000 (payroll penalty) + $3,000 (charitable contributions) + $5,000 (unreasonable compensation).*

\*\* *$4,000 (tax-exempt interest) + $5,000 (life insurance proceeds).*

**Effect of Terminating the S Election.** Normally, distributions to shareholders from a C corporation are taxed as dividends to the extent of E & P. However, any distribution of *cash* by a C corporation to shareholders during a one-year period[38] following an S election termination receives special treatment. Such a distribution is treated as a tax-free recovery of stock basis to the extent that it does not exceed the AAA.[39] Since *only* cash distributions reduce the AAA during this *postelection termination period*, a corporation should not make property distributions during this time. Instead, the entity should sell property and distribute the proceeds to shareholders.

**EXAMPLE 20**

Quinn, the sole shareholder of Azalea, Inc., a calendar year S corporation, decides during 2006 to terminate the S election, effective January 1, 2007. As of the end of 2006, Azalea has an AAA of $1,300. Quinn can receive a nontaxable distribution of cash during the post-termination period to the extent of Azalea's AAA. Cash distributions of $1,300 during 2007 are nontaxable to Quinn, but they reduce the adjusted basis of his stock. ■

---

[38] § 1377(b).

[39] § 1371(e). Termination-period distributions from the OAA are taxed as capital gains.

## The Accumulated Adjustments Account

FRAMEWORK FOCUS: TAX RATE

STRATEGY ➤ AVOID DOUBLE TAXATION.

The AAA is needed to determine the tax treatment of distributions from S corporations with AEP *and* distributions made during the post-termination election period. Therefore, it is important for all S corporations (even those with no AEP) to maintain the AAA balance. Without an accurate AAA balance, distributions could needlessly be classified as taxable dividends. Alternatively, it will be costly to reconstruct the AAA after the S election terminates.

Distributions should be made when AAA is positive. If future years bring operating losses, AAA is reduced, and shareholder exposure to AEP and taxable dividends increases.

### TAX TREATMENT OF PROPERTY DISTRIBUTIONS BY THE CORPORATION

An S corporation recognizes a gain on any distribution of appreciated property (other than in a reorganization) in the same manner as if the asset had been sold to the shareholder at its fair market value.[40] The corporate gain is passed through to the shareholders. There is an important reason for this rule. Without it, property might be distributed tax-free (other than for certain recapture items) and later sold without income recognition to the shareholder because the shareholder's basis equals the asset's fair market value. The character of the gain—capital gain or ordinary income—depends upon the type of asset being distributed.

The S corporation does not recognize a loss when distributing assets that are worth less than their basis. As with gain property, the shareholder's basis is equal to the asset's fair market value. Thus, the potential loss is postponed until the shareholder sells the stock of the S corporation. Since loss property receives a step-down in basis without any loss recognition by the S corporation, distributions of loss property should be avoided. See Concept Summary 11–2.

**EXAMPLE 21**

Yarrow, Inc., an S corporation for 10 years, distributes a tract of land held as an investment to one of its shareholders. The land was purchased for $22,000 many years ago and is currently worth $82,000. Yarrow recognizes a capital gain of $60,000, which increases the AAA by $60,000. The gain flows through proportionately to Yarrow's shareholders and is taxed to them.

Then a tax-free property distribution reduces AAA and shareholder stock basis by $82,000 (fair market value). The tax consequences are the same for appreciated property, whether it is distributed to the shareholders and they dispose of it, or the corporation sells the property and distributes the proceeds to the shareholders. ■

**EXAMPLE 22**

Continue with the facts of Example 21. If the land had been purchased for $82,000 and was currently worth $22,000, the shareholder would take a $22,000 basis in the land. The $60,000 realized loss is not recognized at the corporate level. The loss does not reduce Yarrow's AAA. Only when the S corporation sells the asset does it recognize the loss and reduce AAA. ■

---

[40]§ 311(b).

## CONCEPT SUMMARY 11-2

### Distribution of Property In-Kind

|  | Appreciated Property | Depreciated Property |
| --- | --- | --- |
| S corporation | Realized gain is recognized by the corporation, which passes it through to the shareholders. Such gain increases a shareholder's stock basis, generating a basis in the property equal to FMV. On the distribution, the shareholder's stock basis is reduced by the FMV of the property (but not below zero). | Realized loss is not recognized. The shareholder assumes an FMV basis in the property. |
| C corporation | Realized gain is recognized under § 311(b) and increases E & P (net of tax). The shareholder has a taxable dividend to the extent of E & P. | Realized loss is not recognized. The shareholder assumes an FMV basis in the property. |
| Partnership | No gain to the partnership or partner. The partner takes a carryover basis in the asset, but the asset basis is limited to the partner's basis in the partnership. | Realized loss is not recognized. The partner takes a carryover basis in the asset, but the asset basis is limited to the partner's basis in the partnership. |

**EXAMPLE 23**

Assume the same facts as in Examples 21 and 22, except that Yarrow is a C corporation (E & P balance of $1 million) or a partnership. Assume the partner's basis in the partnership interest is $100,000 and ignore any corporate-level taxes. Compare the results.

|  | Appreciated Property | | |
| --- | --- | --- | --- |
|  | S Corporation | C Corporation | Partnership |
| Entity gain/loss | $60,000 | $60,000 | $ –0– |
| Owner's gain/loss/dividend | 60,000 | 82,000 | –0– |
| Owner's basis in land | 82,000 | 82,000 | 22,000 |

|  | Property That Has Declined in Value | | |
| --- | --- | --- | --- |
|  | S Corporation | C Corporation | Partnership |
| Entity gain/loss | $ –0– | $ –0– | $ –0– |
| Owner's gain/loss/dividend | –0– | 22,000 | –0– |
| Owner's basis in land | 22,000 | 22,000 | 82,000 |

**LO.6**

Calculate a shareholder's basis in S corporation stock.

### SHAREHOLDER'S BASIS

The calculation of the initial tax basis of stock in an S corporation is similar to that for the basis of stock in a C corporation and depends upon the manner in which the shares are acquired (e.g., gift, inheritance, purchase, exchange under § 351). Once the initial tax basis is determined, various transactions during the life of the corporation affect the shareholder's basis in the stock. Although each shareholder is required to compute his or her own basis in the S shares, neither Form 1120S nor Schedule K–1 provides a place for tracking this amount.

A shareholder's basis is increased by stock purchases and capital contributions. Operations during the year cause the following additional upward adjustments to basis.[41]

- Nonseparately computed income.
- Separately stated income items (e.g., nontaxable income).

Basis then is reduced by distributions not reported as income by the shareholder (e.g., an AAA or PTI distribution). Next, the following items reduce basis (but not below zero).

- Nondeductible expenses of the corporation (e.g., fines, penalties, illegal kickbacks).
- Nonseparately computed loss.
- Separately stated loss and deduction items.

As under the partnership rules, basis first is increased by income items; then it is decreased by distributions and finally by losses.[42] In most cases, this *losses last* rule is advantageous.

**EXAMPLE 24**

In its first year of operations, Iris, Inc., a calendar year S corporation, earns income of $2,000. On February 2 in its second year of operations, Iris distributes $2,000 to Marty, its sole shareholder. During the remainder of the second year, the corporation incurs a $2,000 loss.

Under the S corporation ordering rules, the $2,000 distribution is tax-free AAA to Marty. The distribution is accounted for before the loss. The $2,000 loss is *not* passed through, though, because stock basis cannot be reduced below zero. ■

A shareholder's basis in S corporation stock can never be reduced below zero. Once stock basis is zero, any additional basis reductions (losses or deductions, but *not* distributions) decrease (but not below zero) the shareholder's basis in loans made to the S corporation. Any excess of losses or deductions over both stock and loan bases is not deductible in the current year. Losses can be deducted only to the extent that they offset stock or loan basis. Thus, until additional basis is created due to capital contributions or flow-through income, the loss deductions are suspended.

When there is a capital contribution or an item of flow-through income, basis is first restored to the shareholder loans, up to the original principal amount.[43] Then, basis in the stock is restored.

**EXAMPLE 25**

Stacey, a sole shareholder, has a $7,000 stock basis and a $2,000 basis in a loan that she made to a calendar year S corporation. At the beginning of the year, the corporation's AAA and OAA balances are $0. Subchapter S ordinary income for the year is $8,200. During the year, the corporation also received $2,000 of tax-exempt interest income.

Cash of $17,300 is distributed to Stacey on November 15. As a result, Stacey recognizes only a $100 capital gain.

| | Corporate AAA | Corporate OAA | Stacey's Stock Basis | Stacey's Loan Basis |
|---|---|---|---|---|
| Beginning balance | $   –0– | $    –0– | $ 7,000 | $2,000 |
| Ordinary income | 8,200 | | 8,200 | |
| Tax-exempt income | | 2,000 | 2,000 | |
| Subtotal | $ 8,200 | $ 2,000 | $17,200 | $2,000 |

---

[41]§ 1367(a).

[42]Reg. § 1.1367–1(f).

[43]§ 1367(b)(2).

| | Corporate AAA | Corporate OAA | Stacey's Stock Basis | Stacey's Loan Basis |
|---|---|---|---|---|
| Distribution ($17,300) | | | | |
| From AAA | (8,200) | | (8,200) | |
| From OAA | | (2,000) | (2,000) | |
| From stock basis | | | (7,000) | |
| Ending balance | $ –0– | $ –0– | $ –0– | $2,000 |
| Distribution in excess of stock basis (capital gain) | | | $ 100 | |

Pass-through losses can reduce loan basis, but distributions do not. Stock basis cannot be reduced below zero, but the $100 excess distribution does not reduce Stacey's loan basis. ■

The basis rules for S corporation stock are similar to the rules for determining a partner's basis in a partnership interest. However, a partner's basis in the partnership interest includes the partner's direct investment plus a *ratable share* of partnership liabilities.[44] If a partnership borrows from a partner, the partner receives a basis increase as if the partnership had borrowed from an unrelated third party.[45] In contrast, except for loans from the shareholder to the corporation, corporate borrowing has no effect on S corporation shareholder basis. Loans from a shareholder to the S corporation have a tax basis only for the shareholder making the loan.

If a loan's basis has been reduced and is not restored, income is recognized when the corporation repays the loan. If the corporation issued a note as evidence of the debt, repayment constitutes an amount received in exchange for a capital asset, and the amount that exceeds the shareholder's basis is capital gain.[46] However, if the loan is made on open account, the repayment constitutes ordinary income to the extent that it exceeds the shareholder's basis in the loan. Thus, a note should be given to ensure capital gain treatment for the income that results from a loan's repayment.

**EXAMPLE 26**

Phil is the sole shareholder of Falcon, a valid S corporation. At the beginning of 2006, Phil's basis in his stock was $10,000. During 2006, he made a $4,000 loan to the corporation, using a written debt instrument and market interest rates. Falcon has no other outstanding debt.

Falcon generated a $13,000 taxable loss for 2006. Thus, at the beginning of 2007, Phil's stock basis was zero, and the basis in his loan to Falcon was $1,000.

Falcon repaid the loan in full on March 1, 2007. Phil recognized a $3,000 capital gain on the repayment. ■

 DIGGING DEEPER 4    *Find more information on this topic at our Web site: http://wft-entities.swlearning.com.*

 **PLANNING STRATEGIES**

## Working with Suspended Losses

**FRAMEWORK FOCUS: INCOME AND EXCLUSIONS**

**STRATEGY ➤ AVOID INCOME RECOGNITION.**

Distributions made to shareholders with suspended losses usually create capital gain income because there is no stock or debt basis to offset. Usually, distributions should be deferred until the shareholder creates stock basis in some form. In this way, no gross income is recognized until the suspended losses are fully used.

---

[44]§ 752(a).
[45]Reg. § 1.752–1(e).

[46]*Joe M. Smith,* 48 T.C. 872 (1967), *aff'd* and *rev'd* in 70–1 USTC ¶9327, 25 AFTR2d 70–936, 424 F.2d 219 (CA–9, 1970); Rev.Rul. 64–162, 1964–1 C.B. 304.

**EXAMPLE 27**

Continue with the facts of Example 26 except that Falcon's loss cannot be deducted by Phil because of the lack of basis. Phil purchases $5,000 of additional stock in Falcon. Phil gets an immediate deduction for his investment, due to his $13,000 in suspended losses. Alternatively, if Falcon shows a $5,000 profit for the year,

Phil pays no tax on the flow-through income, due to his $13,000 in suspended losses.

However, if Falcon distributes $5,000 to Phil in 2007 without earning any profit for the year, and prior to any capital contribution by him, Phil recognizes a $5,000 capital gain, because his stock basis is zero. ■

---

**LO.7**

Explain the tax effects of losses on S shareholders.

## TREATMENT OF LOSSES

**Net Operating Loss.**   One major advantage of an S election is the ability to pass through any net operating loss (NOL) of the corporation directly to the shareholders. A shareholder can deduct an NOL for the year in which the S corporation's tax year ends. The corporation is not entitled to any deduction for the NOL. A shareholder's basis in the stock is reduced to the extent of any pass-through of the NOL, and the shareholder's AAA is reduced by the same deductible amount.[47]

Deductions for an S corporation's NOL pass-through cannot exceed a shareholder's adjusted basis in the stock *plus* the basis of any loans made by the shareholder to the corporation.[48] A shareholder is entitled to carry forward a loss to the extent that the loss for the year exceeds basis. Any loss carried forward may be deducted *only* by the *same* shareholder if and when the basis in the stock of or loans to the corporation is restored.[49]

DIGGING DEEPER ⑤   *Find more information on this topic at our Web site: http://wft-entities.swlearning.com.*

**EXAMPLE 28**

Ginny owns 10% of the stock of Pilot, a calendar year S corporation. Her basis in the shares is $10,000 at the beginning of 2004. The indicated events are accounted for under the S corporation rules as follows.

| Tax Year | Event | Tax Consequences |
|---|---|---|
| 2004 | Ginny's share of Pilot's operating loss is $15,000. | Ginny deducts $10,000. Her stock basis is reduced to zero. She holds a $5,000 suspended loss. |
| 2005 | Ginny's share of Pilot's operating loss is $4,000. | No deduction for the loss, as Ginny has no stock basis to offset. Her suspended loss is now $9,000. |
| 2006 | Ginny's share of Pilot's operating loss is $7,000. She purchases an additional $10,000 of stock from Pilot. | The purchase creates $10,000 of stock basis. Ginny deducts $10,000—the current $7,000 loss and $3,000 of the suspended loss. Stock basis again is zero, and the new suspended loss is $6,000. |
| 2007 | Ginny sells all of her Pilot shares to Christina on January 1. | The $6,000 suspended loss disappears—it cannot be transferred to Christina. ■ |

---

[47]§§ 1368(a)(1)(A) and (e)(1)(A).
[48]See *Donald J. Sauvigne,* 30 TCM 123, T.C.Memo. 1971–30.
[49]§ 1366(d).

## Loss Considerations

**FRAMEWORK FOCUS: DEDUCTIONS**

STRATEGY ➤ MAXIMIZE DEDUCTIBLE AMOUNTS.

A loss in excess of tax basis may be carried forward and deducted only by the same shareholder in succeeding years. Thus, before disposing of the stock, a shareholder should increase stock/loan basis to flow through the loss. The next shareholder cannot acquire the loss carryover.

The NOL provisions create a need for sound tax planning during the last election year and the post-termination transition period. If it appears that the S corporation is going to sustain an NOL or use up any loss carryover, each shareholder's basis should be analyzed to determine if it can absorb the owner's share of the loss. If basis is insufficient to absorb the loss, further investments should be considered before the end of the post-termination period. Such investments can be accomplished through additional stock purchases from the corporation, or from other shareholders, to increase basis.

### EXAMPLE 29

A calendar year C corporation has an NOL of $20,000 in 2005. The corporation makes a valid S election in 2006 and has another $20,000 NOL in that year. At all times during 2006, the stock of the corporation was owned by the same 10 shareholders, each of whom owned 10% of the stock. Tim, one of the shareholders, has an adjusted basis in his stock of $1,800 at the beginning of 2006. None of the 2005 NOL may be carried forward into the S year. Although Tim's share of the 2006 NOL is $2,000, his deduction for the loss is limited to $1,800 in 2006 with a $200 carryover to 2007. ■

**At-Risk Rules.**  S corporation shareholders, like partners, are limited in the amount of loss that they may deduct by their "at-risk" amounts. The rules for determining at-risk amounts are similar, but not identical, to the partnership at-risk rules.

An amount at risk is determined separately for each shareholder. The amount of the corporate losses that are passed through and deductible by the shareholders is not affected by the amount the corporation has at risk. A shareholder usually is considered at risk with respect to an activity to the extent of cash and the adjusted basis of other property contributed to the electing corporation, any amount borrowed for use in the activity for which the taxpayer has personal liability for payment from personal assets, and the net fair market value of personal assets that secure nonrecourse borrowing. Any losses that are suspended under the at-risk rules are carried forward and are available during the post-termination period. The S stock basis limitations and at-risk limitations are applied before the passive activity limitations (see below).

**EXAMPLE 30**

Carl has a basis of $35,000 in his S corporation stock. He takes a $15,000 nonrecourse loan from a relative and lends the proceeds to the S corporation. Carl now has a stock basis of $35,000 and a loan basis of $15,000. However, due to the at-risk limitation, he can deduct only $35,000 of losses from the S corporation. ■

**Passive Losses and Credits.**  Net passive losses and credits are not deductible when incurred and must be carried over to a year when there is passive income. Thus, one must be aware of three major classes of income, losses, and credits—active, portfolio, and passive. S corporations are not directly subject to the passive activity limits, but corporate rental activities are inherently passive, and other activities of an S corporation may be passive unless the shareholder(s) materially participate(s) in operating the business. An S corporation may engage in more than one such activity.

## CONCEPT SUMMARY 11–3

### Treatment of S Corporation Losses

Step 1.   Allocate total loss to the shareholder on a daily basis, based upon stock ownership.

Step 2.   If the shareholder's loss exceeds his or her stock basis, apply any excess to the adjusted basis of indebtedness to the shareholder. Loss allocations do not reduce stock or loan basis below zero.

Step 3.   Where a flow-through loss exceeds the stock and loan basis, any excess is suspended and carried over to succeeding tax years.

Step 4.   In succeeding tax years, any net increase in basis restores the debt basis first, up to its original amount.

Step 5.   Once debt basis is restored, any remaining net increase restores stock basis.

Step 6.   Any suspended loss from a previous year now reduces stock basis first and debt basis second.

Step 7.   If the S election terminates, any suspended loss carryover may be deducted during the post-termination period to the extent of the stock basis at the end of this period. Any loss remaining at the end of this period is lost forever.

If the corporate activity is rental or the shareholders do not materially participate, any passive losses or credits flow through. The shareholders are able to apply the losses or credits only against their income from other passive activities. An S shareholder's stock basis is reduced by passive losses that flow through to the shareholder, even though the shareholder may not be entitled to a current deduction due to the passive loss limitations.

**LO.8**

Compute the entity-level taxes on S corporations.

*\*Definition
Built-in Gains Tax
– Page C-3*

**EXAMPLE 31**

### TAX ON PRE-ELECTION BUILT-IN GAIN

Normally, an S corporation does *not* pay an income tax, since all items flow through to the shareholders. But an S corporation that was previously a C corporation may be required to pay a built-in gains tax, a LIFO recapture tax, or a passive investment income tax.

Without the **built-in gains tax,** it would be possible to avoid the corporate double tax on a disposition of appreciated property, by electing S corporation status.

Zinnia, Inc., a C corporation, owns a single asset with a basis of $100,000 and a fair market value of $500,000. If Zinnia sells this asset and distributes the cash to its shareholders, there are two levels of tax, one at the corporate level and one at the shareholder level. Alternatively, if Zinnia distributes the asset to its shareholders as a dividend, a double tax still results. In an attempt to avoid the double tax, Zinnia elects S corporation status. It then sells the asset and distributes the proceeds to shareholders. Without the built-in gains tax, the gain would be taxed only once, at the shareholder level. The distribution of the sales proceeds would be a tax-free reduction of the AAA. ■

The built-in gains tax generally applies to C corporations converting to S status after 1986. It is a *corporate-level* tax on any built-in gain recognized when the S corporation disposes of an asset in a taxable disposition within 10 calendar years after the date on which the S election took effect. The steps in computing the tax are summarized in Concept Summary 11–4.

**General Rules.**   The base for the built-in gains tax includes any unrealized gain on appreciated assets (e.g., real estate, cash basis receivables, goodwill) held by a corporation on the day it elects S status. The highest corporate tax rate (currently 35 percent) is applied to the unrealized gain when any of the assets are sold. Any

## CONCEPT SUMMARY 11–4

### Calculation of the Built-in Gains Tax Liability

Step 1.    Select the smaller of built-in gain or taxable income.*

Step 2.    Deduct unexpired NOLs and capital losses from C corporation tax years.

Step 3.    Multiply the tax base obtained in step 2 by the top corporate income tax rate.

Step 4.    Deduct any business credit carryforwards and AMT credit carryforwards arising in a C corporation tax year from the amount obtained in step 3.

Step 5.    The corporation pays any tax resulting in step 4.

*Any net recognized built-in gain in excess of taxable income is carried forward to the next year within the 10-year recognition period.

gain from the sale (net of the § 1374 tax)[50] also passes through as a taxable gain to shareholders.

**EXAMPLE 32**

Assume the same facts as in the preceding example. Section 1374 imposes a corporate-level built-in gains tax that must be paid by Zinnia if it sells the asset after electing S status. Upon sale of the asset, the corporation owes a tax of $140,000 ($400,000 × 35%). In addition, the shareholders report a $260,000 taxable gain ($400,000 − $140,000). Hence, the built-in gains tax effectively imposes a double tax on Zinnia and its shareholders. ∎

*Find more information on this topic at our Web site: **http://wft-entities.swlearning.com**.*

The amount of built-in gain recognized in any year is limited to an *as if* taxable income for the year, computed as if the corporation were a C corporation. Any built-in gain that escapes taxation due to the taxable income limitation is carried forward and recognized in future tax years. Thus, a corporation can defer a built-in gain tax liability whenever it has a low or negative taxable income.

**EXAMPLE 33**

Vinca's recognized built-in gain for 2006 is $400,000. If Vinca were a C corporation, its 2006 taxable income would be $300,000. The amount of built-in gain subject to tax in 2006 is $300,000. The excess built-in gain of $100,000 is carried forward and taxed in 2007 (assuming adequate C corporation taxable income in that year). There is no statutory limit on the carryforward period, but the gain would effectively expire at the end of the 10-year recognition period applicable to all built-in gains.[51] ∎

Normally, tax attributes of a C corporation do not carry over to a converted S corporation. For purposes of the built-in gains tax, however, certain carryovers are allowed. In particular, an S corporation can offset built-in gains with unexpired NOLs or capital losses from C corporation years.

**EXAMPLE 34**

An S corporation has a built-in gain of $100,000 and taxable income of $90,000. The built-in gains tax liability is calculated as follows, applying the indicated loss carryforwards.

---

[50]§ 1366(f)(2).
[51]§ 1374(d)(7); Notice 90–27, 1990–1 C.B. 336.

| | |
|---|---:|
| Lesser of taxable income or built-in gain | $ 90,000 |
| Less: NOL carryforward from C year | (12,000) |
| Capital loss carryforward from C year | (8,000) |
| Tax base | $ 70,000 |
| Highest corporate income tax rate | × 0.35 |
| Tentative tax | $ 24,500 |
| Less: Business credit carryforward from C year | (4,000) |
| Built-in gains tax liability | $ 20,500 |

The $10,000 realized (but not taxed) built-in gain in excess of taxable income is carried forward to the next year, as long as the next year is within the 10-year recognition period. ■

## PLANNING STRATEGIES   Managing the Built-in Gains Tax

FRAMEWORK FOCUS: INCOME AND EXCLUSIONS

STRATEGY ➤ AVOID INCOME RECOGNITION.
➤ POSTPONE RECOGNITION OF INCOME TO ACHIEVE TAX DEFERRAL.

Although limitations exist on contributions of loss property to the corporation before electing S status, it still is possible for a corporation to minimize built-in gains and maximize built-in losses prior to the S election. A cash basis S corporation can accomplish this by reducing receivables, accelerating payables, and accruing compensation costs.

To further reduce or defer the tax, the corporation may take advantage of the taxable income limitation by shifting income and deductions to minimize taxable income in years when built-in gain is recognized. Although the postponed built-in gain is carried forward to future years, the time value of money makes the postponement beneficial. For example, paying compensation to shareholder-employees in place of a distribution creates a deduction that reduces taxable income and postpones the built-in gains tax.

holders. If Tulip pays at least $120,000 in salaries to the shareholders (rather than making a distribution), its taxable income drops to zero, and the built-in gains tax is postponed. Thus, Tulip needs to keep the salaries as high as possible to postpone the built-in gains tax in future years and reap a benefit from the time value of money. Of course, paying the salaries may increase the payroll tax burden if the salaries are initially below FICA and FUTA limits. ■

Giving built-in gain property to a charitable organization does not trigger the built-in gains tax. Built-in *loss* property may be sold in the same year that built-in gain property is sold to reduce or eliminate the built-in gains tax. Generally, the taxpayer should sell built-in loss property in a year when an equivalent amount of built-in gain property is sold. Otherwise, the built-in loss could be wasted.

### EXAMPLE 35

Tulip, Inc., an S corporation, has built-in gain of $110,000 and taxable income of $120,000 before payment of salaries to its share-

**LIFO Recapture Tax.** When a corporation uses the FIFO method for its last year before making the S election, any built-in gain is recognized and taxed as the inventory is sold. A LIFO-basis corporation does not recognize this gain unless the corporation invades the LIFO layer during the 10-year built-in gains tax period. To preclude deferral of gain recognition under LIFO, any LIFO recapture amount at the time of the S election is subject to a corporate-level tax.

The taxable LIFO recapture amount equals the excess of the inventory's value under FIFO over the LIFO value. The resulting tax is payable in four equal installments,

## NO DOUBLE TAXATION?

**S** corporations paid almost $400 million in Federal corporate-level taxes for tax year 2001, a significant level of collections from "tax-exempt" entities.

| Federal Income Taxes Paid by S Corporations ($M) | | |
|---|---|---|
| | **2000** | **2001** |
| Built-in gains, LIFO recapture taxes | $468 | $303 |
| Passive investment income penalty tax | 25 | 9 |
| Audit adjustments, other | 182 | 57 |
| Totals | $675 | $369 |

For 2001, corporate-level Federal income taxes were reported by about 7,250 S corporations, about 0.50 percent of all S returns filed.

with the first payment due on or before the due date for the corporate return for the last C corporation year (without regard to any extensions). The remaining three installments must be paid on or before the due dates of the succeeding corporate returns. No interest is due if payments are made by the due dates, and no estimated taxes are due on the four tax installments. No refund is allowed if the LIFO value is higher than the FIFO value.

**EXAMPLE 36**

Daffodil Corporation converts from a C corporation to an S corporation at the beginning of 2006. Daffodil used the LIFO inventory method in 2005 and had an ending LIFO inventory of $110,000 (FIFO value of $190,000). Daffodil must add $80,000 of LIFO recapture amount to its 2005 taxable income, resulting in an increased tax liability of $28,000 ($80,000 × 35%). Daffodil must pay one-fourth of the tax (or $7,000) with its 2005 corporate tax return. The three succeeding installments of $7,000 each are paid with Daffodil's 2006–2008 tax returns. ■

## PASSIVE INVESTMENT INCOME PENALTY TAX

A tax is imposed on the excess passive income of S corporations that possess AEP from C corporation years. The tax rate is the highest corporate income tax rate for the year. The rate is applied to excess net passive income (ENPI), which is determined using the following formula.

$$\text{Excess net passive income} = \frac{\text{Passive investment income in excess of 25\% of gross receipts for the year}}{\text{Passive investment income for the year}} \times \text{Net passive investment income for the year}$$

Passive investment income (PII) includes gross receipts derived from royalties, rents, dividends, interest, annuities, and sales and exchanges of stocks and securities.[52] Only the net gain from the disposition of capital assets (other than stocks and securities) is taken into account in computing gross receipts. Net passive income is passive income reduced by any deductions directly connected with the production of that income. Any passive income tax reduces the amount the shareholders must take into income.

The excess net passive income cannot exceed a hypothetical C corporate taxable income for the year, before considering special C corporation deductions (like the dividends received deduction) or an NOL carryover.[53]

**EXAMPLE 37**

Lilac Corporation, an electing S corporation, has gross receipts totaling $264,000 (of which $110,000 is PII). Expenditures directly connected to the production of the PII total $30,000. Therefore, Lilac has net PII of $80,000 ($110,000 − $30,000), and its PII exceeds 25% of its gross receipts by $44,000 [$110,000 PII − (25% × $264,000)]. Excess net passive income (ENPI) is $32,000, calculated as follows.

$$\text{ENPI} = \frac{\$44,000}{\$110,000} \times \$80,000 = \$32,000$$

Lilac's PII tax is $11,200 ($32,000 × 35%). ■

**PLANNING STRATEGIES**

## Avoid the PII Tax

**FRAMEWORK FOCUS: TAX RATE**

**STRATEGY ➤ AVOID DOUBLE TAXATION.**

Watch for a possible violation of the PII limitation. Avoid a consecutive third year with excess passive income when the corporation has accumulated E & P from C corporation years. In this connection, assets that produce passive income (e.g., stocks and bonds, certain rental assets) might be retained by the shareholders in their individual capacities and kept out of the corporation.

## OTHER OPERATIONAL RULES

Several other points may be made about the possible effects of various Code provisions on S corporations.

- An S corporation must make estimated tax payments with respect to any recognized built-in gain and excess passive investment income tax.
- An S corporation may own stock in another corporation, but an S corporation may not have a C corporation shareholder. An S corporation is *not* eligible for a dividends received deduction.
- An S corporation is *not* subject to the 10 percent of taxable income limitation applicable to charitable contributions made by a C corporation.
- Any family member who renders services or furnishes capital to an S corporation must be paid reasonable compensation. Otherwise, the IRS can make adjustments to reflect the value of the services or capital. This rule may make it more difficult for related parties to shift Subchapter S taxable income to children or other family members.

---

[52]§ 1362(d)(3)(C)(i).

[53]§§ 1374(d)(4), and 1375(a) and (b).

- Although § 1366(a)(1) provides for a flow-through of S items to a shareholder, this amount is not self-employment income and is not subject to the self-employment tax.[54] Compensation for services rendered to an S corporation is, however, subject to FICA taxes.

**EXAMPLE 38**

Cody and Dana each own one-third of a fast-food restaurant, and their 14-year-old son owns the other shares. Both parents work full-time in the restaurant operations, but the son works infrequently. Neither parent receives a salary this year, when the taxable income of the S corporation is $160,000. The IRS can require that reasonable compensation be deemed as paid to the parents to prevent the full one-third of the $160,000 from being taxed to the son. Otherwise, this would be an effective technique to shift earned income to a family member to reduce the total family tax burden. Furthermore, low or zero salaries can reduce FICA taxes due to the Federal government. ■

- An S corporation is placed on the cash method of accounting for purposes of deducting business expenses and interest owed to a cash basis related party.[55] Thus, the timing of the shareholder's income and the corporate deduction must match.
- The S election is not recognized by the District of Columbia and several states, including Louisiana, New Hampshire, and Tennessee. Thus, some or all of the entity's income may be subject to a state-level income tax.
- An S corporation may issue § 1244 stock to its shareholders to obtain ordinary loss treatment.
- Losses may be disallowed due to a lack of a profit motive. If the activities at the corporate level are not profit motivated, the losses may be disallowed under the hobby loss rules of § 183 (see Chapter 16).[56]

## Summary

The S corporation rules are elective and can be used to benefit a number of owners of small businesses.

- When the business is profitable, the S corporation election removes the threat of double taxation on corporate profits.
- When the business is generating losses, deductions for allocable losses are immediately available to the shareholders.

Over one-half of all U.S. corporations operate under the S rules. Flow-through income is taxed to the shareholders, who increase basis in their corporate stock accordingly. In this manner, subsequent distributions to shareholders can be made tax-free. Flow-through losses reduce stock and debt basis, but loss deductions are suspended when basis reaches zero. Flow-through items that could be treated differently by various shareholders are separately stated on Schedule K–1 of the Form 1120S.

Corporate-level taxes are seldom assessed on S corporations, but they guard against abuses of the S rules, such as shifting appreciated assets from higher C corporation rates to lower individual rates (the built-in gains tax) or doing the same with investment assets (the tax on excessive PII).

---

[54]Rev.Rul. 59–221, 1959–1 C.B. 225. Recall from Chapter 10 that flow-through ordinary income is self-employment income to a partner or LLC member.

[55]§ 267(b).

[56]*Michael J. Houston*, 69 TCM 2360, T.C.Memo. 1995–159; *Mario G. De Mendoza, III*, 68 TCM 42, T.C.Memo. 1994–314.

⊙ **T A X   F A C T**

### THE S CORPORATION ECONOMY

**T**otal assets controlled by even the smallest S corporations make up a significant part of the economy. The 3 million S corporations filing returns, representing over 5 million shareholders, employ $1.88 trillion in assets in their investments and operations.

**Assets Controlled ($B) by S Corporations, by Number of Shareholders, 2001 Tax Year**

| Number of Shareholders | One | Two | Three | Four to Ten | More than Ten |
|---|---|---|---|---|---|
| Assets ($B) | 584 | 389 | 183 | 415 | 307 |

The S rules are designed for closely held businesses with simple capital structures. Eligibility rules are not oppressive, and they do not include any limitations on the corporation's capitalization value, sales, number or distribution of employees, or other operating measures. The S election process can be complex, though, and maintenance of S status must be monitored on an ongoing basis.

## Suggested Further Readings

Donald Cunningham and Paul Erickson, "Employment Taxes and the Entity Choice Decision," *Business Entities Online*, July/August 2004.

James P. Dawson and David W. LaRue, "Eluding the LIFO Recapture Provisions of Subchapter S," *Business Entities*, September/October 2003, pp. 22–30.

Charles M. Steines, "S Corporation Distribution Subject to City Earnings Tax," *Journal of Multistate Taxation and Incentives*, October 2002, pp. 38–40.

## KEY TERMS

| | | |
|---|---|---|
| Accumulated adjustments account (AAA), 11–16 | Passive investment income (PII), 11–10 | Small business corporation, 11–5 |
| Built-in gains tax, 11–25 | S corporation, 11–2 | Subchapter S, 11–2 |
| | | Voluntary revocation, 11–9 |

## PROBLEM MATERIALS

### Problems

1. What are some tax differences between a partnership and an S corporation?

*Issue ID*

2. On March 2, the two 50% shareholders of a calendar year corporation decide to elect S status. One of the shareholders, Terry, purchased her stock from a previous shareholder (a nonresident alien) on January 18 of the same year. Identify any potential problems for Terry or the corporation.

*Ethics*

3. Burt is the custodian at Quaker Inn, an S corporation that has paid him bonuses over the years in the form of shares in the corporation. Burt now holds 276 shares in Quaker Inn.

   While listening to a television debate about a national health care plan, Burt decides that the company's health coverage is unfair. He is concerned about this because his wife, Dora, is seriously ill.

   During the second week in December, Burt informs Quaker's president that he would like a Christmas bonus of $75,000 cash, or else he will sell 10 shares of his stock to one of his relatives, a nonresident alien. The resulting loss of the S election would trigger about $135,000 in Federal corporate income taxes for the current year alone. Can you defend Burt's position?

4. Ninety-nine individuals own all of the shares of Woodpecker Corporation. Hal and Mary Jones want to buy into the corporation, and then to direct the entity to make an S election. Can Woodpecker so elect? How many signatures must appear on the consent form making the S election?

*Issue ID*

5. Lynch's share of her S corporation's net operating loss is $41,000, but her stock basis is only $29,000. Point out any tax consequences to Lynch.

6. Zebra, Inc., a calendar year S corporation, incurred the following items. Sammy is a 40% shareholder in Zebra throughout the year.

| | |
|---|---|
| Sales | $100,000 |
| Cost of goods sold | 40,000 |
| Depreciation expense | 10,000 |
| Administrative expenses | 5,000 |
| § 1231 gain | 21,000 |
| § 1250 gain | 20,000 |
| Short-term capital loss from stock sale | 6,000 |
| Long-term capital loss from stock sale | 4,000 |
| Long-term capital gain from stock sale | 15,000 |
| Charitable contributions | 4,500 |

   a. Calculate Sammy's share of nonseparately computed income.
   b. Calculate Sammy's share of any net long-term capital gain.

7. An S corporation's profit and loss statement shows net profits of $90,000 (book income). The corporation has three equal shareholders. From supplemental data, you obtain the following information about the corporation. All of the indicated items are included in book income.

| | |
|---|---|
| Selling expenses | $21,200 |
| Municipal bond interest income | 2,000 |
| Dividends received on IBM stock | 9,000 |
| § 1231 gain | 6,000 |
| § 1250 gain | 12,000 |
| Recovery of bad debts | 4,000 |
| Long-term capital losses | 6,000 |
| Salary paid to owners (each) | 10,000 |
| Cost of goods sold | 95,000 |

a. Determine nonseparately computed income or loss.
b. What would be the portion of taxable income or loss for Chang, one of the shareholders?

8. Ramos, Inc., a calendar year S corporation, incurred the following items this year.

| | |
|---|---|
| Sales | $130,000 |
| Municipal bond interest income | 7,000 |
| § 1250 gain | 12,000 |
| Short-term capital gain | 30,000 |
| Cost of goods sold | 42,000 |
| Administrative expenses | 15,000 |
| Depreciation expense | 17,000 |
| Charitable contributions | 14,000 |

Calculate Ramos's nonseparately computed income.

9. Polly has been the sole shareholder of a calendar year S corporation since its inception. Polly's stock basis is $15,500, and she receives a distribution of $19,000. Corporate-level accounts are as follows.

AAA    $6,000        AEP    $500

How is Polly taxed on the distribution?

10. Suresh, Inc., an S corporation, has a beginning AAA balance of $782,000. During the year, the following items occur.

| | |
|---|---|
| Operating income | $472,000 |
| Interest income | 6,500 |
| Dividend income | 14,050 |
| Municipal bond interest income | 6,000 |
| Long-term capital loss from sale of land | (7,400) |
| § 179 expense | (6,000) |
| Charitable contributions | (19,000) |
| Cash distributions | 57,000 |

Calculate Suresh's ending AAA balance.

Issue ID

11. Berger, Inc., a calendar year S corporation, is owned equally by three individuals: Adam, Bonnie, and Charlene. The company owns a plot of land, purchased for $110,000 three years ago. When the land is worth $170,000, it is distributed to Charlene. Assuming

Charlene's stock basis is $300,000 on the distribution date, what are the potential tax ramifications?

**Decision Making** 12. Goblins, Inc., a calendar year S corporation, has $90,000 of AEP. Tobias, the sole shareholder, has an adjusted basis of $80,000 in his stock with a zero balance in the AAA.
   a. Determine the tax aspects if a $90,000 salary is paid to Tobias.
   b. Same as (a), except that Tobias receives a cash distribution of $90,000.

13. At the beginning of the year, Malcolm, a 50% shareholder of a calendar year S corporation, has a stock basis of $22,000. During the year, the corporation has taxable income of $32,000. The following data are obtained from supplemental sources.

| | |
|---|---:|
| Dividends received from IBM | $12,000 |
| Municipal bond interest income | 18,000 |
| Short-term capital gain | 6,000 |
| § 1245 gain | 10,000 |
| § 1231 gain | 7,000 |
| Charitable contributions | 5,000 |
| Political contributions | 8,000 |
| Short-term capital loss | 12,000 |
| Distribution to Malcolm | 6,000 |
| Selling expense | 14,000 |
| Beginning AAA | 40,000 |

   a. Compute Malcolm's ending stock basis.
   b. Compute ending AAA.

**Decision Making** 14. Adam and Bonnie form an S corporation, with Adam contributing cash of $100,000 for a 50% interest and Bonnie contributing appreciated ordinary income property with an adjusted basis of $20,000 and a fair market value of $100,000.
   a. Determine Bonnie's initial basis in her stock, assuming that she receives a 50% corporate ownership interest.
   b. The S corporation sells the property for $120,000. Determine Adam's and Bonnie's stock basis after the sale.

**Issue ID** 15. Red Dragon, Inc., is an S corporation with a sizable amount of AEP from a C corporation year. The S corporation has $300,000 of investment income and $300,000 of investment expenses. The company makes cash distributions to enable its sole shareholder to pay her taxes. What are the tax aspects to consider?

16. On January 1, Bobby and Alicia own equally all of the stock of an electing S corporation called Prairie Dirt Delight. The company has a $60,000 loss for the year (not a leap year). On the 219th day of the year, Bobby sells his half of the stock to his son, Bubba. How much of the $60,000 loss, if any, is allocated to Bubba?

**Communications** 17. A calendar year S corporation has a taxable loss of $80,000 and a capital loss of $20,000. Ms. Muhammad owns 30% of the corporate stock and has a $24,000 basis in her stock. Determine the amounts of the taxable loss and capital loss, if any, that flow through to Ms. Muhammad. Prepare a tax memo for the files.

18. Money, Inc., a calendar year S corporation, has two unrelated shareholders, each owning 50% of the stock. Both shareholders have a $400,000 stock basis as of January 1, and Money has AAA of $300,000 and AEP of $600,000. During the year, Money has operating income of $100,000. At the end of the year, Money distributes securities worth $1 million, with an adjusted basis of $800,000. Determine the tax effects of these transactions.

**Decision Making** 19. Assume the same facts as in Problem 18, except that the two shareholders consent to an AAA bypass election (i.e., to distribute AEP first).

20. An S corporation's Form 1120S shows taxable income of $88,000 for the year. Daniel owns 40% of the stock throughout the year. The following information is obtained from the corporate records.

| | |
|---|---|
| Salary paid to Daniel | $52,000 |
| Tax-exempt interest income | 3,000 |
| Charitable contributions | 6,000 |
| Dividends received from a non-U.S. corporation | 5,000 |
| Long-term capital loss | 6,000 |
| § 1245 gain | 11,000 |
| Refund of prior state income taxes | 5,000 |
| Cost of goods sold | 72,000 |
| Short-term capital loss | 7,000 |
| Administrative expenses | 18,000 |
| Short-term capital gain | 14,000 |
| Selling expenses | 11,000 |
| Daniel's beginning stock basis | 32,000 |
| Daniel's additional stock purchases | 9,000 |
| Beginning AAA | 31,000 |
| Daniel's loan to corporation | 20,000 |

a. Compute book income or loss.
b. Compute Daniel's ending stock basis.
c. Calculate ending corporate AAA.

21. Cloris owns 35% of the stock of an S corporation and lends the corporation $7,000 during the year. Her stock basis in the corporation at the end of the year is $25,000. If the corporation sustains a $110,000 operating loss during the year, what amount, if any, can Cloris deduct with respect to the operating loss?

**Communications**
22. Candy owns 40% of the stock of Park, a valid S corporation. Her stock basis is $25,000, and she loaned $8,000 to the corporation during the year. How much of Park's $110,000 operating loss can Candy deduct for this year? Show your computation of the tax consequences in spreadsheet form and include them in a memo to your manager.

23. Crew Corporation elected S status effective for tax year 2004. As of January 1, 2004, Crew's assets were appraised as follows.

| | **Adjusted Basis** | **Fair Market Value** |
|---|---|---|
| Cash | $ 16,010 | $ 16,010 |
| Accounts receivable | –0– | 55,400 |
| Investment in land | 110,000 | 215,000 |
| Building | 220,000 | 275,000 |
| Goodwill | –0– | 93,000 |

In each of the following situations, calculate any built-in gains tax, assuming that the highest corporate tax rate is 35%. C corporation taxable income would have been $100,000.
a. During 2004, Crew collects $40,000 of the accounts receivable.
b. In 2005, Crew sells the land held for investment for $203,000.
c. In 2006, the building is sold for $270,000.

24. Chris Valletta, the sole shareholder of Taylor, Inc., elects to terminate the S election, effective at the end of the year. As of the end of the year, Taylor, Inc., has AAA of $120,000 and OAA of $13,000. This amount reflects the fact that Chris received a cash dividend of $130,000 on January 15. If his stock basis was $220,000 before the distribution, calculate his taxable amount and his ending stock basis.

25. Opal, the owner of *all* of the shares of an S corporation in Richmond, Virginia, transfers all of the stock to Will at the middle of the tax year. There is a $200,000 NOL for the entire year, but $130,000 of the loss occurs during the first half of the year. With a short-year election, how much of the loss is allocated to Will?

26. An S corporation in Polly Beach, South Carolina, has a recognized built-in gain of $95,000 and taxable income of $80,000. It holds a $7,000 NOL carryforward and a $9,000 business credit carryforward from a C corporation year. There are no earnings and profits from C corporation years. Calculate the built-in gains tax liability.

27. Ruff Ltd., an S corporation in Flint, Michigan, recognizes an $80,000 built-in gain and a $10,000 built-in loss. Ruff also holds an $8,000 unexpired NOL from a C corporation year. Currently, Ruff generates ordinary income of $65,000. Calculate any built-in gains tax.

28. Lejeune, Inc., an S corporation in Boone, North Carolina, has operating revenues of $400,000, taxable interest of $380,000, operating expenses of $250,000, and deductions attributable to the interest income of $140,000. Lejeune's accumulated E & P amounts to $2 million. Calculate any penalty tax payable by this S corporation or its shareholders.

29. Brew, an S corporation, has gross receipts of $190,000 and gross income of $170,000. Brew has $22,000 of accumulated earnings and profits and taxable income of $30,000. It reports passive investment income of $100,000, with $40,000 of expenses directly related to the production of passive investment income. Calculate Brew's excess net passive income and any penalty tax liability.

Issue ID

30. Bonnie and Clyde each own one-third of a fast-food restaurant, and their 13-year-old daughter owns the other shares. Both parents work full-time in the restaurant, but the daughter works infrequently. Neither Bonnie nor Clyde receives a salary during the year, when the taxable income of the S corporation is $180,000. An IRS agent estimates that reasonable salaries for Bonnie, Clyde, and the daughter are $30,000, $35,000, and $10,000, respectively. What adjustments would you expect the IRS to impose upon these taxpayers?

Issue ID

31. Friedman, Inc., an S corporation, holds some highly appreciated land and inventory, and some marketable securities that have declined in value. It anticipates a sale of these assets and a complete liquidation of the company over the next two years. Arnold Schwartz, the CFO, calls you, asking how to treat these transactions. Prepare a tax memo indicating what you told Arnold over the phone.

32. Blue Corporation elects S status effective for calendar year 2006. As of January 1, 2006, Blue holds two assets.

| | Adjusted Basis | Fair Market Value |
|---|---|---|
| Land | $50,000 | $110,000 |
| IBM stock | 55,000 | 40,000 |

Blue sells the land in 2007 for $120,000. Calculate Blue's recognized built-in gain, if any, in 2007.

**EXTENDER**

33. Claude Bergeron sold 1,000 shares of Ditta, Inc., an S corporation located in Concord, North Carolina, for $9,000. He has a stock basis of $107,000 in the shares. Assuming that Claude is single and that he is the original owner of these § 1244 stock shares, calculate the appropriate tax treatment of any gain or loss. If he sold the stock for $201,000, could he obtain a 50% exclusion under § 1202 for one-half of the gain?

**EXTENDER**

Decision Making

34. Gert is the owner of all of the shares of an S corporation. In 2005, Gert is considering receiving a salary of $80,000 from the business. She will pay 7.65% FICA taxes on the salary, and the S corporation will pay the same amount of FICA tax. If Gert reduces her salary to $60,000 and takes an additional $20,000 as a distribution, how much total tax could be saved?

35. One of your clients, Sweet Tea Corporation, is considering electing S status. Both of Sweet Tea's equal shareholders paid $30,000 for their stock. As of the beginning of 2004, Sweet Tea's Subchapter C NOL carryforward is $110,000. Its taxable income projections for the next few years are as follows.

| 2004 | $40,000 |
|------|---------|
| 2005 | 25,000 |
| 2006 | 25,000 |
| 2007 | 25,000 |

Will you counsel Sweet Tea to make the S election?

36. C&C Properties is an S corporation and owns two rental real estate undertakings: Carrot Plaza and Cantaloupe Place. Both properties produce an annual $10,000 operating loss. C&C's Schedule K aggregates the results of the two locations into one number.

Dan and Marta, C&C's two equal shareholders, both hold a $7,000 stock basis in C&C as of the beginning of the year. Marta actively participates in the Cantaloupe location, but not at Carrot. Dan actively participates at neither location. Determine the amount of the available loss pass-throughs for both shareholders.

## Comprehensive Tax Return Problem

37. John Martin (Social Security number 234–10–5214) and Stan Mitchell (Social Security number 244–58–8695) are 55% and 45% owners of Ram, Inc. (74–8265910), a small textile manufacturing company located at 1011 Wright Avenue, Kannapolis, NC 28083. The company's first S election was made on January 1, 1984. The following information was taken from the income statement for 2004.

| | | |
|---|---|---:|
| Other income (active) | $ | 380 |
| Interest income | | 267 |
| Gross sales | | 1,376,214 |
| Beginning inventory | | 7,607 |
| Direct labor | | 303,102 |
| Direct materials purchased | | 278,143 |
| Direct other costs | | 149,356 |
| Ending inventory | | 13,467 |
| Taxes | | 39,235 |
| Contributions to United Fund | | 445 |
| Contributions to Senator Brown's campaign | | 5,000 |
| Fines on illegal activities | | 34 |
| Life insurance premiums (the corporation is the beneficiary) | | 98 |
| Compensation to shareholder/officers (proportionate to ownership) | | 34,934 |
| Salaries and wages | | 62,103 |
| Interest | | 17,222 |
| Repairs | | 16,106 |
| Depreciation | | 16,154 |
| Advertising | | 3,246 |
| Pension plan contributions | | 6,000 |
| Employee benefit programs | | 2,875 |
| Other deductions | | 63,784 |
| Net income | | 384,884 |

A comparative balance sheet appears below.

|  | January 1, 2004 | December 31, 2004 |
|---|---|---|
| Cash | $ 47,840 | $ 61,242 |
| Accounts receivable | 93,100 | 153,136 |
| Inventories | 7,607 | 13,467 |
| Prepaid expenses | 10,333 | 7,582 |
| Loans to shareholders | 313 | 727 |
| Building and trucks | 138,203 | 244,348 |
| Accumulated depreciation | (84,235) | (100,389) |
| Land | 1,809 | 16,513 |
| Life insurance | 11,566 | 18,344 |
|  | $ 226,536 | $ 414,970 |
| Accounts payable | $ 52,404 | $ 82,963 |
| Notes payable (less than one year) | 5,122 | 8,989 |
| Loans from shareholders | 155,751 | 191,967 |
| Notes payable (more than one year) | 21,821 | 33,835 |
| Loan on life insurance | 5,312 | 16,206 |
| Capital stock | 1,003 | 1,003 |
| Paid-in capital | 9,559 | 9,559 |
| Retained earnings (unappropriated) | (8,314) | ? |
| Accumulated adjustments account | –0– | ? |
| Other adjustments account | –0– | ? |
| Treasury stock | (16,122) | (16,122) |
|  | $ 226,536 | $ 414,970 |

Ram's accounting firm provides the follow additional information.

| Dividends paid to shareholders | $290,000 |
|---|---|
| AMT depreciation adjustment | (1,075) |
| AMT interest on private activity bonds preference | 11,070 |

Using the above information, prepare a complete Form 1120S and a Schedule K–1 for John Martin (596 Lane Street, Kannapolis, NC 28083). If any information is missing, make realistic assumptions and list them.

**BRIDGE DISCIPLINE**

1. Using an online research service, determine whether your state:
   a. Allows flow-through treatment for Federal S corporations.
   b. Requires any state-specific form to elect or elect out of S treatment at the state level.
   c. Places any additional withholding tax burdens on out-of-state U.S. shareholders or on non-U.S. shareholders of an S corporation.
   d. Requires any additional information disclosures or compliance deadlines for S corporations operating in the state *other than* to the revenue department (e.g., a report that must be filed with the secretary of state).

## Research Problems

*Note: Solutions to Research Problems can be prepared by using the **RIA Checkpoint® Student Edition** online research product, which is available to accompany this text. It is also possible to prepare solutions to the Research Problems by using tax research materials found in a standard tax library.*

**Decision Making**

**Research Problem 1.** Eel Corporation, in Spivey Corners, North Carolina, has filed a Form 1120S for six years, and the local office of the IRS has sent the company a letter requesting an audit next month. Carrie, who is in charge of tax matters at Eel, cannot find a copy of the original S election, Form 2553.

The original shareholders and officers all agree that a local accountant filed the form, but he passed away last year. Several of the shareholders instruct Carrie to prepare a backdated Form 2553, which they will sign. Carrie could then copy the form and tell the agent that this was a copy of the original Form 2553. What should Carrie do? She estimates that any proposed deficiency would be in the range of $625,000.

*Partial list of research aids:*
§§ 1362(b)(5) and (f).
Rev.Proc. 97–48, 1997–2 C.B. 521.
Ltr.Rul. 9748033.

**Research Problem 2.** Ewing Ballman owned a major league baseball team (the Rattlers), an S corporation. In 1993, Ballman sold 49% of his stock to Avon Fogel. Fogel also bought an option to purchase more of the stock. In 1997, Fogel purchased 2% more of the shares of the team, but later he encountered financial problems. In 2006, Ballman loaned $34 million to the team; then the Rattlers lent the money to Fogel, secured by his stock shares. Fogel's stock was auctioned off, but no acceptable bids were obtained.

Fogel defaulted on the $34 million loan and signed a waiver allowing the Rattlers to take his stock and options. The Rattlers claimed that the collateral had no value and deducted the full amount of the loan. Ballman deducted the losses on his 2007 tax return. Do you agree with Ballman's action?

**Research Problem 3.** Charles, Inc., was a closely held C corporation engaged in the real estate rental business in 2005. The company had $6 million in passive activity losses. In 2006, Charles elected to be taxed as an S corporation, and the company sold a number of rental properties. May these suspended passive activity losses (PAL) be claimed as deductions under § 469(g)(1)(A)?

Recall that § 1371(b)(1) prohibits an S corporation from using any carryforwards from a year in which it was a C corporation. If the PAL deductions are disallowed, may Charles increase its cost basis in the sold property?

**Internet Activity**

*Use the tax resources of the Internet to address the following questions. Do not restrict your search to the World Wide Web, but include a review of newsgroups and general reference materials, practitioner sites and resources, primary sources of the tax law, chat rooms and discussion groups, and other opportunities.*

**Communications**

**Research Problem 4.** Go to the Internet site of a newspaper or business magazine and find a case study of how to start a small business and choose the best tax entity (e.g., C corporation, S corporation, etc.). Summarize your findings in an e-mail to your instructor.

**Research Problem 5.** Go to the sites of both the U.S. Tax Court and the U.S. Court of Appeals for your circuit and find a recent decision involving an S corporation. Prepare a summary of the decision.

**Communications**

**Research Problem 6.** Use a spreadsheet program to graph the growth in the number of S corporation returns filed. Obtain data for these years: 1975, 1980, 1985, 1990, 1995, 2000, and projected 2005. In a note to your instructor, explain the trends that you found in S returns filed.

**Communications**

**Research Problem 7.** Which types of trusts can own S corporation stock? Summarize your findings in a PowerPoint presentation for your classmates.

# Special Business Topics

Part V covers several topics that are relevant to all types of business entities. Business entities operate in both the international arena and state arenas. Therefore, multijurisdictional taxation is addressed from both a multinational business perspective and a multistate business perspective. A very important component of the basic tax model, tax credits, is presented next. This is followed by a discussion of the alternative tax system applicable to certain C corporations, that is, the AMT. Part V concludes with a comparative analysis of the different types of business entities previously discussed. This analysis recognizes the relevance of each of the three life cycle components in selecting a business entity form.

http://wft.swlearning.com

# Multijurisdictional Taxation

## LEARNING OBJECTIVES

*After completing Chapter 12, you should be able to:*

### L O . 1
Recognize the computational and compliance issues that arise when a taxpayer operates in more than one taxing jurisdiction.

### L O . 2
Identify the sources of tax law applicable to a taxpayer operating in more than one country.

### L O . 3
Outline the U.S. tax effects related to the offshore operations of a U.S. taxpayer.

### L O . 4
Describe the tax effects related to the U.S. operations of a non-U.S. taxpayer.

### L O . 5
Identify the sources of tax law applicable to a taxpayer operating in more than one U.S. state.

### L O . 6
Apply computational principles designed for a taxpayer operating in more than one U.S. state.

### L O . 7
Synthesize the international and multistate tax systems and recognize common issues faced by both systems.

http://wft.swlearning.com

## OUTLINE

---

**TAX TALK**

*Don't tax you, don't tax me; tax the fellow behind the tree.*

—*Russell B. Long*

*Don't tax you, don't tax me; tax the companies across the sea.*

—*Dan Rostenkowski*

---

**O**ne of the tax planning principles that has been discussed throughout this text relates to the use of favorable tax jurisdictions—moving income into lower-taxed districts and deductions into higher-taxed ones. Many individuals dream of moving all of their income and wealth to a tax-friendly state or a proverbial island in the tropics, never to be taxed again. This chapter examines the temptations that attract taxpayers to this idea and various ways in which this goal can and cannot be accomplished.

**LO.1**

Recognize the computational and compliance issues that arise when a taxpayer operates in more than one taxing jurisdiction.

# The Multijurisdictional Taxpayer

Companies large and small must deal with the consequences of earning income through activities in different jurisdictions. A small business may have its center of operations in a single city but have customers in many states and countries. Consider the typical U.S. multinational corporation. Its assets, employees, customers, suppliers, lenders, and owners are located in numerous locations, crossing city, county, state, national, and even "virtual" borders.

**EXAMPLE 1**

RobotCo, a corporation created and organized in Delaware, produces and sells robotic manufacturing equipment. It holds its valuable patents and intangible property in Delaware and Bermuda. The company has manufacturing operations in Ireland, Singapore, Germany, Texas, and New Jersey. It has distribution centers in Canada, the United Kingdom, Germany, Hong Kong, Texas, New Jersey, Georgia, California, Illinois, and Arizona. RobotCo's sales force spends time in Europe, Asia, Mexico, Canada, and almost every state in the union. RobotCo's engineers likewise provide technical service to customers wherever they may be located. And in recent years, RobotCo has developed a substantial Web presence.

RobotCo must determine its potential exposure to tax in each of these jurisdictions. Such exposure usually is based on RobotCo's nexus (or economic connection) to the various locations. Unfortunately for all concerned, each of these taxing jurisdictions uses a different

**Bridge to International Law**

Many of the provisions of the U.S. tax law relating to international transactions are thinly disguised extensions of a principle of international law—the ability of sovereign countries to protect the safety and privacy of their citizens abroad.

For instance, U.S. tax auditors often have difficulty obtaining or reviewing the documentation supporting deductions claimed by U.S. taxpayers operating overseas. Banking, credit card, and other records that are available (in the course of business or forcibly by summons) for strictly U.S. transactions are not available once those same transactions cross national borders.

How could the U.S. tax base include rental and royalty income of a U.S. investor operating through a corporation in another country when property ownership and taxation records are not available for substantiation or audit outside the country of the investment? Perhaps this explains why the U.S. tax base typically excludes such items.

Conversely, when the taxing agencies of multiple countries are allowed by law to trade among themselves information about business operations and taxpayers, the fairness and completeness of the taxing process may improve. But such lengthening of the reach of the taxing authorities results from diplomatic negotiations among the countries, not from the passage of legislation.

---

taxing system and methods, imposes taxes under differing structures, and even defines the tax base differently. How does RobotCo divide its income among the various jurisdictions that want a piece of the tax pie, determine its tax costs, mitigate any potential double taxation, and file the appropriate information returns with this diverse set of taxing authorities? Such questions and more must be addressed by modern-day businesses. ■

Thousands of state and local jurisdictions are involved in the taxation of interstate transactions through income, property, sales, or other taxes. State and local taxes make up over one-third of all taxes collected in the United States. Global trade also represents a major portion of the U.S. economy. In recent years, U.S. exports of goods and services have averaged over $1 trillion a year, with imports reaching $1.5 trillion. As of the beginning of 2004, U.S. companies had direct investments abroad exceeding $2 trillion, and foreign companies had invested $1.6 trillion in U.S. businesses. Hundreds of countries and many more political subdivisions participated in the taxation of these transactions. These interstate and international trade flows, along with cross-state and cross-country investments, create significant Federal, state, and local tax consequences for both U.S. and foreign entities.

# U.S. Taxation of Multinational Transactions

Cross-country transactions create the need for special tax considerations for both the United States and its trading partners. From a U.S. perspective, international tax laws should promote the global competitiveness of U.S. enterprises and at the same time protect the tax revenue base of the United States. These two objectives sometimes conflict, however. The need to deal with both objectives contributes to the complexity of the rules governing the U.S. taxation of cross-border transactions.

■ **FIGURE 12–1**
U.S. Taxation of International
Transactions

|  | **U.S. Person** | **Foreign Person** |
|---|---|---|
| **U.S.-Source Income** | Domestic taxation only | "Inbound" taxation |
| **Foreign-Source Income** | "Outbound" taxation | Limited U.S. authority to tax |

**EXAMPLE 2**

U.S. persons engage in activities outside the United States for many different reasons. Consider two U.S. corporations that have established sales subsidiaries in foreign countries. Dedalus, Inc., operates in Germany, a high-tax country, because customers demand local attention from sales agents. Mulligan, Inc., operates in the Cayman Islands, a tax haven country, simply to shift income outside the United States. U.S. tax law must fairly address both situations with the same law. ■

U.S. international tax provisions are concerned primarily with two types of potential taxpayers: U.S. persons earning income from outside the United States and non-U.S. persons earning income from inside the United States.[1] U.S. persons earning income only from inside the United States do not create any international tax issues and are taxed under the purely domestic provisions of the Internal Revenue Code. Foreign persons earning income from outside the United States are not within the taxing jurisdiction of the United States (unless this income is somehow directly connected to U.S. operations).

The U.S. taxation of international transactions can be organized in terms of "outbound" and "inbound" taxation. **Outbound taxation** refers to the U.S. taxation of foreign-source income earned by U.S. taxpayers. **Inbound taxation** refers to the U.S. taxation of U.S.-source income earned by foreign taxpayers. Figure 12–1 summarizes these concepts.

## LO.2

Identify the sources of tax law applicable to a taxpayer operating in more than one country.

## SOURCES OF LAW

U.S. individuals and companies operating across national borders are subject to both U.S. law and the laws of the other jurisdictions in which they operate or invest. Accordingly, the source of law depends on the nature of a taxpayer's connection with a particular country. For U.S. persons, the Internal Revenue Code addresses the tax consequences of earning income anywhere in the world. However, U.S. persons must also comply with the local tax law of the other nations in which they operate. For non-U.S. persons, U.S. statutory law is relevant to income they earn that is connected to U.S. income-producing activities, whether those activities involve a passive investment or an active trade or business. Whether non-U.S. persons are also subject to potential tax in their home countries on their U.S. income depends on their own local tax law.

It is difficult for the United States (or any country) to craft local tax laws that equitably address all of the potential issues that arise when two countries attempt to tax the same income. Furthermore, any uncertainty as to tax consequences can be an impediment to global business investment. Consequently, countries enter into **income tax treaties** with each other to provide more certainty to taxpayers.

Tax treaties are the result of specific negotiations with each treaty partner, so each treaty is unique. Nevertheless, all tax treaties are organized in the same way

---

[1]The term "person" includes an individual, corporation, partnership, trust, estate, or association. § 7701(a)(1). The terms "domestic" and "foreign" are defined in §§ 7701(a)(4) and (5).

---

## TAX FACT

### U.S. INCOME TAX TREATIES IN FORCE

The United States has entered into income tax treaties with the following nations:

| | | | |
|---|---|---|---|
| Australia | France | Latvia | Russia |
| Austria | Germany | Lithuania | Slovak Republic |
| Barbados | Greece | Luxembourg | Slovenia |
| Belgium | Hungary | Mexico | South Africa |
| Canada | Iceland | Morocco | Spain |
| China | India | Netherlands | Sweden |
| Commonwealth of | Indonesia | New Zealand | Switzerland |
|     Independent States* | Ireland | Norway | Thailand |
| Cyprus | Israel | Pakistan | Trinidad and Tobago |
| Czech Republic | Italy | Philippines | Tunisia |
| Denmark | Jamaica | Poland | Turkey |
| Egypt | Japan | Portugal | United Kingdom |
| Estonia | Kazakhstan | Romania | Venezuela |
| Finland | Korea | | |

*The income tax treaty between the United States and the former Soviet Union applies to the countries of Armenia, Azerbaijan, Belarus, Georgia, Kyrgyzstan, Moldova, Tajikistan, Turkmenistan, Ukraine, and Uzbekistan. The Commonwealth of Independent States is an association of many of the former constituent republics of the Soviet Union.

---

and address similar issues. For example, all treaties include provisions regarding the taxation of investment income, business profits from a **permanent establishment (PE),** personal service income, and exceptions for certain persons (e.g., athletes, entertainers, students, and teachers). Treaty provisions generally override the treatment otherwise called for under the Internal Revenue Code or foreign tax statutes.

Permanent establishment (PE) is an important concept that is defined in all income tax treaties. A person has a PE within a country when its activities within that country rise beyond a minimal level. Tax treaties outline the activities that create a PE, including an office, plant, or other fixed place of business. Treaties also specify specific activities that do not create a PE (e.g., maintaining goods in a warehouse or a temporary construction project). Once a person has a PE within a country, the business profits associated with the PE become subject to tax in that country.

**EXAMPLE 3**

Amelia, Inc., a U.S. corporation, sells boating supplies to customers in the United States and Canada. Amelia has no assets in Canada. All Canadian sales transactions are conducted via the Internet or telephone from Amelia's Florida office. Because Amelia does not have any assets in Canada or conduct any activities within Canada, it does not have a Canadian PE. Consequently, Canada does not impose an income tax on the profit associated with Amelia's Canadian sales. However, if Amelia opens a sales office in Canada, a PE will exist, and Canada will tax the profits associated with the PE. ■

Although the United States has entered into more than 50 income tax treaties, many jurisdictions where U.S. taxpayers operate are not covered by a treaty. Where there is no tax treaty, the more subjective test of whether a person is "engaged in a trade or business" within a country replaces the PE determination. Both the PE concept and the engaged in a trade or business concept are closely related to the determination of whether a person has nexus within a jurisdiction for state and local tax purposes.

## Treaty Shopping

**FRAMEWORK FOCUS: TAX RATE**

STRATEGY ➤ AVOID DOUBLE TAXATION.

U.S. taxpayers with operations in countries that do not have a treaty with the United States may attempt to arrange their activities to take advantage of other countries' tax treaties. In some cases, structuring a company's global operations in this way is simply good tax planning. In other cases, attempts to benefit from tax treaties constitute unwarranted treaty shopping.

USCo, a domestic corporation, owns subsidiaries in Country A and Country B. The U.S. parent wants to obtain a loan from its A subsidiary. The United States does not have a tax treaty with A, but it does have a tax treaty with B. Countries A and B have a tax treaty with each other. The home tax laws of all three countries impose a withholding tax on payments of interest to persons outside the country. However, the existing tax treaties exempt interest payments from withholding.

If the U.S. parent borrows money directly from its A subsidiary, any interest paid to the subsidiary is subject to a 30 percent withholding tax under the Internal Revenue Code (loan

option 1). If the U.S. parent instead borrows money from its B subsidiary, any interest paid to the subsidiary is not subject to withholding under the treaty (loan option 2). Thus, USCo's choice of obtaining the loan from its A subsidiary or its B subsidiary possesses major tax consequences. Making such decisions is part of an appropriate global tax plan.

Alternatively, the U.S. parent could use the B subsidiary as a mere conduit by funneling A funds to B via a loan and then having the B subsidiary lend these funds to the U.S. parent (loan option 3). In this case, however, the ability of the U.S. parent to benefit from the tax treaty with B may be restricted by the provisions of the treaty itself or by U.S. tax law. The United States is likely to take an anti-treaty-shopping position. In such case, it would ignore the intermediate payment to the B subsidiary and treat the interest as being paid directly to the A subsidiary, resulting in a 30 percent withholding tax.

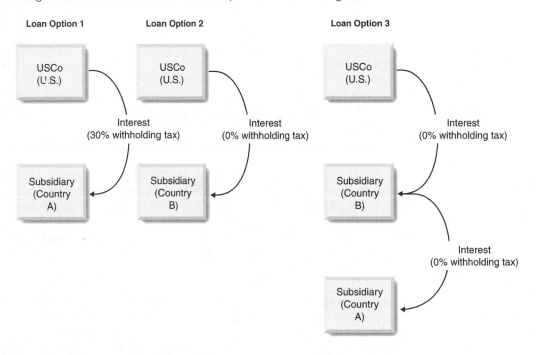

**LO.3**

Outline the U.S. tax effects related to the offshore operations of a U.S. taxpayer.

## TAX ISSUES

**Authority to Tax.** The United States taxes the worldwide income of U.S. taxpayers.[2] The United States claims the right to tax all of a U.S. person's income because of the protection of U.S. law provided to a person connected to the United States through citizenship, residency, or place of organization.

Because non-U.S. governments may also tax some of the U.S. person's income when it is earned within their borders, U.S. taxpayers may be subjected to double taxation. There are two broad methods of mitigating this double taxation problem. Under the territorial approach, a country simply exempts from tax the income derived from sources outside its borders. Some European and Asian countries have adopted this approach.[3] The second approach, and the one adopted by the United States, is to provide a **foreign tax credit** against home country taxes for taxes paid to other countries on the same income. The United States allows its taxpayers to reduce their U.S. tax liability by some or all of the foreign income taxes paid on income earned outside the United States.

**EXAMPLE 4**

Gator Enterprises, Inc., a U.S. corporation, operates a manufacturing branch in Italy because of customer demand in Italy, local availability of raw materials, and the high cost of shipping finished goods. This branch income is taxed in the United States as part of Gator's worldwide income, but it is also taxed in Italy. Without the availability of a foreign tax credit to mitigate this double taxation, Gator Enterprises would suffer an excessive tax burden and could not compete with local Italian companies. ■

The United States does adopt the territorial approach in taxing foreign persons. Such "inbound" taxpayers generally are subject to tax only on income earned within U.S. borders.

**EXAMPLE 5**

Purdie, Ltd., a corporation based in the United Kingdom, operates in the United States. Although not a U.S. person, Purdie is taxed in the United States on its U.S.-source business income. If Purdie, Ltd., could operate free of U.S. tax, its U.S.-based competitors would face a serious disadvantage. ■

**Income Sourcing.** Determining the source of net income is a critical component in calculating the U.S. tax consequences to both U.S. and foreign persons. A number of specific provisions contained in §§ 861 through 865 address the income-sourcing rules for all types of income, including interest, dividends, rents, royalties, services, and sales of assets. Although sometimes complex and subject to various special exceptions, these sourcing rules generally assign income to a geographic source based on the location where the economic activity producing the income took place. In some cases, this relationship is clear, and in others the connection is more obscure.

**EXAMPLE 6**

Wickless, Inc., a U.S. corporation, provides scuba diving lessons to customers in Florida and in the Bahamas. These services are sourced based on the place where the activity is performed. The services performed in Florida are U.S.-source income, and those performed in the Bahamas are foreign-source income. Because Wickless, Inc., is a U.S. person, all the income, U.S. and foreign, is subject to U.S. taxation. But the foreign-source portion is important in determining any available foreign tax credits for Wickless. ■

---

[2]Gross income for a U.S. person includes all income from whatever source derived. "Source" in this context means not only type of income (e.g., wages or interest) but geographic source as well (e.g., the United States or Belgium). § 61.

[3]In some cases, countries allow the territorial exemption from home country taxation only if the income has been subject to tax in another country. Other countries, however, exempt such income even if no source country tax is imposed.

### EXPORT INCENTIVES FADE AWAY AFTER 2004

To improve the U.S. balance of trade, Congress has used various export tax incentives to encourage exports of U.S.-produced property. In the late 1970s, Congress created the domestic international sales corporation (DISC) provisions, allowing a DISC to defer the tax on a portion of its export income until actual repatriation of the earnings. After the General Agreement on Tariffs and Trade (GATT) charged that the DISC provisions were a prohibited *export subsidy,* the provisions were curtailed. As an alternative, in 1984 the foreign sales corporation (FSC) provisions (§§ 921–927) were enacted to provide similar tax incentives to U.S. exporters while appeasing the GATT members. FSCs were not allowed to defer the tax on export income. Instead, a certain percentage of export income was permanently exempt from U.S. taxation. In 2000, the United States was forced to repeal the FSC provisions after the World Trade Organization (WTO) found that the FSC benefits constituted an illegal export subsidy. Congress replaced the FSC with a benefit that excluded extraterritorial income from U.S. taxation.

The new extraterritorial income (ETI) regime preserved the basic incentives provided by the FSC rules. Consequently, it is not surprising that the WTO found that the ETI provisions also violated its rules. After losing its appeal to the WTO, the United States repealed the ETI rules in October 2004, but provided a transition rule that allows partial ETI benefits for 2005 and 2006. Congress did not replace the ETI benefit with a new tax benefit for U.S. exporters. Instead, it created a new broad-based "domestic production deduction" for U.S. manufacturers and certain other domestic producers equal to 9 percent of the taxpayer's *qualified production activities income* subject to several limitations. The deduction is phased in, beginning with a 3 percent deduction for tax years beginning in 2005 or 2006, a 6 percent deduction for tax years beginning in 2007, 2008, or 2009, and a 9 percent deduction for tax years thereafter. This manufacturers' deduction replacement for ETI is no longer an "international tax" issue, as the deduction does not require exporting or any other activity outside the United States.

**EXAMPLE 7**

Brown, Inc., a U.S. corporation, receives dividend income from Takeda Corporation, a Japanese corporation, based on its ownership of Takeda common stock. Brown purchased the stock in the United States and receives all payments in the United States. At first glance, it appears that all of the activities related to earning the dividend income take place in the United States. Nevertheless, the dividend income is treated as foreign source because it is paid by a foreign corporation.[4] ■

In addition to sourcing income, the U.S. rules require taxpayers to assign deductions to U.S.- or foreign-source categories. Deductions that are directly related to an activity or property are first allocated to classes of income to which they directly relate. This is followed by an apportionment between the U.S. and foreign groupings using some reasonable basis (e.g., revenue, gross profit, assets, units sold, time spent). If a deduction is not definitely related to any class of gross income, the deduction is first assigned to all classes of gross income and then apportioned between U.S.- and foreign-source income.

---

[4]Section 861(a)(2) establishes that if a foreign corporation earns significant U.S.-source income, a portion of the dividend could be treated as U.S.-source income. After 2004, though, the U.S.-source portion is exempt from any U.S. withholding tax.

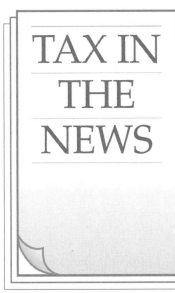

## TAX IN THE NEWS

### SOURCING INCOME IN CYBERSPACE

The use of the Internet in more consumer and business transactions is posing problems for the taxing authorities. Consumers purchase books, music, clothing, and food from Internet retailers. Businesses negotiate with suppliers via online auctions of products and services. Consultants provide services to their clients over the Web. Very few transactions do not have a counterpart that takes place in cyberspace. The existing income-sourcing rules were developed long before the existence of the Internet, and taxing authorities are finding it challenging to apply these rules to Internet transactions.

Where does a sale take place when the Web server is in the Cayman Islands, the seller is in Singapore, and the customer is in Texas? Where is a service performed when all activities take place over the Web? These questions and more must be answered by the United States and its trading partners as the Internet economy grows in size and importance.

**EXAMPLE 8**

Ace, Inc., a domestic corporation, has $2 million of gross income and a $50,000 expense, all related to real estate sales and rental activities. The expense is allocated and apportioned using gross income as a basis.

|  | Gross Income | | | Apportionment | |
|---|---|---|---|---|---|
|  | **Foreign** | **U.S.** | **Allocation** | **Foreign** | **U.S.** |
| Sales | $1,000,000 | $500,000 | $37,500* | $25,000 | $12,500** |
| Rentals | 400,000 | 100,000 | 12,500 | 10,000 | 2,500*** |
|  |  |  | $50,000 | $35,000 | $15,000 |

  *$50,000 × ($1,500,000/$2,000,000).
 **$37,500 × ($500,000/$1,500,000).
***$12,500 × ($100,000/$500,000).

If Ace could show that $45,000 of the expense was directly related to sales income, the $45,000 would be allocated directly to that class of gross income, with the remainder allocated and apportioned between U.S. and foreign source ratably based on gross income. ∎

Many deductions may be allocated and apportioned based on any reasonable method the taxpayer chooses.[5] However, the U.S. tax rules impose a specific method for certain types of deductions, including interest and research and experimentation expenses. Interest expense is allocated and apportioned based on the theory that money is fungible. For example, if a taxpayer borrows to support its manufacturing activity, this frees up other funds for use to support its investment activities. Accordingly, the tax rules require that interest expense be allocated and apportioned to all the activities and property of the taxpayer, regardless of the specific purpose for incurring the debt on which interest is paid. Taxpayers must allocate and apportion interest expense on the basis of asset location, using either the fair market value or the tax book value of the assets.

---

[5]Reg. § 1.861–8.

Fisher, Inc., a domestic corporation, generates both U.S.-source and foreign-source gross income for the current year. Fisher's assets (tax book value) are as follows.

| | |
|---|---:|
| Assets generating U.S.-source income | $18,000,000 |
| Assets generating foreign-source income | 5,000,000 |
| | $23,000,000 |

Fisher incurs interest expense of $800,000 for the current year. Using the tax book value method, interest expense is apportioned to foreign-source income as follows.

$$\frac{\$5,000,000 \text{ (foreign assets)}}{\$23,000,000 \text{ (total assets)}} \times \$800,000 \text{ (interest expense)} = \$173,913. \ \blacksquare$$

**PLANNING STRATEGIES**

## Sourcing Income from Sales of Inventory

**FRAMEWORK FOCUS: TAX RATE**

**STRATEGY ➤ CONTROL THE CHARACTER OF INCOME AND DEDUCTIONS.**

Generally, income from the sale of personal property is sourced according to the residence of the seller under § 865. Several important exceptions exist for inventory. Income from the sale of purchased inventory is sourced in the country in which the sale takes place under the "title passage" rule. This rule provides the taxpayer with flexibility with regard to sourcing and allows for the creation of zero-taxed foreign-source income.

USCo, a domestic corporation, purchases inventory for resale from unrelated parties and sells the inventory to customers in the United States and Brazil. If title on the Brazilian sales passes in the United States (i.e., risks of loss shift to the Brazilian customers at the shipping point), the inventory income is U.S. source. If title passes outside the United States (e.g., at the customer's warehouse in Brazil), the inventory income is foreign source. Although the Code identifies the income item as foreign source, this income likely is not subject to any Brazilian tax because USCo has no employees, assets, or activities in Brazil. Although the income is subject

to U.S. tax in either case (as it represents taxable income to USCo), in the latter case USCo has generated foreign-source income with no corresponding foreign income tax. This will prove very useful in managing USCo's ability to use foreign tax credits, as discussed later in this chapter.

When a taxpayer both produces and sells inventory, the income is apportioned between the country of production and the country of sale. Taxpayers often use a 50–50 allocation method as allowed by § 863(b), where 50 percent of the profits from the sale are automatically assigned to the location of the production assets, and 50 percent of the profits are assigned to the location where title passes.

Assume that USCo manufactures inventory in its Texas plant and sells the inventory to customers in Mexico. Regardless of the actual economic profit relationship between the manufacturing and selling activities, 50 percent of the profit on the Mexican sales can be assigned to foreign-source income by simply passing title outside the United States.

**The Foreign Tax Credit.**   As discussed earlier, the United States retains the right to tax its citizens and residents on their worldwide taxable income. This approach can result in double taxation, presenting a potential problem to U.S. persons who operate abroad. To reduce the possibility of double taxation, Congress created the foreign tax credit (FTC). A qualified taxpayer is allowed a tax credit for foreign income taxes paid or accrued. The credit is a dollar-for-dollar reduction of U.S. income tax liability. For the most recent years data are available, corporations filing U.S. tax returns claimed $41 billion in FTCs, and individuals claimed $6.3 billion in FTCs. Income receipts on U.S. direct investment abroad were $164.7 billion. Without the benefit of the FTC, much of this income would have been subject to double taxation.

○ **T A X   F A C T**

## INCOME SUBJECT TO U.S. TAX, FOREIGN-SOURCE TAXABLE INCOME, CURRENT-YEAR FOREIGN TAXES, AND FOREIGN TAX CREDIT: TAX YEARS 1994–1999

The following table shows some of the most recent data available on the foreign tax credit. Amounts are in millions of dollars.

| Tax Year | Number of U.S. Corporation Returns | Income Subject to U.S. Tax | U.S. Income Tax before Credits | | Foreign-Source Taxable Income (Less Loss) | | Current-Year Foreign Taxes | | Foreign Tax Credit Claimed | |
|---|---|---|---|---|---|---|---|---|---|---|
| | | | Amount | As a Percentage of Income Subject to U.S. Tax | Amount | As a Percentage of Income Subject to U.S. Tax | Amount | As a Percentage of Foreign-Source Taxable Income | Amount | As a Percentage of U.S. Income Tax before Credits |
| 1994 | 7,199 | $255,439 | $ 90,786 | 35.5% | $101,521 | 39.7% | $26,470 | 26.1% | $25,419 | 28.0% |
| 1995 | 6,710 | 303,308 | 107,996 | 35.6 | 120,518 | 39.7 | 30,930 | 25.7 | 30,416 | 28.2 |
| 1996 | 6,100 | 370,049 | 130,748 | 35.3 | 150,826 | 40.8 | 41,177 | 27.3 | 40,255 | 30.8 |
| 1997 | 6,569 | 410,126 | 144,779 | 35.3 | 157,989 | 38.5 | 45,080 | 28.5 | 42,223 | 29.2 |
| 1998 | 5,927 | 377,129 | 132,740 | 35.2 | 147,129 | 35.9 | 47,576 | 32.3 | 37,338 | 28.1 |
| 1999 | 5,789 | 385,832 | 135,855 | 35.2 | 165,713 | 42.9 | 41,309 | 24.9 | 38,271 | 28.2 |

**Source:** IRS, *Statistics of Income Bulletin*, Fall 2003. Publication 1136 (Rev. 12–2003), Figure F.

**EXAMPLE 10**

Caulkin Tools, Inc., a U.S. corporation, has a branch operation in Mexico from which it earns taxable income of $750,000 for the current year. Caulkin pays income tax of $150,000 on these earnings to the Mexican tax authorities. Caulkin must also include the $750,000 in gross income for U.S. tax purposes. Before considering the FTC, Caulkin owes $255,000 in U.S. income taxes on this foreign-source income. Thus, total taxes on the $750,000 could equal $405,000 ($150,000 + $255,000), a 54% effective rate. But Caulkin takes an FTC of $150,000 against its U.S. tax liability on the foreign-source income. Caulkin's total taxes on the $750,000 now are $255,000 ($150,000 + $105,000), a 34% effective rate. ■

The FTC is elective for any particular tax year. If the taxpayer does not "choose" to take the FTC, § 164 allows a deduction for foreign taxes paid or incurred. A taxpayer cannot take a credit and a deduction for the same foreign income taxes, and in most situations the FTC is more valuable to the taxpayer.

U.S. taxpayers may claim FTCs for foreign taxes they pay directly or through withholding as so-called direct credits. In addition, U.S. corporate taxpayers may claim FTCs for foreign taxes paid indirectly. If a U.S. corporation operates in a foreign country through a branch, the direct credit is available for foreign taxes paid. If, however, a U.S. corporation operates in a country through a foreign subsidiary, the direct credit is not available for foreign taxes paid by the foreign corporation. An indirect or **deemed-paid credit** is available to U.S. corporate taxpayers that receive actual or constructive dividends from foreign corporations that have paid foreign income taxes.[6] These foreign taxes are deemed paid by the corporate shareholders

---

[6]U.S. corporations must meet certain minimum ownership requirements under § 902 to claim a deemed-paid credit.

in the same proportion as the dividends actually or constructively received bear to the foreign corporation's post-1986 undistributed E & P.

$$\text{Deemed-paid credit} = \frac{\text{Actual or constructive dividend}}{\text{Post-1986 undistributed E \& P}} \times \frac{\text{Post-1986}}{\text{foreign taxes}}$$

If a U.S. taxpayer claims a deemed-paid credit, § 78 requires the corporation to *gross up* (add to income) the dividend income by the amount of the deemed-paid credit.

---

**EXAMPLE 11**

Wren, Inc., a domestic corporation, owns 50% of Finch, Inc., a foreign corporation. Wren receives a dividend of $120,000 from Finch. Finch paid foreign taxes of $500,000 on post-1986 E & P, which totals $1.2 million. Wren's deemed-paid foreign taxes for FTC purposes are $50,000.

| | |
|---|---|
| Cash dividend from Finch | $120,000 |
| Deemed-paid foreign taxes | |
| [($120,000/$1,200,000) × $500,000] | 50,000 |
| Gross income to Wren | $170,000 |

Wren includes $170,000 in gross income for the year. As a result of the dividend received, Wren can claim a credit for the $50,000 in deemed-paid foreign taxes. ∎

---

The United States does not automatically grant an FTC for all foreign taxes paid, and there are limits on the amount of foreign taxes that can be taken as a credit. First, only foreign *income* taxes are potentially creditable. Second, the FTC allowed in any tax year is limited to the U.S. tax imposed on the foreign-source income included on the U.S. tax return.[7] Thus, taxpayers are allowed a credit for the lesser of the foreign income taxes paid or accrued, or the following limitation.

$$\text{FTC limit} = \frac{\text{Foreign-source taxable income}}{\text{Worldwide taxable income}} \times \text{U.S. tax liability before FTC}$$

Worldwide taxable income is the total taxable income reported on the taxpayer's U.S. tax return, not the total worldwide income of a group of related domestic and foreign entities. Any potential FTCs disallowed because of the FTC limitation may be carried back one year or forward 10 years, subject to the FTC limits in those tax years.

---

**EXAMPLE 12**

Lassaline, Inc., a domestic corporation, invests in the bonds of non-U.S. corporations. Lassaline's worldwide taxable income for the tax year is $1.2 million, consisting of $1 million of profits from U.S. sales and $200,000 of interest income from foreign sources. Foreign taxes of $90,000 were withheld on these interest payments. Lassaline's U.S. tax before the FTC is $420,000. Its FTC is limited to $70,000 [($200,000/$1,200,000) × $420,000]. Thus, Lassaline's net U.S. tax liability is $350,000 after allowing the $70,000 FTC. The remaining $20,000 of FTCs may be carried back or forward. ∎

---

[7]Sections 901, 902, and 903 provide definitions of creditable foreign taxes. Section 904 contains the FTC limitation rules.

## Utilizing the Foreign Tax Credit

**FRAMEWORK FOCUS: TAX CREDITS**

STRATEGY ➤ MAXIMIZE TAX CREDITS.

The FTC limitation can prevent the total amount of foreign taxes paid in high-tax jurisdictions from being credited. Taxpayers can overcome this problem by generating additional foreign-source income that is subject to no, or low, foreign taxation. A U.S. taxpayer's ability to use FTCs is directly related to its level of foreign-source income relative to its total taxable income. To the extent that a U.S. taxpayer can keep the average tax rate on its foreign-source income at or below the U.S. tax rate on such income, the foreign taxes will be fully creditable. Consequently, combining high- and low-tax foreign-source income is an important planning objective.

Compare the two situations at the right where a U.S. corporation's FTC situations differ depending on its ability to mix high- and low-taxed income. In the first scenario, the corporation has only $500,000 of highly taxed foreign-source income. In the second scenario, the corporation also has $100,000 of low-taxed foreign-source interest income.

|  | Only Highly Taxed Income | With Low-Taxed Interest Income |
|---|---|---|
| Foreign-source income | $500,000 | $600,000 |
| Foreign taxes | 275,000 | 280,000 |
| U.S.-source income | 700,000 | 700,000 |
| U.S. taxes (34%) | 408,000 | 442,000 |
| FTC limitation | 170,000* | 204,000** |

*($500,000/$1,200,000) × $408,000.
**($600,000/$1,300,000) × $442,000.

The corporation's actual foreign taxes increase by only $5,000 ($280,000 versus $275,000), but its FTC limitation increases by $34,000 (from $170,000 to $204,000). The ability to "cross-credit" high- and low-taxed foreign income is available only when the foreign-source income is all classified within the same category.

To limit the ability of U.S. taxpayers to cross-credit foreign taxes, the FTC rules provide for several **separate foreign tax credit limitation categories** (or baskets). In any tax year, taxpayers are allowed to credit the lesser of foreign income taxes paid or accrued or the FTC limit *within each separate basket*. The separate FTC limitation categories for different types of income each use this same basic FTC limitation formula. The separate limitation categories affect the amount of FTC that can be taken by generally segregating income subject to a high level of foreign tax from lower-taxed foreign income.

Figure 12–2 summarizes the current separate income categories. Any income that does not fit into one of the specific categories falls into the general (or residual) category. The general limitation basket is where most active income is classified and provides the best opportunity for combining high- and low-taxed foreign-source income. For tax years beginning after 2006, only two baskets exist: passive income and all other (general). Any FTC carryforwards into post-2006 years will be assigned to one of these two categories.

**EXAMPLE 13**

BenCo, Inc., a U.S. corporation, has a foreign branch in Germany that earns taxable income of $1.5 million from manufacturing operations and $600,000 from passive activities. BenCo also earns German-source high withholding tax interest of $100,000. BenCo pays foreign taxes of $600,000 (40%), $300,000 (50%), and $15,000 (15%), respectively, on this foreign-source income. The corporation also earns $4 million of U.S.-source taxable income, resulting in worldwide taxable income of $6.2 million. BenCo's U.S. taxes before the FTC are $2,108,000 (at 34%). The following table illustrates the effect of the separate limitation baskets on cross-crediting in pre-2007 years.

■ **FIGURE 12–2**
Foreign Tax Credit: Separate
Income Limitations for Tax Years
Beginning before 2007

**Note:** DISCs are domestic international sales corporations; FSCs are foreign sales corporations.

| Separate Foreign Income Category | Net Taxable Amount | Foreign Taxes | U.S. Tax before FTC at 34% | FTC Allowed with Separate Limits |
|---|---|---|---|---|
| Manufacturing | $1,500,000 | $600,000 | $510,000 | $510,000 |
| Passive | 600,000 | 300,000 | 204,000 | 204,000 |
| High withholding tax interest | 100,000 | 15,000 | 34,000 | 15,000 |
| Total | $2,200,000 | $915,000 | $748,000 | $729,000 |

Without the separate limitation provisions, the FTC would be the lesser of (1) $915,000 foreign taxes or (2) $748,000 share of U.S. tax [($2,200,000/$6,200,000) × $2,108,000]. The separate limitation provisions reduce the FTC by $19,000 ($748,000 versus $729,000). The effect of the separate limitation rules is that the foreign-source income taxed at the foreign tax rates of 40% and 50% cannot be aggregated with foreign-source income taxed at only 15%. The reduction in the number of baskets in post-2006 years will be helpful to BenCo. ■

*Find more information on this topic at our Web site: **http://wft-entities.swlearning.com**.*

**Controlled Foreign Corporations.** Foreign corporations—even those controlled by U.S. shareholders—generally are not included in a U.S. consolidated income tax return. Consequently, in the absence of some other provision, the income of a foreign corporation is included on the U.S. shareholder's U.S. income tax return only when dividend income is received. To minimize current U.S. tax liability, taxpayers often attempt to defer the recognition of taxable income. One way to do this is to shift the income-generating activity to a foreign entity where the income earned will not be subject to U.S. tax until repatriated.

For example, a U.S. person can create a foreign holding company to own the stock of foreign operating affiliates or intangible assets, such as patents and trademarks. Thus, the income generated by these foreign holdings would escape current U.S. taxation. A non-U.S. corporation can also be used to accumulate income

---

**●T A X   F A C T**

## TAXING THE EARNINGS OF CONTROLLED FOREIGN CORPORATIONS: A TALE OF TWO JFKS

The current Subpart F regime had its genesis as the centerpiece of a major reform of U.S. international tax rules in 1962. President John F. Kennedy and his administration sought to limit the ability of U.S. companies to easily shift income out of the United States into lower tax countries with the creation of the Subpart F regime. Over 40 years later, another JFK wanted to further limit the ability of U.S. corporations to move income offshore. Presidential candidate John F. Kerry made tightening the Subpart F rules a major plank in his 2004 campaign.

---

from sales or service activities by acting as an intermediary between the U.S. corporation and an offshore customer. The foreign subsidiary corporation would be used to purchase goods from the U.S. parent or domestic affiliates and then resell the goods to foreign customers or provide services on behalf of the U.S. parent or affiliates.

In some cases, the use of intermediate foreign subsidiaries is based on a substantive business purpose. In other cases, they are employed only to reduce tax costs. Because of this potential for abuse, Congress has enacted various provisions to limit the availability of deferral.

The most important of these antideferral provisions are those affecting **controlled foreign corporations (CFCs)**. Subpart F, §§ 951–964 of the Code, provides that certain types of "tainted" income generated by CFCs are currently included in gross income by the U.S. shareholders without regard to actual distributions. U.S. shareholders must include in gross income their pro rata share of **Subpart F income**. This rule applies to U.S. shareholders who own stock in the corporation on the last day of the tax year or on the last day the foreign corporation is a CFC.

**EXAMPLE 14**

Jordan, Ltd., a calendar year foreign corporation, is a CFC for the entire tax year. Taylor, Inc., a U.S. corporation, owns 60% of Jordan's one class of stock for the entire year. Jordan earned $100,000 of Subpart F income for the year and makes no actual distributions during the year. Taylor, a calendar year taxpayer, includes $60,000 in gross income as a constructive dividend for the tax year. To the extent Jordan has paid any foreign income taxes, Taylor may claim a deemed-paid foreign tax credit for the portion of the foreign taxes related to the $60,000 constructive dividend.  ■

A CFC is any foreign corporation in which more than 50 percent of the total combined voting power of all classes of stock entitled to vote or the total value of the stock of the corporation is owned by U.S. shareholders on any day during the taxable year of the foreign corporation. The foreign subsidiaries of most multinational U.S. parent corporations are CFCs.

For purposes of determining if a foreign corporation is a CFC, a **U.S. shareholder** is defined as a U.S. person who owns, or is considered to own, 10 percent or more of the total combined voting power of all classes of voting stock of the foreign corporation. Stock owned directly, indirectly, and constructively is counted. Indirect ownership involves stock held through a foreign entity, such as a foreign corporation, foreign partnership, or foreign trust. This stock is considered to be actually owned proportionately by the shareholders, partners, or beneficiaries. Constructive ownership rules, with certain modifications, apply in determining if a U.S. person is a U.S. shareholder, in determining whether a foreign corporation is a CFC, and for certain related-party provisions of Subpart F.

A U.S. shareholder of a CFC does not necessarily lose the ability to defer U.S. taxation of income earned by the CFC. Only certain income earned by the CFC triggers immediate U.S. taxation as a constructive dividend. This tainted income, referred to as Subpart F income, can be characterized as income that is easily shifted or has little or no economic connection with the CFC's country of incorporation. Examples include:

- Passive income such as interest, dividends, rents, and royalties.
- Sales income where neither the manufacturing activity nor the customer base is in the CFC's country and either the property supplier or the customer is related to the CFC.
- Service income where the CFC is providing services on behalf of its U.S. owners outside the CFC's country.

**EXAMPLE 15**

Collins, Inc., a domestic corporation, sells $1 million of its products to customers in Europe. All manufacturing and sales activities take place in the United States. Collins has no employees, assets, or operations in Europe and thus is not subject to income tax in any European jurisdiction.

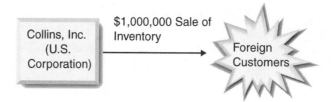

Collins reported the following tax consequences from these inventory sales.

| | |
|---|---|
| Sales revenue | $1,000,000 |
| Cost of goods sold | (600,000) |
| Net income | $ 400,000 |
| U.S. tax at 35% | $ 140,000 |

Assume that Collins instead creates a wholly owned foreign subsidiary in the Cayman Islands, where no income taxes are imposed on corporate income. Collins then sells the inventory to the subsidiary at an intercompany transfer price of $700,000, and the subsidiary sells the inventory to the ultimate European customers for $1 million. The subsidiary does not further process the inventory and is only minimally involved in the sales function, as Collins' employees arrange the transactions with the ultimate customers. In essence, the sale to the subsidiary is simply a "paper" transaction.

## A BOOST TO DOMESTIC INVESTMENT OR A TAX AMNESTY FOR OUTSOURCERS?

The American Jobs Creation Act of 2004 provided a temporary incentive to repatriate foreign profits back to the United States. Section 965 allows domestic corporations to elect to take a one-time 85 percent dividends received deduction for certain cash dividends received from controlled foreign corporations for either the taxpayer's last tax year that began before October 22, 2004, or the first tax year that began after October 22, 2004. Such dividends must be reinvested in the United States, and the eligible dividend amount is based on a calculation that considers prior-year average dividends and the amount of earnings considered "permanently reinvested" abroad under financial accounting principles. The intent was to provide a tax benefit only for earnings that would not otherwise have been repatriated to the United States. With an 85 percent dividends received deduction, the effective U.S. corporate tax rate on such dividends is 5.25 percent (35% corporate tax rate × 15% taxable amount).

Supporters of this measure argued that the inflow of cash back to the United States, along with the requirement for reinvestment here, will provide a boost to the domestic economy. The dividend income is lightly taxed but would otherwise never have been taxed in the United States. Critics argue that the tax break is simply a giveaway to U.S. multinational corporations and rewards outsourcing. They fear that with this precedent, U.S. multinationals may simply outsource more profits to low-tax countries and wait for future tax breaks before repatriating profits.

If there were no tax law restrictions, this structure would create the following tax consequences.

|                    | Collins, Inc. | Foreign Subsidiary |
|--------------------|---------------|--------------------|
| Sales revenue      | $ 700,000     | $1,000,000         |
| Cost of goods sold | (600,000)     | (700,000)          |
| Net income         | $ 100,000     | $ 300,000          |
| U.S. tax at 35%    | $ 35,000      |                    |
| Foreign tax at 0%  |               | $ –0–              |

Because the Cayman Island subsidiary is not engaged in a U.S. trade or business, it is not subject to any U.S. tax on its income. So long as the subsidiary's profits are kept outside the United States, Collins believes it can avoid any U.S. income tax on these profits (i.e., the deferral privilege). Thus, at first glance it appears that using the foreign subsidiary significantly reduces Collins' current tax cost from $140,000 to $35,000.

However, Collins will find this strategy attacked by the U.S. taxing authorities on two fronts, either of which results in the loss of all or most of the tax savings.

First, the IRS may use the transfer pricing rules of § 482 to claim that the $700,000 intercompany transfer price between Collins and its subsidiary is not a correct **arm's length price**. The IRS may claim that the transfer price should be $1 million because the subsidiary does not add any value to the inventory through further processing or sales activities and all the risks of the transaction are borne by Collins. With this transfer pricing adjustment,

### WHO ARE THESE CFCS?

**T**he 7,500 largest CFCs accounted for $4.4 trillion of the assets and more than $2.2 trillion of the gross receipts of all CFCs during the latest year for which complete data are available. These CFCs were engaged primarily in manufacturing (29 percent), services (26 percent), or finance, insurance, or real estate (23 percent). Although these 7,500 CFCs were incorporated in over 100 different countries, CFCs in Europe, Canada, and Japan accounted for over 80 percent of the gross receipts. In 2000, CFCs distributed $95 billion of profits to their U.S. parents and other shareholders. A "large" CFC is one having $500 million or more in assets.

**Source:** *Statistics of Income Bulletin*, Summer 2004, Publication 1136 (Rev. 09–2004).

Collins will have a $400,000 profit from the sales and the same $140,000 tax cost as if it had not used the foreign subsidiary as an intermediary.

Determining a correct transfer price is a very subjective exercise. Accordingly, Congress enacted the Subpart F provisions to create more certainty in the effort to prevent unwarranted tax benefits from accruing to U.S. taxpayers using offshore subsidiaries to shield profits from the reach of the U.S. tax authorities. Under the Subpart F rules, the subsidiary's $300,000 income creates a constructive dividend for Collins, thus producing a $105,000 tax cost ($300,000 × 35%). Combined with its original $35,000 tax, Collins' total tax cost for the sales is $140,000 ($35,000 + $105,000), and the use of the foreign subsidiary does not achieve any tax savings. ■

**EXAMPLE 16**

Assume that in Example 15 Collins' foreign subsidiary instead was incorporated in Ireland, where the tax rate on such sales income is 12.5%. The subsidiary purchases raw materials from Collins and performs substantial manufacturing activity in Ireland before selling the inventory to customers in Hong Kong. In this case, the sales income is not Subpart F income. Even without the manufacturing activity, sales to customers within Ireland would not produce Subpart F income. In both instances, there is economic substance to the non-U.S. subsidiary earning the income. The fact that the Irish subsidiary pays a substantially lower tax rate than the U.S. parent does not by itself trigger a constructive dividend. However, Collins must still document the appropriateness of its intercompany transfer price on raw material sales to its Irish subsidiary. ■

The Subpart F provisions are quite complex and subject to numerous exceptions. But, in general, any time a CFC earns income that has little economic connection to its local country, the income is potentially tainted income under Subpart F and will generate a constructive dividend to the CFC's U.S. shareholders. Alternatively, if the CFC is actively generating the income, it is likely not Subpart F income. Unfortunately, the mechanistic application required by the Subpart F provisions sometimes catches active foreign corporations within the Subpart F web.

**EXAMPLE 17**

Murphy, Inc., a U.S. corporation owns all of GreenCo, Ltd., an Irish manufacturing corporation, and SwissCo, a Swiss distribution corporation. Both GreenCo and SwissCo are CFCs. GreenCo sells its inventory production to SwissCo. SwissCo sells the inventory to unrelated customers located in Switzerland, Italy, and Germany. Because SwissCo does not manufacture the inventory and acquires it from a related supplier, any sales to customers outside

Switzerland will produce Subpart F income and a constructive dividend to Murphy, Inc. This is true even though SwissCo is engaged in an active business and is not merely a "paper" corporation. To avoid Subpart F treatment, Murphy, Inc., should create a distribution company within each country where it operates to sell to customers only within that country. ■

## Avoiding Constructive Dividends

**FRAMEWORK FOCUS: DEDUCTIONS**

**STRATEGY ➤ MAXIMIZE DEDUCTIBLE AMOUNTS.**

To defer U.S. taxes on foreign income, U.S. taxpayers often create separate foreign subsidiaries to hold their foreign operations. This approach is successful so long as the foreign subsidiaries do not pay dividends to the U.S. owners and do not earn Subpart F income that creates constructive dividends. U.S. companies often set up foreign holding companies in tax-favorable jurisdictions to hold the foreign operating subsidiaries.

For example, a U.S. parent might create a CFC holding company to hold its two operating subsidiaries. The subsidiaries both pay interest to the holding company on intercompany loans. The interest is deductible by the operating subsidiaries at a high tax rate (providing tax savings in those countries) and is taxed to the holding company at a relatively low tax rate. This approach provides a net tax savings to the foreign group. However, the interest payments to the holding company may constitute Subpart F income and trigger a constructive dividend back to the U.S. parent. If so, the tax savings related to the intercompany loans are offset by the U.S. taxes on the Subpart F income.

Fortunately, a mechanism exists that allows the holding company to avoid Subpart F treatment for the interest in-

come. The **check-the-box** Regulations under § 7701 provide a great deal of flexibility for U.S.-based multinational corporations. For example, corporations are allowed to elect (i.e., check the box on a form) to treat certain foreign subsidiaries as unincorporated branches for U.S. purposes rather than separate legal entities. This election does not change the treatment of the entities under local tax law.

Using the check-the-box rules, the U.S. parent can elect to treat the foreign subsidiaries as branches for U.S. purposes. In this case, the two foreign subsidiaries are treated as mere divisions of the holding company. Accordingly, the intercompany loans do not exist from a U.S. perspective, and there is no interest income because the interest payments are treated as simply fund transfers within a single corporation. Without the interest income, there is no Subpart F income and thus no constructive dividends. However, the foreign tax savings still exist because the interest payments do exist from a foreign tax perspective and continue to provide interest deductions at the subsidiary level.

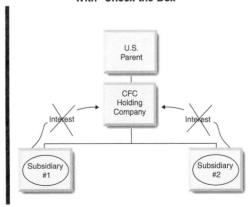

LO.4

Describe the tax effects related to the U.S. operations of a non-U.S. taxpayer.

**Inbound Issues.**   Generally, only the U.S.-source income of nonresident alien individuals and foreign corporations is subject to U.S. taxation. This reflects the reach of the U.S. tax jurisdiction. This constraint, however, does not prevent the United States from also taxing the foreign-source income of nonresident alien individuals and foreign corporations when that income is effectively connected with the conduct of a U.S. trade or business.

A **nonresident alien (NRA)** is an individual who is not a citizen or resident of the United States. Citizenship is determined under the immigration and naturalization laws of the United States. Residency is determined under § 7701(b). A person is treated as a resident of the United States for income tax purposes if he or she meets either the green card test or the substantial presence test. If either of these tests is met for the calendar year, the individual is deemed a U.S. resident for the year. Section 7701(a)(5) defines a foreign corporation as one that is not domestic.

Two important definitions determine the U.S. tax consequences to foreign persons with U.S.-source income: "the conduct of a U.S. trade or business" and "**effectively connected income.**" Specifically, for a foreign person's noninvestment income to be subject to U.S. taxation, the foreign person must be considered engaged in a U.S. trade or business and must earn income effectively connected with that business. General criteria for determining if a U.S. trade or business exists include the location of production activities, management, distribution activities, and other business functions. The Code does not explicitly define a U.S. trade or business, but case law has described the concept as activities carried on in the United States that are regular, substantial, and continuous. Once a foreign person is considered engaged in a U.S. trade or business, all U.S.-source income other than investment and capital gain income is considered effectively connected to that trade or business and is therefore subject to U.S. taxation. Effectively connected income is taxed at the same rates that apply to U.S. persons, and deductions for expenses attributable to that income are allowed.

Certain U.S.-source income that is *not* effectively connected with the conduct of a U.S. trade or business is subject to a flat 30 percent tax. This income includes dividends, interest, rents, royalties, certain compensation, premiums, annuities, and other fixed, determinable, annual or periodic (**FDAP**) income. This tax generally is levied by a withholding mechanism that requires the payors of the income to withhold 30 percent of gross amounts (or a lower rate as established by a treaty). This method eliminates the problems of assuring payment by nonresidents and foreign corporations.

**EXAMPLE 18**

Robert, a citizen and resident of New Zealand, produces wine for export. During the current year, Robert earns $500,000 from exporting wine to unrelated wholesalers in the United States. The title to the wine passes to the U.S. wholesalers in New York. Robert has no offices or employees in the United States. The income from the wine sales is U.S.-source income, but because Robert is not engaged in a U.S. trade or business, the income is not subject to taxation in the United States.

Robert begins operating a hot dog cart in New York City. This activity constitutes a U.S. trade or business. Consequently, all U.S.-source income other than FDAP or capital gain income is taxed in the United States as income effectively connected with a U.S. trade or business. Thus, both the hot dog cart profits and the $500,000 in wine income are taxed in the United States. ■

Several exceptions exempt foreign persons from U.S. taxation on their U.S. investment income that is not connected with a U.S. business. For example, certain U.S.-sourced portfolio debt investments and capital gains (other than gains on U.S. real property investments) are exempt from U.S. tax for most foreign investors. Gains from investments in U.S. real property (held directly or indirectly through other entities) are subject to U.S. taxation. Concept Summary 12–1 summarizes the U.S. taxation of foreign persons.

## CONCEPT SUMMARY 12–1

### U.S. Tax Treatment of Foreign Person's Income

| Type of Income | Tax Rate |
| --- | --- |
| U.S.-source fixed, determinable, annual, or periodic (FDAP) income (not effectively connected to a U.S. business) | Generally 30% withholding on gross amount (or lower treaty rate) with certain limited exceptions. |
| U.S.-source income effectively connected with a U.S. business | Regular individual or corporate rates applied against net income (after deductions). |
| Gain on U.S. real property (direct or indirect interest) | Taxed as if effectively connected to a U.S. trade or business. |
| Capital gains (other than on U.S. real property) not effectively connected to a U.S. business | • Foreign corporation: Not subject to U.S. tax.<br>• Individual: Generally not taxed but may be subject to a 30% U.S. tax if taxpayer physically present in the United States for 183 days or more in a taxable year. |
| Foreign-source business income | Generally not subject to U.S. taxation unless attributable to a U.S. office or fixed place of business. |

(DIGGING DEEPER ②)   *Find more information on this topic at our Web site: **http://wft-entities.swlearning.com**.*

# Crossing State Lines: State and Local Income Taxation in the United States

Very few taxpayers sell goods and services solely in the state in which they are based. Sales in other states are attractive for a variety of business reasons, including the expansion of market share and the achievement of economies of scale. By extending its operations into other states, a firm may be able to lower its labor and distribution costs, obtain additional sources of long-term debt and equity, and perhaps find a more favorable tax climate.

Many of the same issues discussed earlier in the chapter concerning international operations are encountered when a multistate operation is in place. Both international and multistate operations raise basic questions such as where did the transaction occur and who is liable for the collection of the tax.

However, as state and local income taxation has evolved within the United States, differences in terminology, definitions, and scope of the tax have arisen. Although prior knowledge of the U.S. international tax regime can be helpful in studying the state and local income tax structure, there still is much to learn. In addition, the sheer number of income taxing districts at the state and local level make an encounter with the state and local income tax laws of the United States a challenging experience.

**LO.5**

Identify the sources of tax law applicable to a taxpayer operating in more than one U.S. state.

## SOURCES OF LAW

Think of how complicated a tax professional's work would be if there were several hundred different Internal Revenue Codes, each with its own Regulations, rulings, and court decisions. That description is hardly an exaggeration of the state and local income tax law faced by a taxpayer operating in more than one jurisdiction. Unless a firm's salable goods or services are designed, made, and sold strictly within one taxing jurisdiction, the multistate regime comes into effect.

Almost every U.S. state taxes the business income of proprietors, corporations, and other entities that have a presence in the state.[8] Those states all have constitutional provisions allowing an income tax and aggregated legislation defining the tax base, specifying when the tax is due and from whom, and otherwise administering the tax. A separate revenue department interprets the law and administers the annual taxing process.

Every one of these systems is distinct and different in multiple ways—the name and location of the chief tax official, the definitions of what is taxable and deductible and what is not, the due dates and filing requirements applicable to the tax, and the taxpayer-friendliness of the audit and appeals system.

Despite the no-new-taxes pledge of many politicians on election day, income taxes are still popular in the United States. Income taxes are levied by states, cities, counties, villages, commuter districts, stadium boards, and numerous other bodies that have been granted taxing authority by their states. And politicians think that they can gain economic development advantages over their neighbors by granting special tax breaks—"Locate your assembly plant here and we'll exempt one-half of your employees' wages from the state income tax"—so the laws are constantly changing. By one estimate, a business taxpayer might be exposed to almost 500 different income taxing jurisdictions in the United States.

The Federal government has stayed out of the fray and has not attempted to force states and localities to use a single common tax formula and administrative organization. Only in **Public Law 86–272** has Congress attempted to bring order to the multistate income tax process. This 1957 pro-interstate commerce provision exempts from state and local taxation a sale of tangible personal property where the only contact with the state was the **solicitation** activity of the taxpayer.

In the past 20 or 30 years, the states have taken some steps to coordinate their activities. Several groups of states exchange information as to the seller and purchase price for cross-border sales, so that income and sales/use tax obligations can be computed and collected properly. A few states have reciprocity arrangements with their neighbors so as to straighten out the complications that can arise when an employee lives in one jurisdiction but works in another.

**EXAMPLE 19**     Harry works at the Illinois plant of Big Corporation, but he lives in Iowa. His wages are subject to Iowa tax. If Illinois and Iowa had a reciprocity agreement in place, either (1) Big would collect and remit income tax at Iowa's rates and remit the tax to the Iowa revenue department, or (2) Big would collect Illinois tax, and that state would keep the withholdings paid, in full satisfaction of Harry's Iowa tax obligations for the year. ■

About half of the states are members of the **Multistate Tax Commission (MTC)**, a body that proposes legislation to the states and localities and issues its own regulations and informational materials. A majority of the non-MTC members follow the agency's rules virtually without exception. The Uniform Division of Income for Tax Purposes Act (UDITPA) is made available to states and localities interested in a coherent set of income assignment rules, and it forms the basis for the income tax statutes in most of the MTC member states.

The MTC, which provides very specific formulas and definitions to be used in computing state taxable income, is as close as the states have come so far to a multilateral tax treaty process. If all states and localities followed all of the MTC rules, taxpayers would be unable to gain any "border advantages" or disadvantages. But political concerns will keep this coordinated result from ever happening.

---

[8]Some states tax the investment income of individuals, but those taxes are not addressed in this chapter. Nevada, South Dakota, Washington, and Wyoming do not have a corporate income tax. Washington uses a business and occupation tax, Michigan uses a form of value added tax, and several states impose a tax on the gross receipts of a business.

## BRITNEY, YOU NEED TO PAY YOUR TAX

The state and local taxation of athletes, entertainers, and other high-income taxpayers who travel to numerous locations during the tax year has become a point of contention among the jurisdictions, the taxpayers, and policymakers. When Britney Spears comes to town for a major concert appearance, she often leaves behind thousands of dollars in state and local income taxes. California, a high-tax state with a sizable budget deficit, enforces these rules aggressively and collects over $100 million per year just from professional athletes.

The 2003 major league baseball All-Star Game was played at the home of the Chicago White Sox. Illinois is one of the few states that does not assess special taxes on visiting athletes and entertainers, as long as the athlete's home state does not tax Illinois-based professionals. This means that a player from Florida, Texas, or Washington State does not owe any Illinois income tax, but those from most other states do. Thus, as a Tax Foundation economist noted, "When Florida Marlin Dontrelle Willis replaced Los Angeles Dodger Kevin Brown in the All-Star lineup, baseball was happy, but Illinois lost over $2,200 in revenue."

Illinois does not treat its own professional athletes favorably. When income is earned in another state, say, at an away game, Illinois does not allow a tax credit for sums paid to the other state. Thus, when Chicago Cub Sammy Sosa played in the 2002 All-Star Game in Milwaukee, he was liable for both Wisconsin and Illinois income tax.

"Jock taxes" such as these have come under fire for being poorly targeted and arbitrary. States seldom apply, for instance, a special "CEO tax" or "consultant tax" for those in other businesses who must work in multiple states. Plus, the administrative burden on the tax advisers for these high-income taxpayers can be mind-boggling.

And even city-level taxes can be expensive for the professional athlete or entertainer. Philadelphia and New York City were the first to pursue such tax collections almost two decades ago, and about a half-dozen more large cities now have their hands out.

## TAX ISSUES

The key issues facing a state or locality in drafting and implementing an income tax model are the same as those facing the international tax community. The results of the deliberative process, though, have produced somewhat different sets of rules and terminology.

**Authority to Tax.**   A business is taxable in the state in which it is resident, organized, or incorporated. Tax liabilities also arise in other jurisdictions where **nexus** exists; that is, a sufficient presence in the other state has been established on an ongoing basis. Such presence might come about because the corporation was organized there, the proprietor lives there, an in-state customer made a purchase, or the business employed people or equipment within the borders of the state. The precise activities that create nexus vary from jurisdiction to jurisdiction, although most of the taxing states follow the broad rules of Public Law 86–272 and the regulations of the MTC.[9]

When a taxpayer operates in more than one state, total taxable income for the year is split among the jurisdictions in which the operations take place. Portions

---

[9]Income and sales/use tax regimes use different nexus standards. Generally, it has been "easier" to establish nexus for sales/use tax purposes; most states have a separate set of rules to determine the taxability of income or a transaction. But recent U.S. Supreme Court cases seem to apply a "physical presence" test for the sales/use tax, a somewhat stricter and smokestack-industry test than the income tax nexus rules of the MTC. This chapter concentrates on income tax nexus provisions for the most part.

of the total income amount are assigned to each of the business locations, so several tax returns and payments will be due. For a taxpayer considering an expansion of operations, the tax adviser can make an important contribution in helping to decide with which state(s) nexus will be created.

## PLANNING STRATEGIES

## Nexus: To Have or Have Not

### FRAMEWORK FOCUS: TAX RATE

STRATEGY ➤ SHIFT NET INCOME FROM HIGH-TAX JURISDICTIONS TO LOW-TAX JURISDICTIONS.

Most taxpayers try to avoid establishing nexus in a new state, for example, by providing a sales representative with a cash auto allowance rather than a company car, by restricting the situs of inventory to only a few states, or by limiting a sales person's activities to those that are protected by the solicitation standard of Public Law 86–272. This effort to avoid nexus stems in part from the additional compliance burden that falls upon the taxpayer when a new set of income tax returns, information forms, and deadlines must be dealt with in the new state.

Another concern is that the marginal tax rate that applies to the net taxable income generated by the taxpayer may increase. Such a tax increase occurs, of course, only when the applicable tax rate in the new state is higher than the rate that would apply in the home state. If a business is already based in a tax-friendly state such as Alabama or Illinois or in a no-tax state such as Nevada, its aggregate tax liability is sure to increase.

Still, nexus is not necessarily a bad thing. Consider what happens if a business based in Minnesota, Massachusetts, Wisconsin, or another high-tax jurisdiction purposely creates nexus in a low- or no-tax state. If the new state applies a lower marginal rate than is available in the home state, or offers special exemptions or exclusions that match the taxpayer's operations, the aggregate tax bill can decrease. Then the planning efforts include determining which activities will *create* nexus in the new jurisdiction and meeting or maintaining that standard.

For instance, an entertainer based in Manhattan is subject to the relatively high income taxes of New York City and New York State. By establishing a permanent office in Tennessee, nexus will be created, and some portion of the taxpayer's income will subject to taxation there, instead of in New York. These are permanent savings, accruing immediately to after-tax income and the share price of the stock of the taxpayer.

---

Notice that the nexus rules of state/local taxation serve much the same function as do the permanent establishment provisions of international taxation. The PE standards are based in the language of the applicable tax treaty and interpretive court decisions. They look for real estate holdings and manufacturing equipment. Permanent establishment is found when an office in the host country participates significantly in the making of a sales or service contract.

*Find more information on this topic at our Web site: **http://wft-entities.swlearning.com.***

### LO.6
Apply computational principles designed for a taxpayer operating in more than one U.S. state.

**Income Sourcing.**  The multistate business, like its international counterpart, must divide up the taxable income generated for the year among the states in which it operates. Then tax liability is computed for the states in which nexus has been established. The computational template illustrated in Figure 12–3 indicates how most states derive their shares of the entity's aggregate taxable income. Usually, the starting point for this computation is Federal taxable income.

State modification items come about because each state creates its own tax base in the legislative process, and some of the rules adopted may differ from those used in the Internal Revenue Code. The modification items reflect such differences in the tax base. For example, modifications might be created to reflect the following differences between state and Federal taxable income.

■ **FIGURE 12–3**
Computing State Income Tax
Liability

```
                  Federal taxable income
              ±   State modification items

                  State tax base
              ±   Nonbusiness income/loss (for allocation)

                  Business income (for apportionment)
              ×   Apportionment percentage for the state

                  Taxable income apportioned to the state
              ±   Taxable income/loss allocated to the state

                  State taxable income/loss

                  State tax, per tax table or rate schedule
              −   State's tax credits

                  Net state tax liability
```

- The state might allow a different cost recovery schedule.
- The state might tax interest income from its own bonds or from those of other states.
- The state might allow a deduction for Federal income taxes paid.
- The state might disallow a deduction for payment of its own income taxes.
- The state might allow a net operating loss (NOL) deduction only for losses generated in the state.
- The state's NOL deduction might reflect different carryover periods than Federal law allows.

State tax modifications are made even if the taxpayer operates only in its home state.

The next step in computing state taxable income is to **allocate** items of nonbusiness income and loss to the states in which such items are derived. For instance, a Kansas entity might recognize some net income from the rental of a Missouri office building to a tenant. The net rental amount is in Federal taxable income, but it must appear only and fully in Missouri taxable income. So, by means of the modification process, the rents are removed from the taxable income for both states and then added back into Missouri taxable income. The allocation process is very much like the income-sourcing procedures employed in international taxation.

**EXAMPLE 20**

HammerCo reports $400,000 in taxable income for the year from its sales operations, based exclusively in Mississippi and Arkansas. HammerCo recognized net rent income of $60,000 from a building it owns in Mississippi. It earned $20,000 in interest income from Arkansas bonds. This amount is excluded from Federal taxable income, and it is taxed by Mississippi but not Arkansas. HammerCo also claimed a Federal NOL carryforward of $75,000 from a prior period. Mississippi follows Federal law for NOLs, but Arkansas does not allow such carryovers at all. The modifications to the state tax base are as follows.

| Mississippi | | Arkansas | |
|---|---|---|---|
| **Amount** | **Modification** | **Amount** | **Modification** |
| −$60,000 | Total nonbusiness income | −$60,000 | Total nonbusiness income |
| +$20,000 | Municipal bond interest income | +$75,000 | Remove Federal NOL deduction |
| +$60,000 | Net rent income from Mississippi rentals | | |

The business income of the taxpayer is **apportioned** among the states in which it operates. The apportionment percentage for the state is multiplied times the business income of the taxpayer to measure the extent of the taxpayer's exposure to the state's income tax. The application of the apportionment percentage is illustrated in Figure 12–3.

Most states apply an apportionment procedure involving three factors, each meant to estimate the taxpayer's relative activities in the state.

* The **sales factor** = In-state sales/total sales.
* The **payroll factor** = In-state payroll/total payroll.
* The **property factor** = In-state property/total property.

The state's apportionment percentage is the average of these three factors. This three-factor apportionment can be traced to the earliest days of state income taxation. Today, most states add additional weight to the sales factor, believing it to be the most accurate and measurable reflection of the taxpayer's in-state activities. It is common to "double-weight" the sales factor. A few states use only the sales factor in the apportionment procedure.

**EXAMPLE 21**

LinkCo, Inc., operates in two states. It reports the following results for the year. LinkCo's apportionment percentages for both states are computed as shown. Amounts are stated in millions of dollars.

|  | State A | State B | Totals |
|---|---|---|---|
| Sales | $30 | $20 | $50 |
| Payroll | 40 | 20 | 60 |
| Property | 45 | 5 | 50 |
| Sales factor | $30/$50 = .6 | $20/$50 = .4 | |
| Payroll factor | $40/$60 = .67 | $20/$60 = .33 | |
| Property factor | $45/$50 = .9 | $5/$50 = .1 | |
| Apportionment percentage | (.6 + .67 + .9)/3 = .72 | (.4 + .33 + .1)/3 = .28 | |

Note that 100% of the business income is apportioned between the two states: 72% to State A and 28% to State B. ■

**EXAMPLE 22**

Continue with the facts of Example 21, but now assume that State A double-weights the sales factor. LinkCo's apportionment percentages are computed as follows.

|  | State A | State B | Totals |
|---|---|---|---|
| Sales | $30 | $20 | $50 |
| Payroll | 40 | 20 | 60 |
| Property | 45 | 5 | 50 |
| Sales factor | $30/$50 = .6 | $20/$50 = .4 | |
| Payroll factor | $40/$60 = .67 | $20/$60 = .33 | |
| Property factor | $45/$50 = .9 | $5/$50 = .1 | |
| Apportionment percentage | (.6 + .6 + .67 + .9)/4 = .69 | (.4 + .33 + .1)/3 = .28 | |

State B's apportionment computations are not affected by A's double-weighting of the sales factor. The percentages now do not total to 100%. The effect of the special weighting is to reduce LinkCo's tax liability in A. This is likely LinkCo's "home state" given the location of its personnel and plant and equipment. ■

## TAX IN THE NEWS

### STATE DEFICITS CHANGE HOW REVENUE DEPARTMENTS WORK

The current crunch in state budget making has lasted for several years, and with a U.S. president who is inclined to hold Federal taxes steady and push down to lower-level governments the fiscal obligations for large programs such as Medicare and welfare entitlements, new sources of revenue and new attitudes toward enforcement are prime goals of state and local operations.

Much of this budget squeeze has been felt in the increased attention toward sales and use taxes, with many states now dedicating more resources toward those taxes than toward the individual and corporate income taxes. Collecting unpaid use taxes on Internet and mail-order sales and finding new taxpayers to add to the income and sales/use tax rolls are prime enforcement targets for many states.

But a sustained revenue shortfall tends to make some revenue departments either more desperate or more creative. In either event, we can observe the use of new or recycled approaches to tax enforcement that can surprise the taxpayer who has not been paying attention. Some of the techniques observed lately include the following.

- Applying local business and occupation taxes, payroll taxes, and license fees to telecommuters and work-at-home entrepreneurs and creative workers.
- Increasing audit staff and travel resources, resulting in increased and better-targeted auditing of returns.
- Temporary increases in underpayment and nonfiling fines and penalties, and reductions in grace periods for late filing or payment.
- Denial of other licenses and permits (like hunting and boating permissions, driver's licenses, and professional certifications) where income and sales/use taxes are underpaid.
- Adding "unpaid use tax" lines to the income tax return. This does result in some revenue collected from taxpayers who have guilty consciences or high levels of integrity, but mainly it sets up the taxpayer for penalties on a later audit, when the sworn-to-be-complete income tax return shows a zero balance on the use tax line.
- Refusing legislatively to adopt certain Federal tax breaks, such as the 30 and 50 percent additional first-year cost recovery elections or the increases in deductible or tax-deferred retirement and education allowances.
- Increased use of private collection agencies to find delinquent taxpayers and produce dollars for the state treasury.

**EXAMPLE 23**

Continue with the facts of Example 22, but now assume that State B uses a "sales-factor-only" weighting. The A apportionment percentage is .69, and the B percentage is .4. Now the apportionment percentages *exceed* 100%. ■

Most states follow the regulations of the MTC and the outline of the UDITPA in defining and applying the apportionment factors. But because the states do not follow identical rules in the makeup of the factors, the apportionment percentages seldom total precisely to 100 percent. Some other aspects of the three-factor approach include the following.

- Sales are assigned using the tax accounting methods of the taxpayer. Sales are assigned using the "ultimate destination" concept; that is, a sale is usually assigned to the state of the purchaser.
- If a sale is made into a state with no income tax or a state with which the taxpayer has not established nexus, tax is likely escaped. But about a third of the states apply a **throwback rule** that causes the sale to be sourced to the state of the seller.

## CONCEPT SUMMARY 12–2

### Multistate Income Taxation

1. A taxpayer is subject to income tax in the state in which it resides or is organized.
2. A taxpayer is subject to income tax in states where it has a business presence and enjoys the resources of the host state in conducting its operations.
3. A multistate taxpayer must divide its aggregate taxable income for the year among the states in which it conducts business.
4. Nonbusiness income is allocated to the state in which it is generated.
5. Business income is apportioned among the states in which the taxpayer has nexus.
6. Apportionment usually is conducted using a formula based on the relative sales, employment, and asset holdings in the various states.
7. The sales factor uses a destination test, while the payroll and property factors use a source test.
8. Most states weight the sales factor higher than the other apportionment factors.
9. Some states apply a special apportionment formula for certain industries, when the traditional three-factor formula could distort the income division procedure in some way.
10. About a dozen states employ the unitary theory in deriving the apportionment factors, using the data from a group of corporations to compute the apportionment formula. Other states allow or require a consolidated return from a conglomerate.

- Payroll is assigned to the state in which the employee's services primarily are performed. Payroll includes wages, bonuses, commissions, and taxable fringe benefits. Some states exclude officer compensation because it can distort the computations. Some states exclude contributions to a § 401(k) plan.
- The property factor uses an average historical cost basis, net of accumulated depreciation. Idle property is ignored, but construction in progress is included. Property in transit is assigned to the state of its presumed destination.
- Property leased but not owned by the taxpayer is included in the property factor at eight times the annual rentals paid.

Many states use specialized apportionment percentages for industries whose sales and asset profile is not properly reflected in the traditional three-factor formula. For instance, the airline industry might divide its income based on passenger-miles beginning and ending in the state. Truckers might be able to divide taxable income among the states based on in-state vehicle-trips or tons-per-day. Communications companies might use the in-state miles of cable or number of wireless devices to make up an apportionment formula.

About a dozen states use a **unitary approach** to computing the apportionment factors. Conglomerates are required, or can elect, to base their computations on the data for all of their affiliated corporations, not just the legal entities that do business with the state. Affiliates included under the unitary theory share a majority ownership with a parent or group of shareholders. They also often share data processing, sales force, and marketing resources.

The *combined return* that the unitary business files includes much more data than might be expected on a separate-entity basis, but the taxing jurisdictions often believe that the unitary figures offer a more accurate reflection of the taxpayer's activity within the state and that, therefore, a more accurate tax liability can be derived.

**EXAMPLE 24**

Kipp Industries is a holding company for three subsidiaries: GrapeCo operating in California, PotatoCo operating in Idaho, and BratCo operating in Germany. Only GrapeCo has nexus with California. But because California is a unitary state, the California apportionment percentage is computed also using PotatoCo and BratCo data. ■

## PLANNING STRATEGIES

## Where Should My Income Go?

**FRAMEWORK FOCUS: TAX RATE**

**STRATEGY ➤ SHIFT NET INCOME FROM HIGH-TAX JURISDICTIONS TO LOW-TAX JURISDICTIONS.**

Every state defines its apportionment factors in a slightly different manner. The multistate taxpayer needs to keep track of these differences and place activities in the state that will serve them best.

Planning with the sales factor includes a detailed analysis of the destination point of the product shipments for the year, especially when the firm has customers in low- and no-tax states. The property factor should include only assets that are used in the taxpayer's trade or business, not the investment, leasing, or research functions. Permanently idle property is excluded from the property factor as well. The payroll factor can be manipulated by hiring independent contractors to carry out certain sales and distribution work, or by relocating highly paid managers to low-tax states.

By setting up an investment holding company in a no- or low-tax state, such as Delaware or Nevada, and transferring

income-producing securities and intangible assets to that entity, significant tax reductions can be obtained. When the net investment income is paid back to the parent corporation, the dividends received deduction eliminates the tax liability there.

The unitary system does not always result in a tax increase, although the additional record-keeping burden of operating in a unitary state cannot be understated. If the affiliates make available less profitable operations or a presence in low- or no-tax states or countries, the current tax liability may be reduced. The record-keeping burden can be reduced if the taxpayer makes a **waters'-edge election**, which allows it to include only affiliate data from within the boundaries of the United States.

---

**EXAMPLE 25**

Return to the facts of Example 24. If Kipp Industries files a waters'-edge election, the unitary group that files a California income tax return can be limited to GrapeCo and PotatoCo. ■

*Find more information on this topic at our Web site:* ***http://wft-entities.swlearning.com.***

---

# Common Challenges

Practical and policy issues facing the U.S. states, developed countries, and the taxpayers operating in all of them show a great degree of similarity between the multistate and international tax regimes. Terminology may differ, and the evolution of tax solutions may take radically different paths, but the key issues that face the multijurisdictional community are at once challenging and rewarding.

**LO.7**

Synthesize the international and multistate tax systems and recognize common issues faced by both systems.

## AUTHORITY TO TAX

The old-economy orientation of the nexus and permanent establishment rules presents great difficulty in today's economy, as jurisdictions attempt to describe the income and sales/use tax base fairly. An electronic presence also exploits the resources of the host country and should trigger a tax in the visited jurisdiction. Mathematically, the apportionment and sourcing rules should result in only a modest tax liability in the host jurisdiction, but to maintain that no presence exists

## STATES IN A BIND ON SALES/USE TAX ON INTERNET SALES

In the mid-1960s, the Supreme Court held in *National Bellas Hess* that the seller had no sales/use tax nexus with a state into which a sale was made using catalogs and other general advertising materials. In the early 1990s, the Court's decision in *Quill* extended this no-nexus holding to 800 telephone numbers and Internet sales. As a result, states find it difficult to collect taxes on remote sales of personal property, electronic goods and software downloads, and services that clearly are taxable under existing law.

This issue addresses who should collect the tax, not whether a tax is due, or the amount of the liability. Existing law allows the states to collect a tax, but they have found it impossible to chase down all the Internet sellers around the world who deal with local residents, get them to register for the sales/use tax, and remit the tax liability due. Aware of this difficulty, most sellers today still charge no use tax on out-of-state transactions, with little to fear from understaffed state and local tax audit staffs. Correcting this problem does not constitute a tax increase, but it does require a new approach to enforcement and collection.

The stakes are extremely high. Internet sales are estimated at $60 billion for 2005, and are projected to reach $105 billion by 2007. This situation is not just a battle between the "bricks" and "clicks" economies—it is a problem in which we all share as taxpayers and recipients of government goods and services.

The court battles that will follow any state that forces sellers to start collecting use tax on its cross-border Internet sales are "worth it" in terms of the future revenues that any victory would bring. The counterargument that appearing to increase taxes on e-commerce will hurt business and economic development forces a political dispute. Should a politician come down on the side of $200 million per year in new Internet sales tax collections or a $200 million cut in public health care for lower-income citizens?

and no tax should be paid in the context of an 800 telephone number or Internet sale is improper.

But perhaps the notion of *presence* is becoming less important over time, and the level of resource usage in the host jurisdiction also is declining. For example, just-in-time manufacturing and purchasing strategies reduce the need for warehousing by some taxpayers. Human capital can be dispersed through telecommuting, video conferencing, and project rotation using work-group software that provides acceptable levels of data security. If the future is to a great degree wireless, perhaps the standard of presence will diminish, as the buyer and the seller are both "everywhere."

## DIVISION OF INCOME

The multistate apportionment procedure could use an overhaul. The fact that a majority of states change the weighting of the sales factor indicates that some other income division method might better serve taxpayers and governments. Three-factor apportionment was designed for an age of traveling sales representatives and sales of built, grown, and manufactured goods. Sales reps were assigned territories that they could drive through on short notice, so they usually lived close to their customer base. In that case, the sales and payroll factors could be highly

**○ T A X   F A C T**

## THE OECD'S TAX HAVEN BLACKLIST

In 2000, the OECD identified these jurisdictions as tax havens that had not cooperated with its campaign to stop harmful global tax practices. As of 2004, only the countries marked with an asterisk remained on the list.

| | | |
|---|---|---|
| Andorra* | Guernsey | Panama |
| Anguilla | Isle of Man | Samoa |
| Antigua and Barbuda | Jersey | Seychelles |
| Aruba | Liberia* | St. Christopher |
| Bahamas | Liechtenstein* | and Nevis |
| Bahrain | Maldives | St. Lucia |
| Barbados | Marshall Islands* | St. Vincent and the |
| Belize | Monaco* | Grenadines |
| British Virgin Islands | Montserrat | Tonga |
| Cook Island | Nauru | Turks and Caicos Islands |
| Dominica | Netherlands Antilles | U.S. Virgin Islands |
| Gibraltar | Niue | Vanuatu |
| Grenada | | |

**Sources:** Organization for Economic Cooperation and Development (OECD), *Towards Global Tax Cooperation: Progress in Identifying and Eliminating Harmful Tax Practices*, 2000; OECD News Release, April 18, 2002; and the OECD's *Project on Harmful Tax Practices: The 2004 Progress Report*, February 4, 2004.

redundant. Today, with communication and distribution systems more highly developed, the sales factor appears incrementally to be the preferred income-sourcing device. Sales of goods and services should be assigned based on a destination test so that the transaction is assigned to the state of the purchaser.

The three-factor formula further breaks down for income derived from specialized industries, as evidenced by the special computational methods allowed by many states. Perhaps the economy is so specialized today that income simply cannot be assigned by the use of one simple formula. Nonetheless, more uniformity among the states as to definitions and computational rules for the factors would be welcome.

The U.S. Treasury has held hearings in the last decade concerning the adoption of an apportionment approach to the sourcing of international taxable income. Although a formulary apportionment would represent a more reliable and predictable method of dividing multinational income and deduction amounts, the data collection burden that such a system would create may be too much to expect from most of the trading partners in the short term. Moreover, the model treaties developed by the United States and the Organization for Economic Cooperation and Development (OECD) include language relating to the income-sourcing rules and transfer pricing at arm's length, not an apportionment approach.

## TRANSFER PRICING

The transfer pricing system used in international trade requires the taxpayer to keep a database of comparable prices and transactions, even though often no such comparability exists. Especially when dealing with proprietary goods and design, it may be impossible to find comparable goods and, therefore, an acceptable transfer

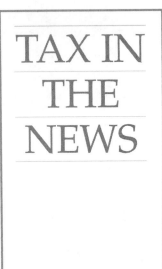

### A MOVE TO THE BEACH FOR U.S. CORPORATIONS SEEKING A VACATION FROM U.S. TAX RULES

A number of U.S.-based companies have decided to cast their lot on the golden shores of Bermuda, reincorporating as Bermuda companies and enjoying Bermuda's low-tax environment. Recent examples include such well-known companies as Fruit of the Loom, Cooper Industries, Foster Wheeler, and Ingersoll Rand. Even Accenture, formerly Andersen Consulting, established itself in Bermuda. Many of these companies argue that U.S. international tax policy compromises their ability to compete in the global marketplace. The stock market often rewarded these so-called inversion transactions (i.e., conversion from U.S. to foreign based) with increased stock prices.

Although an inversion transaction often entailed a current tax cost, the long-term tax benefits were considered more important. For example, with a Bermuda parent company rather than a U.S. parent company, many of the lower-tier foreign subsidiaries would not constitute CFCs. Many other companies were preparing to invert when Congress began developing anti-inversion legislation and the public began reacting negatively to these corporate expatriates. Toolmaker Stanley Works called off its previously announced, and very controversial, inversion plans, and subsequent years saw very few inversions of U.S. companies. The 2004 Jobs Act contained provisions that further curtailed the benefits of moving offshore.

price for them. One solution to this situation would be to allow additional definitions of comparable goods, or of ranges of acceptable transfer prices, perhaps subjected to audit on a rotating five-year basis. The use of advance pricing agreements further allows a greater degree of control by the governments in data collection and analysis, ideally prior to the undertaking of the sales or manufacturing transactions.

### TAX HAVENS

When taxpayers perceive effective tax rates as too high, planning usually includes seeking out a tax haven. If income-producing securities or profitable service operations can be moved to another jurisdiction, ideally one with significantly lower marginal tax rates on that type of income, permanent tax savings can be achieved.

When a government witnesses a loss of its tax base due to the transfer of assets and income out of the jurisdiction, anti-tax-haven legislation becomes attractive. The U.S. international tax regime shows several distinct attempts to find and tax income moved offshore, but those taxes collect few dollars in the typical tax year. The investment holding company structure currently used by multistate taxpayers has been met with little effective restrictive legislation from the states, probably out of fear of being branded "anti-business."

Perhaps a separate set of nexus rules could be created to address the most portable types of income, such as that from interest and dividends. But this difficult problem likely needs a multilateral solution, which is unlikely to be found in the short term among states and countries, each with unique revenue shortfalls and political profiles.

**PLANNING STRATEGIES**

## Holding Companies Make Other States Angry

**FRAMEWORK FOCUS: TAX RATE**

**STRATEGY ▶ SHIFT NET INCOME FROM HIGH-TAX JURISDICTIONS TO LOW-TAX JURISDICTIONS.**

A tax dollar saved in one state is a tax dollar lost in another. That's how some state tax administrators and observers view the use of the **passive investment holding company**. A spokesman for the Multistate Tax Commission asserts that the average state income tax rate paid by larger conglomerates has fallen from about 9.6 percent in 1980 to about 5.2 percent today. And the Secretary of Revenue in North Carolina says it's not fair that corporate tax savings must be recovered from income and sales/use taxes on individuals.

The Delaware version of the investment holding company is the great offender being blamed here. By isolating intangible assets like trademarks, and investment assets generating

income, in tax-friendly states like Delaware, corporate giants can achieve major tax reductions.

These savings may not be easily obtained for long, however. State tax authorities have worked hard to target the holding companies operated by such familiar names as Home Depot, Circuit City, Staples, The Gap and The Limited, and Burger King. Tax advisers tell their clients to comply with the tax laws, but they also devise strategies to use holding companies and other "nowhere income" devices. Passive investment companies seem to be here to stay until Congress or the courts force a change.

## INTERJURISDICTIONAL AGREEMENTS

Treaties are documents that address many issues other than the taxable income computation. They involve several players within the governmental structure, and they take several years to draft and adopt. Treaties involving the United States tend to be only bilateral, meaning that it is difficult to anticipate and coordinate the interaction of several treaties as they apply to a single taxpayer.

At the multistate level, the Federal government has been slow to take up issues involving a synchronization of the income tax systems used by the states. Although this reluctance may be partly for strictly constitutional reasons, it is largely because of the difficulties presented by the lack of uniformity among the states' tax laws and enforcement efforts.

But the future must hold a greater degree of cooperation among various taxing jurisdictions, at least in the trading of information and the coordination of enforcement efforts. The United States must create additional treaties or information-sharing agreements with countries in South America and Africa. And the future of the European Union probably holds a series of highly developed agreements addressing tax issues with the United States.

Procedural developments may accomplish the same result. For instance, block filing by S corporations and their shareholders with various states accomplishes a number of income division and information-sharing goals. Applying the same approach to partnerships and limited liability entities, and perhaps C corporations with a small number of shareholders, would be an important step forward. Including the multinational activities of such flow-through and closely held entities would also allow for a more coordinated result. Sharing data, while still respecting the confidentiality needs of the taxpayer and requirements of the governments, represents a technologically sound method of collecting taxes in today's multijurisdictional economy.

DIGGING DEEPER ⑤ *Find more information on this topic at our Web site:* ***http://wft-entities.swlearning.com.***

# Suggested Further Readings

Bruce Bartlett, "Tax Advice for Mr. Bush: Consider the VAT," Fortune.com, December 1, 2004.

Walter Hellerstein, "Federal Statutory Restraints on State Tax Nexus Generate Continuing Controversy," *Journal of Taxation*, November 2002, pp. 290–296.

John Mongan and Amrit Johal, "Tax Planning with European Holding Companies," *Journal of International Taxation*, January 2005.

Michael S. Schadewald and William A. Raabe, "Present and Future Directions in Federal and State Taxation of Income from Cross Border Trade," *TAXES*, April 1997, pp. 218–229.

David E. Spencer, "OECD Model Agreement Is a Major Advance in Information Exchange," *Journal of International Taxation*, November 2002, pp. 10–46.

William Zink, "Shrinking World Expands Relevance of International Tax Concepts," *Taxation for Accountants*, September 1998.

## KEY TERMS

Allocate, 12–25

Apportion, 12–26

Arm's length price, 12–17

Check-the-box, 12–19

Controlled foreign corporation (CFC), 12–15

Deemed-paid credit, 12–11

Effectively connected income, 12–20

FDAP, 12–20

Foreign tax credit, 12–7

Inbound taxation, 12–4

Income tax treaties, 12–4

Multistate Tax Commission (MTC), 12–22

Nexus, 12–23

Nonresident alien (NRA), 12–20

Outbound taxation, 12–4

Passive investment holding company, 12–33

Payroll factor, 12–26

Permanent establishment (PE), 12–5

Property factor, 12–26

Public Law 86–272, 12–22

Sales factor, 12–26

Separate foreign tax credit limitation category, 12–13

Solicitation, 12–22

Subpart F income, 12–15

Throwback rule, 12–27

Unitary approach, 12–28

U.S. shareholder, 12–15

Waters'-edge election, 12–29

## PROBLEM MATERIALS

### Problems

1. Evaluate this statement: It is unfair that the United States taxes its citizens and residents on their worldwide income.

2. Explain why an income tax treaty between the United States and Germany can be very favorable to a U.S. person who earns investment or business income from Germany.

3. Describe the different approaches used by countries to tax the earnings of their citizens and residents generated outside the borders of the country.

4. Determine the source (U.S. or foreign) of the following items of income.
   a. Interest income paid by a U.S. corporation.
   b. Dividend income paid by a foreign corporation that has no U.S. operations.
   c. Dividend income paid by a foreign corporation that has U.S. operations that historically produce 76% of the corporation's income.
   d. Income from providing consulting services to clients with 12% of the services provided to clients on-site in Canada.

**Decision Making**

5. ERP, Inc., produces inventory in its foreign manufacturing plants for sale in the United States. Its foreign manufacturing assets have a tax book value of $3 million and a fair market value of $8 million. Its assets related to the sales activity have a tax book value of $400,000 and a fair market value of $100,000. ERP's interest expense totaled $50,000 for the current year.

   a. What amount of interest expense is allocated and apportioned to foreign-source income using the tax book value method? What amount of interest expense is allocated and apportioned to foreign-source income using the fair market value method?

   b. If ERP wishes to maximize its FTC, which method should it use?

6. Lynn, Inc., a domestic corporation, operates in both Mexico and the United States. This year, the business generated taxable income of $600,000 from foreign sources and $200,000 from U.S. sources. All of Lynn's foreign-source income is in the general limitation basket. Lynn's total worldwide taxable income is $800,000. Lynn pays Mexican taxes of $300,000. What is Lynn's allowed FTC for the tax year? Assume a 35% U.S. income tax rate.

7. Drake, Inc., a U.S. corporation, operates a branch sales office in Turkey. During the current year, Drake earned $500,000 in taxable income from U.S. sources and $100,000 in taxable income from sources within Turkey. Drake paid $40,000 in income taxes to Turkey. All the income is characterized as general limitation income. Compute Drake's U.S. income tax liability after consideration of any foreign tax credit. Drake's U.S. tax rate is 35%.

8. Crank, Inc., a U.S. corporation, operates a branch sales office in Ghana. During the current year, Crank earned $200,000 in taxable income from U.S. sources and $50,000 in taxable income from sources within Ghana. Crank paid $5,000 in income taxes to Ghana. All the income is characterized as general limitation income. Compute Crank's U.S. income tax liability after consideration of any foreign tax credit. Crank's U.S. tax rate is 35%.

9. Harold, Inc., a domestic corporation, earned $500,000 from foreign manufacturing activities on which it paid $150,000 of foreign income taxes. Harold's foreign sales income is taxed at a 45% foreign tax rate. Both sales and manufacturing income are assigned to the general limitation basket. What amount of foreign sales income can Harold earn without generating any excess FTCs for the current year? Assume a 35% U.S. rate.

10. Food, Inc., a domestic corporation, owns 70% of the stock of Drink, Inc., a foreign corporation. For the current year, Food receives a dividend of $20,000 from Drink. Drink's post-1986 E & P (after taxes) and foreign taxes are $6 million and $800,000, respectively. What is Food's total gross income from receipt of this dividend if it elects to claim the FTC for deemed-paid foreign taxes?

11. Hightower, Inc., a U.S. corporation, has foreign-source income and pays foreign taxes as follows.

| | Income | Taxes |
|---|---|---|
| Shipping category | $ 50,000 | $ 10,000 |
| Passive category | 100,000 | 3,000 |
| General category | 300,000 | 150,000 |

   Hightower's worldwide taxable income is $600,000, and U.S. taxes before the FTC are $210,000 (assume a 35% rate). What is Hightower's U.S. tax liability after the FTC?

**Issue ID**

12. Discuss the policy reasons for the existence of the Subpart F rules. Give two examples of Subpart F income.

13. Snowball Enterprises, a domestic corporation, owns 100% of Aussie, Ltd., an Australian corporation. Determine whether any of the following transactions produce Subpart F gross income for the current year.

- Aussie earned $300,000 from sales of products purchased from Snowball and sold to customers outside Australia.

- Aussie earned $500,000 from sales of products purchased from Snowball and sold to customers in Australia.

- Aussie earned $200,000 from sales of products purchased from unrelated suppliers and sold to customers in Ireland.

- Aussie purchased raw materials from Snowball, used these materials to manufacture finished goods, and sold these goods to customers in New Zealand. Aussie earned $100,000 from these sales.

- Aussie earned $60,000 for the performance of warranty services on behalf of Snowball. These services were performed in Japan for customers located in Japan.

- Aussie earned $30,000 in dividend income from passive investments.

14. Ames, Inc., a U.S. corporation, owns 100% of Boone, Ltd., a United Kingdom corporation. Boone purchases finished inventory from Ames and sells the inventory to customers in the U.K. and Germany. During the current year, Ames earned $600,000 in profits from sales to U.K. customers and $400,000 in profits from sales to German customers. Boone operates a sales office in London with 12 full-time employees. How much of Boone's $1 million in profits will be characterized as Subpart F income?

15. Explain the purpose of determining whether a foreign person is engaged in a U.S. trade or business.

16. Evaluate the following statement: Foreign persons are never subject to U.S. taxation on U.S.-source investment income so long as they are not engaged in a U.S. trade or business.

**EXTENDER**

17. Lili, Inc., a domestic corporation, operates a branch in France. The earnings record of the branch is as follows.

| Year | Taxable Income (Loss) | Foreign Taxes Paid |
|------|------|------|
| 2003 | ($ 25,000) | $ –0– |
| 2004 | (40,000) | –0– |
| 2005 | (10,000) | –0– |
| 2006 | 120,000 | 40,000 |

For 2003–2006, Lili, Inc., has U.S.-source taxable income of $500,000 each year. What is the allowed FTC for 2006? Assume a 35% U.S. tax rate.

18. Evaluate this statement: A state can tax only its resident individuals and the corporations and partnerships that are organized in-state.

19. What is the function of the Multistate Tax Commission? Why have some U.S. states not joined the MTC?

**Decision Making**

20. Considering only the aggregate state income tax liability, how should a taxpayer, resident in State A and selling widgets, deploy its sales force? Assume the following flat income tax rates for the indicated states, which entail the entire customer base of the taxpayer.

State A    5%
State B    3
State C    6
State D    0

**Ethics**

21. Continue to consider the case of the taxpayer in Problem 20. Is it acceptable to you if the taxpayer purposely shifts its sales force among the states so as to reduce its tax liabilities?

22. Compute state taxable income for HippCo, Inc. Its Federal taxable income for the year is $1 million. Its operations are confined to Oregon and Montana. HippCo generates only business and interest income for the year.

    • Federal cost recovery deductions totaled $200,000. Montana used this amount, but Oregon allowed only $140,000.

    • Interest income of $45,000 from Oregon bonds was excluded from Federal taxable income. Oregon taxes all municipal bond income, while Montana taxes all such interest except that from its own bonds.

    • Interest income from Treasury bonds that was recognized on the Federal return came to $46,000. Neither state taxes such income.

23. Continue with the facts of Problem 22. Using the format of Figure 12–3, compute state taxable income for HippCo, assuming also that the taxpayer recognized $225,000 net rent income during the year from a warehouse building in Montana. Federal taxable income still is $1 million.

24. PinkCo, Inc., operates in two states. It reports the following results for the year. Compute the apportionment percentage for both states. Amounts are stated in millions of dollars.

| | State A | State B | Totals |
|---|---|---|---|
| Sales | $25 | $75 | $100 |
| Payroll | 10 | 40 | 50 |
| Property | 10 | 90 | 100 |

25. Repeat the computations of Problem 24, but now assume that State B uses a double-weighted sales factor in its apportionment formula.

26. Repeat the computations of Problem 24, but now assume that State A is a sales-factor-only state and that State B uses the following weights: sales .70, payroll .15, and property .15.

27. Diagram the creation of an investment subsidiary in Delaware, by Parent, a Massachusetts corporation conducting all of its current sales activities through a single subsidiary, Junior, Inc.

**EXTENDER** 28. Determine for your state and two of its neighbors:
    a. Whether a Federal affiliated group is allowed to file a consolidated return with the state.
    b. What the return is called (i.e., a "combined," "consolidated," or other type of return).
    c. Whether any special rules apply to the use of consolidated returns in the state (e.g., a special election is required, a limitation on deductible losses applies, a specified term exists during which the election to consolidate is binding).

**EXTENDER** 29. The administrators of many of the U.S. states have developed model legislation for determining sales/use tax nexus for Internet sales. Look for a discussion of the Streamlined Sales Tax in various newspapers and Web sites and state whether:
    a. Your state is a participant in the Streamlined Sales Tax movement.
    b. You believe that the legislation needed to implement a Streamlined Sales Tax will be in place by the scheduled date. What issues might slow down the adoption date?

**BRIDGE DISCIPLINE**

1. What type of information-sharing agreements does the IRS have with the revenue agency of the Bahamas? Canada? Germany?

## Research Problems

**Internet Activity**

*Use the tax resources of the Internet to address the following questions. Do not restrict your search to the World Wide Web, but include a review of newsgroups and general reference materials, practitioner sites and resources, primary sources of the tax law, chat rooms and discussion groups, and other opportunities.*

**Communications**

**Research Problem 1.**   Review the last six months' archive of articles in one of the newspapers that you read. Use search terms such as "expatriate" and "tax haven" to look for articles that examine the ability of a taxpayer to move U.S. income offshore. Summarize two of the articles in an e-mail sent to your instructor.

**Research Problem 2.**   Make a list of the countries with which the United States currently has an income tax treaty. Then make a list of the countries with which the United States currently is negotiating an income tax treaty. For the second list, include the date on which negotiations started and the current status of the negotiations.

**Communications**

**Research Problem 3.**   Locate the most recent financial statements of four different publicly traded U.S. companies. Examine their tax footnotes and determine (1) the percentage of total income before taxes earned from foreign sources, (2) the overall effective tax rate, and (3) the effect, if any, on the effective tax rate of earning income outside the United States. Summarize this information in an e-mail to your instructor.

**Research Problem 4.**   Shane, plc. is a corporation created and organized in France. All of Shane's owners are French citizens and residents. Most of Shane's income is derived from active business operations within France. During the current year, Shane invested excess cash into bonds issued by a U.S. corporation. Under Article 11 of the U.S.-French tax treaty, the interest income from the bonds is exempt from withholding. The U.S. corporation has requested that Shane complete a Form W-8BEN to document this treatment. Shane's address is 25 Rue Blomet, Paris, France, 75015. Visit the IRS Web site, locate a Form W-8BEN, complete Shane's form online using the "fill in" function of the IRS form, and print the completed form.

**Research Problem 5.**   Determine which, if any, of the multistate information-sharing groups your state has joined, as to either income or sales/use tax transactions.

**Communications**

**Research Problem 6.**   For your state and one of its neighbors, determine the following. (Place your data in a chart and e-mail it to your professor.)
  a. To what extent does it follow the rulings of the Multistate Tax Commission?
  b. When are income tax estimated payments due?
  c. What are the factors and weightings of the income tax apportionment formula?
  d. What apportionment factors and weightings apply to an airline operator, like Delta?

**Communications**

**Research Problem 7.**   Read the "tax footnote" of five publicly traded U.S. corporations. Find the effective state/local income tax rates of each. Create a PowerPoint presentation for your instructor, summarizing the search and reporting the findings.

**Communications**

**Research Problem 8.**   Use **http://taxsites.com** or some other index to find a state/local tax organization (e.g., the Council on State Taxation). Read its current newsletter. In an e-mail to your instructor, summarize a major article at the site.

# Business Tax Credits and Corporate Alternative Minimum Tax

CHAPTER

13

LEARNING OBJECTIVES

## LEARNING OBJECTIVES

*After completing Chapter 13, you should be able to:*

### L O . 1
Explain how tax credits are used as a tool of Federal tax policy.

### L O . 2
Work with various business-related tax credits.

### L O . 3
Explain the reason for the alternative minimum tax.

### L O . 4
Identify and calculate the tax preferences that are included in determining the AMT.

### L O . 5
Identify and calculate AMT adjustments.

### L O . 6
Understand the function of adjusted current earnings (ACE).

### L O . 7
Compute the AMT liability for corporations.

http://wft.swlearning.com

---

**TAX TALK**

*A government which robs Peter to pay Paul can always count on the support of Paul.*

—*George Bernard Shaw*

---

**L0.1**

Explain how tax credits are used as a tool of Federal tax policy.

# Tax Policy and Tax Credits

**F**ederal tax law often serves other purposes besides merely raising revenue for the government. Evidence of equity, social, and economic considerations, among others, is found throughout the tax law. These considerations also have considerable import in the area of **tax credits.** Congress has generally used tax credits to promote social or economic objectives or to work toward greater tax equity among different types of taxpayers. For example, the disabled access credit was enacted to accomplish a social objective: to encourage taxpayers to renovate older buildings so they would be in compliance with the Americans with Disabilities Act. This Act requires businesses and institutions to make their facilities more accessible to persons with various types of disabilities. As another example, the foreign tax credit, which has been a part of the law for decades, has as its chief purpose the economic and equity objectives of mitigating the burden of multiple taxation on a single stream of income.

A tax credit should not be confused with an income tax deduction. Certain expenditures (e.g., business expenses) are permitted as deductions from gross income in arriving at taxable income. While the tax benefit received from a tax deduction depends on the tax rate, a tax credit is not affected by the tax rate of the taxpayer. All taxpayers can benefit equally when a tax credit is used.

**EXAMPLE 1**

Assume Congress wishes to encourage a certain type of expenditure. One way to accomplish this objective is to allow a tax credit of 25% for such expenditures. Another way is to allow a deduction for the expenditures. Assume Red Corporation's tax rate is 15%, while Blue

## WHERE HAVE ALL THE CREDITS GONE?

The number of individual income tax returns claiming tax credits has fluctuated substantially over the years as indicated below.

| Year | Returns Claiming Credits (in Millions) |
|------|----------------------------------------|
| 1975 | 65.9 |
| 1980 | 19.7 |
| 1985 | 21.0 |
| 1990 | 12.5 |
| 1995 | 15.2 |
| 2000 | 17.1 |

The probable cause of the decline between 1975 and 1980 was tax reform legislation enacted in 1976. Likewise the probable cause of the decline between 1985 and 1990 was tax reform legislation enacted in 1986.

**Source:** IRS Tax Statistics.

Corporation's tax rate is 34%. The following tax benefits are available to each corporation for a $1,000 expenditure.

| | Red | Blue |
|---|---|---|
| Tax benefit if a 25% credit is allowed | $250 | $250 |
| Tax benefit if a deduction is allowed | 150 | 340 |

As these results indicate, tax credits can provide benefits on a more equitable basis than tax deductions often do. ■

**LO.2**

Work with various business-related tax credits.

# Specific Business-Related Tax Credit Provisions

## GENERAL BUSINESS CREDIT

As shown in Exhibit 13–1, the **general business credit** is comprised of a number of other credits, each of which is computed separately under its own set of rules. The general business credit combines these credits into one amount to limit the annual credit that can be used to offset a taxpayer's income tax liability. The idea behind combining the credits is to prevent a taxpayer from completely avoiding an income tax liability in any one year by offsetting it with several business credits that would otherwise be available.

Two special rules apply to the general business credit. First, any unused credit must be carried back 1 year, then forward 20 years. Second, for any tax year, the

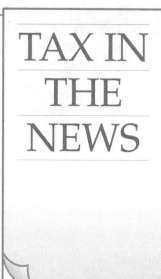

## A CREDIT THAT WENT UP IN SMOKE

In 1997, Congress passed a special $50 billion tax credit for the tobacco industry to subsidize the cost of a proposed multibillion dollar national settlement between tobacco companies and the 50 states. Several state attorneys general had previously sued tobacco companies in an attempt to recover billions of state Medicaid dollars spent on tobacco-related health problems. Once tobacco industry foes became aware of the significant savings that would accrue to tobacco companies from the tobacco tax credit, Congress was under considerable pressure to cut out the tax break. Less than a month after the credit's passage, legislation was introduced to repeal the controversial credit. As a result, the tobacco credit goes on record as one of the shortest-lived credits in tax history.

As several news reports suggested, repeal of the tobacco tax credit may have signaled a change in congressional sentiment concerning special interest legislation for the tobacco industry. In fact, subsequent budget proposals included provisions that would increase the price of tobacco products.

general business credit is limited to the taxpayer's *net income tax* reduced by the greater of:[1]

- The *tentative minimum tax* (see the discussion of AMT later in this chapter).
- 25 percent of *net regular tax liability* that exceeds $25,000.[2]

To understand these general business credit limitations, several terms need defining.

- *Net income tax* is the sum of the regular tax liability and the alternative minimum tax reduced by certain nonrefundable tax credits.
- *Tentative minimum tax* (discussed later in this chapter) is reduced by any foreign tax credit allowed, as specified in Exhibit 13–2.

■ **EXHIBIT 13–1**
Principal Components of the General Business Credit

The general business credit combines (but is not limited to) the following.

- Tax credit for rehabilitation expenditures
- Work opportunity tax credit*
- Welfare-to-work credit*
- Research activities credit**
- Low-income housing credit
- Disabled access credit
- Credit for small employer pension plan startup costs
- Credit for employer-provided child care

---

*Not available for employees hired after December 31, 2005.
**Scheduled to expire after December 31, 2005.

---

[1]§ 38(c). This rule works to keep the general business credit from completely eliminating the tax liability for many taxpayers.

[2]§ 38(c)(3)(B). The $25,000 amount is apportioned among the members of a controlled group.

**Bridge to Finance**

When calculating the cash-flow benefit of particular tax attributes and making a decision based on this analysis, an inappropriate decision can be made unless present value analysis is incorporated into the calculation.

The general business credit and the related carryback and carryover provisions can be used to illustrate the cash-flow impact.

Blonde, Inc.'s general business credit for 2005 is $400,000. However, the amount that may be used to reduce the current-year tax liability is only $280,000. None can be used in 2004 (the carryback year), so the $120,000 is carried forward. The $120,000 of unused general business credit is expected to offset Blonde's future tax liability as follows.

| | |
|---|---|
| **2006** | $20,000 |
| **2007** | 40,000 |
| **2008** | 60,000 |

It appears that the cash-flow benefit to Blonde is $400,000. In nominal dollars, this result is correct. However, when the present value concept is applied, the cash-flow benefit is only $376,280 (assuming Blonde's discount rate is 10 percent).

| | | | |
|---|---|---|---|
| **2005** | $280,000 × 1.0 | = | $280,000 |
| **2006** | 20,000 × .909 | = | 18,180 |
| **2007** | 40,000 × .826 | = | 33,040 |
| **2008** | 60,000 × .751 | = | 45,060 |
| | | | $376,280 |

The carryforward period for the general business credit is 20 years. Using a 10 percent discount rate, one dollar in 20 years is worth $0.149 ($1 × .149) today. So it behooves the taxpayer to use the general business credit to offset tax liability as rapidly as possible.

---

- *Regular tax liability* is determined from the appropriate tax table or tax rate schedule, based on taxable income. However, the regular tax liability does not include certain taxes (e.g., alternative minimum tax).
- *Net regular tax liability* is the regular tax liability reduced by certain nonrefundable credits (e.g., foreign tax credit).

**EXAMPLE 2**

Tanager Corporation's general business credit for the current year is $70,000. Tanager's net income tax is $150,000, tentative minimum tax is $130,000, and net regular tax liability is $150,000. Tanager has no other tax credits. The general business credit allowed for the tax year is computed as follows.

| | |
|---|---|
| Net income tax | $ 150,000 |
| Less: The greater of— | |
| • $130,000 (tentative minimum tax) | |
| • $31,250 [25% × ($150,000 − $25,000)] | (130,000) |
| Amount of general business credit allowed for tax year | $ 20,000 |

Tanager then has $50,000 ($70,000 − $20,000) of unused general business credits that may be carried back or forward. ■

**Treatment of Unused General Business Credits.**   Unused general business credits are initially carried back one year and reduce the tax liability of that year. Thus, the taxpayer may receive a tax refund as a result of the carryback. Any remaining unused credits are then carried forward 20 years.[3]

A FIFO method is applied to the carryback, carryovers, and utilization of credits earned during a particular year. The oldest credits are used first in determining the amount of the general business credit. The FIFO method minimizes the potential for loss of a general business credit benefit due to the expiration of credit carryovers and generally works to the taxpayer's benefit.

**EXAMPLE 3**

This example illustrates the use of general business credit carryovers for the taxpayer's 2005 tax year.

| | | |
|---|---:|---:|
| General business credit carryovers (unused in prior tax years) | | |
| 2002 | $ 4,000 | |
| 2003 | 6,000 | |
| 2004 | 2,000 | |
| Total carryovers | $12,000 | |
| 2005 general business credit | | $ 40,000 |
| Total credit allowed in 2005 (based on tax liability) | $50,000 | |
| Less: Carryovers used | | |
| 2002 | (4,000) | |
| 2003 | (6,000) | |
| 2004 | (2,000) | |
| Remaining credit allowed in 2005 | $38,000 | |
| 2005 general business credit used | | (38,000) |
| 2005 unused amount carried forward to 2006 | | $ 2,000 |

Most of the various credits that make up the general business credit are discussed in the paragraphs below.

## TAX CREDIT FOR REHABILITATION EXPENDITURES

Taxpayers are allowed a tax credit for expenditures incurred to rehabilitate older industrial and commercial buildings and certified historic structures. The **rehabilitation expenditures credit** is intended to discourage businesses from moving from economically distressed areas (e.g., an inner city) to outlying locations and to encourage the preservation of historic structures. The current operating features of this credit follow.[4]

| Rate of the Credit for Rehabilitation Expenses | Nature of the Property |
|:---:|---|
| 10% | Nonresidential buildings and residential rental property, other than certified historic structures, originally placed in service before 1936 |
| 20% | Nonresidential and residential certified historic structures |

Taxpayers who claim the rehabilitation credit must reduce the basis of the rehabilitated building by the credit allowed.[5]

---

[3]§ 39(a)(1).
[4]§ 47.

[5]§ 50(c).

■ **TABLE 13–1**
Recapture Calculation for
Rehabilitation Expenditures
Credit

| If the Property Is Held for | The Recapture Percentage Is |
| --- | --- |
| Less than 1 year | 100 |
| One year or more but less than 2 years | 80 |
| Two years or more but less than 3 years | 60 |
| Three years or more but less than 4 years | 40 |
| Four years or more but less than 5 years | 20 |
| Five years or more | 0 |

**EXAMPLE 4**

Grosbeak, Inc., spent $60,000 to rehabilitate a building (adjusted basis of $40,000) that originally had been placed in service in 1932. Grosbeak is allowed a credit of $6,000 (10% × $60,000) for rehabilitation expenditures. The corporation then increases the basis of the building by $54,000 [$60,000 (rehabilitation expenditures) – $6,000 (credit allowed)]. If the building were a historic structure, the credit allowed would be $12,000 (20% × $60,000), and the building's depreciable basis would increase by $48,000 [$60,000 (rehabilitation expenditures) – $12,000 (credit allowed)]. ■

To qualify for the credit, buildings must be substantially rehabilitated. A building has been *substantially rehabilitated* if qualified rehabilitation expenditures exceed the *greater of*:

- the adjusted basis of the property before the rehabilitation expenditures, or
- $5,000.

Qualified rehabilitation expenditures do not include the cost of acquiring a building, the cost of facilities related to a building (such as a parking lot), and the cost of enlarging an existing building. Stringent rules apply concerning the retention of the building's original internal and external walls.

**Recapture of Tax Credit for Rehabilitation Expenditures.**   The rehabilitation credit taken is recaptured if the rehabilitated property is disposed of prematurely or if it ceases to be qualifying property. The **rehabilitation expenditures credit recapture** is added to the taxpayer's regular tax liability in the recapture year. The recapture amount also is *added* to the adjusted basis of the building.

The portion of the credit recaptured is a specified percentage of the credit that was taken by the taxpayer. This percentage is based on the period the property was held by the taxpayer, as shown in Table 13–1. If the property is held at least five years, no recapture can result.

**EXAMPLE 5**

On March 15, 2002, Chickadee Corporation rehabilitated a building qualifying for the 10% credit. The company spent $30,000 in qualifying rehabilitation expenditures and claimed a $3,000 credit ($30,000 × 10%). The basis of the building was increased by $27,000 ($30,000 – $3,000).

Chickadee sold the building on December 15, 2005. Chickadee recaptures a portion of the rehabilitation credit based on the schedule in Table 13–1. Because Chickadee held the rehabilitated property for more than three years but less than four, 40% of the credit, or $1,200, is added to the company's 2005 income tax liability. In addition, the adjusted basis of the building is increased by the $1,200 recapture amount. ■

## WORK OPPORTUNITY TAX CREDIT

The **work opportunity tax credit**[6] was enacted to encourage employers to hire individuals from a variety of targeted and economically disadvantaged groups. To qualify, the employer must hire the individual by December 31, 2005. Examples of such targeted persons include qualified ex-felons, high-risk youths, food stamp recipients, veterans, summer youth employees, and persons receiving certain welfare benefits.

### Computation of the Work Opportunity Tax Credit: General.

The credit generally is equal to 40 percent of the first $6,000 of wages (per eligible employee) for the first 12 months of employment. The credit is not available for wages paid to an employee after the *first year* of employment. If the employee's first year overlaps two of the employer's tax years, however, the employer may take the credit over two tax years. If the credit is claimed, the employer's tax deduction for wages is reduced by the amount of the credit.

To qualify an employer for the 40 percent credit, the employee must (1) be certified by a designated local agency as being a member of one of the targeted groups and (2) have completed at least 400 hours of service to the employer. If an employee meets the first condition but not the second, the credit is reduced to 25 percent, provided the employee has completed a minimum of 120 hours of service to the employer.

(DIGGING DEEPER 1)

*Find more information on this topic at our Web site: **http://wft-entities.swlearning.com**.*

**EXAMPLE 6**

In January 2005, Green hires four individuals who are certified to be members of a qualifying targeted group. Each employee works 1,000 hours and is paid wages of $8,000 during the year. Green's work opportunity credit is $9,600 [($6,000 × 40%) × 4 employees]. If the tax credit is taken, Green reduces its deduction for wages paid by $9,600. No credit is available for wages paid to these employees after their first year of employment. ■

**EXAMPLE 7**

On June 1, 2005, Maria, a calendar year taxpayer, hires Joe, a member of a targeted group, and obtains the required certification to qualify Maria for the work opportunity credit. During his seven months of work in 2005, Joe is paid $3,500 for 500 hours of work. Maria is allowed a credit of $1,400 ($3,500 × 40%) for 2005.

Joe continues to work for Maria in 2006 and is paid $7,000 through May 31, 2006. Because up to $6,000 of first-year wages are eligible for the credit, Maria is also allowed a 40% credit on $2,500 [$6,000 − $3,500 (wages paid in 2005)] of 2006 wages paid, or $1,000 ($2,500 × 40%). None of Joe's wages paid after May 31, 2006, the end of the first year of employment, is eligible for the credit. ■

## WELFARE-TO-WORK CREDIT

The **welfare-to-work credit**[7] is available to employers hiring individuals who have been long-term recipients of family assistance welfare benefits. In general, *long-term recipients* are those individuals who are certified by a designated local agency as being members of a family receiving assistance under a public aid program for the 18-month period ending on the hiring date. Unlike the work opportunity credit, which applies only to first-year wages paid to qualified individuals, the welfare-to-work credit is available for qualified wages paid in the first *two years* of employment. If an employee's first and second work years overlap two or more of the employer's tax years, the employer may take the credit during the applicable tax years. If the

---

[6]§ 51.                              [7]§ 51A.

welfare-to-work credit is taken, the employer's tax deduction for wages is reduced by the amount of the credit.

An employer is prohibited from taking both the work opportunity credit and the welfare-to-work credit for wages paid to a qualified employee in a given tax year. The welfare-to-work credit is not available for employees hired after December 31, 2005.

**Maximum Credit.** The credit is equal to 35 percent of the first $10,000 of qualified wages paid to an employee in the first year of employment, plus 50 percent of the first $10,000 of qualified wages in the second year of employment, resulting in a maximum credit per qualified employee of $8,500 [$3,500 (year 1) + $5,000 (year 2)]. The credit rate is higher for second-year wages to encourage employers to retain qualified individuals, thereby promoting the overall welfare-to-work goal.

**EXAMPLE 8**

In April 2005, Blue hired three individuals who are certified as long-term family assistance recipients. Each employee is paid $12,000 during 2005. Two of the three individuals continue to work for Blue in 2006, earning $9,000 each during the year. Blue's welfare-to-work credit is $10,500 [(35% × $10,000) × 3 employees] for 2005 and $9,000 [(50% × $9,000) × 2 employees] for 2006. ■

## RESEARCH ACTIVITIES CREDIT

To encourage research and development (R & D) in the U.S. business community, a credit is allowed for certain qualifying expenditures paid or incurred not later than December 31, 2005. The **research activities credit** is the *sum* of two components: (1) an incremental research activities credit and (2) a basic research credit.[8]

**Incremental Research Activities Credit.** The incremental research activities credit applies at a 20 percent rate to the *excess* of qualified research expenses for the taxable year (the credit year) over a base amount.

In general, *research expenditures* qualify if the research relates to discovering technological information that is intended for use in the development of a new or improved business component of the taxpayer. Such expenses qualify fully if the research is performed in-house (by the taxpayer or its employees). If the research is conducted by persons outside the taxpayer's business (under contract), only 65 percent of the amount paid qualifies for the credit.[9]

**EXAMPLE 9**

Bobwhite Company incurs the following research expenditures during May 2005.

| | |
|---|---|
| In-house wages, supplies, computer time | $50,000 |
| Payment to Cutting Edge Scientific Foundation for research | 30,000 |

Bobwhite's qualified research expenditures are $69,500 [$50,000 + ($30,000 × 65%)]. ■

Beyond the general guidelines described above, the Code does not give specific examples of qualifying research. However, the credit is *not* allowed for research that falls into certain categories, including the following.[10]

- Research conducted after the beginning of commercial production of the business component.
- Surveys and studies such as market research, testing, and routine data collection.

---

[8]§ 41.

[9]§ 41(b)(3)(A). In the case of payments to a qualified research consortium, 75% of the amount paid qualifies for the credit.

[10]§ 41(d).

- Research conducted *outside* the United States (other than research undertaken in Puerto Rico and possessions of the United States).
- Research in the social sciences, arts, or humanities.

Determining the *base amount* involves a relatively complex series of computations, meant to approximate recent historical levels of research activity by the taxpayer. Thus, the credit is allowed only for increases in research expenses.

**EXAMPLE 10**

Hawk, Inc., a calendar year taxpayer, incurs qualifying research expenditures of $200,000 during January 2005. If the base amount is $100,000, the incremental research activities credit is $20,000 [($200,000 – $100,000) × 20%]. ■

Qualified research and experimentation expenditures are not only eligible for the 20 percent credit, but can also be *expensed* in the year incurred. In this regard, a taxpayer has two choices.[11]

- Use the full credit and reduce the expense deduction for research expenses by 100 percent of the credit.
- Retain the full expense deduction and reduce the credit by the product of 100 percent of the credit times the maximum corporate tax rate (35 percent).

As an alternative to the expense deduction, the taxpayer may *capitalize* the research expenses and *amortize* them over 60 months or more. In this case, the amount capitalized and subject to amortization is reduced by the full amount of the credit *only* if the credit exceeds the amount allowable as a deduction.

**EXAMPLE 11**

This year, Thin Corporation's potential incremental research activities credit is $20,000. The amounts that Thin can deduct and the credit amount are computed as follows.

|  | Credit Amount | Deduction Amount |
| --- | --- | --- |
| • Full credit and reduced deduction | | |
| $20,000 – $0 | $20,000 | |
| $200,000 – $20,000 | | $180,000 |
| • Reduced credit and full deduction | | |
| $20,000 – [(1.00 × $20,000) × .35] | 13,000 | |
| $200,000 – $0 | | 200,000 |
| • Full credit and capitalize and elect to amortize costs over 60 months | | |
| $20,000 – $0 | 20,000 | |
| ($200,000/60) × 12 | | 40,000 |

The value of the deduction depends on Thin's marginal tax rates. ■

**Basic Research Credit.**  Corporations (other than S corporations or personal service corporations) are allowed an additional 20 percent credit for basic research expenditures incurred not later than December 31, 2005, in *excess* of a base amount.[12] This credit is not available to individual taxpayers. *Basic research expenditures* are defined as amounts paid in cash to a qualified basic research organization, such

---

[11]§§ 174 and 280C(c). Recall the discussion of rules for deducting research and experimental expenditures in Chapter 4.

[12]§ 41(e).

as a college or university or a tax-exempt organization operated primarily to conduct scientific research.

*Basic research* is defined generally as any original investigation for the advancement of scientific knowledge not having a specific commercial objective. The definition excludes basic research conducted outside the United States and basic research in the social sciences, arts, or humanities.

## DISABLED ACCESS CREDIT

The **disabled access credit** is designed to encourage small businesses to make their facilities more accessible to disabled individuals. The credit is available for any eligible access expenditures paid or incurred by an eligible small business. The credit is calculated at the rate of 50 percent of the eligible expenditures that exceed $250 but do not exceed $10,250. Thus, the maximum amount for the credit is $5,000 ($10,000 × 50%).[13]

An *eligible small business* is one that during the previous year either had gross receipts of $1 million or less or had no more than 30 full-time employees. A sole proprietorship, partnership, regular corporation, or S corporation can qualify as such an entity.

*Eligible access expenditures* generally include any reasonable and necessary amounts that are paid or incurred to make certain changes to facilities. These changes must involve the removal of architectural, communication, physical, or transportation barriers that would otherwise make a business inaccessible to disabled and handicapped individuals. Examples of qualifying projects include installing ramps, widening doorways, and adding raised markings on elevator control buttons. However, the improved facility must have been placed into service prior to the enactment of the credit (i.e., November 5, 1990).

To the extent a disabled access credit is available, no deduction or credit is allowed under any other provision of the tax law. The asset's adjusted basis is reduced by the amount of the credit.

**EXAMPLE 12**

This year Red, Inc., an eligible business, makes $11,000 of capital improvements to business realty that had been placed in service in June 1990. The expenditures are intended to make Red's business more accessible to the disabled and are considered eligible expenditures for purposes of the disabled access credit. The amount of the credit is $5,000 [($10,250 maximum – $250 floor) × 50%]. The depreciable basis of the capital improvement is $6,000 [$11,000 (cost) – $5,000 (amount of the credit)]. ∎

DIGGING DEEPER ②

*Find more information on this topic at our Web site:* ***http://wft-entities.swlearning.com***.

## CREDIT FOR SMALL EMPLOYER PENSION PLAN STARTUP COSTS

Small businesses are entitled to a nonrefundable credit for administrative costs associated with establishing and maintaining certain qualified retirement plans.[14] While such costs (e.g., payroll system changes, consulting fees) generally are deductible as ordinary and necessary business expenses, the credit is intended to lower the after-tax cost of establishing a qualified retirement program and thereby to encourage qualifying businesses to offer retirement plans for their employees.

---

[13]§ 44.
[14]§ 45E. Currently, this credit is scheduled to expire for years after December 31, 2010.

The **credit for small employer pension plan startup costs** is available for eligible employers at the rate of 50 percent of qualified startup costs. An eligible employer is one with fewer than 100 employees who have earned at least $5,000 of compensation. Qualified startup costs include ordinary and necessary expenses incurred in connection with establishing or maintaining an employer pension plan and retirement-related education costs.[15] The maximum credit is $500 (based on a maximum $1,000 of qualifying expenses), and the deduction for the startup costs incurred is reduced by the amount of the credit. The credit can be claimed for qualifying costs incurred in each of the three years beginning with the tax year in which the retirement plan becomes effective (maximum total credit of $1,500).

**EXAMPLE 13**

Maple Company decides to establish a qualified retirement plan for its employees. In the process, it pays consulting fees of $1,200 to a firm that will provide educational seminars to Maple's employees and will assist the payroll department in making necessary changes to the payroll system. Maple may claim a credit for the pension plan startup costs of $500 ($1,200 of qualifying costs, limited to $1,000 × 50%), and its deduction for these expenses is reduced to $700 ($1,200 – $500). ■

## CREDIT FOR EMPLOYER-PROVIDED CHILD CARE

The scope of § 162 trade or business expenses includes an employer's expenditures incurred to provide for the care of children of employees as ordinary and necessary business expenses. Another option now available permits employers to claim a credit for qualifying expenditures incurred while providing child care facilities to their employees during normal working hours.[16]

The **credit for employer-provided child care**, limited annually to $150,000, is composed of the aggregate of two components: 25 percent of qualified child care expenses and 10 percent of qualified child care resource and referral services. *Qualified child care expenses* include the costs of acquiring, constructing, rehabilitating, expanding, and operating a child care facility. *Child care resource and referral services* include amounts paid or incurred under a contract to provide child care resource and referral services to an employee.

To prevent an employer from obtaining a double benefit by claiming a credit and the associated deductions on the same expenditures, any qualifying expenses otherwise deductible by the taxpayer must be reduced by the amount of the credit. In addition, the taxpayer's basis for any property acquired or constructed and used for qualifying purposes is reduced by the amount of the credit. If within 10 years of being placed in service, a child care facility ceases to be used for a qualified use, the taxpayer will be required to recapture a portion of the credit previously claimed.[17]

**EXAMPLE 14**

During the year, Tan Company constructed a child care facility for $400,000 to be used by its employees who have preschool-aged children in need of child care services while their parents are at work. In addition, Tan incurred salaries for child care workers and other administrative costs associated with the facility of $100,000 during the year. As a result, Tan's credit for employer-provided child care is $125,000 [($400,000 + $100,000) × 25%]. Correspondingly, the basis of the facility is reduced to $300,000 ($400,000 – $100,000), and the deduction for salaries and administrative costs is reduced to $75,000 ($100,000 – $25,000). ■

*Find more information on this topic at our Web site:* **http://wft-entities.swlearning.com.**

---

[15]§§ 45E(c) and (d)(1).

[16]§ 45F. Currently, this credit is scheduled to expire for years after December 31, 2010.

[17]§ 45F(d).

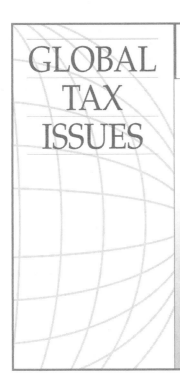

GLOBAL TAX ISSUES

### SOURCING INCOME IN CYBERSPACE—GETTING IT RIGHT WHEN CALCULATING THE FOREIGN TAX CREDIT

The overall limitation on the foreign tax credit plays a critical role in restricting the amount of the credit available to a taxpayer. In the overall limitation formula, the taxpayer must characterize the year's taxable income as either earned (or sourced) inside the United States or earned from sources outside the United States. As a general rule, a relatively greater percentage of foreign-source income in the formula will lead to a larger foreign tax credit. Therefore, determining the source of various types of income is critical in the proper calculation of the credit. However, classifying income as either foreign or U.S. source is not always a simple matter.

For example, consumers and business are using the Internet to conduct more and more commerce involving both products and services. The problem is that the existing income-sourcing rules were developed long before the existence of the Internet, and taxing authorities are finding it challenging to apply these rules to Internet transactions. Where does a sale take place when the Web server is in Scotland, the seller is in India, and the customer is in Illinois? Where is a service performed when all activities take place over the Net? These questions and more will have to be answered by the United States and its trading partners as the Internet economy grows in size and importance.

## FOREIGN TAX CREDIT

Both individual taxpayers and corporations may claim a credit for foreign income tax paid on income earned and subject to tax in another country or a U.S. possession.[18] The purpose of the **foreign tax credit (FTC)** is to reduce the possibility of double taxation of foreign income.

**EXAMPLE 15**

Ace Tools, Inc., a U.S. corporation, has a branch operation in Mexico, from which it earns taxable income of $750,000 for the current year. Ace pays income tax of $150,000 on these earnings to the Mexican tax authorities. Ace must also include the $750,000 in gross income for U.S. tax purposes. Assume that, before considering the FTC, Ace would owe $255,000 in U.S. income taxes on this foreign-source income. Thus, total taxes on the $750,000 could equal $405,000 ($150,000 + $255,000), a 54% effective rate. But Ace takes the FTC of $150,000 against its U.S. tax liability on the foreign-source income. Ace Tools' total taxes on the $750,000 now are $255,000 ($150,000 + $105,000), a 34% effective rate. ■

The tax year's FTC equals the *lesser* of the foreign taxes imposed or the *overall limitation* determined according to the following formula. Thus, where applicable foreign tax rates exceed those of the United States, the credit offsets no more than the marginal U.S. tax on the double-taxed income.

$$\frac{\text{Foreign-source taxable income}}{\text{Worldwide taxable income}} \times \text{U.S. tax before FTC}$$

Foreign taxes paid but not allowed as a credit due to the overall limitation are carried back 1 tax year and then forward 10 years.[19]

---

[18]§ 27 provides for the credit, but the qualifications and calculation procedure for the credit are contained in §§ 901–908. Alternatively, the taxpayer can *deduct* the foreign taxes paid.

[19]This treatment of unused FTCs applies to tax years ending after October 22, 2004. Prior law provided a two-year carryback and a five-year carryforward.

**EXAMPLE 16**

Oriole, Inc., a U.S. corporation, conducts business in a foreign country. Oriole's worldwide taxable income for the tax year is $120,000, consisting of $100,000 in income from U.S. operations and $20,000 of income from the foreign source. Foreign tax of $6,000 was paid to foreign tax authorities on the $20,000. Before the FTC, Oriole's U.S. tax on the $120,000 is $30,050. The corporation's FTC is $5,008 {lesser of $6,000 paid or $5,008 limitation [$30,050 × ($20,000/$120,000)]}. Oriole's net U.S. tax liability is $25,042 ($30,050 − $5,008). Thus, Oriole carries over (back 1 year and forward 10 years) $992 FTC ($6,000 − $5,008) because of the overall limitation. ■

**LO.3**

Explain the reason for the alternative minimum tax.

# Corporate Alternative Minimum Tax

A perception that many large corporations were not paying their fair share of Federal income tax was especially widespread in the early 1980s. A study released in 1986 reported that 130 of the 250 largest corporations in the United States (e.g., Reynolds Metals, General Dynamics, Georgia Pacific, and Texas Commerce Bankshares) paid no Federal tax, or received refunds, in at least one year between 1981 and 1985. Political pressure subsequently led to the adoption of an **alternative minimum tax (AMT)** to ensure that corporations with substantial economic income pay at least a minimum amount of Federal taxes.

The AMT limits the tax savings for some taxpayers who are seen as gaining "too much" from exclusions, deductions, and credits available under the law. A separate tax system with a proportional tax rate is applied each year to a corporation's economic income. If the tentative AMT is greater than the regular corporate income tax, then the corporation must pay the regular tax plus this excess, the AMT.

Since its inception, the AMT has been vulnerable to criticisms that it is too complex. Smaller corporations especially find that the imposition of a second tax structure unduly increases their compliance burdens. Thus, proposals to cut back or even repeal the AMT were considered by Congress throughout the 1990s. A special exemption from the AMT finally was adopted in 1997. For tax years beginning after 1997, most smaller corporations are not subject to the AMT at all. A corporation is exempted from the AMT if it meets the following tests.

- *Initial test.* The corporation must report average annual gross receipts of no more than $5 million for the three-year period beginning after December 1993.
- *Ongoing test.* If the initial test is passed, the corporation is exempt from the AMT as long as its average annual gross receipts for the three-year period preceding the current tax year and any intervening three-year periods do not exceed $7.5 million.

A corporation that fails the initial test *never* (other than the first year exception below) can be exempt from the AMT. Furthermore, if the ongoing test is failed, the taxpayer is subject to the AMT provisions for that year and all subsequent tax years. Congress estimates that this provision will exempt up to 95 percent of all C corporations from the AMT. A corporation *automatically* is classified as a small corporation in the first tax year of existence.

## THE AMT FORMULA

The AMT is imposed in addition to the regular corporate income tax, but is computed in a manner wholly separate and independent from it.[20] The AMT is a parallel income tax system that generally uses more conservative accounting methods than

---

[20]The AMT provisions are contained in §§ 55 through 59.

## CONCEPT SUMMARY 13–1

### Tax Credits

| Credit | Computation | Comments |
|---|---|---|
| General business (§ 38) | May not exceed net income tax minus the greater of tentative minimum tax or 25% of net regular tax liability that exceeds $25,000. | Components include tax credit for rehabilitation expenditures, work opportunity tax credit, welfare-to-work credit, research activities credit, low-income housing credit, disabled access credit, credit for small employer pension plan startup costs, and credit for employer-provided child care. Unused credit may be carried back 1 year and forward 20 years. FIFO method applies to carrybacks, carryovers, and credits earned during current year. |
| Investment (§ 46) | Qualifying investment times rehabilitation percentage, depending on type of property. Part of general business credit and subject to its limitations. | Part of general business credit and therefore subject to same carryback, carryover, and FIFO rules. Regular rehabilitation rate is 10%; rate for certified historic structures is 20%. |
| Work opportunity (§ 51) | Credit is limited to 40% of the first $6,000 of wages paid to each eligible employee. Under current law, the employee must begin work by December 31, 2005. | Part of the general business credit and therefore subject to the same carryback, carryover, and FIFO rules. Purpose is to encourage employment of members of economically disadvantaged groups. |
| Welfare-to-work (§ 51A) | Credit is limited to 35% of first $10,000 of wages paid to eligible employee in first year of employment, plus 50% of first $10,000 of wages paid to same employee in second year of employment. Under current law, the employee must begin work by December 31, 2005. | Part of general business credit and therefore subject to same carryback, carryover, and FIFO rules. Purpose is to encourage employment of long-term recipients of family assistance welfare benefits. |
| Research activities (§ 41) | Incremental credit is 20% of excess of computation-year expenditures over a base amount. Basic research credit is allowed to certain corporations for 20% of cash payments to qualified organizations that exceed a specially calculated base amount. To qualify for the credit under current law, research expenditures must be made not later than December 31, 2005. | Part of general business credit and therefore subject to same carryback, carryover, and FIFO rules. Purpose is to encourage high-tech research in the United States. |
| Low-income housing (§ 42) | Appropriate rate times eligible basis (portion of project attributable to low-income units). | Part of general business credit and therefore subject to same carryback, carryover, and FIFO rules. Recapture may apply. Purpose is to encourage construction of housing for low-income individuals. Credit is available each year for 10 years. |
| Disabled access (§ 44) | Credit is 50% of eligible access expenditures that exceed $250, but do not exceed $10,250. Maximum credit is $5,000. | Part of general business credit and therefore subject to same carryback, carryover, and FIFO rules. Purpose is to encourage small businesses to become more accessible to disabled individuals. Available only to eligible small businesses. |

| Credit | Computation | Comments |
|---|---|---|
| Credit for small employer pension plan startup costs (§ 45E) | The credit equals 50% of qualified startup costs incurred by eligible employers. Maximum annual credit is $500. Deduction for related expenses is reduced by the amount of the credit. | Part of general business credit and therefore subject to same carryback, carryover, and FIFO rules. Purpose is to encourage small employers to establish qualified retirement plans for their employees. |
| Credit for employer-provided child care (§ 45F) | Credit is equal to 25% of qualified child care expenses plus 10% of qualified expenses for child care resource and referral services. Maximum credit is $150,000. Deduction for related expenses or basis must be reduced by the amount of the credit. | Part of general business credit and therefore subject to same carryback, carryover, and FIFO rules. Purpose is to encourage employers to provide child care for their employees' children during normal working hours. |
| Foreign tax (§ 27) | Foreign taxable income/total worldwide taxable income × U.S. tax = overall limitation. Lesser of foreign taxes imposed or overall limitation. | Unused credits may be carried back 1 year and forward 10 years. Purpose is to reduce double taxation of foreign income. |

the regular income tax. Typically, more items are subject to tax under AMT rules, some gross income items are accelerated, and some deductions are deferred.

The formula for determining the AMT liability of corporate taxpayers appears in Exhibit 13–2 and follows the format of Form 4626 (Alternative Minimum Tax—Corporations).

The base for the AMT, **alternative minimum taxable income (AMTI),** begins with regular taxable income before any deductions for net operating losses (NOLs). A series of adjustments are then made. Most AMT adjustments relate to *timing differences* that arise because of separate regular income tax and AMT treatments. Adjustments that are caused by timing differences eventually reverse; that is, positive adjustments are offset by negative adjustments in the future, and vice versa.

The adjustments related to *circulation expenditures* illustrate this concept. Circulation expenditures include expenses incurred to establish, maintain, or increase the circulation of a newspaper, magazine, or other periodical.

In computing *taxable income*, corporations that are personal holding companies are allowed to deduct circulation expenditures in the year incurred. In computing

■ **EXHIBIT 13–2**
AMT Formula for Corporations

> Regular taxable income before NOL deduction
>
> **Plus/minus:** AMT adjustments (except ACE adjustment)
>
> **Plus:** Tax preferences
>
> **Equals:** AMTI before AMT NOL deduction and ACE adjustment
>
> **Plus/minus:** ACE adjustment
>
> **Equals:** AMTI before AMT NOL deduction
>
> **Minus:** AMT NOL deduction (limited to 90%)
>
> **Equals:** Alternative minimum taxable income (AMTI)
>
> **Minus:** Exemption
>
> **Equals:** AMT base
>
> **Times:** 20% rate
>
> **Equals:** Tentative AMT before AMT foreign tax credit
>
> **Minus:** AMT foreign tax credit
>
> **Equals:** Tentative minimum tax
>
> **Minus:** Regular income tax liability before credits minus regular foreign tax credit
>
> **Equals:** Alternative minimum tax (AMT) if positive

## TAX FACT

### THE REACH OF THE AMT

The total number of returns subject to the AMT is projected to increase as follows.

| Year | Number of Returns |
|------|-------------------|
| 2000 | 1,300,000 |
| 2005 | 3,100,000 |
| 2011 | 35,500,000 |

Tax year 2000 is representative of the increases that are likely to occur because of the AMT unless the Code is modified.

| | |
|---|---|
| Number of returns with AMT | 1,300,000 |
| Percentage increase in number of returns with AMT over prior year | 28.1% |
| Percentage increase in AMT liability over prior year | 48.2% |
| Revenue generated by AMT | $9 billion |

The revenue generated by the corporate AMT as a percentage of corporate tax liabilities, however, is declining. The probable cause for this decline is the exemption from the AMT for small corporations.

| Year | AMT as Percentage of Corporate Tax Liabilities |
|------|------------------------------------------------|
| 1990 | 8.0% |
| 2000 | 1.8% |

**Source:** IRS Tax Statistics.

AMTI, however, these expenditures must be capitalized and amortized ratably over the three-year period beginning with the year in which the expenditures were made.

**EXAMPLE 17**

Bobwhite, Inc., a personal holding company, incurred circulation expenditures of $30,000 in 2005. For regular income tax purposes, Bobwhite deducts $30,000 in 2005. For AMT purposes, the corporation is required to capitalize the expenditures and amortize them over a three-year period. Therefore, the deduction for AMT purposes is only $10,000. The AMT adjustment for 2005 is computed as follows.

| | |
|---|---|
| Circulation expenditures deducted for regular income tax purposes | $ 30,000 |
| Circulation expenditures deducted for AMT purposes | (10,000) |
| AMT adjustment (positive) | $ 20,000 |

**EXAMPLE 18**

Assume the same facts as in Example 17. The timing difference that gave rise to the positive adjustment in 2005 will reverse in the future. For AMT purposes, Bobwhite will deduct $10,000 in 2006 and $10,000 in 2007. The regular income tax deduction for circulation

## THE AMT: FROM 155 TO 35.5 MILLION

Sometimes the law changes in response to the demands of society (e.g., raising the legal drinking age to 21). On other occasions, the law is changed to prevent or reduce certain perceived abuses. Such was the case when the AMT was enacted in 1969. The identifiable perceived abuse was that 155 individual taxpayers had zero Federal income tax liability despite having incomes in excess of $200,000.

The original idea behind the AMT was one of fairness, based on the premise that taxpayers with significant economic income should pay at least a minimum amount of tax. That same concept of fairness later led Nina Olsen, the IRS's Taxpayer Advocate, to identify the expanding scope of the AMT as the number one problem facing taxpayers that needs to be legislatively addressed.

What has caused this shift in what is deemed fair? The idea that taxpayers with significant economic income should pay at least a minimum amount of tax has not changed. What is new is the number of taxpayers subject to the AMT—an estimated 35.5 million taxpayers in 2011 if the law is not changed. Thus, a tax that was perceived as fair when it affected only a "few" now is perceived as unfair because it affects "many."

SOURCE: Adapted from Catina Downey-Stroble, "Alternative Minimum Tax: Freedom and Taxes for All," *Disclosures*, May/June 2004, pp. 7 and 8.

---

expenditures in each of those years will be $0, because the entire $30,000 expenditure was deducted in 2005. This results in a negative AMT adjustment of $10,000 each in 2006 and 2007. The AMT adjustments over the three-year period are summarized below.

| Year | Regular Income Tax Deduction | AMT Deduction | AMT Adjustment |
|---|---|---|---|
| 2005 | $30,000 | $10,000 | $ 20,000 |
| 2006 | –0– | 10,000 | (10,000) |
| 2007 | –0– | 10,000 | (10,000) |
| Totals | $30,000 | $30,000 | $    –0– |

Timing differences eventually reverse. Thus, positive AMT adjustments can be offset later by negative adjustments. ■

## LO.4

Identify and calculate the tax preferences that are included in determining the AMT.

## TAX PREFERENCES

AMTI includes designated **tax preference items.** In many cases, this part of the AMT formula has the effect of subjecting otherwise nontaxable income to the AMT. Tax preferences always increase AMTI. Some of the principal tax preferences are discussed below.

**Percentage Depletion.**   Congress originally enacted the percentage depletion rules to provide taxpayers with incentives to invest in the development of specified natural resources. Percentage depletion is computed by multiplying a rate specified in the Code times the gross income from the property (refer to Chapter 4). The

### DISTINGUISHING BETWEEN TAXABLE AND EXEMPT BONDS FOR AMT PURPOSES

Interest on state and local bonds generally is exempt from the regular income tax, but it may be subject to the AMT.

If the state or local bond is a private activity bond, then the interest is a tax preference for AMT purposes. According to the Bond Market Association, interest from almost 8.7 percent of the $1.9 trillion municipal bond market is subject to the AMT. The association's Web site (**http://www.investinginbonds.com**) provides a primer on the AMT's effect on municipal bonds and explains how to determine if the related interest is subject to the AMT.

SOURCE: Adapted from Tom Herman, "A Website Can Help Demystify the AMT's Impact on Municipal-Bond Investors, *Wall Street Journal*, June 17, 2004, p. D2.

percentage rate is based on the type of mineral involved. The basis of the property is reduced by the amount of depletion taken until the basis reaches zero. However, once the basis of the property reaches zero, taxpayers are allowed to continue taking percentage depletion deductions. Thus, over the life of the property, depletion deductions may greatly exceed the cost of the property.

The percentage depletion preference is equal to the excess of the regular income tax deduction for percentage depletion over the adjusted basis of the property at the end of the taxable year.[21] Basis is determined without regard to the depletion deduction for the taxable year. This preference item is figured separately for each piece of property for which the taxpayer is claiming depletion.

**EXAMPLE 19**

Finch, Inc., owns a mineral property that qualifies for a 22% depletion rate. The basis of the property at the beginning of the year is $10,000. Gross income from the property for the year is $100,000. For regular income tax purposes, Finch's percentage depletion deduction (assume it is not limited by taxable income from the property) is $22,000. For AMT purposes, Finch has a tax preference of $12,000 ($22,000 – $10,000). ◼

**Interest on Private Activity Bonds.**   Income from private activity bonds is not included in taxable income, and expenses related to carrying such bonds are not deductible for regular income tax purposes. However, interest on private activity bonds is included as a preference in computing AMTI. Expenses incurred in carrying the bonds are offset against the interest income in computing the tax preference.[22]

The Code contains a lengthy, complex definition of **private activity bonds.**[23] In general, such debt is issued by states or municipalities, but more than 10 percent of the proceeds are used to benefit private business. For example, a bond issued by a city whose proceeds are used to construct a factory that is leased to a private business at a favorable rate is a private activity bond.

*Find more information on this topic at our Web site:* **http://wft-entities.swlearning.com.**

---

[21]§ 57(a)(1). Percentage depletion on oil and gas wells taken by independent producers and royalty owners does not create an AMT preference. See § 613A(c).

[22]§ 57(a)(5).
[23]§ 141.

**LO.5**

Identify and calculate AMT adjustments.

## AMT ADJUSTMENTS

As Exhibit 13–2 indicates, the starting point for computing AMTI is the taxable income of the corporation before any NOL deduction. Certain *adjustments* must be made to this amount. Unlike tax preference items, which always increase AMTI, the adjustments may be either increases or decreases to taxable income.

Although NOLs are separately stated in Exhibit 13–2, they are actually negative adjustments. They are separately stated in Exhibit 13–2 and on Form 4626 because they may not exceed more than 90 percent of AMTI. Thus, such adjustments cannot be determined until all other adjustments and tax preference items are considered.

**Computing Adjustments.**   It is necessary to determine not only the amount of an adjustment, but also whether the adjustment is positive or negative. Careful study of Examples 17 and 18 reveals the following pattern with regard to *deductions*.

- If the deduction allowed for regular income tax purposes exceeds the deduction allowed for AMT purposes, the difference is a positive adjustment.
- If the deduction allowed for AMT purposes exceeds the deduction allowed for regular income tax purposes, the difference is a negative adjustment.

Conversely, the direction of an adjustment attributable to an *income* item can be determined as follows.

- If the income reported for regular income tax purposes exceeds the income reported for AMT purposes, the difference is a negative adjustment.
- If the income reported for AMT purposes exceeds the income reported for regular income tax purposes, the difference is a positive adjustment.

The principal AMT adjustments are discussed below. The adjustment for circulation expenditures was discussed previously.

**Depreciation of Post-1986 Real Property.**   Tax legislation enacted in 1997 eliminated the AMT depreciation adjustment for real property by providing that the MACRS recovery periods (see Table 4–3) used in calculating the regular income tax apply in calculating the AMT. Note, however, that this AMT recovery period conformity provision applies only to property placed in service after December 31, 1998.[24] Thus, the AMT depreciation adjustment discussed below does apply for real property placed in service before January 1, 1999.

For real property placed in service after 1986 (MACRS property) and before January 1, 1999, AMT depreciation is computed under the alternative depreciation system (ADS), which uses the straight-line method over a 40-year life. The depreciation lives for regular income tax purposes are 27.5 years for residential rental property and 39 years for all other real property.[25] The difference between AMT depreciation and regular income tax depreciation is treated as an adjustment in computing the AMT. The differences will be positive during the regular income tax life of the asset because the cost is written off over a shorter period for regular income tax purposes. For example, during the 27.5-year income tax life of residential real property, the regular income tax depreciation will exceed the AMT depreciation because AMT depreciation is computed over a 40-year period.

Table 4–3 is used to compute regular income tax depreciation on real property placed in service after 1986. For AMT purposes, depreciation on real property placed in service after 1986 and before January 1, 1999, is computed under the ADS (refer to Table 4–7).

---

[24]§ 56(a)(1)(A)(i).

[25]The 39-year life generally applies to nonresidential real property placed in service on or after May 13, 1993.

**EXAMPLE 20**

In January 1998, Robin Rentals placed in service a residential building that cost $100,000. Regular income tax depreciation, AMT depreciation, and the AMT adjustment are as follows:

| | Depreciation | | |
|---|---|---|---|
| Year | Regular Income Tax | AMT | AMT Adjustment |
| 1998 | $3,485[1] | $2,396[2] | $1,089 |
| 1999 | 3,636[3] | 2,500[4] | 1,136 |
| 2000 | 3,636 | 2,500 | 1,136 |
| 2001 | 3,636 | 2,500 | 1,136 |
| 2002 | 3,636 | 2,500 | 1,136 |
| 2003 | 3,636 | 2,500 | 1,136 |
| 2004 | 3,636 | 2,500 | 1,136 |
| 2005 | 3,636 | 2,500 | 1,136 |

[1]$100,000 cost × 3.485% (Table 4–3) = $3,485
[2]$100,000 cost × 2.396% (Table 4–7) = $2,396
[3]$100,000 cost × 3.636% (Table 4–3) = $3,636
[4]$100,000 cost × 2.500% (Table 4–7) = $2,500

If the building had been placed in service after 1998, there would have been no AMT depreciation adjustment for the tax year it is placed in service or for subsequent years. The depreciation for the tax year the building was placed in service for both regular income tax purposes and AMT purposes would have been $3,485 ($100,000 × 3.485%). ■

After real property placed in service before 1999 has been held for the entire depreciation period for regular income tax purposes, the asset will be fully depreciated. However, the depreciation period under the ADS is 41 years due to application of the mid-month convention, so depreciation will continue for AMT purposes. This causes negative adjustments after the property has been fully depreciated for regular income tax purposes.

**EXAMPLE 21**

Assume the same facts as in the previous example for the building placed in service in 1998. Regular income tax depreciation in the year 2026 (the twenty-ninth year of the asset's life) is zero (refer to Table 4–3). AMT depreciation is $2,500 ($100,000 cost × 2.500% from Table 4–7). Therefore, Robin has a negative AMT adjustment of $2,500 ($0 regular income tax depreciation – $2,500 AMT depreciation). ■

After real property is fully depreciated for both regular income tax and AMT purposes, the positive and negative adjustments that have been made for AMT purposes will net to zero.

**Depreciation of Post-1986 Personal Property.** For most personal property placed in service after 1986 (MACRS property), the MACRS deduction for regular income tax purposes is based on the 200 percent declining-balance method with a switch to straight-line when that method produces a larger depreciation deduction for the asset. Refer to Table 4–1 for computing regular income tax depreciation.

For AMT purposes, the taxpayer must use the ADS for such property placed in service before 1999. This method is based on the 150 percent declining-balance method with a similar switch to straight-line for all personal property.[26] Refer to Table 4–5 for percentages to be used in computing AMT depreciation.

---

[26]§ 56(a)(1).

The MACRS deduction for personal property is larger than the ADS deduction in the early years of an asset's life. However, the ADS deduction is larger in the later years. This is so because ADS lives are sometimes longer than MACRS lives and use less accelerated depreciation methods.[27] Over the ADS life of the asset, the same aggregate amount of depreciation is deducted for both regular income tax and AMT purposes. In the same manner as other timing adjustments, the AMT adjustments for depreciation will net to zero over the ADS life of the asset.

The taxpayer may elect to use the ADS for regular income tax purposes. If this election is made, no AMT adjustment is required because the depreciation deduction is the same for regular income tax and for the AMT. The election eliminates the burden of maintaining two sets of tax depreciation records at the cost of a higher regular tax liability.

Tax legislation enacted in 1997 either reduces or eliminates the AMT adjustment for the depreciation of personal property. Prior to the effective date of this provision, the difference between regular income tax depreciation and AMT depreciation was caused by longer recovery periods for the AMT (class life versus MACRS recovery periods) and more accelerated depreciation methods for the regular income tax (200 percent declining balance rather than 150 percent declining balance).

Now, MACRS recovery periods are used in calculating AMT depreciation. Thus, if the taxpayer elects to use the 150 percent declining-balance method for regular income tax purposes, there are no AMT adjustments. Conversely, if the taxpayer uses the 200 percent declining-balance method for regular income tax purposes, there is an AMT adjustment for depreciation. This AMT recovery period conformity provision applies only to property placed in service after 1998. Thus, the adjustment continues to apply for personal property placed in service before 1999.

**Pollution Control Facilities.**   For regular income tax purposes, the cost of certified pollution control facilities may be amortized over a period of 60 months. For AMT purposes, the cost of these facilities placed in service after 1986 and before 1999 is depreciated under the ADS over the appropriate class life, determined as explained above for depreciation of post-1986 property.[28] The required adjustment for AMTI is the difference between the amortization deduction allowed for regular income tax purposes and the depreciation deduction computed under the ADS. The adjustment may be positive or negative.

The AMT adjustment for pollution control facilities is reduced for property placed in service after 1998. This reduction is achieved by providing conformity in the recovery periods used for regular income tax purposes and AMT purposes (MACRS recovery periods).

*Find more information on this topic at our Web site: **http://wft-entities.swlearning.com**.*

**Use of Completed Contract Method of Accounting.**   For a long-term contract, taxpayers are required to use the percentage of completion method for AMT purposes.[29] However, in limited circumstances, taxpayers can use the completed contract method for regular income tax purposes.[30] The resulting AMT adjustment is equal to the difference between income reported under the percentage of completion method and the amount reported using the completed contract method.[31] The adjustment can be either positive or negative, depending on the amount of income recognized under the different methods.

---

[27]Class lives and recovery periods are established for all assets in Rev.Proc. 87–56, 1987–2 C.B. 674.

[28]§ 56(a)(5).

[29]§ 56(a)(3).

[30]See Chapter 12 of *Advanced Business Entity Taxation* for a detailed discussion of the completed contract and percentage of completion methods of accounting.

[31]§ 56(a)(3).

A taxpayer can avoid an AMT adjustment on long-term contracts by using the percentage of completion method for regular income tax purposes rather than the completed contract method.

**Adjusted Gain or Loss.** When property is sold during the year or a casualty occurs to business or income-producing property, gain or loss reported for regular income tax may be different than gain or loss determined for the AMT. This difference occurs because the adjusted basis of the property for AMT purposes must reflect any current and prior AMT adjustments for the following.[32]

- Depreciation.
- Circulation expenditures.
- Amortization of certified pollution control facilities.

A negative gain or loss adjustment is required if:

- the gain for AMT purposes is less than the gain for regular income tax purposes;
- the loss for AMT purposes is more than the loss for regular income tax purposes; or
- a loss is computed for AMT purposes and a gain is computed for regular income tax purposes.

Otherwise, the AMT gain or loss adjustment is positive.

**EXAMPLE 22**

In January 1998, Cardinal Corporation paid $100,000 for a duplex acquired for rental purposes. Regular income tax depreciation, AMT depreciation, and the AMT adjustment are as follows:

| Year | Depreciation | | AMT Adjustment |
| | Regular Income Tax | AMT | |
| --- | --- | --- | --- |
| 1998 | $3,485[1] | $2,396[2] | $1,089 |
| 1999 | 3,636[3] | 2,500[4] | 1,136 |
| 2000 | 3,636 | 2,500 | 1,136 |
| 2001 | 3,636 | 2,500 | 1,136 |
| 2002 | 3,636 | 2,500 | 1,136 |
| 2003 | 3,636 | 2,500 | 1,136 |
| 2004 | 3,636 | 2,500 | 1,136 |

[1]$100,000 cost × 3.485% (Table 4–3) = $3,485
[2]$100,000 cost × 2.396% (Table 4–7) = $2,396
[3]$100,000 cost × 3.636% (Table 4–3) = $3,636
[4]$100,000 cost × 2.500% (Table 4–7) = $2,500

Cardinal then sold the duplex on December 20, 2005, for $105,000. Regular income tax depreciation for 2005 is $3,485 [($100,000 cost × 3.636% from Table 4–3) × ($11.5/12$)]. AMT depreciation for 2005 is $2,396 [($100,000 cost × 2.500% from Table 4–7) × ($11.5/12$)]. Cardinal's positive AMT adjustment for 2005 is $1,089 ($3,485 regular income tax depreciation − $2,396 AMT depreciation).

Because depreciation on the duplex differs for regular income tax and AMT purposes, Cardinal's adjusted basis for the property is different for regular income tax and AMT purposes. Consequently, the gain or loss on disposition of the duplex is different for regular income tax and AMT purposes.

[32]§ 56(a)(6).

The adjusted basis for Cardinal's duplex for regular income tax purposes is $71,214 and for AMT purposes is $80,208.

|  | **Regular Income Tax** | **AMT** |
|---|---|---|
| Cost | $100,000 | $100,000 |
| Depreciation: |  |  |
| 1998 | (3,485) | (2,396) |
| 1999 | (3,636) | (2,500) |
| 2000 | (3,636) | (2,500) |
| 2001 | (3,636) | (2,500) |
| 2002 | (3,636) | (2,500) |
| 2003 | (3,636) | (2,500) |
| 2004 | (3,636) | (2,500) |
| 2005 | (3,485) | (2,396) |
| Adjusted basis | $ 71,214 | $ 80,208 |

The regular income tax gain is $33,786 and the AMT gain is $24,792.

|  | **Regular Income Tax** | **AMT** |
|---|---|---|
| Amount realized | $105,000 | $105,000 |
| Adjusted basis | (71,214) | (80,208) |
| Recognized gain | $ 33,786 | $ 24,792 |

Because the regular income tax and AMT gain on the sale of the duplex differ, Cardinal makes a negative AMT adjustment of $8,994 ($33,786 regular income tax gain − $24,792 AMT gain). The negative adjustment matches the $8,994 total of the eight positive adjustments for depreciation ($1,089 in 1998 + $1,136 in 1999 + $1,136 in 2000 + $1,136 in 2001 + $1,136 in 2002 + $1,136 in 2003 + $1,136 in 2004 + $1,089 in 2005). ■

**Passive Activity Losses.**   Net losses on passive activities are not deductible in computing either the regular income tax or the AMT for closely held C corporations (cannot offset portfolio income) and personal service corporations (cannot offset either active income or portfolio income).[33] This does not, however, eliminate the possibility of adjustments attributable to passive activities.

The rules for computing taxable income differ from the rules for computing AMTI. It follows, then, that the rules for computing a loss for regular income tax purposes differ from the AMT rules for computing a loss. Therefore, any *passive loss* computed for regular income tax purposes may differ from the passive loss computed for AMT purposes.

**EXAMPLE 23**

Robin, Inc., a personal service corporation, acquired two passive activities in 2005. Robin received net passive income of $10,000 from Activity A and had no AMT adjustments or preferences in connection with the activity. Activity B had gross income of $27,000 and operating expenses (not affected by AMT adjustments or preferences) of $19,000. Robin claimed MACRS depreciation of $20,000 for Activity B; depreciation under the ADS would have been $15,000. In addition, Robin deducted $10,000 of percentage depletion in excess of basis. The following comparison illustrates the differences in the computation of the passive loss for regular income tax and AMT purposes for Activity B.

[33]§ 469(a).

|  | **Regular Income Tax** | **AMT** |
|---|---|---|
| Gross income | $ 27,000 | $ 27,000 |
| Deductions: |  |  |
|    Operating expenses | ($ 19,000) | ($ 19,000) |
|    Depreciation | (20,000) | (15,000) |
|    Depletion | (10,000) | –0– |
| Total deductions | ($ 49,000) | ($ 34,000) |
| Passive loss | ($ 22,000) | ($ 7,000) |

Because the adjustment for depreciation ($5,000) applies and the preference for depletion ($10,000) is not taken into account in computing AMTI, the regular income tax passive activity loss of $22,000 for Activity B is reduced by these amounts, resulting in a passive activity loss of $7,000 for AMT purposes.

For regular income tax purposes, Robin would offset the $10,000 of net passive income from Activity A with $10,000 of the passive loss from Activity B. For AMT purposes, the corporation would offset the $10,000 of net passive income from Activity A with the $7,000 passive activity loss allowed from Activity B, resulting in passive activity income of $3,000. Thus, in computing AMTI, Robin makes a positive passive loss adjustment of $3,000 [$10,000 (passive activity loss allowed for regular income tax) – $7,000 (passive activity loss allowed for the AMT)].[34]

For regular income tax purposes, Robin, Inc., has a suspended passive loss of $12,000 [$22,000 (amount of loss) – $10,000 (used in 2005)]. This suspended passive loss can offset passive income in the future or can offset active or portfolio income when the corporation disposes of the loss activity (refer to Chapter 5). For AMT purposes, Robin's suspended passive loss is $0 [$7,000 (amount of loss) – $7,000 (amount used in 2005)]. ■

**PLANNING STRATEGIES**

## Avoiding Preferences and Adjustments

**FRAMEWORK FOCUS: TAX RATE**

**STRATEGY ▶ CONTROL THE CHARACTER OF INCOME AND DEDUCTIONS.**

Investments in state and local bonds are attractive for income tax purposes because the interest is not included in gross income. Some of these bonds (private activity bonds) are issued to generate funds that are not used for an essential function of the government (e.g., to provide infrastructure for shopping malls or industrial parks or to build sports facilities). The interest on such bonds is a tax preference item and could lead to the imposition of the AMT. When the AMT applies, investors should take this factor into account. Perhaps an investment in regular tax-exempt bonds or even fully taxed private-sector bonds might yield a higher after-tax rate of return.

For a corporation anticipating AMT problems, capitalizing rather than expensing certain costs can avoid generating preferences and adjustments. The decision should be based on the present discounted value of after-tax cash flows under the available alternatives. Costs that may be capitalized and amortized, rather than expensed, include circulation expenditures, mining exploration and development costs, and research and experimentation expenditures.

[34]The depreciation adjustment and depletion preference are combined as part of the passive loss adjustment and are *not* reported separately.

■ **FIGURE 13–1**
Determining the ACE
Adjustment*

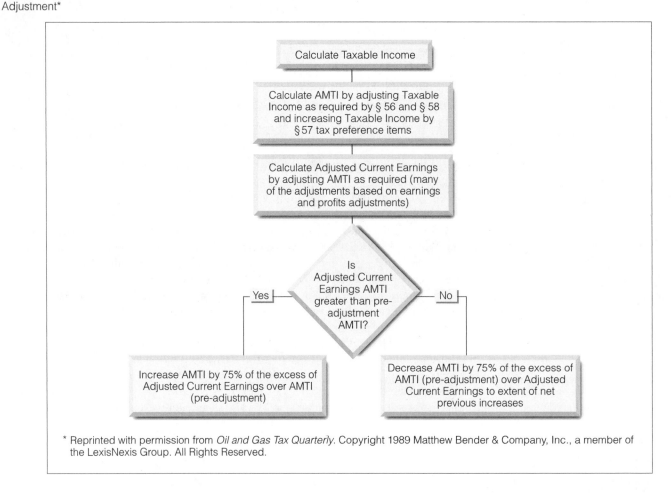

* Reprinted with permission from *Oil and Gas Tax Quarterly*. Copyright 1989 Matthew Bender & Company, Inc., a member of the LexisNexis Group. All Rights Reserved.

LO.6

Understand the function of
adjusted current earnings
(ACE).

## ADJUSTED CURRENT EARNINGS (ACE)

The **adjusted current earnings (ACE)** rules make up a third, separate tax system, parallel to both AMT and taxable income. S corporations, real estate investment trusts, regulated investment companies, and real estate mortgage investment conduits are not subject to the ACE provisions.

The purpose of the ACE adjustment is to ensure that the mismatching of financial statement income and taxable income will not produce inequitable results. ACE represents another attempt by Congress to assure that large corporations with significant financial accounting income pay a fair share of Federal corporate income tax.

The ACE adjustment is tax-based and can be negative or positive. AMTI is increased by 75 percent of the excess of ACE over unadjusted AMTI, or AMTI is reduced by 75 percent of the excess of unadjusted AMTI over ACE. Any negative ACE adjustment is limited to the aggregate of the positive adjustments under ACE for prior years reduced by the previously claimed negative adjustments (see Figure 13–1).[35] Any unused negative adjustment is lost forever.

---

[35]§§ 56(g)(1) and (2). *Unadjusted AMTI* is AMTI before the ACE adjustment and the AMT NOL deduction.

## CONCEPT SUMMARY 13–2

### Impact of Various Transactions on ACE and E & P

| | Effect on Unadjusted AMTI in Arriving at ACE | Effect on Taxable Income in Arriving at E & P |
|---|---|---|
| Tax-exempt income (net of expenses) | Add | Add |
| Federal income tax | No effect | Subtract |
| Dividends received deduction (80% and 100% rules) | No effect | Add |
| Dividends received deduction (70% rule) | Add | Add |
| Exemption amount of $40,000 | No effect | No effect |
| Key employee insurance proceeds | Add | Add |
| Excess charitable contribution | No effect | Subtract |
| Excess capital losses | No effect | Subtract |
| Disallowed meals and entertainment expenses | No effect | Subtract |
| Penalties and fines | No effect | Subtract |
| Intangible drilling costs deducted currently | Add | Add |
| Deferred gain on installment sales | Add | Add |
| Realized (not recognized) gain on an involuntary conversion | No effect | No effect |
| Loss on sale between related parties | No effect | Subtract |
| Gift received | No effect | No effect |
| Net buildup on life insurance policy | Add | Add |
| Organization expense amortization | Add | Add |

**EXAMPLE 24**

A calendar year corporation reports the following.

| | 2004 | 2005 | 2006 |
|---|---|---|---|
| Unadjusted AMTI | $3,000,000 | $3,000,000 | $3,100,000 |
| Adjusted current earnings | 4,000,000 | 3,000,000 | 2,000,000 |

In 2004, since ACE exceeds unadjusted AMTI by $1 million, $750,000 (75% × $1,000,000) is the positive ACE adjustment. No adjustment is necessary for 2005. Unadjusted AMTI exceeds ACE by $1,100,000 in 2006, so there is a potential negative ACE adjustment of $825,000. Since the total increases to AMTI for prior years equal $750,000 (and there are no negative adjustments), only $750,000 of the potential negative ACE adjustment reduces AMTI for 2006. Further, $75,000 of negative ACE is lost forever. ■

The starting point for computing ACE is AMTI, which is regular taxable income after AMT adjustments (other than the NOL and ACE adjustments) and tax preferences.[36] Pre-NOL AMTI is adjusted for certain items to determine ACE. See Concept Summary 13–2.

*Find more information on this topic at our Web site:* ***http://wft-entities.swlearning.com.***

---

[36]§ 56(g)(3).

**EXAMPLE 25**

Crimson Corporation makes the ACE adjustment calculation as follows.

| | | |
|---|---:|---:|
| AMTI | | $ 5,780,000 |
| Plus: | | |
| Municipal bond interest | $210,000 | |
| Installment gain | 140,000 | |
| 70% dividends received deduction | 300,000 | |
| Income element in cash surrender life insurance | 60,000 | |
| Organization expense amortization | 70,000 | 780,000 |
| Subtotal | | $ 6,560,000 |
| Less: | | |
| Related-party loss disallowance | $240,000 | (240,000) |
| Adjusted current earnings | | $ 6,320,000 |
| AMTI | | (5,780,000) |
| Base amount | | $ 540,000 |
| Times | | .75 |
| ACE adjustment (positive) | | $ 405,000 |

ACE should not be confused with current E & P. Many items are treated in the same manner, but certain items that are deductible in computing E & P (but are not deductible in calculating taxable income) generally are not deductible in computing ACE (e.g., Federal income taxes). Concept Summary 13–2 compares the impact various transactions will have on the determination of ACE and E & P.

## LO.7

Compute the AMT liability for corporations.

## COMPUTING ALTERNATIVE MINIMUM TAXABLE INCOME

The following example illustrates the effect of tax preferences and adjustments in arriving at AMTI.

**EXAMPLE 26**

For 2005, Tan Corporation (a calendar year company) had the following transactions.

| | |
|---|---:|
| Taxable income | $4,250,000 |
| Income deferred by using completed contract method (versus percentage of completion method) | 450,000 |
| Percentage depletion claimed (the property has a zero adjusted basis) | 1,575,000 |
| Interest on City of Elmira (Michigan) private activity bonds | 1,175,000 |

Tan Corporation's AMTI for 2005 is determined as follows.

| | | |
|---|---:|---:|
| Taxable income | | $4,250,000 |
| Adjustments | | |
| Income deferred by using completed contract method (versus percentage of completion method) | | 450,000 |
| Tax preferences | | |
| Excess depletion deduction | $1,575,000 | |
| Interest on private activity municipal bonds | 1,175,000 | 2,750,000 |
| AMTI | | $7,450,000 |

## Optimum Use of the AMT and Regular Corporate Income Tax Rate Difference

**FRAMEWORK FOCUS: TAX RATE**

STRATEGY ➤ SHIFT NET INCOME FROM HIGH-BRACKET YEARS TO LOW-BRACKET YEARS.

A corporation that cannot avoid the AMT in a particular year often can save taxes by taking advantage of the difference between the AMT and the regular income tax rates. In general, a corporation that expects to be subject to the AMT should consider accelerating income and deferring deductions for the remainder of the year. Since the difference between the regular income tax rate and the AMT rate may be as much as 14 or 15 percentage points, this strategy may result in the income being taxed at less than it would be if reported in the next year (a non-AMT year). If the same corporation expects to be subject to the AMT for the next year (or years) and is not subject to AMT this year, this technique should be reversed.

### EXAMPLE 27

Falcon Corporation expects to be in the 34% regular income tax bracket in 2006, but is subject to the AMT in 2005. In late 2005, Falcon is contemplating selling a tract of unimproved land (basis of $200,000 and fair market value of $1 million), which is classified as inventory. Under these circumstances, it may be preferable to sell the land in 2005. The gain of $800,000 ($1,000,000 − $200,000) generates a tax of $160,000 [$800,000 (recognized gain) × 20% (AMT rate)]. However, if the land is sold in 2006, the resulting tax is $272,000 [$800,000 (recognized gain) × 34% (regular corporate income tax rate)]. A nominal savings of $112,000 ($272,000 − $160,000) materializes by making the sale in 2005. ■

Whenever one accelerates income or defers deductions, a present value analysis should be conducted. This technique to accelerate gross income is attractive only if it reduces the present value of tax liabilities.

## AMT RATE AND EXEMPTION

The AMT rate is 20 percent. The rate is applied to the *AMT base*, which is AMTI reduced by the *AMT exemption*. The exemption amount for a corporation is $40,000 reduced by 25 percent of the amount by which AMTI exceeds $150,000. The exemption phases out entirely when AMTI reaches $310,000.

**EXAMPLE 28**

Beige Corporation has AMTI of $180,000. Since the exemption amount is reduced by $7,500 [25% × ($180,000 − $150,000)], the amount remaining is $32,500 ($40,000 − $7,500). Thus, Beige Corporation's alternative minimum tax base (refer to Exhibit 13–2) is $147,500 ($180,000 − $32,500). ■

## Controlling the Timing of Preferences and Adjustments

**FRAMEWORK FOCUS: TAX RATE**

STRATEGY ➤ CONTROL THE CHARACTER OF INCOME AND DEDUCTIONS.

In many situations, corporations with modest levels of income may be able to avoid the AMT by making use of the exemption. To maximize the exemption, taxpayers should attempt to avoid bunching positive adjustments and tax preferences in any one year. Rather, net these items against negative adjustments to keep AMTI low. When the expenditure is largely within the control of the taxpayer, timing to avoid bunching is more easily accomplished.

**Bridge to Finance**

For entities other than C corporations, each year more taxpayers are subject to the AMT. In addition, for taxpayers who are paying the AMT, the amount of AMT increases annually, even when both the total Federal taxable income and the tentative AMT are constant. This increase is even more noticeable in light of the statutory tax rate decreases for individual taxpayers provided for in the Tax Relief Reconciliation Act of 2001 commencing in 2002. The next scheduled decrease in the individual income tax rates under the 2001 Act was to be effective for 2004. However, the reduced tax rates for 2004 and thereafter were accelerated into 2003 by the Jobs Growth and Tax Relief Reconciliation Act of 2003 (JGTRRA of 2003).

Rose, Inc., an S corporation, has one shareholder, Jack, who is single. In 2002 and 2003, Rose has taxable income of $100,000, which is reported to Jack each year on a Schedule K–1. Jack's taxable income, excluding the $100,000 from Rose, is $300,000 each year. Jack's tentative AMT each year is $150,000.

Jack's regular income tax liability, AMT, and total Federal income tax liability for 2002 and 2003 are as follows.

| **2002** | | |
|---|---|---|
| Regular income tax liability | | |
| Tax on $307,050 | = | $ 94,720 |
| 92,950 × 38.6% | = | 35,879 |
| $400,000 | | $130,599 |
| AMT ($150,000 − $130,599) | | $ 19,401 |
| Regular income tax | | $130,599 |
| AMT | | 19,401 |
| Total tax liability | | $150,000 |

| **2003** | | |
|---|---|---|
| Regular income tax liability | | |
| Tax on $311,950 | = | $ 90,514 |
| 88,050 × 35% | = | 30,818 |
| $400,000 | | $121,332 |
| AMT ($150,000 − $121,332) | | $ 28,668 |
| Regular income tax | | $121,332 |
| AMT | | 28,668 |
| Total tax liability | | $150,000 |

When Jack's taxable income remains the same each year, why does the AMT increase by $9,267 ($28,668 − $19,401)? The reasons are as follows: (1) the tax rates used in calculating the regular income tax (§ 1) are indexed for the effect of inflation each year, while the AMT tax rates (§ 55) are not subject to indexing, and (2) the statutory tax rates for the regular income tax for 2002 versus 2003 have been reduced by the JGTRRA of 2003 while the AMT rates have not changed. Note that if the tax years being compared were 2004 and 2005, only the indexing effect would be present. That is, the 2004 and 2005 statutory tax rates are the same.

The inflation effect could easily be fixed by indexing the AMT tax rates. Corporations are not subject to inflation-caused effects because neither the regular income tax rates (§ 11) nor the AMT rates (§ 55) are indexed. In addition, the Tax Relief Reconciliation Act of 2001 did not modify either the regular income tax rates or the AMT rates for C corporations.

## MINIMUM TAX CREDIT

The **minimum tax credit** acts to make the AMT merely a *prepayment of tax* for corporations. Essentially, the AMT paid in one tax year may be carried forward indefinitely and used as a credit against the corporation's future *regular* tax liability that exceeds its tentative minimum tax. The minimum tax credit may not be carried back and may not be offset against any future AMT liability.

**EXAMPLE 29**

Return to the facts of Example 26. AMTI exceeds $310,000, so there is no exemption amount. The tentative minimum tax is $1,490,000 (20% of $7,450,000). Since Tan's regular income tax liability for 2005 is $1,445,000, the AMT liability is $45,000 ($1,490,000 – $1,445,000). The minimum tax credit carried forward is $45,000, the current year's AMT. The credit can be used to reduce regular income tax liability in future years (but not below the tentative alternative minimum tax). ■

## OTHER ASPECTS OF THE AMT

In addition to paying their regular income tax liability, corporations must make estimated tax payments of the AMT liability. Even corporations that prepare quarterly financial statements may find this requirement adds to compliance costs.

The only credit that can be used to offset the AMT is the foreign tax credit (FTC). The general business credit and other credits discussed earlier in the chapter are unavailable in AMT years.

The corporate AMT is computed and reported by completing Form 4626.

**PLANNING STRATEGIES**

### The Subchapter S Option

**FRAMEWORK FOCUS: TAX RATE**

**STRATEGY ➤ AVOID DOUBLE TAXATION.**

Corporations that make the S election are not subject to the corporate AMT. As noted in Chapter 11, however, various AMT adjustments and preferences pass through to the individual shareholders. But one troublesome adjustment, the one involving the ACE adjustment, is avoided since it does not apply to individual taxpayers.

# Individual Alternative Minimum Tax

The AMT applicable to individuals is similar to the corporate AMT. Most of the adjustments and preferences discussed above apply equally to individuals and corporations. However, there are several important differences.

- The individual AMT rates are slightly progressive, with rates at 26 percent on the first $175,000 of AMTI and at 28 percent on any additional AMTI.
- The alternative rate on net capital gain of 5 or 15 percent applies.
- The AMT exemption and phaseout amounts are tied to the individual's filing status for the year. The exemption phases out at a rate of $1 for every $4 of AMTI.[37]

| Filing Status | Initial Exemption Amount in 2005 | Phaseout Range | |
| --- | --- | --- | --- |
| | | Begins at | Ends at |
| Married, joint | $58,000 | $150,000 | $382,000 |
| Married, separate | 29,000 | 75,000 | 191,000 |
| Single, head of household | 40,250 | 112,500 | 273,500 |

---

[37]§§ 55(d)(1) and (3). For tax years beginning in 2006 and thereafter, the exemption amount is reduced to the following amounts: married taxpayers filing jointly—$45,000, single taxpayers—$33,750, married taxpayers filing separately—$22,500.

- Individuals make no AMT adjustment for ACE.
- Some additional adjustments apply to individual taxpayers. Taxes and miscellaneous itemized deductions subject to the 2 percent-of-AGI floor are not allowed as deductions for AMTI. Medical expenses are allowed only to the extent that they exceed 10 percent of AGI (instead of a 7.5 percent limitation for regular income tax purposes). Interest expense deductions are limited to qualified residence interest, interest on certain student loans, and investment interest (subject to limitations). Finally, the standard deduction and personal and dependency exemptions are not allowed as deductions when computing AMTI. Other individual-specific adjustments also exist, including an adjustment accelerating the taxation of incentive stock options.
- Determination of the minimum tax credit is more complex for individual taxpayers. The credit applies only to AMT generated as a result of *timing* differences.

Although there are several computational differences, the individual AMT and the corporate AMT have the same objective: to force taxpayers who have more economic income than that reflected in taxable income to pay a fair share of Federal income tax.

## Suggested Further Readings

Steven D. Arkin and James M. Eberle, "The New Research Credit Final Regs.—What's Gone, What's New, and What's Missing," *Journal of Taxation,* March 2004, pp. 144–151.

Albert B. Ellentuck, "Case Study: Avoiding the AMT Depreciation Adjustment," *The Tax Adviser,* January 2003, pp. 54–55.

John O. Everett and Cherie J. O'Neil, "AMT Planning Strategies," *The Tax Adviser,* November 2000, pp. 788–799.

Matt Given, "Aim to Take Advantage of Various Targeted Tax Credits," *Practical Tax Strategies,* April 2004, pp. 220–235.

Joseph R. Oliver, "Research Credit Potentially Available for Internal-Use Software," *Practical Tax Strategies,* September 2002, pp. 153–160.

Michael I. Sanders, "The New Markets Tax Credit: Stimulating Investment While Facilitating Economic Development," *Journal of Taxation*, November 2002, pp. 94–101.

## KEY TERMS

Adjusted current earnings (ACE), 13–26

Alternative minimum tax (AMT), 13–14

Alternative minimum taxable income (AMTI), 13–16

Credit for employer-provided child care, 13–12

Credit for small employer pension plan startup costs, 13–12

Disabled access credit, 13–11

Foreign tax credit (FTC), 13–13

General business credit, 13–3

Minimum tax credit, 13–30

Private activity bonds, 13–19

Rehabilitation expenditures credit, 13–6

Rehabilitation expenditures credit recapture, 13–7

Research activities credit, 13–9

Tax credits, 13–2

Tax preference items, 13–18

Welfare-to-work credit, 13–8

Work opportunity tax credit, 13–8

## Problems

1. Canary, Inc., has a tentative general business credit of $85,000 for 2005. Canary's net regular tax liability before the general business credit is $95,000, and its tentative minimum tax is $90,000. Compute Canary's allowable general business credit for the year.

2. Burt Corporation has the following general business credit carryovers.

| | |
|---|---|
| 2001 | $ 5,000 |
| 2002 | 15,000 |
| 2003 | 5,000 |
| 2004 | 20,000 |
| Total carryovers | $45,000 |

   If the general business credit generated by activities during 2005 equals $45,000 and the total credit allowed during the current year is $80,000 (based on tax liability), what amounts of the current general business credit and carryovers can Burt use against its 2005 income tax liability? What is the amount of unused credit carried forward to 2006?

**Issue ID**

3. Clint, a self-employed engineering consultant, is contemplating purchasing an old building for renovation. After the work is completed, Clint plans to rent out two-thirds of the floor space to businesses and to live and work in the remaining portion. Identify the relevant tax issues for Clint.

4. In January 2004, Iris Corporation purchased and placed into service a 1933 building that houses retail businesses. The cost was $200,000, of which $25,000 applied to the land. In modernizing the facility, Iris Corporation incurred $250,000 of renovation costs of the type that qualify for the rehabilitation credit. These improvements were placed into service in October 2005.
   a. Compute Iris Corporation's rehabilitation tax credit for 2005.
   b. Calculate the cost recovery deductions for the building and the renovation costs for 2005.

**Decision Making**

**Communications**

5. In the current year, Diane Lawson (127 Peachtree Drive, Savannah, GA 31419) acquires a qualifying historic structure for $250,000 (excluding the cost of land) with full intentions of substantially rehabilitating the building. Write a letter to Diane and a memo to the tax files explaining the computation that determines the rehabilitation tax credit available to her and the impact on the depreciable basis, assuming she incurs either $200,000 or $400,000 for the rehabilitation project.

**Ethics**

6. The tax credit for rehabilitation expenditures is available to help offset the costs related to substantially rehabilitating certain buildings. The credit is calculated on the rehabilitation expenditures incurred and not on the acquisition cost of the building itself.

   You are a developer who buys, sells, and does construction work on real estate in the inner city of your metropolitan area. A potential customer approaches you about acquiring one of your buildings that easily could qualify for the 20% rehabilitation credit on historic structures. The stated sales price of the structure is $100,000 (based on appraisals ranging from $80,000 to $120,000), and the rehabilitation expenditures, if the job is done correctly, would be about $150,000.

   Your business has been slow recently due to the sluggish real estate market in your area, and the potential customer makes the following proposal: if you reduce the sales price of the building to $75,000, he will pay you $175,000 to perform the rehabilitation work. Although the buyer's total expenditures would be the same, he would benefit from this approach by obtaining a larger tax credit ($25,000 increased rehabilitation costs × 20% = $5,000).

   It has been a long time since you have sold any of your real estate. How will you respond?

7. Red Company hires six individuals on January 15, 2005, qualifying Red for the work opportunity tax credit. Three of these individuals receive wages of $9,000 each during 2005, for working 900 hours each. The other three receive wages of $2,500 each, for working 325 hours each.
   a. Calculate the amount of Red's work opportunity tax credit for 2005.
   b. Assume Red pays total wages of $175,000 to its employees during the year. How much of this amount is deductible in 2005 if the work opportunity tax credit is taken?

8. In March 2005, Wren Corporation hired three individuals, Trent, Bernice, and Benita, all of whom are certified as long-term family assistance recipients. Each employee is paid $11,000 during 2005. Only Bernice continued to work for Wren in 2006, earning $13,500. In February 2006, Wren hired Cassie, who was also certified as a long-term family assistance recipient. During 2006, Cassie earned $11,000. Wren does not claim the work opportunity credit with respect to any employees hired in 2005 or 2006.
   a. Compute Wren's welfare-to-work credit for 2005 and 2006.
   b. Wren pays total wages of $325,000 to its employees during 2005 and $342,000 during 2006. How much may Wren claim as a wage deduction for 2005 and 2006 if the welfare-to-work credit is claimed in both years?

**Decision Making**

9. Martin, Inc., a calendar year taxpayer, informs you that during the year it incurs expenditures of $50,000 that qualify for the incremental research activities credit. In addition, it is determined that the corporation's base amount for the year is $35,000.
   a. Determine Martin's incremental research activities credit for the year.
   b. Martin is in the 25% tax bracket. Determine which approach to the research expenditures and the research activities credit would provide the greatest tax benefit to Martin.

**Communications**

10. Ahmed Zinna (16 Southside Drive, Charlotte, NC 28204), one of your clients, owns two restaurants in downtown Charlotte and has come to you seeking advice concerning the tax consequences of complying with the Americans with Disabilities Act. He understands that he needs to install various features at his businesses (e.g., ramps, doorways, and restrooms that are handicapped accessible) to make them more accessible to disabled individuals. He inquires whether any tax credits are available to help offset the cost of the necessary changes. He estimates the cost of the planned changes to his facilities as follows.

| Location | Projected Cost |
| --- | --- |
| Calvin Street | $22,000 |
| Stowe Avenue | 8,500 |

He reminds you that the Calvin Street restaurant was constructed in 2001 while the Stowe Avenue restaurant is in a building that was constructed in 1986. Ahmed operates his business as a sole proprietorship and has approximately eight employees at each location. Write a letter to Ahmed in which you summarize your conclusions concerning the tax consequences of his proposed capital improvements.

11. Blue Corporation, a U.S. corporation, is a manufacturing concern that sells most of its products in the United States. It also does some business in Europe through various branches. During the current year, Blue Corporation has taxable income of $500,000, of which $350,000 is U.S.-sourced and $150,000 is foreign-sourced. Foreign income taxes paid are $55,000. Blue's U.S. income tax liability before any foreign tax credit is $170,000.
   a. What is Blue Corporation's U.S. income tax liability net of the allowable foreign tax credit?
   b. What is the amount of Blue's foreign tax credit carryback and carryover?

12. Aqua, Inc., a calendar year corporation, has the following gross receipts and taxable income for 1993–2005.

| Year | Gross Receipts | Taxable Income |
|------|---------------|----------------|
| 1993 | $11,000,000 | $3,000,000 |
| 1994 | 4,800,000 | 900,000 |
| 1995 | 5,300,000 | 1,500,000 |
| 1996 | 4,600,000 | 700,000 |
| 1997 | 8,200,000 | 1,200,000 |
| 1998 | 8,500,000 | 1,900,000 |
| 1999 | 5,200,000 | 1,300,000 |
| 2000 | 8,000,000 | 1,500,000 |
| 2001 | 6,000,000 | 1,450,000 |
| 2002 | 6,200,000 | 1,375,000 |
| 2003 | 6,100,000 | 1,425,000 |
| 2004 | 10,000,000 | 1,400,000 |
| 2005 | 9,000,000 | 1,312,000 |

    a.  When is Aqua first exempt from the AMT as a small corporation?

    b.  Is Aqua subject to the AMT for 2005?

13.  Falcon, Inc., owns a silver mine that it purchased several years ago for $925,000. The adjusted basis at the beginning of the year is $400,000. For the year, Falcon deducts depletion of $700,000 (greater of cost depletion of $290,000 or percentage depletion of $700,000) for regular income tax purposes.

    a.  Calculate Falcon's AMT adjustment.

    b.  Calculate Falcon's adjusted basis for regular income tax purposes.

    c.  Calculate Falcon's adjusted basis for AMT purposes.

**Decision Making**

**Communications**

14.  In March 2005, Grackle, Inc., acquired used equipment for its business at a cost of $300,000. The equipment is five-year class property for regular income tax purposes and for AMT purposes.

    a.  If Grackle depreciates the equipment using the method that will produce the greatest deduction for 2005 for regular income tax purposes, what is the amount of the AMT adjustment? Grackle does not elect §179 limited expensing.

    b.  How can Grackle reduce the AMT adjustment to $0? What circumstances would motivate Grackle to do so?

    c.  Draft a letter to Helen Carlon, Grackle's controller, regarding the choice of depreciation methods. Helen's address is 500 Monticello Avenue, Glendale, AZ 85306.

15.  Rust Company is a real estate construction company with average annual gross receipts of $3 million. Rust uses the completed contract method on a contract that requires 16 months to complete. The contract is for $500,000 with estimated costs of $300,000. At the end of 2005, $180,000 of costs had been incurred. The contract is completed in 2006 with the total cost being $295,000. Determine the amount of adjustments for AMT purposes for 2005 and 2006.

**Ethics**

16.  Allie, who was an accounting major in college, is the controller of a medium-size construction corporation. She prepares the corporate tax return each year. Due to reporting a home construction contract using the completed contract method, the corporation is subject to the AMT in 2005. Allie files the 2005 corporate tax return in early February 2006. The total tax liability is $58,000 ($53,000 regular income tax liability + $5,000 AMT).

    In early March, Allie reads an article on minimizing income taxes. Based on this article, she decides that it would be beneficial for the corporation to report the home construction contract using the percentage of completion method on its 2005 return. Although this will increase the corporation's 2005 income tax liability, it will minimize the total income tax liability over the two-year construction period. Therefore, Allie files an amended return on March 14, 2006. Evaluate Allie's actions from both a tax avoidance and an ethical perspective.

17. Buford sells an apartment building for $580,000. His adjusted basis is $312,000 for regular income tax purposes and $345,000 for AMT purposes. Calculate Buford's:
    a. Gain for regular income tax purposes.
    b. Gain for AMT purposes.
    c. AMT adjustment, if any.

**Issue ID**

18. Pheasant, Inc., is going to be subject to the AMT in 2005. The corporation owns an investment building and is considering disposing of it and investing in other realty. Based on an appraisal of the building's value, the realized gain would be $85,000. Ed has offered to purchase the building from Pheasant with the closing date being December 29, 2005. Ed wants to close the transaction in 2005 because certain beneficial tax consequences will result only if the transaction is closed prior to the beginning of 2006. Abby has offered to purchase the building with the closing date being January 2, 2006. The building has a $95,000 greater AMT adjusted basis. For regular income tax purposes, Pheasant expects to be in the 34% tax bracket. What are the relevant tax issues that Pheasant faces in making its decision?

19. Flicker, Inc., a closely held corporation, acquired a passive activity in 2005. Gross income from operations of the activity was $160,000. Operating expenses, not including depreciation, were $122,000. Regular income tax depreciation of $49,750 was computed under MACRS. AMT depreciation, computed under ADS, was $41,000. Compute Flicker's passive loss deduction and passive loss suspended for regular income tax purposes and for AMT purposes.

20. Maize Corporation (a calendar year corporation) reports the following information for the years listed:

|                           | 2003        | 2004        | 2005        |
| ------------------------- | ----------- | ----------- | ----------- |
| Adjusted current earnings | $5,000,000  | $5,000,000  | $7,000,000  |
| Unadjusted AMTI           | 8,000,000   | 5,000,000   | 3,000,000   |

    Compute the ACE adjustment for each year.

21. Based upon the following facts, calculate adjusted current earnings (ACE).

| | |
| --- | --- |
| Alternative minimum taxable income (AMTI) | $5,120,000 |
| Municipal bond interest | 630,000 |
| Expenses related to municipal bonds | 50,000 |
| Key employee life insurance proceeds in excess of cash surrender value | 2,000,000 |
| Organization expense amortization | 100,000 |
| Cost of goods sold | 6,220,000 |
| Advertising expenses | 760,000 |
| Loss between related parties | 260,000 |
| Life insurance expense | 300,000 |

22. Purple Corporation, a calendar year taxpayer, reported the following amounts. Calculate Purple's positive and negative ACE adjustments.

|       | **Preadjusted AMTI** | **ACE**      |
| ----- | -------------------- | ------------ |
| 2004  | $80,000,000          | $70,000,000  |
| 2005  | 60,000,000           | 90,000,000   |
| 2006  | 50,000,000           | 40,000,000   |
| 2007  | 60,000,000           | 20,000,000   |

23. Determine whether each of the following transactions is a preference (P), an adjustment (A), or not applicable (NA) for purposes of the corporate AMT.
    a. Depletion in excess of basis taken by Giant Oil Company.
    b. Accelerated depreciation on property.
    c. Charitable contributions of cash.
    d. Adjusted current earnings.
    e. Tax-exempt interest on private activity bonds.
    f. Untaxed appreciation on property donated to charity.
    g. Dividends received deduction.

24. In each of the following *independent* situations, determine the tentative minimum tax. Assume the company is not in small corporation status.

    |  | AMTI (Before the Exemption Amount) |
    | --- | --- |
    | Quincy Corporation | $150,000 |
    | Redland Corporation | 160,000 |
    | Tanzen Corporation | 320,000 |

25. For 2005, Peach Corporation (a calendar year company) had the following transactions.

    | | |
    | --- | --- |
    | Taxable income | $5,000,000 |
    | Regular tax depreciation on realty in excess of ADS (placed in service in 1990) | 1,700,000 |
    | Amortization of certified pollution control facilities (in excess of ADS amortization) | 200,000 |
    | Tax-exempt interest on private activity bonds | 300,000 |
    | Percentage depletion in excess of the property's adjusted basis | 700,000 |

    a. Determine Peach Corporation's AMTI.
    b. Determine the tentative minimum tax base (refer to Exhibit 13–2).
    c. Determine the tentative AMT.
    d. What is the amount of the AMT?

26. Included in Alice's regular taxable income and in her AMT base is a $200,000 capital gain on the sale of stocks that she owned for three years. Alice is in the 35% tax bracket for regular income tax purposes. In calculating her regular income tax liability, she uses the appropriate alternative tax rate on net capital gain of 15%.
    a. What rate should Alice use in calculating her tentative AMT?
    b. What is Alice's AMT adjustment?
    c. How would your answers in (a) and (b) change if the taxpayer were a C corporation in the 34% tax bracket for regular income tax purposes?

**EXTENDER**  27. Calculate the AMT for the following cases in 2005. The taxpayer reports regular taxable income of $525,000 and no tax credits.

| | Tentative AMT | |
| --- | --- | --- |
| Filing Status | Case 1 | Case 2 |
| Single | $194,000 | $175,000 |
| Married, filing jointly | 194,000 | 175,000 |

**EXTENDER**  28. Grayson, who is single with no dependents and does not itemize, provides you with the following information for 2005.

| | |
| --- | --- |
| Short-term capital loss | $ 4,000 |
| Long-term capital gain | 19,000 |
| Municipal bond interest received on private activity bonds acquired in 1995 | 13,000 |

| | |
|---|---|
| Dividends from General Motors | $ 6,500 |
| Excess of FMV over cost for incentive stock options (the rights became freely transferable and not subject to a substantial risk of forfeiture in 2005) | 36,000 |
| Charitable contributions | 10,000 |

What are Grayson's tax preference items and AMT adjustments for 2005?

**BRIDGE DISCIPLINE**

1. Balm, Inc., has a general business credit for 2005 of $90,000. Balm's regular income tax liability before credits is $140,000, and its tentative AMT is $132,000.
   a. Calculate the amount of general business credit that Balm can use in 2005 and calculate its general business credit carryback and carryforward, if any.
   b. Balm projects a $140,000 regular 2006 income tax liability. Its tentative AMT will be $132,000. Balm is considering making an investment early in 2006 that annually will produce $45,000 of tax-exempt income. Balm is trying to decide between two alternatives. The first alternative is a tax-exempt bond that is a private activity bond. The second alternative is a tax-exempt bond that is not a private activity bond. Advise Balm on the preferable investment.

2. Cooper Partnership, a calendar year partnership, made qualifying rehabilitation expenditures to a building that it has used in its business for eight years. These improvements were placed in service on January 5, 2004. The amount of the rehabilitation expenditures credit was $40,000.

   Cooper is negotiating to sell the building in either December 2005 or January 2006. The sales price will be $600,000, and the recognized gain will be $100,000. Provide support for the CFO's position that Cooper should delay the sale until 2006.

3. For many years, Saul's sole proprietorship and his related Form 1040 have had a number of AMT tax preferences and AMT adjustments. He has made the AMT calculation each year, but the calculated amount always has been $0. Saul's regular taxable income and the AMT adjustments and preferences for 2005 are the same as for last year. Yet he must pay AMT this year. Explain how this could happen.

## Research Problems

*Note: Solutions to Research Problems can be prepared by using the **RIA Checkpoint® Student Edition** online research product, which is available to accompany this text. It is also possible to prepare solutions to the Research Problems by using tax research materials found in a standard tax library.*

**Research Problem 1.**   Miriam, an admirer of early twentieth-century architecture, discovers a 1920s-era house in the countryside outside Mobile, Alabama, during a recent Sunday excursion. She desires not only to purchase and renovate this particular house, but also to move the structure into Mobile so her community can enjoy its architectural features. Being aware of the availability of the tax credit for rehabilitation expenditures, she wishes to maximize her use of the provision, if it is available in this case, once the renovation work begins in Mobile. However, Miriam also informs you that she will pursue the purchase, relocation, and renovation of the house only if the tax credit is available. Comment on Miriam's decision and whether any renovation expenditures incurred will qualify for the tax credit for rehabilitation expenditures.

*Partial list of research aids:*
*George S. Nalle, III, 99 T.C. 187 (1992).*

**Communications**

**Research Problem 2.** Oriole Corporation is a large wholesaler of office products. To remain successful in a fiercely competitive industry, Oriole has automated and computerized many of its business operations. Specifically, the corporation has developed several new software programs to:

- Maintain files of customer histories.
- Create a paperless invoicing system.
- Develop a computer-to-computer order entry system.
- Monitor inventory levels more closely.

Oriole estimates that it spent more than $1 million to develop and test the new software programs that are used throughout the business. To date, Oriole has not sold the software programs to the public, but it is contemplating doing so. Oriole has claimed a research and experimentation deduction for the costs associated with developing the software programs. The corporation also wants to claim the research activities credit relating to the software development. Can Oriole do so? Write a memo to the tax research file summarizing your conclusions.

**Communications**

**Research Problem 3.** Your ophthalmologist, Dr. Hunter Francis (55 Wheatland Drive, Hampton, CT 06247), has been very pleased with the growth of his practice in the 15 years he has been in business. This growth has resulted, at least in part, because he has aggressively marketed his services and tried to accommodate clients with various needs. This year Dr. Francis purchased a sophisticated piece of equipment that enables him to diagnose persons with mental handicaps, hearing impairments, and physical disabilities without having to go through a series of questions. In addition, he can treat his patients who are not disabled much more accurately and efficiently by using this equipment.

Since purchasing the machine this year for $9,500, Dr. Francis has used it on many occasions. Unfortunately, he has not been able to attract any disabled patients, even though previously he referred such people to other ophthalmologists who owned the necessary equipment. Therefore, the primary purpose for acquiring the equipment (i.e., to attract disabled patients) has not been realized, but he has put it to good use in treating other patients. Write a letter to Dr. Francis explaining whether he may claim the disabled access credit for this acquisition.

**Research Problem 4.** Parrot, Inc., receives tax-exempt interest of $20,000 on bonds that are classified as private activity bonds. The corporation appropriately excludes the $20,000 from its gross income for regular income tax purposes under § 103(a) and § 103(b)(1). Parrot has asked you for advice on the treatment of the $20,000 for AMT purposes. Find the Code Section that addresses the AMT treatment for private activity bond interest. Provide Parrot with the advice it has requested.

**Research Problem 5.** Teal, Inc., owns two warehouses that were placed in service before 1987. Accelerated depreciation for 2005 on Warehouse A is $36,000 (straight-line depreciation would have been $30,000). On Warehouse B, accelerated depreciation was $16,000 (straight-line depreciation would have been $20,000). What is the amount of Teal's tax preference for excess depreciation in 2005?

**Internet Activity**

*Use the tax resources of the Internet to address the following questions. Do not restrict your search to the World Wide Web, but include a review of newsgroups and general reference materials, practitioner sites and resources, primary sources of the tax law, chat rooms and discussion groups, and other opportunities.*

**Research Problem 6.** The foreign tax credit is especially valuable when a U.S. business earns income in a country whose income tax rates exceed those of the United States. List five countries whose tax rates on business income exceed those of the United States, and five where the corresponding U.S. rates are higher.

**Research Problem 7.** Some parties believe that many corporations are paying little, if any, corporate income tax and blame the AMT for being ineffective. Examine both government and press sites on the Internet and summarize these complaints.

# Comparative Forms of Doing Business

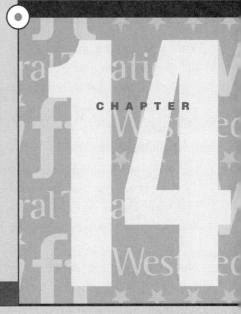

## LEARNING OBJECTIVES

*After completing Chapter 14, you should be able to:*

### L O . 1
Identify the principal legal and tax forms for conducting a business.

### L O . 2
Appreciate the relative importance of nontax factors in business decisions.

### L O . 3
Distinguish between the forms for conducting a business according to whether they are subject to single taxation or double taxation.

### L O . 4
Identify techniques for avoiding double taxation.

### L O . 5
Understand and apply the conduit and entity concepts as they affect operations, capital changes, and distributions.

### L O . 6
Analyze the effects of the disposition of a business on the owners and the entity for each of the forms for conducting a business.

http://wft.swlearning.com

## O U T L I N E

---

## TAX TALK

*[My law firm] had a rule—at least it seemed to be a rule—that everybody that came had to spend at least a year working on taxes. The general rationale for the rule as I could understand it was that taxes were so important to everything that you do, whatever the kind of case you are handling, you have to know something about the tax consequences of things.*

—*Charles A. Horsky*

**A** variety of factors, both tax and nontax, can affect the choice of the form of business entity. The form that is appropriate at one point in the life of an entity and its owners may not be appropriate at a different time.

**EXAMPLE 1**

Eva is a tax practitioner in Kentwood, the Dairy Center of the South. Many of her clients are dairy farmers. She recently had tax planning discussions with two of her clients, Jesse, a Line Creek dairy farmer, and Larry, a Spring Creek dairy farmer.

Jesse recently purchased his dairy farm. He is 52 years old and just retired after 30 years of service as a chemical engineer at an oil refinery in Baton Rouge. Eva recommended that he incorporate his dairy farm and elect S corporation status for Federal income tax purposes.

Larry has owned his dairy farm since 1999. He inherited it from his father. At that time, Larry retired after 20 years of service in the U.S. Air Force. He has a master's degree in Agricultural Economics from LSU. His farm is incorporated, and shortly after the date of incorporation, Eva had advised him to elect S corporation status. She now advises him to revoke the S election. ■

## SHOULD YOU CHECK THAT BOX?

The check-the-box rules have been evolving since their introduction into the Regulations in late 1996. They are designed to remove tax considerations from the owners' choice of the legal form in which to conduct business. These provisions act to reduce the owners' exposure to the double taxation of taxable business profits. But taxpayers considering the use of these rules have run into several complications.

- Changing tax entity classifications from year to year comes at a cost. Changing the business form from a corporation to a partnership might trigger taxes for both the entity and its owners, defeating the purpose of the entity change.
- State income tax laws do not always match those of the Code. Several states have been slow to adopt the check-the-box rules, and others have modified the rules in some way. For instance, in several states a one-member limited liability company does not receive the expected tax treatment as a partnership, but is reclassified as a corporation or sole proprietorship. Uncertainty as to the state income tax treatment of a check-the-box selection alone may keep the owners from exercising their supposed freedom of choice of tax entity.

Example 1 raises a number of interesting questions. Does Eva advise all of her dairy farmer clients to elect S corporation status initially? Why has she advised Larry to revoke his S election? Will she advise Jesse to revoke his S election at some time in the future? Will she advise Larry to make another S election at some time in the future? Why did she not advise Larry to dissolve his corporation outright? Could Larry and Jesse have achieved the same tax consequences for their dairy farms if they had operated the farms as limited liability entities or partnerships instead of incorporating? Does the way the farm is acquired (e.g., purchase versus inheritance) affect the choice of business entity for tax purposes?

This chapter provides the basis for comparing and analyzing the tax consequences of business decisions for various types of tax entities (sole proprietorship, partnership, corporation, limited liability entity, and S corporation). Understanding the comparative tax consequences for the different types of entities and being able to apply them effectively to specific fact patterns will result in effective tax planning, which is exactly what Eva was doing with her two clients. As the following discussion illustrates, a variety of potential answers may exist for each of the questions raised by Eva's advice.

### LO.1

Identify the principal legal and tax forms for conducting a business.

# Forms of Doing Business

## PRINCIPAL FORMS

The principal *legal* forms for conducting a business entity are the sole proprietorship, partnership, limited liability entity, and corporation.[1] From a *Federal income tax* perspective, these same forms are available, but the corporate form can be taxed

---

[1]A business entity can also be conducted in the form of a trust or estate.

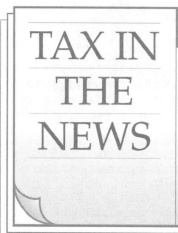

## PROFESSIONAL SERVICE FIRMS AND ORGANIZATIONAL FORM

Many professional service firms (e.g., accountants, architects, lawyers) have chosen to become limited liability partnerships. In the accounting profession, this includes all of the Big 4 (i.e., Deloitte, Ernst & Young, KPMG, and PricewaterhouseCoopers) and most regional and local accounting firms.

An LLP helps to provide protection for the purely personal assets of the partners. Under the LLP organizational structure, the only partners whose personal assets are at risk to pay a judgment are those actually involved in the negligence or wrongdoing at issue. Note, however, that the entity is still responsible for the full judgment. Thus, the capital of the entity is still at risk.

in either of two ways (S corporation and C or regular corporation). In most instances, the legal form and the tax form are the same.

The taxpayer generally is bound for tax purposes by the legal form that is selected. A major statutory exception to this is the ability of an S corporation to receive tax treatment similar to that of a partnership.[2] In addition, taxpayers sometimes can control which set of tax rules will apply to their business operations. The "check-the-box" Regulations provide an elective procedure that enables certain entities to be classified as partnerships for Federal income tax purposes even though they have corporate characteristics.[3] These Regulations have greatly simplified the determination of entity classification. See Chapter 8 for a more detailed discussion of the check-the-box provisions.

An individual conducting a sole proprietorship files Schedule C of Form 1040. If more than one trade or business is conducted, a separate Schedule C is filed for each trade or business. A partnership files Form 1065. A corporation files Form 1120, and an S corporation files Form 1120S.

About 4.5 million corporations file U.S. income tax returns every year, and about 2 million of these use S corporation status. About 1.5 million partnership returns are filed every year, and more than 16 million individuals report sole proprietorship activities on Schedule C in a typical tax year.[4] The business entity forms that are growing in number the fastest are the sole proprietorship (twice as many as 15 years ago) and the partnership (perhaps due to the popularity of the new limited liability entities).

### LIMITED LIABILITY COMPANIES

*Definition
Limited Liability
Company
– page C-10*

A **limited liability company (LLC)** is a hybrid business form that combines the corporate characteristic of limited liability for the owners with the tax characteristics of a partnership.[5] All of the states now permit this legal form for conducting a business.

The most frequently cited nontax benefit of an LLC is the limited liability of the owners. Compared to the other forms of ownership, LLCs offer additional benefits over other forms of business, including the following.

---

[2]§§ 1361 and 1362. See Chapter 11.
[3]Reg. §§ 301.7701–1 through –4, and –6. Note that if the business has only one owner, the elective procedure enables the entity to be classified as a sole proprietorship.

[4]*Statistics of Income Bulletin*, Summer 2003.
[5]Depending on state law, an LLC may be organized as a limited liability corporation or a limited liability partnership.

---

### ⊙ T A X   F A C T

## REVENUE RELEVANCE OF CORPORATE VERSUS INDIVIDUAL TAXPAYERS

Federal income taxes (FIT) provide over half of the Federal budget receipts. As indicated below, the portion provided by individual taxpayers (which includes the effect of flow-through entities) far exceeds that provided by corporate taxpayers.

|                                       | 2001 | 2002 | 2003 | 2004 | 2005 |
|---------------------------------------|------|------|------|------|------|
| % of budget receipts from FIT         | 58%  | 60%  | 57%  | 53%  | 54%  |
| % of FIT from individual taxpayers    | 83%  | 83%  | 88%  | 83%  | 80%  |
| % of FIT from corporate taxpayers     | 17%  | 17%  | 12%  | 17%  | 20%  |

**Source:** Federal Budget of the United States.

---

*Advantages over S corporations*

- Greater flexibility in terms of the number of owners, types of owners, special allocation opportunities, and capital structure.
- Inclusion of entity debt in the owner's basis for an ownership interest.
- More liberal deferral of gain recognition on contributions of appreciated property by an owner (determined under § 721 rather than § 351).
- For securities law purposes, an ownership interest in an LLC is not necessarily a security.

*Advantages over C corporations*

- Ability to pass tax attributes through to the owners.
- Absence of double taxation.

*Advantages over limited partnerships*

- Right of all owners to participate in the management of the business.
- Ability of all owners to have limited liability (no need for a general partner).
- For securities law purposes, an ownership interest in an LLC is not necessarily a security (the interest of a limited partner normally is classified as a security).

*Advantages over general partnerships*

- Limited liability for owners.
- Greater continuity of life.
- Limitation on an owner's ability to withdraw from the business.

Among the disadvantages associated with LLCs are the following.

- Absence of a developed body of case law on LLCs.
- Requirement in most states that there be at least two owners.
- Inability to qualify for § 1244 ordinary loss treatment.

**LO.2**

Appreciate the relative importance of nontax factors in business decisions.

# Nontax Factors

Taxes are only one of many factors to consider when making a business decision. Above all, any business decision should make economic sense.

**EXAMPLE 2**

Walter is considering investing $10,000 in a limited partnership. He projects that he will be able to deduct the $10,000 capital contribution within the next two years (as his share of partnership losses). Since Walter's marginal tax rate is 35%, the deductions will produce a positive cash-flow effect of $3,500 ($10,000 × 35%). However, there is a substantial risk that he will not recover any of his original investment. If this occurs, his negative cash flow from the investment in the limited partnership is $6,500 ($10,000 − $3,500). Walter must decide if the investment makes economic sense. ■

## CAPITAL FORMATION

The ability of an entity to raise capital is a factor that must be considered. A sole proprietorship has the narrowest capital base. Compared to the sole proprietorship, the partnership has a greater opportunity to raise funds through the pooling of owner resources.

**EXAMPLE 3**

Adam and Beth decide to form a partnership, AB. Adam contributes cash of $200,000, and Beth contributes land with an adjusted basis of $60,000 and a fair market value of $200,000. The partnership is going to construct an apartment building at a cost of $800,000. AB pledges the land and the building to secure a loan of $700,000. ■

The limited partnership offers even greater potential than the general partnership form because a limited partnership can secure funds from investors (i.e., future limited partners).

**EXAMPLE 4**

Carol and Dave form a limited partnership, CD. Carol contributes cash of $200,000, and Dave contributes land with an adjusted basis of $60,000 and a fair market value of $200,000. The partnership is going to construct a shopping center at a cost of $5 million. Included in this cost is the purchase price of $800,000 for land adjacent to that contributed by Dave. Thirty limited partnership interests are sold for $100,000 each to raise $3 million. CD then pledges the shopping center (including the land) and obtains nonrecourse creditor financing of another $2 million. ■

Both the at-risk limitations and the passive activity loss provisions reduce the tax attractiveness of investments in real estate, particularly in the limited partnership form. In effect, the tax rules themselves place a severe curb on the economic consequences. Chapter 5 presents these loss rules and their critical interaction.

Of the different business entities, the corporate form offers the greatest ease and potential for obtaining owner financing because it can issue additional shares of stock. The ultimate examples of this form are the large public companies that are listed on the stock exchanges.

## LIMITED LIABILITY

A corporation offers its owners limited liability under state law. This absence of personal liability on the part of the owners is the most frequently cited advantage of the corporate form.

■ **FIGURE 14–1**
Limited Partnership with a
Corporate General Partner

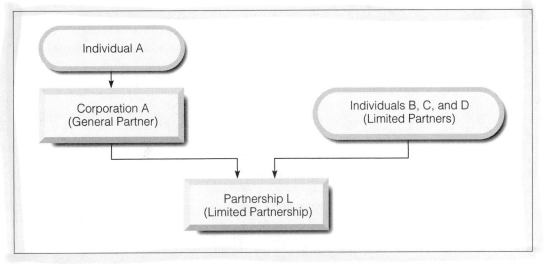

EXAMPLE 5

Ed, Fran, and Gabriella each invest $25,000 for all the shares of stock of Brown Corporation. Brown obtains creditor financing of $100,000. Brown is the defendant in a personal injury suit resulting from an accident involving one of its delivery trucks. The court awards a judgment of $2.5 million to the plaintiff. The award exceeds Brown's insurance coverage by $1.5 million. Even though the judgment probably will result in Brown's bankruptcy, the shareholders will have no personal liability for the unpaid corporate debts. ■

Limited liability is not available to all corporations. For many years, state laws did not permit professional individuals (e.g., accountants, attorneys, architects, and physicians) to incorporate. Even though professionals now are allowed to incorporate, the statutes do not provide limited liability for the performance of professional services.

Even if state law provides for limited liability, the shareholders of small corporations may forgo this benefit. Quite often, a corporation may be unable to obtain external financing (e.g., a bank loan) at reasonable interest rates unless the shareholders guarantee the loan.

The limited partnership form provides limited liability to the limited partners. Their liability is limited to the amount invested. In contrast, a general partner has unlimited liability.

EXAMPLE 6

Hazel, the general partner, invests $250,000 in HIJ, a limited partnership. Iris and Jane, the limited partners, each invest $50,000. While the potential loss for Iris and Jane is limited to $50,000 each, Hazel's liability is unlimited. ■

Indirectly, it may be possible to provide the general partner with limited liability by establishing a corporation as the general partner (see Figure 14–1). When a venture is structured this way, the general partner (the corporation) has limited its liability under the corporate statutes. In the figure, Individual A is protected from personal liability by being merely the shareholder of Corporation A.

**Bridge to Business Law and Financial Accounting**

When a business entity is created and assets are transferred to the business entity by the owners, the tax balance sheet and the financial accounting balance sheet generally will contain different amounts for the assets. The balance sheet amounts are a function of whether conduit theory or entity theory is applied.

Conduit theory, also referred to as aggregate theory or proprietary theory, assumes that the business entity is merely an extension of the owners. Therefore, the transfer of the assets by the owners to the entity is not a taxable event. The owners' basis for their ownership interests is a carryover basis. The business entity's basis for its assets is a carryover basis.

Entity theory assumes that the business entity is separate and apart from the owners. Therefore, the transfer of assets by the owners to the entity is a taxable event. The owners' basis for their ownership interests is a new basis (i.e., fair market value). The business entity's basis for its assets is a new basis (i.e., fair market value).

Financial accounting uses entity theory. Thus, the critical value is the fair market value of each asset contributed by an owner to the business entity. Tax generally uses conduit theory. Thus, the critical value is the owner's adjusted basis for the contributed assets.

## OTHER FACTORS

Other nontax factors may be significant in selecting an organization form, such as:

- Estimated life of the business.
- Number of owners and their roles in the management of the business.
- Freedom of choice in transferring ownership interests.
- Organizational formality, including the related cost and extent of government regulation.

**LO.3**

Distinguish between the forms for conducting a business according to whether they are subject to single taxation or double taxation.

# Single versus Double Taxation

## OVERALL IMPACT ON ENTITY AND OWNERS

The sole proprietorship, limited liability entity, and partnership are subject to *single* taxation. This result occurs because the owner(s) and the business generally are not considered separate entities for tax purposes. Therefore, the tax liability is levied at the owner level rather than at the entity level.

In contrast, a corporation and its owners can be subject to *double* taxation. This is frequently cited as the major tax disadvantage of the corporate form. The entity is taxed on the earnings of the corporation, and the owners are taxed on distributions to the extent they are made from corporate earnings.

The S corporation provides a way to avoid double taxation and possibly subject corporate earnings to a lower tax rate (the individual tax rate may be lower than the corporate tax rate). However, the ownership structure of an S corporation is restricted in both the number and type of shareholders. In addition, statutory exceptions subject the entity to taxation in certain circumstances.[6] To the extent these corporate-level taxes apply, double taxation results. Finally, the distribution policy of the S corporation may create difficulties under the *wherewithal to pay* concept.

---

[6]Recall the Chapter 11 discussions of the taxes on an S corporation's built-in gains, LIFO recapture, and investment income.

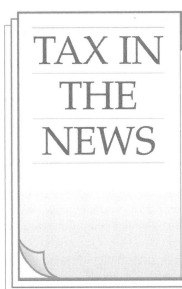

### DO CORPORATIONS PAY TAXES?

A disadvantage of being a C corporation is the potential for double taxation. This potential disappears, however, if the taxable income of the corporation is zero or negative.

A recent Government Accountability Office study indicates that for the period 1996–2000, more than 60 percent of U.S. corporations did not owe or pay any Federal income taxes. Neither did 70 percent of foreign-owned corporations doing business in the United States. By 2003, corporate tax receipts had fallen to 7.4 percent of overall Federal receipts, the lowest percentage since 1983.

Senator Carl Levin (who requested the GAO study) along with Senator Byron Dorgan, both Democrats, concluded that "too many corporations are finagling ways to dodge paying Uncle Sam, despite the benefits they receive from doing business in this country."

SOURCE: Adapted from John D. McKinnon, "Many Companies Avoided Taxes Even as Profits Soared in Boom," *Wall Street Journal*, April 6, 2004, p. A1.

**EXAMPLE 7**

Hawk Corporation has been operating as an S corporation since it began its business two years ago. For both of the prior years, Hawk incurred a tax loss. Hawk has taxable income of $75,000 this year and expects that its earnings will increase each year in the foreseeable future. Part of this earnings increase results from Hawk's expansion into other communities in the state. Since most of this expansion will be financed internally, no dividend distributions will be made to Hawk's shareholders.

Assuming all of Hawk's shareholders are in the 33% tax bracket, their tax liability on corporate earnings will be $24,750 ($75,000 × 33%). Even though Hawk will not distribute any cash to the shareholders, they still will be required to pay the tax liability. This creates a wherewithal to pay problem. In addition, the corporate tax liability would have been less if Hawk had not been an S corporation [(15% × $50,000) + (25% × $25,000) = $13,750].

The shareholders' wherewithal to pay problem could be resolved by terminating the S corporation election. The tax liability would then be imposed at the corporate level. Since Hawk does not intend to make any dividend distributions, double taxation at the present time would be avoided. Terminating the election also reduces the overall shareholder-corporation tax liability by $11,000 ($24,750 − $13,750).[7]

In making the decision about the form of business entity, Hawk's shareholders should consider more than the current taxable year. If the S election is terminated, another election might not be available for five years. Thus, the decision to revoke the election should be made using at least a five-year planning horizon. Perhaps a better solution would be to retain the election and distribute enough dividends to the S corporation shareholders to enable them to pay the shareholder tax liability. ■

Two other variables that relate to the adverse effect of double taxation are the timing and form of corporate distributions. If no distributions are made, then only single taxation occurs in the short run.[8] To the extent that double taxation does occur in the future, the cash-flow effect should be discounted to its present value. Second, when the distribution is made, is it in the form of a dividend or a return

---

[7]The absence of distributions to shareholders could create an accumulated earnings tax (AET) problem under § 531. However, as long as earnings are used to finance expansion, the "reasonable needs" provision will be satisfied, and the corporation will avoid any AET. Refer to the discussion of the AET in Chapter 9.

[8]This assumes there is no accumulated earnings tax problem. See especially Example 10 in the subsequent discussion of distributions in Minimizing Double Taxation.

of capital?[9] The owners likely would prefer to receive long-term capital gain (subject to lower tax rates) instead of ordinary income. Proper structuring of the distribution can accomplish this result. Note that for distributions made in 2003 and thereafter the availability of the 15%/5% rate for qualified dividends reduces the potential negative impact of double taxation (see Chapter 3).

## ALTERNATIVE MINIMUM TAX

All of the forms of business are directly or indirectly subject to the alternative minimum tax (AMT).[10] For the sole proprietorship and the C corporation, the effect is direct (the AMT liability calculation is attached to the tax form that reports the entity's taxable income—Form 1040 or Form 1120). For the partnership, limited liability entity, and S corporation, the effect is indirect; the tax preferences and adjustments pass through from the entity to the owners, and the AMT liability calculation is *not* assessed on the tax form that reports the entity's taxable income—Form 1065 or Form 1120S.

When compared to other entities, the C corporation appears to have a slight advantage. The corporate AMT rate of 20 percent is less the individual AMT rates of 26 and 28 percent. An even better perspective is provided by comparing the maximum AMT rate with the maximum regular rate for both the individual and the corporation. For the individual, the AMT rate is 80 percent (28%/35%) of the maximum regular rate. The AMT rate for the corporation is 57 percent (20%/35%) of the maximum regular rate. Therefore, on the basis of comparative rates, the C corporation appears to offer lower AMT tax burdens. In addition, as presented below, under certain circumstances, a C corporation is exempt from the AMT.

The apparent corporate AMT rate advantage may be more than offset by the ACE adjustment, which applies only to C corporations.[11] If the ACE adjustment continually causes the C corporation to be subject to the AMT, the owners should consider electing S corporation status (if eligibility requirements can be satisfied). Since the S corporation does not compute an ACE adjustment, it may be possible to reduce the tax liability.

The AMT does not apply to modest-sized C corporations. To be exempt from the tax, the corporation must meet both of the following tests.

- Average annual gross receipts of not more than $5 million for the three tax years after 1993.
- Average annual gross receipts of not more than $7.5 million for every subsequent three-tax-year period.

**PLANNING STRATEGIES**

## Planning for the AMT

**FRAMEWORK FOCUS: TAX RATE**

**STRATEGY ▶ SHIFT NET INCOME FROM HIGH-BRACKET YEARS TO LOW-BRACKET YEARS.**

If the AMT will apply in the current year, the entity should consider accelerating income and delaying deductions, so that current-year taxable income is taxed at the lower AMT rate. For a C corporation, the potential rate differential is 15 percentage points (20 percent AMT rate versus 35 percent regular tax rate). For an individual (i.e., as a sole proprietor, as a partner, or as an S corporation shareholder), the potential tax rate differential is 7 percentage points (28 percent highest AMT rate versus 35 percent regular tax rate). A present value analysis should be used to assure that the income acceleration and deduction deferral do not increase actual tax liabilities.

---

[9]Redemptions of stock and corporate liquidations may be taxed as a sale of stock to shareholders (i.e., as capital gain or loss). See § 302 and Chapter 9.

[10]§ 55.

[11]§§ 56(c)(1) and (f). Refer to the discussion of the corporate AMT in Chapter 13.

A corporation automatically is classified as a small corporation in the first year of existence. About 95 percent of all C corporations are likely to meet these tests and be exempt from the AMT in the future.

### STATE TAXATION

In selecting a form for doing business, the determination of the tax consequences should not be limited to Federal income taxes. Consideration also should be given to state income taxes and, if applicable, local income taxes.

The S corporation provides a good illustration of this point. Suppose that the forms of business being considered are a limited partnership or a corporation. An operating loss is projected for the next several years. The owners decide to operate the business in the corporate form. The principal nontax criterion for the decision is the limited liability attribute of the corporation. The owners consent to an S corporation election, so the corporate losses can be passed through to the shareholders to deduct on their individual tax returns. However, assume that state law does not permit the S corporation election. Thus, the owners will not receive the tax benefits of the loss deductions that would have been available on their state income tax returns if they had chosen the limited partnership form. As a result of providing limited liability to the owner who would have been the general partner for the limited partnership, the loss deduction at the state level is forgone.

---

**LO.4**

Identify techniques for avoiding double taxation.

# Minimizing Double Taxation

Only the corporate form is potentially subject to double taxation. Several techniques are available for eliminating or at least reducing the second layer of taxation.

- Making distributions to the shareholders that are deductible to the corporation.
- Not making distributions to the shareholders.
- Making distributions that qualify for return of capital treatment at the shareholder level.
- Making the S corporation election.

### MAKING DEDUCTIBLE DISTRIBUTIONS

The following are typical distribution forms that will result in a deduction to the corporation.

- Salary payments to shareholder-employees.
- Lease or rental payments to shareholder-lessors.
- Interest payments to shareholder-creditors.

Recognizing the potential for abuse, the IRS scrutinizes these types of distributions carefully. All three forms are evaluated in terms of *reasonableness*.[12] In addition, interest payments to shareholders may lead to reclassification of some or all of the debt as equity.[13] IRS success with either approach raises the specter of double taxation.

---

[12]§ 162(a)(1). *Mayson Manufacturing Co. v. Comm.*, 49–2 USTC ¶9467, 38 AFTR 1028, 178 F.2d 115 (CA–6, 1949); *Harolds Club v. Comm.*, 65–1 USTC ¶9198, 15 AFTR2d 241, 340 F.2d 861 (CA–9, 1965).

[13]§ 385; Rev.Rul. 83–98, 1983–2 C.B. 40; *Bauer v. Comm.*, 84–2 USTC ¶9996, 55 AFTR2d 85–433, 748 F.2d 1365 (CA–9, 1984).

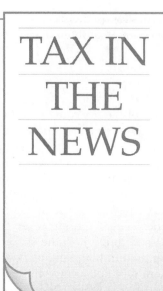

## WHO PAYS CORPORATE AMT?

One of the issues often raised in debates over tax legislation is whether the corporate AMT should be repealed. Among the topics discussed are the revenue generated, the related compliance costs, and the number of corporations subject to the AMT.

According to the IRS, nearly 6 million corporate tax returns were filed in 2003. Of these returns, under 15,000 included any AMT.

Proponents of the corporate AMT argue that these statistics show that the AMT is being paid by corporations targeted by the law (i.e., large corporations). Opponents argue that the same statistics show that the compliance costs borne by the mass of corporations do not justify the continuation of this tax system.

The exemption from the AMT for small corporations may be providing the needed solution. Large corporations must make minimal Federal income tax payments when the AMT applies. Most C corporations no longer need to compute the tax.

SOURCE: IRS Tax Stats.

---

**EXAMPLE 8**

Donna owns all the stock of Green Corporation and is also the chief executive officer. Green's taxable income before salary payments to Donna is as follows.

| 2003 | 2004 | 2005 |
|------|------|------|
| $80,000 | $50,000 | $250,000 |

During the year, Donna receives a monthly salary of $3,000. In December of each year, Donna reviews the operations for the year and determines the year-end bonus she is to receive. Donna's yearly bonuses are as follows.

| 2003 | 2004 | 2005 |
|------|------|------|
| $44,000 | $14,000 | $214,000 |

The apparent purpose of Green's bonus program is to reduce the corporate taxable income to zero and thereby avoid double taxation. An examination of Green's tax return by the IRS would likely result in a deduction disallowance for **unreasonable compensation.** ■

---

**EXAMPLE 9**

Tom and Vicki each contribute $20,000 to TV Corporation for all of its stock. In addition, they each lend $80,000 to TV. The loan is documented by formal notes, the interest rate is 8%, and the maturity date is 10 years from the date of the loan.

The notes provide the opportunity for the corporation to make payments of $6,400 each year to both Tom and Vicki and for the payments not to be subject to double taxation. This happens because the interest payments are includible in the gross income of Tom and Vicki, but are deductible by TV in calculating its taxable income. At the time of repayment in 10 years, neither Tom nor Vicki recognizes gross income from the repayment; the $80,000 amount realized is equal to the basis for the note of $80,000.

If the IRS succeeded in reclassifying the notes as equity, Tom and Vicki still would have gross income of $6,400, but the interest would be reclassified as dividend income (which may be taxed at the 15% rate). Because dividend payments are not deductible by TV, the corporation's taxable income would increase by $12,800 ($6,400 × 2). To make matters worse, the repayment of the notes in 10 years would not qualify as a recovery of capital, resulting in additional dividend income for Tom and Vicki. ■

Note that for distributions made in 2003 and thereafter the availability of the 15%/5% rate for qualified dividends reduces the potential negative impact of double taxation (see Chapter 3).

## NOT MAKING DISTRIBUTIONS

Double taxation will not occur unless the corporation makes (actual or deemed) distributions to the shareholders. A closely held corporation that does not make distributions may eventually encounter an accumulated earnings tax problem unless the reasonable needs requirement is satisfied. When making distribution decisions each year, the board of directors should be apprised of any potential accumulated earnings tax problem and take the appropriate steps to eliminate it. The accumulated earnings tax rate of 15 percent in 2005 is the same as the 15 percent rate for qualified dividends for individual taxpayers.[14]

**EXAMPLE 10**

According to an internal calculation made by Dolphin Corporation, its accumulated taxable income is $400,000. The board of directors would prefer not to declare any dividends, but is considering a dividend declaration of $400,000 to avoid the accumulated earnings tax. All of the shareholders are in the 35% bracket.

If a dividend of $400,000 is declared, the tax cost to the shareholders is $60,000 ($400,000 × 15%, assuming the dividends are qualified dividends). If a dividend is not declared and the IRS assesses the accumulated earnings tax, the tax cost to the corporation for the accumulated earnings tax also would be $60,000 ($400,000 × 15%).

To make matters worse, Dolphin will have incurred the accumulated earnings tax cost without getting any funds out of the corporation to the shareholders. If the unwise decision were now made to distribute the remaining $340,000 ($400,000 – $60,000) to the shareholders, the additional tax cost at the shareholder level would be $51,000 ($340,000 × 15%). Therefore, the combined shareholder-corporation tax cost would be $111,000 ($60,000 + $51,000). This is 185% ($111,000/$60,000) of the tax cost that would have resulted from an initial dividend distribution of $400,000. ■

Assuming that the accumulated earnings tax can be avoided (e.g., a growth company whose reasonable needs justify its failure to pay dividends), a policy of no distributions to shareholders can avoid the second layer of taxation on corporate earnings. The retained earnings will drive the value of the shares upward, equal to the accumulated after-tax cash. As a result of the step-up in basis rules for inherited property, the basis of the stock for the beneficiaries will be the fair market value at the date of the decedent's death rather than the decedent's basis.

## RETURN OF CAPITAL DISTRIBUTIONS

The exposure to double taxation can be reduced if the corporate distributions to the shareholders can qualify for return of capital rather than dividend treatment. This can occur when the corporation's earnings and profits (E & P) are low or

---

[14]§ 531. Refer to the discussion of the accumulated earnings tax in Chapter 9.

BRIDGE DISCIPLINE

**Bridge to Economics**

Corporations such as General Motors, IBM, Microsoft, Wal-Mart, and ExxonMobil are major players not only in their industries, but also in the world economy. However, people are also attracted to "mom and pop type stores," which cumulatively play a major role in the economy.

In recognition of the important role of small businesses and their size competitive disadvantage at times, Congress has provided small businesses with beneficial tax treatment that is not available to major business entities. Included among such beneficial treatments are the following.

- § 11 beneficial tax rates.
- § 44 disabled access credit.
- § 55(e) exemption from the AMT for small corporations.
- § 179 limited expensing for tangible personal property.
- § 1244 ordinary loss treatment.

Each of these provisions defines "small" in a different way. Sometimes, however, when beneficial tax treatment is provided for a business entity, the term "small" may be used inappropriately. The classic example is the small business corporation of Subchapter S. Some S corporations hold billions of dollars of assets. They are "small" only in the sense that the number of shareholders cannot exceed 100 unrelated shareholders.

---

negative in amount. Review Example 1 in Chapter 9. In some cases, the stock redemption provisions offer an opportunity to avoid dividend treatment altogether. Under these rules, the distribution may be treated as a sale of the shareholder's stock, resulting in a tax-free recovery of basis and then recognition of low-tax long-term capital gain.

## ELECTING S CORPORATION STATUS

Electing S corporation status generally eliminates double taxation. Several factors, listed below, should be considered when making this election.

- Are all the shareholders willing to consent to the election?
- Can the qualification requirements under § 1361 be satisfied at the time of the election?
- Can the S corporation requirements continue to be satisfied?
- For what period will the conditions that make the election beneficial continue to prevail?
- Will the corporate distribution policy create wherewithal to pay problems at the shareholder level?

**EXAMPLE 11**

Emerald Corporation commenced business in January 2005. The two shareholders, Diego and Jaime, are both in the 28% tax bracket. The following operating results are projected for the first five years of operations.

| 2005 | 2006 | 2007 | 2008 | 2009 |
|------|------|------|------|------|
| ($50,000) | $400,000 | $600,000 | $800,000 | $1,000,000 |

### TAX FACT

## NUMBER OF INCOME TAX RETURNS FILED BY DIFFERENT TYPES OF TAXPAYERS (IN MILLIONS)

| Type of Taxpayer | 1980 | 1985 | 1990 | 1995 | 2000 | 2004 |
|---|---|---|---|---|---|---|
| Individual | 93.1 | 99.5 | 112.3 | 116.1 | 126.9 | 131.6 |
| Partnership | 1.4 | 1.8 | 1.8 | 1.6 | 2.1 | 2.5 |
| C corporation | 2.1 | 2.4 | 2.3 | 2.2 | 2.2 | 2.5 |
| S corporation | .5 | .7 | 1.5 | 2.2 | 2.8 | 3.5 |

The number of S corporation returns has increased dramatically since 1980. In addition, the number of S corporation returns now exceeds the number of C corporation returns. Since LLCs normally file as partnerships, it will be interesting to see what effect the popularity of this entity form will have on the number of partnership returns filed.

**Source:** IRS Tax Stats.

The corporation plans to expand rapidly. Therefore, no distributions will be made to shareholders. In addition, beginning in 2006, preferred stock will be offered to a substantial number of investors to help finance the expansion.

If the S corporation election is made for 2005, the $50,000 loss can be passed through to Diego and Jaime. The loss will generate a positive cash-flow effect of $14,000 ($50,000 × 28%). Assume that the election is either revoked or is involuntarily terminated at the beginning of 2006 as a result of the issuance of the preferred stock. The corporate tax liability for 2006 is $136,000 ($400,000 × 34%).

If the S corporation election is not made for 2005, the $50,000 loss is a net operating loss. The amount can be carried forward to reduce the 2006 corporate taxable income to $350,000 ($400,000 − $50,000). The resultant tax liability is $119,000 ($350,000 × 34%).

Should the S corporation election be made for just the one-year period? The answer is unclear. With an assumed after-tax rate of return to Diego and Jaime of 10%, the value of the $14,000 one year hence is $15,400 ($14,000 × 110%). Even considering the time value of money, the combined corporation-shareholder negative cash-flow effect of $120,600 ($136,000 − $15,400) in the case of an S election is not significantly different from the $119,000 corporate tax liability that would result for a C corporation. ∎

---

**LO.5**

Understand and apply the conduit and entity concepts as they affect operations, capital changes, and distributions.

## Conduit versus Entity Treatment

Under the **conduit concept,** the entity is viewed as merely an extension of the owners. Under the **entity concept,** the entity is regarded as being separate and distinct from its owners. The effects of the conduit and entity concepts extend to a variety of tax rules, including the following.

- Recognition at time of contribution to the entity.
- Basis of ownership interest.

*Definitions
Conduit concept
- page 14
Entity concept
- page 14

- Results of operations.
- Recognition at time of distribution.
- Passive activity losses.
- At-risk rules.
- Special allocations.

The sole proprietorship is not analyzed separately because the owner and the business are the same tax entity. In one circumstance, however, a tax difference can result. Income recognition does not occur when an owner contributes an asset to a sole proprietorship. Thus, the business generally takes a carryover basis. However, if the asset is a personal-use asset, the sole proprietorship's basis is the *lower of* the adjusted basis or the fair market value at the date of contribution. If a personal-use asset is contributed to a partnership or corporation, this same *lower-of* rule applies.

## EFFECT ON RECOGNITION AT TIME OF CONTRIBUTION TO THE ENTITY

Since the conduit approach applies to partnerships, § 721 provides for no recognition on the contribution of property to a partnership in exchange for a partnership interest. Section 721 protects both a contribution associated with the formation of the partnership and later contributions. The partnership takes a carryover basis in the contributed property, and the partners have a carryover basis in their partnership interests.[15]

Since the entity approach applies to corporations, the transfer of property to a corporation in exchange for its stock is a taxable event. However, if the § 351 control requirement is satisfied, no gain or loss is recognized. In this case, both the corporate property and the shareholders' stock have a carryover basis.[16] This control requirement makes it possible for shareholders who contribute appreciated property to the corporation *after* its formation to recognize gain.

To the extent that the fair market value of property contributed to the entity at the time of formation is not equal to the property's adjusted basis, a special allocation may be desirable. With a special allocation, the owner contributing the property receives the tax benefit or detriment for any recognized gain or loss that subsequently results because of the initial difference between the adjusted basis and the fair market value. For the partnership, this special allocation treatment is mandatory. No such allocation is available for a C corporation because the gain or loss is recognized at the corporation level rather than at the shareholder level. As with a C corporation, no such allocation is available for an S corporation. The recognized gain or loss is reported on the shareholders' tax returns according to their stock ownership.

**EXAMPLE 12**

Khalid contributes land with an adjusted basis of $10,000 and a fair market value of $50,000 for a 50% ownership interest. At the same time, Tracy contributes cash of $50,000 for the remaining 50% ownership interest. Because the entity is unable to obtain the desired zoning, it subsequently sells the land for $50,000.

If the entity is a C corporation, Khalid has a realized gain of $40,000 ($50,000 − $10,000) and a recognized gain of $0 resulting from the contribution. His basis in the stock is $10,000, and the corporation has a basis in the land of $10,000. The corporation realizes and recognizes a gain of $40,000 ($50,000 − $10,000) when it sells the land. Thus, what should have been

---

[15]Refer to the pertinent discussion in Chapter 10.

[16]Refer to the pertinent discussion in Chapter 8.

Khalid's recognized gain is now the corporation's taxable gain. There is no way that the corporation can allocate the recognized gain directly to Khalid. The corporation could distribute the land to Khalid and let him sell it, but such a distribution is likely to be taxable to Khalid as a dividend, and gain on the distribution is also recognized at the corporate level.

If the entity is a partnership or limited liability entity, the tax consequences are the same as for the C corporation, except for the $40,000 recognized gain on the sale of the land. The partnership realizes and recognizes a gain of $40,000 ($50,000 − $10,000). However, even though Khalid's share of profits and losses is only 50%, all of the $40,000 recognized gain is allocated to him. If the entity is an S corporation, the tax consequences are the same as for the C corporation, except that Khalid reports $20,000 of the recognized gain on his tax return and Tracy reports $20,000. ∎

## EFFECT ON BASIS OF OWNERSHIP INTEREST

In a partnership or limited liability entity, since the owner is the taxpayer, profits and losses of the partnership affect the owner's basis in the entity interest. Likewise, the owner's basis is increased by the share of entity liability increases and is decreased by the share of liability decreases. Accordingly, ownership basis changes frequently.[17]

Because a C corporation is a taxpaying entity, the shareholder's basis for the stock is not affected by corporate profits and losses or corporate liability changes.

The treatment of an S corporation shareholder falls between that of the partner and the C corporation shareholder. The S corporation shareholder's stock basis is increased by the share of profits and decreased by the share of losses, but it usually is not affected by corporate liability increases or decreases.[18]

**EXAMPLE 13**

Peggy contributes cash of $100,000 to an entity for a 30% ownership interest. The entity borrows $50,000 and repays $20,000 of this amount by the end of the taxable year. The profits for the year are $90,000.

If the entity is a partnership or limited liability entity, Peggy's basis at the end of the period is $136,000 ($100,000 investment + $9,000 share of net liability increase + $27,000 share of profits). If Peggy is a C corporation shareholder instead, her stock basis is $100,000 ($100,000 original investment). If the corporation is an S corporation, Peggy's stock basis is $127,000 ($100,000 + $27,000). ∎

## EFFECT ON RESULTS OF OPERATIONS

The entity concept is responsible for producing potential double taxation for the C corporation if the corporation is taxed on its earnings, and the shareholders are taxed on the distribution of earnings. Thus, from the perspective of taxing the results of operations, the entity concept appears to provide a disadvantage to corporations. However, whether the entity concept actually produces disadvantageous results depends on the following.

- Whether the corporation generates positive taxable income.
- The tax rates that apply to the corporation and to the shareholders.
- The distribution policy of the corporation.

---

[17]§§ 705 and 752.

[18]Recall from Chapter 11 that pass-through S losses can reduce a *shareholder's* basis in loans to the entity.

As discussed previously, techniques exist for getting cash out of the corporation to the shareholders without incurring double taxation (e.g., compensation payments to shareholder-employees, lease payments to shareholder-lessors, and interest payments to shareholder-creditors). Since these payments are deductible to the corporation, they reduce corporate taxable income. If the payments can be used to reduce corporate taxable income to zero, the corporation will have no tax liability.

The maximum individual tax rate currently is the same as the maximum corporate tax rate (35 percent). However, in a specific situation, the corporate tax rates that apply may be greater than or less than the applicable individual tax rates.

Double taxation occurs only if distributions (actual or constructive) are made to the shareholders. Thus, if no distributions (actual or constructive) are made and if the entity can avoid the accumulated earnings tax (e.g., based on the statutory credit or the reasonable needs adjustment) and the personal holding company tax (e.g., the corporation primarily generates active income), only one current level of taxation will occur. If the distribution can qualify for return of capital rather than dividend treatment, the shareholder tax liability is decreased. Finally, taxation of the earnings at the shareholder level can be avoided permanently if the stock passes through the decedent shareholder's estate.[19]

Application of the entity concept causes income and deductions to lose any unique tax characteristics when they are passed through to shareholders in the form of dividends. This may produce a negative result for capital gains. Since capital gains lose their identity when passed through in the form of dividends, they cannot be used to offset capital losses at the shareholder level. An even more negative result is produced when dividends are paid out of tax-exempt income. Tax-exempt income is excludible in calculating corporate taxable income, but is included in calculating current earnings and profits. Thus, exclusions from income may be taxed because of the entity concept.

Partnerships, limited liability entities, and S corporations use the conduit concept in reporting the results of operations. Any item that is subject to special treatment on the taxpayer-owner's tax return is reported separately to the owner. Other items are aggregated and reported as taxable income. Thus, taxable income merely represents the sum of income and deductions that are not subject to special treatment.[20]

Many of the problems that the entity concept may produce for the C corporation form are not present in pass-through entities. In particular, pass-through entities are not subjected to double taxation, problems with the reasonableness requirement, or loss of identity of the income or expense item at the owner level.

Only partnerships and limited liability entities completely apply the conduit concept when reporting the results of operations. In several circumstances, the S corporation is subject to taxation at the corporate level, including the tax on built-in gains. This limited application of the entity concept necessitates additional planning to attempt to avoid taxation at the corporate level.

## EFFECT ON RECOGNITION AT TIME OF DISTRIBUTION

The application of the conduit concept results in distributions not being taxed to the owners. The application of the entity concept produces the opposite result. Therefore, tax-free distributions can be made to owners of flow-through entities, whereas distributions to C corporation shareholders may be taxable.

---

[19]Recall Chapter 6's analysis of the basis step-up rules for property acquired from a decedent.

[20]§§ 701, 702, 1363, and 1366.

A combination entity/conduit concept applies to property distributions from S corporations. The conduit concept applies with respect to the shareholder. However, if the distributed property has appreciated in value, any realized gain is recognized at the corporate level.[21] This is the same treatment received by C corporations. Thus, corporate-level gain recognition is an application of the entity concept, whereas the pass-through of the gain to shareholders is an application of the conduit concept.

**EXAMPLE 14**

Tan, an S corporation, is equally owned by Leif and Matt. Tan distributes two parcels of land to Leif and Matt. Tan has a basis of $10,000 for each parcel. Each parcel has a fair market value of $15,000. The distribution results in a $10,000 ($30,000 − $20,000) recognized gain for Tan. Leif and Matt each report $5,000 of the gain on their individual income tax returns. ■

Stock redemptions and complete liquidations receive identical treatment whether a C or an S corporation is involved.[22]

## EFFECT ON PASSIVE ACTIVITY LOSSES

The passive activity loss rules apply to flow-through entities, personal service corporations, and closely held C corporations. A *closely held C corporation* exists when more than 50 percent of the value of the outstanding stock at any time during the last half of the taxable year is owned by or for not more than five individuals. A corporation is classified as a *personal service corporation* if the following requirements are satisfied.[23]

* The principal activity of the corporation is the performance of personal services.
* The services are substantially performed by owner-employees.
* Owner-employees own more than 10 percent in value of the stock of the corporation.

The general passive activity loss rules apply to personal service corporations. Therefore, passive activity losses can be offset only against passive activity income. For closely held corporations, the application of the passive activity rules is less harsh. Passive activity losses can be offset against both active and passive income.

Since the conduit concept applies to partnerships, S corporations, and limited liability entities, the passive activity results are separately stated at the entity level and are passed through to the owners with their passive character maintained.

## EFFECT OF AT-RISK RULES

The at-risk rules apply to all flow-through entities and to closely held C corporations. The rules produce a harsher result for partnerships and limited liability entities than for S corporations. This occurs because of the way liabilities affect partners' basis.

**EXAMPLE 15**

Walt is the general partner, and Ira and Vera are the limited partners in the WIV limited partnership. Walt contributes land with an adjusted basis of $40,000 and a fair market value

---

[21]§ 311(b).
[22]§§ 302, 331, and 336.

[23]§ 469, derived from the definition in § 269A.

○ **T A X   F A C T**

## PARTNERSHIP INCOME TAX RETURNS: PROFITS VERSUS LOSSES

During the period from 1980 to 2000, the number of partnership income tax returns increased by 50 percent (i.e., from 1.4 million returns to 2.1 million returns). The beneficial tax treatment of LLCs is expected to cause this trend to continue. While the partnership provides a tax shelter opportunity by passing losses through to the partner, a majority of partnerships are profitable.

|  | 1980 | 1985 | 1990 | 1995 | 2000 |
|---|---|---|---|---|---|
| % of returns with profits | 57% | 53% | 56% | 63% | 60% |
| % of returns with losses | 43% | 47% | 44% | 37% | 40% |

**Source:** IRS Tax Stats.

of $50,000 for his partnership interest, and Ira and Vera each contribute cash of $100,000 for their partnership interests. They agree to share profits and losses equally. To finance construction of an apartment building, the partnership obtains $600,000 of nonrecourse financing [not qualified nonrecourse financing under § 465(b)(6)] using the land and the building as the pledged assets. Each partner's basis for the partnership interest is as follows.

|  | Walt | Ira | Vera |
|---|---|---|---|
| Contribution | $ 40,000 | $100,000 | $100,000 |
| Share of nonrecourse debt | 200,000 | 200,000 | 200,000 |
| Basis | $240,000 | $300,000 | $300,000 |

Without the at-risk rules, Ira and Vera could pass through losses up to $300,000 each even though they invested only $100,000 and have no personal liability for the nonrecourse debt. However, the at-risk rules limit the loss pass-through to the at-risk basis, which is $100,000 for Ira and $100,000 for Vera.

The at-risk rules also affect the general partner. Since Walt is not at risk for the nonrecourse debt, his at-risk basis is $40,000. If the mortgage were recourse debt, his at-risk basis would be $640,000 ($40,000 + $600,000).

If, instead, the entity were an S corporation and Walt received 20% of the stock and Ira and Vera each received 40%, the basis for their stock would be as follows.

| Walt | Ira | Vera |
|---|---|---|
| $40,000 | $100,000 | $100,000 |

In S corporations, nonrecourse debt does not affect the calculation of stock basis. The stock basis for each shareholder would remain the same even if the debt were recourse debt. Only direct loans by the shareholders increase the ceiling on loss pass-through. ▪

## EFFECT OF SPECIAL ALLOCATIONS

An advantage of the conduit concept over the entity concept is the ability to make special allocations. Special allocations are not permitted in C corporations. Indirectly, however, the corporate form may be able to achieve results similar to those produced by special allocations through payments to owners (e.g., salary payments, lease rental payments, and interest payments) and through different classes of stock (e.g., preferred and common). However, even in these cases, the breadth of the treatment and the related flexibility are far less than that achievable under the conduit concept.

Although S corporations generally operate as conduits, they are treated more like C corporations than partnerships with respect to special allocations. This treatment results from the application of the per-share and per-day allocation rule in § 1377(a). Although S corporations are limited to one class of stock, they still can use salary, interest, and rental payments to owners to shift income to the desired recipient. However, the IRS has the authority to reallocate income among members of a family if fair returns are not provided for services rendered or capital invested.[24]

**EXAMPLE 16**

The stock of an S corporation is owned by Debra (50%), Helen (25%), and Joyce (25%). Helen and Joyce are Debra's adult children. Debra is subject to a 35% marginal tax rate, and Helen and Joyce have a 15% marginal tax rate. Only Debra is an employee of the corporation. She is paid an annual salary of $20,000, whereas employees with similar responsibilities in other corporations earn $100,000. The corporation generates earnings of approximately $200,000 each year.

It appears that the reason Debra is paid a low salary is to enable more of the earnings of the S corporation to be taxed to Helen and Joyce, who are in lower tax brackets. Thus, the IRS could use its statutory authority to allocate a larger salary to Debra. ■

Partnerships and limited liability entities have many opportunities to use special allocations, including the following (refer to Chapter 10).

- The ability to share profits and losses differently from the share in capital.
- The ability to share profits and losses differently.
- A required special allocation for the difference between the adjusted basis and the fair market value of contributed property.
- The special allocation of some items if a substantial economic effect rule is satisfied.

**LO.6**

Analyze the effects of the disposition of a business on the owners and the entity for each of the forms for conducting a business.

# Disposition of a Business or an Ownership Interest

A key factor in evaluating the tax consequences of a business disposition is whether the disposition is viewed as the sale of an ownership interest or as a sale of assets. Generally, the tax consequences are more favorable to the seller if the transaction is treated as a sale of the ownership interest.

---

[24]§ 1366(e).

## SOLE PROPRIETORSHIPS

Regardless of the form of the transaction, the sale of a sole proprietorship is treated as the sale of individual assets. Thus, gains and losses must be calculated separately for each asset. Classification as capital gain or ordinary income depends on the nature and holding period of the individual assets. Ordinary income property such as inventory will result in ordinary gains and losses. Section 1231 property such as land, buildings, and machinery used in the business will produce § 1231 gains and losses (subject to depreciation recapture under §§ 1245 and 1250). Capital assets such as investment land and stocks qualify for capital gain or loss treatment.

If the amount realized exceeds the fair market value of the identifiable assets, the excess is allocated to goodwill, which produces capital gain for the seller. If instead the excess payment is allocated to a covenant not to compete, the related gain is classified as ordinary income rather than capital gain. Both goodwill and covenants are amortized over a 15-year statutory period.[25]

**EXAMPLE 17**

Seth, who is in the 35% tax bracket, sells his sole proprietorship to Wilma for $600,000. The identifiable assets are as follows.

|                          | Adjusted Basis | Fair Market Value |
|--------------------------|---------------:|------------------:|
| Inventory                | $ 20,000       | $ 25,000          |
| Accounts receivable      | 40,000         | 40,000            |
| Machinery and equipment* | 125,000        | 150,000           |
| Buildings**              | 175,000        | 250,000           |
| Land                     | 40,000         | 100,000           |
|                          | $400,000       | $565,000          |

*Potential § 1245 recapture of $50,000.
**Potential § 1250 recapture of $20,000.

The sale produces the following results for Seth.

|                          | Gain (Loss) | Ordinary Income | § 1231 Gain | Capital Gain |
|--------------------------|------------:|----------------:|------------:|-------------:|
| Inventory                | $ 5,000     | $ 5,000         |             |              |
| Accounts receivable      | –0–         |                 |             |              |
| Machinery and equipment  | 25,000      | 25,000          |             |              |
| Buildings                | 75,000      | 20,000          | $ 55,000    |              |
| Land                     | 60,000      |                 | 60,000      |              |
| Goodwill                 | 35,000      |                 |             | $35,000      |
|                          | $200,000    | $50,000         | $115,000    | $35,000      |

If the sale is structured this way, Wilma can deduct the $35,000 paid for goodwill over a 15-year period. If instead Wilma paid the $35,000 to Seth for a covenant not to compete for a period of seven years, she still would amortize the $35,000 over a 15-year period. However, Seth's $35,000 capital gain would now be taxed to him as ordinary income. If the covenant

---

[25]§ 197.

has no legal relevance to Wilma, in exchange for treating the payment as a goodwill payment, she should negotiate for a price reduction that reflects Seth's benefit from the lower capital gains tax. ■

## PARTNERSHIPS AND LIMITED LIABILITY ENTITIES

The sale of a partnership or limited liability entity can be structured as the sale of assets or as the sale of an ownership interest. If the transaction takes the form of an asset sale, it is treated the same as for a sole proprietorship. The sale of an ownership interest is treated as the sale of a capital asset, although ordinary income potential exists for unrealized receivables and substantially appreciated inventory. Thus, if capital gain treatment can produce beneficial results for the taxpayer (e.g., he or she has capital losses to offset or has beneficially treated net capital gain), the sale of an ownership interest is preferable.

From a buyer's perspective, tax consequences are not affected by the form of the transaction. If the transaction is an asset purchase, the basis for the assets equals the amount paid. If a buyer intends to continue to operate as an LLC or a partnership, the assets can be contributed to the entity under § 721. Therefore, the owner's basis in the entity interest is equal to the purchase price for the assets. Likewise, if ownership interests are purchased, the owner's basis is the purchase price paid. The partnership's basis for the assets is the purchase price since the original partnership will have terminated.[26]

When the inside and outside basis of a partner's ownership interest differ (see Chapter 10), an election can be made to step up the partner's share of the entity's asset bases.[27] This tax-free basis step-up applies to all such exchanges by all of the partners as long as the election is in effect. The election allows asset basis to reflect increases in fair market value and the goodwill that a new partner has purchased.

**EXAMPLE 18**

Roz buys a one-third interest in the RST Partnership for $50,000 (outside basis). All of the entity's assets are depreciable, and their basis to the partnership (inside basis) is $90,000. If a § 754 election is in effect, the partnership can step up the basis of its depreciable assets by $20,000, the difference between Roz's outside and inside basis amounts [$50,000 − (⅓ × $90,000)]. All of the "new" asset basis is allocated to Roz. ■

## C CORPORATIONS

The sale of a business held by a C corporation can be structured as either an asset sale or a stock sale. The stock sale has the dual advantage to the seller of being less complex both as a legal transaction and as a tax transaction. It also has the advantage of providing a way to avoid double taxation. Finally, any gain or loss on the sale of the stock is treated as a capital gain or loss to the shareholder.

**EXAMPLE 19**

Jane and Zina each own 50% of the stock of Purple Corporation. They have owned the business for 10 years. Jane's basis in her stock is $40,000, and Zina's basis in her stock is $60,000. They agree to sell the stock to Rex for $300,000. Jane recognizes a long-term capital gain of $110,000 ($150,000 − $40,000), and Zina recognizes a long-term capital gain of $90,000 ($150,000 − $60,000). Rex has a basis in his stock of $300,000. Purple's basis in its assets does not change as a result of the stock sale. ■

---

[26]§ 708(b)(1)(B).

[27]§ 754.

## Selling Stock or Assets

**FRAMEWORK FOCUS: TAX RATE**

STRATEGY ➤ AVOID DOUBLE TAXATION.

Structuring the sale of the business as a stock sale may produce detrimental tax results for the purchaser. As Example 19 illustrates, the basis of the corporation's assets is not affected by the stock sale. If the fair market value of the stock exceeds the corporation's adjusted basis for its assets, the purchaser is denied the opportunity to step up the basis of the assets to reflect the amount in effect paid for them through the stock acquisition—no § 754 election is available to C corporations.

For an asset sale, the seller of the business can be either the corporation or its shareholders. If the seller is the corporation, the corporation sells the business (the assets), pays any debts not transferred, and makes a liquidating distribution to the shareholders. If the sellers are the shareholders, the corporation pays any debts that will not be transferred and makes a liquidating distribution to the shareholders; then the shareholders sell the business.

Regardless of the approach used for an asset sale, double taxation will occur. The corporation is taxed on the actual sale of the assets and is taxed as if it had sold the assets when it makes the liquidating distribution to the shareholders

who then sell the distributed assets. The shareholders are taxed when they receive cash or assets distributed in-kind by the corporation.

The asset sale resolves the purchaser's problem of not being able to step up the basis of the assets to their fair market value. The basis for each asset is its purchase price. To operate in corporate form (assuming the purchaser is not a corporation), the purchaser needs to transfer the property to a corporation in a § 351 transaction.

From the perspective of the seller, the ideal form of the transaction is a stock sale. Conversely, from the purchaser's perspective, the ideal form is an asset purchase. Double taxation seldom can be avoided in either case. Therefore, the bargaining ability of the seller and the purchaser to structure the sale as a stock sale or an asset sale, respectively, is critical.

Rather than selling the entire business, an owner may sell only his or her ownership interest. Since the form of the transaction is a stock sale, the results for the selling shareholder will be the same as if all the shareholders had sold their stock (i.e., capital gain or capital loss).

### S CORPORATIONS

Since the S corporation is a corporation, it is subject to the provisions for a C corporation discussed previously. Either an asset sale at the corporate level or a liquidating distribution of assets produces recognition at the corporate level. However, under the conduit concept applicable to the S corporation, the recognized amount is taxed at the shareholder level. Therefore, double taxation is avoided directly (only the shareholder is involved) for a stock sale and indirectly (the conduit concept ignores the involvement of the corporation) for an asset sale.

Double taxation might seem to be avoided by making an S corporation election prior to the liquidation of a C corporation, but the built-in gains tax closes this loophole; taxation occurs at the corporate level, and double taxation results.

Concept Summary 14–1 summarizes the tax consequences of business dispositions.

## Overall Comparison of Forms of Doing Business

Concept Summary 14–2 provides a detailed comparison of the tax consequences of the various forms of doing business.

| CONCEPT SUMMARY 14–1 |
| --- |

## Tax Treatment of Disposition of a Business

| Form of Entity | Form of Transaction | Tax Consequences | |
| --- | --- | --- | --- |
| | | Seller | Buyer |
| Sole proprietorship | Sale of individual assets. | Gain or loss is calculated separately for the individual assets. Classification as capital or ordinary depends on the nature and holding period of the individual assets. If amount realized exceeds the fair market value of the identifiable assets, the excess is allocated to goodwill (except to the extent identified with a covenant not to compete), which is a capital asset. | Basis for individual assets is the allocated cost. Prefers that any excess of purchase price over the fair market value of identifiable assets be identified with a covenant not to compete if the covenant has legal utility. Otherwise, the buyer is neutral since both goodwill and covenants are amortized over a 15-year statutory period. |
| | Sale of the business. | Treated as a sale of the individual assets (as above). | Treated as a purchase of the individual assets (as above). |
| Partnership and limited liability entity | Sale of individual assets. | Treatment is the same as for the sole proprietorship. | Treatment is the same as for the sole proprietorship. If the intent is to operate in partnership form, the assets can be contributed to a partnership under § 721. |
| | Sale of ownership interest. | Entity interest is treated as the sale of a capital asset (subject to ordinary income potential for unrealized receivables and substantially appreciated inventory). | Basis for new owner's ownership interest is the cost. The new entity's basis for the assets is also the pertinent cost (i.e., contributed to the entity under § 721), since the original entity will have terminated. |
| C corporation | Sale of corporate assets by corporation (i.e., corporation sells assets, pays debts, and makes liquidating distribution to the shareholders). | Double taxation occurs. Corporation is taxed on the sale of the assets with the gain or loss determination and the classification as capital or ordinary treated the same as for the sole proprietorship. Shareholders calculate gain or loss as the difference between the stock basis and the amount received from the corporation in the liquidating distribution. Capital gain or loss usually results, since stock typically is a capital asset. | Basis for individual assets is the allocated cost. If the intent is to operate in corporate form, the assets can be contributed to a corporation under § 351. |
| | Sale of corporate assets by the shareholders (i.e., corporation pays debts and makes liquidating distribution to the shareholders). | Double taxation occurs. At the time of the liquidating distribution to the shareholders, the corporation is taxed as if it had sold the assets. Shareholders calculate gain or loss as the difference between the stock basis and the fair market value of the assets received from the corporation in the liquidating distribution. Capital gain or loss usually results, since stock typically is a capital asset. | Same as corporate asset sale. |

| Form of Entity | Form of Transaction | Tax Consequences | |
|---|---|---|---|
| | | Seller | Buyer |
| | Sale of corporate stock. | Enables double taxation to be avoided. Since the corporation is not a party to the transaction, there are no tax consequences at the corporate level. Shareholders calculate gain or loss as the difference between the stock basis and the amount received for the stock. Capital gain or loss usually results, since stock typically is a capital asset. | Basis for the stock is its cost. The basis for the corporate assets is not affected by the stock purchase. |
| S corporation | Sale of corporate assets by corporation. | Recognition occurs at the corporate level on the sale of the assets, with the gain or loss determination and the classification as capital or ordinary treated the same as for the sole proprietorship. Conduit concept applicable to the S corporation results in the recognized amount being taxed at the shareholder level. Double taxation associated with the asset sale is avoided, because the shareholder's stock basis is increased by the amount of gain recognition and decreased by the amount of loss recognition. Shareholders calculate gain or loss as the difference between the stock basis and the amount received from the corporation in the liquidating distribution. Capital gain or loss usually results, since stock typically is a capital asset. | Basis for individual assets is the allocated cost. If the intent is to operate in corporate form (i.e., as an S corporation), the assets can be contributed to a corporation under § 351. |
| | Sale of corporate assets by the shareholders. | At the time of the liquidating distribution to the shareholders, recognition occurs at the corporation level as if the corporation had sold the assets. The resultant tax consequences for the shareholders and the corporation are the same as for the sale of corporate assets by the S corporation. | Same as corporate asset sale by the corporation. |
| | Sale of corporate stock. | Same as the treatment for the sale of stock of a C corporation. | Same as the treatment for the purchase of stock of a C corporation. |

## CONCEPT SUMMARY 14–2

### Tax Attributes of Different Forms of Business (Assume Partners and Shareholders Are All Individuals)

| | Sole Proprietorship | Partnership/Limited Liability Entity | S Corporation | C Corporation |
|---|---|---|---|---|
| Restrictions on type or number of owners | One owner. The owner must be an individual. | Must have at least 2 owners. | Only individuals, estates, certain trusts, and certain tax-exempt entities can be owners. Maximum number of shareholders limited to 100.* | None, except some states require a minimum of 2 shareholders. |
| Incidence of tax | Sole proprietorship's income and deductions are reported on Schedule C of the individual's Form 1040. A separate Schedule C is prepared for each business. | Entity not subject to tax. Owners in their separate capacity subject to tax on their distributive share of income. Entity files Form 1065. | Except for certain built-in gains and passive investment income when earnings and profits are present from C corporation tax years, entity not subject to Federal income tax. S corporation files Form 1120S. Shareholders are subject to tax on income attributable to their stock ownership. | Income subject to double taxation. Entity subject to tax, and shareholder subject to tax on any corporate dividends received. Corporation files Form 1120. |
| Highest tax rate | 35% at individual level. | 35% at owner level. | 35% at shareholder level. | 35% at corporate level plus 15%/5% on any corporate dividends at shareholder level (if qualified dividends; otherwise 35%). |
| Choice of tax year | Same tax year as owner. | Selection generally restricted to coincide with tax year of majority owners or principal owners, or to tax year determined under the least aggregate deferral method. | Restricted to a calendar year unless IRS approves a different year for business purposes or other exceptions apply. | Unrestricted selection allowed at time of filing first tax return. |
| Timing of taxation | Based on owner's tax year. | Owners report their share of income in their tax year within which the entity's tax year ends. Owners in their separate capacities are subject to payment of estimated taxes. | Shareholders report their shares of income in their tax year within which the corporation's tax year ends. Generally, the corporation uses a calendar year, but see "Choice of tax year." Shareholders may be subject to payment of estimated taxes. Corporation may be subject to payment of estimated taxes for the taxes imposed at the corporate level. | Corporation subject to tax at close of its tax year. May be subject to payment of estimated taxes. Dividends are subject to tax at the shareholder level in the tax year received. |

*Spouses and family members can be treated as 1 shareholder.

| | Sole Proprietorship | Partnership/Limited Liability Entity | S Corporation | C Corporation |
|---|---|---|---|---|
| Basis for allocating income to owners | Not applicable (only one owner). | Profit and loss sharing agreement. Cash basis items of cash basis entities are allocated on a daily basis. Other entity items are allocated after considering varying interests of owners. | Pro rata share based on stock ownership. Shareholder's pro rata share is determined on a daily basis, according to the number of shares of stock held on each day'of the corporation's tax year. | Not applicable. |
| Contribution of property to the entity | Not a taxable transaction. | Generally not a taxable transaction. | Is a taxable transaction unless the § 351 requirements are satisfied. | Is a taxable transaction unless the § 351 requirements are satisfied. |
| Character of income taxed to owners | Retains source characteristics. | Conduit—retains source characteristics. | Conduit—retains source characteristics. | All source characteristics are lost when income is distributed to owners. |
| Basis for allocating a net operating loss to owners | Not applicable (only one owner). | Profit and loss sharing agreement. Cash basis items of cash basis entities are allocated on a daily basis. Other entity items are allocated after considering varying interests of owners. | Prorated among shareholders on a daily basis. | Not applicable. |
| Limitation on losses deductible by owners | Investment plus liabilities. | Owner's investment plus share of liabilities. | Shareholder's investment plus loans made by shareholder to corporation. | Not applicable. |
| Subject to at-risk rules? | Yes, at the owner level. Indefinite carryover of excess loss. | Yes, at the owner level. Indefinite carryover of excess loss. | Yes, at the shareholder level. Indefinite carryover of excess loss. | Yes, for closely held corporations. Indefinite carryover of excess loss. |
| Subject to passive activity loss rules? | Yes, at the owner level. Indefinite carryover of excess loss. | Yes, at the owner level. Indefinite carryover of excess loss. | Yes, at the shareholder level. Indefinite carryover of excess loss. | Yes, for closely held corporations and personal service corporations. Indefinite carryover of excess loss. |
| Tax consequences of earnings retained by entity | Taxed to owner when earned and increases his or her investment in the sole proprietorship. | Taxed to owners when earned and increases their respective interest bases in the entity. | Taxed to shareholders when earned and increases their respective interest bases in stock. | Taxed to corporation when earned and may be subject to penalty tax if accumulated unreasonably. |

| | Sole Proprietorship | Partnership/Limited Liability Entity | S Corporation | C Corporation |
|---|---|---|---|---|
| Nonliquidating distributions to owners | Not taxable. | Not taxable unless money received exceeds recipient owner's basis in entity interest. Existence of § 751 assets may cause recognition of ordinary income. | Generally not taxable unless the distribution exceeds the shareholder's AAA or stock basis. Existence of accumulated earnings and profits could cause some distributions to be dividends. | Taxable in year of receipt to extent of earnings and profits or if exceeds basis in stock. |
| Capital gains | Taxed at owner level using maximum rate of 5%, 15%, 25%, or 28%. | Conduit—owners must account for their respective shares. Taxed at owner level. | Conduit, with certain exceptions (a possible penalty tax)—shareholders must account for their respective shares. Tax treatment determined at shareholder level. | Taxed at corporate level with a maximum 35% rate. No other benefits. |
| Capital losses | Only $3,000 of capital losses can be offset each tax year against ordinary income. Indefinite carryover. | Conduit—owners must account for their respective shares. Tax treatment determined at owner level. | Conduit—shareholders must account for their respective shares. Tax treatment determined at shareholder level. | Carried back three years and carried forward five years. Deductible only to the extent of capital gains. |
| § 1231 gains and losses | Taxable or deductible at owner level. Five-year lookback rule for § 1231 losses. | Conduit—owners must account for their respective shares. Tax treatment determined at owner level. | Conduit—shareholders must account for their respective shares. Tax treatment determined at shareholder level. | Taxable or deductible at corporate level only. Five-year lookback rule for § 1231 losses. |
| Foreign tax credits | Available at owner level. | Conduit—tax payments passed through to owners. | Generally conduit—tax payments passed through to shareholders. | Available at corporate level only. |
| § 1244 treatment of loss on sale of interest | Not applicable. | Not applicable. | Available. | Available. |
| Basis treatment of entity liabilities | Not applicable. | Includible in interest basis. | Not includible in stock basis. | Not includible in stock basis. |
| Built-in gains | Not applicable. | Not applicable. | Possible corporate tax. | Not applicable. |
| Special allocations to owners | Not applicable (only one owner). | Available if supported by substantial economic effect. | Not available. | Not applicable. |
| Availability of fringe benefits to owners | None. | None. | None unless a 2% or less shareholder. | Available within antidiscrimination rules. |
| Effect of liquidation/ redemption/ reorganization on basis of entity assets | Not applicable. | Usually carried over from entity to owner. | Taxable step-up to fair market value. | Taxable step-up to fair market value. |

| | Sole Proprietorship | Partnership/Limited Liability Entity | S Corporation | C Corporation |
|---|---|---|---|---|
| Sale of ownership interest | Treated as the sale of individual assets. Classification of recognized gain or loss depends on the nature of the individual assets. | Treated as the sale of an entity interest. Recognized gain or loss is classified as capital, although appreciated inventory and receivables are subject to ordinary income treatment. | Treated as the sale of corporate stock. Recognized gain is classified as capital gain. Recognized loss is classified as capital loss, subject to ordinary loss treatment under § 1244. | Treated as the sale of corporate stock. Recognized gain is classified as capital gain. Recognized loss is classified as capital loss, subject to ordinary loss treatment under § 1244. |
| Distribution of appreciated property | Not taxable. | No recognition at the entity level. | Recognition at the corporate level to the extent of the appreciation. Conduit—amount of recognized gain is passed through to shareholders. | Taxable at the corporate level to the extent of the appreciation. |
| Splitting of income among family members | Not applicable (only one owner). | Difficult—IRS will not recognize a family member as an owner unless certain requirements are met. | Rather easy—gift of stock will transfer tax on a pro rata share of income to the donee. However, IRS can make adjustments to reflect adequate compensation for services. | Same as an S corporation, except that donees will be subject to tax only on earnings actually or constructively distributed to them. Other than unreasonable compensation, IRS generally cannot make adjustments to reflect adequate compensation for services and capital. |
| Organizational costs | Start-up expenditures are eligible for $5,000 limited expensing (subject to phaseout) and amortizing balance over 180 months. | Organization costs are eligible for $5,000 limited expensing (subject to phaseout) and amortizing balance over 180 months. | Same as partnership. | Same as partnership. |
| Charitable contributions | Limitations apply at owner level. | Conduit—owners are subject to deduction limitations in their own capacities. | Conduit—shareholders are subject to deduction limitations in their own capacities. | Limited to 10% of taxable income before certain deductions. |
| Alternative minimum tax | Applies at owner level. AMT rates are 26% and 28%. | Applies at the owner level rather than at the entity level. AMT preferences and adjustments are passed through from the entity to the owners. | Applies at the shareholder level rather than at the corporate level. AMT preferences and adjustments are passed through from the S corporation to the shareholders. | Applies at the corporate level. AMT rate is 20%. Modest-sized C corporations are exempt. |
| ACE adjustment | Does not apply. | Does not apply. | Does not apply. | The adjustment is made in calculating AMTI. The adjustment is 75% of the excess of adjusted current earnings over unadjusted AMTI. If the unadjusted AMTI exceeds adjusted current earnings, the adjustment may be negative. |

**PLANNING STRATEGIES**

## Choosing a Business Form: Case Study

**FRAMEWORK FOCUS: TAX RATE**

STRATEGY ➤ AVOID DOUBLE TAXATION.
➤ SHIFT NET INCOME FROM HIGH-BRACKET TAXPAYERS TO LOW-BRACKET TAXPAYERS.

The chapter began with an example that illustrated the relationship between tax planning and the choice of business form; it also raised a variety of questions about the advice given by the tax practitioner. By this time, one should be able to develop various scenarios supporting the tax advice given. The actual fact situations that produced the tax adviser's recommendations were as follows.

- Jesse's experience in the dairy industry consists of raising a few heifers during the final five years of his employment. Eva anticipates that Jesse will generate tax losses for the indeterminate future. In addition, Jesse indicated that he and his wife must have limited liability associated with the dairy farm.
- Larry was born and raised on his father's dairy farm. Both his education and his Air Force managerial experience provide him with useful tools for managing his business. However, Larry inherited his farm when milk prices were at a low for the modern era. Since none of her dairy farm clients were profitable, Eva anticipated Larry would operate his dairy farm at a loss. Larry, like Jesse, felt that limited liability was imperative. Thus, he incorporated the dairy farm and made the S corporation election.
- For the first two years, Larry's dairy farm produced tax losses. Since then, the dairy farm has produced tax

profits large enough to absorb the losses. Larry anticipates that his profits will remain relatively stable in the $50,000 to $75,000 range in the future. Since he is subject to a 28 percent marginal tax rate and anticipates that no dividend distributions will be made, his tax liability associated with the dairy farm will be reduced if he terminates the S corporation election.

As Jesse and Larry's example illustrates, selection of the proper business form can result in both nontax and tax advantages. Both of these factors should be considered in making the selection decision. Furthermore, this choice should be reviewed periodically, since a proper business form at one point in time may not be the proper form at a different time. Note that another business form Eva could have considered for Jesse is the limited liability entity.

In looking at the tax attributes, consideration should be given to the tax consequences of the following.

- Contribution of assets to the entity by the owners at the time the entity is created and at later dates.
- Taxation of the results of operations.
- Distributions to owners.
- Disposition of an ownership interest.
- Termination of the entity.

# Suggested Further Readings

Bruce D. Bernard, "Improve Tax Consequences of Business Purchase and Sale," *Practical Tax Strategies*, January 2002, pp. 4–7.

George Jackson III and David M. Maloney, "Buy-Sell Agreements—An Invaluable Tool," *The Tax Adviser*, April 2003, pp. 200–204 and May 2003, pp. 284–286.

Richard M. Lipton and Steven R. Dixon, "When Is a Partner Not a Partner? When Does a Partnership Exist?" *Journal of Taxation*, February 2004, pp. 73–84.

Christian M. McBurney, "Conversion of Start-Up Corporations to LLCs Could Provide Tax Benefit to Investors," *Journal of Taxation*, November 2002, pp. 298–305.

Mark A. Turner, "Excessive Involvement May Affect Benefits of Entity Choice," *Practical Tax Strategies*, March 2002, pp. 136–140.

Robert Willens, "IRS Alters the Landscape with Respect to the 351 'Control Immediately After' Requirement," *Journal of Taxation*, June 2003, pp. 325–332.

## KEY TERMS

| | | |
|---|---|---|
| Conduit concept, 14–15 | Limited liability company (LLC), 14–4 | Unreasonable compensation, 14–12 |
| Entity concept, 14–15 | | |

## PROBLEM MATERIALS

### Problems

1. Using the legend provided, indicate which form of business entity each of the following characteristics describes. Some of the characteristics may apply to more than one form of business entity.

   **Legend**

   SP = Applies to sole proprietorship
   P  = Applies to partnership and LLC
   S  = Applies to S corporation
   C  = Applies to C corporation

   a. Has limited liability.
   b. Greatest ability to raise capital.
   c. Subject to double taxation.
   d. Subject to accumulated earnings tax.
   e. Limit on types and number of shareholders.
   f. Has unlimited liability.
   g. Sale of the business can be subject to double taxation.
   h. Contribution of property to the entity in exchange for an ownership interest can result in the nonrecognition of realized gain.
   i. Profits and losses affect the basis for an ownership interest.
   j. Entity liabilities affect the basis for an ownership interest.
   k. Distributions of earnings are taxed as dividend income to the owners.

2. Using the legend provided, indicate which form of business entity each of the following characteristics describes. Some of the characteristics may apply to more than one form of business entity.

   **Legend**

   P = Applies to partnership and LLC
   S = Applies to S corporation
   C = Applies to C corporation

   a. Basis for an ownership interest is increased by an investment by the owner.
   b. Basis for an ownership interest is decreased by a distribution to the owner.
   c. Basis for an ownership interest is increased by entity profits.
   d. Basis for an ownership interest is decreased by entity losses.
   e. Basis for an ownership interest is increased as the entity's liabilities increase.
   f. Basis for an ownership interest is decreased as the entity's liabilities decrease.

3. A business entity has the following assets and liabilities on its balance sheet.

| | **Net Book Value** | **Fair Market Value** |
|---|---|---|
| Assets | $675,000 | $950,000 |
| Liabilities | 100,000 | 100,000 |

The business entity has just lost a product liability suit with damages of $5 million being awarded to the plaintiff. Although the business entity will appeal the judgment, legal counsel indicates the judgment is highly unlikely to be overturned by the appellate court. The product liability insurance carried by the business has a policy ceiling of $3 million. What is the amount of liability of the entity and its owners if the form of the business entity is:

   a. A sole proprietorship?
   b. A partnership or LLC?
   c. A C corporation?
   d. An S corporation?

**Ethics**

4. Bryan operates his business as a C corporation. He is the only shareholder. The accumulated E & P is $800,000. Starting next year, he plans on distributing $200,000. In future years, he intends to distribute all of the annual earnings. Recognizing that the distribution would be taxed as dividend income, he has developed the following tax strategy:

   • Sell the corporate assets to himself for the fair market value.

   • Have the corporation invest the sales proceeds in a mutual fund.

   • Contribute the assets to an LLC and operate his business in this legal form.

   Evaluate Bryan's proposal to avoid double taxation.

5. Red, White, Blue, and Orange generate taxable income as follows.

| **Corporation** | **Taxable Income** |
|---|---|
| Red | $ 92,000 |
| White | 325,000 |
| Blue | 800,000 |
| Orange | 40,000,000 |

   a. Calculate the marginal and effective tax rates for each of the C corporations.
   b. Explain why the marginal tax rate for a C corporation can exceed 35%, but the effective tax rate cannot do so.

**Decision Making**

**Communications**

6. Amy and Jeff Barnes are going to operate their florist shop as a partnership or as an S corporation. Their mailing address is 5700 Richmond Highway, Alexandria, VA 22300. After paying salaries of $80,000 to each of the owners, the shop's earnings are projected to be about $100,000. The earnings are to be invested in the growth of the business. Write a letter to Amy and Jeff advising them of which of the two entity forms they should select.

**Decision Making**

7. Gary is an entrepreneur who likes to be actively involved in his business ventures. He is going to invest $400,000 in a business that he projects will produce a tax loss of approximately $75,000 per year in the short run. However, once consumers become aware of the new product being sold by the business and the quality of the service it provides, he is confident the business will generate a profit of at least $100,000 per year. Gary has substantial other income (from both business ventures and investment activities) each year. Advise Gary on the business form he should select for the short run. He will be the sole owner.

**Decision Making**

8. Jack, an unmarried taxpayer, is going to establish a manufacturing business. He anticipates that the business will be profitable immediately due to a patent that he holds. He anticipates that profits for the first year will be about $200,000 and will increase at

a rate of about 20% per year for the foreseeable future. He will be the sole owner of the business. Advise Jack on the form of business entity he should select. Jack will be in the 35% tax bracket.

**Decision Making**

9. Clay Corporation will begin operations on January 1. Earnings for the next five years are projected to be relatively stable at about $90,000 per year. The shareholders of Clay are in the 33% tax bracket.
   a. Clay will reinvest its after-tax earnings in the growth of the company. Should Clay operate as a C corporation or as an S corporation?
   b. Clay will distribute its after-tax earnings each year to its shareholders. Should Clay operate as a C corporation or as an S corporation?

10. Mabel and Alan, who are in the 35% tax bracket, recently acquired a fast-food franchise. Both of them will work in the business and receive a salary of $100,000. They anticipate that the annual profits of the business, after deducting salaries, will be approximately $300,000. The entity will distribute enough cash each year to Mabel and Alan to cover their Federal income taxes associated with the franchise.
    a. What amount will the entity distribute if the franchise operates as a C corporation?
    b. What amount will the entity distribute if the franchise operates as an S corporation?
    c. What will be the amount of the combined entity/owner tax liability in (a) and (b)?

11. Parrott is a closely held corporation owned by 10 shareholders (each has 10% of the stock). Selected financial information provided by Parrott follows.

| | |
|---|---|
| Taxable income | $5,250,000 |
| Positive AMT adjustments (excluding ACE adjustment) | 425,000 |
| Negative AMT adjustments | (30,000) |
| Tax preferences | 6,000,000 |
| Retained earnings | 850,000 |
| Accumulated E & P | 775,000 |
| ACE adjustment | 720,000 |

   a. Calculate Parrott's tax liability as a C corporation.
   b. Calculate Parrott's tax liability as an S corporation.
   c. How would your answers in (a) and (b) change if Parrott is not closely held (e.g., 5,000 shareholders with no shareholder owning more than 2% of the stock)?

**Decision Making**

**Communications**

12. Pelican Corporation, an offshore drilling company, is going to sell land and an equipment warehouse that it no longer needs. The real estate is located at 200 Brando Row, Grand Isle, LA 70535. The adjusted basis for the real estate is $400,000 ($700,000 − $300,000 straight-line depreciation), and the fair market value is $500,000. ADS straight-line depreciation would have been $275,000. The buyer of the real estate would like to close the transaction prior to the end of the calendar year. Pelican is uncertain whether the tax consequences would be better if it sold the real estate this year or next year and is considering the following options.

   • $500,000 in cash payable on December 31, 2005.

   • The sale will be closed on December 31, 2005, with the consideration being a $500,000 note issued by the buyer. The maturity date of the note is January 2, 2006, with the real estate being pledged as security.

   Pelican projects its taxable income for 2005 and 2006 to be $600,000 (gross receipts of $8.5 million) without the sale of the real estate. Pelican's accounting period is the calendar year. Determine the tax consequences to Pelican under either option and recommend which option Pelican should select. Send your recommendation to Corey Longwell, Pelican's tax director, whose office is at the warehouse.

**Ethics**

13. Heron Corporation has been in operation for 10 years. Since Heron's creation, all of the stock has been owned by Andy, who initially invested $200,000 in the corporation. Heron has been successful far beyond Andy's expectations, and the current fair market value of the stock is $10 million. While he has been paid a salary of $200,000 per year by the corporation, all of Heron's earnings have been reinvested in the growth of the corporation.

Heron is currently being audited by the IRS. One of the issues raised by the IRS agent is the possibility of the assessment of the accumulated earnings tax. Andy is not concerned about this issue because he believes Heron can easily justify the accumulations based on its past rapid expansion by opening new outlets. The expansion program is fully documented in the minutes of Heron's board of directors. Andy has provided this information to the IRS agent.

Two years ago, Andy decided that he would curtail any further expansion into new markets by Heron. In his opinion, further expansion would exceed his ability to manage the corporation effectively. Since the tax year under audit is three years ago, Andy sees no reason to provide the IRS agent with this information.

Heron will continue its policy of no dividend payments into the foreseeable future. Andy believes that if the accumulated earnings issue is satisfactorily resolved on this audit, it probably will not be raised again on any subsequent audits. Thus, double taxation in the form of the tax on dividends at the shareholder level or the accumulated earnings tax at the corporate level can be avoided.

What is Heron's responsibility to disclose to the IRS agent the expected change in its growth strategy? Are Andy's beliefs regarding future accumulated earnings tax issues realistic?

**EXTENDER**

14. Two unmarried brothers own and operate a farm. The live on the farm and take their meals on the farm for the "convenience of the employer." The fair market value of their lodging is $20,000, and the fair market value of their meals is $12,000. The meals are prepared for them by the farm cook who prepares their meals along with those of the five other farm employees.
    a. Determine the tax consequences of the meals and lodging to the brothers if the farm is incorporated.
    b. Determine the tax consequences of the meals and lodging to the brothers if the farm is not incorporated.

**EXTENDER**

15. A business entity's taxable income before the cost of certain fringe benefits paid to owners and other employees is $400,000. The amounts paid for these fringe benefits are as follows:

| | Owners | Other Employees |
|---|---|---|
| Group term life insurance | $20,000 | $40,000 |
| Meals and lodging incurred for the convenience of the employer | 50,000 | 75,000 |
| Pension plan | 30,000* | 90,000 |

*H.R. 10 (Keogh) plan for partnership and S corporation.

The business entity is equally owned by four owners.
    a. Calculate the taxable income of the business entity if the entity is a partnership, a C corporation, or an S corporation.
    b. Determine the effect on the owners for each of the three business forms.

16. Beaver, a C corporation, has taxable income of $300,000 before paying salaries to the two equal shareholder-employees, Gerald and Joanie. Beaver follows a policy of distributing all after-tax earnings to the shareholders.
    a. Determine the tax consequences for Beaver, Gerald, and Joanie if the corporation pays salaries to Gerald and Joanie as follows.

| Option 1 | | Option 2 | |
|---|---|---|---|
| Gerald | $180,000 | Gerald | $60,000 |
| Joanie | 120,000 | Joanie | 40,000 |

    b. Is Beaver likely to encounter any tax problems associated with either option?

17. Swallow, a C corporation, is owned by Sandra (50%) and Fran (50%). Sandra is the president, and Fran is the vice president for sales. Late in 2004, Swallow encounters working capital difficulties. Thus, Sandra and Fran each loan the corporation $300,000 on a 6% note that is due in five years with interest payable annually.
    a. Determine the tax consequences to Swallow, Sandra, and Fran for 2005 if the notes are classified as debt.
    b. Determine the tax consequences to Swallow, Sandra, and Fran for 2005 if the notes are classified as equity.

**Decision Making**

**Communications**

18. Laurie Gladin owns land and a building that she has been using in her sole proprietorship. She is going to incorporate her sole proprietorship as a C corporation. Laurie must decide whether to contribute the land and building to the corporation or to lease them to the corporation. The net income of the sole proprietorship for the past five years has averaged $250,000. Advise Laurie on the tax consequences. Summarize your analysis in a memo to the tax file.

**Decision Making**

19. Marci and Jennifer each own 50% of the stock of Lavender, a C corporation. After paying each of them a "reasonable" salary of $150,000, the taxable income of Lavender is normally around $800,000. The corporation is about to purchase a $2 million shopping mall ($1,500,000 allocated to the building and $500,000 allocated to the land). The mall will be rented to tenants at a net rental rate (including rental commissions, depreciation, etc.) of $600,000 annually. Marci and Jennifer will contribute $1 million each to the corporation to provide the cash required for the acquisition. Their CPA has suggested that Marci and Jennifer purchase the shopping mall as individuals and lease it to Lavender for a fair rental of $400,000. Both Marci and Jennifer are in the 35% tax bracket. The acquisition will occur on January 2, 2005. Determine whether the shopping mall should be acquired by Lavender or by Marci and Jennifer in accordance with their CPA's recommendation. Depreciation on the shopping mall in 2005 is $37,000.

20. Petal, Inc., has taxable income of $625,000 for 2005. Petal has been in business for many years and long ago used up the accumulated earnings credit. Petal has no additional "reasonable needs of the business" for the current tax year.
    a. Determine the total potential tax liability for Petal if it declares no dividends.
    b. Determine the total potential tax liability for Petal if it declares and pays dividends equal to the after-tax earnings.
    c. Determine the total potential tax liability for Petal in (a) and (b) if Petal is an S corporation.

21. Frank owns 600 shares of the stock of Autumn, Inc., and Grace owns the remaining 400 shares. Frank's stock basis is $60,000, and Grace's is $40,000. As part of a stock redemption, Frank redeems 100 of his shares for $50,000, and Grace redeems 300 of her shares for $150,000.
    a. Determine the tax consequences to Autumn, Inc., to Frank, and to Grace if Autumn, Inc., is a C corporation.
    b. Determine the tax consequences to Autumn, Inc., to Frank, and to Grace if Autumn, Inc., is an S corporation.

**Issue ID**

22. Oscar created Lavender Corporation four years ago. The C corporation has paid Oscar as president a salary of $200,000 each year. Annual earnings after taxes approximate $700,000 each year. Lavender has not paid any dividends nor does it intend to do so in the future. Instead, Oscar wants his heirs to receive the stock with a step-up in stock basis when he dies. Identify the relevant tax issues.

**Issue ID**

23. Tammy and Arnold own 40% of the stock of Roadrunner, an S corporation. The other 60% is owned by 99 other shareholders, all of whom are single and unrelated. Tammy and Arnold have agreed to a divorce and are in the process of negotiating a property settlement. Identify the relevant tax issues for Tammy and Arnold.

**Decision Making**

24. Eagle Corporation has been an electing S corporation since its incorporation 10 years ago. During the first three years of operations, it incurred total losses of $250,000. Since then Eagle has generated earnings of approximately $150,000 each year. None of the

earnings have been distributed to the three equal shareholders, Claire, Lynn, and Todd, because the corporation has been in an expansion mode. At the beginning of 2005, Claire sells her stock to Nell for $400,000. Nell has reservations about the utility of the S election. Therefore, Lynn, Todd, and Nell are discussing whether the election should be continued. They expect the earnings to remain at approximately $150,000 each year. However, since they perceive that the company's expansion period is over and Eagle has adequate working capital, they may start distributing the earnings to the shareholders. All of the shareholders are in the 33% tax bracket. Advise the three shareholders on whether the S election should be maintained.

**Communications**

25. Bob Bentz and Carl Pierce each own 50% of the stock of Deer, Inc., a C corporation. When the corporation was organized, Bob contributed cash of $200,000, and Carl contributed land with an adjusted basis of $125,000 and a fair market value of $240,000. Deer assumed Carl's $40,000 mortgage on the land. In addition to the capital contributions, Bob and Carl each loaned the corporation $75,000. The maturity date of the loan is in 10 years, and the interest rate is 8%, the same as the Federal rate.
    a. Determine the tax consequences to Bob, Carl, and Deer of the initial contribution of assets, the shareholder loans, and the annual interest payments if the loans are classified as debt.
    b. Determine the tax consequences if the loans are reclassified as equity.
    c. You met with Bob at lunch to discuss the tax consequences of the capital contributions and loans made by Carl and him to Deer, Inc. Prepare a memo for the files on your discussion.

26. Agnes, Becky, and Carol form a business entity with each contributing the following.

| | Adjusted Basis | Fair Market Value |
| --- | --- | --- |
| Agnes: Cash | $100,000 | $100,000 |
| Becky: Land | 60,000 | 120,000 |
| Carol: Services | | 50,000 |

Their ownership percentages will be as follows.

| | |
| --- | --- |
| Agnes | 40% |
| Becky | 40% |
| Carol | 20% |

Becky's land has a $20,000 mortgage that is assumed by the entity. Carol is an attorney who receives her ownership interest in exchange for legal services. Determine the recognized gain to the owners, the basis for their ownership interests, and the entity's basis for its assets if the entity is:
    a. A partnership.
    b. A C corporation.
    c. An S corporation.

27. Alicia contributes $180,000 to a business entity in exchange for a 30% ownership interest. During the first year of operations, the entity earns a profit of $160,000. At the end of that year, the entity has liabilities of $60,000.
    a. Calculate Alicia's basis for her stock if the entity is a C corporation.
    b. Calculate Alicia's basis for her stock if the entity is an S corporation.
    c. Calculate Alicia's basis for her partnership interest if the entity is a partnership.

28. An entity has the following income for the current year:

| | |
| --- | --- |
| Operations | $92,000 |
| Tax-exempt interest income | 19,000 |
| Long-term capital gain | 60,000 |

The entity has earnings and profits (AAA for an S corporation) of $900,000 at the beginning of the year. A distribution of $200,000 is made to the owners.
a. Calculate the taxable income if the entity is (1) a C corporation and (2) an S corporation.
b. Determine the effect of the distribution on the shareholders if the entity is (1) a C corporation and (2) an S corporation.

29. Amber holds a 20% interest in a business to which she contributed $100,000 as part of the initial ownership group. During the life of the business, the following have occurred.

    * $200,000 cumulative losses, first three tax years.

    * $150,000 operating profit in the fourth tax year.

    * $75,000 distribution to owners at the end of the third tax year.

    * $60,000 payment to redeem 25% of Amber's ownership interest at the end of the fourth year. No other ownership redemptions have occurred.

    Determine the tax consequences to Amber if the entity is:
    a. A partnership.
    b. An S corporation.
    c. A C corporation.

**Decision Making**

30. On January 1, 2005, John contributes assets with an adjusted basis of $80,000 and a fair market value of $212,000 for a 40% ownership interest in an interior design business. Maria contributes $300,000 cash for a 60% ownership interest. The entity assumes a $12,000 mortgage attributable to one of the assets contributed by John. During 2005, the business earns $130,000. In addition, the entity makes a $35,000 cash distribution to John and a $52,500 cash distribution to Maria during the year. John and Maria are each in the 33% tax bracket.
    a. If the business entity is a C corporation, determine each of the following.

       * Recognized gain to the owners and the business entity on the creation of the business entity.

       * Original basis for John's and Maria's ownership interests.

       * Effect of the business entity earnings on the entity, John, and Maria.

       * Effect of the distributions on John and Maria.

       * Adjusted basis for John's and Maria's ownership interest at the end of the year.

    b. Determine each of the above if the business entity is an S corporation.
    c. If the objective is to minimize the income tax liability, should the business entity be a C corporation or an S corporation? Assume 2005 is a representative year.

31. JK is a partnership that is owned by James and Karen. James's basis for his partnership interest is $60,000, and Karen's basis is $80,000. JK distributes $50,000 to James and $60,000 to Karen.
    a. Determine the tax consequences of the distribution to James, Karen, and JK.
    b. Assume that JK is a C corporation rather than a partnership. JK's earnings and profits are $200,000. James's basis for his stock is $60,000, and Karen's stock basis is $80,000. Determine the tax consequences of the distribution to James, Karen, and JK.

32. Beige, Inc., a personal service corporation, has the following types of income and losses.

| | |
|---|---|
| Active income | $212,000 |
| Portfolio income | 20,000 |
| Passive activity losses | 216,000 |

    a. Calculate Beige's taxable income.
    b. Assume that instead of being a personal service corporation, Beige is a closely held corporation. Calculate Beige's taxable income.

33. Rosa contributes $50,000 to a business entity in exchange for a 10% ownership interest. Rosa materially participates in the business. The business entity incurs a loss of $900,000

for 2005. The entity liabilities at the end of 2005 are $700,000. Of this amount, $150,000 is for recourse debt, and $550,000 is for nonrecourse debt.

a. Assume the business entity is a partnership. How much of Rosa's share of the loss can be deducted on her 2005 individual tax return? What is Rosa's basis for her partnership interest at the end of 2005?

b. Assume the business entity is a C corporation. How much of Rosa's share of the loss can be deducted on her 2005 individual tax return? What is Rosa's basis for her stock at the end of 2005?

34. Sanford contributes land to a business entity in January 2005 for a 35% ownership interest. Sanford's basis for the land is $83,000, and the fair market value is $120,000. The business entity was formed three years ago by Pam and Rene, who have equal ownership. The entity is unsuccessful in getting the land rezoned from agricultural to residential use. In August 2005, the land is sold for $140,000. Determine the tax consequences of the sale of the land for the business entity and the three owners if the organization is:

a. A C corporation.
b. An S corporation.
c. A partnership.

35. Abby and Velma are equal owners of the AV Partnership. Abby invests $75,000 cash in the partnership. Velma contributes land and a building (basis to her of $50,000, fair market value of $75,000). The entity then borrows $200,000 cash using recourse financing and $100,000 using nonrecourse financing.

a. Compute the outside basis in the partnership interest for Abby and Velma.
b. Compute the at-risk amount for Abby and Velma.

36. Indicate which of the following special allocations are available for a partnership (P), a C corporation (C), and an S corporation (S).

a. Share profits and losses differently from the share in capital.
b. Share profits in a different percentage than losses.
c. Special allocation of precontribution gain.
d. Special allocation supported by substantial economic effect.
e. Allocation to eliminate difference between inside and outside basis.
f. Special allocation of precontribution loss.

37. Sanjay contributes land to a business entity in January 2005 for a 30% ownership interest. Sanjay's basis for the land is $60,000, and the fair market value is $100,000. The business entity was formed three years ago by Polly and Rita, who have equal ownership. The entity is unsuccessful in getting the land rezoned from agricultural to residential. In October 2005, the land is sold for $110,000.

Determine the tax consequences of the sale of the land for the entity and its owners if the entity is:

a. A C corporation.
b. An S corporation.
c. A partnership.

38. Emily and Freda are negotiating with George to purchase the business that he operates in corporate form (Pelican, Inc.). The assets of Pelican, Inc., a C corporation, are as follows.

| Asset | Basis | FMV |
| --- | --- | --- |
| Cash | $ 20,000 | $ 20,000 |
| Accounts receivable | 50,000 | 50,000 |
| Inventory | 100,000 | 110,000 |
| Furniture and fixtures | 150,000 | 170,000* |
| Building | 200,000 | 250,000** |
| Land | 40,000 | 150,000 |

*Potential depreciation recapture under § 1245 is $45,000.
**The straight-line method was used to depreciate the building. Accumulated depreciation is $340,000.

George's basis for the stock of Pelican, Inc., is $560,000. George is subject to a 35% marginal tax rate, and Pelican, Inc., faces a 34% marginal tax rate.

a. Emily and Freda purchase the *stock* of Pelican, Inc., from George for $908,000. Determine the tax consequences to Emily and Freda, Pelican, Inc., and George.

b. Emily and Freda purchase the *assets* from Pelican, Inc., for $908,000. Determine the tax consequences to Emily and Freda, Pelican, Inc., and George.

c. The purchase price is $550,000 because the fair market value of the building is $150,000, and the fair market value of the land is $50,000. No amount is assigned to goodwill. Emily and Freda purchase the *stock* of Pelican, Inc., from George. Determine the tax consequences to Emily and Freda, Pelican, Inc., and George.

**Decision Making** 39. Linda is the owner of a sole proprietorship. The entity has the following assets.

| Asset | Basis | FMV |
|---|---|---|
| Cash | $10,000 | $10,000 |
| Accounts receivable | –0– | 25,000 |
| Office furniture and fixtures* | 15,000 | 17,000 |
| Building** | 75,000 | 90,000 |
| Land | 60,000 | 80,000 |

*Potential depreciation recapture under § 1245 of $5,000.
**The straight-line method has been used to depreciate the building.

Linda sells the business for $260,000 to Juan.

a. Determine the tax consequences to Linda, including the classification of any recognized gain or loss.

b. Determine the tax consequences to Juan.

c. Advise Juan on how the purchase agreement could be modified to produce more beneficial tax consequences for him.

**Decision Making** 40. Gail and Harry own the GH Partnership. They have conducted the business as a partnership for 10 years. The bases for their partnership interests are as follows.

| Gail | Harry |
|---|---|
| $100,000 | $150,000 |

GH Partnership holds the following assets.

| Asset | Basis | FMV |
|---|---|---|
| Cash | $ 10,000 | $ 10,000 |
| Accounts receivable | 30,000 | 28,000 |
| Inventory | 25,000 | 26,000 |
| Building* | 100,000 | 150,000 |
| Land | 250,000 | 400,000 |

*The straight-line method has been used to depreciate the building. Accumulated depreciation is $70,000.

Gail and Harry sell their partnership interests to Keith and Liz for $307,000 each.

a. Determine the tax consequences of the sale to Gail, Harry, and GH Partnership.

b. From a tax perspective, should it matter to Keith and Liz whether they purchase Gail and Harry's partnership interests or the partnership assets from GH Partnership?

41. Ted Jamison and Skip Arnold are going to purchase the Carp Partnership, as equal partners, from Jan and Gail for $800,000. Because of your negotiations on behalf of Ted and Skip, the transaction will be structured as a purchase of the partnership, not of its individual assets. Carp's inside basis in its assets is $625,000. Write a letter to Ted at 50 Lake Shore Drive, Erie, PA 16501, explaining the following.
    a. What outside basis do Ted and Skip take in the partnership?
    b. Can Carp change its inside asset basis as a result of the purchase of the entity?

42. Vladimir owns all the stock of Ruby Corporation. The fair market value of the stock (and Ruby's assets) is about four times his adjusted basis for the stock. Vladimir is negotiating with an investor group for the sale of the corporation. Identify the relevant tax issues for Vladimir.

43. Bill Evans will purchase either the stock or the assets of Dane Corporation. All of the Dane stock is owned by Chuck. Bill and Chuck agree that Dane is worth $750,000. The tax basis for Dane's assets is $410,000. Write a letter to Bill advising him on whether he should negotiate to purchase the stock or the assets. Bill's address is 100 Village Green, Chattanooga, TN 37403.

**BRIDGE DISCIPLINE**

1.  Parchment, Inc., is created with the following asset and liability contributions. Jake and Fran each receive 100 shares of Parchment common stock.

| Shareholder | Assets | Basis | Fair Market Value |
| --- | --- | --- | --- |
| Jake | Cash | $100,000 | $100,000 |
| Fran | Land | 40,000 | 120,000* |

*The land has a mortgage of $20,000 that Parchment assumes.

    a. Prepare a financial accounting balance sheet. Discuss the relevance of conduit theory and entity theory.
    b. Prepare a tax balance sheet. Discuss the relevance of conduit theory and entity theory.
    c. Assume Parchment sells the land four months after the creation of the corporation for $150,000. Discuss the effect on the financial accounting balance sheet and the tax balance sheet.

2.  Assume that Parchment in the preceding problem elects S corporation status at the time of its creation. Respond to (a), (b), and (c).

3.  Assume that Parchment in (1) is a general partnership rather than a corporation. Respond to (a), (b), and (c). Would your answer change if Parchment were an LLC that "checked the box" to be taxed as a partnership?

4.  Teal, Inc., has total assets of $100 million and annual revenues of $700 million. Lavender, Inc., has total assets of $12 million and annual revenues of $900,000. Both have been in existence for three years.
    a. Explain why neither Teal nor Lavender need make an AMT calculation for its first tax year.
    b. Explain why Teal must make an AMT calculation and why Lavender is not required to do so.
    c. Do you think that this different tax treatment for Teal and Lavender is equitable?

## Research Problems

*Note: Solutions to Research Problems can be prepared by using the **RIA Checkpoint® Student Edition** online research product, which is available to accompany this text. It is also possible to prepare solutions to the Research Problems by using tax research materials found in a standard tax library.*

**Research Problem 1.** The stock of Ebony, Inc., is owned as follows:

| | **Percent Ownership** | **Basis** | **FMV** |
|---|---|---|---|
| Alma | 30% | $2,700 | $270,000 |
| Ben | 30 | 2,700 | 270,000 |
| Debbie | 20 | 1,800 | 180,000 |
| Clyde | 20 | 1,800 | 180,000 |

Alma and Ben are the parents of Debbie and Clyde. Managerial positions in Ebony are as follows: Alma is the chief executive officer (CEO), Ben is the chief operating officer (COO), Debbie is the chief financial officer (CFO), and Clyde is the vice president for human resources. Alma and Ben have owned their stock for 30 years, and Debbie and Clyde have owned their stock for 10 years. Alma and Ben are considering disposing of their stock and would like to use the funds to acquire a more lucrative investment. Their initial plan was to have Ebony redeem their stock. However, their accountant has indicated that since they intend to retain their positions as officers, the redemption will not qualify under § 302(b)(3). The accountant suggests that they sell their stock to several outsiders who wish to acquire an interest in Ebony. As Debbie and Clyde expect to move into the CEO and COO positions in a few years, they oppose a sale to outsiders. They are concerned about the loss of family control that would result.

How can this family dilemma be resolved?

**Internet Activity**

*Use the tax resources of the Internet to address the following questions. Do not restrict your search to the World Wide Web, but include a review of newsgroups and general reference materials, practitioner sites and resources, primary sources of the tax law, chat rooms and discussion groups, and other opportunities.*

**Research Problem 2.** Find an anecdote about a professional consulting firm that recently converted to LLP status. Are the firm and its competition and clients agreeable to the conversion of operating status?

**Research Problem 3.** When did your state adopt LLC legislation? When did it receive IRS approval to apply partnership tax law to the entities?

**Research Problem 4.** Find an article describing how a specific business put together its employee fringe benefit package in light of the limitations presented by the tax law and its form of operation.

**Research Problem 5.** Determine whether your state income tax system permits an S corporation election.

**Research Problem 6.** Find a company that provides a service of identifying investment properties that are producing passive activity income.

# Taxation of Individuals

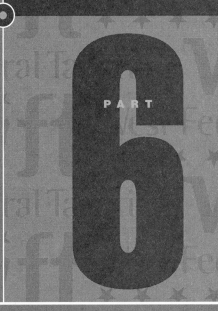

**PART 6**

The primary orientation of this text is toward basic tax concepts as they apply to business entities. Although many of these concepts also apply to the individual taxpayer, numerous tax concepts have been designed to apply specifically to the individual taxpayer. The components of the basic tax model provide the framework for the presentation of these specifically designed tax concepts for the individual taxpayer.

**CHAPTER 15**

Introduction to the Taxation of Individuals

**CHAPTER 16**

Individuals as Employees and Proprietors

http://wft.swlearning.com

# Introduction to the Taxation of Individuals

## LEARNING OBJECTIVES

*After completing Chapter 15, you should be able to:*

### LO.1
Understand and apply the components of the Federal income tax formula for individuals.

### LO.2
Apply the rules for arriving at personal and dependency exemptions.

### LO.3
Use the proper method for determining the tax liability.

### LO.4
Identify and work with kiddie tax situations.

### LO.5
Recognize filing requirements and proper filing status.

### LO.6
Identify specific inclusions and exclusions applicable to individuals.

### LO.7
Determine an individual's allowable itemized deductions.

### LO.8
Understand the adoption expenses credit, child tax credit, education tax credits, credit for child and dependent care expenses, and earned income credit.

## OUTLINE

---

**TAX TALK**

*I'm proud of paying taxes in the United States. The only thing is—I could be just as proud for half the money.*

—*Arthur Godfrey*

---

**T**he individual income tax accounts for approximately 37 percent of Federal budget receipts, compared to approximately 6 percent for the corporate income tax. The tax laws affecting individuals have become increasingly more complex in recent years as the government adds new laws to protect or increase this important source of revenue. Taxpayers respond to each new tax act with techniques to exploit loopholes, and the government responds with loophole-closing provisions, making the individual income tax law even more complex.[1]

---

[1]Refer to the discussion of tax complexity in Chapter 1.

**TAX FACT**

### THE GOVERNMENT'S INTEREST IN OUR WORK

How much of the typical American's eight-hour work day goes to pay Federal, state, and local taxes? According to the Tax Foundation, the answer is 2 hours and 14 minutes. However, the required effort also depends on where the individual lives. In high-tax jurisdictions such as Connecticut and New York, people need to work on average nearly 3 hours, while in Alabama and Alaska, only about 2 hours are required.

**Source:** Tax Foundation, 2004.

**LO.1**

Understand and apply the components of the Federal income tax formula for individuals.

# The Individual Tax Formula

Individuals are subject to Federal income tax based on taxable income. This chapter explains how taxable income and the income tax of an individual taxpayer are determined. To compute taxable income, it is necessary to understand the tax formula in Figure 15–1.

Although the tax formula is rather simple, determining an individual's taxable income can be quite complex because of the numerous provisions that govern the determination of gross income and allowable deductions.

After computing taxable income, the appropriate rates must be applied. This requires a determination of the individual's filing status, since different rates apply for single taxpayers, married taxpayers, and heads of household. The individual tax rate structure is progressive, with rates for 2005 ranging from 10 percent to

■ **FIGURE 15–1**
Individual Income Tax Formula

| | |
|---|---|
| Income (broadly conceived) | $xx,xxx |
| Less: Exclusions | (x,xxx) |
| Gross income | $xx,xxx |
| Less: Deductions *for* adjusted gross income | (x,xxx) |
| Adjusted gross income (AGI) | $xx,xxx |
| Less: The greater of— | |
|     Total itemized deductions *or* | |
|     Standard deduction | (x,xxx) |
| Less: Personal and dependency exemptions | (x,xxx) |
| Taxable income | $xx,xxx |
| | |
| Tax on taxable income (see Tax Tables or Tax Rate Schedules) | $ x,xxx |
| Less: Tax credits (including income taxes withheld and prepaid) | (xxx) |
| Tax due (or refund) | $ xxx |

■ **EXHIBIT 15–1**
Partial List of Exclusions from
Gross Income

*Leave out completely!*

Accident and health insurance proceeds

Annuity payments (to the extent proceeds represent a recovery of the taxpayer's investment)

Child support payments

Damages for personal injury or sickness

Fringe benefits of employees:

- Educational assistance payments provided by employer
- Employer-provided accident and health insurance
- Group term life insurance (for coverage up to $50,000)
- Meals and lodging (if furnished for convenience of employer)
- Tuition reductions for employees of educational institutions
- Miscellaneous benefits

Gains from sale of principal residence (subject to statutory ceiling)

Gifts and inheritances received

Interest from state and local bonds

Life insurance paid on death of insured

Scholarship grants (to a limited extent)

Social Security benefits (to a limited extent)

Workers' compensation benefits

35 percent.[2] For comparison, the lowest rate structure, which was in effect from 1913 to 1915, ranged from 1 to 7 percent, and the highest, in effect during 1944–1945, ranged from 23 to 94 percent.

Once the individual's tax has been computed, prepayments and credits are subtracted to determine whether the taxpayer owes additional tax or is entitled to a refund.

## COMPONENTS OF THE TAX FORMULA

Before illustrating the application of the tax formula, a brief discussion of each of its components is helpful.

**Income (Broadly Conceived).**   This includes all the taxpayer's income, both taxable and nontaxable. Although it is essentially equivalent to gross receipts, it does not include a return of capital or receipt of borrowed funds. Nor does gross income include unrealized appreciation in the value of a taxpayer's assets.

**EXAMPLE 1**

Dave needed money to purchase a house. He sold 5,000 shares of stock for $100,000. He had paid $40,000 for the stock. In addition, he borrowed $75,000 from a bank. Dave has income that is taxable of $60,000 from the sale of the stock ($100,000 selling price – $40,000 return of capital). He has no income from the $75,000 borrowed from the bank because he has an obligation to repay that amount. ■

**Exclusions.**   For various reasons, Congress has chosen to exclude certain types of income from the income tax base. The principal income exclusions are listed in Exhibit 15–1. The exclusions most commonly encountered by individual taxpayers (employee fringe benefits) are discussed in detail in Chapter 16.

---

[2]Prior to the Tax Relief Reconciliation Act of 2001, the tax rates ranged from 15% to 39.6%. The Act established 10% as the new lowest bracket. Later legislation lowered the top tax rate to 35%.

**■ EXHIBIT 15–2**

Partial List of Gross Income Items

*Decide whether to add or subtract and put under economic income.*

| | |
|---|---|
| Alimony | Interest |
| Bargain purchase from employer | Jury duty fees |
| Bonuses | Partnership income |
| Breach of contract damages | Pensions |
| Business income | Prizes (with some exceptions) |
| Commissions | Professional fees |
| Compensation for services | Punitive damages |
| Debts forgiven (with some exceptions) | Rents |
| Dividends | Rewards |
| Embezzled funds | Royalties |
| Farm income | Salaries |
| Fees | Severance pay |
| Gains from illegal activities | Strike and lockout benefits |
| Gains from sale of property | Tips and gratuities |
| Gambling winnings | Unemployment compensation |
| Hobby income | Wages |

**Gross Income.** The Internal Revenue Code defines gross income broadly as "except as otherwise provided . . . all income from whatever source derived."[3] The "except as otherwise provided" refers to exclusions. Gross income includes, but is not limited to, the items in Exhibit 15–2.

**EXAMPLE 2**

Beth received the following amounts during the year:

| | |
|---|---|
| Salary | $30,000 |
| Interest on savings account | 900 |
| Gift from her aunt | 10,000 |
| Prize won in state lottery | 1,000 |
| Alimony from ex-husband | 12,000 |
| Child support from ex-husband | 6,000 |
| Damages for injury in auto accident | 25,000 |
| Increase in the value of stock held for investment | 5,000 |

Review Exhibits 15–1 and 15–2 to determine the amount Beth must include in the computation of taxable income and the amount she may exclude. Then check your answer in footnote 4.[4] ■

**Deductions for Adjusted Gross Income.** Individual taxpayers have two categories of deductions: (1) deductions *for* adjusted gross income (deductions to arrive at adjusted gross income) and (2) deductions *from* adjusted gross income. Deductions *for* adjusted gross income (AGI) include the following:[5]

- Ordinary and necessary expenses incurred in a trade or business.
- One-half of self-employment tax paid.
- Alimony paid.

---

[3] § 61(a).

[4] Beth must include $43,900 in computing taxable income ($30,000 salary + $900 interest + $1,000 lottery prize + $12,000 alimony). She can exclude $41,000 ($10,000 gift from aunt + $6,000 child support + $25,000 damages). The unrealized gain of $5,000 on the stock held for investment is not included in gross income. Such gain will be included in gross income only when it is realized upon disposition of the stock.

[5] See § 62 for a comprehensive list of items that are deductible *for* AGI. Deductions *for* AGI are sometimes known as *above-the-line* deductions because on the tax return they are taken before the "line" designating AGI.

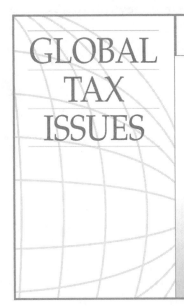

**GLOBAL TAX ISSUES**

### CITIZENSHIP IS NOT TAX-FREE

Gross income from "whatever source derived" includes income from both U.S. and foreign sources. This approach to taxation, where the government taxes its citizens and residents on their worldwide income regardless of where earned, is referred to as a *global* system. Income earned by U.S. citizens outside the United States can be subject to additional taxes, however, because all countries maintain the right to tax income earned within their borders. Consequently, the U.S. tax law includes various mechanisms to alleviate the double taxation that arises when income is subject to tax in multiple jurisdictions. These mechanisms include the foreign tax deduction, the foreign tax credit, the foreign earned income exclusion for U.S. citizens and residents working abroad, and various tax treaty provisions.

Most industrialized countries use variants of the global system. An alternative approach is the *territorial* system, where a government taxes only the income earned within its borders. Hong Kong and Guatemala, for example, use a territorial approach.

* Certain payments to traditional Individual Retirement Accounts and Health Savings Accounts.
* Moving expenses.
* The capital loss deduction (limited to $3,000).

The principal deductions *for* AGI are discussed later in this chapter.

**Adjusted Gross Income (AGI).**   AGI is an important subtotal that serves as the basis for computing percentage limitations on certain itemized deductions, such as medical expenses, charitable contributions, and certain casualty losses. For example, medical expenses are deductible only to the extent they exceed 7.5 percent of AGI, and charitable contribution deductions may not exceed 50 percent of AGI. These limitations might be described as a 7.5 percent *floor* under the medical expense deduction and a 50 percent *ceiling* on the charitable contribution deduction.

**EXAMPLE 3**

Keith earned a salary of $24,000 in the current tax year. He contributed $4,000 to his traditional Individual Retirement Account (IRA) and sustained a $1,000 capital loss on the sale of Wren Corporation stock. His AGI is computed as follows:

| | | |
|---|---|---|
| Gross income | | |
|    Salary | | $24,000 |
| Less: Deductions *for* AGI | | |
|    IRA contribution | $4,000 | |
|    Capital loss | 1,000 | (5,000) |
| AGI | | $19,000 |

**EXAMPLE 4**

Assume the same facts as in Example 3, and that Keith also had medical expenses of $1,800. Medical expenses may be included in his itemized deductions to the extent they exceed 7.5% of AGI. In computing his itemized deductions, Keith may include medical expenses of $375 [$1,800 medical expenses – $1,425 (7.5% × $19,000 AGI)]. ∎

**Itemized Deductions.**   As a general rule, personal expenditures are disallowed as deductions in arriving at taxable income. However, Congress has chosen to

■ **TABLE 15–1**
Basic Standard Deduction
Amounts

| Filing Status | 2004 | 2005 |
|---|---|---|
| Single | $4,850 | $ 5,000 |
| Married, filing jointly | 9,700 | 10,000 |
| Surviving spouse | 9,700 | 10,000 |
| Head of household | 7,150 | 7,300 |
| Married, filing separately | 4,850 | 5,000 |

allow specific personal expenses as **itemized deductions.** Such expenditures include medical expenses, certain taxes and interest, and charitable contributions. Itemized deductions are discussed in detail later in this chapter.

**EXAMPLE 5**

Leo is the owner and operator of a video game arcade. All allowable expenses he incurs in connection with the arcade business are deductions *for* AGI. In addition, Leo paid medical expenses, mortgage interest, state income tax, and charitable contributions. These personal expenses are allowable as itemized deductions. ■

**Standard Deduction.** The **standard deduction** is used by taxpayers who do not have itemized deductions in excess of the allowable standard deduction amount. The standard deduction is a specified amount that depends on the filing status of the taxpayer (e.g., single, married filing jointly, married filing separately). In the past, Congress has attempted to set the amount of the standard deduction at a level that would exempt poverty-level taxpayers from the income tax,[6] but it has not always been consistent in doing so.

The standard deduction is the sum of two components: a *basic* standard deduction and an *additional* standard deduction.[7] Taxpayers who are allowed a *basic* standard deduction are entitled to the applicable amount listed in Table 15–1. The standard deduction amounts are subject to adjustment for inflation each year. Currently, about 70 percent of all individual taxpayers choose to use the standard deduction in lieu of itemizing deductions. However, certain taxpayers are not allowed to claim *any* standard deduction, and the standard deduction is *limited* for others.[8]

A taxpayer who is age 65 or over *or* blind qualifies for an *additional standard deduction* of $1,000 or $1,250, depending on filing status (see amounts in Table 15–2). Two additional standard deductions are allowed for a taxpayer who is age 65 or over *and* blind. The additional standard deduction provisions also apply for a qualifying spouse who is age 65 or over or blind, but a taxpayer may not claim an additional standard deduction for a dependent.

To determine whether to itemize, the taxpayer compares the *total* standard deduction (the sum of the basic standard deduction and any additional standard deductions) to total itemized deductions. Taxpayers are allowed to deduct the *greater* of itemized deductions or the standard deduction. Taxpayers whose itemized deductions are less than the standard deduction compute their taxable income using the standard deduction rather than itemizing.

---

[6] S.Rep. No. 92–437, 92nd Cong., 1st Sess., 1971, p. 54. Another purpose of the standard deduction was discussed in Chapter 1 under Influence of the Internal Revenue Service—Administrative Feasibility. The size of the standard deduction has a direct bearing on the number of taxpayers who are in a position to itemize deductions.

Reducing the number of taxpayers who itemize also reduces the audit effort required from the IRS.
[7] § 63(c)(1).
[8] § 63(c)(6).

■ **TABLE 15–2**
Amount of Each Additional
Standard Deduction

| Filing Status | 2004 | 2005 |
|---|---|---|
| Single | $1,200 | $1,250 |
| Married, filing jointly | 950 | 1,000 |
| Surviving spouse | 950 | 1,000 |
| Head of household | 1,200 | 1,250 |
| Married, filing separately | 950 | 1,000 |

**EXAMPLE 6**

Sara, who is single, is 66 years old. She had total itemized deductions of $5,900 during 2005. Her total standard deduction is $6,250 ($5,000 basic standard deduction plus $1,250 additional standard deduction). Sara should compute her taxable income for 2005 using the standard deduction ($6,250), since it exceeds her itemized deductions ($5,900). ■

**Personal and Dependency Exemptions.**   Exemptions are allowed for the taxpayer, for the taxpayer's spouse, and for each dependent of the taxpayer. The exemption amount is $3,100 in 2004 and $3,200 in 2005.

## APPLICATION OF THE TAX FORMULA

The tax formula shown in Figure 15–1 is illustrated in Example 7.

**EXAMPLE 7**

Grace, age 25, is single and has no dependents. She is a high school teacher and earned a $30,000 salary in 2005. Her other income consisted of a $1,000 prize won in a sweepstakes contest and $500 of interest on municipal bonds received as a graduation gift in 2002. During 2005, she sustained a deductible capital loss of $1,000. Her itemized deductions are $5,400. Grace's taxable income for the year is computed as follows:

| | | |
|---|---|---|
| Income (broadly conceived) | | |
|    Salary | | $30,000 |
|    Prize | | 1,000 |
|    Interest on municipal bonds | | 500 |
| Total income | | $31,500 |
| Less: Exclusion— | | |
|      Interest on municipal bonds | | (500) |
| Gross income | | $31,000 |
| Less: Deduction *for* adjusted gross income— | | |
|    Capital loss | | (1,000) |
| Adjusted gross income (AGI) | | $30,000 |
| Less: The *greater* of— | | |
|    Total itemized deductions | $5,400 | |
|    *or* the standard deduction | 5,000 | (5,400) |
| Less: Personal and dependency exemptions | | |
|    (1 × $3,200) | | (3,200) |
| Taxable income | | $21,400 |

■

*Find more information on this topic at our Web site:* ***http://wft-entities.swlearning.com.***

## SPECIAL LIMITATIONS FOR INDIVIDUALS WHO CAN BE CLAIMED AS DEPENDENTS

Special rules apply to the standard deduction and personal exemption of an individual who can be claimed as a dependent on another person's tax return.

When filing his or her own tax return, a *dependent's* basic standard deduction in 2005 is limited to the greater of $800 or the sum of the individual's earned income for the year plus $250.[9] However, if the sum of the individual's earned income plus $250 exceeds the normal standard deduction, the standard deduction is limited to the appropriate amount shown in Table 15–1. These limitations apply only to the basic standard deduction. A dependent who is 65 or over or blind or both is also allowed the additional standard deduction amount on his or her own return (refer to Table 15–2). These provisions are illustrated in Examples 8 through 11.

**EXAMPLE 8**

Susan, who is 17 years old and single, is claimed as a dependent on her parents' tax return. During 2005, she received $1,200 of interest (unearned income) on a savings account. She also earned $300 from a part-time job. When Susan files her own tax return, her standard deduction is $800 (the greater of $800 or the sum of earned income of $300 plus $250). ■

**EXAMPLE 9**

Assume the same facts as in Example 8, except that Susan is 67 years old and is claimed as a dependent on her son's tax return. In this case, when Susan files her own tax return, her standard deduction is $2,050 [$800 (the greater of $800 or the sum of earned income of $300 plus $250) + $1,250 (the additional standard deduction allowed because Susan is age 65 or over)]. ■

**EXAMPLE 10**

Peggy, who is 16 years old and single, earned $600 from a summer job and had no unearned income during 2005. She is claimed as a dependent on her parents' tax return. Her standard deduction is $850 (the greater of $800 or the sum of earned income of $600 plus $250). ■

**EXAMPLE 11**

Jack, who is a 20-year-old, single, full-time college student, is claimed as a dependent on his parents' tax return. He worked as a musician during the summer of 2005, earning $5,300. Jack's standard deduction is $5,000 (the greater of $800 or the sum of earned income of $5,300 plus $250, but limited to the $5,000 standard deduction for a single taxpayer). ■

A taxpayer who claims an individual as a dependent is allowed to claim an exemption for the dependent. The dependent cannot claim a personal exemption on his or her own return. Based on the tax formula, Jack in Example 11 would have taxable income of $300, determined as follows:

| | |
|---|---|
| Gross income | $ 5,300 |
| Less: Standard deduction | (5,000) |
| Personal exemption | (–0–) |
| Taxable income | $ 300 |

---

[9]§ 63(c)(5). Both the $800 amount and the $250 amount are subject to adjustment for inflation each year. The amounts were also $800 and $250, respectively, for 2004.

LO.2

Apply the rules for arriving at personal and dependency exemptions.

# Personal and Dependency Exemptions

The use of exemptions in the tax system is based in part on the idea that a taxpayer with a small amount of income should be exempt from income taxation. An exemption frees a specified amount of income from tax ($3,100 in 2004 and $3,200 in 2005). The exemption amount is indexed (adjusted) annually for inflation. An individual who is not claimed as a dependent by another taxpayer is allowed to claim his or her own personal exemption. In addition, a taxpayer may claim an exemption for each dependent.

**EXAMPLE 12**

Bonnie, who is single, supports her mother and father, who have no income of their own, and claims them as dependents on her tax return. Bonnie may claim a personal exemption for herself plus an exemption for each dependent. On her 2005 tax return, Bonnie may deduct $9,600 for exemptions ($3,200 per exemption × 3 exemptions). ■

## PERSONAL EXEMPTIONS

The Code provides a **personal exemption** for the taxpayer and an exemption for the spouse if a joint return is filed. However, when separate returns are filed, a married taxpayer cannot claim an exemption for his or her spouse *unless* the spouse has no gross income and is not claimed as the dependent of another taxpayer.

The determination of marital status generally is made at the end of the taxable year, except when a spouse dies during the year. Spouses who enter into a legal separation under a decree of divorce or separate maintenance before the end of the year are considered to be unmarried at the end of the taxable year. The following summary illustrates the effect of death or divorce upon marital status:

| Description | Marital Status and Personal Exemptions |
| --- | --- |
| • Walt is the widower of Helen who died on January 3, 2005. | Walt and Helen are considered to be married for purposes of filing the 2005 return. Walt may claim two exemptions on his 2005 return. |
| • Bill and Jane entered into a divorce decree that becomes effective on December 31, 2005. | Bill and Jane are considered to be unmarried for purposes of filing the 2005 return. Bill and Jane each may claim a personal exemption on their separate returns. |

For *Federal* tax purposes, the law does not recognize same-sex marriages. By virtue of the Defense of Marriage Act (P.L. 104–199), a marriage means a legal union only between a man and a woman as husband and wife.

## DEPENDENCY EXEMPTIONS—PRIOR TO 2005

The Working Families Tax Relief Act of 2004 has modified the rules applicable to dependency exemptions. Because the new rules do not become effective until 2005, preexisting law remains applicable through 2004. Consequently, preexisting law will govern tax returns filed in 2005 for calendar year 2004. As will be pointed out later, many of the old rules dealing with dependency exemptions remain unchanged under the new law. A **dependency exemption** may be claimed for each individual for whom the following five tests are met:[10]

- Support.
- Relationship or member of the household.
- Gross income.
- Joint return.
- Citizenship or residency.

**Support Test.** Over one-half of the support of the individual must be furnished by the taxpayer. Support includes food, shelter, clothing, medical and dental care, education, etc. However, a scholarship received by a student is not included for purposes of determining whether the taxpayer furnished more than half of the child's support.[11]

**EXAMPLE 13**

Hal contributed $3,400 (consisting of food, clothing, and medical care) toward the support of his cousin, Sam, who lives with him. Sam earned $1,500 from a part-time job and received a $2,000 scholarship to attend a local university. Assuming that the other dependency tests are met, Hal can claim Sam as a dependent since he has contributed more than half of Sam's support. The $2,000 scholarship is not included as support for purposes of this test. ■

If an individual does not spend funds that have been received from any source, the unspent amounts are not counted for purposes of the support test.

**EXAMPLE 14**

Emily contributed $3,000 to her father's support during the year. In addition, her father received $2,400 in Social Security benefits, $200 of interest, and wages of $600. Her father deposited the Social Security benefits, interest, and wages in his own savings account and did not use any of the funds for his support. Thus, the Social Security benefits, interest, and wages are not considered to be support provided by Emily's father. Emily may claim her father as a dependent if the other tests are met. ■

Capital expenditures for items such as furniture, appliances, and automobiles are included for purposes of the support test if the item does, in fact, constitute support.[12]

**EXAMPLE 15**

Norm purchased a television set costing $250 and gave it to his mother who lives with him. The television set was placed in the mother's bedroom and was used exclusively by her. Norm should include the cost of the television set in determining the support of his mother. ■

An exception to the support test involves a **multiple support agreement.** A multiple support agreement permits one of a group of taxpayers who furnish support for an individual to claim a dependency exemption for that individual even if no one person provides more than 50 percent of the support.[13] The group together must provide more than 50 percent of the support. Any person who contributed *more than 10 percent* of the support is entitled to claim the exemption if each person in the group who contributed more than 10 percent files a written consent. This provision frequently enables one of the children of aged dependent parents to claim an exemption when none of the children meets the 50 percent support test. Each person who is a party to the multiple support agreement must meet all other requirements (except the support requirement) for claiming the exemption. A person who does not meet the relationship or member-of-the-household test, for instance, cannot claim the dependency exemption under a

---

[10]§§ 151 and 152.
[11]Reg. § 1.152–1(c).

[12]Rev.Rul. 57–344, 1957–2 C.B. 112; Rev.Rul. 58–419, 1958–2 C.B. 57.
[13]§ 152(d)(3).

multiple support agreement. It does not matter if he or she contributes more than 10 percent of the individual's support.

**EXAMPLE 16**

Wanda, who resides with her son, Adam, received $12,000 from various sources during the year. This constituted her entire support for the year. She received support from the following individuals:

|  | Amount | Percentage of Total |
|---|---|---|
| Adam, a son | $ 5,760 | 48 |
| Bob, a son | 1,200 | 10 |
| Carol, a daughter | 3,600 | 30 |
| Diane, a friend | 1,440 | 12 |
|  | $12,000 | 100 |

If Adam and Carol file a multiple support agreement, either may claim the dependency exemption for Wanda. Bob may not claim Wanda because he did not contribute more than 10% of her support. Bob's consent is not required in order for Adam and Carol to file a multiple support agreement. Diane does not meet the relationship or member-of-the-household test and cannot be a party to the agreement. The decision as to who claims Wanda rests with Adam and Carol. It is possible for Carol to claim Wanda, even though Adam furnished more of Wanda's support. ■

*Find more information on this topic at our Web site:* ***http://wft-entities.swlearning.com.***

## Multiple Support Agreements and the Medical Expense Deduction

**FRAMEWORK FOCUS: DEDUCTIONS**

STRATEGY ➤ MAXIMIZE DEDUCTIBLE AMOUNTS.

Generally, medical expenses are deductible only if they are paid on behalf of the taxpayer, his or her spouse, and their dependents.[14] Since deductibility may rest on dependency status, planning is important in arranging multiple support agreements.

**EXAMPLE 17**

During the year, Zelda will be supported by her two sons (Vern and Vito) and her daughter (Maria). Each will furnish approximately one-third of the required support. If the parties decide that the depen-

dency exemption should be claimed by Maria under a multiple support agreement, any medical expenses incurred by Zelda should be paid by Maria. ■

In planning a multiple support agreement, take into account which of the parties is most likely to exceed the 7.5 percent limitation. In Example 17, for instance, Maria might be a poor choice if she and her family do not expect to incur many medical expenses of their own.

---

[14]See the discussion of medical expenses later in this chapter.

A special rule applies for a child of parents who are divorced or separated under a decree of separate maintenance. For decrees executed after 1984, the custodial parent is allowed to claim the exemption unless that parent agrees in writing not to claim a dependency exemption for the child.[15] Thus, claiming the exemption is dependent on whether a written agreement exists, *not* on meeting the support test.

**EXAMPLE 18**

Ira and Rita obtained a divorce decree in 1994. In 2005, their two children are in Rita's custody. Ira contributed over half of the support for each child. In the absence of a written agreement on the dependency exemptions, Rita (the custodial parent) is entitled to the exemptions in 2005. However, Ira may claim the exemptions if Rita agrees in writing. ■

*Find more information on this topic at our Web site: **http://wft-entities.swlearning.com**.*

**Relationship or Member-of-the-Household Test.**    To be claimed as a dependent, an individual must be either a relative of the taxpayer or a member of the taxpayer's household. The Code contains a detailed listing of the various blood and marriage relationships that qualify. Note, however, that the relationship test is met if the individual is a qualifying relative of either spouse. Once established by marriage, a relationship continues regardless of subsequent changes in marital status.[16]

*Find more information on this topic at our Web site: **http://wft-entities.swlearning.com**.*

**Gross Income Test.**    The dependent's gross income must be less than the exemption amount ($3,100 in 2004 and $3,200 in 2005).[17] The gross income test is measured by income that is taxable. In the case of scholarships, for example, it excludes the nontaxable portion (e.g., amounts received for books and tuition) but includes the taxable portion (e.g., amounts received for room and board).

A parent may claim a dependency exemption for his or her child in 2004, even when the child's gross income is $3,100 or more, if the parent provided over half of the child's support and the child, at year-end, is under age 19 or is a full-time student under age 24. If the parent claims a dependency exemption, the dependent child may *not* claim a personal exemption on his or her own income tax return.

A child is defined as a son, stepson, daughter, stepdaughter, adopted son, or adopted daughter and may include a foster child.[18] For the child to qualify as a student for purposes of the dependency exemption, he or she must be a full-time student at an educational institution during some part of five calendar months of the year.[19] This exception to the gross income test for dependent children who are (1) under age 19 or (2) full-time students under age 24 (applicable to 2004 and prior years) permits a child or college student to earn money from part-time or summer jobs without penalizing the parent with the loss of the dependency exemption.

**Joint Return Test.**    If a dependent is married, the supporting taxpayer (e.g., the parent of a married child) generally is not permitted a dependency exemption if

---

[15]§ 152(e).

[16]§ 152(d)(2). However, under § 152(f)(3), a taxpayer may not claim someone who is a member of his or her household as a dependent if their relationship is in violation of local law. For example, the dependency exemption was denied because the taxpayer's relationship to the person claimed as a dependent constituted *cohabitation*,

a crime under applicable state law. *Cassius L. Peacock, III,* 37 TCM 177, T.C.Memo. 1978–30.

[17]§ 151(c)(1).

[18]Reg. § 1.151–3(a).

[19]Reg. §§ 1.151–3(b) and (c).

the married individual files a joint return with his or her spouse.[20] The joint return rule does not apply, however, if the following conditions are met:

- The reason for filing is to claim a refund for tax withheld.
- No tax liability would exist for either spouse on separate returns.
- Neither spouse is required to file a return.

**EXAMPLE 19**

Paul provides over half of the support of his son, Quinn. He also provides over half of the support of Vera, who is Quinn's wife. During the year, both Quinn and Vera had part-time jobs. To recover the taxes withheld, they file a joint return. If Quinn and Vera have income low enough that they are not *required* to file a return, Paul is allowed to claim both as dependents. ■

## Problems with a Joint Return

**FRAMEWORK FOCUS: DEDUCTIONS**

STRATEGY ➤ MAXIMIZE DEDUCTIBLE AMOUNTS.

A married person who files a joint return generally cannot be claimed as a dependent by another taxpayer. If a joint return has been filed, the damage may be undone if separate returns are substituted on a timely basis (on or before the due date of the return).

**EXAMPLE 20**

While preparing a client's 2004 income tax return on April 8, 2005, a tax practitioner discovered that the client's daughter had filed a joint return with her husband in late January of 2005. Presuming the daughter otherwise qualifies as the client's dependent, the exemption is not lost if she and her husband file separate returns on or before April 15, 2005. ■

**Citizenship or Residency Test.**   To be a dependent, the individual must be either a U.S. citizen, a U.S. resident, or a resident of Canada or Mexico for some part of the calendar year in which the taxpayer's tax year begins.

### DEPENDENCY EXEMPTIONS—AFTER 2004

One of the objectives of the Working Families Tax Relief Act of 2004 was to establish a uniform definition of qualifying child for purposes of the dependency exemption, the child tax credit, the earned income credit, the credit for child and dependent care expenses, and head-of-household filing status. This would resolve the confusion that existed with varying definitions of "child" applying to the different Code provisions. One effect of the new uniform definition is to modify the existing rules governing dependency exemptions.

Under the new law, a dependent is one who is either a qualifying child *or* a qualifying relative.[21]

**Qualifying Child.**   A **qualifying child** must meet the tests of relationship, domicile, and age.[22] For the relationship test, the child must be the taxpayer's son, daughter, stepson, stepdaughter, brother, sister, stepbrother, stepsister, half brother, half sister, or a descendant of such individual (e.g., grandchildren, nephews, nieces). A child

---

[20]§ 151(c)(2).
[21]§§ 152(a)(1) and (2).

[22]§ 152(c)(1).

who has been adopted, or whose adoption is pending, qualifies. Under certain circumstances, a foster child also can qualify.[23]

Under the domicile test, the child must have the same principal place of abode as the taxpayer for more than half of the taxable year. In satisfying this requirement, temporary absences from the household due to special circumstances (e.g., illness, education) are not considered.

The last test for qualifying child status pertains to age. The child must be under age 19 (or under age 24 in the case of a full-time student). An exception provides that individuals who are disabled[24] are not subject to any limitations as to age.

Except in one situation, the definition of qualifying child makes the support of an individual irrelevant. The one case where support becomes relevant involves self-support. A child who provides more than one-half of his or her own support cannot be claimed as a dependent.[25]

In the event that a child satisfies the requirements of a qualified child for more than one taxpayer, the following tie-breaking rules apply:[26]

- If one of the individuals eligible to claim the child is a parent, that person prevails.
- If both parents qualify (separate returns are filed), then the parent with whom the child resides the longest during the year prevails. If the residence period is the same (or is not ascertainable), then the parent with the highest AGI prevails.
- If no parents are involved, the claimant with the highest AGI prevails.

**EXAMPLE 21**

Tim, age 15, lives in the same household with Mike, his father, and Aaron, his uncle. Since Tim is a qualified child to both Mike and Aaron, as a parent Mike prevails. ■

**EXAMPLE 22**

Assume the same facts as in Example 21, except that Mike is an uncle and not a parent. If Aaron has a higher AGI than Mike, he gets to claim Tim as a dependent. ■

Resorting to the tie-breaking rules is not necessary if the party who would prevail does not claim the exemption. Thus, in Example 21, Aaron can claim Tim if Mike does not. Likewise, in Example 22, Aaron can make the exemption available to Mike by not claiming Tim as a dependent on his own return.

Although the gross income and support tests are inapplicable to the status of a qualifying child (but note the self-support exception previously discussed), other dependency tests apply. In the case of a married child, for example, the joint return test may come into play. Barring the usual refund exception, qualifying child status excludes a married child who files a joint return with his or her spouse.[27]

With one minor exception, the citizenship or residency test also applies. Under the exception, an adopted child need not be a citizen or resident of the United States (or a contiguous country) as long as his or her principal abode is with a U.S. citizen.[28]

**EXAMPLE 23**

Esther is a U.S. citizen who lives and works in Spain. She has adopted Benito, a four-year-old Italian national, who lives with her and is a member of her household. Although Benito does not meet the usual citizenship or residency test, he is covered by the exception. Benito is a qualifying child, and Esther can claim him as a dependent. ■

In the case of divorced or legally separated parents with children, the custodian rules continue to apply. Thus, the dependency exemption for a child (or children)

---

[23]An eligible foster child is an individual who is placed with the taxpayer by an authorized placement agency or by judgment, decree, or other order of any court of competent jurisdiction.
[24]Within the meaning of § 22(a)(3).

[25]§ 152(c)(1)(D).
[26]§ 152(c)(4).
[27]§ 152(b)(2).
[28]§ 152(b)(3).

## CONCEPT SUMMARY 15–1

### Tests for Dependency Exemption after 2004

| Category | |
| --- | --- |
| **Qualifying Child** | **Qualifying Relative[1]** |
| Relationship[2] | Support |
| Domicile[3] | Relationship[4] or member of household[3] |
| Age | Gross income |
| Joint return[5] | Joint return[5] |
| Citizenship or residency[6] | Citizenship or residency[6] |

[1]These rules are largely the same as those applicable to pre-2005 years.
[2]Children, siblings, and their descendants.
[3]The rules for domicile are the same as for member of the household.
[4]Children and their descendants, siblings and their children, parents and their ascendants, uncles and aunts, stepparents and stepsiblings, and certain in-laws.
[5]The joint return rules are the same for each category.
[6]The citizenship or residency rules are the same for each category.

belongs to whichever parent has custody. The exemption can be shifted to the non-custodial parent if the custodial parent issues the appropriate waiver.

**Qualifying Relative.**   Under the **qualifying relative** category for the dependency exemption, individuals must also satisfy the gross income and support tests.[29] In large part, therefore, the pre-2005 rules are carried over. A comparison of the tests governing the qualifying child and the qualifying relative categories appears in Concept Summary 15–1.

The designation "qualifying relative" is somewhat misleading in that a "relative" need not be involved. An unrelated individual who is a member of the taxpayer's household can qualify if the other dependency tests are satisfied. Also, not every "relative" is eligible; only those who meet the relationship test set forth in the Code qualify.[30]

**EXAMPLE 24**

Andy provides all of the support of an unrelated family friend who lives with him for the entire tax year. He also supports a cousin who lives elsewhere. The family friend can qualify as Andy's dependent, but the cousin cannot. The family friend meets the member-of-the-household test, whereas the cousin satisfies neither the relationship test nor the member-of-the-household test. ■

Though the relationship test under the qualifying relative category includes those covered by the qualifying child definition, it is more expansive. Also included are lineal ascendants (e.g., parents, grandparents), collateral ascendants (e.g., uncles and aunts), and certain in-laws (son-, daughter-, father-, mother-, brother-, and sister-in-law). A son or daughter who is not a qualifying child can be a dependent.

**EXAMPLE 25**

Greta furnished more than half of the support of her father who lives with her and of a daughter (age 26) who lives elsewhere. Presuming the other tests are met (i.e., gross income, etc.), Greta can claim both the father and the daughter as her dependents. [Note: The daughter is not a qualifying child because she does not meet the abode and age tests.] ■

---

[29]§§ 152(d)(1)(B) and (C).          [30]§ 152(d)(2).

# TAX IN THE NEWS

## HOW TO SUBTLY PLUCK THE CHICKEN

No government likes to admit that it is enacting new taxes or even raising the rates on existing taxes. Needless to say, this is particularly true of the U.S. Congress. But there are more subtle ways to raise revenue (or to curtail revenue loss). The most popular way is to use a so-called *stealth tax*. A stealth tax is not really a tax at all. Instead, it is a means of depriving higher-income taxpayers of the benefits of certain tax provisions thought to be available to all.

The heart and soul of the stealth tax is the phaseout approach. Thus, as income increases, the tax benefit thought to be derived from a particular relief provision decreases. Since the phaseout is gradual and not drastic, many affected taxpayers are unaware of what has happened. Although the tax law is rampant with phaseouts, the two most flagrant limit the deductibility of personal and dependency exemptions and itemized deductions. (The itemized deduction phaseout is discussed later in this chapter.)

However, perhaps Congress has had some misgivings about the stealth tax imposed on personal and dependency exemptions. These misgivings cannot be too severe, though, as any scheduled relief does not even *start* until year 2006 and is not *completed* until year 2010!

## PHASEOUT OF EXEMPTIONS

Several provisions of the tax law are intended to increase the tax liability of more affluent taxpayers who might otherwise enjoy some benefit from having some of their taxable income subject to the lower income tax brackets (e.g., 10 percent, 15 percent, 25 percent). One such provision phases out personal and dependency exemptions as AGI exceeds specified threshold amounts. For 2004 and 2005, the phaseout *begins* at the following threshold amounts (which are indexed annually for inflation):

| Filing Status | 2004 | 2005 |
| --- | --- | --- |
| Joint return/surviving spouse | $214,050 | $218,950 |
| Head of household | 178,350 | 182,450 |
| Single | 142,700 | 145,950 |
| Married, filing separately | 107,025 | 109,475 |

Exemptions are phased out by 2 percent for each $2,500 (or fraction thereof) by which the taxpayer's AGI exceeds the threshold amounts. For a married taxpayer filing separately, the phaseout is 2 percent for each $1,250 or fraction thereof.

The allowable exemption amount can be determined with the following steps:

1. AGI – threshold amount = excess amount.
2. Excess amount/$2,500 = reduction factor [rounded up to the next whole increment (e.g., 18.1 = 19)] × 2 = phaseout percentage.
3. Phaseout percentage (from step 2) × exemption amount = amount of exemptions phased out.
4. Exemption amount – phaseout amount = allowable exemption deduction.

**EXAMPLE 26**

Frederico is married but files a separate return. His 2005 AGI is $129,475. He is entitled to one personal exemption.

1. $129,475 – $109,475 = $20,000 excess amount.
2. [($20,000/$1,250) × 2] = 32% (phaseout percentage).

3. 32% × $3,200 = $1,024 amount of exemption phased out.
4. $3,200 – $1,024 = $2,176 allowable exemption deduction.

Note that the exemption amount is completely phased out when the taxpayer's AGI exceeds the threshold amount by more than $122,500 ($61,250 for a married taxpayer filing a separate return), calculated as follows:

$122,501/$2,500 = 49.0004, rounded to 50 and multiplied by 2 = 100% (phaseout percentage). ▪

Under the Tax Relief Reconciliation Act of 2001, the exemption phaseout is repealed as to post-2009 years. The repeal takes place over a five-year period beginning in year 2006.

**L0.3**

Use the proper method for determining the tax liability.

# Tax Determination

## TAX TABLE METHOD

The tax liability is computed using either the Tax Table method or the Tax Rate Schedule method. Most taxpayers compute their tax using the Tax Table. Eligible taxpayers compute taxable income (as shown in Figure 15–1) and *must* determine their tax by reference to the **Tax Table**.[31]

**DIGGING DEEPER 5**

*Find more information on this topic at our Web site: **http://wft-entities.swlearning.com**.*

Although the Tax Table is derived by using the Tax Rate Schedules (discussed below), the tax calculated using the two methods may vary slightly. This variation occurs because the tax for a particular income range in the Tax Table is based on the midpoint amount.

**EXAMPLE 27**

Linda is single and has taxable income of $30,000 for calendar year 2004. To determine Linda's tax using the Tax Table, find the $30,000 to $30,050 income line. The tax of $4,244 is actually the tax the Tax Rate Schedules would yield on taxable income of $30,025 (i.e., the midpoint amount between $30,000 and $30,050). ▪

## TAX RATE SCHEDULE METHOD

Prior to 2001 tax legislation, the **Tax Rate Schedules** contained rates of 15, 28, 31, 36, and 39.6 percent. These rates were scheduled to be reduced to 10, 15, 25, 28, 33, and 35 percent by year 2006. The Jobs and Growth Tax Relief Reconciliation Act of 2003 (JGTRRA of 2003), however, accelerated the phase-in and made the new rates effective as of January 1, 2003.[32] A sunset provision reinstates the original rates (pre-2001) after 2010.

The 2005 rate schedule for single taxpayers is reproduced in Table 15–3. This schedule is used to illustrate the tax computations in Examples 28, 29, and 30.

**EXAMPLE 28**

Pat is single and had $5,870 of taxable income in 2005. His tax is $587 ($5,870 × 10%). ▪

**EXAMPLE 29**

Chris is single and had taxable income of $50,000 in 2005. Her tax is $9,165 [$4,090 + 25% ($50,000 – $29,700)]. ▪

---

[31]The 2004 Tax Table is located at **http://wft-entities.swlearning.com**. This table will be used to illustrate the tax computation. The 2005 Tax Table was not available at the date of publication of this text.

[32]§ 1(i).

**■ TABLE 15–3**
2005 Tax Rate Schedule for Single Taxpayers

| If Taxable Income Is . . . | | The Tax Is: | Of the Amount Over |
|---|---|---|---|
| Over | But Not Over | | |
| $ –0– | $ 7,300 | 10% | $ –0– |
| 7,300 | 29,700 | $ 730.00 + 15% | 7,300 |
| 29,700 | 71,950 | 4,090.00 + 25% | 29,700 |
| 71,950 | 150,150 | 14,652.50 + 28% | 71,950 |
| 150,150 | 326,450 | 36,548.50 + 33% | 150,150 |
| 326,450 | | 94,727.50 + 35% | 326,450 |

Note that $4,090, which is the starting point in the tax computation in Example 29, is 10 percent of the $7,300 taxable income in the first bracket + 15 percent of the $22,400 ($29,700 – $7,300) taxable income in the second bracket. Chris's income in excess of $29,700 is taxed at the 25 percent rate. This reflects the *progressive* (or *graduated*) rate structure on which the U.S. income tax system is based. A tax is progressive if a higher rate of tax applies as the tax base increases.

*EXAMPLE 30*

Carl is single and had taxable income of $80,000 in 2005. His tax is $16,906.50 [$14,652.50 + 28% ($80,000 – $71,950)]. Note that the effect of this computation is to tax part of Carl's income at 10%, part at 15%, part at 25%, and part at 28%. An alternative computational method provides a clearer illustration of the progressive rate structure of the individual income tax:

| | |
|---|---|
| Tax on $7,300 at 10% | $ 730.00 |
| Tax on $29,700 – $7,300 at 15% | 3,360.00 |
| Tax on $71,950 – $29,700 at 25% | 10,562.50 |
| Tax on $80,000 – $71,950 at 28% | 2,254.00 |
| Total | $16,906.50 |

Carl's marginal rate (refer to Chapter 1) is 28%, and his average rate is 21.1% ($16,906.50 tax/$80,000 taxable income). ■

A special computation limits the effective tax rate on qualified dividends (see Chapter 3) and net long-term capital gain (see Chapter 7).

**PLANNING STRATEGIES**

## Shifting Income and Deductions across Time

**FRAMEWORK FOCUS: TAX RATE**

**STRATEGY ➤ SHIFT NET INCOME FROM HIGH-BRACKET YEARS TO LOW-BRACKET YEARS.**

It is natural for taxpayers to be concerned about the tax rates they are paying. How does a tax practitioner communicate information about rates to clients? There are several possibilities. For example, a taxpayer who is in the 15 percent bracket this year and expects to be in the 28 percent bracket next year should, if possible, defer payment of deductible expenses until next year to maximize the tax benefit of the deduction.

A note of caution is in order with respect to shifting income and expenses between years. Congress has recognized the tax planning possibilities of such shifting and has enacted many provisions to limit a taxpayer's ability to do so. Some of these limitations on the shifting of income and deductions are discussed in Chapters 3 through 5.

**◉ T A X   F A C T**

## THE TIGHTENING TAX SQUEEZE

Ｈow has the total tax burden changed over time? Many Americans would likely assert that more of their income than ever goes just to pay taxes. The Tax Foundation contends that such assertion is correct. It reports that the percentage of income claimed by Federal, state, and local taxes has increased from 5.9 percent in 1900 to 27.8 percent in 2004.

**Source:** Tax Foundation, 2004.

## COMPUTATION OF NET TAXES PAYABLE OR REFUND DUE

The pay-as-you-go feature of the Federal income tax system requires payment of all or part of the taxpayer's income tax liability during the year. These payments take the form of Federal income tax withheld by employers or estimated tax paid by the taxpayer or both.[33] The payments are applied against the tax from the Tax Table or Tax Rate Schedules to determine whether the taxpayer will get a refund or pay additional tax.

Employers are required to withhold income tax on compensation paid to their employees and to pay this tax over to the government. The employer notifies the employee of the amount of income tax withheld on Form W–2 (Wage and Tax Statement). The employee should receive this form by January 31 after the year in which the income tax is withheld.

If taxpayers receive income that is not subject to withholding or income from which insufficient tax is withheld, they must pay estimated tax. These individuals must file Form 1040–ES (Estimated Tax for Individuals) and pay in quarterly installments the income tax and self-employment tax estimated to be due.

The income tax from the Tax Table or the Tax Rate Schedules also is reduced by the individual's tax credits. There is an important distinction between tax credits and tax deductions. Tax credits (including tax withheld) reduce the tax liability dollar-for-dollar. Tax deductions reduce taxable income on which the tax liability is based.

**EXAMPLE 31**

Gail is a taxpayer in the 25% tax bracket. As a result of incurring $1,000 in child care, she is entitled to a $200 credit for child and dependent care expenses ($1,000 child care expenses × 20% credit rate). She also contributed $1,000 to the American Cancer Society and included this amount in her itemized deductions. The credit for child and dependent care expenses results in a $200 reduction of Gail's tax liability for the year. The contribution to the American Cancer Society reduces taxable income by $1,000 and results in a $250 reduction in Gail's tax liability ($1,000 reduction in taxable income × 25% tax rate). ■

Selected tax credits for individuals are discussed later in this chapter. The following are some of the more common credits available to individuals:

* Child tax credit.
* Credit for child and dependent care expenses.
* Earned income credit.

**EXAMPLE 32**

Kelly, age 30, is a head of household whose 12-year-old daughter lives with him. During 2005, Kelly had the following: taxable income, $30,000; income tax withheld, $2,450; estimated

---

[33]See § 3402 for withholding and § 6654 for estimated payments.

tax payments, $600; and child tax credit, $1,000. Kelly's net tax payable (refund due) is computed as follows:

| | | |
|---|---:|---:|
| Income tax (from 2005 Tax Rate Schedule) | | $ 3,978 |
| Less: Tax credits and prepayments— | | |
| Child tax credit | $1,000 | |
| Income tax withheld | 2,450 | |
| Estimated tax payments | 600 | (4,050) |
| Net taxes payable (refund due if negative) | | ($ 72) |

**LO.4**

Identify and work with kiddie tax situations.

## UNEARNED INCOME OF CHILDREN UNDER AGE 14 TAXED AT PARENTS' RATE

Most individuals compute taxable income using the tax formula shown in Figure 15–1. Special provisions govern the computation of taxable income and the tax liability for children under age 14 who have **unearned income** in excess of specified amounts.

Recall that individuals who are claimed as dependents by other taxpayers cannot claim an exemption on their own return. This prevents parents from shifting the tax on investment income (such as interest and dividends) to a child by transferring ownership of the assets producing the income. Without this provision, the child would pay no tax on the income to the extent that it was sheltered by the child's exemption.

Current tax law also reduces or eliminates the possibility of saving taxes by shifting income from parents to children by taxing the net unearned income of children under age 14 as if it were the parents' income.[34] Unearned income includes such income as taxable interest, dividends, capital gains, rents, royalties, pension and annuity income, and income (other than earned income) received as the beneficiary of a trust.

This provision, commonly referred to as the **kiddie tax,** applies to any child for any taxable year if the child has not reached age 14 by the close of the taxable year, has at least one living parent, and has unearned income of more than $1,600. The kiddie tax provision does not apply to a child age 14 or older. However, the limitation on the use of the standard deduction and the unavailability of the personal exemption do apply to such a child as long as he or she is eligible to be claimed as a dependent by a parent.

**Net Unearned Income.**   Net unearned income of a dependent child is computed as follows:

Unearned income
Less: $800
Less: The *greater* of
    $800 of the standard deduction *or*
    The amount of allowable itemized deductions directly connected with
       the production of the unearned income
Equals: Net unearned income

If net unearned income is zero (or negative), the child's tax is computed without using the parents' rate. If the amount of net unearned income (regardless of source) is positive, the net unearned income will be taxed at the parents' rate. The $800 amounts in the preceding formula are subject to adjustment for inflation each year.

---

[34]§ 1(g).

*Find more information on this topic at our Web site: **http://wft-entities.swlearning.com**.*

**Election to Report Certain Unearned Income on Parent's Return.**   If a child under age 14 is required to file a tax return and meets all of the following requirements, the parent may elect to report the child's unearned income that exceeds $1,600 on the parent's own tax return:

- Gross income is from interest and dividends only.
- Gross income is more than $800 but less than $8,000.
- No estimated tax has been paid in the name and Social Security number of the child, and the child is not subject to backup withholding.

If the parental election is made, the child is treated as having no gross income and then is not required to file a tax return.

The parent(s) must also pay an additional tax equal to the smaller of $80 or 10 percent of the child's gross income over $800. Parents who have substantial itemized deductions based on AGI may find that making the parental election increases total taxes for the family unit. Taxes should be calculated both with the parental election and without it to determine the appropriate choice.

### Income of Minor Children

**FRAMEWORK FOCUS: TAX RATE**

**STRATEGY ➤ SHIFT NET INCOME FROM HIGH-BRACKET TAXPAYERS TO LOW-BRACKET TAXPAYERS.**

Taxpayers can use several strategies to avoid or minimize the effect of the rules that tax the unearned income of certain minor children at the parents' rate. The kiddie tax rules do not apply once a child reaches age 14. Parents should consider giving a younger child assets that defer the inclusion in gross income until the child reaches age 14. For example, U.S. government Series EE savings bonds can be used to defer income until the bonds are cashed in.

Growth stocks typically pay little in the way of dividends. However, the unrealized appreciation on an astute investment may more than offset the lack of dividends. The child can hold the growth stock until he or she reaches age 14. If the stock is sold then at a profit, the profit is taxed at the child's low rates.

Taxpayers in a position to do so can employ their children in their business and pay them a reasonable wage for the work they actually perform (e.g., light office help, such as filing). The child's earned income is sheltered by the standard deduction, and the parents' business is allowed a deduction for the wages. The kiddie tax rules have no effect on earned income, even if it is earned from the parents' business.

## LO.5

Recognize filing requirements and proper filing status.

# Filing Considerations

Under the category of filing considerations, the following questions need to be resolved:

- Is the taxpayer required to file an income tax return?
- If so, which form should be used?
- When and how should the return be filed?
- In computing the tax liability, which column of the Tax Table or which Tax Rate Schedule should be used?

The first three questions are discussed under Filing Requirements, and the last is treated under Filing Status.

## FILING REQUIREMENTS

**General Rules.**   An individual must file a tax return if certain minimum amounts of gross income have been received. The general rule is that a tax return is required for every individual who has gross income that equals or exceeds the sum of the exemption amount plus the applicable standard deduction.[35] For example, a single taxpayer under age 65 must file a tax return in 2005 if gross income equals or exceeds $8,200 ($3,200 exemption plus $5,000 standard deduction).[36]

*Find more information on this topic at our Web site: **http://wft-entities.swlearning.com**.*

The additional standard deduction for being age 65 or older is considered in determining the gross income filing requirements. For example, the 2005 filing requirement for a single taxpayer age 65 or older is $9,450 ($5,000 basic standard deduction + $1,250 additional standard deduction + $3,200 exemption).

A self-employed individual with net earnings of $400 or more from a business or profession must file a tax return regardless of the amount of gross income.

Even though an individual has gross income below the filing level amounts and therefore does not owe any tax, he or she must file a return to obtain a tax refund of amounts withheld by employers. A return is also necessary to obtain the benefits of the earned income credit allowed to taxpayers with little or no tax liability.

**Filing Requirements for Dependents.**   Computation of the gross income filing requirement for an individual who can be claimed as a dependent on another person's tax return is subject to more complex rules. For example, such an individual must file a return if he or she has earned income only and it is more than the total standard deduction (including any additional standard deduction) that the individual is allowed for the year.

*Find more information on this topic at our Web site: **http://wft-entities.swlearning.com**.*

**Selecting the Proper Form.**   Although a variety of forms are available to individual taxpayers, the use of some of these forms is restricted. For example, Form 1040EZ cannot be used if the:

- Taxpayer claims any dependents;
- Taxpayer (or spouse) is 65 or older or blind; or
- Taxable income is $100,000 or more.

Taxpayers who desire to itemize deductions *from* AGI cannot use Form 1040A, but must file Form 1040 (the long form).

**The E-File Approach.**   In addition to traditional paper returns, the **e-file** program is an increasingly popular alternative. Here, the required tax information is transmitted to the IRS electronically either directly from the taxpayer (i.e., an "e-file online return") or indirectly through an electronic return originator (ERO). EROs are tax professionals who have been accepted into the electronic filing program by the IRS. Such parties hold themselves out to the general public as "authorized IRS e-file providers." Providers often are also the preparers of the return.

The e-file approach has two major advantages. First, compliance with the format required by the IRS eliminates many errors that would otherwise occur. Second, the time required for processing a refund usually is reduced to three weeks or less.

---

[35]The exemption and standard deduction amounts for determining whether a tax return must be filed are adjusted for inflation each year.

[36]§ 6012(a)(1).

## WHAT FORM OF TAX COMPLIANCE IS RIGHT FOR YOU?

**B**ased on recent projections from the IRS, when preparing over 134 million individual income tax returns expected to be filed in 2005, taxpayers mostly will be using Forms 1040, 1040A, and 1040EZ. But importantly, the IRS expects the level of electronically filed returns to be at an all-time high.

|  | Percentage |
|---|---|
| Paper individual returns | 49.95 |
| Electronically filed individual returns | 50.05 |
|  | 100.00 |

**Source:** Projections of Returns to Be Filed in Calendar Years 2004–2010, *SOI Bulletin*, Winter 2003–2004.

**When and Where to File.**   Tax returns of individuals are due on or before the fifteenth day of the fourth month following the close of the tax year. For the calendar year taxpayer, the usual filing date is on or before April 15 of the following year.[37] When the due date falls on a Saturday, Sunday, or legal holiday, the last day for filing falls on the next business day.

If a taxpayer is unable to file the return by the specified due date, an automatic four-month extension of time can be obtained.[38] Further extensions may be granted by the IRS upon a showing of good cause by the taxpayer.

Although obtaining an extension excuses a taxpayer from a penalty for failure to file, it does not insulate against the penalty for failure to pay. If more tax is owed, the extension request should be accompanied by an additional payment to cover the balance due. The return should be sent or delivered to the Regional Service Center listed in the instructions for each type of return or contained in software applications.[39]

**Mode of Payment.**   Usually, payment is made by check. However, the IRS may now accept debit, credit, or charge cards for the payment of Federal income taxes. The entity providing the credit will charge the taxpayer a fee based on the size of the payment.

### FILING STATUS

The amount of tax will vary considerably depending on which filing status is used. This is illustrated in the following example.

**EXAMPLE 33**

The following amounts of tax (rounded to the nearest dollar) are computed using the 2005 Tax Rate Schedules (inside the front cover of this text). The taxpayer (or taxpayers in the case of a joint return) is assumed to have $40,000 of taxable income.

---

[37]§ 6072(a).

[38]Reg. § 1.6081–4.

[39]The Regional Service Centers and the geographic area each covers can also be found at **http://www.irs.gov/file** or in the tax forms packages.

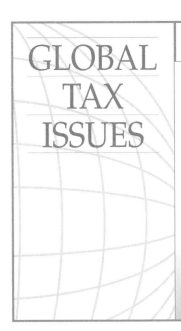

GLOBAL TAX ISSUES

## FILING A JOINT RETURN

John Garth is a U.S. citizen and resident, but spends a lot of time in London where his employer sends him on frequent assignments. John is married to Victoria, a citizen and resident of the United Kingdom.

Can John and Victoria file a joint return for U.S. Federal income tax purposes? Although § 6013(a)(1) specifically precludes the filing of a joint return if one spouse is a nonresident alien, another Code provision permits an exception. Under § 6013(g), the parties can elect to treat the nonqualifying spouse as a "resident" of the United States. This election would allow John and Victoria to file jointly.

But should John and Victoria make this election? If Victoria has considerable income of her own (from non-U.S. sources), the election could be ill-advised. As a nonresident alien, Victoria's non-U.S. source income *would not* be subject to the U.S. income tax. If she is treated as a U.S. resident, however, her non-U.S. source income *will be subject to U.S. tax.* Under the U.S. global approach to taxation, all income (regardless of where earned) of anyone who is a *resident* or *citizen* of the United States is subject to tax.

| Filing Status | Amount of Tax |
|---|---|
| Single | $6,665 |
| Married, filing joint return | 5,270 |
| Married, filing separate return | 6,665 |
| Head of household | 5,498 |

**Rates for Single Taxpayers.**   A taxpayer who is unmarried or separated from his or her spouse by a decree of divorce or separate maintenance and does not qualify for another filing status must use the rates for single taxpayers. Marital status is determined as of the last day of the tax year, except when a spouse dies during the year. In that case, marital status is determined as of the date of death.

**Rates for Married Individuals.**   The joint filing status was originally enacted to establish equity between married taxpayers in common law states and those in community property states. Before the joint return rates were enacted, taxpayers in community property states were in an advantageous position relative to taxpayers in common law states because they could split their income.

Taxpayers in common law states did not have this income-splitting option, so their taxable income was subject to higher marginal rates. This inconsistency in treatment was remedied by the joint return provisions. The progressive rates in the joint return Tax Rate Schedule are constructed based on the assumption that income is earned equally by the two spouses.

If married individuals elect to file separate returns, each reports only his or her own income, exemptions, deductions, and credits, and each must use the Tax Rate Schedule applicable to married taxpayers filing separately. It is generally advantageous for married individuals to file a joint return, since the combined amount of tax is lower. However, special circumstances (e.g., significant medical expenses incurred by one spouse subject to the 7.5 percent limitation) may warrant

**Bridge to Equity or Fairness**

Much has been made in the press and in political circles in recent years concerning the so-called marriage penalty tax. This marriage penalty refers to the additional income tax that married couples pay over and above the aggregate amount two single individuals would pay with equal amounts of income. The marriage penalty arose because of the nature of the income tax rate structure that applied to individual taxpayers.

Relevant policy and ethical issues related to this dilemma are:

- Should the income tax system contain a bias against marriage?
- Should the income tax system require two people of economic means equal to that of two other people to pay a different amount of income taxes?
- Should the income tax system encourage two individuals to cohabit outside the commitment of marriage?

Long aware of the inequity of the marriage penalty, Congress reduced the effect of the problem in the JGTRRA of 2003. Beginning in 2003, the standard deduction available to married filers increased to 200 percent of that applicable to single persons. Furthermore and also beginning in 2003, the 15 percent bracket for joint filers increased to 200 percent of the size of that applicable to single filers.

---

the election to file separate returns. It may be necessary to compute the tax under both assumptions to determine the most advantageous filing status.

When Congress enacted the joint return filing status, the result was to favor married taxpayers. In certain situations, however, the parties would incur less tax if they were not married and filed separate returns. The additional tax that a joint return caused, commonly called the **marriage penalty,** developed when *both* spouses had significant taxable incomes.

*Find more information on this topic at our Web site: **http://wft-entities.swlearning.com**.*

The joint return rates also apply for two years following the death of one's spouse, if the **surviving spouse** maintains a household for a dependent child.[40] This is referred to as surviving spouse status.

**Rates for Heads of Household.**   Unmarried individuals who maintain a household for a dependent (or dependents) are entitled to use the **head-of-household** rates.[41] The tax liability resulting from the head-of-household rates falls between the liability using the joint return Tax Rate Schedule and the liability using the Tax Rate Schedule for single taxpayers.

To qualify for head-of-household rates, a taxpayer must pay more than half the cost of maintaining a household as his or her home. The household must also be the principal home of a dependent. As a general rule, the dependent must live in the taxpayer's household for over half the year.

*Find more information on this topic at our Web site: **http://wft-entities.swlearning.com**.*

---

[40]§ 2(a). The IRS label for surviving spouse status is "Qualifying Widow(er) with Dependent Child."   [41]§ 2(b).

**Bridge to Economics and Finance**

As is the case for business entities, a primary financial goal for individual taxpayers should entail maximizing the *after-tax value* of their assets over time. This approach requires not only selecting the best investment alternatives, but also choosing those investments with the most favorable tax attributes. Fundamental to this notion is recognizing the key role that the government plays in all economic activity through its taxing authority. As a result, an investor should consider economically sound strategies that minimize the extent to which government can stake a claim to his or her success. For example, taxpayers can reduce the government's share of their wealth accumulations by deferring the payment of taxes until future years and by taking advantage of investment strategies for which tax incentives are available. Taxpayers should choose the investment alternatives that provide the best after-tax return over time and not necessarily the ones that lead to the least amount of taxation.

These points can be illustrated by examining two classic strategies. One of the best ways for individuals to maximize their personal wealth is to invest to the extent possible in qualifying retirement savings programs [e.g., traditional Individual Retirement Accounts, § 401(k) accounts]. Not only do current additions to such accounts provide a current tax deduction, but earnings within the account are not subject to taxation until they are withdrawn, which, in most cases, is during the retirement years of the owner. Postponing the tax in these two ways reduces the present value of the tax cost, which increases the after-tax value of the investment. Another strategy involves investing in tax-free municipal bonds, which produce interest income that is free of Federal income tax. The returns from such investments, however, should be compared with the after-tax returns flowing from available taxable debt securities. For example, a relevant question is how the implicit tax (see Chapter 1) associated with a municipal bond compares with the explicit tax associated with a taxable bond.

---

**LO.6**

Identify specific inclusions and exclusions applicable to individuals.

# Overview of Income Provisions Applicable to Individuals

As indicated earlier in this chapter, the definition of gross income is broad enough to include almost all receipts of money, property, or services. However, the tax law provides for exclusion of many types of income. The following income provisions, which apply to all taxpayers (including individuals), were discussed in Chapter 3:

- Interest from state and local bonds.
- Life insurance paid on death of the insured.
- Imputed interest on below-market loans.
- Income from discharge of indebtedness.
- Income included under the tax benefit rule.

Most *exclusions* available only to individuals are for *fringe benefits* received by *employees* (refer to Exhibit 15–1). Fringe benefits are discussed in Chapter 16. Other specific inclusions and exclusions for individuals are discussed below.

# Specific Inclusions Applicable to Individuals

The general principles of gross income determination as applied by the IRS and the courts have on occasion yielded results Congress found unacceptable. Consequently, Congress has provided more specific rules for determining the amount of gross income from certain sources. Some of these special rules appear in §§ 71–90 of the Code. The following provisions applicable to individuals are covered in this chapter:

- Alimony and separate maintenance payments.
- Prizes and awards.
- Unemployment compensation.
- Social Security benefits.

## ALIMONY AND SEPARATE MAINTENANCE PAYMENTS

When a married couple divorce or become legally separated, state law generally requires a division of the property accumulated during the marriage. In addition, one spouse may have a legal obligation to support the other spouse. The Code distinguishes between the support payments (alimony or separate maintenance) and the property division in terms of the tax consequences.

**Alimony and separate maintenance payments** are deductible by the party making the payments and are includible in the gross income of the party receiving the payments.[42] Thus, taxation of the income is shifted from the income earner to the income beneficiary.

**EXAMPLE 34**

Pete and Tina are divorced, and Pete is required to pay Tina $15,000 of alimony each year. Pete earns $50,000 a year. Therefore, Tina must include the $15,000 in her gross income, and Pete is allowed to deduct $15,000 from his gross income. ■

A transfer of property other than cash to a former spouse under a divorce decree or agreement is not a taxable event. The transferor is not entitled to a deduction and does not recognize gain or loss on the transfer. The transferee does not recognize income and has a cost basis equal to the transferor's basis.[43]

**EXAMPLE 35**

Paul transfers stock to Rosa as part of a 2005 divorce settlement. The cost of the stock to Paul is $12,000, and the stock's fair market value at the time of the transfer is $15,000. Rosa later sells the stock for $16,000. Paul is not required to recognize gain from the transfer of the stock to Rosa, and Rosa has a realized *and* recognized gain of $4,000 ($16,000 − $12,000) when she sells the stock. ■

In the case of cash payments, however, it is often difficult to distinguish between support payments (alimony) and property settlements. In 1984, Congress developed objective rules to classify these payments.[44]

*Find more information on this topic at our Web site: **http://wft-entities.swlearning.com**.*

---

[42]§§ 71 and 215.
[43]Section 1041 was added to the Code in 1984 to repeal the rule of *U.S. v. Davis*, 62–2 USTC ¶9509, 9 AFTR2d 1625, 82 S.Ct. 1190 (USSC, 1962). Under the *Davis* rule, which applied to pre-1985 divorces, a property transfer incident to divorce was a taxable event.

[44]More complex rules existed for determining the nature of payments under pre-1985 agreements.

**Child Support.** While alimony is taxable, a taxpayer does *not* report income from the receipt of child support payments made by his or her former spouse. This result occurs because the money is received subject to the duty to use the money for the child's benefit. The payor is not allowed to deduct the child support payments because the payments are made to satisfy the payor's legal obligation to support the child.

In many cases, it is difficult to determine whether an amount received is alimony or child support. If the amount of the payments would be reduced upon the happening of a contingency related to a child (e.g., the child attains age 21 or dies), the amount of the future reduction in the payment is deemed child support.[45]

**EXAMPLE 36**

A divorce agreement provides that Matt is required to make periodic alimony payments of $500 per month to Grace. However, when Matt and Grace's child reaches age 21, marries, or dies (whichever occurs first), the payments will be reduced to $300 per month. Child support payments are $200 each month, and alimony is $300 each month. ■

## PRIZES AND AWARDS

The fair market value of prizes and awards must be included in gross income.[46] Therefore, TV giveaway prizes, magazine publisher prizes, door prizes, and awards from an employer to an employee in recognition of performance are fully taxable to the recipient.

A narrow exception permits a prize or award to be excluded from gross income if *all* of the following requirements are satisfied:

- The prize or award is received in recognition of religious, charitable, scientific, educational, artistic, literary, or civic achievement (e.g., Nobel Prize, Pulitzer Prize).
- The recipient was selected without taking any action to enter the contest or proceeding.
- The recipient is not required to render substantial future services as a condition for receiving the prize or award.[47]
- The recipient arranges for the prize or award to be paid *directly* to a qualified governmental unit or nonprofit organization.

Another exception is provided to allow exclusion of certain employee achievement awards in the form of tangible personal property (e.g., a gold watch). The awards must be made in recognition of length of service or safety achievement. Generally, the ceiling on the excludible amount for an employee is $400 per taxable year. However, if the award is a *qualified plan award,* the ceiling on the exclusion is $1,600 per taxable year.[48]

## UNEMPLOYMENT COMPENSATION

The unemployment compensation program is sponsored and operated by the states and Federal government to provide a source of income for people who have been employed and are temporarily out of work. In a series of rulings over a period of 40 years, the IRS exempted unemployment benefits from tax. These payments were considered social benefit programs for the promotion of the general welfare. After experiencing dissatisfaction with the IRS's treatment of unemployment compensation, Congress amended the Code to provide that the benefits are taxable.[49]

---

[45]§ 71(c)(2).
[46]§ 74.
[47]§ 74(b).

[48]§§ 74(c) and 274(j).
[49]§ 85.

## SOCIAL SECURITY BENEFITS

If a taxpayer's income exceeds a specified base amount, as much as 50 or 85 percent of Social Security retirement benefits must be included in gross income. The taxable amount of benefits is determined through the application of one of two complex formulas described in § 86.

*Find more information on this topic at our Web site: **http://wft-entities.swlearning.com**.*

# Specific Exclusions Applicable to Individuals

### GIFTS AND INHERITANCES

Beginning with the Income Tax Act of 1913 and continuing to the present, Congress has allowed the recipient of a **gift** to exclude the value of the property from gross income. The exclusion applies to gifts made during the life of the donor (*inter vivos* gifts) and transfers that take effect upon the death of the donor (bequests and inheritances).[50] However, the recipient of a gift of income-producing property is subject to tax on the income subsequently earned from the property. Also, as discussed in Chapter 1, the donor or the decedent's estate may be subject to gift or estate taxes on such transfers.

In numerous cases, gifts are made in a business setting. For example, a salesperson gives a purchasing agent free samples; an employee receives cash from his or her employer on retirement; a corporation makes payments to employees who were victims of a natural disaster; a corporation makes a cash payment to a deceased employee's spouse. In these and similar instances, it is frequently unclear whether the payment was a gift or whether it represents compensation for past, present, or future services.

The courts have defined a gift as "a voluntary transfer of property by one to another without adequate consideration or compensation therefrom."[51] If the payment is intended to be for services rendered, it is not a gift, even though the payment is made without legal or moral obligation and the payor receives no economic benefit from the transfer. To qualify as a gift, the payment must be made "out of affection, respect, admiration, charity or like impulses."[52] Thus, the cases on this issue have been decided on the basis of the donor's intent.[53]

In the case of cash or other property received by an employee from his or her employer, Congress has eliminated any ambiguity. Transfers from an employer to an employee cannot be excluded as a gift.[54]

*Find more information on this topic at our Web site: **http://wft-entities.swlearning.com**.*

### SCHOLARSHIPS

**General Information.**   Payments or benefits received by a student at an educational institution may be (1) compensation for services, (2) a gift, or (3) a scholarship. If the payments or benefits are received as compensation for services (past or

---

[50]§ 102.
[51]*Estate of D. R. Daly*, 3 B.T.A. 1042 (1926).
[52]*Robertson v. U.S.*, 52–1 USTC ¶9343, 41 AFTR 1053, 72 S.Ct. 994 (USSC, 1952).

[53]See, for example, *Comm. v. Duberstein*, 60–2 USTC ¶9515, 5 AFTR2d 1626, 80 S.Ct. 1190 (USSC, 1960).
[54]§ 102(c).

### BEGGING AS A TAX-DISFAVORED OCCUPATION

In five recent decisions, the Tax Court ruled that amounts received from begging are nontaxable gifts. In a reversal of the normal roles, the beggars contended that the amounts received were earned income while the IRS argued that the taxpayers had merely received gifts. The beggars wanted the fruit of their efforts to be treated as earned income in order to qualify them for the earned income credit.

present), the fact that the recipient is a student generally does not render the amounts received nontaxable.[55]

**EXAMPLE 37**

State University waives tuition for all graduate teaching assistants. The tuition waived is intended as compensation for services and is therefore included in the graduate assistant's gross income. ∎

The **scholarship** rules are intended to provide exclusion treatment for education-related benefits that cannot qualify as gifts but are not compensation for services. According to the Regulations, "a scholarship is an amount paid or allowed to, or for the benefit of, an individual to aid such individual in the pursuit of study or research."[56] The recipient must be a candidate for a degree (either undergraduate or graduate) at an educational institution.[57]

**EXAMPLE 38**

Terry enters a contest sponsored by a local newspaper. Each contestant is required to submit an essay on local environmental issues. The prize is one year's tuition at State University. Terry wins the contest. The newspaper has a legal obligation to Terry (as the contest winner). Thus, the benefits are not a gift. However, since the tuition payment aids Terry in pursuing her studies and is not compensation for services, the payment is a scholarship. ∎

A scholarship recipient may exclude from gross income the amount used for tuition and related expenses (fees, books, supplies, and equipment required for courses), provided the conditions of the grant do not require that the funds be used for other purposes.[58] Amounts received for room and board are taxable and are treated as earned income for purposes of calculating the standard deduction for a taxpayer who is another taxpayer's dependent.[59]

**EXAMPLE 39**

Kelly receives a scholarship of $9,500 from State University to be used to pursue a bachelor's degree. She spends $4,000 on tuition, $3,000 on books and supplies, and $2,500 for room and board. Kelly may exclude $7,000 ($4,000 + $3,000) from gross income. The $2,500 spent for room and board is includible in Kelly's gross income.

Kelly's only source of income. Her parents provide more than 50% of Kelly's support and claim her as a dependent. Kelly's standard deduction of $2,750 ($2,500 + $250) exceeds her $2,500 gross income. Thus, she has no taxable income. ∎

---

[55]Reg. § 1.117–2(a). See *C. P. Bhalla,* 35 T.C. 13 (1960), for a discussion of the distinction between a scholarship and compensation. See also *Bingler v. Johnson,* 69–1 USTC ¶9348, 23 AFTR2d 1212, 89 S.Ct. 1439 (USSC, 1969). For potential exclusion treatment, see the discussion of qualified tuition reductions in Chapter 16.

[56]Prop.Reg. § 1.117–6(c)(3)(i).
[57]§ 117(a).
[58]§ 117(b).
[59]Prop.Reg. § 1.117–6(h).

**Timing Issues.**   Frequently, the scholarship recipient is a cash basis taxpayer who receives the money in one tax year but pays the educational expenses in a subsequent year. The amount eligible for exclusion may not be known at the time the money is received. In that case, the transaction is held open until the educational expenses are paid.[60]

**EXAMPLE 40**

In August 2005, Sanjay received $10,000 as a scholarship for the academic year 2005–2006. Sanjay's expenditures for tuition, books, and supplies were as follows:

| | |
|---|---|
| August–December 2005 | $3,000 |
| January–May 2006 | 4,500 |
| | $7,500 |

Sanjay's gross income for 2006 includes $2,500 ($10,000 – $7,500) that is not excludible as a scholarship. None of the scholarship is included in his gross income in 2005. ■

**Disguised Compensation.**   Some employers make scholarships available solely to the children of key employees. The tax objective of these plans is to provide a nontaxable fringe benefit to the executives by making the payment to the child in the form of an excludible scholarship. However, the IRS has ruled that the payments are generally includible by the parent-employee as compensation for services.[61]

## DAMAGES

A person who suffers harm caused by another is often entitled to **compensatory damages.** The tax consequences of the receipt of damages depend on the type of harm the taxpayer has experienced. The taxpayer may seek recovery for (1) a loss of income, (2) expenses incurred, (3) property destroyed, or (4) personal injury.

Generally, reimbursement for a loss of income is taxed in the same manner as the income replaced (see the exception under Personal Injury below). Damages that are a recovery of expenses previously deducted by the taxpayer are generally taxable under the tax benefit rule (refer to Chapter 3).

*Recovery of capital →* A payment for damaged or destroyed property is treated as an amount received in a sale or exchange of the property. Thus, the taxpayer has a realized gain if the damage payments received exceed the property's basis. Damages for personal injuries receive special treatment under the Code.

**Personal Injury.**   The legal theory of personal injury damages is that the amount received is intended "to make the plaintiff [the injured party] whole as before the injury."[62] It follows that if the damage payments received were subject to tax, the after-tax amount received would be less than the actual damages incurred and the injured party would not be "whole as before the injury."

With regard to personal injury damages, a distinction is made between compensatory damages and **punitive damages.** Under specified circumstances, compensatory damages may be excluded from gross income. Under no circumstances may punitive damages be excluded from gross income.

Compensatory damages are intended to compensate the taxpayer for the damages incurred. Only those compensatory damages received on account of *physical personal injury or sickness* can be excluded from gross income.[63] Such exclusion

---

[60]Prop.Reg. § 1.117–6(b)(2).
[61]Rev.Rul. 75–448, 1975–2 C.B. 55 and *Richard T. Armantrout*, 67 T.C. 996 (1977).

[62]*C. A. Hawkins*, 6 B.T.A. 1023 (1928).
[63]§ 104(a)(2).

## Concept Summary 15–2

### Taxation of Damages

| Type of Claim | Taxation of Award or Settlement |
| --- | --- |
| Breach of contract (generally loss of income) | Taxable. |
| Property damages | Recovery of cost; gain to the extent of the excess over basis. A loss is deductible for business property and investment property to the extent of basis over the amount realized. A loss may be deductible for personal-use property (see discussion of casualty losses in Chapter 5). |
| Personal injury | |
| Physical | All compensatory amounts are excluded unless previously deducted (e.g., medical expenses). Amounts received as punitive damages are included in gross income. |
| Nonphysical | Compensatory damages and punitive damages are included in gross income. |

treatment includes amounts received for loss of income associated with the physical personal injury or physical sickness. Compensatory damages awarded on account of emotional distress are not received on account of physical injury or sickness and thus cannot be excluded from gross income (except to the extent of any amount received for medical care). Likewise, any amounts received for age discrimination or injury to one's reputation cannot be excluded.

Punitive damages are amounts the party that caused the harm must pay to the victim as punishment for outrageous conduct. Punitive damages are not intended to compensate the victim, but rather to punish the party that caused the harm. Thus, it follows that amounts received as punitive damages may actually place the victim in a better economic position than before the harm was experienced. Logically, punitive damages are thus included in gross income.

**EXAMPLE 41**

Tom, a television announcer, was dissatisfied with the manner in which Ron, an attorney, was defending the television station in a libel case. Tom stated on the air that Ron was botching the case. Ron sued Tom for slander, claiming damages for loss of income from clients and potential clients who heard Tom's statement. Ron's claim is for damages to his business reputation, and the amounts received are taxable.

Ron collected on the suit against Tom and was on his way to a party to celebrate his victory when a negligent driver, Norm, drove a truck into Ron's automobile, injuring Ron. Ron filed suit for the physical personal injuries and claimed as damages the loss of income for the period he was unable to work as a result of the injuries. Ron also collected punitive damages that were awarded because of Norm's extremely negligent behavior. Ron's wife also collected damages for the emotional distress she experienced as a result of the accident. Ron may exclude the amounts he received for damages, except the punitive damages. Ron's wife must include the amounts she received for damages in gross income because the amounts were not received because of physical personal injuries or sickness. ■

### WORKERS' COMPENSATION

State workers' compensation laws require the employer to pay fixed amounts for specific job-related injuries. The state laws were enacted so that the employee will not have to go through the ordeal of a lawsuit (and possibly not collect damages because of some defense available to the employer) to recover the damages. Although the payments are intended, in part, to compensate for a loss of future income, Congress has specifically exempted workers' compensation benefits from inclusion in gross income.[64]

## ACCIDENT AND HEALTH INSURANCE BENEFITS

The income tax treatment of **accident and health insurance benefits** depends on whether the policy providing the benefits was purchased by the taxpayer or the taxpayer's employer. Benefits collected under an accident and health insurance policy purchased by the taxpayer are excludible. In this case, benefits collected under the taxpayer's insurance policy are excluded even though the payments are a substitute for income.[65]

**EXAMPLE 42**

Bonnie purchases a medical and disability insurance policy. The insurance company pays Bonnie $1,000 per week to replace wages she loses while in the hospital. Although the payments serve as a substitute for income, the amounts received are tax-exempt benefits collected under Bonnie's insurance policy. ■

**EXAMPLE 43**

Joe's injury results in a partial paralysis of his left foot. He receives $20,000 for the injury from his accident insurance company under a policy he had purchased. The $20,000 accident insurance proceeds are tax-exempt. ■

A different set of rules applies if the accident and health insurance protection was purchased by the individual's employer, as discussed in Chapter 16.

## EDUCATIONAL SAVINGS BONDS

The cost of a college education has risen dramatically during the past 15 years. The U.S. Department of Education estimates that by the year 2007, the cost of attending a publicly supported university for four years will exceed $60,000. For a private university, the cost is expected to exceed $200,000. Consequently, Congress has attempted to assist low- to middle-income parents in saving for their children's college education.

The assistance is in the form of an interest income exclusion on **educational savings bonds.**[66] The interest on U.S. government Series EE savings bonds may be excluded from gross income if the bond proceeds are used to pay qualified higher education expenses. The exclusion applies only if both of the following requirements are satisfied:

- The savings bonds are issued after December 31, 1989.
- The savings bonds are issued to an individual who is at least 24 years old at the time of issuance.

The redemption proceeds must be used to pay qualified higher education expenses. Qualified higher education expenses consist of tuition and fees paid to an eligible educational institution for the taxpayer, spouse, or dependent. In calculating qualified higher education expenses, the tuition and fees paid are reduced by excludible scholarships and veterans' benefits received. If the redemption proceeds (both principal and interest) exceed the qualified higher education expenses, only a pro rata portion of the interest will qualify for exclusion treatment.

**EXAMPLE 44**

Tracy's redemption proceeds from qualified savings bonds during the taxable year are $6,000 (principal of $4,000 and interest of $2,000). Tracy's qualified higher education expenses are

---

[64]§ 104(a)(1).
[65]§ 104(a)(3).

[66]§ 135.

$5,000. Since the redemption proceeds exceed the qualified higher education expenses, only $1,667 [($5,000/$6,000) × $2,000] of the interest is excludible. ■

The exclusion is limited by the application of the wherewithal to pay concept. That is, once the *modified AGI (MAGI)* exceeds a threshold amount, the phaseout of the exclusion begins. The threshold amounts are adjusted for inflation each year. For 2005, the phaseout begins at $61,200 ($91,850 on a joint return).[67] The phaseout is completed when MAGI exceeds the threshold amount by more than $15,000 ($30,000 on a joint return). The otherwise excludible interest is reduced by the amount calculated as follows:

$$\frac{MAGI - \$61,200}{\$15,000} \times \frac{\text{Excludible interest}}{\text{before phaseout}} = \frac{\text{Reduction in}}{\text{excludible interest}}$$

On a joint return, $91,850 is substituted for $61,200 (in 2005), and $30,000 is substituted for $15,000.

**EXAMPLE 45**

Assume the same facts as in Example 44, except that Tracy's MAGI for 2005 is $70,000. The phaseout results in Tracy's interest exclusion being reduced by $978 {[($70,000 − $61,200)/ $15,000] × $1,667}. Therefore, Tracy's exclusion is $689 ($1,667 − $978). ■

**LO.7**

Determine an individual's allowable itemized deductions.

# Itemized Deductions

Taxpayers are allowed to deduct specified expenditures as itemized deductions. Itemized deductions, which are reported on Schedule A, can be classified as follows:

- Expenses that are purely *personal* in nature.
- Expenses incurred by *employees* in connection with their employment activities.
- Expenses related to (1) the *production or collection of income* and (2) the *management of property* held for the production of income.[68]

Expenses in the third category, sometimes referred to as *nonbusiness expenses*, differ from trade or business expenses (discussed previously). Trade or business expenses, which are deductions *for* AGI, must be incurred in connection with a trade or business. Nonbusiness expenses, on the other hand, are expenses incurred in connection with an income-producing activity that does not qualify as a trade or business. If the nonbusiness expense is incurred in connection with rent or royalty property, it is classified as a deduction *for* AGI. Otherwise, it is classified as a deduction *from* AGI. Itemized deductions include, but are not limited to, the expenses listed in Exhibit 15–3.

Allowable itemized deductions are deductible *from* AGI in arriving at taxable income if the taxpayer elects to itemize. The election to itemize is appropriate when total itemized deductions exceed the standard deduction based on the taxpayer's filing status. The more important itemized deductions are discussed below.

## MEDICAL EXPENSES

**Medical Expenses Defined.** **Medical expenses** paid for the care of the taxpayer, spouse, and dependents are allowed as an itemized deduction to the extent

---

[67]The indexed amounts for 2004 are $59,850 and $89,750.
[68]Section 212 allows itemized deductions for these types of activities. However, expenses related to the production of *rental or royalty*

*income* are deductions *for* AGI, not itemized deductions, under § 62(a)(4).

■ **EXHIBIT 15–3**
Partial List of Itemized
Deductions

---

**Personal Expenditures**

Medical expenses (in excess of 7.5% of AGI)

State and local income taxes or sales taxes

Real estate taxes

Personal property taxes

Interest on home mortgage

Charitable contributions (limited to a maximum of 50% of AGI)

Casualty and theft losses (in excess of 10% of AGI)

Tax return preparation fee (in excess of 2% of AGI)

**Expenditures Related to Employment (in Excess of 2% of AGI)**

Union dues

Professional dues and subscriptions

Certain educational expenses

Unreimbursed employee business expenses

**Expenditures Related to Income-Producing Activities**

Investment interest (to the extent of investment income)

Investment counsel fees (in excess of 2% of AGI)

Other investment expenses (in excess of 2% of AGI)

---

the expenses are not reimbursed. The medical expense deduction is limited to the amount by which such expenses exceed 7.5 percent of the taxpayer's AGI.

**EXAMPLE 46**

During the year, Iris had medical expenses of $4,800, of which $1,000 was reimbursed by her insurance company. If her AGI for the year is $40,000, the itemized deduction for medical expenses is limited to $800 [$4,800 − $1,000 = $3,800 − (7.5% × $40,000)]. ■

The term *medical care* includes expenditures incurred for the "diagnosis, cure, mitigation, treatment, or prevention of disease, or for the purpose of affecting any structure or function of the body."[69] Medical expense also includes premiums paid for health care insurance, prescribed drugs and insulin, and lodging while away from home for the purpose of obtaining medical care. Examples of deductible and nondeductible medical expenses appear in Exhibit 15–4.

**Cosmetic Surgery.**   Amounts paid for unnecessary cosmetic surgery are not deductible medical expenses. However, if cosmetic surgery is deemed necessary, it is deductible as a medical expense. Cosmetic surgery is necessary when it ameliorates (1) a deformity arising from a congenital abnormality, (2) a personal injury, or (3) a disfiguring disease.

**Nursing Home Care.**   The cost of care in a nursing home or home for the aged, including meals and lodging, can be included in deductible medical expenses if the primary reason for being in the home is to get medical care. If the primary reason for being there is personal, any costs for medical or nursing care can be included in deductible medical expenses, but the cost of meals and lodging must be excluded.

**Capital Expenditures.**   The treatment of certain illnesses may require expenditures for equipment, special structures, or modification of the taxpayer's residence.

---

[69]§ 213(d).

■ **EXHIBIT 15–4**
Examples of Deductible and Nondeductible Medical Expenses

| Deductible | Nondeductible |
|---|---|
| Medical (including dental, mental, and hospital) care | Funeral, burial, or cremation expenses |
| Prescription drugs | Nonprescription drugs (except insulin) |
| Special equipment | Bottled water |
|    Wheelchairs | Diaper service, maternity clothes |
|    Crutches | Programs for the general improvement of health |
|    Artificial limbs |    Weight reduction |
|    Eyeglasses (including contact lenses) |    Health spas |
|    Hearing aids | Social activities (e.g., dancing and swimming lessons) |
| Transportation for medical care | Unnecessary cosmetic surgery |
| Medical and hospital insurance premiums | |
| Long-term care insurance premiums (subject to limitations) | |
| Cost of alcohol and drug rehabilitation | |
| Certain costs to stop smoking | |
| Weight reduction programs related to obesity | |

Some examples of capital expenditures for medical purposes are swimming pools if the taxpayer does not have access to a neighborhood pool and air conditioners if they do not become permanent improvements (e.g., window units).[70] Other examples include dust elimination systems,[71] elevators,[72] and a room built to house an iron lung. These expenditures are medical in nature if they are incurred as a medical necessity upon the advice of a physician, the facility is used primarily by the patient alone, and the expense is reasonable.

Capital expenditures normally are adjustments to basis and are deductible only through depreciation. However, both a capital expenditure for a permanent improvement and expenditures made for the operation or maintenance of the improvement may qualify as medical expenses. If a capital expenditure qualifies as a medical expense, the allowable amount is deductible in the *year incurred*. The allowable amount is the excess of the cost of the capital expenditure over the increase in the value of the related property.

**Medical Expenses for Spouse and Dependents.** In computing the medical expense deduction, a taxpayer may include medical expenses for a spouse and for a person who was a dependent at the time the expenses were paid or incurred. Of the five requirements that normally apply in determining dependency status, neither the gross income nor the joint return test applies in determining dependency status for medical expense deduction purposes.

**Transportation and Lodging.** Payments for transportation to and from a hospital or other medical facility for medical care are deductible as medical expenses (subject to the 7.5 percent floor). Transportation expenses for medical care include bus, taxi, train, or plane fare, charges for ambulance service, and out-of-pocket

---

[70]Rev.Rul. 55–261, 1955–1 C.B. 307, modified by Rev.Rul. 68–212, 1968–1 C.B. 91.
[71]*F. S. Delp,* 30 T.C. 1230 (1958).

[72]*Riach v. Frank,* 62–1 USTC ¶9419, 9 AFTR2d 1263, 302 F.2d 374 (CA–9, 1962).

## THE PRESIDENT AND VICE PRESIDENT ITEMIZE

Approximately two-thirds of all individual taxpayers take the standard deduction each year rather than itemize. President George W. Bush and Vice President Richard B. Cheney are among the one-third who itemize. Both the President and Vice President, who file joint returns with their wives, released their 2003 tax returns to the public. Their itemized deductions, along with certain other information from their tax returns, are shown below.

|  | **President Bush** | **Vice President Cheney** |
|---|---|---|
| Gross income | $822,126 | $1,273,334* |
| Adjusted gross income | $822,126 | $1,267,915 |
| Itemized deductions: |  |  |
|    Medical expenses | $    –0– | $    –0– |
|    Taxes | 21,352 | 44,728 |
|    Interest | –0– | –0– |
|    Charitable contributions | 68,360 | 321,141 |
|    Job expenses and most other<br>    miscellaneous deductions | 25,810 | 122,632 |
|    Total itemized deductions | $115,522 | $ 488,501 |

*It is interesting to note that Vice President Cheney also reported tax-exempt interest of $627,005 on his return.

expenses for the use of an automobile. A mileage allowance of 15 cents per mile[73] may be used instead of actual out-of-pocket automobile expenses. Whether the taxpayer chooses to claim out-of-pocket automobile expenses or the 15 cents per mile automatic mileage option, related parking fees and tolls can also be deducted. The cost of meals while en route to obtain medical care is not deductible.

*Find more information on this topic at our Web site: **http://wft-entities.swlearning.com**.*

**Health Savings Accounts.**   In December 2003, President Bush signed legislation creating **Health Savings Accounts (HSAs)** as a replacement for Archer Medical Savings Accounts (MSAs).[74] A taxpayer can use an HSA in conjunction with a high-deductible medical insurance policy to help reduce the overall cost of medical coverage.

A high-deductible policy provides coverage for extraordinary medical expenses (in excess of the deductible), and expenses not covered by the policy can be paid with funds withdrawn from the HSA.

**EXAMPLE 47**

Sanchez, who is married and has three dependent children, carries a high-deductible medical insurance policy with a deductible of $4,400. He rolls over the balance in his Archer MSA into the HSA and contributes the maximum allowable amount to the HSA in 2005. During 2005, the Sanchez family incurs medical expenses of $12,000. The high-deductible policy covers $7,600 of the expenses ($12,000 expenses – $4,400 deductible). Sanchez may withdraw $4,400 from the HSA to pay the medical expenses not covered by the high-deductible policy. ∎

[73]This amount is adjusted periodically. The amount in 2004 was 14 cents per mile.

[74]§ 223.

*High-Deductible Plans.*   High-deductible policies are less expensive than low-deductible policies, so taxpayers with low medical costs can benefit from the lower premiums and use funds from the HSA to pay costs not covered by the high-deductible policy. A plan must meet two requirements to qualify as a high-deductible plan.[75]

1. The annual deductible is not less than $1,000 for self-only coverage ($2,000 for family coverage).
2. The sum of the annual deductible and other out-of-pocket costs (excluding the premiums) under the plan does not exceed $5,100 for self-only coverage ($10,200 for family coverage).

*Tax Treatment of HSA Contributions and Distributions.*   To establish an HSA, a taxpayer contributes funds to a tax-exempt trust.[76] As illustrated in the preceding example, funds can be withdrawn from an HSA to pay medical expenses that are not covered by the high-deductible policy. The following general tax rules apply to HSAs:

1. Contributions made by the taxpayer to an HSA are deductible from gross income to arrive at AGI (deduction *for* AGI). Thus, the taxpayer does not need to itemize in order to take the deduction.
2. Earnings on HSAs are not subject to taxation unless distributed, in which case taxability depends on the way the funds are used.[77]
   * Distributions from HSAs are excluded from gross income if they are used to pay for medical expenses not covered by the high-deductible policy.
   * Distributions that are not used to pay for medical expenses are included in gross income and are subject to an additional 10 percent penalty if made before age 65, death, or disability. Such distributions made by reason of death or disability and distributions made after the HSA beneficiary becomes eligible for Medicare are taxed but not penalized.

HSAs have at least two other attractive features. First, an HSA is portable. Taxpayers who switch jobs can take their HSAs with them. Second, coverage is more widely available under the HSA rules than under the previous Archer MSA rules. Generally, anyone under age 65 who has a high-deductible plan and is not covered by another policy that is not a high-deductible plan can establish an HSA.

*Deductible Amount.*   The annual deduction for contributions to an HSA is limited to the sum of the monthly limitations. The monthly limitation is calculated for each month that the individual is an eligible individual. The monthly deduction is not allowed after the individual becomes eligible for Medicare coverage.

The amount of the monthly limitation for an individual who has self-only coverage in 2005 is the *lesser* of one-twelfth of the annual deductible under the high-deductible plan or $2,650. An individual who has family coverage in 2005 is limited to the *lesser* of one-twelfth of the annual deductible under the high-deductible plan or $5,250.[78] For an eligible taxpayer who in 2005 has attained the age of 55 by the end of the tax year, the limit on annual contributions is increased by $600. These amounts are subject to annual cost-of-living adjustments.

| EXAMPLE 48 | Liu, who is married and self-employed, carries a high-deductible medical insurance policy with a deductible of $4,000. In addition, he has established an HSA. Liu's maximum annual contribution to the HSA is $4,000 (the lesser of $5,250 or the annual deductible). ∎ |

---

[75]§ 223(c)(2).
[76]§ 223(d).

[77]§ 223(f).
[78]§ 223(b)(2).

■ **EXHIBIT 15–5**
Deductible and Nondeductible
Taxes

| Deductible | Nondeductible |
|---|---|
| State, local, and foreign real property taxes | Federal income taxes |
| | FICA taxes imposed on employees |
| State and local personal property taxes | Employer FICA taxes paid on domestic household workers |
| State and local income taxes *or* sales/use taxes | Estate, inheritance, and gift taxes |
| Foreign income taxes | Federal, state, and local excise taxes (e.g., gasoline, tobacco, spirits) |
| The environmental tax | Taxes on real property to the extent such taxes are to be apportioned and treated as imposed on another taxpayer |
| | Special assessments for streets, sidewalks, curbing, and other similar improvements |

**EXAMPLE 49**

During 2005, Adam, who is self-employed, made 12 monthly payments of $700 for an HSA contract that provides medical insurance coverage with a $3,600 deductible. The plan covers Adam, his wife, and their two children. Of the $700 monthly fee, $400 was for the high-deductible policy, and $300 was deposited into an HSA. The deductible monthly contribution to the HSA is calculated as follows:

| | |
|---|---|
| Amount of the annual deductible under the plan | $3,600 |
| Maximum annual deduction for family coverage | 5,250 |
| Monthly limitation (1/12 of $3,600) | 300 |

Because Adam is self-employed, he can deduct $4,800 of the amount paid for the high-deductible policy ($400 per month × 12 months) as a deduction *for* AGI (refer to Chapter 16). In addition, he can deduct the $3,600 ($300 × 12) paid to the HSA as a deduction *for* AGI. ■

## TAXES

A deduction is allowed for certain state and local taxes paid or accrued by a taxpayer.[79] The deduction was created to relieve the burden of multiple taxes upon the same source of revenue.

Deductible taxes must be distinguished from nondeductible fees. Fees for special privileges or services are not deductible as itemized deductions if personal in nature. Examples include fees for dog licenses, automobile inspection, automobile titles and registration, hunting and fishing licenses, bridge and highway tolls, drivers' licenses, parking meter deposits, postage, etc. These items, however, could be deductible if incurred as a business expense or for the production of income (refer to Chapter 4). Deductible and nondeductible taxes for purposes of computing itemized deductions are summarized in Exhibit 15–5.

**Personal Property Taxes.**  Deductible personal property taxes must be *ad valorem* (assessed in relation to the value of the property). Therefore, a motor vehicle tax based on weight, model, year, or horsepower is not an ad valorem tax. In contrast, a motor vehicle tax based on the value of the car is deductible.

---

[79]Most deductible taxes are listed in § 164, while the nondeductible items are included in § 275.

## DEDUCTIBILITY OF FOREIGN TAXES

Josef, a citizen of the United States who works primarily in New York, also works several months each year in Austria. He owns a residence in Austria and pays income taxes to Austria on the income he earns there. Both the property tax he pays on his Austrian residence and the income tax he pays on his Austrian income are deductible in computing U.S. taxable income.

**EXAMPLE 50**

A state imposes a motor vehicle registration tax on 4% of the value of the vehicle plus 40 cents per hundredweight. Belle, a resident of the state, owns a car having a value of $4,000 and weighing 3,000 pounds. Belle pays an annual registration fee of $172. Of this amount, $160 (4% of $4,000) is deductible as a personal property tax. The remaining $12, based on the weight of the car, is not deductible. ■

**Real Estate Taxes.** Real estate taxes of individuals are generally deductible. Taxes on personal-use property and investment property are deductible as itemized deductions. Taxes on business property are deductible as business expenses. Real property taxes on property that is sold during the year must be allocated between the buyer and the seller (refer to Chapter 4).

**State and Local Income Taxes and Sales Taxes.** The position of the IRS is that state and local *income* taxes imposed upon an individual are deductible only as itemized deductions, even if the taxpayer's sole source of income is from a business, rents, or royalties.

Cash basis taxpayers are entitled to deduct state income taxes withheld by the employer in the year the taxes are withheld. In addition, estimated state income tax payments are deductible in the year the payment is made by cash basis taxpayers even if the payments relate to a prior or subsequent year.[80] If the taxpayer overpays state income taxes because of excessive withholdings or estimated tax payments, the refund received is included in gross income of the following year to the extent that the deduction reduced the taxable income in the prior year.

**EXAMPLE 51**

Leona, a cash basis, unmarried taxpayer, had $800 of state income tax withheld during 2005. Additionally in 2005, Leona paid $100 that was due when she filed her 2004 state income tax return in 2005 and made estimated payments of $300 on her 2005 state income tax. When Leona files her 2005 Federal income tax return in April 2006, she elects to itemize deductions, which amount to $5,500, including the $1,200 of state income tax payments and withholdings. The itemized deductions reduce her taxable income.

As a result of overpaying her 2005 state income tax, Leona receives a refund of $200 early in 2006. She will include this amount in her 2006 gross income in computing her Federal income tax. It does not matter whether Leona received a check from the state for $200 or applied the $200 toward her 2006 state income tax. ■

Individuals can elect to deduct either their state and local income taxes *or* their sales/use taxes paid as an itemized deduction on Schedule A of Form 1040. This American Jobs Creation Act provision is effective beginning with 2004 returns. The new, annual election can reflect actual sales/use tax payments *or* an amount from

---

[80]Rev.Rul. 71–190, 1971–1 C.B. 70. See also Rev.Rul. 82–208, 1982–2 C.B. 58, where a deduction is not allowed when the taxpayer cannot, in good faith, reasonably determine that there is additional state income tax liability.

an IRS table. The amount from the table may be increased by sales tax paid on the purchase of motor vehicles, boats, and other specified items. Most likely, the sales tax deduction will be elected by those living in states with no individual income tax (e.g., Texas and Washington).

## PLANNING STRATEGIES    Timing the Payment of Deductible Taxes

### FRAMEWORK FOCUS: DEDUCTIONS

STRATEGY ➤ ACCELERATE RECOGNITION OF DEDUCTIONS TO ACHIEVE TAX DEFERRAL.

It is sometimes possible to defer or accelerate the payment of certain deductible taxes, such as state income tax, real property tax, and personal property tax. For instance, the final installment of estimated state income tax is generally due after the end of a given tax year. However, accelerating the payment of the final installment could result in larger itemized deductions for the current year.

## INTEREST

For Federal income tax purposes, interest must be divided into five categories: business interest, personal interest, interest on qualified education loans, qualified residence interest, and investment interest. Business interest is fully deductible as an ordinary and necessary expense. Personal (consumer) interest is not deductible. This includes credit card interest, interest on car loans, and any other interest that is not interest on qualified education loans, business interest, qualified residence interest, or investment interest. Interest on qualified education loans, investment interest, and qualified residence (home mortgage) interest are deductible, subject to limits discussed below.

**Interest on Qualified Education Loans.**   Taxpayers who pay interest on a qualified education loan may deduct the interest as a deduction *for* AGI. A qualified education loan does not include indebtedness to certain related parties. The maximum deduction is $2,500. The deduction is phased out for taxpayers with modified AGI (MAGI) between $50,000 and $65,000 ($105,000 and $135,000 on joint returns). The deduction is not available for taxpayers who are claimed as dependents or for married taxpayers filing separately.[81]

**Investment Interest.**   Taxpayers frequently borrow funds that they use to acquire investment assets. When the interest expense is large relative to the income from the investments, substantial tax benefits could result. Congress has therefore limited the deductibility of interest on funds borrowed for the purpose of purchasing or continuing to hold investment property. **Investment interest** expense is limited to **net investment income** for the year.[82]

Investment income is gross income from interest, dividends (see below), annuities, and royalties not derived in the ordinary course of a trade or business. Income from a passive activity and income from a real estate activity in which the taxpayer actively participates are not included in investment income (see Chapter 5).

---

[81]§ 221. See § 221(b)(2)(C) for the definition of MAGI. The phaseout amounts are subject to adjustments for inflation. The $2,500 limitation and the phaseout amounts apply to tax returns for 2005. For

2004, the amounts were the same except for joint returns ($100,000 and $130,000).
[82]§ 163(d).

The following types of income are not included in investment income unless the taxpayer *elects* to do so.

- Net capital gain attributable to the disposition of (a) property producing the types of income just enumerated or (b) property held for investment purposes.
- Qualified dividends that are taxed at the same marginal rate that is applicable to a net capital gain.

A taxpayer may include net capital gains and qualified dividends as investment income by electing to do so. The election is available only if the taxpayer agrees to reduce amounts qualifying for the 15 percent (five percent for low income taxpayers) rates that otherwise apply to net capital gain (see Chapter 7) and qualified dividends (refer to Chapter 3) by an equivalent amount.

**EXAMPLE 52**

Terry incurred $13,000 of interest expense related to her investments during the year. Her investment income included $4,000 of interest, $2,000 of qualified dividends, and a $5,000 net capital gain on the sale of investment securities. If Terry does not make the election to include the net capital gain and qualified dividends in investment income, her investment income for purposes of computing the investment income limitation is $4,000 (interest income). If she does make the election, her investment income is $11,000 ($4,000 interest + $2,000 qualified dividends + $5,000 net capital gain). ■

Net investment income is the excess of investment income over investment expenses. Investment expenses are those deductible expenses directly connected with the production of investment income. Investment expenses do not include investment interest expense.

*Find more information on this topic at our Web site: **http://wft-entities.swlearning.com**.*

**Qualified Residence Interest.** **Qualified residence interest** is interest paid or accrued during the taxable year on indebtedness (subject to limitations) secured by any property that is a qualified residence of the taxpayer. Qualified residence interest falls into two categories: (1) interest on **acquisition indebtedness** and (2) interest on **home equity loans.** Before discussing each of these categories, however, the term *qualified residence* must be defined.

A qualified residence includes the taxpayer's principal residence and one other residence of the taxpayer or spouse. The principal residence is one that meets the requirement for nonrecognition of gain upon sale under § 121 (see Chapter 6). The one other residence, or second residence, refers to one that is used as a residence if not rented or, if rented, meets the requirements for a personal residence under the rental of vacation home rules. A taxpayer who has more than one second residence can make the selection each year of which one is the qualified second residence. A residence includes, in addition to a house in the ordinary sense, cooperative apartments, condominiums, and mobile homes and boats that have living quarters (sleeping accommodations and toilet and cooking facilities).

Although in most cases interest paid on a home mortgage is fully deductible, there are limitations.[83] Interest paid or accrued during the tax year on aggregate acquisition indebtedness of $1 million or less ($500,000 for married persons filing separate returns) is deductible as qualified residence interest. *Acquisition indebtedness* refers to amounts incurred in acquiring, constructing, or substantially improving a qualified residence of the taxpayer.

Qualified residence interest also includes interest on home equity loans. These loans utilize the personal residence of the taxpayer as security. Because the funds from home equity loans can be used for personal purposes (e.g., auto purchases,

---

[83]§ 163(h)(3).

medical expenses), what would otherwise have been nondeductible consumer interest becomes deductible qualified residence interest. However, interest is deductible only on the portion of a home equity loan that does not exceed the lesser of:

- The fair market value of the residence, reduced by the acquisition indebtedness, or
- $100,000 ($50,000 for married persons filing separate returns).

**EXAMPLE 53**

Larry owns a personal residence with a fair market value of $150,000 and an outstanding first mortgage of $120,000. Therefore, his equity in his home is $30,000 ($150,000 – $120,000). Larry issues a lien on the residence and in return borrows $15,000 to purchase a new family automobile. All interest on the $135,000 of debt is treated as qualified residence interest. ■

**EXAMPLE 54**

Leon and Pearl, married taxpayers, took out a mortgage on their home for $200,000 in 1989. In March of the current year, when the home has a fair market value of $400,000 and they owe $195,000 on the mortgage, Leon and Pearl take out a home equity loan for $120,000. They use the funds to purchase an airplane to be used for recreational purposes. On a joint return, Leon and Pearl can deduct all of the interest on the first mortgage since it is acquisition indebtedness. Of the $120,000 home equity loan, only the interest on the first $100,000 is deductible. The interest on the remaining $20,000 is not deductible because it exceeds the statutory ceiling of $100,000. ■

**Interest Paid for Services.**   Mortgage loan companies commonly charge a fee for finding, placing, or processing a mortgage loan. Such fees are often called **points** and are expressed as a percentage of the loan amount. Borrowers often have to pay points to obtain the necessary financing. To qualify as deductible interest, the points must be considered compensation to a lender solely for the use or forbearance of money. The points cannot be a form of service charge or payment for specific services if they are to qualify as deductible interest.[84]

Points must be capitalized and are amortized and deductible ratably over the life of the loan. A special exception permits the purchaser of a personal residence to deduct qualifying points in the year of payment.[85] The exception also covers points paid to obtain funds for home improvements.

**EXAMPLE 55**

During 2005, Thelma purchases a new residence for $130,000 and pays points of $2,600 to obtain mortgage financing. At Thelma's election, the $2,600 can be claimed as an interest deduction for 2005. ■

Points paid to refinance an existing home mortgage cannot be immediately expensed, but must be capitalized and amortized as interest expense over the life of the new loan.[86]

**EXAMPLE 56**

Sandra purchased her residence several years ago, obtaining a 30-year mortgage at an annual interest rate of 9%. In the current year, Sandra refinances the mortgage in order to reduce the interest rate to 6%. To obtain the refinancing, she has to pay points of $2,600. The $2,600 paid comes under the usual rule applicable to points. That is, the $2,600 must be capitalized and amortized over the life of the mortgage. ■

**Prepayment Penalty.**   When a mortgage or loan is paid off in full in a lump sum before its term, the lending institution may require an additional payment of a certain percentage applied to the unpaid amount at the time of prepayment. This is known as a prepayment penalty and is considered to be interest (e.g., personal,

[84]Rev.Rul. 67–297, 1967–2 C.B. 87.
[85]§ 461(g)(2).

[86]Rev.Rul. 87–22, 1987–1 C.B. 146.

## CONCEPT SUMMARY 15–3

### Deductibility of Personal, Education, Investment, and Mortgage Interest

| Type | Deductible | Comments |
|------|-----------|----------|
| Personal (consumer) interest | No | Includes any interest that is not home mortgage interest, interest on qualified education loans, investment interest, or business interest. Examples include car loans, credit cards, etc. |
| Qualified education interest | Yes | Deduction *for* AGI; subject to limitations. |
| Investment interest (*not* related to rental or royalty property) | Yes | Itemized deduction; limited to net investment income for the year; disallowed interest can be carried over to future years. |
| Investment interest (related to rental or royalty property) | Yes | Deduction *for* AGI; limited to net investment income for the year; disallowed interest can be carried over to future years. |
| Qualified residence interest on acquisition indebtedness | Yes | Deductible as an itemized deduction; limited to indebtedness of $1 million. |
| Qualified residence interest on home equity indebtedness | Yes | Deductible as an itemized deduction; limited to indebtedness equal to lesser of $100,000 or FMV of residence minus acquisition indebtedness. |

qualified residence, investment) in the year paid. The general rules for deductibility of interest also apply to prepayment penalties.

**Interest Paid to Related Parties.**   Nothing prevents the deduction of interest paid to a related party as long as the payment actually took place and the interest meets the requirements for deductibility. However, a special rule applies for related taxpayers when the debtor uses the accrual basis and the related creditor is on the cash basis. If this rule is applicable, interest that has been accrued but not paid at the end of the debtor's tax year is not deductible until payment is made and the income is reportable by the cash basis recipient.

**Tax-Exempt Securities.**   The tax law provides that no deduction is allowed for interest on debt incurred to purchase or carry tax-exempt securities.[87] A major problem for the courts has been to determine what is meant by the words "to purchase or carry." Refer to Chapter 4 for a detailed discussion of these issues.

**Prepaid Interest.**   Accrual method reporting is imposed on cash basis taxpayers for interest prepayments that extend beyond the end of the taxable year.[88] Such payments must be allocated to the tax years to which the interest payments relate. These provisions are intended to prevent cash basis taxpayers from *manufacturing* tax deductions before the end of the year by prepaying interest.

**Classification of Interest Expense.**   Whether interest is deductible *for* AGI or as an itemized deduction depends on whether the indebtedness has a business, investment, or personal purpose. If the indebtedness is incurred in relation to a business (other than performing services as an employee) or for the production of rent or royalty income, the interest is deductible *for* AGI. If the indebtedness is incurred for personal use, such as qualified residence interest, any deduction allowed is reported on Schedule A of Form 1040 if the taxpayer elects to itemize. If

[87]§ 265(a)(2).

[88]§ 461(g)(1).

the taxpayer is an employee who incurs debt in relation to his or her employment, the interest is considered to be personal, or consumer, interest. Business expenses appear on Schedule C of Form 1040, and expenses related to rents or royalties are reported on Schedule E.

## CHARITABLE CONTRIBUTIONS

As noted in Chapter 4, individuals are allowed to deduct contributions made to qualified domestic organizations.[89] Contributions to qualified charitable organizations serve certain social welfare needs and thus relieve the government of the cost of providing these needed services to the community.

**Criteria for a Gift.**   A **charitable contribution** is defined as a gift made to a qualified organization.[90] The major elements needed to qualify a contribution as a gift are a donative intent, the absence of consideration, and acceptance by the donee. Consequently, the taxpayer has the burden of establishing that the transfer was made from motives of disinterested generosity as established by the courts.[91] This test is quite subjective and has led to problems of interpretation (refer to the discussion of gifts in Chapter 3).

**Benefit Received Rule.**   When a donor derives a tangible benefit from a contribution, he or she cannot deduct the value of the benefit.

*E X A M P L E   5 7*

Ralph purchases a ticket at $100 for a special performance of the local symphony (a qualified charity). If the price of a ticket to a symphony concert is normally $35, Ralph is allowed only $65 as a charitable contribution. ▪

An exception to this benefit rule provides for the deduction of an automatic percentage of the amount paid for the right to purchase athletic tickets from colleges and universities.[92] Under this exception, 80 percent of the amount paid to or for the benefit of the institution qualifies as a charitable contribution deduction.

**Contribution of Services.**   No deduction is allowed for the value of one's services contributed to a qualified charitable organization. However, unreimbursed expenses related to the services rendered may be deductible. For example, the cost of a uniform (without general utility) that is required to be worn while performing services may be deductible, as are certain out-of-pocket transportation costs incurred for the benefit of the charity. In lieu of these out-of-pocket costs for an automobile, a standard mileage rate of 14 cents per mile is allowed.[93] Deductions are permitted for transportation, reasonable expenses for lodging, and the cost of meals while away from home incurred in performing the donated services. The travel expenses are not deductible if the travel involves a significant element of personal pleasure, recreation, or vacation.[94]

**Nondeductible Items.**   In addition to the benefit received rule and the restrictions placed on contribution of services, the following items may not be deducted as charitable contributions:

- Dues, fees, or bills paid to country clubs, lodges, fraternal orders, or similar groups.
- Cost of raffle, bingo, or lottery tickets.

---

[89]§ 170.
[90]§ 170(c).
[91]*Comm. v. Duberstein,* 60–2 USTC ¶9515, 5 AFTR2d 1626, 80 S.Ct. 1190 (USSC, 1960).

[92]§ 170(l).
[93]§ 170(i).
[94]§ 170(j).

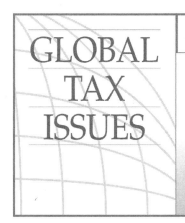

**CHOOSE THE CHARITY WISELY**

Ibrahim, a U.S. citizen of Turkish descent, was distressed by the damage caused by a major earthquake in Turkey. He donated $100,000 to the Earthquake Victims' Relief Fund, a Turkish charitable organization that was set up to help victims of the earthquake. Ahmed, also a U.S. citizen of Turkish descent, donated $200,000 to help with the relief effort. However, Ahmed's contribution went to his mosque, which sent the proceeds of a fund drive to the Earthquake Victims' Relief Fund in Turkey. Ibrahim's contribution is not deductible, but Ahmed's is. Why? Contributions to charitable organizations are not deductible unless the organization is a U.S. charity.

* Cost of tuition.
* Value of blood given to a blood bank.
* Donations to homeowners associations.
* Gifts to individuals.
* Rental value of property used by a qualified charity.

**Time of Deduction.**   A charitable contribution generally is deducted in the year the payment is made. This rule applies to both cash and accrual basis individuals. A contribution is ordinarily deemed to have been made on the date of delivery of the property to the donee. A contribution made by check is considered delivered on the date of mailing. Thus, a check mailed on December 31, 2005, is deductible on the taxpayer's 2005 tax return. If the contribution is charged on a bank credit card, the date the charge is made determines the year of deduction.

**Record-Keeping Requirements.**   No deduction is allowed for contributions of $250 or more unless the taxpayer obtains written substantiation of the contribution from the charitable organization. Additional information is required if the value of the donated property is over $500 but not over $5,000. For noncash contributions with a claimed value in excess of $5,000 ($10,000 in the case of nonpublicly traded stock), the taxpayer must obtain a qualified appraisal. Failure to comply with these reporting rules may result in disallowance of the charitable contribution deduction.[95]

*Find more information on this topic at our Web site: **http://wft-entities.swlearning.com**.*

**Valuation Requirements.**   Property donated to a charity is generally valued at fair market value at the time the gift is made. The Code and Regulations give very little guidance on the measurement of the fair market value except to say, "The fair market value is the price at which the property would change hands between a willing buyer and a willing seller, neither being under any compulsion to buy or sell and both having reasonable knowledge of relevant facts."

Generally, charitable organizations do not attest to the fair market value of the donated property. Nevertheless, the taxpayer must maintain reliable written evidence as to its value.

*Find more information on this topic at our Web site: **http://wft-entities.swlearning.com**.*

---

[95]The amounts discussed in this section ($250, $500, $5,000, and $10,000) apply to 2004 tax returns. Amounts for 2005 had not been announced at the time of this writing.

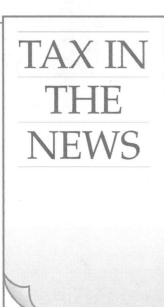

## TAX IN THE NEWS

### SPRING CLEANING AND CHARITABLE CONTRIBUTIONS

Two events that are usually unrelated normally occur in the spring: people clean their houses and file their tax returns. Spring housecleaning can result in a tax deduction for those who donate their unneeded items to charity. Taxpayers can load their old clothes in bags and take them to Goodwill or the Salvation Army. Instead of throwing away old furniture and appliances, these items can be donated to Empty Tomb or Habitat for Humanity. Such generosity can result in a substantial tax deduction. First, however, the taxpayer will have to determine how much to deduct. How much are old clothes worth? What value should be placed on a used sofa?

A prominent software company has created a product to help taxpayers solve the valuation problem. Based on numerous visits to thrift shops around the country, the developer of the software has compiled a list of values for almost 1,000 clothing and household items. Purchasers of the software can purchase an audit protection warranty. If the IRS denies values based on the use of the product, the warranty covers any related penalties and interest.

**Limitations on Charitable Contribution Deduction.**   The potential charitable contribution deduction is the total of all donations, both money and property, that qualify for the deduction. After this determination is made, the actual amount of the charitable contribution deduction that is allowed for individuals for the tax year is limited as follows:

- If the qualifying contributions for the year total 20 percent or less of AGI, they are fully deductible.
- If the qualifying contributions are more than 20 percent of AGI, the deductible amount may be limited to either 20 percent, 30 percent, or 50 percent of AGI, depending on the type of property given and the type of organization to which the donation is made.
- In any case, the maximum charitable contribution deduction may not exceed 50 percent of AGI for the tax year.

To understand the complex rules for computing the amount of a charitable contribution, it is necessary to understand the distinction between **capital gain property** and **ordinary income property.** These rules, which were discussed in Chapter 4, are summarized in Concept Summary 15–4.

In addition, it is necessary to understand when the 50 percent, 30 percent, and 20 percent limitations apply. If a taxpayer's contributions for the year exceed the applicable percentage limitations, the excess contributions may be carried forward and deducted during a five-year carryover period. These topics are discussed in the sections that follow.

**Fifty Percent Ceiling.**   Contributions made to public charities may not exceed 50 percent of an individual's AGI for the year. Excess contributions may be carried over to the next five years.[96] The 50 percent ceiling on contributions applies to the following types of public charities:

---

[96]§ 170(d); Reg. § 1.170A–10.

## CONCEPT SUMMARY 15–4

### Determining the Deduction for Contributions of Property by Individuals

| If the Type of Property Contributed Is: | And the Property Is Contributed to: | The Contribution Is Measured by: | But the Deduction Is Limited to: |
|---|---|---|---|
| Capital gain property | A 50% organization | Fair market value of the property | 30% of AGI |
| Ordinary income property | A 50% organization | The basis of the property* | 50% of AGI |
| Capital gain property (and the property is tangible personal property put to an unrelated use by the donee) | A 50% organization | The basis of the property* | 50% of AGI |
| Capital gain property (and the reduced deduction is elected) | A 50% organization | The basis of the property | 50% of AGI |
| Capital gain property | A private nonoperating foundation that is not a 50% organization | The basis of the property* | The lesser of: 1. 20% of AGI 2. 50% of AGI minus other contributions to 50% organizations |
| Ordinary income property | A private nonoperating foundation that is not a 50% organization | The basis of the property* | 30% of AGI |

*If the FMV of the property is less than the adjusted basis (i.e., the property has declined in value instead of appreciating), the FMV is used.

- A church or a convention or association of churches.
- An educational organization that maintains a regular faculty and curriculum.
- A hospital or medical school.
- An organization supported by the government that holds property or investments for the benefit of a college or university.
- A Federal, state, or local governmental unit.
- An organization normally receiving a substantial part of its support from the public or a governmental unit.

The 50 percent ceiling also applies to contributions to the following organizations:

- All private operating foundations.
- Certain private nonoperating foundations that distribute the contributions they receive to public charities and private operating foundations within two and one-half months following the year they receive the contributions.
- Certain private nonoperating foundations in which the contributions are pooled in a common fund and the income and principal sum are paid to public charities.

In the remaining discussion of charitable contributions, public charities and private foundations (both operating and nonoperating) that qualify for the 50 percent ceiling will be referred to as 50 percent organizations.

**Thirty Percent Ceiling.** A 30 percent ceiling applies to contributions of cash and ordinary income property to private nonoperating foundations that are not

50 percent organizations. The 30 percent ceiling also applies to contributions of appreciated capital gain property to 50 percent organizations unless the taxpayer makes a special election (see Example 59 below).

In the event the contributions for any one tax year involve both 50 percent and 30 percent property, the allowable deduction comes first from the 50 percent property.

**EXAMPLE 58**

During the year, Lisa makes the following donations to her church: cash of $2,000 and unimproved land worth $30,000. Lisa had purchased the land four years ago for $22,000 and held it as an investment. Therefore, it is long-term capital gain property. Lisa's AGI for the year is $60,000. Disregarding percentage limitations, Lisa's potential deduction is $32,000 [$2,000 (cash) + $30,000 (fair market value of land)].

In applying the percentage limitations, however, the current deduction for the land is limited to $18,000 [30% (limitation applicable to long-term capital gain property) × $60,000 (AGI)]. Thus, the total deduction is $20,000 ($2,000 cash + $18,000 land). Note that the total deduction does not exceed $30,000, which is 50% of Lisa's AGI. ■

Under a special election, a taxpayer may choose to forgo a deduction of the appreciation on capital gain property. Referred to as the reduced deduction election, this enables the taxpayer to move from the 30 percent limitation to the 50 percent limitation.

**EXAMPLE 59**

Assume the same facts as in Example 58, except that Lisa makes the reduced deduction election. Now the deduction becomes $24,000 [$2,000 (cash) + $22,000 (basis in land)] because both donations fall under the 50% limitation. Thus, by making the election, Lisa has increased her current charitable contribution deduction by $4,000 [$24,000 − $20,000 (Example 58)]. ■

Although the reduced deduction election appears attractive, it should be considered carefully. The election sacrifices a deduction for the appreciation on long-term capital gain property that might eventually be allowed. Note that in Example 58, the potential deduction was $32,000, yet in Example 59 only $24,000 is allowed. The reason the potential deduction is decreased by $8,000 ($32,000 − $24,000) is that no carryover is allowed for the amount sacrificed by the election.

**Twenty Percent Ceiling.**    A 20 percent ceiling applies to contributions of appreciated long-term capital gain property to private nonoperating foundations that are not 50 percent organizations. Also, recall from Chapter 4 that only the basis of the contributed property is allowed as a deduction.

**Contribution Carryovers.**    Contributions that exceed the percentage limitations for the current year can be carried over for five years. In the carryover process, such contributions do not lose their identity for limitation purposes. Thus, if the contribution originally involved 30 percent property, the carryover will continue to be classified as 30 percent property in the carryover year.

**EXAMPLE 60**

Assume the same facts as in Example 58. Because only $18,000 of the $30,000 value of the land is deducted in the current year, the balance of $12,000 may be carried over to the following year. But the carryover will still be treated as long-term capital gain property and will be subject to the 30%-of-AGI limitation. ■

In applying the percentage limitations, current charitable contributions must be claimed first before any carryovers can be considered. If carryovers involve more than one year, they are utilized in a first-in, first-out order.

## MISCELLANEOUS ITEMIZED DEDUCTIONS SUBJECT TO TWO PERCENT FLOOR

No deduction is allowed for personal, living, or family expenses.[97] However, a taxpayer may incur a number of expenditures related to employment. If an employee or outside salesperson incurs unreimbursed business expenses or expenses that are reimbursed under a nonaccountable plan (see Chapter 16), including travel and transportation, the expenses are deductible as **miscellaneous itemized deductions.**[98] Certain other expenses also fall into the special category of miscellaneous itemized deductions. Some are deductible only to the extent they exceed 2 percent of the taxpayer's AGI. These miscellaneous itemized deductions include the following:

- Professional dues to membership organizations.
- Uniforms or other clothing that cannot be used for normal wear.
- Fees incurred for the preparation of one's tax return or fees incurred for tax litigation before the IRS or the courts.
- Job-hunting costs.
- Fee paid for a safe deposit box used to store papers and documents relating to taxable income-producing investments.
- Investment expenses that are deductible under § 212 as discussed previously in this chapter.
- Appraisal fees to determine the amount of a casualty loss or the fair market value of donated property.
- Hobby losses up to the amount of hobby income (see Chapter 16).
- Unreimbursed employee expenses (see Chapter 16).

Certain employee business expenses that are reimbursed are not itemized deductions, but are deducted *for* AGI. Employee business expenses are discussed in depth in Chapter 16.

## OTHER MISCELLANEOUS DEDUCTIONS

Certain expenses and losses do not fall into any category of itemized deductions already discussed but are nonetheless deductible. The following expenses and losses are deductible on Schedule A as Other Miscellaneous Deductions:

- Gambling losses up to the amount of gambling winnings.
- Impairment-related work expenses of a handicapped person.
- Federal estate tax on income in respect of a decedent.
- Deduction for repayment of amounts under a claim of right if more than $3,000.

Unlike the expenses and losses discussed previously under Miscellaneous Itemized Deductions, the above expenses and losses are not subject to the 2 percent-of-AGI floor.

## OVERALL LIMITATION ON CERTAIN ITEMIZED DEDUCTIONS

Congress has enacted several provisions limiting tax benefits for high-income taxpayers. These limitations include the exemption phaseout (discussed earlier in this chapter) and a phaseout of itemized deductions. For 2005, the phaseout of itemized deductions (also referred to as a *cutback adjustment*) applies to taxpayers whose AGI

---

[97]§ 262.
[98]Actors and performing artists who meet certain requirements are not subject to this rule.

exceeds $145,950 ($72,975 for married taxpayers filing separately).[99] The limitation applies to the following frequently encountered itemized deductions:[100]

- Taxes.
- Home mortgage interest, including points.
- Charitable contributions.
- Unreimbursed employee expenses subject to the 2 percent-of-AGI floor.
- All other expenses subject to the 2 percent-of-AGI floor.

The following deductions are *not* subject to the limitation on itemized deductions:

- Medical and dental expenses.
- Investment interest expense.
- Nonbusiness casualty and theft losses.
- Gambling losses.

Taxpayers subject to the limitation must reduce itemized deductions by the lesser of:

- 3 percent of the amount by which AGI exceeds $145,950 ($72,975 if married filing separately).
- 80 percent of itemized deductions that are affected by the limit.

The overall limitation is applied after applying all other limitations to itemized deductions that are affected by the overall limitation. Other limitations apply to charitable contributions, certain meals and entertainment expenses, and certain miscellaneous itemized deductions.

**EXAMPLE 61**

Herman, who is single, had AGI of $200,000 for 2005. He incurred the following expenses and losses during the year:

| | |
|---|---:|
| Medical expenses before the 7.5%-of-AGI limitation | $16,000 |
| State and local income taxes | 3,200 |
| Real estate taxes | 2,800 |
| Home mortgage interest | 7,200 |
| Charitable contributions | 2,000 |
| Casualty loss (after $100 floor, before 10%-of-AGI limitation) | 21,500 |
| Unreimbursed employee expenses subject to 2%-of-AGI limitation | 4,300 |
| Gambling losses (Herman had $3,000 gambling income) | 7,000 |

Herman's itemized deductions before the overall limitation are computed as follows:

| | |
|---|---:|
| Medical expenses [$16,000 − (7.5% × $200,000)] | $ 1,000 |
| State and local income taxes | 3,200 |
| Real estate taxes | 2,800 |
| Home mortgage interest | 7,200 |
| Charitable contributions | 2,000 |
| Casualty loss [$21,500 − (10% × $200,000)] | 1,500 |
| Unreimbursed employee expenses [$4,300 − (2% × $200,000)] | 300 |
| Gambling losses (limited to $3,000 of gambling income) | 3,000 |
| Total itemized deductions before overall limitation | $21,000 |

[99]For 2004, the limitation applied if AGI exceeded $142,700 ($71,350 for married taxpayers filing separately). The overall limitation applicable to itemized deductions will be phased out over a four-year period, beginning in 2006. The limitation will no longer exist for taxable years beginning after 2009.

[100]Other deductions subject to the limitation include Federal estate tax on income in respect of a decedent, certain amortizable bond premiums, the deduction for repayment of certain amounts, certain unrecovered investments in an annuity, and impairment-related work expenses.

Herman's itemized deductions subject to the overall limitation are as follows:

| | |
|---|---:|
| State and local income taxes | $ 3,200 |
| Real estate taxes | 2,800 |
| Home mortgage interest | 7,200 |
| Charitable contributions | 2,000 |
| Unreimbursed employee expenses | 300 |
| Total itemized deductions before overall limitation | $15,500 |

Herman must reduce this amount by the smaller of the following:

| | |
|---|---:|
| • 3% ($200,000 AGI – $145,950) | $ 1,622 |
| • 80% of itemized deductions subject to limitation ($15,500 × 80%) | 12,400 |

Therefore, the amount of the reduction is $1,622, and Herman has $19,378 of deductible itemized deductions, computed as follows:

| | |
|---|---:|
| Deductible itemized deductions subject to overall limitation ($15,500 – $1,622) | $13,878 |
| Itemized deductions not subject to overall limitation: | |
| Medical expenses | 1,000 |
| Casualty loss | 1,500 |
| Gambling losses | 3,000 |
| Deductible itemized deductions | $19,378 |

**PLANNING STRATEGIES**

## Effective Utilization of Itemized Deductions

**FRAMEWORK FOCUS: DEDUCTIONS**

**STRATEGY ➤ MAXIMIZE DEDUCTIBLE AMOUNTS.**

An individual may use the standard deduction in one year and itemize deductions in another year. Therefore, it is frequently possible to obtain maximum benefit by shifting itemized deductions from one year to another. For example, if a taxpayer's itemized deductions and the standard deduction are approximately the same for each year of a two-year period, the taxpayer should use the standard deduction in one year and shift itemized deductions (to the extent permitted by law) to the other year. The individual could, for example, prepay a church pledge for a particular year or avoid paying end-of-the-year medical expenses to shift the deduction to the following year.

**LO.8**

Understand the adoption expenses credit, child tax credit, education tax credits, credit for child and dependent care expenses, and earned income credit.

# Individual Tax Credits

## ADOPTION EXPENSES CREDIT

Adoption expenses paid or incurred by a taxpayer may give rise to the **adoption expenses credit**.[101] The provision is intended to assist taxpayers who incur nonrecurring costs directly associated with the adoption process, such as adoption fees, attorney fees, court costs, social service review costs, and transportation costs.

---

[101]§ 23.

In 2005, up to $10,630 of costs incurred to adopt an eligible child qualify for the credit. An eligible child is one who is:

* under 18 years of age at the time of the adoption, or
* physically or mentally incapable of taking care of himself or herself.

A taxpayer may claim the credit in the year qualifying expenses were paid or incurred if they were paid or incurred during or after the tax year in which the adoption was finalized. For qualifying expenses paid or incurred in a tax year prior to the year when the adoption was finalized, the credit must be claimed in the tax year following the tax year during which the expenses are paid or incurred. A married couple must file a joint return in order to claim the credit.

**EXAMPLE 62**

In late 2004, Sam and Martha pay $4,000 in legal fees, adoption fees, and other expenses directly related to the adoption of an infant daughter, Susan. In 2005, the year in which the adoption becomes final, they pay an additional $8,000. Sam and Martha are eligible for a $10,630 credit in 2005 (for expenses, limited by the $10,630 ceiling, paid in 2004 and 2005). ■

The amount of the credit that is otherwise available is subject to phaseout for taxpayers whose AGI (modified for this purpose) exceeds $159,450 in 2005, and is phased out completely when AGI reaches $199,450. The resulting credit is calculated by reducing the allowable credit (determined without this reduction) by the amount determined using the following formula:

$$\text{Allowable credit} \times \frac{\text{AGI} - \$159,450}{\$40,000}$$

**EXAMPLE 63**

Assume the same facts as in the previous example, except that Sam and Martha's AGI is $184,450 in 2005. As a result, their available credit in 2005 is reduced from $10,630 to $3,986 {$10,630 − [$10,630 × ($25,000/$40,000)]}. ■

The credit is nonrefundable and is available to taxpayers only in a year in which this credit and the other nonrefundable credits do not exceed the taxpayer's tax liability. However, any unused adoption expenses credit may be carried over for up to five years, being utilized on a first-in, first-out basis.

## CHILD TAX CREDIT

The **child tax credit** provision allows individual taxpayers to take a tax credit based solely on the *number* of their qualifying children. This credit is one of several "family-friendly" provisions that currently are part of our tax law. To be eligible for the credit, the child must be under age 17, a U.S. citizen, and claimed as a dependent on the taxpayer's return.

**Maximum Credit and Phaseouts.**   Under current law, the maximum credit available is $1,000 per child.[102] The available credit is phased out for higher-income taxpayers beginning when AGI reaches $110,000 for joint filers ($55,000 for married taxpayers filing separately) and $75,000 for single taxpayers. The credit is phased out by $50 for each $1,000 (or part thereof) of AGI above the threshold amounts.[103] Since the maximum credit available to taxpayers depends on the number of qualifying children, the income level at which the credit is phased out completely also depends on the number of children qualifying for the credit.

---

[102]§ 24. The maximum credit per child is scheduled to remain at $1,000 through 2010.

[103]AGI is modified for purposes of this calculation. The threshold amounts are *not* indexed for inflation. See §§ 24(a) and (b).

**EXAMPLE 64**

Juanita and Alberto are married and file a joint tax return claiming their two children, ages six and eight, as dependents. Their AGI is $122,400. Juanita and Alberto's available child tax credit is $1,350, computed as their maximum credit of $2,000 ($1,000 × 2 children) reduced by a $650 phaseout. Since Juanita and Alberto's AGI is in excess of the $110,000 threshold, the maximum credit must be reduced by $50 for every $1,000 (or part thereof) above the threshold amount {$50 × [($122,400 − $110,000)/$1,000]}. Thus, the credit reduction equals $650 [$50 × 13 (rounded up from 12.4)]. Therefore, Juanita and Alberto's child tax credit is $1,350. ■

## CREDIT FOR CHILD AND DEPENDENT CARE EXPENSES

A credit is allowed to taxpayers who incur employment-related expenses for child or dependent care.[104] The **credit for child and dependent care expenses** is a specified percentage of expenses incurred to enable the taxpayer to work or to seek employment. Expenses on which the credit for child and dependent care expenses is based are subject to limitations.

**Eligibility.**   To be eligible for the credit, an individual must have either of the following:

* A dependent under age 13.
* A dependent or spouse who is physically or mentally incapacitated and who lives with the taxpayer for more than one-half of the year.

Generally, married taxpayers must file a joint return to obtain the credit.

**Eligible Employment-Related Expenses.**   Eligible expenses include amounts paid for household services and care of a qualifying individual that are incurred to enable the taxpayer to be employed. Child and dependent care expenses include expenses incurred in the home, such as payments for a housekeeper. Out-of-the-home expenses incurred for the care of a dependent under the age of 13 also qualify for the credit. In addition, out-of-the-home expenses incurred for an older dependent or spouse who is physically or mentally incapacitated qualify for the credit if that person regularly spends at least eight hours each day in the taxpayer's household. This makes the credit available to taxpayers who keep handicapped older children and elderly relatives in the home instead of institutionalizing them. Out-of-the-home expenses incurred for services provided by a dependent care center will qualify only if the center complies with all applicable laws and regulations of a state or unit of local government.

Child care payments to a relative are eligible for the credit unless the relative is a child (under age 19) of the taxpayer.

**Earned Income Ceiling.**   The total for qualifying employment-related expenses is limited to an individual's earned income. For married taxpayers, this limitation applies to the spouse with the lesser amount of earned income. Special rules are provided for taxpayers with nonworking spouses who are disabled or are full-time students. If a nonworking spouse is physically or mentally disabled or is a full-time student, he or she is deemed to have earned income for purposes of this limitation. The deemed amount is $250 per month if there is one qualifying individual in the household or $500 per month if there are two or more qualifying individuals in the household. In the case of a student-spouse, the student's income is deemed to be earned only for the months that the student is enrolled on a full-time basis at an educational institution.[105]

---

[104]§ 21.

[105]§ 21(d).

**Calculation of the Credit.**   In general, the credit is equal to a percentage of unreimbursed employment-related expenses up to $3,000 for one qualifying individual and $6,000 for two or more individuals. The credit rate varies between 20 percent and 35 percent, depending on the taxpayer's AGI. The following chart shows the applicable percentage for taxpayers as AGI increases:

| **Adjusted Gross Income** | | |
| --- | --- | --- |
| **Over** | **But Not Over** | **Applicable Rate of Credit** |
| $     0 | $15,000 | 35% |
| 15,000 | 17,000 | 34% |
| 17,000 | 19,000 | 33% |
| 19,000 | 21,000 | 32% |
| 21,000 | 23,000 | 31% |
| 23,000 | 25,000 | 30% |
| 25,000 | 27,000 | 29% |
| 27,000 | 29,000 | 28% |
| 29,000 | 31,000 | 27% |
| 31,000 | 33,000 | 26% |
| 33,000 | 35,000 | 25% |
| 35,000 | 37,000 | 24% |
| 37,000 | 39,000 | 23% |
| 39,000 | 41,000 | 22% |
| 41,000 | 43,000 | 21% |
| 43,000 | No limit | 20% |

**EXAMPLE 65**

Nancy, who has two children under age 13, worked full-time while her spouse, Ron, attended college for 10 months during the year. Nancy earned $22,000 and incurred $6,200 of child care expenses. Ron is deemed to be fully employed and to have earned $500 for each of the 10 months (or a total of $5,000). Since Nancy and Ron have AGI of $22,000, they are allowed a credit rate of 31%. Nancy and Ron are limited to $5,000 in qualified child care expenses (the lesser of $6,000 or $5,000). Therefore, they are entitled to a tax credit of $1,550 (31% × $5,000) for the year. ■

## EDUCATION TAX CREDITS

The **HOPE scholarship credit** and the **lifetime learning credit**[106] are available to help qualifying low- and middle-income individuals defray the cost of higher education. The credits, both of which are nonrefundable, are available for qualifying tuition and related expenses incurred by students pursuing undergraduate or graduate degrees or vocational training. Room, board, and book costs are ineligible for the credits.

**Maximum Credit.**   The HOPE scholarship credit permits a maximum credit of $1,500 per year (100 percent of the first $1,000 of tuition expenses plus 50 percent of the next $1,000 of tuition expenses) for the *first two years* of postsecondary

---

[106]§ 25A.

education.[107] The lifetime learning credit permits a credit of 20 percent of qualifying expenses (up to $10,000 per year) incurred in a year in which the HOPE scholarship credit is not claimed with respect to a given student. Generally, the lifetime learning credit is used for individuals who are beyond the first two years of postsecondary education.

**Eligible Individuals.**   Both education credits are available for qualified expenses incurred by a taxpayer, taxpayer's spouse, or taxpayer's dependent. The HOPE scholarship credit is available per eligible student, while the lifetime learning credit is calculated per taxpayer. To be eligible for the HOPE scholarship credit, a student must take at least one-half the full-time course load for at least one academic term at a qualifying educational institution. No comparable requirement exists for the lifetime learning credit. Therefore, taxpayers who are seeking new job skills or maintaining existing skills through graduate training or continuing education are eligible for the lifetime learning credit. Taxpayers who are married must file joint returns in order to claim either education credit.

**Income Limitations.**   Both education credits are subject to income limitations and are combined for purposes of the limitation calculation. The allowable credit amount is phased out, beginning when the taxpayer's AGI reaches $43,000 ($87,000 for married taxpayers filing jointly). The reduction in 2005 is equal to the extent to which AGI exceeds $43,000 ($87,000 for married filing jointly) as a percentage of the $10,000 ($20,000 for married filing jointly) phaseout range. The credits are completely eliminated when AGI reaches $53,000 ($107,000 for married filing jointly).

**EXAMPLE 66**

Dean and Audry are married, file a joint tax return, have modified AGI under $87,000 and have two children, Raymond and Kelsey. During fall 2005, Raymond is beginning his freshman year at State University, and Kelsey is beginning her senior year. During the prior semester, Kelsey completed her junior year. Both Raymond and Kelsey are full-time students and may be claimed as dependents on their parents' tax return. Raymond's qualifying expenses total $4,300 for the fall semester while Kelsey's qualifying expenses total $10,200 for the prior and current semesters. For 2005, Dean and Audry may claim a $1,500 HOPE scholarship credit [(100% × $1,000) + (50% × $1,000)] relating to Raymond's expenses and a $2,000 lifetime learning credit (20% × $10,000) relating to Kelsey's expenses. Kelsey's tuition expenses are ineligible for the HOPE scholarship credit because she is beyond her first two years of postsecondary education. ■

**EXAMPLE 67**

Assume the same facts as in Example 66, except that Dean and Audry's modified AGI for 2005 is $99,000. Dean and Audry are eligible to claim $1,400 in total education credits for 2005. Their available credits totaling $3,500 ($1,500 HOPE scholarship credit + $2,000 lifetime learning credit) must be reduced because their AGI exceeds the $87,000 limit for married taxpayers. The percentage reduction is computed as the amount by which modified AGI exceeds the limit, expressed as a percentage of the phaseout range, or [($99,000 − $87,000)/$20,000], resulting in a 60% reduction. Therefore, the maximum available credit for 2005 is $1,400 ($3,500 × 40% allowable portion). ■

**Restrictions on Double Tax Benefit.**   Taxpayers are prohibited from receiving a double tax benefit associated with qualifying educational expenses. Therefore,

---

[107]The $1,000 qualifying expense base for the HOPE scholarship credit is subject to inflation adjustment. The base was $1,000 for 2004 and remains at the same level for 2005.

taxpayers who claim an education credit may not deduct the expenses, nor may they claim the credit for amounts that are otherwise excluded from gross income (e.g., scholarships, employer-paid educational assistance). However, a taxpayer may claim an education tax credit and exclude from gross income amounts distributed from a Coverdell Education Savings Account (CESA) as long as the distribution is not used for the same expenses for which the credit is claimed.

## EARNED INCOME CREDIT

The **earned income credit,** which has been a part of the law for many years, has been justified as a means of providing tax equity to the working poor. In addition, the credit has been designed to help offset regressive taxes that are a part of our tax system, such as the gasoline and Social Security taxes. Further, the credit is intended to encourage economically disadvantaged individuals to become contributing members of the workforce.[108]

**Eligibility Requirements.**   Eligibility for the credit may depend not only on the taxpayer meeting the earned income and AGI thresholds, but also on whether he or she has a qualifying child. The term *qualifying child* generally has the same meaning here as it does for purposes of determining who qualifies as a dependent.

In addition to being available for taxpayers with qualifying children, the earned income credit is also available to certain workers without children. However, this provision is available only to such taxpayers aged 25 through 64 who cannot be claimed as a dependent on another taxpayer's return.

**Amount of the Credit.**   In 2005, the earned income credit is determined by multiplying a maximum amount of earned income by the appropriate credit percentage. Generally, earned income includes employee compensation and net earnings from self-employment but excludes items such as interest, dividends, pension benefits, nontaxable employee compensation, and alimony. If a taxpayer has children, the credit percentage used in the calculation depends on the number of qualifying children. Thus, in 2005, the maximum earned income credit for a taxpayer with one qualifying child is $2,662 ($7,830 × 34%) and $4,400 ($11,000 × 40%) for a taxpayer with two or more qualifying children. However, the maximum earned income credit is phased out completely if the taxpayer's earned income or AGI exceeds certain thresholds. To the extent that the greater of earned income or AGI exceeds $16,370 in 2005 for married taxpayers filing a joint return ($14,370 for other taxpayers), the difference, multiplied by the appropriate phaseout percentage, is subtracted from the maximum earned income credit.

It is not necessary for the taxpayer to actually compute the earned income credit. To simplify the compliance process, the IRS issues an Earned Income Credit Table for the determination of the appropriate amount of the credit. This table and a worksheet are included in the instructions available to individual taxpayers.

**Advance Payment.**   The earned income credit is a form of negative income tax (a refundable credit for taxpayers who do not have a tax liability). An eligible individual may elect to receive advance payments of the earned income credit from his or her employer (rather than receiving the credit from the IRS upon filing the tax return). The amount that can be received in advance is limited to 60 percent of the credit that is available to a taxpayer with only one qualifying child. If this election is made, the taxpayer must file a certificate of eligibility (Form W–5) with his or her employer and must file a tax return for the year the income is earned.

---

[108]§ 32. This credit is subject to indexation.

# Suggested Further Readings

Ellen D. Cook, "Innocent Spouse Provisions Evolve as IRS Clarifies Equitable Relief," *Practical Tax Strategies,* October 2004, pp. 196–209.

Karyn Bybee Friske and Darlene Pulliam, "The Marriage Penalty after the JGTRRA," *The Tax Adviser,* May 2004, pp. 284–288.

David Lavin, Myron S. Lubell, and Angela F. Moree, "Tax Savings Ease the Task of Saving for College Tuition," *Practical Tax Strategies,* May 2004, pp. 283–297.

Jill M. Lockwood and Leslie B. Fletcher, "An Array of Rules Govern Charitable Contributions," *Practical Tax Strategies,* February 2004, pp. 87–98.

Susan L. Megaard, "Recent Rulings Expand Definition of Medical Care But Tax Benefits May Remain Limited for Many," *Journal of Taxation,* July 2003, pp. 38–44.

## KEY TERMS

Accident and health insurance benefits, 15–34

Acquisition indebtedness, 15–43

Adoption expenses credit, 15–53

Alimony and separate maintenance payments, 15–28

Capital gain property, 15–48

Charitable contribution, 15–46

Child tax credit, 15–54

Compensatory damages, 15–32

Credit for child and dependent care expenses, 15–55

Dependency exemption, 15–11

Earned income credit, 15–58

Educational savings bonds, 15–34

e-file, 15–23

Gift, 15–30

Head of household, 15–26

Health Savings Accounts (HSAs), 15–38

Home equity loans, 15–43

HOPE scholarship credit, 15–56

Investment interest, 15–42

Itemized deductions, 15–7

Kiddie tax, 15–21

Lifetime learning credit, 15–56

Marriage penalty, 15–26

Medical expenses, 15–35

Miscellaneous itemized deductions, 15–51

Multiple support agreement, 15–11

Net investment income, 15–42

Ordinary income property, 15–48

Personal exemption, 15–10

Points, 15–44

Punitive damages, 15–32

Qualified residence interest, 15–43

Qualifying child, 15–14

Qualifying relative, 15–16

Scholarship, 15–31

Standard deduction, 15–7

Surviving spouse, 15–26

Tax Rate Schedules, 15–18

Tax Table, 15–18

Unearned income, 15–21

## PROBLEM MATERIALS

### Problems

1. Compute the taxable income for 2005 in each of the following independent situations:
   a. Sidney and Cora, ages 39 and 37, are married and file a joint return. In addition to two dependent children, they have AGI of $55,000 and itemized deductions of $8,300.
   b. Kay, age 66, is unmarried and supports her two dependent parents who live in their own home. She has AGI of $70,000 and itemized deductions of $8,100.
   c. Colin, age 60, is an abandoned spouse. The household he maintains includes two unmarried stepdaughters, ages 16 and 17, who qualify as his dependents. He has AGI of $81,000 and itemized deductions of $7,900.

d. Angel, age 33, is a surviving spouse and maintains a household for her four dependent children. She has AGI of $48,000 and itemized deductions of $8,200.

e. Dale, age 42, is divorced but maintains the home in which he and his daughter, Jill, live. Jill is single and qualifies as Dale's dependent. Dale has AGI of $54,000 and itemized deductions of $6,900.

2. Compute the taxable income for 2005 for Quincy on the basis of the following information. His filing status is head of household.

| | |
|---|---:|
| Salary | $40,000 |
| Interest income from bonds issued by General Motors Corporation | 1,200 |
| Child support payments made | 3,600 |
| Alimony payments made | 2,400 |
| Contribution to traditional IRA | 4,000 |
| Gift from grandparents | 30,000 |
| Capital loss from stock investment | 4,000 |
| Amount won in football office pool (sports gambling is against the law where Quincy lives) | 3,200 |
| Number of dependents (parents, ages 66 and 68) | 2 |
| Age | 40 |

3. Compute the taxable income for 2005 for Vivian on the basis of the following information. Her filing status is head of household.

| | |
|---|---:|
| Salary | $70,000 |
| Interest on City of Chicago bonds *Already taxed* | 2,000 |
| Insurance proceeds (Vivian was the named beneficiary of her uncle's life insurance) *Already been taxed* | 50,000 |
| Damages awarded for personal injuries Vivian suffered when she was struck by a delivery truck | 90,000 |
| Cash prize won from a radio call-in contest | 5,000 |
| Interest on home mortgage | 4,800 |
| Property taxes on personal residence | 3,600 |
| Number of dependents (children, ages 12, 14, and 16) | 3 |
| Age | 42 |

4. Determine the amount of the standard deduction allowed for 2005 in the following independent situations. In each case, assume the taxpayer is claimed as another person's dependent.

a. Hollis, age 17, has income as follows: $500 interest from a certificate of deposit and $4,800 from repairing cars. (15-9)

b. Sheila, age 18, has income as follows: $400 cash dividends from a stock investment and $3,300 from handling a paper route.

c. Ernest, age 15, has income as follows: $1,200 interest on a bank savings account and $400 for painting a neighbor's fence.

d. Viola, age 15, has income as follows: $300 cash dividends from a stock investment and $600 from grooming pets.

e. Molly, age 66 and a widow, has income as follows: $900 from a bank savings account and $1,800 from baby-sitting.

5. For tax year 2005, determine the number of personal and dependency exemptions in each of the following independent situations:

a. Leo and Amanda (ages 48 and 46) are husband and wife and furnish more than 50% of the support of their two children, Elton (age 18) and Trista (age 24). During the year, Elton earns $4,500 providing transportation for elderly persons with disabilities, and Trista receives a $5,000 scholarship for tuition at the law school she attends.

b. Audry (age 65) is divorced and lives alone. She maintains a household in which her ex-husband, Clint, and his mother, Olive, live and furnishes more than 50% of their support. Olive is age 82 and blind.

c. Jacque (age 52) furnishes more than 50% of the support of his married daughter, Carin, and her husband, Pierce, who live with him. Both Carin and Pierce are age 18. During the year, Pierce earned $4,000 from a part-time job. All parties live in New York (a common law state).

d. Assume the same facts as in (c), except that all parties live in Nevada (a community property state).

**Ethics**

6. For the six years prior to his death in late 2005, Jesse lived with his daughter, Hannah. Because he had no source of income, Jesse was supported by equal contributions from Hannah and his two sons, Bill and Bob. At Jesse's funeral, his surviving children are amazed to discover that none of them has been claiming Jesse as a dependent. Upon the advice of the director of the funeral home, they decide to divide, among themselves, the dependency exemptions for the past six years. Multiple Forms 2120 are executed, and each of the three children files amended returns for different past years. As Jesse died before the end of the current year, no deduction is planned for 2005.

   Comment on the tax expectations of the parties involved.

7. Dudley and Keri North are married and file a joint return. Transactions for 2005 are summarized below:

| Salaries (Dudley, $46,000; Keri, $51,000) | | $97,000 |
|---|---|---|
| Interest income— | | |
| General Motors Corporation bonds | $2,100 | |
| City of San Francisco bonds | 900 | 3,000 |
| Contribution to traditional IRAs (Keri, $4,000; Dudley, $4,000) | | 8,000 |
| Cash gift from Keri's parents | | 24,000 |
| Loss from the sale of an RV (previously used by the Norths on their vacations) | | 16,000 |

The Norths provide more than half of the support of Demi, Kevin, and Homer. Demi (age 22) is their daughter and is a full-time student at a medical school. She earns $3,400 during the year tutoring college athletes. Kevin (age 18) is their son; he does not go to school but earns $8,000 as a part-time security guard. Homer (age 70) is Dudley's father. His only income is $7,200 of Social Security benefits. If the Norths have $11,500 in itemized deductions, what is their taxable income for 2005?

**Decision Making**

8. Don is a wealthy executive who has taxable income of $200,000 in 2005. He is considering transferring title in a duplex he owns to his son Sam, age 16. Sam has no other income and is claimed as a dependent by Don. Net rent income from the duplex is $10,000 a year, which Sam will be encouraged to place in a savings account. Will the family save income taxes in 2005 if Don transfers title in the duplex to Sam? Explain.

9. Using the Tax Rate Schedules, compute the 2005 tax liability for each taxpayer:
   a. Hector (age 42) is a surviving spouse and provides all of the support of his three minor children who live with him. He also maintains the household in which his parents live and furnished 60% of their support. Besides interest on City of Flint bonds in the amount of $1,200, Hector's father received $2,400 from a part-time job. Hector has a salary of $70,000, a short-term capital loss of $4,000, a cash prize of $2,000 from a church raffle, and itemized deductions of $9,500.
   b. Penny (age 45) is single and provides more than 50% of the support of Rosalyn (a family friend), Flo (a niece, age 18), and Jerold (a nephew, age 18). Both Rosalyn and Flo live with Penny, but Jerold (a French citizen) lives in Canada. Penny earns a salary of $80,000, contributes $4,000 to a traditional IRA, and receives sales proceeds of $15,000 for an RV that cost $40,000 and was used for vacations. She has $8,000 in itemized deductions.

10. Which of the following taxpayers must file a Federal income tax return for 2005?
    a. Ben, age 19, is a full-time college student. He is claimed as a dependent by his parents. He earned $5,100 in wages during the year.
    b. Anita, age 12, is claimed as a dependent by her parents. She earned interest income of $1,200 during the year.
    c. Earl, age 16, is claimed as a dependent by his parents. He earned wages of $2,700 and interest of $1,100 during the year.
    d. Karen, age 16 and blind, is claimed as a dependent by her parents. She earned wages of $2,600 and interest of $1,200 during the year.
    e. Pat, age 17, is claimed as a dependent by her parents. She earned interest of $300 during the year. In addition, she earned $550 during the summer operating her own business at the beach, where she painted caricatures of her customers.

**Decision Making**

11. Amelia is a cash basis, single taxpayer with no dependents. In December 2005, she furnishes you with the following information:

| | 2005 | 2006 |
|---|---|---|
| AGI | $60,000 | $61,000 |
| Property taxes on residence | 1,300 | 1,300 |
| Interest on home mortgage | 1,100 | 1,000 |
| Church pledges | 2,400 | 2,400 |

Amelia wants to know if she can save on taxes over a two-year period by prepaying her 2006 church pledge in December 2005. In providing an answer, use the Tax Rate Schedules, standard deduction, and personal exemption amount applicable to 2005 for both years.

12. Under the terms of their divorce agreement, Barry is to transfer common stock (cost of $25,000, market value of $60,000) to Sandra. Barry and Sandra have a 14-year-old child. Sandra will have custody of the child, and Barry is to pay $300 per month as child support. In addition, Sandra is to receive $1,000 per month for 10 years. However, the payments will be reduced to $750 per month when their child reaches age 21. In the first year under the agreement, Sandra receives the common stock and the correct cash payments for six months. How will the terms of the agreement affect Sandra's gross income?

13. For each of the following, determine the amount that should be included in gross income:
    a. Joe was selected as the most valuable player in the Super Bowl. In recognition of this, he was awarded a sports car worth $60,000 plus $150,000 in cash.
    b. Wanda won the Mrs. America beauty contest. She received various prizes valued at $100,000. None of the $100,000 was for a scholarship or travel expenses.
    c. George was awarded the Nobel Peace Prize. He directed the Nobel committee to pay the $900,000 prize to State University, his alma mater.

**EXTENDER**

**Decision Making**

14. Linda and Don are married and file a joint return. In 2005, they received $9,000 in Social Security benefits and $35,000 in taxable pension benefits and interest.
    a. Compute the couple's adjusted gross income on a joint return.
    b. Don would like to know whether they should sell for $100,000 (at no gain or loss) a corporate bond that pays 8% in interest each year and use the proceeds to buy a $100,000 nontaxable State of Virginia bond that will pay $6,000 in interest each year.
    c. If Linda in (a) works part-time and earns $30,000, how much would Linda and Don's adjusted gross income increase?

15. Alejandro was awarded an academic scholarship to State University for the 2005–2006 academic year. He received $5,000 in August and $6,000 in December 2005. Alejandro had enough personal savings to pay all expenses as they came due. Alejandro's expenditures for the relevant period were as follows:

| Tuition, August 2005 | $3,300 |
|---|---|
| Tuition, December 2005 | 3,400 |
| Room and board | |
| August–December 2005 | 3,000 |
| January–May 2006 | 2,400 |
| Books and educational supplies | |
| August–December 2005 | 1,000 |
| January–May 2006 | 1,200 |

Determine the effect on Alejandro's gross income for 2005 and 2006.

16. Liz sued an overzealous bill collector and received the following settlement:

| Damage to her automobile the collector attempted to repossess | $ 1,000 |
|---|---|
| Physical damage to her arm caused by the collector | 8,000 |
| Loss of income while her arm was healing | 6,000 |
| Punitive damages | 30,000 |

a. What effect does the settlement have on Liz's gross income?
b. Assume Liz also collected $40,000 of damages for slander to her personal reputation caused by the bill collector misrepresenting the facts to Liz's employer and other creditors. Is this $40,000 included in Liz's gross income?

17. Rita is employed as a computer consultant. For calendar year 2005, she had AGI of $200,000 and paid the following medical expenses:

| Medical insurance premiums | $ 7,400 |
|---|---|
| Doctor and dentist bills for Larry and Shirley (Rita's parents) | 7,700 |
| Doctor and dentist bills for Rita | 10,500 |
| Prescription medicines for Rita | 1,450 |
| Nonprescription insulin for Rita | 550 |

Larry and Shirley would qualify as Rita's dependents except that they file a joint return. Rita's medical insurance policy does not cover them. Rita filed a claim for reimbursement of $6,000 of her own expenses with her insurance company in December 2005 and received the reimbursement in January 2006. What is Rita's maximum allowable medical expense deduction for 2005?

**Ethics**

18. Steven, age 37, had his nose broken in a high school football game 20 years ago. As a result, his nose is slightly crooked. In addition, he thinks his nose is too long. In March, he scheduled an appointment with Dr. Keane to discuss surgery to improve his appearance, primarily to shorten his nose. Dr. Keane presented him with computer simulations showing several different possibilities for the size and shape of his nose. Steven selected a nose that was much shorter and completely straight.

Steven called his CPA to ask if the cost of the surgery would be deductible. His CPA told him that unnecessary cosmetic surgery is not deductible, but hinted that most doctors can come up with a medical reason that would make such surgery deductible.

Steven discussed the tax issue with Dr. Keane on his next visit, and the doctor indicated that the surgery would be necessary to repair Steven's deviated septum, which was caused by his football injury. Dr. Keane said that he would be willing to write a letter for Steven's files, stating that the surgery was medically necessary. Is Steven justified in taking a deduction for the cosmetic surgery?

**Issue ID**

19. A local ophthalmologist's advertising campaign included a certificate for a free radial keratotomy for the lucky winner of a drawing. Ahmad held the winning ticket, which was drawn in December 2004. Ahmad had no vision problems and was uncertain what he should do with the prize. In February 2005, Ahmad's daughter, who lives with his former wife, was diagnosed with a vision problem that could be treated with either

prescription glasses or a radial keratotomy. The divorce decree requires that Ahmad pay for all medical expenses incurred for his daughter. Identify the relevant tax issues for Ahmad.

20. Jung suffers from heart problems and, upon the recommendation of a physician, has an elevator installed in his personal residence. In connection with the elevator, Jung incurs and pays the following amounts during the current year:

| | |
|---|---|
| Elevator and cost of installation | $15,500 |
| Increase in utility bills due to the elevator | 750 |
| Cost of certified appraisal | 500 |

The system has an estimated useful life of 20 years. The appraisal was to determine the value of Jung's residence with and without the system. The appraisal states that the system increased the value of Jung's residence by $2,000. How much of these expenses qualifies for the medical expense deduction in the current year?

21. Daniel is a self-employed, calendar year taxpayer. He reports on the cash basis. Daniel made the following estimated state income tax payments:

| Date | Amount |
|---|---|
| January 15, 2005 | $1,200 (4th payment for 2004) |
| April 15, 2005 | 1,500 (1st payment for 2005) |
| June 15, 2005 | 1,500 (2nd payment for 2005) |
| September 15, 2005 | 1,500 (3rd payment for 2005) |
| January 15, 2006 | 1,500 (4th payment for 2005) |

Daniel had a tax overpayment of $800 on his 2004 state income tax return and, rather than requesting a refund, had the overpayment applied to his 2005 state income taxes. What is the amount of Daniel's state income tax itemized deduction for his 2005 Federal income tax return?

**Decision Making**

**Communications**

22. Carol Sharp incurred $29,250 of interest expense related to her investments in 2005. Her investment income included $7,000 of interest, $5,500 of qualified dividends, and a $12,750 net capital gain on the sale of securities. Carol has asked you to compute the amount of her deduction for investment interest, taking into consideration any options she might have. In addition, she has asked for your suggestions as to any tax planning alternatives that might be available. Write a letter to her that contains your advice. Carol lives at 208 Lone Tree Circle, Napa, CA 94558.

23. Helena borrowed $300,000 to acquire a parcel of land to be held for investment purposes. During 2005, she paid interest of $30,000 on the loan. She had AGI of $75,000 for the year. Other items related to Helena's investments include the following:

| | |
|---|---|
| Investment income | $21,150 |
| Investment counsel fees | 2,250 |

Helena is unmarried and elects to itemize her deductions. She has no miscellaneous itemized deductions other than the investment counsel fees.
   a. Determine Helena's investment interest deduction for 2005.
   b. Discuss the treatment of the portion of Helena's investment interest that is disallowed in 2005.
   c. Assume Helena has a long-term capital gain of $8,250 from the sale of investment land, and she elects to treat it as investment income. How would this affect her investment interest deduction and her tax computation for 2005?

24. In 1997, Huseyin, who is single, purchased a personal residence for $170,000 and took out a mortgage of $100,000 on the property. In May of the current year, when the

residence had a fair market value of $220,000 and Huseyin owed $70,000 on the mortgage, he took out a home equity loan for $110,000. He used the funds to purchase a Jaguar for himself and a Cadillac SUV for his wife. For both vehicles, 100% of the use is personal. What is the maximum amount on which Huseyin can deduct home equity interest?

**Decision Making**

**Communications**

25. Pedro contributes a painting to an art museum in 2005. He has owned the painting for 12 years, and it is worth $130,000 at the time of the donation. Pedro's adjusted basis for the painting is $90,000, and his AGI for 2005 is $250,000. Pedro has asked you whether he should make the reduced deduction election for this contribution. Write a letter to Pedro Valdez at 1289 Greenway Avenue, Foster City, CA 94404 and advise him on this matter.

**Decision Making**

**Communications**

26. In December each year, Alice Young contributes 10% of her gross income to the United Way (a 50% organization). Alice, who is in the 35% marginal tax bracket, is considering the following alternatives as charitable contributions in December 2005:

| | **Fair Market Value** |
|---|---|
| (1) Cash donation | $21,000 |
| (2) Unimproved land held for six years ($3,000 basis) | 21,000 |
| (3) Blue Corporation stock held for eight months ($3,000 basis) | 21,000 |
| (4) Gold Corporation stock held for two years ($26,000 basis) | 21,000 |

Alice has asked you to help her decide which of the potential contributions listed above will be most advantageous taxwise. Evaluate the four alternatives, and write a letter to Alice to communicate your advice to her. Her address is 2622 Bayshore Drive, Berkeley, CA 94709.

**Issue ID**

27. The Skins Game, which involves four of the top golfers on the PGA Tour, is held each year on the weekend after Thanksgiving. Total prize money amounts to $1 million, and the leading money winner also receives an automobile as a prize. Twenty percent of the money won by each player goes to charity. In addition, on the par three holes, the winner of the hole receives the keys to an automobile, which goes to the player's favorite charity. Identify the relevant tax issues for the players. Consider the following possibilities with respect to the car won by the leading money winner: (1) he might keep the car for his own use and sell his present car; (2) he might sell the new car; (3) he might give the car to a friend or relative; (4) he might donate the car to charity; or (5) he might give the car to his caddy.

28. Charles, who is single, had an AGI of $400,000 during 2005. He incurred the following expenses and losses during the year:

| | |
|---|---|
| Medical expenses before 7.5%-of-AGI limitation | $39,500 |
| State and local income taxes | 5,200 |
| Real estate taxes | 4,400 |
| Home mortgage interest | 5,400 |
| Charitable contributions | 4,800 |
| Casualty loss before 10% limitation (after $100 floor) | 47,000 |
| Unreimbursed employee expenses subject to 2%-of-AGI limitation | 8,900 |
| Gambling losses (Charles had $7,400 of gambling income) | 9,800 |

Compute Charles's itemized deductions before and after the overall limitation.

29. Ann and Bill were on the list of a local adoption agency for several years seeking to adopt a child. Finally, in 2004, good news comes their way and an adoption seems imminent. They pay qualified adoption expenses of $4,000 in 2004 and $9,000 in 2005. Assume the adoption becomes final in 2005. Ann and Bill always file a joint income tax return.

    a. Determine the amount of the adoption expenses credit available to Ann and Bill assuming their combined annual income is $50,000. In what year(s) will they benefit from the credit?

    b. Assuming Ann and Bill's modified AGI in 2004 and 2005 is $175,000, calculate the amount of the adoption expenses credit.

30. Kevin and Jane are husband and wife and have one dependent child, age 9. Kevin is a full-time student for all of the current year, while Jane earns $36,000 as a nurse's aide. To provide care for their child while Kevin attends classes and Jane works, they pay Sara (Jane's 17-year-old sister) $2,900. Sara is not a dependent of Kevin and Jane. Assuming Kevin and Jane file a joint return, what, if any, is their credit for child and dependent care expenses?

31. Ralph and Jill are husband and wife and have two dependent children under the age of 13. They both are gainfully employed and during the current year earn salaries as follows: $22,500 (Ralph) and $5,000 (Jill). To care for their children while they work, they pay Megan (Ralph's mother) $5,600. Assuming Ralph and Jill file a joint return, what, if any, is their credit for child and dependent care expenses?

**Communications**

32. Bernadette, a longtime client of yours, is an architect and president of the local Rotary chapter. To keep up to date with the latest developments in her profession, she attends continuing education seminars offered by the architecture school at State University. During 2005, Bernadette spends $2,000 on course tuition to attend such seminars. She also spends another $400 on architecture books during the year. Bernadette's son is a senior majoring in engineering at the University of the Midwest. During the 2005 calendar year, Bernadette's son incurs the following expenses: $8,200 for tuition ($4,100 per semester) and $750 for books and supplies. Bernadette's son, whom she claims as a dependent, lives at home while attending school full-time. Bernadette is married, files a joint return, and has a combined AGI with her husband of $95,000.

    a. Calculate Bernadette's education tax credit for 2005.

    b. In her capacity as president of the local Rotary chapter, Bernadette has asked you to make a 30–45 minute speech outlining the different ways the tax law helps defray (1) the cost of higher education and (2) the cost of continuing education once someone is in the workforce. Prepare an outline of possible topics for presentation. A tentative title for your presentation is "How Can the Tax Law Help Pay for College and Continuing Professional Education?"

33. Briefly discuss the requirements that must be satisfied for a taxpayer to qualify for the earned income tax credit.

**Ethics**

34. For many years, Loretta Johnson, a single mother of three children, has been struggling to make ends meet by working at two jobs that pay barely the minimum wage and together provide just over $15,000. Fortunately, her housing and food costs have been partially subsidized through various government programs. In addition, she has been able to take advantage of the earned income credit, which has provided around $3,000 annually to help her with living expenses. The credit has truly made a difference in the lives of Loretta and her family by helping them keep their creditors at bay. She is proud that she has worked hard and provided for her family for many years without having to accept welfare.

    Now, however, Loretta faces a problem as her children have grown up and moved out of her home. With no qualified children in her household, she no longer qualifies for the earned income credit. Although she will continue working at her two jobs, such a significant loss to her household budget cuts into her ability to be self-reliant. As a survival strategy and as a way of keeping the earned income credit, Loretta arranges to have one of her grandchildren live with her for just over six months every year. This enables a significant percentage of her household budget to be secure. How do you react to Loretta's strategy?

**EXTENDER**

**Decision Making**

35. Joyce, a widow, lives in an apartment with her two minor children (ages 8 and 10) whom she supports. Joyce earns $32,000 during 2005. She uses the standard deduction.

a. Calculate the amount, if any, of Joyce's earned income credit.

b. During the year, Joyce is offered a new job that has greater future potential than her current job. If she accepts the job offer, her earnings for the year would be $36,000; however, she will not qualify for the earned income credit. Using after-tax cash-flow calculations, determine whether Joyce should accept the new job offer.

## Cumulative Problems

**Tax Return Problem**

36. Gary and Tracy Wilmot live at 4682 Spring Road, Reno, NV 89557. Gary is a lab technician at the county hospital, and Tracy is the office manager for a local orthopedic clinic. During 2005, Gary and Tracy had the following transactions:

| | | |
|---|---|---|
| Salaries ($48,000 + $49,000) | | $ 97,000 |
| Income tax withheld ($6,000 + $6,200) | | 12,200 |
| Interest income— | | |
| City of Reno bonds | $ 300 | |
| CD at Wells Fargo Bank | 600 | |
| Money market account at Sparks State Bank | 400 | 1,300 |
| Qualified dividend from SBC stock | | 3,200 |
| Gift from Tracy's parents | | 22,000 |
| Bequest from Gary's father | | 160,000 |
| Prudential life insurance policy | | 50,000 |
| Proceeds from sale of property— | | |
| Garage sale | $ 4,800 | |
| Houseboat | 11,000 | |
| Clark County land | 31,000 | 46,800 |
| Interest on home mortgage | | (6,600) |
| Property taxes | | (5,100) |
| Payment on church pledge (receipts maintained) | | (2,400) |
| Medical expenses (including insurance premiums) net of insurance reimbursements | | (3,100) |
| Sales taxes paid (receipts maintained) | | (1,800) |

Gary's father died in 2004, and the estate was settled and distributed in 2005. Gary was the designated beneficiary of a life insurance policy his father had purchased from Prudential.

The garage sale involved used clothing, toys, furniture, and other household items. Gary and Tracy estimate that the items sold originally cost $12,000. The houseboat was built by Gary in his spare time over a period of four years. Gary has receipts reflecting that the materials used in the construction cost $8,500. As one of their sons is afraid of water, the Wilmots decided to sell the boat. Tracy acquired the Clark County property in 1998 for $35,000. She had high expectations as to its investment potential, but restricted water rights proved to be a deterrent to its appreciation in value. She feels fortunate to have recovered as much as $31,000 of her cost.

The Wilmots have three children whom they support: Cole (age 18), Robyn (age 19), and Henry (age 21). Henry is a full-time student, while Cole and Robyn are taking time off prior to attending college. All of the Wilmot children are employed by the Reno Convention Bureau in various part-time capacities, and each earns in excess of $5,000 (which he or she saves). The Wilmots also furnish more than 50% of the support of Faye, Gary's 85-year-old mother, who is in a nursing home.

Compute the Wilmots' tax liability for 2005. Suggested software: TurboTax.

**Tax Return Problem**

**Decision Making**

37. Alice and Bruce Byrd are married taxpayers, ages 47 and 45, who file a joint return. Their Social Security numbers are 034–48–4382 and 016–50–9556, respectively. They live at 473 Revere Avenue, Ames, MA 01850. Alice is the office manager for a dental clinic

and earns an annual salary of $46,200. Bruce is the manager of a fast-food outlet owned and operated by Plymouth Corporation. His annual salary is $58,300.

The Byrds have two children, Cynthia (age 24 and Social Security number 017–44–9126) and John (age 22 and Social Security number 017–27–4148), who live with them. Both children are full-time students at a nearby college.

During 2004, the Byrds furnished one-third of the total support of Bruce's widower father, Sam Byrd (age 70 and Social Security number 034–82–8583). Sam lived alone and received the rest of his support from Bruce's sister and brother (one-third each). They have signed a multiple support agreement allowing Bruce to claim Sam as a dependent for 2004. Sam died in November, and Bruce received life insurance proceeds of $600,000 on December 28.

The Byrds had the following expenses relating to their personal residence during 2004:

| | |
|---|---|
| Property taxes | $6,840 |
| Interest on home mortgage | 8,580 |
| Repairs to roof | 2,920 |
| Utilities | 3,960 |
| Fire and theft insurance | 1,870 |

Medical expenses for 2004 include:

| | |
|---|---|
| Medical insurance premiums | $7,810 |
| Doctor bill for Sam incurred in 2003 and not paid until 2004 | 3,080 |
| Operation for Sam | 6,710 |

The operation for Sam represents the one-third Bruce contributed toward his father's support.

Other relevant information follows:

- Alice and Bruce had $4,870 ($1,980 for Alice and $2,890 for Bruce) withheld from their salaries for state income taxes. When they filed their 2003 state return in 2004, they paid additional state income tax of $880.

- During 2004, Alice and Bruce attended a dinner dance sponsored by the Ames Police Disability Association (a qualified charitable organization). The Byrds paid $220 for the tickets. Cost of comparable entertainment would normally be $90. The Byrds contributed $4,290 to their church and gave used clothing (cost of $1,100 and fair market value of $495) to the Salvation Army. All donations are supported by receipts.

- In 2004, the Byrds received interest income of $2,695 from a savings account they maintained.

- Alice's employer requires that all employees wear uniforms to work. During 2004, Alice spent $407 on new uniforms and $189 on laundry charges. Bruce paid $275 for an annual subscription to the *Journal of Franchise Management*. Neither Alice's nor Bruce's employer reimburses for employee expenses.

- The Byrds do not keep the receipts for the sales taxes they paid. The amount from the sales tax table is $974.

- Alice and Bruce had $10,570 ($4,180 for Alice and $6,390 for Bruce) of Federal income tax withheld in 2004, and they paid no estimated Federal income tax. Neither Alice nor Bruce wishes to designate $3 to the Presidential Election Campaign Fund.

*Part 1—Tax Computation*

Compute net tax payable or refund due for Alice and Bruce Byrd for 2004. If they have overpaid, the amount is to be refunded. If you use tax forms for your computations, you will need Form 1040 and Schedules A and B. Suggested software: TurboTax.

*Part 2—Tax Planning*

Alice and Bruce are planning some significant changes for 2005. They have provided you with the following information and asked you to project their taxable income and tax liability for 2005.

- The Byrds will use $200,000 of the life insurance proceeds they received as a result of Sam's death and pay off their mortgage in early January 2005. They will invest the remaining $400,000 in short-term certificates of deposit (CDs) and use the interest for living expenses during 2005.

- They expect to earn total interest of $16,000 on the CDs. Bruce has been awarded a 10% raise for 2005, and state and Federal tax withholdings on his salary will increase accordingly.

- Alice, who has health problems, will take a leave of absence from work during 2005, so none of her job-related expenses or withholdings will continue.

- The Byrds do not expect to owe additional state income tax when they file their 2004 return, but they do expect their charitable contributions and medical insurance premiums to continue at the 2004 level.

- Assume all other income and deduction items will continue at the same level in 2005 unless you have information that indicates otherwise.

**Tax Return Problem**

38. Paul and Donna Decker are married taxpayers, ages 44 and 42, who file a joint return for 2005. The Deckers live at 1121 College Avenue, Carmel, IN 46032. Paul is an assistant manager at Carmel Motor Inn, and Donna is a teacher at Carmel Elementary School. They present you with W–2 Forms that reflect the following information:

|  | **Paul** | **Donna** |
| --- | --- | --- |
| Salary | $58,000 | $56,000 |
| Federal tax withheld | 10,300 | 9,700 |
| State income tax withheld | 900 | 800 |
| FICA (Social Security and Medicare) withheld | 4,437 | 4,284 |
| Social Security numbers | 222–11–4567 | 333–11–9872 |

Donna is the custodial parent of two children from a previous marriage who reside with the Deckers through the school year. The children, Larry and Jane Parker, reside with their father, Bob, during the summer. Relevant information for the children follows:

|  | **Larry** | **Jane** |
| --- | --- | --- |
| Age | 17 | 18 |
| Social Security numbers | 305–11–4567 | 303–11–9872 |
| Months spent with Deckers | 9 | 9 |

Under the divorce decree, Bob pays child support of $150 per month per child during the nine months the children live with the Deckers. Bob says he spends $200 per month per child during the three summer months they reside with him. Donna and Paul can document that they provide $2,000 of support per child per year. The divorce decree is silent as to which parent can claim the exemption for the children.

In August, Paul and Donna added a suite to their home to provide more comfortable accommodations for Hannah Snyder (Social Security number 263–33–4738), Donna's mother, who had moved in with them in February 2004 after the death of Donna's father. Not wanting to borrow money for this addition, Paul sold 300 shares of Acme Corporation stock for $50 per share on May 3, 2005, and used the proceeds of $15,000 to cover construction costs. The Deckers had purchased the stock on April 29, 2001, for $25 per share. They received dividends of $750 on the jointly owned stock a month before the sale.

Hannah, who is 66 years old, received $7,500 in Social Security benefits during the year, of which she gave the Deckers $2,000 to use toward household expenses and deposited the remainder in her personal savings account. The Deckers determine that they have spent $2,500 of their own money for food, clothing, medical expenses, and other items for Hannah. They do not know what the rental value of Hannah's suite would be, but they estimate it would be at least $300 per month.

Interest paid during the year included the following:

| | |
|---|---|
| Home mortgage interest (paid to Carmel Federal Savings and Loan) | $7,890 |
| Interest on an automobile loan (paid to Carmel National Bank) | 1,490 |
| Interest on Citibank Visa card | 870 |

In July, Paul hit a submerged rock while boating. Fortunately, he was thrown from the boat, landed in deep water, and was uninjured. However, the boat, which was uninsured, was destroyed. Paul had paid $25,000 for the boat in June 2004, and its value was appraised at $18,000 on the date of the accident.

The Deckers paid doctor and hospital bills of $8,700 and were reimbursed $2,000 by their insurance company. They spent $640 for prescription drugs and medicines and $2,810 for premiums on their health insurance policy. They have filed additional claims of $1,200 with their insurance company and have been told they will receive payment for that amount in January 2006. Included in the amounts paid for doctor and hospital bills were payments of $380 for Hannah and $850 for the children.

Additional information of potential tax consequence follows:

| | |
|---|---|
| Real estate taxes paid | $3,700 |
| Sales taxes paid (per table) | 1,379 |
| Cash contributions to church | 2,100 |
| Appraised value of books donated to public library | 740 |
| Paul's unreimbursed employee expenses to attend hotel management convention: | |
|     Airfare | 340 |
|     Hotel | 170 |
|     Meals | 95 |
|     Registration fee | 340 |
| Refund of state income tax for 2004 (the Deckers itemized on their 2004 Federal tax return) | 1,520 |

Compute net tax payable or refund due for the Deckers for 2005. If they have overpaid, the amount is to be credited toward their taxes for 2006. Suggested software: TurboTax.

**BRIDGE DISCIPLINE**

1. George comes to you asking for your advice. He wishes to invest $10,000 either in a debt security or in an equity investment. His choices are as shown below:

   • Redbreast Corporation bond, annual coupon rate of 7.50%.

   • City of Philadelphia general obligation bond, coupon rate of 6.00%.

   • Blue Corporation 7.50% preferred stock (produces qualified dividend income).

   These alternatives are believed to carry comparable risk. Assuming George is in the 35% marginal tax bracket, which investment alternative could be expected to produce the superior annual after-tax rate of return?

2. Assume the same facts as in Problem 1, except that George is a C corporation rather than an individual and is in the 34% marginal tax bracket. Which investment strategy would maximize George, Inc.'s annual return?

## Research Problems

*Note: Solutions to Research Problems can be prepared by using the **RIA Checkpoint® Student Edition** online research product, which is available to accompany this text. It is also possible to prepare solutions to the Research Problems by using tax research materials found in a standard tax library.*

**Communications**

**Research Problem 1.** John and Marge Hudgens were married 26 years ago and have one child, Monica. Sometime in January 2004, after a particularly fierce argument, John packed his clothes and left for parts unknown. Marge has neither seen nor heard from him since.

Marge is employed and maintains the house where she and Monica live. Monica is a full-time student and will graduate from law school on May 9, 2005. During 2004 and 2005, Monica (age 22) earned over $9,000 each year from part-time jobs. She deposited part of her earnings in a savings account under her name and used the rest for her support. The remainder of Monica's support was provided by Marge.

Marge contacts you in March 2005 regarding tax advice. Specifically, she is interested in the answers to the following questions for tax year 2004 and 2005:

* What is her filing status?

* Can she claim Monica as a dependent?

a. Write a letter to Marge addressing her concerns. Marge lives at 1349 Center Street, Warrensburg, MO 64093.
b. Also prepare a memo for your firm's client files.

**Research Problem 2.** Bart and Arlene Keating are husband and wife and live in Mineola, Oregon. They have been married for 18 years and have four children, all of whom are teenagers. After the birth of her last child, Arlene took a job as a city clerk and, over the years, has become city treasurer. Since graduating from high school, Bart has worked as a dispatcher for the city fire and ambulance departments. As Arlene has some college training in finance and accounting, she handles the family's financial affairs, including reconciling the bank account, paying bills, and preparing all tax returns. She also takes care of major purchases (e.g., autos, furniture) and servicing of debt (e.g., home mortgage, auto loans, charge accounts).

The Keatings themselves maintain a modest lifestyle, but Arlene is quite generous with the children. All are well-dressed, attend summer camp, and have their own cars. Bart believes Arlene obtains any additional funds for the children's support through credit card financing and bank loans.

The Keatings filed joint returns for 2001 and 2002 that reflected their salary income. Arlene prepared the returns, and Bart signed them without reviewing them first. The returns did not show the $90,000 Arlene had embezzled from her employer over this two-year period.

The City of Mineola discovers the theft, and Arlene is tried and convicted of grand larceny. Due to the adverse publicity generated by these events, the Keatings are divorced, and Arlene moves to another state.

In 2005, the IRS assesses a deficiency against Bart for the income taxes that would have resulted if the embezzled amounts had been reported as income.

What are the rights of the parties?

*Partial list of research aids:*
§§ 6013(d)(3) and 6015.
*Kathryn Cheshire,* 115 T.C. 183 (2000).
*Evelyn M. Martin,* 80 TCM 665, T.C.Memo. 2000–346.

**Research Problem 3.** Your client, a resident of Hannibal, Missouri, was recently divorced. Under the divorce agreement, he is to pay his former wife five annual payments of $25,000 each. The divorce agreement was approved by the state court. Your client has been informed by his former wife that she does not intend to treat the payments as alimony on her tax return. Her attorney says the payments are not alimony because the agreement does not specify that the payments will cease upon her death. Your supervisor thinks the Tax Court recently decided a case with similar facts involving a Missouri couple, but he does not remember the name of the case or the court's conclusion. Locate the relevant authority to advise your client as to whether he can deduct the payments to his former wife.

**Research Problem 4.**   Tom and Mary Smith, whose son was found murdered in a parking garage, offered a $100,000 reward for the city police to use to obtain information leading to the arrest and conviction of the murderer. As a result of the reward, a person who had overheard the murderer telling a friend about the crime reported the conversation to the police. The murderer was arrested and convicted, and the Smiths contributed the money to the police department, which gave the reward to the informant. Can the Smiths treat the payment as an itemized deduction?

**Internet Activity**

*Use the tax resources of the Internet to address the following questions. Do not restrict your search to the World Wide Web, but include a review of newsgroups and general reference materials, practitioner sites and resources, primary sources of the tax law, chat rooms and discussion groups, and other opportunities.*

**Research Problem 5.**   A nonresident alien earns money in the United States that is subject to Federal income tax. What guidance does the IRS provide on what tax form needs to be used and on when it should be filed? In terms of the proper filing date, does it matter whether the earnings were subject to income tax withholding?

**Research Problem 6.**   Find several news reports concerning the government's effort to extend the use of the earned income credit to more of the taxpayers who qualify for it. Which agencies in your area are involved in this effort?

# Individuals as Employees and Proprietors

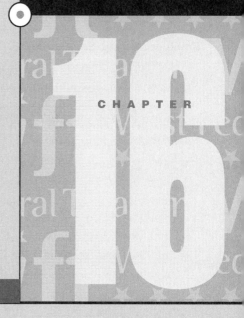

## LEARNING OBJECTIVES

*After completing Chapter 16, you should be able to:*

### L O . 1
Distinguish between employee and self-employed status.

### L O . 2
Understand the exclusions from income available to employees who receive fringe benefits.

### L O . 3
Apply the rules for computing deductible expenses of employees including transportation, travel, moving, education, and entertainment expenses.

### L O . 4
Appreciate the difference between accountable and nonaccountable employee plans.

### L O . 5
Understand the tax provisions applicable to proprietors.

### L O . 6
Distinguish between business and hobby activities and apply the rules limiting the deduction of hobby losses.

## OUTLINE

## TAX TALK

*The taxpayer—that's someone who works for the Federal government but doesn't have to take a civil service examination.*

*—Ronald Reagan*

**A**n individual may be an employee or may be self-employed. The terms *proprietor* and *independent contractor* are both used to describe self-employed individuals. These terms are used interchangeably throughout this chapter.

In many cases, it is difficult to distinguish between employees and self-employed individuals. This chapter begins with a discussion of the factors that must be considered in determining whether an individual is an employee or is self-employed. This is followed by a discussion of tax provisions applicable to employees and then by a discussion of tax provisions related to self-employed individuals.

**LO.1**

Distinguish between employee and self-employed status.

# Employee versus Self-Employed

When one person performs services for another, the person performing the service is either an employee or self-employed (i.e., an **independent contractor**). Failure to recognize employee status can have serious consequences. Not only can interest and penalties result, but career opportunities, such as possible political opportunities or elected positions, can disappear in the wake of extensive negative media coverage.

The determination of employment status is already controversial and can be expected to become an even greater problem in the future. As a means for achieving greater flexibility and cost control, businesses are increasingly relying on self-employed persons (i.e., independent contractors) rather than employees for many services.

The IRS is very much aware that businesses have a tendency to wrongly classify workers as self-employed rather than as employees. In some cases, misclassification is unintentional and results from difficulty in applying the complex set of rules related to employee versus independent contractor status. In other cases, misclassification may be an intentional strategy to avoid certain costs that are associated with employees. Unlike employees, self-employed persons do not have to be included in various fringe benefit programs and retirement plans. Furthermore, employers are not required to pay FICA and unemployment taxes (refer to Chapter 1) on compensation paid to independent contractors.

In terms of tax consequences, employment status also makes a great deal of difference to the worker. Allowable business expenses of self-employed taxpayers are classified as deductions *for* AGI and are reported on Schedule C (Profit or Loss from Business) of Form 1040.[1] On the other hand, unreimbursed business expenses incurred by employees are classified as itemized deductions and are deductible on Schedule A (as itemized deductions) only to the extent that the sum of certain miscellaneous itemized deductions exceeds 2 percent of the taxpayer's AGI. Unreimbursed employee expenses are reported on Form 2106 (Employee Business Expenses) and Schedule A (Itemized Deductions) of Form 1040.

Employee expenses that are reimbursed under an **accountable plan** (covered later in this chapter) are also reported as deductions *for* AGI. Employee expenses that are not reimbursed under an accountable plan are treated in the same way as unreimbursed expenses—deductible *from* AGI and limited to the excess over 2 percent of AGI.[2]

## FACTORS CONSIDERED IN CLASSIFICATION

The pivotal issue in classifying an individual as an independent contractor or an employee is whether an employer-employee relationship exists. The IRS has created a complex *20-factor test* for determining whether a worker is an employee or an independent contractor. The courts, which have focused on a small number of these factors, generally hold that an individual is an employee if the individual or business acquiring the services:[3]

- has the right to specify the end result and the ways and means by which that result is to be attained,
- can exert will and control over the person providing the services with respect not only to *what* shall be done but also to *how* it shall be done,
- has the right to discharge, without legal liability, the person performing the service,
- furnishes tools or a place to work, and
- bases payment on time spent rather than the task performed.

---

[1]§§ 62(a)(1) and 162(a).
[2]§ 67(a).

[3]Reg. § 31.3401(c)–(1)(b).

BRIDGE DISCIPLINE

**Bridge to Equity or Fairness and Business Law**

Max performs services for Calico, Inc. Amy performs services for Amber, Inc. They perform basically the same service. Yet Max is classified as an employee, and Amy is classified as an independent contractor. Does such a legal classification produce equitable results in terms of the effects it has on Max and Amy?

Employee status produces a number of potential perks. Included are coverage in the employer's fringe benefits programs such as medical insurance, group term life insurance, and § 132 fringe benefits. For an employee, the tax rate for Social Security is 6.2 percent and for Medicare, the rate is 1.45 percent (i.e., the employer is responsible for matching the employee amounts). For a self-employed person, the tax rates for Social Security and Medicare are 12.4 percent and 2.9 percent, respectively.

In distinguishing between an employee and an independent contractor, the overriding theme of common law is that the employee is subject to the will and control of the employer both as to what is to be done and as to how it is to be done. Put in more legal terminology, an employer has the right to control and direct the individual who performs the services, not only as to the result to be accomplished by the work but also as to the details and means by which the result is accomplished. Among the factors generally considered in determining whether this right exists are the following:

- Degree of control exercised over the details of the work.
- Provision of facilities used in the work.
- Opportunity for profit or loss.
- Right to discharge.
- Whether work is part of regular business.
- Permanency of the relationship.
- Relationship the parties believe they are creating.
- Manner of payment, by the job or by the hour.
- Skill required.
- Offering of the services to the general public rather than to one individual or entity.
- Distinct occupation or recognized trade or calling involved.
- Custom in the trade.

Each case is tested on its own merits, and the right to control the means and methods of accomplishment is the definitive test. Generally, physicians, lawyers, dentists, contractors, subcontractors, and others who offer services to the public are not classified as employees.

DIGGING DEEPER 1

*Find more information on this topic at our Web site:* ***http://wft-entities.swlearning.com.***

EXAMPLE 1

Arnold is a lawyer whose major client accounts for 60% of his billings. He does the routine legal work and income tax returns at the client's request. He is paid a monthly retainer in addition to amounts charged for extra work. Arnold is a self-employed individual. Even though most of his income comes from one client, he still has the right to determine *how* the end result of his work is attained. ■

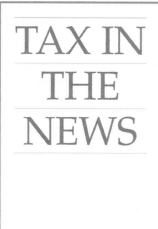

## SELF-EMPLOYED OR EMPLOYED? MISCLASSIFICATION CAN BE COSTLY!

Approximately a decade ago, the media sensation was the number of prominent persons who had run afoul of the so-called nanny tax. Simply stated, this meant not complying with payroll procedures applicable to domestics, baby sitters, and other household employees. This failure to comply with the tax law forced a President Clinton nominee for U.S. Attorney General, Zoe Baird, to withdraw from consideration. The publicity generated by this case, and others like it, had a sobering effect on the taxpaying public. By 1997, as many as 310,000 nanny tax forms (Schedule H , Form 1040) were being filed. Since then, however, the number of such returns has steadily declined. In 2001, for example, a new low of 263,000 was reached. This downward trend has continued with another new low of 239,810 nanny tax returns being filed in 2003. The nanny tax issue was one of the reasons that Bernard Kerik withdrew in December 2004 from being President Bush's nominee for Secretary of Homeland Security.

What does this decline signify? Does it mean that a greater number of these household helpers are now self-employed (i.e., independent contractors) so as to be exempt from employee payroll procedures? Or does it mean that many taxpayers have forgotten about Zoe Baird and her costly lesson? Will Bernard Kerik's situation help them to remember in 2005 and thereafter?

---

**EXAMPLE 2**

Ellen is a lawyer hired by Arnold to assist him in the performance of services for the client mentioned in Example 1. Ellen is under Arnold's supervision; he reviews her work and pays her an hourly fee. Ellen is Arnold's employee. ∎

*Find more information on this topic at our Web site: **http://wft-entities.swlearning.com**.*

---

## Self-Employed Individuals

**FRAMEWORK FOCUS: DEDUCTIONS**

**STRATEGY ➤ MAXIMIZE DEDUCTIBLE AMOUNTS.**

Some taxpayers have the flexibility to be classified as either employees or self-employed individuals. Examples include real estate agents and direct sellers. These taxpayers should carefully consider all factors and not automatically assume that self-employed status is preferable.

It is advantageous to deduct one's business expenses *for* AGI and avoid the 2 percent floor for miscellaneous itemized deductions. However, a self-employed individual may incur additional expenses, such as local gross receipts taxes, license fees, franchise fees, personal property taxes, and occupation taxes. Record-keeping and filing requirements can also be quite burdensome.

One of the most expensive considerations is the **self-employment tax** imposed on independent contractors

and other self-employed individuals. For an employee in 2005, for example, the Social Security tax applies at a rate of 6.2 percent on a base amount of wages of $90,000, and the Medicare tax applies at a rate of 1.45 percent with no limit on the base amount. For self-employed persons, the rate, but not the base amount, for each tax doubles. Even though a deduction *for* AGI is allowed for one-half of the self-employment tax paid, an employee and a self-employed individual are not in the same tax position on equal amounts of earnings. For the applicability of these taxes to workers, see Chapter 1.

After analyzing all these factors, taxpayers in many cases may decide that employee status is preferable to self-employed status.

LO.2

Understand the exclusions from income available to employees who receive fringe benefits.

# Exclusions Available to Employees

Several exclusions that are available to *all taxpayers* were discussed in Chapter 3; these include interest on obligations of state and local governments, life insurance proceeds, and income from discharge of indebtedness. Other exclusions, available only to *individuals*, were discussed in Chapter 15; these exclusions include gifts and inheritances, scholarships, and compensation for injuries and sickness. Exclusions available only to *employees* are discussed below.

## ADVANTAGES OF QUALIFIED FRINGE BENEFITS

Exclusions available only to *employees* are generally referred to as *qualified fringe benefits*. The popularity of fringe benefits is attributable to the fact that the cost of such benefits is deductible by employers and excludible by employees.

**EXAMPLE 3**

Cardinal Corporation, which has a marginal tax rate of 35%, provides health insurance coverage to employees at a cost of $1,000 per employee. Because Cardinal can deduct the health insurance premiums paid to provide this coverage, the net cost to the corporation is $650 per employee ($1,000 cost − $350 tax savings). The employee is allowed to exclude the value of this fringe benefit, so there is no tax cost to the employee.

The average employee of Cardinal Corporation is in the 28% bracket. If Cardinal did not provide the health insurance coverage and the employee paid a $1,000 premium, the employee would have to use after-tax dollars to acquire the coverage. The employee would have to earn $1,389 to pay for the coverage [$1,389 wages − ($1,389 × 28% tax)]. The after-tax cost to the corporation of $1,389 in wages is $903 ($1,389 wages − $486 corporate tax savings). Thus, the cost of health insurance coverage is $253 less per employee ($903 − $650) because it is both deductible by the corporation and excludible by the employee. ■

## EMPLOYER-SPONSORED ACCIDENT AND HEALTH PLANS

Congress encourages employers to provide employees, retired former employees, and their dependents with accident and health benefits, disability insurance, and long-term care plans. The *premiums* are deductible by the employer and are excluded from the employee's gross income.[4] Although § 105(a) provides the general rule that the employee has includible income when he or she collects the insurance *benefits*, two exceptions are provided.

Section 105(b) generally excludes payments received for medical care of the employee, spouse, and dependents. However, if the payments are for expenses that do not meet the Code's definition of medical care,[5] the amount received must be included in gross income. In addition, the taxpayer must include in gross income any amounts received for medical expenses that were deducted by the taxpayer on a prior return.

**EXAMPLE 4**

In 2005, Tab's employer-sponsored health insurance plan paid $4,000 for hair transplants that did not meet the Code's definition of medical care. Tab must include the $4,000 in his gross income for 2005. ■

Section 105(c) excludes payments for the permanent loss or the loss of the use of a member or function of the body or the permanent disfigurement of the employee,

---

[4]§ 106, Reg. § 1.106–1, and Rev.Rul. 82–196, 1982–1 C.B. 106.

[5]See the discussion of medical care in Chapter 15.

**Bridge to Economic and Societal Needs**

The media frequently report on the plight of our "senior citizens." Organizations such as the AARP effectively lobby for the rights of senior citizens through direct lobbying in Washington and through grassroots efforts throughout the country. With the graying of America, these concerns and lobbying efforts are likely to be magnified.

Congress, in the 1930s, enacted Social Security to partially provide for the retirement needs of our senior citizens. In the 1960s, Congress enacted Medicare to partially provide for the medical needs of our senior citizens.

The Internal Revenue Code contains a number of provisions that are "senior citizen friendly." Among these are the following:

- General exclusion, except for the "rich," of Social Security benefits from gross income (§ 86).
- Exclusion of life insurance proceeds from the gross income of the recipient (§ 101).
- Exclusion of medical insurance premiums and benefits from gross income (§ 105 and § 106).
- Limited exclusion from gross income of gain on the sale of a principal residence (§ 121).
- Limited exclusion from gross income of long-term care insurance premiums and benefits (§ 7702B).
- Beneficial treatment of retirement plans (Subchapter D).

spouse, or a dependent. However, payments that are a substitute for salary (e.g., related to the period of time absent) are included in income.

**EXAMPLE 5**

Jill lost an eye in an automobile accident unrelated to her work. As a result of the accident, Jill incurred $2,000 of medical expenses, which she deducted on her return. She collected $10,000 from an accident insurance policy carried by her employer. The benefits were paid according to a schedule of amounts that varied with the part of the body injured (e.g., $10,000 for loss of an eye, $20,000 for loss of a hand). Because the payment was for loss of a *member or function of the body*, the $10,000 is excluded from Jill's gross income. Jill was absent from work for a week as a result of the accident. Her employer also provided her with insurance that reimbursed her for the loss of income due to illness or injury. Jill collected $500, which is includible in her gross income. ■

## MEDICAL REIMBURSEMENT PLANS

As noted above, the amounts received through the insurance coverage (insured plan benefits) are excluded from gross income under § 105. Unfortunately, because of cost considerations, the insurance companies that issue this type of policy usually require a broad coverage of employees. An alternative is to have a plan that is not funded with insurance (a self-insured arrangement). Under a self-insured plan, the employer reimburses employees directly for any medical expenses. The benefits received under a self-insured plan can be excluded from the employee's gross income, if the plan does not discriminate in favor of highly compensated employees.

Archer **Medical Savings Accounts (MSAs)** provided an alternative means of accomplishing a medical reimbursement plan. The MSA had two parts: catastrophic insurance coverage that kicked in after the deductible had been paid, and a savings account that could be tapped to pay the deductible and any uncovered medical expenses.

Legislation enacted in 2003 created the **Health Savings Account (HSA),** which broadened the concept of MSAs and extended it to a larger set of taxpayers.[6] See additional discussion in Chapter 15.

## LONG-TERM CARE BENEFITS

Generally, long-term care insurance, which covers expenses such as the cost of care in a nursing home, is treated the same as accident and health insurance benefits. Thus, the employee does not recognize income when the employer pays the premiums. When benefits are received from the policy, whether the employer or the individual purchased the policy, the exclusion from gross income is limited to the *greater* of the following amounts:

- $240 (indexed amount for 2005) for each day the patient receives the long-term care.
- The actual cost of the care.

The excludible amount is reduced by any amounts received from other third parties (e.g., damages received).[7]

**EXAMPLE 6**

Hazel, who suffers from Alzheimer's disease, was a patient in a nursing home for the last 30 days of 2005. While in the nursing home, she incurred total costs of $7,500. Medicare paid $3,200 of the costs. Hazel received $4,500 from her long-term care insurance policy (which paid $150 per day while she was in the facility). The amount Hazel may exclude is calculated as follows:

| | | |
|---|---:|---:|
| Greater of: | | |
| Daily statutory amount of $240 ($240 × 30 days) | $7,200 | |
| Actual cost of the care | 7,500 | $ 7,500 |
| Less: Amount received from Medicare | | (3,200) |
| Amount of exclusion | | $ 4,300 |

Therefore, Hazel must include $200 ($4,500 − $4,300) of the long-term care benefits received in her gross income. ∎

The exclusion for long-term care insurance is not available if it is provided as part of a cafeteria plan or a flexible spending plan (discussed later in this chapter).

## MEALS AND LODGING FURNISHED FOR THE CONVENIENCE OF THE EMPLOYER

Income can take any form, including meals and lodging. However, § 119 excludes from gross income the value of meals and lodging provided to the employee and the employee's spouse and dependents under the following conditions:[8]

---

[6]§ 223.
[7]§ 7702B.

[8]§ 119(a). The value of meals and lodging is also excluded from FICA and FUTA tax. *Rowan Companies, Inc. v. U.S.*, 81–1 USTC ¶9479, 48 AFTR2d 81–5115, 101 S.Ct. 2288 (USSC, 1981).

- The meals and/or lodging are *furnished by the employer*, on the employer's *business premises*, for the *convenience of the employer*.
- In the case of lodging, the *employee is required* to accept the lodging as a condition of employment.

The courts have construed these requirements strictly, as discussed below.

**Furnished by the Employer.** The following two questions have been raised with regard to the *furnished by the employer* requirement:

- Who is considered an *employee*?
- What is meant by *furnished*?

For the employee issue, the IRS and some courts have reasoned that because a partner is not an employee, the exclusion does not apply to a partner. However, the Tax Court and the Fifth Circuit Court of Appeals have ruled in favor of the taxpayer on this issue.[9]

On the issue of whether meals and lodging are *furnished* by the employer, the Supreme Court held that a *cash meal allowance* was ineligible for the exclusion because the employer did not actually furnish the meals.[10] Similarly, one court denied the exclusion where the employer paid for the food and supplied the cooking facilities but the employee prepared the meal.[11]

**On the Employer's Business Premises.** The *on the employer's business premises* requirement, applicable to both meals and lodging, has resulted in much litigation. The Regulations define business premises as simply "the place of employment of the employee."[12] Thus, the Sixth Circuit Court of Appeals held that a residence, owned by the employer and occupied by an employee, located two blocks from the motel that the employee managed was not part of the business premises.[13] However, the Tax Court considered an employer-owned house located across the street from the hotel that was managed by the taxpayer to be on the business premises of the employer.[14] Perhaps these two cases can be reconciled by comparing the distance from the lodging facilities to the place where the employer's business was conducted. The closer the lodging to the business operations, the more likely the convenience of the employer is served.

**For the Convenience of the Employer.** The *convenience of the employer* test is intended to focus on the employer's motivation for furnishing the meals and lodging rather than on the benefits received by the employee. If the employer furnishes the meals and lodging primarily to enable the employee to perform his or her duties properly, it does not matter that the employee considers these benefits to be a part of his or her compensation.

The Regulations give the following examples in which the tests for excluding meals are satisfied:[15]

- A waitress is required to eat her meals on the premises during the busy lunch and breakfast hours.

---

[9]Rev.Rul. 80, 1953–1 C.B. 62; *Comm. v. Doak,* 56–2 USTC ¶9708, 49 AFTR 1491, 234 F.2d 704 (CA–4, 1956); but see *G. A. Papineau,* 16 T.C. 130 (1951); *Armstrong v. Phinney,* 68–1 USTC ¶9355, 21 AFTR2d 1260, 394 F.2d 661 (CA–5, 1968).

[10]*Comm. v. Kowalski,* 77–2 USTC ¶9748, 40 AFTR2d 6128, 98 S.Ct. 315 (USSC, 1977).

[11]*Tougher v. Comm.,* 71–1 USTC ¶9398, 27 AFTR2d 1301, 441 F.2d 1148 (CA–9, 1971).

[12]Reg. § 1.119–1(c)(1).

[13]*Comm. v. Anderson,* 67–1 USTC ¶9136, 19 AFTR2d 318, 371 F.2d 59 (CA–6, 1966).

[14]*J. B. Lindeman,* 60 T.C. 609 (1973).

[15]Reg. § 1.119–1(f).

- A bank furnishes a teller meals on the premises to limit the time the employee is away from his or her booth during the busy hours.
- A worker is employed at a construction site in a remote part of Alaska. The employer must furnish meals and lodging due to the inaccessibility of other facilities.

If more than half of the meals provided to employees are furnished for the convenience of the employer, then all such employee meals are treated as provided for the convenience of the employer. Thus, in this situation, all employees are treated the same (either all of the employees are allowed exclusion treatment, or none of the employees can exclude the meals from gross income).

**EXAMPLE 7**

Allison's Restaurant has a restaurant area and a bar. Nine employees work in the restaurant and three work in the bar. All of the employees are provided one meal per day. In the case of the restaurant workers, the meals are provided for the convenience of the employer. The meals provided to the bar employees do not satisfy the convenience of the employer requirement. Because more than half of the employees receive their meal for the convenience of the employer, all 12 employees qualify for exclusion treatment. ▪

**Required as a Condition of Employment.**  The *required as a condition of employment* test applies only to lodging. If the employee's use of the housing would serve the convenience of the employer, but the employee is not required to use the housing, the exclusion is not available.

**EXAMPLE 8**

VEP, a utilities company, has all of its service personnel on 24-hour call for emergencies. The company encourages its employees to live near the plant so they can respond quickly to emergency calls. Company-owned housing is available rent-free. Only 10 of the employees live in the company housing because it is not suitable for families.

Although the company-provided housing serves the convenience of the employer, it is not required. Therefore, the employees who live in the company housing must include its value in gross income. ▪

In addition, if the employee has the option of cash or lodging, the employer-required test is not satisfied.

**EXAMPLE 9**

Khalid is the manager of a large apartment complex. The employer gives Khalid the option of rent-free housing (value of $9,600 per year) or an additional $7,500 per year. Khalid selects the housing option. Therefore, he must include $9,600 in gross income. ▪

Other housing exclusions are available for certain employees of educational institutions, ministers of the gospel, and military personnel.

## GROUP TERM LIFE INSURANCE

For many years, the IRS did not attempt to tax the value of life insurance protection provided to an employee by the employer. Some companies took undue advantage of the exclusion by providing large amounts of insurance protection for key executives. In response, Congress enacted § 79, which created a limited exclusion for group term life insurance. Current law allows an exclusion of premiums on the first $50,000 of group term life insurance protection.

The benefits of this exclusion are available only to employees. Proprietors and partners are not considered employees. Moreover, the Regulations generally require broad-scale coverage of employees to satisfy the group requirement (e.g., shareholder-employees would not constitute a qualified group). The exclusion applies only to term insurance (protection for a period of time but with no cash

■ **TABLE 16–1**

Uniform Premiums for $1,000 of Group Term Life Insurance Protection

| 5-Year Age Bracket | Cost of $1,000 of Protection for a One-Month Period* |
|---|---|
| Under 25 | $ .05 |
| 25–29 | .06 |
| 30–34 | .08 |
| 35–39 | .09 |
| 40–44 | .10 |
| 45–49 | .15 |
| 50–54 | .23 |
| 55–59 | .43 |
| 60–64 | .66 |
| 65–69 | 1.27 |
| 70 and above | 2.06 |

*Reg. § 1.79–3, effective for coverage after June 30, 1999.

surrender value) and not to ordinary life insurance (lifetime protection plus a cash surrender value that can be drawn upon before death).

As mentioned, the exclusion applies to the first $50,000 of group term life insurance protection. For each $1,000 of coverage in excess of $50,000, the employee must include the amounts indicated in Table 16–1 in gross income.[16]

*Find more information on this topic at our Web site: **http://wft-entities.swlearning.com**.*

**EXAMPLE 10**

Finch Corporation has a group term life insurance policy with coverage equal to the employee's annual salary. Keith, age 52, is president of the corporation and receives an annual salary of $75,000. Keith must include $69 in gross income from the insurance protection for the year.

$$[(\$75,000 - \$50,000)/\$1,000] \times \$0.23 \times 12 \text{ months} = \$69$$ ■

If the plan discriminates in favor of certain key employees (e.g., officers), the key employees are not eligible for the exclusion. In such a case, the key employees must include in gross income the *greater* of actual premiums paid by the employer or the amount calculated from the Uniform Premiums table in Table 16–1. The other employees are still eligible for the $50,000 exclusion and continue to use the Uniform Premiums table to compute the income from excess insurance protection.[17]

## QUALIFIED TUITION REDUCTION PLANS

Employees (including retired and disabled former employees) of nonprofit educational institutions are allowed to exclude a tuition waiver from gross income, if the waiver is pursuant to a qualified tuition reduction plan.[18] The plan may not discriminate in favor of highly compensated employees. The exclusion applies to the employee, the employee's spouse, and the employee's dependent children. The exclusion also extends to tuition reductions granted by any nonprofit educational institution to employees of any other nonprofit educational institution (reciprocal agreements).

---

[16]Reg. § 1.79–3(d)(2).
[17]§ 79(d).

[18]§ 117(d).

**EXAMPLE 11**

ABC University allows the dependent children of XYZ University employees to attend ABC University with no tuition charge. XYZ University grants reciprocal benefits to the children of ABC University employees. The dependent children can also attend tuition-free the university where their parents are employed. Employees who take advantage of these benefits are not required to recognize gross income. ∎

Generally, the exclusion is limited to undergraduate tuition waivers. However, in the case of teaching or research assistants, graduate tuition waivers may also qualify for exclusion treatment. According to the Proposed Regulations, the exclusion is limited to the value of the benefit in excess of the employee's reasonable compensation.[19] Thus, a tuition reduction that is a substitute for cash compensation cannot be excluded.

**EXAMPLE 12**

Susan is a graduate research assistant. She receives a $5,000 salary for 500 hours of service over a nine-month period. This pay, $10 per hour, is reasonable compensation for Susan's services. In addition, Susan receives a waiver of $6,000 for tuition. Susan may exclude the tuition waiver from gross income. ∎

## OTHER SPECIFIC EMPLOYEE FRINGE BENEFITS

Congress has enacted exclusions to encourage employers to (1) finance and make available child care facilities, (2) provide athletic facilities for employees, (3) finance certain education expenses of employees, and (4) assist employees who adopt children. These provisions are summarized as follows:

- The employee can exclude from gross income the value of child and dependent care services paid for by the employer and incurred to enable the employee to work. The exclusion cannot exceed $5,000 per year ($2,500 if married and filing separately). For a married couple, the annual exclusion cannot exceed the earned income of the spouse who has the lesser amount of earned income. For an unmarried taxpayer, the exclusion cannot exceed the taxpayer's earned income.[20]
- The value of the use of a gymnasium or other athletic facilities by employees, their spouses, and their dependent children may be excluded from an employee's gross income. The facilities must be on the employer's premises, and substantially all of the use of the facilities must be by employees and their family members.[21]
- Qualified employer-provided educational assistance (tuition, fees, books, and supplies) at the undergraduate and graduate levels is excludible from gross income. The exclusion is limited to a maximum of $5,250 annually.[22]
- The employee can exclude from gross income up to $10,630 of expenses incurred to adopt a child where the adoption expenses are paid or reimbursed by the employer under a qualified adoption assistance program.[23] The limit on the exclusion is the same even if the child has special needs (is not physically or mentally capable of caring for himself or herself). The exclusion is phased out over the AGI range from $159,450 to $199,450.

---

[19]Prop.Reg. § 1.117–6(d).
[20]§ 129. The exclusion applies to the same types of expenses that, if paid by the employee (and not reimbursed by the employer), would be eligible for the credit for child and dependent care expenses, discussed in Chapter 15.

[21]§ 132(j)(4).
[22]§ 127.
[23]§ 137.

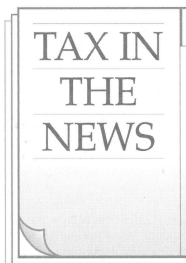

## TAX IN THE NEWS

### EMPLOYEES LOSE SOME UNDER "USE OR LOSE PLANS"

Over 21 million Americans lose between $125 and $200 every year as a result of overfunding their flexible benefit accounts. If the employee overestimates the amount required to provide the flexible benefits, and thus the reduction in the employee's salary, the unused portion of the fund is forfeited to the employer. The total forfeited amounts exceed $2 billion annually. Thus, employees appear to be substantial losers under these "use-it-or-lose-it" plans. Even though employees can still be net beneficiaries from the portion of the accounts that is actually used, the employees simply are not maximizing the benefits.

Tax legislation has been proposed on several occasions recently to allow any unused amount in a flexible benefit account to be transferred to various types of employee retirement accounts or to otherwise carry over for the employee's benefit. To date, none of these proposals has been enacted.

### CAFETERIA PLANS

Generally, if an employee is offered a choice between cash and some other form of compensation, the employee is deemed to have constructively received the cash even when the noncash option is elected. Thus, the employee has gross income regardless of the option chosen.

An exception to this constructive receipt treatment is provided under the cafeteria plan rules. Under such a plan, the employee is permitted to choose between cash and nontaxable benefits (e.g., group term life insurance, health and accident protection, and child care). If the employee chooses the otherwise nontaxable benefits, the cafeteria plan rules allow the benefits to be excluded from the employee's gross income.[24] **Cafeteria plans** provide tremendous flexibility in tailoring the employee pay package to fit individual needs. Some employees (usually the younger group) prefer cash, while others (usually the older group) will opt for the fringe benefit program. However, long-term care insurance cannot be part of a cafeteria plan. Thus, an employer that wishes to provide long-term care benefits must provide such benefits separate from the cafeteria plan.[25]

**EXAMPLE 13**

Hawk Corporation offers its employees (on a nondiscriminatory basis) a choice of any one or all of the following benefits:

| Benefit | Cost |
| --- | --- |
| Group term life insurance | $ 200 |
| Hospitalization insurance for family members | 2,400 |
| Child care payments | 1,800 |
| | $4,400 |

If a benefit is not selected, the employee receives cash equal to the cost of the benefit.

---

[24]§ 125.                                    [25]§ 125(f).

Kay, an employee, has a spouse who works for another employer that provides hospitalization insurance but no child care payments. Kay elects to receive the group term life insurance, the child care payments, and $2,400 of cash. Only the $2,400 must be included in Kay's gross income. ■

## FLEXIBLE SPENDING PLANS

**Flexible spending plans** (often referred to as flexible benefit plans) operate much like cafeteria plans. Under these plans, the employee accepts lower cash compensation in return for the employer's agreement to pay certain costs that the employer can pay without the employee recognizing gross income. For example, assume the employer's health insurance policy does not cover dental expenses. The employee could estimate his or her dental expenses for the upcoming year and agree to a salary reduction equal to the estimated dental expenses. The employer then pays or reimburses the employee for the actual dental expenses incurred, up to the amount of the salary reduction. If the employee's actual dental expenses are less than the reduction in cash compensation, the employee cannot recover the difference. Hence, these plans are often referred to as *use or lose* plans. As is the case for cafeteria plans, flexible spending plans cannot be used to pay long-term care insurance premiums.

## GENERAL CLASSES OF EXCLUDED BENEFITS

An employer can provide a variety of economic benefits to employees. Under the all-inclusive concept of income, the benefits are taxable unless one of the provisions previously discussed specifically excludes the item from gross income. The amount of the income is the fair market value of the benefit. This reasoning can lead to results that Congress considers unacceptable, as illustrated in the following example.

**EXAMPLE 14**

Vern is employed in New York as a ticket clerk for Trans National Airlines. Vern would like to visit his mother, who lives in Miami, Florida, but he has no money for plane tickets. Trans National has daily flights from New York to Miami that often leave with empty seats. The cost of a round-trip ticket is $500, and Vern is in the 25% tax bracket. If Trans National allows Vern to fly without charge to Miami, under the general gross income rules, Vern has income equal to the value of a ticket. Therefore, Vern must pay $125 tax (.25 × $500) on a trip to Miami. Because Vern does not have $125, he cannot visit his mother, and the airplane flies with another empty seat. ■

If Trans National in Example 14 will allow employees to use resources that would otherwise be wasted, why should the tax laws interfere with the employee's decision to take advantage of the available benefit? Thus, to avoid the economic inefficiency that occurs in Example 14 and in similar situations, as well as to create uniform rules for fringe benefits, Congress established seven broad classes of nontaxable employee benefits:[26]

- No-additional-cost services.
- Qualified employee discounts.
- Working condition fringes.
- *De minimis* fringes.

---

[26]See, generally, § 132.

- Qualified transportation fringes.
- Qualified moving expense reimbursements.
- Qualified retirement planning services.

**No-Additional-Cost Services.** Example 14 illustrates a no-additional-cost fringe benefit. **No-additional-cost services** are excluded from an employee's gross income if all of the following conditions are satisfied:

- The employee receives services, as opposed to property.
- The employer does not incur substantial additional costs, including forgone revenue, in providing the services to the employee.
- The services must be from the same line of business in which the employee works.
- The services are offered to customers in the ordinary course of the business in which the employee works.[27]

**EXAMPLE 15**

Assume that Vern in Example 14 can fly without charge only if the airline cannot fill the seats with paying customers. That is, Vern must fly on standby. Although the airplane may burn slightly more fuel because Vern is aboard and Vern may receive the same meal as paying customers, the additional costs would not be substantial. Thus, the trip could qualify as a no-additional-cost service.

On the other hand, assume that Vern is given a reserved seat on a flight that is frequently full. The employer would be forgoing revenue to allow Vern to fly. This forgone revenue would be a substantial additional cost, and thus the benefit would be taxable to Vern. ■

*Find more information on this topic at our Web site: **http://wft-entities.swlearning.com**.*

The no-additional-cost exclusion extends to the employee's spouse and dependent children and to retired and disabled former employees. In the Regulations, the IRS has conceded that partners who perform services for the partnership are employees for purposes of the exclusion.[28] However, the exclusion is not extended to highly compensated employees unless the benefit is available on a nondiscriminatory basis.

**Qualified Employee Discounts.** When the employer sells goods or services (other than no-additional-cost benefits just discussed) to the employee for a price that is less than the price charged regular customers, the employee ordinarily recognizes income equal to the discount. However, **qualified employee discounts** can be excluded from the gross income of the employee, subject to the following conditions and limitations:

- The exclusion is not available for discounted sales of real property (e.g., a house) or for personal property of the type commonly held for investment (e.g., common stocks).
- The property or services must be from the same line of business in which the employee works.
- In the case of property, the exclusion cannot exceed the gross profit component of the price to customers.
- In the case of services, the exclusion is limited to 20 percent of the customer price.[29]

---

[27]Reg. § 1.132–2.
[28]Reg. § 1.132–1(b).

[29]§ 132(c).

**EXAMPLE 16**

Silver Corporation, which operates a department store, sells a television set to a store employee for $300. The regular customer price is $500, and the gross profit rate is 25%. The corporation also sells the employee a service contract for $100. The regular customer price for the contract is $150. The employee must recognize income of $95, computed as follows:

| | | |
|---|---:|---:|
| Customer price for property | $ 500 | |
| Less: Qualifying discount (25% gross profit × $500 price) | (125) | |
| | $ 375 | |
| Employee price | (300) | |
| Excess discount recognized as income | | $75 |
| Customer price for service | $ 150 | |
| Less: Qualifying discount (20%) | (30) | |
| | $ 120 | |
| Employee price | (100) | |
| Excess discount recognized as income | | 20 |
| Total income recognized | | $95 |

**EXAMPLE 17**

Assume the same facts as in Example 16, except that the employee is a clerk in a hotel operated by Silver Corporation. Because the line of business requirement is not met, the employee must recognize $200 of income ($500 – $300) from the discount on the television and $50 of income ($150 – $100) from the service contract. ■

As in the case of no-additional-cost benefits, the exclusion applies to employees, their spouses and dependent children, and retired and disabled former employees. However, the exclusion does not extend to highly compensated individuals unless the discount is available on a nondiscriminatory basis.

**Working Condition Fringes.** Generally, an employee may exclude the cost of property or services provided by the employer if the employee could deduct the cost of those items if he or she had actually paid for them.[30] These benefits are called **working condition fringes.**

**EXAMPLE 18**

Mitch is a certified public accountant employed by an accounting firm. The employer pays Mitch's annual dues to professional organizations. Mitch is not required to include the payment of the dues in gross income because if he had paid the dues, he would have been allowed to deduct the amount as an employee business expense (as discussed later in this chapter). ■

In many cases, this exclusion merely avoids reporting income and an offsetting deduction. However, in two specific situations, the working condition fringe benefit rules allow an exclusion where the expense would not be deductible if paid by the employee:

- Some automobile salespeople are allowed to exclude the value of certain personal use of company demonstrators (e.g., commuting to and from work).[31]
- The employee business expense would be eliminated by the 2 percent floor on miscellaneous itemized deductions under § 67 (refer to Chapter 15).

Unlike the other fringe benefits discussed previously, working condition fringes can be made available on a discriminatory basis and still qualify for the exclusion.

---

[30]§ 132(d).

[31]§ 132(j)(3).

*De Minimis* **Fringes.** As the term suggests, *de minimis* **fringe benefits** are so small that accounting for them is impractical.[32] The House Report contains the following examples of *de minimis* fringes:

- The typing of a personal letter by a company secretary, occasional personal use of a company copying machine, occasional company cocktail parties or picnics for employees, occasional supper money or taxi fare for employees because of overtime work, and certain holiday gifts of property with a low fair market value are excluded.
- The value of meals consumed in a subsidized eating facility (e.g., an employees' cafeteria) operated by the employer is excluded if the facility is located on or near the employer's business premises, if revenue equals or exceeds direct operating costs, and if nondiscrimination requirements are met.

When taxpayers venture beyond the specific examples contained in the House Report and the Regulations, there is obviously much room for disagreement as to what is *de minimis*. However, note that except in the case of subsidized eating facilities, *de minimis* fringe benefits can be granted in a manner that favors highly compensated employees.

**Qualified Transportation Fringes.** The intent of the exclusion for **qualified transportation fringes** is to encourage the use of mass transit for commuting to and from work. Qualified transportation fringes encompass the following transportation benefits provided by the employer to the employee:[33]

1. Transportation in a commuter highway vehicle between the employee's residence and the place of employment.
2. A transit pass.
3. Qualified parking.

Statutory dollar limits are placed on the amount of the exclusion. Categories (1) and (2) above are combined for purposes of applying the limit. In this case, the limit on the exclusion for 2005 is $105 per month. Category (3) has a separate limit. For qualified parking, the limit on the exclusion for 2005 is $200 per month. Both of these dollar limits are indexed annually for inflation.

A commuter highway vehicle is any highway vehicle with a seating capacity of at least six adults (excluding the driver). In addition, at least 80 percent of the vehicle's use must be for transporting employees between their residences and place of employment.

Qualified parking includes the following:

- Parking provided to an employee on or near the employer's business premises.
- Parking provided to an employee on or near a location from which the employee commutes to work via mass transit, in a commuter highway vehicle, or in a carpool.

Qualified transportation fringes may be provided directly by the employer or may be in the form of cash reimbursements.

**EXAMPLE 19**

Gray Corporation's offices are located in the center of a large city. The company pays for parking spaces to be used by the company officers. Steve, a vice president, receives $250 of such benefits each month. The parking space rental qualifies as a qualified transportation fringe. Of the $250 benefit received each month by Steve, $200 is excludible from gross

---

[32]§ 132(e).

[33]§ 132(f).

income. The balance of $50 is included in his gross income. The same result would occur if Steve paid for the parking and was reimbursed by his employer. ■

**Qualified Moving Expense Reimbursements.**   Qualified moving expenses that are reimbursed or paid by the employer are excludible from gross income. A qualified moving expense is one that would be deductible under § 217. See the discussion of moving expenses later in this chapter.

**Qualified Retirement Planning Services.**   Qualified retirement planning services include any retirement planning advice or information provided by an employer who maintains a qualified retirement plan to an employee or the spouse.[34] Congress decided to exclude the value of such services from gross income because they are a key part of retirement income planning. Such an exclusion should motivate more employers to provide retirement planning services to their employees.

**Nondiscrimination Provisions.**   For no-additional-cost services, qualified employee discounts, and qualified retirement planning services, if the plan is discriminatory in favor of *highly compensated employees*,[35] these key employees are denied exclusion treatment. However, any non-highly compensated employees who receive these benefits can still enjoy exclusion treatment.[36]

**EXAMPLE 20**

Dove Company's officers are allowed to purchase goods from the company at a 25% discount. Other employees are allowed only a 15% discount. The company's gross profit margin on these goods is 30%.

Peggy, an officer in the company, purchased goods from the company for $750 when the price charged to customers was $1,000. Peggy must include $250 in gross income because the plan is discriminatory.

Leo, an employee of the company who is not an officer, purchased goods for $850 when the customer price was $1,000. Leo is not required to recognize income because he received a qualified employee discount. ■

*De minimis* fringe benefits (except for subsidized eating facilities) and working condition fringe benefits can be provided on a discriminatory basis. Likewise, the qualified transportation fringe and the qualified moving expense reimbursement can be provided on a discriminatory basis.

 DIGGING DEEPER ⑤    *Find more information on this topic at our Web site:* ***http://wft-entities.swlearning.com.***

## TAXABLE FRINGE BENEFITS

If fringe benefits cannot qualify for any of the specific exclusions or do not fit into any of the general classes of excluded benefits, the employee must recognize gross income equal to the fair market value of the benefits received. Obviously, problems are frequently encountered in determining values. To help taxpayers cope with these problems, the IRS has issued extensive Regulations addressing the valuation of personal use of an employer's automobiles and meals provided at an employer-operated eating facility.[37]

---

[34]§§ 132(a)(7) and (m).
[35]See § 414(q) for the definition of highly compensated employee.
[36]§§ 61, 132(j)(1), and 132(m)(2).
[37]Reg. § 1.61–2T(j). Generally, the income from the personal use of the employer's automobile is based on the lease value of the automobile

(what it would have cost the employee to lease the automobile). Meals are valued at 150% of the employer's direct costs (e.g., food and labor) of preparing the meals.

If a fringe benefit plan discriminates in favor of highly compensated employees, generally those employees are not allowed to exclude the benefits they receive that other employees do not enjoy. However, the highly compensated employees, as well as the other employees, are generally allowed to exclude the nondiscriminatory benefits.[38]

**EXAMPLE 21**

MED Company has a medical reimbursement plan that reimburses officers for 100% of their medical expenses, but reimburses all other employees for only 80% of their medical expenses. Cliff, the president of the company, was reimbursed $1,000 during the year for medical expenses. Cliff must include $200 in gross income [(1 − .80) × $1,000 = $200]. Mike, an employee who is not an officer, received $800 (80% of his actual medical expenses) under the medical reimbursement plan. None of the $800 is includible in his gross income. ■

## FOREIGN EARNED INCOME

A U.S. citizen is generally subject to U.S. tax on his or her income regardless of the income's geographic origin. The income may also be subject to tax in the foreign country, and thus the taxpayer must carry a double tax burden. Out of a sense of fairness and to encourage U.S. citizens to work abroad (so that exports might be increased), Congress has provided alternative forms of relief from taxes on foreign earned income. The taxpayer can elect *either* (1) to include the foreign income in his or her taxable income and then claim a credit for foreign taxes paid or (2) to exclude the foreign earnings from his or her U.S. gross income (the **foreign earned income exclusion**).[39] The foreign tax credit option is discussed in Chapter 13, but as is apparent from the following discussion, most taxpayers will choose the exclusion.

*Foreign earned income* consists of the earnings from the individual's personal services rendered in a foreign country (other than as an employee of the U.S. government). To qualify for the exclusion, the taxpayer must be either of the following:

- A bona fide resident of the foreign country (or countries).
- Present in a foreign country (or countries) for at least 330 days during any 12 consecutive months.

**EXAMPLE 22**

Sandra's trips to and from a foreign country in connection with her work were as follows:

| Arrived in Foreign Country | Arrived in United States |
| --- | --- |
| March 10, 2004 | February 1, 2005 |
| March 7, 2005 | June 1, 2005 |

During the 12 consecutive months ending on March 10, 2005, Sandra was present in the foreign country for at least 330 days (365 days less 28 days in February and 7 days in March 2005). Therefore, all income earned in the foreign country through March 10, 2005, is eligible for the exclusion. The income earned from March 11, 2005, through May 31, 2005, is also eligible for the exclusion because Sandra was present in the foreign country for 330 days during the 12 consecutive months ending on May 31, 2005. ■

The exclusion is *limited* to $80,000. For married persons, both of whom have foreign earned income, the exclusion is computed separately for each spouse.

---

[38]§§ 79(d), 105(h), 127(b)(2), and 132(j)(1).  [39]§ 911.

Community property rules do not apply (the community property spouse is not deemed to have earned one-half of the other spouse's foreign earned income). If all the days in the tax year are not qualifying days, then the taxpayer must compute the maximum exclusion on a daily basis ($80,000 divided by the number of days in the entire year and multiplied by the number of qualifying days).

**EXAMPLE 23**

Keith qualifies for the foreign earned income exclusion. He was present in France for all of 2005. Keith's salary for 2005 is $90,000. Since all of the days in 2005 are qualifying days, Keith can exclude $80,000 of his $90,000 salary.

Assume instead that only 335 days were qualifying days. Then, Keith's exclusion is limited to $73,425, computed as follows:

$$\$80,000 \times \frac{335 \text{ days in foreign country}}{365 \text{ days in the year}} = \$73,425$$

**LO.3**

Apply the rules for computing deductible expenses of employees including transportation, travel, moving, education, and entertainment expenses.

# Employee Expenses

Once the employment relationship is established, employee expenses fall into one of the following categories:

* Transportation.
* Travel.
* Moving.
* Education.
* Entertainment.
* Other.

These expenses are discussed below in the order presented. Keep in mind, however, that these expenses are not necessarily limited to employees. A deduction for business transportation, for example, is equally available to taxpayers who are self-employed.

## TRANSPORTATION EXPENSES

**Qualified Expenditures.**   An employee may deduct unreimbursed employment-related **transportation expenses** as an itemized deduction *from* AGI. Transportation expenses include only the cost of transporting the employee from one place to another when the employee is not away from home in travel status. Such costs include taxi fares, automobile expenses, tolls, and parking.

**Commuting Expenses.**   Commuting between home and one's place of employment is a personal, nondeductible expense. The fact that one employee drives 30 miles to work and another employee walks six blocks is of no significance.[40]

**EXAMPLE 24**

Geraldo is employed by Sparrow Corporation. He drives 22 miles each way to work. The 44 miles he drives each workday are nondeductible commuting expenses. ■

The expenses of getting from one job to another job or from one work station to another work station are deductible transportation expenses rather than nondeductible commuting expenses.

 DIGGING DEEPER 6   *Find more information on this topic at our Web site: **http://wft-entities.swlearning.com**.*

---

[40]*Tauferner v. U.S.*, 69–1 USTC ¶9241, 23 AFTR2d 69–1025, 407 F.2d 243 (CA–10, 1969).

## CONCEPT SUMMARY 16–1

### General Classes of Fringe Benefits

| Benefit | Description and Examples | Coverage Allowed | Effect of Discrimination |
|---|---|---|---|
| 1. No-additional-cost services | The employee takes advantage of the employer's excess capacity (e.g., free passes for airline employees). | Current, retired, and disabled employees; their spouses and dependent children; spouses of deceased employees. Partners are treated as employees. | No exclusion for highly compensated employees. |
| 2. Qualified discounts on goods | The employee is allowed a discount no greater than the gross profit margin on goods sold to customers. | Same as (1) above. | Same as (1) above. |
| 3. Qualified discounts on services | The employee is allowed a discount (maximum of 20%) on services the employer offers to customers. | Same as (1) above. | Same as (1) above. |
| 4. Working condition fringes | Expenses paid by the employer that would be deductible if paid by the employee (e.g., a mechanic's tools). Also, includes auto salesperson's use of a car held for sale. | Current employees, partners, directors, and independent contractors. | No effect. |
| 5. De minimis items | Expenses so immaterial that accounting for them is not warranted (e.g., occasional supper money, personal use of the copy machine). | Any recipient of a fringe benefit. | No effect. |
| 6. Qualified transportation fringes | Transportation benefits provided by the employer to employees, including commuting in a commuter highway vehicle, a transit pass, and qualified parking. | Current employees. | No effect. |
| 7. Qualified moving expense reimbursements | Qualified moving expenses that are paid or reimbursed by the employer. A qualified moving expense is one that would be deductible under § 217. | Current employees. | No effect. |
| 8. Qualified retirement planning services | Qualified retirement planning services that are provided by the employer. | Current employees and spouses. | Same as (1) above. |

EXAMPLE 25

In the current year, Cynthia holds two jobs, a full-time job with Blue Corporation and a part-time job with Wren Corporation. During the 250 days that she works (adjusted for weekends, vacation, and holidays), Cynthia customarily leaves home at 7:30 A.M. and drives 30 miles to the Blue Corporation plant, where she works until 5:00 P.M. After dinner at a nearby café, Cynthia drives 20 miles to Wren Corporation and works from 7:00 to 11:00 P.M. The distance from the second job to Cynthia's home is 40 miles. Her deduction is based on 20 miles (the distance between jobs). ■

**Computation of Automobile Expenses.**   A taxpayer has two choices in computing deductible automobile expenses. The actual operating cost, which includes depreciation (refer to Chapter 4), gas, oil, repairs, licenses, and insurance, may be used. Records must be kept that detail the automobile's personal and business use. Only the percentage allocable to business transportation and travel is allowed as a deduction.

Use of the **automatic mileage method** is the second alternative. For 2005, the deduction is based on 40.5 cents per mile for business miles.[41] Parking fees and tolls are allowed in addition to expenses computed using the automatic mileage method.

Generally, a taxpayer may elect either method for any particular year. However, the following restrictions apply:

- The vehicle must be owned or leased by the taxpayer.
- If five or more vehicles are in use (for business purposes) at the *same* time (not alternately), a taxpayer may not use the automatic mileage method.
- Use of the automatic mileage method in the first year the auto is placed in service is considered an election not to use the MACRS method of depreciation (refer to Chapter 4).
- A taxpayer may not switch to the automatic mileage method if the MACRS statutory percentage method or the election to expense under § 179 has been used.

*Find more information on this topic at our Web site: **http://wft-entities.swlearning.com**.*

### TRAVEL EXPENSES

**Definition of Travel Expenses.**   An itemized deduction is allowed for *unreimbursed* **travel expenses** related to a taxpayer's employment. Travel expenses are more broadly defined in the Code than are transportation expenses. Travel expenses include transportation expenses and meals and lodging while away from home in the pursuit of a trade or business. Meals cannot be lavish or extravagant. A deduction for meals and lodging is available only if the taxpayer is away from his or her tax home. Deductible travel expenses also include reasonable laundry and incidental expenses.

*Find more information on this topic at our Web site: **http://wft-entities.swlearning.com**.*

**Away-from-Home Requirement.**   The crucial test for the deductibility of travel expenses is whether the employee is away from home overnight. "Overnight" need not be a 24-hour period, but it must be a period substantially longer than an ordinary day's work and must require rest, sleep, or a relief-from-work period.[42]

---

[41]Rev.Proc. 2004–64, I.R.B. No. 49, 898. For 2004, the rate was 37.5 cents per mile for business miles.

[42]*U.S. v. Correll*, 68–1 USTC ¶9101, 20 AFTR2d 5845, 88 S.Ct 445 (USSC, 1967); Rev.Rul. 75–168, 1975–1 C.B. 58.

## RELIEF FOR MEMBERS OF THE ARMED FORCES RESERVES

In the Military Family Tax Relief Act of 2003, Congress provided various tax benefits for reservists, one of which deals with the classification of travel expenses. Members of the Reserves or National Guard who travel to drills and other service-related activities may claim the expenses as deductions *for* AGI. Previously, the expenses were not deductible unless the taxpayer itemized. (As miscellaneous itemized deductions, they were subject to the 2 percent-of-AGI floor.) To qualify for the deduction *for* AGI classification, the trip must be more than 100 miles from home and include an overnight stay. Any deduction is limited to the Federal per diem rates applicable to the area involved.

A one-day business trip is not travel status, and meals and lodging for such a trip are not deductible.

**Temporary Assignments.**    The employee must be away from home for a temporary period. If the taxpayer-employee is reassigned to a new post for an indefinite period of time, that new post becomes his or her tax home. Temporary indicates that the assignment's termination is expected within a reasonably short period of time. The position of the IRS is that the tax home is the business location, post, or station of the taxpayer. Thus, travel expenses are not deductible if a taxpayer is reassigned for an indefinite period and does not move his or her place of residence to the new location.

**EXAMPLE 26**    Malcolm's employer opened a branch office in San Diego. Malcolm was assigned to the new office for three months to train a new manager and to assist in setting up the new office. He tried commuting from his home in Los Angeles for a week and decided that he could not continue driving several hours a day. He rented an apartment in San Diego, where he lived during the week. He spent weekends with his wife and children at their home in Los Angeles. Malcolm's rent, meals, laundry, incidentals, and automobile expenses in San Diego are deductible. To the extent that Malcolm's transportation expense related to his weekend trips home exceeds what his cost of meals and lodging would have been, the excess is personal and nondeductible. ■

**EXAMPLE 27**    Assume that Malcolm in Example 26 was transferred to the new location to become the new manager permanently. His wife and children continued to live in Los Angeles until the end of the school year. Malcolm is no longer "away from home" because the assignment is not temporary. His travel expenses are not deductible. ■

To curtail controversy in this area, the Code specifies that a taxpayer "shall not be treated as temporarily away from home during any period of employment if such period exceeds 1 year."[43]

**Determining the Tax Home.**    Under ordinary circumstances, determining the location of a taxpayer's tax home does not present a problem. The tax home is the area in which the taxpayer derives his or her principal source of income; when the taxpayer has more than one place of employment, the tax home is based on the amount of time spent in each area.

---

[43]§ 162(a).

It is possible for a taxpayer never to be away from his or her tax home. In other words, the tax home follows the taxpayer.[44] Under such circumstances, all meals and lodging remain personal and are not deductible.

**EXAMPLE 28**

Bill is employed as a long-haul truck driver. He is single, stores his clothes and other belongings at his parents' home, and stops there for periodic visits. Most of the time, Bill is on the road, sleeping in his truck and in motels. It is likely that Bill is never in travel status, as he is not away from home. Consequently, none of his meals and lodging are deductible. ■

**Combined Business and Pleasure Travel.**   To be deductible, travel expenses need not be incurred in the performance of specific job functions. Travel expenses incurred to attend a professional convention are deductible by an employee if attendance is connected with services as an employee. For example, an employee of a law firm can deduct travel expenses incurred to attend a meeting of the American Bar Association.

Travel deductions have been used in the past by persons who claimed a tax deduction for what was essentially a personal vacation. As a result, several provisions have been enacted to restrict deductions associated with combined business and pleasure trips. If the business/pleasure trip is from one point in the United States to another point in the United States (*domestic travel*), the transportation expenses are deductible only if the trip is primarily for business.[45] If the trip is primarily for pleasure, no transportation expenses qualify as a deduction. Meals, lodging, and other expenses are allocated between business and personal days.

*Find more information on this topic at our Web site: **http://wft-entities.swlearning.com**.*

**EXAMPLE 29**

In the current year, Hana travels from Seattle to New York primarily for business. She spends five days conducting business and three days sightseeing and attending shows. Her plane and taxi fare amounts to $560. Her meals amount to $100 per day, and lodging and incidental expenses are $150 per day. She can deduct the transportation expenses of $560, since the trip is primarily for business (five days of business versus three days of sightseeing). Deductible meals are limited to five days and are subject to the 50% cutback (discussed later in the chapter) for a total of $250 [5 days × ($100 × 50%)], and other deductions are limited to $750 (5 days × $150). If Hana is an employee, the unreimbursed travel expenses are miscellaneous itemized deductions subject to the 2%-of-AGI floor. ■

When the trip is outside the United States (*foreign travel*), special rules apply.[46] Transportation expenses must be allocated between business and personal days *unless* (1) the taxpayer is away from home for seven days or less or (2) less than 25 percent of the time was for personal purposes. No allocation is required if the taxpayer has no substantial control over arrangements for the trip or the desire for a vacation is not a major factor in taking the trip. If the trip is primarily for pleasure, no transportation charges are deductible. Days devoted to travel are considered business days. Weekends, legal holidays, and intervening days are considered business days, provided that both the preceding and succeeding days were business days.

*Find more information on this topic at our Web site: **http://wft-entities.swlearning.com**.*

---

[44]*Moses Mitnick*, 13 T.C. 1 (1949).
[45]Reg. § 1.162–2(b)(1).

[46]§ 274(c) and Reg. § 1.274–4. For purposes of the seven-days-or-less exception, the departure travel day is not counted.

**EXAMPLE 30**

In the current year, Robert takes a trip from New York to Japan primarily for business purposes. He is away from home from June 10 through June 19. He spends three days vacationing and seven days conducting business (including two travel days). His airfare is $2,500, his meals amount to $100 per day, and lodging and incidental expenses are $160 per day. Since Robert is away from home for more than seven days and more than 25% of his time is devoted to personal purposes, only 70% (7 days business/10 days total) of the transportation is deductible. His deductions are as follows:

| | | |
|---|---:|---:|
| Transportation (70% × $2,500) | | $1,750 |
| Lodging ($160 × 7) | | 1,120 |
| Meals ($100 × 7) | $ 700 | |
| Less: 50% cutback (discussed later in this chapter) | (350) | 350 |
| Total deductions | | $3,220 |

If Robert is gone the same period of time but spends only two days (less than 25% of the total) vacationing, no allocation of transportation is required. Since the pleasure portion of the trip is less than 25% of the total, all of the airfare qualifies for the travel deduction. ■

The foreign convention rules do not operate to bar a deduction to an employer if the expense is *compensatory* in nature. For example, a trip to Rome won by a top salesperson is included in the gross income of the employee and is fully deductible by the employer.

**PLANNING STRATEGIES**

## Transportation and Travel Expenses

**FRAMEWORK FOCUS: DEDUCTIONS**

STRATEGY ▶ MAXIMIZE DEDUCTIBLE AMOUNTS.

Adequate detailed records of all transportation and travel expenses should be kept. Since the regular mileage allowance often is modest in amount, a new, expensive automobile used primarily for business may generate a higher expense based on actual cost. The election to expense part of the cost of the automobile under § 179, MACRS depreciation, insurance, repairs and maintenance, automobile club dues, and other related costs may result in automobile expenses greater than the automatic mileage allowance.

If a taxpayer wishes to sightsee or vacation on a business trip, it would be beneficial to schedule business on both a Friday and a Monday to turn the weekend into business days for allocation purposes. It is especially crucial to schedule appropriate business days when foreign travel is involved.

### MOVING EXPENSES

**Moving expenses** are deductible for moves in connection with the commencement of work at a new principal place of work.[47] Both employees and self-employed individuals can deduct these expenses. To be eligible for a moving expense deduction, a taxpayer must meet two basic tests: distance and time.

**Distance Test.**  To meet the distance test, the taxpayer's new job location must be at least 50 miles farther from the taxpayer's old residence than the old residence was from the former place of employment. In this regard, the location of the

---

[47]§ 217(a).

new residence is not relevant. This eliminates a moving expense deduction for (1) taxpayers who purchase a new home in the same general area without changing their place of employment and (2) taxpayers who accept a new job in the same area as their old job.

**EXAMPLE 31**

Harry is permanently transferred to a new job location. The distance from Harry's former home to his new job (80 miles) exceeds the distance from his former home to his old job (30 miles) by at least 50 miles. Harry has met the distance test for a moving expense deduction.

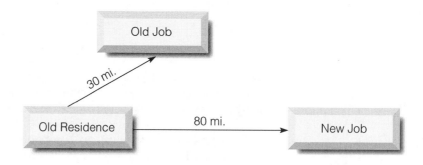

If Harry is not employed before the move, his new job must be at least 50 miles from his former residence. In this instance, Harry has also met the distance test if he was not previously employed. ■

**Time Test.**    To meet the time test, an employee must be employed on a full-time basis at the new location for 39 weeks in the 12-month period following the move. If the taxpayer is a self-employed individual, he or she must work in the new location for 78 weeks during the two years following the move. The first 39 weeks must be in the first 12 months. The time test is suspended if the taxpayer dies, becomes disabled, or is discharged or transferred by the new employer through no fault of the employee.

  *Find more information on this topic at our Web site: **http://wft-entities.swlearning.com**.*

**Treatment of Moving Expenses.**    *Qualified moving expenses* include reasonable expenses of:

* Moving household goods and personal effects.
* Traveling from the former residence to the new place of residence.

For this purpose, traveling includes lodging, but not meals, for the taxpayer and members of the household.[48] It does not include the cost of moving servants or others who are not members of the household. The taxpayer can elect to use actual auto expenses (no depreciation is allowed) or the automatic mileage method. In this case, moving expense mileage is limited in 2005 to 15 cents per mile (14 cents in 2004) for each car. These expenses are also limited by the reasonableness standard. For example, if one moves from Texas to Florida via Maine and takes six weeks to do so, the transportation and lodging must be allocated between personal and moving expenses.

---

[48]§ 217(b).

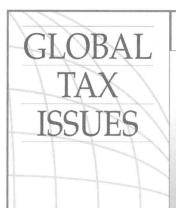

## EXPATRIATES AND THE MOVING EXPENSE DEDUCTION

Expatriates, U.S. persons who accept work assignments overseas, enjoy several favorable tax advantages regarding foreign moves. First, the cost of storing household goods qualifies as a moving expense. This could lead to a major tax saving since expatriates do not ship most of their household effects to the foreign location. Furthermore, the cost of storage, particularly in a climate-controlled facility, is not insignificant.

The second advantage expatriates may enjoy is an exemption from the time test. Those who return to the United States to retire are absolved from the 39-week or 78-week work requirement. Thus, the return home expenses are treated as qualified moving expenses.

---

**EXAMPLE 32**

Jill is transferred by her employer from the Atlanta office to the San Francisco office. In this connection, she spends the following amounts:

| | |
|---|---|
| Cost of moving furniture | $2,800 |
| Transportation | 700 |
| Meals | 200 |
| Lodging | 300 |

Jill's total qualified moving expense is $3,800 ($2,800 + $700 + $300). ∎

The moving expense deduction is allowed regardless of whether the employee is transferred by the existing employer or is employed by a new employer. It is allowed if the employee moves to a new area and obtains employment or switches from self-employed status to employee status (and vice versa). The moving expense deduction is also allowed if an individual is unemployed before obtaining employment in a new area.

 *Find more information on this topic at our Web site: **http://wft-entities.swlearning.com**.*

---

## Moving Expenses

**FRAMEWORK FOCUS: DEDUCTIONS**

**STRATEGY ▸ MAXIMIZE DEDUCTIBLE AMOUNTS.**

Persons who retire and move to a new location incur personal nondeductible moving expenses. If the retired person accepts a full-time job in the new location before moving and meets the time and distance requirements, the moving expenses are deductible.

**EXAMPLE 33**

At the time of his retirement from the national office of a major accounting firm, Gordon had an annual salary of $220,000. He moves from New York City to Seattle to retire, and accepts a full-time teaching position at a Seattle junior college at an annual salary of $15,000. If Gordon satisfies the 39-week test, his moving expenses are deductible. The disparity between the two salaries (previous and current) is of no consequence. ∎

## EDUCATION EXPENSES

**General Requirements.**   Employees *and* self-employed individuals can deduct expenses incurred for education as ordinary and necessary business expenses, provided the expenses are incurred to maintain or improve existing skills required in the present job. An employee can also deduct expenses incurred to meet the express requirements of the employer or the requirements imposed by law to retain his or her employment status.

**Education expenses** are not deductible if the education is for either of the following purposes (except as discussed below under A Limited Deduction Approach):

- To meet the minimum educational standards for qualification in the taxpayer's existing job.
- To qualify the taxpayer for a new trade or business.[49]

Thus, fees incurred for professional exams (the bar exam, for example) and fees for review courses (such as a CPA review course) are not deductible.[50] If the education incidentally results in a promotion or raise, the deduction still can be taken as long as the education maintained and improved existing skills and did not qualify the person for a new trade or business. A change in duties is not always fatal to the deduction if the new duties involve the same general work. For example, the IRS has ruled that a practicing dentist's education expenses incurred to become an orthodontist are deductible.[51]

**Requirements Imposed by Law or by the Employer for Retention of Employment.**   Taxpayers are permitted to deduct education expenses if additional courses are required by the employer or are imposed by law. Many states require a minimum of a bachelor's degree and a specified number of additional courses to retain a teaching job. In addition, some public school systems have imposed a master's degree requirement and require teachers to make satisfactory progress toward a master's degree in order to keep their positions. If the required education is the minimum degree required for the job, no deduction is allowed.

Professionals (such as physicians, attorneys, and CPAs) may deduct expenses incurred to meet continuing professional education requirements imposed by states as a condition for retaining a license to practice.

**EXAMPLE 34**

In order to meet continuing professional education requirements imposed by the State Board of Public Accountancy for maintaining her CPA license, Nancy takes an auditing course sponsored by a local college. The cost of the education is deductible. ■

*Find more information on this topic at our Web site:* ***http://wft-entities.swlearning.com***.

**Maintaining or Improving Existing Skills.**   The *maintaining or improving existing skills* requirement in the Code has been difficult for both taxpayers and the courts to interpret. For example, a business executive is permitted to deduct the costs of obtaining an MBA on the grounds that the advanced management education is undertaken to maintain and improve existing management skills. The executive is eligible to deduct the costs of specialized, nondegree management courses that are taken for continuing education or to maintain or improve existing skills. Expenses incurred by the executive to obtain a law degree are not deductible, however,

---

[49]Reg. §§ 1.162–5(b)(2) and (3).
[50]Reg. § 1.212–1(f) and Rev.Rul. 69–292, 1969–1 C.B. 84.

[51]Rev.Rul. 74–78, 1974–1 C.B. 44.

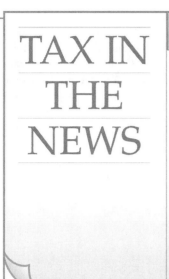

## IS AN MBA DEGREE DEDUCTIBLE?

Education that maintains or improves existing skills is deductible, but education that qualifies a taxpayer for a new field is not. But how do these basic rules apply to a conventional (i.e., nonspecialized) MBA degree? Does being a manager or a consultant require an MBA degree? Generally, the answer has always been that it does not. In this regard, therefore, the education does not create a new skill, so its cost should be deductible.

Several recent holdings, however, have found that an MBA degree can lead to qualifying for a new trade or business. But these holdings involved situations where the education resulted in a job change and satisfied different minimum requirements set by the employer. In one case, for example, the taxpayer moved from the position of investment analyst to become an investment banker, and the latter position required an MBA degree. Under these circumstances, the cost of the education was held to be nondeductible.

But barring a change to a job where the degree is required, the cost of an MBA degree should be deductible as merely improving existing managerial skills.

because the education constitutes training for a new trade or business. The Regulations deny a self-employed accountant a deduction for expenses relating to law school.[52]

## Education Expenses

### FRAMEWORK FOCUS: DEDUCTIONS

STRATEGY ➤ MAXIMIZE DEDUCTIBLE AMOUNTS.

Education expenses are treated as nondeductible personal items unless the individual is employed or is engaged in a trade or business. A temporary leave of absence for further education is one way to assure that the taxpayer is still treated as being engaged in a trade or business. An individual was permitted to deduct education expenses even though he resigned from his job, returned to school full-time for two years, and accepted another job in the same field upon graduation. The court held that the student had merely suspended active participation in his field.[53]

If the time out of the field is too long, education expense deductions will be disallowed. For example, a teacher who left the field for four years to raise her child and curtailed her employment searches and writing activities was denied a deduction for education expenses. She was no longer actively engaged in the trade or business of being an educator.[54]

To secure the deduction, an individual should arrange his or her work situation to preserve employee or business status.

As discussed below under *A Limited Deduction Approach*, a limited exception is available for taxpayers who do not meet the above requirements.

**Classification of Specific Items.**   Education expenses include books, tuition, typing, transportation (e.g., from the office to night school), and travel (e.g., meals and lodging while away from home at summer school).

---

[52]Reg. § 1.162–5(b)(3)(ii) Example (1).
[53]*Stephen G. Sherman*, 36 TCM 1191, T.C.Memo. 1977–301.

[54]*Brian C. Mulherin*, 42 TCM 834, T.C.Memo. 1981–454; *George A. Baist*, 56 TCM 778, T.C.Memo. 1988–554.

**EXAMPLE 35**

Bill, who holds a bachelor of education degree, is a secondary education teacher in the Los Angeles school system. The school board recently raised its minimum education requirement for new teachers from four years of college training to five. A grandfather clause allows teachers with only four years of college to continue to qualify if they show satisfactory progress toward a graduate degree. Bill enrolls at the University of Washington during the summer and takes three graduate courses. His unreimbursed expenses for this purpose are as follows:

| | |
|---|---:|
| Books and tuition | $2,600 |
| Lodging while in travel status (June–August) | 1,150 |
| Meals while in travel status | 800 |
| Laundry while in travel status | 220 |
| Transportation | 600 |

Bill has an itemized deduction as follows:

| | |
|---|---:|
| Books and tuition | $2,600 |
| Lodging | 1,150 |
| Meals less 50% cutback (discussed later in this chapter) | 400 |
| Laundry | 220 |
| Transportation | 600 |
| | $4,970 |

## A LIMITED DEDUCTION APPROACH

One of the major shortcomings of the education deduction, previously discussed, is that it is unavailable for taxpayers obtaining a basic skill. Thus, a taxpayer working for an accounting firm cannot deduct the cost of earning a bachelor in accounting degree. Under 2001 tax legislation, this shortcoming has been partly resolved with the **deduction for qualified tuition and related expenses.**

A deduction *for* AGI is allowed for qualified tuition and related expenses involving higher education (i.e., postsecondary). The maximum amount of the deduction varies depending on the year involved. Further, the deduction is unavailable if the taxpayer's AGI exceeds a prescribed amount.[55] The phase-ins and limitations are summarized in Table 16–2.

Various aspects of the new higher education tuition deduction are summarized below:

- Qualified tuition and related expenses include whatever is required for enrollment at the institution. Usually, student activity fees, books, and room and board are not included.[56]
- The expense need not be employment related, although it can be.
- The deduction is not available for married persons who file separate returns.[57]
- To avoid a "double benefit," the deduction must be coordinated with other education provisions (i.e., HOPE and lifetime learning credits). Along this same line, no deduction is allowed for a taxpayer who qualifies as another's dependent.[58]
- The deduction *for* AGI classification avoids the 2 percent-of-AGI floor on miscellaneous itemized deductions. See Chapter 15.[59]

---

[55]§ 222(b)(2).
[56]§ 222(d)(1).
[57]§ 222(d)(4).

[58]§ 222(c).
[59]§§ 61(a)(18) and 67.

■ **TABLE 16–2**
Phase-in Rules for Qualified
Tuition Deduction

| Tax Years Involved | Filing Status | AGI Limit | Maximum Deduction Allowed |
|---|---|---|---|
| 2002–2003 | Single | $ 65,000* | } $3,000 |
| | Married | 130,000* | |
| 2004–2005 | Single | 65,000 | } 4,000 |
| | Married | 130,000 | |
| | Single | 65,001 to 80,000* | } 2,000 |
| | Married | 130,001 to 160,000* | } 2,000 |

*No deduction at all is available if AGI exceeds this amount.

*EXAMPLE 36*

Tina is single and a full-time employee of a CPA firm. During 2005, she attends law school at night and incurs the following expenses: $4,200 for tuition and $340 for books and supplies. Presuming she satisfies the AGI limitation (see Table 16–2), she can claim $4,000 as a deduction *for* AGI. If she itemizes her deductions for the year, can she claim the $540 not allowed under § 222 ($200 tuition in excess of $4,000 + $340 for books and supplies) as an education expense eligible for itemized deduction treatment? No, because obtaining a law degree leads to a new trade or business. ■

Another deduction item relating to education is the limited deduction of interest on education loans, which is covered in Chapter 15.[60]

## ENTERTAINMENT EXPENSES

Many taxpayers attempt to deduct personal **entertainment expenses** as business expenses. For this reason, the tax law restricts the deductibility of entertainment expenses. The Code contains strict record-keeping requirements and provides restrictive tests for the deduction of certain types of entertainment expenses.

**The Fifty Percent Cutback.** Only 50 percent of meal and entertainment expenses is deductible.[61] The limitation applies to employees, employers, and self-employed individuals. Although the 50 percent cutback can apply to either the employer or the employee, it will not apply twice. The cutback applies to the one who really pays (economically) for the meals or entertainment.

*Find more information on this topic at our Web site: **http://wft-entities.swlearning.com**.*

*EXAMPLE 37*

Jane, an employee of Pelican Corporation, entertains one of her clients. If Pelican Corporation does not reimburse Jane, she is subject to the cutback. If, however, Pelican Corporation reimburses Jane (or pays for the entertainment directly), Pelican suffers the cutback. ■

Transportation expenses are not affected by the cutback rule—only meals and entertainment expenses are reduced. The cutback also applies to taxes and tips relating to meals and entertainment. Cover charges, parking fees at an entertainment

---

[60]§ 221.

[61]§ 274(n).

location, and room rental fees for a meal or cocktail party are also subject to the 50 percent cutback.

*Find more information on this topic at our Web site: **http://wft-entities.swlearning.com**.*

**EXAMPLE 38**

Joe pays a $30 cab fare to meet his client for dinner. The meal costs $120, and Joe leaves a $20 tip. His deduction is $100 [($120 + $20) × 50% + $30 cab fare]. ■

**Classification of Expenses.**   Entertainment expenses are classified either as *directly related* to business or *associated with* business.[62] Directly related expenses are related to an actual business meeting or discussion. These expenses are distinguished from entertainment expenses that are incurred to promote goodwill, such as maintaining existing customer relations. To obtain a deduction for directly related entertainment, it is not necessary to show that actual benefit resulted from the expenditure as long as there was a reasonable expectation of benefit. To qualify as directly related, the expense should be incurred in a business setting. If there is little possibility of engaging in the active conduct of a trade or business due to the nature of the social facility, it is difficult to qualify the expenditure as directly related to business.

Expenses associated with, rather than directly related to, business entertainment must serve a specific business purpose, such as obtaining new business or continuing existing business. These expenditures qualify only if the expenses directly precede or follow a bona fide business discussion. Entertainment occurring on the same day as the business discussion is considered associated with business.

**EXAMPLE 39**

Jerry, a manufacturers' representative, took his client to play a round of golf during the afternoon. They had dinner the same evening, during which time business was discussed. After dinner, they went to a nightclub to have drinks and listen to a jazz band. The business dinner qualifies as directly related entertainment. The golf outing and the visit to the nightclub qualify as associated with entertainment. ■

## Entertainment Expenses

**FRAMEWORK FOCUS: DEDUCTIONS**

STRATEGY ➤ MAXIMIZE DEDUCTIBLE AMOUNTS.

Taxpayers should maintain detailed records of amounts, time, place, business purpose, and business relationships. A credit card receipt details the place, date, and amount of the expense. A notation made on the receipt of the names of the person(s) attending, the business relationship, and the topic of discussion should constitute sufficient documentation.[63] Failure to provide sufficient documentation could lead to disallowance of entertainment expense deductions.

Associated with or goodwill entertainment requires a business discussion to be conducted immediately before or after the entertainment. Furthermore, a business purpose must exist for the entertainment. Taxpayers should arrange for a business discussion before or after such entertainment. They also must document the business purpose, such as obtaining new business from a prospective customer.

---

[62]§ 274(a)(1)(A).
[63]*Kenneth W. Guenther,* 54 TCM 382, T.C.Memo. 1987–440.

**Restrictions upon Deductibility of Business Meals.** Business meals are deductible only if:[64]

- the meal is directly related to or associated with the active conduct of a trade or business,
- the expense is not lavish or extravagant under the circumstances, and
- the taxpayer (or an employee) is present at the meal.

A business meal with a business associate or customer is not deductible unless business is discussed before, during, or after the meal. This requirement does not apply to meals consumed while away from home in travel status.

**EXAMPLE 40**

Lacy travels to San Francisco for a business convention. She pays for dinner with three colleagues and is not reimbursed by her employer. They do not discuss business. She can deduct 50% of the cost of her meal. However, she cannot deduct the cost of her colleagues' meals. ■

**EXAMPLE 41**

Lance, a party to a contract negotiation, buys dinner for other parties to the negotiation but does not attend the dinner. No deduction is allowed because Lance was not present. ■

**Restrictions upon Deductibility of Club Dues.** The Code provides that "No deduction shall be allowed . . . for amounts paid or incurred for membership in any club organized for business, pleasure, recreation, or other social purpose."[65] Although this prohibition seems quite broad, it does not apply to clubs whose primary purpose is public service and community volunteerism (e.g., Kiwanis, Lions, Rotary). Although *dues* are not deductible, actual entertainment at a club may qualify.

**EXAMPLE 42**

During the current year, Vincent spent $1,400 on business lunches at the Lakeside Country Club. The annual membership fee was $6,000, and Vincent used the facility 60% of the time for business. Presuming the lunches meet the business meal test, Vincent may claim $700 (50% cutback × $1,400) as a deduction. None of the club dues are deductible. ■

 DIGGING DEEPER 16

*Find more information on this topic at our Web site: **http://wft-entities.swlearning.com**.*

**Business Gifts.** Business gifts are deductible to the extent of $25 per donee per year.[66] An exception is made for gifts costing $4 or less (e.g., pens with the employee's or company's name on them) or promotional materials. Such items are not treated as business gifts subject to the $25 limitation. In addition, incidental costs such as engraving of jewelry and nominal charges for gift-wrapping, mailing, and delivery are not included in the cost of the gift in applying the limitation. Gifts to superiors and employers are not deductible. Records must be maintained to substantiate business gifts.

## OTHER EMPLOYEE EXPENSES

**Office in the Home.** Employees and self-employed individuals are not allowed a deduction for **office in the home expenses** unless a portion of the residence is used *exclusively and on a regular basis* as either:

- The principal place of business for any trade or business of the taxpayer.
- A place of business used by clients, patients, or customers.

---

[64]§ 274(k).
[65]§ 274(a)(3).

[66]§ 274(b)(1).

Employees must meet an additional test: The use must be for the convenience of the employer rather than merely being "appropriate and helpful."[67]

The precise meaning of "principal place of business" has been the subject of considerable controversy.[68] Congress ultimately resolved the controversy by amending the Code.[69]

The term "principal place of business" now includes a place of business that satisfies the following requirements:

* The office is used by the taxpayer to conduct administrative or management activities of a trade or business.
* There is no other fixed location of the trade or business where the taxpayer conducts these activities.

**EXAMPLE 43**

Dr. Smith is a self-employed anesthesiologist. During the year, he spends 30 to 35 hours per week administering anesthesia and postoperative care to patients in three hospitals, none of which provides him with an office. He also spends two or three hours per day in a room in his home that he uses exclusively as an office. He does not meet patients there, but he performs a variety of tasks related to his medical practice (e.g., contacting surgeons, bookkeeping, reading medical journals). A deduction will be allowed since he uses the office in the home to conduct administrative or management activities of his trade or business, and there is no other fixed location where these activities can be carried out. ∎

The exclusive use requirement means that a specific part of the home must be used solely for business purposes. A deduction, if permitted, requires an allocation of total expenses of operating the home between business and personal use based on floor space or number of rooms.

Even if the taxpayer meets the above requirements, the allowable home office expenses cannot exceed the gross income from the business less all other business expenses attributable to the activity. That is, the home office deduction cannot create a loss. Furthermore, the home office expenses that are allowed as itemized deductions anyway (e.g., mortgage interest and real estate taxes) must be deducted first. All home office expenses of an employee are miscellaneous itemized deductions, except those (such as interest and taxes) that qualify as other personal itemized deductions. Home office expenses of a self-employed individual are trade or business expenses and are deductible *for* AGI. Any disallowed home office expenses are carried forward and used in future years subject to the same limitations.

*Find more information on this topic at our Web site: **http://wft-entities.swlearning.com**.*

**EXAMPLE 44**

Rick is a certified public accountant employed by a regional CPA firm as a tax manager. He operates a separate business in which he refinishes furniture in his home. For this business, he uses two rooms in the basement of his home exclusively and regularly. The floor space of the two rooms constitutes 10% of the floor space of his residence. Gross income from the business totals $8,000. Expenses of the business (other than home office expenses) are $6,500. Rick incurs the following home office expenses:

| | |
|---|---:|
| Real property taxes on residence | $4,000 |
| Interest expense on residence | 7,500 |
| Operating expenses of residence | 2,000 |
| Depreciation on residence (related to 10% business use) | 250 |

---

[67]§ 280A(c)(1).
[68]See the restrictive interpretation arrived at in *Comm. v. Soliman*, 93–1 USTC ¶50,014, 71 AFTR2d 93–463, 113 S.Ct. 701 (USSC, 1993).

[69]§ 280A(c)(1) as modified by TRA of 1997.

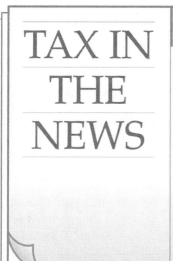

## ONE SIDE EFFECT OF 9/11

Telecommuting (or working at home) has always had its advantages. For the employee, it offers flexibility as to working hours and particularly in metropolitan areas, it avoids an often horrendous commute. For the employer, it offers the cost savings of not having to provide office space.

The tragedy of September 11 has added new variables to consider when evaluating the telecommuting approach. For the employee, there is the peace of mind that comes from the safety of the home. Although no place is entirely safe, the downtown high rise office building is clearly a more likely target of a terrorist attack. From an employer's standpoint, the "at home workplace" guarantees employee accessibility and precludes the complete destruction of job-related business data.

As working at home becomes more popular, an obvious result is the increased use of the office in the home deduction.

Rick's deductions are determined as follows:

| | | |
|---|---:|---:|
| Business income | | $ 8,000 |
| Less: Other business expenses | | (6,500) |
| | | $ 1,500 |
| Less: Allocable taxes ($4,000 × 10%) | $400 | |
| Allocable interest ($7,500 × 10%) | 750 | (1,150) |
| | | $ 350 |
| Less: Allocable operating expenses of the residence | | |
| ($2,000 × 10%) | | (200) |
| | | $ 150 |
| Less: Allocable depreciation ($250, limited to remaining income) | | (150) |
| | | $ –0– |

Rick has a carryover deduction of $100 (the unused excess depreciation). Because he is self-employed, the allocable taxes and interest ($1,150), the other deductible office expenses ($200 + $150), and $6,500 of other business expenses are deductible *for* AGI. ■

**Certain Expenses for Teachers.** The Job Creation and Worker Assistance Act of 2002 provided for a deduction *for* AGI for certain expenses of elementary and secondary school teachers.[70] Such teachers may deduct the costs they incur for books, supplies, computer equipment and related software and services, other equipment, and supplementary materials that they use in the classroom. The annual statutory ceiling on the deduction *for* AGI classification was $250 and applied for the 2002 and 2003 tax years. The Working Families Tax Relief Act of 2004 extended the provision through 2005.

**Miscellaneous Employee Expenses.** Deductible miscellaneous employee expenses include special clothing and its upkeep, union dues, and professional expenses. Also deductible are professional dues, professional meetings, and employment agency fees for seeking new employment in the taxpayer's current trade or business, whether or not a new job is secured.

---

[70]§ 62(a)(2)(D).

To be deductible, *special clothing* must be both specifically required as a condition of employment and not adaptable for regular wear. For example, a police officer's uniform is not suitable for off-duty activities. An exception is clothing used to the extent that it takes the place of regular clothing (e.g., some military uniforms).

EXAMPLE 45

Captain Roberts is on active duty in the U.S. Army. The cost of his regular uniforms is not deductible since such clothing is suitable for regular wear. Captain Roberts, however, spends over $1,100 to purchase "dress blues." Under military regulations, dress uniforms may be worn only during ceremonial functions (e.g., official events, parades). The $1,100 cost, to the extent it exceeds any clothing allowance, qualifies as a deduction. ■

The current position of the IRS is that expenses incurred in *seeking employment* are deductible if the taxpayer is seeking employment in the same trade or business. The deduction is allowed whether or not the attempts to secure employment are successful. An unemployed taxpayer can take a deduction providing there has been no substantial lack of continuity between the last job and the search for a new one. No deduction is allowed for persons seeking their first job or seeking employment in a new trade or business.

## LO.4

Appreciate the difference between accountable and nonaccountable employee plans.

## CLASSIFICATION OF EMPLOYEE EXPENSES

If employee expenses are reimbursed by the employer under an accountable plan, they are not reported by the employee at all. In effect, this result is equivalent to reporting the reimbursement as income and treating the expenses as deductions *for* AGI.[71] Alternatively, if the expenses are reimbursed under a nonaccountable plan or are not reimbursed at all, then they are classified as deductions *from* AGI and can be claimed only if the taxpayer itemizes (subject to the 2 percent-of-AGI floor). Exceptions are made for moving expenses and the employment-related expenses of a qualified performing artist, where a deduction *for* AGI is allowed. Thus, the tax treatment of reimbursements under accountable and nonaccountable plans differs significantly.

**Accountable Plans.**   An accountable plan requires the employee to:

- Adequately account for (substantiate) the expenses. An employee renders an *adequate accounting* by submitting a record, with receipts and other substantiation, to the employer.[72]
- Return any excess reimbursement or allowance. An "excess reimbursement or allowance" is any amount that the employee does not adequately account for as an ordinary and necessary business expense.

The law provides that no deduction is allowed for any travel, entertainment, business gift, or listed property (automobiles, computers) expenditure unless properly substantiated by adequate records. The records should contain the following information:[73]

- The amount of the expense.
- The time and place of travel or entertainment (or date of gift).
- The business purpose of the expense.
- The business relationship of the taxpayer to the person entertained (or receiving the gift).

This means the taxpayer must maintain an account book or diary in which the above information is recorded at the time of the expenditure. Documentary evidence, such as itemized receipts, is required to support any expenditure for lodging while

---

[71]§ 62(a)(2).
[72]Reg. § 1.162–17(b)(4).

[73]§ 274(d).

traveling away from home and for any other expenditure of $75 or more. If a taxpayer fails to keep adequate records, each expense must be established by a written or oral statement of the exact details of the expense and by other corroborating evidence.[74]

*Find more information on this topic at our Web site: **http://wft-entities.swlearning.com**.*

**EXAMPLE 46**

Bertha has travel expenses substantiated only by canceled checks. The checks establish the date, place, and amount of the expenditure. Because neither the business relationship nor the business purpose is established, the deduction is disallowed.[75] ∎

**EXAMPLE 47**

Dwight has travel and entertainment expenses substantiated by a diary showing the time, place, and amount of the expenditure. His oral testimony provides the business relationship and business purpose; however, since he has no receipts, any expenditures of $75 or more are disallowed.[76] ∎

**Nonaccountable Plans.** A **nonaccountable plan** is one in which an adequate accounting or return of excess amounts, or both, is not required. All reimbursements of expenses are reported in full as wages on the employee's Form W–2. Any allowable expenses are deductible in the same manner as are unreimbursed expenses.

An employer may have an accountable plan and require employees to return excess reimbursements or allowances, but an employee may fail to follow the rules of the plan. In that case, the expenses and reimbursements are subject to nonaccountable plan treatment.

**Unreimbursed Expenses.** Unreimbursed employee expenses are treated in a straightforward manner. Meals and entertainment expenses are subject to the 50 percent limit. Total unreimbursed employee business expenses are usually reported as miscellaneous itemized deductions subject to the 2 percent-of-AGI floor (refer to Chapter 15). If the employee could have received, but did not seek, reimbursement for whatever reason, none of the employment-related expenses are deductible.

*Find more information on this topic at our Web site: **http://wft-entities.swlearning.com**.*

**PLANNING STRATEGIES**

## Unreimbursed Employee Business Expenses

**FRAMEWORK FOCUS: DEDUCTIONS**

**STRATEGY ▶ MAXIMIZE DEDUCTIBLE AMOUNTS.**

The 2 percent floor for unreimbursed employee business expenses offers a tax planning opportunity for married couples. If one spouse has high miscellaneous expenses subject to the floor, it may be beneficial for the couple to file separate returns. If they file jointly, the 2 percent floor is based on the adjusted gross incomes of both. Filing separately lowers the reduction to 2 percent of only one spouse's adjusted gross income.

Other provisions of the law should be considered, however. For example, filing separately could cost a couple losses of up to $25,000 from self-managed rental units under the passive activity loss rules (discussed in Chapter 5).

Another possibility is to negotiate a salary reduction with one's employer in exchange for the 100 percent reimbursement of employee expenses. The employee is better off because the 2 percent floor does not apply. The employer is better off because certain expense reimbursements are not subject to Social Security and other payroll taxes.

---

[74]Reg. § 1.274–5T(c)(3).
[75]*William T. Whitaker*, 56 TCM 47, T.C.Memo. 1988–418.

[76]*W. David Tyler*, 43 TCM 927, T.C.Memo. 1982–160.

■ **TABLE 16–3**
Phaseout of Traditional IRA
Deduction of an Active
Participant in 2005

| AGI Filing Status | Phaseout Begins* | Phaseout Ends |
|---|---|---|
| Single and head of household | $50,000 | $60,000 |
| Married, filing joint return | 70,000 | 80,000 |
| Married, filing separate return | –0– | 10,000 |

*The starting point for the phaseout is increased each year through 2007 for married filing jointly and through 2005 for other filing statuses.

## CONTRIBUTIONS TO INDIVIDUAL RETIREMENT ACCOUNTS

**Traditional IRAs.**  Employees not covered by another qualified plan can establish their own tax-deductible **Individual Retirement Accounts (IRAs)**. The contribution ceiling is the smaller of $4,000 (or $8,000 for spousal IRAs) for years 2005–2007 or 100 percent of compensation.[77] If the taxpayer is an active participant in a qualified plan, the traditional IRA deduction limitation is phased out *proportionately* between certain AGI ranges, as shown in Table 16–3.[78]

An individual who attains the age of 50 by the end of the tax year can make additional catch-up IRA contributions. The maximum contribution limit is increased by $500 for the period 2002–2005 and by $1,000 for years after 2005.

AGI is calculated taking into account any § 469 passive losses and § 86 taxable Social Security benefits and ignoring any § 911 foreign income exclusion, § 135 savings bonds interest exclusion, and the IRA deduction. There is a $200 floor on the IRA deduction limitation for individuals whose AGI is not above the phaseout range.

**EXAMPLE 48**

Dan, who is single, has compensation income of $56,000 in 2005. He is an active participant in his employer's qualified retirement plan. Dan contributes $4,000 to a traditional IRA. The deductible amount is reduced from $4,000 by $2,400 because of the phaseout mechanism:

$$\frac{\$6,000}{\$10,000} \times \$4,000 = \$2,400 \text{ reduction.}$$

Therefore, of the $4,000 contribution, Dan can deduct only $1,600 ($4,000 − $2,400).  ■

**EXAMPLE 49**

Ben, an unmarried individual, is an active participant in his employer's qualified retirement plan. With AGI of $59,800, he would normally have an IRA deduction limit of $80 {$4,000 − [($59,800 − $50,000)/$10,000 × $4,000]}. However, because of the special floor provision, Ben is allowed a $200 IRA deduction.  ■

An individual is not considered an active participant in a qualified plan merely because the individual's spouse is an active participant in such a plan for any part of a plan year. Thus, most homemakers may take a full $4,000 deduction regardless of the participation status of their spouse, unless the couple has AGI above $150,000. If their AGI is above $150,000, the phaseout of the deduction begins at $150,000 and ends at $160,000 (phaseout over the $10,000 range) rather than beginning and ending at the phaseout amounts in Table 16–3.[79]

**EXAMPLE 50**

Nell is covered by a qualified employer retirement plan at work. Her husband, Nick, is not an active participant in a qualified plan. If Nell and Nick's combined AGI is $135,000, Nell

---

[77]§§ 219(b)(1) and (c)(2). The ceiling was $3,000 for 2002–2004. It is increased to $5,000 for 2008. After 2008, the limit is adjusted annually for inflation in $500 increments.

[78]§ 219(g).

[79]§ 219(g)(7).

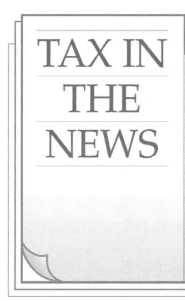

### ROLLING OVER YOUR § 401(K) PLAN?

When you change jobs, what should you do with your § 401(k) plan? If you are a savvy investor, transfer your account into an IRA where you will be free to invest in a variety of products. If you are not a confident investor or don't have your finances under control, leave your investment in your old employer's § 401(k) plan or roll it over to your new company's § 401(k) plan.

There is an estate tax advantage to transferring the amount to an IRA. If the money remains in a § 401(k) plan and you leave it to someone other than your spouse (e.g., children), your heirs could face a huge immediate tax bill because your employer will probably insist that the § 401(k) be cashed out immediately. But if the money in an IRA is left to your kids, they can pull out the money over a lifetime, obtaining years of tax-deferred growth.

SOURCE: Adapted from Jonathan Clements, "Rolling Over Your 401(k) into an IRA Can Boost Returns and Trim Your Taxes," *Wall Street Journal*, August 19, 2004, p. D1.

cannot make a deductible IRA contribution because she exceeds the income threshold for an active participant. However, since Nick is not an active participant, and their combined AGI does not exceed $150,000, he can make a deductible contribution of $4,000 to an IRA. ■

To the extent that an individual is ineligible to make a deductible contribution to an IRA, *nondeductible contributions* can be made to separate accounts. The nondeductible contributions are subject to the same dollar limits as deductible contributions ($4,000 of earned income, $8,000 for a spousal IRA). Income in the account accumulates tax-free until distributed. Only the account earnings are taxed upon distribution because the account basis equals the contributions made by the taxpayer. A taxpayer may elect to treat deductible IRA contributions as nondeductible. If an individual has no taxable income for the year after taking into account other deductions, the election would be beneficial. The election is made on the individual's tax return for the taxable year to which the designation relates.

**Roth IRAs.** A Roth IRA is a *nondeductible* alternative to the traditional deductible IRA. Introduced by Congress to encourage individual savings, earnings inside a Roth IRA are not taxable, and all qualified distributions from a Roth IRA are tax-free.[80] The maximum allowable annual contribution to a Roth IRA is the smaller of $4,000 ($8,000 for spousal IRAs) or 100 percent of the individual's compensation for the year. Contributions to a Roth IRA must be made by the due date (excluding extensions) of the taxpayer's tax return. Roth IRAs are not subject to the minimum distribution rules that apply to traditional IRAs.

A taxpayer can make tax-free withdrawals from a Roth IRA after an initial five-year holding period if any of the following requirements is satisfied:

* The distribution is made on or after the date on which the participant attains age 59½.
* The distribution is made to a beneficiary (or the participant's estate) on or after the participant's death.
* The participant becomes disabled.
* The distribution is used to pay for qualified first-time homebuyer's expenses.

[80]§ 408A.

## TAX FACT

### THE VACILLATING POPULARITY OF IRAS

Individual Retirement Accounts (IRAs) became part of the tax law in 1974. The number of individual income tax returns indicating IRA contributions has varied over time, as the following table shows.

| Year | Number of Returns (in Millions) |
| --- | --- |
| 1975 | 1.2 |
| 1980 | 2.6 |
| 1985 | 16.2 |
| 1990 | 5.2 |
| 1995 | 4.3 |
| 2000 | 5.8 |
| 2002 | 3.3 |

What probably caused the substantial decline between 1985 and 1990? Tax legislation enacted in 1986 applied the *wherewithal to pay* concept in providing for the phaseout of the IRA deduction once an AGI threshold was reached. In addition, the legislation substantially reduced tax rates for the individual taxpayer.

**Source:** IRS Tax Stats.

---

**EXAMPLE 51**

Edith establishes a Roth IRA at age 42 and contributes $3,000 per year for 20 years. The account is now worth $116,400, consisting of $60,000 of nondeductible contributions and $56,400 in accumulated earnings that have not been taxed. Edith may withdraw the $116,400 tax-free from the Roth IRA because she is over age 59½ and has met the five-year holding period requirement. ■

If the taxpayer receives a distribution from a Roth IRA and does not satisfy the aforementioned requirements, the distribution may be taxable. If the distribution represents a return of capital, it is not taxable. Conversely, if the distribution represents a payout of earnings, it is taxable. Under the ordering rules for Roth IRA distributions, distributions are treated as first made from contributions (return of capital).

**EXAMPLE 52**

Assume the same facts as in Example 51, except that Edith is only age 50 and receives a distribution of $55,000. Since her adjusted basis for the Roth IRA is $60,000 (contributions made), the distribution is tax-free, and her adjusted basis is reduced to $5,000 ($60,000 − $55,000). ■

Roth IRAs are subject to income limits. The maximum annual contribution of $4,000 is phased out beginning at AGI of $95,000 for single taxpayers and $150,000 for married couples who file a joint return. The phaseout range is $10,000 for married filing jointly and $15,000 for single taxpayers. For a married taxpayer filing separately, the contribution is phased out over a range beginning with AGI of $0 and ending with $10,000.

**EXAMPLE 53**

Bev, who is single, would like to contribute $4,000 to her Roth IRA. However, her AGI is $105,000, so her contribution is limited to $1,333 ($4,000 – $2,667) calculated as follows:

$$\frac{\$10,000}{\$15,000} \times \$4,000 = \$2,667 \text{ reduction.}$$

**Coverdell Education Savings Accounts (CESAs).** Distributions from a **Coverdell Education Savings Account (CESA)** to pay for qualified education expenses receive favorable tax treatment.[81] Qualified education expenses include tuition, fees, books, supplies, and related equipment. Room and board qualify if the student's course load is at least one-half of the full-time course load. If the CESA is used to pay the qualified education expenses of the designated beneficiary, the withdrawals are tax-free. To the extent the distributions during a tax year exceed qualified education expenses, part of the excess is treated as a return of capital (the contributions), and part is treated as a distribution of earnings under the § 72 annuity rules. Thus, the distribution is presumed to be pro rata from each category. The exclusion for the distribution of earnings part is calculated as follows:

$$\frac{\text{Qualified education expenses}}{\text{Total distributions}} \times \text{Earnings} = \text{Exclusion.}$$

**EXAMPLE 54**

Meg receives a $2,500 distribution from her CESA. She uses $2,000 to pay for qualified education expenses. On the date of the distribution, Meg's CESA balance is $10,000, $6,000 of which represents her contributions. Since 60% ($6,000/$10,000) of her account balance represents her contributions, $1,500 ($2,500 × 60%) of the distribution is a return of capital, and $1,000 ($2,500 × 40%) is a distribution of earnings. The excludible amount of the earnings is calculated as follows:

$$\frac{\$2,000}{\$2,500} \times \$1,000 = \$800$$

Thus, Meg must include $200 ($1,000 – $800) in her gross income.

The maximum amount that can be contributed annually to a CESA for a beneficiary is $2,000 ($500 before 2002). A beneficiary must be an individual and cannot be a group of children or an unborn child. The contributions are not deductible. A CESA is subject to income limits. The maximum annual contribution is phased out beginning at $95,000 for single taxpayers and $190,000 for married couples who file a joint return. The phaseout range is $30,000 for married filing jointly and $15,000 for single taxpayers. Contributions cannot be made to a CESA after the date on which the designated beneficiary attains age 18. Thus, a total of up to $36,000 can be contributed for each beneficiary—$2,000 in the year of birth and in each of the 17 following years.

A 6 percent excise tax is imposed on excess contributions to a CESA. A 10 percent excise tax is imposed on any distributions that are included in gross income.

The balance in a CESA must be distributed within 30 days after the death of a beneficiary or within 30 days after a beneficiary reaches age 30. Any balance at the close of either 30-day period is considered to be distributed at such time, and the earnings portion is included in the beneficiary's gross income. Before a beneficiary reaches age 30, any balance can be rolled over tax-free into another CESA for a member of the beneficiary's family who is under age 30.

The CESA exclusion may be available in a tax year in which the beneficiary claims the HOPE credit or the lifetime learning credit (see Chapter 15). However, any excluded amount of the CESA distribution cannot be used for the same educational expenses for which the HOPE credit or the lifetime learning credit is claimed.

---

[81]§ 530.

Contributions cannot be made to a beneficiary's CESA during any year in which contributions are made to a qualified tuition program on behalf of the same beneficiary.

## LO.5

Understand the tax provisions applicable to proprietors.

# Individuals as Proprietors

## THE PROPRIETORSHIP AS A BUSINESS ENTITY

A sole proprietorship is *not* a taxable entity separate from the individual who owns the proprietorship. A sole proprietor reports the results of business operations of the proprietorship on Schedule C of Form 1040. The net profit or loss from the proprietorship is then transferred from Schedule C to Form 1040, which is used by the taxpayer to determine tax liability. The proprietor reports all of the net profit or net loss from the business, regardless of the amount actually withdrawn from the proprietorship during the year.

Income and expenses of the proprietorship retain their character when reported by the proprietor. For example, ordinary income of the proprietorship is treated as ordinary income when reported by the proprietor, and capital gain of the proprietorship is treated as capital gain by the proprietor.

**EXAMPLE 55**

George is the sole proprietor of George's Record Shop. Gross income of the business in 2005 is $200,000, and operating expenses are $110,000. George also sells a capital asset held by the business for a $10,000 long-term capital gain. During 2005, he withdraws $60,000 from the business for living expenses. George reports the operating income and expenses of the business on Schedule C, resulting in net profit (ordinary income) of $90,000 ($200,000 − $110,000). Even though he withdrew only $60,000, George reports all of the $90,000 net profit from the business on Form 1040, where he computes taxable income and tax liability for the year. He also reports a $10,000 long-term capital gain on his personal tax return (Schedule D of Form 1040). ■

## INCOME OF A PROPRIETORSHIP

The broad definition of gross income in § 61(a) applies equally to individuals and business entities, including proprietorships, corporations, and partnerships. Thus, it is assumed that asset inflows into a proprietorship are to be treated as income. Certain items may be excluded from gross income. Many of the exclusions available to an individual are related to the individual as an employee. Refer to Chapter 3 for a detailed discussion of gross income.

## DEDUCTIONS RELATED TO A PROPRIETORSHIP

**Ordinary and Necessary Business Expenses.**  The provisions that govern business deductions also are general, and not entity specific. The § 162 requirement that trade or business expenses be *ordinary and necessary* (refer to Chapter 4) applies to proprietorships as well as corporations, partnerships, and other business entities. However, certain specific deductions are available only to self-employed taxpayers. These deductions are covered in detail below.

**Health Insurance Premiums.**  A self-employed taxpayer may deduct 100 percent of insurance premiums paid for medical coverage as a deduction *for*

AGI.[82] The deduction is allowed for premiums paid on behalf of the taxpayer, the taxpayer's spouse, and dependents of the taxpayer. The deduction is not allowed to any taxpayer who is eligible to participate in a subsidized health plan maintained by any employer of the taxpayer or of the taxpayer's spouse.

This deduction is reported in the Adjusted Gross Income section of Form 1040 rather than on Schedule C. Premiums paid for medical coverage of the *employees* of a self-employed taxpayer are deductible as business expenses on Schedule C, however.

**EXAMPLE 56**

Ellen, a sole proprietor of a restaurant, has two dependent children. During 2005, she paid health insurance premiums of $1,800 for her own coverage and $1,000 for coverage of her two children. Ellen can deduct $2,800 as a deduction *for* AGI. ■

**Self-Employment Tax.** The tax on self-employment income is levied to provide Social Security and Medicare benefits (old age, survivors, and disability insurance and hospital insurance) for self-employed individuals. Individuals with net earnings of $400 or more from self-employment are subject to the self-employment tax.[83] For 2005, the self-employment tax is 12.4 percent of self-employment earnings up to a $90,000 *ceiling amount* (for the Social Security portion) plus 2.9 percent of the *total* amount of self-employment earnings (for the Medicare portion). Thus, the combined self-employment tax rate on earnings up to $90,000 is 15.3 percent. The ceiling amount is adjusted periodically for inflation.

For purposes of computing the *self-employment tax*, self-employed taxpayers are allowed a deduction from net earnings equal to one-half of the self-employment tax rate.[84] This deduction of 7.65 percent (one-half of the 15.3 percent rate) is reflected by multiplying net earnings from self-employment by 92.35 percent (100% − 7.65%), as shown in Example 57. For purposes of computing *taxable income*, an income tax deduction is allowed for one-half the amount of self-employment tax paid.[85]

Example 57 illustrates the computation of the self-employment tax, as well as the income tax deduction for one-half of self-employment tax paid. For income tax purposes, the amount to be reported on Schedule C is net earnings from self-employment *before* the deduction for one-half of the self-employment tax. The deduction of one-half of the self-employment tax paid is reported separately on Form 1040 as a deduction *for* AGI.

**EXAMPLE 57**

Computation of the self-employment tax is determined using the steps below. The self-employment tax is determined for two taxpayers with net earnings from self-employment for 2005 as follows: Ned, $55,000 and Terry, $100,000.

| Computation of Self-Employment Tax for Ned | |
| --- | ---: |
| 1. Net earnings | $55,000.00 |
| 2. Multiply line 1 by 92.35%. | $50,792.50 |
| 3. If the amount on line 2 is $90,000 or less, multiply the line 2 amount by 15.3%. This is the self-employment tax. | $ 7,771.25 |
| 4. If the amount on line 2 is more than $90,000, multiply the excess over $90,000 by 2.9% and add $13,770. This is the self-employment tax. | |

---

[82]§ 162(l).
[83]§ 6017.

[84]§ 1402(a)(12).
[85]§ 164(f).

| **Computation of Self-Employment Tax for Terry** | |
| --- | --- |
| 1. Net earnings | $100,000.00 |
| 2. Multiply line 1 by 92.35%. | $ 92,350.00 |
| 3. If the amount on line 2 is $90,000 or less, multiply the line 2 amount by 15.3%. This is the self-employment tax. | |
| 4. If the amount on line 2 is more than $90,000, multiply the excess over $90,000 by 2.9% and add $13,770. This is the self-employment tax. | $ 13,838.15 |

For income tax purposes, Ned has net earnings from self-employment of $55,000 and a deduction *for* AGI of $3,885.63 (one-half of $7,771.25). Terry has net earnings from self-employment of $100,000 and a deduction *for* AGI of $6,919.08 (one-half of $13,838.15). Both taxpayers benefit from the deduction for one-half of the self-employment tax paid. ■

Wages of employees also are subject to Social Security and Medicare taxes. The total tax rate is also 15.3 percent, with 7.65 percent being withheld from the employee's wages and the employer paying at a 7.65 percent rate. If an individual who is self-employed also receives wages from working as an employee of another organization, the ceiling amount of the Social Security portion on which the self-employment tax is computed is reduced. Thus, the self-employment tax may be reduced if a self-employed individual also receives Social Security wages in excess of the ceiling amount.

Net earnings from self-employment include gross income from a trade or business less allowable trade or business deductions, the distributive share of any partnership income or loss derived from a trade or business activity, and net income from rendering personal services as an independent contractor. Gain or loss from the disposition of property (including involuntary conversions) is excluded from the computation of self-employment income unless the property involved is inventory.

## RETIREMENT PLANS FOR SELF-EMPLOYED INDIVIDUALS

Self-employed individuals have several options for retirement funding. Individual Retirement Accounts (discussed earlier in this chapter) are available to both employees and self-employed individuals. Other options for self-employed individuals include, but are not limited to, H.R. 10 (Keogh) plans and SIMPLE plans, both of which are discussed below.

**Keogh Plans.**   Self-employed individuals (e.g., partners and sole proprietors) are eligible to establish and receive qualified retirement benefits under **Keogh plans** (also known as H.R. 10 plans). Self-employed individuals who establish Keogh plans for themselves are also required to cover their *employees* under the plan.

Keogh investments can include a variety of funding vehicles, such as mutual funds, annuities, real estate shares, certificates of deposit, debt instruments, commodities, securities, and personal properties. When an individual decides to make all investment decisions, a *self-directed retirement plan* is established. Investment in most collectibles is not allowed in a self-directed plan.

A Keogh plan may be either a *defined contribution* plan or a *defined benefit* plan. In a defined contribution plan, the amount that can be contributed each year is subject to limitations. Retirement benefits depend on the amount contributed and the amount earned by the plan. In a defined benefit plan, the amount of retirement

---

**TAX FACT**

## INCREASING POPULARITY OF KEOGH PLANS

Keogh plans are an increasingly popular retirement savings device for self-employed taxpayers. The number of individual income tax returns that included Keogh contributions is indicated below.

| Year | Number of Returns (in Thousands) |
|------|----------------------------------|
| 1975 | 596 |
| 1980 | 569 |
| 1985 | 676 |
| 1990 | 824 |
| 1995 | 1,032 |
| 2000 | 1,228 |
| 2002 | 1,181 |

**Source:** IRS Tax Statistics.

---

income is fixed and is determined on the basis of the employee's compensation while working, the number of years in the plan, and age on retirement.

A self-employed individual may annually contribute the smaller of $42,000 (in 2005) or 100 percent of earned income to a defined contribution Keogh plan.[86] If the defined contribution plan is a profit sharing plan or stock bonus plan, however, a 25 percent deduction limit applies. Under a defined benefit Keogh plan, the annual benefit is limited to the smaller of $170,000 (in 2005) or 100 percent of the average net earnings for the three highest years.[87]

Earned income refers to net earnings from self-employment.[88] Net earnings from self-employment means the gross income derived by an individual from any trade or business carried on by that individual, less appropriate deductions, plus the distributive share of income or loss from a partnership.[89] Earned income is reduced by contributions to a Keogh plan on the individual's behalf and by 50 percent of any self-employment tax.[90]

**EXAMPLE 58**

Pat, a partner, has earned income of $150,000 in 2005 (after the deduction for one-half of self-employment tax, but before any Keogh contribution). The maximum contribution Pat may make to a defined contribution Keogh plan is $42,000, the lesser of $150,000 or $42,000. ■

For discrimination purposes, the 25 percent limitation on the employee contribution to a profit sharing plan or stock bonus plan is computed on the first $210,000 (in 2005) of earned income. Thus, the maximum contribution in 2005 is $42,000 ($210,000 − .25X = X; X = $168,000). Therefore, $210,000 − $168,000 = $42,000. Alternatively, this can be calculated by multiplying $210,000 by 20 percent.

**EXAMPLE 59**

Terry, a self-employed accountant, has a profit sharing plan with a contribution rate of 15% of compensation. Terry's earned income after the deduction of one-half of self-employment

---

[86]§ 415(c)(1).
[87]§ 415(b)(1). The amount is indexed annually.
[88]§ 401(c)(2).

[89]§ 1402(a).
[90]§§ 401(c)(2)(A)(v) and 164(f).

tax, but before the Keogh contribution, is $250,000. Terry's contribution is limited to $27,391 ($210,000 − .15X = X), since X = $182,609 and .15 × $182,609 = $27,391. ■

Although a Keogh plan must be established before the end of the year in question, contributions may be made up to the normal filing date for that year.

## Important Dates Related to IRAs and Keogh Plans

**FRAMEWORK FOCUS: DEDUCTIONS**

**STRATEGY ➤ ACCELERATE RECOGNITION OF DEDUCTIONS TO ACHIEVE TAX DEFERRAL.**

A Keogh or IRA participant may make a deductible contribution for a tax year up to the time prescribed for filing the individual's tax return for that tax year. A Keogh plan must have been *established* by the end of the *prior* tax year (e.g., December 31, 2004) to obtain a deduction on the 2004 income tax return for the contribution made in the *current* year (2005). An individual can establish an IRA during the *current* tax year (up to the normal filing date) and still receive a deduction on the prior-year income tax return for the contribution made in the *current* year.

**SIMPLE Plans.**   Employers with 100 or fewer employees who do not maintain another qualified retirement plan may establish a *savings incentive match plan for employees* (SIMPLE plan).[91] The plan can be in the form of a § 401(k) plan or an IRA. The SIMPLE plan is not subject to the nondiscrimination rules that are normally applicable to § 401(k) plans.

All employees who received at least $5,000 in compensation from the employer during any two preceding years and who reasonably expect to receive at least $5,000 in compensation during the current year must be eligible to participate in the plan. The decision to participate is up to the employee. A *self-employed individual* may also participate in the plan.

The contributions made by the employee (a salary reduction approach) must be expressed as a percentage of compensation rather than as a fixed dollar amount. The plan must not permit the elective employee contribution for the year to exceed $10,000 (in 2005).[92] The elective deferral limit is increased under the catch-up provision for employees age 50 and over. The amount is $500 for 2002, $1,000 for 2003, $1,500 for 2004, $2,000 for 2005, and $2,500 for 2006 and thereafter. The $2,500 amount is indexed for inflation in $500 increments beginning in 2007. Generally, the employer must either match elective employee contributions up to 3 percent of the employee's compensation or provide nonmatching contributions of 2 percent of compensation for each eligible employee. Thus, the maximum amount that may be contributed to the plan for 2005 is $16,300 [$10,000 employee contributions + $6,300 ($210,000 compensation ceiling × 3%) employer match].

No other contributions may be made to the plan other than the employee elective contribution and the required employer matching contribution (or nonmatching contribution under the 2 percent rule). All contributions are fully vested.

---

[91]§ 408(p).

[92]For 2004, the limit was $9,000. The $10,000 amount for 2005 is indexed for inflation in $500 increments in 2006 and thereafter.

An employer is required to make contributions to a SIMPLE § 401(k) plan once it is established, whereas an employer's contributions to a traditional § 401(k) plan are optional.

An employer's deduction for contributions to a SIMPLE § 401(k) plan is limited to the greater of 25 percent of the compensation paid or accrued or the amount that the employer is required to contribute to the plan. Thus, an employer may deduct contributions to a SIMPLE § 401(k) plan in excess of 25 percent of the $210,000 salary cap. A traditional § 401(k) plan is limited to 25 percent of the total compensation of plan participants for the year.

An employer is allowed a deduction for matching contributions only if the contributions are made by the due date (including extensions) for the employer's tax return. Contributions to a SIMPLE plan are excludible from the employee's gross income, and the SIMPLE plan is tax-exempt.

**EXAMPLE 60**

The Mauve Company has a SIMPLE plan for its employees under which it provides non-matching contributions of 2% of compensation for each eligible employee. The maximum amount that can be added to each participant's account in 2005 is $14,200, composed of the $10,000 employee salary reduction plus an employer contribution of $4,200 ($210,000 × 2%). ■

Distributions from a SIMPLE plan are taxed under the IRA rules. Tax-free rollovers can be made from one SIMPLE account to another. A SIMPLE account can be rolled over to an IRA tax-free after the expiration of a two-year period since the individual first participated in the plan. Withdrawals of contributions during the two-year period beginning on the date an employee first participates in the SIMPLE plan are subject to a 25 percent early withdrawal tax rather than the 10 percent early withdrawal tax that otherwise would apply.

**PLANNING STRATEGIES**

## Factors Affecting Retirement Plan Choices

**FRAMEWORK FOCUS: DEDUCTIONS**

**STRATEGY ➤ MAXIMIZE DEDUCTIBLE AMOUNTS.**

An IRA might not be the best retirement plan option for many self-employed taxpayers. The maximum amount that can be deducted is $4,000 per year ($8,000 for a spousal plan), which may be too low to provide funding for an adequate level of retirement income. Other options such as Keogh plans and SIMPLE plans allow larger contributions and larger deductions. However, a self-employed individual who establishes either a Keogh or a SIMPLE plan is required to cover employees under such plans. This can result in substantial expenditures, not only for the required contributions, but also for expenses of administering the plan. An advantage of an IRA is that coverage of employees is not required.

## ACCOUNTING PERIODS AND METHODS

Proprietors may choose among accounting methods, just as other business entities do (refer to Chapter 3 and Chapter 4). The cash method is commonly used by proprietorships that provide services, while the accrual or hybrid method generally is required if inventory is a material income-producing factor.

The accounting period rules for proprietorships generally are much simpler than the rules for partnerships and S corporations. Because a proprietorship is not an entity separate from the proprietor, the proprietorship must use the same tax year-end as the proprietor. This does not preclude the use of a fiscal year for a proprietorship, but most proprietorships use the calendar year.

## ESTIMATED TAX PAYMENTS

Although the following discussion largely centers on self-employed taxpayers, some of the procedures may be applicable to employed persons. In many cases, for example, employed persons may be required to pay estimated tax if they have income that is not subject to withholding (e.g., income from rentals, dividends, or interest).

**Estimated Tax for Individuals.**   **Estimated tax** is the amount of tax (including alternative minimum tax and self-employment tax) an individual expects to owe for the year after subtracting tax credits and income tax withheld. Any individual who has estimated tax for the year of $1,000 or more and whose withholding does not equal or exceed the required annual payment (discussed below) must make quarterly payments.[93] Otherwise, a penalty may be assessed. No quarterly payments are required, and no penalty will apply on an underpayment, if the taxpayer's estimated tax is under $1,000. No penalty will apply if the taxpayer had no tax liability for the preceding tax year, the preceding tax year was a taxable year of 12 months, and the taxpayer was a citizen or resident for the entire preceding tax year. In this regard, having no tax liability is not the same as having no additional tax to pay.

The required annual payment must first be computed. This is the smaller of the following amounts:

- Ninety percent of the tax shown on the current year's return.
- One hundred percent of the tax shown on the preceding year's return (the return must cover the full 12 months of the preceding year). If the AGI on the preceding year's return exceeds $150,000 ($75,000 if married filing separately), the 100 percent requirement is increased to 110 percent.

In general, one-fourth of this required annual payment is due on April 15, June 15, and September 15 of the tax year and January 15 of the following year. Thus, the quarterly installment of the required annual payment reduced by the applicable withholding is the estimated tax to be paid. An equal part of withholding is deemed paid on each due date, even if a taxpayer's earnings fluctuate widely during the year. Payments are to be accompanied by the payment voucher from Form 1040–ES for the appropriate date.

**Penalty on Underpayments.**   A nondeductible penalty is imposed on the amount of underpayment of estimated tax. The rate for this penalty is the same as the rate for underpayments of tax and is adjusted quarterly to reflect changes in the average prime rate.

An *underpayment* occurs when any quarterly payment (the sum of estimated tax paid and income tax withheld) is less than 25 percent of the required annual payment. The penalty is applied to the amount of the underpayment for the period of the underpayment.[94]

**EXAMPLE 61**

Marta made the following payments of estimated tax for 2005 and had no income tax withheld:

---

[93]§ 6654(c)(1).    [94]§ 6654(b)(2).

| April 15, 2005 | $1,400 |
| June 15, 2005 | 2,300 |
| September 15, 2005 | 1,500 |
| January 16, 2006 | 1,800 |

Marta's actual tax for 2005 is $8,000, and her tax in 2004 was $10,000. Therefore, each installment should have been at least $1,800 [($8,000 × 90%) × 25%]. Of the payment on June 15, $400 will be credited to the unpaid balance of the first quarterly installment due on April 15,[95] thereby effectively stopping the underpayment penalty for the first quarterly period. Of the remaining $1,900 payment on June 15, $100 is credited to the September 15 payment, resulting in this third quarterly payment being $200 short. Then $200 of the January 16 payment is credited to the September 15 shortfall, ending the period of underpayment for that portion due. The January 16, 2006 installment is now underpaid by $200, and a penalty will apply from January 16, 2006, to April 17, 2006 (unless paid sooner). Marta's underpayments for the periods of underpayment are as follows:

| 1st installment due: | $400 from April 15 to June 15 |
| 2nd installment due: | Paid in full |
| 3rd installment due: | $200 from September 15, 2005 to January 16, 2006 |
| 4th installment due: | $200 from January 16, 2006 to April 17, 2006 |

If a possible underpayment of estimated tax is indicated, Form 2210 should be filed to compute the penalty due or to justify that no penalty applies.

<table>
<tr><td>

**LO.6**

Distinguish between business and hobby activities and apply the rules limiting the deduction of hobby losses.
</td></tr>
</table>

# Hobby Losses

Employee deductions and deductions related to a proprietorship were discussed in previous sections of this chapter. Employees are allowed to deduct certain expenditures incurred in connection with their work activities. Expenses incurred by a self-employed taxpayer are deductible only if the taxpayer can show that the activity was entered into for the purpose of making a profit.

Certain activities may have either profit-seeking or personal attributes, depending upon individual circumstances. Examples include raising horses and operating a farm that is also used as a weekend residence. While personal losses are not deductible, losses attributable to profit-seeking activities may be deducted and used to offset a taxpayer's other income. For this reason, losses generated by hobbies are not deductible.

## GENERAL RULES

If an individual can show that an activity has been conducted with the intent to earn a profit, losses from the activity are fully deductible. The hobby loss rules apply only if the activity is not engaged in for profit. Hobby expenses are deductible only to the extent of hobby income.[96]

The Regulations stipulate that the following nine factors should be considered in determining whether an activity is profit seeking or a hobby:[97]

- Whether the activity is conducted in a businesslike manner.
- The expertise of the taxpayers or their advisers.
- The time and effort expended.

---

[95]Payments are credited to unpaid installments in the order in which the installments are required to be paid. § 6654(b)(3).

[96]§ 183(b)(2).
[97]Reg. §§ 1.183–2(b)(1) through (9).

- The expectation that the assets of the activity will appreciate in value.
- The taxpayer's previous success in conducting similar activities.
- The history of income or losses from the activity.
- The relationship of profits earned to losses incurred.
- The financial status of the taxpayer (e.g., if the taxpayer does not have substantial amounts of other income, this may indicate that the activity is engaged in for profit).
- Elements of personal pleasure or recreation in the activity.

The presence or absence of a factor is not by itself determinative of whether the activity is profit seeking or a hobby. Rather, the decision is a subjective one that is based on an analysis of the facts and circumstances.

## PRESUMPTIVE RULE OF § 183

The Code provides a rebuttable presumption that an activity is profit seeking if the activity shows a profit in at least three of any five prior consecutive years.[98] If the activity involves horses, a profit in at least two of seven consecutive years meets the presumptive rule. If these profitability tests are met, the activity is presumed to be a trade or business rather than a personal hobby. In this situation, the burden of proof shifts from the taxpayer to the IRS. That is, the IRS bears the burden of proving that the activity is personal rather than trade or business related.

**EXAMPLE 62**

Camille, an executive for a large corporation, is paid a salary of $200,000. Her husband is a collector of antiques. Several years ago, he opened an antique shop in a local shopping center and spends most of his time buying and selling antiques. He occasionally earns a small profit from this activity but more frequently incurs substantial losses. If the losses are business related, they are fully deductible against Camille's salary income on a joint return. The following approach should be considered in resolving this issue:

- Initially determine whether the antique activity has met the three-out-of-five-years profit test.
- If the presumption is not met, the activity may nevertheless qualify as a business if the taxpayer can show that the intent is to engage in a profit-seeking activity. It is not necessary to show actual profits.
- Attempt to fit the operation within the nine criteria prescribed in the Regulations and listed above. These criteria are the factors considered in trying to rebut the § 183 presumption. ■

## DETERMINING THE AMOUNT OF THE DEDUCTION

If an activity is deemed to be a hobby, the expenses are deductible only to the extent of the gross income from the hobby. These expenses must be deducted in the following order:

- Amounts deductible under other Code Sections without regard to the nature of the activity, such as property taxes and home mortgage interest.
- Amounts deductible under other Code Sections if the activity had been engaged in for profit, but only if those amounts do not affect adjusted basis. Examples include maintenance, utilities, and supplies.
- Amounts that affect adjusted basis and would be deductible under other Code Sections if the activity had been engaged in for profit.[99] Examples include depreciation, amortization, and depletion.

---

[98]§ 183(d).

[99]Reg. § 1.183–1(b)(1).

These deductions are deductible *from* AGI as itemized deductions to the extent they exceed 2 percent of AGI.[100] If the taxpayer uses the standard deduction rather than itemizing, all hobby loss deductions are wasted.

**EXAMPLE 63**

Jim, the vice president of an oil company, has AGI of $80,000. He decides to pursue painting in his spare time. He uses a home studio, comprising 10% of the home's square footage. During the current year, Jim incurs the following expenses:

| | |
|---|---:|
| Frames | $ 350 |
| Art supplies | 300 |
| Fees paid to models | 1,000 |
| Expenses related to home: | |
| Total property taxes | 900 |
| Total home mortgage interest | 10,000 |
| Total home maintenance and utilities | 3,600 |
| Depreciation on 10% of home used as studio | 500 |

During the year, Jim sold paintings for a total of $3,200. If the activity is held to be a hobby, Jim is allowed deductions as follows:

| | | |
|---|---:|---:|
| Gross income | | $ 3,200 |
| Deduct: Taxes and interest (10% of $10,900) | | (1,090) |
| Remainder | | $ 2,110 |
| Deduct: Frames | $ 350 | |
| Art supplies | 300 | |
| Models' fees | 1,000 | |
| Maintenance and utilities (10%) | 360 | (2,010) |
| Remainder | | $ 100 |
| Depreciation ($500, but limited to $100) | | (100) |
| Net income | | $ –0– |

Jim includes the $3,200 of income in AGI, making his AGI $83,200. The taxes and interest are itemized deductions, deductible in full. Assuming Jim has no other miscellaneous itemized deductions, the remaining expenses of $2,110 are reduced by 2% of his AGI ($1,664); so the net deduction is $446. Since the property taxes and home mortgage interest are deductible anyway, the net effect is a $2,754 ($3,200 less $446) increase in taxable income. ■

**EXAMPLE 64**

If Jim's activity in Example 63 were held to be a business, he could deduct expenses totaling $3,600 *for* AGI, as shown below. All these expenses would be trade or business expenses. His reduction in AGI would be as follows:

| | | |
|---|---:|---:|
| Gross income | | $ 3,200 |
| Deduct: Taxes and interest | $1,090 | |
| Other business expenses | 2,010 | |
| Depreciation | 500 | (3,600) |
| Reduction in AGI | | ($ 400) |

As in Example 63, Jim can deduct the remaining property taxes and home mortgage interest of $9,810 ($10,900 − $1,090) as itemized deductions. ■

---

[100]Reg. § 1.67–1T(a)(1)(iv) and Rev.Rul. 75–14, 1975–1 C.B. 90.

## Suggested Further Readings

Shelton I. Banoff and Richard M. Lipton, Editors (Shop Talk), "Oprah's Audience Gets Another Lesson in Taxes," *Journal of Taxation*, January 2005, pp. 63–64.

Stanley D. Baum, "The Advantages of Health Savings Accounts—The Code's Newest Healthcare Arrangement," *Journal of Taxation*, February 2004, pp. 101–110.

William J. Kenny and Anne L. Chrisensen, "Accountable Plans, Reimbursements, and Per-Diem Allowances," *The Tax Adviser*, July 2003, pp. 408–413.

Dennis Lassila, "Cafeteria Plans Can Serve Up Flexibility and Tax Services," *Practical Tax Strategies*, May 2002, pp. 285–294.

John B. Truskowski, "Tax Consequences of Renting Out a Second Home May Turn on How Often the Taxpayer Makes Use of It," *Journal of Taxation*, July 2004, pp. 26–40.

Donald T. Williamson, "Opportunities in Using the Office-in-Home Deduction for Code Sec. 280A," *Taxes—The Tax Magazine*, January 2002, pp. 19–32.

## KEY TERMS

| | | |
|---|---|---|
| Accountable plan, 16–3 | Foreign earned income exclusion, 16–19 | Nonaccountable plan, 16–37 |
| Automatic mileage method, 16–22 | Health Savings Account (HSA), 16–8 | Office in the home expenses, 16–33 |
| Cafeteria plan, 16–13 | Independent contractor, 16–2 | Qualified employee discounts, 16–15 |
| Coverdell Education Savings Account (CESA), 16–41 | Individual Retirement Account (IRA), 16–38 | Qualified transportation fringes, 16–17 |
| *De minimis* fringe benefits, 16–17 | Keogh plan, 16–44 | Self-employment tax, 16–5 |
| Deduction for qualified tuition and related expenses, 16–30 | Medical Savings Account (MSA), 16–8 | Transportation expenses, 16–20 |
| Education expenses, 16–28 | Moving expenses, 16–25 | Travel expenses, 16–22 |
| Entertainment expenses, 16–31 | No-additional-cost services, 16–15 | Working condition fringes, 16–16 |
| Estimated tax, 16–48 | | |
| Flexible spending plan, 16–14 | | |

## PROBLEM MATERIALS

### Problems

1. In determining whether someone who performs services for another is an employee or is self-employed, several factors are considered. In each of the *independent* situations appearing below, which classification is indicated? In all cases, assume Heath performs services for Melvin.
   a. Melvin pays Heath based on units produced.
   b. Melvin sets Heath's working hours.
   c. Heath has his own tools.
   d. At any time he desires, Melvin has the right to terminate Heath's services.

2. Rex, age 45, is an officer of Blue Company, which provides him with the following nondiscriminatory fringe benefits in 2005:

- Hospitalization insurance premiums for Rex and his dependents. The cost of the coverage for Rex is $2,700 per year, and the additional cost for his dependents is $3,600 per year. The plan has a $2,000 deductible, but his employer contributed $1,500 to Rex's Health Savings Account. Rex withdrew only $800 from the HSA, and the account earned $50 interest during the year.

- Long-term care insurance premiums for Rex, at a cost of $3,600 per year.

- Insurance premiums of $840 for salary continuation payments. Under the plan, Rex will receive his regular salary in the event he is unable to work due to illness. Rex collected $4,500 on the policy to replace lost wages while he was ill during the year.

- Rex is a part-time student working on his bachelor's degree in engineering. His employer reimbursed his $5,200 tuition under a plan available to all full-time employees.

Determine the amount Rex must include in gross income.

**Decision Making**

3. Mauve Corporation has a group hospitalization insurance plan that has a $200 deductible amount for hospital visits and a $15 deductible for doctor visits and prescriptions. The deductible portion paid by its employees who have children has become substantial for some employees. The company is considering adopting a medical reimbursement plan or a flexible benefits plan to cover the deductible amounts. Either of these plans can be tailored to meet the needs of the employees. What are the cost considerations to the employer that should be considered in choosing between these plans?

4. Bertha spent the last 60 days of 2005 in a nursing home. The cost of the services provided to her was $12,000. Medicare paid $7,100 toward the cost of her stay. Bertha also received $8,000 of benefits under a long-term care insurance policy she purchased. What is the effect on Bertha's gross income?

5. Does the taxpayer recognize gross income in the following situations?
   a. Ann is a registered nurse working in a community hospital. She is not required to take her lunch on the hospital premises, but she can eat in the cafeteria at no charge. The hospital adopted this policy to encourage employees to stay on the premises and be available in case of emergencies. During the year, Ann ate most of her meals on the premises. The total value of those meals was $750.
   b. Ira is the manager of a hotel. His employer will allow him to live in one of the rooms rent-free or receive a $600 per month cash allowance for rent. Ira elected to live in the hotel.
   c. Seth is a forest ranger and lives in his employer's cabin in the forest. He is required to live there, and because there are no restaurants nearby, the employer supplies Seth with groceries that he cooks and eats on the premises.
   d. Rocky is a partner in the BAR Ranch (a partnership). He is the full-time manager of the ranch. BAR has a business purpose for Rocky's living on the ranch.

6. Sally and Bill are married and file joint returns. In 2005, Bill, an accountant, has a salary of $75,000, and Sally receives a salary of $25,000 as an apartment manager. What are the tax consequences of the following benefits that Bill and Sally's employers provide?
   a. Bill receives a reimbursement of $5,000 for child care expenses. Sally and Bill have three children who are not yet school age.
   b. Bill and Sally are provided a free membership at a local fitness and exercise club that allows them to attend three aerobic exercise sessions per week. The value of this type of membership is $1,600 per year.
   c. Bill is provided free parking at work. The value of the parking is $1,800 per year.
   d. Sally is provided with a free apartment. Living in this apartment is a condition of her employment. Similar apartments rent for $1,200 per month.

**Communications**

7. Finch Construction Company provides its employees who are carpenters with all of the required tools. However, the company believes that this has led to some employees not taking care of the tools and to the mysterious disappearance of some of the tools. The company is considering requiring all of its employees to provide their own tools. Employees' salaries would be increased by $1,500 to compensate for their additional costs. Write a letter to Finch's management explaining the tax consequences of this plan to the carpenters. Finch's address is 300 Harbor Drive, Vermillion, SD 57069.

Online quizzing @ http://wft.swlearning.com

**Decision Making**

8. Tara's employer provides a flexible benefits plan. Under the plan, medical and dental expenses incurred during the year that are not covered by the company's group health insurance plan will be paid by the flexible benefits plan. At the first of each year, the employee must set the amount to be covered by the plan. The employee's monthly salary is reduced by one-twelfth of the identified flexible benefit amount for the year. Tara thinks it is highly unlikely that she can accurately estimate her medical and dental expenses not covered by the company's group health insurance plan, but she feels these costs will probably be in the range of $1,500 to $2,500. She expects to be in the 25% marginal tax bracket. Tara would like your advice regarding how much she should reduce her salary in exchange for the expanded dental and medical benefits.

9. Canary Corporation would like you to review its employee fringe benefits program with regard to the tax consequences of the plan for the company's president (Polly), who is also the majority shareholder:
   a. All executives receive free tickets to State University football games. Polly is not a football fan and usually gives her tickets to another employee. The cost to the employer for Polly's tickets for the year was $600.
   b. The company owns a parking garage that is used by customers, employees, and the general public. Only the general public is required to pay for parking. The charge to the general public for Polly's parking for the year would have been $2,700 (a $225 monthly rate).
   c. All employees are allowed to use the company's fixed charge long-distance telephone services, as long as the privilege is not abused. Although no one has kept track of the actual calls, Polly's use of the telephone had a value (what she would have paid on her personal telephone) of approximately $600.
   d. The company owns a condominium at the beach, which it uses to entertain customers. Employees are allowed to use the facility without charge when the company has no scheduled events. Polly used the facility 10 days during the year. Her use had a rental value of $1,000.
   e. The company is in the household moving business. Employees are allowed to ship goods without charge whenever there is excess space on a truck. Polly purchased a dining room suite for her daughter. Company trucks delivered the furniture to the daughter. Normal freight charges would have been $750.
   f. The company has a storage facility for household goods. Officers are allowed a 20% discount on charges for storing their goods. All other employees are allowed a 10% discount. Polly's discounts for the year totaled $900.

**Ethics**

10. Tom works for Roadrunner Motors, a company that manufactures automobiles. Tom purchased a new automobile from Roadrunner at the company's cost of $10,000. The retail selling price for the automobile is $15,000. Sue works for Coyote, Inc., an auto dealership, which sells the car manufactured by Roadrunner. Sue purchased an automobile identical to Tom's from Coyote. The price Sue pays is equal to Coyote's cost of the automobile ($13,500). Tom and Sue each receive a salary of $40,000 per year. Considering only the above information, do Tom and Sue have equal ability to pay income taxes for the year, and does equitable treatment occur? If not, how should the tax law be changed to produce equitable treatment?

**Issue ID**

11. Several of Egret Company's employees have asked the company to create a hiking trail that employees could use during their lunch hours. The company owns vacant land that is being held for future expansion, but would have to spend approximately $50,000 if it were to make a trail. Nonemployees would be allowed to use the facility as part of the company's effort to build strong community support. What are the relevant tax issues for the employees?

12. Redbird, Inc., does not provide its employees with any tax-exempt fringe benefits. The company is considering adopting a hospital and medical benefits insurance plan that will cost approximately $7,000 per employee. In order to adopt this plan, the company may have to reduce salaries and/or lower future salary increases. Redbird is in the 35% (combined Federal and state rates) income tax bracket. Redbird is also responsible for matching the Social Security and Medicare taxes withheld on employees' salaries. The benefits insurance plans will not be subject to the Social Security and Medicare taxes. The employees generally fall into three marginal tax rate groups:

| Income Tax | Social Security and Medicare Tax | Total |
|---|---|---|
| .15 | .0765 | .2265 |
| .25 | .0765 | .3265 |
| .35 | .0145 | .3645 |

The company has asked you to assist in its financial planning for the benefits insurance plan by computing the following:

a. How much taxable compensation is the equivalent to $7,000 of exempt compensation for each of the three classes of employees?

b. What is the company's after-tax cost of the taxable compensation computed in (a) above?

c. What is the company's after-tax cost of the exempt compensation?

d. Briefly explain your conclusions from the above analysis.

13. George is a U.S. citizen who is employed by Hawk Enterprises, a global company. Beginning on July 1, 2005, George began working in London. He worked there until January 31, 2006, when he transferred to Paris. He worked in Paris the remainder of 2006. His salary for the first six months of 2005 was $95,000, and it was earned in the United States. His salary for the remainder of 2005 was $135,000, and it was earned in London. George's 2006 salary from Hawk was $275,000, with part being earned in London and part being earned in Paris. What is George's gross income in 2005 and 2006?

14. Dena is the regional sales manager for the Burger Hut fast-food chain. Generally, she drives her personal automobile from her residence to the regional office, works for eight hours, and returns home. On many occasions, however, she leaves the office early and visits the four local outlets (starting with No. 1 through No. 4) as part of the workday. Relevant mileage is as follows:

| | Miles |
|---|---|
| Residence to regional office | 20 |
| Regional office to Burger Hut No. 1 | 10 |
| Burger Hut No. 1 to Burger Hut No. 2 | 15 |
| Burger Hut No. 2 to Burger Hut No. 3 | 12 |
| Burger Hut No. 3 to Burger Hut No. 4 | 16 |
| Burger Hut No. 4 to residence | 30 |

Dena works 230 days in 2005. Of these, 75 days involve visits to the outlets. If she uses the automatic mileage method, what is her deduction for the year?

15. Larry went from Cleveland to New York on business. His time was spent as follows:

| | |
|---|---|
| Thursday | Travel |
| Friday | Business |
| Saturday and Sunday | Sightseeing |
| Monday and Tuesday | Business |
| Wednesday | Travel |

During the trip, Larry incurred and paid expenses of $180 per day for lodging from Thursday night through Tuesday night and $110 per day for meals from Friday through Tuesday. Round-trip airfare was $400. Larry is a self-employed attorney who practices law in Cleveland.

a. How much can Larry deduct for the New York trip?

b. How will any deduction be classified?

16. In June of this year, Dr. and Mrs. Alvin Lord traveled to Memphis to attend a three-day conference sponsored by the American Society of Implant Dentistry. Alvin, a practicing oral surgeon, participated in scheduled technical sessions dealing with the latest developments in surgical procedures. On two days, Mrs. Lord attended group meetings where various aspects of family tax planning were discussed. On the other day, she went sightseeing. Mrs. Lord does not work for her husband, but she does their tax returns and handles the family investments. Expenses incurred in connection with the conference are summarized below:

| | |
|---|---|
| Airfare (two tickets) | $1,040 |
| Lodging (single and double occupancy are the same rate—$220 each day) | 660 |
| Meals ($200 × 3 days)* | 600 |
| Conference registration fee (includes $120 for Family Tax Planning sessions) | 520 |
| Car rental | 240 |

*Split equally between Dr. and Mrs. Lord.

How much, if any, of these expenses can the Lords deduct?

17. On Thursday, Justin flies from Baltimore (his home office) to Cadiz (Spain). He conducts business on Friday and Tuesday; vacations on Saturday, Sunday, and Monday (a legal holiday in Spain); and returns to Baltimore on Thursday. Justin was scheduled to return home on Wednesday, but all flights were canceled due to bad weather. Therefore, he spent Wednesday watching floor shows at a local casino.
   a. For tax purposes, what portion of Justin's trip is regarded as being for business?
   b. Suppose Monday had not been a legal holiday. Would this change your answer to part (a)?
   c. Under either (a) or (b), how much of Justin's airfare qualifies as a deductible business expense?

**Ethics**

18. Veronica is a key employee of Perdiz Corporation, an aerospace engineering concern located in Seattle. Perdiz would like to establish an office on the east coast of Florida and wants Veronica to be in charge of the branch. Veronica is hesitant about making the move because she fears she will have to sell her residence in Seattle at a loss. Perdiz buys the house from Veronica for $420,000, its cost to her. She has owned and occupied the house as her principal residence for eight years. One year later, Perdiz resells the property for $370,000. Nothing regarding the sale of the residence is ever reflected on Veronica's income tax returns. Needless to say, Perdiz absorbs all of Veronica's moving expenses. Do you have any qualms as to the way these matters have been handled for income tax purposes?

19. Cole is both a CPA and an attorney. For several years, he has practiced law as an employee of a large law firm in Dallas. In 2005, Cole decides to quit his job and move to El Paso, Texas. Four months after arriving in El Paso, Cole establishes a private practice as a CPA. Expenses in moving from Dallas to El Paso are as follows:

| | |
|---|---|
| Cost of moving household effects | $6,500 |
| Meals | 225 |
| Lodging | 240 |

The total mileage on two personal autos involved in the move is 1,250.
   a. How much, if any, can Cole deduct as a moving expense?
   b. How is the deduction, if any, classified (*for* or *from* AGI)?

20. Marvin is employed as a full-time high school teacher. The school district for which he works recently instituted a policy requiring all of its teachers to start working on a master's degree. Pursuant to this new rule, Marvin spent most of the summer of 2005 taking graduate courses at an out-of-town university. His expenses are as follows:

| Tuition | $4,300 |
| --- | --- |
| Books and course materials | 650 |
| Lodging | 1,200 |
| Meals | 1,600 |
| Laundry and dry cleaning | 220 |
| Campus parking | 300 |

In addition, Marvin drove his personal automobile 1,500 miles in connection with the education. He uses the automatic mileage method.
   a.  How much, if any, of these expenses might qualify as a deduction *for* AGI?
   b.  How much, if any, of these expenses might qualify as a deduction *from* AGI?

21.  In each of the following independent situations, determine how much, if any, qualifies as a deduction *for* AGI under § 222 (qualified tuition and related expenses):
   a.  Ruby is single and is employed as a nurse practitioner. During 2005, she spent $4,200 in tuition to attend law school at night. Her AGI is $64,000.
   b.  Jacque is single and is employed as a pharmacist. During 2005, he spent $2,100 ($1,900 for tuition and $200 for books) to take a course in herbal supplements at a local university. His AGI is $70,000.
   c.  How much, if any, of the above amounts *not allowed under § 222* might otherwise qualify as a deduction *from* AGI?

22.  Elvis is a salesman who works for Crane Sales, Inc. Typically, Elvis spends several days out of town each week. Crane provides Elvis with a travel allowance of $1,100 per month, but requires no accountability. For the current year, Elvis had the following job-related travel expenses:

| Meals | $ 5,040 |
| --- | --- |
| Lodging | 10,080 |
| Transportation | 1,400 |

   a.  What amount qualifies as a deductible travel expense?
   b.  What is the classification of any such deduction?

23.  Brittany is a broker who works full-time for a national brokerage firm. She also maintains an office in her home for her sole proprietorship, which she uses to provide financial planning services to clients. Expenses of the business (other than home office expenses) are $3,200. Brittany's home expenses are as follows:

| Real property taxes | $4,000 |
| --- | --- |
| Interest on home mortgage | 5,000 |
| Operating expenses of home | 1,000 |
| Depreciation (based on 20% business use) | 1,500 |

Brittany's gross income from the consulting activity is $5,500.
   a.  Compute Brittany's office in the home deduction.
   b.  How are these items classified?

24.  Victor has AGI of $94,000 during the year and the following expenses related to his employment:

| Lodging while in travel status | $3,400 |
| --- | --- |
| Meals during travel | 3,200 |
| Business transportation | 5,200 |
| Entertainment of clients | 2,200 |
| Professional dues and subscriptions | 900 |

Victor is reimbursed $10,000 under his employer's accountable plan. What are Victor's deductions *for* and *from* AGI?

25. Molly is unmarried and is an active participant in a qualified deductible (traditional) IRA plan. Her modified AGI is $55,000 in 2005.
    a. Calculate the amount that Molly can contribute to the IRA and the amount she can deduct.
    b. Assume instead that Molly is a participant in a SIMPLE IRA and that she elects to contribute 4% of her compensation to the account, while her employer contributes 3%. What amount will be contributed for 2005? What amount will be vested?

26. Karli and Jacob have been married for 12 years and are both active participants in employer qualified retirement plans. Their total AGI in 2005 is $156,000, and they earn salaries of $78,000 and $72,000, respectively.
    a. What amount can Karli and Jacob contribute to traditional IRAs?
    b. What amount can Karli and Jacob deduct for their contributions in (a)?
    c. What amount can Karli and Jacob contribute to Roth IRAs?
    d. What amount can Karli and Jacob deduct for their contributions in (c)?
    e. What amount can they contribute to Coverdell Education Savings Accounts for their two children?

27. Monica, age 51, has a traditional deductible IRA with an account balance of $102,000. Of this amount, $72,000 represents contributions, and $30,000 represents earnings. In 2005, she converts her IRA into a Roth IRA. What amount must Monica include in her gross income in 2005?

28. In 2013, Joyce receives a $4,000 distribution from her Coverdell Education Savings Account (CESA) which has a fair market value of $10,000. Total contributions to her CESA have been $7,000. Joyce's AGI is $25,000.
    a. Joyce uses the entire $4,000 to pay for qualified education expenses. What amount should she include in her gross income?
    b. Assume instead that Joyce uses only $2,500 of the $4,000 distribution for qualified education expenses. What amount should she include in her gross income?

29. In 2005, Susan's sole proprietorship earns $210,000 of self-employment net income (after the deduction for one-half of self-employment tax).
    a. Calculate the maximum amount that Susan can deduct for contributions to a defined contribution Keogh plan.
    b. Suppose Susan contributes more than the allowable amount to the Keogh plan. What are the tax consequences to her?
    c. Can Susan retire and begin receiving Keogh payments at age 55 without incurring a penalty?

30. Patricia is a self-employed accountant with earned income from the business of $140,000 (after the deduction for one-half of any self-employment tax). She has a profit sharing plan (i.e., defined contribution Keogh plan). What is the maximum amount Patricia can contribute to her retirement plan?

**EXTENDER** 31. In each of the following *independent* situations, determine the amount of FICA (Social Security and Medicare) that should be withheld from the employee's 2005 salary by the employer.
    a. Harry earns a $50,000 salary, files a joint return, and claims four withholding allowances.
    b. Hazel earns a $100,000 salary, files a joint return, and claims four withholding allowances.
    c. Tracey earns a $180,000 salary, files a joint return, and claims four withholding allowances.
    d. Alicia's 17-year-old son, Carlos, earns $10,000 at the family business.

**EXTENDER** 32. During 2005, Helen, the owner of a store, has the following income and expenses:

| | |
|---|---|
| Gross profit on sales | $73,000 |
| Income from part-time job (subject to FICA) | 40,000 |
| Business expenses (related to store) | 15,000 |

| | |
|---|---|
| Fire loss on store building | $ 1,200 |
| Dividend income | 200 |
| Long-term capital gain on the sale of a stock investment | 2,000 |

*—No effect on earned income*

Compute Helen's self-employment tax and allowable income tax deduction for the self-employment tax paid.

33. Samantha is an executive with an AGI of $100,000 before consideration of income or loss from her miniature horse business. Her other income comes from winning horse shows, stud fees, and sales of yearlings. Her home is on 20 acres, 10 of which she uses to pasture the horses and upon which she has erected stables, paddocks, fences, tack houses, and so forth.

Samantha uses an office in her home that is 10% of the square footage of the house. She uses the office exclusively for keeping records of breeding lines, histories, and show and veterinary records. Her records show the following income and expenses for the current year.

| | |
|---|---|
| Income from fees, prizes, and sales | $22,000 |
| Expenses | |
| Entry fees | 1,000 |
| Feed and veterinary bills | 4,000 |
| Supplies | 900 |
| Publications and dues | 500 |
| Travel to horse shows (no meals) | 2,300 |
| Salaries and wages of employees | 8,000 |
| Depreciation on horse equipment | 3,000 |
| Depreciation on horse farm improvements | 7,000 |
| Depreciation on 10% of home | 1,000 |
| Total home mortgage interest | 24,000 |
| Total property taxes on home | 2,200 |
| Total property taxes on horse farm improvements | 800 |

The mortgage interest is only on her home. The horse farm improvements are not mortgaged.
  a. How must Samantha treat the income and expenses of the operation if the miniature horse activity is held to be a hobby?
  b. How would your answer in (a) differ if the horse operation was held to be a business?

## Comprehensive Tax Return Problem

**Tax Return Problem**

34. Beth R. Jordan lives at 2322 Skyview Road, Mesa, AZ 85202. She is a tax accountant with Mesa Manufacturing Company. She also writes computer software programs for tax practitioners and has a part-time tax practice. Beth, age 35, is single and has no dependents. Her Social Security number is 111–35–2222. She wants to contribute $3 to the Presidential Election Campaign Fund.

During 2004, Beth earned a salary of $63,000 from her employer. She received interest of $1,300 from Home Federal Savings and Loan and $400 from Home State Bank. She received dividends of $500 from Gray Corporation, $400 from Blue Corporation, and $1,200 from Orange Corporation.

Beth received a $1,600 income tax refund from the state of Arizona on May 12, 2004. On her 2003 Federal income tax return, she reported total itemized deductions of $7,700, which included $2,400 of state income tax withheld by her employer.

Fees earned from her part-time tax practice in 2004 totaled $3,800. She paid $600 to have the tax returns processed by a computerized tax return service.

On February 1, 2004, Beth bought 500 shares of Gray Corporation common stock for $17.60 a share. On July 16, she sold the stock for $14 a share.

Beth bought a used sports utility vehicle for $3,000 on June 5, 2004. She purchased the vehicle from her brother-in-law, who was unemployed and was in need of cash. On November 2, 2004, she sold the vehicle to a friend for $3,400.

On January 2, 2004, Beth acquired 100 shares of Blue Corporation common stock for $30 a share. She sold the stock on December 19, 2004, for $55 a share.

During 2004, Beth received royalties of $16,000 on a software program she had written. Beth incurred the following expenditures in connection with her software-writing activities:

| | |
|---|---|
| Cost of microcomputer (100% business use) | $7,000 |
| Cost of printer (100% business use) | 2,000 |
| Office furniture | 3,000 |
| Supplies | 650 |
| Fee paid to computer consultant | 3,500 |

Beth elected to expense the maximum portion of the cost of the microcomputer, printer, and furniture allowed under the provisions of § 179. This equipment and furniture were placed in service on January 15, 2004.

Although her employer suggested that Beth attend a convention on current developments in corporate taxation, Beth was not reimbursed for the travel expenses of $1,420 she incurred in attending the convention. The $1,420 included $200 for the cost of meals.

During 2004, Beth paid $300 for prescription medicines and $2,875 in doctor bills, hospital bills, and medical insurance premiums. Her employer withheld state income tax of $1,650. Beth paid real property taxes of $1,766 on her home. Interest on her home mortgage was $3,845, and interest to credit card companies was $320. Beth contributed $30 each week to her church and $10 each week to the United Way. Professional dues and subscriptions totaled $350. Beth maintained her sales tax receipts. The total is $1,954.

Beth's employer withheld Federal income taxes of $11,000 during 2004. Beth paid estimated taxes of $1,000. What is the amount of Beth's net tax payable or refund due for 2004? If Beth has a tax refund due, she wants to have it credited toward her 2005 income tax. If you use tax forms for your solution, you will need Forms 1040, 2106–EZ, and 4562 and Schedules A, B, C, D, and SE. Suggested software: TurboTax.

**Tax Return Problem**

35. Brenda Luce, age 39 and single, lives at 1329 Yorkchester Drive, Spring Valley, TX 77024. Her Social Security number is 444–00–1111. She is the regional sales manager for Style-Smart, a national chain of retail outlets specializing in women's clothing. As such, she oversees the sales performance of the stores in her territory, handles employee relations, and resolves customer disputes. Style-Smart pays Brenda an annual salary of $70,000 plus a bonus based on performance. She also receives a yearly travel and entertainment allowance of $24,000. Style-Smart expects its employees to use the allowance to absorb their employment-related expenses but does not require them to submit any accounting or repay any excess amounts. Federal income tax withheld was $11,000. The appropriate amount was withheld for FICA taxes.

Brenda's expenses during 2005 that relate to her work are summarized below.

| | |
|---|---|
| Airfare (includes European trip) | $11,200 |
| Meals | 3,100 |
| Lodging | 3,900 |
| Entertainment | 3,800 |
| Taxis, limousines, and car rentals | 1,200 |
| Valet service | 420 |
| Professional dues and subscriptions | 390 |
| Business gifts | 400 |
| Online self-study course | 240 |

During the summer of 2005, Brenda went to France and Italy to visit various fashion houses and attend several style shows. During the trip, she spent one week on business and two weeks vacationing. Her plane ticket cost $3,300 (business class). She could have saved $1,200 by flying coach but declined to do so. The fashion houses she visited paid for the one-week business portion of her meals and lodging.

The business gifts consisted of a box of Godiva chocolates given to each of 10 store managers at Christmas. The candy cost $36 plus $4 for wrapping and shipping. The online self-study course, "Creative Fashion Displays," is part of a home study series sponsored by the National Retail Association. Brenda has a college degree in marketing and is not pursuing any further postsecondary education.

Brenda's performance bonus for 2005 turned out to be $15,000 and was paid to her in January 2006. In the past, Style-Smart always paid the bonus in the year awarded. Thus, Brenda received her $12,000 bonus for 2004 in December 2004. In 2005, however, Style-Smart changed its policy in order to improve its year-end cash flow.

In connection with her work, Brenda drives her own car. She uses the actual expense method based on 80% business/20% personal use. She purchased her present car in June 2004 at a cost of $40,000 (no trade-in was involved). She uses MACRS accelerated depreciation (200% declining-balance assuming half-year convention) and took the additional first-year allowance of 50% but no § 179 deduction. Depreciation previously claimed was $8,488 ($10,610 × 80%) for 2004. Expenses relating to the automobile are as follows:

| | |
|---|---:|
| Insurance | $1,300 |
| Registration, inspection, license | 70 |
| Gasoline and oil | 1,500 |
| Tire replacement | 300 |
| Tolls and parking (business related) | 620 |
| Mechanical repairs | 410 |
| Traffic fines (business related) | 320 |

During the year, Brenda had the following additional expenditures:

| | |
|---|---:|
| Contribution to a traditional IRA | $4,000 |
| Premiums on policy covering Brenda's life (Brenda is the owner of the policy, and her parents are the designated beneficiaries.) | 1,200 |
| Premiums on medical insurance policy (sponsored by Style-Smart for its employees) | 900 |
| Contribution to the reelection campaign of the mayor of Spring Valley | 200 |
| Dental bills (not covered by insurance) | 9,200 |
| Property taxes on residence | 2,800 |
| Sales taxes (receipts available) | 1,200 |
| Interest on home mortgage | 2,200 |
| Interest on loan to purchase City of Dallas bonds | 600 |
| Charitable contributions | 1,300 |

Besides employment-related income, Brenda had the following receipts during 2005:

| | | |
|---|---:|---:|
| Federal income tax refund (for year 2004) | | $  180 |
| Interest income— | | |
| City of Dallas bonds | $1,410 | |
| Interest on CD issued by Spring Valley State Bank | 800 | |
| Interest on bonds issued by General Motors Corporation | 360 | 2,570 |
| Qualified dividends on stock investment in General Electric Company | | 940 |

Brenda buys all of her clothing from Style-Smart stores. Pursuant to the employer's policy, employees receive a 30% discount from the listed price (gross profit rate is 20%). In 2005, this enabled Brenda to purchase clothes listed at $3,000 for $2,100.

Based on the information given, determine Brenda's tax liability for 2005 and the related additional tax payable or refund due. Suggested software: TurboTax.

**BRIDGE DISCIPLINE**

1. Justin performs services for Partridge, Inc., and receives compensation of $85,000 for the year. Determine the tax consequences of Social Security and Medicare on Justin's take-home pay if:
   a. Justin is classified as an employee of Partridge.
   b. Justin is classified as an independent contractor.

2. Amanda has been an employee of Robin, Inc., for almost five years. She is a participant in Robin's defined contribution pension plan (money purchase plan). The total contributions made by Robin to the money purchase plan for Amanda are $60,000, and the balance in Amanda's account is $89,000. Amanda is considering accepting a job with a competitor of Robin's at an annual salary $7,000 higher than that received from Robin. Her boss, who is trying to convince her to stay, points out that she will not be vested in the money purchase plan until she has been employed by Robin for at least five years. In addition, she will have to start a new vesting schedule with the competitor.
   a. What is vesting, and how does it affect Amanda and her decision based on the information provided?
   b. What have been the tax consequences to Amanda of Robin's annual contribution of $14,000 to its money purchase plan for her?
   c. What effect would it have on Amanda's decision if the competitor does not provide retirement benefits?

3. The Code contains provisions that are "friendly" to specific groups of taxpayers. Among these are the following:

   • Seniors.

   • Married taxpayers.

   • Employed taxpayers.

   • Taxpayers with children.

   • Self-employed individuals.

   Provide justification for the special treatment for each of the above groups, and give an example of such special treatment for each group.

## Research Problems

*Note: Solutions to Research Problems can be prepared by using the **RIA Checkpoint**® **Student Edition** online research product, which is available to accompany this text. It is also possible to prepare solutions to the Research Problems by using tax research materials found in a standard tax library.*

**Communications**

**Research Problem 1.**  Tom Roberts, a chemical engineer, is a long-time employee of Teal Chemical Corporation. Tom's specialty is the design and construction of special-purpose chemical processing plants. Teal has decided to expand its presence in France and plans to transfer Tom to Paris on a three-year assignment. The planned foreign assignment will take Tom to age 65, Teal's normal retirement age.

Tom has been advised regarding the major income tax ramifications of working abroad. He has not, however, been told about the treatment of moving expenses. Since Teal

Corporation pays its employees a substantial foreign service salary increment, it reimburses for moving expenses. In connection with the move, Tom plans to sell his residence and place most of his furniture in storage. Probabilities are good that the sale of the residence will result in a loss.

a. Write a letter to Tom regarding the income tax treatment of his moving expenses. Tom's address is 1389 Wilson Drive, Trent, NJ 08102. Be sure to include in the discussion the move from France back to the United States.

b. Prepare a memo for your firm's client files.

**Communications**

**Research Problem 2.** Rick Beam has been an independent sales representative for various textile manufacturers for many years. His products consist of soft goods, such as tablecloths, curtains, and drapes. Rick's customers are clothing store chains, department stores, and smaller specialty stores. The employees of these companies who are responsible for purchasing merchandise are known as buyers. These companies generally prohibit their buyers from accepting gifts from manufacturers' sales representatives.

Each year Rick gives cash gifts (never more than $25) to most of the buyers who are his customers. Generally, he cashes a large check in November and gives the money personally to the buyers around Christmas. Rick says, "This is one of the ways that I maintain my relationship with my buyers." He maintains adequate substantiation of all the gifts.

Rick's deductions for these gifts have been disallowed by the IRS, based on § 162(c)(2). Rick is confused and comes to you, a CPA, for advice.

a. Write a letter to Rick concerning his tax position on this issue. Rick's address is 948 Octavia Street, New Orleans, LA 70113.

b. Prepare a memo for your files supporting the advice you have given.

**Research Problem 3.** Al Hardee has been employed as a salesman by Robin Chevrolet at its Milwaukee dealership. In early May 2002, Al and the general manager of the office had a serious dispute over job procedures. When it became clear that the two could no longer work together amicably, Al contacted Robin's CEO regarding a possible solution. As the general manager planned to retire in five months, it was decided that Al would spend this period working at the Green Bay branch. After the manager's retirement, Al was to rejoin the Milwaukee office.

Al's residence is only a few blocks from the Milwaukee office, but it is 96 miles (one-way) from the Green Bay worksite. During the next five months (i.e., May to October), Al made 120 trips driving from his home in Milwaukee to the Green Bay job. His only records of his trips are a wall calendar with the workdays circled and the credit card receipts he received from gasoline purchases. The employee records of the Green Bay dealership can, however, support Al's on-the-job presence.

Upon termination of the five-month assignment and after the retirement of the general manager, Al requested a transfer back to the Milwaukee office. The CEO turned down the request on the grounds that Al was no longer needed in Milwaukee. During his absence and unknown to Al, his job position in Milwaukee had been eliminated. However, the CEO offered to make the Green Bay assignment permanent. Hurt and disgusted, Al quit and took a job with a competing Milwaukee car dealership.

On his Federal income tax return for 2002, Al claimed a deduction of $8,410 for employee transportation expenses, computed as follows: 120 (number of trips) × 192 (round-trip mileage) × $0.365 (automatic mileage rate for 2002) = $8,410 (rounded). The IRS disallowed the deduction on two grounds. First, Al's job status in Green Bay was *permanent*, not *temporary*. Thus, his tax home had changed from Milwaukee to Green Bay. This, in turn, made his transportation expenses nondeductible commuting expenses. Second, even if the transportation was warranted, the expenses were not properly substantiated. Consequently, the lack of substantiation precludes any deduction.

Should Al be allowed a deduction for his transportation expenses? Explain.

*Partial list of research aids:*
Reg. § 1.162–2(e).
Reg. § 1.274–5T(c)(3).
Rev.Rul. 99–7, 1999–1 C.B. 363.
*Teresita T. Diaz,* 84 TCM 148, T.C.Memo. 2002–192.
*Richard M. Brockman,* 85 TCM 733, T.C.Memo. 2003–3.

**Research Problem 4.**   Herron, Inc., previously gave all of its employees a ham for Christmas. However, many of the employees do not eat ham. Therefore, Herron has decided to give each employee a coupon for $35 that can be redeemed (for food or cash) any time between December 1 and January 31 of the following year. Herron has asked you whether the coupons can be excluded from the employees' gross income as a *de minimis* fringe benefit.

**Research Problem 5.**   You recently read an article in your school newspaper about Professor Rodney Taylor, one of your favorite professors in the religious studies department. According to the article, he and the university have been negotiating an early retirement package and have reached a stumbling block. Under the agreement, Professor Taylor is to receive a lump-sum payment equal to one year's salary in exchange for his retirement and the release of any and all rights associated with his tenure status. While recognizing that the payment would be subject to income tax, Taylor contends that the amount is not earned income and thus should not be subject to the FICA tax. The university negotiators say that they are not aware of any authority that supports Taylor's view. In fact, they have learned that other universities in the state system have been withholding amounts for FICA for years in situations involving early retirement buyout packages for high-level administrators. The university's position is that lacking the authority to not withhold for FICA and given the precedent of similar early retirement packages at other universities, they are obligated to withhold FICA from the payment. You want to come to the aid of Professor Taylor. Obviously, if the payments are considered wages subject to the FICA tax, the value of the offer to Professor Taylor will be significantly reduced. Can you find any authority for his position?

**Internet Activity**

*Use the tax resources of the Internet to address the following questions. Do not restrict your search to the World Wide Web, but include a review of newsgroups and general reference materials, practitioner sites and resources, primary sources of the tax law, chat rooms and discussion groups, and other opportunities.*

**Research Problem 6.**   An employer allows its employees limited personal use of one of the corporate executive jets. Does the IRS provide any guidelines as to how much income the employee should recognize due to such use?

**Research Problem 7.**   Check with a major CPA firm in your area. Does the firm provide office space for all of its field auditors? If so, what arrangements are made? If not, what workplace does the firm expect the staff to use?

# Tax Rate Schedules and Tables

(The 2005 Tax Tables and 2005 Sales Tax Tables can be accessed at the IRS web site [http://www.irs.gov] when released.)

# 2004 Tax Rate Schedules

## Single—Schedule X

| If taxable income is: Over— | But not over— | The tax is: | of the amount over— |
|---|---|---|---|
| $0 | $ 7,150 | .........10% | $0 |
| 7,150 | 29,050 | $ 715.00 + 15% | 7,150 |
| 29,050 | 70,350 | 4,000.00 + 25% | 29,050 |
| 70,350 | 146,750 | 14,325.00 + 28% | 70,350 |
| 146,750 | 319,100 | 35,717.00 + 33% | 146,750 |
| 319,100 | ....... | 92,592.50 + 35% | 319,100 |

## Head of household—Schedule Z

| If taxable income is: Over— | But not over— | The tax is: | of the amount over— |
|---|---|---|---|
| $0 | $ 10,200 | .........10% | $0 |
| 10,200 | 38,900 | $ 1,020.00 + 15% | 10,200 |
| 38,900 | 100,500 | 5,325.00 + 25% | 38,900 |
| 100,500 | 162,700 | 20,725.00 + 28% | 100,500 |
| 162,700 | 319,100 | 38,141.00 + 33% | 162,700 |
| 319,100 | ....... | 89,753.00 + 35% | 319,100 |

## Married filing jointly or Qualifying widow(er)—Schedule Y–1

| If taxable income is: Over— | But not over— | The tax is: | of the amount over— |
|---|---|---|---|
| $0 | $ 14,300 | .........10% | $0 |
| 14,300 | 58,100 | $ 1,430.00 + 15% | 14,300 |
| 58,100 | 117,250 | 8,000.00 + 25% | 58,100 |
| 117,250 | 178,650 | 22,787.50 + 28% | 117,250 |
| 178,650 | 319,100 | 39,979.50 + 33% | 178,650 |
| 319,100 | ....... | 86,328.00 + 35% | 319,100 |

## Married filing separately—Schedule Y–2

| If taxable income is: Over— | But not over— | The tax is: | of the amount over— |
|---|---|---|---|
| $0 | $ 7,150 | .........10% | $0 |
| 7,150 | 29,050 | $ 715.00 + 15% | 7,150 |
| 29,050 | 58,625 | 4,000.00 + 25% | 29,050 |
| 58,625 | 89,325 | 11,393.75 + 28% | 58,625 |
| 89,325 | 159,550 | 19,989.75 + 33% | 89,325 |
| 159,550 | ....... | 43,164.00 + 35% | 159,550 |

# 2005 Tax Rate Schedules

## Single—Schedule X

| If taxable income is: Over— | But not over— | The tax is: | of the amount over— |
|---|---|---|---|
| $0 | $ 7,300 | .........10% | $0 |
| 7,300 | 29,700 | $ 730.00 + 15% | 7,300 |
| 29,700 | 71,950 | 4,090.00 + 25% | 29,700 |
| 71,950 | 150,150 | 14,652.50 + 28% | 71,950 |
| 150,150 | 326,450 | 36,548.50 + 33% | 150,150 |
| 326,450 | ....... | 94,727.50 + 35% | 326,450 |

## Head of household—Schedule Z

| If taxable income is: Over— | But not over— | The tax is: | of the amount over— |
|---|---|---|---|
| $0 | $ 10,450 | .........10% | $0 |
| 10,450 | 39,800 | $ 1,045.00 + 15% | 10,450 |
| 39,800 | 102,800 | 5,447.50 + 25% | 39,800 |
| 102,800 | 166,450 | 21,197.50 + 28% | 102,800 |
| 166,450 | 326,450 | 39,019.50 + 33% | 166,450 |
| 326,450 | ....... | 91,819.50 + 35% | 326,450 |

## Married filing jointly or Qualifying widow(er)—Schedule Y–1

| If taxable income is: Over— | But not over— | The tax is: | of the amount over— |
|---|---|---|---|
| $0 | $ 14,600 | .........10% | $0 |
| 14,600 | 59,400 | $ 1,460.00 + 15% | 14,600 |
| 59,400 | 119,950 | 8,180.00 + 25% | 59,400 |
| 119,950 | 182,800 | 23,317.50 + 28% | 119,950 |
| 182,800 | 326,450 | 40,915.50 + 33% | 182,800 |
| 326,450 | ....... | 88,320.00 + 35% | 326,450 |

## Married filing separately—Schedule Y–2

| If taxable income is: Over— | But not over— | The tax is: | of the amount over— |
|---|---|---|---|
| $0 | $ 7,300 | .........10% | $0 |
| 7,300 | 29,700 | $ 730.00 + 15% | 7,300 |
| 29,700 | 59,975 | 4,090.00 + 25% | 29,700 |
| 59,975 | 91,400 | 11,658.75 + 28% | 59,975 |
| 91,400 | 163,225 | 20,457.75 + 33% | 91,400 |
| 163,225 | ....... | 44,160.00 + 35% | 163,225 |

# 2004 Tax Table

See the instructions for line 43 that begin on page 33 to see if you must use the Tax Table below to figure your tax.

**Example.** Mr. and Mrs. Brown are filing a joint return. Their taxable income on Form 1040, line 42, is $25,300. First, they find the $25,300–25,350 taxable income line. Next, they find the column for married filing jointly and read down the column. The amount shown where the taxable income line and filing status column meet is $3,084. This is the tax amount they should enter on Form 1040, line 43.

**Sample Table**

| At least | But less than | Single | Married filing jointly * | Married filing separately | Head of a household |
|---|---|---|---|---|---|
| | | | Your tax is— | | |
| 25,200 | 25,250 | 3,426 | 3,069 | 3,426 | 3,274 |
| 25,250 | 25,300 | 3,434 | 3,076 | 3,434 | 3,281 |
| 25,300 | 25,350 | 3,441 | (3,084) | 3,441 | 3,289 |
| 25,350 | 25,400 | 3,449 | 3,091 | 3,449 | 3,296 |

| If line 42 (taxable income) is— | | And you are— | | | |
|---|---|---|---|---|---|
| At least | But less than | Single | Married filing jointly * | Married filing separately | Head of a household |
| | | | Your tax is— | | |
| 0 | 5 | 0 | 0 | 0 | 0 |
| 5 | 15 | 1 | 1 | 1 | 1 |
| 15 | 25 | 2 | 2 | 2 | 2 |
| 25 | 50 | 4 | 4 | 4 | 4 |
| 50 | 75 | 6 | 6 | 6 | 6 |
| 75 | 100 | 9 | 9 | 9 | 9 |
| 100 | 125 | 11 | 11 | 11 | 11 |
| 125 | 150 | 14 | 14 | 14 | 14 |
| 150 | 175 | 16 | 16 | 16 | 16 |
| 175 | 200 | 19 | 19 | 19 | 19 |
| 200 | 225 | 21 | 21 | 21 | 21 |
| 225 | 250 | 24 | 24 | 24 | 24 |
| 250 | 275 | 26 | 26 | 26 | 26 |
| 275 | 300 | 29 | 29 | 29 | 29 |
| 300 | 325 | 31 | 31 | 31 | 31 |
| 325 | 350 | 34 | 34 | 34 | 34 |
| 350 | 375 | 36 | 36 | 36 | 36 |
| 375 | 400 | 39 | 39 | 39 | 39 |
| 400 | 425 | 41 | 41 | 41 | 41 |
| 425 | 450 | 44 | 44 | 44 | 44 |
| 450 | 475 | 46 | 46 | 46 | 46 |
| 475 | 500 | 49 | 49 | 49 | 49 |
| 500 | 525 | 51 | 51 | 51 | 51 |
| 525 | 550 | 54 | 54 | 54 | 54 |
| 550 | 575 | 56 | 56 | 56 | 56 |
| 575 | 600 | 59 | 59 | 59 | 59 |
| 600 | 625 | 61 | 61 | 61 | 61 |
| 625 | 650 | 64 | 64 | 64 | 64 |
| 650 | 675 | 66 | 66 | 66 | 66 |
| 675 | 700 | 69 | 69 | 69 | 69 |
| 700 | 725 | 71 | 71 | 71 | 71 |
| 725 | 750 | 74 | 74 | 74 | 74 |
| 750 | 775 | 76 | 76 | 76 | 76 |
| 775 | 800 | 79 | 79 | 79 | 79 |
| 800 | 825 | 81 | 81 | 81 | 81 |
| 825 | 850 | 84 | 84 | 84 | 84 |
| 850 | 875 | 86 | 86 | 86 | 86 |
| 875 | 900 | 89 | 89 | 89 | 89 |
| 900 | 925 | 91 | 91 | 91 | 91 |
| 925 | 950 | 94 | 94 | 94 | 94 |
| 950 | 975 | 96 | 96 | 96 | 96 |
| 975 | 1,000 | 99 | 99 | 99 | 99 |

**1,000**

| At least | But less than | Single | Married filing jointly * | Married filing separately | Head of a household |
|---|---|---|---|---|---|
| 1,000 | 1,025 | 101 | 101 | 101 | 101 |
| 1,025 | 1,050 | 104 | 104 | 104 | 104 |
| 1,050 | 1,075 | 106 | 106 | 106 | 106 |
| 1,075 | 1,100 | 109 | 109 | 109 | 109 |
| 1,100 | 1,125 | 111 | 111 | 111 | 111 |
| 1,125 | 1,150 | 114 | 114 | 114 | 114 |
| 1,150 | 1,175 | 116 | 116 | 116 | 116 |
| 1,175 | 1,200 | 119 | 119 | 119 | 119 |
| 1,200 | 1,225 | 121 | 121 | 121 | 121 |
| 1,225 | 1,250 | 124 | 124 | 124 | 124 |
| 1,250 | 1,275 | 126 | 126 | 126 | 126 |
| 1,275 | 1,300 | 129 | 129 | 129 | 129 |

| If line 42 (taxable income) is— | | And you are— | | | |
|---|---|---|---|---|---|
| At least | But less than | Single | Married filing jointly * | Married filing separately | Head of a household |
| | | | Your tax is— | | |
| 1,300 | 1,325 | 131 | 131 | 131 | 131 |
| 1,325 | 1,350 | 134 | 134 | 134 | 134 |
| 1,350 | 1,375 | 136 | 136 | 136 | 136 |
| 1,375 | 1,400 | 139 | 139 | 139 | 139 |
| 1,400 | 1,425 | 141 | 141 | 141 | 141 |
| 1,425 | 1,450 | 144 | 144 | 144 | 144 |
| 1,450 | 1,475 | 146 | 146 | 146 | 146 |
| 1,475 | 1,500 | 149 | 149 | 149 | 149 |
| 1,500 | 1,525 | 151 | 151 | 151 | 151 |
| 1,525 | 1,550 | 154 | 154 | 154 | 154 |
| 1,550 | 1,575 | 156 | 156 | 156 | 156 |
| 1,575 | 1,600 | 159 | 159 | 159 | 159 |
| 1,600 | 1,625 | 161 | 161 | 161 | 161 |
| 1,625 | 1,650 | 164 | 164 | 164 | 164 |
| 1,650 | 1,675 | 166 | 166 | 166 | 166 |
| 1,675 | 1,700 | 169 | 169 | 169 | 169 |
| 1,700 | 1,725 | 171 | 171 | 171 | 171 |
| 1,725 | 1,750 | 174 | 174 | 174 | 174 |
| 1,750 | 1,775 | 176 | 176 | 176 | 176 |
| 1,775 | 1,800 | 179 | 179 | 179 | 179 |
| 1,800 | 1,825 | 181 | 181 | 181 | 181 |
| 1,825 | 1,850 | 184 | 184 | 184 | 184 |
| 1,850 | 1,875 | 186 | 186 | 186 | 186 |
| 1,875 | 1,900 | 189 | 189 | 189 | 189 |
| 1,900 | 1,925 | 191 | 191 | 191 | 191 |
| 1,925 | 1,950 | 194 | 194 | 194 | 194 |
| 1,950 | 1,975 | 196 | 196 | 196 | 196 |
| 1,975 | 2,000 | 199 | 199 | 199 | 199 |

**2,000**

| At least | But less than | Single | Married filing jointly * | Married filing separately | Head of a household |
|---|---|---|---|---|---|
| 2,000 | 2,025 | 201 | 201 | 201 | 201 |
| 2,025 | 2,050 | 204 | 204 | 204 | 204 |
| 2,050 | 2,075 | 206 | 206 | 206 | 206 |
| 2,075 | 2,100 | 209 | 209 | 209 | 209 |
| 2,100 | 2,125 | 211 | 211 | 211 | 211 |
| 2,125 | 2,150 | 214 | 214 | 214 | 214 |
| 2,150 | 2,175 | 216 | 216 | 216 | 216 |
| 2,175 | 2,200 | 219 | 219 | 219 | 219 |
| 2,200 | 2,225 | 221 | 221 | 221 | 221 |
| 2,225 | 2,250 | 224 | 224 | 224 | 224 |
| 2,250 | 2,275 | 226 | 226 | 226 | 226 |
| 2,275 | 2,300 | 229 | 229 | 229 | 229 |
| 2,300 | 2,325 | 231 | 231 | 231 | 231 |
| 2,325 | 2,350 | 234 | 234 | 234 | 234 |
| 2,350 | 2,375 | 236 | 236 | 236 | 236 |
| 2,375 | 2,400 | 239 | 239 | 239 | 239 |
| 2,400 | 2,425 | 241 | 241 | 241 | 241 |
| 2,425 | 2,450 | 244 | 244 | 244 | 244 |
| 2,450 | 2,475 | 246 | 246 | 246 | 246 |
| 2,475 | 2,500 | 249 | 249 | 249 | 249 |
| 2,500 | 2,525 | 251 | 251 | 251 | 251 |
| 2,525 | 2,550 | 254 | 254 | 254 | 254 |
| 2,550 | 2,575 | 256 | 256 | 256 | 256 |
| 2,575 | 2,600 | 259 | 259 | 259 | 259 |
| 2,600 | 2,625 | 261 | 261 | 261 | 261 |
| 2,625 | 2,650 | 264 | 264 | 264 | 264 |
| 2,650 | 2,675 | 266 | 266 | 266 | 266 |
| 2,675 | 2,700 | 269 | 269 | 269 | 269 |

| If line 42 (taxable income) is— | | And you are— | | | |
|---|---|---|---|---|---|
| At least | But less than | Single | Married filing jointly * | Married filing separately | Head of a household |
| | | | Your tax is— | | |
| 2,700 | 2,725 | 271 | 271 | 271 | 271 |
| 2,725 | 2,750 | 274 | 274 | 274 | 274 |
| 2,750 | 2,775 | 276 | 276 | 276 | 276 |
| 2,775 | 2,800 | 279 | 279 | 279 | 279 |
| 2,800 | 2,825 | 281 | 281 | 281 | 281 |
| 2,825 | 2,850 | 284 | 284 | 284 | 284 |
| 2,850 | 2,875 | 286 | 286 | 286 | 286 |
| 2,875 | 2,900 | 289 | 289 | 289 | 289 |
| 2,900 | 2,925 | 291 | 291 | 291 | 291 |
| 2,925 | 2,950 | 294 | 294 | 294 | 294 |
| 2,950 | 2,975 | 296 | 296 | 296 | 296 |
| 2,975 | 3,000 | 299 | 299 | 299 | 299 |

**3,000**

| At least | But less than | Single | Married filing jointly * | Married filing separately | Head of a household |
|---|---|---|---|---|---|
| 3,000 | 3,050 | 303 | 303 | 303 | 303 |
| 3,050 | 3,100 | 308 | 308 | 308 | 308 |
| 3,100 | 3,150 | 313 | 313 | 313 | 313 |
| 3,150 | 3,200 | 318 | 318 | 318 | 318 |
| 3,200 | 3,250 | 323 | 323 | 323 | 323 |
| 3,250 | 3,300 | 328 | 328 | 328 | 328 |
| 3,300 | 3,350 | 333 | 333 | 333 | 333 |
| 3,350 | 3,400 | 338 | 338 | 338 | 338 |
| 3,400 | 3,450 | 343 | 343 | 343 | 343 |
| 3,450 | 3,500 | 348 | 348 | 348 | 348 |
| 3,500 | 3,550 | 353 | 353 | 353 | 353 |
| 3,550 | 3,600 | 358 | 358 | 358 | 358 |
| 3,600 | 3,650 | 363 | 363 | 363 | 363 |
| 3,650 | 3,700 | 368 | 368 | 368 | 368 |
| 3,700 | 3,750 | 373 | 373 | 373 | 373 |
| 3,750 | 3,800 | 378 | 378 | 378 | 378 |
| 3,800 | 3,850 | 383 | 383 | 383 | 383 |
| 3,850 | 3,900 | 388 | 388 | 388 | 388 |
| 3,900 | 3,950 | 393 | 393 | 393 | 393 |
| 3,950 | 4,000 | 398 | 398 | 398 | 398 |

**4,000**

| At least | But less than | Single | Married filing jointly * | Married filing separately | Head of a household |
|---|---|---|---|---|---|
| 4,000 | 4,050 | 403 | 403 | 403 | 403 |
| 4,050 | 4,100 | 408 | 408 | 408 | 408 |
| 4,100 | 4,150 | 413 | 413 | 413 | 413 |
| 4,150 | 4,200 | 418 | 418 | 418 | 418 |
| 4,200 | 4,250 | 423 | 423 | 423 | 423 |
| 4,250 | 4,300 | 428 | 428 | 428 | 428 |
| 4,300 | 4,350 | 433 | 433 | 433 | 433 |
| 4,350 | 4,400 | 438 | 438 | 438 | 438 |
| 4,400 | 4,450 | 443 | 443 | 443 | 443 |
| 4,450 | 4,500 | 448 | 448 | 448 | 448 |
| 4,500 | 4,550 | 453 | 453 | 453 | 453 |
| 4,550 | 4,600 | 458 | 458 | 458 | 458 |
| 4,600 | 4,650 | 463 | 463 | 463 | 463 |
| 4,650 | 4,700 | 468 | 468 | 468 | 468 |
| 4,700 | 4,750 | 473 | 473 | 473 | 473 |
| 4,750 | 4,800 | 478 | 478 | 478 | 478 |
| 4,800 | 4,850 | 483 | 483 | 483 | 483 |
| 4,850 | 4,900 | 488 | 488 | 488 | 488 |
| 4,900 | 4,950 | 493 | 493 | 493 | 493 |
| 4,950 | 5,000 | 498 | 498 | 498 | 498 |

*(Continued on next page)*

* This column must also be used by a qualifying widow(er).

## 2004 Tax Table—Continued

Column headers for each section: **If line 42 (taxable income) is— At least / But less than** and **And you are— Single / Married filing jointly* / Married filing separately / Head of a household** — **Your tax is—**

### 5,000

| At least | But less than | Single | Married filing jointly* | Married filing separately | Head of a household |
|---|---|---|---|---|---|
| 5,000 | 5,050 | 503 | 503 | 503 | 503 |
| 5,050 | 5,100 | 508 | 508 | 508 | 508 |
| 5,100 | 5,150 | 513 | 513 | 513 | 513 |
| 5,150 | 5,200 | 518 | 518 | 518 | 518 |
| 5,200 | 5,250 | 523 | 523 | 523 | 523 |
| 5,250 | 5,300 | 528 | 528 | 528 | 528 |
| 5,300 | 5,350 | 533 | 533 | 533 | 533 |
| 5,350 | 5,400 | 538 | 538 | 538 | 538 |
| 5,400 | 5,450 | 543 | 543 | 543 | 543 |
| 5,450 | 5,500 | 548 | 548 | 548 | 548 |
| 5,500 | 5,550 | 553 | 553 | 553 | 553 |
| 5,550 | 5,600 | 558 | 558 | 558 | 558 |
| 5,600 | 5,650 | 563 | 563 | 563 | 563 |
| 5,650 | 5,700 | 568 | 568 | 568 | 568 |
| 5,700 | 5,750 | 573 | 573 | 573 | 573 |
| 5,750 | 5,800 | 578 | 578 | 578 | 578 |
| 5,800 | 5,850 | 583 | 583 | 583 | 583 |
| 5,850 | 5,900 | 588 | 588 | 588 | 588 |
| 5,900 | 5,950 | 593 | 593 | 593 | 593 |
| 5,950 | 6,000 | 598 | 598 | 598 | 598 |

### 6,000

| At least | But less than | Single | Married filing jointly* | Married filing separately | Head of a household |
|---|---|---|---|---|---|
| 6,000 | 6,050 | 603 | 603 | 603 | 603 |
| 6,050 | 6,100 | 608 | 608 | 608 | 608 |
| 6,100 | 6,150 | 613 | 613 | 613 | 613 |
| 6,150 | 6,200 | 618 | 618 | 618 | 618 |
| 6,200 | 6,250 | 623 | 623 | 623 | 623 |
| 6,250 | 6,300 | 628 | 628 | 628 | 628 |
| 6,300 | 6,350 | 633 | 633 | 633 | 633 |
| 6,350 | 6,400 | 638 | 638 | 638 | 638 |
| 6,400 | 6,450 | 643 | 643 | 643 | 643 |
| 6,450 | 6,500 | 648 | 648 | 648 | 648 |
| 6,500 | 6,550 | 653 | 653 | 653 | 653 |
| 6,550 | 6,600 | 658 | 658 | 658 | 658 |
| 6,600 | 6,650 | 663 | 663 | 663 | 663 |
| 6,650 | 6,700 | 668 | 668 | 668 | 668 |
| 6,700 | 6,750 | 673 | 673 | 673 | 673 |
| 6,750 | 6,800 | 678 | 678 | 678 | 678 |
| 6,800 | 6,850 | 683 | 683 | 683 | 683 |
| 6,850 | 6,900 | 688 | 688 | 688 | 688 |
| 6,900 | 6,950 | 693 | 693 | 693 | 693 |
| 6,950 | 7,000 | 698 | 698 | 698 | 698 |

### 7,000

| At least | But less than | Single | Married filing jointly* | Married filing separately | Head of a household |
|---|---|---|---|---|---|
| 7,000 | 7,050 | 703 | 703 | 703 | 703 |
| 7,050 | 7,100 | 708 | 708 | 708 | 708 |
| 7,100 | 7,150 | 713 | 713 | 713 | 713 |
| 7,150 | 7,200 | 719 | 718 | 719 | 718 |
| 7,200 | 7,250 | 726 | 723 | 726 | 723 |
| 7,250 | 7,300 | 734 | 728 | 734 | 728 |
| 7,300 | 7,350 | 741 | 733 | 741 | 733 |
| 7,350 | 7,400 | 749 | 738 | 749 | 738 |
| 7,400 | 7,450 | 756 | 743 | 756 | 743 |
| 7,450 | 7,500 | 764 | 748 | 764 | 748 |
| 7,500 | 7,550 | 771 | 753 | 771 | 753 |
| 7,550 | 7,600 | 779 | 758 | 779 | 758 |
| 7,600 | 7,650 | 786 | 763 | 786 | 763 |
| 7,650 | 7,700 | 794 | 768 | 794 | 768 |
| 7,700 | 7,750 | 801 | 773 | 801 | 773 |
| 7,750 | 7,800 | 809 | 778 | 809 | 778 |
| 7,800 | 7,850 | 816 | 783 | 816 | 783 |
| 7,850 | 7,900 | 824 | 788 | 824 | 788 |
| 7,900 | 7,950 | 831 | 793 | 831 | 793 |
| 7,950 | 8,000 | 839 | 798 | 839 | 798 |

### 8,000

| At least | But less than | Single | Married filing jointly* | Married filing separately | Head of a household |
|---|---|---|---|---|---|
| 8,000 | 8,050 | 846 | 803 | 846 | 803 |
| 8,050 | 8,100 | 854 | 808 | 854 | 808 |
| 8,100 | 8,150 | 861 | 813 | 861 | 813 |
| 8,150 | 8,200 | 869 | 818 | 869 | 818 |
| 8,200 | 8,250 | 876 | 823 | 876 | 823 |
| 8,250 | 8,300 | 884 | 828 | 884 | 828 |
| 8,300 | 8,350 | 891 | 833 | 891 | 833 |
| 8,350 | 8,400 | 899 | 838 | 899 | 838 |
| 8,400 | 8,450 | 906 | 843 | 906 | 843 |
| 8,450 | 8,500 | 914 | 848 | 914 | 848 |
| 8,500 | 8,550 | 921 | 853 | 921 | 853 |
| 8,550 | 8,600 | 929 | 858 | 929 | 858 |
| 8,600 | 8,650 | 936 | 863 | 936 | 863 |
| 8,650 | 8,700 | 944 | 868 | 944 | 868 |
| 8,700 | 8,750 | 951 | 873 | 951 | 873 |
| 8,750 | 8,800 | 959 | 878 | 959 | 878 |
| 8,800 | 8,850 | 966 | 883 | 966 | 883 |
| 8,850 | 8,900 | 974 | 888 | 974 | 888 |
| 8,900 | 8,950 | 981 | 893 | 981 | 893 |
| 8,950 | 9,000 | 989 | 898 | 989 | 898 |

### 9,000

| At least | But less than | Single | Married filing jointly* | Married filing separately | Head of a household |
|---|---|---|---|---|---|
| 9,000 | 9,050 | 996 | 903 | 996 | 903 |
| 9,050 | 9,100 | 1,004 | 908 | 1,004 | 908 |
| 9,100 | 9,150 | 1,011 | 913 | 1,011 | 913 |
| 9,150 | 9,200 | 1,019 | 918 | 1,019 | 918 |
| 9,200 | 9,250 | 1,026 | 923 | 1,026 | 923 |
| 9,250 | 9,300 | 1,034 | 928 | 1,034 | 928 |
| 9,300 | 9,350 | 1,041 | 933 | 1,041 | 933 |
| 9,350 | 9,400 | 1,049 | 938 | 1,049 | 938 |
| 9,400 | 9,450 | 1,056 | 943 | 1,056 | 943 |
| 9,450 | 9,500 | 1,064 | 948 | 1,064 | 948 |
| 9,500 | 9,550 | 1,071 | 953 | 1,071 | 953 |
| 9,550 | 9,600 | 1,079 | 958 | 1,079 | 958 |
| 9,600 | 9,650 | 1,086 | 963 | 1,086 | 963 |
| 9,650 | 9,700 | 1,094 | 968 | 1,094 | 968 |
| 9,700 | 9,750 | 1,101 | 973 | 1,101 | 973 |
| 9,750 | 9,800 | 1,109 | 978 | 1,109 | 978 |
| 9,800 | 9,850 | 1,116 | 983 | 1,116 | 983 |
| 9,850 | 9,900 | 1,124 | 988 | 1,124 | 988 |
| 9,900 | 9,950 | 1,131 | 993 | 1,131 | 993 |
| 9,950 | 10,000 | 1,139 | 998 | 1,139 | 998 |

### 10,000

| At least | But less than | Single | Married filing jointly* | Married filing separately | Head of a household |
|---|---|---|---|---|---|
| 10,000 | 10,050 | 1,146 | 1,003 | 1,146 | 1,003 |
| 10,050 | 10,100 | 1,154 | 1,008 | 1,154 | 1,008 |
| 10,100 | 10,150 | 1,161 | 1,013 | 1,161 | 1,013 |
| 10,150 | 10,200 | 1,169 | 1,018 | 1,169 | 1,018 |
| 10,200 | 10,250 | 1,176 | 1,023 | 1,176 | 1,024 |
| 10,250 | 10,300 | 1,184 | 1,028 | 1,184 | 1,031 |
| 10,300 | 10,350 | 1,191 | 1,033 | 1,191 | 1,039 |
| 10,350 | 10,400 | 1,199 | 1,038 | 1,199 | 1,046 |
| 10,400 | 10,450 | 1,206 | 1,043 | 1,206 | 1,054 |
| 10,450 | 10,500 | 1,214 | 1,048 | 1,214 | 1,061 |
| 10,500 | 10,550 | 1,221 | 1,053 | 1,221 | 1,069 |
| 10,550 | 10,600 | 1,229 | 1,058 | 1,229 | 1,076 |
| 10,600 | 10,650 | 1,236 | 1,063 | 1,236 | 1,084 |
| 10,650 | 10,700 | 1,244 | 1,068 | 1,244 | 1,091 |
| 10,700 | 10,750 | 1,251 | 1,073 | 1,251 | 1,099 |
| 10,750 | 10,800 | 1,259 | 1,078 | 1,259 | 1,106 |
| 10,800 | 10,850 | 1,266 | 1,083 | 1,266 | 1,114 |
| 10,850 | 10,900 | 1,274 | 1,088 | 1,274 | 1,121 |
| 10,900 | 10,950 | 1,281 | 1,093 | 1,281 | 1,129 |
| 10,950 | 11,000 | 1,289 | 1,098 | 1,289 | 1,136 |

### 11,000

| At least | But less than | Single | Married filing jointly* | Married filing separately | Head of a household |
|---|---|---|---|---|---|
| 11,000 | 11,050 | 1,296 | 1,103 | 1,296 | 1,144 |
| 11,050 | 11,100 | 1,304 | 1,108 | 1,304 | 1,151 |
| 11,100 | 11,150 | 1,311 | 1,113 | 1,311 | 1,159 |
| 11,150 | 11,200 | 1,319 | 1,118 | 1,319 | 1,166 |
| 11,200 | 11,250 | 1,326 | 1,123 | 1,326 | 1,174 |
| 11,250 | 11,300 | 1,334 | 1,128 | 1,334 | 1,181 |
| 11,300 | 11,350 | 1,341 | 1,133 | 1,341 | 1,189 |
| 11,350 | 11,400 | 1,349 | 1,138 | 1,349 | 1,196 |
| 11,400 | 11,450 | 1,356 | 1,143 | 1,356 | 1,204 |
| 11,450 | 11,500 | 1,364 | 1,148 | 1,364 | 1,211 |
| 11,500 | 11,550 | 1,371 | 1,153 | 1,371 | 1,219 |
| 11,550 | 11,600 | 1,379 | 1,158 | 1,379 | 1,226 |
| 11,600 | 11,650 | 1,386 | 1,163 | 1,386 | 1,234 |
| 11,650 | 11,700 | 1,394 | 1,168 | 1,394 | 1,241 |
| 11,700 | 11,750 | 1,401 | 1,173 | 1,401 | 1,249 |
| 11,750 | 11,800 | 1,409 | 1,178 | 1,409 | 1,256 |
| 11,800 | 11,850 | 1,416 | 1,183 | 1,416 | 1,264 |
| 11,850 | 11,900 | 1,424 | 1,188 | 1,424 | 1,271 |
| 11,900 | 11,950 | 1,431 | 1,193 | 1,431 | 1,279 |
| 11,950 | 12,000 | 1,439 | 1,198 | 1,439 | 1,286 |

### 12,000

| At least | But less than | Single | Married filing jointly* | Married filing separately | Head of a household |
|---|---|---|---|---|---|
| 12,000 | 12,050 | 1,446 | 1,203 | 1,446 | 1,294 |
| 12,050 | 12,100 | 1,454 | 1,208 | 1,454 | 1,301 |
| 12,100 | 12,150 | 1,461 | 1,213 | 1,461 | 1,309 |
| 12,150 | 12,200 | 1,469 | 1,218 | 1,469 | 1,316 |
| 12,200 | 12,250 | 1,476 | 1,223 | 1,476 | 1,324 |
| 12,250 | 12,300 | 1,484 | 1,228 | 1,484 | 1,331 |
| 12,300 | 12,350 | 1,491 | 1,233 | 1,491 | 1,339 |
| 12,350 | 12,400 | 1,499 | 1,238 | 1,499 | 1,346 |
| 12,400 | 12,450 | 1,506 | 1,243 | 1,506 | 1,354 |
| 12,450 | 12,500 | 1,514 | 1,248 | 1,514 | 1,361 |
| 12,500 | 12,550 | 1,521 | 1,253 | 1,521 | 1,369 |
| 12,550 | 12,600 | 1,529 | 1,258 | 1,529 | 1,376 |
| 12,600 | 12,650 | 1,536 | 1,263 | 1,536 | 1,384 |
| 12,650 | 12,700 | 1,544 | 1,268 | 1,544 | 1,391 |
| 12,700 | 12,750 | 1,551 | 1,273 | 1,551 | 1,399 |
| 12,750 | 12,800 | 1,559 | 1,278 | 1,559 | 1,406 |
| 12,800 | 12,850 | 1,566 | 1,283 | 1,566 | 1,414 |
| 12,850 | 12,900 | 1,574 | 1,288 | 1,574 | 1,421 |
| 12,900 | 12,950 | 1,581 | 1,293 | 1,581 | 1,429 |
| 12,950 | 13,000 | 1,589 | 1,298 | 1,589 | 1,436 |

### 13,000

| At least | But less than | Single | Married filing jointly* | Married filing separately | Head of a household |
|---|---|---|---|---|---|
| 13,000 | 13,050 | 1,596 | 1,303 | 1,596 | 1,444 |
| 13,050 | 13,100 | 1,604 | 1,308 | 1,604 | 1,451 |
| 13,100 | 13,150 | 1,611 | 1,313 | 1,611 | 1,459 |
| 13,150 | 13,200 | 1,619 | 1,318 | 1,619 | 1,466 |
| 13,200 | 13,250 | 1,626 | 1,323 | 1,626 | 1,474 |
| 13,250 | 13,300 | 1,634 | 1,328 | 1,634 | 1,481 |
| 13,300 | 13,350 | 1,641 | 1,333 | 1,641 | 1,489 |
| 13,350 | 13,400 | 1,649 | 1,338 | 1,649 | 1,496 |
| 13,400 | 13,450 | 1,656 | 1,343 | 1,656 | 1,504 |
| 13,450 | 13,500 | 1,664 | 1,348 | 1,664 | 1,511 |
| 13,500 | 13,550 | 1,671 | 1,353 | 1,671 | 1,519 |
| 13,550 | 13,600 | 1,679 | 1,358 | 1,679 | 1,526 |
| 13,600 | 13,650 | 1,686 | 1,363 | 1,686 | 1,534 |
| 13,650 | 13,700 | 1,694 | 1,368 | 1,694 | 1,541 |
| 13,700 | 13,750 | 1,701 | 1,373 | 1,701 | 1,549 |
| 13,750 | 13,800 | 1,709 | 1,378 | 1,709 | 1,556 |
| 13,800 | 13,850 | 1,716 | 1,383 | 1,716 | 1,564 |
| 13,850 | 13,900 | 1,724 | 1,388 | 1,724 | 1,571 |
| 13,900 | 13,950 | 1,731 | 1,393 | 1,731 | 1,579 |
| 13,950 | 14,000 | 1,739 | 1,398 | 1,739 | 1,586 |

* This column must also be used by a qualifying widow(er).

(Continued on next page)

**2004 Tax Table**—*Continued*

| At least | But less than | Single | Married filing jointly * | Married filing separately | Head of a household |
|---|---|---|---|---|---|
| **14,000** | | | | | |
| 14,000 | 14,050 | 1,746 | 1,403 | 1,746 | 1,594 |
| 14,050 | 14,100 | 1,754 | 1,408 | 1,754 | 1,601 |
| 14,100 | 14,150 | 1,761 | 1,413 | 1,761 | 1,609 |
| 14,150 | 14,200 | 1,769 | 1,418 | 1,769 | 1,616 |
| 14,200 | 14,250 | 1,776 | 1,423 | 1,776 | 1,624 |
| 14,250 | 14,300 | 1,784 | 1,428 | 1,784 | 1,631 |
| 14,300 | 14,350 | 1,791 | 1,434 | 1,791 | 1,639 |
| 14,350 | 14,400 | 1,799 | 1,441 | 1,799 | 1,646 |
| 14,400 | 14,450 | 1,806 | 1,449 | 1,806 | 1,654 |
| 14,450 | 14,500 | 1,814 | 1,456 | 1,814 | 1,661 |
| 14,500 | 14,550 | 1,821 | 1,464 | 1,821 | 1,669 |
| 14,550 | 14,600 | 1,829 | 1,471 | 1,829 | 1,676 |
| 14,600 | 14,650 | 1,836 | 1,479 | 1,836 | 1,684 |
| 14,650 | 14,700 | 1,844 | 1,486 | 1,844 | 1,691 |
| 14,700 | 14,750 | 1,851 | 1,494 | 1,851 | 1,699 |
| 14,750 | 14,800 | 1,859 | 1,501 | 1,859 | 1,706 |
| 14,800 | 14,850 | 1,866 | 1,509 | 1,866 | 1,714 |
| 14,850 | 14,900 | 1,874 | 1,516 | 1,874 | 1,721 |
| 14,900 | 14,950 | 1,881 | 1,524 | 1,881 | 1,729 |
| 14,950 | 15,000 | 1,889 | 1,531 | 1,889 | 1,736 |
| **15,000** | | | | | |
| 15,000 | 15,050 | 1,896 | 1,539 | 1,896 | 1,744 |
| 15,050 | 15,100 | 1,904 | 1,546 | 1,904 | 1,751 |
| 15,100 | 15,150 | 1,911 | 1,554 | 1,911 | 1,759 |
| 15,150 | 15,200 | 1,919 | 1,561 | 1,919 | 1,766 |
| 15,200 | 15,250 | 1,926 | 1,569 | 1,926 | 1,774 |
| 15,250 | 15,300 | 1,934 | 1,576 | 1,934 | 1,781 |
| 15,300 | 15,350 | 1,941 | 1,584 | 1,941 | 1,789 |
| 15,350 | 15,400 | 1,949 | 1,591 | 1,949 | 1,796 |
| 15,400 | 15,450 | 1,956 | 1,599 | 1,956 | 1,804 |
| 15,450 | 15,500 | 1,964 | 1,606 | 1,964 | 1,811 |
| 15,500 | 15,550 | 1,971 | 1,614 | 1,971 | 1,819 |
| 15,550 | 15,600 | 1,979 | 1,621 | 1,979 | 1,826 |
| 15,600 | 15,650 | 1,986 | 1,629 | 1,986 | 1,834 |
| 15,650 | 15,700 | 1,994 | 1,636 | 1,994 | 1,841 |
| 15,700 | 15,750 | 2,001 | 1,644 | 2,001 | 1,849 |
| 15,750 | 15,800 | 2,009 | 1,651 | 2,009 | 1,856 |
| 15,800 | 15,850 | 2,016 | 1,659 | 2,016 | 1,864 |
| 15,850 | 15,900 | 2,024 | 1,666 | 2,024 | 1,871 |
| 15,900 | 15,950 | 2,031 | 1,674 | 2,031 | 1,879 |
| 15,950 | 16,000 | 2,039 | 1,681 | 2,039 | 1,886 |
| **16,000** | | | | | |
| 16,000 | 16,050 | 2,046 | 1,689 | 2,046 | 1,894 |
| 16,050 | 16,100 | 2,054 | 1,696 | 2,054 | 1,901 |
| 16,100 | 16,150 | 2,061 | 1,704 | 2,061 | 1,909 |
| 16,150 | 16,200 | 2,069 | 1,711 | 2,069 | 1,916 |
| 16,200 | 16,250 | 2,076 | 1,719 | 2,076 | 1,924 |
| 16,250 | 16,300 | 2,084 | 1,726 | 2,084 | 1,931 |
| 16,300 | 16,350 | 2,091 | 1,734 | 2,091 | 1,939 |
| 16,350 | 16,400 | 2,099 | 1,741 | 2,099 | 1,946 |
| 16,400 | 16,450 | 2,106 | 1,749 | 2,106 | 1,954 |
| 16,450 | 16,500 | 2,114 | 1,756 | 2,114 | 1,961 |
| 16,500 | 16,550 | 2,121 | 1,764 | 2,121 | 1,969 |
| 16,550 | 16,600 | 2,129 | 1,771 | 2,129 | 1,976 |
| 16,600 | 16,650 | 2,136 | 1,779 | 2,136 | 1,984 |
| 16,650 | 16,700 | 2,144 | 1,786 | 2,144 | 1,991 |
| 16,700 | 16,750 | 2,151 | 1,794 | 2,151 | 1,999 |
| 16,750 | 16,800 | 2,159 | 1,801 | 2,159 | 2,006 |
| 16,800 | 16,850 | 2,166 | 1,809 | 2,166 | 2,014 |
| 16,850 | 16,900 | 2,174 | 1,816 | 2,174 | 2,021 |
| 16,900 | 16,950 | 2,181 | 1,824 | 2,181 | 2,029 |
| 16,950 | 17,000 | 2,189 | 1,831 | 2,189 | 2,036 |
| **17,000** | | | | | |
| 17,000 | 17,050 | 2,196 | 1,839 | 2,196 | 2,044 |
| 17,050 | 17,100 | 2,204 | 1,846 | 2,204 | 2,051 |
| 17,100 | 17,150 | 2,211 | 1,854 | 2,211 | 2,059 |
| 17,150 | 17,200 | 2,219 | 1,861 | 2,219 | 2,066 |
| 17,200 | 17,250 | 2,226 | 1,869 | 2,226 | 2,074 |
| 17,250 | 17,300 | 2,234 | 1,876 | 2,234 | 2,081 |
| 17,300 | 17,350 | 2,241 | 1,884 | 2,241 | 2,089 |
| 17,350 | 17,400 | 2,249 | 1,891 | 2,249 | 2,096 |
| 17,400 | 17,450 | 2,256 | 1,899 | 2,256 | 2,104 |
| 17,450 | 17,500 | 2,264 | 1,906 | 2,264 | 2,111 |
| 17,500 | 17,550 | 2,271 | 1,914 | 2,271 | 2,119 |
| 17,550 | 17,600 | 2,279 | 1,921 | 2,279 | 2,126 |
| 17,600 | 17,650 | 2,286 | 1,929 | 2,286 | 2,134 |
| 17,650 | 17,700 | 2,294 | 1,936 | 2,294 | 2,141 |
| 17,700 | 17,750 | 2,301 | 1,944 | 2,301 | 2,149 |
| 17,750 | 17,800 | 2,309 | 1,951 | 2,309 | 2,156 |
| 17,800 | 17,850 | 2,316 | 1,959 | 2,316 | 2,164 |
| 17,850 | 17,900 | 2,324 | 1,966 | 2,324 | 2,171 |
| 17,900 | 17,950 | 2,331 | 1,974 | 2,331 | 2,179 |
| 17,950 | 18,000 | 2,339 | 1,981 | 2,339 | 2,186 |
| **18,000** | | | | | |
| 18,000 | 18,050 | 2,346 | 1,989 | 2,346 | 2,194 |
| 18,050 | 18,100 | 2,354 | 1,996 | 2,354 | 2,201 |
| 18,100 | 18,150 | 2,361 | 2,004 | 2,361 | 2,209 |
| 18,150 | 18,200 | 2,369 | 2,011 | 2,369 | 2,216 |
| 18,200 | 18,250 | 2,376 | 2,019 | 2,376 | 2,224 |
| 18,250 | 18,300 | 2,384 | 2,026 | 2,384 | 2,231 |
| 18,300 | 18,350 | 2,391 | 2,034 | 2,391 | 2,239 |
| 18,350 | 18,400 | 2,399 | 2,041 | 2,399 | 2,246 |
| 18,400 | 18,450 | 2,406 | 2,049 | 2,406 | 2,254 |
| 18,450 | 18,500 | 2,414 | 2,056 | 2,414 | 2,261 |
| 18,500 | 18,550 | 2,421 | 2,064 | 2,421 | 2,269 |
| 18,550 | 18,600 | 2,429 | 2,071 | 2,429 | 2,276 |
| 18,600 | 18,650 | 2,436 | 2,079 | 2,436 | 2,284 |
| 18,650 | 18,700 | 2,444 | 2,086 | 2,444 | 2,291 |
| 18,700 | 18,750 | 2,451 | 2,094 | 2,451 | 2,299 |
| 18,750 | 18,800 | 2,459 | 2,101 | 2,459 | 2,306 |
| 18,800 | 18,850 | 2,466 | 2,109 | 2,466 | 2,314 |
| 18,850 | 18,900 | 2,474 | 2,116 | 2,474 | 2,321 |
| 18,900 | 18,950 | 2,481 | 2,124 | 2,481 | 2,329 |
| 18,950 | 19,000 | 2,489 | 2,131 | 2,489 | 2,336 |
| **19,000** | | | | | |
| 19,000 | 19,050 | 2,496 | 2,139 | 2,496 | 2,344 |
| 19,050 | 19,100 | 2,504 | 2,146 | 2,504 | 2,351 |
| 19,100 | 19,150 | 2,511 | 2,154 | 2,511 | 2,359 |
| 19,150 | 19,200 | 2,519 | 2,161 | 2,519 | 2,366 |
| 19,200 | 19,250 | 2,526 | 2,169 | 2,526 | 2,374 |
| 19,250 | 19,300 | 2,534 | 2,176 | 2,534 | 2,381 |
| 19,300 | 19,350 | 2,541 | 2,184 | 2,541 | 2,389 |
| 19,350 | 19,400 | 2,549 | 2,191 | 2,549 | 2,396 |
| 19,400 | 19,450 | 2,556 | 2,199 | 2,556 | 2,404 |
| 19,450 | 19,500 | 2,564 | 2,206 | 2,564 | 2,411 |
| 19,500 | 19,550 | 2,571 | 2,214 | 2,571 | 2,419 |
| 19,550 | 19,600 | 2,579 | 2,221 | 2,579 | 2,426 |
| 19,600 | 19,650 | 2,586 | 2,229 | 2,586 | 2,434 |
| 19,650 | 19,700 | 2,594 | 2,236 | 2,594 | 2,441 |
| 19,700 | 19,750 | 2,601 | 2,244 | 2,601 | 2,449 |
| 19,750 | 19,800 | 2,609 | 2,251 | 2,609 | 2,456 |
| 19,800 | 19,850 | 2,616 | 2,259 | 2,616 | 2,464 |
| 19,850 | 19,900 | 2,624 | 2,266 | 2,624 | 2,471 |
| 19,900 | 19,950 | 2,631 | 2,274 | 2,631 | 2,479 |
| 19,950 | 20,000 | 2,639 | 2,281 | 2,639 | 2,486 |
| **20,000** | | | | | |
| 20,000 | 20,050 | 2,646 | 2,289 | 2,646 | 2,494 |
| 20,050 | 20,100 | 2,654 | 2,296 | 2,654 | 2,501 |
| 20,100 | 20,150 | 2,661 | 2,304 | 2,661 | 2,509 |
| 20,150 | 20,200 | 2,669 | 2,311 | 2,669 | 2,516 |
| 20,200 | 20,250 | 2,676 | 2,319 | 2,676 | 2,524 |
| 20,250 | 20,300 | 2,684 | 2,326 | 2,684 | 2,531 |
| 20,300 | 20,350 | 2,691 | 2,334 | 2,691 | 2,539 |
| 20,350 | 20,400 | 2,699 | 2,341 | 2,699 | 2,546 |
| 20,400 | 20,450 | 2,706 | 2,349 | 2,706 | 2,554 |
| 20,450 | 20,500 | 2,714 | 2,356 | 2,714 | 2,561 |
| 20,500 | 20,550 | 2,721 | 2,364 | 2,721 | 2,569 |
| 20,550 | 20,600 | 2,729 | 2,371 | 2,729 | 2,576 |
| 20,600 | 20,650 | 2,736 | 2,379 | 2,736 | 2,584 |
| 20,650 | 20,700 | 2,744 | 2,386 | 2,744 | 2,591 |
| 20,700 | 20,750 | 2,751 | 2,394 | 2,751 | 2,599 |
| 20,750 | 20,800 | 2,759 | 2,401 | 2,759 | 2,606 |
| 20,800 | 20,850 | 2,766 | 2,409 | 2,766 | 2,614 |
| 20,850 | 20,900 | 2,774 | 2,416 | 2,774 | 2,621 |
| 20,900 | 20,950 | 2,781 | 2,424 | 2,781 | 2,629 |
| 20,950 | 21,000 | 2,789 | 2,431 | 2,789 | 2,636 |
| **21,000** | | | | | |
| 21,000 | 21,050 | 2,796 | 2,439 | 2,796 | 2,644 |
| 21,050 | 21,100 | 2,804 | 2,446 | 2,804 | 2,651 |
| 21,100 | 21,150 | 2,811 | 2,454 | 2,811 | 2,659 |
| 21,150 | 21,200 | 2,819 | 2,461 | 2,819 | 2,666 |
| 21,200 | 21,250 | 2,826 | 2,469 | 2,826 | 2,674 |
| 21,250 | 21,300 | 2,834 | 2,476 | 2,834 | 2,681 |
| 21,300 | 21,350 | 2,841 | 2,484 | 2,841 | 2,689 |
| 21,350 | 21,400 | 2,849 | 2,491 | 2,849 | 2,696 |
| 21,400 | 21,450 | 2,856 | 2,499 | 2,856 | 2,704 |
| 21,450 | 21,500 | 2,864 | 2,506 | 2,864 | 2,711 |
| 21,500 | 21,550 | 2,871 | 2,514 | 2,871 | 2,719 |
| 21,550 | 21,600 | 2,879 | 2,521 | 2,879 | 2,726 |
| 21,600 | 21,650 | 2,886 | 2,529 | 2,886 | 2,734 |
| 21,650 | 21,700 | 2,894 | 2,536 | 2,894 | 2,741 |
| 21,700 | 21,750 | 2,901 | 2,544 | 2,901 | 2,749 |
| 21,750 | 21,800 | 2,909 | 2,551 | 2,909 | 2,756 |
| 21,800 | 21,850 | 2,916 | 2,559 | 2,916 | 2,764 |
| 21,850 | 21,900 | 2,924 | 2,566 | 2,924 | 2,771 |
| 21,900 | 21,950 | 2,931 | 2,574 | 2,931 | 2,779 |
| 21,950 | 22,000 | 2,939 | 2,581 | 2,939 | 2,786 |
| **22,000** | | | | | |
| 22,000 | 22,050 | 2,946 | 2,589 | 2,946 | 2,794 |
| 22,050 | 22,100 | 2,954 | 2,596 | 2,954 | 2,801 |
| 22,100 | 22,150 | 2,961 | 2,604 | 2,961 | 2,809 |
| 22,150 | 22,200 | 2,969 | 2,611 | 2,969 | 2,816 |
| 22,200 | 22,250 | 2,976 | 2,619 | 2,976 | 2,824 |
| 22,250 | 22,300 | 2,984 | 2,626 | 2,984 | 2,831 |
| 22,300 | 22,350 | 2,991 | 2,634 | 2,991 | 2,839 |
| 22,350 | 22,400 | 2,999 | 2,641 | 2,999 | 2,846 |
| 22,400 | 22,450 | 3,006 | 2,649 | 3,006 | 2,854 |
| 22,450 | 22,500 | 3,014 | 2,656 | 3,014 | 2,861 |
| 22,500 | 22,550 | 3,021 | 2,664 | 3,021 | 2,869 |
| 22,550 | 22,600 | 3,029 | 2,671 | 3,029 | 2,876 |
| 22,600 | 22,650 | 3,036 | 2,679 | 3,036 | 2,884 |
| 22,650 | 22,700 | 3,044 | 2,686 | 3,044 | 2,891 |
| 22,700 | 22,750 | 3,051 | 2,694 | 3,051 | 2,899 |
| 22,750 | 22,800 | 3,059 | 2,701 | 3,059 | 2,906 |
| 22,800 | 22,850 | 3,066 | 2,709 | 3,066 | 2,914 |
| 22,850 | 22,900 | 3,074 | 2,716 | 3,074 | 2,921 |
| 22,900 | 22,950 | 3,081 | 2,724 | 3,081 | 2,929 |
| 22,950 | 23,000 | 3,089 | 2,731 | 3,089 | 2,936 |

* This column must also be used by a qualifying widow(er).

*(Continued on next page)*

## 2004 Tax Table—*Continued*

| If line 42 (taxable income) is— | | And you are— | | | | If line 42 (taxable income) is— | | And you are— | | | | If line 42 (taxable income) is— | | And you are— | | | |
|---|---|---|---|---|---|---|---|---|---|---|---|---|---|---|---|---|---|
| At least | But less than | Single | Married filing jointly * | Married filing separately | Head of a household | At least | But less than | Single | Married filing jointly * | Married filing separately | Head of a household | At least | But less than | Single | Married filing jointly * | Married filing separately | Head of a household |
| | | Your tax is— | | | | | | Your tax is— | | | | | | Your tax is— | | | |
| **23,000** | | | | | | **26,000** | | | | | | **29,000** | | | | | |
| 23,000 | 23,050 | 3,096 | 2,739 | 3,096 | 2,944 | 26,000 | 26,050 | 3,546 | 3,189 | 3,546 | 3,394 | 29,000 | 29,050 | 3,996 | 3,639 | 3,996 | 3,844 |
| 23,050 | 23,100 | 3,104 | 2,746 | 3,104 | 2,951 | 26,050 | 26,100 | 3,554 | 3,196 | 3,554 | 3,401 | 29,050 | 29,100 | 4,006 | 3,646 | 4,006 | 3,851 |
| 23,100 | 23,150 | 3,111 | 2,754 | 3,111 | 2,959 | 26,100 | 26,150 | 3,561 | 3,204 | 3,561 | 3,409 | 29,100 | 29,150 | 4,019 | 3,654 | 4,019 | 3,859 |
| 23,150 | 23,200 | 3,119 | 2,761 | 3,119 | 2,966 | 26,150 | 26,200 | 3,569 | 3,211 | 3,569 | 3,416 | 29,150 | 29,200 | 4,031 | 3,661 | 4,031 | 3,866 |
| 23,200 | 23,250 | 3,126 | 2,769 | 3,126 | 2,974 | 26,200 | 26,250 | 3,576 | 3,219 | 3,576 | 3,424 | 29,200 | 29,250 | 4,044 | 3,669 | 4,044 | 3,874 |
| 23,250 | 23,300 | 3,134 | 2,776 | 3,134 | 2,981 | 26,250 | 26,300 | 3,584 | 3,226 | 3,584 | 3,431 | 29,250 | 29,300 | 4,056 | 3,676 | 4,056 | 3,881 |
| 23,300 | 23,350 | 3,141 | 2,784 | 3,141 | 2,989 | 26,300 | 26,350 | 3,591 | 3,234 | 3,591 | 3,439 | 29,300 | 29,350 | 4,069 | 3,684 | 4,069 | 3,889 |
| 23,350 | 23,400 | 3,149 | 2,791 | 3,149 | 2,996 | 26,350 | 26,400 | 3,599 | 3,241 | 3,599 | 3,446 | 29,350 | 29,400 | 4,081 | 3,691 | 4,081 | 3,896 |
| 23,400 | 23,450 | 3,156 | 2,799 | 3,156 | 3,004 | 26,400 | 26,450 | 3,606 | 3,249 | 3,606 | 3,454 | 29,400 | 29,450 | 4,094 | 3,699 | 4,094 | 3,904 |
| 23,450 | 23,500 | 3,164 | 2,806 | 3,164 | 3,011 | 26,450 | 26,500 | 3,614 | 3,256 | 3,614 | 3,461 | 29,450 | 29,500 | 4,106 | 3,706 | 4,106 | 3,911 |
| 23,500 | 23,550 | 3,171 | 2,814 | 3,171 | 3,019 | 26,500 | 26,550 | 3,621 | 3,264 | 3,621 | 3,469 | 29,500 | 29,550 | 4,119 | 3,714 | 4,119 | 3,919 |
| 23,550 | 23,600 | 3,179 | 2,821 | 3,179 | 3,026 | 26,550 | 26,600 | 3,629 | 3,271 | 3,629 | 3,476 | 29,550 | 29,600 | 4,131 | 3,721 | 4,131 | 3,926 |
| 23,600 | 23,650 | 3,186 | 2,829 | 3,186 | 3,034 | 26,600 | 26,650 | 3,636 | 3,279 | 3,636 | 3,484 | 29,600 | 29,650 | 4,144 | 3,729 | 4,144 | 3,934 |
| 23,650 | 23,700 | 3,194 | 2,836 | 3,194 | 3,041 | 26,650 | 26,700 | 3,644 | 3,286 | 3,644 | 3,491 | 29,650 | 29,700 | 4,156 | 3,736 | 4,156 | 3,941 |
| 23,700 | 23,750 | 3,201 | 2,844 | 3,201 | 3,049 | 26,700 | 26,750 | 3,651 | 3,294 | 3,651 | 3,499 | 29,700 | 29,750 | 4,169 | 3,744 | 4,169 | 3,949 |
| 23,750 | 23,800 | 3,209 | 2,851 | 3,209 | 3,056 | 26,750 | 26,800 | 3,659 | 3,301 | 3,659 | 3,506 | 29,750 | 29,800 | 4,181 | 3,751 | 4,181 | 3,956 |
| 23,800 | 23,850 | 3,216 | 2,859 | 3,216 | 3,064 | 26,800 | 26,850 | 3,666 | 3,309 | 3,666 | 3,514 | 29,800 | 29,850 | 4,194 | 3,759 | 4,194 | 3,964 |
| 23,850 | 23,900 | 3,224 | 2,866 | 3,224 | 3,071 | 26,850 | 26,900 | 3,674 | 3,316 | 3,674 | 3,521 | 29,850 | 29,900 | 4,206 | 3,766 | 4,206 | 3,971 |
| 23,900 | 23,950 | 3,231 | 2,874 | 3,231 | 3,079 | 26,900 | 26,950 | 3,681 | 3,324 | 3,681 | 3,529 | 29,900 | 29,950 | 4,219 | 3,774 | 4,219 | 3,979 |
| 23,950 | 24,000 | 3,239 | 2,881 | 3,239 | 3,086 | 26,950 | 27,000 | 3,689 | 3,331 | 3,689 | 3,536 | 29,950 | 30,000 | 4,231 | 3,781 | 4,231 | 3,986 |
| **24,000** | | | | | | **27,000** | | | | | | **30,000** | | | | | |
| 24,000 | 24,050 | 3,246 | 2,889 | 3,246 | 3,094 | 27,000 | 27,050 | 3,696 | 3,339 | 3,696 | 3,544 | 30,000 | 30,050 | 4,244 | 3,789 | 4,244 | 3,994 |
| 24,050 | 24,100 | 3,254 | 2,896 | 3,254 | 3,101 | 27,050 | 27,100 | 3,704 | 3,346 | 3,704 | 3,551 | 30,050 | 30,100 | 4,256 | 3,796 | 4,256 | 4,001 |
| 24,100 | 24,150 | 3,261 | 2,904 | 3,261 | 3,109 | 27,100 | 27,150 | 3,711 | 3,354 | 3,711 | 3,559 | 30,100 | 30,150 | 4,269 | 3,804 | 4,269 | 4,009 |
| 24,150 | 24,200 | 3,269 | 2,911 | 3,269 | 3,116 | 27,150 | 27,200 | 3,719 | 3,361 | 3,719 | 3,566 | 30,150 | 30,200 | 4,281 | 3,811 | 4,281 | 4,016 |
| 24,200 | 24,250 | 3,276 | 2,919 | 3,276 | 3,124 | 27,200 | 27,250 | 3,726 | 3,369 | 3,726 | 3,574 | 30,200 | 30,250 | 4,294 | 3,819 | 4,294 | 4,024 |
| 24,250 | 24,300 | 3,284 | 2,926 | 3,284 | 3,131 | 27,250 | 27,300 | 3,734 | 3,376 | 3,734 | 3,581 | 30,250 | 30,300 | 4,306 | 3,826 | 4,306 | 4,031 |
| 24,300 | 24,350 | 3,291 | 2,934 | 3,291 | 3,139 | 27,300 | 27,350 | 3,741 | 3,384 | 3,741 | 3,589 | 30,300 | 30,350 | 4,319 | 3,834 | 4,319 | 4,039 |
| 24,350 | 24,400 | 3,299 | 2,941 | 3,299 | 3,146 | 27,350 | 27,400 | 3,749 | 3,391 | 3,749 | 3,596 | 30,350 | 30,400 | 4,331 | 3,841 | 4,331 | 4,046 |
| 24,400 | 24,450 | 3,306 | 2,949 | 3,306 | 3,154 | 27,400 | 27,450 | 3,756 | 3,399 | 3,756 | 3,604 | 30,400 | 30,450 | 4,344 | 3,849 | 4,344 | 4,054 |
| 24,450 | 24,500 | 3,314 | 2,956 | 3,314 | 3,161 | 27,450 | 27,500 | 3,764 | 3,406 | 3,764 | 3,611 | 30,450 | 30,500 | 4,356 | 3,856 | 4,356 | 4,061 |
| 24,500 | 24,550 | 3,321 | 2,964 | 3,321 | 3,169 | 27,500 | 27,550 | 3,771 | 3,414 | 3,771 | 3,619 | 30,500 | 30,550 | 4,369 | 3,864 | 4,369 | 4,069 |
| 24,550 | 24,600 | 3,329 | 2,971 | 3,329 | 3,176 | 27,550 | 27,600 | 3,779 | 3,421 | 3,779 | 3,626 | 30,550 | 30,600 | 4,381 | 3,871 | 4,381 | 4,076 |
| 24,600 | 24,650 | 3,336 | 2,979 | 3,336 | 3,184 | 27,600 | 27,650 | 3,786 | 3,429 | 3,786 | 3,634 | 30,600 | 30,650 | 4,394 | 3,879 | 4,394 | 4,084 |
| 24,650 | 24,700 | 3,344 | 2,986 | 3,344 | 3,191 | 27,650 | 27,700 | 3,794 | 3,436 | 3,794 | 3,641 | 30,650 | 30,700 | 4,406 | 3,886 | 4,406 | 4,091 |
| 24,700 | 24,750 | 3,351 | 2,994 | 3,351 | 3,199 | 27,700 | 27,750 | 3,801 | 3,444 | 3,801 | 3,649 | 30,700 | 30,750 | 4,419 | 3,894 | 4,419 | 4,099 |
| 24,750 | 24,800 | 3,359 | 3,001 | 3,359 | 3,206 | 27,750 | 27,800 | 3,809 | 3,451 | 3,809 | 3,656 | 30,750 | 30,800 | 4,431 | 3,901 | 4,431 | 4,106 |
| 24,800 | 24,850 | 3,366 | 3,009 | 3,366 | 3,214 | 27,800 | 27,850 | 3,816 | 3,459 | 3,816 | 3,664 | 30,800 | 30,850 | 4,444 | 3,909 | 4,444 | 4,114 |
| 24,850 | 24,900 | 3,374 | 3,016 | 3,374 | 3,221 | 27,850 | 27,900 | 3,824 | 3,466 | 3,824 | 3,671 | 30,850 | 30,900 | 4,456 | 3,916 | 4,456 | 4,121 |
| 24,900 | 24,950 | 3,381 | 3,024 | 3,381 | 3,229 | 27,900 | 27,950 | 3,831 | 3,474 | 3,831 | 3,679 | 30,900 | 30,950 | 4,469 | 3,924 | 4,469 | 4,129 |
| 24,950 | 25,000 | 3,389 | 3,031 | 3,389 | 3,236 | 27,950 | 28,000 | 3,839 | 3,481 | 3,839 | 3,686 | 30,950 | 31,000 | 4,481 | 3,931 | 4,481 | 4,136 |
| **25,000** | | | | | | **28,000** | | | | | | **31,000** | | | | | |
| 25,000 | 25,050 | 3,396 | 3,039 | 3,396 | 3,244 | 28,000 | 28,050 | 3,846 | 3,489 | 3,846 | 3,694 | 31,000 | 31,050 | 4,494 | 3,939 | 4,494 | 4,144 |
| 25,050 | 25,100 | 3,404 | 3,046 | 3,404 | 3,251 | 28,050 | 28,100 | 3,854 | 3,496 | 3,854 | 3,701 | 31,050 | 31,100 | 4,506 | 3,946 | 4,506 | 4,151 |
| 25,100 | 25,150 | 3,411 | 3,054 | 3,411 | 3,259 | 28,100 | 28,150 | 3,861 | 3,504 | 3,861 | 3,709 | 31,100 | 31,150 | 4,519 | 3,954 | 4,519 | 4,159 |
| 25,150 | 25,200 | 3,419 | 3,061 | 3,419 | 3,266 | 28,150 | 28,200 | 3,869 | 3,511 | 3,869 | 3,716 | 31,150 | 31,200 | 4,531 | 3,961 | 4,531 | 4,166 |
| 25,200 | 25,250 | 3,426 | 3,069 | 3,426 | 3,274 | 28,200 | 28,250 | 3,876 | 3,519 | 3,876 | 3,724 | 31,200 | 31,250 | 4,544 | 3,969 | 4,544 | 4,174 |
| 25,250 | 25,300 | 3,434 | 3,076 | 3,434 | 3,281 | 28,250 | 28,300 | 3,884 | 3,526 | 3,884 | 3,731 | 31,250 | 31,300 | 4,556 | 3,976 | 4,556 | 4,181 |
| 25,300 | 25,350 | 3,441 | 3,084 | 3,441 | 3,289 | 28,300 | 28,350 | 3,891 | 3,534 | 3,891 | 3,739 | 31,300 | 31,350 | 4,569 | 3,984 | 4,569 | 4,189 |
| 25,350 | 25,400 | 3,449 | 3,091 | 3,449 | 3,296 | 28,350 | 28,400 | 3,899 | 3,541 | 3,899 | 3,746 | 31,350 | 31,400 | 4,581 | 3,991 | 4,581 | 4,196 |
| 25,400 | 25,450 | 3,456 | 3,099 | 3,456 | 3,304 | 28,400 | 28,450 | 3,906 | 3,549 | 3,906 | 3,754 | 31,400 | 31,450 | 4,594 | 3,999 | 4,594 | 4,204 |
| 25,450 | 25,500 | 3,464 | 3,106 | 3,464 | 3,311 | 28,450 | 28,500 | 3,914 | 3,556 | 3,914 | 3,761 | 31,450 | 31,500 | 4,606 | 4,006 | 4,606 | 4,211 |
| 25,500 | 25,550 | 3,471 | 3,114 | 3,471 | 3,319 | 28,500 | 28,550 | 3,921 | 3,564 | 3,921 | 3,769 | 31,500 | 31,550 | 4,619 | 4,014 | 4,619 | 4,219 |
| 25,550 | 25,600 | 3,479 | 3,121 | 3,479 | 3,326 | 28,550 | 28,600 | 3,929 | 3,571 | 3,929 | 3,776 | 31,550 | 31,600 | 4,631 | 4,021 | 4,631 | 4,226 |
| 25,600 | 25,650 | 3,486 | 3,129 | 3,486 | 3,334 | 28,600 | 28,650 | 3,936 | 3,579 | 3,936 | 3,784 | 31,600 | 31,650 | 4,644 | 4,029 | 4,644 | 4,234 |
| 25,650 | 25,700 | 3,494 | 3,136 | 3,494 | 3,341 | 28,650 | 28,700 | 3,944 | 3,586 | 3,944 | 3,791 | 31,650 | 31,700 | 4,656 | 4,036 | 4,656 | 4,241 |
| 25,700 | 25,750 | 3,501 | 3,144 | 3,501 | 3,349 | 28,700 | 28,750 | 3,951 | 3,594 | 3,951 | 3,799 | 31,700 | 31,750 | 4,669 | 4,044 | 4,669 | 4,249 |
| 25,750 | 25,800 | 3,509 | 3,151 | 3,509 | 3,356 | 28,750 | 28,800 | 3,959 | 3,601 | 3,959 | 3,806 | 31,750 | 31,800 | 4,681 | 4,051 | 4,681 | 4,256 |
| 25,800 | 25,850 | 3,516 | 3,159 | 3,516 | 3,364 | 28,800 | 28,850 | 3,966 | 3,609 | 3,966 | 3,814 | 31,800 | 31,850 | 4,694 | 4,059 | 4,694 | 4,264 |
| 25,850 | 25,900 | 3,524 | 3,166 | 3,524 | 3,371 | 28,850 | 28,900 | 3,974 | 3,616 | 3,974 | 3,821 | 31,850 | 31,900 | 4,706 | 4,066 | 4,706 | 4,271 |
| 25,900 | 25,950 | 3,531 | 3,174 | 3,531 | 3,379 | 28,900 | 28,950 | 3,981 | 3,624 | 3,981 | 3,829 | 31,900 | 31,950 | 4,719 | 4,074 | 4,719 | 4,279 |
| 25,950 | 26,000 | 3,539 | 3,181 | 3,539 | 3,386 | 28,950 | 29,000 | 3,989 | 3,631 | 3,989 | 3,836 | 31,950 | 32,000 | 4,731 | 4,081 | 4,731 | 4,286 |

\* This column must also be used by a qualifying widow(er).

(Continued on next page)

**2004 Tax Table**—*Continued*

| If line 42 (taxable income) is— | | And you are— | | | |
|---|---|---|---|---|---|
| At least | But less than | Single | Married filing jointly * | Married filing separately | Head of a household |
| | | Your tax is— | | | |

### 32,000

| At least | But less than | Single | Married filing jointly | Married filing separately | Head of a household |
|---|---|---|---|---|---|
| 32,000 | 32,050 | 4,744 | 4,089 | 4,744 | 4,294 |
| 32,050 | 32,100 | 4,756 | 4,096 | 4,756 | 4,301 |
| 32,100 | 32,150 | 4,769 | 4,104 | 4,769 | 4,309 |
| 32,150 | 32,200 | 4,781 | 4,111 | 4,781 | 4,316 |
| 32,200 | 32,250 | 4,794 | 4,119 | 4,794 | 4,324 |
| 32,250 | 32,300 | 4,806 | 4,126 | 4,806 | 4,331 |
| 32,300 | 32,350 | 4,819 | 4,134 | 4,819 | 4,339 |
| 32,350 | 32,400 | 4,831 | 4,141 | 4,831 | 4,346 |
| 32,400 | 32,450 | 4,844 | 4,149 | 4,844 | 4,354 |
| 32,450 | 32,500 | 4,856 | 4,156 | 4,856 | 4,361 |
| 32,500 | 32,550 | 4,869 | 4,164 | 4,869 | 4,369 |
| 32,550 | 32,600 | 4,881 | 4,171 | 4,881 | 4,376 |
| 32,600 | 32,650 | 4,894 | 4,179 | 4,894 | 4,384 |
| 32,650 | 32,700 | 4,906 | 4,186 | 4,906 | 4,391 |
| 32,700 | 32,750 | 4,919 | 4,194 | 4,919 | 4,399 |
| 32,750 | 32,800 | 4,931 | 4,201 | 4,931 | 4,406 |
| 32,800 | 32,850 | 4,944 | 4,209 | 4,944 | 4,414 |
| 32,850 | 32,900 | 4,956 | 4,216 | 4,956 | 4,421 |
| 32,900 | 32,950 | 4,969 | 4,224 | 4,969 | 4,429 |
| 32,950 | 33,000 | 4,981 | 4,231 | 4,981 | 4,436 |

### 33,000

| At least | But less than | Single | Married filing jointly | Married filing separately | Head of a household |
|---|---|---|---|---|---|
| 33,000 | 33,050 | 4,994 | 4,239 | 4,994 | 4,444 |
| 33,050 | 33,100 | 5,006 | 4,246 | 5,006 | 4,451 |
| 33,100 | 33,150 | 5,019 | 4,254 | 5,019 | 4,459 |
| 33,150 | 33,200 | 5,031 | 4,261 | 5,031 | 4,466 |
| 33,200 | 33,250 | 5,044 | 4,269 | 5,044 | 4,474 |
| 33,250 | 33,300 | 5,056 | 4,276 | 5,056 | 4,481 |
| 33,300 | 33,350 | 5,069 | 4,284 | 5,069 | 4,489 |
| 33,350 | 33,400 | 5,081 | 4,291 | 5,081 | 4,496 |
| 33,400 | 33,450 | 5,094 | 4,299 | 5,094 | 4,504 |
| 33,450 | 33,500 | 5,106 | 4,306 | 5,106 | 4,511 |
| 33,500 | 33,550 | 5,119 | 4,314 | 5,119 | 4,519 |
| 33,550 | 33,600 | 5,131 | 4,321 | 5,131 | 4,526 |
| 33,600 | 33,650 | 5,144 | 4,329 | 5,144 | 4,534 |
| 33,650 | 33,700 | 5,156 | 4,336 | 5,156 | 4,541 |
| 33,700 | 33,750 | 5,169 | 4,344 | 5,169 | 4,549 |
| 33,750 | 33,800 | 5,181 | 4,351 | 5,181 | 4,556 |
| 33,800 | 33,850 | 5,194 | 4,359 | 5,194 | 4,564 |
| 33,850 | 33,900 | 5,206 | 4,366 | 5,206 | 4,571 |
| 33,900 | 33,950 | 5,219 | 4,374 | 5,219 | 4,579 |
| 33,950 | 34,000 | 5,231 | 4,381 | 5,231 | 4,586 |

### 34,000

| At least | But less than | Single | Married filing jointly | Married filing separately | Head of a household |
|---|---|---|---|---|---|
| 34,000 | 34,050 | 5,244 | 4,389 | 5,244 | 4,594 |
| 34,050 | 34,100 | 5,256 | 4,396 | 5,256 | 4,601 |
| 34,100 | 34,150 | 5,269 | 4,404 | 5,269 | 4,609 |
| 34,150 | 34,200 | 5,281 | 4,411 | 5,281 | 4,616 |
| 34,200 | 34,250 | 5,294 | 4,419 | 5,294 | 4,624 |
| 34,250 | 34,300 | 5,306 | 4,426 | 5,306 | 4,631 |
| 34,300 | 34,350 | 5,319 | 4,434 | 5,319 | 4,639 |
| 34,350 | 34,400 | 5,331 | 4,441 | 5,331 | 4,646 |
| 34,400 | 34,450 | 5,344 | 4,449 | 5,344 | 4,654 |
| 34,450 | 34,500 | 5,356 | 4,456 | 5,356 | 4,661 |
| 34,500 | 34,550 | 5,369 | 4,464 | 5,369 | 4,669 |
| 34,550 | 34,600 | 5,381 | 4,471 | 5,381 | 4,676 |
| 34,600 | 34,650 | 5,394 | 4,479 | 5,394 | 4,684 |
| 34,650 | 34,700 | 5,406 | 4,486 | 5,406 | 4,691 |
| 34,700 | 34,750 | 5,419 | 4,494 | 5,419 | 4,699 |
| 34,750 | 34,800 | 5,431 | 4,501 | 5,431 | 4,706 |
| 34,800 | 34,850 | 5,444 | 4,509 | 5,444 | 4,714 |
| 34,850 | 34,900 | 5,456 | 4,516 | 5,456 | 4,721 |
| 34,900 | 34,950 | 5,469 | 4,524 | 5,469 | 4,729 |
| 34,950 | 35,000 | 5,481 | 4,531 | 5,481 | 4,736 |

### 35,000

| At least | But less than | Single | Married filing jointly | Married filing separately | Head of a household |
|---|---|---|---|---|---|
| 35,000 | 35,050 | 5,494 | 4,539 | 5,494 | 4,744 |
| 35,050 | 35,100 | 5,506 | 4,546 | 5,506 | 4,751 |
| 35,100 | 35,150 | 5,519 | 4,554 | 5,519 | 4,759 |
| 35,150 | 35,200 | 5,531 | 4,561 | 5,531 | 4,766 |
| 35,200 | 35,250 | 5,544 | 4,569 | 5,544 | 4,774 |
| 35,250 | 35,300 | 5,556 | 4,576 | 5,556 | 4,781 |
| 35,300 | 35,350 | 5,569 | 4,584 | 5,569 | 4,789 |
| 35,350 | 35,400 | 5,581 | 4,591 | 5,581 | 4,796 |
| 35,400 | 35,450 | 5,594 | 4,599 | 5,594 | 4,804 |
| 35,450 | 35,500 | 5,606 | 4,606 | 5,606 | 4,811 |
| 35,500 | 35,550 | 5,619 | 4,614 | 5,619 | 4,819 |
| 35,550 | 35,600 | 5,631 | 4,621 | 5,631 | 4,826 |
| 35,600 | 35,650 | 5,644 | 4,629 | 5,644 | 4,834 |
| 35,650 | 35,700 | 5,656 | 4,636 | 5,656 | 4,841 |
| 35,700 | 35,750 | 5,669 | 4,644 | 5,669 | 4,849 |
| 35,750 | 35,800 | 5,681 | 4,651 | 5,681 | 4,856 |
| 35,800 | 35,850 | 5,694 | 4,659 | 5,694 | 4,864 |
| 35,850 | 35,900 | 5,706 | 4,666 | 5,706 | 4,871 |
| 35,900 | 35,950 | 5,719 | 4,674 | 5,719 | 4,879 |
| 35,950 | 36,000 | 5,731 | 4,681 | 5,731 | 4,886 |

### 36,000

| At least | But less than | Single | Married filing jointly | Married filing separately | Head of a household |
|---|---|---|---|---|---|
| 36,000 | 36,050 | 5,744 | 4,689 | 5,744 | 4,894 |
| 36,050 | 36,100 | 5,756 | 4,696 | 5,756 | 4,901 |
| 36,100 | 36,150 | 5,769 | 4,704 | 5,769 | 4,909 |
| 36,150 | 36,200 | 5,781 | 4,711 | 5,781 | 4,916 |
| 36,200 | 36,250 | 5,794 | 4,719 | 5,794 | 4,924 |
| 36,250 | 36,300 | 5,806 | 4,726 | 5,806 | 4,931 |
| 36,300 | 36,350 | 5,819 | 4,734 | 5,819 | 4,939 |
| 36,350 | 36,400 | 5,831 | 4,741 | 5,831 | 4,946 |
| 36,400 | 36,450 | 5,844 | 4,749 | 5,844 | 4,954 |
| 36,450 | 36,500 | 5,856 | 4,756 | 5,856 | 4,961 |
| 36,500 | 36,550 | 5,869 | 4,764 | 5,869 | 4,969 |
| 36,550 | 36,600 | 5,881 | 4,771 | 5,881 | 4,976 |
| 36,600 | 36,650 | 5,894 | 4,779 | 5,894 | 4,984 |
| 36,650 | 36,700 | 5,906 | 4,786 | 5,906 | 4,991 |
| 36,700 | 36,750 | 5,919 | 4,794 | 5,919 | 4,999 |
| 36,750 | 36,800 | 5,931 | 4,801 | 5,931 | 5,006 |
| 36,800 | 36,850 | 5,944 | 4,809 | 5,944 | 5,014 |
| 36,850 | 36,900 | 5,956 | 4,816 | 5,956 | 5,021 |
| 36,900 | 36,950 | 5,969 | 4,824 | 5,969 | 5,029 |
| 36,950 | 37,000 | 5,981 | 4,831 | 5,981 | 5,036 |

### 37,000

| At least | But less than | Single | Married filing jointly | Married filing separately | Head of a household |
|---|---|---|---|---|---|
| 37,000 | 37,050 | 5,994 | 4,839 | 5,994 | 5,044 |
| 37,050 | 37,100 | 6,006 | 4,846 | 6,006 | 5,051 |
| 37,100 | 37,150 | 6,019 | 4,854 | 6,019 | 5,059 |
| 37,150 | 37,200 | 6,031 | 4,861 | 6,031 | 5,066 |
| 37,200 | 37,250 | 6,044 | 4,869 | 6,044 | 5,074 |
| 37,250 | 37,300 | 6,056 | 4,876 | 6,056 | 5,081 |
| 37,300 | 37,350 | 6,069 | 4,884 | 6,069 | 5,089 |
| 37,350 | 37,400 | 6,081 | 4,891 | 6,081 | 5,096 |
| 37,400 | 37,450 | 6,094 | 4,899 | 6,094 | 5,104 |
| 37,450 | 37,500 | 6,106 | 4,906 | 6,106 | 5,111 |
| 37,500 | 37,550 | 6,119 | 4,914 | 6,119 | 5,119 |
| 37,550 | 37,600 | 6,131 | 4,921 | 6,131 | 5,126 |
| 37,600 | 37,650 | 6,144 | 4,929 | 6,144 | 5,134 |
| 37,650 | 37,700 | 6,156 | 4,936 | 6,156 | 5,141 |
| 37,700 | 37,750 | 6,169 | 4,944 | 6,169 | 5,149 |
| 37,750 | 37,800 | 6,181 | 4,951 | 6,181 | 5,156 |
| 37,800 | 37,850 | 6,194 | 4,959 | 6,194 | 5,164 |
| 37,850 | 37,900 | 6,206 | 4,966 | 6,206 | 5,171 |
| 37,900 | 37,950 | 6,219 | 4,974 | 6,219 | 5,179 |
| 37,950 | 38,000 | 6,231 | 4,981 | 6,231 | 5,186 |

### 38,000

| At least | But less than | Single | Married filing jointly | Married filing separately | Head of a household |
|---|---|---|---|---|---|
| 38,000 | 38,050 | 6,244 | 4,989 | 6,244 | 5,194 |
| 38,050 | 38,100 | 6,256 | 4,996 | 6,256 | 5,201 |
| 38,100 | 38,150 | 6,269 | 5,004 | 6,269 | 5,209 |
| 38,150 | 38,200 | 6,281 | 5,011 | 6,281 | 5,216 |
| 38,200 | 38,250 | 6,294 | 5,019 | 6,294 | 5,224 |
| 38,250 | 38,300 | 6,306 | 5,026 | 6,306 | 5,231 |
| 38,300 | 38,350 | 6,319 | 5,034 | 6,319 | 5,239 |
| 38,350 | 38,400 | 6,331 | 5,041 | 6,331 | 5,246 |
| 38,400 | 38,450 | 6,344 | 5,049 | 6,344 | 5,254 |
| 38,450 | 38,500 | 6,356 | 5,056 | 6,356 | 5,261 |
| 38,500 | 38,550 | 6,369 | 5,064 | 6,369 | 5,269 |
| 38,550 | 38,600 | 6,381 | 5,071 | 6,381 | 5,276 |
| 38,600 | 38,650 | 6,394 | 5,079 | 6,394 | 5,284 |
| 38,650 | 38,700 | 6,406 | 5,086 | 6,406 | 5,291 |
| 38,700 | 38,750 | 6,419 | 5,094 | 6,419 | 5,299 |
| 38,750 | 38,800 | 6,431 | 5,101 | 6,431 | 5,306 |
| 38,800 | 38,850 | 6,444 | 5,109 | 6,444 | 5,314 |
| 38,850 | 38,900 | 6,456 | 5,116 | 6,456 | 5,321 |
| 38,900 | 38,950 | 6,469 | 5,124 | 6,469 | 5,331 |
| 38,950 | 39,000 | 6,481 | 5,131 | 6,481 | 5,344 |

### 39,000

| At least | But less than | Single | Married filing jointly | Married filing separately | Head of a household |
|---|---|---|---|---|---|
| 39,000 | 39,050 | 6,494 | 5,139 | 6,494 | 5,356 |
| 39,050 | 39,100 | 6,506 | 5,146 | 6,506 | 5,369 |
| 39,100 | 39,150 | 6,519 | 5,154 | 6,519 | 5,381 |
| 39,150 | 39,200 | 6,531 | 5,161 | 6,531 | 5,394 |
| 39,200 | 39,250 | 6,544 | 5,169 | 6,544 | 5,406 |
| 39,250 | 39,300 | 6,556 | 5,176 | 6,556 | 5,419 |
| 39,300 | 39,350 | 6,569 | 5,184 | 6,569 | 5,431 |
| 39,350 | 39,400 | 6,581 | 5,191 | 6,581 | 5,444 |
| 39,400 | 39,450 | 6,594 | 5,199 | 6,594 | 5,456 |
| 39,450 | 39,500 | 6,606 | 5,206 | 6,606 | 5,469 |
| 39,500 | 39,550 | 6,619 | 5,214 | 6,619 | 5,481 |
| 39,550 | 39,600 | 6,631 | 5,221 | 6,631 | 5,494 |
| 39,600 | 39,650 | 6,644 | 5,229 | 6,644 | 5,506 |
| 39,650 | 39,700 | 6,656 | 5,236 | 6,656 | 5,519 |
| 39,700 | 39,750 | 6,669 | 5,244 | 6,669 | 5,531 |
| 39,750 | 39,800 | 6,681 | 5,251 | 6,681 | 5,544 |
| 39,800 | 39,850 | 6,694 | 5,259 | 6,694 | 5,556 |
| 39,850 | 39,900 | 6,706 | 5,266 | 6,706 | 5,569 |
| 39,900 | 39,950 | 6,719 | 5,274 | 6,719 | 5,581 |
| 39,950 | 40,000 | 6,731 | 5,281 | 6,731 | 5,594 |

### 40,000

| At least | But less than | Single | Married filing jointly | Married filing separately | Head of a household |
|---|---|---|---|---|---|
| 40,000 | 40,050 | 6,744 | 5,289 | 6,744 | 5,606 |
| 40,050 | 40,100 | 6,756 | 5,296 | 6,756 | 5,619 |
| 40,100 | 40,150 | 6,769 | 5,304 | 6,769 | 5,631 |
| 40,150 | 40,200 | 6,781 | 5,311 | 6,781 | 5,644 |
| 40,200 | 40,250 | 6,794 | 5,319 | 6,794 | 5,656 |
| 40,250 | 40,300 | 6,806 | 5,326 | 6,806 | 5,669 |
| 40,300 | 40,350 | 6,819 | 5,334 | 6,819 | 5,681 |
| 40,350 | 40,400 | 6,831 | 5,341 | 6,831 | 5,694 |
| 40,400 | 40,450 | 6,844 | 5,349 | 6,844 | 5,706 |
| 40,450 | 40,500 | 6,856 | 5,356 | 6,856 | 5,719 |
| 40,500 | 40,550 | 6,869 | 5,364 | 6,869 | 5,731 |
| 40,550 | 40,600 | 6,881 | 5,371 | 6,881 | 5,744 |
| 40,600 | 40,650 | 6,894 | 5,379 | 6,894 | 5,756 |
| 40,650 | 40,700 | 6,906 | 5,386 | 6,906 | 5,769 |
| 40,700 | 40,750 | 6,919 | 5,394 | 6,919 | 5,781 |
| 40,750 | 40,800 | 6,931 | 5,401 | 6,931 | 5,794 |
| 40,800 | 40,850 | 6,944 | 5,409 | 6,944 | 5,806 |
| 40,850 | 40,900 | 6,956 | 5,416 | 6,956 | 5,819 |
| 40,900 | 40,950 | 6,969 | 5,424 | 6,969 | 5,831 |
| 40,950 | 41,000 | 6,981 | 5,431 | 6,981 | 5,844 |

* This column must also be used by a qualifying widow(er).

(Continued on next page)

## 2004 Tax Table—*Continued*

**41,000 – 43,950**

| At least | But less than | Single | Married filing jointly * | Married filing separately | Head of a household |
|---|---|---|---|---|---|
| 41,000 | 41,050 | 6,994 | 5,439 | 6,994 | 5,856 |
| 41,050 | 41,100 | 7,006 | 5,446 | 7,006 | 5,869 |
| 41,100 | 41,150 | 7,019 | 5,454 | 7,019 | 5,881 |
| 41,150 | 41,200 | 7,031 | 5,461 | 7,031 | 5,894 |
| 41,200 | 41,250 | 7,044 | 5,469 | 7,044 | 5,906 |
| 41,250 | 41,300 | 7,056 | 5,476 | 7,056 | 5,919 |
| 41,300 | 41,350 | 7,069 | 5,484 | 7,069 | 5,931 |
| 41,350 | 41,400 | 7,081 | 5,491 | 7,081 | 5,944 |
| 41,400 | 41,450 | 7,094 | 5,499 | 7,094 | 5,956 |
| 41,450 | 41,500 | 7,106 | 5,506 | 7,106 | 5,969 |
| 41,500 | 41,550 | 7,119 | 5,514 | 7,119 | 5,981 |
| 41,550 | 41,600 | 7,131 | 5,521 | 7,131 | 5,994 |
| 41,600 | 41,650 | 7,144 | 5,529 | 7,144 | 6,006 |
| 41,650 | 41,700 | 7,156 | 5,536 | 7,156 | 6,019 |
| 41,700 | 41,750 | 7,169 | 5,544 | 7,169 | 6,031 |
| 41,750 | 41,800 | 7,181 | 5,551 | 7,181 | 6,044 |
| 41,800 | 41,850 | 7,194 | 5,559 | 7,194 | 6,056 |
| 41,850 | 41,900 | 7,206 | 5,566 | 7,206 | 6,069 |
| 41,900 | 41,950 | 7,219 | 5,574 | 7,219 | 6,081 |
| 41,950 | 42,000 | 7,231 | 5,581 | 7,231 | 6,094 |
| 42,000 | 42,050 | 7,244 | 5,589 | 7,244 | 6,106 |
| 42,050 | 42,100 | 7,256 | 5,596 | 7,256 | 6,119 |
| 42,100 | 42,150 | 7,269 | 5,604 | 7,269 | 6,131 |
| 42,150 | 42,200 | 7,281 | 5,611 | 7,281 | 6,144 |
| 42,200 | 42,250 | 7,294 | 5,619 | 7,294 | 6,156 |
| 42,250 | 42,300 | 7,306 | 5,626 | 7,306 | 6,169 |
| 42,300 | 42,350 | 7,319 | 5,634 | 7,319 | 6,181 |
| 42,350 | 42,400 | 7,331 | 5,641 | 7,331 | 6,194 |
| 42,400 | 42,450 | 7,344 | 5,649 | 7,344 | 6,206 |
| 42,450 | 42,500 | 7,356 | 5,656 | 7,356 | 6,219 |
| 42,500 | 42,550 | 7,369 | 5,664 | 7,369 | 6,231 |
| 42,550 | 42,600 | 7,381 | 5,671 | 7,381 | 6,244 |
| 42,600 | 42,650 | 7,394 | 5,679 | 7,394 | 6,256 |
| 42,650 | 42,700 | 7,406 | 5,686 | 7,406 | 6,269 |
| 42,700 | 42,750 | 7,419 | 5,694 | 7,419 | 6,281 |
| 42,750 | 42,800 | 7,431 | 5,701 | 7,431 | 6,294 |
| 42,800 | 42,850 | 7,444 | 5,709 | 7,444 | 6,306 |
| 42,850 | 42,900 | 7,456 | 5,716 | 7,456 | 6,319 |
| 42,900 | 42,950 | 7,469 | 5,724 | 7,469 | 6,331 |
| 42,950 | 43,000 | 7,481 | 5,731 | 7,481 | 6,344 |
| 43,000 | 43,050 | 7,494 | 5,739 | 7,494 | 6,356 |
| 43,050 | 43,100 | 7,506 | 5,746 | 7,506 | 6,369 |
| 43,100 | 43,150 | 7,519 | 5,754 | 7,519 | 6,381 |
| 43,150 | 43,200 | 7,531 | 5,761 | 7,531 | 6,394 |
| 43,200 | 43,250 | 7,544 | 5,769 | 7,544 | 6,406 |
| 43,250 | 43,300 | 7,556 | 5,776 | 7,556 | 6,419 |
| 43,300 | 43,350 | 7,569 | 5,784 | 7,569 | 6,431 |
| 43,350 | 43,400 | 7,581 | 5,791 | 7,581 | 6,444 |
| 43,400 | 43,450 | 7,594 | 5,799 | 7,594 | 6,456 |
| 43,450 | 43,500 | 7,606 | 5,806 | 7,606 | 6,469 |
| 43,500 | 43,550 | 7,619 | 5,814 | 7,619 | 6,481 |
| 43,550 | 43,600 | 7,631 | 5,821 | 7,631 | 6,494 |
| 43,600 | 43,650 | 7,644 | 5,829 | 7,644 | 6,506 |
| 43,650 | 43,700 | 7,656 | 5,836 | 7,656 | 6,519 |
| 43,700 | 43,750 | 7,669 | 5,844 | 7,669 | 6,531 |
| 43,750 | 43,800 | 7,681 | 5,851 | 7,681 | 6,544 |
| 43,800 | 43,850 | 7,694 | 5,859 | 7,694 | 6,556 |
| 43,850 | 43,900 | 7,706 | 5,866 | 7,706 | 6,569 |
| 43,900 | 43,950 | 7,719 | 5,874 | 7,719 | 6,581 |
| 43,950 | 44,000 | 7,731 | 5,881 | 7,731 | 6,594 |

**44,000 – 46,950**

| At least | But less than | Single | Married filing jointly * | Married filing separately | Head of a household |
|---|---|---|---|---|---|
| 44,000 | 44,050 | 7,744 | 5,889 | 7,744 | 6,606 |
| 44,050 | 44,100 | 7,756 | 5,896 | 7,756 | 6,619 |
| 44,100 | 44,150 | 7,769 | 5,904 | 7,769 | 6,631 |
| 44,150 | 44,200 | 7,781 | 5,911 | 7,781 | 6,644 |
| 44,200 | 44,250 | 7,794 | 5,919 | 7,794 | 6,656 |
| 44,250 | 44,300 | 7,806 | 5,926 | 7,806 | 6,669 |
| 44,300 | 44,350 | 7,819 | 5,934 | 7,819 | 6,681 |
| 44,350 | 44,400 | 7,831 | 5,941 | 7,831 | 6,694 |
| 44,400 | 44,450 | 7,844 | 5,949 | 7,844 | 6,706 |
| 44,450 | 44,500 | 7,856 | 5,956 | 7,856 | 6,719 |
| 44,500 | 44,550 | 7,869 | 5,964 | 7,869 | 6,731 |
| 44,550 | 44,600 | 7,881 | 5,971 | 7,881 | 6,744 |
| 44,600 | 44,650 | 7,894 | 5,979 | 7,894 | 6,756 |
| 44,650 | 44,700 | 7,906 | 5,986 | 7,906 | 6,769 |
| 44,700 | 44,750 | 7,919 | 5,994 | 7,919 | 6,781 |
| 44,750 | 44,800 | 7,931 | 6,001 | 7,931 | 6,794 |
| 44,800 | 44,850 | 7,944 | 6,009 | 7,944 | 6,806 |
| 44,850 | 44,900 | 7,956 | 6,016 | 7,956 | 6,819 |
| 44,900 | 44,950 | 7,969 | 6,024 | 7,969 | 6,831 |
| 44,950 | 45,000 | 7,981 | 6,031 | 7,981 | 6,844 |
| 45,000 | 45,050 | 7,994 | 6,039 | 7,994 | 6,856 |
| 45,050 | 45,100 | 8,006 | 6,046 | 8,006 | 6,869 |
| 45,100 | 45,150 | 8,019 | 6,054 | 8,019 | 6,881 |
| 45,150 | 45,200 | 8,031 | 6,061 | 8,031 | 6,894 |
| 45,200 | 45,250 | 8,044 | 6,069 | 8,044 | 6,906 |
| 45,250 | 45,300 | 8,056 | 6,076 | 8,056 | 6,919 |
| 45,300 | 45,350 | 8,069 | 6,084 | 8,069 | 6,931 |
| 45,350 | 45,400 | 8,081 | 6,091 | 8,081 | 6,944 |
| 45,400 | 45,450 | 8,094 | 6,099 | 8,094 | 6,956 |
| 45,450 | 45,500 | 8,106 | 6,106 | 8,106 | 6,969 |
| 45,500 | 45,550 | 8,119 | 6,114 | 8,119 | 6,981 |
| 45,550 | 45,600 | 8,131 | 6,121 | 8,131 | 6,994 |
| 45,600 | 45,650 | 8,144 | 6,129 | 8,144 | 7,006 |
| 45,650 | 45,700 | 8,156 | 6,136 | 8,156 | 7,019 |
| 45,700 | 45,750 | 8,169 | 6,144 | 8,169 | 7,031 |
| 45,750 | 45,800 | 8,181 | 6,151 | 8,181 | 7,044 |
| 45,800 | 45,850 | 8,194 | 6,159 | 8,194 | 7,056 |
| 45,850 | 45,900 | 8,206 | 6,166 | 8,206 | 7,069 |
| 45,900 | 45,950 | 8,219 | 6,174 | 8,219 | 7,081 |
| 45,950 | 46,000 | 8,231 | 6,181 | 8,231 | 7,094 |
| 46,000 | 46,050 | 8,244 | 6,189 | 8,244 | 7,106 |
| 46,050 | 46,100 | 8,256 | 6,196 | 8,256 | 7,119 |
| 46,100 | 46,150 | 8,269 | 6,204 | 8,269 | 7,131 |
| 46,150 | 46,200 | 8,281 | 6,211 | 8,281 | 7,144 |
| 46,200 | 46,250 | 8,294 | 6,219 | 8,294 | 7,156 |
| 46,250 | 46,300 | 8,306 | 6,226 | 8,306 | 7,169 |
| 46,300 | 46,350 | 8,319 | 6,234 | 8,319 | 7,181 |
| 46,350 | 46,400 | 8,331 | 6,241 | 8,331 | 7,194 |
| 46,400 | 46,450 | 8,344 | 6,249 | 8,344 | 7,206 |
| 46,450 | 46,500 | 8,356 | 6,256 | 8,356 | 7,219 |
| 46,500 | 46,550 | 8,369 | 6,264 | 8,369 | 7,231 |
| 46,550 | 46,600 | 8,381 | 6,271 | 8,381 | 7,244 |
| 46,600 | 46,650 | 8,394 | 6,279 | 8,394 | 7,256 |
| 46,650 | 46,700 | 8,406 | 6,286 | 8,406 | 7,269 |
| 46,700 | 46,750 | 8,419 | 6,294 | 8,419 | 7,281 |
| 46,750 | 46,800 | 8,431 | 6,301 | 8,431 | 7,294 |
| 46,800 | 46,850 | 8,444 | 6,309 | 8,444 | 7,306 |
| 46,850 | 46,900 | 8,456 | 6,316 | 8,456 | 7,319 |
| 46,900 | 46,950 | 8,469 | 6,324 | 8,469 | 7,331 |
| 46,950 | 47,000 | 8,481 | 6,331 | 8,481 | 7,344 |

**47,000 – 49,950**

| At least | But less than | Single | Married filing jointly * | Married filing separately | Head of a household |
|---|---|---|---|---|---|
| 47,000 | 47,050 | 8,494 | 6,339 | 8,494 | 7,356 |
| 47,050 | 47,100 | 8,506 | 6,346 | 8,506 | 7,369 |
| 47,100 | 47,150 | 8,519 | 6,354 | 8,519 | 7,381 |
| 47,150 | 47,200 | 8,531 | 6,361 | 8,531 | 7,394 |
| 47,200 | 47,250 | 8,544 | 6,369 | 8,544 | 7,406 |
| 47,250 | 47,300 | 8,556 | 6,376 | 8,556 | 7,419 |
| 47,300 | 47,350 | 8,569 | 6,384 | 8,569 | 7,431 |
| 47,350 | 47,400 | 8,581 | 6,391 | 8,581 | 7,444 |
| 47,400 | 47,450 | 8,594 | 6,399 | 8,594 | 7,456 |
| 47,450 | 47,500 | 8,606 | 6,406 | 8,606 | 7,469 |
| 47,500 | 47,550 | 8,619 | 6,414 | 8,619 | 7,481 |
| 47,550 | 47,600 | 8,631 | 6,421 | 8,631 | 7,494 |
| 47,600 | 47,650 | 8,644 | 6,429 | 8,644 | 7,506 |
| 47,650 | 47,700 | 8,656 | 6,436 | 8,656 | 7,519 |
| 47,700 | 47,750 | 8,669 | 6,444 | 8,669 | 7,531 |
| 47,750 | 47,800 | 8,681 | 6,451 | 8,681 | 7,544 |
| 47,800 | 47,850 | 8,694 | 6,459 | 8,694 | 7,556 |
| 47,850 | 47,900 | 8,706 | 6,466 | 8,706 | 7,569 |
| 47,900 | 47,950 | 8,719 | 6,474 | 8,719 | 7,581 |
| 47,950 | 48,000 | 8,731 | 6,481 | 8,731 | 7,594 |
| 48,000 | 48,050 | 8,744 | 6,489 | 8,744 | 7,606 |
| 48,050 | 48,100 | 8,756 | 6,496 | 8,756 | 7,619 |
| 48,100 | 48,150 | 8,769 | 6,504 | 8,769 | 7,631 |
| 48,150 | 48,200 | 8,781 | 6,511 | 8,781 | 7,644 |
| 48,200 | 48,250 | 8,794 | 6,519 | 8,794 | 7,656 |
| 48,250 | 48,300 | 8,806 | 6,526 | 8,806 | 7,669 |
| 48,300 | 48,350 | 8,819 | 6,534 | 8,819 | 7,681 |
| 48,350 | 48,400 | 8,831 | 6,541 | 8,831 | 7,694 |
| 48,400 | 48,450 | 8,844 | 6,549 | 8,844 | 7,706 |
| 48,450 | 48,500 | 8,856 | 6,556 | 8,856 | 7,719 |
| 48,500 | 48,550 | 8,869 | 6,564 | 8,869 | 7,731 |
| 48,550 | 48,600 | 8,881 | 6,571 | 8,881 | 7,744 |
| 48,600 | 48,650 | 8,894 | 6,579 | 8,894 | 7,756 |
| 48,650 | 48,700 | 8,906 | 6,586 | 8,906 | 7,769 |
| 48,700 | 48,750 | 8,919 | 6,594 | 8,919 | 7,781 |
| 48,750 | 48,800 | 8,931 | 6,601 | 8,931 | 7,794 |
| 48,800 | 48,850 | 8,944 | 6,609 | 8,944 | 7,806 |
| 48,850 | 48,900 | 8,956 | 6,616 | 8,956 | 7,819 |
| 48,900 | 48,950 | 8,969 | 6,624 | 8,969 | 7,831 |
| 48,950 | 49,000 | 8,981 | 6,631 | 8,981 | 7,844 |
| 49,000 | 49,050 | 8,994 | 6,639 | 8,994 | 7,856 |
| 49,050 | 49,100 | 9,006 | 6,646 | 9,006 | 7,869 |
| 49,100 | 49,150 | 9,019 | 6,654 | 9,019 | 7,881 |
| 49,150 | 49,200 | 9,031 | 6,661 | 9,031 | 7,894 |
| 49,200 | 49,250 | 9,044 | 6,669 | 9,044 | 7,906 |
| 49,250 | 49,300 | 9,056 | 6,676 | 9,056 | 7,919 |
| 49,300 | 49,350 | 9,069 | 6,684 | 9,069 | 7,931 |
| 49,350 | 49,400 | 9,081 | 6,691 | 9,081 | 7,944 |
| 49,400 | 49,450 | 9,094 | 6,699 | 9,094 | 7,956 |
| 49,450 | 49,500 | 9,106 | 6,706 | 9,106 | 7,969 |
| 49,500 | 49,550 | 9,119 | 6,714 | 9,119 | 7,981 |
| 49,550 | 49,600 | 9,131 | 6,721 | 9,131 | 7,994 |
| 49,600 | 49,650 | 9,144 | 6,729 | 9,144 | 8,006 |
| 49,650 | 49,700 | 9,156 | 6,736 | 9,156 | 8,019 |
| 49,700 | 49,750 | 9,169 | 6,744 | 9,169 | 8,031 |
| 49,750 | 49,800 | 9,181 | 6,751 | 9,181 | 8,044 |
| 49,800 | 49,850 | 9,194 | 6,759 | 9,194 | 8,056 |
| 49,850 | 49,900 | 9,206 | 6,766 | 9,206 | 8,069 |
| 49,900 | 49,950 | 9,219 | 6,774 | 9,219 | 8,081 |
| 49,950 | 50,000 | 9,231 | 6,781 | 9,231 | 8,094 |

* This column must also be used by a qualifying widow(er).

*(Continued on next page)*

**2004 Tax Table—**_Continued_

| If line 42 (taxable income) is— | | And you are— | | | | If line 42 (taxable income) is— | | And you are— | | | | If line 42 (taxable income) is— | | And you are— | | | |
|---|---|---|---|---|---|---|---|---|---|---|---|---|---|---|---|---|---|
| At least | But less than | Single | Married filing jointly * | Married filing sepa-rately | Head of a house-hold | At least | But less than | Single | Married filing jointly * | Married filing sepa-rately | Head of a house-hold | At least | But less than | Single | Married filing jointly * | Married filing sepa-rately | Head of a house-hold |
| | | Your tax is— | | | | | | Your tax is— | | | | | | Your tax is— | | | |
| **50,000** | | | | | | **53,000** | | | | | | **56,000** | | | | | |
| 50,000 | 50,050 | 9,244 | 6,789 | 9,244 | 8,106 | 53,000 | 53,050 | 9,994 | 7,239 | 9,994 | 8,856 | 56,000 | 56,050 | 10,744 | 7,689 | 10,744 | 9,606 |
| 50,050 | 50,100 | 9,256 | 6,796 | 9,256 | 8,119 | 53,050 | 53,100 | 10,006 | 7,246 | 10,006 | 8,869 | 56,050 | 56,100 | 10,756 | 7,696 | 10,756 | 9,619 |
| 50,100 | 50,150 | 9,269 | 6,804 | 9,269 | 8,131 | 53,100 | 53,150 | 10,019 | 7,254 | 10,019 | 8,881 | 56,100 | 56,150 | 10,769 | 7,704 | 10,769 | 9,631 |
| 50,150 | 50,200 | 9,281 | 6,811 | 9,281 | 8,144 | 53,150 | 53,200 | 10,031 | 7,261 | 10,031 | 8,894 | 56,150 | 56,200 | 10,781 | 7,711 | 10,781 | 9,644 |
| 50,200 | 50,250 | 9,294 | 6,819 | 9,294 | 8,156 | 53,200 | 53,250 | 10,044 | 7,269 | 10,044 | 8,906 | 56,200 | 56,250 | 10,794 | 7,719 | 10,794 | 9,656 |
| 50,250 | 50,300 | 9,306 | 6,826 | 9,306 | 8,169 | 53,250 | 53,300 | 10,056 | 7,276 | 10,056 | 8,919 | 56,250 | 56,300 | 10,806 | 7,726 | 10,806 | 9,669 |
| 50,300 | 50,350 | 9,319 | 6,834 | 9,319 | 8,181 | 53,300 | 53,350 | 10,069 | 7,284 | 10,069 | 8,931 | 56,300 | 56,350 | 10,819 | 7,734 | 10,819 | 9,681 |
| 50,350 | 50,400 | 9,331 | 6,841 | 9,331 | 8,194 | 53,350 | 53,400 | 10,081 | 7,291 | 10,081 | 8,944 | 56,350 | 56,400 | 10,831 | 7,741 | 10,831 | 9,694 |
| 50,400 | 50,450 | 9,344 | 6,849 | 9,344 | 8,206 | 53,400 | 53,450 | 10,094 | 7,299 | 10,094 | 8,956 | 56,400 | 56,450 | 10,844 | 7,749 | 10,844 | 9,706 |
| 50,450 | 50,500 | 9,356 | 6,856 | 9,356 | 8,219 | 53,450 | 53,500 | 10,106 | 7,306 | 10,106 | 8,969 | 56,450 | 56,500 | 10,856 | 7,756 | 10,856 | 9,719 |
| 50,500 | 50,550 | 9,369 | 6,864 | 9,369 | 8,231 | 53,500 | 53,550 | 10,119 | 7,314 | 10,119 | 8,981 | 56,500 | 56,550 | 10,869 | 7,764 | 10,869 | 9,731 |
| 50,550 | 50,600 | 9,381 | 6,871 | 9,381 | 8,244 | 53,550 | 53,600 | 10,131 | 7,321 | 10,131 | 8,994 | 56,550 | 56,600 | 10,881 | 7,771 | 10,881 | 9,744 |
| 50,600 | 50,650 | 9,394 | 6,879 | 9,394 | 8,256 | 53,600 | 53,650 | 10,144 | 7,329 | 10,144 | 9,006 | 56,600 | 56,650 | 10,894 | 7,779 | 10,894 | 9,756 |
| 50,650 | 50,700 | 9,406 | 6,886 | 9,406 | 8,269 | 53,650 | 53,700 | 10,156 | 7,336 | 10,156 | 9,019 | 56,650 | 56,700 | 10,906 | 7,786 | 10,906 | 9,769 |
| 50,700 | 50,750 | 9,419 | 6,894 | 9,419 | 8,281 | 53,700 | 53,750 | 10,169 | 7,344 | 10,169 | 9,031 | 56,700 | 56,750 | 10,919 | 7,794 | 10,919 | 9,781 |
| 50,750 | 50,800 | 9,431 | 6,901 | 9,431 | 8,294 | 53,750 | 53,800 | 10,181 | 7,351 | 10,181 | 9,044 | 56,750 | 56,800 | 10,931 | 7,801 | 10,931 | 9,794 |
| 50,800 | 50,850 | 9,444 | 6,909 | 9,444 | 8,306 | 53,800 | 53,850 | 10,194 | 7,359 | 10,194 | 9,056 | 56,800 | 56,850 | 10,944 | 7,809 | 10,944 | 9,806 |
| 50,850 | 50,900 | 9,456 | 6,916 | 9,456 | 8,319 | 53,850 | 53,900 | 10,206 | 7,366 | 10,206 | 9,069 | 56,850 | 56,900 | 10,956 | 7,816 | 10,956 | 9,819 |
| 50,900 | 50,950 | 9,469 | 6,924 | 9,469 | 8,331 | 53,900 | 53,950 | 10,219 | 7,374 | 10,219 | 9,081 | 56,900 | 56,950 | 10,969 | 7,824 | 10,969 | 9,831 |
| 50,950 | 51,000 | 9,481 | 6,931 | 9,481 | 8,344 | 53,950 | 54,000 | 10,231 | 7,381 | 10,231 | 9,094 | 56,950 | 57,000 | 10,981 | 7,831 | 10,981 | 9,844 |
| **51,000** | | | | | | **54,000** | | | | | | **57,000** | | | | | |
| 51,000 | 51,050 | 9,494 | 6,939 | 9,494 | 8,356 | 54,000 | 54,050 | 10,244 | 7,389 | 10,244 | 9,106 | 57,000 | 57,050 | 10,994 | 7,839 | 10,994 | 9,856 |
| 51,050 | 51,100 | 9,506 | 6,946 | 9,506 | 8,369 | 54,050 | 54,100 | 10,256 | 7,396 | 10,256 | 9,119 | 57,050 | 57,100 | 11,006 | 7,846 | 11,006 | 9,869 |
| 51,100 | 51,150 | 9,519 | 6,954 | 9,519 | 8,381 | 54,100 | 54,150 | 10,269 | 7,404 | 10,269 | 9,131 | 57,100 | 57,150 | 11,019 | 7,854 | 11,019 | 9,881 |
| 51,150 | 51,200 | 9,531 | 6,961 | 9,531 | 8,394 | 54,150 | 54,200 | 10,281 | 7,411 | 10,281 | 9,144 | 57,150 | 57,200 | 11,031 | 7,861 | 11,031 | 9,894 |
| 51,200 | 51,250 | 9,544 | 6,969 | 9,544 | 8,406 | 54,200 | 54,250 | 10,294 | 7,419 | 10,294 | 9,156 | 57,200 | 57,250 | 11,044 | 7,869 | 11,044 | 9,906 |
| 51,250 | 51,300 | 9,556 | 6,976 | 9,556 | 8,419 | 54,250 | 54,300 | 10,306 | 7,426 | 10,306 | 9,169 | 57,250 | 57,300 | 11,056 | 7,876 | 11,056 | 9,919 |
| 51,300 | 51,350 | 9,569 | 6,984 | 9,569 | 8,431 | 54,300 | 54,350 | 10,319 | 7,434 | 10,319 | 9,181 | 57,300 | 57,350 | 11,069 | 7,884 | 11,069 | 9,931 |
| 51,350 | 51,400 | 9,581 | 6,991 | 9,581 | 8,444 | 54,350 | 54,400 | 10,331 | 7,441 | 10,331 | 9,194 | 57,350 | 57,400 | 11,081 | 7,891 | 11,081 | 9,944 |
| 51,400 | 51,450 | 9,594 | 6,999 | 9,594 | 8,456 | 54,400 | 54,450 | 10,344 | 7,449 | 10,344 | 9,206 | 57,400 | 57,450 | 11,094 | 7,899 | 11,094 | 9,956 |
| 51,450 | 51,500 | 9,606 | 7,006 | 9,606 | 8,469 | 54,450 | 54,500 | 10,356 | 7,456 | 10,356 | 9,219 | 57,450 | 57,500 | 11,106 | 7,906 | 11,106 | 9,969 |
| 51,500 | 51,550 | 9,619 | 7,014 | 9,619 | 8,481 | 54,500 | 54,550 | 10,369 | 7,464 | 10,369 | 9,231 | 57,500 | 57,550 | 11,119 | 7,914 | 11,119 | 9,981 |
| 51,550 | 51,600 | 9,631 | 7,021 | 9,631 | 8,494 | 54,550 | 54,600 | 10,381 | 7,471 | 10,381 | 9,244 | 57,550 | 57,600 | 11,131 | 7,921 | 11,131 | 9,994 |
| 51,600 | 51,650 | 9,644 | 7,029 | 9,644 | 8,506 | 54,600 | 54,650 | 10,394 | 7,479 | 10,394 | 9,256 | 57,600 | 57,650 | 11,144 | 7,929 | 11,144 | 10,006 |
| 51,650 | 51,700 | 9,656 | 7,036 | 9,656 | 8,519 | 54,650 | 54,700 | 10,406 | 7,486 | 10,406 | 9,269 | 57,650 | 57,700 | 11,156 | 7,936 | 11,156 | 10,019 |
| 51,700 | 51,750 | 9,669 | 7,044 | 9,669 | 8,531 | 54,700 | 54,750 | 10,419 | 7,494 | 10,419 | 9,281 | 57,700 | 57,750 | 11,169 | 7,944 | 11,169 | 10,031 |
| 51,750 | 51,800 | 9,681 | 7,051 | 9,681 | 8,544 | 54,750 | 54,800 | 10,431 | 7,501 | 10,431 | 9,294 | 57,750 | 57,800 | 11,181 | 7,951 | 11,181 | 10,044 |
| 51,800 | 51,850 | 9,694 | 7,059 | 9,694 | 8,556 | 54,800 | 54,850 | 10,444 | 7,509 | 10,444 | 9,306 | 57,800 | 57,850 | 11,194 | 7,959 | 11,194 | 10,056 |
| 51,850 | 51,900 | 9,706 | 7,066 | 9,706 | 8,569 | 54,850 | 54,900 | 10,456 | 7,516 | 10,456 | 9,319 | 57,850 | 57,900 | 11,206 | 7,966 | 11,206 | 10,069 |
| 51,900 | 51,950 | 9,719 | 7,074 | 9,719 | 8,581 | 54,900 | 54,950 | 10,469 | 7,524 | 10,469 | 9,331 | 57,900 | 57,950 | 11,219 | 7,974 | 11,219 | 10,081 |
| 51,950 | 52,000 | 9,731 | 7,081 | 9,731 | 8,594 | 54,950 | 55,000 | 10,481 | 7,531 | 10,481 | 9,344 | 57,950 | 58,000 | 11,231 | 7,981 | 11,231 | 10,094 |
| **52,000** | | | | | | **55,000** | | | | | | **58,000** | | | | | |
| 52,000 | 52,050 | 9,744 | 7,089 | 9,744 | 8,606 | 55,000 | 55,050 | 10,494 | 7,539 | 10,494 | 9,356 | 58,000 | 58,050 | 11,244 | 7,989 | 11,244 | 10,106 |
| 52,050 | 52,100 | 9,756 | 7,096 | 9,756 | 8,619 | 55,050 | 55,100 | 10,506 | 7,546 | 10,506 | 9,369 | 58,050 | 58,100 | 11,256 | 7,996 | 11,256 | 10,119 |
| 52,100 | 52,150 | 9,769 | 7,104 | 9,769 | 8,631 | 55,100 | 55,150 | 10,519 | 7,554 | 10,519 | 9,381 | 58,100 | 58,150 | 11,269 | 8,006 | 11,269 | 10,131 |
| 52,150 | 52,200 | 9,781 | 7,111 | 9,781 | 8,644 | 55,150 | 55,200 | 10,531 | 7,561 | 10,531 | 9,394 | 58,150 | 58,200 | 11,281 | 8,019 | 11,281 | 10,144 |
| 52,200 | 52,250 | 9,794 | 7,119 | 9,794 | 8,656 | 55,200 | 55,250 | 10,544 | 7,569 | 10,544 | 9,406 | 58,200 | 58,250 | 11,294 | 8,031 | 11,294 | 10,156 |
| 52,250 | 52,300 | 9,806 | 7,126 | 9,806 | 8,669 | 55,250 | 55,300 | 10,556 | 7,576 | 10,556 | 9,419 | 58,250 | 58,300 | 11,306 | 8,044 | 11,306 | 10,169 |
| 52,300 | 52,350 | 9,819 | 7,134 | 9,819 | 8,681 | 55,300 | 55,350 | 10,569 | 7,584 | 10,569 | 9,431 | 58,300 | 58,350 | 11,319 | 8,056 | 11,319 | 10,181 |
| 52,350 | 52,400 | 9,831 | 7,141 | 9,831 | 8,694 | 55,350 | 55,400 | 10,581 | 7,591 | 10,581 | 9,444 | 58,350 | 58,400 | 11,331 | 8,069 | 11,331 | 10,194 |
| 52,400 | 52,450 | 9,844 | 7,149 | 9,844 | 8,706 | 55,400 | 55,450 | 10,594 | 7,599 | 10,594 | 9,456 | 58,400 | 58,450 | 11,344 | 8,081 | 11,344 | 10,206 |
| 52,450 | 52,500 | 9,856 | 7,156 | 9,856 | 8,719 | 55,450 | 55,500 | 10,606 | 7,606 | 10,606 | 9,469 | 58,450 | 58,500 | 11,356 | 8,094 | 11,356 | 10,219 |
| 52,500 | 52,550 | 9,869 | 7,164 | 9,869 | 8,731 | 55,500 | 55,550 | 10,619 | 7,614 | 10,619 | 9,481 | 58,500 | 58,550 | 11,369 | 8,106 | 11,369 | 10,231 |
| 52,550 | 52,600 | 9,881 | 7,171 | 9,881 | 8,744 | 55,550 | 55,600 | 10,631 | 7,621 | 10,631 | 9,494 | 58,550 | 58,600 | 11,381 | 8,119 | 11,381 | 10,244 |
| 52,600 | 52,650 | 9,894 | 7,179 | 9,894 | 8,756 | 55,600 | 55,650 | 10,644 | 7,629 | 10,644 | 9,506 | 58,600 | 58,650 | 11,394 | 8,131 | 11,394 | 10,256 |
| 52,650 | 52,700 | 9,906 | 7,186 | 9,906 | 8,769 | 55,650 | 55,700 | 10,656 | 7,636 | 10,656 | 9,519 | 58,650 | 58,700 | 11,406 | 8,144 | 11,408 | 10,269 |
| 52,700 | 52,750 | 9,919 | 7,194 | 9,919 | 8,781 | 55,700 | 55,750 | 10,669 | 7,644 | 10,669 | 9,531 | 58,700 | 58,750 | 11,419 | 8,156 | 11,422 | 10,281 |
| 52,750 | 52,800 | 9,931 | 7,201 | 9,931 | 8,794 | 55,750 | 55,800 | 10,681 | 7,651 | 10,681 | 9,544 | 58,750 | 58,800 | 11,431 | 8,169 | 11,436 | 10,294 |
| 52,800 | 52,850 | 9,944 | 7,209 | 9,944 | 8,806 | 55,800 | 55,850 | 10,694 | 7,659 | 10,694 | 9,556 | 58,800 | 58,850 | 11,444 | 8,181 | 11,450 | 10,306 |
| 52,850 | 52,900 | 9,956 | 7,216 | 9,956 | 8,819 | 55,850 | 55,900 | 10,706 | 7,666 | 10,706 | 9,569 | 58,850 | 58,900 | 11,456 | 8,194 | 11,464 | 10,319 |
| 52,900 | 52,950 | 9,969 | 7,224 | 9,969 | 8,831 | 55,900 | 55,950 | 10,719 | 7,674 | 10,719 | 9,581 | 58,900 | 58,950 | 11,469 | 8,206 | 11,478 | 10,331 |
| 52,950 | 53,000 | 9,981 | 7,231 | 9,981 | 8,844 | 55,950 | 56,000 | 10,731 | 7,681 | 10,731 | 9,594 | 58,950 | 59,000 | 11,481 | 8,219 | 11,492 | 10,344 |

* This column must also be used by a qualifying widow(er).

(Continued on next page)

## 2004 Tax Table—Continued

**59,000**

| If line 42 (taxable income) is— At least | But less than | And you are— Single | Married filing jointly * | Married filing separately | Head of a household |
|---|---|---|---|---|---|
| | | Your tax is— | | | |
| 59,000 | 59,050 | 11,494 | 8,231 | 11,506 | 10,356 |
| 59,050 | 59,100 | 11,506 | 8,244 | 11,520 | 10,369 |
| 59,100 | 59,150 | 11,519 | 8,256 | 11,534 | 10,381 |
| 59,150 | 59,200 | 11,531 | 8,269 | 11,548 | 10,394 |
| 59,200 | 59,250 | 11,544 | 8,281 | 11,562 | 10,406 |
| 59,250 | 59,300 | 11,556 | 8,294 | 11,576 | 10,419 |
| 59,300 | 59,350 | 11,569 | 8,306 | 11,590 | 10,431 |
| 59,350 | 59,400 | 11,581 | 8,319 | 11,604 | 10,444 |
| 59,400 | 59,450 | 11,594 | 8,331 | 11,618 | 10,456 |
| 59,450 | 59,500 | 11,606 | 8,344 | 11,632 | 10,469 |
| 59,500 | 59,550 | 11,619 | 8,356 | 11,646 | 10,481 |
| 59,550 | 59,600 | 11,631 | 8,369 | 11,660 | 10,494 |
| 59,600 | 59,650 | 11,644 | 8,381 | 11,674 | 10,506 |
| 59,650 | 59,700 | 11,656 | 8,394 | 11,688 | 10,519 |
| 59,700 | 59,750 | 11,669 | 8,406 | 11,702 | 10,531 |
| 59,750 | 59,800 | 11,681 | 8,419 | 11,716 | 10,544 |
| 59,800 | 59,850 | 11,694 | 8,431 | 11,730 | 10,556 |
| 59,850 | 59,900 | 11,706 | 8,444 | 11,744 | 10,569 |
| 59,900 | 59,950 | 11,719 | 8,456 | 11,758 | 10,581 |
| 59,950 | 60,000 | 11,731 | 8,469 | 11,772 | 10,594 |

**60,000**

| At least | But less than | Single | Married filing jointly * | Married filing separately | Head of a household |
|---|---|---|---|---|---|
| 60,000 | 60,050 | 11,744 | 8,481 | 11,786 | 10,606 |
| 60,050 | 60,100 | 11,756 | 8,494 | 11,800 | 10,619 |
| 60,100 | 60,150 | 11,769 | 8,506 | 11,814 | 10,631 |
| 60,150 | 60,200 | 11,781 | 8,519 | 11,828 | 10,644 |
| 60,200 | 60,250 | 11,794 | 8,531 | 11,842 | 10,656 |
| 60,250 | 60,300 | 11,806 | 8,544 | 11,856 | 10,669 |
| 60,300 | 60,350 | 11,819 | 8,556 | 11,870 | 10,681 |
| 60,350 | 60,400 | 11,831 | 8,569 | 11,884 | 10,694 |
| 60,400 | 60,450 | 11,844 | 8,581 | 11,898 | 10,706 |
| 60,450 | 60,500 | 11,856 | 8,594 | 11,912 | 10,719 |
| 60,500 | 60,550 | 11,869 | 8,606 | 11,926 | 10,731 |
| 60,550 | 60,600 | 11,881 | 8,619 | 11,940 | 10,744 |
| 60,600 | 60,650 | 11,894 | 8,631 | 11,954 | 10,756 |
| 60,650 | 60,700 | 11,906 | 8,644 | 11,968 | 10,769 |
| 60,700 | 60,750 | 11,919 | 8,656 | 11,982 | 10,781 |
| 60,750 | 60,800 | 11,931 | 8,669 | 11,996 | 10,794 |
| 60,800 | 60,850 | 11,944 | 8,681 | 12,010 | 10,806 |
| 60,850 | 60,900 | 11,956 | 8,694 | 12,024 | 10,819 |
| 60,900 | 60,950 | 11,969 | 8,706 | 12,038 | 10,831 |
| 60,950 | 61,000 | 11,981 | 8,719 | 12,052 | 10,844 |

**61,000**

| At least | But less than | Single | Married filing jointly * | Married filing separately | Head of a household |
|---|---|---|---|---|---|
| 61,000 | 61,050 | 11,994 | 8,731 | 12,066 | 10,856 |
| 61,050 | 61,100 | 12,006 | 8,744 | 12,080 | 10,869 |
| 61,100 | 61,150 | 12,019 | 8,756 | 12,094 | 10,881 |
| 61,150 | 61,200 | 12,031 | 8,769 | 12,108 | 10,894 |
| 61,200 | 61,250 | 12,044 | 8,781 | 12,122 | 10,906 |
| 61,250 | 61,300 | 12,056 | 8,794 | 12,136 | 10,919 |
| 61,300 | 61,350 | 12,069 | 8,806 | 12,150 | 10,931 |
| 61,350 | 61,400 | 12,081 | 8,819 | 12,164 | 10,944 |
| 61,400 | 61,450 | 12,094 | 8,831 | 12,178 | 10,956 |
| 61,450 | 61,500 | 12,106 | 8,844 | 12,192 | 10,969 |
| 61,500 | 61,550 | 12,119 | 8,856 | 12,206 | 10,981 |
| 61,550 | 61,600 | 12,131 | 8,869 | 12,220 | 10,994 |
| 61,600 | 61,650 | 12,144 | 8,881 | 12,234 | 11,006 |
| 61,650 | 61,700 | 12,156 | 8,894 | 12,248 | 11,019 |
| 61,700 | 61,750 | 12,169 | 8,906 | 12,262 | 11,031 |
| 61,750 | 61,800 | 12,181 | 8,919 | 12,276 | 11,044 |
| 61,800 | 61,850 | 12,194 | 8,931 | 12,290 | 11,056 |
| 61,850 | 61,900 | 12,206 | 8,944 | 12,304 | 11,069 |
| 61,900 | 61,950 | 12,219 | 8,956 | 12,318 | 11,081 |
| 61,950 | 62,000 | 12,231 | 8,969 | 12,332 | 11,094 |

**62,000**

| If line 42 (taxable income) is— At least | But less than | And you are— Single | Married filing jointly * | Married filing separately | Head of a household |
|---|---|---|---|---|---|
| | | Your tax is— | | | |
| 62,000 | 62,050 | 12,244 | 8,981 | 12,346 | 11,106 |
| 62,050 | 62,100 | 12,256 | 8,994 | 12,360 | 11,119 |
| 62,100 | 62,150 | 12,269 | 9,006 | 12,374 | 11,131 |
| 62,150 | 62,200 | 12,281 | 9,019 | 12,388 | 11,144 |
| 62,200 | 62,250 | 12,294 | 9,031 | 12,402 | 11,156 |
| 62,250 | 62,300 | 12,306 | 9,044 | 12,416 | 11,169 |
| 62,300 | 62,350 | 12,319 | 9,056 | 12,430 | 11,181 |
| 62,350 | 62,400 | 12,331 | 9,069 | 12,444 | 11,194 |
| 62,400 | 62,450 | 12,344 | 9,081 | 12,458 | 11,206 |
| 62,450 | 62,500 | 12,356 | 9,094 | 12,472 | 11,219 |
| 62,500 | 62,550 | 12,369 | 9,106 | 12,486 | 11,231 |
| 62,550 | 62,600 | 12,381 | 9,119 | 12,500 | 11,244 |
| 62,600 | 62,650 | 12,394 | 9,131 | 12,514 | 11,256 |
| 62,650 | 62,700 | 12,406 | 9,144 | 12,528 | 11,269 |
| 62,700 | 62,750 | 12,419 | 9,156 | 12,542 | 11,281 |
| 62,750 | 62,800 | 12,431 | 9,169 | 12,556 | 11,294 |
| 62,800 | 62,850 | 12,444 | 9,181 | 12,570 | 11,306 |
| 62,850 | 62,900 | 12,456 | 9,194 | 12,584 | 11,319 |
| 62,900 | 62,950 | 12,469 | 9,206 | 12,598 | 11,331 |
| 62,950 | 63,000 | 12,481 | 9,219 | 12,612 | 11,344 |

**63,000**

| At least | But less than | Single | Married filing jointly * | Married filing separately | Head of a household |
|---|---|---|---|---|---|
| 63,000 | 63,050 | 12,494 | 9,231 | 12,626 | 11,356 |
| 63,050 | 63,100 | 12,506 | 9,244 | 12,640 | 11,369 |
| 63,100 | 63,150 | 12,519 | 9,256 | 12,654 | 11,381 |
| 63,150 | 63,200 | 12,531 | 9,269 | 12,668 | 11,394 |
| 63,200 | 63,250 | 12,544 | 9,281 | 12,682 | 11,406 |
| 63,250 | 63,300 | 12,556 | 9,294 | 12,696 | 11,419 |
| 63,300 | 63,350 | 12,569 | 9,306 | 12,710 | 11,431 |
| 63,350 | 63,400 | 12,581 | 9,319 | 12,724 | 11,444 |
| 63,400 | 63,450 | 12,594 | 9,331 | 12,738 | 11,456 |
| 63,450 | 63,500 | 12,606 | 9,344 | 12,752 | 11,469 |
| 63,500 | 63,550 | 12,619 | 9,356 | 12,766 | 11,481 |
| 63,550 | 63,600 | 12,631 | 9,369 | 12,780 | 11,494 |
| 63,600 | 63,650 | 12,644 | 9,381 | 12,794 | 11,506 |
| 63,650 | 63,700 | 12,656 | 9,394 | 12,808 | 11,519 |
| 63,700 | 63,750 | 12,669 | 9,406 | 12,822 | 11,531 |
| 63,750 | 63,800 | 12,681 | 9,419 | 12,836 | 11,544 |
| 63,800 | 63,850 | 12,694 | 9,431 | 12,850 | 11,556 |
| 63,850 | 63,900 | 12,706 | 9,444 | 12,864 | 11,569 |
| 63,900 | 63,950 | 12,719 | 9,456 | 12,878 | 11,581 |
| 63,950 | 64,000 | 12,731 | 9,469 | 12,892 | 11,594 |

**64,000**

| At least | But less than | Single | Married filing jointly * | Married filing separately | Head of a household |
|---|---|---|---|---|---|
| 64,000 | 64,050 | 12,744 | 9,481 | 12,906 | 11,606 |
| 64,050 | 64,100 | 12,756 | 9,494 | 12,920 | 11,619 |
| 64,100 | 64,150 | 12,769 | 9,506 | 12,934 | 11,631 |
| 64,150 | 64,200 | 12,781 | 9,519 | 12,948 | 11,644 |
| 64,200 | 64,250 | 12,794 | 9,531 | 12,962 | 11,656 |
| 64,250 | 64,300 | 12,806 | 9,544 | 12,976 | 11,669 |
| 64,300 | 64,350 | 12,819 | 9,556 | 12,990 | 11,681 |
| 64,350 | 64,400 | 12,831 | 9,569 | 13,004 | 11,694 |
| 64,400 | 64,450 | 12,844 | 9,581 | 13,018 | 11,706 |
| 64,450 | 64,500 | 12,856 | 9,594 | 13,032 | 11,719 |
| 64,500 | 64,550 | 12,869 | 9,606 | 13,046 | 11,731 |
| 64,550 | 64,600 | 12,881 | 9,619 | 13,060 | 11,744 |
| 64,600 | 64,650 | 12,894 | 9,631 | 13,074 | 11,756 |
| 64,650 | 64,700 | 12,906 | 9,644 | 13,088 | 11,769 |
| 64,700 | 64,750 | 12,919 | 9,656 | 13,102 | 11,781 |
| 64,750 | 64,800 | 12,931 | 9,669 | 13,116 | 11,794 |
| 64,800 | 64,850 | 12,944 | 9,681 | 13,130 | 11,806 |
| 64,850 | 64,900 | 12,956 | 9,694 | 13,144 | 11,819 |
| 64,900 | 64,950 | 12,969 | 9,706 | 13,158 | 11,831 |
| 64,950 | 65,000 | 12,981 | 9,719 | 13,172 | 11,844 |

**65,000**

| If line 42 (taxable income) is— At least | But less than | And you are— Single | Married filing jointly * | Married filing separately | Head of a household |
|---|---|---|---|---|---|
| | | Your tax is— | | | |
| 65,000 | 65,050 | 12,994 | 9,731 | 13,186 | 11,856 |
| 65,050 | 65,100 | 13,006 | 9,744 | 13,200 | 11,869 |
| 65,100 | 65,150 | 13,019 | 9,756 | 13,214 | 11,881 |
| 65,150 | 65,200 | 13,031 | 9,769 | 13,228 | 11,894 |
| 65,200 | 65,250 | 13,044 | 9,781 | 13,242 | 11,906 |
| 65,250 | 65,300 | 13,056 | 9,794 | 13,256 | 11,919 |
| 65,300 | 65,350 | 13,069 | 9,806 | 13,270 | 11,931 |
| 65,350 | 65,400 | 13,081 | 9,819 | 13,284 | 11,944 |
| 65,400 | 65,450 | 13,094 | 9,831 | 13,298 | 11,956 |
| 65,450 | 65,500 | 13,106 | 9,844 | 13,312 | 11,969 |
| 65,500 | 65,550 | 13,119 | 9,856 | 13,326 | 11,981 |
| 65,550 | 65,600 | 13,131 | 9,869 | 13,340 | 11,994 |
| 65,600 | 65,650 | 13,144 | 9,881 | 13,354 | 12,006 |
| 65,650 | 65,700 | 13,156 | 9,894 | 13,368 | 12,019 |
| 65,700 | 65,750 | 13,169 | 9,906 | 13,382 | 12,031 |
| 65,750 | 65,800 | 13,181 | 9,919 | 13,396 | 12,044 |
| 65,800 | 65,850 | 13,194 | 9,931 | 13,410 | 12,056 |
| 65,850 | 65,900 | 13,206 | 9,944 | 13,424 | 12,069 |
| 65,900 | 65,950 | 13,219 | 9,956 | 13,438 | 12,081 |
| 65,950 | 66,000 | 13,231 | 9,969 | 13,452 | 12,094 |

**66,000**

| At least | But less than | Single | Married filing jointly * | Married filing separately | Head of a household |
|---|---|---|---|---|---|
| 66,000 | 66,050 | 13,244 | 9,981 | 13,466 | 12,106 |
| 66,050 | 66,100 | 13,256 | 9,994 | 13,480 | 12,119 |
| 66,100 | 66,150 | 13,269 | 10,006 | 13,494 | 12,131 |
| 66,150 | 66,200 | 13,281 | 10,019 | 13,508 | 12,144 |
| 66,200 | 66,250 | 13,294 | 10,031 | 13,522 | 12,156 |
| 66,250 | 66,300 | 13,306 | 10,044 | 13,536 | 12,169 |
| 66,300 | 66,350 | 13,319 | 10,056 | 13,550 | 12,181 |
| 66,350 | 66,400 | 13,331 | 10,069 | 13,564 | 12,194 |
| 66,400 | 66,450 | 13,344 | 10,081 | 13,578 | 12,206 |
| 66,450 | 66,500 | 13,356 | 10,094 | 13,592 | 12,219 |
| 66,500 | 66,550 | 13,369 | 10,106 | 13,606 | 12,231 |
| 66,550 | 66,600 | 13,381 | 10,119 | 13,620 | 12,244 |
| 66,600 | 66,650 | 13,394 | 10,131 | 13,634 | 12,256 |
| 66,650 | 66,700 | 13,406 | 10,144 | 13,648 | 12,269 |
| 66,700 | 66,750 | 13,419 | 10,156 | 13,662 | 12,281 |
| 66,750 | 66,800 | 13,431 | 10,169 | 13,676 | 12,294 |
| 66,800 | 66,850 | 13,444 | 10,181 | 13,690 | 12,306 |
| 66,850 | 66,900 | 13,456 | 10,194 | 13,704 | 12,319 |
| 66,900 | 66,950 | 13,469 | 10,206 | 13,718 | 12,331 |
| 66,950 | 67,000 | 13,481 | 10,219 | 13,732 | 12,344 |

**67,000**

| At least | But less than | Single | Married filing jointly * | Married filing separately | Head of a household |
|---|---|---|---|---|---|
| 67,000 | 67,050 | 13,494 | 10,231 | 13,746 | 12,356 |
| 67,050 | 67,100 | 13,506 | 10,244 | 13,760 | 12,369 |
| 67,100 | 67,150 | 13,519 | 10,256 | 13,774 | 12,381 |
| 67,150 | 67,200 | 13,531 | 10,269 | 13,788 | 12,394 |
| 67,200 | 67,250 | 13,544 | 10,281 | 13,802 | 12,406 |
| 67,250 | 67,300 | 13,556 | 10,294 | 13,816 | 12,419 |
| 67,300 | 67,350 | 13,569 | 10,306 | 13,830 | 12,431 |
| 67,350 | 67,400 | 13,581 | 10,319 | 13,844 | 12,444 |
| 67,400 | 67,450 | 13,594 | 10,331 | 13,858 | 12,456 |
| 67,450 | 67,500 | 13,606 | 10,344 | 13,872 | 12,469 |
| 67,500 | 67,550 | 13,619 | 10,356 | 13,886 | 12,481 |
| 67,550 | 67,600 | 13,631 | 10,369 | 13,900 | 12,494 |
| 67,600 | 67,650 | 13,644 | 10,381 | 13,914 | 12,506 |
| 67,650 | 67,700 | 13,656 | 10,394 | 13,928 | 12,519 |
| 67,700 | 67,750 | 13,669 | 10,406 | 13,942 | 12,531 |
| 67,750 | 67,800 | 13,681 | 10,419 | 13,956 | 12,544 |
| 67,800 | 67,850 | 13,694 | 10,431 | 13,970 | 12,556 |
| 67,850 | 67,900 | 13,706 | 10,444 | 13,984 | 12,569 |
| 67,900 | 67,950 | 13,719 | 10,456 | 13,998 | 12,581 |
| 67,950 | 68,000 | 13,731 | 10,469 | 14,012 | 12,594 |

* This column must also be used by a qualifying widow(er).

(Continued on next page)

**2004 Tax Table**—*Continued*

| If line 42 (taxable income) is— At least | But less than | Single | Married filing jointly * | Married filing separately | Head of a household |
|---|---|---|---|---|---|
| **68,000** | | | | | |
| 68,000 | 68,050 | 13,744 | 10,481 | 14,026 | 12,606 |
| 68,050 | 68,100 | 13,756 | 10,494 | 14,040 | 12,619 |
| 68,100 | 68,150 | 13,769 | 10,506 | 14,054 | 12,631 |
| 68,150 | 68,200 | 13,781 | 10,519 | 14,068 | 12,644 |
| 68,200 | 68,250 | 13,794 | 10,531 | 14,082 | 12,656 |
| 68,250 | 68,300 | 13,806 | 10,544 | 14,096 | 12,669 |
| 68,300 | 68,350 | 13,819 | 10,556 | 14,110 | 12,681 |
| 68,350 | 68,400 | 13,831 | 10,569 | 14,124 | 12,694 |
| 68,400 | 68,450 | 13,844 | 10,581 | 14,138 | 12,706 |
| 68,450 | 68,500 | 13,856 | 10,594 | 14,152 | 12,719 |
| 68,500 | 68,550 | 13,869 | 10,606 | 14,166 | 12,731 |
| 68,550 | 68,600 | 13,881 | 10,619 | 14,180 | 12,744 |
| 68,600 | 68,650 | 13,894 | 10,631 | 14,194 | 12,756 |
| 68,650 | 68,700 | 13,906 | 10,644 | 14,208 | 12,769 |
| 68,700 | 68,750 | 13,919 | 10,656 | 14,222 | 12,781 |
| 68,750 | 68,800 | 13,931 | 10,669 | 14,236 | 12,794 |
| 68,800 | 68,850 | 13,944 | 10,681 | 14,250 | 12,806 |
| 68,850 | 68,900 | 13,956 | 10,694 | 14,264 | 12,819 |
| 68,900 | 68,950 | 13,969 | 10,706 | 14,278 | 12,831 |
| 68,950 | 69,000 | 13,981 | 10,719 | 14,292 | 12,844 |
| **69,000** | | | | | |
| 69,000 | 69,050 | 13,994 | 10,731 | 14,306 | 12,856 |
| 69,050 | 69,100 | 14,006 | 10,744 | 14,320 | 12,869 |
| 69,100 | 69,150 | 14,019 | 10,756 | 14,334 | 12,881 |
| 69,150 | 69,200 | 14,031 | 10,769 | 14,348 | 12,894 |
| 69,200 | 69,250 | 14,044 | 10,781 | 14,362 | 12,906 |
| 69,250 | 69,300 | 14,056 | 10,794 | 14,376 | 12,919 |
| 69,300 | 69,350 | 14,069 | 10,806 | 14,390 | 12,931 |
| 69,350 | 69,400 | 14,081 | 10,819 | 14,404 | 12,944 |
| 69,400 | 69,450 | 14,094 | 10,831 | 14,418 | 12,956 |
| 69,450 | 69,500 | 14,106 | 10,844 | 14,432 | 12,969 |
| 69,500 | 69,550 | 14,119 | 10,856 | 14,446 | 12,981 |
| 69,550 | 69,600 | 14,131 | 10,869 | 14,460 | 12,994 |
| 69,600 | 69,650 | 14,144 | 10,881 | 14,474 | 13,006 |
| 69,650 | 69,700 | 14,156 | 10,894 | 14,488 | 13,019 |
| 69,700 | 69,750 | 14,169 | 10,906 | 14,502 | 13,031 |
| 69,750 | 69,800 | 14,181 | 10,919 | 14,516 | 13,044 |
| 69,800 | 69,850 | 14,194 | 10,931 | 14,530 | 13,056 |
| 69,850 | 69,900 | 14,206 | 10,944 | 14,544 | 13,069 |
| 69,900 | 69,950 | 14,219 | 10,956 | 14,558 | 13,081 |
| 69,950 | 70,000 | 14,231 | 10,969 | 14,572 | 13,094 |
| **70,000** | | | | | |
| 70,000 | 70,050 | 14,244 | 10,981 | 14,586 | 13,106 |
| 70,050 | 70,100 | 14,256 | 10,994 | 14,600 | 13,119 |
| 70,100 | 70,150 | 14,269 | 11,006 | 14,614 | 13,131 |
| 70,150 | 70,200 | 14,281 | 11,019 | 14,628 | 13,144 |
| 70,200 | 70,250 | 14,294 | 11,031 | 14,642 | 13,156 |
| 70,250 | 70,300 | 14,306 | 11,044 | 14,656 | 13,169 |
| 70,300 | 70,350 | 14,319 | 11,056 | 14,670 | 13,181 |
| 70,350 | 70,400 | 14,332 | 11,069 | 14,684 | 13,194 |
| 70,400 | 70,450 | 14,346 | 11,081 | 14,698 | 13,206 |
| 70,450 | 70,500 | 14,360 | 11,094 | 14,712 | 13,219 |
| 70,500 | 70,550 | 14,374 | 11,106 | 14,726 | 13,231 |
| 70,550 | 70,600 | 14,388 | 11,119 | 14,740 | 13,244 |
| 70,600 | 70,650 | 14,402 | 11,131 | 14,754 | 13,256 |
| 70,650 | 70,700 | 14,416 | 11,144 | 14,768 | 13,269 |
| 70,700 | 70,750 | 14,430 | 11,156 | 14,782 | 13,281 |
| 70,750 | 70,800 | 14,444 | 11,169 | 14,796 | 13,294 |
| 70,800 | 70,850 | 14,458 | 11,181 | 14,810 | 13,306 |
| 70,850 | 70,900 | 14,472 | 11,194 | 14,824 | 13,319 |
| 70,900 | 70,950 | 14,486 | 11,206 | 14,838 | 13,331 |
| 70,950 | 71,000 | 14,500 | 11,219 | 14,852 | 13,344 |

| If line 42 (taxable income) is— At least | But less than | Single | Married filing jointly * | Married filing separately | Head of a household |
|---|---|---|---|---|---|
| **71,000** | | | | | |
| 71,000 | 71,050 | 14,514 | 11,231 | 14,866 | 13,356 |
| 71,050 | 71,100 | 14,528 | 11,244 | 14,880 | 13,369 |
| 71,100 | 71,150 | 14,542 | 11,256 | 14,894 | 13,381 |
| 71,150 | 71,200 | 14,556 | 11,269 | 14,908 | 13,394 |
| 71,200 | 71,250 | 14,570 | 11,281 | 14,922 | 13,406 |
| 71,250 | 71,300 | 14,584 | 11,294 | 14,936 | 13,419 |
| 71,300 | 71,350 | 14,598 | 11,306 | 14,950 | 13,431 |
| 71,350 | 71,400 | 14,612 | 11,319 | 14,964 | 13,444 |
| 71,400 | 71,450 | 14,626 | 11,331 | 14,978 | 13,456 |
| 71,450 | 71,500 | 14,640 | 11,344 | 14,992 | 13,469 |
| 71,500 | 71,550 | 14,654 | 11,356 | 15,006 | 13,481 |
| 71,550 | 71,600 | 14,668 | 11,369 | 15,020 | 13,494 |
| 71,600 | 71,650 | 14,682 | 11,381 | 15,034 | 13,506 |
| 71,650 | 71,700 | 14,696 | 11,394 | 15,048 | 13,519 |
| 71,700 | 71,750 | 14,710 | 11,406 | 15,062 | 13,531 |
| 71,750 | 71,800 | 14,724 | 11,419 | 15,076 | 13,544 |
| 71,800 | 71,850 | 14,738 | 11,431 | 15,090 | 13,556 |
| 71,850 | 71,900 | 14,752 | 11,444 | 15,104 | 13,569 |
| 71,900 | 71,950 | 14,766 | 11,456 | 15,118 | 13,581 |
| 71,950 | 72,000 | 14,780 | 11,469 | 15,132 | 13,594 |
| **72,000** | | | | | |
| 72,000 | 72,050 | 14,794 | 11,481 | 15,146 | 13,606 |
| 72,050 | 72,100 | 14,808 | 11,494 | 15,160 | 13,619 |
| 72,100 | 72,150 | 14,822 | 11,506 | 15,174 | 13,631 |
| 72,150 | 72,200 | 14,836 | 11,519 | 15,188 | 13,644 |
| 72,200 | 72,250 | 14,850 | 11,531 | 15,202 | 13,656 |
| 72,250 | 72,300 | 14,864 | 11,544 | 15,216 | 13,669 |
| 72,300 | 72,350 | 14,878 | 11,556 | 15,230 | 13,681 |
| 72,350 | 72,400 | 14,892 | 11,569 | 15,244 | 13,694 |
| 72,400 | 72,450 | 14,906 | 11,581 | 15,258 | 13,706 |
| 72,450 | 72,500 | 14,920 | 11,594 | 15,272 | 13,719 |
| 72,500 | 72,550 | 14,934 | 11,606 | 15,286 | 13,731 |
| 72,550 | 72,600 | 14,948 | 11,619 | 15,300 | 13,744 |
| 72,600 | 72,650 | 14,962 | 11,631 | 15,314 | 13,756 |
| 72,650 | 72,700 | 14,976 | 11,644 | 15,328 | 13,769 |
| 72,700 | 72,750 | 14,990 | 11,656 | 15,342 | 13,781 |
| 72,750 | 72,800 | 15,004 | 11,669 | 15,356 | 13,794 |
| 72,800 | 72,850 | 15,018 | 11,681 | 15,370 | 13,806 |
| 72,850 | 72,900 | 15,032 | 11,694 | 15,384 | 13,819 |
| 72,900 | 72,950 | 15,046 | 11,706 | 15,398 | 13,831 |
| 72,950 | 73,000 | 15,060 | 11,719 | 15,412 | 13,844 |
| **73,000** | | | | | |
| 73,000 | 73,050 | 15,074 | 11,731 | 15,426 | 13,856 |
| 73,050 | 73,100 | 15,088 | 11,744 | 15,440 | 13,869 |
| 73,100 | 73,150 | 15,102 | 11,756 | 15,454 | 13,881 |
| 73,150 | 73,200 | 15,116 | 11,769 | 15,468 | 13,894 |
| 73,200 | 73,250 | 15,130 | 11,781 | 15,482 | 13,906 |
| 73,250 | 73,300 | 15,144 | 11,794 | 15,496 | 13,919 |
| 73,300 | 73,350 | 15,158 | 11,806 | 15,510 | 13,931 |
| 73,350 | 73,400 | 15,172 | 11,819 | 15,524 | 13,944 |
| 73,400 | 73,450 | 15,186 | 11,831 | 15,538 | 13,956 |
| 73,450 | 73,500 | 15,200 | 11,844 | 15,552 | 13,969 |
| 73,500 | 73,550 | 15,214 | 11,856 | 15,566 | 13,981 |
| 73,550 | 73,600 | 15,228 | 11,869 | 15,580 | 13,994 |
| 73,600 | 73,650 | 15,242 | 11,881 | 15,594 | 14,006 |
| 73,650 | 73,700 | 15,256 | 11,894 | 15,608 | 14,019 |
| 73,700 | 73,750 | 15,270 | 11,906 | 15,622 | 14,031 |
| 73,750 | 73,800 | 15,284 | 11,919 | 15,636 | 14,044 |
| 73,800 | 73,850 | 15,298 | 11,931 | 15,650 | 14,056 |
| 73,850 | 73,900 | 15,312 | 11,944 | 15,664 | 14,069 |
| 73,900 | 73,950 | 15,326 | 11,956 | 15,678 | 14,081 |
| 73,950 | 74,000 | 15,340 | 11,969 | 15,692 | 14,094 |

| If line 42 (taxable income) is— At least | But less than | Single | Married filing jointly * | Married filing separately | Head of a household |
|---|---|---|---|---|---|
| **74,000** | | | | | |
| 74,000 | 74,050 | 15,354 | 11,981 | 15,706 | 14,106 |
| 74,050 | 74,100 | 15,368 | 11,994 | 15,720 | 14,119 |
| 74,100 | 74,150 | 15,382 | 12,006 | 15,734 | 14,131 |
| 74,150 | 74,200 | 15,396 | 12,019 | 15,748 | 14,144 |
| 74,200 | 74,250 | 15,410 | 12,031 | 15,762 | 14,156 |
| 74,250 | 74,300 | 15,424 | 12,044 | 15,776 | 14,169 |
| 74,300 | 74,350 | 15,438 | 12,056 | 15,790 | 14,181 |
| 74,350 | 74,400 | 15,452 | 12,069 | 15,804 | 14,194 |
| 74,400 | 74,450 | 15,466 | 12,081 | 15,818 | 14,206 |
| 74,450 | 74,500 | 15,480 | 12,094 | 15,832 | 14,219 |
| 74,500 | 74,550 | 15,494 | 12,106 | 15,846 | 14,231 |
| 74,550 | 74,600 | 15,508 | 12,119 | 15,860 | 14,244 |
| 74,600 | 74,650 | 15,522 | 12,131 | 15,874 | 14,256 |
| 74,650 | 74,700 | 15,536 | 12,144 | 15,888 | 14,269 |
| 74,700 | 74,750 | 15,550 | 12,156 | 15,902 | 14,281 |
| 74,750 | 74,800 | 15,564 | 12,169 | 15,916 | 14,294 |
| 74,800 | 74,850 | 15,578 | 12,181 | 15,930 | 14,306 |
| 74,850 | 74,900 | 15,592 | 12,194 | 15,944 | 14,319 |
| 74,900 | 74,950 | 15,606 | 12,206 | 15,958 | 14,331 |
| 74,950 | 75,000 | 15,620 | 12,219 | 15,972 | 14,344 |
| **75,000** | | | | | |
| 75,000 | 75,050 | 15,634 | 12,231 | 15,986 | 14,356 |
| 75,050 | 75,100 | 15,648 | 12,244 | 16,000 | 14,369 |
| 75,100 | 75,150 | 15,662 | 12,256 | 16,014 | 14,381 |
| 75,150 | 75,200 | 15,676 | 12,269 | 16,028 | 14,394 |
| 75,200 | 75,250 | 15,690 | 12,281 | 16,042 | 14,406 |
| 75,250 | 75,300 | 15,704 | 12,294 | 16,056 | 14,419 |
| 75,300 | 75,350 | 15,718 | 12,306 | 16,070 | 14,431 |
| 75,350 | 75,400 | 15,732 | 12,319 | 16,084 | 14,444 |
| 75,400 | 75,450 | 15,746 | 12,331 | 16,098 | 14,456 |
| 75,450 | 75,500 | 15,760 | 12,344 | 16,112 | 14,469 |
| 75,500 | 75,550 | 15,774 | 12,356 | 16,126 | 14,481 |
| 75,550 | 75,600 | 15,788 | 12,369 | 16,140 | 14,494 |
| 75,600 | 75,650 | 15,802 | 12,381 | 16,154 | 14,506 |
| 75,650 | 75,700 | 15,816 | 12,394 | 16,168 | 14,519 |
| 75,700 | 75,750 | 15,830 | 12,406 | 16,182 | 14,531 |
| 75,750 | 75,800 | 15,844 | 12,419 | 16,196 | 14,544 |
| 75,800 | 75,850 | 15,858 | 12,431 | 16,210 | 14,556 |
| 75,850 | 75,900 | 15,872 | 12,444 | 16,224 | 14,569 |
| 75,900 | 75,950 | 15,886 | 12,456 | 16,238 | 14,581 |
| 75,950 | 76,000 | 15,900 | 12,469 | 16,252 | 14,594 |
| **76,000** | | | | | |
| 76,000 | 76,050 | 15,914 | 12,481 | 16,266 | 14,606 |
| 76,050 | 76,100 | 15,928 | 12,494 | 16,280 | 14,619 |
| 76,100 | 76,150 | 15,942 | 12,506 | 16,294 | 14,631 |
| 76,150 | 76,200 | 15,956 | 12,519 | 16,308 | 14,644 |
| 76,200 | 76,250 | 15,970 | 12,531 | 16,322 | 14,656 |
| 76,250 | 76,300 | 15,984 | 12,544 | 16,336 | 14,669 |
| 76,300 | 76,350 | 15,998 | 12,556 | 16,350 | 14,681 |
| 76,350 | 76,400 | 16,012 | 12,569 | 16,364 | 14,694 |
| 76,400 | 76,450 | 16,026 | 12,581 | 16,378 | 14,706 |
| 76,450 | 76,500 | 16,040 | 12,594 | 16,392 | 14,719 |
| 76,500 | 76,550 | 16,054 | 12,606 | 16,406 | 14,731 |
| 76,550 | 76,600 | 16,068 | 12,619 | 16,420 | 14,744 |
| 76,600 | 76,650 | 16,082 | 12,631 | 16,434 | 14,756 |
| 76,650 | 76,700 | 16,096 | 12,644 | 16,448 | 14,769 |
| 76,700 | 76,750 | 16,110 | 12,656 | 16,462 | 14,781 |
| 76,750 | 76,800 | 16,124 | 12,669 | 16,476 | 14,794 |
| 76,800 | 76,850 | 16,138 | 12,681 | 16,490 | 14,806 |
| 76,850 | 76,900 | 16,152 | 12,694 | 16,504 | 14,819 |
| 76,900 | 76,950 | 16,166 | 12,706 | 16,518 | 14,831 |
| 76,950 | 77,000 | 16,180 | 12,719 | 16,532 | 14,844 |

* This column must also be used by a qualifying widow(er).

(Continued on next page)

## 2004 Tax Table—*Continued*

### 77,000 / 78,000 / 79,000

| At least | But less than | Single | Married filing jointly * | Married filing separately | Head of a household |
|---|---|---|---|---|---|
| **77,000** | | | | | |
| 77,000 | 77,050 | 16,194 | 12,731 | 16,546 | 14,856 |
| 77,050 | 77,100 | 16,208 | 12,744 | 16,560 | 14,869 |
| 77,100 | 77,150 | 16,222 | 12,756 | 16,574 | 14,881 |
| 77,150 | 77,200 | 16,236 | 12,769 | 16,588 | 14,894 |
| 77,200 | 77,250 | 16,250 | 12,781 | 16,602 | 14,906 |
| 77,250 | 77,300 | 16,264 | 12,794 | 16,616 | 14,919 |
| 77,300 | 77,350 | 16,278 | 12,806 | 16,630 | 14,931 |
| 77,350 | 77,400 | 16,292 | 12,819 | 16,644 | 14,944 |
| 77,400 | 77,450 | 16,306 | 12,831 | 16,658 | 14,956 |
| 77,450 | 77,500 | 16,320 | 12,844 | 16,672 | 14,969 |
| 77,500 | 77,550 | 16,334 | 12,856 | 16,686 | 14,981 |
| 77,550 | 77,600 | 16,348 | 12,869 | 16,700 | 14,994 |
| 77,600 | 77,650 | 16,362 | 12,881 | 16,714 | 15,006 |
| 77,650 | 77,700 | 16,376 | 12,894 | 16,728 | 15,019 |
| 77,700 | 77,750 | 16,390 | 12,906 | 16,742 | 15,031 |
| 77,750 | 77,800 | 16,404 | 12,919 | 16,756 | 15,044 |
| 77,800 | 77,850 | 16,418 | 12,931 | 16,770 | 15,056 |
| 77,850 | 77,900 | 16,432 | 12,944 | 16,784 | 15,069 |
| 77,900 | 77,950 | 16,446 | 12,956 | 16,798 | 15,081 |
| 77,950 | 78,000 | 16,460 | 12,969 | 16,812 | 15,094 |
| **78,000** | | | | | |
| 78,000 | 78,050 | 16,474 | 12,981 | 16,826 | 15,106 |
| 78,050 | 78,100 | 16,488 | 12,994 | 16,840 | 15,119 |
| 78,100 | 78,150 | 16,502 | 13,006 | 16,854 | 15,131 |
| 78,150 | 78,200 | 16,516 | 13,019 | 16,868 | 15,144 |
| 78,200 | 78,250 | 16,530 | 13,031 | 16,882 | 15,156 |
| 78,250 | 78,300 | 16,544 | 13,044 | 16,896 | 15,169 |
| 78,300 | 78,350 | 16,558 | 13,056 | 16,910 | 15,181 |
| 78,350 | 78,400 | 16,572 | 13,069 | 16,924 | 15,194 |
| 78,400 | 78,450 | 16,586 | 13,081 | 16,938 | 15,206 |
| 78,450 | 78,500 | 16,600 | 13,094 | 16,952 | 15,219 |
| 78,500 | 78,550 | 16,614 | 13,106 | 16,966 | 15,231 |
| 78,550 | 78,600 | 16,628 | 13,119 | 16,980 | 15,244 |
| 78,600 | 78,650 | 16,642 | 13,131 | 16,994 | 15,256 |
| 78,650 | 78,700 | 16,656 | 13,144 | 17,008 | 15,269 |
| 78,700 | 78,750 | 16,670 | 13,156 | 17,022 | 15,281 |
| 78,750 | 78,800 | 16,684 | 13,169 | 17,036 | 15,294 |
| 78,800 | 78,850 | 16,698 | 13,181 | 17,050 | 15,306 |
| 78,850 | 78,900 | 16,712 | 13,194 | 17,064 | 15,319 |
| 78,900 | 78,950 | 16,726 | 13,206 | 17,078 | 15,331 |
| 78,950 | 79,000 | 16,740 | 13,219 | 17,092 | 15,344 |
| **79,000** | | | | | |
| 79,000 | 79,050 | 16,754 | 13,231 | 17,106 | 15,356 |
| 79,050 | 79,100 | 16,768 | 13,244 | 17,120 | 15,369 |
| 79,100 | 79,150 | 16,782 | 13,256 | 17,134 | 15,381 |
| 79,150 | 79,200 | 16,796 | 13,269 | 17,148 | 15,394 |
| 79,200 | 79,250 | 16,810 | 13,281 | 17,162 | 15,406 |
| 79,250 | 79,300 | 16,824 | 13,294 | 17,176 | 15,419 |
| 79,300 | 79,350 | 16,838 | 13,306 | 17,190 | 15,431 |
| 79,350 | 79,400 | 16,852 | 13,319 | 17,204 | 15,444 |
| 79,400 | 79,450 | 16,866 | 13,331 | 17,218 | 15,456 |
| 79,450 | 79,500 | 16,880 | 13,344 | 17,232 | 15,469 |
| 79,500 | 79,550 | 16,894 | 13,356 | 17,246 | 15,481 |
| 79,550 | 79,600 | 16,908 | 13,369 | 17,260 | 15,494 |
| 79,600 | 79,650 | 16,922 | 13,381 | 17,274 | 15,506 |
| 79,650 | 79,700 | 16,936 | 13,394 | 17,288 | 15,519 |
| 79,700 | 79,750 | 16,950 | 13,406 | 17,302 | 15,531 |
| 79,750 | 79,800 | 16,964 | 13,419 | 17,316 | 15,544 |
| 79,800 | 79,850 | 16,978 | 13,431 | 17,330 | 15,556 |
| 79,850 | 79,900 | 16,992 | 13,444 | 17,344 | 15,569 |
| 79,900 | 79,950 | 17,006 | 13,456 | 17,358 | 15,581 |
| 79,950 | 80,000 | 17,020 | 13,469 | 17,372 | 15,594 |

### 80,000 / 81,000 / 82,000

| At least | But less than | Single | Married filing jointly * | Married filing separately | Head of a household |
|---|---|---|---|---|---|
| **80,000** | | | | | |
| 80,000 | 80,050 | 17,034 | 13,481 | 17,386 | 15,606 |
| 80,050 | 80,100 | 17,048 | 13,494 | 17,400 | 15,619 |
| 80,100 | 80,150 | 17,062 | 13,506 | 17,414 | 15,631 |
| 80,150 | 80,200 | 17,076 | 13,519 | 17,428 | 15,644 |
| 80,200 | 80,250 | 17,090 | 13,531 | 17,442 | 15,656 |
| 80,250 | 80,300 | 17,104 | 13,544 | 17,456 | 15,669 |
| 80,300 | 80,350 | 17,118 | 13,556 | 17,470 | 15,681 |
| 80,350 | 80,400 | 17,132 | 13,569 | 17,484 | 15,694 |
| 80,400 | 80,450 | 17,146 | 13,581 | 17,498 | 15,706 |
| 80,450 | 80,500 | 17,160 | 13,594 | 17,512 | 15,719 |
| 80,500 | 80,550 | 17,174 | 13,606 | 17,526 | 15,731 |
| 80,550 | 80,600 | 17,188 | 13,619 | 17,540 | 15,744 |
| 80,600 | 80,650 | 17,202 | 13,631 | 17,554 | 15,756 |
| 80,650 | 80,700 | 17,216 | 13,644 | 17,568 | 15,769 |
| 80,700 | 80,750 | 17,230 | 13,656 | 17,582 | 15,781 |
| 80,750 | 80,800 | 17,244 | 13,669 | 17,596 | 15,794 |
| 80,800 | 80,850 | 17,258 | 13,681 | 17,610 | 15,806 |
| 80,850 | 80,900 | 17,272 | 13,694 | 17,624 | 15,819 |
| 80,900 | 80,950 | 17,286 | 13,706 | 17,638 | 15,831 |
| 80,950 | 81,000 | 17,300 | 13,719 | 17,652 | 15,844 |
| **81,000** | | | | | |
| 81,000 | 81,050 | 17,314 | 13,731 | 17,666 | 15,856 |
| 81,050 | 81,100 | 17,328 | 13,744 | 17,680 | 15,869 |
| 81,100 | 81,150 | 17,342 | 13,756 | 17,694 | 15,881 |
| 81,150 | 81,200 | 17,356 | 13,769 | 17,708 | 15,894 |
| 81,200 | 81,250 | 17,370 | 13,781 | 17,722 | 15,906 |
| 81,250 | 81,300 | 17,384 | 13,794 | 17,736 | 15,919 |
| 81,300 | 81,350 | 17,398 | 13,806 | 17,750 | 15,931 |
| 81,350 | 81,400 | 17,412 | 13,819 | 17,764 | 15,944 |
| 81,400 | 81,450 | 17,426 | 13,831 | 17,778 | 15,956 |
| 81,450 | 81,500 | 17,440 | 13,844 | 17,792 | 15,969 |
| 81,500 | 81,550 | 17,454 | 13,856 | 17,806 | 15,981 |
| 81,550 | 81,600 | 17,468 | 13,869 | 17,820 | 15,994 |
| 81,600 | 81,650 | 17,482 | 13,881 | 17,834 | 16,006 |
| 81,650 | 81,700 | 17,496 | 13,894 | 17,848 | 16,019 |
| 81,700 | 81,750 | 17,510 | 13,906 | 17,862 | 16,031 |
| 81,750 | 81,800 | 17,524 | 13,919 | 17,876 | 16,044 |
| 81,800 | 81,850 | 17,538 | 13,931 | 17,890 | 16,056 |
| 81,850 | 81,900 | 17,552 | 13,944 | 17,904 | 16,069 |
| 81,900 | 81,950 | 17,566 | 13,956 | 17,918 | 16,081 |
| 81,950 | 82,000 | 17,580 | 13,969 | 17,932 | 16,094 |
| **82,000** | | | | | |
| 82,000 | 82,050 | 17,594 | 13,981 | 17,946 | 16,106 |
| 82,050 | 82,100 | 17,608 | 13,994 | 17,960 | 16,119 |
| 82,100 | 82,150 | 17,622 | 14,006 | 17,974 | 16,131 |
| 82,150 | 82,200 | 17,636 | 14,019 | 17,988 | 16,144 |
| 82,200 | 82,250 | 17,650 | 14,031 | 18,002 | 16,156 |
| 82,250 | 82,300 | 17,664 | 14,044 | 18,016 | 16,169 |
| 82,300 | 82,350 | 17,678 | 14,056 | 18,030 | 16,181 |
| 82,350 | 82,400 | 17,692 | 14,069 | 18,044 | 16,194 |
| 82,400 | 82,450 | 17,706 | 14,081 | 18,058 | 16,206 |
| 82,450 | 82,500 | 17,720 | 14,094 | 18,072 | 16,219 |
| 82,500 | 82,550 | 17,734 | 14,106 | 18,086 | 16,231 |
| 82,550 | 82,600 | 17,748 | 14,119 | 18,100 | 16,244 |
| 82,600 | 82,650 | 17,762 | 14,131 | 18,114 | 16,256 |
| 82,650 | 82,700 | 17,776 | 14,144 | 18,128 | 16,269 |
| 82,700 | 82,750 | 17,790 | 14,156 | 18,142 | 16,281 |
| 82,750 | 82,800 | 17,804 | 14,169 | 18,156 | 16,294 |
| 82,800 | 82,850 | 17,818 | 14,181 | 18,170 | 16,306 |
| 82,850 | 82,900 | 17,832 | 14,194 | 18,184 | 16,319 |
| 82,900 | 82,950 | 17,846 | 14,206 | 18,198 | 16,331 |
| 82,950 | 83,000 | 17,860 | 14,219 | 18,212 | 16,344 |

### 83,000 / 84,000 / 85,000

| At least | But less than | Single | Married filing jointly * | Married filing separately | Head of a household |
|---|---|---|---|---|---|
| **83,000** | | | | | |
| 83,000 | 83,050 | 17,874 | 14,231 | 18,226 | 16,356 |
| 83,050 | 83,100 | 17,888 | 14,244 | 18,240 | 16,369 |
| 83,100 | 83,150 | 17,902 | 14,256 | 18,254 | 16,381 |
| 83,150 | 83,200 | 17,916 | 14,269 | 18,268 | 16,394 |
| 83,200 | 83,250 | 17,930 | 14,281 | 18,282 | 16,406 |
| 83,250 | 83,300 | 17,944 | 14,294 | 18,296 | 16,419 |
| 83,300 | 83,350 | 17,958 | 14,306 | 18,310 | 16,431 |
| 83,350 | 83,400 | 17,972 | 14,319 | 18,324 | 16,444 |
| 83,400 | 83,450 | 17,986 | 14,331 | 18,338 | 16,456 |
| 83,450 | 83,500 | 18,000 | 14,344 | 18,352 | 16,469 |
| 83,500 | 83,550 | 18,014 | 14,356 | 18,366 | 16,481 |
| 83,550 | 83,600 | 18,028 | 14,369 | 18,380 | 16,494 |
| 83,600 | 83,650 | 18,042 | 14,381 | 18,394 | 16,506 |
| 83,650 | 83,700 | 18,056 | 14,394 | 18,408 | 16,519 |
| 83,700 | 83,750 | 18,070 | 14,406 | 18,422 | 16,531 |
| 83,750 | 83,800 | 18,084 | 14,419 | 18,436 | 16,544 |
| 83,800 | 83,850 | 18,098 | 14,431 | 18,450 | 16,556 |
| 83,850 | 83,900 | 18,112 | 14,444 | 18,464 | 16,569 |
| 83,900 | 83,950 | 18,126 | 14,456 | 18,478 | 16,581 |
| 83,950 | 84,000 | 18,140 | 14,469 | 18,492 | 16,594 |
| **84,000** | | | | | |
| 84,000 | 84,050 | 18,154 | 14,481 | 18,506 | 16,606 |
| 84,050 | 84,100 | 18,168 | 14,494 | 18,520 | 16,619 |
| 84,100 | 84,150 | 18,182 | 14,506 | 18,534 | 16,631 |
| 84,150 | 84,200 | 18,196 | 14,519 | 18,548 | 16,644 |
| 84,200 | 84,250 | 18,210 | 14,531 | 18,562 | 16,656 |
| 84,250 | 84,300 | 18,224 | 14,544 | 18,576 | 16,669 |
| 84,300 | 84,350 | 18,238 | 14,556 | 18,590 | 16,681 |
| 84,350 | 84,400 | 18,252 | 14,569 | 18,604 | 16,694 |
| 84,400 | 84,450 | 18,266 | 14,581 | 18,618 | 16,706 |
| 84,450 | 84,500 | 18,280 | 14,594 | 18,632 | 16,719 |
| 84,500 | 84,550 | 18,294 | 14,606 | 18,646 | 16,731 |
| 84,550 | 84,600 | 18,308 | 14,619 | 18,660 | 16,744 |
| 84,600 | 84,650 | 18,322 | 14,631 | 18,674 | 16,756 |
| 84,650 | 84,700 | 18,336 | 14,644 | 18,688 | 16,769 |
| 84,700 | 84,750 | 18,350 | 14,656 | 18,702 | 16,781 |
| 84,750 | 84,800 | 18,364 | 14,669 | 18,716 | 16,794 |
| 84,800 | 84,850 | 18,378 | 14,681 | 18,730 | 16,806 |
| 84,850 | 84,900 | 18,392 | 14,694 | 18,744 | 16,819 |
| 84,900 | 84,950 | 18,406 | 14,706 | 18,758 | 16,831 |
| 84,950 | 85,000 | 18,420 | 14,719 | 18,772 | 16,844 |
| **85,000** | | | | | |
| 85,000 | 85,050 | 18,434 | 14,731 | 18,786 | 16,856 |
| 85,050 | 85,100 | 18,448 | 14,744 | 18,800 | 16,869 |
| 85,100 | 85,150 | 18,462 | 14,756 | 18,814 | 16,881 |
| 85,150 | 85,200 | 18,476 | 14,769 | 18,828 | 16,894 |
| 85,200 | 85,250 | 18,490 | 14,781 | 18,842 | 16,906 |
| 85,250 | 85,300 | 18,504 | 14,794 | 18,856 | 16,919 |
| 85,300 | 85,350 | 18,518 | 14,806 | 18,870 | 16,931 |
| 85,350 | 85,400 | 18,532 | 14,819 | 18,884 | 16,944 |
| 85,400 | 85,450 | 18,546 | 14,831 | 18,898 | 16,956 |
| 85,450 | 85,500 | 18,560 | 14,844 | 18,912 | 16,969 |
| 85,500 | 85,550 | 18,574 | 14,856 | 18,926 | 16,981 |
| 85,550 | 85,600 | 18,588 | 14,869 | 18,940 | 16,994 |
| 85,600 | 85,650 | 18,602 | 14,881 | 18,954 | 17,006 |
| 85,650 | 85,700 | 18,616 | 14,894 | 18,968 | 17,019 |
| 85,700 | 85,750 | 18,630 | 14,906 | 18,982 | 17,031 |
| 85,750 | 85,800 | 18,644 | 14,919 | 18,996 | 17,044 |
| 85,800 | 85,850 | 18,658 | 14,931 | 19,010 | 17,056 |
| 85,850 | 85,900 | 18,672 | 14,944 | 19,024 | 17,069 |
| 85,900 | 85,950 | 18,686 | 14,956 | 19,038 | 17,081 |
| 85,950 | 86,000 | 18,700 | 14,969 | 19,052 | 17,094 |

\* This column must also be used by a qualifying widow(er).

(Continued on next page)

**2004 Tax Table**—*Continued*

| If line 42 (taxable income) is— | | And you are— | | | |
|---|---|---|---|---|---|
| At least | But less than | Single | Married filing jointly * | Married filing separately | Head of a household |
| | | Your tax is— | | | |

### 86,000

| At least | But less than | Single | MFJ * | MFS | HoH |
|---|---|---|---|---|---|
| 86,000 | 86,050 | 18,714 | 14,981 | 19,066 | 17,106 |
| 86,050 | 86,100 | 18,728 | 14,994 | 19,080 | 17,119 |
| 86,100 | 86,150 | 18,742 | 15,006 | 19,094 | 17,131 |
| 86,150 | 86,200 | 18,756 | 15,019 | 19,108 | 17,144 |
| 86,200 | 86,250 | 18,770 | 15,031 | 19,122 | 17,156 |
| 86,250 | 86,300 | 18,784 | 15,044 | 19,136 | 17,169 |
| 86,300 | 86,350 | 18,798 | 15,056 | 19,150 | 17,181 |
| 86,350 | 86,400 | 18,812 | 15,069 | 19,164 | 17,194 |
| 86,400 | 86,450 | 18,826 | 15,081 | 19,178 | 17,206 |
| 86,450 | 86,500 | 18,840 | 15,094 | 19,192 | 17,219 |
| 86,500 | 86,550 | 18,854 | 15,106 | 19,206 | 17,231 |
| 86,550 | 86,600 | 18,868 | 15,119 | 19,220 | 17,244 |
| 86,600 | 86,650 | 18,882 | 15,131 | 19,234 | 17,256 |
| 86,650 | 86,700 | 18,896 | 15,144 | 19,248 | 17,269 |
| 86,700 | 86,750 | 18,910 | 15,156 | 19,262 | 17,281 |
| 86,750 | 86,800 | 18,924 | 15,169 | 19,276 | 17,294 |
| 86,800 | 86,850 | 18,938 | 15,181 | 19,290 | 17,306 |
| 86,850 | 86,900 | 18,952 | 15,194 | 19,304 | 17,319 |
| 86,900 | 86,950 | 18,966 | 15,206 | 19,318 | 17,331 |
| 86,950 | 87,000 | 18,980 | 15,219 | 19,332 | 17,344 |

### 87,000

| At least | But less than | Single | MFJ * | MFS | HoH |
|---|---|---|---|---|---|
| 87,000 | 87,050 | 18,994 | 15,231 | 19,346 | 17,356 |
| 87,050 | 87,100 | 19,008 | 15,244 | 19,360 | 17,369 |
| 87,100 | 87,150 | 19,022 | 15,256 | 19,374 | 17,381 |
| 87,150 | 87,200 | 19,036 | 15,269 | 19,388 | 17,394 |
| 87,200 | 87,250 | 19,050 | 15,281 | 19,402 | 17,406 |
| 87,250 | 87,300 | 19,064 | 15,294 | 19,416 | 17,419 |
| 87,300 | 87,350 | 19,078 | 15,306 | 19,430 | 17,431 |
| 87,350 | 87,400 | 19,092 | 15,319 | 19,444 | 17,444 |
| 87,400 | 87,450 | 19,106 | 15,331 | 19,458 | 17,456 |
| 87,450 | 87,500 | 19,120 | 15,344 | 19,472 | 17,469 |
| 87,500 | 87,550 | 19,134 | 15,356 | 19,486 | 17,481 |
| 87,550 | 87,600 | 19,148 | 15,369 | 19,500 | 17,494 |
| 87,600 | 87,650 | 19,162 | 15,381 | 19,514 | 17,506 |
| 87,650 | 87,700 | 19,176 | 15,394 | 19,528 | 17,519 |
| 87,700 | 87,750 | 19,190 | 15,406 | 19,542 | 17,531 |
| 87,750 | 87,800 | 19,204 | 15,419 | 19,556 | 17,544 |
| 87,800 | 87,850 | 19,218 | 15,431 | 19,570 | 17,556 |
| 87,850 | 87,900 | 19,232 | 15,444 | 19,584 | 17,569 |
| 87,900 | 87,950 | 19,246 | 15,456 | 19,598 | 17,581 |
| 87,950 | 88,000 | 19,260 | 15,469 | 19,612 | 17,594 |

### 88,000

| At least | But less than | Single | MFJ * | MFS | HoH |
|---|---|---|---|---|---|
| 88,000 | 88,050 | 19,274 | 15,481 | 19,626 | 17,606 |
| 88,050 | 88,100 | 19,288 | 15,494 | 19,640 | 17,619 |
| 88,100 | 88,150 | 19,302 | 15,506 | 19,654 | 17,631 |
| 88,150 | 88,200 | 19,316 | 15,519 | 19,668 | 17,644 |
| 88,200 | 88,250 | 19,330 | 15,531 | 19,682 | 17,656 |
| 88,250 | 88,300 | 19,344 | 15,544 | 19,696 | 17,669 |
| 88,300 | 88,350 | 19,358 | 15,556 | 19,710 | 17,681 |
| 88,350 | 88,400 | 19,372 | 15,569 | 19,724 | 17,694 |
| 88,400 | 88,450 | 19,386 | 15,581 | 19,738 | 17,706 |
| 88,450 | 88,500 | 19,400 | 15,594 | 19,752 | 17,719 |
| 88,500 | 88,550 | 19,414 | 15,606 | 19,766 | 17,731 |
| 88,550 | 88,600 | 19,428 | 15,619 | 19,780 | 17,744 |
| 88,600 | 88,650 | 19,442 | 15,631 | 19,794 | 17,756 |
| 88,650 | 88,700 | 19,456 | 15,644 | 19,808 | 17,769 |
| 88,700 | 88,750 | 19,470 | 15,656 | 19,822 | 17,781 |
| 88,750 | 88,800 | 19,484 | 15,669 | 19,836 | 17,794 |
| 88,800 | 88,850 | 19,498 | 15,681 | 19,850 | 17,806 |
| 88,850 | 88,900 | 19,512 | 15,694 | 19,864 | 17,819 |
| 88,900 | 88,950 | 19,526 | 15,706 | 19,878 | 17,831 |
| 88,950 | 89,000 | 19,540 | 15,719 | 19,892 | 17,844 |

### 89,000

| At least | But less than | Single | MFJ * | MFS | HoH |
|---|---|---|---|---|---|
| 89,000 | 89,050 | 19,554 | 15,731 | 19,906 | 17,856 |
| 89,050 | 89,100 | 19,568 | 15,744 | 19,920 | 17,869 |
| 89,100 | 89,150 | 19,582 | 15,756 | 19,934 | 17,881 |
| 89,150 | 89,200 | 19,596 | 15,769 | 19,948 | 17,894 |
| 89,200 | 89,250 | 19,610 | 15,781 | 19,962 | 17,906 |
| 89,250 | 89,300 | 19,624 | 15,794 | 19,976 | 17,919 |
| 89,300 | 89,350 | 19,638 | 15,806 | 19,990 | 17,931 |
| 89,350 | 89,400 | 19,652 | 15,819 | 20,006 | 17,944 |
| 89,400 | 89,450 | 19,666 | 15,831 | 20,023 | 17,956 |
| 89,450 | 89,500 | 19,680 | 15,844 | 20,039 | 17,969 |
| 89,500 | 89,550 | 19,694 | 15,856 | 20,056 | 17,981 |
| 89,550 | 89,600 | 19,708 | 15,869 | 20,072 | 17,994 |
| 89,600 | 89,650 | 19,722 | 15,881 | 20,089 | 18,006 |
| 89,650 | 89,700 | 19,736 | 15,894 | 20,105 | 18,019 |
| 89,700 | 89,750 | 19,750 | 15,906 | 20,122 | 18,031 |
| 89,750 | 89,800 | 19,764 | 15,919 | 20,138 | 18,044 |
| 89,800 | 89,850 | 19,778 | 15,931 | 20,155 | 18,056 |
| 89,850 | 89,900 | 19,792 | 15,944 | 20,171 | 18,069 |
| 89,900 | 89,950 | 19,806 | 15,956 | 20,188 | 18,081 |
| 89,950 | 90,000 | 19,820 | 15,969 | 20,204 | 18,094 |

### 90,000

| At least | But less than | Single | MFJ * | MFS | HoH |
|---|---|---|---|---|---|
| 90,000 | 90,050 | 19,834 | 15,981 | 20,221 | 18,106 |
| 90,050 | 90,100 | 19,848 | 15,994 | 20,237 | 18,119 |
| 90,100 | 90,150 | 19,862 | 16,006 | 20,254 | 18,131 |
| 90,150 | 90,200 | 19,876 | 16,019 | 20,270 | 18,144 |
| 90,200 | 90,250 | 19,890 | 16,031 | 20,287 | 18,156 |
| 90,250 | 90,300 | 19,904 | 16,044 | 20,303 | 18,169 |
| 90,300 | 90,350 | 19,918 | 16,056 | 20,320 | 18,181 |
| 90,350 | 90,400 | 19,932 | 16,069 | 20,336 | 18,194 |
| 90,400 | 90,450 | 19,946 | 16,081 | 20,353 | 18,206 |
| 90,450 | 90,500 | 19,960 | 16,094 | 20,369 | 18,219 |
| 90,500 | 90,550 | 19,974 | 16,106 | 20,386 | 18,231 |
| 90,550 | 90,600 | 19,988 | 16,119 | 20,402 | 18,244 |
| 90,600 | 90,650 | 20,002 | 16,131 | 20,419 | 18,256 |
| 90,650 | 90,700 | 20,016 | 16,144 | 20,435 | 18,269 |
| 90,700 | 90,750 | 20,030 | 16,156 | 20,452 | 18,281 |
| 90,750 | 90,800 | 20,044 | 16,169 | 20,468 | 18,294 |
| 90,800 | 90,850 | 20,058 | 16,181 | 20,485 | 18,306 |
| 90,850 | 90,900 | 20,072 | 16,194 | 20,501 | 18,319 |
| 90,900 | 90,950 | 20,086 | 16,206 | 20,518 | 18,331 |
| 90,950 | 91,000 | 20,100 | 16,219 | 20,534 | 18,344 |

### 91,000

| At least | But less than | Single | MFJ * | MFS | HoH |
|---|---|---|---|---|---|
| 91,000 | 91,050 | 20,114 | 16,231 | 20,551 | 18,356 |
| 91,050 | 91,100 | 20,128 | 16,244 | 20,567 | 18,369 |
| 91,100 | 91,150 | 20,142 | 16,256 | 20,584 | 18,381 |
| 91,150 | 91,200 | 20,156 | 16,269 | 20,600 | 18,394 |
| 91,200 | 91,250 | 20,170 | 16,281 | 20,617 | 18,406 |
| 91,250 | 91,300 | 20,184 | 16,294 | 20,633 | 18,419 |
| 91,300 | 91,350 | 20,198 | 16,306 | 20,650 | 18,431 |
| 91,350 | 91,400 | 20,212 | 16,319 | 20,666 | 18,444 |
| 91,400 | 91,450 | 20,226 | 16,331 | 20,683 | 18,456 |
| 91,450 | 91,500 | 20,240 | 16,344 | 20,699 | 18,469 |
| 91,500 | 91,550 | 20,254 | 16,356 | 20,716 | 18,481 |
| 91,550 | 91,600 | 20,268 | 16,369 | 20,732 | 18,494 |
| 91,600 | 91,650 | 20,282 | 16,381 | 20,749 | 18,506 |
| 91,650 | 91,700 | 20,296 | 16,394 | 20,765 | 18,519 |
| 91,700 | 91,750 | 20,310 | 16,406 | 20,782 | 18,531 |
| 91,750 | 91,800 | 20,324 | 16,419 | 20,798 | 18,544 |
| 91,800 | 91,850 | 20,338 | 16,431 | 20,815 | 18,556 |
| 91,850 | 91,900 | 20,352 | 16,444 | 20,831 | 18,569 |
| 91,900 | 91,950 | 20,366 | 16,456 | 20,848 | 18,581 |
| 91,950 | 92,000 | 20,380 | 16,469 | 20,864 | 18,594 |

### 92,000

| At least | But less than | Single | MFJ * | MFS | HoH |
|---|---|---|---|---|---|
| 92,000 | 92,050 | 20,394 | 16,481 | 20,881 | 18,606 |
| 92,050 | 92,100 | 20,408 | 16,494 | 20,897 | 18,619 |
| 92,100 | 92,150 | 20,422 | 16,506 | 20,914 | 18,631 |
| 92,150 | 92,200 | 20,436 | 16,519 | 20,930 | 18,644 |
| 92,200 | 92,250 | 20,450 | 16,531 | 20,947 | 18,656 |
| 92,250 | 92,300 | 20,464 | 16,544 | 20,963 | 18,669 |
| 92,300 | 92,350 | 20,478 | 16,556 | 20,980 | 18,681 |
| 92,350 | 92,400 | 20,492 | 16,569 | 20,996 | 18,694 |
| 92,400 | 92,450 | 20,506 | 16,581 | 21,013 | 18,706 |
| 92,450 | 92,500 | 20,520 | 16,594 | 21,029 | 18,719 |
| 92,500 | 92,550 | 20,534 | 16,606 | 21,046 | 18,731 |
| 92,550 | 92,600 | 20,548 | 16,619 | 21,062 | 18,744 |
| 92,600 | 92,650 | 20,562 | 16,631 | 21,079 | 18,756 |
| 92,650 | 92,700 | 20,576 | 16,644 | 21,095 | 18,769 |
| 92,700 | 92,750 | 20,590 | 16,656 | 21,112 | 18,781 |
| 92,750 | 92,800 | 20,604 | 16,669 | 21,128 | 18,794 |
| 92,800 | 92,850 | 20,618 | 16,681 | 21,145 | 18,806 |
| 92,850 | 92,900 | 20,632 | 16,694 | 21,161 | 18,819 |
| 92,900 | 92,950 | 20,646 | 16,706 | 21,178 | 18,831 |
| 92,950 | 93,000 | 20,660 | 16,719 | 21,194 | 18,844 |

### 93,000

| At least | But less than | Single | MFJ * | MFS | HoH |
|---|---|---|---|---|---|
| 93,000 | 93,050 | 20,674 | 16,731 | 21,211 | 18,856 |
| 93,050 | 93,100 | 20,688 | 16,744 | 21,227 | 18,869 |
| 93,100 | 93,150 | 20,702 | 16,756 | 21,244 | 18,881 |
| 93,150 | 93,200 | 20,716 | 16,769 | 21,260 | 18,894 |
| 93,200 | 93,250 | 20,730 | 16,781 | 21,277 | 18,906 |
| 93,250 | 93,300 | 20,744 | 16,794 | 21,293 | 18,919 |
| 93,300 | 93,350 | 20,758 | 16,806 | 21,310 | 18,931 |
| 93,350 | 93,400 | 20,772 | 16,819 | 21,326 | 18,944 |
| 93,400 | 93,450 | 20,786 | 16,831 | 21,343 | 18,956 |
| 93,450 | 93,500 | 20,800 | 16,844 | 21,359 | 18,969 |
| 93,500 | 93,550 | 20,814 | 16,856 | 21,376 | 18,981 |
| 93,550 | 93,600 | 20,828 | 16,869 | 21,392 | 18,994 |
| 93,600 | 93,650 | 20,842 | 16,881 | 21,409 | 19,006 |
| 93,650 | 93,700 | 20,856 | 16,894 | 21,425 | 19,019 |
| 93,700 | 93,750 | 20,870 | 16,906 | 21,442 | 19,031 |
| 93,750 | 93,800 | 20,884 | 16,919 | 21,458 | 19,044 |
| 93,800 | 93,850 | 20,898 | 16,931 | 21,475 | 19,056 |
| 93,850 | 93,900 | 20,912 | 16,944 | 21,491 | 19,069 |
| 93,900 | 93,950 | 20,926 | 16,956 | 21,508 | 19,081 |
| 93,950 | 94,000 | 20,940 | 16,969 | 21,524 | 19,094 |

### 94,000

| At least | But less than | Single | MFJ * | MFS | HoH |
|---|---|---|---|---|---|
| 94,000 | 94,050 | 20,954 | 16,981 | 21,541 | 19,106 |
| 94,050 | 94,100 | 20,968 | 16,994 | 21,557 | 19,119 |
| 94,100 | 94,150 | 20,982 | 17,006 | 21,574 | 19,131 |
| 94,150 | 94,200 | 20,996 | 17,019 | 21,590 | 19,144 |
| 94,200 | 94,250 | 21,010 | 17,031 | 21,607 | 19,156 |
| 94,250 | 94,300 | 21,024 | 17,044 | 21,623 | 19,169 |
| 94,300 | 94,350 | 21,038 | 17,056 | 21,640 | 19,181 |
| 94,350 | 94,400 | 21,052 | 17,069 | 21,656 | 19,194 |
| 94,400 | 94,450 | 21,066 | 17,081 | 21,673 | 19,206 |
| 94,450 | 94,500 | 21,080 | 17,094 | 21,689 | 19,219 |
| 94,500 | 94,550 | 21,094 | 17,106 | 21,706 | 19,231 |
| 94,550 | 94,600 | 21,108 | 17,119 | 21,722 | 19,244 |
| 94,600 | 94,650 | 21,122 | 17,131 | 21,739 | 19,256 |
| 94,650 | 94,700 | 21,136 | 17,144 | 21,755 | 19,269 |
| 94,700 | 94,750 | 21,150 | 17,156 | 21,772 | 19,281 |
| 94,750 | 94,800 | 21,164 | 17,169 | 21,788 | 19,294 |
| 94,800 | 94,850 | 21,178 | 17,181 | 21,805 | 19,306 |
| 94,850 | 94,900 | 21,192 | 17,194 | 21,821 | 19,319 |
| 94,900 | 94,950 | 21,206 | 17,206 | 21,838 | 19,331 |
| 94,950 | 95,000 | 21,220 | 17,219 | 21,854 | 19,344 |

* This column must also be used by a qualifying widow(er).

(Continued on next page)

## 2004 Tax Table— *Continued*

| If line 42 (taxable income) is— | | And you are— | | | | If line 42 (taxable income) is— | | And you are— | | | |
|---|---|---|---|---|---|---|---|---|---|---|---|
| At least | But less than | Single | Married filing jointly * | Married filing separately | Head of a household | At least | But less than | Single | Married filing jointly * | Married filing separately | Head of a household |
| | | Your tax is— | | | | | | Your tax is— | | | |

### 95,000

| At least | But less than | Single | MFJ* | MFS | HoH |
|---|---|---|---|---|---|
| 95,000 | 95,050 | 21,234 | 17,231 | 21,871 | 19,356 |
| 95,050 | 95,100 | 21,248 | 17,244 | 21,887 | 19,369 |
| 95,100 | 95,150 | 21,262 | 17,256 | 21,904 | 19,381 |
| 95,150 | 95,200 | 21,276 | 17,269 | 21,920 | 19,394 |
| 95,200 | 95,250 | 21,290 | 17,281 | 21,937 | 19,406 |
| 95,250 | 95,300 | 21,304 | 17,294 | 21,953 | 19,419 |
| 95,300 | 95,350 | 21,318 | 17,306 | 21,970 | 19,431 |
| 95,350 | 95,400 | 21,332 | 17,319 | 21,986 | 19,444 |
| 95,400 | 95,450 | 21,346 | 17,331 | 22,003 | 19,456 |
| 95,450 | 95,500 | 21,360 | 17,344 | 22,019 | 19,469 |
| 95,500 | 95,550 | 21,374 | 17,356 | 22,036 | 19,481 |
| 95,550 | 95,600 | 21,388 | 17,369 | 22,052 | 19,494 |
| 95,600 | 95,650 | 21,402 | 17,381 | 22,069 | 19,506 |
| 95,650 | 95,700 | 21,416 | 17,394 | 22,085 | 19,519 |
| 95,700 | 95,750 | 21,430 | 17,406 | 22,102 | 19,531 |
| 95,750 | 95,800 | 21,444 | 17,419 | 22,118 | 19,544 |
| 95,800 | 95,850 | 21,458 | 17,431 | 22,135 | 19,556 |
| 95,850 | 95,900 | 21,472 | 17,444 | 22,151 | 19,569 |
| 95,900 | 95,950 | 21,486 | 17,456 | 22,168 | 19,581 |
| 95,950 | 96,000 | 21,500 | 17,469 | 22,184 | 19,594 |

### 96,000

| At least | But less than | Single | MFJ* | MFS | HoH |
|---|---|---|---|---|---|
| 96,000 | 96,050 | 21,514 | 17,481 | 22,201 | 19,606 |
| 96,050 | 96,100 | 21,528 | 17,494 | 22,217 | 19,619 |
| 96,100 | 96,150 | 21,542 | 17,506 | 22,234 | 19,631 |
| 96,150 | 96,200 | 21,556 | 17,519 | 22,250 | 19,644 |
| 96,200 | 96,250 | 21,570 | 17,531 | 22,267 | 19,656 |
| 96,250 | 96,300 | 21,584 | 17,544 | 22,283 | 19,669 |
| 96,300 | 96,350 | 21,598 | 17,556 | 22,300 | 19,681 |
| 96,350 | 96,400 | 21,612 | 17,569 | 22,316 | 19,694 |
| 96,400 | 96,450 | 21,626 | 17,581 | 22,333 | 19,706 |
| 96,450 | 96,500 | 21,640 | 17,594 | 22,349 | 19,719 |
| 96,500 | 96,550 | 21,654 | 17,606 | 22,366 | 19,731 |
| 96,550 | 96,600 | 21,668 | 17,619 | 22,382 | 19,744 |
| 96,600 | 96,650 | 21,682 | 17,631 | 22,399 | 19,756 |
| 96,650 | 96,700 | 21,696 | 17,644 | 22,415 | 19,769 |
| 96,700 | 96,750 | 21,710 | 17,656 | 22,432 | 19,781 |
| 96,750 | 96,800 | 21,724 | 17,669 | 22,448 | 19,794 |
| 96,800 | 96,850 | 21,738 | 17,681 | 22,465 | 19,806 |
| 96,850 | 96,900 | 21,752 | 17,694 | 22,481 | 19,819 |
| 96,900 | 96,950 | 21,766 | 17,706 | 22,498 | 19,831 |
| 96,950 | 97,000 | 21,780 | 17,719 | 22,514 | 19,844 |

### 97,000

| At least | But less than | Single | MFJ* | MFS | HoH |
|---|---|---|---|---|---|
| 97,000 | 97,050 | 21,794 | 17,731 | 22,531 | 19,856 |
| 97,050 | 97,100 | 21,808 | 17,744 | 22,547 | 19,869 |
| 97,100 | 97,150 | 21,822 | 17,756 | 22,564 | 19,881 |
| 97,150 | 97,200 | 21,836 | 17,769 | 22,580 | 19,894 |
| 97,200 | 97,250 | 21,850 | 17,781 | 22,597 | 19,906 |
| 97,250 | 97,300 | 21,864 | 17,794 | 22,613 | 19,919 |
| 97,300 | 97,350 | 21,878 | 17,806 | 22,630 | 19,931 |
| 97,350 | 97,400 | 21,892 | 17,819 | 22,646 | 19,944 |
| 97,400 | 97,450 | 21,906 | 17,831 | 22,663 | 19,956 |
| 97,450 | 97,500 | 21,920 | 17,844 | 22,679 | 19,969 |
| 97,500 | 97,550 | 21,934 | 17,856 | 22,696 | 19,981 |
| 97,550 | 97,600 | 21,948 | 17,869 | 22,712 | 19,994 |
| 97,600 | 97,650 | 21,962 | 17,881 | 22,729 | 20,006 |
| 97,650 | 97,700 | 21,976 | 17,894 | 22,745 | 20,019 |
| 97,700 | 97,750 | 21,990 | 17,906 | 22,762 | 20,031 |
| 97,750 | 97,800 | 22,004 | 17,919 | 22,778 | 20,044 |
| 97,800 | 97,850 | 22,018 | 17,931 | 22,795 | 20,056 |
| 97,850 | 97,900 | 22,032 | 17,944 | 22,811 | 20,069 |
| 97,900 | 97,950 | 22,046 | 17,956 | 22,828 | 20,081 |
| 97,950 | 98,000 | 22,060 | 17,969 | 22,844 | 20,094 |

### 98,000

| At least | But less than | Single | MFJ* | MFS | HoH |
|---|---|---|---|---|---|
| 98,000 | 98,050 | 22,074 | 17,981 | 22,861 | 20,106 |
| 98,050 | 98,100 | 22,088 | 17,994 | 22,877 | 20,119 |
| 98,100 | 98,150 | 22,102 | 18,006 | 22,894 | 20,131 |
| 98,150 | 98,200 | 22,116 | 18,019 | 22,910 | 20,144 |
| 98,200 | 98,250 | 22,130 | 18,031 | 22,927 | 20,156 |
| 98,250 | 98,300 | 22,144 | 18,044 | 22,943 | 20,169 |
| 98,300 | 98,350 | 22,158 | 18,056 | 22,960 | 20,181 |
| 98,350 | 98,400 | 22,172 | 18,069 | 22,976 | 20,194 |
| 98,400 | 98,450 | 22,186 | 18,081 | 22,993 | 20,206 |
| 98,450 | 98,500 | 22,200 | 18,094 | 23,009 | 20,219 |
| 98,500 | 98,550 | 22,214 | 18,106 | 23,026 | 20,231 |
| 98,550 | 98,600 | 22,228 | 18,119 | 23,042 | 20,244 |
| 98,600 | 98,650 | 22,242 | 18,131 | 23,059 | 20,256 |
| 98,650 | 98,700 | 22,256 | 18,144 | 23,075 | 20,269 |
| 98,700 | 98,750 | 22,270 | 18,156 | 23,092 | 20,281 |
| 98,750 | 98,800 | 22,284 | 18,169 | 23,108 | 20,294 |
| 98,800 | 98,850 | 22,298 | 18,181 | 23,125 | 20,306 |
| 98,850 | 98,900 | 22,312 | 18,194 | 23,141 | 20,319 |
| 98,900 | 98,950 | 22,326 | 18,206 | 23,158 | 20,331 |
| 98,950 | 99,000 | 22,340 | 18,219 | 23,174 | 20,344 |

### 99,000

| At least | But less than | Single | MFJ* | MFS | HoH |
|---|---|---|---|---|---|
| 99,000 | 99,050 | 22,354 | 18,231 | 23,191 | 20,356 |
| 99,050 | 99,100 | 22,368 | 18,244 | 23,207 | 20,369 |
| 99,100 | 99,150 | 22,382 | 18,256 | 23,224 | 20,381 |
| 99,150 | 99,200 | 22,396 | 18,269 | 23,240 | 20,394 |
| 99,200 | 99,250 | 22,410 | 18,281 | 23,257 | 20,406 |
| 99,250 | 99,300 | 22,424 | 18,294 | 23,273 | 20,419 |
| 99,300 | 99,350 | 22,438 | 18,306 | 23,290 | 20,431 |
| 99,350 | 99,400 | 22,452 | 18,319 | 23,306 | 20,444 |
| 99,400 | 99,450 | 22,466 | 18,331 | 23,323 | 20,456 |
| 99,450 | 99,500 | 22,480 | 18,344 | 23,339 | 20,469 |
| 99,500 | 99,550 | 22,494 | 18,356 | 23,356 | 20,481 |
| 99,550 | 99,600 | 22,508 | 18,369 | 23,372 | 20,494 |
| 99,600 | 99,650 | 22,522 | 18,381 | 23,389 | 20,506 |
| 99,650 | 99,700 | 22,536 | 18,394 | 23,405 | 20,519 |
| 99,700 | 99,750 | 22,550 | 18,406 | 23,422 | 20,531 |
| 99,750 | 99,800 | 22,564 | 18,419 | 23,438 | 20,544 |
| 99,800 | 99,850 | 22,578 | 18,431 | 23,455 | 20,556 |
| 99,850 | 99,900 | 22,592 | 18,444 | 23,471 | 20,569 |
| 99,900 | 99,950 | 22,606 | 18,456 | 23,488 | 20,581 |
| 99,950 | 100,000 | 22,620 | 18,469 | 23,504 | 20,594 |

**$100,000 or over — use the Tax Rate Schedules on page A–2**

* This column must also be used by a qualifying widow(er).

# Income Tax Rates—Estates and Trusts

## TAX YEAR 2004

| Taxable Income | | The Tax Is: | Of the Amount Over— |
|---|---|---|---|
| Over— | But not Over— | | |
| $ 0 | $1,950 | 15% | $ 0 |
| 1,950 | 4,600 | . $ 292.50 + 25% | 1,950 |
| 4,600 | 7,000 | 955.00 + 28% | 4,600 |
| 7,000 | 9,550 | 1,627.00 + 33% | 7,000 |
| 9,550 | ......... | 2,468.50 + 35% | 9,550 |

## TAX YEAR 2005

| Taxable Income | | The Tax Is: | Of the Amount Over— |
|---|---|---|---|
| Over— | But not Over— | | |
| $ 0 | $2,000 | 15% | $ 0 |
| 2,000 | 4,700 | $ 300 + 25% | 2,000 |
| 4,700 | 7,150 | 975 + 28% | 4,700 |
| 7,150 | 9,750 | 1,661 + 33% | 7,150 |
| 9,750 | ......... | 2,519 + 35% | 9,750 |

# Income Tax Rates—Corporations

| Taxable Income | | The Tax Is: | Of the Amount Over— |
|---|---|---|---|
| Over— | But not Over— | | |
| $ 0 | $ 50,000 | 15% | $ 0 |
| 50,000 | 75,000 | $ 7,500 + 25% | 50,000 |
| 75,000 | 100,000 | 13,750 + 34% | 75,000 |
| 100,000 | 335,000 | 22,250 + 39% | 100,000 |
| 335,000 | 10,000,000 | 113,900 + 34% | 335,000 |
| 10,000,000 | 15,000,000 | 3,400,000 + 35% | 10,000,000 |
| 15,000,000 | 18,333,333 | 5,150,000 + 38% | 15,000,000 |
| 18,333,333 | ............. | 35% | 0 |

# Unified Transfer Tax Rates

## FOR GIFTS MADE AND FOR DEATHS AFTER 1983 AND BEFORE 2002

| If the Amount with Respect to Which the Tentative Tax to Be Computed Is: | The Tentative Tax Is: |
| --- | --- |
| Not over $10,000 | 18 percent of such amount. |
| Over $10,000 but not over $20,000 | $1,800, plus 20 percent of the excess of such amount over $10,000. |
| Over $20,000 but not over $40,000 | $3,800, plus 22 percent of the excess of such amount over $20,000. |
| Over $40,000 but not over $60,000 | $8,200, plus 24 percent of the excess of such amount over $40,000. |
| Over $60,000 but not over $80,000 | $13,000, plus 26 percent of the excess of such amount over $60,000. |
| Over $80,000 but not over $100,000 | $18,200, plus 28 percent of the excess of such amount over $80,000. |
| Over $100,000 but not over $150,000 | $23,800, plus 30 percent of the excess of such amount over $100,000. |
| Over $150,000 but not over $250,000 | $38,800, plus 32 percent of the excess of such amount over $150,000. |
| Over $250,000 but not over $500,000 | $70,800, plus 34 percent of the excess of such amount over $250,000. |
| Over $500,000 but not over $750,000 | $155,800, plus 37 percent of the excess of such amount over $500,000. |
| Over $750,000 but not over $1,000,000 | $248,300, plus 39 percent of the excess of such amount over $750,000. |
| Over $1,000,000 but not over $1,250,000 | $345,800, plus 41 percent of the excess of such amount over $1,000,000. |
| Over $1,250,000 but not over $1,500,000 | $448,300, plus 43 percent of the excess of such amount over $1,250,000. |
| Over $1,500,000 but not over $2,000,000 | $555,800, plus 45 percent of the excess of such amount over $1,500,000. |
| Over $2,000,000 but not over $2,500,000 | $780,800, plus 49 percent of the excess of such amount over $2,000,000. |
| Over $2,500,000 but not over $3,000,000 | $1,025,800, plus 53 percent of the excess of such amount over $2,500,000. |
| Over $3,000,000* | $1,290,800, plus 55 percent of the excess of such amount over $3,000,000. |

*For large taxable transfers (generally in excess of $10 million) there is a phaseout of the graduated rates and the unified tax credit.

# Unified Transfer Tax Rates

## FOR GIFTS MADE AND FOR DEATHS IN 2002

| If the Amount with Respect to Which the Tentative Tax to Be Computed Is: | The Tentative Tax Is: |
| --- | --- |
| Not over $10,000 | 18 percent of such amount. |
| Over $10,000 but not over $20,000 | $1,800, plus 20 percent of the excess of such amount over $10,000. |
| Over $20,000 but not over $40,000 | $3,800, plus 22 percent of the excess of such amount over $20,000. |
| Over $40,000 but not over $60,000 | $8,200, plus 24 percent of the excess of such amount over $40,000. |
| Over $60,000 but not over $80,000 | $13,000, plus 26 percent of the excess of such amount over $60,000. |
| Over $80,000 but not over $100,000 | $18,200, plus 28 percent of the excess of such amount over $80,000. |
| Over $100,000 but not over $150,000 | $23,800, plus 30 percent of the excess of such amount over $100,000. |
| Over $150,000 but not over $250,000 | $38,800, plus 32 percent of the excess of such amount over $150,000. |
| Over $250,000 but not over $500,000 | $70,800, plus 34 percent of the excess of such amount over $250,000. |
| Over $500,000 but not over $750,000 | $155,800, plus 37 percent of the excess of such amount over $500,000. |
| Over $750,000 but not over $1,000,000 | $248,300, plus 39 percent of the excess of such amount over $750,000. |
| Over $1,000,000 but not over $1,250,000 | $345,800, plus 41 percent of the excess of such amount over $1,000,000. |
| Over $1,250,000 but not over $1,500,000 | $448,300, plus 43 percent of the excess of such amount over $1,250,000. |
| Over $1,500,000 but not over $2,000,000 | $555,800, plus 45 percent of the excess of such amount over $1,500,000. |
| Over $2,000,000 but not over $2,500,000 | $780,800, plus 49 percent of the excess of such amount over $2,000,000. |
| Over $2,500,000 | $1,025,800, plus 50 percent of the excess of such amount over $2,500,000. |

# Unified Transfer Tax Rates

## FOR GIFTS MADE AND FOR DEATHS IN 2003

| If the Amount with Respect to Which the Tentative Tax to Be Computed Is: | The Tentative Tax Is: |
| --- | --- |
| Not over $10,000 | 18 percent of such amount. |
| Over $10,000 but not over $20,000 | $1,800, plus 20 percent of the excess of such amount over $10,000. |
| Over $20,000 but not over $40,000 | $3,800, plus 22 percent of the excess of such amount over $20,000. |
| Over $40,000 but not over $60,000 | $8,200, plus 24 percent of the excess of such amount over $40,000. |
| Over $60,000 but not over $80,000 | $13,000, plus 26 percent of the excess of such amount over $60,000. |
| Over $80,000 but not over $100,000 | $18,200, plus 28 percent of the excess of such amount over $80,000. |
| Over $100,000 but not over $150,000 | $23,800, plus 30 percent of the excess of such amount over $100,000. |
| Over $150,000 but not over $250,000 | $38,800, plus 32 percent of the excess of such amount over $150,000. |
| Over $250,000 but not over $500,000 | $70,800, plus 34 percent of the excess of such amount over $250,000. |
| Over $500,000 but not over $750,000 | $155,800, plus 37 percent of the excess of such amount over $500,000. |
| Over $750,000 but not over $1,000,000 | $248,300, plus 39 percent of the excess of such amount over $750,000. |
| Over $1,000,000 but not over $1,250,000 | $345,800, plus 41 percent of the excess of such amount over $1,000,000. |
| Over $1,250,000 but not over $1,500,000 | $448,300, plus 43 percent of the excess of such amount over $1,250,000. |
| Over $1,500,000 but not over $2,000,000 | $555,800, plus 45 percent of the excess of such amount over $1,500,000. |
| Over $2,000,000 | $780,800, plus 49 percent of the excess of such amount over $2,000,000. |

# Unified Transfer Tax Rates

## FOR GIFTS MADE AND FOR DEATHS IN 2004

| If the Amount with Respect to Which the Tentative Tax to Be Computed Is: | The Tentative Tax Is: |
| --- | --- |
| Not over $10,000 | 18 percent of such amount. |
| Over $10,000 but not over $20,000 | $1,800, plus 20 percent of the excess of such amount over $10,000. |
| Over $20,000 but not over $40,000 | $3,800, plus 22 percent of the excess of such amount over $20,000. |
| Over $40,000 but not over $60,000 | $8,200, plus 24 percent of the excess of such amount over $40,000. |
| Over $60,000 but not over $80,000 | $13,000, plus 26 percent of the excess of such amount over $60,000. |
| Over $80,000 but not over $100,000 | $18,200, plus 28 percent of the excess of such amount over $80,000. |
| Over $100,000 but not over $150,000 | $23,800, plus 30 percent of the excess of such amount over $100,000. |
| Over $150,000 but not over $250,000 | $38,800, plus 32 percent of the excess of such amount over $150,000. |
| Over $250,000 but not over $500,000 | $70,800, plus 34 percent of the excess of such amount over $250,000. |
| Over $500,000 but not over $750,000 | $155,800, plus 37 percent of the excess of such amount over $500,000. |
| Over $750,000 but not over $1,000,000 | $248,300, plus 39 percent of the excess of such amount over $750,000. |
| Over $1,000,000 but not over $1,250,000 | $345,800, plus 41 percent of the excess of such amount over $1,000,000. |
| Over $1,250,000 but not over $1,500,000 | $448,300, plus 43 percent of the excess of such amount over $1,250,000. |
| Over $1,500,000 but not over $2,000,000 | $555,800, plus 45 percent of the excess of such amount over $1,500,000. |
| Over $2,000,000 | $780,800, plus 48 percent of the excess of such amount over $2,000,000. |

# Unified Transfer Tax Rates

## FOR GIFTS MADE AND FOR DEATHS IN 2005

| If the Amount with Respect to Which the Tentative Tax to Be Computed Is: | The Tentative Tax Is: |
|---|---|
| Not over $10,000 | 18 percent of such amount. |
| Over $10,000 but not over $20,000 | $1,800, plus 20 percent of the excess of such amount over $10,000. |
| Over $20,000 but not over $40,000 | $3,800, plus 22 percent of the excess of such amount over $20,000. |
| Over $40,000 but not over $60,000 | $8,200, plus 24 percent of the excess of such amount over $40,000. |
| Over $60,000 but not over $80,000 | $13,000, plus 26 percent of the excess of such amount over $60,000. |
| Over $80,000 but not over $100,000 | $18,200, plus 28 percent of the excess of such amount over $80,000. |
| Over $100,000 but not over $150,000 | $23,800, plus 30 percent of the excess of such amount over $100,000. |
| Over $150,000 but not over $250,000 | $38,800, plus 32 percent of the excess of such amount over $150,000. |
| Over $250,000 but not over $500,000 | $70,800, plus 34 percent of the excess of such amount over $250,000. |
| Over $500,000 but not over $750,000 | $155,800, plus 37 percent of the excess of such amount over $500,000. |
| Over $750,000 but not over $1,000,000 | $248,300, plus 39 percent of the excess of such amount over $750,000. |
| Over $1,000,000 but not over $1,250,000 | $345,800, plus 41 percent of the excess of such amount over $1,000,000. |
| Over $1,250,000 but not over $1,500,000 | $448,300, plus 43 percent of the excess of such amount over $1,250,000. |
| Over $1,500,000 but not over $2,000,000 | $555,800, plus 45 percent of the excess of such amount over $1,500,000. |
| Over $2,000,000 | $780,800, plus 47 percent of the excess of such amount over $2,000,000. |

# Table for Computation of Maximum Credit for State Death Taxes**

| (A)<br><br>Adjusted Taxable Estate* Equal to or More Than | (B)<br><br>Adjusted Taxable Estate* Less Than | (C)<br><br>Credit on Amount in Column (A) | (D)<br>Rate of Credit on Excess Over Amount in Column (A) (Percentage) |
|---|---|---|---|
| 0 | $ 40,000 | 0 | None |
| $ 40,000 | 90,000 | 0 | 0.8 |
| 90,000 | 140,000 | $ 400 | 1.6 |
| 140,000 | 240,000 | 1,200 | 2.4 |
| 240,000 | 440,000 | 3,600 | 3.2 |
| 440,000 | 640,000 | 10,000 | 4.0 |
| 640,000 | 840,000 | 18,000 | 4.8 |
| 840,000 | 1,040,000 | 27,600 | 5.6 |
| 1,040,000 | 1,540,000 | 38,800 | 6.4 |
| 1,540,000 | 2,040,000 | 70,800 | 7.2 |
| 2,040,000 | 2,540,000 | 106,800 | 8.0 |
| 2,540,000 | 3,040,000 | 146,800 | 8.8 |
| 3,040,000 | 3,540,000 | 190,800 | 9.6 |
| 3,540,000 | 4,040,000 | 238,800 | 10.4 |
| 4,040,000 | 5,040,000 | 290,800 | 11.2 |
| 5,040,000 | 6,040,000 | 402,800 | 12.0 |
| 6,040,000 | 7,040,000 | 522,800 | 12.8 |
| 7,040,000 | 8,040,000 | 650,800 | 13.6 |
| 8,040,000 | 9,040,000 | 786,800 | 14.4 |
| 9,040,000 | 10,040,000 | 930,800 | 15.2 |
| 10,040,000 | | 1,082,800 | 16.0 |

*Adjusted Taxable Estate = Taxable Estate − $60,000.

**Although the § 2011 credit has been completely phased out for Federal estate tax purposes, the schedule continues to be used by some states as the measure of state death tax imposed.

# Scheduled phaseout:

| Year | | Percentage Allowed |
|---|---|---|
| 2002 | ............................. | 75 |
| 2003 | ............................. | 50 |
| 2004 | ............................. | 25 |
| 2005 | ............................. | 0 |

# 2004 Optional Sales Tax Tables

**When Used.**   The election to deduct state and local general sales taxes requires that the taxpayer forgo any deduction for state and local income taxes. Further, the use of the optional sales tax tables means that the actual expense method is not chosen. The actual expense method cannot be used when the amount claimed is not supported by actual receipts.

**Adjustments Necessary.**   The optional sales tax tables are based on a number of assumptions that require adjustments to be made. As the starting point for the use of the tables is AGI, nontaxable receipts have not been included. Examples of receipts that should be added include: tax-exempt interest, veterans' benefits, workers' compensation, nontaxable social security and other retirement benefits. But do not include any large nontaxable items that are not likely to be spent. For example, a $100,000 inheritance should not be added if it was invested in a certificate of deposit.

Because the tables are based on the state general sales tax rate, an adjustment has to be made for any local (city, county, transit authority, etc.) tax imposed.

The tables represent the sales tax on the average (and recurring) expenditures based on level of income by family size and do not include exceptional purchases. Therefore, add to the table amount any sales taxes on major purchases (such as motor vehicles, aircraft, boats, and home building materials, etc.).

**Use Illustrated.**

> EXAMPLE.   The Archers file a joint return for 2004 reflecting AGI of $88,000 and claiming three exemptions. They have tax-exempt interest of $3,000, and during the year, they incurred sales tax of $1,650 on the purchase of an automobile for their dependent teenage son. They live in Bellaire, Texas, where the general sales tax rates are 6.25% (0.0625) for state and 2% (0.02) for local.

Using the Worksheet appearing below, the general sales tax deduction is $3,062. As Texas imposes no state or local income tax, no choice is necessary, and the $3,062 can be claimed by the Archers as an itemized deduction on Schedule A.

## Sales Tax Deduction Worksheet

| | |
|---|---|
| Adjusted Gross Income (AGI) as listed on line 37 of Form 1040 | 88,000 |
| Add nontaxable items | 3,000 |
| Table income to be used for purposes of line 1 below | 91,000 |
| 1. Use table income to determine table amount—go to state of residence and find applicable range of table income and exemption column* for *state* sales tax | 1,070 |
| 2a. Enter local general sales tax rate                     0.02 | |
| 2b. Enter state general sales tax rate**                  0.0625 | |
| 2c. Divide 2a by 2b                                            0.32 | |
| 2d. Multiply line 1 by line 2c for the local sales tax | 342 |
| 3. Enter general sales tax on large purchases | 1,650 |
| 4. Deduction for general sales tax (add lines 1 + 2d + 3) and report on line 5 of Schedule A of Form 1040 | 3,062 |

*Use total of personal and dependency exemptions as reported in item 6d of Form 1040.

**Due to change in rates during 2004 use: .059 for Arkansas, .061 for California, and .037 for Virginia.

# 2004 Optional State Sales Tax Tables

**Alaska residents only.** If you paid any local sales taxes, you must use your actual expenses to figure your deduction.

## Alabama

| Income (At least – But less than) | 1 | 2 | 3 | 4 | 5 | Over 5 |
|---|---|---|---|---|---|---|
| $0 – $20,000 | 288 | 344 | 381 | 410 | 434 | 468 |
| 20,000 – 30,000 | 366 | 434 | 481 | 517 | 547 | 590 |
| 30,000 – 40,000 | 416 | 494 | 547 | 587 | 621 | 669 |
| 40,000 – 50,000 | 460 | 545 | 602 | 647 | 684 | 736 |
| 50,000 – 60,000 | 498 | 590 | 652 | 700 | 740 | 796 |
| 60,000 – 70,000 | 532 | 630 | 695 | 747 | 789 | 849 |
| 70,000 – 80,000 | 565 | 667 | 737 | 791 | 835 | 898 |
| 80,000 – 90,000 | 593 | 701 | 773 | 830 | 877 | 942 |
| 90,000 – 100,000 | 621 | 733 | 809 | 868 | 916 | 985 |
| 100,000 – 120,000 | 657 | 775 | 855 | 917 | 968 | 1040 |
| 120,000 – 140,000 | 706 | 832 | 916 | 982 | 1037 | 1114 |
| 140,000 – 160,000 | 749 | 881 | 971 | 1040 | 1098 | 1179 |
| 160,000 – 180,000 | 789 | 928 | 1022 | 1095 | 1155 | 1240 |
| 180,000 – 200,000 | 827 | 972 | 1070 | 1146 | 1209 | 1298 |
| 200,000 or more | 995 | 1166 | 1281 | 1371 | 1445 | 1549 |

## Arizona

| Income (At least – But less than) | 1 | 2 | 3 | 4 | 5 | Over 5 |
|---|---|---|---|---|---|---|
| $0 – $20,000 | 332 | 374 | 402 | 422 | 439 | 463 |
| 20,000 – 30,000 | 430 | 485 | 520 | 547 | 568 | 598 |
| 30,000 – 40,000 | 496 | 558 | 599 | 629 | 654 | 688 |
| 40,000 – 50,000 | 552 | 621 | 666 | 699 | 727 | 765 |
| 50,000 – 60,000 | 603 | 678 | 726 | 763 | 792 | 833 |
| 60,000 – 70,000 | 648 | 728 | 780 | 819 | 851 | 895 |
| 70,000 – 80,000 | 690 | 776 | 831 | 872 | 906 | 952 |
| 80,000 – 90,000 | 728 | 818 | 876 | 920 | 955 | 1004 |
| 90,000 – 100,000 | 765 | 859 | 920 | 965 | 1003 | 1054 |
| 100,000 – 120,000 | 814 | 913 | 977 | 1026 | 1065 | 1119 |
| 120,000 – 140,000 | 878 | 985 | 1054 | 1106 | 1148 | 1206 |
| 140,000 – 160,000 | 935 | 1048 | 1122 | 1177 | 1222 | 1283 |
| 160,000 – 180,000 | 990 | 1109 | 1186 | 1244 | 1292 | 1357 |
| 180,000 – 200,000 | 1041 | 1166 | 1247 | 1308 | 1357 | 1425 |
| 200,000 or more | 1267 | 1417 | 1514 | 1587 | 1647 | 1728 |

## Arkansas

| Income (At least – But less than) | 1 | 2 | 3 | 4 | 5 | Over 5 |
|---|---|---|---|---|---|---|
| $0 – $20,000 | 430 | 510 | 564 | 605 | 640 | 688 |
| 20,000 – 30,000 | 542 | 641 | 708 | 760 | 803 | 863 |
| 30,000 – 40,000 | 616 | 727 | 802 | 860 | 908 | 976 |
| 40,000 – 50,000 | 678 | 800 | 882 | 945 | 998 | 1072 |
| 50,000 – 60,000 | 734 | 864 | 952 | 1021 | 1077 | 1157 |
| 60,000 – 70,000 | 783 | 922 | 1015 | 1088 | 1148 | 1232 |
| 70,000 – 80,000 | 829 | 976 | 1074 | 1150 | 1214 | 1302 |
| 80,000 – 90,000 | 871 | 1023 | 1126 | 1206 | 1272 | 1365 |
| 90,000 – 100,000 | 910 | 1070 | 1177 | 1260 | 1328 | 1425 |
| 100,000 – 120,000 | 962 | 1130 | 1242 | 1330 | 1402 | 1503 |
| 120,000 – 140,000 | 1031 | 1210 | 1330 | 1422 | 1499 | 1607 |
| 140,000 – 160,000 | 1093 | 1280 | 1407 | 1504 | 1585 | 1699 |
| 160,000 – 180,000 | 1151 | 1347 | 1479 | 1582 | 1667 | 1785 |
| 180,000 – 200,000 | 1205 | 1410 | 1548 | 1654 | 1743 | 1866 |
| 200,000 or more | 1443 | 1684 | 1846 | 1971 | 2074 | 2220 |

## California

| Income (At least – But less than) | 1 | 2 | 3 | 4 | 5 | Over 5 |
|---|---|---|---|---|---|---|
| $0 – $20,000 | 363 | 416 | 451 | 477 | 499 | 529 |
| 20,000 – 30,000 | 469 | 537 | 581 | 615 | 643 | 681 |
| 30,000 – 40,000 | 540 | 617 | 668 | 706 | 738 | 782 |
| 40,000 – 50,000 | 600 | 685 | 741 | 784 | 819 | 867 |
| 50,000 – 60,000 | 654 | 747 | 807 | 854 | 892 | 944 |
| 60,000 – 70,000 | 702 | 801 | 866 | 916 | 956 | 1012 |
| 70,000 – 80,000 | 748 | 853 | 922 | 974 | 1017 | 1077 |
| 80,000 – 90,000 | 789 | 899 | 971 | 1027 | 1072 | 1134 |
| 90,000 – 100,000 | 828 | 944 | 1019 | 1077 | 1124 | 1189 |
| 100,000 – 120,000 | 880 | 1002 | 1082 | 1143 | 1193 | 1262 |
| 120,000 – 140,000 | 949 | 1080 | 1166 | 1232 | 1285 | 1359 |
| 140,000 – 160,000 | 1010 | 1149 | 1240 | 1310 | 1366 | 1445 |
| 160,000 – 180,000 | 1069 | 1215 | 1311 | 1384 | 1444 | 1526 |
| 180,000 – 200,000 | 1123 | 1277 | 1377 | 1454 | 1516 | 1602 |
| 200,000 or more | 1365 | 1549 | 1669 | 1761 | 1835 | 1939 |

## Colorado

| Income (At least – But less than) | 1 | 2 | 3 | 4 | 5 | Over 5 |
|---|---|---|---|---|---|---|
| $0 – $20,000 | 160 | 183 | 197 | 208 | 217 | 230 |
| 20,000 – 30,000 | 209 | 238 | 257 | 271 | 283 | 299 |
| 30,000 – 40,000 | 242 | 275 | 297 | 313 | 327 | 345 |
| 40,000 – 50,000 | 271 | 307 | 331 | 349 | 364 | 384 |
| 50,000 – 60,000 | 296 | 336 | 362 | 382 | 398 | 420 |
| 60,000 – 70,000 | 319 | 362 | 390 | 411 | 428 | 452 |
| 70,000 – 80,000 | 341 | 386 | 416 | 438 | 457 | 482 |
| 80,000 – 90,000 | 360 | 408 | 439 | 463 | 482 | 509 |
| 90,000 – 100,000 | 379 | 429 | 462 | 487 | 507 | 535 |
| 100,000 – 120,000 | 404 | 457 | 492 | 518 | 539 | 569 |
| 120,000 – 140,000 | 437 | 494 | 531 | 560 | 583 | 614 |
| 140,000 – 160,000 | 466 | 527 | 567 | 597 | 621 | 655 |
| 160,000 – 180,000 | 494 | 559 | 600 | 632 | 658 | 694 |
| 180,000 – 200,000 | 521 | 588 | 632 | 665 | 693 | 730 |
| 200,000 or more | 638 | 720 | 773 | 813 | 846 | 891 |

## Connecticut

| Income (At least – But less than) | 1 | 2 | 3 | 4 | 5 | Over 5 |
|---|---|---|---|---|---|---|
| $0 – $20,000 | 338 | 387 | 419 | 444 | 464 | 492 |
| 20,000 – 30,000 | 440 | 503 | 545 | 577 | 603 | 639 |
| 30,000 – 40,000 | 509 | 581 | 629 | 665 | 695 | 736 |
| 40,000 – 50,000 | 567 | 647 | 700 | 740 | 773 | 819 |
| 50,000 – 60,000 | 620 | 707 | 764 | 808 | 844 | 894 |
| 60,000 – 70,000 | 667 | 760 | 822 | 869 | 907 | 960 |
| 70,000 – 80,000 | 712 | 811 | 876 | 926 | 966 | 1023 |
| 80,000 – 90,000 | 751 | 856 | 924 | 976 | 1019 | 1079 |
| 90,000 – 100,000 | 790 | 899 | 971 | 1026 | 1071 | 1133 |
| 100,000 – 120,000 | 840 | 956 | 1032 | 1090 | 1138 | 1204 |
| 120,000 – 140,000 | 908 | 1032 | 1114 | 1177 | 1228 | 1298 |
| 140,000 – 160,000 | 968 | 1100 | 1187 | 1253 | 1307 | 1382 |
| 160,000 – 180,000 | 1025 | 1164 | 1256 | 1325 | 1383 | 1462 |
| 180,000 – 200,000 | 1079 | 1225 | 1320 | 1394 | 1454 | 1536 |
| 200,000 or more | 1315 | 1491 | 1606 | 1694 | 1766 | 1866 |

## District of Columbia

| Income (At least – But less than) | 1 | 2 | 3 | 4 | 5 | Over 5 |
|---|---|---|---|---|---|---|
| $0 – $20,000 | 327 | 375 | 407 | 431 | 451 | 478 |
| 20,000 – 30,000 | 428 | 490 | 531 | 563 | 588 | 624 |
| 30,000 – 40,000 | 496 | 568 | 615 | 651 | 680 | 721 |
| 40,000 – 50,000 | 555 | 635 | 687 | 727 | 759 | 805 |
| 50,000 – 60,000 | 608 | 695 | 752 | 795 | 831 | 880 |
| 60,000 – 70,000 | 655 | 748 | 810 | 856 | 894 | 947 |
| 70,000 – 80,000 | 700 | 799 | 864 | 914 | 954 | 1011 |
| 80,000 – 90,000 | 740 | 845 | 913 | 966 | 1008 | 1067 |
| 90,000 – 100,000 | 779 | 889 | 961 | 1016 | 1060 | 1122 |
| 100,000 – 120,000 | 831 | 947 | 1023 | 1082 | 1129 | 1195 |
| 120,000 – 140,000 | 900 | 1025 | 1107 | 1170 | 1221 | 1292 |
| 140,000 – 160,000 | 961 | 1094 | 1181 | 1248 | 1302 | 1377 |
| 160,000 – 180,000 | 1019 | 1160 | 1252 | 1322 | 1380 | 1459 |
| 180,000 – 200,000 | 1074 | 1222 | 1319 | 1393 | 1453 | 1536 |
| 200,000 or more | 1319 | 1498 | 1615 | 1704 | 1777 | 1877 |

## Florida

| Income (At least – But less than) | 1 | 2 | 3 | 4 | 5 | Over 5 |
|---|---|---|---|---|---|---|
| $0 – $20,000 | 394 | 450 | 487 | 515 | 537 | 569 |
| 20,000 – 30,000 | 509 | 580 | 627 | 662 | 691 | 731 |
| 30,000 – 40,000 | 585 | 666 | 720 | 760 | 793 | 838 |
| 40,000 – 50,000 | 650 | 740 | 799 | 843 | 880 | 930 |
| 50,000 – 60,000 | 709 | 806 | 870 | 918 | 957 | 1012 |
| 60,000 – 70,000 | 761 | 865 | 933 | 984 | 1027 | 1085 |
| 70,000 – 80,000 | 810 | 920 | 992 | 1047 | 1092 | 1153 |
| 80,000 – 90,000 | 854 | 970 | 1045 | 1103 | 1150 | 1215 |
| 90,000 – 100,000 | 896 | 1018 | 1097 | 1157 | 1206 | 1274 |
| 100,000 – 120,000 | 952 | 1080 | 1164 | 1228 | 1280 | 1351 |
| 120,000 – 140,000 | 1026 | 1164 | 1254 | 1322 | 1378 | 1455 |
| 140,000 – 160,000 | 1092 | 1238 | 1333 | 1406 | 1465 | 1546 |
| 160,000 – 180,000 | 1155 | 1309 | 1409 | 1485 | 1547 | 1633 |
| 180,000 – 200,000 | 1214 | 1375 | 1480 | 1560 | 1625 | 1714 |
| 200,000 or more | 1474 | 1667 | 1792 | 1888 | 1965 | 2073 |

## Georgia

| Income (At least – But less than) | 1 | 2 | 3 | 4 | 5 | Over 5 |
|---|---|---|---|---|---|---|
| $0 – $20,000 | 247 | 285 | 310 | 330 | 345 | 367 |
| 20,000 – 30,000 | 328 | 377 | 410 | 435 | 455 | 484 |
| 30,000 – 40,000 | 382 | 439 | 477 | 506 | 529 | 562 |
| 40,000 – 50,000 | 429 | 493 | 535 | 567 | 593 | 630 |
| 50,000 – 60,000 | 471 | 541 | 587 | 622 | 651 | 691 |
| 60,000 – 70,000 | 509 | 584 | 634 | 672 | 703 | 746 |
| 70,000 – 80,000 | 545 | 625 | 678 | 719 | 752 | 798 |
| 80,000 – 90,000 | 578 | 662 | 718 | 761 | 796 | 844 |
| 90,000 – 100,000 | 609 | 698 | 757 | 802 | 838 | 889 |
| 100,000 – 120,000 | 651 | 746 | 808 | 855 | 894 | 949 |
| 120,000 – 140,000 | 707 | 809 | 876 | 927 | 969 | 1028 |
| 140,000 – 160,000 | 757 | 865 | 937 | 991 | 1036 | 1099 |
| 160,000 – 180,000 | 804 | 919 | 995 | 1053 | 1100 | 1166 |
| 180,000 – 200,000 | 849 | 970 | 1050 | 1110 | 1160 | 1230 |
| 200,000 or more | 1049 | 1196 | 1293 | 1367 | 1428 | 1512 |

## Hawaii

| Income (At least – But less than) | 1 | 2 | 3 | 4 | 5 | Over 5 |
|---|---|---|---|---|---|---|
| $0 – $20,000 | 325 | 386 | 428 | 460 | 487 | 525 |
| 20,000 – 30,000 | 416 | 493 | 545 | 586 | 620 | 667 |
| 30,000 – 40,000 | 476 | 564 | 623 | 669 | 707 | 761 |
| 40,000 – 50,000 | 527 | 624 | 689 | 739 | 781 | 840 |
| 50,000 – 60,000 | 573 | 677 | 747 | 802 | 847 | 911 |
| 60,000 – 70,000 | 614 | 725 | 800 | 858 | 906 | 974 |
| 70,000 – 80,000 | 652 | 770 | 849 | 910 | 961 | 1033 |
| 80,000 – 90,000 | 687 | 809 | 892 | 957 | 1010 | 1085 |
| 90,000 – 100,000 | 720 | 848 | 935 | 1002 | 1058 | 1136 |
| 100,000 – 120,000 | 763 | 899 | 990 | 1061 | 1120 | 1202 |
| 120,000 – 140,000 | 821 | 966 | 1063 | 1139 | 1202 | 1290 |
| 140,000 – 160,000 | 873 | 1025 | 1129 | 1209 | 1275 | 1368 |
| 160,000 – 180,000 | 921 | 1082 | 1190 | 1274 | 1344 | 1442 |
| 180,000 – 200,000 | 967 | 1135 | 1248 | 1336 | 1409 | 1511 |
| 200,000 or more | 1169 | 1368 | 1502 | 1607 | 1693 | 1814 |

## Idaho

| Income (At least – But less than) | 1 | 2 | 3 | 4 | 5 | Over 5 |
|---|---|---|---|---|---|---|
| $0 – $20,000 | 405 | 482 | 535 | 575 | 609 | 657 |
| 20,000 – 30,000 | 519 | 615 | 681 | 732 | 775 | 835 |
| 30,000 – 40,000 | 594 | 703 | 777 | 835 | 883 | 951 |
| 40,000 – 50,000 | 658 | 778 | 859 | 923 | 976 | 1050 |
| 50,000 – 60,000 | 715 | 845 | 933 | 1001 | 1058 | 1138 |
| 60,000 – 70,000 | 767 | 904 | 998 | 1071 | 1131 | 1216 |
| 70,000 – 80,000 | 815 | 960 | 1059 | 1136 | 1200 | 1290 |
| 80,000 – 90,000 | 858 | 1010 | 1114 | 1194 | 1261 | 1355 |
| 90,000 – 100,000 | 900 | 1059 | 1166 | 1250 | 1320 | 1418 |
| 100,000 – 120,000 | 954 | 1122 | 1236 | 1324 | 1398 | 1501 |
| 120,000 – 140,000 | 1027 | 1206 | 1327 | 1422 | 1500 | 1611 |
| 140,000 – 160,000 | 1092 | 1281 | 1409 | 1508 | 1591 | 1708 |
| 160,000 – 180,000 | 1153 | 1352 | 1486 | 1591 | 1677 | 1800 |
| 180,000 – 200,000 | 1211 | 1418 | 1558 | 1668 | 1758 | 1886 |
| 200,000 or more | 1467 | 1711 | 1877 | 2006 | 2113 | 2264 |

## Illinois

| Income (At least – But less than) | 1 | 2 | 3 | 4 | 5 | Over 5 |
|---|---|---|---|---|---|---|
| $0 – $20,000 | 480 | 578 | 644 | 696 | 740 | 801 |
| 20,000 – 30,000 | 603 | 723 | 806 | 870 | 924 | 999 |
| 30,000 – 40,000 | 683 | 819 | 911 | 983 | 1043 | 1128 |
| 40,000 – 50,000 | 751 | 899 | 999 | 1078 | 1144 | 1236 |
| 50,000 – 60,000 | 812 | 970 | 1078 | 1163 | 1233 | 1332 |
| 60,000 – 70,000 | 866 | 1034 | 1148 | 1237 | 1312 | 1417 |
| 70,000 – 80,000 | 916 | 1093 | 1213 | 1308 | 1386 | 1496 |
| 80,000 – 90,000 | 961 | 1146 | 1272 | 1370 | 1452 | 1567 |
| 90,000 – 100,000 | 1005 | 1197 | 1327 | 1430 | 1515 | 1635 |
| 100,000 – 120,000 | 1061 | 1263 | 1401 | 1508 | 1597 | 1723 |
| 120,000 – 140,000 | 1137 | 1351 | 1497 | 1611 | 1706 | 1840 |
| 140,000 – 160,000 | 1203 | 1429 | 1583 | 1703 | 1803 | 1943 |
| 160,000 – 180,000 | 1266 | 1503 | 1664 | 1789 | 1893 | 2041 |
| 180,000 – 200,000 | 1326 | 1572 | 1739 | 1870 | 1979 | 2132 |
| 200,000 or more | 1585 | 1874 | 2069 | 2222 | 2349 | 2529 |

*(Continued)*

## 2004 Optional State Sales Tax Tables (Continued)

### Indiana

| Income At least | But less than | 1 | 2 | 3 | 4 | 5 | Over 5 |
|---|---|---|---|---|---|---|---|
| $0 | $20,000 | 375 | 431 | 467 | 495 | 518 | 550 |
| 20,000 | 30,000 | 489 | 561 | 608 | 644 | 673 | 714 |
| 30,000 | 40,000 | 566 | 648 | 702 | 743 | 776 | 823 |
| 40,000 | 50,000 | 631 | 722 | 782 | 828 | 865 | 917 |
| 50,000 | 60,000 | 691 | 789 | 854 | 904 | 944 | 1001 |
| 60,000 | 70,000 | 744 | 849 | 919 | 972 | 1015 | 1076 |
| 70,000 | 80,000 | 794 | 906 | 980 | 1036 | 1082 | 1146 |
| 80,000 | 90,000 | 839 | 957 | 1035 | 1094 | 1142 | 1210 |
| 90,000 | 100,000 | 882 | 1006 | 1088 | 1150 | 1200 | 1271 |
| 100,000 | 120,000 | 940 | 1071 | 1157 | 1223 | 1277 | 1351 |
| 120,000 | 140,000 | 1016 | 1157 | 1250 | 1321 | 1379 | 1459 |
| 140,000 | 160,000 | 1085 | 1234 | 1333 | 1408 | 1469 | 1554 |
| 160,000 | 180,000 | 1150 | 1308 | 1411 | 1490 | 1555 | 1645 |
| 180,000 | 200,000 | 1211 | 1377 | 1485 | 1568 | 1636 | 1730 |
| 200,000 or more | | 1483 | 1682 | 1813 | 1913 | 1994 | 2107 |

### Iowa

| Income At least | But less than | 1 | 2 | 3 | 4 | 5 | Over 5 |
|---|---|---|---|---|---|---|---|
| $0 | $20,000 | 304 | 348 | 377 | 399 | 417 | 442 |
| 20,000 | 30,000 | 400 | 457 | 494 | 523 | 546 | 578 |
| 30,000 | 40,000 | 465 | 530 | 573 | 606 | 632 | 669 |
| 40,000 | 50,000 | 520 | 593 | 641 | 677 | 707 | 748 |
| 50,000 | 60,000 | 570 | 650 | 702 | 741 | 774 | 819 |
| 60,000 | 70,000 | 616 | 701 | 757 | 799 | 834 | 882 |
| 70,000 | 80,000 | 658 | 749 | 808 | 854 | 891 | 942 |
| 80,000 | 90,000 | 696 | 792 | 855 | 902 | 941 | 995 |
| 90,000 | 100,000 | 734 | 834 | 900 | 950 | 991 | 1047 |
| 100,000 | 120,000 | 783 | 889 | 959 | 1012 | 1056 | 1116 |
| 120,000 | 140,000 | 848 | 963 | 1038 | 1095 | 1142 | 1207 |
| 140,000 | 160,000 | 906 | 1029 | 1109 | 1169 | 1219 | 1288 |
| 160,000 | 180,000 | 962 | 1091 | 1176 | 1240 | 1293 | 1365 |
| 180,000 | 200,000 | 1015 | 1150 | 1239 | 1307 | 1362 | 1438 |
| 200,000 or more | | 1249 | 1413 | 1520 | 1602 | 1669 | 1761 |

### Kansas

| Income At least | But less than | 1 | 2 | 3 | 4 | 5 | Over 5 |
|---|---|---|---|---|---|---|---|
| $0 | $20,000 | 390 | 464 | 514 | 553 | 585 | 631 |
| 20,000 | 30,000 | 496 | 589 | 652 | 700 | 741 | 798 |
| 30,000 | 40,000 | 566 | 671 | 742 | 797 | 843 | 907 |
| 40,000 | 50,000 | 626 | 741 | 819 | 879 | 929 | 999 |
| 50,000 | 60,000 | 679 | 803 | 887 | 952 | 1006 | 1082 |
| 60,000 | 70,000 | 727 | 858 | 948 | 1017 | 1074 | 1155 |
| 70,000 | 80,000 | 771 | 910 | 1004 | 1078 | 1138 | 1223 |
| 80,000 | 90,000 | 811 | 957 | 1055 | 1132 | 1195 | 1284 |
| 90,000 | 100,000 | 849 | 1001 | 1104 | 1184 | 1250 | 1343 |
| 100,000 | 120,000 | 900 | 1060 | 1168 | 1252 | 1322 | 1420 |
| 120,000 | 140,000 | 966 | 1138 | 1253 | 1343 | 1417 | 1521 |
| 140,000 | 160,000 | 1026 | 1206 | 1328 | 1423 | 1501 | 1611 |
| 160,000 | 180,000 | 1082 | 1272 | 1399 | 1499 | 1581 | 1696 |
| 180,000 | 200,000 | 1135 | 1333 | 1466 | 1570 | 1656 | 1776 |
| 200,000 or more | | 1367 | 1601 | 1759 | 1881 | 1983 | 2125 |

### Kentucky

| Income At least | But less than | 1 | 2 | 3 | 4 | 5 | Over 5 |
|---|---|---|---|---|---|---|---|
| $0 | $20,000 | 337 | 388 | 421 | 446 | 467 | 496 |
| 20,000 | 30,000 | 441 | 507 | 549 | 582 | 609 | 646 |
| 30,000 | 40,000 | 511 | 586 | 635 | 673 | 704 | 747 |
| 40,000 | 50,000 | 572 | 655 | 709 | 751 | 785 | 833 |
| 50,000 | 60,000 | 626 | 716 | 776 | 821 | 858 | 910 |
| 60,000 | 70,000 | 675 | 772 | 835 | 884 | 924 | 979 |
| 70,000 | 80,000 | 721 | 824 | 892 | 943 | 986 | 1045 |
| 80,000 | 90,000 | 762 | 871 | 942 | 997 | 1041 | 1103 |
| 90,000 | 100,000 | 802 | 916 | 991 | 1048 | 1095 | 1160 |
| 100,000 | 120,000 | 855 | 976 | 1055 | 1116 | 1166 | 1234 |
| 120,000 | 140,000 | 925 | 1056 | 1141 | 1206 | 1260 | 1334 |
| 140,000 | 160,000 | 988 | 1127 | 1217 | 1287 | 1343 | 1422 |
| 160,000 | 180,000 | 1048 | 1194 | 1290 | 1363 | 1423 | 1506 |
| 180,000 | 200,000 | 1104 | 1258 | 1359 | 1436 | 1498 | 1585 |
| 200,000 or more | | 1355 | 1541 | 1662 | 1755 | 1831 | 1936 |

### Louisiana

| Income At least | But less than | 1 | 2 | 3 | 4 | 5 | Over 5 |
|---|---|---|---|---|---|---|---|
| $0 | $20,000 | 216 | 247 | 268 | 283 | 296 | 313 |
| 20,000 | 30,000 | 282 | 322 | 349 | 369 | 385 | 408 |
| 30,000 | 40,000 | 327 | 373 | 403 | 426 | 445 | 470 |
| 40,000 | 50,000 | 365 | 416 | 449 | 475 | 496 | 524 |
| 50,000 | 60,000 | 399 | 455 | 491 | 519 | 541 | 573 |
| 60,000 | 70,000 | 430 | 489 | 528 | 558 | 582 | 616 |
| 70,000 | 80,000 | 459 | 522 | 564 | 595 | 621 | 657 |
| 80,000 | 90,000 | 485 | 551 | 595 | 628 | 656 | 693 |
| 90,000 | 100,000 | 510 | 580 | 626 | 661 | 689 | 728 |
| 100,000 | 120,000 | 543 | 617 | 666 | 703 | 733 | 775 |
| 120,000 | 140,000 | 587 | 667 | 719 | 759 | 792 | 837 |
| 140,000 | 160,000 | 626 | 711 | 767 | 809 | 844 | 892 |
| 160,000 | 180,000 | 664 | 754 | 812 | 857 | 893 | 944 |
| 180,000 | 200,000 | 699 | 793 | 855 | 902 | 940 | 993 |
| 200,000 or more | | 855 | 969 | 1043 | 1100 | 1146 | 1209 |

### Maine

| Income At least | But less than | 1 | 2 | 3 | 4 | 5 | Over 5 |
|---|---|---|---|---|---|---|---|
| $0 | $20,000 | 264 | 301 | 325 | 344 | 359 | 379 |
| 20,000 | 30,000 | 352 | 400 | 432 | 456 | 475 | 502 |
| 30,000 | 40,000 | 411 | 467 | 504 | 532 | 554 | 586 |
| 40,000 | 50,000 | 463 | 525 | 566 | 597 | 623 | 658 |
| 50,000 | 60,000 | 509 | 578 | 622 | 656 | 684 | 723 |
| 60,000 | 70,000 | 551 | 625 | 673 | 710 | 740 | 781 |
| 70,000 | 80,000 | 591 | 670 | 721 | 760 | 792 | 836 |
| 80,000 | 90,000 | 627 | 710 | 765 | 806 | 840 | 886 |
| 90,000 | 100,000 | 662 | 749 | 806 | 850 | 885 | 934 |
| 100,000 | 120,000 | 708 | 801 | 862 | 908 | 946 | 998 |
| 120,000 | 140,000 | 770 | 870 | 936 | 986 | 1027 | 1083 |
| 140,000 | 160,000 | 825 | 932 | 1002 | 1056 | 1099 | 1159 |
| 160,000 | 180,000 | 878 | 992 | 1066 | 1122 | 1168 | 1232 |
| 180,000 | 200,000 | 928 | 1047 | 1126 | 1185 | 1233 | 1300 |
| 200,000 or more | | 1151 | 1297 | 1392 | 1465 | 1524 | 1605 |

### Maryland

| Income At least | But less than | 1 | 2 | 3 | 4 | 5 | Over 5 |
|---|---|---|---|---|---|---|---|
| $0 | $20,000 | 241 | 280 | 306 | 326 | 343 | 366 |
| 20,000 | 30,000 | 326 | 378 | 413 | 440 | 462 | 493 |
| 30,000 | 40,000 | 384 | 445 | 486 | 517 | 543 | 579 |
| 40,000 | 50,000 | 435 | 504 | 549 | 585 | 614 | 654 |
| 50,000 | 60,000 | 481 | 557 | 607 | 646 | 678 | 722 |
| 60,000 | 70,000 | 523 | 605 | 659 | 701 | 736 | 784 |
| 70,000 | 80,000 | 563 | 650 | 709 | 754 | 791 | 842 |
| 80,000 | 90,000 | 599 | 692 | 753 | 801 | 840 | 895 |
| 90,000 | 100,000 | 634 | 732 | 797 | 847 | 888 | 946 |
| 100,000 | 120,000 | 680 | 785 | 854 | 908 | 952 | 1014 |
| 120,000 | 140,000 | 743 | 856 | 932 | 990 | 1038 | 1105 |
| 140,000 | 160,000 | 799 | 920 | 1001 | 1063 | 1114 | 1186 |
| 160,000 | 180,000 | 852 | 981 | 1067 | 1133 | 1188 | 1264 |
| 180,000 | 200,000 | 903 | 1039 | 1130 | 1200 | 1257 | 1337 |
| 200,000 or more | | 1131 | 1299 | 1411 | 1497 | 1568 | 1667 |

### Massachusetts

| Income At least | But less than | 1 | 2 | 3 | 4 | 5 | Over 5 |
|---|---|---|---|---|---|---|---|
| $0 | $20,000 | 279 | 315 | 339 | 357 | 372 | 392 |
| 20,000 | 30,000 | 370 | 418 | 449 | 473 | 492 | 519 |
| 30,000 | 40,000 | 432 | 487 | 524 | 551 | 573 | 604 |
| 40,000 | 50,000 | 485 | 547 | 588 | 618 | 643 | 677 |
| 50,000 | 60,000 | 534 | 602 | 646 | 679 | 706 | 744 |
| 60,000 | 70,000 | 578 | 651 | 698 | 734 | 763 | 804 |
| 70,000 | 80,000 | 619 | 697 | 748 | 786 | 817 | 860 |
| 80,000 | 90,000 | 656 | 739 | 792 | 832 | 865 | 911 |
| 90,000 | 100,000 | 692 | 779 | 835 | 878 | 912 | 960 |
| 100,000 | 120,000 | 740 | 832 | 892 | 937 | 974 | 1025 |
| 120,000 | 140,000 | 804 | 904 | 968 | 1017 | 1057 | 1112 |
| 140,000 | 160,000 | 861 | 967 | 1036 | 1088 | 1131 | 1189 |
| 160,000 | 180,000 | 916 | 1028 | 1101 | 1156 | 1201 | 1263 |
| 180,000 | 200,000 | 967 | 1086 | 1162 | 1221 | 1268 | 1333 |
| 200,000 or more | | 1198 | 1342 | 1436 | 1506 | 1564 | 1643 |

### Michigan

| Income At least | But less than | 1 | 2 | 3 | 4 | 5 | Over 5 |
|---|---|---|---|---|---|---|---|
| $0 | $20,000 | 349 | 396 | 426 | 450 | 469 | 495 |
| 20,000 | 30,000 | 448 | 507 | 545 | 575 | 599 | 632 |
| 30,000 | 40,000 | 514 | 580 | 624 | 657 | 684 | 722 |
| 40,000 | 50,000 | 570 | 643 | 691 | 727 | 757 | 798 |
| 50,000 | 60,000 | 621 | 699 | 751 | 790 | 822 | 867 |
| 60,000 | 70,000 | 666 | 749 | 804 | 846 | 880 | 927 |
| 70,000 | 80,000 | 708 | 796 | 854 | 898 | 934 | 984 |
| 80,000 | 90,000 | 746 | 838 | 899 | 945 | 983 | 1035 |
| 90,000 | 100,000 | 783 | 879 | 942 | 990 | 1030 | 1084 |
| 100,000 | 120,000 | 831 | 933 | 999 | 1050 | 1091 | 1148 |
| 120,000 | 140,000 | 896 | 1004 | 1074 | 1128 | 1173 | 1234 |
| 140,000 | 160,000 | 953 | 1067 | 1141 | 1198 | 1245 | 1309 |
| 160,000 | 180,000 | 1007 | 1127 | 1205 | 1265 | 1313 | 1381 |
| 180,000 | 200,000 | 1059 | 1183 | 1264 | 1327 | 1378 | 1448 |
| 200,000 or more | | 1285 | 1431 | 1527 | 1600 | 1660 | 1744 |

### Minnesota

| Income At least | But less than | 1 | 2 | 3 | 4 | 5 | Over 5 |
|---|---|---|---|---|---|---|---|
| $0 | $20,000 | 379 | 429 | 462 | 487 | 508 | 536 |
| 20,000 | 30,000 | 495 | 561 | 603 | 636 | 662 | 698 |
| 30,000 | 40,000 | 573 | 649 | 698 | 735 | 765 | 806 |
| 40,000 | 50,000 | 640 | 724 | 778 | 820 | 853 | 899 |
| 50,000 | 60,000 | 701 | 792 | 851 | 896 | 933 | 983 |
| 60,000 | 70,000 | 755 | 853 | 916 | 964 | 1003 | 1057 |
| 70,000 | 80,000 | 806 | 910 | 978 | 1029 | 1071 | 1128 |
| 80,000 | 90,000 | 852 | 962 | 1033 | 1087 | 1130 | 1191 |
| 90,000 | 100,000 | 896 | 1011 | 1086 | 1142 | 1188 | 1252 |
| 100,000 | 120,000 | 955 | 1077 | 1156 | 1216 | 1265 | 1332 |
| 120,000 | 140,000 | 1033 | 1164 | 1250 | 1314 | 1367 | 1439 |
| 140,000 | 160,000 | 1102 | 1242 | 1333 | 1401 | 1457 | 1534 |
| 160,000 | 180,000 | 1168 | 1316 | 1412 | 1484 | 1543 | 1624 |
| 180,000 | 200,000 | 1231 | 1386 | 1486 | 1562 | 1624 | 1710 |
| 200,000 or more | | 1507 | 1695 | 1816 | 1908 | 1983 | 2085 |

### Mississippi

| Income At least | But less than | 1 | 2 | 3 | 4 | 5 | Over 5 |
|---|---|---|---|---|---|---|---|
| $0 | $20,000 | 510 | 607 | 673 | 724 | 766 | 826 |
| 20,000 | 30,000 | 643 | 762 | 844 | 907 | 959 | 1033 |
| 30,000 | 40,000 | 729 | 864 | 955 | 1026 | 1085 | 1167 |
| 40,000 | 50,000 | 802 | 949 | 1049 | 1126 | 1191 | 1281 |
| 50,000 | 60,000 | 868 | 1026 | 1133 | 1216 | 1285 | 1381 |
| 60,000 | 70,000 | 926 | 1093 | 1207 | 1295 | 1368 | 1470 |
| 70,000 | 80,000 | 980 | 1157 | 1276 | 1369 | 1446 | 1554 |
| 80,000 | 90,000 | 1029 | 1213 | 1338 | 1434 | 1515 | 1628 |
| 90,000 | 100,000 | 1075 | 1267 | 1397 | 1498 | 1581 | 1699 |
| 100,000 | 120,000 | 1137 | 1338 | 1475 | 1580 | 1668 | 1792 |
| 120,000 | 140,000 | 1208 | 1421 | 1577 | 1690 | 1783 | 1914 |
| 140,000 | 160,000 | 1290 | 1515 | 1668 | 1786 | 1885 | 2023 |
| 160,000 | 180,000 | 1358 | 1594 | 1754 | 1878 | 1981 | 2125 |
| 180,000 | 200,000 | 1421 | 1668 | 1834 | 1963 | 2070 | 2221 |
| 200,000 or more | | 1701 | 1990 | 2185 | 2336 | 2461 | 2637 |

### Missouri

| Income At least | But less than | 1 | 2 | 3 | 4 | 5 | Over 5 |
|---|---|---|---|---|---|---|---|
| $0 | $20,000 | 323 | 385 | 427 | 460 | 488 | 527 |
| 20,000 | 30,000 | 409 | 487 | 539 | 580 | 614 | 662 |
| 30,000 | 40,000 | 466 | 553 | 612 | 658 | 697 | 751 |
| 40,000 | 50,000 | 514 | 609 | 674 | 724 | 766 | 825 |
| 50,000 | 60,000 | 557 | 660 | 729 | 783 | 828 | 892 |
| 60,000 | 70,000 | 595 | 704 | 778 | 836 | 883 | 951 |
| 70,000 | 80,000 | 631 | 746 | 824 | 885 | 935 | 1006 |
| 80,000 | 90,000 | 663 | 783 | 865 | 928 | 981 | 1055 |
| 90,000 | 100,000 | 694 | 819 | 904 | 970 | 1025 | 1102 |
| 100,000 | 120,000 | 735 | 866 | 955 | 1025 | 1083 | 1164 |
| 120,000 | 140,000 | 789 | 929 | 1024 | 1098 | 1159 | 1246 |
| 140,000 | 160,000 | 837 | 984 | 1084 | 1162 | 1227 | 1318 |
| 160,000 | 180,000 | 882 | 1037 | 1141 | 1223 | 1290 | 1386 |
| 180,000 | 200,000 | 925 | 1086 | 1195 | 1280 | 1350 | 1450 |
| 200,000 or more | | 1112 | 1301 | 1429 | 1529 | 1612 | 1728 |

### Nebraska

| Income At least | But less than | 1 | 2 | 3 | 4 | 5 | Over 5 |
|---|---|---|---|---|---|---|---|
| $0 | $20,000 | 318 | 363 | 392 | 414 | 432 | 457 |
| 20,000 | 30,000 | 417 | 475 | 513 | 541 | 565 | 597 |
| 30,000 | 40,000 | 484 | 550 | 594 | 627 | 654 | 691 |
| 40,000 | 50,000 | 541 | 615 | 663 | 700 | 730 | 771 |
| 50,000 | 60,000 | 593 | 674 | 726 | 766 | 799 | 844 |
| 60,000 | 70,000 | 639 | 726 | 782 | 825 | 860 | 908 |
| 70,000 | 80,000 | 683 | 775 | 835 | 881 | 918 | 970 |
| 80,000 | 90,000 | 723 | 820 | 883 | 931 | 970 | 1024 |
| 90,000 | 100,000 | 761 | 863 | 929 | 980 | 1021 | 1078 |
| 100,000 | 120,000 | 811 | 920 | 990 | 1044 | 1087 | 1147 |
| 120,000 | 140,000 | 879 | 995 | 1071 | 1129 | 1176 | 1241 |
| 140,000 | 160,000 | 939 | 1063 | 1143 | 1205 | 1255 | 1324 |
| 160,000 | 180,000 | 996 | 1127 | 1212 | 1277 | 1330 | 1403 |
| 180,000 | 200,000 | 1050 | 1187 | 1277 | 1345 | 1400 | 1477 |
| 200,000 or more | | 1289 | 1456 | 1564 | 1647 | 1714 | 1806 |

### Nevada

| Income At least | But less than | 1 | 2 | 3 | 4 | 5 | Over 5 |
|---|---|---|---|---|---|---|---|
| $0 | $20,000 | 304 | 355 | 389 | 415 | 437 | 467 |
| 20,000 | 30,000 | 406 | 472 | 517 | 551 | 579 | 619 |
| 30,000 | 40,000 | 474 | 551 | 603 | 643 | 675 | 721 |
| 40,000 | 50,000 | 534 | 620 | 677 | 722 | 758 | 810 |
| 50,000 | 60,000 | 588 | 682 | 745 | 794 | 834 | 890 |
| 60,000 | 70,000 | 636 | 738 | 806 | 858 | 901 | 961 |
| 70,000 | 80,000 | 682 | 791 | 863 | 919 | 965 | 1029 |
| 80,000 | 90,000 | 724 | 838 | 915 | 974 | 1022 | 1090 |
| 90,000 | 100,000 | 764 | 884 | 965 | 1027 | 1078 | 1149 |
| 100,000 | 120,000 | 817 | 945 | 1031 | 1097 | 1151 | 1228 |
| 120,000 | 140,000 | 888 | 1027 | 1120 | 1191 | 1250 | 1332 |
| 140,000 | 160,000 | 952 | 1100 | 1198 | 1275 | 1337 | 1425 |
| 160,000 | 180,000 | 1012 | 1169 | 1274 | 1355 | 1421 | 1514 |
| 180,000 | 200,000 | 1070 | 1235 | 1345 | 1430 | 1500 | 1597 |
| 200,000 or more | | 1326 | 1528 | 1662 | 1765 | 1851 | 1970 |

### New Jersey

| Income At least | But less than | 1 | 2 | 3 | 4 | 5 | Over 5 |
|---|---|---|---|---|---|---|---|
| $0 | $20,000 | 317 | 367 | 400 | 425 | 446 | 475 |
| 20,000 | 30,000 | 418 | 482 | 525 | 558 | 585 | 623 |
| 30,000 | 40,000 | 485 | 560 | 610 | 647 | 679 | 722 |
| 40,000 | 50,000 | 544 | 627 | 682 | 724 | 759 | 807 |
| 50,000 | 60,000 | 597 | 688 | 748 | 794 | 831 | 884 |
| 60,000 | 70,000 | 644 | 742 | 806 | 856 | 896 | 953 |
| 70,000 | 80,000 | 689 | 793 | 862 | 914 | 957 | 1017 |
| 80,000 | 90,000 | 730 | 839 | 911 | 967 | 1012 | 1076 |
| 90,000 | 100,000 | 769 | 884 | 960 | 1018 | 1066 | 1132 |
| 100,000 | 120,000 | 821 | 943 | 1023 | 1085 | 1136 | 1206 |
| 120,000 | 140,000 | 890 | 1021 | 1108 | 1175 | 1229 | 1305 |
| 140,000 | 160,000 | 951 | 1091 | 1184 | 1255 | 1313 | 1394 |
| 160,000 | 180,000 | 1010 | 1158 | 1256 | 1331 | 1392 | 1478 |
| 180,000 | 200,000 | 1066 | 1222 | 1324 | 1403 | 1467 | 1557 |
| 200,000 or more | | 1313 | 1502 | 1626 | 1722 | 1800 | 1908 |

### New Mexico

| Income At least | But less than | 1 | 2 | 3 | 4 | 5 | Over 5 |
|---|---|---|---|---|---|---|---|
| $0 | $20,000 | 371 | 439 | 484 | 519 | 548 | 589 |
| 20,000 | 30,000 | 471 | 555 | 611 | 655 | 691 | 742 |
| 30,000 | 40,000 | 536 | 631 | 695 | 744 | 785 | 842 |
| 40,000 | 50,000 | 592 | 696 | 766 | 820 | 864 | 927 |
| 50,000 | 60,000 | 641 | 753 | 829 | 887 | 935 | 1003 |
| 60,000 | 70,000 | 686 | 805 | 885 | 947 | 998 | 1069 |
| 70,000 | 80,000 | 727 | 853 | 937 | 1002 | 1056 | 1132 |
| 80,000 | 90,000 | 764 | 896 | 984 | 1052 | 1109 | 1188 |
| 90,000 | 100,000 | 800 | 937 | 1029 | 1100 | 1159 | 1241 |
| 100,000 | 120,000 | 847 | 991 | 1088 | 1163 | 1225 | 1312 |
| 120,000 | 140,000 | 909 | 1063 | 1166 | 1246 | 1312 | 1405 |
| 140,000 | 160,000 | 964 | 1126 | 1235 | 1320 | 1389 | 1487 |
| 160,000 | 180,000 | 1016 | 1187 | 1301 | 1389 | 1462 | 1564 |
| 180,000 | 200,000 | 1065 | 1243 | 1362 | 1454 | 1531 | 1637 |
| 200,000 or more | | 1281 | 1491 | 1631 | 1740 | 1830 | 1955 |

### New York

| Income At least | But less than | 1 | 2 | 3 | 4 | 5 | Over 5 |
|---|---|---|---|---|---|---|---|
| $0 | $20,000 | 224 | 262 | 287 | 306 | 322 | 344 |
| 20,000 | 30,000 | 296 | 345 | 378 | 403 | 424 | 453 |
| 30,000 | 40,000 | 345 | 401 | 439 | 468 | 492 | 526 |
| 40,000 | 50,000 | 387 | 450 | 492 | 524 | 551 | 588 |
| 50,000 | 60,000 | 425 | 494 | 540 | 575 | 604 | 645 |
| 60,000 | 70,000 | 459 | 533 | 582 | 620 | 652 | 696 |
| 70,000 | 80,000 | 491 | 570 | 623 | 663 | 697 | 743 |
| 80,000 | 90,000 | 520 | 604 | 659 | 702 | 737 | 786 |
| 90,000 | 100,000 | 549 | 636 | 694 | 739 | 776 | 828 |
| 100,000 | 120,000 | 586 | 679 | 741 | 788 | 828 | 883 |
| 120,000 | 140,000 | 635 | 736 | 802 | 854 | 896 | 956 |
| 140,000 | 160,000 | 680 | 786 | 858 | 912 | 958 | 1021 |
| 160,000 | 180,000 | 722 | 835 | 910 | 968 | 1016 | 1083 |
| 180,000 | 200,000 | 762 | 881 | 960 | 1021 | 1071 | 1141 |
| 200,000 or more | | 940 | 1084 | 1180 | 1254 | 1315 | 1399 |

### North Carolina

| Income At least | But less than | 1 | 2 | 3 | 4 | 5 | Over 5 |
|---|---|---|---|---|---|---|---|
| $0 | $20,000 | 269 | 304 | 327 | 344 | 358 | 377 |
| 20,000 | 30,000 | 350 | 395 | 424 | 445 | 463 | 488 |
| 30,000 | 40,000 | 403 | 455 | 488 | 513 | 533 | 561 |
| 40,000 | 50,000 | 449 | 506 | 543 | 571 | 593 | 624 |
| 50,000 | 60,000 | 491 | 552 | 592 | 622 | 647 | 681 |
| 60,000 | 70,000 | 528 | 594 | 636 | 669 | 695 | 731 |
| 70,000 | 80,000 | 563 | 633 | 678 | 712 | 740 | 778 |
| 80,000 | 90,000 | 594 | 668 | 715 | 751 | 781 | 821 |
| 90,000 | 100,000 | 624 | 701 | 751 | 789 | 820 | 862 |
| 100,000 | 120,000 | 664 | 746 | 799 | 839 | 871 | 916 |
| 120,000 | 140,000 | 717 | 805 | 862 | 905 | 940 | 988 |
| 140,000 | 160,000 | 764 | 857 | 918 | 963 | 1000 | 1051 |
| 160,000 | 180,000 | 809 | 907 | 971 | 1019 | 1058 | 1112 |
| 180,000 | 200,000 | 851 | 954 | 1021 | 1072 | 1112 | 1169 |
| 200,000 or more | | 1038 | 1162 | 1242 | 1303 | 1352 | 1420 |

### North Dakota

| Income At least | But less than | 1 | 2 | 3 | 4 | 5 | Over 5 |
|---|---|---|---|---|---|---|---|
| $0 | $20,000 | 291 | 331 | 357 | 377 | 393 | 415 |
| 20,000 | 30,000 | 383 | 434 | 468 | 494 | 514 | 543 |
| 30,000 | 40,000 | 444 | 503 | 542 | 572 | 596 | 629 |
| 40,000 | 50,000 | 497 | 563 | 606 | 639 | 665 | 702 |
| 50,000 | 60,000 | 544 | 617 | 664 | 699 | 728 | 768 |
| 60,000 | 70,000 | 587 | 665 | 715 | 753 | 784 | 828 |
| 70,000 | 80,000 | 627 | 710 | 764 | 804 | 838 | 883 |
| 80,000 | 90,000 | 664 | 751 | 807 | 850 | 885 | 934 |
| 90,000 | 100,000 | 699 | 790 | 850 | 895 | 931 | 982 |
| 100,000 | 120,000 | 745 | 842 | 905 | 953 | 992 | 1046 |
| 120,000 | 140,000 | 807 | 912 | 980 | 1031 | 1073 | 1131 |
| 140,000 | 160,000 | 862 | 973 | 1046 | 1101 | 1145 | 1207 |
| 160,000 | 180,000 | 915 | 1032 | 1109 | 1167 | 1214 | 1279 |
| 180,000 | 200,000 | 964 | 1088 | 1168 | 1229 | 1279 | 1347 |
| 200,000 or more | | 1185 | 1335 | 1432 | 1505 | 1566 | 1648 |

### Ohio

| Income At least | But less than | 1 | 2 | 3 | 4 | 5 | Over 5 |
|---|---|---|---|---|---|---|---|
| $0 | $20,000 | 364 | 412 | 443 | 467 | 486 | 512 |
| 20,000 | 30,000 | 475 | 536 | 576 | 606 | 631 | 665 |
| 30,000 | 40,000 | 549 | 619 | 665 | 699 | 727 | 766 |
| 40,000 | 50,000 | 612 | 690 | 741 | 779 | 810 | 853 |
| 50,000 | 60,000 | 670 | 754 | 809 | 851 | 885 | 932 |
| 60,000 | 70,000 | 721 | 812 | 871 | 915 | 951 | 1001 |
| 70,000 | 80,000 | 769 | 866 | 928 | 976 | 1014 | 1067 |
| 80,000 | 90,000 | 813 | 914 | 980 | 1030 | 1071 | 1126 |
| 90,000 | 100,000 | 855 | 961 | 1030 | 1083 | 1125 | 1184 |
| 100,000 | 120,000 | 911 | 1023 | 1096 | 1152 | 1197 | 1259 |
| 120,000 | 140,000 | 985 | 1106 | 1185 | 1244 | 1292 | 1359 |
| 140,000 | 160,000 | 1051 | 1180 | 1263 | 1326 | 1377 | 1448 |
| 160,000 | 180,000 | 1114 | 1250 | 1338 | 1404 | 1458 | 1533 |
| 180,000 | 200,000 | 1173 | 1316 | 1408 | 1478 | 1534 | 1612 |
| 200,000 or more | | 1437 | 1608 | 1719 | 1803 | 1871 | 1965 |

*(Continued)*

## 2004 Optional State Sales Tax Tables *(Continued)*

### Oklahoma

| Income At least | But less than | 1 | 2 | 3 | 4 | 5 | Over 5 |
|---|---|---|---|---|---|---|---|
| $0 | $20,000 | 327 | 388 | 430 | 462 | 489 | 527 |
| 20,000 | 30,000 | 412 | 487 | 539 | 578 | 612 | 658 |
| 30,000 | 40,000 | 468 | 552 | 609 | 654 | 691 | 744 |
| 40,000 | 50,000 | 515 | 607 | 669 | 718 | 759 | 816 |
| 50,000 | 60,000 | 557 | 656 | 723 | 775 | 818 | 879 |
| 60,000 | 70,000 | 595 | 699 | 770 | 825 | 871 | 936 |
| 70,000 | 80,000 | 630 | 739 | 814 | 872 | 920 | 988 |
| 80,000 | 90,000 | 661 | 775 | 853 | 913 | 964 | 1035 |
| 90,000 | 100,000 | 691 | 810 | 891 | 954 | 1006 | 1080 |
| 100,000 | 120,000 | 731 | 855 | 940 | 1006 | 1061 | 1139 |
| 120,000 | 140,000 | 784 | 915 | 1005 | 1075 | 1134 | 1216 |
| 140,000 | 160,000 | 830 | 968 | 1063 | 1136 | 1198 | 1284 |
| 160,000 | 180,000 | 874 | 1019 | 1117 | 1194 | 1258 | 1348 |
| 180,000 | 200,000 | 916 | 1066 | 1168 | 1248 | 1315 | 1409 |
| 200,000 or more | | 1098 | 1272 | 1391 | 1484 | 1561 | 1670 |

### Pennsylvania

| Income At least | But less than | 1 | 2 | 3 | 4 | 5 | Over 5 |
|---|---|---|---|---|---|---|---|
| $0 | $20,000 | 284 | 328 | 357 | 380 | 398 | 424 |
| 20,000 | 30,000 | 382 | 440 | 478 | 508 | 532 | 566 |
| 30,000 | 40,000 | 448 | 516 | 561 | 595 | 623 | 663 |
| 40,000 | 50,000 | 506 | 582 | 632 | 671 | 702 | 746 |
| 50,000 | 60,000 | 558 | 642 | 697 | 739 | 774 | 822 |
| 60,000 | 70,000 | 605 | 696 | 755 | 801 | 838 | 890 |
| 70,000 | 80,000 | 650 | 747 | 811 | 859 | 899 | 955 |
| 80,000 | 90,000 | 691 | 793 | 860 | 912 | 954 | 1013 |
| 90,000 | 100,000 | 730 | 838 | 909 | 963 | 1008 | 1070 |
| 100,000 | 120,000 | 782 | 897 | 973 | 1031 | 1079 | 1145 |
| 120,000 | 140,000 | 852 | 977 | 1059 | 1122 | 1173 | 1245 |
| 140,000 | 160,000 | 915 | 1048 | 1135 | 1203 | 1258 | 1335 |
| 160,000 | 180,000 | 975 | 1116 | 1209 | 1280 | 1339 | 1420 |
| 180,000 | 200,000 | 1031 | 1180 | 1278 | 1354 | 1415 | 1501 |
| 200,000 or more | | 1285 | 1468 | 1588 | 1681 | 1756 | 1862 |

### Rhode Island

| Income At least | But less than | 1 | 2 | 3 | 4 | 5 | Over 5 |
|---|---|---|---|---|---|---|---|
| $0 | $20,000 | 302 | 342 | 368 | 387 | 403 | 425 |
| 20,000 | 30,000 | 403 | 455 | 489 | 515 | 536 | 565 |
| 30,000 | 40,000 | 472 | 532 | 571 | 601 | 625 | 659 |
| 40,000 | 50,000 | 531 | 598 | 642 | 676 | 703 | 740 |
| 50,000 | 60,000 | 585 | 658 | 706 | 743 | 773 | 814 |
| 60,000 | 70,000 | 633 | 712 | 764 | 803 | 835 | 880 |
| 70,000 | 80,000 | 678 | 763 | 819 | 861 | 895 | 942 |
| 80,000 | 90,000 | 719 | 809 | 868 | 912 | 948 | 998 |
| 90,000 | 100,000 | 759 | 854 | 915 | 962 | 1000 | 1053 |
| 100,000 | 120,000 | 812 | 913 | 978 | 1028 | 1068 | 1124 |
| 120,000 | 140,000 | 882 | 991 | 1062 | 1116 | 1160 | 1220 |
| 140,000 | 160,000 | 945 | 1061 | 1137 | 1194 | 1241 | 1306 |
| 160,000 | 180,000 | 1005 | 1128 | 1208 | 1269 | 1319 | 1387 |
| 180,000 | 200,000 | 1062 | 1191 | 1276 | 1340 | 1392 | 1464 |
| 200,000 or more | | 1314 | 1472 | 1575 | 1653 | 1717 | 1805 |

### South Carolina

| Income At least | But less than | 1 | 2 | 3 | 4 | 5 | Over 5 |
|---|---|---|---|---|---|---|---|
| $0 | $20,000 | 379 | 449 | 496 | 533 | 563 | 606 |
| 20,000 | 30,000 | 481 | 568 | 627 | 672 | 710 | 763 |
| 30,000 | 40,000 | 547 | 646 | 712 | 764 | 806 | 866 |
| 40,000 | 50,000 | 604 | 712 | 785 | 841 | 888 | 953 |
| 50,000 | 60,000 | 655 | 771 | 849 | 910 | 960 | 1031 |
| 60,000 | 70,000 | 700 | 823 | 906 | 971 | 1024 | 1099 |
| 70,000 | 80,000 | 742 | 872 | 960 | 1028 | 1085 | 1164 |
| 80,000 | 90,000 | 780 | 916 | 1008 | 1079 | 1138 | 1221 |
| 90,000 | 100,000 | 816 | 958 | 1054 | 1128 | 1190 | 1276 |
| 100,000 | 120,000 | 864 | 1014 | 1114 | 1193 | 1257 | 1348 |
| 120,000 | 140,000 | 927 | 1087 | 1194 | 1278 | 1347 | 1443 |
| 140,000 | 160,000 | 983 | 1152 | 1265 | 1353 | 1426 | 1527 |
| 160,000 | 180,000 | 1036 | 1213 | 1332 | 1424 | 1500 | 1607 |
| 180,000 | 200,000 | 1086 | 1271 | 1395 | 1491 | 1570 | 1682 |
| 200,000 or more | | 1306 | 1523 | 1670 | 1783 | 1876 | 2008 |

### South Dakota

| Income At least | But less than | 1 | 2 | 3 | 4 | 5 | Over 5 |
|---|---|---|---|---|---|---|---|
| $0 | $20,000 | 263 | 319 | 358 | 388 | 414 | 450 |
| 20,000 | 30,000 | 344 | 417 | 466 | 505 | 538 | 585 |
| 30,000 | 40,000 | 399 | 482 | 539 | 584 | 621 | 674 |
| 40,000 | 50,000 | 446 | 537 | 601 | 650 | 692 | 751 |
| 50,000 | 60,000 | 488 | 588 | 656 | 711 | 756 | 820 |
| 60,000 | 70,000 | 526 | 633 | 706 | 764 | 813 | 882 |
| 70,000 | 80,000 | 562 | 675 | 753 | 815 | 867 | 940 |
| 80,000 | 90,000 | 594 | 713 | 796 | 860 | 915 | 991 |
| 90,000 | 100,000 | 625 | 750 | 836 | 904 | 961 | 1042 |
| 100,000 | 120,000 | 666 | 799 | 890 | 962 | 1022 | 1108 |
| 120,000 | 140,000 | 721 | 864 | 962 | 1039 | 1104 | 1195 |
| 140,000 | 160,000 | 770 | 921 | 1025 | 1107 | 1176 | 1273 |
| 160,000 | 180,000 | 816 | 976 | 1086 | 1172 | 1245 | 1347 |
| 180,000 | 200,000 | 860 | 1028 | 1143 | 1234 | 1310 | 1417 |
| 200,000 or more | | 1055 | 1257 | 1395 | 1504 | 1596 | 1725 |

### Tennessee

| Income At least | But less than | 1 | 2 | 3 | 4 | 5 | Over 5 |
|---|---|---|---|---|---|---|---|
| $0 | $20,000 | 506 | 601 | 666 | 717 | 758 | 817 |
| 20,000 | 30,000 | 628 | 745 | 824 | 886 | 937 | 1008 |
| 30,000 | 40,000 | 708 | 838 | 926 | 995 | 1052 | 1132 |
| 40,000 | 50,000 | 775 | 916 | 1012 | 1086 | 1148 | 1235 |
| 50,000 | 60,000 | 835 | 986 | 1088 | 1168 | 1233 | 1326 |
| 60,000 | 70,000 | 887 | 1047 | 1155 | 1239 | 1309 | 1407 |
| 70,000 | 80,000 | 937 | 1105 | 1218 | 1306 | 1379 | 1482 |
| 80,000 | 90,000 | 981 | 1155 | 1273 | 1365 | 1441 | 1548 |
| 90,000 | 100,000 | 1023 | 1204 | 1327 | 1422 | 1501 | 1612 |
| 100,000 | 120,000 | 1078 | 1268 | 1397 | 1496 | 1579 | 1695 |
| 120,000 | 140,000 | 1151 | 1353 | 1489 | 1594 | 1682 | 1805 |
| 140,000 | 160,000 | 1216 | 1427 | 1570 | 1681 | 1773 | 1902 |
| 160,000 | 180,000 | 1277 | 1498 | 1647 | 1762 | 1858 | 1993 |
| 180,000 | 200,000 | 1334 | 1563 | 1718 | 1838 | 1938 | 2078 |
| 200,000 or more | | 1583 | 1850 | 2030 | 2169 | 2284 | 2446 |

### Texas

| Income At least | But less than | 1 | 2 | 3 | 4 | 5 | Over 5 |
|---|---|---|---|---|---|---|---|
| $0 | $20,000 | 375 | 427 | 461 | 487 | 509 | 538 |
| 20,000 | 30,000 | 488 | 555 | 599 | 633 | 660 | 697 |
| 30,000 | 40,000 | 564 | 641 | 691 | 730 | 761 | 804 |
| 40,000 | 50,000 | 629 | 714 | 770 | 812 | 847 | 895 |
| 50,000 | 60,000 | 687 | 780 | 841 | 887 | 925 | 976 |
| 60,000 | 70,000 | 740 | 840 | 904 | 954 | 994 | 1049 |
| 70,000 | 80,000 | 789 | 895 | 964 | 1017 | 1059 | 1118 |
| 80,000 | 90,000 | 834 | 945 | 1018 | 1073 | 1118 | 1180 |
| 90,000 | 100,000 | 877 | 994 | 1070 | 1127 | 1174 | 1239 |
| 100,000 | 120,000 | 933 | 1057 | 1138 | 1199 | 1249 | 1318 |
| 120,000 | 140,000 | 1009 | 1142 | 1229 | 1294 | 1348 | 1422 |
| 140,000 | 160,000 | 1076 | 1217 | 1309 | 1379 | 1436 | 1515 |
| 160,000 | 180,000 | 1140 | 1289 | 1386 | 1460 | 1520 | 1603 |
| 180,000 | 200,000 | 1200 | 1357 | 1459 | 1536 | 1599 | 1686 |
| 200,000 or more | | 1467 | 1656 | 1779 | 1872 | 1948 | 2052 |

### Utah

| Income At least | But less than | 1 | 2 | 3 | 4 | 5 | Over 5 |
|---|---|---|---|---|---|---|---|
| $0 | $20,000 | 345 | 411 | 456 | 491 | 521 | 562 |
| 20,000 | 30,000 | 437 | 520 | 576 | 620 | 657 | 708 |
| 30,000 | 40,000 | 498 | 592 | 655 | 705 | 746 | 804 |
| 40,000 | 50,000 | 550 | 652 | 722 | 776 | 821 | 884 |
| 50,000 | 60,000 | 596 | 707 | 781 | 840 | 888 | 956 |
| 60,000 | 70,000 | 637 | 755 | 834 | 896 | 947 | 1020 |
| 70,000 | 80,000 | 676 | 800 | 884 | 949 | 1003 | 1079 |
| 80,000 | 90,000 | 711 | 840 | 928 | 996 | 1053 | 1132 |
| 90,000 | 100,000 | 744 | 879 | 970 | 1041 | 1100 | 1183 |
| 100,000 | 120,000 | 787 | 929 | 1026 | 1100 | 1163 | 1250 |
| 120,000 | 140,000 | 845 | 997 | 1099 | 1179 | 1245 | 1339 |
| 140,000 | 160,000 | 897 | 1056 | 1164 | 1248 | 1318 | 1416 |
| 160,000 | 180,000 | 945 | 1113 | 1226 | 1314 | 1387 | 1490 |
| 180,000 | 200,000 | 991 | 1166 | 1284 | 1376 | 1452 | 1559 |
| 200,000 or more | | 1192 | 1398 | 1537 | 1645 | 1735 | 1861 |

### Vermont

| Income At least | But less than | 1 | 2 | 3 | 4 | 5 | Over 5 |
|---|---|---|---|---|---|---|---|
| $0 | $20,000 | 259 | 300 | 327 | 348 | 365 | 389 |
| 20,000 | 30,000 | 352 | 406 | 442 | 470 | 493 | 525 |
| 30,000 | 40,000 | 416 | 479 | 521 | 554 | 581 | 618 |
| 40,000 | 50,000 | 471 | 543 | 590 | 627 | 657 | 699 |
| 50,000 | 60,000 | 522 | 601 | 653 | 693 | 726 | 772 |
| 60,000 | 70,000 | 568 | 653 | 710 | 753 | 789 | 839 |
| 70,000 | 80,000 | 612 | 703 | 764 | 810 | 849 | 902 |
| 80,000 | 90,000 | 651 | 748 | 812 | 862 | 902 | 959 |
| 90,000 | 100,000 | 690 | 792 | 859 | 912 | 955 | 1014 |
| 100,000 | 120,000 | 741 | 850 | 922 | 978 | 1024 | 1088 |
| 120,000 | 140,000 | 809 | 928 | 1006 | 1067 | 1117 | 1186 |
| 140,000 | 160,000 | 871 | 998 | 1082 | 1147 | 1200 | 1274 |
| 160,000 | 180,000 | 930 | 1065 | 1154 | 1223 | 1280 | 1359 |
| 180,000 | 200,000 | 986 | 1128 | 1223 | 1296 | 1355 | 1439 |
| 200,000 or more | | 1238 | 1414 | 1531 | 1620 | 1694 | 1797 |

### Virginia

| Income At least | But less than | 1 | 2 | 3 | 4 | 5 | Over 5 |
|---|---|---|---|---|---|---|---|
| $0 | $20,000 | 270 | 322 | 357 | 385 | 408 | 440 |
| 20,000 | 30,000 | 345 | 411 | 455 | 490 | 519 | 559 |
| 30,000 | 40,000 | 395 | 470 | 520 | 559 | 592 | 638 |
| 40,000 | 50,000 | 438 | 520 | 575 | 618 | 654 | 704 |
| 50,000 | 60,000 | 476 | 564 | 624 | 670 | 709 | 763 |
| 60,000 | 70,000 | 510 | 604 | 667 | 717 | 758 | 816 |
| 70,000 | 80,000 | 542 | 641 | 708 | 761 | 804 | 865 |
| 80,000 | 90,000 | 571 | 675 | 745 | 800 | 845 | 909 |
| 90,000 | 100,000 | 598 | 707 | 780 | 837 | 885 | 952 |
| 100,000 | 120,000 | 635 | 749 | 827 | 887 | 937 | 1007 |
| 120,000 | 140,000 | 683 | 805 | 888 | 952 | 1006 | 1081 |
| 140,000 | 160,000 | 726 | 855 | 942 | 1010 | 1067 | 1146 |
| 160,000 | 180,000 | 767 | 902 | 994 | 1065 | 1125 | 1208 |
| 180,000 | 200,000 | 805 | 947 | 1043 | 1117 | 1179 | 1266 |
| 200,000 or more | | 974 | 1142 | 1256 | 1344 | 1417 | 1520 |

### Washington

| Income At least | But less than | 1 | 2 | 3 | 4 | 5 | Over 5 |
|---|---|---|---|---|---|---|---|
| $0 | $20,000 | 389 | 439 | 471 | 496 | 516 | 543 |
| 20,000 | 30,000 | 500 | 564 | 605 | 636 | 662 | 696 |
| 30,000 | 40,000 | 574 | 647 | 694 | 729 | 758 | 797 |
| 40,000 | 50,000 | 637 | 717 | 769 | 808 | 840 | 883 |
| 50,000 | 60,000 | 694 | 780 | 836 | 879 | 913 | 960 |
| 60,000 | 70,000 | 744 | 837 | 896 | 942 | 978 | 1029 |
| 70,000 | 80,000 | 791 | 890 | 953 | 1001 | 1040 | 1093 |
| 80,000 | 90,000 | 834 | 937 | 1004 | 1054 | 1095 | 1151 |
| 90,000 | 100,000 | 875 | 983 | 1052 | 1105 | 1148 | 1206 |
| 100,000 | 120,000 | 929 | 1043 | 1116 | 1172 | 1217 | 1279 |
| 120,000 | 140,000 | 1000 | 1123 | 1201 | 1261 | 1309 | 1376 |
| 140,000 | 160,000 | 1064 | 1193 | 1277 | 1340 | 1391 | 1462 |
| 160,000 | 180,000 | 1124 | 1261 | 1349 | 1415 | 1469 | 1543 |
| 180,000 | 200,000 | 1181 | 1324 | 1416 | 1485 | 1542 | 1619 |
| 200,000 or more | | 1431 | 1602 | 1712 | 1795 | 1862 | 1955 |

### West Virginia

| Income At least | But less than | 1 | 2 | 3 | 4 | 5 | Over 5 |
|---|---|---|---|---|---|---|---|
| $0 | $20,000 | 493 | 585 | 646 | 694 | 734 | 789 |
| 20,000 | 30,000 | 622 | 736 | 812 | 872 | 921 | 990 |
| 30,000 | 40,000 | 706 | 835 | 921 | 988 | 1043 | 1121 |
| 40,000 | 50,000 | 778 | 918 | 1013 | 1086 | 1146 | 1231 |
| 50,000 | 60,000 | 842 | 993 | 1094 | 1173 | 1238 | 1329 |
| 60,000 | 70,000 | 899 | 1059 | 1166 | 1250 | 1319 | 1416 |
| 70,000 | 80,000 | 952 | 1121 | 1234 | 1322 | 1395 | 1497 |
| 80,000 | 90,000 | 999 | 1176 | 1294 | 1386 | 1462 | 1569 |
| 90,000 | 100,000 | 1045 | 1229 | 1352 | 1448 | 1527 | 1639 |
| 100,000 | 120,000 | 1105 | 1298 | 1428 | 1529 | 1612 | 1729 |
| 120,000 | 140,000 | 1184 | 1390 | 1528 | 1636 | 1725 | 1849 |
| 140,000 | 160,000 | 1254 | 1471 | 1617 | 1730 | 1824 | 1955 |
| 160,000 | 180,000 | 1320 | 1548 | 1701 | 1819 | 1917 | 2055 |
| 180,000 | 200,000 | 1383 | 1620 | 1779 | 1903 | 2005 | 2148 |
| 200,000 or more | | 1656 | 1935 | 2123 | 2268 | 2388 | 2556 |

### Wisconsin

| Income At least | But less than | 1 | 2 | 3 | 4 | 5 | Over 5 |
|---|---|---|---|---|---|---|---|
| $0 | $20,000 | 293 | 334 | 360 | 380 | 396 | 419 |
| 20,000 | 30,000 | 388 | 440 | 475 | 501 | 522 | 551 |
| 30,000 | 40,000 | 452 | 513 | 552 | 582 | 607 | 641 |
| 40,000 | 50,000 | 507 | 575 | 619 | 652 | 680 | 718 |
| 50,000 | 60,000 | 557 | 631 | 679 | 716 | 746 | 787 |
| 60,000 | 70,000 | 602 | 681 | 733 | 773 | 805 | 849 |
| 70,000 | 80,000 | 644 | 729 | 785 | 827 | 861 | 908 |
| 80,000 | 90,000 | 683 | 772 | 831 | 875 | 911 | 961 |
| 90,000 | 100,000 | 720 | 814 | 875 | 922 | 960 | 1012 |
| 100,000 | 120,000 | 769 | 869 | 934 | 983 | 1024 | 1080 |
| 120,000 | 140,000 | 834 | 942 | 1013 | 1066 | 1110 | 1170 |
| 140,000 | 160,000 | 893 | 1008 | 1083 | 1140 | 1186 | 1250 |
| 160,000 | 180,000 | 949 | 1071 | 1150 | 1210 | 1259 | 1327 |
| 180,000 | 200,000 | 1001 | 1130 | 1213 | 1276 | 1328 | 1399 |
| 200,000 or more | | 1237 | 1392 | 1494 | 1571 | 1633 | 1720 |

### Wyoming

| Income At least | But less than | 1 | 2 | 3 | 4 | 5 | Over 5 |
|---|---|---|---|---|---|---|---|
| $0 | $20,000 | 337 | 401 | 445 | 479 | 507 | 547 |
| 20,000 | 30,000 | 428 | 508 | 563 | 605 | 640 | 689 |
| 30,000 | 40,000 | 487 | 578 | 640 | 687 | 727 | 783 |
| 40,000 | 50,000 | 538 | 637 | 705 | 757 | 800 | 861 |
| 50,000 | 60,000 | 583 | 690 | 763 | 819 | 866 | 932 |
| 60,000 | 70,000 | 623 | 737 | 814 | 874 | 924 | 994 |
| 70,000 | 80,000 | 661 | 781 | 863 | 926 | 978 | 1052 |
| 80,000 | 90,000 | 695 | 821 | 906 | 972 | 1026 | 1104 |
| 90,000 | 100,000 | 727 | 858 | 947 | 1016 | 1073 | 1153 |
| 100,000 | 120,000 | 770 | 908 | 1001 | 1074 | 1134 | 1219 |
| 120,000 | 140,000 | 826 | 974 | 1073 | 1150 | 1215 | 1305 |
| 140,000 | 160,000 | 876 | 1032 | 1137 | 1218 | 1286 | 1381 |
| 160,000 | 180,000 | 924 | 1087 | 1197 | 1282 | 1353 | 1453 |
| 180,000 | 200,000 | 969 | 1138 | 1253 | 1342 | 1416 | 1520 |
| 200,000 or more | | 1164 | 1365 | 1500 | 1605 | 1692 | 1814 |

# APPENDIX B
# Tax Forms

(Tax forms can be obtained from the IRS web site: **http://www.irs.gov**)

Form **1040**

Department of the Treasury—Internal Revenue Service

**U.S. Individual Income Tax Return** **2004** (99) IRS Use Only—Do not write or staple in this space.

For the year Jan. 1–Dec. 31, 2004, or other tax year beginning _____, 2004, ending _____, 20____    OMB No. 1545-0074

**Label** (See instructions on page 16.)

**Use the IRS label.** Otherwise, please print or type.

| | |
|---|---|
| Your first name and initial | Last name |
| If a joint return, spouse's first name and initial | Last name |
| Home address (number and street). If you have a P.O. box, see page 16. | Apt. no. |
| City, town or post office, state, and ZIP code. If you have a foreign address, see page 16. | |

Your social security number

Spouse's social security number

▲ **Important!** ▲

You **must** enter your SSN(s) above.

**Presidential Election Campaign** (See page 16.)

**Note.** Checking "Yes" will not change your tax or reduce your refund.

Do you, or your spouse if filing a joint return, want $3 to go to this fund? . . . ▶

You: ☐ Yes ☐ No   Spouse: ☐ Yes ☐ No

**Filing Status**

Check only one box.

1 ☐ Single
2 ☐ Married filing jointly (even if only one had income)
3 ☐ Married filing separately. Enter spouse's SSN above and full name here. ▶
4 ☐ Head of household (with qualifying person). (See page 17.) If the qualifying person is a child but not your dependent, enter this child's name here. ▶
5 ☐ Qualifying widow(er) with dependent child (see page 17)

**Exemptions**

6a ☐ **Yourself.** If someone can claim you as a dependent, **do not** check box 6a . . . .
b ☐ **Spouse** . . . . . . . . . . . . . . . . . . . . . . . . . . .

c Dependents:

| (1) First name   Last name | (2) Dependent's social security number | (3) Dependent's relationship to you | (4) ✓ if qualifying child for child tax credit (see page 18) |
|---|---|---|---|
| | | | ☐ |
| | | | ☐ |
| | | | ☐ |
| | | | ☐ |

If more than four dependents, see page 18.

Boxes checked on 6a and 6b ____

No. of children on 6c who:
- lived with you ____
- did not live with you due to divorce or separation (see page 18) ____

Dependents on 6c not entered above ____

Add numbers on lines above ▶ ____

d Total number of exemptions claimed . . . . . . . . . .

**Income**

**Attach Form(s) W-2 here. Also attach Forms W-2G and 1099-R if tax was withheld.**

If you did not get a W-2, see page 19.

Enclose, but do not attach, any payment. Also, please use Form 1040-V.

| | | |
|---|---|---|
| 7 | Wages, salaries, tips, etc. Attach Form(s) W-2 . . . . . | 7 |
| 8a | **Taxable** interest. Attach Schedule B if required . . . . | 8a |
| b | **Tax-exempt** interest. **Do not** include on line 8a . . . 8b | |
| 9a | Ordinary dividends. Attach Schedule B if required . . . | 9a |
| b | Qualified dividends (see page 20) . . . . . . 9b | |
| 10 | Taxable refunds, credits, or offsets of state and local income taxes (see page 20) . . | 10 |
| 11 | Alimony received . . . . . . . . . . . | 11 |
| 12 | Business income or (loss). Attach Schedule C or C-EZ . . . . . . | 12 |
| 13 | Capital gain or (loss). Attach Schedule D if required. If not required, check here ▶ ☐ | 13 |
| 14 | Other gains or (losses). Attach Form 4797 . . . . . . | 14 |
| 15a | IRA distributions . . 15a _____ b Taxable amount (see page 22) | 15b |
| 16a | Pensions and annuities 16a _____ b Taxable amount (see page 22) | 16b |
| 17 | Rental real estate, royalties, partnerships, S corporations, trusts, etc. Attach Schedule E | 17 |
| 18 | Farm income or (loss). Attach Schedule F . . . . . | 18 |
| 19 | Unemployment compensation . . . . . . . . | 19 |
| 20a | Social security benefits 20a _____ b Taxable amount (see page 24) | 20b |
| 21 | Other income. List type and amount (see page 24) _____ | 21 |
| 22 | Add the amounts in the far right column for lines 7 through 21. This is your **total income** ▶ | 22 |

**Adjusted Gross Income**

| | | |
|---|---|---|
| 23 | Educator expenses (see page 26) . . . . . . | 23 |
| 24 | Certain business expenses of reservists, performing artists, and fee-basis government officials. Attach Form 2106 or 2106-EZ | 24 |
| 25 | IRA deduction (see page 26) . . . . . | 25 |
| 26 | Student loan interest deduction (see page 28) . . . . | 26 |
| 27 | Tuition and fees deduction (see page 29) . . . | 27 |
| 28 | Health savings account deduction. Attach Form 8889 . | 28 |
| 29 | Moving expenses. Attach Form 3903 . . . . | 29 |
| 30 | One-half of self-employment tax. Attach Schedule SE . | 30 |
| 31 | Self-employed health insurance deduction (see page 30) | 31 |
| 32 | Self-employed SEP, SIMPLE, and qualified plans . . . | 32 |
| 33 | Penalty on early withdrawal of savings . . . . . | 33 |
| 34a | Alimony paid b Recipient's SSN ▶ _____ | 34a |
| 35 | Add lines 23 through 34a . . . . . . . . . . | 35 |
| 36 | Subtract line 35 from line 22. This is your **adjusted gross income** . . . . ▶ | 36 |

**For Disclosure, Privacy Act, and Paperwork Reduction Act Notice, see page 75.**    Cat. No. 11320B    Form **1040** (2004)

Form 1040 (2004)

**Tax and Credits**

| | 37 | Amount from line 36 (adjusted gross income) . . . . . . . . | 37 | |
|---|---|---|---|---|

| | 38a | Check if: { ☐ **You** were born before January 2, 1940, ☐ Blind. ☐ **Spouse** was born before January 2, 1940, ☐ Blind. } Total boxes checked ▶ 38a | | |

**Standard Deduction for—**

- People who checked any box on line 38a or 38b **or** who can be claimed as a dependent, see page 31.

- All others:

Single or Married filing separately, $4,850

Married filing jointly or Qualifying widow(er), $9,700

Head of household, $7,150

| | b | If your spouse itemizes on a separate return or you were a dual-status alien, see page 31 and check here ▶ 38b ☐ | | |
|---|---|---|---|---|
| | 39 | **Itemized deductions** (from Schedule A) **or** your **standard deduction** (see left margin) . . | 39 | |
| | 40 | Subtract line 39 from line 37 . . . . . . . . . . . | 40 | |
| | 41 | If line 37 is $107,025 or less, multiply $3,100 by the total number of exemptions claimed on line 6d. If line 37 is over $107,025, see the worksheet on page 33 . . . . . . . | 41 | |
| | 42 | **Taxable income.** Subtract line 41 from line 40. If line 41 is more than line 40, enter -0- . | 42 | |
| | 43 | **Tax** (see page 33). Check if any tax is from: **a** ☐ Form(s) 8814 **b** ☐ Form 4972 . . . | 43 | |
| | 44 | **Alternative minimum tax** (see page 35). Attach Form 6251 . . . . . . . | 44 | |
| | 45 | Add lines 43 and 44 . . . . . . . . . . . . . . . ▶ | 45 | |

| | 46 | Foreign tax credit. Attach Form 1116 if required . . . | 46 | |
|---|---|---|---|---|
| | 47 | Credit for child and dependent care expenses. Attach Form 2441 | 47 | |
| | 48 | Credit for the elderly or the disabled. Attach Schedule R . | 48 | |
| | 49 | Education credits. Attach Form 8863 . . . . . | 49 | |
| | 50 | Retirement savings contributions credit. Attach Form 8880. | 50 | |
| | 51 | Child tax credit (see page 37) . . . . . . . | 51 | |
| | 52 | Adoption credit. Attach Form 8839 . . . . . . | 52 | |
| | 53 | Credits from: **a** ☐ Form 8396 **b** ☐ Form 8859 . | 53 | |
| | 54 | Other credits. Check applicable box(es): **a** ☐ Form 3800 **b** ☐ Form 8801 **c** ☐ Specify _____ | 54 | |
| | 55 | Add lines 46 through 54. These are your **total credits** . . . . . . . | 55 | |
| | 56 | Subtract line 55 from line 45. If line 55 is more than line 45, enter -0- . . . . . ▶ | 56 | |

**Other Taxes**

| | 57 | Self-employment tax. Attach Schedule SE . . . . . | 57 | |
|---|---|---|---|---|
| | 58 | Social security and Medicare tax on tip income not reported to employer. Attach Form 4137 . . | 58 | |
| | 59 | Additional tax on IRAs, other qualified retirement plans, etc. Attach Form 5329 if required . | 59 | |
| | 60 | Advance earned income credit payments from Form(s) W-2 . . . . . . . | 60 | |
| | 61 | Household employment taxes. Attach Schedule H . . . . . . . . | 61 | |
| | 62 | Add lines 56 through 61. This is your **total tax** . . . . . . . . . ▶ | 62 | |

**Payments**

If you have a qualifying child, attach Schedule EIC.

| | 63 | Federal income tax withheld from Forms W-2 and 1099 . . | 63 | |
|---|---|---|---|---|
| | 64 | 2004 estimated tax payments and amount applied from 2003 return | 64 | |
| | 65a | **Earned income credit (EIC)** . . . . . . . . | 65a | |
| | b | Nontaxable combat pay election ▶ 65b | | |
| | 66 | Excess social security and tier 1 RRTA tax withheld (see page 54) | 66 | |
| | 67 | Additional child tax credit. Attach Form 8812 . . . . | 67 | |
| | 68 | Amount paid with request for extension to file (see page 54) | 68 | |
| | 69 | Other payments from: **a** ☐ Form 2439 **b** ☐ Form 4136 **c** ☐ Form 8885 . | 69 | |
| | 70 | Add lines 63, 64, 65a, and 66 through 69. These are your **total payments** . . . . . ▶ | 70 | |

**Refund**

Direct deposit? See page 54 and fill in 72b, 72c, and 72d.

| | 71 | If line 70 is more than line 62, subtract line 62 from line 70. This is the amount you **overpaid** | 71 | |
|---|---|---|---|---|
| ▶ | 72a | Amount of line 71 you want **refunded to you** . . . . . . . . . . ▶ | 72a | |
| ▶ | b | Routing number | | ▶ **c** Type: ☐ Checking ☐ Savings |
| ▶ | d | Account number | | |
| | 73 | Amount of line 71 you want **applied to your 2005 estimated tax** ▶ 73 | | |

**Amount You Owe**

| | 74 | **Amount you owe.** Subtract line 70 from line 62. For details on how to pay, see page 55 ▶ | 74 | |
|---|---|---|---|---|
| | 75 | Estimated tax penalty (see page 55) . . . . . . . | 75 | |

**Third Party Designee**

Do you want to allow another person to discuss this return with the IRS (see page 56)? ☐ **Yes.** Complete the following. ☐ **No**

Designee's name ▶

Phone no. ▶ ( )

Personal identification number (PIN) ▶

**Sign Here**

Joint return? See page 17.

Keep a copy for your records.

Under penalties of perjury, I declare that I have examined this return and accompanying schedules and statements, and to the best of my knowledge and belief, they are true, correct, and complete. Declaration of preparer (other than taxpayer) is based on all information of which preparer has any knowledge.

Your signature | Date | Your occupation | Daytime phone number ( )

Spouse's signature. If a joint return, **both** must sign. | Date | Spouse's occupation

**Paid Preparer's Use Only**

Preparer's signature ▶ | Date | Check if self-employed ☐ | Preparer's SSN or PTIN

Firm's name (or yours if self-employed), address, and ZIP code ▶ | EIN

Phone no. ( )

Form **1040** (2004)

| SCHEDULE C | Profit or Loss From Business | OMB No. 1545-0074 |
|---|---|---|

**SCHEDULE C**
**(Form 1040)**

Department of the Treasury
Internal Revenue Service

# Profit or Loss From Business
### (Sole Proprietorship)
▶ **Partnerships, joint ventures, etc., must file Form 1065 or 1065-B.**
▶ **Attach to Form 1040 or 1041.**    ▶ **See Instructions for Schedule C (Form 1040).**

OMB No. 1545-0074

20**04**

Attachment
Sequence No. **09**

| Name of proprietor | Social security number (SSN) |
|---|---|

**A**  Principal business or profession, including product or service (see page C-2 of the instructions)

**B**  Enter code from pages C-7, 8, & 9
▶

**C**  Business name. If no separate business name, leave blank.

**D**  Employer ID number (EIN), if any

**E**  Business address (including suite or room no.) ▶
City, town or post office, state, and ZIP code

**F**  Accounting method:  **(1)** ☐ Cash  **(2)** ☐ Accrual  **(3)** ☐ Other (specify) ▶

**G**  Did you "materially participate" in the operation of this business during 2004? If "No," see page C-3 for limit on losses   ☐ Yes  ☐ No

**H**  If you started or acquired this business during 2004, check here  . . . . . . . . . . . . . . . . . . ▶ ☐

## Part I  Income

| | | | |
|---|---|---|---|
| 1 | Gross receipts or sales. **Caution.** If this income was reported to you on Form W-2 and the "Statutory employee" box on that form was checked, see page C-3 and check here . . . . . ▶ ☐ | 1 | |
| 2 | Returns and allowances . . . . . . . . . . | 2 | |
| 3 | Subtract line 2 from line 1 . . . . . . . . | 3 | |
| 4 | Cost of goods sold (from line 42 on page 2) . . . . . . . | 4 | |
| 5 | **Gross profit.** Subtract line 4 from line 3 . . . . . . | 5 | |
| 6 | Other income, including Federal and state gasoline or fuel tax credit or refund (see page C-3) . . . . | 6 | |
| 7 | **Gross income.** Add lines 5 and 6 . . . . . . . . . . . . ▶ | 7 | |

## Part II  Expenses. Enter expenses for business use of your home **only** on line 30.

| | | | | | | | |
|---|---|---|---|---|---|---|---|
| 8 | Advertising . . . . . | 8 | | 19 | Pension and profit-sharing plans | 19 | |
| 9 | Car and truck expenses (see page C-3) . . . . . . | 9 | | 20 | Rent or lease (see page C-5): | | |
| 10 | Commissions and fees . . | 10 | | | **a** Vehicles, machinery, and equipment | 20a | |
| 11 | Contract labor (see page C-4) | 11 | | | **b** Other business property . . | 20b | |
| 12 | Depletion . . . . . | 12 | | 21 | Repairs and maintenance . . | 21 | |
| 13 | Depreciation and section 179 expense deduction (not included in Part III) (see page C-4) . . . . | 13 | | 22 | Supplies (not included in Part III) | 22 | |
| | | | | 23 | Taxes and licenses . . . . | 23 | |
| | | | | 24 | Travel, meals, and entertainment: | | |
| | | | | | **a** Travel . . . . . . . . | 24a | |
| 14 | Employee benefit programs (other than on line 19) . . | 14 | | | **b** Meals and entertainment | | |
| 15 | Insurance (other than health) . | 15 | | | **c** Enter nondeductible amount included on line 24b (see page C-5) | | |
| 16 | Interest: | | | | | | |
| **a** | Mortgage (paid to banks, etc.) | 16a | | | **d** Subtract line 24c from line 24b | 24d | |
| **b** | Other . . . . . . . | 16b | | 25 | Utilities . . . . . . . | 25 | |
| 17 | Legal and professional services . . . . . . | 17 | | 26 | Wages (less employment credits) . | 26 | |
| 18 | Office expense . . . . . | 18 | | 27 | Other expenses (from line 48 on page 2) . . . . . . . | 27 | |

| | | | |
|---|---|---|---|
| 28 | **Total expenses** before expenses for business use of home. Add lines 8 through 27 in columns . . ▶ | 28 | |
| 29 | Tentative profit (loss). Subtract line 28 from line 7 . . . . . . . . . . | 29 | |
| 30 | Expenses for business use of your home. Attach **Form 8829** . . . . . . | 30 | |
| 31 | **Net profit or (loss).** Subtract line 30 from line 29. | | |

**31**
- If a profit, enter on **Form 1040, line 12,** and **also** on **Schedule SE, line 2** (statutory employees, see page C-6). Estates and trusts, enter on Form 1041, line 3.
- If a loss, you **must** go to line 32.

| 31 | |
|---|---|

**32**  If you have a loss, check the box that describes your investment in this activity (see page C-6).
- If you checked 32a, enter the loss on **Form 1040, line 12,** and **also** on **Schedule SE, line 2** (statutory employees, see page C-6). Estates and trusts, enter on Form 1041, line 3.
- If you checked 32b, you **must** attach **Form 6198.**

**32a** ☐ All investment is at risk.
**32b** ☐ Some investment is not at risk.

For Paperwork Reduction Act Notice, see Form 1040 instructions.    Cat. No. 11334P    Schedule C (Form 1040) 2004

**Part III** **Cost of Goods Sold** (see page C-6)

33 Method(s) used to
value closing inventory: **a** ☐ Cost **b** ☐ Lower of cost or market **c** ☐ Other (attach explanation)

34 Was there any change in determining quantities, costs, or valuations between opening and closing inventory? If
"Yes," attach explanation . . . . . . . . . . . . . . . . . . . . . . . . . ☐ **Yes** ☐ **No**

| | | |
|---|---|---|
| 35 Inventory at beginning of year. If different from last year's closing inventory, attach explanation . . | 35 | |
| 36 Purchases less cost of items withdrawn for personal use . . . . . . . . | 36 | |
| 37 Cost of labor. Do not include any amounts paid to yourself . . . . . . . | 37 | |
| 38 Materials and supplies . . . . . . . . . . . . | 38 | |
| 39 Other costs . . . . . . . . . . . . . | 39 | |
| 40 Add lines 35 through 39 . . . . . . . . . . | 40 | |
| 41 Inventory at end of year . . . . . . . . . . . | 41 | |
| 42 **Cost of goods sold.** Subtract line 41 from line 40. Enter the result here and on page 1, line 4 . . | 42 | |

**Part IV** **Information on Your Vehicle.** Complete this part **only** if you are claiming car or truck expenses on line 9 and are not required to file Form 4562 for this business. See the instructions for line 13 on page C-4 to find out if you must file Form 4562.

43 When did you place your vehicle in service for business purposes? (month, day, year) ▶ ......... / ......... / ......... .

44 Of the total number of miles you drove your vehicle during 2004, enter the number of miles you used your vehicle for:

**a** Business ......................... **b** Commuting ......................... **c** Other .........................

45 Do you (or your spouse) have another vehicle available for personal use? . . . . . . . . . . . ☐ **Yes** ☐ **No**

46 Was your vehicle available for personal use during off-duty hours? . . . . . . . . . ☐ **Yes** ☐ **No**

47a Do you have evidence to support your deduction? . . . . . . . . . . . . . . . ☐ **Yes** ☐ **No**

**b** If "Yes," is the evidence written? . . . . . . . . . . . . . . . . . . . . . . ☐ **Yes** ☐ **No**

**Part V** **Other Expenses.** List below business expenses not included on lines 8–26 or line 30.

| | | |
|---|---|---|
| | | |
| | | |
| | | |
| | | |
| | | |
| | | |
| | | |
| | | |
| 48 **Total other expenses.** Enter here and on page 1, line 27 . . . . . . . . . | 48 | |

**Form 1065**

Department of the Treasury
Internal Revenue Service

## U.S. Return of Partnership Income

For calendar year 2004, or tax year beginning .......... , 2004, and ending .......... , 20...... .
▶ See separate instructions.

OMB No. 1545-0099

**2004**

| | | | |
|---|---|---|---|
| **A** Principal business activity | Use the IRS label. Other-wise, print or type. | Name of partnership | **D** Employer identification number |
| **B** Principal product or service | | Number, street, and room or suite no. If a P.O. box, see page 14 of the instructions. | **E** Date business started |
| **C** Business code number | | City or town, state, and ZIP code | **F** Total assets (see page 14 of the instructions) $ |

**G** Check applicable boxes: **(1)** ☐ Initial return  **(2)** ☐ Final return  **(3)** ☐ Name change  **(4)** ☐ Address change  **(5)** ☐ Amended return

**H** Check accounting method: **(1)** ☐ Cash  **(2)** ☐ Accrual  **(3)** ☐ Other (specify) ▶ .............................

**I** Number of Schedules K-1. Attach one for each person who was a partner at any time during the tax year ▶ .............................

**Caution:** *Include **only** trade or business income and expenses on lines 1a through 22 below. See the instructions for more information.*

### Income

| | | | |
|---|---|---|---|
| **1a** Gross receipts or sales | **1a** | | |
| **b** Less returns and allowances | **1b** | **1c** | |
| **2** Cost of goods sold (Schedule A, line 8) | | **2** | |
| **3** Gross profit. Subtract line 2 from line 1c | | **3** | |
| **4** Ordinary income (loss) from other partnerships, estates, and trusts *(attach schedule)* | | **4** | |
| **5** Net farm profit (loss) *(attach Schedule F (Form 1040))* | | **5** | |
| **6** Net gain (loss) from Form 4797, Part II, line 17 | | **6** | |
| **7** Other income (loss) *(attach statement)* | | **7** | |
| **8** **Total income (loss).** Combine lines 3 through 7 | | **8** | |

### Deductions (see page 16 of the instructions for limitations)

| | | | |
|---|---|---|---|
| **9** Salaries and wages (other than to partners) (less employment credits) | | **9** | |
| **10** Guaranteed payments to partners | | **10** | |
| **11** Repairs and maintenance | | **11** | |
| **12** Bad debts | | **12** | |
| **13** Rent | | **13** | |
| **14** Taxes and licenses | | **14** | |
| **15** Interest | | **15** | |
| **16a** Depreciation *(if required, attach Form 4562)* | **16a** | | |
| **b** Less depreciation reported on Schedule A and elsewhere on return | **16b** | **16c** | |
| **17** Depletion **(Do not deduct oil and gas depletion.)** | | **17** | |
| **18** Retirement plans, etc. | | **18** | |
| **19** Employee benefit programs | | **19** | |
| **20** Other deductions *(attach statement)* | | **20** | |
| **21** **Total deductions.** Add the amounts shown in the far right column for lines 9 through 20 | | **21** | |
| **22** **Ordinary business income (loss).** Subtract line 21 from line 8 | | **22** | |

### Sign Here

Under penalties of perjury, I declare that I have examined this return, including accompanying schedules and statements, and to the best of my knowledge and belief, it is true, correct, and complete. Declaration of preparer (other than general partner or limited liability company member) is based on all information of which preparer has any knowledge.

▶ _____        ▶ _____
Signature of general partner or limited liability company member manager        Date

May the IRS discuss this return with the preparer shown below (see instructions)? ☐ Yes ☐ No

### Paid Preparer's Use Only

| | | | | |
|---|---|---|---|---|
| Preparer's signature | | Date | Check if self-employed ▶ ☐ | Preparer's SSN or PTIN |
| Firm's name (or yours if self-employed), address, and ZIP code ▶ | | | EIN ▶ | |
| | | | Phone no. ( ) | |

**For Privacy Act and Paperwork Reduction Act Notice, see separate instructions.**        Cat. No. 11390Z        Form **1065** (2004)

Form 1065 (2004)

Page **2**

## Schedule A — Cost of Goods Sold (see page 19 of the instructions)

| | | | |
|---|---|---|---|
| 1 | Inventory at beginning of year | 1 | |
| 2 | Purchases less cost of items withdrawn for personal use | 2 | |
| 3 | Cost of labor | 3 | |
| 4 | Additional section 263A costs *(attach statement)* | 4 | |
| 5 | Other costs *(attach statement)* | 5 | |
| 6 | **Total.** Add lines 1 through 5 | 6 | |
| 7 | Inventory at end of year | 7 | |
| 8 | **Cost of goods sold.** Subtract line 7 from line 6. Enter here and on page 1, line 2 | 8 | |

**9a** Check all methods used for valuing closing inventory:

   **(i)** ☐ Cost as described in Regulations section 1.471-3

   **(ii)** ☐ Lower of cost or market as described in Regulations section 1.471-4

   **(iii)** ☐ Other (specify method used and attach explanation) ▶ ........................................................................

  **b** Check this box if there was a writedown of "subnormal" goods as described in Regulations section 1.471-2(c) . . . ▶ ☐

  **c** Check this box if the LIFO inventory method was adopted this tax year for any goods *(if checked, attach Form 970)*. . ▶ ☐

  **d** Do the rules of section 263A (for property produced or acquired for resale) apply to the partnership? . . ☐ **Yes** ☐ **No**

  **e** Was there any change in determining quantities, cost, or valuations between opening and closing inventory? ☐ **Yes** ☐ **No** If "Yes," attach explanation.

## Schedule B — Other Information

| | | Yes | No |
|---|---|---|---|
| 1 | What type of entity is filing this return? Check the applicable box: | | |

  **a** ☐ Domestic general partnership      **b** ☐ Domestic limited partnership

  **c** ☐ Domestic limited liability company      **d** ☐ Domestic limited liability partnership

  **e** ☐ Foreign partnership      **f** ☐ Other ▶ ........................................................................

| | | Yes | No |
|---|---|---|---|
| 2 | Are any partners in this partnership also partnerships? | | |
| 3 | During the partnership's tax year, did the partnership own any interest in another partnership or in any foreign entity that was disregarded as an entity separate from its owner under Regulations sections 301.7701-2 and 301.7701-3? If yes, see instructions for required attachment | | |
| 4 | Did the partnership file Form 8893, Election of Partnership Level Tax Treatment, or an election statement under section 6231(a)(1)(B)(ii) for partnership-level tax treatment, that is in effect for this tax year? See Form 8893 for more details | | |
| 5 | Does this partnership meet all three of the following requirements? | | |
| a | The partnership's total receipts for the tax year were less than $250,000; | | |
| b | The partnership's total assets at the end of the tax year were less than $600,000; and | | |
| c | Schedules K-1 are filed with the return and furnished to the partners on or before the due date (including extensions) for the partnership return. | | |
| | If "Yes," the partnership is not required to complete Schedules L, M-1, and M-2; Item F on page 1 of Form 1065; or Item N on Schedule K-1. | | |
| 6 | Does this partnership have any foreign partners? If "Yes," the partnership may have to file Forms 8804, 8805 and 8813. See page 20 of the instructions | | |
| 7 | Is this partnership a publicly traded partnership as defined in section 469(k)(2)? | | |
| 8 | Has this partnership filed, or is it required to file, Form 8264, Application for Registration of a Tax Shelter? | | |
| 9 | At any time during calendar year 2004, did the partnership have an interest in or a signature or other authority over a financial account in a foreign country (such as a bank account, securities account, or other financial account)? See page 20 of the instructions for exceptions and filing requirements for Form TD F 90-22.1. If "Yes," enter the name of the foreign country. ▶ ........................................... | | |
| 10 | During the tax year, did the partnership receive a distribution from, or was it the grantor of, or transferor to, a foreign trust? If "Yes," the partnership may have to file Form 3520. See page 21 of the instructions | | |
| 11 | Was there a distribution of property or a transfer (e.g., by sale or death) of a partnership interest during the tax year? If "Yes," you may elect to adjust the basis of the partnership's assets under section 754 by attaching the statement described under *Elections Made By the Partnership* on page 9 of the instructions | | |
| 12 | Enter the number of Forms 8865, Return of U.S. Persons With Respect to Certain Foreign Partnerships, attached to this return ▶ | | |

**Designation of Tax Matters Partner** (see page 21 of the instructions)

Enter below the general partner designated as the tax matters partner (TMP) for the tax year of this return:

| Name of designated TMP ▶ | | Identifying number of TMP ▶ | |
|---|---|---|---|
| Address of designated TMP ▶ | | | |

Form **1065** (2004)

Form 1065 (2004) Page **3**

| Schedule K | Partners' Distributive Share Items | | Total amount | |
|---|---|---|---|---|

<table>
<tr><td rowspan="18">Income (Loss)</td><td>1</td><td>Ordinary business income (loss) (page 1, line 22) . . . . . . . . .</td><td></td><td>1</td><td></td></tr>
<tr><td>2</td><td>Net rental real estate income (loss) (attach Form 8825) . . . . . . .</td><td></td><td>2</td><td></td></tr>
<tr><td>3a</td><td>Other gross rental income (loss) . . . . . . . . .</td><td>3a</td><td></td><td></td></tr>
<tr><td>b</td><td>Expenses from other rental activities (attach statement). . . .</td><td>3b</td><td></td><td></td></tr>
<tr><td>c</td><td>Other net rental income (loss). Subtract line 3b from line 3a . . . . .</td><td></td><td>3c</td><td></td></tr>
<tr><td>4</td><td>Guaranteed payments . . . . . . . . . . . . . .</td><td></td><td>4</td><td></td></tr>
<tr><td>5</td><td>Interest income . . . . . . . . . . . . . . . .</td><td></td><td>5</td><td></td></tr>
<tr><td>6</td><td>Dividends: a Ordinary dividends . . . . . . . . . .</td><td></td><td>6a</td><td></td></tr>
<tr><td></td><td>b Qualified dividends . . . . . . . . .</td><td>6b</td><td></td><td></td></tr>
<tr><td>7</td><td>Royalties . . . . . . . . . . . . . . . . . .</td><td></td><td>7</td><td></td></tr>
<tr><td>8</td><td>Net short-term capital gain (loss) (attach Schedule D (Form 1065)) . . .</td><td></td><td>8</td><td></td></tr>
<tr><td>9a</td><td>Net long-term capital gain (loss) (attach Schedule D (Form 1065)) . . .</td><td></td><td>9a</td><td></td></tr>
<tr><td>b</td><td>Collectibles (28%) gain (loss) . . . . . . . .</td><td>9b</td><td></td><td></td></tr>
<tr><td>c</td><td>Unrecaptured section 1250 gain (attach statement) . . . .</td><td>9c</td><td></td><td></td></tr>
<tr><td>10</td><td>Net section 1231 gain (loss) (attach Form 4797) . . . . . .</td><td></td><td>10</td><td></td></tr>
<tr><td>11</td><td>Other income (loss) (attach statement) . . . . . . . . . .</td><td></td><td>11</td><td></td></tr>
<tr><td rowspan="6">Deductions</td><td>12</td><td>Section 179 deduction (attach Form 4562) . . . . . . . . .</td><td></td><td>12</td><td></td></tr>
<tr><td>13a</td><td>Contributions . . . . . . . . . . . . . . . .</td><td></td><td>13a</td><td></td></tr>
<tr><td>b</td><td>Deductions related to portfolio income (attach statement) . . . .</td><td></td><td>13b</td><td></td></tr>
<tr><td>c</td><td>Investment interest expense . . . . . . . . . . . .</td><td></td><td>13c</td><td></td></tr>
<tr><td>d</td><td>Section 59(e)(2) expenditures: (1) Type ▶ _____ (2) Amount ▶</td><td></td><td>13d(2)</td><td></td></tr>
<tr><td>e</td><td>Other deductions (attach statement) . . . . . . . . . . .</td><td></td><td>13e</td><td></td></tr>
<tr><td rowspan="3">Self-Employment</td><td>14a</td><td>Net earnings (loss) from self-employment . . . . . . . . .</td><td></td><td>14a</td><td></td></tr>
<tr><td>b</td><td>Gross farming or fishing income . . . . . . . . . . .</td><td></td><td>14b</td><td></td></tr>
<tr><td>c</td><td>Gross nonfarm income . . . . . . . . . . . . .</td><td></td><td>14c</td><td></td></tr>
<tr><td rowspan="6">Credits & Credit Recapture</td><td>15a</td><td>Low-income housing credit (section 42(j)(5)) . . . . . . . .</td><td></td><td>15a</td><td></td></tr>
<tr><td>b</td><td>Low-income housing credit (other) . . . . . . . . . . .</td><td></td><td>15b</td><td></td></tr>
<tr><td>c</td><td>Qualified rehabilitation expenditures (rental real estate) (attach Form 3468).</td><td></td><td>15c</td><td></td></tr>
<tr><td>d</td><td>Other rental real estate credits . . . . . . . . . . .</td><td></td><td>15d</td><td></td></tr>
<tr><td>e</td><td>Other rental credits . . . . . . . . . . . . . .</td><td></td><td>15e</td><td></td></tr>
<tr><td>f</td><td>Other credits and credit recapture (attach statement) . . . . .</td><td></td><td>15f</td><td></td></tr>
<tr><td rowspan="12">Foreign Transactions</td><td>16a</td><td>Name of country or U.S. possession ▶ _____</td><td></td><td></td><td></td></tr>
<tr><td>b</td><td>Gross income from all sources . . . . . . . . . . .</td><td></td><td>16b</td><td></td></tr>
<tr><td>c</td><td>Gross income sourced at partner level . . . . . . . . .</td><td></td><td>16c</td><td></td></tr>
<tr><td></td><td colspan="2">Foreign gross income sourced at partnership level</td><td></td><td></td></tr>
<tr><td>d</td><td>Passive ▶ _____ e Listed categories (attach statement) ▶ _____ f General limitation ▶</td><td></td><td>16f</td><td></td></tr>
<tr><td></td><td colspan="2">Deductions allocated and apportioned at partner level</td><td></td><td></td></tr>
<tr><td>g</td><td>Interest expense ▶ _____ h Other . . . . . . . ▶</td><td></td><td>16h</td><td></td></tr>
<tr><td></td><td colspan="2">Deductions allocated and apportioned at partnership level to foreign source income</td><td></td><td></td></tr>
<tr><td>i</td><td>Passive ▶ _____ j Listed categories (attach statement) ▶ _____ k General limitation ▶</td><td></td><td>16k</td><td></td></tr>
<tr><td>l</td><td>Foreign taxes: (1) Paid ▶ _____ (2) Accrued . . . . . ▶</td><td></td><td>16l(2)</td><td></td></tr>
<tr><td>m</td><td>Reduction in taxes available for credit (attach statement) . . . . .</td><td></td><td>16m</td><td></td></tr>
<tr><td rowspan="6">Alternative Minimum Tax (AMT) Items</td><td>17a</td><td>Post-1986 depreciation adjustment . . . . . . . . . .</td><td></td><td>17a</td><td></td></tr>
<tr><td>b</td><td>Adjusted gain or loss . . . . . . . . . . . . .</td><td></td><td>17b</td><td></td></tr>
<tr><td>c</td><td>Depletion (other than oil and gas) . . . . . . . . . .</td><td></td><td>17c</td><td></td></tr>
<tr><td>d</td><td>Oil, gas, and geothermal properties—gross income . . . . . .</td><td></td><td>17d</td><td></td></tr>
<tr><td>e</td><td>Oil, gas, and geothermal properties—deductions . . . . . .</td><td></td><td>17e</td><td></td></tr>
<tr><td>f</td><td>Other AMT items (attach statement) . . . . . . . . . .</td><td></td><td>17f</td><td></td></tr>
<tr><td rowspan="8">Other Information</td><td>18a</td><td>Tax-exempt interest income . . . . . . . . . . . .</td><td></td><td>18a</td><td></td></tr>
<tr><td>b</td><td>Other tax-exempt income . . . . . . . . . . . .</td><td></td><td>18b</td><td></td></tr>
<tr><td>c</td><td>Nondeductible expenses . . . . . . . . . . . .</td><td></td><td>18c</td><td></td></tr>
<tr><td>19a</td><td>Distributions of cash and marketable securities . . . . . . .</td><td></td><td>19a</td><td></td></tr>
<tr><td>b</td><td>Distributions of other property . . . . . . . . . . .</td><td></td><td>19b</td><td></td></tr>
<tr><td>20a</td><td>Investment income . . . . . . . . . . . . . .</td><td></td><td>20a</td><td></td></tr>
<tr><td>b</td><td>Investment expenses . . . . . . . . . . . . .</td><td></td><td>20b</td><td></td></tr>
<tr><td>c</td><td>Other items and amounts (attach statement) . . . . . . . .</td><td></td><td></td><td></td></tr>
</table>

Form **1065** (2004)

Form 1065 (2004)                                                                                            Page **4**

## Analysis of Net Income (Loss)

**1** Net income (loss). Combine Schedule K, lines 1 through 11. From the result, subtract the sum of Schedule K, lines 12 through 13e, 16l(1), and 16l(2) . . . . . . . . . . . . . . . . . . **1**

| **2** Analysis by partner type: | **(i)** Corporate | **(ii)** Individual (active) | **(iii)** Individual (passive) | **(iv)** Partnership | **(v)** Exempt organization | **(vi)** Nominee/Other |
|---|---|---|---|---|---|---|
| **a** General partners | | | | | | |
| **b** Limited partners | | | | | | |

**Note:** Schedules L, M-1, and M-2 are not required if Question 5 of Schedule B is answered "Yes."

| Schedule L | **Balance Sheets per Books** | Beginning of tax year | | End of tax year | |
|---|---|---|---|---|---|
| **Assets** | | **(a)** | **(b)** | **(c)** | **(d)** |
| **1** Cash . . . . . . . . . . | | | | | |
| **2a** Trade notes and accounts receivable . . . . | | | | | |
| **b** Less allowance for bad debts . . . . . . | | | | | |
| **3** Inventories . . . . . . . . | | | | | |
| **4** U.S. government obligations . . . . . . | | | | | |
| **5** Tax-exempt securities . . . . . . . | | | | | |
| **6** Other current assets (attach statement) . . . | | | | | |
| **7** Mortgage and real estate loans . . . . . | | | | | |
| **8** Other investments (attach statement) . . . . | | | | | |
| **9a** Buildings and other depreciable assets. . . . | | | | | |
| **b** Less accumulated depreciation . . . . . | | | | | |
| **10a** Depletable assets . . . . . . | | | | | |
| **b** Less accumulated depletion . . . . . | | | | | |
| **11** Land (net of any amortization). . . . . . | | | | | |
| **12a** Intangible assets (amortizable only) . . . . | | | | | |
| **b** Less accumulated amortization . . . . . | | | | | |
| **13** Other assets (attach statement) . . . . . | | | | | |
| **14** Total assets . . . . . . . . | | | | | |
| **Liabilities and Capital** | | | | | |
| **15** Accounts payable . . . . . . . | | | | | |
| **16** Mortgages, notes, bonds payable in less than 1 year . | | | | | |
| **17** Other current liabilities (attach statement) . . . | | | | | |
| **18** All nonrecourse loans . . . . . . | | | | | |
| **19** Mortgages, notes, bonds payable in 1 year or more . | | | | | |
| **20** Other liabilities (attach statement) . . . . | | | | | |
| **21** Partners' capital accounts . . . . . | | | | | |
| **22** Total liabilities and capital . . . . . . | | | | | |

| Schedule M-1 | **Reconciliation of Income (Loss) per Books With Income (Loss) per Return** |
|---|---|

| | | | | |
|---|---|---|---|---|
| **1** | Net income (loss) per books . . . . | | **6** Income recorded on books this year not included on Schedule K, lines 1 through 11 (itemize): | |
| **2** | Income included on Schedule K, lines 1, 2, 3c, 5, 6a, 7, 8, 9a, 10, and 11, not recorded on books this year (itemize): _____ | | **a** Tax-exempt interest $ _____ | |
| | | | _____ | |
| **3** | Guaranteed payments (other than health insurance) . . . . . . . . . | | **7** Deductions included on Schedule K, lines 1 through 13e, 16l(1), and 16l(2), not charged against book income this year (itemize): | |
| **4** | Expenses recorded on books this year not included on Schedule K, lines 1 through 13e, 16l(1), and 16l(2) (itemize): | | **a** Depreciation $ _____ | |
| **a** | Depreciation $ _____ | | _____ | |
| **b** | Travel and entertainment $ _____ | | **8** Add lines 6 and 7 . . . . . . . . | |
| | _____ | | **9** Income (loss) (Analysis of Net Income (Loss), line 1). Subtract line 8 from line 5 . . . . | |
| **5** | Add lines 1 through 4 . . . . . . | | | |

| Schedule M-2 | **Analysis of Partners' Capital Accounts** |
|---|---|

| | | | | |
|---|---|---|---|---|
| **1** | Balance at beginning of year . . . . | | **6** Distributions: **a** Cash . . . . . . . . | |
| **2** | Capital contributed: **a** Cash . . . . | | **b** Property . . . . . . | |
| | **b** Property . . . | | **7** Other decreases (itemize): _____ | |
| **3** | Net income (loss) per books . . . . | | _____ | |
| **4** | Other increases (itemize): _____ | | | |
| | _____ | | **8** Add lines 6 and 7 . . . . . . . . | |
| **5** | Add lines 1 through 4 . . . . . . | | **9** Balance at end of year. Subtract line 8 from line 5 | |

Form **1065** (2004)

6511

☐ Final K-1    ☐ Amended K-1    OMB No. 1545-0099

**Schedule K-1**
**(Form 1065)**

20**04**

Department of the Treasury
Internal Revenue Service

Tax year beginning _____ , 2004
and ending _____ , 20___

**Partner's Share of Income, Deductions,**
**Credits, etc.** ▶ See back of form and separate instructions.

| Part I | Information About the Partnership |
|---|---|

**A** Partnership's employer identification number

**B** Partnership's name, address, city, state, and ZIP code

**C** IRS Center where partnership filed return

**D** ☐ Check if this is a publicly traded partnership (PTP)
**E** ☐ Tax shelter registration number, if any _____
**F** ☐ Check if Form 8271 is attached

| Part II | Information About the Partner |
|---|---|

**G** Partner's identifying number

**H** Partner's name, address, city, state, and ZIP code

**I** ☐ General partner or LLC member-manager    ☐ Limited partner or other LLC member

**J** ☐ Domestic partner    ☐ Foreign partner

**K** What type of entity is this partner? _____

**L** Partner's share of profit, loss, and capital:

|  | Beginning | Ending |
|---|---|---|
| Profit | % | % |
| Loss | % | % |
| Capital | % | % |

**M** Partner's share of liabilities at year end:

Nonrecourse . . . . . . . . $ _____
Qualified nonrecourse financing . . $ _____
Recourse . . . . . . . . $ _____

**N** Partner's capital account analysis:

Beginning capital account . . . . $ _____
Capital contributed during the year . $ _____
Current year increase (decrease) . . $ _____
Withdrawals & distributions . . . $ ( _____ )
Ending capital account . . . . $ _____

☐ Tax basis    ☐ GAAP    ☐ Section 704(b) book
☐ Other (explain)

| Part III | Partner's Share of Current Year Income, Deductions, Credits, and Other Items |
|---|---|

| | | | |
|---|---|---|---|
| **1** | Ordinary business income (loss) | **15** | Credits & credit recapture |
| **2** | Net rental real estate income (loss) | | |
| **3** | Other net rental income (loss) | **16** | Foreign transactions |
| **4** | Guaranteed payments | | |
| **5** | Interest income | | |
| **6a** | Ordinary dividends | | |
| **6b** | Qualified dividends | | |
| **7** | Royalties | | |
| **8** | Net short-term capital gain (loss) | | |
| **9a** | Net long-term capital gain (loss) | **17** | Alternative minimum tax (AMT) items |
| **9b** | Collectibles (28%) gain (loss) | | |
| **9c** | Unrecaptured section 1250 gain | | |
| **10** | Net section 1231 gain (loss) | **18** | Tax-exempt income and nondeductible expenses |
| **11** | Other income (loss) | | |
| | | **19** | Distributions |
| **12** | Section 179 deduction | | |
| **13** | Other deductions | **20** | Other information |
| **14** | Self-employment earnings (loss) | | |

*See attached statement for additional information.

For IRS Use Only

**This list identifies the codes used on Schedule K-1 for all partners and provides summarized reporting information for partners who file Form 1040. For detailed reporting and filing information, see the separate Partner's Instructions for Schedule K-1 and the instructions for your income tax return.**

1. **Ordinary business income (loss).** You must first determine whether the income (loss) is passive or nonpassive. Then enter on your return as follows:

| | *Enter on* |
|---|---|
| Passive loss | See the Partner's Instructions |
| Passive income | Schedule E, line 28, column (g) |
| Nonpassive loss | Schedule E, line 28, column (h) |
| Nonpassive income | Schedule E, line 28, column (j) |

2. **Net rental real estate income (loss)** — See the Partner's Instructions

3. **Other net rental income (loss)**

| | |
|---|---|
| Net income | Schedule E, line 28, column (g) |
| Net loss | See the Partner's Instructions |

4. **Guaranteed payments** — Schedule E, line 28, column (j)

5. **Interest income** — Form 1040, line 8a

6a. **Ordinary dividends** — Form 1040, line 9a

6b. **Qualified dividends** — Form 1040, line 9b

7. **Royalties** — Schedule E, line 4

8. **Net short-term capital gain (loss)** — Schedule D, line 5, column (f)

9a. **Net long-term capital gain (loss)** — Schedule D, line 12, column (f)

9b. **Collectibles (28%) gain (loss)** — 28% Rate Gain Worksheet, line 4 (Schedule D Instructions)

9c. **Unrecaptured section 1250 gain** — See the Partner's Instructions

10. **Net section 1231 gain (loss)** — See the Partner's Instructions

11. **Other income (loss)**

*Code*

| A | Other portfolio income (loss) | See the Partner's Instructions |
|---|---|---|
| B | Involuntary conversions | See the Partner's Instructions |
| C | Sec. 1256 contracts & straddles | Form 6781, line 1 |
| D | Mining exploration costs recapture | See Pub. 535 |
| E | Cancellation of debt | Form 1040, line 21 or Form 982 |
| F | Other income (loss) | See the Partner's Instructions |

12. **Section 179 deduction** — See the Partner's Instructions

13. **Other deductions**

| A | Cash contributions (50%) | Schedule A, line 15 |
|---|---|---|
| B | Cash contributions (30%) | Schedule A, line 15 |
| C | Noncash contributions (50%) | Schedule A, line 16 |
| D | Noncash contributions (30%) | Schedule A, line 16 |
| E | Capital gain property to a 50% organization (30%) | Schedule A, line 16 |
| F | Capital gain property (20%) | Schedule A, line 16 |
| G | Deductions—portfolio (2% floor) | Schedule A, line 22 |
| H | Deductions—portfolio (other) | Schedule A, line 27 |
| I | Investment interest expense | Form 4952, line 1 |
| J | Deductions—royalty income | Schedule E, line 18 |
| K | Section 59(e)(2) expenditures | See Partner's Instructions |
| L | Amounts paid for medical insurance | Schedule A, line 1 or Form 1040, line 31 |
| M | Educational assistance benefits | See the Partner's Instructions |
| N | Dependent care benefits | Form 2441, line 12 |
| O | Preproductive period expenses | See the Partner's Instructions |
| P | Commercial revitalization deduction from rental real estate activities | See Form 8582 Instructions |
| Q | Penalty on early withdrawal of savings | Form 1040, line 33 |
| R | Pensions and IRAs | See the Partner's Instructions |
| S | Reforestation expense deduction | See the Partner's Instructions |
| T | Other deductions | See the Partner's Instructions |

14. **Self-employment earnings (loss)**

**Note.** *If you have a section 179 deduction or any partner-level deductions, see the Partner's Instructions before completing Schedule SE.*

| A | Net earnings (loss) from self-employment | Schedule SE, Section A or B |
|---|---|---|
| B | Gross farming or fishing income | See the Partner's Instructions |
| C | Gross non-farm income | See the Partner's Instructions |

15. **Credits & credit recapture**

| A | Low-income housing credit (section 42(j)(5)) | Form 8586, line 5 |
|---|---|---|
| B | Low-income housing credit (other) | Form 8586, line 5 |
| C | Qualified rehabilitation expenditures (rental real estate) | Form 3468, line 1 |
| D | Qualified rehabilitation expenditures (other than rental real estate) | Form 3468, line 1 |
| E | Basis of energy property | Form 3468, line 2 |
| F | Qualified timber property | Form 3468, line 3 |
| G | Other rental real estate credits | See the Partner's Instructions |
| H | Other rental credits | See the Partner's Instructions |

| | | *Code* | | *Enter on* |
|---|---|---|---|---|

| I | Undistributed capital gains credit | Form 1040, line 69, box a |
|---|---|---|
| J | Work opportunity credit | Form 5884, line 3 |
| K | Welfare-to-work credit | Form 8861, line 3 |
| L | Disabled access credit | Form 8826, line 7 |
| M | Empowerment zone and renewal community employment credit | Form 8844, line 3 |
| N | New York Liberty Zone business employee credit | Form 8884, line 3 |
| O | New markets credit | Form 8874, line 2 |
| P | Credit for employer social security and Medicare taxes | Form 8846, line 5 |
| Q | Backup withholding | Form 1040, line 63 |
| R | Recapture of low-income housing credit (section 42(j)(5)) | Form 8611, line 8 |
| S | Recapture of low-income housing credit (other) | Form 8611, line 8 |
| T | Recapture of investment credit | See Form 4255 |
| U | Other credits | See the Partner's Instructions |
| V | Recapture of other credits | See the Partner's Instructions |

16. **Foreign transactions**

| A | Name of country or U.S. possession | Form 1116, Part I |
|---|---|---|
| B | Gross income from all sources | Form 1116, Part I |
| C | Gross income sourced at partner level | Form 1116, Part I |

*Foreign gross income sourced at partnership level*

| D | Passive | Form 1116, Part I |
|---|---|---|
| E | Listed categories | Form 1116, Part I |
| F | General limitation | Form 1116, Part I |

*Deductions allocated and apportioned at partner level*

| G | Interest expense | Form 1116, Part I |
|---|---|---|
| H | Other | Form 1116, Part I |

*Deductions allocated and apportioned at partnership level to foreign source income*

| I | Passive | Form 1116, Part I |
|---|---|---|
| J | Listed categories | Form 1116, Part I |
| K | General limitation | Form 1116, Part I |

*Other information*

| L | Total foreign taxes paid | Form 1116, Part II |
|---|---|---|
| M | Total foreign taxes accrued | Form 1116, Part II |
| N | Reduction in taxes available for credit | Form 1116, line 12 |
| O | Foreign trading gross receipts | Form 8873 |
| P | Extraterritorial income exclusion | Form 8873 |
| Q | Other foreign transactions | See the Partner's Instructions |

17. **Alternative minimum tax (AMT) items**

| A | Post-1986 depreciation adjustment | |
|---|---|---|
| B | Adjusted gain or loss | See the Partner's Instructions and the Instructions for Form 6251 |
| C | Depletion (other than oil & gas) | |
| D | Oil, gas, & geothermal—gross income | |
| E | Oil, gas, & geothermal—deductions | |
| F | Other AMT items | |

18. **Tax-exempt income and nondeductible expenses**

| A | Tax-exempt interest income | Form 1040, line 8b |
|---|---|---|
| B | Other tax-exempt income | See the Partner's Instructions |
| C | Nondeductible expenses | See the Partner's Instructions |

19. **Distributions**

| A | Cash and marketable securities | See the Partner's Instructions |
|---|---|---|
| B | Other property | See the Partner's Instructions |

20. **Other information**

| A | Investment income | Form 4952, line 4a |
|---|---|---|
| B | Investment expenses | Form 4952, line 5 |
| C | Fuel tax credit information | Form 4136 |
| D | Look-back interest—completed long-term contracts | Form 8697 |
| E | Look-back interest—income forecast method | Form 8866 |
| F | Dispositions of property with section 179 deductions | |
| G | Recapture of section 179 deduction | |
| H | Special basis adjustments | |
| I | Section 453(l)(3) information | |
| J | Section 453A(c) information | |
| K | Section 1260(b) information | See the Partner's Instructions |
| L | Interest allocable to production expenditures | |
| M | CCF nonqualified withdrawals | |
| N | Information needed to figure depletion—oil and gas | |
| O | Amortization of reforestation costs | |
| P | Unrelated business taxable income | |
| Q | Other information | |

# Form 1120

Department of the Treasury
Internal Revenue Service

## U.S. Corporation Income Tax Return

For calendar year 2004 or tax year beginning ............... , 2004, ending ............... , 20 ....
▶ See separate instructions.

OMB No. 1545-0123

**2004**

**A** Check if:

1 Consolidated return (attach Form 851) ☐
2 Personal holding co. (attach Sch. PH) ☐
3 Personal service corp. (see instructions) ☐
4 Schedule M-3 required (attach Sch. M-3) ☐

Use IRS label. Otherwise, print or type.

Name

Number, street, and room or suite no. If a P.O. box, see page 9 of instructions.

City or town, state, and ZIP code

**B** Employer identification number

**C** Date incorporated

**D** Total assets (see page 8 of instructions)

$

**E** Check if: **(1)** ☐ Initial return  **(2)** ☐ Final return  **(3)** ☐ Name change  **(4)** ☐ Address change

| | | |
|---|---|---|
| Income | 1a Gross receipts or sales [____] **b** Less returns and allowances [____] **c** Bal ▶ | 1c |
| | 2 Cost of goods sold (Schedule A, line 8) | 2 |
| | 3 Gross profit. Subtract line 2 from line 1c | 3 |
| | 4 Dividends (Schedule C, line 19) | 4 |
| | 5 Interest | 5 |
| | 6 Gross rents | 6 |
| | 7 Gross royalties | 7 |
| | 8 Capital gain net income (attach Schedule D (Form 1120)) | 8 |
| | 9 Net gain or (loss) from Form 4797, Part II, line 17 (attach Form 4797) | 9 |
| | 10 Other income (see page 11 of instructions—attach schedule) | 10 |
| | 11 **Total income.** Add lines 3 through 10 ▶ | 11 |

| | | |
|---|---|---|
| Deductions (See instructions for limitations on deductions.) | 12 Compensation of officers (Schedule E, line 4) | 12 |
| | 13 Salaries and wages (less employment credits) | 13 |
| | 14 Repairs and maintenance | 14 |
| | 15 Bad debts | 15 |
| | 16 Rents | 16 |
| | 17 Taxes and licenses | 17 |
| | 18 Interest | 18 |
| | 19 Charitable contributions (see page 14 of instructions for 10% limitation) | 19 |
| | 20 Depreciation (attach Form 4562) [20] | |
| | 21 Less depreciation claimed on Schedule A and elsewhere on return [21a] | 21b |
| | 22 Depletion | 22 |
| | 23 Advertising | 23 |
| | 24 Pension, profit-sharing, etc., plans | 24 |
| | 25 Employee benefit programs | 25 |
| | 26 Other deductions (attach schedule) | 26 |
| | 27 **Total deductions.** Add lines 12 through 26 ▶ | 27 |
| | 28 Taxable income before net operating loss deduction and special deductions. Subtract line 27 from line 11 | 28 |
| | 29 **Less:** **a** Net operating loss deduction (see page 16 of instructions) [29a] | |
| | **b** Special deductions (Schedule C, line 20) [29b] | 29c |

| | | |
|---|---|---|
| Tax and Payments | 30 **Taxable income.** Subtract line 29c from line 28 (see instructions if Schedule C, line 12, was completed) | 30 |
| | 31 **Total tax** (Schedule J, line 11) | 31 |
| | 32 **Payments: a** 2003 overpayment credited to 2004. [32a] | |
| | **b** 2004 estimated tax payments [32b] | |
| | **c** Less 2004 refund applied for on Form 4466 [32c] ( ) **d** Bal ▶ [32d] | |
| | **e** Tax deposited with Form 7004 [32e] | |
| | **f** Credit for tax paid on undistributed capital gains (attach Form 2439) [32f] | |
| | **g** Credit for Federal tax on fuels (attach Form 4136). See instructions. [32g] | 32h |
| | 33 Estimated tax penalty (see page 17 of instructions). Check if Form 2220 is attached ▶ ☐ | 33 |
| | 34 **Tax due.** If line 32h is smaller than the total of lines 31 and 33, enter amount owed | 34 |
| | 35 **Overpayment.** If line 32h is larger than the total of lines 31 and 33, enter amount overpaid | 35 |
| | 36 Enter amount of line 35 you want: **Credited to 2005 estimated tax** ▶  **Refunded** ▶ | 36 |

**Sign Here** ▶

Under penalties of perjury, I declare that I have examined this return, including accompanying schedules and statements, and to the best of my knowledge and belief, it is true, correct, and complete. Declaration of preparer (other than taxpayer) is based on all information of which preparer has any knowledge.

_____  _____  _____
Signature of officer     Date          Title

May the IRS discuss this return with the preparer shown below (see instructions)? ☐ **Yes** ☐ **No**

**Paid Preparer's Use Only**

| | | | |
|---|---|---|---|
| Preparer's signature ▶ | | Date | Check if self-employed ☐ |
| Firm's name (or yours if self-employed), address, and ZIP code ▶ | | EIN | |
| | | Phone no. ( ) | |

Preparer's SSN or PTIN

For Privacy Act and Paperwork Reduction Act Notice, see separate instructions.     Cat. No. 11450Q     Form **1120** (2004)

Form 1120 (2004)

## Schedule A — Cost of Goods Sold (see page 17 of instructions)

| | | | |
|---|---|---|---|
| 1 | Inventory at beginning of year | 1 | |
| 2 | Purchases | 2 | |
| 3 | Cost of labor | 3 | |
| 4 | Additional section 263A costs (attach schedule) | 4 | |
| 5 | Other costs (attach schedule) | 5 | |
| 6 | **Total.** Add lines 1 through 5 | 6 | |
| 7 | Inventory at end of year | 7 | |
| 8 | **Cost of goods sold.** Subtract line 7 from line 6. Enter here and on page 1, line 2 | 8 | |

**9a** Check all methods used for valuing closing inventory:

    *(i)* ☐ Cost as described in Regulations section 1.471-3

    *(ii)* ☐ Lower of cost or market as described in Regulations section 1.471-4

    *(iii)* ☐ Other (Specify method used and attach explanation.) ▶ ------------------------------

  **b** Check if there was a writedown of subnormal goods as described in Regulations section 1.471-2(c) . . . . . . . ▶ ☐

  **c** Check if the LIFO inventory method was adopted this tax year for any goods (if checked, attach Form 970) . . . . . . ▶ ☐

  **d** If the LIFO inventory method was used for this tax year, enter percentage (or amounts) of closing inventory computed under LIFO . . . . . . . . . . . . . . . . . . . . | 9d |

  **e** If property is produced or acquired for resale, do the rules of section 263A apply to the corporation? . . . . . ☐ Yes ☐ No

  **f** Was there any change in determining quantities, cost, or valuations between opening and closing inventory? If "Yes," attach explanation . . . . . . . . . . . . . . . . . . . . . . . . . . . . . . ☐ Yes ☐ No

## Schedule C — Dividends and Special Deductions (see page 18 of instructions)

| | | (a) Dividends received | (b) % | (c) Special deductions (a) × (b) |
|---|---|---|---|---|
| 1 | Dividends from less-than-20%-owned domestic corporations that are subject to the 70% deduction (other than debt-financed stock) | | 70 | |
| 2 | Dividends from 20%-or-more-owned domestic corporations that are subject to the 80% deduction (other than debt-financed stock) | | 80 | |
| 3 | Dividends on debt-financed stock of domestic and foreign corporations (section 246A) | | see instructions | |
| 4 | Dividends on certain preferred stock of less-than-20%-owned public utilities | | 42 | |
| 5 | Dividends on certain preferred stock of 20%-or-more-owned public utilities | | 48 | |
| 6 | Dividends from less-than-20%-owned foreign corporations and certain FSCs that are subject to the 70% deduction | | 70 | |
| 7 | Dividends from 20%-or-more-owned foreign corporations and certain FSCs that are subject to the 80% deduction | | 80 | |
| 8 | Dividends from wholly owned foreign subsidiaries subject to the 100% deduction (section 245(b)) | | 100 | |
| 9 | **Total.** Add lines 1 through 8. See page 19 of instructions for limitation | | | |
| 10 | Dividends from domestic corporations received by a small business investment company operating under the Small Business Investment Act of 1958 | | 100 | |
| 11 | Dividends from affiliated group members and certain FSCs that are subject to the 100% deduction | | 100 | |
| 12 | Dividends from controlled foreign corporations subject to the 85% deduction (attach Form 8895) | | 85 | |
| 13 | Other dividends from foreign corporations not included on lines 3, 6, 7, 8, 11, or 12 | | | |
| 14 | Income from controlled foreign corporations under subpart F (attach Form(s) 5471) | | | |
| 15 | Foreign dividend gross-up (section 78) | | | |
| 16 | IC-DISC and former DISC dividends not included on lines 1, 2, or 3 (section 246(d)) | | | |
| 17 | Other dividends | | | |
| 18 | Deduction for dividends paid on certain preferred stock of public utilities | | | |
| 19 | **Total dividends.** Add lines 1 through 17. Enter here and on page 1, line 4 ▶ | | | |
| 20 | **Total special deductions.** Add lines 9, 10, 11, 12, and 18. Enter here and on page 1, line 29b ▶ | | | |

## Schedule E — Compensation of Officers (see instructions for page 1, line 12, on page 13 of instructions)

**Note:** *Complete Schedule E only if total receipts (line 1a plus lines 4 through 10 on page 1) are $500,000 or more.*

| | (a) Name of officer | (b) Social security number | (c) Percent of time devoted to business | Percent of corporation stock owned | | (f) Amount of compensation |
|---|---|---|---|---|---|---|
| | | | | (d) Common | (e) Preferred | |
| 1 | | | % | % | % | |
| | | | % | % | % | |
| | | | % | % | % | |
| | | | % | % | % | |
| | | | % | % | % | |
| 2 | Total compensation of officers | | | | | |
| 3 | Compensation of officers claimed on Schedule A and elsewhere on return | | | | | |
| 4 | Subtract line 3 from line 2. Enter the result here and on page 1, line 12 | | | | | |

Form **1120** (2004)

Form 1120 (2004)　　　　　　　　　　　　　　　　　　　　　　　　　　　　　　　　　　　　　　　　Page **3**

## Schedule J　Tax Computation (see page 20 of instructions)

1　Check if the corporation is a member of a controlled group (see sections 1561 and 1563). . . . . ▶ ☐

**Important:** Members of a controlled group, see page 20 of instructions.

2a　If the box on line 1 is checked, enter the corporation's share of the $50,000, $25,000, and $9,925,000 taxable income brackets (in that order):

(1) $ _____ | (2) $ _____ | (3) $ _____

b　Enter the corporation's share of: (1) Additional 5% tax (not more than $11,750)　　$ _____

　　　　　　　　　　　　　　　　(2) Additional 3% tax (not more than $100,000)　　$ _____

| | |
|---|---|
| 3　Income tax. Check if a qualified personal service corporation under section 448(d)(2) (see page 21) . ▶ ☐ | 3 |
| 4　Alternative minimum tax (attach Form 4626) . . . . . . . . . . . | 4 |
| 5　Add lines 3 and 4 . . . . . . . . . . . . . . . . . | 5 |
| 6a　Foreign tax credit (attach Form 1118) . . . . . . . . 6a | |
| b　Possessions tax credit (attach Form 5735) . . . . . . 6b | |
| c　Check: ☐ Nonconventional source fuel credit ☐ QEV credit (attach Form 8834) 6c | |
| d　General business credit. Check box(es) and indicate which forms are attached: | |
| 　　☐ Form 3800 　☐ Form(s) (specify) ▶ .................... 6d | |
| e　Credit for prior year minimum tax (attach Form 8827) . . . . 6e | |
| f　Qualified zone academy bond credit (attach Form 8860) . . . . 6f | |
| 7　**Total credits.** Add lines 6a through 6f . . . . . . . . . . . | 7 |
| 8　Subtract line 7 from line 5 . . . . . . . . . . . | 8 |
| 9　Personal holding company tax (attach Schedule PH (Form 1120)) . . . . . . | 9 |
| 10　Other taxes. Check if from: ☐ Form 4255 ☐ Form 8611 ☐ Form 8697 | |
| 　　　　　　　　　　　☐ Form 8866 ☐ Other (attach schedule) . . . . . | 10 |
| 11　**Total tax.** Add lines 8 through 10. Enter here and on page 1, line 31 . . . . . | 11 |

## Schedule K　Other Information (see page 23 of instructions)

| | Yes | No |
|---|---|---|
| 1　Check accounting method: a ☐ Cash | | |
| 　b ☐ Accrual c ☐ Other (specify) ▶ .............. | | |
| 2　See page 25 of the instructions and enter the: | | |
| a　Business activity code no. ▶ .............. | | |
| b　Business activity ▶ .............. | | |
| c　Product or service ▶ .............. | | |
| 3　At the end of the tax year, did the corporation own, directly or indirectly, 50% or more of the voting stock of a domestic corporation? (For rules of attribution, see section 267(c).) . . . . . . . . . . | | |

If "Yes," attach a schedule showing: (a) name and employer identification number (EIN), (b) percentage owned, and (c) taxable income or (loss) before NOL and special deductions of such corporation for the tax year ending with or within your tax year.

| | Yes | No |
|---|---|---|
| 4　Is the corporation a subsidiary in an affiliated group or a parent-subsidiary controlled group? . . . . . | | |

If "Yes," enter name and EIN of the parent corporation ▶ ..............
..............

5　At the end of the tax year, did any individual, partnership, corporation, estate, or trust own, directly or indirectly, 50% or more of the corporation's voting stock? (For rules of attribution, see section 267(c).) . . . . . .
If "Yes," attach a schedule showing name and identifying number. (Do not include any information already entered in **4** above.) Enter percentage owned ▶ ..............

6　During this tax year, did the corporation pay dividends (other than stock dividends and distributions in exchange for stock) in excess of the corporation's current and accumulated earnings and profits? (See sections 301 and 316.) . .

If "Yes," file **Form 5452,** Corporate Report of Nondividend Distributions.

If this is a consolidated return, answer here for the parent corporation and on **Form 851,** Affiliations Schedule, for each subsidiary.

| | Yes | No |
|---|---|---|
| 7　At any time during the tax year, did one foreign person own, directly or indirectly, at least 25% of (a) the total voting power of all classes of stock of the corporation entitled to vote or (b) the total value of all classes of stock of the corporation? . . . . . . . . | | |

If "Yes," enter: (a) Percentage owned ▶ ..............
and (b) Owner's country ▶ ..............

c　The corporation may have to file **Form 5472,** Information Return of a 25% Foreign-Owned U.S. Corporation or a Foreign Corporation Engaged in a U.S. Trade or Business. Enter number of Forms 5472 attached ▶ ..............

8　Check this box if the corporation issued publicly offered debt instruments with original issue discount . ▶ ☐

If checked, the corporation may have to file **Form 8281,** Information Return for Publicly Offered Original Issue Discount Instruments.

9　Enter the amount of tax-exempt interest received or accrued during the tax year ▶ $ ..............

10　Enter the number of shareholders at the end of the tax year (if 75 or fewer) ▶ ..............

11　If the corporation has an NOL for the tax year and is electing to forego the carryback period, check here ▶ ☐

If the corporation is filing a consolidated return, the statement required by Temporary Regulations section 1.1502-21T(b)(3)(i) or (ii) must be attached or the election will not be valid.

12　Enter the available NOL carryover from prior tax years (Do not reduce it by any deduction on line 29a.) ▶ $ ..............

| | Yes | No |
|---|---|---|
| 13　Are the corporation's total receipts (line 1a plus lines 4 through 10 on page 1) for the tax year **and** its total assets at the end of the tax year less than $250,000? . . . | | |

If "Yes," the corporation is not required to complete Schedules L, M-1, and M-2 on page 4. Instead, enter the total amount of cash distributions and the book value of property distributions (other than cash) made during the tax year. ▶ $ ..............

**Note:** *If the corporation, at any time during the tax year, had assets or operated a business in a foreign country or U.S. possession, it may be required to attach **Schedule N (Form 1120)**, Foreign Operations of U.S. Corporations, to this return. See Schedule N for details.*

Form 1120 (2004)

Page **4**

**Note:** *The corporation is not required to complete Schedules L, M-1, and M-2 if Question 13 on Schedule K is answered "Yes."*

| Schedule L | Balance Sheets per Books | Beginning of tax year | | End of tax year | |
|---|---|---|---|---|---|
| | **Assets** | **(a)** | **(b)** | **(c)** | **(d)** |
| 1 | Cash | | | | |
| 2a | Trade notes and accounts receivable | | | | |
| b | Less allowance for bad debts | ( ) | | ( ) | |
| 3 | Inventories | | | | |
| 4 | U.S. government obligations | | | | |
| 5 | Tax-exempt securities (see instructions) | | | | |
| 6 | Other current assets (attach schedule) | | | | |
| 7 | Loans to shareholders | | | | |
| 8 | Mortgage and real estate loans | | | | |
| 9 | Other investments (attach schedule) | | | | |
| 10a | Buildings and other depreciable assets | | | | |
| b | Less accumulated depreciation | ( ) | | ( ) | |
| 11a | Depletable assets | | | | |
| b | Less accumulated depletion | ( ) | | ( ) | |
| 12 | Land (net of any amortization) | | | | |
| 13a | Intangible assets (amortizable only) | | | | |
| b | Less accumulated amortization | ( ) | | ( ) | |
| 14 | Other assets (attach schedule) | | | | |
| 15 | Total assets | | | | |
| | **Liabilities and Shareholders' Equity** | | | | |
| 16 | Accounts payable | | | | |
| 17 | Mortgages, notes, bonds payable in less than 1 year | | | | |
| 18 | Other current liabilities (attach schedule) | | | | |
| 19 | Loans from shareholders | | | | |
| 20 | Mortgages, notes, bonds payable in 1 year or more | | | | |
| 21 | Other liabilities (attach schedule) | | | | |
| 22 | Capital stock: **a** Preferred stock | | | | |
| | **b** Common stock | | | | |
| 23 | Additional paid-in capital | | | | |
| 24 | Retained earnings—Appropriated (attach schedule) | | | | |
| 25 | Retained earnings—Unappropriated | | | | |
| 26 | Adjustments to shareholders' equity (attach schedule) | | | | |
| 27 | Less cost of treasury stock | | ( ) | | ( ) |
| 28 | Total liabilities and shareholders' equity | | | | |

| Schedule M-1 | Reconciliation of Income (Loss) per Books With Income per Return (see page 24 of instructions) |
|---|---|

| 1 | Net income (loss) per books | | 7 | Income recorded on books this year not included on this return (itemize): | |
| 2 | Federal income tax per books | | | | |
| 3 | Excess of capital losses over capital gains | | | Tax-exempt interest $ | |
| 4 | Income subject to tax not recorded on books this year (itemize): | | | | |
| | | | 8 | Deductions on this return not charged against book income this year (itemize): | |
| 5 | Expenses recorded on books this year not deducted on this return (itemize): | | a | Depreciation $ | |
| a | Depreciation $ | | b | Charitable contributions $ | |
| b | Charitable contributions $ | | | | |
| c | Travel and entertainment $ | | 9 | Add lines 7 and 8 | |
| 6 | Add lines 1 through 5 | | 10 | Income (page 1, line 28)—line 6 less line 9 | |

| Schedule M-2 | Analysis of Unappropriated Retained Earnings per Books (Line 25, Schedule L) |
|---|---|

| 1 | Balance at beginning of year | | 5 | Distributions: **a** Cash | |
| 2 | Net income (loss) per books | | | **b** Stock | |
| 3 | Other increases (itemize): | | | **c** Property | |
| | | | 6 | Other decreases (itemize): | |
| | | | 7 | Add lines 5 and 6 | |
| 4 | Add lines 1, 2, and 3 | | 8 | Balance at end of year (line 4 less line 7) | |

Form **1120** (2004)

| Form **1120S** | **U.S. Income Tax Return for an S Corporation** | OMB No. 1545-0130 |
|---|---|---|

Department of the Treasury
Internal Revenue Service

► Do not file this form unless the corporation has timely filed
Form 2553 to elect to be an S corporation.
► See separate instructions.

**2004**

For calendar year 2004, or tax year beginning _____ , 2004, and ending _____ , 20____

| **A** Effective date of S election | **Use the IRS label. Otherwise, print or type.** | Name | **C** Employer identification number |
|---|---|---|---|
| | | Number, street, and room or suite no. (If a P.O. box, see page 12 of the instructions.) | **D** Date incorporated |
| **B** Business code number (see pages 36–38 of the Insts.) | | City or town, state, and ZIP code | **E** Total assets (see page 12 of instructions) $ |

**F** Check applicable boxes:  (1) ☐ Initial return  (2) ☐ Final return  (3) ☐ Name change  (4) ☐ Address change  (5) ☐ Amended return
**G** Enter number of shareholders in the corporation at end of the tax year . . . . . . . . . . . . . . ►

**Caution:** Include **only** trade or business income and expenses on lines 1a through 21. See page 13 of the instructions for more information.

**Income**

| | | |
|---|---|---|
| **1a** Gross receipts or sales _____ **b** Less returns and allowances _____ **c** Bal ► | **1c** | |
| **2** Cost of goods sold (Schedule A, line 8) . . . . . . . . . . . . . | **2** | |
| **3** Gross profit. Subtract line 2 from line 1c . . . . . . . . . . . . | **3** | |
| **4** Net gain (loss) from Form 4797, Part II, line 17 (attach Form 4797) . . . | **4** | |
| **5** Other income (loss) (attach schedule) . . . . . . . . . . . . | **5** | |
| **6** **Total income (loss).** Add lines 3 through 5. . . . . . . . . . . ► | **6** | |

**Deductions (see page 14 of the instructions for limitations)**

| | | |
|---|---|---|
| **7** Compensation of officers . . . . . . . . . . . . . . . . . | **7** | |
| **8** Salaries and wages (less employment credits) . . . . . . . . . | **8** | |
| **9** Repairs and maintenance . . . . . . . . . . . . . . . . | **9** | |
| **10** Bad debts . . . . . . . . . . . . . . . . . . . . . | **10** | |
| **11** Rents. . . . . . . . . . . . . . . . . . . . . . . | **11** | |
| **12** Taxes and licenses . . . . . . . . . . . . . . . . . . | **12** | |
| **13** Interest . . . . . . . . . . . . . . . . . . . . . . | **13** | |
| **14a** Depreciation (attach Form 4562) . . . . . **14a** | | |
| **b** Depreciation claimed on Schedule A and elsewhere on return . . **14b** | | |
| **c** Subtract line 14b from line 14a . . . . . . . . . . . . . | **14c** | |
| **15** Depletion (**Do not deduct oil and gas depletion.**) . . . . . . . | **15** | |
| **16** Advertising . . . . . . . . . . . . . . . . . . . . . | **16** | |
| **17** Pension, profit-sharing, etc., plans . . . . . . . . . . . . . | **17** | |
| **18** Employee benefit programs. . . . . . . . . . . . . . . . | **18** | |
| **19** Other deductions (attach schedule) . . . . . . . . . . . . . | **19** | |
| **20** **Total deductions.** Add the amounts shown in the far right column for lines 7 through 19 ► | **20** | |
| **21** Ordinary business income (loss). Subtract line 20 from line 6 . . . . . | **21** | |

**Tax and Payments**

| | | |
|---|---|---|
| **22 Tax:  a** Excess net passive income tax (attach schedule) . . **22a** | | |
| **b** Tax from Schedule D (Form 1120S) . . . . . . . . **22b** | | |
| **c** Add lines 22a and 22b (see page 18 of the instructions for additional taxes) . . . . . | **22c** | |
| **23 Payments: a** 2004 estimated tax payments and amount applied from 2003 return  **23a** | | |
| **b** Tax deposited with Form 7004. . . . . . . . . . **23b** | | |
| **c** Credit for Federal tax paid on fuels (attach Form 4136) . . . . **23c** | | |
| **d** Add lines 23a through 23c . . . . . . . . . . . . . . . | **23d** | |
| **24** Estimated tax penalty (see page 18 of instructions). Check if Form 2220 is attached. . . ► ☐ | **24** | |
| **25** **Tax due.** If line 23d is smaller than the total of lines 22c and 24, enter amount owed. . . . | **25** | |
| **26** **Overpayment.** If line 23d is larger than the total of lines 22c and 24, enter amount overpaid . | **26** | |
| **27** Enter amount of line 26 you want: **Credited to 2005 estimated tax** ►_____ Refunded ► | **27** | |

**Sign Here** ►

Under penalties of perjury, I declare that I have examined this return, including accompanying schedules and statements, and to the best of my knowledge and belief, it is true, correct, and complete. Declaration of preparer (other than taxpayer) is based on all information of which preparer has any knowledge.

_____    _____    _____
Signature of officer              Date         Title

May the IRS discuss this return with the preparer shown below (see instructions)? ☐ Yes ☐ No

**Paid Preparer's Use Only**

| Preparer's signature ► | | Date | Check if self-employed ☐ | Preparer's SSN or PTIN |
|---|---|---|---|---|
| Firm's name (or yours if self-employed), address, and ZIP code ► | | | EIN | |
| | | | Phone no. ( ) | |

**For Privacy Act and Paperwork Reduction Act Notice, see the separate instructions.**          Cat. No. 11510H          Form **1120S** (2004)

Form 1120S (2004)                                                                        Page **2**

## Schedule A    Cost of Goods Sold (see page 18 of the instructions)

| | | | |
|---|---|---|---|
| 1 | Inventory at beginning of year | **1** | |
| 2 | Purchases | **2** | |
| 3 | Cost of labor | **3** | |
| 4 | Additional section 263A costs *(attach schedule)* | **4** | |
| 5 | Other costs *(attach schedule)* | **5** | |
| 6 | **Total.** Add lines 1 through 5 | **6** | |
| 7 | Inventory at end of year | **7** | |
| 8 | **Cost of goods sold.** Subtract line 7 from line 6. Enter here and on page 1, line 2 | **8** | |

9a   Check all methods used for valuing closing inventory:    *(i)* ☐ Cost as described in Regulations section 1.471-3

     *(ii)* ☐ Lower of cost or market as described in Regulations section 1.471-4

     *(iii)* ☐ Other (specify method used and attach explanation) ▶ ----------------------------------------

   b   Check if there was a writedown of subnormal goods as described in Regulations section 1.471-2(c)   .   .   .   .   . ▶ ☐

   c   Check if the LIFO inventory method was adopted this tax year for any goods (if checked, attach Form 970)   .   .   .   . ▶ ☐

   d   If the LIFO inventory method was used for this tax year, enter percentage (or amounts) of closing
      inventory computed under LIFO   .   .   .   .   .   .   .   .   .   .   .   .    **9d** |

   e   If property is produced or acquired for resale, do the rules of Section 263A apply to the corporation?   .   .   . ☐ Yes   ☐ No

   f   Was there any change in determining quantities, cost, or valuations between opening and closing inventory?   .   . ☐ Yes   ☐ No
      If "Yes," attach explanation.

## Schedule B    Other Information (see page 19 of instructions)

| | | Yes | No |
|---|---|---|---|
| 1 | Check method of accounting:   **(a)** ☐ Cash    **(b)** ☐ Accrual    **(c)** ☐ Other (specify) ▶ ------------------ | | |
| 2 | See pages 36 through 38 of the instructions and enter the: | | |
| | **(a)** Business activity ▶ ---------------------------    **(b)** Product or service ▶ ---------------------- | | |
| 3 | At the end of the tax year, did the corporation own, directly or indirectly, 50% or more of the voting stock of a domestic corporation? (For rules of attribution, see section 267(c).) If "Yes," attach a schedule showing: **(a)** name, address, and employer identification number and **(b)** percentage owned   .   .   .   .   .   . | | |
| 4 | Was the corporation a member of a controlled group subject to the provisions of section 1561?   .   .   .   . | | |
| 5 | Check this box if the corporation has filed or is required to file **Form 8264,** Application for Registration of a Tax Shelter ▶ ☐ | | |
| 6 | Check this box if the corporation issued publicly offered debt instruments with original issue discount   .   . ▶ ☐ | | |
| | If checked, the corporation may have to file **Form 8281,** Information Return for Publicly Offered Original Issue Discount Instruments. | | |
| 7 | If the corporation: **(a)** was a C corporation before it elected to be an S corporation **or** the corporation acquired an asset with a basis determined by reference to its basis (or the basis of any other property) in the hands of a C corporation **and (b)** has net unrealized built-in gain (defined in section 1374(d)(1)) in excess of the net recognized built-in gain from prior years, enter the net unrealized built-in gain reduced by net recognized built-in gain from prior years   .   .   .   .   .   .   . ▶ $ --------------------- | | |
| 8 | Check this box if the corporation had accumulated earnings and profits at the close of the tax year   .   . ▶ ☐ | | |
| 9 | Are the corporation's total receipts (see page 19 of the instructions) for the tax year **and** its total assets at the end of the tax year less than $250,000? If "Yes," the corporation is not required to complete Schedules L and M-1. | | |

**Note:** *If the corporation had assets or operated a business in a foreign country or U.S. possession, it may be required to attach* **Schedule N (Form 1120),** *Foreign Operations of U.S. Corporations, to this return. See Schedule N for details.*

## Schedule K    Shareholders' Shares of Income, Deductions, Credits, etc.

| | Shareholders' Pro Rata Share Items | | | Total amount |
|---|---|---|---|---|
| | **1** Ordinary business income (loss) (page 1, line 21) | | **1** | |
| | **2** Net rental real estate income (loss) *(attach Form 8825)* | | **2** | |
| | **3a** Other gross rental income (loss) | **3a** | | |
| |    **b** Expenses from other rental activities *(attach schedule)* | **3b** | | |
| Income (Loss) |    **c** Other net rental income (loss). Subtract line 3b from line 3a | | **3c** | |
| | **4** Interest income | | **4** | |
| | **5** Dividends: **a** Ordinary dividends | | **5a** | |
| |         **b** Qualified dividends | **5b** | | |
| | **6** Royalties | | **6** | |
| | **7** Net short-term capital gain (loss) | | **7** | |
| | **8a** Net long-term capital gain (loss) | | **8a** | |
| |    **b** Collectibles (28%) gain (loss) | **8b** | | |
| |    **c** Unrecaptured section 1250 gain *(attach schedule)* | **8c** | | |
| | **9** Net section 1231 gain (loss) (attach Form 4797) | | **9** | |
| | **10** Other income (loss) *(attach schedule)* | | **10** | |

Form **1120S** (2004)

| | Shareholders' Pro Rata Share Items (continued) | | Total amount | |
|---|---|---|---|---|
| **Deductions** | 11 Section 179 deduction *(attach Form 4562)* | 11 | | |
| | 12a Contributions | 12a | | |
| | b Deductions related to portfolio income *(attach schedule)* | 12b | | |
| | c Investment interest expense | 12c | | |
| | d Section 59(e)(2) expenditures  (1) Type ▶_____  (2) Amount ▶ | 12d(2) | | |
| | e Other deductions *(attach schedule)* | 12e | | |
| **Credits & Credit Recapture** | 13a Low-income housing credit (section 42(j)(5)) | 13a | | |
| | b Low-income housing credit (other) | 13b | | |
| | c Qualified rehabilitation expenditures (rental real estate) *(attach Form 3468)* | 13c | | |
| | d Other rental real estate credits | 13d | | |
| | e Other rental credits | 13e | | |
| | f Credit for alcohol used as fuel *(attach Form 6478)* | 13f | | |
| | g Other credits and credit recapture *(attach schedule)* | 13g | | |
| **Foreign Transactions** | 14a Name of country or U.S. possession ▶_____ | | | |
| | b Gross income from all sources | 14b | | |
| | c Gross income sourced at shareholder level | 14c | | |
| | *Foreign gross income sourced at corporate level:* | | | |
| | d Passive | 14d | | |
| | e Listed categories *(attach schedule)* | 14e | | |
| | f General limitation | 14f | | |
| | *Deductions allocated and apportioned at shareholder level:* | | | |
| | g Interest expense | 14g | | |
| | h Other | 14h | | |
| | *Deductions allocated and apportioned at corporate level to foreign source income:* | | | |
| | i Passive | 14i | | |
| | j Listed categories *(attach schedule)* | 14j | | |
| | k General limitation | 14k | | |
| | *Other information:* | | | |
| | l Foreign taxes paid | 14l | | |
| | m Foreign taxes accrued | 14m | | |
| | n Reduction in taxes available for credit *(attach schedule)* | 14n | | |
| **Alternative Minimum Tax (AMT) Items** | 15a Post-1986 depreciation adjustment | 15a | | |
| | b Adjusted gain or loss | 15b | | |
| | c Depletion (other than oil and gas) | 15c | | |
| | d Oil, gas, and geothermal properties—gross income | 15d | | |
| | e Oil, gas, and geothermal properties—deductions | 15e | | |
| | f Other AMT items *(attach schedule)* | 15f | | |
| **Items Affecting Shareholder Basis** | 16a Tax-exempt interest income | 16a | | |
| | b Other tax-exempt income | 16b | | |
| | c Nondeductible expenses | 16c | | |
| | d Property distributions | 16d | | |
| | e Repayment of loans from shareholders | 16e | | |
| **Other Information** | 17a Investment income | 17a | | |
| | b Investment expenses | 17b | | |
| | c Dividend distributions paid from accumulated earnings and profits | 17c | | |
| | d Other items and amounts *(attach schedule)* | | | |
| | e **Income/loss reconciliation.** (Required only if Schedule M-1 must be completed.) Combine the amounts on lines 1 through 10 in the far right column. From the result, subtract the sum of the amounts on lines 11 through 12e and lines 14l or 14m, whichever applies | 17e | | |

Form **1120S** (2004)

**Note:** The corporation is not required to complete Schedules L and M-1 if question 9 of Schedule B is answered "Yes."

| Schedule L | Balance Sheets per Books | Beginning of tax year | | End of tax year | |
|---|---|---|---|---|---|
| | **Assets** | (a) | (b) | (c) | (d) |
| 1 | Cash | | | | |
| 2a | Trade notes and accounts receivable | | | | |
| b | Less allowance for bad debts | | | | |
| 3 | Inventories | | | | |
| 4 | U.S. government obligations | | | | |
| 5 | Tax-exempt securities | | | | |
| 6 | Other current assets (attach schedule) | | | | |
| 7 | Loans to shareholders | | | | |
| 8 | Mortgage and real estate loans | | | | |
| 9 | Other investments (attach schedule) | | | | |
| 10a | Buildings and other depreciable assets | | | | |
| b | Less accumulated depreciation | | | | |
| 11a | Depletable assets | | | | |
| b | Less accumulated depletion | | | | |
| 12 | Land (net of any amortization) | | | | |
| 13a | Intangible assets (amortizable only) | | | | |
| b | Less accumulated amortization | | | | |
| 14 | Other assets (attach schedule) | | | | |
| 15 | Total assets | | | | |
| | **Liabilities and Shareholders' Equity** | | | | |
| 16 | Accounts payable | | | | |
| 17 | Mortgages, notes, bonds payable in less than 1 year | | | | |
| 18 | Other current liabilities (attach schedule) | | | | |
| 19 | Loans from shareholders | | | | |
| 20 | Mortgages, notes, bonds payable in 1 year or more | | | | |
| 21 | Other liabilities (attach schedule) | | | | |
| 22 | Capital stock | | | | |
| 23 | Additional paid-in capital | | | | |
| 24 | Retained earnings | | | | |
| 25 | Adjustments to shareholders' equity (attach schedule) | | | | |
| 26 | Less cost of treasury stock | | ( ) | | ( ) |
| 27 | Total liabilities and shareholders' equity | | | | |

| Schedule M-1 | Reconciliation of Income (Loss) per Books With Income (Loss) per Return | |
|---|---|---|
| 1 | Net income (loss) per books | | 5 | Income recorded on books this year not included on Schedule K, lines 1 through 10 (itemize): | |
| 2 | Income included on Schedule K, lines 1, 2, 3c, 4, 5a, 6, 7, 8a, 9, and 10, not recorded on books this year (itemize): | | a | Tax-exempt interest $ | |
| 3 | Expenses recorded on books this year not included on Schedule K, lines 1 through 12, and 14l or (14m) (itemize): | | 6 | Deductions included on Schedule K, lines 1 through 12, and 14l or (14m), not charged against book income this year (itemize): | |
| a | Depreciation $ | | a | Depreciation $ | |
| b | Travel and entertainment $ | | | | |
| | | | 7 | Add lines 5 and 6 | |
| 4 | Add lines 1 through 3 | | 8 | Income (loss) (Schedule K, line 17e). Line 4 less line 7 | |

| Schedule M-2 | Analysis of Accumulated Adjustments Account, Other Adjustments Account, and Shareholders' Undistributed Taxable Income Previously Taxed (see page 32 of the instructions) | | |
|---|---|---|---|
| | | (a) Accumulated adjustments account | (b) Other adjustments account | (c) Shareholders' undistributed taxable income previously taxed |
| 1 | Balance at beginning of tax year | | | |
| 2 | Ordinary income from page 1, line 21 | | | |
| 3 | Other additions | | | |
| 4 | Loss from page 1, line 21 | ( ) | | |
| 5 | Other reductions | ( ) | ( ) | |
| 6 | Combine lines 1 through 5 | | | |
| 7 | Distributions other than dividend distributions | | | |
| 8 | Balance at end of tax year. Subtract line 7 from line 6 | | | |

6711

## Schedule K-1
### (Form 1120S)
Department of the Treasury
Internal Revenue Service

**20**04

Tax year beginning _____ , 2004

and ending _____ , 20__

## Shareholder's Share of Income, Deductions, Credits, etc.
▶ See back of form and separate instructions.

☐ Final K-1    ☐ Amended K-1    OMB No. 1545-0130

| **Part III** | **Shareholder's Share of Current Year Income, Deductions, Credits, and Other Items** |
|---|---|

| | | | |
|---|---|---|---|
| **1** | Ordinary business income (loss) | **13** | Credits & credit recapture |
| **2** | Net rental real estate income (loss) | | |
| **3** | Other net rental income (loss) | | |
| **4** | Interest income | | |
| **5a** | Ordinary dividends | | |
| **5b** | Qualified dividends | **14** | Foreign transactions |
| **6** | Royalties | | |
| **7** | Net short-term capital gain (loss) | | |
| **8a** | Net long-term capital gain (loss) | | |
| **8b** | Collectibles (28%) gain (loss) | | |
| **8c** | Unrecaptured section 1250 gain | | |
| **9** | Net section 1231 gain (loss) | | |
| **10** | Other income (loss) | **15** | Alternative minimum tax (AMT) items |
| | | | |
| | | | |
| **11** | Section 179 deduction | **16** | Items affecting shareholder basis |
| **12** | Other deductions | | |
| | | | |
| | | | |
| | | | |
| | | | |
| | | **17** | Other information |
| | | | |
| | | | |
| | | | |
| | | | |

\* See attached statement for additional information.

| **Part I** | **Information About the Corporation** |
|---|---|

**A**   Corporation's employer identification number

**B**   Corporation's name, address, city, state, and ZIP code

**C**   IRS Center where corporation filed return

**D** ☐   Tax shelter registration number, if any _____

**E** ☐   Check if Form 8271 is attached

| **Part II** | **Information About the Shareholder** |
|---|---|

**F**   Shareholder's identifying number

**G**   Shareholder's name, address, city, state and ZIP code

**H**   Shareholder's percentage of stock ownership for tax year . . . . . . . . . _____ %

For IRS Use Only

For Privacy Act and Paperwork Reduction Act Notice, see Instructions for Form 1120S.      Cat. No. 11520D      **Schedule K-1 (Form 1120S) 2004**

**This list identifies the codes used on Schedule K-1 for all shareholders and provides summarized reporting information for shareholders who file Form 1040. For detailed reporting and filing information, see the separate Shareholder's Instructions for Schedule K-1 and the instructions for your income tax return.**

**1. Ordinary business income (loss).** You must first determine whether the income (loss) is passive or nonpassive. Then enter on your return as follows:

| | Enter on |
|---|---|
| Passive loss | See the Shareholder's Instructions |
| Passive income | Schedule E, line 28, column (g) |
| Nonpassive loss | Schedule E, line 28, column (h) |
| Nonpassive income | Schedule E, line 28, column (j) |

**2. Net rental real estate income (loss)**  See the Shareholder's Instructions

**3. Other net rental income (loss)**

| | |
|---|---|
| Net income | Schedule E, line 28, column (g) |
| Net loss | See the Shareholder's Instructions |

**4. Interest income**  Form 1040, line 8a

**5a. Ordinary dividends**  Form 1040, line 9a

**5b. Qualified dividends**  Form 1040, line 9b

**6. Royalties**  Schedule E, line 4

**7. Net short-term capital gain (loss)**  Schedule D, line 5, column (f)

**8a. Net long-term capital gain (loss)**  Schedule D, line 12, column (f)

**8b. Collectibles (28%) gain (loss)**  28% Rate Gain Worksheet, line 4 (Schedule D instructions)

**8c. Unrecaptured section 1250 gain**  See the Shareholder's Instructions

**9. Net section 1231 gain (loss)**  See the Shareholder's Instructions

**10. Other income (loss)**

Code
| | | |
|---|---|---|
| A | Other portfolio income (loss) | See the Shareholder's Instructions |
| B | Involuntary conversions | See the Shareholder's Instructions |
| C | 1256 contracts & straddles | Form 6781, line 1 |
| D | Mining exploration costs recapture | See Pub. 535, Chap. 8 |
| E | Other income (loss) | See the Shareholder's Instructions |

**11. Section 179 deduction**  See the Shareholder's Instructions

**12. Other deductions**

| | | |
|---|---|---|
| A | Cash contributions (50%) | Schedule A, line 15 |
| B | Cash contributions (30%) | Schedule A, line 15 |
| C | Noncash contributions (50%) | Schedule A, line 16 |
| D | Noncash contributions (30%) | Schedule A, line 16 |
| E | Capital gain property to a 50% organization (30%) | Schedule A, line 16 |
| F | Capital gain property (20%) | Schedule A, line 16 |
| G | Deductions—portfolio (2% floor) | Schedule A, line 22 |
| H | Deductions—portfolio (other) | Schedule A, line 27 |
| I | Investment interest expense | Form 4952, line 1 |
| J | Deductions—royalty income | Schedule E, line 18 |
| K | Section 59(e)(2) expenditures | See the Shareholder's Instructions |
| L | Reforestation expense deduction | See the Shareholder's Instructions |
| M | Preproductive period expenses | See the Shareholder's Instructions |
| N | Commercial revitalization deduction from rental real estate activities | See Form 8582 Instructions |
| O | Penalty on early withdrawal of savings | Form 1040, line 33 |
| P | Other deductions | See the Shareholder's Instructions |

**13. Credits & credit recapture**

| | | |
|---|---|---|
| A | Low-income housing credit (section 42(j)(5)) | Form 8586, line 5 |
| B | Low-income housing credit (other) | Form 8586, line 5 |
| C | Qualified rehabilitation expenditures (rental real estate) | Form 3468, line 1 |
| D | Qualified rehabilitation expenditures (other than rental real estate) | Form 3468, line 1 |
| E | Basis of energy property | Form 3468, line 2 |
| F | Qualified timber property | Form 3468, line 3 |
| G | Other rental real estate credits | See the Shareholder's Instructions |
| H | Other rental credits | See the Shareholder's Instructions |
| I | Undistributed capital gains credit | Form 1040, line 69, box a |
| J | Work opportunity credit | Form 5884, line 3 |
| K | Welfare-to-Work credit | Form 8861, line 3 |

| Code | | Enter on |
|---|---|---|
| L | Disabled access credit | Form 8826, line 7 |
| M | Empowerment zone and renewal community employment credit | Form 8844, line 3 |
| N | New York Liberty Zone business employee credit | Form 8884, line 3 |
| O | New markets credit | Form 8874, line 2 |
| P | Credit for employer social security and Medicare taxes | Form 8846, line 5 |
| Q | Backup withholding | Form 1040, line 63 |
| R | Credit for alcohol used as fuel | Form 6478, line 10 |
| S | Recapture of low-income housing credit (section 42(j)(5)) | Form 8611, line 8 |
| T | Recapture of low-income housing credit (other) | Form 8611, line 8 |
| U | Recapture of investment credit | See Form 4255 |
| V | Other credits | See the Shareholder's Instructions |
| W | Recapture of other credits | See the Shareholder's Instructions |

**14. Foreign transactions**

| | | |
|---|---|---|
| A | Name of country or U.S. possession | Form 1116, Part I |
| B | Gross income from all sources | Form 1116, Part I |
| C | Gross income sourced at shareholder level | Form 1116, Part I |

Foreign gross income sourced at corporate level
| | | |
|---|---|---|
| D | Passive | Form 1116, Part I |
| E | Listed categories | Form 1116, Part I |
| F | General limitation | Form 1116, Part I |

Deductions allocated and apportioned at shareholder level
| | | |
|---|---|---|
| G | Interest expense | Form 1116, Part I |
| H | Other | Form 1116, Part I |

Deductions allocated and apportioned at corporate level to foreign source income
| | | |
|---|---|---|
| I | Passive | Form 1116, Part I |
| J | Listed categories | Form 1116, Part I |
| K | General limitation | Form 1116, Part I |

Other information
| | | |
|---|---|---|
| L | Total foreign taxes paid | Form 1116, Part II |
| M | Total foreign taxes accrued | Form 1116, Part II |
| N | Reduction in taxes available for credit | Form 1116, line 12 |
| O | Foreign trading gross receipts | Form 8873 |
| P | Extraterritorial income exclusion | Form 8873 |
| Q | Other foreign transactions | See the Shareholder's Instructions |

**15. Alternative minimum tax (AMT) items**

| | |
|---|---|
| A | Post-1986 depreciation adjustment |
| B | Adjusted gain or loss |
| C | Depletion (other than oil & gas) |
| D | Oil, gas, & geothermal properties—gross income |
| E | Oil, gas, & geothermal properties—deductions |
| F | Other AMT items |

See the Shareholder's Instructions and the instructions for Form 6251

**16. Items affecting shareholder basis**

| | | |
|---|---|---|
| A | Tax-exempt interest income | Form 1040, line 8b |
| B | Other tax-exempt income | See the Shareholder's Instructions |
| C | Nondeductible expenses | See the Shareholder's Instructions |
| D | Property distributions | See the Shareholder's Instructions |
| E | Repayment of loans from shareholders | See the Shareholder's Instructions |

**17. Other information**

| | | |
|---|---|---|
| A | Investment income | Form 4952, line 4a |
| B | Investment expenses | Form 4952, line 5 |
| C | Look-back interest—completed long-term contracts | See Form 8697 |
| D | Look-back interest—income forecast method | See Form 8866 |
| E | Dispositions of property with section 179 deductions | See the Shareholder's Instructions |
| F | Recapture of section 179 deduction | See the Shareholder's Instructions |
| G | Section 453(l)(3) information | See the Shareholder's Instructions |
| H | Section 453A(c) information | See the Shareholder's Instructions |
| I | Section 1260(b) information | See the Shareholder's Instructions |
| J | Interest allocable to production expenditures | See the Shareholder's Instructions |
| K | CCF nonqualified withdrawal | See the Shareholder's Instructions |
| L | Information needed to figure depletion—oil and gas | See the Shareholder's Instructions |
| M | Amortization of reforestation costs | See the Shareholder's Instructions |
| N | Other information | See the Shareholder's Instructions |

Form **2553**
(Rev. December 2002)

Department of the Treasury
Internal Revenue Service

# Election by a Small Business Corporation
(Under section 1362 of the Internal Revenue Code)
▶ See Parts II and III on back and the separate instructions.
▶ **The corporation may either send or fax this form to the IRS. See page 2 of the instructions.**

OMB No. 1545-0146

**Notes:** 1. *Do not* file *Form 1120S,* U.S. Income Tax Return for an S Corporation, for any tax year before the year the election takes effect.

2. *This election to be an S corporation can be accepted only if all the tests are met under **Who May Elect** on page 1 of the instructions; all shareholders have signed the consent statement; and the exact name and address of the corporation and other required form information are provided.*

3. *If the corporation was in existence before the effective date of this election, see **Taxes an S Corporation May Owe** on page 1 of the instructions.*

---

| Part I | **Election Information** | |
|---|---|---|

**Please Type or Print**

| Name of corporation (see instructions) | **A** Employer identification number |
|---|---|
| Number, street, and room or suite no. (If a P.O. box, see instructions.) | **B** Date incorporated |
| City or town, state, and ZIP code | **C** State of incorporation |

**D** Check the applicable box(es) if the corporation, after applying for the EIN shown in **A** above, changed its name ☐ or address ☐

**E** Election is to be effective for tax year beginning (month, day, year) . . . . . . . . . . . . . . . . . ▶   /  /

**F** Name and title of officer or legal representative who the IRS may call for more information      **G** Telephone number of officer or legal representative

(    )

**H** If this election takes effect for the first tax year the corporation exists, enter month, day, and year of the **earliest** of the following: (1) date the corporation first had shareholders, (2) date the corporation first had assets, or (3) date the corporation began doing business . . . . . . . . . . . . . . . . . . . . . . . ▶   /  /

**I** Selected tax year: Annual return will be filed for tax year ending (month and day) ▶ . . . . . . . . . . . . . . . . . . . . . . . . . .

If the tax year ends on any date other than December 31, except for a 52–53-week tax year ending with reference to the month of December, you **must** complete Part II on the back. If the date you enter is the ending date of a 52–53-week tax year, write "52–53-week year" to the right of the date.

| **J** Name and address of each shareholder; shareholder's spouse having a community property interest in the corporation's stock; and each tenant in common, joint tenant, and tenant by the entirety. (A husband and wife (and their estates) are counted as one shareholder in determining the number of shareholders without regard to the manner in which the stock is owned.) | **K** Shareholders' Consent Statement. Under penalties of perjury, we declare that we consent to the election of the above-named corporation to be an S corporation under section 1362(a) and that we have examined this consent statement, including accompanying schedules and statements, and to the best of our knowledge and belief, it is true, correct, and complete. We understand our consent is binding and may not be withdrawn after the corporation has made a valid election. (Shareholders sign and date below.) | | **L** Stock owned | | **M** Social security number or employer identification number (see instructions) | **N** Share-holder's tax year ends (month and day) |
|---|---|---|---|---|---|---|
| | Signature | Date | Number of shares | Dates acquired | | |
| | | | | | | |
| | | | | | | |
| | | | | | | |
| | | | | | | |
| | | | | | | |

Under penalties of perjury, I declare that I have examined this election, including accompanying schedules and statements, and to the best of my knowledge and belief, it is true, correct, and complete.

Signature of officer ▶        Title ▶        Date ▶

**For Paperwork Reduction Act Notice, see page 4 of the instructions.**      Cat. No. 18629R      Form **2553** (Rev. 12-2002)

**Part II**  **Selection of Fiscal Tax Year** (All corporations using this part must complete item O and item P, Q, or R.)

**O**  Check the applicable box to indicate whether the corporation is:

   **1.** ☐ A new corporation adopting the tax year entered in item I, Part I.

   **2.** ☐ An existing corporation retaining the tax year entered in item I, Part I.

   **3.** ☐ An existing corporation changing to the tax year entered in item I, Part I.

**P**  Complete item P if the corporation is using the automatic approval provisions of Rev. Proc. 2002-38, 2002-22 I.R.B. 1037, to request **(1)** a natural business year (as defined in section 5.05 of Rev. Proc. 2002-38) or **(2)** a year that satisfies the ownership tax year test (as defined in section 5.06 of Rev. Proc. 2002-38). Check the applicable box below to indicate the representation statement the corporation is making.

   **1. Natural Business Year** ▶ ☐ I represent that the corporation is adopting, retaining, or changing to a tax year that qualifies as its natural business year as defined in section 5.05 of Rev. Proc. 2002-38 and has attached a statement verifying that it satisfies the 25% gross receipts test (see instructions for content of statement). I also represent that the corporation is not precluded by section 4.02 of Rev. Proc. 2002-38 from obtaining automatic approval of such adoption, retention, or change in tax year.

   **2. Ownership Tax Year** ▶ ☐ I represent that shareholders (as described in section 5.06 of Rev. Proc. 2002-38) holding more than half of the shares of the stock (as of the first day of the tax year to which the request relates) of the corporation have the same tax year or are concurrently changing to the tax year that the corporation adopts, retains, or changes to per item I, Part I, and that such tax year satisfies the requirement of section 4.01(3) of Rev. Proc. 2002-38. I also represent that the corporation is not precluded by section 4.02 of Rev. Proc. 2002-38 from obtaining automatic approval of such adoption, retention, or change in tax year.

**Note:** *If you do not use item P and the corporation wants a fiscal tax year, complete either item Q or R below. Item Q is used to request a fiscal tax year based on a business purpose and to make a back-up section 444 election. Item R is used to make a regular section 444 election.*

**Q**  Business Purpose—To request a fiscal tax year based on a business purpose, you must check box Q1. See instructions for details including payment of a user fee. You may also check box Q2 and/or box Q3.

   **1.** Check here ▶ ☐ if the fiscal year entered in item I, Part I, is requested under the prior approval provisions of Rev. Proc. 2002-39, 2002-22 I.R.B. 1046. Attach to Form 2553 a statement describing the relevant facts and circumstances and, if applicable, the gross receipts from sales and services necessary to establish a business purpose. See the instructions for details regarding the gross receipts from sales and services. If the IRS proposes to disapprove the requested fiscal year, do you want a conference with the IRS National Office?
   ☐ Yes    ☐ No

   **2.** Check here ▶ ☐ to show that the corporation intends to make a back-up section 444 election in the event the corporation's business purpose request is not approved by the IRS. (See instructions for more information.)

   **3.** Check here ▶ ☐ to show that the corporation agrees to adopt or change to a tax year ending December 31 if necessary for the IRS to accept this election for S corporation status in the event (1) the corporation's business purpose request is not approved and the corporation makes a back-up section 444 election, but is ultimately not qualified to make a section 444 election, or (2) the corporation's business purpose request is not approved and the corporation did not make a back-up section 444 election.

**R**  Section 444 Election—To make a section 444 election, you must check box R1 and you may also check box R2.

   **1.** Check here ▶ ☐ to show the corporation will make, if qualified, a section 444 election to have the fiscal tax year shown in item I, Part I. To make the election, you must complete **Form 8716**, Election To Have a Tax Year Other Than a Required Tax Year, and either attach it to Form 2553 or file it separately.

   **2.** Check here ▶ ☐ to show that the corporation agrees to adopt or change to a tax year ending December 31 if necessary for the IRS to accept this election for S corporation status in the event the corporation is ultimately not qualified to make a section 444 election.

**Part III**  **Qualified Subchapter S Trust (QSST) Election Under Section 1361(d)(2)***

| Income beneficiary's name and address | Social security number |
|---|---|
| | |
| Trust's name and address | Employer identification number |
| | |

Date on which stock of the corporation was transferred to the trust (month, day, year) . . . . . . . . . ▶    /    /

In order for the trust named above to be a QSST and thus a qualifying shareholder of the S corporation for which this Form 2553 is filed, I hereby make the election under section 1361(d)(2). Under penalties of perjury, I certify that the trust meets the definitional requirements of section 1361(d)(3) and that all other information provided in Part III is true, correct, and complete.

_____     _____

Signature of income beneficiary or signature and title of legal representative or other qualified person making the election    Date

*Use Part III to make the QSST election only if stock of the corporation has been transferred to the trust on or before the date on which the corporation makes its election to be an S corporation. The QSST election must be made and filed separately if stock of the corporation is transferred to the trust after the date on which the corporation makes the S election.

# Form 4562

**Depreciation and Amortization**

**(Including Information on Listed Property)**

Department of the Treasury
Internal Revenue Service

► See separate instructions.    ► Attach to your tax return.

OMB No. 1545-0172

**2004**

Attachment
Sequence No. **67**

| Name(s) shown on return | Business or activity to which this form relates | Identifying number |
|---|---|---|

## Part I — Election To Expense Certain Property Under Section 179

**Note:** *If you have any listed property, complete Part V before you complete Part I.*

| | | | |
|---|---|---|---|
| 1 | Maximum amount. See page 2 of the instructions for a higher limit for certain businesses | **1** | $102,000 |
| 2 | Total cost of section 179 property placed in service (see page 3 of the instructions) | **2** | |
| 3 | Threshold cost of section 179 property before reduction in limitation | **3** | $410,000 |
| 4 | Reduction in limitation. Subtract line 3 from line 2. If zero or less, enter -0- | **4** | |
| 5 | Dollar limitation for tax year. Subtract line 4 from line 1. If zero or less, enter -0-. If married filing separately, see page 3 of the instructions. | **5** | |

| (a) Description of property | (b) Cost (business use only) | (c) Elected cost | |
|---|---|---|---|
| **6** | | | |
| | | | |

| | | | |
|---|---|---|---|
| 7 | Listed property. Enter the amount from line 29 . . . . . . . . . . | **7** | |
| 8 | Total elected cost of section 179 property. Add amounts in column (c), lines 6 and 7 | **8** | |
| 9 | Tentative deduction. Enter the **smaller** of line 5 or line 8. | **9** | |
| 10 | Carryover of disallowed deduction from line 13 of your 2003 Form 4562 | **10** | |
| 11 | Business income limitation. Enter the smaller of business income (not less than zero) or line 5 (see instructions) | **11** | |
| 12 | Section 179 expense deduction. Add lines 9 and 10, but do not enter more than line 11 | **12** | |
| 13 | Carryover of disallowed deduction to 2005. Add lines 9 and 10, less line 12 ► | **13** | |

**Note:** *Do not use Part II or Part III below for listed property. Instead, use Part V.*

## Part II — Special Depreciation Allowance and Other Depreciation (Do not include listed property.)

| | | | |
|---|---|---|---|
| 14 | Special depreciation allowance for qualified property (other than listed property) placed in service during the tax year (see page 3 of the instructions) | **14** | |
| 15 | Property subject to section 168(f)(1) election (see page 4 of the instructions) | **15** | |
| 16 | Other depreciation (including ACRS) (see page 4 of the instructions) | **16** | |

## Part III — MACRS Depreciation (Do not include listed property.) (See page 5 of the instructions.)

### Section A

| | | | |
|---|---|---|---|
| 17 | MACRS deductions for assets placed in service in tax years beginning before 2004 | **17** | |
| 18 | If you are electing under section 168(i)(4) to group any assets placed in service during the tax year into one or more general asset accounts, check here . . . . . . . . . ► ☐ | | |

### Section B—Assets Placed in Service During 2004 Tax Year Using the General Depreciation System

| (a) Classification of property | (b) Month and year placed in service | (c) Basis for depreciation (business/investment use only—see instructions) | (d) Recovery period | (e) Convention | (f) Method | (g) Depreciation deduction |
|---|---|---|---|---|---|---|
| **19a** 3-year property | | | | | | |
| **b** 5-year property | | | | | | |
| **c** 7-year property | | | | | | |
| **d** 10-year property | | | | | | |
| **e** 15-year property | | | | | | |
| **f** 20-year property | | | | | | |
| **g** 25-year property | | | 25 yrs. | | S/L | |
| **h** Residential rental property | | | 27.5 yrs. | MM | S/L | |
| | | | 27.5 yrs. | MM | S/L | |
| **i** Nonresidential real property | | | 39 yrs. | MM | S/L | |
| | | | | MM | S/L | |

### Section C—Assets Placed in Service During 2004 Tax Year Using the Alternative Depreciation System

| | | | | | | |
|---|---|---|---|---|---|---|
| **20a** Class life | | | | | S/L | |
| **b** 12-year | | | 12 yrs. | | S/L | |
| **c** 40-year | | | 40 yrs. | MM | S/L | |

## Part IV — Summary (see page 8 of the instructions)

| | | | |
|---|---|---|---|
| 21 | Listed property. Enter amount from line 28 . . . . . . . . . | **21** | |
| 22 | **Total.** Add amounts from line 12, lines 14 through 17, lines 19 and 20 in column (g), and line 21. Enter here and on the appropriate lines of your return. Partnerships and S corporations—see instr. | **22** | |
| 23 | For assets shown above and placed in service during the current year, enter the portion of the basis attributable to section 263A costs . . | **23** | |

**For Paperwork Reduction Act Notice, see separate instructions.**    Cat. No. 12906N    Form **4562** (2004)

Form 4562 (2004)

**Part V** **Listed Property** (Include automobiles, certain other vehicles, cellular telephones, certain computers, and property used for entertainment, recreation, or amusement.)

Note: *For any vehicle for which you are using the standard mileage rate or deducting lease expense, complete only 24a, 24b, columns (a) through (c) of Section A, all of Section B, and Section C if applicable.*

**Section A—Depreciation and Other Information (Caution:** *See page 9 of the instructions for limits for passenger automobiles.***)**

**24a** Do you have evidence to support the business/investment use claimed? ☐ **Yes** ☐ **No**   **24b** If "Yes," is the evidence written? ☐ **Yes** ☐ **No**

| (a) Type of property (list vehicles first) | (b) Date placed in service | (c) Business/ investment use percentage | (d) Cost or other basis | (e) Basis for depreciation (business/investment use only) | (f) Recovery period | (g) Method/ Convention | (h) Depreciation deduction | (i) Elected section 179 cost |
|---|---|---|---|---|---|---|---|---|
| **25** Special depreciation allowance for qualified listed property placed in service during the tax year and used more than 50% in a qualified business use (see page 8 of the instructions) | | | | **25** | | | | |
| **26** Property used more than 50% in a qualified business use (see page 8 of the instructions): | | | | | | | | |
| | | % | | | | | | |
| | | % | | | | | | |
| | | % | | | | | | |
| **27** Property used 50% or less in a qualified business use (see page 8 of the instructions): | | | | | | | | |
| | | % | | | | S/L – | | |
| | | % | | | | S/L – | | |
| | | % | | | | S/L – | | |
| **28** Add amounts in column (h), lines 25 through 27. Enter here and on line 21, page 1. | | | | | **28** | | | |
| **29** Add amounts in column (i), line 26. Enter here and on line 7, page 1. | | | | | | | **29** | |

**Section B—Information on Use of Vehicles**

Complete this section for vehicles used by a sole proprietor, partner, or other "more than 5% owner," or related person.
If you provided vehicles to your employees, first answer the questions in Section C to see if you meet an exception to completing this section for those vehicles.

| | | (a) Vehicle 1 | | (b) Vehicle 2 | | (c) Vehicle 3 | | (d) Vehicle 4 | | (e) Vehicle 5 | | (f) Vehicle 6 | |
|---|---|---|---|---|---|---|---|---|---|---|---|---|---|
| **30** | Total business/investment miles driven during the year (**do not** include commuting miles—See page 2 of the instructions) | | | | | | | | | | | | |
| **31** | Total commuting miles driven during the year | | | | | | | | | | | | |
| **32** | Total other personal (noncommuting) miles driven | | | | | | | | | | | | |
| **33** | Total miles driven during the year. Add lines 30 through 32 | | | | | | | | | | | | |
| **34** | Was the vehicle available for personal use during off-duty hours? | Yes | No | Yes | No | Yes | No | Yes | No | Yes | No | Yes | No |
| **35** | Was the vehicle used primarily by a more than 5% owner or related person? | | | | | | | | | | | | |
| **36** | Is another vehicle available for personal use? | | | | | | | | | | | | |

**Section C—Questions for Employers Who Provide Vehicles for Use by Their Employees**

Answer these questions to determine if you meet an exception to completing Section B for vehicles used by employees who **are not** more than 5% owners or related persons (see page 10 of the instructions).

| | | Yes | No |
|---|---|---|---|
| **37** | Do you maintain a written policy statement that prohibits all personal use of vehicles, including commuting, by your employees? | | |
| **38** | Do you maintain a written policy statement that prohibits personal use of vehicles, except commuting, by your employees? See page 10 of the instructions for vehicles used by corporate officers, directors, or 1% or more owners | | |
| **39** | Do you treat all use of vehicles by employees as personal use? | | |
| **40** | Do you provide more than five vehicles to your employees, obtain information from your employees about the use of the vehicles, and retain the information received? | | |
| **41** | Do you meet the requirements concerning qualified automobile demonstration use? (See page 10 of the instructions.) | | |

Note: *If your answer to 37, 38, 39, 40, or 41 is "Yes," do not complete Section B for the covered vehicles.*

**Part VI** **Amortization**

| (a) Description of costs | (b) Date amortization begins | (c) Amortizable amount | (d) Code section | (e) Amortization period or percentage | (f) Amortization for this year |
|---|---|---|---|---|---|
| **42** Amortization of costs that begins during your 2004 tax year (see page 11 of the instructions): | | | | | |
| | | | | | |
| | | | | | |
| **43** Amortization of costs that began before your 2004 tax year. | | | **43** | | |
| **44** **Total.** Add amounts in column (f). See page 12 of the instructions for where to report. | | | **44** | | |

Form **4562** (2004)

Form **4626**

Department of the Treasury
Internal Revenue Service

## Alternative Minimum Tax—Corporations

▶ See separate instructions.
▶ Attach to the corporation's tax return.

OMB No. 1545-0175

**2004**

Name

Employer identification number

**Note:** See page 1 of the instructions to find out if the corporation is a small corporation exempt from the alternative minimum tax (AMT) under section 55(e).

| | | |
|---|---|---|
| 1 | Taxable income or (loss) before net operating loss deduction | 1 |
| 2 | **Adjustments and preferences:** | |
| a | Depreciation of post-1986 property | 2a |
| b | Amortization of certified pollution control facilities | 2b |
| c | Amortization of mining exploration and development costs | 2c |
| d | Amortization of circulation expenditures (personal holding companies only) | 2d |
| e | Adjusted gain or loss | 2e |
| f | Long-term contracts | 2f |
| g | Merchant marine capital construction funds | 2g |
| h | Section 833(b) deduction (Blue Cross, Blue Shield, and similar type organizations only) | 2h |
| i | Tax shelter farm activities (personal service corporations only) | 2i |
| j | Passive activities (closely held corporations and personal service corporations only) | 2j |
| k | Loss limitations | 2k |
| l | Depletion | 2l |
| m | Tax-exempt interest income from specified private activity bonds | 2m |
| n | Intangible drilling costs | 2n |
| o | Other adjustments and preferences | 2o |
| 3 | Pre-adjustment alternative minimum taxable income (AMTI). Combine lines 1 through 2o | 3 |
| 4 | **Adjusted current earnings (ACE) adjustment:** | |
| a | ACE from line 10 of the worksheet on page 11 of the instructions | 4a |
| b | Subtract line 3 from line 4a. If line 3 exceeds line 4a, enter the difference as a negative amount. See examples on page 6 of the instructions | 4b |
| c | Multiply line 4b by 75% (.75). Enter the result as a positive amount | 4c |
| d | Enter the excess, if any, of the corporation's total increases in AMTI from prior year ACE adjustments over its total reductions in AMTI from prior year ACE adjustments (see page 6 of the instructions). **Note:** You **must** enter an amount on line 4d (even if line 4b is positive) | 4d |
| e | ACE adjustment. <br> • If line 4b is zero or more, enter the amount from line 4c <br> • If line 4b is less than zero, enter the **smaller** of line 4c or line 4d as a negative amount | 4e |
| 5 | Combine lines 3 and 4e. If zero or less, stop here; the corporation does not owe any AMT | 5 |
| 6 | Alternative tax net operating loss deduction (see page 7 of the instructions) | 6 |
| 7 | **Alternative minimum taxable income.** Subtract line 6 from line 5. If the corporation held a residual interest in a REMIC, see page 7 of the instructions | 7 |
| 8 | **Exemption phase-out** (if line 7 is $310,000 or more, skip lines 8a and 8b and enter -0- on line 8c): | |
| a | Subtract $150,000 from line 7 (if completing this line for a member of a controlled group, see page 7 of the instructions). If zero or less, enter -0- | 8a |
| b | Multiply line 8a by 25% (.25) | 8b |
| c | Exemption. Subtract line 8b from $40,000 (if completing this line for a member of a controlled group, see page 7 of the instructions). If zero or less, enter -0- | 8c |
| 9 | Subtract line 8c from line 7. If zero or less, enter -0- | 9 |
| 10 | Multiply line 9 by 20% (.20) | 10 |
| 11 | Alternative minimum tax foreign tax credit (AMTFTC) (see page 7 of the instructions) | 11 |
| 12 | Tentative minimum tax. Subtract line 11 from line 10 | 12 |
| 13 | Regular tax liability before all credits except the foreign tax credit and possessions tax credit | 13 |
| 14 | **Alternative minimum tax.** Subtract line 13 from line 12. If zero or less, enter -0-. Enter here and on Form 1120, Schedule J, line 4, or the appropriate line of the corporation's income tax return | 14 |

**For Paperwork Reduction Act Notice, see page 10 of the instructions.**      Cat. No. 12955I      Form **4626** (2004)

| Form **4797** | **Sales of Business Property** | OMB No. 1545-0184 |
|---|---|---|
| Department of the Treasury<br>Internal Revenue Service (99) | (Also Involuntary Conversions and Recapture Amounts<br>Under Sections 179 and 280F(b)(2))<br>▶Attach to your tax return. ▶See separate instructions. | 20**04**<br>Attachment<br>Sequence No. **27** |

Name(s) shown on return | Identifying number

**1** Enter the gross proceeds from sales or exchanges reported to you for 2004 on Form(s) 1099-B or 1099-S (or substitute statement) that you are including on line 2, 10, or 20 (see instructions) . . . . . . . . . . . . . . **1**

**Part I  Sales or Exchanges of Property Used in a Trade or Business and Involuntary Conversions From Other Than Casualty or Theft—Most Property Held More Than 1 Year** (see instructions)

| (a) Description of property | (b) Date acquired (mo., day, yr.) | (c) Date sold (mo., day, yr.) | (d) Gross sales price | (e) Depreciation allowed or allowable since acquisition | (f) Cost or other basis, plus improvements and expense of sale | (g) Gain or (loss) Subtract (f) from the sum of (d) and (e) |
|---|---|---|---|---|---|---|
| **2** | | | | | | |
| | | | | | | |
| | | | | | | |
| | | | | | | |

**3** Gain, if any, from Form 4684, line 39 . . . . . . . . . . . . . . **3**

**4** Section 1231 gain from installment sales from Form 6252, line 26 or 37 . . . . . . . . . **4**

**5** Section 1231 gain or (loss) from like-kind exchanges from Form 8824 . . . . . . . . **5**

**6** Gain, if any, from line 32, from other than casualty or theft . . . . . . . . . . **6**

**7** Combine lines 2 through 6. Enter the gain or (loss) here and on the appropriate line as follows: . . . . . **7**

**Partnerships (except electing large partnerships) and S corporations.** Report the gain or (loss) following the instructions for Form 1065, Schedule K, line 10, or Form 1120S, Schedule K, line 9. Skip lines 8, 9, 11, and 12 below.

**All others.** If line 7 is zero or a loss, enter the amount from line 7 on line 11 below and skip lines 8 and 9. If line 7 is a gain and you did not have any prior year section 1231 losses, or they were recaptured in an earlier year, enter the gain from line 7 as a long-term capital gain on Schedule D and skip lines 8, 9, 11, and 12 below.

**8** Nonrecaptured net section 1231 losses from prior years (see instructions) . . . . . . . . . **8**

**9** Subtract line 8 from line 7. If zero or less, enter -0-. If line 9 is zero, enter the gain from line 7 on line 12 below. If line 9 is more than zero, enter the amount from line 8 on line 12 below and enter the gain from line 9 as a long-term capital gain on Schedule D (see instructions) . . . . . . . . . . . . . . . . . . . **9**

**Part II  Ordinary Gains and Losses**

**10** Ordinary gains and losses not included on lines 11 through 16 (include property held 1 year or less):

| | | | | | | |
|---|---|---|---|---|---|---|
| | | | | | | |
| | | | | | | |
| | | | | | | |

**11** Loss, if any, from line 7 . . . . . . . . . . . **11** ( )

**12** Gain, if any, from line 7 or amount from line 8, if applicable . . . . . . . . . **12**

**13** Gain, if any, from line 31 . . . . . . . . . . . . . . . . **13**

**14** Net gain or (loss) from Form 4684, lines 31 and 38a . . . . . . . . . . **14**

**15** Ordinary gain from installment sales from Form 6252, line 25 or 36 . . . . . . . **15**

**16** Ordinary gain or (loss) from like-kind exchanges from Form 8824 . . . . . . . . **16**

**17** Combine lines 10 through 16 . . . . . . . . . . . . . . . **17**

**18** For all except individual returns, enter the amount from line 17 on the appropriate line of your return and skip lines a and b below. For individual returns, complete lines a and b below:

**a** If the loss on line 11 includes a loss from Form 4684, line 35, column (b)(ii), enter that part of the loss here. Enter the part of the loss from income-producing property on Schedule A (Form 1040), line 27, and the part of the loss from property used as an employee on Schedule A (Form 1040), line 22. Identify as from "Form 4797, line 18a." See instructions . . . . . . . . . . . . . . . . . . **18a**

**b** Redetermine the gain or (loss) on line 17 excluding the loss, if any, on line 18a. Enter here and on Form 1040, line 14 . . . . . . . . . . . . . . . . . . . . . . **18b**

**For Paperwork Reduction Act Notice, see page 8 of the instructions.** Cat. No. 13086I Form **4797** (2004)

**Part III** **Gain From Disposition of Property Under Sections 1245, 1250, 1252, 1254, and 1255**

| 19 | (a) Description of section 1245, 1250, 1252, 1254, or 1255 property: | (b) Date acquired (mo., day, yr.) | (c) Date sold (mo., day, yr.) |
|---|---|---|---|
| A | | | |
| B | | | |
| C | | | |
| D | | | |

| | These columns relate to the properties on lines 19A through 19D. ▶ | | Property A | Property B | Property C | Property D |
|---|---|---|---|---|---|---|
| 20 | Gross sales price (**Note:** *See line 1 before completing.*) | 20 | | | | |
| 21 | Cost or other basis plus expense of sale | 21 | | | | |
| 22 | Depreciation (or depletion) allowed or allowable | 22 | | | | |
| 23 | Adjusted basis. Subtract line 22 from line 21 | 23 | | | | |
| 24 | Total gain. Subtract line 23 from line 20 | 24 | | | | |
| 25 | **If section 1245 property:** | | | | | |
| a | Depreciation allowed or allowable from line 22 | 25a | | | | |
| b | Enter the **smaller** of line 24 or 25a | 25b | | | | |
| 26 | **If section 1250 property:** If straight line depreciation was used, enter -0- on line 26g, except for a corporation subject to section 291. | | | | | |
| a | Additional depreciation after 1975 (see instructions) | 26a | | | | |
| b | Applicable percentage multiplied by the **smaller** of line 24 or line 26a (see instructions) | 26b | | | | |
| c | Subtract line 26a from line 24. If residential rental property **or** line 24 is not more than line 26a, skip lines 26d and 26e | 26c | | | | |
| d | Additional depreciation after 1969 and before 1976 | 26d | | | | |
| e | Enter the **smaller** of line 26c or 26d | 26e | | | | |
| f | Section 291 amount (corporations only) | 26f | | | | |
| g | Add lines 26b, 26e, and 26f | 26g | | | | |
| 27 | **If section 1252 property:** Skip this section if you did not dispose of farmland or if this form is being completed for a partnership (other than an electing large partnership). | | | | | |
| a | Soil, water, and land clearing expenses | 27a | | | | |
| b | Line 27a multiplied by applicable percentage (see instructions) | 27b | | | | |
| c | Enter the **smaller** of line 24 or 27b | 27c | | | | |
| 28 | **If section 1254 property:** | | | | | |
| a | Intangible drilling and development costs, expenditures for development of mines and other natural deposits, and mining exploration costs (see instructions) | 28a | | | | |
| b | Enter the **smaller** of line 24 or 28a | 28b | | | | |
| 29 | **If section 1255 property:** | | | | | |
| a | Applicable percentage of payments excluded from income under section 126 (see instructions) | 29a | | | | |
| b | Enter the **smaller** of line 24 or 29a (see instructions) | 29b | | | | |

**Summary of Part III Gains.** Complete property columns A through D through line 29b before going to line 30.

| 30 | Total gains for all properties. Add property columns A through D, line 24 | 30 | |
|---|---|---|---|
| 31 | Add property columns A through D, lines 25b, 26g, 27c, 28b, and 29b. Enter here and on line 13 | 31 | |
| 32 | Subtract line 31 from line 30. Enter the portion from casualty or theft on Form 4684, line 33. Enter the portion from other than casualty or theft on Form 4797, line 6 | 32 | |

**Part IV** **Recapture Amounts Under Sections 179 and 280F(b)(2) When Business Use Drops to 50% or Less** (see instructions)

| | | | (a) Section 179 | (b) Section 280F(b)(2) |
|---|---|---|---|---|
| 33 | Section 179 expense deduction or depreciation allowable in prior years | 33 | | |
| 34 | Recomputed depreciation. See instructions | 34 | | |
| 35 | Recapture amount. Subtract line 34 from line 33. See the instructions for where to report | 35 | | |

Form **6251**

Department of the Treasury
Internal Revenue Service (99)

**Alternative Minimum Tax—Individuals**

▶ See separate instructions.

▶ Attach to Form 1040 or Form 1040NR.

OMB No. 1545-0227

20**04**

Attachment
Sequence No. **32**

Name(s) shown on Form 1040

Your social security number

**Part I   Alternative Minimum Taxable Income** (See instructions for how to complete each line.)

| | | | |
|---|---|---|---|
| 1 | If filing Schedule A (Form 1040), enter the amount from Form 1040, line 40, and go to line 2. Otherwise, enter the amount from Form 1040, line 37, and go to line 7. (If less than zero, enter as a negative amount.) | **1** | |
| 2 | Medical and dental. Enter the **smaller** of Schedule A (Form 1040), line 4, **or** 2½% of Form 1040, line 37 . | **2** | |
| 3 | Taxes from Schedule A (Form 1040), line 9 . . . . . . . . . . . . . . . . . . . . | **3** | |
| 4 | Enter the home mortgage interest adjustment, if any, from line 6 of the worksheet on page 2 of the instructions | **4** | |
| 5 | Miscellaneous deductions from Schedule A (Form 1040), line 26 . . . . . . . . . . . . | **5** | |
| 6 | If Form 1040, line 37, is over $142,700 (over $71,350 if married filing separately), enter the amount from line 9 of the **Itemized Deductions Worksheet** on page B-1 of the Instructions for Schedules A & B (Form 1040) | **6** ( | ) |
| 7 | Tax refund from Form 1040, line 10 or line 21 . . . . . . . . . . . . . . . . . | **7** ( | ) |
| 8 | Investment interest expense (difference between regular tax and AMT) . . . . . . . . . . | **8** | |
| 9 | Depletion (difference between regular tax and AMT) . . . . . . . . . . . . . . . | **9** | |
| 10 | Net operating loss deduction from Form 1040, line 21. Enter as a positive amount . . . . . | **10** | |
| 11 | Interest from specified private activity bonds exempt from the regular tax . . . . . . . . | **11** | |
| 12 | Qualified small business stock (7% of gain excluded under section 1202) . . . . . . . . | **12** | |
| 13 | Exercise of incentive stock options (excess of AMT income over regular tax income) . . . . . | **13** | |
| 14 | Estates and trusts (amount from Schedule K-1 (Form 1041), line 9) . . . . . . . . . . | **14** | |
| 15 | Electing large partnerships (amount from Schedule K-1 (Form 1065-B), box 6) . . . . . . . | **15** | |
| 16 | Disposition of property (difference between AMT and regular tax gain or loss) . . . . . . . | **16** | |
| 17 | Depreciation on assets placed in service after 1986 (difference between regular tax and AMT) . . . | **17** | |
| 18 | Passive activities (difference between AMT and regular tax income or loss) . . . . . . . . | **18** | |
| 19 | Loss limitations (difference between AMT and regular tax income or loss) . . . . . . . . | **19** | |
| 20 | Circulation costs (difference between regular tax and AMT) . . . . . . . . . . . . . | **20** | |
| 21 | Long-term contracts (difference between AMT and regular tax income) . . . . . . . . . | **21** | |
| 22 | Mining costs (difference between regular tax and AMT) . . . . . . . . . . . . . . | **22** | |
| 23 | Research and experimental costs (difference between regular tax and AMT) . . . . . . . . | **23** | |
| 24 | Income from certain installment sales before January 1, 1987 . . . . . . . . . . . . | **24** ( | ) |
| 25 | Intangible drilling costs preference . . . . . . . . . . . . . . . . . . . . | **25** | |
| 26 | Other adjustments, including income-based related adjustments . . . . . . . . . . . | **26** | |
| 27 | Alternative tax net operating loss deduction . . . . . . . . . . . . . . . . . | **27** ( | ) |
| 28 | **Alternative minimum taxable income.** Combine lines 1 through 27. (If married filing separately and line 28 is more than $191,000, see page 6 of the instructions.) . . . . . . . . . . . . . . | **28** | |

**Part II   Alternative Minimum Tax**

| | | | |
|---|---|---|---|
| 29 | Exemption. (If this form is for a child under age 14, see page 6 of the instructions.) | | |

| IF your filing status is . . . | AND line 28 is not over . . . | THEN enter on line 29 . . . | |
|---|---|---|---|
| Single or head of household . . . . . . | $112,500 . . . . . . . | $40,250 | |
| Married filing jointly or qualifying widow(er) . . | 150,000 . . . . . . . | 58,000 | **29** |
| Married filing separately . . . . . | 75,000 . . . . . . . | 29,000 | |

If line 28 is **over** the amount shown above for your filing status, see page 6 of the instructions.

| | | | |
|---|---|---|---|
| 30 | Subtract line 29 from line 28. If zero or less, enter -0- here and on lines 33 and 35 and stop here . . | **30** | |
| 31 | ● If you reported capital gain distributions directly on Form 1040, line 13; you reported qualified dividends on Form 1040, line 9b; **or** you had a gain on both lines 15 and 16 of Schedule D (Form 1040) (as refigured for the AMT, if necessary), complete Part III on the back and enter the amount from line 55 here. ● **All others:** If line 30 is $175,000 or less ($87,500 or less if married filing separately), multiply line 30 by 26% (.26). Otherwise, multiply line 30 by 28% (.28) and subtract $3,500 ($1,750 if married filing separately) from the result. | **31** | |
| 32 | Alternative minimum tax foreign tax credit (see page 7 of the instructions) . . . . . . . . | **32** | |
| 33 | Tentative minimum tax. Subtract line 32 from line 31 . . . . . . . . . . . . . . | **33** | |
| 34 | Tax from Form 1040, line 43 (minus any tax from Form 4972 and any foreign tax credit from Form 1040, line 46). If you used Schedule J to figure your tax, the amounts for lines 43 and 46 of Form 1040 must be refigured without using Schedule J (see page 8 of the instructions) . . . . . . . . . . | **34** | |
| 35 | **Alternative minimum tax.** Subtract line 34 from line 33. If zero or less, enter -0-. Enter here and on Form 1040, line 44 . . . . . . . . . . . . . . . . . . . . . . . . . . | **35** | |

**For Paperwork Reduction Act Notice, see page 8 of the instructions.**          Cat. No. 13600G          Form **6251** (2004)

**Part III**   **Tax Computation Using Maximum Capital Gains Rates**

| | | | |
|---|---|---|---|
| 36 | Enter the amount from Form 6251, line 30 . . . . . . . . . . . . . . . | **36** | |

37   Enter the amount from line 6 of the Qualified Dividends and Capital Gain Tax Worksheet in the instructions for Form 1040, line 43, or the amount from line 13 of the Schedule D Tax Worksheet on page D-9 of the instructions for Schedule D (Form 1040), whichever applies (as refigured for the AMT, if necessary) (see page 8 of the instructions) . . . . . . . . . .   **37**

38   Enter the amount from Schedule D (Form 1040), line 19 (as refigured for the AMT, if necessary) (see page 8 of the instructions) . . . . . . . .   **38**

39   If you did not complete a Schedule D Tax Worksheet for the regular tax or the AMT, enter the amount from line 37. Otherwise, add lines 37 and 38, and enter the **smaller** of that result or the amount from line 10 of the Schedule D Tax Worksheet (as refigured for the AMT, if necessary) . . . . . .   **39**

| | | | |
|---|---|---|---|
| 40 | Enter the **smaller** of line 36 or line 39 . . . . . . . . . . . . . . | **40** | |
| 41 | Subtract line 40 from line 36 . . . . . . . . . . . . . . . . . | **41** | |

42   If line 41 is $175,000 or less ($87,500 or less if married filing separately), multiply line 41 by 26% (.26). Otherwise, multiply line 41 by 28% (.28) and subtract $3,500 ($1,750 if married filing separately) from the result . . . . . . . . . . . . . . . . . . . . . . . . . . . . ▶   **42**

43   Enter:
  • $58,100 if married filing jointly or qualifying widow(er),
  • $29,050 if single or married filing separately, or       } . . . . .   **43**
  • $38,900 if head of household.

44   Enter the amount from line 7 of the Qualified Dividends and Capital Gain Tax Worksheet in the instructions for Form 1040, line 43, or the amount from line 14 of the Schedule D Tax Worksheet on page D-9 of the instructions for Schedule D (Form 1040), whichever applies (as figured for the regular tax). If you did not complete either worksheet for the regular tax, enter -0- . . . .   **44**

45   Subtract line 44 from line 43. If zero or less, enter -0- . . . . . . .   **45**

46   Enter the **smaller** of line 36 or line 37 . . . . . . . . . .   **46**

47   Enter the **smaller** of line 45 or line 46 . . . . . . . . . .   **47**

| | | | |
|---|---|---|---|
| 48 | Multiply line 47 by 5% (.05) . . . . . . . . . . . . . . . . ▶ | **48** | |
| 49 | Subtract line 47 from line 46 . . . . . . . . . . . **49** | | |
| 50 | Multiply line 49 by 15% (.15) . . . . . . . . . . . . . . . . ▶ | **50** | |

**If line 38 is zero or blank, skip lines 51 and 52 and go to line 53. Otherwise, go to line 51.**

| | | | |
|---|---|---|---|
| 51 | Subtract line 46 from line 40 . . . . . . . . . . . . **51** | | |
| 52 | Multiply line 51 by 25% (.25) . . . . . . . . . . . . . . . . ▶ | **52** | |
| 53 | Add lines 42, 48, 50, and 52 . . . . . . . . . . . . . . . . | **53** | |

54   If line 36 is $175,000 or less ($87,500 or less if married filing separately), multiply line 36 by 26% (.26). Otherwise, multiply line 36 by 28% (.28) and subtract $3,500 ($1,750 if married filing separately) from the result . . . . . . . . . . . . . . . . . . . . . . . . . . . .   **54**

55   Enter the **smaller** of line 53 or line 54 here and on line 31 . . . . . . . . . . . . .   **55**

Form **6251** (2004)

| Form **8582** | **Passive Activity Loss Limitations** | OMB No. 1545-1008 |
|---|---|---|
| Department of the Treasury Internal Revenue Service   (99) | ► See separate instructions.<br>► Attach to Form 1040 or Form 1041. | **2004** Attachment Sequence No. **88** |

Name(s) shown on return | Identifying number

## Part I   2004 Passive Activity Loss

**Caution:** *See the instructions for Worksheets 1, 2, and 3 on pages 7 and 8 before completing Part I.*

**Rental Real Estate Activities With Active Participation** (For the definition of active participation see **Special Allowance for Rental Real Estate Activities** on page 3 of the instructions.)

**1a** Activities with net income (enter the amount from Worksheet 1, column (a)) . . . . . . . . . . . . . . . .  **1a**

**b** Activities with net loss (enter the amount from Worksheet 1, column (b)) . . . . . . . . . . . . . . . .  **1b** (               )

**c** Prior years unallowed losses (enter the amount from Worksheet 1, column (c)) . . . . . . . . . . . . . . . .  **1c** (               )

**d** Combine lines 1a, 1b, and 1c. . . . . . . . . . . . . . . .  **1d**

**Commercial Revitalization Deductions From Rental Real Estate Activities**

**2a** Commercial revitalization deductions from Worksheet 2, column (a)  **2a** (               )

**b** Prior year unallowed commercial revitalization deductions from Worksheet 2, column (b) . . . . . . . . . . . .  **2b** (               )

**c** Add lines 2a and 2b. . . . . . . . . . . . . . . .  **2c** (               )

**All Other Passive Activities**

**3a** Activities with net income (enter the amount from Worksheet 3, column (a)) . . . . . . . . . . . . . . . .  **3a**

**b** Activities with net loss (enter the amount from Worksheet 3, column (b)) . . . . . . . . . . . . . . . .  **3b** (               )

**c** Prior years unallowed losses (enter the amount from Worksheet 3, column (c)) . . . . . . . . . . . . . . . .  **3c** (               )

**d** Combine lines 3a, 3b, and 3c. . . . . . . . . . . . . . .  **3d**

**4** Combine lines 1d, 2c, and 3d. If the result is net income or zero, all losses are allowed, including any prior year unallowed losses entered on line 1c, 2b, or 3c. **Do not** complete Form 8582. Report the losses on the forms and schedules normally used . . . . . . . . . . . .  **4**

If line 4 is a loss and:  • Line 1d is a loss, go to Part II.
  • Line 2c is a loss (and line 1d is zero or more), skip Part II and go to Part III.
  • Line 3d is a loss (and lines 1d and 2c are zero or more), skip Parts II and III and go to line 15.

**Caution:** *If your filing status is married filing separately and you lived with your spouse at any time during the year, **do not** complete Part II or Part III. Instead, go to line 15.*

## Part II   Special Allowance for Rental Real Estate With Active Participation

**Note:** *Enter all numbers in Part II as positive amounts. See page 8 for an example.*

**5** Enter the **smaller** of the loss on line 1d or the loss on line 4 . . . . . . . . . . . .  **5**

**6** Enter $150,000. If married filing separately, see page 8 . . .  **6**

**7** Enter modified adjusted gross income, but not less than zero (see page 8)  **7**

**Note:** *If line 7 is greater than or equal to line 6, skip lines 8 and 9, enter -0- on line 10. Otherwise, go to line 8.*

**8** Subtract line 7 from line 6 . . . . . . . . . . . . . . .  **8**

**9** Multiply line 8 by 50% (.5). **Do not** enter more than $25,000. If married filing separately, see page 8  **9**

**10** Enter the **smaller** of line 5 or line 9. . . . . . . . . . . .  **10**

If line 2c is a loss, go to Part III. Otherwise, go to line 15.

## Part III   Special Allowance for Commercial Revitalization Deductions From Rental Real Estate Activities

**Note:** *Enter all numbers in Part III as positive amounts. See the example for Part II on page 8.*

**11** Enter $25,000 reduced by the amount, if any, on line 10. If married filing separately, see instructions  **11**

**12** Enter the loss from line 4 . . . . . . . . . . . . . . . .  **12**

**13** Reduce line 12 by the amount on line 10 . . . . . . . . .  **13**

**14** Enter the **smallest** of line 2c (treated as a positive amount), line 11, or line 13 . . . . . .  **14**

## Part IV   Total Losses Allowed

**15** Add the income, if any, on lines 1a and 3a and enter the total. . . . . . . . . . .  **15**

**16** **Total losses allowed from all passive activities for 2004.** Add lines 10, 14, and 15. See pages 10 and 11 of the instructions to find out how to report the losses on your tax return .  **16**

**For Paperwork Reduction Act Notice, see page 12 of the instructions.**       Cat. No. 63704F       Form **8582** (2004)

Form 8582 (2004)                                                                                    Page **2**

**Caution:** *The worksheets must be filed with your tax return. Keep a copy for your records.*

**Worksheet 1—For Form 8582, Lines 1a, 1b, and 1c** (See page 7 of the instructions.)

| Name of activity | Current year | | Prior years | Overall gain or loss | |
|---|---|---|---|---|---|
| | (a) Net income (line 1a) | (b) Net loss (line 1b) | (c) Unallowed loss (line 1c) | (d) Gain | (e) Loss |
| | | | | | |
| | | | | | |
| | | | | | |
| | | | | | |
| **Total. Enter on Form 8582, lines 1a, 1b, and 1c** . . . . . . . . . ▶ | | | | | |

**Worksheet 2—For Form 8582, Lines 2a and 2b** (See pages 7 and 8 of the instructions.)

| Name of activity | (a) Current year deductions (line 2a) | (b) Prior year unallowed deductions (line 2b) | (c) Overall loss |
|---|---|---|---|
| | | | |
| | | | |
| | | | |
| **Total. Enter on Form 8582, lines 2a and 2b** . . . . . . . . . ▶ | | | |

**Worksheet 3—For Form 8582, Lines 3a, 3b, and 3c** (See page 8 of the instructions.)

| Name of activity | Current year | | Prior years | Overall gain or loss | |
|---|---|---|---|---|---|
| | (a) Net income (line 3a) | (b) Net loss (line 3b) | (c) Unallowed loss (line 3c) | (d) Gain | (e) Loss |
| | | | | | |
| | | | | | |
| | | | | | |
| | | | | | |
| **Total. Enter on Form 8582, lines 3a, 3b, and 3c** . . . . . . . . . ▶ | | | | | |

**Worksheet 4—Use this worksheet if an amount is shown on Form 8582, line 10 or 14** (See page 9.)

| Name of activity | Form or schedule and line number to be reported on (see instructions) | (a) Loss | (b) Ratio | (c) Special allowance | (d) Subtract column (c) from column (a) |
|---|---|---|---|---|---|
| | | | | | |
| | | | | | |
| | | | | | |
| | | | | | |
| **Total** . . . . . . . . . . . . . . . . . ▶ | | | 1.00 | | |

**Worksheet 5—Allocation of Unallowed Losses** (See page 9 of the instructions.)

| Name of activity | Form or schedule and line number to be reported on (see instructions) | (a) Loss | (b) Ratio | (c) Unallowed loss |
|---|---|---|---|---|
| | | | | |
| | | | | |
| | | | | |
| | | | | |
| | | | | |
| **Total** . . . . . . . . . . . . . . . . . . . ▶ | | | 1.00 | |

Form **8582** (2004)

## Worksheet 6—Allowed Losses (See pages 9 and 10 of the instructions.)

| Name of activity | Form or schedule and line number to be reported on (see instructions) | (a) Loss | (b) Unallowed loss | (c) Allowed loss |
|---|---|---|---|---|
| | | | | |
| | | | | |
| | | | | |
| | | | | |
| | | | | |
| **Total** . . . . . . . . . . . . . . . . . . ▶ | | | | |

## Worksheet 7—Activities With Losses Reported on Two or More Different Forms or Schedules (See page 10.)

| Name of Activity: | (a) | (b) | (c) Ratio | (d) Unallowed loss | (e) Allowed loss |
|---|---|---|---|---|---|
| **Form or schedule and line number to be reported on (see instructions):** ------------- | | | | | |
| **1a** Net loss plus prior year unallowed loss from form or schedule. ▶ | | | | | |
| **b** Net income from form or schedule . . . . . . ▶ | | | | | |
| **c** Subtract line 1b from line 1a. If zero or less, enter -0- ▶ | | | | | |
| **Form or schedule and line number to be reported on (see instructions):** ------------- | | | | | |
| **1a** Net loss plus prior year unallowed loss from form or schedule. ▶ | | | | | |
| **b** Net income from form or schedule . . . . . . ▶ | | | | | |
| **c** Subtract line 1b from line 1a. If zero or less, enter -0- ▶ | | | | | |
| **Form or schedule and line number to be reported on (see instructions):** ------------- | | | | | |
| **1a** Net loss plus prior year unallowed loss from form or schedule. ▶ | | | | | |
| **b** Net income from form or schedule . . . . . . ▶ | | | | | |
| **c** Subtract line 1b from line 1a. If zero or less, enter -0- ▶ | | | | | |
| **Total** . . . . . . . . . . . . . . . . . . ▶ | | | 1.00 | | |

Form **8832**
(Rev. September 2002)
Department of the Treasury
Internal Revenue Service

## Entity Classification Election

OMB No. 1545-1516

| **Type or Print** | Name of entity | EIN ▶ |
| | Number, street, and room or suite no. If a P.O. box, see instructions. | |
| | City or town, state, and ZIP code. If a foreign address, enter city, province or state, postal code and country. | |

**1 Type of election** (see instructions):

a ☐ Initial classification by a newly-formed entity.

b ☐ Change in current classification.

**2 Form of entity** (see instructions):

a ☐ A domestic eligible entity electing to be classified as an association taxable as a corporation.

b ☐ A domestic eligible entity electing to be classified as a partnership.

c ☐ A domestic eligible entity with a single owner electing to be disregarded as a separate entity.

d ☐ A foreign eligible entity electing to be classified as an association taxable as a corporation.

e ☐ A foreign eligible entity electing to be classified as a partnership.

f ☐ A foreign eligible entity with a single owner electing to be disregarded as a separate entity.

**3 Disregarded entity information** (see instructions):
a Name of owner ▶ ................................................................
b Identifying number of owner ▶ ................................................................
c Country of organization of entity electing to be disregarded (if foreign) ▶ ................................................................

**4** Election is to be effective beginning (month, day, year) (see instructions) . . . . . . . . . . . . . ▶ _____ / _____ / _____

**5** Name and title of person whom the IRS may call for more information | **6** That person's telephone number
( )

### Consent Statement and Signature(s) (see instructions)

Under penalties of perjury, I (we) declare that I (we) consent to the election of the above-named entity to be classified as indicated above, and that I (we) have examined this consent statement, and to the best of my (our) knowledge and belief, it is true, correct, and complete. If I am an officer, manager, or member signing for all members of the entity, I further declare that I am authorized to execute this consent statement on their behalf.

| Signature(s) | Date | Title |
| --- | --- | --- |
| | | |
| | | |
| | | |
| | | |

For Paperwork Reduction Act Notice, see page 4.      Cat. No. 22598R      Form **8832** (Rev. 9-2002)

The key terms in this glossary have been defined to reflect their conventional use in the field of taxation. The definitions may therefore be incomplete for other purposes.

## A

**Accelerated cost recovery system (ACRS).** A method in which the cost of tangible property is recovered over a prescribed period of time. The approach disregards salvage value, imposes a period of cost recovery that depends upon the classification of the asset into one of various recovery periods, and prescribes the applicable percentage of cost that can be deducted each year. § 168.

**Accident and health insurance benefits.** Employee fringe benefits provided by employers through the payment of health and accident insurance premiums or the establishment of employer-funded medical reimbursement plans. Employers generally are entitled to a deduction for such payments, whereas employees generally exclude such fringe benefits from gross income. §§ 105 and 106.

**Accountable plan.** An accountable plan is a type of expense reimbursement plan that requires an employee to render an adequate accounting to the employer and return any excess reimbursement or allowance. If the expense qualifies, it will be treated as a deduction *for* AGI.

**Accounting income.** The accountant's concept of income is generally based upon the realization principle. Financial accounting income may differ from taxable income (e.g., accelerated depreciation might be used for Federal income tax and straight-line depreciation for financial accounting purposes). Differences are included in a reconciliation of taxable and accounting income on Schedule M–1 of Form 1120 for corporations.

**Accounting method.** The method under which income and expenses are determined for tax purposes. Important accounting methods include the cash basis and the accrual basis. Special methods are available for the reporting of gain on installment sales, recognition of income on construction projects (the completed contract and percentage of completion methods), and the valuation of inventories (last-in, first-out and first-in, first-out). §§ 446–474.

**Accounting period.** The period of time, usually a year, used by a taxpayer for the determination of tax liability. Unless a fiscal year is chosen, taxpayers must determine and pay their income tax liability by using the calendar year (January 1 through December 31) as the period of measurement. An example of a fiscal year is July 1 through June 30. A change in accounting period (e.g., from a calendar year to a fiscal year) generally requires the consent of the IRS. Some new taxpayers, such as a newly formed corporation, are free to select either an initial calendar or a fiscal year without the consent of the IRS. §§ 441–444.

**Accrual method.** A method of accounting that reflects expenses incurred and income earned for any one tax year. In contrast to the cash basis of accounting, expenses need not be paid to be deductible, nor need income be received to be taxable. Unearned income (e.g., prepaid interest and rent) generally is taxed in the year of receipt regardless of the method of accounting used by the taxpayer. § 446(c)(2).

**Accumulated adjustments account (AAA).** An account that aggregates an S corporation's post-1982 income, loss, and deductions for the tax year (including nontaxable income and nondeductible losses and expenses). After the year-end income and expense adjustments are made, the account is reduced by distributions made during the tax year. § 1368(e)(1).

**Accumulated earnings and profits.** Net undistributed tax-basis earnings of a corporation aggregated from March 1, 1913, to the end of the prior tax year. Used to determine the amount of dividend income associated with a distribution to shareholders. § 316 and Reg. § 1.316–2.

**Acquiescence.** Agreement by the IRS on the results reached in certain judicial decisions; sometimes abbreviated *Acq.* or *A.*

**Acquisition indebtedness.** Debt incurred in acquiring, constructing, or substantially improving a qualified residence of the taxpayer. The interest on such loans is deductible as qualified residence interest. However, interest on such debt is deductible only on the portion of the indebtedness that does not exceed $1,000,000 ($500,000 for married persons filing separate returns). § 163(h)(3).

**Active income.** Active income includes wages, salary, commissions, bonuses, profits from a trade or business in which the taxpayer is a material participant, gain on the sale or other disposition of assets used in an active trade or business, and income from intangible property if the taxpayer's personal efforts significantly contributed to the creation of the property. The passive activity loss rules require classification of income and losses into three categories with active income being one of them. § 465.

**Ad valorem tax.**   A tax imposed on the value of property. The most common ad valorem tax is that imposed by states, counties, and cities on real estate. Ad valorem taxes can be imposed on personal property as well.

**Additional depreciation.**   The excess of the amount of depreciation actually deducted over the amount that would have been deducted had the straight-line method been used. § 1250(b).

**Adjusted basis.**   The cost or other basis of property reduced by depreciation allowed or allowable and increased by capital improvements. Other special adjustments are provided in § 1016 and the related Regulations.

**Adjusted current earnings (ACE).**   An adjustment in computing corporate alternative minimum taxable income (AMTI), computed at 75 percent of the excess of adjusted current earnings (ACE) over unadjusted AMTI. ACE computations reflect longer and slower cost recovery deductions and other restrictions on the timing of certain recognition events. Exempt interest, life insurance proceeds, and other receipts that are included in earnings and profits but not in taxable income also increase the ACE adjustment. If unadjusted AMTI exceeds ACE, the ACE adjustment is negative. The negative adjustment is limited to the aggregate of the positive adjustments under ACE for prior years, reduced by any previously claimed negative adjustments. § 56(g).

**Adoption expenses credit.**   A provision intended to assist taxpayers who incur nonrecurring costs directly associated with the adoption process such as legal costs, social service review costs, and transportation costs. Up to $10,630 ($10,630 for a child with special needs regardless of the actual adoption expenses) of costs incurred to adopt an eligible child qualify for the credit. A taxpayer may claim the credit in the year qualifying expenses are paid or incurred if the expenses are paid during or after the year in which the adoption is finalized. For qualifying expenses paid or incurred in a tax year prior to the year the adoption is finalized, the credit must be claimed in the tax year following the tax year during which the expenses are paid or incurred. § 23.

**Alimony and separate maintenance payments.**   Alimony deductions result from the payment of a legal obligation arising from the termination of a marital relationship. Payments designated as alimony generally are included in the gross income of the recipient and are deductible *for* AGI by the payer. §§ 62(a)(10), 71, and 215.

**Allocate.**   The assignment of income for various tax purposes. A multistate corporation's nonbusiness income usually is allocated to the state where the nonbusiness assets are located; it is not apportioned with the rest of the entity's income. International taxpayers allocate certain expenses in computing the taxable income from specific activities. Partnerships can allocate specific items of income, deduction, and credit if certain requirements are met.

**Alternative depreciation system (ADS).**   A cost recovery system that produces a smaller deduction than would be calculated under ACRS or MACRS. The alternative system must be used in certain instances and can be elected in other instances. § 168(g).

**Alternative minimum tax (AMT).**   The AMT is a fixed percentage of alternative minimum taxable income (AMTI). AMTI generally starts with the taxpayer's adjusted gross income (for individuals) or taxable income (for other taxpayers). To this amount, the taxpayer (1) adds designated preference items (e.g., tax-exempt interest income on private activity bonds), (2) makes other specified adjustments (e.g., to reflect a longer, straight-line cost recovery deduction), (3) subtracts certain AMT itemized deductions for individuals (e.g., interest incurred on housing but not taxes paid), and (4) subtracts an exemption amount (e.g., $40,000 on a C corporation's return). The taxpayer must pay the greater of the resulting AMT (reduced by only the foreign tax credit) or the regular income tax (reduced by all allowable tax credits). The AMT does not apply to certain small C corporations. AMT preferences and adjustments are assigned to partners and S corporation shareholders. § 55–59.

**Alternative minimum taxable income (AMTI).**   The base (prior to deducting the exemption amount) for computing a taxpayer's alternative minimum tax. This consists of the taxable income for the year modified for AMT adjustments and AMT preferences. § 55(b)(2).

**Amortization.**   The tax deduction for the cost or other basis of an intangible asset over the asset's estimated useful life. Examples of amortizable intangibles include patents, copyrights, and leasehold interests. The intangible goodwill can be amortized for income tax purposes over a 15-year period. § 197.

**Amount realized.**   The amount received by a taxpayer upon the sale or exchange of property. Amount realized is the sum of the cash and the fair market value of any property or services received by the taxpayer, plus any related debt assumed by the buyer. Determining the amount realized is the starting point for arriving at realized gain or loss. § 1001(b).

**Apportion.**   The assignment of the business income of a multistate corporation to specific states for income taxation. Usually, the apportionment procedure accounts for the property, payroll, and sales activity levels of the various states, and a proportionate assignment of the entity's total income is made, using a three-factor apportionment formula. Some states exclude nonbusiness income from the apportionment procedure; they allocate nonbusiness income to the states where the nonbusiness assets are located.

**Arm's length concept.**   The standard under which unrelated parties would carry out a transaction. Suppose Bint Corporation sells property to its sole shareholder for $10,000. In determining whether $10,000 is an arm's length price, one would ascertain the amount for which the corporation could have sold the property to a disinterested third party.

**Arm's length price.**   See *Arm's length concept.*

**Assignment of income.** A procedure whereby a taxpayer attempts to avoid the recognition of income by assigning to another the property that generates the income. Such a procedure will not avoid the recognition of income by the taxpayer making the assignment if it can be said that the income was earned at the point of the transfer. In this case, usually referred to as an anticipatory assignment of income, the income will be taxed to the person who earns it.

**Assumption of liabilities.** In a corporate formation, corporate takeover, or asset purchase, the new owner often takes assets and agrees to assume preexisting debt. Such actions do not create boot received on the transaction for the new shareholder, unless there is no *bona fide* business purpose for the exchange, or the principal purpose of the debt assumption is the avoidance of tax liabilities. Gain is recognized to the extent that liabilities assumed exceed the aggregated bases of the transferred assets. § 357.

**At-risk limitation.** Generally, a taxpayer can deduct losses related to a trade or business, S corporation, partnership, or investment asset only to the extent of the at-risk amount.

**Automatic mileage method.** Automobile expenses are generally deductible only to the extent the automobile is used in business or for the production of income. Personal commuting expenses are not deductible. The taxpayer may deduct actual expenses (including depreciation and insurance), or the standard (automatic) mileage rate may be used (36 cents per mile for 2003, 37.5 cents per mile for 2004, and 40.5 cents per mile for 2005) during any one year. Automobile expenses incurred for medical purposes or in connection with job-related moving expenses are deductible to the extent of actual out-of-pocket expenses or at the rate of 15 cents per mile in 2005 (14 cents per mile in 2004). For charitable activities, the rate is 14 cents per mile.

# B

**Bad debts.** A deduction is permitted if a business account receivable subsequently becomes partially or completely worthless, providing the income arising from the debt previously was included in income. Available methods are the specific charge-off method and the reserve method. However, except for certain financial institutions, TRA of 1986 repealed the use of the reserve method for 1987 and thereafter. If the reserve method is used, partially or totally worthless accounts are charged to the reserve. A nonbusiness bad debt deduction is allowed as a short-term capital loss if the loan did not arise in connection with the creditor's trade or business activities. Loans between related parties (family members) generally are classified as nonbusiness. § 166.

**Basis in partnership interest.** The acquisition cost of the partner's ownership interest in the partnership. Includes purchase price and associated debt acquired from other partners and in the course of the entity's trade or business. § 705.

**Boot.** Cash or property of a type not included in the definition of a nontaxable exchange. The receipt of boot causes an otherwise nontaxable transfer to become taxable to the extent of the lesser of the fair market value of the boot or the realized gain on the transfer. For example, see transfers to controlled corporations under § 351(b) and like-kind exchanges under § 1031(b).

**Brother-sister controlled group.** More than one corporation owned by the same shareholders. If, for example, Chris and Pat each own one-half of the stock in Wren Corporation and Redbird Corporation, Wren and Redbird form a brother-sister controlled group. § 1563(a)(2).

**Built-in gains tax.** A penalty tax designed to discourage a shift of the incidence of taxation on unrealized gains from a C corporation to its shareholders, via an S election. Under this provision, any recognized gain during the first 10 years of S status generates a corporate-level tax on a base not to exceed the aggregate untaxed built-in gains brought into the S corporation upon its election from C corporation taxable years. § 1374.

**Business bad debt.** A tax deduction allowed for obligations obtained in connection with a trade or business that have become either partially or completely worthless. In contrast to nonbusiness bad debts, business bad debts are deductible as business expenses. § 166.

**Buy-sell agreement.** An arrangement, particularly appropriate in the case of a closely held corporation or a partnership, whereby the surviving owners (shareholders or partners) or the entity agrees to purchase the interest of a withdrawing owner. The buy-sell agreement provides for an orderly disposition of an interest in a business and may aid in setting the value of the interest for death tax purposes.

# C

**C corporation.** A separate taxable entity, subject to the rules of Subchapter C of the Code. This business form may create a double taxation effect relative to its shareholders. The entity is subject to the regular corporate tax and a number of penalty taxes at the Federal level.

**Cafeteria plan.** An employee benefit plan under which an employee is allowed to select from among a variety of employer-provided fringe benefits. Some of the benefits may be taxable, and some may be statutory nontaxable benefits (e.g., health and accident insurance and group term life insurance). The employee is taxed only on the taxable benefits selected. A cafeteria benefit plan is also referred to as a flexible benefit plan. § 125.

**Capital account.** The financial accounting analog of a partner's tax basis in the entity.

**Capital asset.** Broadly speaking, all assets are capital except those specifically excluded by the Code. Major categories of noncapital assets include property held for resale in the normal course of business (inventory), trade accounts and notes receivable, and depreciable property and real estate used in a trade or business (§ 1231 assets). § 1221.

**Capital contribution.** Various means by which a shareholder makes additional funds available to the corporation (placed at the risk of the business), sometimes without the receipt of additional stock. If no stock is received, the contributions are added to the basis of the shareholder's existing stock investment and do not generate gross income to the corporation. § 118.

**Capital gain.**   The gain from the sale or exchange of a capital asset.

**Capital gain property.**   Property contributed to a charitable organization that, if sold rather than contributed, would have resulted in long-term capital gain to the donor.

**Capital interest.**   Usually, the percentage of the entity's net assets that a partner would receive on liquidation. Typically determined by the partner's capital sharing ratio.

**Capital loss.**   The loss from the sale or exchange of a capital asset.

**Capital sharing ratio.**   A partner's percentage ownership of the entity's capital.

**Cash receipts method.**   A method of accounting that reflects deductions as paid and income as received in any one tax year. However, deductions for prepaid expenses that benefit more than one tax year (e.g., prepaid rent and prepaid interest) usually must be spread over the period benefited rather than deducted in the year paid. For fixed assets, the cash basis taxpayer claims deductions through depreciation or amortization in the same manner as an accrual basis taxpayer. § 446(c)(1).

**Casualty loss.**   A casualty is defined as "the complete or partial destruction of property resulting from an identifiable event of a sudden, unexpected or unusual nature" (e.g., floods, storms, fires, auto accidents). Individuals may deduct a casualty loss only if the loss is incurred in a trade or business or in a transaction entered into for profit or arises from fire, storm, shipwreck, or other casualty or from theft. Individuals usually deduct personal casualty losses as itemized deductions subject to a $100 nondeductible amount and to an annual floor equal to 10 percent of adjusted gross income that applies after the $100 per casualty floor has been applied. Special rules are provided for the netting of certain casualty gains and losses. § 165(c)(3).

**Charitable contributions.**   Contributions are deductible (subject to various restrictions and ceiling limitations) if made to qualified nonprofit charitable organizations. A cash basis taxpayer is entitled to a deduction solely in the year of payment. Accrual basis corporations may accrue contributions at year-end if payment is properly authorized before the end of the year and payment is made within two and one-half months after the end of the year. § 170.

**Check-the-box Regulation.**   A business entity can elect to be taxed as a partnership, S corporation, or C corporation by indicating its preference on the tax return. Legal structure and operations are irrelevant in this regard. Thus, by using the check-the-box rules prudently, an entity can select the most attractive tax results offered by the Code, without being bound by legal forms. Not available if the entity is incorporated under state law.

**Child tax credit.**   A tax credit based solely on the number of qualifying children under age 17. The maximum credit available is $1,000 per child through 2010. A qualifying child must be claimed as a dependent on a parent's tax return in order to qualify for the credit. Taxpayers who qualify for the child tax credit may also qualify for a supplemental credit. The supplemental credit is treated as a component of the earned income credit and is therefore refundable. The credit is phased out for higher-income taxpayers. § 24.

**Circuit Court of Appeals.**   Any of 13 Federal courts that consider tax matters appealed from the U.S. Tax Court, a U.S. District Court, or the U.S. Court of Federal Claims. Appeal from a U.S. Court of Appeals is to the U.S. Supreme Court by *Certiorari*.

**Citator.**   A tax research resource that presents the judicial history of a court case and traces the subsequent references to the case. When these references include the citing cases' evaluations of the cited case's precedents, the research can obtain some measure of the efficacy and reliability of the original holding.

**Claim of right doctrine.**   A judicially imposed doctrine applicable to both cash and accrual basis taxpayers that holds that an amount is includible in income upon actual or constructive receipt if the taxpayer has an unrestricted claim to the payment. For the tax treatment of amounts repaid when previously included in income under the claim of right doctrine, see § 1341.

**Closely held C corporation.**   A regular corporation (i.e., the S election is not in effect) for which more than 50 percent of the value of its outstanding stock is owned, directly or indirectly, by five or fewer individuals at any time during the tax year. The term is relevant in identifying C corporations that are subject to the passive activity loss provisions. § 469.

**Collectibles.**   A special type of capital asset, the gain from which is taxed at a maximum rate of 28 percent if the holding period is more than one year. Examples include art, rugs, antiques, gems, metals, stamps, some coins and bullion, and alcoholic beverages held for investment. § 1(h).

**Compensatory damages.**   Damages received or paid by the taxpayer can be classified as compensatory damages or as punitive damages. Compensatory damages are those paid to compensate one for harm caused by another. Compensatory damages are excludible from the recipient's gross income. § 104(a)(2).

**Conduit concept.**   An approach assumed by the tax law in the treatment of certain entities and their owners. Specific tax characteristics pass through the entity without losing their identity. For example, items of income and expense, capital gains and losses, tax credits, etc., realized by a partnership pass through the partnership (a conduit) and are subject to taxation at the partner level. Also, in an S corporation, certain items pass through and are reported on the returns of the shareholders.

**Constructive dividend.** A taxable benefit derived by a shareholder from his or her corporation that is not actually called a dividend. Examples include unreasonable compensation, excessive rent payments, bargain purchases of corporate property, and shareholder use of corporate property. Constructive dividends generally are found in closely held corporations.

**Constructive receipt.** If income is unqualifiedly available although not physically in the taxpayer's possession, it is subject to the income tax. An example is accrued interest on a savings account. Under the constructive receipt of income concept, the interest is taxed to a depositor in the year available, rather than the year actually withdrawn. The fact that the depositor uses the cash basis of accounting for tax purposes is irrelevant. See Reg. § 1.451–2.

**Control.** Holding a specified level of stock ownership in a corporation. For § 351, the new shareholder(s) must hold at least 80 percent of the total combined voting power of all voting classes of stock and at least 80 percent of the shares of all nonvoting classes. Other tax provisions require different levels of control to bring about desired effects, such as 50 or 100 percent.

**Controlled foreign corporation (CFC).** A non-U.S. corporation in which more than 50 percent of the total combined voting power of all classes of stock entitled to vote or the total value of the stock of the corporation is owned by "U.S. shareholders" on any day during the taxable year of the foreign corporation. For purposes of this definition, a U.S. shareholder is any U.S. person who owns, or is considered to own, 10 percent or more of the total combined voting power of all classes of voting stock of the foreign corporation. Stock owned directly, indirectly, and constructively is used in this measure. Certain Subpart F income of the CFC is taxed to the U.S. shareholders when it is earned, not when it is later repatriated.

**Controlled group.** A controlled group of corporations is required to share the lower-level corporate tax rates and various other tax benefits among the members of the group. A controlled group may be either a brother-sister or a parent-subsidiary group. §§ 1561 and 1563.

**Cost depletion.** Depletion that is calculated based on the adjusted basis of the asset. The adjusted basis is divided by the expected recoverable units to determine the depletion per unit. The depletion per unit is multiplied by the units sold during the tax year to calculate cost depletion. § 612.

**Cost recovery system.** The system which provides for the write-off of the cost of an asset under ACRS or MACRS. The cost recovery system replaced the depreciation system as the method of writing off the cost of an asset for most capitalized assets placed in service after 1980 (after 1986 for MACRS). § 168.

**Court of Federal Claims.** A trial court (court of original jurisdiction) that decides litigation involving Federal tax matters. Appeal from this court is to the Court of Appeals for the Federal Circuit.

**Court of original jurisdiction.** The Federal courts are divided into courts of original jurisdiction and appellate courts. A dispute between a taxpayer and the IRS is first considered by a court of original jurisdiction (i.e., a trial court). The four Federal courts of original jurisdiction are the U.S. Tax Court, U.S. District Court, the Court of Federal Claims, and the Small Cases Division of the U.S. Tax Court.

**Coverdell Education Savings Account (CESA).** A savings account established to pay for qualified education expenses (i.e., tuition, fees, books, supplies, related equipment, room and board if the student's course load is at least one-half of the full-time course load). The maximum annual contribution to the savings account of a beneficiary is $2,000. The maximum annual contribution is subject to phaseout beginning at $95,000 for single taxpayers and $150,000 for married couples who file a joint return. Contributions are not deductible and cannot be made to a savings account once the beneficiary attains age 18. Distributions used to pay for qualified education expenses for a designated beneficiary are tax-free. § 530.

**Credit for child and dependent care expenses.** A tax credit ranging from 20 percent to 35 percent of employment-related expenses (child and dependent care expenses) for amounts of up to $6,000 is available to individuals who are employed (or deemed to be employed) and maintain a household for a dependent child under age 13, disabled spouse, or disabled dependent. § 21.

**Credit for employer-provided child care.** A nonrefundable credit is available to employers who provided child care facilities to their employees during normal working hours. The credit, limited to $150,000, is comprised of two components. The portion of the credit for qualified child care expenses is equal to 25 percent of these expenses while the portion of the credit for qualified child care resources and referral services is equal to 10 percent of these expenses. Any qualifying expenses otherwise deductible by taxpayer must be reduced by the amount of the credit. In addition, the taxpayer's basis for any property used for qualifying purposes is reduced by the amount of the credit. § 45F.

**Credit for small employer pension plan startup costs.** A nonrefundable credit available to small businesses based on administrative costs associated with establishing and maintaining certain qualified plans. While such qualifying costs generally are deductible as ordinary and necessary business expense, the availability of the credit is intended to lower the costs of starting a qualified retirement program, and therefore encourage qualifying businesses to establish retirement plans for their employees. The credit is available for eligible employers at the rate of 50 percent of qualified startup costs. The maximum credit is $500 (based on a maximum of $1,000 of qualifying expenses). § 45E.

**Current earnings and profits.** Net tax-basis earnings of a corporation aggregated during the current tax year. A corporate distribution is deemed to be first from the entity's current earnings and profits and then from accumulated earnings and profits. Shareholders recognize dividend income to the extent of the earnings and profits of the corporation. A dividend results to the extent of current earnings and profits, even if there is a larger negative balance in accumulated earnings and profits.

# D

**De minimis fringe benefits.** Benefits provided to employees that are too insignificant to warrant the time and effort required to account for the benefits received by each employee and the value of those benefits. Such amounts are excludible from the employee's gross income. § 132.

**Death tax.** A tax imposed on property transferred by the death of the owner.

**Deduction for qualified tuition and related expenses.** Taxpayers are allowed a deduction of up to $4,000 for higher education expenses. Certain taxpayers are not eligible for the deduction: those whose AGI exceeds a specified amount and those who can be claimed as a dependent by another taxpayer. These expenses are classified as a deduction *for* AGI and they need not be employment related. § 222.

**Deemed-paid credit.** A foreign tax credit allowed to a U.S. taxpayer that has received an actual or constructive dividend from a non-U.S. corporation that has paid foreign income taxes. The credit is computed using the proportion of foreign income taxes paid by the payor corporation to its post-1986 undistributed earnings. Under § 78, the U.S. taxpayer claiming a deemed-paid credit includes the same amount in gross income for the tax year.

**Dependency exemption.** The tax law provides an exemption for each individual taxpayer and an additional exemption for the taxpayer's spouse if a joint return is filed. An individual may also claim a dependency exemption for each dependent, provided certain tests are met. The amount of the personal and dependency exemptions is $3,200 in 2005 ($3,100 in 2004). The exemption is subject to phaseout once adjusted gross income exceeds certain statutory threshold amounts.

**Depletion.** The process by which the cost or other basis of a natural resource (e.g., an oil or gas interest) is recovered upon extraction and sale of the resource. The two ways to determine the depletion allowance are the cost and percentage (or statutory) methods. Under cost depletion, each unit of production sold is assigned a portion of the cost or other basis of the interest. This is determined by dividing the cost or other basis by the total units expected to be recovered. Under percentage (or statutory) depletion, the tax law provides a special percentage factor for different types of minerals and other natural resources. This percentage is multiplied by the gross income from the interest to arrive at the depletion allowance. §§ 611–613 and 613A.

**Depreciation rules.** The depreciation system that existed prior to the enactment of the Accelerated Cost Recovery System (ACRS). This system applies to depreciable assets placed in service prior to January 1, 1981, and to certain post-1980 assets that do not qualify for ACRS. § 167.

**Determination letter.** Upon the request of a taxpayer, an IRS Area Director will comment on the tax status of a completed transaction. Determination letters frequently are used to clarify employee status, determine whether a retirement or profit sharing plan qualifies under the Code, and determine the tax-exempt status of certain nonprofit organizations.

**Disabled access credit.** A tax credit designed to encourage small businesses to make their facilities more accessible to disabled individuals. The credit is equal to 50 percent of the eligible expenditures that exceed $250 but do not exceed $10,250. Thus, the maximum amount for the credit is $5,000. The adjusted basis for depreciation is reduced by the amount of the credit. To qualify, the facility must have been placed in service before November 6, 1990. § 44.

**Disaster area loss.** A casualty sustained in an area designated as a disaster area by the President of the United States. In such an event, the disaster loss may be treated as having occurred in the taxable year immediately preceding the year in which the disaster actually occurred. Thus, immediate tax benefits are provided to victims of a disaster. § 165(i).

**Disguised sale.** When a partner contributes property to the entity and soon thereafter receives a distribution from the partnership, the transactions are collapsed, and the distribution is seen as a purchase of the asset by the partnership. § 707(a)(2)(B).

**District Court.** A Federal District Court is a trial court for purposes of litigating (among others) Federal tax matters. It is the only trial court where a jury trial can be obtained.

**Dividend.** A nondeductible distribution by a corporation to a shareholder. A dividend constitutes gross income to the recipient if it is from the current or accumulated earnings and profits of the corporation.

**Dividends received deduction.** A deduction allowed a shareholder that is a corporation for dividends received from a domestic corporation. The deduction usually is 70 percent of the dividends received, but it could be 80 or 100 percent depending upon the ownership percentage held by the recipient corporation. §§ 243–246.

# E

**Earned income credit.** A tax credit designed to provide assistance to certain low-income individuals who generally have a qualifying child. This is a refundable credit. To receive the most beneficial treatment, the taxpayer must have qualifying children. However, it is possible to qualify for the credit without having a child. To calculate the credit for a taxpayer with one or more children for 2005, a statutory rate of 34 percent for one child (40 percent for two or more children) is multiplied by the earned income (subject to a statutory maximum of $7,830 with one qualifying child or $11,000 with two or more qualifying children). Once the earned income exceeds certain thresholds, the credit is phased out using a

15.98 percent rate for one qualifying child and a 21.06 percent rate for two qualifying children. For the qualifying taxpayer without children, the credit is calculated on a maximum earned income of $5,220 applying a 7.65 percent rate with the phaseout beginning later applying the same rate. § 32.

**Earnings and profits (E & P).** Measures the economic capacity of a corporation to make a distribution to shareholders that is not a return of capital. Such a distribution results in dividend income to the shareholders to the extent of the corporation's current and accumulated earnings and profits. §§ 312 and 316.

**Economic effect test.** Requirements that must be met before a special allocation may be used by a partnership. The premise behind the test is that each partner who receives an allocation of income or loss from a partnership bears the economic benefit or burden of the allocation.

**Economic income.** The change in the taxpayer's net worth, as measured in terms of market values, plus the value of the assets the taxpayer consumed during the year. Because of the impracticality of this income model, it is not used for tax purposes.

**Education expenses.** Employees may deduct education expenses that are incurred either (1) to maintain or improve existing job-related skills or (2) to meet the express requirements of the employer or the requirements imposed by law to retain employment status. The expenses are not deductible if the education is required to meet the minimum educational standards for the taxpayer's job or if the education qualifies the individual for a new trade or business. Reg. § 1.162–5.

**Educational savings bonds.** U.S. Series EE bonds whose proceeds are used for qualified higher educational expenses for the taxpayer, the taxpayer's spouse, or a dependent. The interest may be excluded from gross income, provided the taxpayer's adjusted gross income does not exceed certain amounts. § 135.

**Effectively connected income.** Income of a nonresident alien or non-U.S. corporation that is attributable to a trade or business operating in the United States. Income effectively connected to a U.S. trade or business usually is subject to U.S. income taxation, after deductions and allowing other credits, using the appropriate progressive tax rate schedule.

**e-file.** The electronic filing of a tax return. The filing is either direct or indirect. As to direct, the taxpayer goes online using a computer and tax return preparation software. Indirect filing occurs when a taxpayer utilizes an authorized IRS e-file provider. The provider often is the tax return preparer.

**Employment taxes.** Employment taxes are those taxes that an employer must pay on account of its employees. Employment taxes include FICA (Federal Insurance Contributions Act) and FUTA (Federal Unemployment Tax Act) taxes. Employment taxes are paid to the IRS in addition to income tax withholdings at specified intervals. Such taxes can be levied on the employees, the employer, or both. §§ 1401 and 1402.

**Entertainment expenses.** These expenses are deductible only if they are directly related to or associated with a trade or business. Various restrictions and documentation requirements have been imposed upon the deductibility of entertainment expenses to prevent abuses by taxpayers. See, for example, the provision contained in § 274(n) that disallows 50 percent of entertainment expenses. § 274.

**Entity concept.** The theory of partnership taxation under which a partnership is treated as a separate and distinct entity from the partners and has its own tax attributes.

**Estate tax.** A tax imposed on the right to transfer property by death. Thus, an estate tax is levied on the decedent's estate and not on the heir receiving the property. §§ 2001–2058.

**Estimated tax.** The amount of tax (including alternative minimum tax and self-employment tax) a taxpayer expects to owe for the year after subtracting tax credits and income tax withheld. The estimated tax must be paid in installments at designated intervals (e.g., for the individual taxpayer, by April 15, June 15, September 15, and January 15 of the following year). § 6654.

**Excise tax.** A tax on the manufacture, sale, or use of goods; on the carrying on of an occupation or activity; or on the transfer of property. Thus, the Federal estate and gift taxes are, theoretically, excise taxes.

# F

**Fair market value.** The amount at which property would change hands between a willing buyer and a willing seller, neither being under any compulsion to buy or to sell, and both having reasonable knowledge of the relevant facts. Reg. §§ 1.1001–1(a) and 20.2031–1(b).

**FDAP.** Income of a nonresident alien or non-U.S. corporation that is received in the form of dividends, interest, rents, royalties, certain compensation, premiums, annuities, and other "fixed, determinable, annual, or periodic" forms. FDAP income usually is subject to U.S. income taxation at a flat 30 percent tax rate.

**FICA tax.** An abbreviation that stands for Federal Insurance Contributions Act, commonly referred to as the Social Security tax. The FICA tax is comprised of the Social Security tax (old age, survivors, and disability insurance) and the Medicare tax (hospital insurance) and is imposed on both employers and employees. The employer is responsible for withholding from the employee's wages the Social Security tax at a rate of 6.2 percent on a maximum wage base of $90,000 (for 2005) and the Medicare tax at a rate of 1.45 percent (no maximum wage base). The employer is required to match the employee's contribution. § 3101.

**Fifty percent additional first-year depreciation.** This provision, which was effective for property acquired after May 5, 2003, and placed in service before January 1, 2005, provided for an additional cost recovery deduction of 50 percent in the tax year the qualified property was placed in service. Qualified property included most types of new property other than buildings. The taxpayer could elect to forgo this bonus depreciation. The taxpayer also could elect to use 30 percent bonus depreciation rather than the 50 percent bonus depreciation. See also *cost recovery system* and *thirty percent additional first-year depreciation.*

**Final Regulation.** The U.S. Treasury Department Regulations (abbreviated Reg.) represent the position of the IRS as to how the Internal Revenue Code is to be interpreted. Their purpose is to provide taxpayers and IRS personnel with rules of general and specific application to the various provisions of the tax law. Regulations are published in the *Federal Register* and in all tax services.

**Flexible spending plan.** An employee benefit plan that allows the employee to take a reduction in salary in exchange for the employer paying benefits that can be provided by the employer without the employee being required to recognize income (e.g., medical and child care benefits).

**Foreign earned income exclusion.** The foreign earned income exclusion is a relief provision that applies to U.S. citizens working in a foreign country. To qualify for the exclusion, the taxpayer must be either a bona fide resident of the foreign country or present in the foreign country for 330 days during any 12 consecutive months. The exclusion is limited to $80,000 per year. § 911.

**Foreign tax credit.** A U.S. citizen or resident who incurs or pays income taxes to a foreign country on income subject to U.S. tax may be able to claim some or all of these taxes as a credit against the U.S. income tax. §§ 27 and 901–905.

**Franchise.** An agreement that gives the transferee the right to distribute, sell, or provide goods, services, or facilities within a specified area. The cost of obtaining a franchise may be amortized over a statutory period of 15 years. In general, the franchisor's gain on the sale of franchise rights is an ordinary gain because the franchisor retains a significant power, right, or continuing interest in the subject of the franchise. §§ 197 and 1253.

**Franchise tax.** A tax levied on the right to do business in a state as a corporation. Although income considerations may come into play, the tax usually is based on the capitalization of the corporation.

**Fruit and tree metaphor.** The courts have held that an individual who earns income from property or services cannot assign that income to another. For example, a father cannot assign his earnings from commissions to his child and escape income tax on those amounts.

**FUTA tax.** An employment tax levied on employers. Jointly administered by the Federal and state governments, the tax provides funding for unemployment benefits. FUTA applies at a rate of 6.2 percent on the first $7,000 of covered wages paid during the year for each employee. The Federal government allows a credit for FUTA paid (or allowed under a merit rating system) to the state. The credit cannot exceed 5.4 percent of the covered wages. § 3301.

# G

**General business credit.** The summation of various nonrefundable business credits, including the tax credit for rehabilitation expenditures, business energy credit, welfare-to-work credit, work opportunity credit, research activities credit, low-income housing credit, disabled access credit, credit for small employer pension plan startup costs, and credit for employer-provided child care. The amount of general business credit that can be used to reduce the tax liability is limited to the taxpayer's net income tax reduced by the greater of (1) the tentative minimum tax or (2) 25 percent of the net regular tax liability that exceeds $25,000. Unused general business credits can be carried back 1 year and forward 20 years. § 38.

**General partnership.** A partnership that is owned by one or more general partners. Creditors of a general partnership can collect amounts owed them from both the partnership assets and the assets of the partners individually.

**Gift.** A transfer of property for less than adequate consideration. Gifts usually occur in a personal setting (such as between members of the same family). They are excluded from the income tax base but may be subject to a transfer tax.

**Gift tax.** A tax imposed on the transfer of property by gift. The tax is imposed upon the donor of a gift and is based on the fair market value of the property on the date of the gift. §§ 2501–2524.

**Goodwill.** The reputation and built-up business of a company. For accounting purposes, goodwill has no basis unless it is purchased. In the purchase of a business, goodwill generally is the difference between the purchase price and the fair market value of the assets acquired. Since acquired goodwill is a § 197 intangible asset, it is amortized for tax purposes over a 15-year period. Reg. § 1.167(a)–3.

**Gross income.** Income subject to the Federal income tax. Gross income does not include all economic income. That is, certain exclusions are allowed (e.g., interest on municipal bonds). For a manufacturing or merchandising business, gross income usually means gross profit (gross sales or gross receipts less cost of goods sold). § 61 and Reg. § 1.61–3(a).

**Guaranteed payments.** Payments made by a partnership to a partner for services rendered or for the use of capital to the extent that the payments are determined without regard to the income of the partnership. The payments are treated as though they were made to a nonpartner and thus are usually deductible by the entity. § 707(c).

# H

**Half-year convention.** The half-year convention is a cost recovery convention that assumes all property is placed in service at mid-year and thus provides for a half-year's cost recovery for that year.

**Head of household.** An unmarried individual who maintains a household for another and satisfies certain conditions set forth in § 2(b). This status enables the taxpayer to use a set of income tax rates that are lower than those applicable to other unmarried individuals but higher than those applicable to surviving spouses and married persons filing a joint return.

**Health Savings Account (HSA).** A medical savings account created in legislation enacted in December 2003 that is designed to replace and expand Archer Medical Savings Accounts. See also *medical savings account.*

**Holding period.** The period of time during which property has been held for income tax purposes. The holding period is significant in determining whether gain or loss from the sale or exchange of a capital asset is long term or short term. § 1223.

**Home equity loans.** Loans that utilize the personal residence of the taxpayer as security. The interest on such loans is deductible as qualified residence interest. However, interest is deductible only on the portion of the loan that does not exceed the lesser of (1) the fair market value of the residence, reduced by the acquisition indebtedness, or (2) $100,000 ($50,000 for married persons filing separate returns). A major benefit of a home equity loan is that there are no tracing rules regarding the use of the loan proceeds. § 163(h)(3).

**HOPE scholarship credit.** A tax credit for qualifying expenses paid for the first two years of postsecondary education. Room, board, and book costs are ineligible for the credit. The maximum credit available is $1,500 per year per student, computed as 100 percent of the first $1,000 of qualifying expenses, plus 50 percent of the second $1,000 of qualifying expenses. Eligible students include the taxpayer, taxpayer's spouse, and taxpayer's dependents. To qualify for the credit, a student must take at least one-half the full-time course load for at least one academic term at a qualifying educational institution. The credit is phased out for higher-income taxpayers. § 25A.

**Hybrid method.** A combination of the accrual and cash methods of accounting. That is, the taxpayer may account for some items of income on the accrual method (e.g., sales and cost of goods sold) and other items (e.g., interest income) on the cash method.

# I

**Implicit tax.** A tax that is paid through higher prices or lower returns on tax-favored investments rather than being paid directly to the government (i.e., an explicit tax). The value added tax is an example of an implicit tax.

**Inbound taxation.** U.S. tax effects when a non-U.S. person undertakes an investment or business activity in the U.S.

**Income.** For tax purposes, an increase in wealth that has been realized.

**Income tax treaties.** An agreement between the U.S. State Department and another country designed to alleviate potential double taxation and to share administrative information useful to tax agencies in both countries, relative to taxpayers with investment or business activities in both countries.

**Independent contractor.** A self-employed person as distinguished from one who is employed as an employee.

**Individual Retirement Account (IRA).** A type of retirement plan to which an individual with earned income can contribute a maximum of $3,000 ($3,000 each in the case of a married couple with a spousal IRA) per tax year for 2002–2004. The maximum amount increases to $4,000 in 2005 and to $5,000 in 2008. IRAs can be classified as traditional IRAs or Roth IRAs. With a traditional IRA, an individual can contribute and deduct a maximum of $4,000 per tax year in 2005. The deduction is a deduction *for* AGI. However, if the individual is an active participant in another qualified retirement plan, the deduction is phased out proportionally between certain AGI ranges (note that the phaseout limits the amount of the deduction and not the amount of the contribution). With a Roth IRA, an individual can contribute a maximum of $4,000 per tax year in 2005. No deduction is permitted. However, if a five-year holding period requirement is satisfied and if the distribution is a qualified distribution, the taxpayer can make tax-free withdrawals from a Roth IRA. The maximum annual contribution is phased out proportionally between certain AGI ranges. §§ 219 and 408A.

**Inheritance tax.** A tax imposed on the right to receive property from a decedent. Thus, theoretically, an inheritance tax is imposed on the heir. The Federal estate tax is imposed on the estate.

**Inside basis.** A partnership's basis in the assets it owns.

**Intangible drilling and development costs (IDC).** Taxpayers may elect to expense or capitalize (subject to amortization) intangible drilling and development costs. However, ordinary income recapture provisions apply to oil and gas properties on a sale or other disposition if the expense method is elected. §§ 263(c) and 1254(a).

**Interpretive Regulation.** A Regulation issued by the Treasury Department that purports to explain the meaning of a particular Code Section. An interpretive Regulation is given less deference than a legislative Regulation.

**Investment interest.** Payment for the use of funds used to acquire assets that produce investment income. The deduction for investment interest is limited to net investment income for the tax year.

**Involuntary conversion.** The loss or destruction of property through theft, casualty, or condemnation. Any gain realized on an involuntary conversion can, at the taxpayer's election, be deferred for Federal income tax purposes if the owner reinvests the proceeds within a prescribed period of time in property that is similar or related in service or use. § 1033.

**Itemized deductions.** Personal and employee expenditures allowed by the Code as deductions from adjusted gross income. Examples include certain medical expenses, interest on home mortgages, state income taxes, and charitable contributions. Itemized deductions are reported on Schedule A of Form 1040. Certain miscellaneous itemized deductions are reduced by 2 percent of the taxpayer's adjusted gross income. In addition, a taxpayer whose adjusted gross income exceeds a certain level (indexed annually) must reduce the itemized deductions by 3 percent of the excess of adjusted gross income over that level. Medical, casualty and theft, and investment interest deductions are not subject to the 3 percent reduction. The 3 percent reduction may not reduce itemized deductions that are subject to the reduction to below 20 percent of their initial amount. §§ 63(d), 67, and 68.

# K

**Keogh plan.** A retirement plan that is available to self-employed taxpayers; also referred to as an H.R. 10 plan. Under such plans, in 2005, a taxpayer may deduct each year up to either 100 percent of net earnings from self-employment or $42,000, whichever is less. If the plan is a profit sharing plan, the percentage is 25 percent.

**Kiddie tax.** Passive income, such as interest and dividends, that is recognized by a child under age 14 is taxed to him or her at the rates that would have applied had the income been incurred by the child's parents, generally to the extent that the income exceeds $1,600. The additional tax is assessed regardless of the source of the income or the income's underlying property. If the child's parents are divorced, the custodial parent's rates are used. The parents' rates reflect any applicable alternative minimum tax and the phaseouts of lower tax brackets and other deductions. § 1(g).

# L

**Legislative Regulation.** Some Code Sections give the Secretary of the Treasury or his delegate the authority to prescribe Regulations to carry out the details of administration or to otherwise complete the operating rules. Regulations issued pursuant to this type of authority truly possess the force and effect of law. In effect, Congress is almost delegating its legislative powers to the Treasury Department.

**Lessee.** One who rents property from another. In the case of real estate, the lessee is also known as the tenant.

**Lessor.** One who rents property to another. In the case of real estate, the lessor is also known as the landlord.

**Letter ruling.** The written response of the IRS to a taxpayer's request for interpretation of the revenue laws, with respect to a proposed transaction (e.g., concerning the tax-free status of a reorganization). Not to be relied on as precedent by other than the party who requested the ruling.

**Life insurance proceeds.** A specified sum (the face value or maturity value of the policy) paid to the designated beneficiary of the policy by the life insurance company upon the death of the insured.

**Lifetime learning credit.** A tax credit for qualifying expenses for taxpayers pursuing education beyond the first two years of postsecondary education. Individuals who are completing their last two years of undergraduate studies, pursuing graduate or professional degrees, or otherwise seeking new job skills or maintaining existing job skills are all eligible for the credit. Eligible individuals include the taxpayer, taxpayer's spouse, and taxpayer's dependents. The maximum credit is 20 percent of the first $10,000 of qualifying expenses and is computed per taxpayer. The credit is phased out for higher-income taxpayers. § 25A.

**Like-kind exchange.** An exchange of property held for productive use in a trade or business or for investment (except inventory and stocks and bonds) for other investment or trade or business property. Unless non-like-kind property (boot) is received, the exchange is fully nontaxable. § 1031.

**Limited liability company (LLC).** A form of entity allowed by all of the states. The entity is taxed as a partnership in which all members or owners of the LLC are treated much like limited partners. There are no restrictions on ownership, all members may participate in management, and none has personal liability for the entity's debts.

**Limited liability partnership (LLP).** A form of entity allowed by many of the states, where a general partnership registers with the state as an LLP. Owners are general partners, but a partner is not liable for any malpractice committed by other partners. The personal assets of the partners are at risk for the entity's contractual liabilities, such as accounts payable. The personal assets of a specific partner are at risk for his or her own professional malpractice and tort liability, and for malpractice and torts committed by those whom he or she supervises.

**Limited partnership.** A partnership in which some of the partners are limited partners. At least one of the partners in a limited partnership must be a general partner.

**Listed property.** The term listed property includes (1) any passenger automobile, (2) any other property used as a means of transportation, (3) any property of a type generally used for purposes of entertainment, recreation, or amusement, (4) any computer or peripheral equipment (with an exception for exclusive business use), (5) any cellular telephone (or other similar telecommunications equipment), and (6) any other property of a type specified in the Regulations. If listed property is predominantly used for business, the taxpayer is allowed to use the statutory percentage method of cost recovery. Otherwise, the straight-line cost recovery method must be used. § 280F.

**Long-term nonpersonal-use capital assets.** Includes investment property with a long-term holding period. Such property disposed of by casualty or theft may receive § 1231 treatment.

# M

**Manufacturers' deduction.** A deduction allowed to sole proprietors, C corporations, partnerships, S corporations, cooperatives, estates, and trusts for certain production activities. The deduction rate is 3 percent for 2005–2006 and is scheduled to increase to 6 percent for 2007 through 2009 and to 9 percent for 2010 and thereafter. § 199.

**Marriage penalty.** The additional tax liability that results for a married couple when compared with what their tax liability would be if they were not married and filed separate returns.

**Material participation.** If an individual taxpayer materially participates in a nonrental trade or business activity, any loss from that activity is treated as an active loss that can be offset against active income. Material participation is achieved by meeting any one of seven tests provided in the Regulations. § 469(h).

**Medical expenses.** Medical expenses of an individual, spouse, and dependents are allowed as an itemized deduction to the extent that such amounts (less insurance reimbursements) exceed 7.5 percent of adjusted gross income. § 213.

**Medical savings account (MSA).** A plan available to employees of small firms (50 or fewer employees) with high-deductible health insurance. The employee can place money in the fund and then deduct the contributions (within limits) from gross income. If the employer contributes to the fund, the employee can exclude the contribution from gross income. Income earned from the fund and withdrawals for medical care are not subject to tax. See also *Health Savings Account (HSA)*. §§ 106(b) and 220.

**Mid-month convention.** A cost recovery convention that assumes property is placed in service in the middle of the month that it is actually placed in service.

**Mid-quarter convention.** A cost recovery convention that assumes property placed in service during the year is placed in service at the middle of the quarter in which it is actually placed in service. The mid-quarter convention applies if more than 40 percent of the value of property (other than eligible real estate) is placed in service during the last quarter of the year.

**Minimum tax credit (AMT).** When a corporation pays an alternative minimum tax (AMT), a minimum tax credit is created on a dollar-for-dollar basis, to be applied against regular tax liabilities incurred in future years. The credit is carried forward indefinitely, but it is not carried back. The effect of the credit for corporate taxpayers alternating between the AMT and regular tax models is to make the AMT liabilities a prepayment of regular taxes. Noncorporate AMT taxpayers are allowed the credit only with respect to the elements of the AMT that reflect timing differences between the two tax models. § 53.

**Miscellaneous itemized deductions.** A special category of itemized deductions that includes such expenses as professional dues, tax return preparation fees, job-hunting costs, unreimbursed employee business expenses, and certain investment expenses. Such expenses are deductible only to the extent they exceed 2 percent of adjusted gross income. § 67.

**Modified accelerated cost recovery system (MACRS).** A method in which the cost of tangible property is recovered over a prescribed period of time. Enacted by the Economic Recovery Tax Act (ERTA) of 1981 and substantially modified by the Tax Reform Act (TRA) of 1986 (the modified system is referred to as MACRS), the approach disregards salvage value, imposes a period of cost recovery that depends upon the classification of the asset into one of various recovery periods, and prescribes the applicable percentage of cost that can be deducted each year. § 168.

**Moving expenses.** A deduction *for* AGI is permitted to employees and self-employed individuals provided certain tests are met. The taxpayer's new job must be at least 50 miles farther from the old residence than the old residence was from the former place of work. In addition, an employee must be employed on a full-time basis at the new location for 39 weeks in the 12-month period following the move. Deductible moving expenses include the cost of moving the household and personal effects, transportation, and lodging expenses during the move. The cost of meals during the move is not deductible. Qualified moving expenses that are paid (or reimbursed) by the employer can be excluded from the employee's gross income. In this case, the related deduction by the employee is not permitted. §§ 62(a)(15), 132(a)(6), and 217.

**Multiple support agreement.** To qualify for a dependency exemption, the support test must be satisfied. This requires that over 50 percent of the support of the potential dependent be provided by the taxpayer. Where no one person provides more than 50 percent of the support, a multiple support agreement enables a taxpayer to still qualify for the dependency exemption. Any person who contributed more than 10 percent of the support is entitled to claim the exemption if each person in the group who contributed more than 10 percent files a written consent (Form 2120). Each person who is a party to the multiple support agreement must meet all the other requirements for claiming the dependency exemption. § 152(c).

**Multistate corporation.** A corporation that has operations in more than one of the states of the United States. Issues arise relative to the assignment of appropriate amounts of the entity's taxable income to the states in which it has a presence. See also *allocate, apportion,* and *nexus.*

**Multistate Tax Commission (MTC).** A regulatory body of which about half of the U.S. states are members. The MTC develops operating rules and regulations to compute and assign the total taxable income of a multistate taxpayer to specific states.

# N

**Net capital gain.** The excess of the net long-term capital gain for the tax year over the net short-term capital loss. The net capital gain of an individual taxpayer is eligible for the alternative tax. § 1222(11).

**Net capital loss.** The excess of the losses from sales or exchanges of capital assets over the gains from sales or exchanges of such assets. Up to $3,000 per year of the net capital loss may be deductible by noncorporate taxpayers against ordinary income. The excess net capital loss carries over to future tax years. For corporate taxpayers, the net capital loss cannot be offset against ordinary income, but it can be carried back three years and forward five years to offset net capital gains. §§ 1211, 1212, and 1221(10).

**Net investment income.** The excess of investment income over investment expenses. Investment expenses are those deductible expenses directly connected with the production of investment income. Investment expenses do not include investment interest. The deduction for investment interest for the tax year is limited to net investment income. § 163(d).

**Net operating loss.** To mitigate the effect of the annual accounting period concept, § 172 allows taxpayers to use an excess loss of one year as a deduction for certain past or future years. In this regard, a carryback period of 2 years and a carryforward period of 20 years currently are allowed.

**Nexus.** A multistate taxpayer's taxable income can be apportioned to a specific state only if the taxpayer has established a sufficient presence, or nexus with that state. State law, which often follows the UDITPA, specifies various activities that lead to nexus in various states.

**No-additional-cost services.** Services that the employer may provide the employee at no additional cost to the employer. Generally, the benefit is the ability to utilize the employer's excess capacity (e.g., vacant seats on an airliner). Such amounts are excludible from the recipient's gross income. § 132(b).

**Nonaccountable plan.** An expense reimbursement plan that does not have an accountability feature. The result is that employee expenses must be claimed as deductions *from* AGI. An exception is moving expenses that are deductions *for* AGI.

**Nonacquiescence.** Disagreement by the IRS on the result reached in certain judicial decisions. *Nonacq.* or *NA.*

**Nonbusiness bad debt.** A bad debt loss that is not incurred in connection with a creditor's trade or business. The loss is classified as a short-term capital loss and is allowed only in the year the debt becomes entirely worthless. In addition to family loans, many investor losses are nonbusiness bad debts. § 166(d).

**Nonrecourse debt.** Debt secured by the property that it is used to purchase. The purchaser of the property is not personally liable for the debt upon default. Rather, the creditor's recourse is to repossess the related property. Nonrecourse debt generally does not increase the purchaser's at-risk amount.

**Nonresident alien.** An individual who is neither a citizen nor a resident of the United States. Citizenship is determined under the immigration and naturalization laws of the United States. Residency is determined under § 7701(b) of the Internal Revenue Code. Certain activities of the nonresident alien are subject to U.S. taxation.

**Nontaxable exchange.** A transaction in which realized gains or losses are not recognized. The recognition of gain or loss is postponed (deferred) until the property received in the nontaxable exchange is subsequently disposed of in a taxable transaction. Examples are § 1031 like-kind exchanges and § 1033 involuntary conversions.

# O

**Occupational tax.** A tax imposed on various trades or businesses. A license fee that enables a taxpayer to engage in a particular occupation.

**Office in the home expenses.** Employment and business-related expenses attributable to the use of a residence (e.g., den or office) are allowed only if the portion of the residence is exclusively used on a regular basis as a principal place of business of the taxpayer or as a place of business that is used by patients, clients, or customers. If the expenses are incurred by an employee, the use must be for the convenience of the employer as opposed to being merely appropriate and helpful. § 280A.

**Options.** The sale or exchange of an option to buy or sell property results in capital gain or loss if the property is a capital asset. Generally, the closing of an option transaction results in short-term capital gain or loss to the writer of the call and the purchaser of the call option. § 1234.

**Ordinary and necessary.** An ordinary expense is one that is common and accepted in the general industry or type of activity in which the taxpayer is engaged. It comprises one of the tests for the deductibility of expenses incurred or paid in connection with a trade or business; for the production or collection of income; for the management, conservation, or maintenance of property held for the production of income; or in connection with the determination, collection, or refund of any tax. §§ 162(a) and 212. A necessary expense is one that is appropriate and helpful in furthering the taxpayer's business or income-producing activity. §§ 162(a) and 212.

**Ordinary income property.** Property contributed to a charitable organization that, if sold rather than contributed, would have resulted in other than long-term capital gain to the donor (i.e., ordinary income property and short-term capital gain property). Examples are inventory and capital assets held for less than the long-term holding period.

**Organizational expenditures.** Items incurred early in the life of a corporate entity, qualifying for a special treatment under Federal tax law. A corporation can elect to immediately expense the first $5,000 (subject to phaseout) of organizational expenditures and generally amortize the balance over a period of 180 months or more. Amortizable expenditures exclude those incurred to obtain capital (underwriting fees) or assets (subject to cost recovery). Typically, amortizable expenditures include legal and accounting fees and state incorporation payments. Such items must be incurred by the end of the entity's first tax year. § 248.

**Original issue discount.** The difference between the issue price of a debt obligation (e.g., a corporate bond) and the maturity value of the obligation when the issue price is *less than* the maturity value. OID represents interest and must be amortized over the life of the debt obligation using the effective interest method. The difference is not considered to be original issue discount for tax purposes when it is less than one-fourth of 1 percent of the redemption price at maturity multiplied by the number of years to maturity. §§ 1272 and 1273(a)(3).

**Outbound taxation.** U.S. tax effects when a U.S. person undertakes an investment or business activity outside the United States.

**Outside basis.** A partner's basis in his or her partnership interest.

# P

**Parent-subsidiary controlled group.** A controlled or affiliated group of corporations, where at least one corporation is at least 80 percent owned by one or more of the others. The affiliated group definition is more difficult to meet.

**Passive investment holding company.** A means by which a multistate taxpayer can reduce its overall effective tax rate by isolating investment income in a no- or low-tax state.

**Passive investment income (PII).** Gross receipts from royalties, certain rents, dividends, interest, annuities, and gains from the sale or exchange of stock and securities. With certain exceptions, if the passive investment income of an S corporation exceeds 25 percent of the corporation's gross receipts for three consecutive years, S status is lost. In another circumstance, if the S corporation has excessive passive income, a penalty tax is imposed on the S corporation. §§ 1362(d)(3) and 1375.

**Passive loss.** Any loss from (1) activities in which the taxpayer does not materially participate or (2) rental activities (subject to certain exceptions). Net passive losses cannot be used to offset income from nonpassive sources. Rather, they are suspended until the taxpayer either generates net passive income (and a deduction of such losses is allowed) or disposes of the underlying property (at which time the loss deductions are allowed in full). One relief provision allows landlords who actively participate in the rental activities to deduct up to $25,000 of passive losses annually. However, a phaseout of the $25,000 amount commences when the landlord's AGI exceeds $100,000. Another relief provision applies for material participation in a real estate trade or business. § 469.

**Patent.** A patent is an intangible asset that may be amortized over a statutory 15-year period as a § 197 intangible. The sale of a patent usually results in favorable long-term capital gain treatment. §§ 197 and 1235.

**Payroll factor.** The proportion of a multistate corporation's total payroll that is traceable to a specific state. Used in determining the taxable income that is to be apportioned to that state.

**Percentage depletion.** Percentage depletion is depletion based on a statutory percentage applied to the gross income from the property. The taxpayer deducts the greater of cost depletion or percentage depletion. § 613.

**Permanent establishment (PE).** A level of business activity, as defined under an income tax treaty, that subjects the taxpayer to taxation in a country other than that in which the taxpayer is based. Often evidenced by the presence of a plant, office, or other fixed place of business. Inventory storage and temporary activities do not rise to the level of a PE. PE is the treaty's equivalent to nexus.

**Personal exemption.** The tax law provides an exemption for each individual taxpayer and an additional exemption for the taxpayer's spouse if a joint return is filed. An individual may also claim a dependency exemption for each dependent, provided certain tests are met. The amount of the personal and dependency exemptions is $3,200 in 2005 ($3,100 in 2004). The amount is indexed for inflation. The exemption is subject to phaseout once adjusted gross income exceeds certain statutory threshold amounts.

**Personal service corporation (PSC).** A corporation whose principal activity is the performance of personal services (e.g., health, law, engineering, architecture, accounting, actuarial science, performing arts, or consulting) and where such services are substantially performed by the employee-owners. The 35 percent statutory income tax rate applies to PSCs.

**Personalty.** All property that is not attached to real estate (realty) and is movable. Examples of personalty are machinery, automobiles, clothing, household furnishings, inventory, and personal effects.

**Points.** Loan origination fees that may be deductible as interest by a buyer of property. A seller of property who pays points reduces the selling price by the amount of the points paid for the buyer. While the seller is not permitted to deduct this amount as interest, the buyer may do so. § 461(g).

**Portfolio income.** Income from interest, dividends, certain rentals, royalties, capital gains, or other investment sources. Net passive losses cannot be used to offset net portfolio income. § 469.

**Precedent.** A previously decided court decision that is recognized as authority for the disposition of future decisions.

**Precontribution gain or loss.** Partnerships allow for a variety of special allocations of gain or loss among the partners, but gain or loss that is "built in" on an asset contributed to the partnership is assigned specifically to the contributing partner. § 704(c)(1)(A).

**Private activity bond.** Interest on state and local bonds is excludible from gross income. § 103. Certain such bonds are labeled private activity bonds. Although the interest on such bonds is excludible for regular income tax purposes, it is treated as a tax preference in calculating the AMT.

**Procedural Regulation.** A Regulation issued by the Treasury Department that is a housekeeping-type instruction indicating information that taxpayers should provide the IRS as well as information about the internal management and conduct of the IRS itself.

**Profit and loss sharing ratios.** Specified in the partnership agreement and used to determine each partner's allocation of ordinary taxable income and separately stated items. Profits and losses can be shared in different ratios. The ratios can be changed by amending the partnership agreement. § 704(a).

**Profits (loss) interest.** A partner's percentage allocation of partnership operating results, determined by the profit and loss sharing ratios.

**Property.** Assets defined in the broadest legal sense. Property includes the unrealized receivables of a cash basis taxpayer, but not services rendered. § 351.

**Property dividend.** Generally treated in the same manner as a cash distribution, measured by the fair market value of the property on the date of distribution. The portion of the distribution representing E & P is a dividend; any excess is treated as a return of capital. Distribution of appreciated property causes the distributing corporation to recognize gain. The distributing corporation does not recognize loss on property that has depreciated in value. §§ 301 and 311.

**Property factor.** The proportion of a multistate corporation's total property that is traceable to a specific state. Used in determining the taxable income that is to be apportioned to that state.

**Proposed Regulation.** A Regulation issued by the Treasury Department in proposed, rather than final, form. The interval between the proposal of a Regulation and its finalization permits taxpayers and other interested parties to comment on the propriety of the proposal.

**Proprietorship.** A business entity for which there is a single owner. The net profit of the entity is reported on the owner's Federal income tax return (Schedule C of Form 1040).

**Public Law 86–272.** A congressional limit on the ability of the state to force a multistate taxpayer to assign income to that state. Under P.L. 86–272, where orders for tangible personal property are both filled and delivered outside the state, the entity must establish more than the mere solicitation of such orders took place in-state before any income can be apportioned to the state.

**Punitive damages.** Damages received or paid by the taxpayer can be classified as compensatory damages or as punitive damages. Punitive damages are those awarded to punish the defendant for gross negligence or the intentional infliction of harm. Such damages are includible in gross income. § 104(a)(2).

# Q

**Qualified dividend income.** Dividends that are eligible for the beneficial 5 percent or 15 percent tax rate. Excluded are certain dividends from foreign corporations, dividends from tax-exempt entities, and dividends that do not satisfy the holding period requirement. A dividend from a foreign corporation is eligible for qualified dividend status only if one of the following requirements is met: (1) the foreign corporation's stock is traded on an established U.S. securities market, or (2) the foreign corporation is eligible for the benefits of a comprehensive income tax treaty between its country of incorporation and the United States. To satisfy the holding period requirement, the stock on which the dividend is paid must have been held for more than 60 days during the 120-day period beginning 60 days before the ex-dividend date.

**Qualified employee discounts.** Discounts offered employees on merchandise or services that the employer ordinarily sells or provides to customers. The discounts must be generally available to all employees. In the case of property, the discount cannot exceed the employer's gross profit (the sales price cannot be less than the employer's cost). In the case of services, the discounts cannot exceed 20 percent of the normal sales price. § 132.

**Qualified nonrecourse debt.** Debt issued on realty by a bank, retirement plan, or governmental agency. Included in the at-risk amount by the investor. § 465(b)(6).

**Qualified production income.** The base for computing the manufacturers' deduction. It comprises qualified production receipts less allocable cost of goods sold and other deductions. § 199.

**Qualified real property business indebtedness.** Indebtedness that was incurred or assumed by the taxpayer in connection with real property used in a trade or business and is secured by such real property. The taxpayer must not be a C corporation. For qualified real property business indebtedness, the taxpayer may elect to exclude some or all of the income realized from cancellation of debt on qualified real property. If the election is made, the basis of the property must be reduced by the amount excluded. The amount excluded cannot be greater than the excess of the principal amount of the outstanding debt over the fair market value (net of any other debt outstanding on the property) of the property securing the debt. § 108(c).

**Qualified residence interest.** A term relevant in determining the amount of interest expense the individual taxpayer may deduct as an itemized deduction for what otherwise would be disallowed as a component of personal interest (consumer interest). Qualified residence interest consists of interest paid on qualified residences (principal residence and one other residence) of the taxpayer. Debt that qualifies as qualified residence interest is limited to $1 million of debt to acquire, construct, or substantially improve qualified residences (acquisition indebtedness) plus $100,000 of other debt secured by qualified residences (home equity indebtedness). The home equity indebtedness may not exceed the fair market value of a qualified residence reduced by the acquisition indebtedness for that residence. § 163(h)(3).

**Qualified small business stock.** Stock in a qualified small business corporation, purchased as part of an original issue after August 10, 1993. The shareholder may exclude from gross income 50 percent of the realized gain on the sale of the stock, if he or she held the stock for more than five years. § 1202.

**Qualified transportation fringes.** Transportation benefits provided by the employer to the employee. Such benefits include (1) transportation in a commuter highway vehicle between the employee's residence and the place of employment, (2) a transit pass, and (3) qualified parking. Qualified transportation fringes are excludible from the employee's gross income to the extent categories (1) and (2) above do not exceed $105 per month in 2005 and category (3) does not exceed $200 per month in 2005. These amounts are indexed annually for inflation. § 132(f).

**Qualifying child.** An individual who, as to the taxpayer, satisfies the relationship, abode, and age tests. To be claimed as a dependent, such individual must also meet the citizenship and joint return tests and not be self-supporting. §§ 152(a)(1) and (c).

**Qualifying relative.** An individual who, as to the taxpayer, satisfies the relationship, gross income, support, citizenship, and joint return tests. Such an individual can be claimed as a dependent of the taxpayer. §§ 152(a)(2) and (d).

# R

**Realized gain or loss.** The difference between the amount realized upon the sale or other disposition of property and the adjusted basis of the property. § 1001.

**Realty.** Real estate.

**Reasonableness requirement.** The Code includes a reasonableness requirement with respect to the deduction of salaries and other compensation for services. What constitutes reasonableness is a question of fact. If an expense is unreasonable, the amount that is classified as unreasonable is not allowed as a deduction. The question of reasonableness generally arises with respect to closely held corporations where there is no separation of ownership and management. § 162(a)(1).

**Recognized gain or loss.** The portion of realized gain or loss subject to income taxation.

**Recourse debt.** Debt for which the lender may both foreclose on the property and assess a guarantor for any payments due under the loan. A lender may also make a claim against the assets of any general partner in a partnership to which debt is issued, without regard to whether the partner has guaranteed the debt.

**Recovery of capital doctrine.** When a taxable sale or exchange occurs, the seller may be permitted to recover his or her investment (or other adjusted basis) in the property before gain or loss is recognized.

**Regular corporation.** See *C corporation*.

**Rehabilitation expenditures credit.** A credit that is based on expenditures incurred to rehabilitate industrial and commercial buildings and certified historic structures. The credit is intended to discourage businesses from moving from older, economically distressed areas to newer locations and to encourage the preservation of historic structures. § 47.

**Rehabilitation expenditures credit recapture.** When property that qualifies for the rehabilitation expenditures credit is disposed of or ceases to be used in the trade or business of the taxpayer, some or all of the tax credit claimed on the property may be recaptured as additional tax liability. The amount of the recapture is the difference between the amount of the credit claimed originally and what should have been claimed in light of the length of time the property was actually held or used for qualifying purposes. § 50.

**Related corporation.** See *controlled group*.

**Related-party transactions.** Various Code Sections define related parties and often include a variety of persons within this (usually detrimental) category. Generally, related parties are accorded different tax treatment from that applicable to other taxpayers who enter into similar transactions. For instance, realized losses that are generated between related parties are not recognized in the year of the loss (§ 267). However, these deferred losses can be used to offset recognized gains that occur upon the subsequent sale of the asset to a nonrelated party. Other uses of a related-party definition include the conversion of gain upon the sale of a depreciable asset into all ordinary income (§ 1239) and the identification of constructive ownership of stock relative to corporate distributions, redemptions, liquidations, reorganizations, and compensation.

**Rental activity.** Any activity where payments are received principally for the use of tangible property is a rental activity. Temporary Regulations provide that in certain circumstances activities involving rentals of real and personal property are not to be *treated* as rental activities. The Temporary Regulations list six exceptions.

**Research activities credit.** A tax credit whose purpose is to encourage research and development. It consists of two components: the incremental research activities credit and the basic research credit. The incremental research activities credit is equal to 20 percent of the excess qualified research expenditures over the base amount. The basic research credit is equal to 20 percent of the excess of basic research payments over the base amount. § 41.

**Research and experimental expenditures.** The Code provides three alternatives for the tax treatment of research and experimental expenditures. They may be expensed in the year paid or incurred, deferred subject to amortization, or capitalized. If the taxpayer does not elect to expense such costs or to defer them subject to amortization (over 60 months), the expenditures must be capitalized. § 174. Two types of research activities credits are available: the basic research credit and the incremental research activities credit. The rate for each type is 20 percent. § 41.

**Reserve method.** A method of accounting whereby an allowance is permitted for estimated uncollectible accounts. Actual write-offs are charged to the reserve, and recoveries of amounts previously written off are credited to the reserve. The Code permits only certain financial institutions to use the reserve method. § 166.

**Residential rental real estate.** Buildings for which at least 80 percent of the gross rents are from dwelling units (e.g., an apartment building). This type of building is distinguished from nonresidential (commercial or industrial) buildings in applying the recapture of depreciation provisions. The term also is relevant in distinguishing between buildings that are eligible for a 27.5-year life versus a 39-year life for MACRS purposes. Generally, residential buildings receive preferential treatment. § 168(e)(2)(A).

**Revenue Procedure.** A matter of procedural importance to both taxpayers and the IRS concerning the administration of the tax laws is issued as a Revenue Procedure (abbreviated Rev.Proc.). A Revenue Procedure is first published in an *Internal Revenue Bulletin* (I.R.B.) and later transferred to the appropriate *Cumulative Bulletin* (C.B.). Both the *Internal Revenue Bulletins* and the *Cumulative Bulletins* are published by the U.S. Government Printing Office.

**Revenue Ruling.** A Revenue Ruling (abbreviated Rev.Rul.) is issued by the National Office of the IRS to express an official interpretation of the tax law as applied to specific transactions. It is more limited in application than a Regulation. A Revenue Ruling is first published in an *Internal Revenue Bulletin* (I.R.B.) and later transferred to the appropriate *Cumulative Bulletin* (C.B.). Both the *Internal Revenue Bulletins* and the *Cumulative Bulletins* are published by the U.S. Government Printing Office.

# S

**S corporation.** The designation for a small business corporation. See also *Subchapter S*.

**Sale or exchange.** A requirement for the recognition of capital gain or loss. Generally, the seller of property must receive money or relief from debt in order to have sold the property. An exchange involves the transfer of property for other property. Thus, collection of a debt is neither a sale nor an exchange. The term *sale or exchange* is not defined by the Code.

**Sales factor.** The proportion of a multistate corporation's total sales that is traceable to a specific state. Used in determining the taxable income that is to be apportioned to that state.

**Sales tax.** A state- or local-level tax on the retail sale of specified property. Generally, the purchaser pays the tax, but the seller collects it, as an agent for the government. Various taxing jurisdictions allow exemptions for purchases of specific items, including certain food, services, and manufacturing equipment. If the purchaser and seller are in different states, a use tax usually applies.

**Schedule M–1.** On the Form 1120, a reconciliation of book net income with Federal taxable income. Accounts for timing and permanent differences in the two computations, such as depreciation differences, exempt income, and nondeductible items. On Forms 1120S and 1065, the Schedule M–1 reconciles book income with owners' aggregate ordinary taxable income.

**Schedule M–3.** An *expanded* reconciliation of book net income with Federal taxable income (see *Schedule M–1*). Applies to corporations with total assets of $10 million or more.

**Scholarships.** Scholarships are generally excluded from the gross income of the recipient unless the payments are a disguised form of compensation for services rendered. However, the Code imposes restrictions on the exclusion. The recipient must be a degree candidate. The excluded amount is limited to amounts used for tuition, fees, books, supplies, and equipment required for courses of instruction. Amounts received for room and board are not eligible for the exclusion. § 117.

**Section 179 expensing election.** The ability to deduct a capital expenditure in the year an asset is placed in service rather than over the asset's useful life or cost recovery period. The annual ceiling on the deduction is $105,000 for 2005 ($102,000 for 2004). However, the deduction is reduced dollar for dollar when § 179 property placed in service during the taxable year exceeds $420,000 in 2005 ($410,000 in 2004). In addition, the amount expensed under § 179 cannot exceed the aggregate amount of taxable income derived from the conduct of any trade or business by the taxpayer.

**Section 1231 gains and losses.** If the combined gains and losses from the taxable dispositions of § 1231 assets plus the net gain from business involuntary conversions (of both § 1231 assets and long-term capital assets) is a gain, the gains and losses are treated as long-term capital gains and losses. In arriving at § 1231 gains, however, the depreciation recapture provisions (e.g., §§ 1245 and 1250) are first applied to produce ordinary income. If the net result of the combination is a loss, the gains and losses from § 1231 assets are treated as ordinary gains and losses. § 1231(a).

**Section 1231 lookback.** In order for gain to be classified as § 1231 gain, the gain must survive the § 1231 lookback. To the extent of nonrecaptured § 1231 losses for the five prior tax years, the gain is classified as ordinary income. § 1231(c).

**Section 1231 property.** Depreciable assets and real estate used in trade or business and held for the required long-term holding period. Under certain circumstances, the classification also includes timber, coal, domestic iron ore, livestock (held for draft, breeding, dairy, or sporting purposes), and unharvested crops. § 1231(b).

**Section 1245 property.** Property that is subject to the recapture of depreciation under § 1245. For a definition of § 1245 property, see § 1245(a)(3).

**Section 1245 recapture.** Upon a taxable disposition of § 1245 property, all depreciation claimed on the property is recaptured as ordinary income (but not to exceed recognized gain from the disposition).

**Section 1250 property.** Real estate that is subject to the recapture of depreciation under § 1250. For a definition of § 1250 property, see § 1250(c).

**Section 1250 recapture.** Upon a taxable disposition of § 1250 property, some of the depreciation or cost recovery claimed on the property may be recaptured as ordinary income.

**Securities.** Generally, stock, debt, and other financial assets. To the extent securities other than the stock of the transferee corporation are received in a § 351 exchange, the new shareholder realizes a gain.

**Self-employment tax.** In 2005, a tax of 12.4 percent is levied on individuals with net earnings from self-employment (up to $90,000) to provide Social Security benefits (i.e., the old age, survivors, and disability insurance portion) for such individuals. In addition, in 2005, a tax of 2.9 percent is levied on individuals with net earnings from self-employment (with no statutory ceiling) to provide Medicare benefits (i.e., the hospital insurance portion) for such individuals. If a self-employed individual also receives wages from an employer that are subject to FICA, the self-employment tax will be reduced if total income subject to Social Security is more than $90,000 in 2005. A partial deduction is allowed in calculating the self-employment tax. Individuals with net earnings of $400 or more from self-employment are subject to this tax. §§ 1401 and 1402.

**Separate foreign tax credit limitation category.** The foreign tax credit of a taxpayer is computed for each of several types of income sources, as specified by the Code to limit the results of tax planning. FTC income "baskets" include passive, ordinary, and shipping income. The FTC for the year is the sum of the credits as computed within all of the taxpayer's separate FTC baskets used for the tax year.

**Separately stated item.** Any item of a partnership or S corporation that might be taxed differently to any two owners of the entity. These amounts are not included in ordinary income of the entity, but are instead reported separately to the owners; tax consequences are determined at the owner level. §§ 702(a) and 1366(a)(1).

**Short sale.** A short sale occurs when a taxpayer sells borrowed property (usually stock) and repays the lender with substantially identical property either held on the date of the short sale or purchased after the sale. No gain or loss is recognized until the short sale is closed, and such gain or loss is generally short term. § 1233.

**Significant participation activity.** There are seven tests to determine whether an individual has achieved material participation in an activity, one of which is based on more than 500 hours of participation in significant participation activities. A significant participation activity is one in which the individual's participation exceeds 100 hours during the year. Reg. § 1.469–5T.

**Small business corporation.** A corporation that satisfies the definition of § 1361(b), § 1244(c), or both. Satisfaction of § 1361(b) permits an S election, and satisfaction of § 1244 enables the shareholders of the corporation to claim an ordinary loss on the worthlessness of stock.

**Small business stock.** See *small business corporation.*

**Small Cases Division of the U.S. Tax Court.** Jurisdiction is limited to claims of $50,000 or less. There is no appeal from this court.

**Solicitation.** A level of activity brought about by the taxpayer within a specific state. Under Public Law 86–272, certain types of solicitation activities do not create nexus with the state. Exceeding mere solicitation, though, creates nexus.

**Special allocation.** Any amount for which an agreement exists among the partners of a partnership outlining the method used for spreading the item among the partners.

**Specific charge-off method.** A method of accounting for bad debts in which a deduction is permitted only when an account becomes partially or completely worthless.

**Standard deduction.** The individual taxpayer can either itemize deductions or take the standard deduction. The amount of the standard deduction depends on the taxpayer's filing status (single, head of household, married filing jointly, surviving spouse, or married filing separately). For 2005, the amount of the standard deduction ranges from $5,000 (for married, filing separately or unmarried) to $10,000 (for married, filing jointly). Additional standard deductions of either $1,000 (for married taxpayers) or $1,250 (for single taxpayers) are available if the taxpayer is either blind or age 65 or over. Limitations exist on the amount of the standard deduction of a taxpayer who is another taxpayer's dependent. The standard deduction amounts are adjusted for inflation each year. § 63(c).

**Stock dividend.** Not taxable if pro rata distributions of stock or stock rights on common stock. Section 305 governs the taxability of stock dividends and sets out five exceptions to the general rule that stock dividends are nontaxable.

**Stock redemption.** A corporation buys back its own stock from a specified shareholder. Typically, the corporation recognizes any realized gain on the noncash assets that it uses to effect a redemption, and the shareholder obtains a capital gain or loss upon receipt of the purchase price. §§ 301 and 302.

**Subchapter S.** Sections 1361–1379 of the Internal Revenue Code. An elective provision permitting certain small business corporations (§ 1361) and their shareholders (§ 1362) to elect to be treated for income tax purposes in accordance with the operating rules of §§ 1363–1379. S corporations usually avoid the corporate income tax, and corporate losses can be claimed by the shareholders.

**Subpart F income.** Certain income earned by a controlled foreign corporation. Usually, Subpart F income is included in the gross income of a U.S. shareholder of the CFC when the income is earned, not when it is later repatriated.

**Supreme Court.** The highest appellate court or the court of last resort in the Federal court system and in most states. Only a small number of tax decisions of the U.S. Courts of Appeal are reviewed by the U.S. Supreme Court under its certiorari procedure. The Supreme Court usually grants certiorari to resolve a conflict among the Courts of Appeal (e.g., two or more appellate courts have assumed opposing positions on a particular issue) or when the tax issue is extremely important (e.g., size of the revenue loss to the Federal government).

**Surviving spouse.** When a husband or wife predeceases the other spouse, the survivor is known as a surviving spouse. Under certain conditions, a surviving spouse may be entitled to use the income tax rates in § 1(a) (those applicable to married persons filing a joint return) for the two years after the year of death of his or her spouse. § 2.

**Syndication costs.** Incurred in promoting and marketing partnership interests for sale to investors. Examples include legal and accounting fees, printing costs for prospectus and placement documents, and state registration fees. These items are capitalized by the partnership as incurred, with no amortization thereof allowed.

# T

**Tax avoidance.** The minimization of one's tax liability by taking advantage of legally available tax planning opportunities. Tax avoidance can be contrasted with tax evasion, which entails the reduction of tax liability by illegal means.

**Tax benefit rule.** A provision that limits the recognition of income from the recovery of an expense or loss properly deducted in a prior tax year to the amount of the deduction that generated a tax saving. Assume that last year Gary had medical expenses of $3,000 and adjusted gross income of $30,000. Because of the 7.5 percent limitation, Gary could deduct only $750 of these expenses [$3,000 − (7.5% × $30,000)]. If, this year, Gary is reimbursed by his insurance company for $900 of these expenses, the tax benefit rule limits the amount of income from the reimbursement to $750 (the amount previously deducted with a tax saving). § 111.

**Tax Court.** The U.S. Tax Court is one of four trial courts of original jurisdiction that decides litigation involving Federal income, death, or gift taxes. It is the only trial court where the taxpayer must not first pay the deficiency assessed by the IRS. The Tax Court will not have jurisdiction over a case unless a statutory notice of deficiency (90-day letter) has been issued by the IRS and the taxpayer files the petition for hearing within the time prescribed.

**Tax credits.** Tax credits are amounts that directly reduce a taxpayer's tax liability. The tax benefit received from a tax credit is not dependent on the taxpayer's marginal tax rate, whereas the benefit of a tax deduction or exclusion is dependent on the taxpayer's tax bracket.

**Tax evasion.** The reduction of the taxpayer's tax liability through the use of illegal means. Tax evasion can be contrasted with tax avoidance, which entails the reduction of tax liability through the use of legal means.

**Tax preference items.** Various items that may result in the imposition of the alternative minimum tax. §§ 55–58.

**Tax rate schedules.** Rate schedules that are used by upper-income taxpayers and those not permitted to use the tax table. Separate rate schedules are provided for married individuals filing jointly, head of household, single taxpayers, estates and trusts, and married individuals filing separate returns. § 1.

**Tax shelters.** The typical tax shelter generated large losses in the early years of the activity. Investors would offset these losses against other types of income and, therefore, avoid paying income taxes on this income. These tax shelter investments could then be sold after a few years and produce capital gain income, which is taxed at a lower rate than ordinary income. The passive activity loss rules and the at-risk rules now limit tax shelter deductions.

**Tax table.** A tax table that is provided for taxpayers with less than $100,000 of taxable income. Separate columns are provided for single taxpayers, married taxpayers filing jointly, head of household, and married taxpayers filing separately. § 3.

**Taxable year.** The annual period over which income is measured for income tax purposes. Most individuals use a calendar year, but many businesses use a fiscal year based on the natural business year.

**Technical advice memoranda (TAMs).** TAMs are issued by the National Office of the IRS in response to questions raised by IRS field personnel during audits. They deal with completed rather than proposed transactions and are often requested for questions related to exempt organizations and employee plans.

**Temporary Regulation.** A Regulation issued by the Treasury Department in temporary form. When speed is critical, the Treasury Department issues Temporary Regulations that take effect immediately. These Regulations have the same authoritative value as Final Regulations and may be cited as precedent for three years. Temporary Regulations are also issued as proposed Regulations.

**Theft loss.** A loss from larceny, embezzlement, or robbery. It does not include misplacement of items.

**Thin capitalization.** When debt owed by a corporation to the shareholders becomes too large in relation to the corporation's capital structure (i.e., stock and shareholder equity), the IRS may contend that the corporation is thinly capitalized. In effect, this means that some or all of the debt is reclassified as equity. The immediate result is to disallow any interest deduction to the corporation on the reclassified debt. To the extent of the corporation's earnings and profits, interest payments and loan repayments on the reclassified debt are treated as dividends to the shareholders. § 385.

**Thirty percent additional first-year depreciation.** This provision, which was effective for property acquired after September 10, 2001, and before September 11, 2004, provided for an additional cost recovery deduction of 30 percent in the tax year that qualified property was placed in service. Qualified property included most types of new property other than buildings. The property had to be placed in service before January 1, 2005. § 168(k). See also *cost recovery system* and *fifty percent additional first-year depreciation*.

**Throwback rule.** If there is no income tax in the state to which a sale otherwise would be apportioned, the sale essentially is exempt from state income tax, even though the seller is domiciled in a state that levies an income tax. Nonetheless, if the seller's state has adopted a throwback rule, the sale is attributed to the seller's state, and the transaction is subjected to a state-level tax.

**Transportation expenses.** Transportation expenses for an employee include only the cost of transportation (taxi fares, automobile expenses, etc.) in the course of employment when the employee is not away from home in travel status. Commuting expenses are not deductible.

**Travel expenses.** Travel expenses include meals (generally subject to a 50 percent disallowance) and lodging and transportation expenses while away from home in the pursuit of a trade or business (including that of an employee).

## U

**Unearned income.** Income received but not yet earned. Normally, such income is taxed when received, even for accrual basis taxpayers. In certain cases involving advance payments for goods and services, income may be deferred. See Revenue Procedure 2004–34 (I.R.B. No. 22, 991) and Reg. § 1.451-5.

**Unitary approach.** Sales, property, and payroll of related corporations are combined for nexus and apportionment purposes, and the worldwide income of the unitary entity is apportioned to the state. Subsidiaries and other affiliated corporations found to be part of the corporation's unitary business (because they are subject to overlapping ownership, operations, or management) are included in the apportionment procedure. This approach can be limited if a waters'-edge election is in effect.

**Unreasonable compensation.** A deduction is allowed for "reasonable" salaries or other compensation for personal services actually rendered. To the extent compensation is "excessive" ("unreasonable"), no deduction is allowed. The problem of unreasonable compensation usually is limited to closely held corporations, where the motivation is to pay out profits in some form that is deductible to the corporation. Deductible compensation therefore becomes an attractive substitute for nondeductible dividends when the shareholders also are employed by the corporation. § 162(a)(1).

**Unrecaptured § 1250 gain (25 percent gain).** Gain from the sale of depreciable real estate held more than one year. The gain is equal to or less than the depreciation taken on such property and is reduced by § 1245 and § 1250 gain.

**U.S. shareholder.** For purposes of classification of an entity as a controlled foreign corporation, a U.S. person who owns, or is considered to own, 10 percent or more of the total combined voting power of all classes of voting stock of a foreign corporation. Stock owned directly, indirectly, and constructively is counted for this purpose. The U.S. shareholder may be currently taxed on a proportionate share of Subpart F income.

**U.S. trade or business.** A set of activities that is carried on in a regular, continuous, and substantial manner. A non-U.S. taxpayer is subject to U.S. tax on the taxable income that is effectively connected with a U.S. trade or business.

**Use tax.** A sales tax that is collectible by the seller where the purchaser is domiciled in a different state.

## V

**Value added tax (VAT).** A national sales tax that taxes the increment in value as goods move through the production process. A VAT is much used in other countries but has not yet been incorporated as part of the U.S. Federal tax structure.

**Voluntary revocation.** The owners of a majority of shares in an S corporation elect to terminate the S status of the entity, as of a specified date. The day on which the revocation is effective is the first day of the corporation's C tax year.

## W

**Wash sale.** A loss from the sale of stock or securities that is disallowed because the taxpayer, within 30 days before or after the sale, has acquired stock or securities substantially identical to those sold. § 1091.

**Waters'-edge election.** A limitation on the worldwide scope of the unitary approach to computing state taxable income. If a waters'-edge election is in effect, the state can consider only the activities that occur within the boundaries of the United States in the apportionment procedure.

**Welfare-to-work credit.** A tax credit available to employers hiring individuals who have been long-term recipients of family assistance welfare benefits. In general, long-term recipients are those individuals who are certified by a designated local agency as being members of a family receiving assistance under a public aid program for at least an 18-month period ending on the hiring date. The welfare-to-work credit is available for qualified wages paid in the first two years of employment. The maximum credit is equal to $8,500 per qualified employee, computed as 35 percent of the first $10,000 of qualified wages paid in the first year of employment, plus 50 percent of the first $10,000 of qualified wages paid in the second year of employment. § 51A.

**Wherewithal to pay.** This concept recognizes the inequity of taxing a transaction when the taxpayer lacks the means with which to pay the tax. Under it, there is a correlation between the imposition of the tax and the ability to pay the tax. It is particularly suited to situations in which the taxpayer's economic position has not changed significantly as a result of the transaction.

**Work opportunity tax credit.** Employers are allowed a tax credit equal to 40 percent of the first $6,000 of wages (per eligible employee) for the first year of employment. Eligible employees include certain hard-to-employ individuals (e.g., qualified ex-felons, high-risk youth, food stamp recipients, and veterans). The employer's deduction for wages is reduced by the amount of the credit taken. For qualified summer youth employees, the 40 percent rate is applied to the first $3,000 of qualified wages. §§ 51 and 52.

**Working condition fringe.** A type of fringe benefit received by the employee that is excludible from the employee's gross income. It consists of property or services provided (paid or reimbursed) by the employer for which the employee could take a tax deduction if the employee had paid for them. § 132(d).

**Worthless securities.** A loss (usually capital) is allowed for a security that becomes worthless during the year. The loss is deemed to have occurred on the last day of the year. Special rules apply to securities of affiliated companies and small business stock. § 165.

**Writ of Certiorari.** Appeal from a U.S. Court of Appeals to the U.S. Supreme Court is by Writ of Certiorari. The Supreme Court need not accept the appeal, and it usually does not (*cert. den.*) unless a conflict exists among the lower courts that must be resolved or a constitutional issue is involved.

# Table of Code Sections Cited

[See Title 26 U.S.C.A.]

# Table of Cases Cited

# Present Value and Future Value Tables

## Present Value of $1

| N/R | 4% | 5% | 6% | 7% | 8% | 9% | 10% | 11% | 12% | 13% | 14% |
|---|---|---|---|---|---|---|---|---|---|---|---|
| 1 | 0.9615 | 0.9524 | 0.9434 | 0.9346 | 0.9259 | 0.9174 | 0.9091 | 0.9009 | 0.8929 | 0.8850 | 0.8772 |
| 2 | 0.9246 | 0.9070 | 0.8900 | 0.8734 | 0.8573 | 0.8417 | 0.8264 | 0.8116 | 0.7972 | 0.7831 | 0.7695 |
| 3 | 0.8890 | 0.8638 | 0.8396 | 0.8163 | 0.7938 | 0.7722 | 0.7513 | 0.7312 | 0.7118 | 0.6931 | 0.6750 |
| 4 | 0.8548 | 0.8227 | 0.7921 | 0.7629 | 0.7350 | 0.7084 | 0.6830 | 0.6587 | 0.6355 | 0.6133 | 0.5921 |
| 5 | 0.8219 | 0.7835 | 0.7473 | 0.7130 | 0.6806 | 0.6499 | 0.6209 | 0.5935 | 0.5674 | 0.5428 | 0.5194 |
| 6 | 0.7903 | 0.7462 | 0.7050 | 0.6663 | 0.6302 | 0.5963 | 0.5645 | 0.5346 | 0.5066 | 0.4803 | 0.4556 |
| 7 | 0.7599 | 0.7107 | 0.6651 | 0.6227 | 0.5835 | 0.5470 | 0.5132 | 0.4817 | 0.4523 | 0.4251 | 0.3996 |
| 8 | 0.7307 | 0.6768 | 0.6274 | 0.5820 | 0.5403 | 0.5019 | 0.4665 | 0.4339 | 0.4039 | 0.3762 | 0.3506 |
| 9 | 0.7026 | 0.6446 | 0.5919 | 0.5439 | 0.5002 | 0.4604 | 0.4241 | 0.3909 | 0.3606 | 0.3329 | 0.3075 |
| 10 | 0.6756 | 0.6139 | 0.5584 | 0.5083 | 0.4632 | 0.4224 | 0.3855 | 0.3522 | 0.3220 | 0.2946 | 0.2697 |
| 11 | 0.6496 | 0.5847 | 0.5268 | 0.4751 | 0.4289 | 0.3875 | 0.3505 | 0.3173 | 0.2875 | 0.2607 | 0.2366 |
| 12 | 0.6246 | 0.5568 | 0.4970 | 0.4440 | 0.3971 | 0.3555 | 0.3186 | 0.2858 | 0.2567 | 0.2307 | 0.2076 |
| 13 | 0.6006 | 0.5303 | 0.4688 | 0.4150 | 0.3677 | 0.3262 | 0.2897 | 0.2575 | 0.2292 | 0.2042 | 0.1821 |
| 14 | 0.5775 | 0.5051 | 0.4423 | 0.3878 | 0.3405 | 0.2992 | 0.2633 | 0.2320 | 0.2046 | 0.1807 | 0.1597 |
| 15 | 0.5553 | 0.4810 | 0.4173 | 0.3624 | 0.3152 | 0.2745 | 0.2394 | 0.2090 | 0.1827 | 0.1599 | 0.1401 |
| 16 | 0.5339 | 0.4581 | 0.3936 | 0.3387 | 0.2919 | 0.2519 | 0.2176 | 0.1883 | 0.1631 | 0.1415 | 0.1229 |
| 17 | 0.5134 | 0.4363 | 0.3714 | 0.3166 | 0.2703 | 0.2311 | 0.1978 | 0.1696 | 0.1456 | 0.1252 | 0.1078 |
| 18 | 0.4936 | 0.4155 | 0.3503 | 0.2959 | 0.2502 | 0.2120 | 0.1799 | 0.1528 | 0.1300 | 0.1108 | 0.0946 |
| 19 | 0.4746 | 0.3957 | 0.3305 | 0.2765 | 0.2317 | 0.1945 | 0.1635 | 0.1377 | 0.1161 | 0.0981 | 0.0829 |
| 20 | 0.4564 | 0.3769 | 0.3118 | 0.2584 | 0.2145 | 0.1784 | 0.1486 | 0.1240 | 0.1037 | 0.0868 | 0.0728 |

## Present Value of an Ordinary Annuity of $1

| N/R | 4% | 5% | 6% | 7% | 8% | 9% | 10% | 11% | 12% | 13% | 14% |
|---|---|---|---|---|---|---|---|---|---|---|---|
| 1 | 0.9615 | 0.9524 | 0.9434 | 0.9346 | 0.9259 | 0.9174 | 0.9091 | 0.9009 | 0.8929 | 0.8850 | 0.8772 |
| 2 | 1.8861 | 1.8594 | 1.8334 | 1.8080 | 1.7833 | 1.7591 | 1.7355 | 1.7125 | 1.6901 | 1.6681 | 1.6467 |
| 3 | 2.7751 | 2.7232 | 2.6730 | 2.6243 | 2.5771 | 2.5313 | 2.4869 | 2.4437 | 2.4018 | 2.3612 | 2.3216 |
| 4 | 3.6299 | 3.5460 | 3.4651 | 3.3872 | 3.3121 | 3.2397 | 3.1699 | 3.1024 | 3.0373 | 2.9745 | 2.9137 |
| 5 | 4.4518 | 4.3295 | 4.2124 | 4.1002 | 3.9927 | 3.8897 | 3.7908 | 3.6959 | 3.6048 | 3.5172 | 3.4331 |
| 6 | 5.2421 | 5.0757 | 4.9173 | 4.7665 | 4.6229 | 4.4859 | 4.3553 | 4.2305 | 4.1114 | 3.9975 | 3.8887 |
| 7 | 6.0021 | 5.7864 | 5.5824 | 5.3893 | 5.2064 | 5.0330 | 4.8684 | 4.7122 | 4.5638 | 4.4226 | 4.2883 |
| 8 | 6.7327 | 6.4632 | 6.2098 | 5.9713 | 5.7466 | 5.5348 | 5.3349 | 5.1461 | 4.9676 | 4.7988 | 4.6389 |
| 9 | 7.4353 | 7.1078 | 6.8017 | 6.5152 | 6.2469 | 5.9952 | 5.7590 | 5.5370 | 5.3282 | 5.1317 | 4.9464 |
| 10 | 8.1109 | 7.7217 | 7.3601 | 7.0236 | 6.7101 | 6.4177 | 6.1446 | 5.8892 | 5.6502 | 5.4262 | 5.2161 |
| 11 | 8.7605 | 8.3064 | 7.8869 | 7.4987 | 7.1390 | 6.8052 | 6.4951 | 6.2065 | 5.9377 | 5.6869 | 5.4527 |
| 12 | 9.3851 | 8.8633 | 8.3838 | 7.9427 | 7.5361 | 7.1607 | 6.8137 | 6.4924 | 6.1944 | 5.9176 | 5.6603 |
| 13 | 9.9856 | 9.3936 | 8.8527 | 8.3577 | 7.9038 | 7.4869 | 7.1034 | 6.7499 | 6.4235 | 6.1218 | 5.8424 |
| 14 | 10.5631 | 9.8986 | 9.2950 | 8.7455 | 8.2442 | 7.7862 | 7.3667 | 6.9819 | 6.6282 | 6.3025 | 6.0021 |
| 15 | 11.1184 | 10.3797 | 9.7122 | 9.1079 | 8.5595 | 8.0607 | 7.6061 | 7.1909 | 6.8109 | 6.4624 | 6.1422 |
| 16 | 11.6523 | 10.8378 | 10.1059 | 9.4466 | 8.8514 | 8.3126 | 7.8237 | 7.3792 | 6.9740 | 6.6039 | 6.2651 |
| 17 | 12.1657 | 11.2741 | 10.4773 | 9.7632 | 9.1216 | 8.5436 | 8.0216 | 7.5488 | 7.1196 | 6.7291 | 6.3729 |
| 18 | 12.6593 | 11.6896 | 10.8276 | 10.0591 | 9.3719 | 8.7556 | 8.2014 | 7.7016 | 7.2497 | 6.8399 | 6.4674 |
| 19 | 13.1339 | 12.0853 | 11.1581 | 10.3356 | 9.6036 | 8.9501 | 8.3649 | 7.8393 | 7.3658 | 6.9380 | 6.5504 |
| 20 | 13.5903 | 12.4622 | 11.4699 | 10.5940 | 9.8181 | 9.1285 | 8.5136 | 7.9633 | 7.4694 | 7.0248 | 6.6231 |

# Future Value of $1

| N/R | 4% | 5% | 6% | 7% | 8% | 9% | 10% | 11% | 12% | 13% | 14% |
|---|---|---|---|---|---|---|---|---|---|---|---|
| 1 | 1.0400 | 1.0500 | 1.0600 | 1.0700 | 1.0800 | 1.0900 | 1.1000 | 1.1100 | 1.1200 | 1.1300 | 1.1400 |
| 2 | 1.0816 | 1.1025 | 1.1236 | 1.1449 | 1.1664 | 1.1881 | 1.2100 | 1.2321 | 1.2544 | 1.2769 | 1.2996 |
| 3 | 1.1249 | 1.1576 | 1.1910 | 1.2250 | 1.2597 | 1.2950 | 1.3310 | 1.3676 | 1.4049 | 1.4429 | 1.4815 |
| 4 | 1.1699 | 1.2155 | 1.2625 | 1.3108 | 1.3605 | 1.4116 | 1.4641 | 1.5181 | 1.5735 | 1.6305 | 1.6890 |
| 5 | 1.2167 | 1.2763 | 1.3382 | 1.4026 | 1.4693 | 1.5386 | 1.6105 | 1.6851 | 1.7623 | 1.8424 | 1.9254 |
| 6 | 1.2653 | 1.3401 | 1.4185 | 1.5007 | 1.5869 | 1.6771 | 1.7716 | 1.8704 | 1.9738 | 2.0820 | 2.1950 |
| 7 | 1.3159 | 1.4071 | 1.5036 | 1.6058 | 1.7138 | 1.8280 | 1.9487 | 2.0762 | 2.2107 | 2.3526 | 2.5023 |
| 8 | 1.3686 | 1.4775 | 1.5938 | 1.7182 | 1.8509 | 1.9926 | 2.1436 | 2.3045 | 2.4760 | 2.6584 | 2.8526 |
| 9 | 1.4233 | 1.5513 | 1.6895 | 1.8385 | 1.9990 | 2.1719 | 2.3579 | 2.5580 | 2.7731 | 3.0040 | 3.2519 |
| 10 | 1.4802 | 1.6289 | 1.7908 | 1.9672 | 2.1589 | 2.3674 | 2.5937 | 2.8394 | 3.1058 | 3.3946 | 3.7072 |
| 11 | 1.5395 | 1.7103 | 1.8983 | 2.1049 | 2.3316 | 2.5804 | 2.8531 | 3.1518 | 3.4785 | 3.8359 | 4.2262 |
| 12 | 1.6010 | 1.7959 | 2.0122 | 2.2522 | 2.5182 | 2.8127 | 3.1384 | 3.4985 | 3.8960 | 4.3345 | 4.8179 |
| 13 | 1.6651 | 1.8856 | 2.1329 | 2.4098 | 2.7196 | 3.0658 | 3.4523 | 3.8833 | 4.3635 | 4.8980 | 5.4924 |
| 14 | 1.7317 | 1.9799 | 2.2609 | 2.5785 | 2.9372 | 3.3417 | 3.7975 | 4.3104 | 4.8871 | 5.5348 | 6.2613 |
| 15 | 1.8009 | 2.0789 | 2.3966 | 2.7590 | 3.1722 | 3.6425 | 4.1772 | 4.7846 | 5.4736 | 6.2543 | 7.1379 |
| 16 | 1.8730 | 2.1829 | 2.5404 | 2.9522 | 3.4259 | 3.9703 | 4.5950 | 5.3109 | 6.1304 | 7.0673 | 8.1372 |
| 17 | 1.9479 | 2.2920 | 2.6928 | 3.1588 | 3.7000 | 4.3276 | 5.0545 | 5.8951 | 6.8660 | 7.9861 | 9.2765 |
| 18 | 2.0258 | 2.4066 | 2.8543 | 3.3799 | 3.9960 | 4.7171 | 5.5599 | 6.5436 | 7.6900 | 9.0243 | 10.5752 |
| 19 | 2.1068 | 2.5270 | 3.0256 | 3.6165 | 4.3157 | 5.1417 | 6.1159 | 7.2633 | 8.6128 | 10.1974 | 12.0557 |
| 20 | 2.1911 | 2.6533 | 3.2071 | 3.8697 | 4.6610 | 5.6044 | 6.7275 | 8.0623 | 9.6463 | 11.5231 | 13.7435 |

# Future Value of an Ordinary Annuity of $1

| N/R | 4% | 5% | 6% | 7% | 8% | 9% | 10% | 11% | 12% | 13% | 14% |
|---|---|---|---|---|---|---|---|---|---|---|---|
| 1 | 1.0000 | 1.0000 | 1.0000 | 1.0000 | 1.0000 | 1.0000 | 1.0000 | 1.0000 | 1.0000 | 1.0000 | 1.0000 |
| 2 | 2.0400 | 2.0500 | 2.0600 | 2.0700 | 2.0800 | 2.0900 | 2.1000 | 2.1100 | 2.1200 | 2.1300 | 2.1400 |
| 3 | 3.1216 | 3.1525 | 3.1836 | 3.2149 | 3.2464 | 3.2781 | 3.3100 | 3.3421 | 3.3744 | 3.4069 | 3.4396 |
| 4 | 4.2465 | 4.3101 | 4.3746 | 4.4399 | 4.5061 | 4.5731 | 4.6410 | 4.7097 | 4.7793 | 4.8498 | 4.9211 |
| 5 | 5.4163 | 5.5256 | 5.6371 | 5.7507 | 5.8666 | 5.9847 | 6.1051 | 6.2278 | 6.3528 | 6.4803 | 6.6101 |
| 6 | 6.6330 | 6.8019 | 6.9753 | 7.1533 | 7.3359 | 7.5233 | 7.7156 | 7.9129 | 8.1152 | 8.3227 | 8.5355 |
| 7 | 7.8983 | 8.1420 | 8.3938 | 8.6540 | 8.9228 | 9.2004 | 9.4872 | 9.7833 | 10.0890 | 10.4047 | 10.7305 |
| 8 | 9.2142 | 9.5491 | 9.8975 | 10.2598 | 10.6366 | 11.0285 | 11.4359 | 11.8594 | 12.2997 | 12.7573 | 13.2328 |
| 9 | 10.5828 | 11.0266 | 11.4913 | 11.9780 | 12.4876 | 13.0210 | 13.5795 | 14.1640 | 14.7757 | 15.4157 | 16.0853 |
| 10 | 12.0061 | 12.5779 | 13.1808 | 13.8164 | 14.4866 | 15.1929 | 15.9374 | 16.7220 | 17.5487 | 18.4197 | 19.3373 |
| 11 | 13.4864 | 14.2068 | 14.9716 | 15.7836 | 16.6455 | 17.5603 | 18.5312 | 19.5614 | 20.6546 | 21.8143 | 23.0445 |
| 12 | 15.0258 | 15.9171 | 16.8699 | 17.8885 | 18.9771 | 20.1407 | 21.3843 | 22.7132 | 24.1331 | 25.6502 | 27.2707 |
| 13 | 16.6268 | 17.7130 | 18.8821 | 20.1406 | 21.4953 | 22.9534 | 24.5227 | 26.2116 | 28.0291 | 29.9847 | 32.0887 |
| 14 | 18.2919 | 19.5986 | 21.0151 | 22.5505 | 24.2149 | 26.0192 | 27.9750 | 30.0949 | 32.3926 | 34.8827 | 35.5811 |
| 15 | 20.0236 | 21.5786 | 23.2760 | 25.1290 | 27.1521 | 29.3609 | 31.7725 | 34.4054 | 37.2797 | 40.4175 | 43.8424 |
| 16 | 21.8245 | 23.6575 | 25.6725 | 27.8881 | 30.3243 | 33.0034 | 35.9497 | 39.1899 | 42.7533 | 46.6717 | 50.9804 |
| 17 | 23.6975 | 25.8404 | 28.2129 | 30.8402 | 33.7502 | 36.9737 | 40.5447 | 44.5008 | 48.8837 | 53.7391 | 59.1176 |
| 18 | 25.6454 | 28.1324 | 30.9057 | 33.9990 | 37.4502 | 41.3013 | 45.5992 | 50.3959 | 55.7497 | 61.7251 | 68.3941 |
| 19 | 27.6712 | 30.5390 | 33.7600 | 37.3790 | 41.4463 | 46.0185 | 51.1591 | 56.9395 | 63.4397 | 70.7494 | 78.9692 |
| 20 | 29.7781 | 33.0660 | 36.7856 | 40.9955 | 45.7620 | 51.1601 | 57.2750 | 64.2028 | 72.0524 | 80.9468 | 91.0249 |

# Index

# AMT Formula for Individuals

## Regular Taxable Income

| | |
|---|---|
| *Plus or minus:* | Adjustments |
| *Plus:* | Tax preferences |
| *Equals:* | Alternative minimum taxable income |
| *Minus:* | Exemption |
| *Equals:* | Alternative minimum tax base |
| *Times:* | 26% and 28% graduated rates |
| *Equals:* | Tentative minimum tax before foreign tax credit |
| *Minus:* | Alternative minimum tax foreign tax credit |
| *Equals:* | Tentative minimum tax |
| *Minus:* | Regular income tax liability |
| *Equals:* | Alternative minimum tax (if amount is positive) |

# AMT Formula for Corporations

## Regular Taxable Income before NOL Deduction

| | |
|---|---|
| *Plus or minus:* | Adjustments (except ACE adjustment) |
| *Plus:* | Tax preferences |
| *Equals:* | AMTI before ATNOL deduction and ACE adjustment |
| *Plus or minus:* | ACE adjustment |
| *Equals:* | Alternative minimum taxable income (AMTI) before ATNOL deduction |
| *Minus:* | ATNOL deduction (limited to 90% of AMTI before ATNOL deduction) |
| *Equals:* | Alternative minimum taxable income (AMTI) |
| *Minus:* | Exemption |
| *Equals:* | Alternative minimum tax base |
| *Times:* | 20% rate |
| *Equals:* | AMT before AMT foreign tax credit |
| *Minus:* | AMT foreign tax credit |
| *Equals:* | Tentative minimum tax |
| *Minus:* | Regular income tax liability before credits minus regular foreign tax credit |
| *Equals:* | Alternative minimum tax (AMT) if positive |

# Tax Formula for Corporate Taxpayers

| | |
|---|---|
| Income (broadly conceived) ................................................. | $xxx,xxx |
| Less: Exclusions (income that is not subject to tax) ......................... | (xx,xxx) |
| Gross Income ................................................................ | $xxx,xxx |
| Less: Certain business deductions ..................................... | (xx,xxx) |
| Taxable income.............................................................. | $xxx,xxx |
| Federal income tax (see Tax Rate Schedule inside front cover of text) ................................................................ | $ xx,xxx |
| Less: Tax credits (including Federal income tax withheld and other prepayments of Federal income taxes)............................... | (x,xxx) |
| Tax owed (or refund due)................................................. | $ xx,xxx |